Community Health Nursing

Promoting the Health of Aggregates

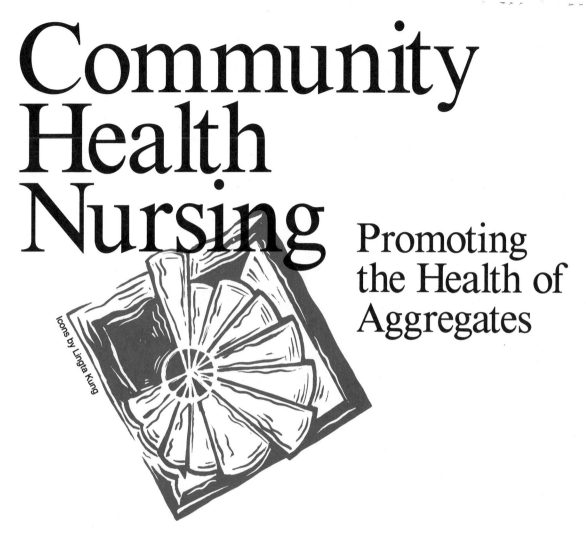

Icons by Lingta Kung

Janice M. Swanson, Ph.D., R.N.
Professor of Nursing
Samuel Merritt College
Department of Nursing
Director of Clinical Nursing Research
Summit Medical Center
Oakland, California

Mary Albrecht, Ph.D., R.N.
Associate Professor,
Department of Community Health and
  Family Nursing, College of Nursing
Joint Appointment,
Department of Preventive Medicine
College of Medicine
University of Tennessee
Memphis, Tennessee

WB SAUNDERS COMPANY
A Division of Harcourt Brace & Company

Philadelphia   London   Toronto
Montreal   Sydney   Tokyo

ABE 5618

WB Saunders Company
A Division of
Harcourt Brace & Company

The Curtis Center
Independence Square West
Philadelphia, Pennsylvania 19106

Library of Congress Cataloging-in-Publication Data
Swanson, Janice E.
Community health nursing : promoting the health of aggregates / Janice M. Swanson, Mary Albrecht. — 1st ed.
p. cm.
ISBN 0-7216-1312-8
1. Community health nursing. 2. Health Promotion. I. Albrecht, Mary. II. Title.
[DNLM: 1. Community Health Nursing. WY 106 S972c]
RT98.S9 1993
610.73′43 — dc20
DNLM/DLC   92-48201

Community Health Nursing: Promoting the Health of Aggregates   ISBN 0-7216-1312-8

Printed in the United States of America.

Last digit is the print number: 9   8   7   6   5   4   3

This book is dedicated to all community health nurses, educators, and students, together with our families—
Richard, Karen, and Betsy Swanson

Jan

and

To my parents, my sisters and brothers, and my nieces and nephews and to friends who continued to be encouraging throughout the process.

Mary

AUTHORS

Janice M. Swanson

Janice M. Swanson, R.N., Ph.D., is Professor, Samuel Merritt College, Department of Nursing, and Director of Clinical Nursing Research, Summit Medical Center, in Oakland, California. Dr. Swanson received her diploma in nursing from Emanuel Hospital School of Nursing in Portland, Oregon; her baccalaureate in nursing from Wayne State University in Detroit, Michigan; and her master of science degree in community health nursing and doctorate in education from the University of Maryland. She completed a postdoctoral research fellowship at the University of California, San Francisco, in medical sociology and nursing. Dr. Swanson has coauthored two books: *Men's Reproductive Health,* with K. Forest, and *From Practice to Grounded Theory: Qualitative Research for Nurses,* with W. C. Chenitz. Her research interests focus on community aspects of reproductive health. Her current project, funded by the National Center for Nursing Research, National Institutes of Health, tests the outcomes of an intervention carried out by nurses in the community with young adults who have genital herpes. Dr. Swanson serves as a member of the Nursing Research Study Section, Division of Research Grants, National Institutes of Health.

Mary Albrecht

Mary Albrecht received her Ph.D. in public health nursing from the University of Illinois, Chicago. She currently holds a joint appointment in the College of Nursing, Department of Community Health and Family Nursing and in the College of Medicine, Department of Preventive Medicine at the University of Tennessee, Memphis. Formerly she was a postdoctoral fellow at the University of Michigan, Ann Arbor. She has had more than 16 years of experience teaching community health nursing to both undergraduate and graduate students. She has also had experience in public health nursing, ranging from official agencies to proprietary agencies. She is associated with the University of Tennessee Center for Prevention and Health Services Research exploring interventions that promote positive health outcomes in the community. She is a site visit coordinator for the Community Health Accreditation Program of the National League for Nursing.

CONTRIBUTORS

Mary Albrecht, Ph.D., R.N.
Associate Professor, Department
of Community Health and
Family Nursing, College of
Nursing, Joint Appointment,
Department of Preventive
Medicine, College of Medicine,
University of Tennessee,
Memphis, Tennessee
Health: A Community View;
Community Health Nursing:
Making a Difference

Mary E. Allen, Ph.D., R.N.,C.S.
Associate Professor and Division
Director, Psychiatric/Mental
Health and Community Health
Nursing, University of
Oklahoma, Oklahoma City,
Oklahoma
Mental Health

Madalon O'Rawe Amenta,
Dr.P.H., R.N.
Editor, The Hospice Journal
Policy, Politics, Legislation, and
Public Health Nursing

Margaret M. Andrews, Ph.D.,
R.N., C.T.N.
Chairperson and Professor,
Department of Nursing,
Nazareth College, Rochester,
New York
Cultural Diversity and
Community Health Nursing;
The African-American
Community

Lucretia Bolin, D.N.S., R.N.
Postdoctoral Fellow,
Department of Social and
Behavorial Sciences, University
of California, San Francisco,
San Francisco, California
The African-American
Community; Substance Abuse

Christine DiMartile Bolla,
M.S., R.N.
Assistant Professor, Nursing,
Samuel Merritt College,
Oakland, California
The Home Visit

Patricia M. Burbank, D.N.Sc., R.N.
Assistant Professor, University
of Rhode Island College of
Nursing, Kingston, Rhode Island
Health Planning

Patricia G. Butterfield, Ph.D., R.N.
Assistant Professor, School of
Nursing, Oregon Health
Sciences University;
Postdoctoral Fellow, Center for
Research on Occupational and
Environmental Toxicology,
Oregon Health Sciences
University, Portland, Oregon
Thinking Upstream:
Conceptualizing Health From a
Population Perspective

Mary Brecht Carpenter,
M.P.H., R.N.
Deputy Director, National
Commission to Prevent Infant
Mortality, Washington, D.C.
Child Health

Holly B. Cassells, Ph.D., M.P.H., R.N.,C.
Associate Professor, Incarnate Word College, San Antonio, Texas
Nursing Process in the Community

Della Dash, M.P.H., B.S.N.
Project Officer, Water and Environmental Sanitation, % UNICEF–Addis Ababa, New York, New York
Communicable Disease

Sandra DeBella, Ed.D., M.S.N., R.N.
Chair, Professor of Nursing, Sonoma State University Department of Nursing, Rohnert Park, California
Health Education

Susan Rumsey Givens, M.P.H., R.N.,C.
Senior Policy Analyst, National Commission to Prevent Infant Mortality, Washington, D.C.
Child Health

Deborah A. Godfrey, M.S., R.N.
Undergraduate Director and Assistant Professor, University of Rhode Island College of Nursing, Kingston, Rhode Island
Health Planning

Joanne M. Hall, Ph.D., R.N.
Postdoctoral Fellow, Department of Mental Health Community and Administrative Nursing, School of Nursing, University of California, San Francisco, San Francisco, California
Substance Abuse; Environmental Health

Peggy Hickman, Ed.D., R.N., C.C.D.
Associate Professor, College of Nursing, University of Kentucky, Lexington, Kentucky
Community Organization

Barbara J. Horn, Ph.D., R.N., F.A.A.N.
Professor, Community Health Care Systems, University of Washington School of Nursing; President, Board of Directors, Community Home Health Care, Seattle, Washington
The Health Care System

Beverly M. Horn, Ph.D., R.N.
Associate Professor, Community Health Care Systems, University of Washington School of Nursing, Seattle, Washington
The Health Care System

Charlene Olivia Lund, M.S.N., R.N.
Division of Public Health Nursing, Fresno County Department of Health, Fresno, California
Rural Health

Jean Cozad Lyon, Ph.D., R.N., C.S.
Assistant Professor, Orvis School of Nursing, University of Nevada–Reno, Reno, Nevada
The Home Visit; Home Health Care

Erika Madrid, D.N.Sc., R.N., C.S.
Assistant Professor, Holy Names College Department of Nursing, Oakland, California
Substance Abuse

Ricardo A. Martinez, M.S., M.P.H., R.N.
Principal Consultant, Medicolegal Consultants; Medicolegal Consultant, Mauzé and Jones Law Firm, San Antonio, Texas; Doctoral Student, University of Texas School of Public Health, University of Texas Health

Sciences at Houston, Houston, Texas
Cultural Influence in the Community: The Mexican-American Community

Cherryl E. McDougall, R.N., C.O.H.N.
Health Services, Digital Equipment Corporation, Shrewsbury, Massachusetts
The Occupational Health Nurse: Roles and Responsibilities, Current and Future Trends

Barbara S. Morgan, Ph.D., R.N.
Dean and Professor, School of Nursing, The City College of the City University of New York, New York, New York
Health Planning

Marjorie A. Muecke, Ph.D., F.A.A.N.
Professor of Nursing, Adjunct Professor of Anthropology, and Adjunct Professor of Health Services, University of Washington, Seattle, Washington
Cultural Influence in the Community: Southeast Asian Refugees

Olive T. Roen, M.S.N., M.P.H., R.N.C.N.P.
Doctoral Student, University of Texas Health Science Center at Houston School of Public Health, Houston, Texas
Senior Health

Theresa M. Stephany, M.S., R.N.,C.S.
Staff Nurse III, Hospice Program, Kaiser Permanente, Haywood, California
Home Health Care

Patricia E. Stevens, Ph.D., R.N.
Postdoctoral Fellow,

Department of Mental Health, Community and Administrative Nursing, School of Nursing, University of California, San Francisco, San Francisco, California
Environmental Health

Ruth F. Stewart, M.S., R.N.
Associate Professor, University of Texas Health Science Center School of Nursing (San Antonio), San Antonio, Texas
Policy, Politics, Legislation, and Public Health Nursing

Janice M. Swanson, Ph.D., R.N.
Professor of Nursing, Samuel Merritt College Department of Nursing; Director of Clinical Nursing Research, Summit Medical Center, Oakland, California
Health: A Community View; Historical Factors: Community Health Nursing in Context; Men's Health; Addressing the Needs of Families; World Health; Community Health Nursing: Making a Difference

Karen A. Swanson, B.A.
Graduate Student, Harvard School of Public Health, Boston, Massachusetts
World Health

Donna Neal Thomas, Ph.D., R.N.,C.
Associate Professor (LOA), University of Wisconsin Oshkosh, College of Nursing, Oshkosh, Wisconsin; Executive Director, Mary Mahoney Memorial Health Center/ Healing Hands Health Services for the Homeless, Oklahoma City, Oklahoma
Women's Health

Patricia Hyland Travers, Sc.M., M.S., R.N., C.O.H.N.
Consultant, Occupational Health Nursing Program, Harvard School of Public Health, Boston, Massachusetts
The Occupational Health Nurse: Roles and Responsibilities, Current and Future Trends

Ann C. Watkins, M.S.N., R.N., C.N.M.
Nursing Consultant II, State of California, Department of Health Services, Maternal and Child Health Branch, Berkeley, California
Family Violence

Roma D. Williams, Ph.D., C.R.N.P.
Assistant Professor, College of Nursing, University of Alabama in Huntsville, Huntsville, Alabama
Women's Health

REVIEWERS

Patrice A. Bartelme, M.S., B.S.N.,
R.N., C.F.N.P.
Assistant Professor
School of Nursing
Alverno College
Milwaukee, Wisconsin

Janlee R. Blosser, M.N., R.N.
Associate Professor
Department of Nursing
Bethel College
North Newton, Kansas

Linda Bugle, Ph.D., R.N.,C.
Assistant Professor
School of Nursing
Southeast Missouri State
University
Cape Girardeau, Missouri

Jacquelyn C. Campbell, Ph.D.,
R.N., F.A.A.N.
Associate Professor
College of Nursing
Wayne State University
Detroit, Michigan

Jeri W. Dunkin, Ph.D., M.S., R.N.
Assistant Professor
College of Nursing
University of North Dakota
Grand Forks, North Dakota

Beth B. Gaul, M.S., R.N.
Assistant Professor
College of Nursing
Grand View College
Des Moines, Iowa

Nancy B. Jones, M.S.N., R.N.
Assistant Professor
School of Nursing
Kent State University
Kent, Ohio

Catherine Malloy, Dr.P.H.
Associate Professor
School of Nursing
George Mason University
Fairfax, Virginia

Melanie McEwen, Ph.D., R.N.
Assistant Professor
School of Nursing
Baylor University
Dallas, Texas

Jane M. Parks, M.S.N., R.N.
Assistant Professor
School of Nursing
Kearney State College
Kearney, Nebraska

Jennan Atkins Phillips,
D.S.N., R.N.
Assistant Professor
School of Nursing
The University of Alabama at
Birmingham
Birmingham, Alabama

Linda Ann Ruest, M.S., R.N.
Assistant Professor
Department of Nursing
St. Joseph's College
North Windham, Maine

Terri Jean Woods, M.S.N., R.N.,C.
Assistant Professor
School of Nursing
Southeast Missouri State
University
Cape Girardeau, Missouri

Nancy C. Zarle, M.S., R.N.
Assistant Professor
School of Nursing
Aurora University
Aurora, Illinois

Community health nurses have traditionally addressed the needs of aggregates such as families and school, work site, clinic, and community groups. Community health nursing texts, however, have traditionally defined the unit of care of the community health nurse generalist, with undergraduate preparation, as limited primarily to the individual and family and the unit of care of the specialist, with graduate preparation, as limited primarily to other aggregates, communities, or populations. If community health nursing is truly a synthesis of nursing and public health practice with the goal of promoting and preserving the health of populations, then all community health nurses carry out this mandate. The "diagnosis and treatment of human responses to actual or potential health problems" (American Nurses' Association Social Policy Statement, 1980) is derived from the nursing component. The ability to prevent disease, prolong life, and promote health through organized community effort is derived from the public health component. Community health nursing practice is responsible to the population as a whole; nursing efforts to promote health and prevent disease are applied to the public, which includes all units in the community, whether a person, a family, other aggregate, community, or population. The generalist is competent to practice at a minimum safe level, whereas the specialist is expected to have developed expert competence through practice over time, expert knowledge, and a higher level of autonomy and freedom.

The purpose of *Community Health Nursing: Promoting the Health of Aggregates* is to highlight an aggregate focus within the traditional areas of family and community health. The primary focus is on promotion of the health of aggregates. Including the family as an aggregate, yet going beyond the traditional home visit to the family, this book also addresses the needs of other aggregates or population subgroups. It not only conceptualizes the individual as a member of a family, but also individuals and families as members of other aggregates including organizations and institutions, and a population within an environment.

The aggregate is made up of a collective of individuals, whether a family or other groups, that combine with others to make up a community. In this book, the aggregate as a unit of focus is emphasized; how aggregates that make up communities promote their own health is also emphasized. The aggregate is presented within the social context of the community, and the opportunity is given to students to define and analyze economic, political, and legal constraints to the health of aggregates experienced by the community.

The student is encouraged to become a student of the community, to learn from families and other aggregates in the community how they define and promote their own health. For example, the use of language or terminology varies in different parts of the country by clients and by agencies, and it may vary from that used by government officials. The contributors of the chapters of this textbook represent a diversity of individuals from various parts of the country. Their terms vary from chapter to chapter, as will those in use in local communities. For example, some authors refer to African-Americans, some to blacks, some to Euro-Americans, some to whites. It is important for the student to be familiar with a range of terms and, most important, to know what is used in his or her local community. The student is exposed to the view that the complexity and rich diversity of the community and evidence of how the community organizes to meet change, are strengths.

Outstanding features of this text include **its provocative nature as it raises consciousness regarding the social injustices** that exist in the United States and how these injustices prevent the realization of health as a right for all. The text is designed to **stimulate critical thinking and challenge** students to question and debate issues. Because complex problems demand complex answers, the student is *expected to synthesize prior biophysical, psychosocial, cultural, and ethical arenas of knowledge.* But experiential knowledge is also necessary, and the student is challenged to enter *new environments within the community* and to gain, firsthand, new sensory, cognitive, and affective experiences. The student is introduced to both individual and aggregate roles of the community health nurse as nurses are described engaging collectively and collaboratively in the community's promotion of its own health.

The text's goals are 1) to provide the student with the ability to assess the complex of factors in the community that affect individual, family, and other aggregate responses to health states and actual or potential health problems and 2) to use this ability to plan, implement, and evaluate community health nursing care to increase contributions to the promotion of the health of populations.

RATIONALE FOR AN AGGREGATE APPROACH

The rationale for an aggregate approach is as follows:

- The concept of the aggregate is common to community health nursing. Individuals are members of groups or aggregates such as families, neighborhoods, schools, churches, and other institutions that are organized to make up communities and populations and receive community health nursing care.
- Community health nurses have inherited a long, rich tradition of giving care at the aggregate level.
- A major criticism of current community health nursing practice is a shift away from the aggregate or community focus to a family caseload focus.
- Since 1983, community health nurse educators at national conferences have acknowledged a need for greater emphasis in the baccalaureate curriculum on a community and aggregate focus rather than on the current family theory and family caseload focus. They express a need for models.
- A national survey by Blank, University of Arizona, and McElmurry, University of Illinois at Chicago, described community health nursing

content included in baccalaureate preparation. Of the 339 National League for Nursing–accredited programs asked to participate, 275 (82%) responded. Of schools that responded, 49% of faculty stated they placed "great" emphasis and 42% stated they placed "some" emphasis on the concept of "aggregates" in baccalaureate nursing education. (Blank, J., and McElmurry, B.: An evaluation of consistency in baccalaureate public health nursing education. Public Health Nurs. 3;171–182, 1986).

- Models that provide undergraduate students with aggregate-focused learning experiences, long absent in the literature, are now appearing in papers and poster sessions at national conferences and in community health nursing journals.
- Community health nursing texts, however, have not yet addressed the need for aggregate-focused learning experiences for the undergraduate student.
- This text addresses the need for aggregate-focused learning experiences for both undergraduate and graduate students. It will be of interest also to community health nurses and administrators and to nurses and administrators who practice in the community setting, to graduate students in other schools of health professions, and, in particular, to students in public health.

This text is built on the following major themes:

- A social justice ethic of health care in contrast to a market justice ethic of health care in keeping with the philosophy of public health as "health for all"
- A population-focused model of community health nursing as necessary to achieve equity in health for the entire population
- Appropriate theoretical frameworks related to chapter topics
- The use of population-focused and other community data to develop an assessment, or profile of health, and potential and actual health needs and capabilities of aggregates
- The application of all steps in the nursing process at the individual, family, and aggregate levels
- A focus on identifying needs of the aggregate from common interactions with individuals, families, and communities in traditional environments
- An orientation toward the application of all three levels of prevention at the individual, family, and aggregate levels
- The experience of the underserved aggregate, particularly the economically disenfranchised, including racial and ethnic groups disproportionately at risk of developing health problems

Themes were developed and related to promoting the health of the aggregate in the following ways:

- The commitment of community health nursing is to an equity model, and as such, community health nurses work toward provision of the unmet health needs of the population, including aggregates, in a system that allows access to care only for those who can pay (Chapters 1, 2, and 3).

- The development of a population-focused model is necessary to close the gap between unmet health care needs and health resources on a geographical basis to the entire population. The contributions of intervention at the aggregate level work toward the realization of such a model (Chapters 4–10).
- Contemporary theories provide frameworks for holistic community health nursing practice that help the student conceptualize the reciprocal impact of various components within the community on the health of aggregates and the population (Chapter 4 and throughout).
- The ability to gather population-focused and other community data in developing an assessment of health is a crucial initial step that precedes the identification of nursing diagnoses and plans to meet aggregate responses to potential and actual health problems (Chapter 5).
- The nursing process includes, in each step, a focus on the aggregate: assessment of the aggregate, nursing diagnosis of the aggregate, planning for the aggregate, and intervention and evaluation at the aggregate level (Chapters 5 and 6 and Units 3 and 4).
- The development of the ability to gather cues about the needs of aggregates from complex environments such as with a home visit, with parents in a waiting room of a well-baby clinic, or with elders receiving hypertension screening, and to promote individual, collective, and political action that addresses the health of aggregates (Units 2, 3, and 4).
- Primary, secondary, and tertiary prevention strategies include a major focus at the aggregate level (Units 1, 2, 3, 4, and 5).
- In addition to offering an extended chapter sequence on cultural influences in the community, the text includes data on the experience of underserved aggregates at high risk of developing health problems, groups most often in need of community health nursing services: low and marginal income, racial, and ethnic groups (Chapters 16, 17, 18, and 19 and throughout).

The book is divided into five units. Unit 1 presents an overview of the concept of health, a perspective of health as evolving and as defined by the community, and the concept of community health nursing as the nursing of aggregates from both historical and contemporary mandates. Health is viewed as an individual and a collective right, brought about through individual and collective/political action. The definitions of public health and community health nursing and their foci are presented. Current crises in public health and in the medical care system and consequences for the health of the public frame implications for community health nursing. The historical evolutions of public health, the health care system, and community health nursing are presented. The evolution of humans from wanderers and food gatherers to those who live in groups and the impact of the group on health contrast with the evolution of a health care system built around the individual person, increasingly fractured into many parts. Community health nurses bring to their practice awareness of the social context; of economic, political, and legal constraints from the larger community; and knowledge of the current health care system and its structural constraints and limitations on the care of populations.

Unit 2 presents the art and science of community health nursing. The theoretical foundations for the book and the rationale for an aggregate approach to community health nursing are presented. The application of the nursing process—assessment, planning, intervention, and evaluation—to aggregates in the community using selected theory bases is presented. The unit addresses the need for a population focus that includes the public health sciences of biostatistics and epidemiology as key in the application of the nursing process to aggregates to promote the health of populations. Application of both the art and the science of community health nursing to meet the needs of aggregates is evident in chapters that focus on health planning, community organization, the home visit, health education, and social advocacy.

Unit 3 presents the application of the community health nursing process to aggregates in community health: infants and children, women, men, families, and elders. The focus is on the major indicators of health (longevity, mortality, and morbidity), types of common health problems, pertinent legislation, health services and resources, selected applications of the community health nursing process to a case study, application of the levels of prevention, selected roles of the community health nurse, and relevant research.

Unit 4 addresses the application of the community health nursing process to special needs of aggregates of increasing importance to the community: needs of culturally diverse populations and needs related to family violence, mental health, substance abuse, communicable disease, the work place, the environment, home health care, and rural areas.

Unit 5 presents the future of community health nursing, including the challenge of attaining world health and a model of population-focused nursing in Cuba, which has reached the World Health Organization's goal of providing "health for all" of its citizens, and an overview of the future. This final chapter emphasizes the need for community health nursing to show that it "makes a difference," which calls for an accountability–creativity link from community health nurses in all settings.

JANICE M. SWANSON

MARY ALBRECHT

ACKNOWLEDGMENTS

Many people—individuals, families, groups, and communities—have contributed to this book, although many of these persons and aggregates were not aware of their contributions. In numerous ways, they motivated us to critically review the practice of community health nursing and to speak out for what we believe. Sincere thanks go to everyone who made significant contributions to the book.

We are indebted to our contributing authors, whose beliefs, untiring work, and patience usher in a new era of community health nursing practice that focuses on preparing the graduate to practice at the individual, family, and aggregate levels. We would like to thank the many community health nursing faculty who served as reviewers of earlier drafts of chapters. We also appreciate the understanding support of fellow work colleagues during the undertaking and writing of this book.

Melanie McEwen, Ph.D., R.N., C.S., Assistant Professor, Baylor University School of Nursing, Dallas, is owed special recognition and thanks for writing the Instructor's Manual and test questions to accompany the text.

Special thanks go to Ilze Rader and editors at W.B. Saunders, whose vision and patience have provided the stimulus and support necessary to complete this text. Ilze Rader's suggestions were invaluable, and her time and efforts were greatly appreciated.

CONTENTS

UNIT 1   *Introduction to Community Health Nursing*   1

Chapter 1   *Health: A Community View*   3
Mary Albrecht
Janice M. Swanson
Definitions of Health   5
Definition and Focus of Public Health/Community Health   6
Preventive Approach to Health   6
Definition and Focus of Public and Community Health Nursing   7

Chapter 2   *Historical Factors: Community Health Nursing in Context*   13
Janice M. Swanson
Evolution of the State of Health of Western Populations   14
Advent of Modern Health Care   21
Consequences for the Health of Aggregates   34
Challenges for Community Health Nursing   35

Chapter 3   *The Health Care System*   41
Barbara J. Horn
Beverly M. Horn
Major Legislation and the Health Care System   42
Health Care System   44
Public Health Subsystem   50
Future of the Health Care System   59

UNIT 2   *The Art and Science of Community Health Nursing*   65

Chapter 4   *Thinking Upstream: Conceptualizing Health From a Population Perspective*   67
Patricia G. Butterfield
Thinking Upstream: Looking Beyond the Individual   68
Definitions of Theory   68
Theory to What End?   69
Microscopic Versus Macroscopic Approach   69
Forced Fit? Assessing a Theory's Scope in Relation to Community Health Nursing   70
Format for Review of Theories   71

Chapter 5	***Nursing Process in the Community***	**81**
	Holly B. Cassells	
	The Nature of Community	82
	Assessing the Community: Sources of Data	84
	Epidemiology	91
	Epidemiological Methods	96
	Application of the Nursing Process	103
Chapter 6	***Health Planning***	**109**
	Barbara S. Morgan	
	Patricia M. Burbank	
	Deborah A. Godfrey	
	Overview of Health Planning	110
	Health Planning Model	113
	Health Planning Projects	117
	Health Planning Legislation	123
	Nursing Implications	126
Chapter 7	***Community Organization***	**129**
	Peggy Hickman	
	Definition of Community Organization Practice	130
	Community Organization in Nursing Practice	131
	Community Organization Concepts	132
	Community Organization Models	134
	Community Organization Strategies for Nurses	135
	Application of the Nursing Process Through Community Organization	137
Chapter 8	***The Home Visit***	**143**
	Christine DiMartile Bolla	
	Jean Cozad Lyon	
	Public Health Nursing	144
	Home Health Care	144
	Conducting a Home Visit Using the Nursing Process	145
	Application of the Nursing Process Through Home Visits	149
Chapter 9	***Health Education***	**163**
	Sandra DeBella	
	Health as a Personal Value Within a Social Context	164
	Community Settings	165
	Healthier Lifestyles	166
	Health as a Cultural Value	166
	Learning Theories and Strategies	167
	Concepts of Teaching and Learning	167
	Teaching Strategies Derived from Theories of Learning	169
	Health Education in a Social Context	172
	Freire's Education Model	172
	Health Education Models	175
	Health Education Resources	179

Health Education Evaluation   180
Application of the Nursing Process   181

Chapter 10   *Policy, Politics, Legislation, and Public Health Nursing*   **187**
                    Ruth F. Stewart
                    Madalon O'Rawe Amenta
Nurses Who Made a Difference   188
Public Policy: Blueprint for Governance   193
Government: The Hallmark of Civilization   197
Nursing and the Health of the Nation: A Social Contract   205

UNIT 3   *Aggregates in the Community*   **209**

Chapter 11   *Child Health*   **211**
                    Mary Brecht Carpenter
                    Susan Rumsey Givens
Indicators of Child Health Status   212
Social Factors Affecting Child Health   216
Costs to Society of Poor Child Health   218
Public Health Programs Targeted to Children   219
Strategies to Improve Child Health   221
Application of the Nursing Process   223

Chapter 12   *Women's Health*   **231**
                    Donna Neal Thomas
                    Roma D. Williams
Major Indicators of Health   232
Life Expectancy   232
Mortality   232
Morbidity   235
Other Factors   238
Types of Problems   239
Major Legislation Affecting Women's Health Services   245
Health and Social Services to Promote the Health of Women   247
Roles of the Community Health Nurse   252
Research in Women's Health   253

Chapter 13   *Men's Health*   **257**
                    Janice M. Swanson
Men's Health Status   258
Use of Medical and Preventive Care   260
Theories That Explain Men's Health   261
Factors That Impede Men's Health   266
Factors That Promote Men's Health   269
Men's Health Care Needs   270
Meeting Men's Health Needs   270

Application of the Nursing Process 273
Roles of the Community Health Nurse 280
Research and Men's Health 281

Chapter 14 *Addressing the Needs of Families* **287**
Janice M. Swanson
The Changing Family 289
Approaches to Meeting the Health Needs of Families 290
The Family Theory Approach to Meeting the Health Needs of Families 295
Extending Family Health Intervention to Larger Aggregates and Social Action 307
Application of the Nursing Process 310

Chapter 15 *Senior Health* **329**
Olive T. Roen
Major Indicators of the Health of the Elderly 330
Problems of the Elderly 337
Support for the Elderly 346
New Concepts of Community Care 351
Application of the Nursing Process 352
Allocation of Resources for Senior Health 363
Research on the Health of the Elderly 364
Roles of the Community Health Nurse 364

UNIT 4 *Special Needs of Aggregates* 369

Chapter 16 *Cultural Diversity and Community Health Nursing* **371**
Margaret M. Andrews
Historical Perspective on Cultural Diversity 372
Family 377
Socioeconomic Factors 378
Culture and Nutrition 380
Religion and Culture 381
Cross-Cultural Communication 383
Health-Related Beliefs and Practices 387
Health, Illness, and Cultural Diversity 390
Cultural Expression of Illness 391
Culture and Treatment 393
Cultural Negotiation 394
Solutions to Health Care Problems in Culturally Diverse Populations 394
Community Health Nursing and Culturally Diverse Populations 398
Role of the Community Health Nurse in Improving Health for Culturally
Diverse People 398
Culturological Assessment 399
Cultural Self-Assessment 402
Increase Knowledge About Local Cultures 402
Recognize Political Aspects 402

Provide Culturally Sensitive Care 402
Recognize Culturally Based Health Practices 403

Chapter 17   *Cultural Influence in the Community: The Mexican-American Community* **407**
Ricardo A. Martinez
Reactions to Illness: Understanding as a Prerequisite 408
A Biological Perspective: Disease Prevalence in the Mexican-American
    Community and Access to Health Care 409
The Mexican-American Family 410
Beliefs of Disease Causation Among Mexican-Americans 412
Use of Herbal Medicine Among Mexican-Americans 415
Cultural Adaptation to Health Care in the Community 416
Improving Health Education and Health Communication 418

Chapter 18   *Cultural Influence in the Community: Southeast Asian Refugees* **421**
Marjorie A. Muecke
Background 422
Caring for Southeast Asian Refugee Patients 423

Chapter 19   *The African-American Community* **433**
Margaret M. Andrews
Lucretia Bolin
The African-American Community 435
Social Justice: An African-American Perspective 438
Communication and Language 439
Health Beliefs and Practices 439
Cultural Healers 441
Indicators of Health in the African-American Population 441
Cancer 444
Cardiovascular Disease 445
Chemical Dependency 446
Diabetes 447
Homicide and Unintentional Injuries 447
Infant Mortality 448
AIDS 449
Nursing Care of African-American Individuals, Families, and Communities 450
Biocultural Variations in Assessing African-Americans 451
Laboratory Tests 455
Cross-Cultural Differences in Communication 455
Cultural Sensitivity 456
Cultural Healers and Health Practices 456

Chapter 20   *Family Violence* **459**
Ann C. Watkins
History of Abuse 460
Scope of the Problem 461
Child Abuse 463

	Abuse of Women	467
	Elderly Abuse	472
	Nursing Care of Victims of Family Violence	473
	Application of the Nursing Process	481

Chapter 21   ***Mental Health***   **487**
Mary E. Allen
Community Mental Health Movement   488
Assessment of Aggregate Mental Health   490
Research in Mental Health   501

Chapter 22   ***Substance Abuse***   **505**
Erika Madrid
Joanne M. Hall
Lucretia Bolin
Conceptualizations of Substance Abuse   506
Modes of Intervention   511
Social Network Involvement   515
Vulnerable Aggregates   517
Nursing Perspective on Substance Abuse   521

Chapter 23   ***Communicable Disease***   **533**
Della Dash
Transmission   535
Vaccine-Preventable Diseases   539
Sexually Transmitted Diseases   549
Application of the Nursing Process   557

Chapter 24   ***Environmental Health***   **567**
Patricia E. Stevens
Joanne M. Hall
A Critical Theory Approach to Environmental Health   569
Areas of Environmental Health   570
Effects of Environmental Hazards   580
Efforts to Control Environmental Health Problems   580
Approaching Environmental Health at the Aggregate Level   582
Critical Community Health Nursing Practice   583

Chapter 25   ***The Occupational Health Nurse: Roles and Responsibilities, Current and Future Trends***   **597**
Patricia Hyland Travers
Cherryl E. McDougall
Emerging Demographic Trends   602
Skills and Competencies   606
Primary, Secondary, and Tertiary Levels of Prevention   607
Impact of Legislation on Occupational Health   613

Professional Liability 616
Multidisciplinary Team Work 616

Chapter 26 *Home Health Care* **625**
Jean Cozad Lyon
Theresa M. Stephany
Purpose of Home Health Services 626
Types of Home Health Agencies 626
Educational Preparation of Home Health Nurses and Nursing Standards 628
Nursing Process Applied to Home Care 629
Documentation of Home Care 631
The Family or Caregiver in Home Care 632
Pain Control and Symptom Management 636

Chapter 27 *Rural Health* **641**
Charlene Olivia Lund
Definition of Rurality 642
Historical Perspective 643
Major Indicators and Problems of Rural Health 644
Action for and by the Community 649
Legislation and Political Action 650
Research in Rural Health 658

U N I T 5 *The Future of Community Health Nursing* **661**

Chapter 28 *World Health* **663**
Janice M. Swanson
Karen A. Swanson
Introduction 664
Nursing in Cuba: Population-Focused Practice 667
The Ethics of Health Care in the United States and Cuba 668
Changes in Health Status Since the Revolution 668
Population-Based Nursing Practice 669
Educational Preparation for Population-Based Nursing 673
Critique of Community Health Nursing Within the Cuban Health Care System 674
Implications for Community Health Nursing in the United States 675

Chapter 29 *Community Health Nursing: Making a Difference* **679**
Mary Albrecht
Janice M. Swanson
Collective Activity for Health 682
Determinants of Health 682
Confusion Regarding Health, Health Care, and Medical Care 682
Health as a Right 684

Appendices

I	Standards of Community Health Nursing Practice	689
II	Standards of Home Health Nursing Practice	690
III	Declaration of Alma-Ata	691
IV	Recommendations of the U.S. Preventive Services Task Force	694
V	Healthy People 2000	711

Index   733

Introduction to Community Health Nursing

Health:
A Community View

Upon completion of this chapter, the reader will be able to:

1. Compare and contrast definitions of health as used in public health nursing.

2. Define and discuss the focus of public health.

3. List the three levels of prevention and give one example of each.

4. Differentiate between the conceptual models of community health nursing as defined by the American Nurses' Association and of public health nursing as defined by the Public Health Nursing Section of the American Public Health Association.

Mary Albrecht
Janice M. Swanson

Public health nurses are in a position to assist the U.S. health care system in a transition from a system that is disease oriented to one that is health oriented. Current costs of the care of the sick account for the majority of the escalating health care dollar, which increased from 5.9% of the gross national product in 1965 to 12.2% in 1990 (National Center for Health Statistics, 1992). National annual health care expenditures reached $666 billion in 1990, or $2,566 per person. U.S. health expenditures reflect a focus on care of the sick. In 1990, $0.38 of each health care dollar was spent on hospital care, and $0.19 was spent on physician services, mostly for care of the sick. In contrast, only $0.03 of every health care dollar was spent on preventive government public health activities. Despite hospital and physician expenditures, U.S. health indices rate far below the health indices of many other countries, a consequence that reflects the severe disproportion of funding for preventive services and social and economic opportunities. Furthermore, the health status of the population within the United States varies markedly among areas of the country and among groups, for example, the economically disadvantaged and many cultural and ethnic groups.

Nurses compose the largest group of health care workers and are instrumental in the evolution of a health care delivery system that will meet the health-oriented needs of the people. According to the Fourth National Sample Survey of Registered Nurses conducted by the Division of Nursing, Bureau of Health Professions, Health Resources and Services Administration, in 1988, about two thirds of the approximately 1.6 million employed registered nurses in the United States worked in hospitals and about 11% (approximately 250,000) worked in community, school, or occupational health settings (U.S. Department of Health and Human Services, 1990). The number of nurses employed in hospitals in 1988 represents an increase of 84% over the number employed in hospitals in 1977, whereas the number of nurses employed in community health areas has increased 26% since 1977. However, it has been predicted that there will be a marked decline in hospital employment of nurses and an increase in the number of nurses working in community settings that focus on health promotion and preventive care. More nurses will be employed by alternative delivery systems that provide ambulatory care to meet cost-containment mandates as well as fulfill a growing proportion of health care needs.

Community health nursing is the synthesis of nursing practice and public health practice. The major goal of community health nursing is the preservation of the health of the community and populations through a focus on health promotion and health maintenance of individuals, families, and groups within the community. Thus, community health nursing is oriented toward health and the identification of populations at risk rather than toward an episodic response to patient demand.

The mission of public health is social justice, which entitles all persons to basic necessities such as adequate income and health protection and accepts collective burdens to make such possible. Public health, with its egalitarian tradition and vision, conflicts with the predominant U.S. model of justice: market justice, or the entitlement of people to only what they have gained through individual efforts. Although individual rights are respected, collective action and obligations are minimal. An overinvestment in technology and curative medical services has cut short the evolution of a health ethic to protect and preserve the health of the population. Current U.S. health policy calls for individuals to change behavior that might predispose them to chronic disease or accident. People are asked to exercise, eat healthfully, and give up smoking or alcohol use. However, to ask the individual to overcome the effects of unhealthy social and physical environments negates the collective behavior necessary to change the many determinants of health stemming from those environments such as air and water pollution and work place hazards. As both lifestyle and disease are a result of the environment in which we live, public health policy seeks to bring about not only lifestyle change but also social and environmental changes.

Community health nurses work within the larger health care system and so probably are influenced to accept a narrow view of public health as activities addressing health problems that are unresolvable by the market model of health care and/or call for collective action at the community level. With the predicted changes in the health care system and increasing employment of nurses in the community setting, greater demands will be made on community health nursing to broaden its view of public health. As nurses leave the hospital setting, they bring to the community expertise in working with individuals and families, as well as the mandate in the American Nurses' Association's (ANA) Social Policy Statement to carry out prevention and health promotion. With the move into the community, then, comes a growing responsibility for community health nurses to claim their right to the full synthesis of nursing and public health practice and to increase their alliance with public health to promote and preserve the health of populations.

In this opening chapter, we establish a perspective of health from a community viewpoint. To do so requires definition of how people identify and describe the focus of health and related concepts. Explored are:

- Definitions of health;
- Definition and focus of public and community health;
- What constitutes a preventive approach to health; and
- Definition and focus of public health and community health nursing.

DEFINITIONS OF HEALTH

World Health Organization Definition

In many disciplines, the definition of health is evolving. A trend to define health in social terms rather than in medical terms is reflected in the World Health Organization's classic definition of health (1947, p. 1) as

"a state of complete physical, mental, and social well-being and not merely the absence of disease or infirmity."

Why define health in social terms? "Social" means "of or having to do with human beings living together as a group in a situation requiring that they have dealings with one another" (*Webster's,* 1979, p. 1094). Social, then, refers to units of persons in communities who interact with each other. Social health is a result of positive interaction among groups within the community, such as sponsoring food banks in churches and civic organizations. Social health promotes community vitality — hence the need to define health in social terms. Social health is negatively affected by interaction that results in poverty, violence, and other problems that stem from lack of opportunity for groups within the community.

Public Health Nursing Definitions of Health

Health has been defined as an "optimal level of functioning" by the client (Archer and Fleshman, 1979); "community competence" (Goeppinger et al., 1980); a "purposeful and integrated method of functioning within an environment" (Hall and Weaver, 1977); "fitness as a result of individual adaptation to stress" (Leahy et al., 1982); and "an orientation toward wellness focusing on the maintenance and promotion of the health of the entire population being served" (Lancaster, 1984). Although this variety of definitions illustrates that health is not easy to define, the major problem involves the unit of analysis. For these authors except Archer et al., Goeppinger et al., and Lancaster, the unit of analysis is the individual, and the community is excluded. Many authors include the concepts of stress, adaptation, and environment in definitions of health. Environment is presented as a given to which one must adapt rather than as something that is changing, something that humans have affected and can affect, change, or modify in the future.

Many nurses use Dunn's (1961) concept of wellness, in which family, community, society, and environment are interrelated and have an impact on health. Illness, health, and peak wellness are considered as being on a continuum, with goals being individual performance at a potential consistent with age and other factors and overall goals set for not only the individual but also the family, the community, and society. Health, then, is seen as a fluid and changing state. The state of health depends on the goals and potentials of individuals, families, communities, and societies within an environment affected by the performance of social units; its purpose is to enhance the potential development of such units.

Community Definition of Health

Social units achieve health in multiple, complex ways to meet the demands of rapidly changing conditions. For example, in a social unit of a couple, the elderly woman who has become the caretaker of her ill husband notes that she has less energy than when her husband first became bedfast;

because caring for his incontinence takes so much of her energy, she now withholds a portion of his diuretic to conserve energy she needs to care for him in other ways.

Another example of a social unit is the Sierra Club, whose members lobby for preservation of natural resource lands, or a group of disabled persons who take over an office building to obtain equal access to not only public buildings but also education, jobs, and transportation.

Each of these social units is striving to realize a level of potential "health" beyond that of past states, which, in turn, will provide the impetus for future changes.

It is important for the community health nurse to recognize how the community defines its health, and definitions should be obtained from families, organizations, various groups, and other aggregates (subgroups) within the community.

Communities have a wide range of values. For some, protection of their economic interests is a primary factor in achieving health; for others, human needs and family closeness are primary factors. From the rich cultural diversity within a community, the community health nurse learns many different definitions and views of health.

DEFINITION AND FOCUS OF PUBLIC HEALTH/COMMUNITY HEALTH

C. E. Winslow is known for his classic definition of public health:

"Public health is the Science and Art of (1) preventing disease, (2) prolonging life, and (3) promoting health and efficiency through organized community effort for

(a) the sanitation of the environment,
(b) the control of communicable infections,
(c) the education of the individual in personal hygiene,
(d) the organization of medical and nursing services for the early diagnosis and preventive treatment of disease, and
(e) the development of the social machinery to insure everyone a standard of living adequate for the maintenance of health, so organizing these benefits as to enable every citizen to realize his birthright of health and longevity" (Hanlon, 1960, p. 23).

The key phrase in this definition of public health is "through organized community effort." "Public health" connotes efforts made through public channels such as government agencies like health departments, which serve the people in accordance with legislation supported by taxes (Spradley, 1981).

The newer term "community health" extends the realm of public health to include organized efforts for health at the community level through both government and private efforts, including private agencies supported by private funds, such as the American Heart Association. A mosaic of private and public structures serves community health efforts.

Public health efforts are aimed at prevention and promotion of the health of populations at federal, state, and local levels. Public health efforts at federal and state levels focus on providing supportive and advisory services to public health structures at the local level. Public health structures at the local level provide direct services to communities through two avenues:

- Community health services to protect the public from hazards such as polluted water or air, tainted food, or unsafe housing, and
- Personal health care services such as immunization, well-baby care, family planning services, or care for persons with sexually transmitted diseases.

Personal health services are a part of public health efforts and are targeted to populations most at risk or most in need of services.

Public health efforts are multidisciplinary as they require people with many different skills. Community health nurses work with a diverse team of public health professionals, including epidemiologists, local health officers, and health educators. Special public health sciences are used to assess the needs of populations, and biostatistics provide a method of measuring characteristics and health indices within a community.

PREVENTIVE APPROACH TO HEALTH

Health Promotion and Levels of Prevention

Health promotion and disease prevention compose the focus of public health efforts. Health promotion activities enhance resources aimed at improving well-being, whereas disease prevention activities protect persons from disease and its consequences. There are three levels of prevention (Fig. 1–1 and Table 1–1):

- Primary prevention activities prevent a problem before it occurs, e.g., immunizations to prevent disease;
- Secondary prevention activities provide early detection and intervention, e.g., screening for sexually transmitted diseases; and
- Tertiary prevention activities correct a disease state and prevent it from further deteriorating, e.g., teaching insulin administration in the home (Leavell and Clark, 1958).

Unfortunately, society resists public funding of preventive health care measures. According to Beauchamp (1986), this resistance is due to a mistaken concept of individual responsibility for health, one that is modeled on the ethics of market justice, which gives people only what they are entitled to through their own efforts. Beauchamp calls for an ethic of social justice, which emphasizes society's rather than the individual's responsibility for the protection of all human life to ensure that all persons have their basic needs met, such as adequate health protection and income. Market justice, claims Beauchamp, ignores socially determined preconditions that strongly influence behavior, particularly involving health.

It is the nature of the private sector, however, to vie for more of the health care dollar. The energy of the private sector pulls money into the corporate health care world, which tends to emphasize expensive equipment and supplies, buildings, and pharmaceuticals and to polarize the domains of prevention and cure.

DEFINITION AND FOCUS OF PUBLIC AND COMMUNITY HEALTH NURSING

Public Health Nursing

Freeman (1963) gives a classic definition of public health nursing:

"Public health nursing may be defined as a field of professional practice in nursing and in public health in which technical nursing, interpersonal, analytical, and organizational skills are applied to problems of health as they affect the community. These skills are applied in concert with those of other persons engaged in health care, through comprehensive nursing care of families and other groups and through measures for evaluation or control of threats to health, for health education of the public, and for mobilization of the public for health action" (p. 34).

Public health nursing is a synthesis of public health and nursing practice, as reflected in two contemporary definitions that provide similar yet

---

Level 1.   Primary Prevention Activities
Prevention of problems before they occur

Example: Immunizations

Level 2.   Secondary Prevention Activities
Early detection and intervention

Example: Screening for sexually transmitted disease

Level 3.   Tertiary Prevention Activities
Correction and prevention of deterioration of a disease state

Example: Teaching insulin administration in the home

Figure 1–1
The three levels of prevention.

Table 1–1			
Examples of Levels of Prevention and Clients Served in Community			
	Level of Prevention		
Definition of Client Served*	**Primary (Health Promotion and Specific Prevention)**	**Secondary (Early Diagnosis and Treatment)**	**Tertiary (Limitation of Disability and Rehabilitation)**
Individual	Dietary teaching during pregnancy Immunizations	HIV testing Screening for cervical cancer	Teaching new client with diabetes how to administer insulin Exercise therapy after stroke Skin care for incontinent patient
Family (two or more individuals bound by kinship, law, or living arrangement and with common emotional ties and obligations [see Chapter 13])	Education regarding smoking, dental care, or nutritional counseling Adequate housing	Dental examinations Tuberculin testing for family at risk	Mental health counseling or referral for family in crisis, e.g., grieving, experiencing a divorce Dietary instructions and monitoring for family with overweight members
Group or aggregate (interacting persons with a common purpose or purposes)	Birthing classes for pregnant teenage mothers AIDS and other sexually transmitted disease education for high school students	Vision screening of first grade class Mammography van for screening of women in a low-income neighborhood Hearing tests at a senior center	Group counseling for grade school children with asthma Swim therapy for physically disabled elders at a senior center Alcoholics Anonymous and other self-help groups Mental health services for military veterans
Community and populations (aggregate of people sharing space over time within a social system [see Chapter 5]; population groups or aggregates with power relations and common needs and/or purposes)	Fluoride water supplementation Environmental sanitation Removal of environmental hazards	Organized screening programs for communities, such as health fairs VDRL screening for marriage license applicants in a city Lead screening for children by school district	Shelter and relocation centers for fire or earthquake victims Emergency medical services Community mental health services for chronically mentally ill Home care services for chronically ill

* Note that terms are used differently in literature of various disciplines. There are no clear-cut definitions; for example, families may be referred to as an aggregate, and a population and subpopulations may exist within a community.

distinctive ideologies, or visions of reality. The first definition is from the American Public Health Association (APHA) Ad Hoc Committee on Public Health Nursing (1981):

"Public health nursing synthesizes the body of knowledge from the public health sciences and professional nursing theories for the purpose of improving the health of the entire community. This goal lies at the heart of primary prevention and health promotion and is the foundation for public health nursing practice. To accomplish this goal, public health nurses work with groups, families, and individuals as well as in multidisciplinary teams and programs. Identifying subgroups (aggregates) within the population which are at high risk of illness, disability, or premature death, and directing resources toward these groups, is the most effective approach for accomplishing the goal of [public health nursing]. Success in reducing the risks and in improving the health of the community depends on the involvement of consumers, especially groups experiencing health risks, and others in the community, in health planning, and in self-help activities" (p. 10).

The second definition is from the ANA (1980):

"Community health nursing is a synthesis of nursing practice and public health practice applied to promoting and preserving the health of populations. The practice is general and comprehensive. It is not limited to a particular age group or diagnosis and is continuing, not episodic. The dominant responsibility is to the population as a whole; nursing directed to individuals, families, or groups contributes to the health of the total population. Health promotion, health maintenance, health education and management, coordination, and continuity of care are utilized in a holistic approach to the management of the health care of individuals, families, and groups in a community" (p. 2).

A common theme of these definitions is the provision of nursing service to the community, or population as a whole. Muecke (1984) notes that while the ANA definition focuses on care to individuals, families, and groups within a community, the APHA definition focuses on care to the community as a whole and considers the individual or family *only* when viewed as members of groups at risk. Both definitions are important for addressing

the health of aggregates. Individual and family health in the community are necessary building blocks to the health of populations, but they represent only one facet of health care provision at the aggregate level.

Historically, the public health nursing tradition, begun in the late 1800s by Lillian Wald and her associates, clearly portrays this important distinction (Wald, 1971) (see Chapter 2). After moving into the immigrant community to provide care to individuals and families, these nurses saw that the true determinants of health were not solely combated by bedside clinical nursing, or even by teaching care of the sick to family members in the home. They saw that the social and environmental determinants of health—child labor, pollution, and poverty—had to be addressed through collective political activity aimed at improving the health of aggregates by improving social and environmental conditions. Community organization, establishment of school nursing, and taking impoverished mothers to testify in Washington were the types of activities engaged in by Wald and her colleagues that had an impact on the health of the community (Wald, 1971).

Today, interventions with families and individuals in the community, although important, are incomplete unless they are extended to intervention at the aggregate level. Aggregate care encompasses care based on the ANA definition of community health nursing as well as care extended to aggregates identified by the APHA.

The distinction between actions based on the two definitions is made clearly by Muecke (1984) in an example involving provision of prenatal care to adolescents. According to Muecke, a nurse subscribing to the ANA definition would focus on each family in the caseload and address the problem of low-birth-weight infants among this population through individual family assessment of nutritional factors, health education related to nutrition and fetal development, and referral to community resources for nutritional services.

The nurse who subscribes to the APHA definition would focus on characteristics of the community as a whole. The nurse would determine the proportion of teenagers in the community and rates of teenage pregnancy, intervene at the community level by assessing teenagers' sources of nutrition, and work politically to make nutritious

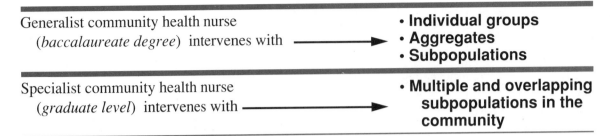

Figure 1–2
Differences in generalist and specialist applications of population focus.

foods available to teenagers in settings such as in food vending machines in schools, or the nurse would lobby for nutritional supplements to be provided to low-income pregnant women in the community. Thus, aggregate care extends the concept of individual and family care to care of the population as a whole.

Population-Focused Practice

Williams (1992) states that community health nurses must use a population-focused approach to move beyond the orientation of providing direct care to individuals and families. Although individuals and organizations may be responsible for a specific subpopulation in the community (e.g., a school may be responsible for its pregnant teenagers), population-focused practice ultimately is concerned with many community subpopulations, both distinct and overlapping. That is, population-focused community health nurses would not limit their interest to one or two subpopulations but rather focus on the many subpopulations that compose the entire community. A population focus involves concern for those who do not receive health services as well as for those who do. A population focus also involves a scientific approach to community health nursing in that an assessment of the community or population is necessary and basic to planning, intervention, and evaluation at the individual, family, aggregate, and population levels.

This text proposes that the difference between the generalist and the specialist application of a population focus is that the generalist community health nurse with baccalaureate preparation is able to plan and intervene with individual groups, aggregates, and subpopulations, whereas the specialist community health nurse with graduate preparation is able to plan and intervene with multiple and overlapping subpopulations within the community (Fig. 1–2). Regardless of the level of practice, however, both generalist and specialist community health nurses must be aware of and use a population focus to aid in assessment, planning, intervention, and evaluation with larger units. A population focus also is needed to plan care required by groups of individuals and groups of families with needs that are not addressed within a community.

According to Williams (1984), a population focus bases assessment and management decisions on the status of a subpopulation. The subpopulation may be made up of a group of individuals (e.g., unmarried, pregnant teenagers), a group of families (e.g., families with high-risk infants less than 1 year old), or a group of "groups" (e.g., children in several age groups or classes in a school).

A scientific approach to, or population focus on, community health nursing practice requires two types of data: the epidemiology, or body of knowledge, of a particular problem and its solution, and information about the community (Williams, 1984). Each type of knowledge and its source are presented in Table 1–2.

Data collection for assessment and management decisions should be ongoing within a community, not episodic, to best determine the overall patterns of health in a population. Many of the data that are needed for surveillance of a community are gathered inadequately or are nonexistent (Miller et al., 1986).

Aggregate-Focused Practice

Community health nurses focus on the care of not only individuals but also aggregates in many settings, including homes, clinics, and schools. In ad-

Table 1–2
Data Required for Population Focus

Body of Knowledge About Problem		Information About the Community	
Definition	Sources	Definition	Sources
Cause or etiology	Epidemiological research	Demographic data	Demographics such as age, sex, and socioeconomic and racial distributions
Groups at high risk	Community health nursing research	Health status of the subpopulations	
Treatment methods			Vital statistics such as mortality and morbidity
Effectiveness of treatment methods	Clinical research in nursing and medicine	Services given to various subpopulations	
	Research in other fields	Measure of effectiveness of services	Annual reports of health care organizations
			Services provided by health planning agencies
			Computerized information systems for monitoring high-risk population

Data from Williams, C. A.: Population-focused practice. *In* Stanhope, M., and Lancaster, J., eds. Community Health Nursing: Process and Practice for Promoting Health. St. Louis: C. V. Mosby, 1984, p. 809.

dition to interviewing clients and assessing individual and family health, community health nurses must be able to assess an aggregate's health needs and resources; to identify its values; to work with the community to identify and implement programs that meet health needs; and to evaluate the effectiveness of programs after their implementation. School nurses, for example, no longer only run first-aid stations but also are actively involved in assessing the needs of their population and in defining programs to meet those needs through activities such as health screening and group health education and promotion. Activities of school nurses may be as varied as designing health curricula with a school/community advisory group, leading support groups for elementary school children with chronic illness, and monitoring the health status of teenage mothers.

Similarly, occupational health nurses are no longer tied to an office or dispensary but are involved in monitoring records of workers' complaints resulting from excessive exposure to physical or chemical risks, or in classes for workers with health-related problems such as alcoholism.

Community health nurses also are employed in private associations such as the American Diabetes Association, where their organizational abilities as well as their health-related skills are used. Other community health nurses work with multidisci-

plinary groups of professionals, serve on boards of voluntary health associations such as the American Heart Association, are members of health planning agencies and councils, and form and work with nursing organizations directed at major public health problems, such as the Nurses' Environmental Health Watch. Education of nurses regarding environmental conditions and threats to the health of populations, such as nuclear armament, is carried out to involve nurses in collective activity aimed at improving environmental conditions at national, state, and local levels (McCarty and Pratt, 1986).

Community health nurses are also involved in the Public Health Nursing Section of the APHA and the Division of Community Health Nursing of the ANA and perform activities such as updating the definition and role of community health nursing. Community health nurses involved in state nurses' associations perform activities such as promoting health-related legislation, promoting the use of safety infant car seats, and serving on state task forces that address health issues.

SUMMARY

Community health nurses have knowledge and skills that enable them to work in diverse community settings, ranging from the isolated rural area to the crowded urban ghetto. To meet the health needs of the population, the community health nurse must work with many individuals and groups within the community. A sensitivity to these groups and a respect for the community and its established method of managing its problems will enable the community health nurse to become more proficient in helping the community improve its health.

Learning Activities

1. Interview several community health nurses and several clients regarding their definitions of health. Share the results with your classmates. Do you agree with their definitions? Why or why not?

2. Interview several community health nurses regarding their opinions on what is the focus of community health nursing. Do you agree?

3. Ask several neighbors or consumers of health care about what they believe is the role of public health and community health nursing. Share your results with your classmates.

REFERENCES

American Nurses' Association: A Conceptual Model of Community Health Nursing. ANA Publication No. CH-10. Kansas City, Missouri, ANA, 1980.

American Public Health Association, Ad Hoc Committee on Public Health Nursing: The definition and role of public health nursing practice in the delivery of health care. The Nation's Health, September 1981.

Archer, S. E., and Fleshman, E. P.: Community Health Nursing Patterns and Practice. 2nd Ed. North Scituate, Massachusetts, Duxbury Press, 1979.

Beauchamp, D. E.: Public health as social justice. In Mappes, T., and Zembaty, J., eds.: Biomedical Ethics. 2nd Ed. New York, McGraw-Hill, 1986, pp. 585–593.

Dunn, H. L.: High Level Wellness. Arlington, Virginia, R. W. Beatty, Ltd., 1961.

Ehrenreich, B., and English, D.: Witches, Midwives, and Nurses: A History of Women Healers. Old Westbury, New York, The Feminist Press, 1973.

Freeman, R. B.: Public Health Nursing Practice. 3rd Ed. Philadelphia, W. B. Saunders, 1963.

Goeppinger, J., Lassiter, P. G., and Wilcox, B.: Community health is community competence. Nurs. Outlook 30;464–467, 1980.

Hall, J. E., and Weaver, B. R.: Distributive Nursing Practice: A Systems Approach to Community Health. Philadelphia, J. B. Lippincott, 1977.

Hanlon, J. J.: Principles of Public Health Administration. 3rd Ed. St. Louis, C. V. Mosby, 1960.

Leahy, K. M., Cobb, M. M., and Jones, M. C.: Community Health Nursing. 4th Ed. New York, McGraw-Hill, 1982.

Leavell, H. R., and Clark, E. G.: Preventive Medicine for the Doctor in His Community. New York, McGraw-Hill, 1958.

McCarty, T. L., and Pratt, M. A.: Nuclear freeze and disarmament: A mandate for community health nursing. Public Health Nurs. 3;71–79, 1986.

Miller, C. A., Fine, A., Adams-Taylor, S., and Schorr, L. B.: Monitoring Children's Health: Key Indicators. Washington, D. C., American Public Health Association Publications Department, 1986.

Muecke, M. A.: Community health diagnosis in nursing. Public Health Nurs. 1;23–35, 1984.

National Center for Health Statistics: Health, United States, 1991. Hyattsville, Maryland: Public Health Service, 1992.

Spradley, B. W.: Community Health Nursing: Concepts and Practice. Boston, Little, Brown, and Co., 1981.

Stanhope, M., and Lancaster, J., eds.: Community Health Nursing: Process and Practice for Promoting Health. St. Louis, C. V. Mosby, 1984.

U.S. Department of Health and Human Services, Health Resources and Services Administration, Bureau of Health Professions, Division of Nursing: The Registered Nurse Population: Findings From the National Sample Survey of Registered Nurses. Springfield, Virginia: National Technical Information Service, 1990.

Wald, L. D.: The House on Henry Street. New York, Dover Publications, Inc., 1971.

Webster, N. Webster's Deluxe Unabridged Dictionary. New York, Simon and Shuster, 1979.

Williams, C. A.: Population-focused practice. In Stanhope, M., and Lancaster, J., eds.: Community Health Nursing: Process and Practice for Promoting Health. St. Louis, C. V. Mosby, 1984, pp. 805–815.

Williams, C. A.: Community-based population-focused practice: The foundation of specialization in public health nursing. In Stanhope, M., and Lancaster, J., eds.: Community Health Nursing. Process and Practice for Promoting Health. 3rd Ed. St. Louis, C. V. Mosby, 1992, pp. 244–252.

World Health Organization: Chronicle of WHO. 1;1–2, 1947. New York, WHO, 1958.

Historical Factors: Community Health Nursing in Context

Upon completion of this chapter, the reader will be able to:

1. Describe the impact of the aggregate on the health of populations from the hunting and gathering stage to the present.

2. Trace approaches to the health of aggregates from prehistoric times to the present.

3. Analyze three historical events that have influenced a holistic approach to the health of populations.

4. Compare the application of the principles of public health to the nation's major health problems at the turn of the century (infectious disease) with that in the 1980s (chronic disease).

5. Describe two leaders in nursing who had a profound impact on addressing the health of aggregates.

6. Discuss two major contemporary issues facing community health nursing, and trace their historical roots to the present.

Janice M. Swanson

This chapter presents an overview of selected historical factors that influenced the evolution of community health nursing and help explain present-day challenges. Areas examined are: 1) evolution of the state of health of Western populations from prehistoric to recent times; 2) the evolution of modern health care, including public health nursing; 3) consequences for the health of aggregates; and 4) challenges for community health nursing.

EVOLUTION OF THE STATE OF HEALTH OF WESTERN POPULATIONS

Historically, the study of the evolution of humankind seldom takes into consideration the interrelationship of an individual's environment and health and the nature and size of the aggregate of which the individual is a member. Medical anthropologists use paleontological records and accounts of disease in primitive societies to base their speculations of the interrelationship among early humans, probable diseases, and environment (Armelagos

and Dewey, 1978). Historians have also documented the existence since prehistoric times of public health activity, i.e., an organized community effort to prevent disease, prolong life, and promote health. The impact on the health of Western populations due to the aggregate and early public health efforts is presented in the following.

Aggregate Impact on Health

Polgar (1964) defines five stages in the disease history of humankind: 1) hunting and gathering, 2) settled villages, 3) preindustrial cities, 4) industrial cities, and 5) the present (Fig. 2–1). In these stages, changes in cultural adaptation occurred as consequences of increased population, increased population density, and the ecological imbalance that results when humans tamper with their environment to accommodate group living. Human tampering, in turn, had a marked consequence on health. Although these stages often have been used to portray the evolution of civilization, it is important to note that they have limitations. First, the stages depict the evolution of Western civilization as chronicled from the perspective of the Western

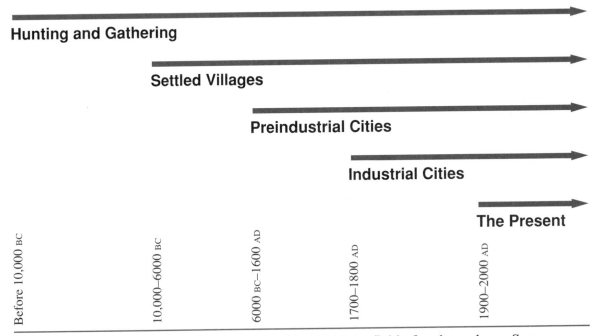

Hunting and Gathering

Settled Villages

Preindustrial Cities

Industrial Cities

The Present

Before 10,000 BC   10,000–6000 BC   6000 BC–1600 AD   1700–1800 AD   1900–2000 AD

Stages overlap and time periods are widely debated in the field of anthropology. Some form of each stage remains evident in the world today.

Figure 2–1
Stages in the disease history of humankind.

world. Second, the stages are not discrete historical time periods but instead overlap; the time periods often associated with the stages are widely debated in the field of anthropology. The stages do provide, however, a frame of reference to aid in determination of the relationship among humans, disease, and environment since before recorded history to the present day. Although the stages chronicle the initiation of each stage in the Western world, it is important to realize that each stage exists in civilization today. For example, Australian aborigines still hunt and gather food, and settled villages are common in many countries, especially Third World countries.

Of importance to the community nurse is awareness that populations from each stage represent a great variety of persons who have distinct cultural traditions and a broad range of health care practices and beliefs. For example, a nurse in a U.S. community may have to plan care for immigrants or refugees from a settled village or preindustrial city. It is important for nurses in the community to

Mexico is accredited with protecting these mothers compared with U.S.-born mothers of Mexican descent, in whom the risk-associated behaviors of drinking and smoking increased. Similarly, the HHANES data showed that acculturation into U.S. society by Mexican-Americans, Puerto Ricans, and Cuban-Americans was associated with an increase in illicit drug use (Amaro et al., 1990). An increase in risk-associated behaviors was attributed to influences of the norms and practices of the dominant U.S. culture.

HUNTING AND GATHERING STAGE

During the Paleolithic period (Old Stone Age), nomadic and seminomadic peoples lived by hunting and gathering food. For 2 million years, small groups (aggregates) wandered in search of food. Armelagos and Dewey (1980) reviewed how the health of hunters and gatherers probably was affected by their size, density, and relationship to the environment. For example, a wide range of foods was eaten, which probably provided a diverse se-

---

Hispanic Health and Nutrition Examination Survey

DATA FROM the Hispanic Health and Nutrition Examination Survey (HHANES) (conducted in 1982–1984) of Mexican-Americans, Puerto Ricans, and Cuban-Americans living in the United States showed that generational differences in perinatal health exist among the Mexican-American population. Low-birth-weight rates were higher among second-generation U.S.-born mothers of Mexican descent than among first-generation Mexico-born mothers. The U.S.-born mothers were at 60% higher risk for having low-birth-weight babies than were mothers born in Mexico. The authors state that a "Mexican cultural orientation protects [the] first genera-

tion" (p. 61). Although second-generation mothers had more education and higher incomes and used health care more than first-generation mothers, behaviors such as smoking and drinking increased in the second-generation mothers (Guendelman et al., 1990).

The HHANES revealed other risk-associated behaviors among Hispanics in the United States as a result of influences by the norms and practices of the dominant U.S. culture. Acculturation into the U.S. society (English language use) was found to be associated with higher rates of use of illicit drugs. This association held for all three Hispanic groups even when demographic variables such as gender, age, income, and education were controlled for (Amaro et al., 1990).

---

recognize not only the health risks faced by each aggregate but also the strengths and contributions made by the host culture and environment to the health status of each particular aggregate. Data from the Hispanic Health and Nutrition Examination Survey (HHANES) (conducted in 1982–1984) show that perinatal outcomes among Mexican-born women worsen corresponding to the length of time lived in the United States (Guendelman et al., 1990). The "cultural orientation" of

lection of nutrients. Hunters and gatherers are thought to have suffered from wounds and from diseases caused by parasites, such as lice and pinworms; from diseases transmitted by insect bites, such as sleeping sickness and relapsing fever; and from diseases caused by eating infected meat, such as trichinosis and tularemia. These people are thought to have had few contagious diseases because the scattered aggregates were not sufficiently large, were not stationary, and were not in contact with other aggregates often enough to sustain the diseases. The disposal of human feces and waste was not perceived of as a great problem as the people were nomadic; caves probably were abandoned as waste accumulated.

SETTLED VILLAGE STAGE

Small settlements are characteristic of the Mesolithic (Middle Stone Age) and Neolithic (New Stone Age) periods. As wandering peoples became sedentary, small encampments and villages were formed. The concentration of people in small areas brought different kinds of problems. For example, the domestication of animals led to living close to herds, which probably transmitted diseases such as salmonella, anthrax, Q fever, and tuberculosis (Polgar, 1964). The domestication of plants probably reduced the range of nutrients compared with that available from gathering days and may have led to diseases of deficiency. Water had to be secured, and wastes had to be disposed of. With the evolution of the agricultural societies, other diseases probably appeared; scrub typhus, for example, increases with cultivation of new ground, and malaria appears with creation of new mosquito breeding areas. With irrigation, schistosomiasis increases; medical anthropologists have found references to such a parasite in ancient Chinese and Mesopotamian literature (Brothwell, 1978).

PREINDUSTRIAL CITIES STAGE

With expanding populations, large urban centers formed in preindustrial times. Preexisting problems increased with even larger populations living in small areas. For example, food and water had to be supplied to a larger population, and greater amounts of waste products had to be removed. Elaborate water systems were developed in some cultures. For example, in Mexico City, the Aztec king Ahuitzutl had a stone pipeline built to transport spring water to the inhabitants (Duran, 1964). However, removal of wastes via the water supply led to diseases such as cholera. With the development of towns, rodent infestation increased and facilitated the spread of plague. Because more people had more frequent contact, the transmission of disease by contact increased, and endemics occurred, such as mumps, measles, influenza, and smallpox (Polgar, 1964). A population must reach a certain size for it to maintain a disease in endemic proportions; for example, approximately 1 million persons are needed to sustain measles at an endemic level (Cockburn, 1967). Different forms of disease also appeared. Syphilis, originally a nonvenereal disease, became a venereal disease because of changes in population density, the family, and sexuality (Hudson, 1965). This and other diseases were carried to other countries by explorers. Occupational threats to health resulted from handling of poisons in mining and metal processing, handling of pottery glazes, and using poisons directly in fishing and hunting (Brothwell, 1978).

INDUSTRIAL CITIES STAGE

With industrialization, urban areas became more dense and heavily populated, and the slum areas expanded. Increased industrial wastes, increased air and water pollution, and harsh working conditions took their toll on health. For example, there was an increase in respiratory diseases such as tuberculosis, pneumonia, and bronchitis; common during the 18th and 19th centuries were epidemics of infectious diseases such as diphtheria, smallpox, typhoid fever, typhus, measles, malaria, and yellow fever (Armelagos and Dewey, 1978). Enactment of imperialism spread epidemics to populations who had no immunity.

PRESENT STAGE

Although infectious diseases no longer account for a majority of mortalities in the Western world, they remain prevalent in the West among low-income populations and in some racial and ethnic groups and account for many mortalities in the non-Western world. Diseases characteristic of Western populations are almost unknown in traditional communities and appear with adaptation to Western customs (Burkitt, 1978). These diseases include large bowel diseases such as cancer, diverticulitis, and ulcerative colitis; venous disorders including varicose veins, thrombosis, pulmonary embolism, and hemorrhoids; heart disease; obesity; diabetes; and gallstones. These diseases occurred infrequently in the Western world until the past 100 years and have increased significantly during the past 50 years. Changes from traditional patterns of life to urban environments appear to be associated with the appearance of these diseases. Epidemiological studies suggest that common factors are changes in diet, especially increases in refined sugar and fats, and lack of fiber; environmental and occupational hazards are also beginning to be identified. An increase in population and density of population also increases mental and behavioral disorders (Garn, 1963).

As wandering, hunting, and gathering aggregates became sedentary and grew into large populations, the disease patterns as well as demands on environment changed. Humans fit reasonably well into the natural world but have had to adapt to an overpopulated, largely urban existence with marked consequences for health, i.e., mortalities that have changed in nature from infectious to chronic. Public health efforts traditionally have been viewed as 18th- and 19th-century activities associated with the Sanitary Revolution. Historians have shown, however, that organized community efforts toward preventing disease, prolonging life, and promoting health have also occurred since prehistoric times.

Evolution of Early Public Health Efforts

Public health efforts have evolved slowly over time. The evolution of organized public health efforts is traced briefly here, highlighting the periods of 1) prehistoric times (before 5000 B.C.); 2) classical times (3000 B.C. to 200 B.C.); 3) Middle Ages (500 A.D. to 1500 A.D.); 4) Renaissance (15th, 16th, and 17th centuries); 5) 18th century; and 6) 19th century. It is important to note, however, that as with the disease history of humankind, public health efforts exist in various stages of development throughout the world. A brief history encapsulates organized public health efforts as viewed by the Western world.

PREHISTORIC TIMES

Early nomadic humans became domesticated and tended to live in ever-larger groups. Episodes of life, health, sickness, and death are inevitably shared by members of aggregates ranging from family to community. Health practices, whether based on superstition or sanitation, evolved as a way for many aggregates to ensure survival. For example, from earliest records, it has been documented that primitive societies have used elements of psychosomatic medicine (e.g., voodoo), isolation (e.g., banishment), and fumigation (e.g., smoke) to manage disease and thus protect the community (Hanlon and Pickett, 1984).

CLASSICAL TIMES

As early as 3000–1400 B.C., the Minoans devised ways to flush water and construct drainage systems. Circa 1000 B.C., the Egyptians constructed elaborate drainage systems, developed pharmaceutical preparations, and embalmed the dead. Pollution has long been a problem; in *Exodus,* it was reported that "All the waters that were in the river stank," and *Leviticus* contains the first written hygiene code, formulated by the Hebrews, which dealt with laws governing both personal and community hygiene, such as contagion, disinfection, and sanitation through the protection of water and food.

GREECE. Greek literature contains accounts of communicable diseases such as diphtheria, mumps, and malaria (Rosen, 1958). The Hippocratic book *Airs, Waters and Places,* a treatise on the balance between humans and their environment, is said to have been the only such volume on this topic until the development of bacteriology in the late 19th century (Rosen, 1958). Diseases that were always present in a population, such as colds and pneumonia, were called *endemic.* Those that were not always present but flared up on occasion, such as diphtheria and malaria, were called *epidemic.* Another important distinction made by the Greeks was their emphasis on the preservation of health, as personified by the goddess Hygeia, or good living, as well as on curative medicine, as personified by the goddess Panacea. Life had to be in balance with the demands of environment, and the importance of factors such as exercise, rest, and nutrition were weighed according to factors such as age, sex, constitution, and climate (Rosen, 1958). However, only the aristocracy could afford to be concerned with maintaining a healthful lifestyle, and the masses, in particular, the slaves who supported the economy, could not afford to maintain "health" (Rosen, 1958).

Disease Definitions

Endemic: Diseases that are always present in a population.
   Examples: colds, pneumonia
Epidemic: Diseases that are not always present in a population but flare up on occasion.
   Examples: Diphtheria, malaria

Pandemic: The existence of disease in a
large proportion of the population.
Example: Outbreaks of annual influenza
type A

ROME. The Romans readily adopted Greek culture but far surpassed the Greeks in engineering ability, as evidenced by massive aqueducts, bathhouses, and sewer systems. For example, records show that at the height of the Roman Empire, Rome provided 40 gallons of water per person per day to its 1 million inhabitants, which is comparable with modern rates of consumption (Rosen, 1958). Inhabitants of the overcrowded Roman slums, however, did not share in such public health amenities as sewer systems and latrines.

Rome Versus California
ROME SUPPLIED an amount of water (40 gallons) per person per day roughly equivalent to that necessary for a California resident. In California in 1991, the San Francisco Bay Area as well as many other areas of the state faced water rationing owing to prolonged drought conditions. Residents of Marin County, north of San Francisco, were restricted to 50 gallons of water per person per day. At the height of the drought, 50 gallons of water per person per day was considered sufficient for table use, bathing, and sewer systems.

The Romans also made mention of occupational health, in particular referring to the pallor of the miners, the danger of suffocation, and "vitriolic fumes" (Rosen, 1958, p. 46). Safeguards were devised and used by the miners in the form of bags, sacks, and masks made of membranes and bladder skins.

Priests dispensed medicine in the early years of the Roman Republic; Greek physicians migrated to Rome. Medical care benefited the aristocracy rather than the poor, who used folk medicine. Public physicians were appointed to towns and paid to care for the poor as well as being allowed to charge a fee for service to those who could pay. As a prototype of a health maintenance organization or group practice, several families paid a set fee for yearly services. Hospitals, surgeries, and infirmaries (for slaves) as well as nursing home–type structures appeared. A hospital for the sick poor was

established by Fabiola, a Christian woman who lived in the 4th century; this model was repeated throughout medieval times.

Romans Provided Public Health Services
ROMANS PROVIDED public health services that included the following (Rosen, 1958):

● A Water Board to maintain the aqueducts
● A supervisor of the public baths
● Street cleaners
● Supervision of the sale of food

MIDDLE AGES

The decline of Rome circa 500 A.D. led to the Middle Ages, during which magic and religion were applied to health problems. Collective activity on behalf of health occurred largely through the monasteries. Measures to protect the public are reflected in reports of wells and fountains, street cleaning, and disposal of refuse. Communicable diseases occurred and included measles, smallpox, diphtheria, leprosy, and bubonic plague. Physicians had little to offer, and the management of leprosy, in particular, was taken over by the church, which used hygienic codes from *Leviticus* and established isolation and leper houses, or leprosaria (Rosen, 1958). Response to the plague (Black Death) of the 14th century, which claimed close to half the world's population at that time, led to the establishment of public health practices such as quarantine of ships, isolation, and disinfection that are still carried out today (Hanlon and Pickett, 1984). Ships without crews were reported drifting about the Mediterranean Sea, infecting ports with which they came into contact. *Pandemic* (the existence of disease in a large proportion of the population) waves of plague and other communicable diseases swept over Europe well into the 18th century. Although bubonic plague ravaged the population and quarantine was used to protect people, the role of fleas and rodents in its existence was not known for centuries.

**Human Plague Case Documented in
the United States**
THE DISEASE human plague is endemic and, on occasion epidemic in Africa, Asia, and South America. There were reports of 770 cases from 11 countries in 1989. A low frequency of human plague occurs in the United

States owing to the usual control of plague in most parts of the world and the immunization of persons at high risk (e.g., military personnel and Peace Corps volunteers). A recorded case of plague in the United States occurred in Washington, D. C., in 1990, in a 47-year-old mammologist from the United States who had been collecting small rats for study in La Paz, Bolivia. She had not received a booster immunization for plague since 1971 (Wolfe et al., 1991).

During the Middle Ages physicians usually were clergymen and treated mostly kings and noblemen. Hospitals were largely small houses in which nursing care was provided by monks and nuns. Hygiene was written about in medieval tracts and addressed such topics as housing, diet, personal cleanliness, and sleep (Rosen, 1958).

THE RENAISSANCE

The Renaissance began in the 14th and 15th centuries and marked an era of expanding trade, population growth, and migration. Interest in human dignity, human rights, and scientific truth was awakening, as seen in discourses by Galileo, Spinoza, and Descartes:

Life in an English Household in the 16th Century
THE WAY life was lived in the 16th century as described in the following account by Erasmus must have affected health; such accounts continued to appear in the literature into the 19th century (Hanlon and Pickett, 1984, p. 26):

"AS TO floors, they are usually made with clay, covered with rushes that grow in the fens and which are so seldom removed that the lower parts remain sometimes for twenty years and has in it a collection of spittle, vomit, urine of dogs and humans, beer, scraps of fish and other filthiness not to be named."

The cause of infectious disease was yet to be discovered. Two events important to public health occurred during this time. In 1546, Girolamo Fracastoro presented a theory of infection as a cause and epidemic a consequence of "seeds of disease." In 1676, Anton van Leeuwenhoek described microscopic organisms but did not associate them with disease (Rosen, 1958).

Measures taken to deal with poverty resulted in the Elizabethan Poor Law, which was enacted in England in 1601 and put the responsibility of providing relief for the poor upon the parishes. This law governed care for the poor for more than two centuries and served as a prototype for later U.S. laws.

18TH CENTURY

GREAT BRITAIN. The 18th century was marked by imperialism and industrialization. Sanitary conditions remained a great problem:

"THE ROADS around London were neither very attractive nor very safe. The land adjoining them was watered with drains and thickly sprinkled by laystalls and refuse heaps. Hogs were kept in large numbers on the outskirts and fed on the garbage of the town. . . . In 1706 it was said of the highways, though they are mended every summer, yet everybody knows that for a mile or two about this City, the same and the ditches hard by are commonly so full of nastiness and stinking dirt, that oftentimes many persons who have occasion to go in or come out of town, are forced to stop their noses to avoid the ill-smell occasioned by it" (George, 1925, cited in Hanlon and Pickett, 1984, p. 27).

During the Industrial Revolution, in which a gradual change in production occurred, lives were sacrificed for profit, particularly the lives of poor children, who were forced into labor. The parishes, which were given responsibility for providing relief for the poor under the Elizabethan Poor Law, established workhouses to employ the poor. Orphaned and poor children, who were wards of the parishes, were placed in parish workhouses, where they were forced to labor for long hours at an early age (George, 1925). Those apprenticed to chimney sweeps were reported to suffer the worst fate—they were forced into chimneys at the risk of being burned and suffocated and made to beg and steal. At 12–14 years of age, children were apprenticed to a master, a worse fate for most, as stated by a writer on the Poor Laws in 1738:

"The master may be a tiger in cruelty, he may beat, abuse, strip naked, starve, or do what he will with the innocent lad, few people take much notice, and the officers who put him out the least of anybody . . ." (Hanlon and Pickett, 1984, p. 24).

A major discovery of the times was inoculation. In 1796, Edward Jenner observed that persons who worked around cattle were less likely to have smallpox. He discovered that immunity to smallpox resulted from inoculation with cowpox virus. Jenner's contribution was significant because during the 18th century, approximately 95% of the population suffered from smallpox, as evidenced by a pocked face, and approximately 10% of the population died of it.

Although liberal views of human nature were being expounded by men such as Hume, Voltaire, and Rousseau in Europe and Adams, Jefferson, and Franklin in America, public health reforms culminating in the Sanitary Revolution were beginning to take place throughout Europe and especially in England. The study of community health problems using the survey method, which dates from Hippocrates, was further developed in the 18th century (Rosen, 1958). Geographical factors related to health and the diseases by region were mapped as "medical topographies." A health education movement provided books and pamphlets on health to the middle and upper classes; it was said to neglect "economic factors" and did not concern the working classes (Rosen, 1958).

19TH CENTURY

Communicable diseases ravaged the population who lived in unsanitary conditions. Each year in the mid-1800s, typhus and typhoid fever claimed twice as many lives as did the battle of Waterloo (Hanlon and Pickett, 1984).

Edwin Chadwick called attention to the cost of the unsanitary conditions which shortened the life span of the laboring class in particular, from whence came the wealth of the nation. The first sanitary legislation was passed in 1837, establishing a National Vaccination Board. However, in 1842, according to Chadwick, death rates were high in large industrial cities such as Liverpool; more than half of all children of working class parents died by age 5. Laborers lived an average of 16 years compared with 22 years for tradesmen and 36 for the upper classes (Richardson, 1887). In 1842, Chadwick published his famous *Report on an Inquiry Into the Sanitary Conditions of the Laboring Population of Great Britain*. One consequence of

the report was the establishment of the General Board of Health for England in 1848. Legislation for social reform followed and was concerned with child welfare, care of elders, the sick, mentally ill, factory management, and education. The appearance of a water supply, sewers, fireplugs, and sidewalks marked the new changes.

Public Health Interventions Used in the Third World Needed in the United States
IN 1991, a conference sponsored by the National Council on International Health and public health organizations in San Francisco, California, urged public health professionals to consider using technology from the Third World to handle Third World health conditions that exist in the United States. For example, each year in the United States about 500 babies die of dehydration, a common problem in the Third World, and about 200,000 are hospitalized for this condition, at a cost of about $500 million a year. Use of a United Nations Children's Fund device to help parents treat dehydration was recommended. The device is a block of wood into which are bored wells that hold the appropriate amounts of sugar and salt to be mixed with water to create a solution to rehydrate the baby. In addition, the conference recommended that funds be shifted from high-technology interventions to hiring more public health nurses to work in needy communities to introduce methods of care that are inexpensive.

Data from State studies Third World solutions. NURSEWEEK, Northern California Edition, March 18, 1991, p. 5.

Social action — bettering the lives of the people through improving economic, social, and environmental conditions — to attack the root social causes of disease was argued for in 1849 by Rudolf Virchow, a pathologist. He proposed ". . . a theory of epidemic disease as a manifestation of social and cultural maladjustment" (Rosen, 1958, p. 86). He further argued that the health of the people was the responsibility of the public, that health and disease were heavily affected by social and economic conditions, that efforts to promote health and fight disease must be social and economic as well as medical, and that the social and economic determinants of health and disease must be studied to yield knowledge to guide appropriate action. These principles were best embodied in a draft for a public health law to the Berlin Society of

Physicians and Surgeons in 1849 by Neumann (Rosen, 1958):

"According to this document, public health has as its objectives (1) the healthy mental and physical development of the citizen; (2) the prevention of all dangers to health; and (3) the control of disease. Public health must care for society as a whole by considering the general physical and social conditions that may adversely affect health, such as soil, industry, food, and housing, and it must protect each individual by considering those conditions that prevent him from caring for his health" (p. 255).

"Conditions" may be considered to be in one of two major categories: conditions such as poverty and infirmity in which the individual has the right to request assistance from the state, and conditions in which the state has the right and the obligation to interfere with the personal liberty of the individual, e.g., transmissible diseases and mental illness.

Another major contribution was made by John Snow, an English physician, anesthetist, and epidemiologist, who demonstrated in 1854 that cholera was transmissible, by removing the pump handle to a well that served as a water resource to a large population afflicted with cholera and keeping track of the decreasing number of new cases (Rosen, 1958).

UNITED STATES. In the United States during the 19th century, waves of epidemics continued and included yellow fever, smallpox, cholera, typhoid fever, and typhus. As cities grew, the poor crowded into inadequate housing with unsanitary conditions, causing illness that took lives. Lemuel Shattuck, a Boston bookseller and publisher with a keen interest in public health and welfare, organized the American Statistical Society in 1839 and issued a *Census of Boston* in 1845. The census showed high overall mortality rates and very high infant and maternal mortality rates. Living conditions of the poor were inadequate, and communicable diseases were widely prevalent (Rosen, 1958). Shattuck's *Report of the Massachusetts Sanitary Commission* (1850) outlined the findings and recommended modern public health reforms that included keeping vital statistics and providing environmental, food, drug, and communicable disease control information. Well-infant and well-child care, school-age child health, vaccination,

mental health, health education, and planning were called for. However, the report fell on deaf ears; the recommendation, for example, for a State Board of Health was not implemented until 19 years later. The newly formed American Medical Association (1847) was asked by the National Institute, a Washington, D.C., scientific organization, to form a committee to uniformly collect vital statistics, which it began in 1848.

The evolution of early public health efforts was making some progress in the mid-19th century in terms of administrative efforts, initial legislation, and debate regarding the determinants and thus approaches to health, whether social, economic, or medical. The advent of what we call "modern" health care occurred about this time, to which nursing made a large contribution. Discussed are the areas of the evolution of modern nursing, the evolution of modern medical care and public health practice, the evolution of the community caregiver, and the establishment of public health nursing.

ADVENT OF MODERN HEALTH CARE
Evolution of Modern Nursing

It was during the mid-19th century that the woman accredited with establishing "modern nursing" appeared. Although she is usually remembered by historians for her contributions to the health of British soldiers during the Crimean War and the establishment of nursing education, Florence Nightingale's remarkable use of public health principles and distinguished scientific contributions to health care reforms have gone unrecognized with few exceptions (Cohen, 1984; Grier and Grier, 1978). This review of Nightingale's work emphasizes her concern for environmental determinants of health; her focus on the aggregate of British soldiers through emphasis on sanitation, community assessment, and analysis; the development of the use of graphically depicted statistics; and the gathering of comparable census data and political advocacy on behalf of the aggregate.

Nightingale was from an established English family and was well educated. Her father tutored her in many subjects, including mathematics. She later studied with and was profoundly influenced by Adolphe Quetelet, a Belgian statistician, from whom she learned the discipline of social inquiry (Goodnow, 1933). She also had a passion for hygiene and health. A proper Englishwoman, she traveled extensively and was allowed finally in 1851 at the age of 31 years to enter a period of training in nursing at Kaiserswerth Hospital in Germany with Pastor Fliedner. She also studied the organization and discipline of the Sisters of Charity, in Paris. She wrote extensively and published her analyses of the many nursing systems she studied in France, Austria, Italy, and Germany (Dock and Stewart, 1925).

In 1854, Nightingale responded to the outbreak of the Crimean War by going to Scutari, in Turkey, with 40 nurses, Roman Catholic and Anglican sisters, and lay nurses in response to distressing accounts of the lack of care for wounded soldiers. She was sponsored by government officials but not officially backed by the army. Her greatest achievement was the overthrow of the British army management method, which had created a horror of horrors and allowed conditions that produced extraordinarily high death rates to persist. Scathing letters of criticism accompanied by constructive recommendations were sent to Secretary of War Sidney Herbert.

Nightingale faced an assignment in The Barrack Hospital, which had been built for 1,700 patients. She found 3,000–4,000 patients in 4 miles of beds only 18 inches apart (Goodnow, 1933):

"THE BEDS were mostly of straw, and many were laid directly on the floor. The few sheets to be had were of canvas, and so rough that the men begged not to have them used. Practically no laundry was being done; there was no hospital clothing, and the patients were still in their uniforms, stiff with blood and covered with filth. There was no soap, no towels, nor basins, very few utensils of any sort. Every place swarmed with vermin. Men ate half-cooked food with their fingers as utensils did not exist" (pp. 55–56).

Cholera and "contagious fever" were rampant. As many men died of the diseases as died of battlefield injuries (Cohen, 1984). Nightingale found that supplies had been allocated but were tied up owing to bureaucratic red tape. For example, supplies were ". . . sent to the wrong ports or were buried under munitions and could not be got" (Goodnow, 1933, p, 86).

Problems were caused by having to work

through eight departments of the army concerned with military affairs related to her assignment. For example, Nightingale sent to London reports of the conditions of the buildings. "A committee had been appointed to investigate the buildings. Miss Nightingale had them repaired before the committee's report was even in" (Goodnow, 1933, p. 87). Nightingale immediately set up a laundry and diet kitchens and provided food, clothing, dressings, and equipment for a laboratory with government money given her and donated funds (Dock and Stewart, 1925). Her nurses provided care only to patients of sympathetic physicians. Major reforms occurred during the first 2 months. Aware of the emerging interest in keeping social statistics, Nightingale realized that her most forceful argument would be statistical in nature. She reorganized the inept methods of keeping statistics. Through the use of careful never-before-used coxcomb graphs of wedges, circles, and squares, shaded and in varying colors, she illustrated the preventable deaths of soldiers in the hospitals during the Crimean War versus the average annual mortality in Manchester and of soldiers in military hospitals in and near London at the time (Fig. 2–2). She also showed through her reforms that by the end of the war, the death rate among ill soldiers during the Crimean War was no higher than that among well soldiers in Britain (Cohen, 1984). Keeping careful statistics, she showed that the death rate for those treated decreased from 42% to 2%. She then established community services and activities to improve the quality of life of the soldiers; these included rest and recreation facilities, a savings fund, an opportunity for study, and a post office. She also organized care for the families of the soldiers (Dock and Stewart, 1925).

Returning to London at the close of the war in 1856 and ill herself, she devoted her efforts to making compelling arguments on behalf of sanitary reform; this probably was her greatest contribution. However, she showed no interest in the emerging germ theory of disease (Cohen, 1984). At home, she surmised that if the sanitary neglect of the army of soldiers existed in the battle area, it probably existed at home in London as well. She prepared statistical tables that backed up her suspicions (Table 2–1). In one study, of a comparison of the mortality of men 25–35 years old in the army barracks in England with the mortality of men the same age in civilian life, she found the mortality of

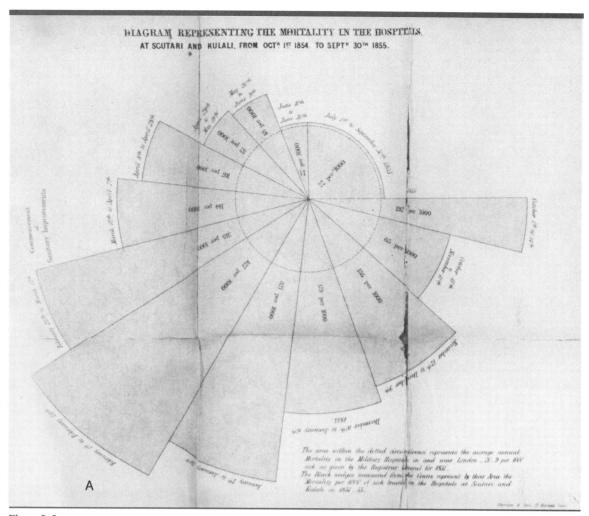

Figure 2–2

A and B, Coxcomb charts by Florence Nightingale from her publication *Notes on Matters Affecting the Health, Efficiency and Hospitalization of the British Army* (London: Harrison and Sons, 1858). These photographs of the large, fold-out charts are from an original preserved at the University of Chicago Library (public domain; courtesy of University of Chicago Library).

Illustration continued on following page

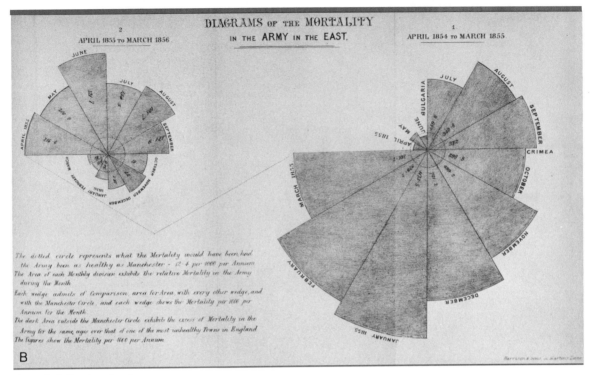

Figure 2–2 *Continued*

Table 2–1
Nightingale's Crimean War Mortality Statistics: Nursing Research That Made a Difference

Year	Deaths That Would Have Occurred in Healthy Districts Among Males of the Soldiers' Ages*	Actual Deaths of Noncommissioned Officers and Men	Excess of Deaths Among Noncommissioned Officers and Men
1839	763	2,914	2,151
1840	829	3,300	2,471
1841	857	4,167	3,310
1842	888	5,052	4,164
1843	914	5,270	4,356
1844	920	3,867	2,947
1845	911	4,587	3,676
1846	930	5,125	4,195
1847	981	4,232	3,251
1848	987	3,213	2,226
1849	954	4,052	3,098
1850	919	3,119	2,200
1851	901	2,729	1,828
1852	915	3,120	2,205
1853	920	3,392	2,472
Total	13,589	58,139	44,550

* The exact mortality in the healthy districts is 0.0077122, the logarithm of which (3.8871801) has been used in making this calculation.

Number of deaths of noncommissioned officers and men showing also the number of deaths that would have occurred if the mortality were 7.7 per 1,000, such as it was among Englishmen of the soldiers' age in healthy districts, in the years 1849–1853, which fairly represent the average mortality.

From Grier, B., and Grier, M.: Contributions of the passionate statistician. Res. Nurs. Health *1*;103–109, 1978. Copyright © 1978 by John Wiley & Sons, Inc. Reprinted by permission of John Wiley & Sons, Inc.

the soldiers to be nearly double that of the civilians. In one of her reports, she stated that she felt it was as criminal to allow the young soldier to die needlessly from unsanitary conditions as to take him out, line him up, and shoot him (Kopf, 1978). "Our soldiers enlist to death in the barracks" she reiterated (Kopf, 1978, p. 95). She was not content to keep her community assessment and analysis to herself and was very political; from her sick bed, she distributed her reports to army medical and commanding officers and to members of Parliament (Kopf, 1978). Her reports were challenged by prominent male leaders of the time; undaunted, she rewrote them in greater depth and redistributed them.

Through her earlier comparative work of hospital systems in European countries, she showed that data kept from each hospital were not comparable and that the names and classification of diseases varied from hospital to hospital. This difference prevented collection of similar statistics from larger geographical areas that would create a health–illness profile of a region and allow a comparison with other regions. She printed common statistical forms that were adopted by some hospitals in London experimentally. A study of the tabulated results revealed the promise of this strategy (Kopf, 1978).

Her development and application of statistical procedures continued, and recognition was won. She was elected a fellow by the Royal Statistical Society in 1858; in 1874, she was made an honorary member of the American Statistical Association (Kopf, 1978).

Nightingale Used Statistical Methods in Community Assessment

AN EXAMPLE of Nightingale's application of her statistical method to the health needs of the community is related to Southeastern Railway's plans to remove St. Thomas' Hospital to increase the railway's right-of-way between London Bridge and Charing Cross. Nightingale conducted a *community assessment,* plotting the cases served by the hospital, analyzing the proportion by distance, and calculating the probable impact on the community should the hospital be relocated to the proposed sites. In her view, hospitals were but a part of the wider community that together served the needs of humanity. This means of health planning, matching resources to the needs of the population, was visionary and, as noted by Kopf (1978), was not reapplied until the 20th century.

In 1861, Nightingale prevailed upon the census officials to add two areas to census taking, as had been done earlier in Ireland: the number of sick and infirm in the population and data depicting the housing of the population (Kopf, 1978). She stated the following:

"The connection between the *health* and the *dwellings* of the population is one of the most important that exists. The 'diseases' can be approximated also. In all the more important—such as smallpox, fevers, measles, heart disease, etc., all those which affect the *national* health, there will be very little error. Where there *is* error, in these things, the error is uniform . . . and corrects itself . . ." (Kopf, 1978, p. 98).

Although they were not adopted, Nightingale's suggestions were, again, visionary. According to Kopf (1978), only a few countries currently gather census data on sickness and housing.

Another of her concerns dealt with the need to make use of statistics at the administrative and political levels to direct health policy. Noting the ignorance of politicians and those who set policy regarding the interpretation and use of statistics, she stressed the need to teach national leaders to use statistical facts.

In addition to her contributions to nursing and the development of nursing education, Nightingale has been credited with using statistics to re-

place the individual case method to provide a grasp of the total environmental situation (Kopf, 1978). An often-neglected contribution, it has marked implications for the development of public health and, later, public health nursing. Grier and Grier (1978) said of her contributions to statistics, "Her name occurs in the index of many texts on the history of probability and statistics . . . in the history of quantitative graphics . . . and in texts on the history of science and mathematics." To be more precise, these authors point out that Nightingale's research occurred *before* later works that defined correlation in 1880, the *t* test in 1908, and χ^2, contingency table analysis, and analysis of variance, which were also developed about this time. These tests were later developed to aid in judging the relevance of data when the numbers were few and the effects were small, neither of which was the case in Nightingale's research. It may be asked why her contributions to current nursing education did not include and build on the need to determine the social and environmental determinants of the health of aggregates by using a sound research base and statistics to determine the need for and effects of nursing practice, as she so aptly demonstrated in her own short but significant period of practice.

Establishment of Modern Medical Care and Public Health Practice

After Nightingale's birth in 1820, other important scientists were born—Louis Pasteur in 1822, Joseph Lister in 1827, and Robert Koch in 1843. Their research also had profound impacts on health care, medicine, and nursing. To place Nightingale's work in perspective, the development of medical care must be considered in light of common education and practice during the latter 19th and early 20th centuries. Goodnow (1933) calls this time a "dark age." Few medical schools existed at the time, so apprenticeship was the route to a medical education. Medical sciences were underdeveloped, and bacteriology was unknown. The majority of physicians believed in the "spontaneous generation" theory of disease causation (Najman, 1980), i.e., that disease organisms grew from nothing. Typical medical treatment included bloodletting, starving, the use of leeches, and large doses of metals such as mercury and antimony (Goodnow, 1933). Even the clinical thermometer was not used until 1850. Nightingale's uniform classification of hospital statistics noted the need not only to tabulate the classification of diseases of patients in the hospital, but also to note diseases contracted by patients while under treatment during hospitalization; these diseases, such as gangrene and septicemia, were later called *iatrogenic* diseases (Kopf, 1978). That infection was rampant is not surprising, as Goodnow (1933) relates:

> "BEFORE AN operation the surgeon turned up the sleeves of his coat to save the coat, and would often not trouble to wash his hands, knowing how soiled they soon would be (!). The area of the operation would sometimes be washed with soap and water, but not always, for the inevitability of corruption made it seem useless. The silk or thread used for stitches or ligatures was hung over a button of the surgeon's coat, and during the operation a convenient place for the knife to rest was between his lips. Instruments . . . used for . . . lancing abcesses were kept in the vest pocket and often only wiped with a piece of rag as the surgeon went from one patient to another" (pp. 471–472).

Pasteur was a chemist, not a physician. While experimenting with wine production in 1854, he proposed the theory of the existence of germs. He was ridiculed, and acknowledgment of his work came later; Koch later applied his theories and developed methods for handing and studying bacteria.

Lister, whose father perfected the microscope, noted the healing processes of compound fractures. When the bone was broken but the skin was not, he noted that recovery was uneventful. When both the bone and the skin were broken, however, fever, infection, and even death were frequent. Only through the work of Pasteur did he find the proposed answer to his observation: that something from outside got into the wound through the broken skin (Goodnow, 1933). His surgical successes eventually improved with the soaking of dressings and instruments in mixtures of carbolic acid and oil.

The discovery of cholera and the tubercle bacillus by Koch (1882) and immunization (1881) and rabies vaccine (1885) by Pasteur were of significance to the development of public health and of medicine. In general, however, such discoveries were slow to be accepted (Rosen, 1958). For example, in late-19th-century America, tuberculosis was a major cause of death that often plagued its victims with chronic illness and disability. A highly stigmatized disease, most physicians of the time thought it was a hereditary, constitutional disease associated with poor environmental conditions. Family members with the disease were hidden, which increased the communicability of the disease, and hospitalization for tuberculosis was rare. Common treatment was a change of climate (Rosen, 1958). Although Koch had announced the discovery of the tubercle bacillus in 1882, it was 10 years before the first organized community campaign against the disease precipitated.

Another example of slow innovation stemming from scientific discoveries is seen in laboratory work by Pasteur that showed that *Streptococcus* caused puerperal (childbirth) fever. It was years before his discovery was accepted, however, and medical practice changed and physicians no longer delivered women without washing their hands after the performance of autopsies on puerperal fever cases (Goodnow, 1933).

The causes of disease were questioned and debated throughout the 19th century; scientific discoveries of organisms during the later part of the century supported those who held to the theory of specific contagious entities that caused disease and challenged most supporters of an earlier, miasmic theory that environment and atmospheric conditions caused disease (Greifinger and Sidel, 1981). The new scientific discoveries had a major impact on the development of both public health and medical practice. The birth of the germ theory of disease encouraged a focus on the individual organism and the individual disease in diagnosis and treatment. The birth of allopathism (treatment of the part) rather than holism (considering the social, economic, and environmental context as a whole as contributing to disease) influenced the direction of public health as well as medical care practitioners of the time.

With new discoveries, state and local governments felt increasingly responsible for controlling the spread of bacteria and other micro-organisms. They also were forced to heed a community outcry for social reform of deplorable living conditions in the cities—overcrowding, filth in the street, no provision for the poor, and inadequate food, water, and housing, as voiced by the populace in the New York City Riots of 1863. Local boards of health were formed and charged with safeguarding water and food and managing sewage and quarantine of victims of contagious diseases (Greifinger and Sidel, 1981). The New York Metropolitan Board of Health was established in 1866. Later, state health departments were formed. States built large public hospitals and treated both tuberculosis and mental disease through rest, diet, and quarantine. In 1889, the New York City Health Department recommended surveillance of tuberculosis and health education regarding tuberculosis, although neither recommendation was well received by physicians (Rosen, 1958). In 1894, the New York City Health Department required reporting of cases of tuberculosis by institutions and, in 1897, by physicians. Although sanitation was largely accomplished in the latter part of the 19th century by organized community effort, this marked the first application of such effort to a disease. The National Tuberculosis Association was formed to control tuberculosis by ". . . enlisting community support and action through a systematic and organized campaign of public health education . . ." (Rosen, 1958, p. 390). Many voluntary health organizations were to follow, and many were organized efforts to ". . . further community health through education, demonstrating ways of improving health services, advancing related research or legislation, as well as guarding and representing the public interest in this field . . ." (Rosen, 1958, p. 384) Rosen further notes the subsequent organization of these agencies largely on behalf of diseases and organs:

"Despite the great multiplicity and variety of such agencies, the voluntary health organizations tend generally to fall into four categories: (1) those concerned with specific diseases, such as tuberculosis, cancer, poliomyelitis, diabetes, and multiple sclerosis; (2) those concerned with disorders of certain organs of the body, such as the heart, defects of vision or hearing, dental defects, and diseases of the locomotor and skeletal systems; (3) those concerned with the health and welfare of special groups in the community such as mothers and children, the aged, or the Negro; and (4) those that dealt with health problems that affect the community as a whole, such as accident prevention, mental health, or planned parenthood" (p. 384).

Although environmental control was bringing about remarkable changes in health on the one hand, the increased use of anesthetics and the increasing awareness of pathology led to the establishment of many medical schools and a focus on one-to-one practice. Greifinger and Sidel (1981) stated the following:

"During the late nineteenth century, as many as 400 medical schools were founded in the United States; most lasted only a short time, but at least 147 medical schools were operating near the end of the century. These were privately owned institutions, and, lacking standardized graduation requirements, they produced physicians and surgeons who had inconsistent and often inadequate education . . ." (p. 130).

In 1883, The Johns Hopkins University Medical School was established in Baltimore, Maryland, on the German model that espoused medical education on principles of scientific discovery, after the great breakthroughs in identifying disease organisms. In the United States, the Carnegie Commission appointed Abraham Flexner to visit medical schools throughout the country and to evaluate them on the basis of the German model. In 1910, the Flexner Report outlined the shortcomings of U.S. medical schools not using this model, and, within a few years, successfully brought about withdrawal of funding of these schools by philanthropic organizations such as the Rockefeller and Carnegie foundations. Thus, the closure of scientifically "inadequate" medical schools occurred (Greifinger and Sidel, 1981). A "new breed" of physicians was promulgated, who adhered to the germ theory of disease causation; consequences included closing schools of midwifery and medical schools for women and blacks. Further consequences are outlined by Greifinger and Sidel (1981):

"**THE EMPHASIS** on the utilization of scientific theory in medical care, especially in a society wedded to the 'single agent theory' of the genesis of illness, developed into a focus on disease and symptoms rather than on therapy, prevention of disability, and caring for the 'whole person.' The old-fashioned family doctor had viewed patients in relation to their families and communities and had apparently been able to help people cope with problems of personal life, family, and society; the vigor with which American medicine adopted science left many of these qualities in the lurch. Science allowed the physician to

> deal with tissues and organs, which were much easier to comprehend than were the dynamics of human relationships, being propounded by Sigmund Freud and Carl Jung, or the complexities of disease prevention. Many physicians made efforts to integrate the various roles; however, the main thrust within society was toward academic science" (p. 132).

Aggregates with special needs for physicians and midwives who were female, nonwhite, and/or poor were forced to do without these practitioners (Ehrenreich and English, 1973).

Philanthropic foundations continued to influence health care efforts. For example, the Rockefeller Sanitary Commission for the Eradication of Hookworm was established in 1909 in conjunction with discovering that preventive efforts to eradicate hookworm, which was an occupational hazard among Southern workers, kept the workers healthy and therefore greatly benefitted industry. The model was so successful that the Rockefeller Foundation established The Johns Hopkins School of Hygiene and Public Health, the first school of public health, in 1916. The focus was on the preservation and improvement of health of individuals and the community and the prevention of disease through multidisciplinary efforts. The faculty came from a broad range of sciences—biological, physical, social, and behavioral. Additional efforts by foundations resulted in an International Health Commission, schools of tropical medicine, and medical research institutes in foreign ports to raise the level of health and, thus, production of the workers who loaded cargo bound for American shores.

Although community caregivers or traditional healers continue to exist, they often have been overlooked in holistic approaches to the provision of health care in the community.

Community Caregiver

Little has been preserved of the traditional role of the community caregiver or the traditional healer. Inferences are made, however, by medical and nurse anthropologists who have studied primitive and Western cultures (Leininger, 1976; Logan and Hunt, 1978).

The traditional healer is common in non-Western, ancient, and primitive societies (Hughes,

1978). The healer may have been manifest in various forms, e.g., shaman, midwife, herbalist, curandero, or priest. Traditional healers have, however, always existed, even in industrialized societies, although they may have a less visible role, or their role may be overlooked by professionals as well as by selected parts of the community. The role of the healer often is integrated with other institutions of society: religion, medicine, and morality, for example. The notion that there is "one" person who serves as healer may be foreign to many societies; healers can be individuals, kin, or even entire societies (Hughes, 1978).

Societies have theories of disease and of the relationship of disease to other aspects of group life. Disease often is considered an expression of one's relationship to the environment (disharmony) rather than as a condition that is caused by a specific "germ."

A "Theory of Disease"
IN COMMON with a great many other people, Tiv do not regard "illness" or "disease" as a completely separate category distinct from misfortunes to compound and farm, from relationship between kin, and from more complicated matters relating to the control of land. But it would be completely erroneous to say that Tiv are not able, in a cognitive sense, to recognize disease. As Bohannan has said, "The concept of a disease is not foreign to the Tiv: mumps, smallpox . . . yaws and gonorrhea are all common and each has a name" (p. 125). What is meant is that disease is seldom viewed in isolation (Price-Williams, 1902).

Both supernatural and empirical theories of disease exist. Many practices are empirically efficacious by public health standards, e.g., the practice of reheating food that has been left overnight to do away with "coldness" also destroys pathogens (Hughes, 1978). With repeated success, folk practices are kept by the society. Many therapeutic and preventive practices exist, and most cultures have a pharmacopoeia. From one fourth to one half of folk medicines are "empirically effective," and many modern drugs are based on the experience of primitive cultures, e.g., eucalyptus, coca, and opium (Hughes, 1978).

Results of folk healing practices not only may benefit the "patient" but also may be socially cohesive; healing rituals and sessions frequently involve not only the patient but also the patient's family and neighbors. A chance to participate in one's own treatment and to involve one's fellows may result in the application of the "treatment" to a whole group, or aggregate (Hughes, 1978).

Other cultural practices affecting the health of the people have occurred since ancient times and include isolation of those who are "unclean" (lepers) and treatment of food, water, and even housing.

An example of the taking of "healing" from the people by modern medicine is provided by midwifery as practiced during the late 19th and early 20th centuries (Ehrenreich and English, 1973; Smith, 1979). Traditional midwifery practices of getting women up within 24 hours of delivery to help "clear" the lochia stood in sharp contrast to medical recommendations keeping women in bed (Smith, 1979).

Modern nursing also developed from caregiving tasks carried out by men and women in the community. Richards' account of village women in America before the Industrial Revolution who gave community and family services is given by Baer (1985):

"LINDA RICHARDS called certain of these women 'born nurses . . . one or more of whom could be found in every village or community. . . .' Identified as a woman's role, the nurse needed to have kindness of heart, give cheerful service, and have '. . . a love for the work and a strong desire to alleviate suffering.' Trained by 'experience . . . the instruction of older women and of the family doctors,' these nurses 'were always subject to call' (Richards, 1911, pp. 3–4).

Both the consumer movement in health, which arose in the 1830s, and the self-help movement have evolved to meet the needs of the community and society for health care and a safe environment.

Another holistic approach that was developing in the late 19th and early 20th centuries was public health nursing. Public health nursing and, later, community health nursing evolved from practice in the home, known as home health care; community organizing; and political intervention on behalf of aggregates.

Establishment of Public Health Nursing and Focus

ENGLAND

Public health nursing developed from two traditions that stem from the Enlightenment: providing nursing care to the sick poor and helping the poor through providing them with information and channels of community organization that enable them to improve their health status.

DISTRICT NURSING. District nursing, based on the first tradition, first developed in England. The Epidemiological Society of London developed a plan between 1854 and 1856 to train selected poor women to provide nursing care in the community to the sick poor. It was theorized that nurses of the same social class as their patients' would be more effective, and that overall, more nurses would be available in the community (Rosen, 1958). Although this particular plan failed, a later plan was carried out in Liverpool in 1859 to provide nursing care to the sick poor.

After experiencing the excellent care given his sick wife by a nurse in his home, William Rathbone, a Quaker, felt strongly that such a plan was needed. He then divided the community into 18 districts, each to be assigned a nurse and a social worker to meet the needs of their communities for nursing, social work, and health education. As the plan was accepted widely in the community, Rathbone needed education for these nurses and consulted Nightingale. She assisted him by providing for the training of district nurses, referring to them as "health nurses." The model was successful and widely adopted, eventually on the national level under voluntary agencies (Rosen, 1958).

HEALTH VISITING. A parallel service — health visiting — was originated in Manchester in 1862 by the Ladies Section of the Manchester and Salford Sanitary Association. Because the distribution of health pamphlets alone had little effect, the purpose of this service was to establish home visitors to give health information to the poor. In 1893, Nightingale pointed out that the district nurse should be a health teacher as well as a nurse for the sick in the home and that "health missioners" should be educated for this purpose. The model that was adopted, however, was that of the district nurse who provided care to the sick in the home and the health visitor who provided health information in the home. Eventually, health visitors were placed under the auspices of government agencies, supervised by the medical health officer, and paid by the municipality. Thus, a collaborative model existed between government and voluntary agencies, which largely exists today in the United States.

UNITED STATES. In the United States, public health nursing similarly developed from district nursing and home nursing. In 1877, the Women's Board of the New York City Mission sent Francis Root, a graduate nurse, into the home to provide care to the sick. The innovation spread, with nursing associations, later called visiting nurse associations, set up in Buffalo (1885) and then in Boston and Philadelphia (1886).

In 1893, Lillian Wald and Mary Brewster, nurses, established a district nursing service known as the House on Henry Street on the Lower East Side of New York, an area teeming with crowded immigrants with minimal resources such as jobs, housing, and health care. This organization, later to become the Visiting Nurse Association of New York City, played an important role in the establishment of public health nursing in the United States. Wald provides a compelling account of her early exposure to the community where she identified public health nursing needs:

Lillian Wald: The House on Henry Street HIGHLIGHTS FROM *The House on Henry Street,* published in 1915, bring Lillian Wald's experience to life:

"A SICK woman in a squalid rear tenement, so wretched and so pitiful that, in all the years since, I have not seen anything more appealing, determined me, within half an hour, to live on the East Side.

"I had spent two years in a New York training-school for nurses. . . . After graduation, I supplemented the theoretical instruction, which was casual and inconsequential in the hospital classes twenty-five years ago, by a period of study at a medical college. It was while at the college that a great opportunity came to me.

"While there, the long hours 'on duty' and the exhausting demands of the ward work scarcely admitted freedom for keeping informed as to what was happening in the world outside. The nurses had no time for general reading; visits to and from friends were brief; we were out of the current and saw little of life save as it flowed into the hospital wards. It is not strange, therefore, that I should have been ignorant of the various movements which reflected the awakening of the social conscience at the time. . . .

"Remembering the families who came to visit patients in the wards, I outlined a course of instruction in home nursing adapted to their needs, and gave it in an old building in Henry Street, then used as a technical school and now part of the settlement. Henry Street then as now was the center of a dense industrial population.

"From the schoolroom where I had been giving a lesson in bedmaking, a little girl led me one drizzling March morning. She had told me of her sick mother, and gathering from her incoherent account that a child had been born, I caught up the paraphernalia of the bedmaking lesson and carried it with me.

"The child led me over broken roadways — there was no asphalt, although its use was well established in other parts of the city,— over dirty mattresses and heaps of refuse, — it was before Colonel Waring had shown the possibility of clean streets even in that quarter,— between tall, reeking houses whose laden fire-escapes, useless for their appointed purpose, bulged with household goods of every description. The rain added to the dismal appearance of the streets and to the discomfort of the crowds which thronged them, intensifying the odors which assailed me from every side. Through Hester and Division street we went to the end of Ludlow; past odorous fishstands, for the streets were a market-place, unregulated, unsupervised, unclean; past evil-smelling, uncovered garbage-cans; and — perhaps worst of all, where so many little children played — past the trucks brought down from more fastidious quarters and stalled on these already overcrowded streets, lending themselves inevitably to many forms of indecency.

"The child led me on through a tenement hallway, across a court where open and unscreened closets were promiscuously used by men and women, up into a rear tenement, by slimy steps whose accumulated dirt was augmented that day by the mud of the streets, and finally into the sickroom.

"All the maladjustments of our social and economic relations seemed epitomized in this brief journey and what was found at the end of it. The family to which the child led me was neither criminal nor vicious. Although the husband was a cripple, one of those who stand on street corners exhibiting deformities to enlist compassion, and masking the begging of alms by a pretense at selling; although the family of seven shared their two rooms with boarders—who were literally boarders, since a piece of timber was placed over the floor for them to sleep on—and although the sick woman lay on a wretched, unclean bed, soiled with a hemorrhage two days old, they were not degraded human beings, judged by any measure of moral values.

"In fact, it was very plain that they were sensitive to their condition, and when, at the end of my ministrations, they kissed my hands (those who have undergone similar experiences will, I am sure, understand), it would have been some solace if by any conviction of the moral unworthiness of the family I could have defended myself as a part of a society which permitted such conditions to exist. Indeed, my subsequent acquaintance with them revealed the fact that, miserable as their state was, they were not without ideals for the family life, and for society, of which they were so unloved and unlovely a part.

"That morning's experience was a baptism of fire. Deserted were the laboratory and the academic work of the college. I never re-turned to them. On my way from the sickroom to my comfortable student quarters my mind was intent on my own responsibility. To my inexperience it seemed certain that conditions such as these were allowed because people did not *know,* and for me there was a challenge to know and to tell. When early morning found me still awake, my naive conviction remained that, if people knew things—and 'things' meant everything implied in the condition of this family—such horrors would cease to exist, and I rejoiced that I had had a training in the care of the sick that in itself would give me an organic relationship to the neighborhood in which this awakening had come.

"To the first sympathetic friend to whom I poured forth my story, I found myself presenting a plan which had been developing almost without conscious mental direction on my part . . .

"Within a day or two a comrade from the training-school, Mary Brewster, agreed to share in the venture. We were to live in the neighborhood as nurses, identify ourselves with it socially, and, in brief, contribute to it our citizenship. . . .

"I should like to make it clear that from the beginning we were most profoundly moved by the wretched industrial conditions which were constantly forced upon us. . . . I hope to tell of the constructive programmes that the people themselves have evolved out of their own hard lives, of the ameliorative measures, ripened out of sympathetic comprehension, and finally, of the social legislation that expresses the new compunction of the community" (pp. 1–9).

From The House on Henry Street, *New York, Henry Holt and Co., 1915; reprinted by Dover Publications, Inc., New York, 1971.*

Wald describes a range of services that evolved from Henry Street. Home visiting was provided by nurses, and patients paid carfare for the nurses or a cursory fee. Physicians were consultants to Henry Street, and families could initiate a visit by calling the nurse directly, or nurses could respond to the call by a physician. The philosophy was one of meeting the health needs of aggregates, broadly defined to include the many evident social, economic, and environmental determinants of health. This, by necessity, involved an aggregate approach, one that empowered people of the community.

Helen Hall, a later director of the House at Henry Street, writes of the settlement's role as ". . . one of helping people to help themselves" (Wald, 1971) through the development of centers of social action aimed at meeting the needs of the community as well as of the individual. Community organizing led to the formation of a great variety of programs for the people such as youth clubs, a program for juveniles, sex education for local school teachers, and support programs for immigrants. A Community Studies Department carried out systematic community assessments (surveys)

". . . so that we could tell our neighbors' story where it would do the most good" (Wald, 1971, p. vi). Mothers from the settlement went to Washington, D. C., and testified regarding the experience of bringing children up in "decaying tenements." Whether it was the need for traffic lights, schools, garbage collection, unemployment insurance, or health care, neighbors of the settlement were drawn into a democratic process that took them from the steps of city hall to the nation's capital to speak out on behalf of the needs of the aggregate that was affected by the condition. Legislation resulting from these efforts and the efforts of others led to the formation of the Children's Bureau and the Social Security Act. As late as 1963, elders' testimonies had an impact on the formation of Medicare.

On the basis of individual observations and interventions, programs were planned for aggregates. One example is that of school nursing. Wald (1971) reports an incident that preceded her later successful trial of school nursing:

"I HAD been downtown only a short time when I met Louis. An open door in a rear tenement revealed a woman standing over a washtub, a fretting baby on her left arm, while with her right she rubbed at the butcher's aprons which she washed for a living.

"Louis, she explained, was 'bad.' He did not 'cure his head,' and what would become of him, for they would not take him into the school because of it? Louis, hanging the offending head, said he had been to the dispensary many times. He knew it was awful for a twelve-year-old boy not to know how to read the names of the streets on the lampposts, but 'every time I go to school Teacher tells me to go home.'

"It needed only intelligent application of the dispensary ointments to cure the affected area, and in September, I had the joy of securing the boy's admittance to school for the first time in his life. The next day, at the noon recess, he fairly rushed up our five flights of stairs in the Jefferson Street tenement to spell the elementary words he had acquired that morning" (pp. 46–47).

Overcrowded schools, an uninformed and uninterested public, and an unaware department of health all contributed to this neglect. Wald and the nursing staff at the settlement kept anecdotal notes

of children they encountered who had been excluded from school owing to illness. One nurse found a boy in school whose skin was desquamating from scarlet fever and took him to the president of the Department of Health in an attempt to have physicians placed in the schools. A later program in which physicians screened children in school for one hour a day suffered from lack of comprehensiveness.

In 1902, Wald talked Dr. Lederle, Commissioner of Health in New York City, into trying a school nursing experiment. A public health nurse, Linda Rogers, from Henry Street was loaned to the New York City Health Department to work in a school (Dock and Stewart, 1925). School nursing was adopted on a widespread basis; school nurses were sometimes hired by the Board of Health and sometimes by the Board of Education. School nurses did physical assessments, treated minor infections, and carried out health teaching with pupils and with parents.

In 1909, Wald mentioned the efficacy of home nursing to one of the officials of the Metropolitan Life Insurance Company. The company decided to provide home nursing to their industrial policyholders; the program proved very successful and was used throughout the United States and Canada (Wald, 1971).

The demand for public health nursing increased and was hard to meet. In 1910, the Department of Nursing and Health was started at the Teachers College of Columbia University in New York. A course in visiting nursing was offered that placed nurses at the Henry Street Settlement for field work. In 1912, the National Organization of Public Health Nursing was formed, and Lillian Wald was elected as president. This organization was open to public health nurses and to others in the community who were interested in public health nursing. In 1913, the Los Angeles Department of Health formed the first Bureau of Public Health Nursing (Rosen, 1958). That same year, the first public health nurse was appointed to the U.S. Public Health Service to do field work in trachoma.

Historical Nursing Research

IN 1909, the Metropolitan Life Insurance Company adopted a program of home visiting by nurses to lower mortality rates and improve the company's image. Originally associated with the Henry Street Settlement House, the Metropolitan Visiting Nurse Service (MVNS) created a system of more than 650 Visiting Nurse Associations throughout the United States. Nurses promoted the health of the policyholders, many of whom were immigrants, by teaching them health habits, including the importance of immunizations, and caring for them at times of illness in their homes. The nurses also carried out projects in selected communities, e.g., a treatment-of-tuberculosis demonstration project in Framingham, an infant mortality study in the Thetford mines, and a study to decrease high rates of mortality in Kingsport, a railroad town. In these projects, "nurses collected baseline health data, initiated health clinics, gave immunizations, established home visits, and taught health to policyholders." Statistics kept by Metropolitan Life documented the lowered mortality rates and increased health of the citizens as an outcome of the nurses' public health and clinical expertise. The MVNS continued to operate until 1953, when rising costs, unquestioned by the nurses, supported the company's decision to close.

Data from Hamilton, D.: Clinical excellence, but too high a cost: The Metropolitan Life Insurance Company Visiting Nurse Service (1909–1953). Public Health Nurs. 5;235–240, 1988.

At first, many public health nursing programs used nurses in specialized areas such as school nursing, tuberculosis nursing, maternal-child health nursing, and communicable disease nursing. A more generalized program has come to be acceptable in which a nurse hired by an official agency covers the entire population of one district and, with the exception of occupational health, provides prevention, health promotion, and health maintenance care. Collaboratively, visiting nurses in voluntary home health agencies such as the Visiting Nurse Association provide care to the homebound ill who are referred by a physician. Combination agencies providing both services also exist but are less available in urban areas.

Conclusions and implications for community health nursing from history cannot be made without considering the consequences of the evolution of health for the health of aggregates.

CONSEQUENCES FOR THE HEALTH OF AGGREGATES

Implications for the health of aggregates are explored in relation to new causes of mortality,

Hygeia versus Panacea, and additional theories of disease causation.

New Causes of Mortality

The causes of mortality in Western societies have changed since the turn of the century from infectious diseases to largely chronic diseases. The decline in death rate from infectious diseases has been attributed mainly to increased food production and better nutrition during the 18th and 19th centuries; other factors include better sanitation through purification of water, sewage disposal, improved care of food, and pasteurization of milk. According to McKeown (1981), medicine and immunization had little effect on health until the 20th century. Improved vaccination programs were begun in the 1920s; powerful antibiotics came into use after 1935. The advent of modern chronic disease in Western populations places selected aggregates at risk. Aggregates at risk of chronic disease need, for example, health education, screening, and programs to ensure occupational and environmental safety. Because of the pursuit of the germ theory of disease, however, health services focus expenditures on treatment of the acutely ill and treat the chronically ill with an acute care approach. Yet, preventive, health promotion, and restorative care are necessary to combat escalating rates of chronic disease.

Hygeia Versus Panacea

The "healthful living" (Hygeia) versus "cure" (Panacea) dichotomy, which originates from Greek times, is still seen today. The change in the nature of health "problems" is identifiable, yet the roles of individual and collective activities in the prevention of illness and premature death are slow to evolve. The focus of medical technology and academic science on the disease organism has created more than 85 medical subspecialties. A consequence is that ". . . complex life-threatening disorders are better understood; on the other hand, few professionals have been trained to specialize in the treatment of the common, uncomplicated health problems that account for 90 percent of visits to doctors" (Lee et al., 1981, p. 197). A coordinated system that addresses the problem holistically, using multiple approaches and planning outcomes for aggregates and populations, is needed. A redistribution of interest and resources to major determinants of health, such as food and the environment, is necessary (McKeown, 1981).

Additional Theories of Disease Causation

The germ theory of disease causation, which evolved in the late 19th century, is a unicausal model. Challenges to the germ theory of disease include that made by Max von Pettenkofer, a German physician and hygienist. In the late 19th century, von Pettenkofer, with his students, defiantly swallowed a large number of cholera bacteria and did not die as a result (Hume, 1927). McKeown's research (1981) also refutes this model. For example, although Koch named the tubercle bacillus in 1882, no treatments were effective until the appearance of streptomycin in 1947. By 1947, however, mortality from tuberculosis was a fraction of what it was in the 19th century because of improved food, nutrition, sanitation, and other environmental factors.

Najman (1980) reviewed two additional theories of disease causation: the multicausal view, which considers environment to have many contributing causes, and the general susceptibility view, which takes into account stress and lifestyle factors. Najman contends that each theory accounts for some disease under some conditions, but no theory can account for largely unexplained phenomena in modern illness patterns and contradictory findings in research such as studies that demonstrate high levels of stress and low cigarette consumption among widows and the opposite among married persons. The continued concentration by medicine and research on specific diseases is a consequence of the laboratory science approach to medical care that has existed since the time of Koch. Studies by Scrimshaw et al. (1969) and McDermott et al. (1972) question the efficacy of public health measures as well as medical measures in non-Western countries beset with infectious diseases. As pointed out by Najman (1980), literacy (Stewart, 1971) and nutrition (Scrimshaw et al., 1969) ". . . may reduce the level of infectious disease morbidity and mortality to a greater extent than do 'medical' interventions" (p. 231). A rethinking of "intervention" at the aggregate level aimed at these larger needs is past due.

CHALLENGES FOR COMMUNITY HEALTH NURSING

Community health nurses face the challenge of promoting the health of populations with the new causes of mortality and underserved populations, who are more likely to experience both infectious and chronic disease in our society. The specialization of medicine has affected not only how medical care is delivered but also how nursing care is delivered. Nurses must be aware of the increased technological advances spawned by the many medical specialties that exist. Nurses are called on to seek increasing specialization to care for the "specialist's" patients. The number of nurses seeking specialized clinical preparation is increasing with medical specialization. The number of master's prepared nurses choosing an advanced clinical specialty over teaching, administration, supervision, or other functional purpose of curriculum increased from 59% in 1976 to 69% in 1984–1985 (American Nurses' Association, 1987). The percentage of nurses employed in public and community health settings increased 26% between 1977 and 1988 but still accounts for only 11% of employed registered nurses (U.S. Department of Health and Human Services, 1990).

In the 1988 National Sample Survey of Registered Nurses (U.S. Department of Health and Human Services, 1990), 37% of the community health nurses reported a baccalaureate degree as their highest educational preparation, and 10.0% reported a master's degree as their highest nursing-related educational preparation. These statistics and trends reflect a phenomenon of concern to community health nursing—the need for education in community health nursing.

The consequences of a bimodal focus on prevention and health promotion versus home care of the ill may become more profound with changing patterns of reimbursement under diagnosis-related groups (DRGs). Holistic care, which requires both dimensions, has suffered and stands to suffer more as funds go into the illness dimension. This phenomenon has been affected by an ideology that favors service in pursuit of the alleviation of illness, which is in keeping with the germ theory of disease causation. An ethnohistorical study of public health nursing in rural New England from the turn of the century examined the cost-benefit ratios of the population-based district nurse that have persisted since 1900 in parts of New England (Dreher, 1984). The district nurse provided preventive, cu-

liams, 1984). A population focus will better enable community health nurses to contribute to the ethic of social justice by emphasizing society's rather

---

A Timely Model of District Nursing
IN AN ethnohistorical study of the development of public health nursing in rural New England, a model of population-based nursing was found, unexpectedly, that holds promise for meeting the nation's current and even future health concerns (Dreher, 1984). Data were collected from public records, the census, interviews with town residents, public officials, medical care providers, active and retired public health nurses, and direct observations. The use of a district nurse, or "town hall" nurse, a health model from the 1920s, was found to exist today. The district nurse described in the findings provided health education and services to persons in four neighboring towns. The district nurse's activities were administered locally and paid for by property tax revenues, not by patients or third-party reimbursement. The district nurse provided a full range of community nursing services to persons in need regard-

less of ability to pay or insurance coverage. The nurse carried out responsibilities in the following areas: school nursing, health promotion and prevention, and home health care. She held office hours weekly in the town halls of the four communities, where she did blood pressure screening and gave routine parenteral medications and health counseling. Mobility was not an issue, as patients who were confined to their homes received home visits from the district nurse. The district nurse conducted routine screening in the schools and planned and carried out programs that addressed identified needs. The annual cost per visit of health services provided by the district nurse was far less than that provided by nurses in a nearby home health agency. The model is recommended as a way of addressing the nation's needy health problems through prevention, promotion, and maintenance care.

---

rative, and health maintenance services. Such a model, proposes Dreher, may better address the nation's health problems.

The need for education in community health nursing raises questions as to the pull from the DRGs for clinical specialization versus an even broader generalist approach which would prepare students to meet the needs of aggregates via community organization, e.g., to promote literacy and nutrition programs. Where to intervene along the health–illness continuum and how to intervene comprehensively are, as Dreher suggests, challenges.

Care and cure have been taken from the hands of many of the people. Medicine has "medicalized" social problems and normal life events, from childbirth to death. Medicine cannot solve today's health problems; nurses must work with and on behalf of aggregates, helping them build a constituency for issues facing them as consumers.

A focus on aggregates will mean many approaches, including the careful gathering of anecdotes (the experience of the people or organization) and statistics, known as a population focus, which addresses the health of all in the population (Wil-

than the individual's responsibility for health (Beauchamp, 1986). Helping aggregates—with the goal being all of them in a community—to help themselves will empower the people and create with the people ways of carrying their concerns forward to help redress the balance.

A knowledge of our history provides insight into the dilemmas faced in contemporary times, which in many ways are not so different from the past. As Duffus (1938) states of Wald's work,

"The 'case' element in these early reports of hers [Wald] got less and less emphasis; she instinctively went behind the symptoms to appraise the whole individual, saw that one could not understand the individual without understanding the family, saw that the family was in the grip of larger social and economic forces which it could not control" (p. 51).

The historians of health care have reconstructed the past from written fragments of "the facts" carefully sifted and weighed and thought to be worthy of mention. Values and theories held by the historian influence the writing of our past. Versluysen

(1980) points out the consequences of the inevitable selectivity of the reconstruction of the history of health care: the history of health care has been written largely from the viewpoint of men, and the history of health care has been narrowly interpreted as the history of medicine.

Nonphysician healers, especially women, traditionally have been viewed by historians as inauthentic "amateurs" who were marginal to ". . . the maintenance of the physical health and well-being of society" (Versluysen, 1980, p. 176). However, throughout history until the late 19th century, healing took place largely in the home by healers, who were invisible yet representative of an extensive system of care delivery. Sources of accounts of home care by healers such as diaries, health manuals, and letters have been overlooked by male historians and are only now being researched by female historians and, often, feminists. Davis (1980) states that Versluysen (1980) implies that we should ask if the study of nursing's history is even appropriate and contends that the history of healers, who usually were women, might be more appropriate.

Another historical trend mentioned by Versluysen (1980) is for historians to mention a few heroines in typical feminine stereotypes. For example, Nightingale's life-long intellectual endeavors and marked achievements expand considerably the profile of this remarkable woman beyond the typical focus on only her limited time (2 years) in the Crimea and the founding of modern nursing education. These achievements include being a health statistician, a prolific writer and scientist, a radical environmental sanitarian, and a reformer of both the British Army medical care system and sanitary policy in India.

In addition, historians have also neglected to a large extent the social and environmental contexts of health and medical care, dimensions that are necessary to place health care in a broader context. Such a context is necessary to grasp the state of the health of the public and public health efforts during specific periods.

SUMMARY

As Western civilization evolved from the Paleolithic Period to the present and people began to live in increasingly closer proximity to each other, the nature of the health problems they experienced also changed.

In the mid-19th and early 20th centuries, public health efforts, including the precursors of modern nursing and public health nursing, began to make progress in improving societal health. Nursing pioneers such as Nightingale in England and Wald in the United States focused on the collection and analysis of statistical data, health care reforms, home nursing, community empowerment, and nursing education and laid the groundwork for the establishment of community health nursing as it exists today.

Modern community health nurses must grapple with an array of philosophical controversies that affect the way they practice. These include differences of opinion about what "intervention" means, focus both on the individual and on the aggregate, and what steps should be taken to best solve the problem of runaway health care costs.

L e a r n i n g
A c t i v i t i e s

1. Research the history of the health department or Visiting Nurse Association in your city or county.

2. Find two recent articles about Florence Nightingale. After reading the articles, analyze and list the contributions made by Nightingale to public health and public health nursing and later, community health nursing, according to the accounts given by the authors.

3. Read Henrik Ibsen's play *The Enemy of the People.* Write a summary of the main points of the play and list the implications of the play for health professionals who want to bring about similar changes in a contemporary community.

RECOMMENDED READINGS: NURSING RESEARCH

Barker, E. R.: Caregivers as casualties: War experiences and the postwar consequences for both Nightingale- and Vietnam-era nurses. West. J. Nurs. Res. *11*;628–631, 1989.

Barnie, D. C.: Evolution of nursing specialties. Gastroenterol. Nurs. *11*;214–216, 1989.

Buhler-Wilkerson, K.: Public health nursing: A photographic study. Turn-of-the-century visiting nurses. Nurs. Outlook *36*;241–243, 1988.

Carr, A. M.: Development of public health nursing literature. Public Health Nurs. 5;81–85, 1988.

Dennis, K. E., and Prescott, P. A.: Florence Nightingale: Yesterday, today, and tomorrow. Adv. Nurs. Sci. 7;66–81, 1985.

Frachel, R. R.: A new profession: The evolution of public health nursing. Public Health Nurs. 5;86–90, 1988.

Grier, B., and Grier, M.: Contributions of the passionate statistician. Res. Nurs. Health *1*;103–109, 1978.

Poslusny, S. M.: Feminist friendship: Isabel Hampton Robb, Lavinia Lloyd Dock and Mary Adelaide Nutting. Image J. Nurs. Scholarship *21*;64–68, 1989.

Silverstein, N. G.: Lillian Wald at Henry Street, 1893–1895. Adv. Nurs. Sci. 7;1–12, 1985.

REFERENCES

Amaro, H., Whitaker, R., Coffman, G., and Heeren T.: Acculturation and marijuana and cocaine use: Findings from HHANES 1982–84. Am. J. Public Health *80*(suppl);54–60, 1990.

American Nurses' Association: Facts About Nursing 82–83. Kansas City, Missouri, ANA, 1983.

American Nurses' Association: Facts About Nursing 86–87. Kansas City, Missouri, ANA, 1987.

Armelagos, G. K., and Dewey, J. R.: Evolutionary response to human infectious diseases. *In* Logan, M. H., and Hunt, E. E., eds.: Health and the Human Condition. North Scituate, Massachusetts, Duxbury Press, 1978, pp. 101–107.

Baer, E. D.: Nursing's divided house—an historical view. Nurs. Res. *34*;32–38, 1985.

Beauchamp, D. E.: Public health as social justice. *In* Mappes, T., and Zembaty, J., eds.: Biomedical Ethics. 2nd Ed. New York, McGraw-Hill, 1986, pp. 585–593.

Brothwell, D.: The question of pollution in earlier and less developed societies. *In* Logan, M. H., and Hunt, E. E., eds.: Health and the Human Condition. North Scituate, Massachusetts, Duxbury Press, 1978, pp. 129–136.

Burkitt, D. P.: Some diseases characteristic of modern western civilization. *In* Logan, M. H., and Hunt, E. E., eds.: Health and the Human Condition. North Scituate, Massachusetts, Duxbury Press, 1978, pp. 137–147.

Cockburn, T. A.: The evolution of human infectious diseases. *In* Cockburn, T., ed.: Infectious Diseases: Their Evolution and Eradication. Springfield, Illinois, Charles C Thomas, 1967, pp. 34–107.

Cohen, I. B.: Florence Nightingale. Sci. Am. *250*;128–137, 1984.

Davies, C.: Rewriting Nursing History. Totowa, New Jersey, Barnes and Noble, 1980.

Dock, L. L., and Stewart, I. M.: A Short History of Nursing: From the Earliest Times to the Present Day. New York, G. P. Putnam's Sons, 1925.

Dreher, M.: District nursing: The cost benefits of a population-based practice. Am. J. Public Health *74*;1107–1111, 1984.

Duffus, R. L.: Lillian Wald—Neighbor and Crusader. New York, Macmillan, 1938.

Duran, F. D.: The Aztecs: The History of the Indies of New Spain. Translated, with notes, by Heyden, D., and Horcasitas, F. New York, Orion Press, 1964.

Ehrenreich, B., and English, D.: Witches, Midwives, and Nurses: A History of Women Healers. Old Westbury, New York, The Feminist Press, 1973.

Garling, J.: Flexner and Goldmark: Why the difference in impact? Nurs. Outlook *33*;26–31, 1985.

Garn, S. M.: Culture and the direction of human evolution. Hum. Biol. *35*;221–236, 1963.

George, M. D.: London Life in the XVIIIth Century. New York, Alfred A. Knopf, 1925.

Goodnow, M.: Outlines of Nursing History. Philadelphia, W. B. Saunders, 1933.

Greifinger, R. B., and Sidel, V. W.: American medicine: Charity begins at home. *In* Lee, P., Brown, N., and Red, I., eds.: The Nation's Health. San Francisco, Boyd and Fraser, 1981, pp. 124–134.

Grier, B., and Grier, M.: Contributions of the passionate statistician. Res. Nurs. Health *1*;103–109, 1978.

Guendelman, S., Gould, J., Hudes, M., and Eskenazi, B.: Generational differences in perinatal health among the Mexican American population: Findings from HHANES 1982–84. Am. J. Public Health *80*(suppl);61–65, 1990.

Hall, H.: Introduction to the Dover edition. *In* Wald, L.: The House on Henry Street. New York, Dover Publications, 1971, pp. v–xiv.

Hanlon, J. J., and Pickett, G. E.: Public Health Administration and Practice. 8th Ed. St. Louis, Times Mirror/Mosby, 1984.

Hudson, E. H.: Treponematosis and man's social evolution. Am. Anthropologist *67*;885–901, 1965.

Hughes, C. C.: Medical care: Ethnomedicine. *In* Logan, M. H., and Hunt, E. E., eds.: Health and the Human Condition. North Scituate, Massachusetts, Duxbury Press, 1978, pp. 150–158.

Hume, E. E.: Max von Pettenkofer. New York, Hoeber, 1927.

Kopf, E. W.: Florence Nightingale as statistician. Res. Nurs. Health *1*;93–102, 1978.

Lee, P. R., Brown, N., and Red, I., eds.: The Nation's Health. San Francisco, Boyd and Fraser, 1981.

Leininger, M.: Transcultural Health Care Issues and Conditions. Philadelphia, F. A. Davis, 1976.

Logan, M. H., and Hunt, E. E., eds.: Health and the Human Condition. North Scituate, Massachusetts, Duxbury Press, 1978.

McDermott, W., Deuschle, K. W., and Barnett, C. R.: Health care experiment at Many Farms. Science *175*;23–31, 1972.

McKeown, T.: Determinants of health. *In* Lee, P., Brown, N., and Red, I., eds.: The Nation's Health. San Francisco, Boyd and Fraser, 1981, pp. 49–57.

Najman, J. M.: Theories of disease causation and the concept of a general susceptibility: A review. Social Sci. Med. *14A*;231–237, 1980.

Polgar, S.: Evolution and the ills of mankind. *In* Tax, S., ed.: Horizons of Anthropology. Chicago, Aldine, 1964, pp. 200–211.

Price-Williams, D. R.: A case study of ideas concerning disease among the Tiv. Africa *32*;123–131, 1962.

Richards, L.: Reminiscences of Linda Richards: America's First Trained Nurse. Boston, Whitcomb and Barrows, 1911.

Richardson, B. W.: The Health of Nations: A Review of the Works of Edwin Chadwick, Vol. 2. London, Longmans, Green and Company, 1887.

Rosen, G.: A History of Public Health. New York, MD Publications, Inc., 1958.

Scrimshaw, N. S., Béhar, M., Guzmán, M. A., et al.: Nutrition and infection field study in Guatemalan villages, 1959–64. Arch. Environ. Health *18*;51–62, 1969.

Smith, F. B.: The People's Health 1830–1910. London, Croom Helm, Ltd., 1979.

Stewart, C. T.: Allocation of resources to health. J. Hum. Res. 6;103–122, 1971.

U.S. Department of Health and Human Services, Health Resources and Services Administration. Bureau of Health Professions, Division of Nursing: The Registered Nurse Population: Findings From the National Sample Survey of Registered Nurses. Springfield, Virginia, National Technical Information Service, 1990.

Versluysen, M. C.: Old wives' tales? Women healers in English history. *In* Davies, C., ed.: Rewriting Nursing History. Totowa, New Jersey, Barnes and Noble, 1980, pp. 175–199.

Wald, L.: The House on Henry Street, New York, Dover Publications, Inc., 1971 (reprint of House on Henry Street, New York, Henry Holt and Company, 1915).

Wales, M.: The Public Health Nurse in Action. New York, Macmillan, 1941, p. xi.

Williams, C. A.: Population-focused practice. *In* Stanhope, M., and Lancaster, J., eds.: Community Health Nursing: Process and Practice for Promoting Health. St. Louis, C. V. Mosby, 1984, pp. 805–815.

3

The Health Care System

Upon completion of this chapter, the reader will be able to:

1. Discuss the four major determinants of health.

2. Describe the current private/public health care system.

3. Describe the organization of the public health care subsystem at the national, state, and local levels.

4. Describe the role of the public health care subsystem at all levels.

5. Describe the goals for health care in the future.

6. Analyze landmark health care legislation and its impact on the delivery system.

Barbara J. Horn
Beverly M. Horn

The health care system of the United States is dynamic, multifaceted, and not comparable to any other health care system in the world. It often is praised for its technological breakthroughs, frequently criticized for its high costs, and difficult to access by those most in need. What is this system, how did it come to be, and how is its viability maintained? This chapter describes landmark health care legislation; determinants of health; and the organization and scope of the private and government health care systems at the federal, state, and local levels and then presents a futuristic perspective.

MAJOR LEGISLATION AND THE HEALTH CARE SYSTEM

To understand the evolution of the U.S. health care system, it is critical to know what major legislative actions have been taken by the federal government that influence health and health care. The U.S. Congress enacted bills, particularly in the 20th century, that had major impacts on both public and private health care sectors. Legislation governing health increased in each decade of the 20th century and was aimed at improving the health of populations. Some of the landmark federal acts that influenced health services are listed.

tive effect on children's health. The Shepard-Towner Act (1921) was aimed specifically at providing funds for the health and welfare of infants. The Hill-Burton Act (1946) authorized federal assistance in construction of hospitals and health centers. As a result, large numbers of hospitals were built in towns and cities throughout the United States. Although health care became available on a widespread basis, the current high cost of health care has forced closure of many of the hospitals built with Hill-Burton funds.

Expansion of services in the areas of health, education, and welfare accelerated after World War I, the Great Depression, and World War II. Coordination of services under several agencies culminated in establishment in 1953 of the Department of Health, Education, and Welfare under President Eisenhower. In 1979, this department was separated into the Department of Education and the Department of Health and Human Services.

The Health Amendments Act of 1956, Title II, authorized funds to allow registered nurses to study administration, supervision, or teaching. In 1963, the Surgeon General's Consultant Group on Nursing noted that there were still too few nursing schools, that nursing personnel were not well utilized, and that limited research was being done in nursing. In 1964, the Nurse Training Act provided funds for loans and scholarships for full-time study

Date	Legislation		
1906	Pure Food and Drugs Act	1970	Occupational Safety and Health Act
1912	Children's Bureau	1972	Social Security Act amendments:
1921	Shepard-Towner Act		Professional Standards Review Organization
1935	Social Security Act		
1946	Hill-Burton Act		Further benefits provided under Medicare/Medicaid, including dialysis
1953	Department of Health, Education, and Welfare established as cabinet-status agency		
		1973	Health Maintenance Organization
		1974	National Health Planning and Resources Act
1964	Nurse Training Act		
1964	Economic Opportunity Act	1981	Omnibus Budget Reconciliation Act
1965	Social Security Act amendments:	1983	Tax Equity and Fiscal Responsibility Act
	Title XVIII Medicare	1988	Family Support Act
	Title XIX Medicaid	1990	Health Objectives Planning Act

The Pure Food and Drugs Act (1906) reflected an early concern for prevention of morbidity and mortality due to environmental influences. The Children's Bureau (1912) was founded to protect children from the unhealthy child labor practices of the time and to enact programs that had a posi-

for nurses as well as funds for nursing school construction.

The Social Security Act (1935) and its subsequent amendments (1965 and 1972) had far-reaching effects by providing welfare for high-risk mothers and children, and benefits were expanded to include health care provisions for the elderly and handicapped (see "Health Care System").

The National Health Planning and Resources Act (1974) established health service areas and was the most influential piece of legislation regarding the roles of citizens in development of state and local health policy (Zimmerman, 1990). The Omnibus Budget Reconciliation Act (1981) was a response to the huge federal deficit and reduced eligibility of poor women and children for welfare and health care. The Family Support Act (1988) expanded coverage for poor women and children and required states to extend Medicaid coverage for 12 months to families with increased earnings who were no longer receiving cash assistance. This act also required states to expand Aid to Families With Dependent Children coverage to two-parent families when the principal wage-earner was unemployed (Cohen, 1990).

The thrust of legislation was either prevention of illness through influence on the environment (Occupational Safety and Health Act, 1970) or provision of funding to support programs that had a direct impact on health care provision (Social Security Act, 1935). Beginning with the Shepard-Towner Act of 1921 and continuing to the present, a pattern of stimulating state and local health departments through federal grants increased the involvement of state and local governments in health care. The involvement of the federal government through provision of funds to state and local governments facilitated programs not previously available. Similar services became available in all states. Funds supporting these services were accompanied by regulations that were applied to all recipients. Many state and local government programs were developed based on availability of funds. Thus, the involvement of the federal government through funding tended to standardize public health policy in the United States (Pickett and Hanlon, 1990).

As health care costs escalated in the 1970s and 1980s, efforts to control costs ensued. Health maintenance organizations (HMOs) were thought to be a potential answer to ever increasing costs. The Tax Equity and Fiscal Responsibility Act (TEFRA, 1983) was necessary because despite HMO proliferation, health care costs continued to escalate. Through TEFRA, a plan for prospective payment was introduced. However, in 1992, health care costs continue to rise despite numerous efforts to contain them.

The 1990 Health Objectives Planning Act was the result of several years of effort by both the private and public sectors. Title XVII of the Public Health Service Act directed the Secretary of Health and Human Services to establish national preventive health goals. In 1979, the Public Health Service identified goals to reduce premature mortality and morbidity for all Americans. The first report was *Healthy People: The Surgeon General's Report on Health Promotion and Disease Prevention* (1979). In 1980, a second report included specific objectives for the year 1990 and was called *Promoting Health, Preventing Disease: Objectives for the Nation.*

The Year 2000 Objectives were developed with considerable input from a wide range of national, state, and local health organizations. The Association of State and Territorial Health Officials (ASTHO) was working to structure a relationship between the national health objectives and state and local public health efforts. ASTHO also was concerned with the functions of public health as presented in the Institute of Medicine report (1988). All 57 state and territorial health departments were invited to participate in the development of the Year 2000 Objectives. Public hearings were conducted in Birmingham, Los Angeles, Houston, Seattle, Denver, Detroit, and New York. These efforts resulted in the Institute of Medicine Report *Healthy People 2000* (U.S. Public Health Service, 1990a). The efforts of ASTHO, as represented in this document, resulted in the introduction in Congress in the Health Objectives Planning Act 2000 in October 1990. The final document, Public Law 101-582, was passed by the 101st Congress on November 15, 1990. According to Scott et al. (1991), the Year 2000 Health Objectives reflect the "second installment of a continuing Federal initiative to adopt 'management by objectives' techniques for health status improvement in the nation" (p. 145). Initial funding authorization ($10 million) was not as much as was requested and did not include funding for health promotion and disease prevention intervention. During the 1991 congressional session, both the House and Senate passed legislation supporting further funding for health promotion and disease prevention. It is hoped that the current reconciliation hearings on the two bills will enable the 1992 Congress to appropriate funds to support these two areas.

HEALTH CARE SYSTEM
Determinants of Health

An effective health care system evolves from an understanding of health. The definition of health is dynamic and has evolved over time; each definition represents the values and beliefs of a given culture at a particular time. Past definitions have served as the basis for the next definition. As discussed in Chapter 1, a definition widely used has been the one stated in the World Health Organization preamble (1944):

"A state of complete physical, mental, and social well being, not merely the absence of disease or infirmity" (p. 29).

Because of the changing nature of health problems of individuals (e.g., the increasing number of persons with chronic disease and of older adults) and the effects of the environment (e.g., pollution) in the population, the WHO definition no longer is adequate. A definition that better reflects current needs and could be used by a health care system is as follows:

"Health is a state characterized by anatomic integrity; ability to perform personally valued family, work, and community roles; ability to deal with physical, biologic, and social stress; a feeling of well-being; and freedom from the risk of disease and untimely death" (Stokes et al., 1982, p. 34).

With this definition, the focus of services changes from unlimited illness care to promoting a safe environment, protecting individuals and communities through immunizations, promoting healthier lifestyles, improving nutrition, and providing health services with known efficacy. Measurable outcomes of a health care system based on this definition include life span, disease, discomfort, participation in health care, health behavior, social behavior, and satisfaction (Blum, 1981).

The outcomes identified in this definition are influenced by a number of factors. For example, Blum (1981) postulated four major inputs (in increasing magnitude of impact) that determine health: heredity, behavior, environment, and health care services. If this is true and evidence

supports this notion, then interventions directed toward education to change lifestyle behaviors and make the environment safer are essential if health is to be achieved (Blum, 1981; Haggerty, 1990; McKeown, 1990).

Blum (1981) suggested the following as appropriate goals of a health care system:

- Promotion of high-level "wellness" or self-fulfillment
- Promotion of high-level satisfaction with the environment
- Minimization of departures from physiological or functional norms for optimal health
- Prolongation of life through prevention of premature death
- Extension of resistance to ill health and creation of reserve capacity
- Minimization of discomfort (illness)
- Minimization of disability (incapacity)
- Increasing capacity for the underprivileged to participate in health matters

In the model proposed by Blum, health care services have less influence on health than do individual personal behavior and habits and the environment (i.e., physical characteristics such as climate, topography, and inadequate housing) (Blum, 1981; Haggerty, 1990; McKeown, 1990). The health care system has been slow in changing to incorporate more recent definitions of health, and the lack of achievement of many of the measurable outcomes is evident in the health of populations. The health care system remains relatively static and continues to focus on illness and disease with less attention paid to health promotion and disease prevention. The following discussion describes the present health care system.

Components of the Health Care System

The health care system has two subsystems: the private health subsystem and the public/environmental health subsystem (Fig. 3–1). The major focus of the private sector is on individuals. The private health care subsystem comprises nonprofit and for-profit sectors and personal care (fee-for-service) by physicians. Also included within the nonprofit sector are voluntary agencies. The public/environmental health subsystem is concerned with the health of populations and the provision of

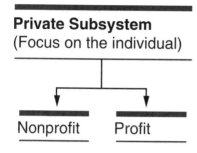

Private Subsystem
(Focus on the individual)

Nonprofit   Profit

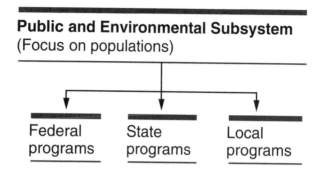

Public and Environmental Subsystem
(Focus on populations)

Federal programs   State programs   Local programs

Figure 3–1
U.S. health care system.

a healthy environment. It is composed of federal, state, and local levels of government programs.

Private Health Care Subsystem

Health care services began within a very simple model. Physicians provided care in their offices and made home visits. Patients were admitted to hospitals for general care if they experienced serious complications during the course of their illness. Today, a variety of highly skilled health care professionals provide comprehensive, preventive, restorative, rehabilitative, and palliative care. A broad array of services, ranging from general to highly specialized with multidelivery configurations, is available.

THE U.S. health care system is complex and is governed by social policies that favor pluralism, free choice, and free enterprise. The private sector personal care subsystem provides the majority of care to individuals. The private sector includes nonprofit and for-profit agencies as well as voluntary organizations. The public health subsystem provides limited personal care services for socially marginal populations but for the most part subsidizes the private sector through Medicare/Medicaid reimbursement for services. In the private sector, personal care services costs are uncontrolled, access to care is not equitable, and the quality of care is uneven.

In this subsystem, personal health care is provided to individuals. Services in this subsystem include health promotion, prevention and early detection of disease, diagnosis and treatment of disease with a focus on cure, rehabilitative and restorative care, and custodial care. These services are provided on an outpatient basis in clinics, physicians' offices, hospital ambulatory centers, and homes; the services are provided on an inpatient basis in hospitals and skilled care facilities. The majority of personal health care services are provided by the private sector. The public health care subsystem provides personal care to citizens who do not have access to the private sector. The majority of these services are provided by health professionals in clinics; public health nurses provide services in the community, home, and schools. However, the scope and amount of services vary among states as well as within each state.

Models of Personal Care

Personal care provided by physicians is delivered under five basic models. The *solo practice* of a physician in an office continues to be present in many communities. The *single-specialty group* model consists of physicians in the same specialty who pool expenses, income, and offices, whereas *multispecialty group practice* provides for interaction across specialty areas. A more recent model is the *integrated health maintenance model,* which has prepaid multispecialty physicians. A fifth model, *community health centers* (developed through federal funds in the 1960s) addresses broader inputs into health such as education and housing.

During the 1960s, health care technology effectively prevented and cured most infectious diseases. Based on the belief that science, knowledge, and technology could treat and cure all health problems, society valued the right of each individual to receive health care. Because societal values translate into public policy and guide and define health services, public policy was directed toward providing all individuals with access to health care.

Medicaid/Medicare

A major government action was the enactment of legislation for Medicare/Medicaid. *Medicare,* Title XVIII Social Security Amendment (1965), is a federal program that pays specified health care services for *all persons over the age of 65 years* who are eligible (approximately 90%) to receive Social Security benefits. Persons with *permanent total disabilities* also are covered. The objective of Medicare is to protect older adults against large medical outlays. The program is funded through a payroll tax for all working citizens. Thus, private funds in the form of payroll tax go to the federal government. Individual providers are reimbursed for health services provided according to Medicare regulations.

Medicare, Part A, pays for institutional care (hospital, nursing home, and skilled home health services). The benefits are the same for all recipients. There is no monthly premium; however, there are copayments and limitations on type and duration of services.

Medicare, Part B, pays for noninstitutional care (physician, outpatient, home health, and ambulatory care). Part B requires a monthly fee and is voluntary (individuals do not have to subscribe). The majority of Medicare dollars spent is for illness care (more than 70% to hospitals and 20% to physicians). Medicare does not cover prescription drugs, preventive services, long-term care, or dental care.

The other major government program for health care is *Medicaid.* Medicaid, Title XIX Social Security Amendment, 1965, is a federal–state program. The purpose of the program is to provide access to *care for the poor and medically needy of all ages.* Each state is allocated federal funds on a matching basis (50% of costs are paid with federal dollars). Each state has the responsibility and right to determine the services to be provided and the amount of funds to be allocated to the program. Basic services (inpatient and outpatient hospital care, physical therapy, laboratory, radiography, and skilled nursing and home health care) are required to be eligible for matching federal funds. States choose from a wide range of optional services, including drugs, eyeglasses, intermediate care, inpatient psychiatric care, and dental care. Limits can and are placed on the amount and duration of service. Unlike Medicare, Medicaid provides long-term care services (e.g., nursing home, home health) and personal care services, (e.g., chores, homemaking). In addition, Medicaid has eligibility criteria that are based on level of income. There is great variability in the services and funds that are provided by each state. For example, Medicaid programs in five states and one territory accounted for 48% of all Medicaid recipients in 1985. In California, New York, Puerto Rico, Michigan, and Pennsylvania, 70% of recipients were in the Aid to Families with Dependent Children category. In addition to the required services for matching of federal dollars, some states and three territories (Georgia, Guam, Mississippi, Puerto Rico, the Virgin Islands, and Wyoming) provide less than 10 additional services. In contrast, Minnesota and California offer 29 additional services, and Michigan, New York, and Wisconsin each offer 26 additional services (Health Care Financing Program Statistics, 1988). Two states, Nevada and Arizona, do not participate in the Medicaid program.

The influx of federal funds through Medicare/Medicaid reimbursement increased the number of persons who had access to and obtained personal care services from the private sector. These funds enabled the private sector of the health care system to provide highly technical personal care services (Fox, 1984; Reinhardt, 1990; Schmitt, 1983). The services provided continued to be based on the biomedical model, which focuses more on treatment than on prevention. Diagnostic practice and treatments continue to depend on the most up-to-date and sophisticated technology. Reliance on expensive laboratory tests and the use of technology for both diagnosis and treatment has increased annually the cost of care. Although some measures have been employed to reduce or stabilize personal care costs, the cost of these services continues to escalate. In 1990, more than $585 billion was spent for personal health care services (National Center for Health Statistics, 1992).

Cost-Containment Concerns

Since the enactment of Medicare/Medicaid, chronic conditions such as heart disease and cancer have replaced the infectious diseases prevalent during the previous decades as major health problems. During the 1970s, chronic diseases placed great demands on the personal health care subsystem with treatments providing "relatively marginal benefits" (Banta, 1990; Rice, 1990; Verbrugge, 1990). For many patients, their health status was not improved significantly.

Schmitt (1983) concluded that consumers' dissatisfaction with the rising costs of service and health benefits that do not meet their expectations caused them to question the right of all individuals to unlimited health care services. Changes in societal values resulted in policy changes that limited access to health care through the use of payment caps and rate regulation. Cost-containment policies were implemented early in the 1980s. A prospective payment system was instituted to control costs and limit use of acute care facilities. The payment system was implemented as diagnosis-related groups. This system controls admissions and length of stays.

Out-of-pocket health care costs increased drastically during the 1980s. It has been estimated that the percentage increase has been as much as 150% in some cases (Estes and Binney, 1988). Persons who can afford insurance are paying more to purchase insurance and receiving less coverage. Millions of Americans with insurance lack adequate coverage and do not have the means to pay for needed health services. In addition, it is estimated that at least 13% of Americans are uninsured (Robert Wood Johnson Foundation, 1991). The rising cost of insurance premiums and health services decreases access to and use of services by those who are unable to purchase or qualify for insurance coverage or pay directly for services.

Although costs continue to increase, and there has not been great success in treating chronic diseases and emerging health problems such as AIDS, smoking, and substance abuse, personal care services, diagnosis, and treatment continue to receive the primary attention and the greatest amount of funds. This support is fostered in part by personal attitudes in which individuals tend to seek care only when it is urgently needed and in part by reimbursement policies geared to care for acute illness. In addition, we attribute recovery to health services received, although evidence supports Scrimshaw's (1974) conclusion that "no matter what is done patients get well most of the time" (p. 794).

During the past decade, privatization of health care has been evolving. After the enactment of the Social Security Act that legislated Medicare/Medicaid, the public sector channeled government funds into the nonprofit sector to provide needed services. The exception was fee-for-services to physicians. During the 1980s, social policy changed from improving access to containing costs. The Omnibus Reconciliation Act (1980) and Omnibus Budget Reconciliation Act (1981) stimulated competition and deregulation. These acts resulted in more public funds allocated to the for-profit sector of the private subsystem to provide services and in fewer funds allocated to the nonprofit sector. Not only was there a shift to for-profit providers, but health care funds did not encourage growth, and allocations for social services were reduced by 20% (Bergthold et al., 1990). The shift toward for-profit providers is based on market principles — ability to pay determines what services are attainable. It is a conscious move away from the equity principle — access for all who are in need of services.

Competition and Fragmentation in the System

The current health care system is pluralistic and competitive. By definition, the system provides fragmented and uncoordinated care. Private care agencies and institutions are in competition with each other for clients, health professionals, and resources. Two hospitals in the same geographic area may compete for the same patients. Hospital home care programs are in direct competition with private home care agencies. Hospitals diversify services to become economically viable and compete with HMOs for the ambulatory market. Public health services can be viewed as competing indirectly for resources (Rice, 1990; Schulz and Johnson, 1990).

Health care agencies function in isolation from each other and provide fragmented services. Although multiple services are available for the wellness-through-serious-illness continuum, coordination is lacking. Services include office or clinic visits, home care, adult day care, acute care institutions, specialized institutions, and skilled nursing facilities. The services provided by one agency or one provider do not help the individual move across boundary lines and receive services offered by others. In addition, the services tend to be geographically separated, and each agency has different criteria for access. The focus of services has not kept pace with the changing needs of individuals and populations, and millions of Americans lack access to health care services and are unable to use available health services due to inadequate financial resources.

Current Efforts to Improve Coordination

Recent efforts to decrease the fragmentation of services, enhance quality of care, and decrease costs include the following:

● Discharge planning
● Case management
● Multiservice models
● Prioritization of health services

DISCHARGE PLANNING

Discharge planning assesses a patient's needs and the resources that are required and available after the patient is discharged from a care setting. The function is most formalized in the acute care setting with designated discharge planners. Effective discharge planning requires knowledge of the client's needs and of resources available within the family and community. The development of a comprehensive plan and implementation to begin immediately after discharge requires collaboration with professionals both within an agency and in other agencies that have or will serve the client after discharge. Communication of these plans to family and providers is essential. Unfortunately, the reimbursement system does not reimburse adequately for development, communication, and evaluation of a comprehensive discharge plan.

CASE MANAGEMENT

To overcome some of the limitations of discharge planning in coordinating care, health care providers instituted case management. In case management, one professional is responsible for assessing needs, targeting services to meet the needs, and monitoring and evaluating client status to ensure that needs are met adequately. The case manager transcends service boundaries and coordinates care throughout the illness trajectory through collaboration with all involved health professionals.

MULTISERVICE MODELS

The development of multiservice models, such as social health maintenance organizations, makes comprehensive coordinated services available within one organization. The range of services encompasses the continuum of care from wellness through illness that includes social services such as meals, housing, and social activities. Several demonstration models are in place; the On Lok Senior Health Services Community Organization (San Francisco) is one example of this model (Kane and Kane, 1987). The On Lok model provides care to frail seniors who meet the criteria for admission to a nursing home. The purpose is to assist them in maintaining their independence and remaining in the community. Currently, this model is being replicated in other geographical localities.

Some multiservice models include residential housing as a component of service. An early model was implemented by nonprofit religious and social organizations. In this model, residents paid an entrance fee as well as a monthly fee. These fees provided the resident with housing and guaranteed health care for life. More recently, for-profit organizations developed similar residential multiservice models. In recent years, these organizations have experienced financial difficulties. Multiple factors make it difficult to remain viable financially. Although individuals enter the facility while able to care for themselves, the longer life span with increasing frailty required more services for a longer time period than were used in the formula that set the original fees. Spiralling health care costs also are an important factor. Currently, the more common residential model is to either buy or rent an apartment or house and then sell or move out when unable to live independently. Care provided in assisted living or skilled care units is funded through Medicare, Medicaid, private insurance, or out of pocket.

PRIORITIZATION OF CARE

Another ongoing experiment is being conducted in Oregon. The Oregon legislature has legislated and outlined strategies to set priorities for state-funded services. The list of services was generated through public forums and reflects both public values and knowledge related to the efficacy of specific interventions. The budgeting process incorporates the prioritized list of services. If budgets need to be reduced, priorities on the lower end of the list are not reimbursed. For example, in a ranking of 13 community values, prevention is first and mental health and chemical dependency are eighth (Capuzzi and Garland, 1990). With severe budget constraints, Oregon would continue to fund prevention but might have to eliminate or set stringent limits on mental health and chemical dependency care.

In summary, the recent efforts have had some impact on improving coordination and provision of services. The lack of standard definitions and common explicit outcomes as well as limited access and adequate funding combine to decrease the effectiveness of these efforts. The public health subsystem must articulate clearly its mission and role and provide leadership in delivering quality care to all citizens in collaboration with the private sector.

Voluntary Agencies

Voluntary or nonofficial agencies are a part of the private health care system and developed at the same time that the government was assuming responsibility for public health. During the first century of the United States, voluntary efforts were virtually nonexistent because early settlers from western Europe were not accustomed to participating in organized charity. Immigration expanded to include slaves from Africa and persons from Eastern Europe, and their well-being received little attention. Toward the end of the 19th century, new immigrants brought a heritage of social

---

Examples of Voluntary Agencies
American Cancer Society
American Heart Association
National Safety Council
American Red Cross
American Nurses' Association
National League for Nursing
American Public Health Association
National Kidney Foundation
National Council on Aging
Planned Parenthood
Rockefeller Foundation
Visiting Nurse Organizations
United Fund

---

protest and reform. Wealthy businesspeople such as the Rockefellers, Carnegies, and Mellons responded to the needs of the poor and set up foundations that provided funds for charitable endeavors. District nurses such as Lillian Wald established nursing practices in the large cities for the poor and destitute.

Proliferation of voluntary agencies continues into the 1990s. According to Hanlon and Pickett (1984), these agencies fall into different categories according to their primary concern: specific diseases (agency examples are the American Diabetes Association, the American Cancer Society, and the Multiple Sclerosis Society); organ or body structures, (e.g., the National Kidney Foundation, and the American Heart Association); health and welfare of special groups (e.g., the National Council on Aging); and particular phases of health (e.g., the Planned Parenthood Federation of America). There are also major philanthropic groups that support research and programs. In addition, there are many professional organizations such as the American Medical Association and the American Nurses' Association (ANA). Voluntary organizations are major sources of assistance in prevention of disease, promotion of health, treatment of illness, and research. For example, private and voluntary organizations support AIDS patients.

There is no central organization for voluntary agencies; as a result, frequent overlapping occurs of services provided by the numerous voluntary and public agencies. Private and public agencies provide a wide array of services, but because of the overlap in services sometimes are not cost effective. However, without both voluntary and official agencies, the array of services would be less than what is currently available.

Future of the Private Health Care System

Although great strides have been made in providing health services that promote health and prevent and treat diseases, many problems remain to be solved. The private sector lacks coordinated, systematic, organized, and sustained efforts directed toward ensuring an environment in which people can be healthy. The system is in disarray. Many gaps exist in care, and large segments of the society are not able to have access to basic care.

The greatest share of resources is channeled into the personal care subsystem and focuses on individuals; this personal care system continues to provide services based on the biomedical model, in which high technology is used for diagnosis and treatment of disease. The public health care subsystem provides limited services for socially marginal populations but continues to subsidize the private sector through Medicare/Medicaid reimbursement.

The debate continues into the 1990s regarding what services should be provided, who should have access to the services, and how the services should be delivered. Changes in the health care system are necessary to meet the changing needs of populations. The personal care subsystem must set limits on the care provided, set criteria for the use of technology, and determine which conditions will be treated, which interventions are effective, and who should receive the care (Banta, 1990). The legal and moral issues involved in setting criteria are just beginning to be addressed.

PUBLIC HEALTH SUBSYSTEM

The role and responsibility of the community health nurse requires understanding the mission, organization, and role of the public health subsystem and the context within which it functions. The public health subsystem, organization, and scope of activities is addressed.

Role of Government

The public health subsystem is mandated by law to address the health of populations. Activities are covered by legal provisions at both state and national levels. At the federal level, Congress enacts laws; rules and regulations are written, and various departments of the executive branch implement and administer them. The U.S. constitution mandates that the federal government "promote the general welfare of its citizens." Interpretations of and amendments to the constitution and Supreme Court decisions have changed and increased the involvement of the federal government in health activities. National policies and practices have had an increasing influence on state and local governments in handling health and social problems. During the past five decades, many laws have been enacted to respond to changing health needs. Two

examples of these laws are the Medicare/Medicaid legislation and the Occupational Safety and Health Act (1970). The former legislation provides funds for health services for older adults and the poor. The latter law addresses working conditions.

Public health with its focus on populations can be described by the following:

"Public health is the effort organized by society to protect, promote, and restore the people's health. The program, services, and institutions involved emphasize the prevention of disease and the health needs of the population as a whole. Public health activities change with changing technology and social values, but the goals remain the same: to reduce the amount of disease, premature death, and disease-produced discomfort and disability" (Sheps, 1976, p. 3).

The activities of the public health subsystem are directed toward the protection of individuals from hazards in their environment. Thus, the focus of public health is threefold: to search for causes of disease, to develop ways to protect the public against disease, and to establish programs to address health problems. The definition of public health has changed over time to reflect the changing health care needs of society. The current values of society, principles that guide actions, knowledge, and social policy determine public health activities. For example, as the population has grown and people live in greater proximity to each other, collective action has become necessary to institute measures to protect people from the hazards of group life (Ellencweig and Yoshpe, 1984).

PRINCIPLE OF SOCIAL JUSTICE

Public health services are predicated on the principle of social justice. The goal of social justice is to decrease preventable death and disability. The social justice model assumes that everyone is entitled equally to valued ends (e.g., status, income, happiness, and health protection). Therefore, the programs and services target groups who lack the resources and ability to obtain needed health care. However, the market justice model is the one that is most prominent in the United States; this model states that persons are entitled to what they can acquire through their own efforts. This belief in individual responsibility affects the health policy of the government health agencies. Efforts remain focused on subsidizing the private sector when significant deficiencies are acknowledged (Beauchamp, 1984). The funds awarded in the form of grants and contracts for education (nurse training) and research, funds for construction of health facilities (Hill-Burton Act), and legislation of Medicare/Medicaid are examples of these efforts. If the social justice model was implemented, health services would be planned and organized with collective action by the private sector and government agencies. Beauchamp (1984) suggests principles that must be in practice for true social justice to occur:

"Controlling hazards of the world to prevent death and disability through organized collective action shared equally by all except where unequal burdens result in increased protection of everyone's health" (p. 309).

Although social justice is the foundation of public health, it has yet to be realized. There are many inequities in access to health care. As previously mentioned, more than 13% of the population is uninsured in the United States. Uninsured persons reflect a wide range of incomes, races, and occupations. In addition, many individuals underuse the health care system: 17% of persons with chronic illness, 15% of those who are in the first trimester of pregnancy, 20% of those who have hypertension, and 38% of those with needs for dental care do not receive any care (Freeman et al., 1990).

Health care expenditures in 1990 were $666.2 billion, which represented 12.2% of the gross national product (National Center for Health Statistics, 1992). In 1987, public health expenditures stabilized and accounted for 40% of total expenditures for health care services (Knickman and Thorpe, 1990). One fifth of public health program expenditures were for health services given in conjunction with supplemental food programs for women, infants, and children. In 1988, only 3% of the health care expenditures were for preventive government public health activities (National Center for Health Statistics, 1991). The increasing allocations of funds have not significantly improved the health status of large segments of our society. For example, in 1989, 58% of native American and 60% of black mothers received care during the first trimester, whereas 79% of white mothers received care (National Center for Health Statistics, 1992). During 1986–1987, infant mortality declined by 3% for white infants but by less than 1% for black infants (U.S. Public Health Service, 1990b).

Three Government Levels

The public health subsystem is organized into multiple levels — federal, state, and local — to provide services more effectively to those who are unable to obtain it without assistance and to establish laws, rules, and regulations to protect the public. The organization of the public health subsystem reflects the values and belief of this country in the separation of powers between the federal government and the states. States are responsible for promulgating laws to protect the public and for providing needed public health services. Each level of government has a distinct role. The public health subsystem is concerned with the health of the population and a healthy environment. The scope of public health is broad and encompasses activities that promote good health. As societal values change, new health and social problems are recognized, and the knowledge and ability to solve perceived problems emerge, programs and services of public health will change.

FEDERAL LEVEL

ORGANIZATION. Most health-related activities are implemented and administered by the Department of Health and Human Services. This department is directed by a secretary and numerous undersecretaries and assistant secretaries. The Surgeon General is the principal deputy to the Assistant Secretary of DHHS.

The DHHS is composed of five major agencies: Office of Human Development Services, Public Health Service, Health Care Financing Administration, Social Security Administration, and Family Support Administration (Fig. 3–2).

The Office of Human Development Services is an umbrella agency that is responsible for programs meeting special needs of the population, such as providing congregate meals to the elderly. The Health Care Financing Administration administers Medicare/Medicaid programs and carries out activities related to assurance of quality care. The Social Security Administration coordinates all activities related to implementing the So-

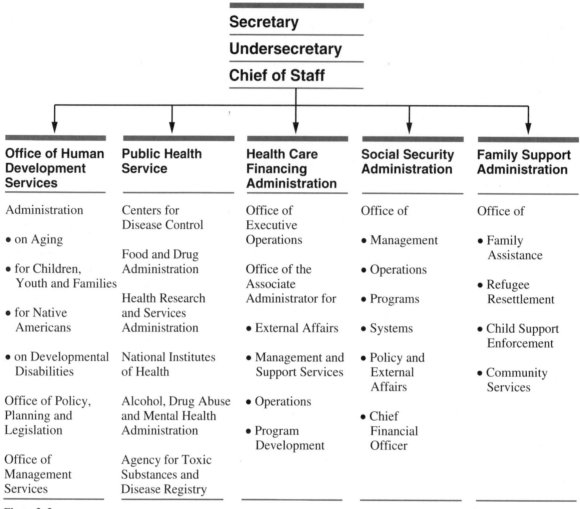

Figure 3–2
Agencies that compose the U.S. Department of Health and Human Services.

cial Security law, including Supplemental Security Income for the Aged, Blind, and Disabled. The Family Support Administration carries out functions to strengthen the family unit.

The U.S. Public Health Service has six units (see Fig. 3–2).

1. *The Centers for Disease Control* conduct and support programs directed to prevent and control infectious diseases and provide assistance to states during epidemics. In addition, they provide services related to health promotion and education and professional development and training.

2. The *Food and Drug Administration* provides surveillance over the safety and efficacy of foods, pharmaceuticals, and other consumer goods.

3. *The Health Resources and Service Administration* is concerned with the development of health services programs and facilities. The Division of Nursing funds grants related to education and training. The Indian Health Service provides health services for Native Americans and Alaskan natives.

4. *The National Institutes of Health* carry out and support research programs. The focus is on developing and extending scientific knowledge

bases. The National Center for Nursing Research is a part of this unit.

5. The *Alcohol, Drug Abuse, and Mental Health Administration* supports research and programs related to substance abuse and mental health.
6. The *Agency for Toxic Substances and Disease Registry* prevents or mitigates adverse health effects of hazardous substances in the environment. A major activity of this unit is the administration of grants and contracts.

Other federal agencies perform activities related to health. For example, the Department of Education is involved with health education and school health, and the Department of Agriculture is involved with inspection of meat and milk and provides funds for the supplemental nutrition program for women, infants, and children; for the food stamp program; and for the school-based nutrition program. The Department of Interior is concerned with mining safety and stream pollution.

To facilitate coordination and provide more direct assistance to the states, there are 10 regional offices of the U.S. Public Health Service (Fig. 3–3). The regional offices carry out selected health programs, activities, and initiatives under the direction of the Assistant Secretary for Health (Last, 1987*b*; Pickett and Hanlon, 1990; Wilner et al., 1978; Wilson and Neuhauser, 1985).

SCOPE. The federal government focuses on the health of the general population, special populations, and the international community. Concern for the health of the general population involves protection against hazards, maintenance of vital and health statistics, advancement of scientific knowledge through research, and provision of disaster relief.

In recent years, public health efforts have been directed toward changing behaviors by encouraging the eating of healthier foods, exercising, and stopping or preventing the use of tobacco, drugs, and alcohol. Other programs have provided nutritional food and foodstamps to individuals and families to reduce the risk of illness due to lowered resistance.

Services for special groups include protection of workers against hazardous occupations and work conditions and provision of health care to veterans, native Americans, Alaskan natives, federal prisoners, and members of the armed services. In addition, special services are provided for children, older adults, the mentally ill, and the vocationally handicapped.

In the international arena, the U.S. government is a member of the World Health Organization and works with other countries and international health organizations to promote various health programs throughout the world (Hanlon and Pickett, 1984; Last, 1987*a*; Wilner et al., 1978; Wilson and Neuhauser, 1985).

STATE LEVEL

ORGANIZATION. States are responsible for the health of their citizens. They are the central authorities in the public health care system. There is wide variation among states in the organization of public health and related activities. In a recent survey in which 46 states responded to the question of organizational type, 25 (50%) indicated that they are independent, cabinet-level public health agencies; 13 (26%) were in a department with other services such as social services; and six (12%) were in integrated human services departments (Scott et al., 1990).

State agencies are directed by a health commissioner or secretary of health who is appointed by the state governor. Each state also has a health officer, usually a physician with a degree and experience in public health. In some states, the health officer directs the health department. Twenty-four states have boards of health that determine policies and priorities for allocation of funds. Staffing of the state agency varies among states; health programs have the largest number of staff. Nurses represent the largest group of professionals providing health services (Hanlon and Pickett, 1984; Last, 1987*b*; Wilner et al., 1978; Wilson and Neuhauser 1985).

SCOPE. Because each state is responsible for their own laws (they cannot violate federal law), there is wide variation in state policy among the 50 states. Factors that affect the level of state services include per capita income, political factors related to division of power between state and local health departments, and competition among officials, providers, and the business community. The three major functions that categorize state activities are assessment, policy development, and assurance

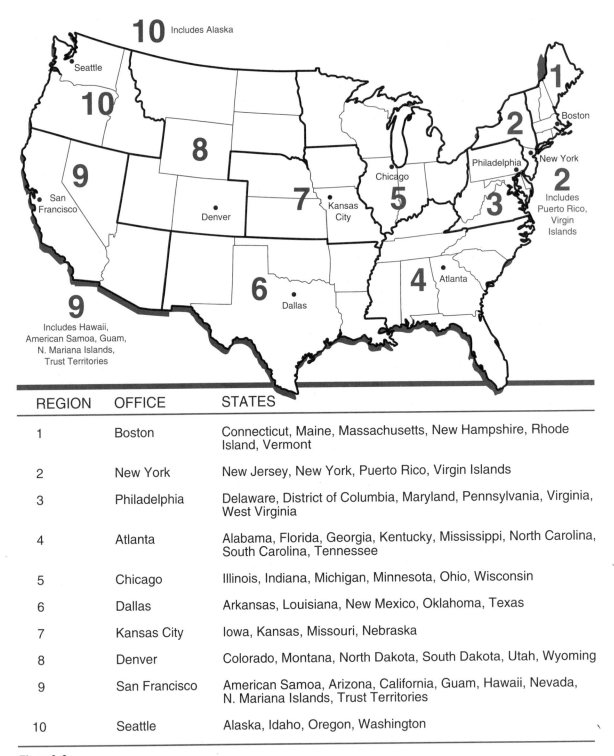

REGION	OFFICE	STATES
1	Boston	Connecticut, Maine, Massachusetts, New Hampshire, Rhode Island, Vermont
2	New York	New Jersey, New York, Puerto Rico, Virgin Islands
3	Philadelphia	Delaware, District of Columbia, Maryland, Pennsylvania, Virginia, West Virginia
4	Atlanta	Alabama, Florida, Georgia, Kentucky, Mississippi, North Carolina, South Carolina, Tennessee
5	Chicago	Illinois, Indiana, Michigan, Minnesota, Ohio, Wisconsin
6	Dallas	Arkansas, Louisiana, New Mexico, Oklahoma, Texas
7	Kansas City	Iowa, Kansas, Missouri, Nebraska
8	Denver	Colorado, Montana, North Dakota, South Dakota, Utah, Wyoming
9	San Francisco	American Samoa, Arizona, California, Guam, Hawaii, Nevada, N. Mariana Islands, Trust Territories
10	Seattle	Alaska, Idaho, Oregon, Washington

Figure 3–3
U.S. Public Health Service regional offices.

(Institute of Medicine, 1988). Assessment activities include collection of data pertaining to vital statistics, health facilities, and manpower; epidemiological activities such as communicable disease control, health screening, and laboratory analyses; and participation in research projects (Institute of Medicine, 1988). In the area of policy development, states formulate goals, develop health plans, and set standards for local health agencies. Assurance activities involve inspection in a variety of areas, licensing, health education, environmental safety, personal health services, and resource development.

In 1984, $308 million was spent for assessment activities; of these funds, communicable disease control activities received the greatest proportion ($160 million). Six million dollars were spent for policy development. Assurance activities received more than $4.5 billion; within this category, maternal child health efforts received $2 billion, and inpatient state institutions received $900 million. Three hundred million dollars were spent for environmental services. During the past few years, the level of total funding at the state level has remained constant (Institute of Medicine, 1988). In 1989, over $15 billion was spent for public health services at the state and local levels (Lazenby and Letsch, 1990).

The Institute of Medicine recommended 13 specific duties for state health departments, as shown in Table 3–1. A survey of 50 state health officers showed that although they agreed that the recommended duties were appropriate (>84%), there was wide variation (26–86%) in actual implementation of these duties. The two activities least frequently performed by states were integration of mental health services and establishment of standards for minimum services provided by the state. The two duties most frequently implemented were provision of subsidies and direct assistance to local health departments and assessment of state health needs. States currently not implementing the duties indicated that they would in the future assess state needs and provide assistance to local health departments (85–100%); fewer states (65%) planned to establish standards, and only 38%

Table 3–1
Number of State Public Health Departments Agreeing With and Implementing Selected Recommendations of the Institute of Medicine Committee on the Future of Public Health—United States, 1989

Recommendation	Agree	Implementing	Plan to Implement
Support local health with subsidies and direct assistance	50	37	11
Educate public on community health needs and policy issues	50	34	14
Revise statutory base to address contemporary health problems	50	33	15
Assess state health needs based on state data	49	40	10
Ensure statewide availability of essential environmental health services	49	27	11
Develop comprehensive strategies to influence health-related behavior	48	21	24
Link with mental health services to improve integration of service delivery	48	13	18
Conduct population-based health research	47	24	16
Be responsible for disease prevention and health promotion	45	35	3
Ensure personal health services for the medically indigent	45	29	14
Establish standards specifying minimum services to be provided by local public health facilities	45	16	22
Be responsible for regulation of health facilities	44	43	0
Be responsible for health planning	42	25	13

From Centers for Disease Control: Strengthening public health practice: Survey of state health officers—United States, 1989. M. M. W. R. *39*;773–776, 1990*a*.

planned to integrate mental health services (Centers for Disease Control, 1990*a*).

LOCAL LEVEL

ORGANIZATION. The day-to-day responsibility for protecting the health of citizens resides in the local health departments. They are responsible for direct delivery of public health services. The authority to conduct these activities is delegated by the state and local governments. Four states — Delaware, Hawaii, Rhode Island, and Vermont — do not have local departments. The other 46 states have a total of 2,262 local health departments. Within the 50 states, there are 3,041 counties, 82,290 units of government (e.g., village, town, or city), and 14,851 school districts that also provide some health-related services (Brecher, 1990); the number of services in each state ranges from 0 to more than 100. The 2,262 local health departments were located in the following jurisdictional units: county (49%), town or township (13%), and city (10%). Twenty percent were combined city and county departments, and 7% were multiple county (National Association of County Health Officials, 1990). Depending on the population density, some areas are not covered by local services (e.g., southwestern South Dakota).

Local health departments are directed by a health officer or administrator appointed by the unit leadership (i.e., mayor, town council, county supervisors). Twenty-one states require the health officer of a local health department to have a medical degree. A multidisciplinary team carries out the activities of the department. Public health nurses and health inspectors represent the two largest groups of professional staff; other professional staff include dentists, social workers, epidemiologists, nutritionists, and health educators.

The organizational structure of local health departments varies within and among states. Some local health departments function as district offices of the state health department; others are responsible to local government and the state; and others are autonomous (large cities). A local health department may be a separate agency or a division within an agency such as a health and human services agency. The population served ranges from a few hundred to hundreds of thousands. The relationship between local health departments and state public health agencies varies in the coopera-

tion and sharing of responsibility for programs (Hanlon and Pickett, 1984; Last, 1987*b*; Wilner et al., 1978; Wilson and Neuhauser, 1985).

SCOPE. Local health departments are responsible for determining the health status and needs of their constituents, identifying unmet needs, and taking action to see that the unmet needs are met adequately. Most services provided to groups and individuals are provided at the local level. These activities fall into four major categories: community health services, environmental health services, mental health services, and personal health services. Community health services include control of communicable diseases (surveillance and immunizations), maternal-child health programs, nutrition, and education. Specific activities include health promotion directed toward changing behavior through eating healthier foods, increasing exercise, and decreasing the use of tobacco, drugs, and alcohol. Other programs provide nutritional food and foodstamps to individuals and families. Preventive screening for potential problems throughout life is a major activity of local health departments. Screening leads to early detection of genetic disorders, developmental delay, behavior disorders, hypertension, diabetes, and cancer (Table 3–2). Environmental health services include food hygiene (inspection of food production and processing and restaurants); protection from hazardous substances; control of waste, air, noise, and water pollution; and occupational health. The objective of these activities is to provide a safe environment.

Mental health activities are focused on primary prevention, diagnosis, and treatment. Personal health services provide care to individuals and families in clinics, schools, jails, and clients' homes. Other activities include disaster planning, programmatic planning within departments and with other agencies, and coordination of programs involving the public and private sectors. The scope of services varies among local health departments. Data reported by local health departments indicated that at least 75% provide services in the categories of immunizations; communicable disease reporting; child health; tuberculosis; health education; sexually transmitted diseases; women, infants, and children; and chronic diseases. At least 40% were involved with family planning, prenatal

Table 3–2
Screening Procedures and Developmental Stages

Prenatal Period (Assess Pregnant Women)

Genetic disorders	Obstetric conditions
Blood group incompatibility	Pelvic disproportion
Sexually transmitted diseases	Recurrent or threatened abortion
Syphilis, gonorrhea, herpes, AIDS	Maternal behavior
Rubella, toxoplasmosis	Alcohol, tobacco use
Birth defects	Neglect, abuse
Neural tube defects, Down's syndrome	
Medical conditions	
Diabetes, hypertension	
Bacteriuria, pyelonephritis	

Infancy (0–18 mo)

Screening routines for	Examination for other defects
Phenylketonuria	Cardiovascular defects
Congenital hip disease	Hearing, visual impairment, strabismus
Hypothyroidism	Developmental delay or abnormalities

Childhood (18 mo–11 yr)

Visual, hearing disorders	Behavior disorders, learning disabilities
Developmental abnormalities	Dental caries

Adolescence (12–15 yr)

Tuberculin test	Sexual maturation
Dental caries	Psychosexual development

Adulthood (16–44 yr)

Hypertension	Cancer of cervix
Diabetes	Family dysfunction
Dental caries	

Adulthood (45–64 yr)

Glaucoma	Cancer
Hypertension	Breast
Diabetes	Cervix
	Colon and rectum
	Prostate
	Oral cavity
	Lung, bladder, stomach

Adulthood (65 yr and older)

Tuberculin test	Cancer
Sensory impairments (vision, hearing)	Nutrition
Motor impairments (hips, feet)	Emotional status
Hypertension	Intellectual status
Diabetes	

From Spitzer, W. O.: Periodic Health Examination: Report of a Task Force to the Deputy Ministers of Health. Ottawa, Canada, Health and Welfare, 1980.

care, AIDS testing and counseling, home health care, handicapped children, laboratory services, and dental health. Less than 25% indicated that they were involved in occupational safety and health, primary care, obstetric care, drug and alcohol use, mental health, emergency medical services, long-term care facilities, and hospitals (Centers for Disease Control, 1990b). Functions and services of local health departments range from the control of communicable disease, environmental health, food hygiene, health education, clinic services, screening programs, home care, disaster planning, and coordination of voluntary service agencies (Table 3–3 and Fig. 3–4).

The services of each local health department are determined by many factors; three critical factors are the values held by constituents, the values of elected officials, and the availability of resources. A major determinant is the needs of the people served. For example, departments on the West Coast are actively involved in providing services related to AIDS testing and counseling, sexually transmitted diseases, immunizations, and tuberculosis; other regions are less active in these functions. To interpret the appropriateness and completeness of the services provided, an understanding of the demographic characteristics and needs of the region is required.

Table 3–3
Percentage of Local Health Departments That Reported Being Active in Selected Functions and Services by Region

Functions and Services	Public Health Service Region									
	1	2	3	4	5	6	7	8	9	10
Reportable disease data collection	75%	92%	97%	94%	87%	88%	80%	77%	96%	96%
Health planning	39%	80%	62%	55%	64%	49%	51%	58%	74%	78%
Food and milk control	83%	82%	94%	81%	66%	73%	42%	49%	73%	70%
Health education	47%	90%	84%	79%	77%	75%	74%	71%	83%	81%
Hazardous waste management	60%	70%	40%	36%	42%	47%	23%	42%	70%	66%
Individual water supply safety	66%	79%	93%	89%	76%	80%	62%	60%	73%	80%
Vector and animal control	57%	85%	81%	77%	77%	70%	41%	57%	77%	72%
AIDS testing and counseling	12%	41%	86%	94%	41%	62%	45%	56%	93%	99%
Child health	35%	96%	92%	99%	86%	94%	89%	83%	91%	93%
Family planning	6%	29%	92%	98%	44%	82%	58%	55%	86%	74%
Immunizations	61%	98%	100%	100%	96%	98%	96%	85%	97%	100%
Prenatal care	10%	50%	76%	93%	53%	77%	43%	59%	52%	82%
Sexually transmitted diseases	20%	77%	97%	99%	68%	92%	55%	63%	99%	95%
Tuberculosis	40%	83%	98%	99%	78%	96%	74%	60%	97%	100%
No. of departments	327	158	124	478	486	239	206	108	69	74

Based on National Association of County Health Officials: NACHO's response to the IOM report: The future of public health. J. Public Health Policy 10;95–98, 1989.

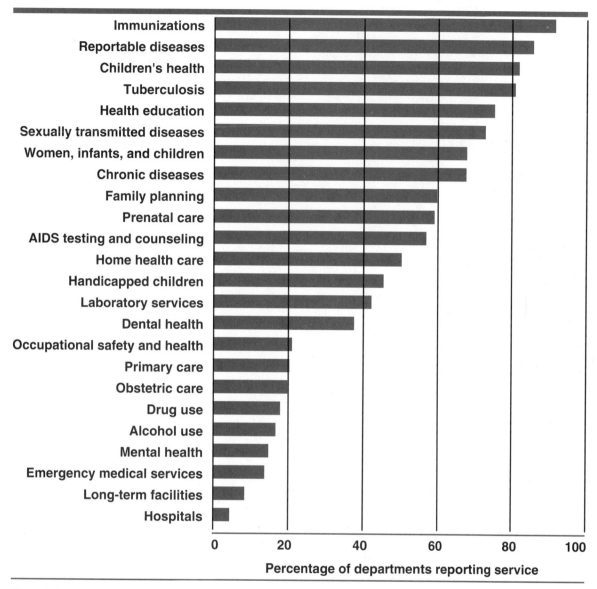

Figure 3–4
Services reported by local health departments. This graph illustrates the information in Table 3–3. It shows that services are provided very unevenly in the 2,262 local health departments reporting (Redrawn from Centers for Disease Control: Health objectives for the nation: Selected characteristics of local health departments—United States, 1989. M. M. W. R. *39*:609, 1990*b*.)

FUTURE OF THE HEALTH CARE SYSTEM

Futurists predict that many changes will occur in the U.S. during the end of the 20th century and the beginning of the 21st century (Arthur Andersen & Co., 1987; Ebert and Ginzberg, 1988; Kovner,

1990). Futurists are influenced by patterns and events they believe will have an increasing impact on the direction of health care, e.g., chronic illness, AIDS, and environmental hazards. The aging of the population, increased consumer involvement, escalating health care costs, increased technology, fewer hospital admissions, and more ambulatory

---

Changing Focus of Public Health

ALTHOUGH THE goals of the public health subsystem do not change, the programs and services provided change to meet the changing needs of the public. The leading causes of death illustrate the changing focus of public health. The incidence of pneumonia, tuberculosis, diarrhea, and diseases of the heart has decreased in the population. Current priorities include activities related to violent and abusive behavior, vitality, independence of older persons, HIV infection prevention, and health education.

---

care are social and scientific patterns that will continue to have profound influences.

Kovner predicted in 1990 that for at least the next 5 years, there would be no national health insurance, fewer large systems of health care (such as HMOs), less medical use per capita, less physician power, and more state regulation regarding cost, quality, and access to health care. Furthermore, Kovner stated that the factors that will contribute to future health care are demographic characteristics of the population, disease patterns, information systematization, and major technological breakthroughs.

Although there are differing opinions concerning how satisfied or dissatisfied Americans are with the current health care system (Blendon, 1989; Ginzberg, 1990), Kovner (1990) does not believe there will be a fundamental break with the current health care system in the 1990s because of the limited political power of the uninsured. He further noted that although there are indicators that the United States has serious problems with the cost, access, and quality of health care, the seriousness of these problems depends on who is answering the questions related to the problems—the poor, minority, and rural Americans or the remainder of the population.

Health care organizations at all levels are promoting health care changes in the areas of access, quality, and cost. Some are advocating changes that would place the major responsibility for health care in the public sector. Others are seeking to combine the public and private sectors in unique ways. Bold efforts are aimed at restructuring and reorienting the entire health care system through reform. For example, the ANA requests a shift from the "predominant focus on illness and cure to an orientation toward wellness and care" (ANA, 1991). In this document, the ANA recommends that a federally defined standard package of essential health care services be available to all, financed through an integration of public and private plans and sources. The development of this plan remains uncertain. Harrington (1990) classified current proposals into three types:

1. Incremental expansion of existing public programs such as Medicaid/Medicare.
2. Mandatory private health insurance provided by employers
3. A comprehensive national health plan similar to the Canadian plan

Ward (1990) points out that the tension between states' rights and federal powers will be reflected in future health care systems. States already have begun to work out a variety of plans and may facilitate the achievement of health insurance for all.

Public Health Subsystem

Two potential influences on the future of the public health subsystem include the Institute of Medicine's report on the future of public health (1988) and the Health Objectives 2000 Act proposed by the Association of State and Territorial Health Officials in 1989. These two documents are expected to have a profound influence on the future and can provide the framework for the structure and function of public health in the 21st century.

The U.S. Conference of Local Health Officers considered the Institute of Medicine's report a valuable planning document that was useful at all levels. They stated that the report "offers a myriad of recommendations that are of value to the future of public health in general and to local public health in particular" (National Association of County Health Officials, 1989, p. 95) (see Table 3–1). Emphasized was the importance of partnership among federal, state, and local levels of government and the building of close networks between public and private agencies. Although the report described the public health subsystem as being in a state of disarray, there is widespread disagreement with this stance. However, the report was accepted for its valuable recommendations and has stimulated self-evaluation by public health agencies at all levels. The report will continue to be used by these agencies in planning for the future.

Prevention of Disease and Promotion of Health

The recognition that social and behavioral factors are vital in the health of the nation has prompted the development of new approaches. Control and eradication of communicable diseases, based on the biomedical model, has dominated the health care system since the late 1900s; because diseases that were a threat in the beginning of this century have been controlled or eradicated, there has been a change in focus toward promotion of health. A

Goals for the Nation in the Year 2000
THE YEAR 2000 Health Objectives identify 298 specific health objectives in 22 priority areas. The objectives are to reduce infant mortality, increase life expectancy, reduce disability caused by chronic conditions, increase years of healthy life, and decrease the disparity in life expectancy between white and minority populations.

---

new set of health problems exists today. Green and Raeburn (1990) refer to a growing international awareness of an ecological model of health promotion that identifies health as the "product of the individual's continuous interaction and interdependence with his or her ecosphere—that is, the family, the community, the culture, the societal structure, and the physical environment" (p. 35). The health promotional approach focuses on the lifestyle of persons and interaction with the eco-structure rather than relying on the biomedical model.

The ecological model also fits more precisely with an international view of health. Two documents that support such a perspective are the *Alma Ata Charter of 1978,* and the *Ottawa Charter for Health Promotion* of 1986. Both documents emphasize living standards as critical to health. The Ottawa charter stated that the fundamental conditions and resources for health are peace, shelter, education, food, income, a stable ecosystem, sustainable resources, social justice, and equity. The document further noted that improvement in health requires a secure foundation in these basic prerequisites. This is an ideal that will take both the

industrial countries and the Third World decades to achieve (Editorial, 1990*a*). Nevertheless, the mandate is clear and will increase in importance during the 1990s.

According to Terris (1990), health promotion in the United States began with a more limited focus. The Surgeon General's report in 1979 defined health promotion as modification of lifestyle to prevent disease, with little attention given to improvement of living standards. Although modification of lifestyle is important, inattention to improvement of living standards is detrimental to health as defined in the broader ecological model.

There are fundamental differences in health promotion between Canada and the United States. Since the Ottawa charter, the Canadian system (which provides health care to all) focuses on the general well-being of populations. For example, major efforts are aimed toward incorporating cultural concepts into all aspects of the health care system. The United States, on the other hand, has continued to focus on lifestyle change, e.g., smoking cessation, safe sexual practices, and exercise.

Future of Public Health and the Health Care System

How does the public health subsystem, an important component of the health care system, fit into a future health care system? Futurists rarely identify the public health subsystem as a component of the health care system, perhaps because of the historical involvement of the public health subsystem with the poor and disenfranchised. The assumptions underlying the ecological model demand that attention be paid to the poor and underserved, but the political aspects of health care frequently demand other foci. Terris (1990) stated that international and domestic political and economic factors play a major role in public health policy and will continue to do so. A major change in policy will require fundamental changes in U.S. ideology and political stance.

Most futurists agree that some type of national or state-by-state medical program will develop within the decade of the 1990s. Health promotion, disease prevention, and medical care are priorities of proposed programs. Whether any of the programs will be conceived within the framework of the ecological model and incorporate attention to living standards remains uncertain. Focus on environmental influences on population is critical for the future health of any nation.

As emphasized in this chapter, the goals for health care reflect the values of society. Last (1987*a*) pointed out that predicting future trends in human values is more difficult than predicting scientific discoveries or disease patterns. However, Koop (1989) stated that the ultimate test of the public health subsystem is whether it effectively serves the people by their measurements, not by those of the public health profession.

SUMMARY

In the 20th century, several major pieces of health and welfare legislation were enacted by the federal government. Current legislative initiatives, cost-containment measures, and health care objectives

for the future are influenced by the increase in chronic disease, the greater number of older people, the importance of preventive interventions, and the impact of environmental factors on health.

The population of the United States is served by the public and private health care subsystems. In the private sector, there is much fragmentation and inconsistency in the way services are provided. In the public sector, services are available in often uncoordinated or disparate ways at the federal, state, and local levels.

Many experts foresee a future health care system in which there will be greater involvement of the public sector—one that will more equitably ensure access to health care. They predict that this approach will include an ecological perspective that will consider family, community, culture, societal structures, and physical environment.

Learning Activities

1. Describe the organization of your state and local health departments.

2. Visit your local health department and learn what services are provided. Compare your health department's services with those listed in Figure 3–4 and identify possible gaps in local services.

3. Identify the regional and state services where you live and compare them with those described in the chapter (see Table 3–3).

4. Visit one voluntary agency; determine the services they offer and how the agency collaborates with the local public health agency.

5. Determine how your state health department has operationalized health goals for the year 2000.

6. Interview a public health nurse regarding perceptions of the Institute of Medicine report on nursing practice.

REFERENCES

Alma Ata World Health Organization and Children's Fund: Primary Health Care: A Joint Report. Geneva, World Health Organization, 1978.

American Nurses' Association: Nursing's Agenda for Health Care Reform. Kansas City, Missouri, ANA, 1991.

Andersen, A., & Co.: The Future of Health Care: Changes and Choices. Chicago, American College of Health Care Executives, 1987.

Banta, H. D.: What is health care? *In* Kovner, A. R., ed.: Health Care Delivery in the United States. 4th Ed. New York, Springer, 1990, pp. 8–30.

Beauchamp, D. E.: Public health as social justice. *In* Lee, P. R., Estes, C. L., and Ramsay, N. B., eds.: The Nation's Health. 2nd Ed. San Francisco, Boyd & Fraser, 1984, pp. 306–313.

Bergthold, L. A., Estes, C. L., and Villanuevae, A.: Public light and private dark: The privatization of home health services for the elderly in the U. S. Home Health Care Serv. Q. *11*;7–33, 1990.

Blendon, R. J.: Three systems: A comparative survey. Health Mgmt. Q. *2*;185–192, 1989.

Blum, H. L.: Planning for health: Development and application of social change theory. *In* Health and the Systems Approach. 2nd Ed. New York, Human Sciences Press, Inc., 1981, pp. 10–38.

Brecher, C.: The government's role in health care. *In* Kovner, A. R., ed.: Health Care Delivery in the United States. 4th Ed. New York, Springer, 1990, pp. 297–323.

Capuzzi, C., and Garland, M.: The Oregon plan: Increasing access to health care. Nurs. Outlook *38*;260–263, 1990.

Centers for Disease Control: Strengthening public health practice: Survey of state health officers—United States, 1989. Morbidity and Mortality Weekly Report *39*;773–776, 1990*a*.

Centers for Disease Control: Health objectives for the nation: Selected characteristics of local health departments—United States, 1989. Morbidity and Mortality Weekly Report *39*;607–610, 1990*b*.

Cohen, S. S.: The politics of Medicaid: 1980–89. Nurs. Outlook *36*;229–233, 1990.

Ebert, R. H., and Ginzberg, E.: The reform of medical education. Health Affairs Suppl. *7*;5–38, 1988.

Editorial: Confusion worse confounded: Health promotion and prevention. J. Public Health Policy *11*;144–145, 1990*a*.

Editorial: The Health Objectives 2000 Act: Our first and foremost legislative goal. J. Public Health Policy *2*;141–143, 1990*b*.

Ellencweig, A. Y., and Yoshpe, R. B.: Definition of public health. Public Health Rev. *12*;65–78, 1984.

Estes, C. L., and Binney, E. A.: Toward a transformation of health and aging policy. Int. J. Health Serv. *18*;69–96, 1988.

Fox, R.: The medicalization and demedicalization of American society. *In* Lee, P. R., Estes, C. L., and Ramsey, N. B., eds.: The Nation's Health. 2nd Ed. San Francisco, Boyd & Fraser, 1984, pp. 143–159.

Freeman, H. E., et al.: Americans report on their access to health care. *In* Lee, P. R., and Estes, C. L., eds.: The Nation's Health. 3rd Ed. Boston, Jones and Bartlett, 1990, pp. 309–319.

Ginzberg, E.: A non-conforming view. Health Mgmt. Q. *12*;20–22, 1990.

Green, L. W., and Raeburn, J.: Contemporary developments in health promotion: Definitions and challenges. *In* Bracht, N., ed.: Health Promotion at the Community Level. Newbury Park, California, Sage Publications, 1990, pp. 29–42.

Haggerty, R. J.: The boundaries of health care. *In* Lee, P. R., and Estes, C. L., eds.: The Nation's Health. 3rd Ed. Boston, Jones and Bartlett, 1990, pp. 112–117.

Hanlon, G., and Pickett, J.: Public Health Administration and Practice. 8th Ed. St. Louis, Times Mirror/Mosby, 1984, pp. 143–156.

Harrington, C.: Policy options for a national health care plan. Nurs. Outlook *38*;223–228, 1990.

Health Objectives 2000 Act, S2056. Washington, D. C., U.S. Government Printing Office, February 1, 1990.

Health Care Financing Administration: Health Care Financing Program Statistics: Medicare and Medicaid Data Book. Washington, D. C., Health Care Financing Administration, Publication no. 03270, 1988, pp. 59–123.

Institute of Medicine: The National Academy of Science: The Future of Public Health. Washington, D. C., The National Academy Press, 1988.

Kane, R. A., and Kalne, R. L.: Long-term Care: Principles, Programs and Policies. New York, Springer, 1987, pp. 306–349.

Knickman, J. R., and Thorpe, K. E.: Financing for health care. *In* Kovner, A. R., ed.: Health Care Delivery in the United States. 4th Ed. New York, Springer, 1990, pp. 240–269.

Koop, C. E.: An agenda for public health. J. Public Health Policy *10*;7–18, 1989.

Kovner, A. R., ed.: Health Care Delivery in the United States. 4th Ed., New York, Springer, 1990.

Last, J. M.: The scope, goals, and methods of public health. *In*: Public Health Human Ecology. East Norwalk, Connecticut, Appleton and Lange, 1987*a*, pp. 1–26.

Last, J. M.: Organization of public health services. *In*: Public Health and Human Ecology. East Norwalk, Connecticut, Appleton and Lange, 1987*b*, pp. 281–300.

Lazenby, H. C., and Letsch, S. W.: National health expenses, 1989. Health Care Financing Review *12*; 1–26, 1990.

McKeown, T.: Determinants of health. *In* Lee, P. R., and Estes, C. L., eds.: The Nation's Health. 3rd Ed. Boston, Jones and Bartlett, 1990, pp. 6–13.

National Association of County Health Officials: NACHO's response to the IOM report: The future of public health. J. Public Health Policy *10*;95–98, 1989.

National Association of County Health Officials: National Profile of Local Health Departments: An Overview of the Nation's Local Public Health System. Washington, D. C., National Association of County Health Officials, 1990, p. 43.

National Center for Health Statistics: Health, United States, 1990. Hyattsville, Maryland, U.S. Public Health Service, 1991.

National Center for Health Statistics: Health, United States, 1991. Hyattsville, Maryland, U.S. Public Health Service, 1992.

Ottawa Charter for Health Promotion 1986. Ottawa, Canadian Public Health Association, 1986.

Pickett, G., and Hanlon, J. J.: Public Health Administration and Practice. 9th Ed. St. Louis, Times Mirror/Mosby, 1990, pp. 97–133.

Reinhardt, U. E.: Rationing the health care surplus: An American tragedy. *In* Lee, P. R., and Estes, C. L., eds.: The Nation's Health. 3rd Ed. Boston, Jones and Bartlett, 1990, pp. 104–111.

Rice, D. P.: The medical care system: Past trends and future projections. *In* Lee, P. R., and Estes, C. L., eds.: The Nation's Health. 3rd Ed. Boston, Jones and Bartlett, 1990, pp. 72–93.

Robert Wood Johnson Foundation: Challenges in Health Care: A Chartbook Perspective. Trenton, New Jersey, RWJF, 1991.

Schmitt, G. H.: How we deliver care. Issues Health Care *4*;8–11, 1983.

Schulz, R., and Johnson, A. C.: Health and the health system. *In* Management of Hospitals and Health Services. 3rd Ed. St. Louis, C. V. Mosby, 1990, pp. 17–33.

Scott, H. D., Tierney, J. T., and Waters, W. J.: The future of public health: A survey of the states. J. Public Health Policy *11*;296–304, 1990.

Scott, H. D., Tierney, J. T., and Waters, W. J.: The year 2,000 national health objectives. J. Public Health Policy *12*;145–147, 1991.

Scrimshaw, N.: Myths and realities in international health planning. Am. J. Public Health *64*;792–797, 1974.

Sheps, C. G.: Higher education for public health. *In*: A Report of the Milbank Memorial Fund Commission. New York, Prodist, 1976, pp. 1–5.

Spitzer, W. O.: Periodic Health Examination: Report of a Task Force to the Deputy Ministers of Health. Health and Welfare, Ottawa, Canada, 1980.

Stokes, J. III, Noren, J. J., and Shindell, S.: Definitions of terms and concepts applicable to clinical preventive medicine. J. Comm. Health *8*;33–41, 1982.

Terris, M.: Public health policy for the 1990's. J. Public Health Policy *11*;281–295, 1990.

Torrens, P. R.: The American Health Care System Issues on Problems. St. Louis, C. V. Mosby, 1978.

U.S. Public Health Service: Healthy People 2,000: National Health Promotion and Disease Prevention Objectives. Washington, D. C., U.S. Government Printing Office, 1990*a*.

U.S. Public Health Service: Healthy People — The Surgeon General's Report on Health Promotion and Disease Preven-tion. Washington, D. C., U.S. Government Printing Office, 1979.

U.S. Public Health Service: Promoting Health, Preventing Dis-ease: Objectives for the Nation. 1980. Washington, D. C., U.S. Government Printing Office, 1980.

U.S. Public Health Service: United States Health and Preven-tion Profile, 1989. Washington, D.C., U.S. Government Printing Office, Publication no. (PHS) 90-1232, 1990*b*, pp. 1–5.

Verbrugge, L. M.: Longer life but worsening health? Trends in health and mortality of middle-aged and older persons. *In* Lee, P. R., and Estes, C. L., eds.: The Nation's Health. 3rd Ed. Boston, Jones and Bartlett, 1990.

Ward, D.: National health insurance: Where do nurses fit in? Nurs. Outlook *38*;206–207, 1990.

Wilner, M., Walkley, R. P., and O'Neill, E. J.: Introduction to Public Health. 7th Ed. New York, Macmillan, 1978, pp. 25–68.

Wilson, F. A., and Neuhauser, D.: Health Services in the United States. 2nd Ed. Cambridge, Massachusetts, Ballinger, 1985, pp. 131–236.

World Health Organization: The constitution of the World Health Organization. WHO Chronicle *I*;29, 1944.

Zimmerman, M. A.: Citizen participation in rural health: A promising resource. J. Public Health Policy *11*;323–340, 1990.

UNIT

2

The Art and Science of Community Health Nursing

Thinking Upstream: Conceptualizing Health From a Population Perspective

Upon completion of this chapter, the reader will be able to:

1. Describe the concept of theoretic scope as it applies to the protection and promotion of health in community health nursing.

2. Differentiate between upstream interventions, which are designed to alter the precursors of poor health, and downstream interventions, which are characterized by efforts to modify individuals' perceptions of their health.

3. Critique a theory in regard to its relevance to facilitating an understanding of population health dynamics.

4. Recognize theory-based practice as the means of meeting community health nursing's responsibilities to protect and promote health in populations.

Patricia G. Butterfield

A thorough understanding of the dynamics of population health is critical to the practice of community health nursing; this is a fundamental principle that differentiates community health nursing from other nursing specialties. For many, this emphasis on population health requires a change in perspective from original orientations to nursing practice. Novice nurses are frequently acculturated to nursing in a hospital or skilled nursing facility; these settings are designed, for the most part, to intervene on behalf of individuals. Although such organizations play an important role in the health care system, their structure does not provide a model for developing an understanding of population health.

The emphasis on the one-to-one relationship in practice has also been reflected in the development of nursing theory. Because nursing practice historically has emphasized the relationship between nurse and patient, many nursing theories that originated during the 1950s and 1960s emphasize the dynamics of nurse–patient interactions. Although not without value, such theories are of limited use in understanding health from a broader perspective; they were simply not designed to incorporate the social and environmental variables on which community health is predicated. Many of the more recent theories of nursing reflect advances in the scope as well as the content of nursing. However, nurses who are not acquainted with a sufficient range of theoretical approaches may select an individual-oriented theory to give them insight into a population-based health problem. The results of such frustrating efforts do a disservice to the theory, which was not designed for such application, as well as to the nurse. A primary goal of this chapter is to enable the selection of theoretical approaches that are compatible with a population-based perspective of health.

This chapter begins with a brief overview of nursing theory and then follows with a discussion of the scope of community health nursing in addressing population health concerns. Next, several theoretical approaches are compared to demonstrate how different conceptualizations can lead to different conclusions about the range of interventions available to nurses. Throughout the text, the analogy of upstream-versus-downstream thinking is used to differentiate among strategies that are population directed and those that are directed toward the individual.

THINKING UPSTREAM: LOOKING BEYOND THE INDIVIDUAL

In his description of the frustrations of medical practice, McKinlay (1979) uses the image of a swiftly flowing river to represent illness. In this analogy, physicians are so caught up with rescuing victims from the river that they have no time to look upstream and see who is pushing their patients into the perilous waters. McKinlay uses this story to demonstrate the ultimate futility of "downstream endeavors," which are characterized by short-term, individual-based interventions, and he challenges health care providers to focus more of their energies "upstream, where the real problems lie" (p. 9). Upstream endeavors focus on modifying economic, political, and environmental factors that have been shown to be the precursors of poor health throughout the world. Although the story cites medical practice, it is equally fitting to describe the dilemmas of nursing practice. And although nursing has a rich history of providing preventive and population-based care, it has been well substantiated that the current health system, which emphasizes episodic and individual-based care, has done little to stem the tide of chronic illness, to which 70% of the U.S. population succumbs.

At several points in the chapter, this analogy will be used to analyze different theories from an upstream-versus-downstream perspective. Although these categories are not mutually exclusive, the use of the term "upstream" can provide a point of reference to evaluate a theory's potential for understanding population health.

DEFINITIONS OF THEORY

Like other abstract concepts, different authors of nursing textbooks have defined and interpreted theory in different ways. Walker (1971) presented a satirical look at the phraseology of nursing theory by noting the following:

"To some it is 'applied' and to others 'basic,' by some it is characterized as 'unique' while by others

---

Portions of this chapter were adapted from Butterfield, P.G.: Thinking upstream: Nurturing a conceptual understanding of the societal context of health care, in Advances in Nursing Science, Vol. 12:2, pp. 1–8, with permission of Aspen Publishers, Inc., © 1990.

it is seen as 'derived and synthesized from other disciplines.' It is called 'prescriptive,' 'normative,' 'situation-producing,' and 'scientific.' Some see it as 'theoretical,' and still others as a body of attributes" (pp. 27–28).

Certainly this myriad of attributes appears to indicate that the concept of a theory of nursing is a troublesome one.

Definitions of Theory

"A SYSTEMATIC vision of reality; a set of interrelated concepts that is useful for prediction and control" (Woods and Catanzaro, 1988, p. 568).

"A conceptual system or framework invented for some purpose; and as the purpose varies so too must the structure and complexity of the system" (Dickoff and James, 1968, p.198).

"A set of concepts, definitions, and propositions that projects a systematic view of phenomena by designating specific interrelationships among concepts for purposes of describing, explaining, and predicting" (Chinn and Jacobs, 1987, pp. 207–208).

"A statement that purports to account or characterize some phenomena. A nursing theory, therefore, attempts to describe or explain the phenomenon called nursing" (Barnum, 1990, p. 1).

"Theory organizes the relationships between the complex events that occur in a nursing situation so that we can assist human beings. Simply stated, theory provides a way of thinking about and looking at the world around us" (Torres, 1986, p. 19).

The various definitions of theory lack uniformity and, although frustrating for the beginner, reflect the evolution of the profession's thinking as well as individual differences in the conceptualization of the relationships among theory, practice, and research. The definitions also reflect the difficulty in describing something as complex and diverse as theory within the constraints of one definition. Reading several definitions can foster an appreciation of the richness of theory as well as help identify one or two definitions that are particularly meaningful. Common themes among the definitions of theory include a set of concepts, propositions or relational statements, a framework or system, and an end or purpose. The theoretical

perspectives presented in this chapter are congruent with a fairly broad definition of theory, one that is in step with the definitions proposed by Dickoff and James (1968), Torres (1986), or Barnum (1990).

THEORY TO WHAT END?

The goal of theory is to improve the practice of nursing. Chinn and Jacobs (1987) stated that this goal is best achieved by using theories or parts of theoretical frameworks to guide practice. Students often perceive theory as intellectually burdensome and cannot see how something so seemingly obtuse can be used to improve the care they provide. However, because theory-based practice guides the process of data collection and interpretation in a clear and organized manner, it is easier to make appropriate diagnoses of problems and then devise methods of addressing those problems. In this way, through integration of theory and practice, it is possible to focus on factors that are critical in understanding the situation at hand. As Barnum (1990) stated, "A theory is like a map of a territory as opposed to an aerial photograph. The map does not give the full terrain (i.e., the full picture); instead it picks out those parts that are important for its given purpose" (p. 1). Using a theoretical perspective to plan nursing care not only guides the assessment of a nursing situation but also "allows you to plan and not get lost in the details or sidetracked in the alleys" (J. Swanson, personal communication).

MICROSCOPIC VERSUS MACROSCOPIC APPROACH

In many ways, an understanding of population health requires a transformation—a new way of seeing and interpreting the complexity of forces that shape the health of a society. This transformation can best be achieved through the integration of population-based practice and theoretical perspectives that conceptualize health from a macroscopic-versus-microscopic perspective.

It is helpful to use the analogy of a target to understand whether an approach is microscopic or macroscopic. Think of individuals with the health problem of interest (e.g., pediatric exposure to lead compounds) as the bull's-eye. In this context, a

---

Microscopic Versus Macroscopic Approaches to the Delineation of Community Health Nursing Problems

Microscopic Approach	*Macroscopic Approach*
● Examines individual (and sometimes family) responses to health and illness	● Examines interfamily and intercommunity themes in health and illness
	● Delineates factors in the population that perpetuate the development of illness or foster the development of health
● Often emphasizes an individual's behavioral responses to illness or lifestyle patterns	● Emphasizes social, economic, and environmental precursors of illness
● Nursing interventions often aimed at modifying an individual's behavior through changing their perceptions of belief system	● Nursing interventions may include modifying social or environmental variables (i.e., working to remove barriers to care, improving sanitation or living conditions)
	● May involve social or political action

---

microscopic approach to assessment would focus exclusively on individual children who have been diagnosed with lead poisoning; nursing interventions would focus on the identification and removal of sources of lead in the home. It is easy to recognize the importance of these nursing activities; it is imperative that all children with elevated serum lead levels be removed as quickly as possible from all suspect sources of exposure. However, there are broader ways in which to view this problem; it is possible to both address the issues relating to health threats to individuals and examine interperson and intercommunity factors in the development and perpetuation of lead poisoning as a national health problem. This approach may be thought of as including the bull's-eye as well as the concentric circles that extend from the center of the target. A macroscopic approach to the problem of lead exposure may include activities such as examining trends in the prevalence of lead poisoning over time, gathering estimates of the percentage of older homes in a neighborhood (which may contain lead pipes or lead-based paint surfaces), and locating industrial sources of lead vapors. Such efforts are not usually addressed by one nurse alone but often involve the cooperative efforts of nurses from school, occupational, and other community settings.

How does a theoretical focus on the individual preclude an understanding of a larger perspective? Dreher (1982) considered a practice to be conservative if it focuses exclusively on intrapatient and nurse–patient factors. She stated that such frameworks often adopt psychological explanations to explain patient behavior. In this mode of thinking,

low compliance, broken appointments, and reluctance to participate in care are attributed to motivational or attitudinal problems on the part of the patient. Nurses are charged with the responsibility of altering patient attitudes toward health rather than altering the system itself, "even though such negative attitudes may well be a realistic appraisal of health care" (p. 505). The nurse who views the world from such a perspective does not entertain the possibility of working to alter the system itself or empowering patients to do so.

FORCED FIT? ASSESSING A THEORY'S SCOPE IN RELATION TO COMMUNITY HEALTH NURSING

The issue of theoretical scope is especially salient to community health nursing because of the many levels of practice within this specialty. For example, a home health nurse who is caring for ill persons after hospitalization has a very different range of practice than does a nurse epidemiologist or health planner. Although it is important that all nurses practice with an understanding of population health, it is most critical for nurses whose practice is founded on interpopulation rather than intrapopulation dynamics. Unless a given theory is broad enough in scope to address health and determinants of health from a population perspective, it will be of limited use to community health nurses. Although there have been many advancements in the development of nursing theory during the past 25 years, there continues to be some lack of clarity about the theoretical foundation of community health nursing (Batra, 1991). The application of the terms "microscopic" and "macroscopic" to health situations may help to fill this void and stimulate theory development in the field of community health nursing.

How does the macroscopic concept relate to the upstream analogy presented at the beginning of the chapter? Although these concepts are similar, macroscopic refers to a broad scope that incorporates many variables to aid in the understanding of a health problem. Upstream thinking falls within this domain; this view of a problem emphasizes variables that precede or play a role in the development of health problems. Consider macroscopic as the broad, umbrella concept and the term "upstream" as a more specific concept located under the umbrella. These related concepts and the meanings they portray can help one develop a critical eye when evaluating a theory's relevance to population health.

FORMAT FOR REVIEW OF THEORIES

The contrast of several theoretical approaches demonstrates how they may lead to very different conclusions about not only the reasons for client behavior but also the range of interventions available to the nurse. Two theories—one that originated within nursing and one based on social psychology—are presented to exemplify individual, microscopic approaches to community health nursing problems. Two other theories—one from nursing and one with its roots in phenomenology—have been selected to demonstrate the examination of nursing problems from a macroscopic perspective. The format for this review is as follows:

1. The individual as locus of change
   a. Orem's self-care deficit theory of nursing
   b. The health belief model
2. Thinking upstream: Society as the locus of change
   a. Milio's framework for prevention
   b. Critical social theory

The Individual as Locus of Change

OREM'S SELF-CARE DEFICIT THEORY OF NURSING

The theoretical foundations of the self-care deficit theory of nursing were based on Dorothea Orem's initial experiences as a staff and private duty nurse and, later, on the faculty at the Catholic University of America. In 1958, Orem began to formalize her insights about why individuals required nursing care and the purpose of nursing activities (Eben et al., 1986). The theory is prefaced with the assumption that self-care needs and activities compose the primary focus of nursing practice. Orem outlines what she refers to as a general theory of nursing and states that this general theory really is a composite of three related constructs:

1. The theory of self-care deficits, which provides criteria for identifying those who need nursing
2. The theory of self-care, which explains self-care and why it is necessary
3. The theory of nursing systems, which specifies the role of nursing in the delivery of care and how persons can be helped through nursing

---

Definitions of Concepts from Orem's Self-Care Deficit Theory (Orem, 1985, p. 31)

SELF-CARE: "THE production of actions directed to self or to the environment in order to regulate one's functioning in the interest of one's life, integrated functioning, and well-being."

Therapeutic self-care demand: "The measures of care required at moments in time in order to meet existent requisites for regulatory action to maintain life and to maintain or promote health and development and general well-being."

Self-care agency: "The complex capability for action that is activated in the performance of the actions or operations of self-care."

Self-care deficit: "A relationship between self-care agency and therapeutic self-care demand in which self-care agency is not adequate to meet the known therapeutic self-care demand."

Nursing agency: "The complex capability for action that is activated by nurses in their determination of needs for, design of, and production of nursing for persons with a range of types of self-care deficits."

Nursing system: "A continuing series of actions produced when nurses link one way or a number of ways of helping to meet their own actions or the actions of persons under care that are directed to meet these person's therapeutic self-care demands or to regulate their self-care agency."

The basic concepts of this theory evolved almost exclusively from observations of the chronology of illness in hospitalized patients. The theory is based on the premise that nursing is a response to one's incapacity to care for one's self because of one's health. Nursing assumes the role of providing some or all self-care activities on behalf of the patient (Orem, 1985). Because of this focus, the content and scope of the theory are more useful to nurses who are practicing within an institutionalized setting, than to those practicing within the community. Although Orem briefly specified the role of nursing for populations (Orem, 1985), the concepts of self-care, self-care deficit, and self-care agency are so embedded in an individual orientation to disease that the application of these concepts to a population can become awkward and trying. (However, Orem's theory is widely applied in nursing; see Chapter 9 for its application to health education.) In this theory, the process of assessing a patient's abilities takes precedence over upstream concepts (e.g., environmental, social, economic) that may explain the development and perpetuation of health problems in the community.

APPLICATION OF SELF-CARE DEFICIT THEORY

In a recent article, Angela Kennedy, a British nurse, lamented the mandate by nursing supervisors that Orem's self-care deficit theory be adopted as the primary theory for her specialty area, occupational health nursing. Her frustration was evident as she argued that many of the model's assumptions were incongruous with the realities of her daily practice. According to Kennedy (1989), the self-care deficit theory assumes that persons are able to exert purposeful control over their environments in the pursuit of health; however, in the workplace, persons may have little control over the physical or social aspects of the work environment. Based on this thesis, she concluded that the self-care model is incompatible with the practice domain of occupational health nursing.

Although it is easy to recognize the salience of Orem's concepts to many arenas of nursing practice, it also is apparent that this gestalt has limited usefulness for understanding antecedents of population health. Kennedy clearly articulated this po-

sition when she stated, "The many facets of the occupational health nurse's role may 'fit in comfortably with Orem's self-care model.' But will Orem's model fit into the many facets of the occupational health nurse's role? That is the key question we should be asking" (p. 354).

THE INDIVIDUAL AS LOCUS OF CHANGE: THE HEALTH BELIEF MODEL

The health belief model evolved from the premise that it is the world of the perceiver that determines what one will do. The model had its inceptions during the late 1950s in the United States after the development of the polio vaccine. Although a life-saving vaccine was available, health professionals were stymied when some people chose not to bring themselves or their children into clinics to be immunized. The health belief model resulted from the efforts of social psychologists and other public health workers, who recognized the need to develop a more complete understanding of the factors that influence preventive health behaviors.

The model's core dimensions were derived primarily from the work of Kurt Lewin, who proposed that behavior is primarily based on the current dynamics confronting an individual rather than on their prior experiences (Maiman and Becker, 1974). Within this framework, diseases are considered regions of negative valence that act to repel the individual. An assumption of the model is that the major determinant of preventive health behavior is the avoidance of disease. Major concepts include perceived susceptibility to disease X, perceived seriousness of disease X, modifying factors, cues to action, perceived benefits minus barriers of preventive health action, perceived threat of disease X, and likelihood of taking a recommended health action; arrows are used to specify relations among concepts. The model was not designed to be generalized across disorders; disease X represents a particular disorder that an individual believes may be prevented by a health action. This means that actions that relate to preventive health behaviors for breast cancer will be different from those relating to measles; for the former, a cue to action may involve a public service advertisement encouraging women to make an appointment for a mammogram, whereas for the latter, the same concept may be operationalized in the form of hearing of a measles outbreak in a neighboring

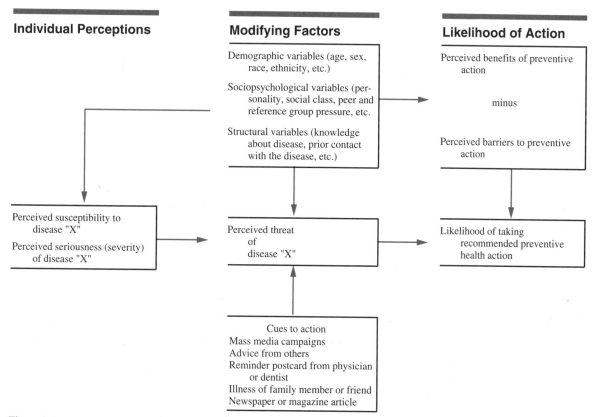

Figure 4–1
Variables and relationships in the health belief model. (Redrawn from Rosenstock, I. M.: Historical origins of the health belief model. *In* Becker, M. H., ed.: The Health Belief Model and Personal Health Behavior. Thorofare, New Jersey: Charles B. Slack, 1974, pp. 1–8.)

town. Figure 4–1 outlines the variables and relationships in the health belief model.

APPLICATION OF THE HEALTH BELIEF MODEL

A number of authors have proposed modifications to the health belief model, both to broaden its scope in addressing health promotion and illness behaviors (Kirscht, 1974; Pender, 1987) and to merge its concepts with other theories that describe health behavior (Cummings et al., 1980). This conceptualization of health and health behaviors represented the author's first encounter with the power of theory-based practice. Perceptions of the strengths and limitations of the model are presented in a brief personal chronology.

A first class in nursing theory followed a format much like that of many other courses throughout the country. Each week, a new theoretical perspective was introduced; the background of the theorist, assumptions of the theory, the theory's concepts and relational statements, and application of the theory to nursing practice were discussed. Like many of the other students, mixed feelings about the class were noted. Most of the content was intellectually interesting, but difficulty was experienced in relating it to the patients seen each week in the neighborhood clinics and during home visits. Several weeks into the class, the health belief model was presented. The interest of the author was immediately piqued; the model soon captured her thoughts in a way that no other framework had.

After the seminar, she went to the library and checked out *The Health Belief Model and Personal Health Behavior* by Marshall Becker (Charles B. Slack, Inc., 1974) and quickly became absorbed in the book.

The model's focus on compliance brought insight into patients' behaviors and helped the nurse organize thoughts about the reasons persons choose to disregard the instructions of well-intended nurses and doctors. The way the model interpreted behaviors from the patient's rather than nurse's perspective was most intriguing. Concepts such as "perceived seriousness," "perceived susceptibility," and "cue to action" brought new insights into the dynamics of health decision making. The health belief model provided answers to problems encountered in practice every day.

An interpretation of the model was used to guide eventual work with some families. One family in particular had an 18-month-old son who had never been immunized. The father owned a health food store and was strongly immersed in a culture in which natural foods and medicines were emphasized and the use of anything considered to be "unnatural" was shunned. Childhood immunizations for diseases such as polio, tetanus, and measles were, in that family's eyes, unnatural. An assessment was made: the failure to immunize the child resulted from the parents' low perceived susceptibility and seriousness of childhood illnesses coupled with modifying factors, such as a reference group who disdained most traditional medical practices. During the next few weeks, a strategy was mapped out: to work toward raising the parents' perceived susceptibility to childhood illnesses by providing them with information about communicable diseases. During the next two or three visits, time was taken to inundate the poor family with literature and pictures that graphically demonstrated the sequelae of diphtheria, polio, and pertussis. These efforts culminated in the parents taking their son to an immunization clinic for his first shot, much to the author's delight.

Twelve years later, mixed feelings arise when this family and the means used to drive their compliance to the accepted standard of pediatric health care are recalled. In the years since this experience, more skill has been gained in the assessment and labeling of patient problems and a better appreciation has been gained of the strengths and limitations of theoretical frameworks.

LIMITATIONS OF THE HEALTH BELIEF MODEL

The health belief model places the burden of action exclusively on the client and assumes that only clients who have distorted or negative perceptions will fail to act. In practice, the use of this model as the foundation for practice results in a focus of the nurse's energies on interventions designed to modify the client's distorted perceptions; this is the approach taken in attempting to change the behavior of these patients.

True to its historical roots, the model offers an explanation of health behaviors that, in many ways, is similar to a mechanical system. From the health belief model, it can easily be concluded that compliance can be induced by using model variables as catalysts to stimulate action. For example, an intervention study based on the health belief model demonstrated increased follow-up in hypertensive clients by increasing their perceptions of the seriousness of hypertension (Jones et al., 1987). In addition, patients received education over the telephone or in the emergency department that was designed to increase their perception of the benefits of follow-up. According to the authors, the interventions resulted in a dramatic increase in compliance. However, they noted several patient groups that failed to respond to the intervention, most notably, a small group of patients who had no available child care. Although this study demonstrates the predictive power of health belief model concepts, it also exemplifies the limitations of the model. The health belief model may be effective in promoting behavior change through alteration of patients' perspectives, but it does not acknowledge the responsibility of the health professional to reduce or ameliorate barriers to health care.

The health belief model is a prototype for the type of theoretical perspective that has dominated nursing education and, thus, nursing practice. The strength of the model—its narrow scope—also is its limitation: one is not drawn outside the scope of the model to the forces that shape the characteristics described by the model.

The Upstream View: Society as the Locus of Change

MILIO'S FRAMEWORK FOR PREVENTION

Nancy Milio's framework for prevention (1976) provided a thought-provoking complement to the health belief model and a mechanism for directing attention upstream and examining opportunities for nursing intervention at the population level (see chapter 9 for its use in health education). Milio outlined six propositions that relate the ability of an individual to improve healthful behavior to a society's ability to provide options for healthy choices that are both accessible and socially affirming. Through these statements, Milio moved the focus of attention upstream by pointing out that it is the range of available health choices rather than the choices made at any one time that is critical in shaping the overall health status of a society. She maintained that the range of choices is shaped, to a large degree, by policy decisions by both government and private organizations. Rather than concentrate efforts on imparting information to change patterns of individual behavior, she considered national level policy-making the most effective means by which to favorably have an impact on the societal health.

economic realities that deprive many Americans of a health-sustaining environment despite the fact that "cigarettes, sucrose, pollutants, and tensions are readily available to the poor" (p 436).

The range of health-promoting or health-damaging choices available to individuals is affected by their personal resources and their societal resources. Personal resources include one's awareness, knowledge, and beliefs and those of one's family and friends as well as money, time, and the urgency of other priorities. Societal resources are influenced strongly by community and national locale and include the availability and cost of health services, environmental protection, safe shelter, and the penalties or rewards given for failure to select the given options.

Milio challenged the commonly held assumption in health education that knowing health-generating behaviors implies acting in accordance with that knowledge, and she cited the lifestyles of health professionals in support of her argument.

Six Propositions of Milio

"THE HEALTH status of populations is the result of deprivation and/or excess of critical health-sustaining resources.

"Behavior patterns of populations are a result of habitual selection from limited choices, and these habits of choice are related to: (a) actual and perceived options available; (b) beliefs and expectations developed and refined over time by socialization, formal learning, and immediate experience.

"Organizational behavior (decisions or policy-choices made by governmental/non-governmental, national/non-national; not-for-profit/for-profit, formal/non-formal organizations) sets the range of options available to individuals for their personal choice-making.

"The choice-making of individuals at a given point in time concerning potentially health-promoting or health-damaging selections is affected by their effort to maximize valued resources.

"Social change may be thought of as changes in patterns of behavior resulting from shifts in the choice-making of significant numbers of people within a population.

"Health education, as the process of teaching and learning health-supporting information, can have little significantly extensive impact on behavior patterns, that is, on personal choice-making of groups of people, without the easy availability of new, or newly-perceived alternative health-promoting options for investing personal resources."

Adapted from Milio N.: A framework for prevention: Changing health-damaging to health-generating life patterns. Am. J. Public Health 66;435–439, 1976.

Milio proposed that health deficits often result from an imbalance between a population's health needs and its health-sustaining resources, with affluent societies afflicted by the diseases associated with excess (e.g., obesity, alcoholism) and poor societies afflicted by diseases that result from inadequate or unsafe food, shelter, and water. Viewing the situation within this context, the poor who live in affluent societies may experience the least desirable combination of factors. Milio cited the socio-

She proposed that "most human beings, professional or nonprofessional, provider or consumer, make the easiest choices available to them most of the time" (p. 435). Therefore, health-promoting choices must be more readily available and less costly than health-damaging options if individuals are to be healthy and a society is to improve its health status. Milio was critical of many traditional approaches to health education that emphasize knowledge acquisition and consequently expect patients to change their behavior. Milio's framework can enable a nurse to reframe this view by understanding the historical play of social forces that have limited the choices available to the involved parties.

COMPARISON OF THE HEALTH BELIEF MODEL WITH MILIO'S CONCEPTUALIZATIONS OF HEALTH

One cannot help but note the similarities between Milio's health resources and the concepts of the health belief model. The purpose of the health belief model is to provide the nurse with an understanding of the dynamics of personal health behaviors; environmental variables, such as the constraints of the health care system, are specified only as they influence the decision-making processes of the individual. In contrast, Milio's framework includes an assessment of community resources and their availability to individuals. This differs from the health belief model, which may assume that everyone has equal health resources and free will. By assessing up front such factors, the nurse is able to gain a more thorough understanding of individuals' actual resources. Milio offered a different set of insights into health-related behaviors by proposing that many low-income individuals are acting within the constraints of their limited resources. Furthermore, she went beyond the downstream focus and the health of populations by examining choices made by significant numbers of people within a population.

Because Milio's framework provides for the inclusion of economic, political, and environmental health determinants, the nurse is given broader range than is allowed with the health belief model in diagnosis and interpretation of health problems. Although the health belief model allows for only a dichotomous, all-or-nothing (i.e., either "acts" or "fails to act according to recommended health action") outcome, Milio's framework encourages the nurse to understand health behaviors in the context of the societal milieu in which they reside.

APPLICATION OF MILIO'S FRAMEWORK FOR PREVENTION

There are opportunities to apply this framework to the extremely prevalent problem of cigarette smoking during pregnancy. As stated previously, the health belief model will lead nurses to conclude that success (smoking cessation) can be achieved by helping patients change their perceptions about smoking during pregnancy; this approach may be very effective with selected patients. However, this view does not recognize the existence of societal factors that influence this problem and result in deleterious health effects to thousands of children. Through its broader scope, Milio's model allows for nursing interventions at many levels by analyzing social and economic factors that may inhibit healthy choices in populations. Population-based interventions may include such diverse activities as mobilizing comprehensive smoking cessation programs in schools and workplaces and encouraging politicians to end federal subsidization of the tobacco industry. Interventions that empower clients as well as those that involve social action on the part of the nurse are addressed within the parameters of Milio's framework.

The opportunities for a society to make healthy choices have been a central theme throughout Milio's work. In a related article (1981), she elaborated on this theme:

"Personal behavior patterns are not simply 'free' choices about 'lifestyle,' isolated from their personal and economic context. Lifestyles are, rather, patterns of choices made from the alternatives that are available to people according to their socioeconomic circumstances and the ease with which they are able to choose certain ones over others" (p. 76).

CRITICAL SOCIAL THEORY

Just as Milio used societal awareness as an aid to understanding health behaviors, critical social theory uses similar means to expose social inequalities that limit people from reaching their full potential. This theoretical approach is based in the belief that life is structured by social meanings that are determined, rather one-sidedly, through social domination. Proponents of this theoretical approach maintain that social exchanges that are not distorted from power imbalances will stimulate the evolution of a more just society (Allen et al., 1986). Critical theory makes the assumption that standards of truth are determined socially and that no form of scientific inquiry is value-free. As Allen et al. stated, "One cannot separate theory and value, as the empiricist claims. Every theory is penetrated by value interests" (p. 34).

APPLICATION OF CRITICAL SOCIAL THEORY

Application of the theory uses one's processes of inductive reasoning; rather than superimposing concepts into a situation, relevant concepts are revealed to the nurse through an ongoing process of data collection and analysis. Interviews with critical informants, news articles, and transcripts of government proceedings may be sources of data. For example, suppose the domain of interest involves child care options for employees of a large microcomputer manufacturer. Data sources initially may include the age and gender distribution of the workers, review of worksite policies on parental leave, and interviews with both workers and administrative officials. Further into the analysis, the nurse may choose to incorporate additional sources of data such as interviews with shift workers regarding their difficulties in accessing evening and night child care or statistics on job turnover among child care workers.

The methodological approaches adopted in critical social theory may also differ from those suggested by other nursing theories. No specific method of analysis is mandated; instead, methods are chosen to be congruent with the focus of study. The dialectic is often used as a methodological tool; this refers to a process in which the investigator seeks understanding by examining contradictions within the phenomena of interest. Continu-

ing with the previous example, the nurse may apply critical social theory to an examination of child care by contrasting an organization's policies with interviews from those workers who have found the organization to be an impediment to achieving quality care for their children. Data analysis may also include an examination of the interests of both workers and administration in promoting social change versus maintaining the status quo.

CHALLENGING ASSUMPTIONS ABOUT PREVENTIVE HEALTH THROUGH CRITICAL SOCIAL THEORY

Both the health belief model and Milio's model for prevention focus on personal health behaviors from a disease avoidance or preventive health perspective; this phenomenon may also be analyzed with critical social theory. Consider the analogy of health care workers who were so busy fishing people out of the river of illness that they had no time to look upstream. In the same article, McKinlay (1979) later uses his upstream analogy to ask the rhetorical question, "How preventive is prevention?" (p. 22). He uses this tactic to critically examine intervention strategies aimed at enhancing preventive behavior. Figure 4–2 presents McKinlay's model of different modes of prevention. He relates both curative and lifestyle modification interventions by health professionals to a downstream con-

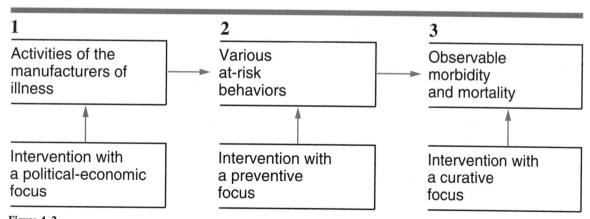

Figure 4–2
Continuum of health behaviors and corresponding intervention foci. (From McKinlay, J. B.: A case for refocusing upstream: The political economy of illness. *In* Proceedings of an AHA Conference: Applying Behavioral Science to Cardiovascular Risk, Seattle, Washington, June 17–19, 1974, pp. 7–17. Reproduced with permission. © Applying Behavioral Science to Cardiovascular Risk 1974. Copyright American Heart Association.)

ceptualization of health; the majority of so-called preventive actions fail to alter the process of illness at its origin. Politicoeconomic interventions remain the most effective method of ameliorating illness at its source.

McKinlay then delineated the activities of the "manufacturers of illness—those individuals, interest groups, and organizations which, in addition to producing material goods and services, also produce, as an inevitable byproduct, widespread morbidity and mortality" (p. 9). Through the embedding of desired behaviors in the dominant cultural norm, the manufacturers of illness foster the habituation of high-risk behavior in the population. Unhealthy consumption patterns become integrated into everyday lives; the holiday dinner table is a stellar example of "the binding of at-riskness to culture" (p. 12). However, the existing health care system misguidedly devotes its efforts to changing the products of the manufacturers of illness rather than the processes that create the products.

Waitzkin (1983) continued with this theme by asserting that our health care system's emphasis on lifestyle diverts attention from important sources of illness in the capitalist industrial environment; "it also puts the burden of health squarely on the individual rather than seeking collective solutions to health problems" (p. 664). Salmon (1987) supported this position by noting that the basic tenets of Western medicine promote understanding of individual factors of health and illness while obscuring the exploration of their social and economic roots. He stated that critical social theory "can aid in uncovering larger dimensions impacting health that are usually unseen or misrepresented by ideological biases. Thus, the social reality of health conditions can be both understood and changed" (p. 75).

Because critical social theory holds that each person is responsible for creating social conditions in which all members of society are able to speak freely, the nurse is challenged, as an individual and a member of the profession, to expose power imbalances that prohibit people from achieving their full potential. Nurses versed in critical theory are equipped to see beyond the perpetuation of status quo ideas and may be able to generate unique ideas that are unencumbered by previous stereotypes (Allen, 1985).

SUMMARY

Long before the term "nursing theory" was coined, community health nurses used theory-based practice to solve problems that threatened the health of societies throughout the world. Community health nurses were responsible for many of the life-saving advances in sanitation, communicable disease containment, and environmental conditions that today are taken for granted. Some nurses continue to be involved in what are considered traditional community health nursing roles; however, the parameters of practice have expanded into new realms such as health planning and the empowerment of vulnerable populations. As nursing has advanced as a profession, so too has the need to formalize the scientific base of nursing practice through the development and dissemination of nursing theories. Not only does the development of nursing theory prevent the loss of valuable knowledge, it also provides the mechanism by which practice can be advanced and refined. Much of the richness of community health nursing comes from the challenge of designing interventions that will enhance the health of not just one but many persons. Similarly, nurses in this area of practice need to be provided with theoretical perspectives that address the social, political, and environmental determinants of population health. Through the integration of population-based theory and practice, nurses are given the means by which to favorably impact the health of all members of our global community.

Learning Activities

1. Select a theory or conceptual model with which you are familiar. Evaluate its potential for understanding health in individuals, families, a population of 400 children in an elementary school, 2,000 workers within a corporate setting, and a community of 50,000 residents.

2. Identify one health problem (i.e., substance abuse, domestic violence, cardiovascular disease) that is prevalent in the community or city in which you live. Analyze the problem using two different theories or conceptual models — one that emphasizes individual determinants of health and one that emphasizes population determinants of health. What are some of the differences in the ways that these two different perspectives inform nursing practice?

3. Review the American Nurses' Association's definition of community health nursing practice and the American Public Health Association's definition of public health nursing practice (see Chapter 1). What do these definitions tell us about the theoretical basis of community health nursing? How is the theoretical basis of community health nursing practice different from that of other specialty areas in nursing?

REFERENCES

Allen, D. G.: Critical social theory as a model for analyzing ethical issues in family and community health. Family Comm. Health *10*;63–72, 1987.

Allen, D. G.: Nursing research and social control: Alternate modes of science that emphasize understanding and emancipation. Image J. Nurs. Scholarship *17*;58–64, 1985.

Allen, D. G., Diekelmann, N., Benner, P.: Three paradigms for nursing research: Methodologic implications. *In* Chinn, P., ed.: Nursing Research Methodology: Issues and Implementation. Rockville, Maryland, Aspen Publishers, 1986, pp. 23–28.

American Nurses' Association: Nursing: A Social Policy Statement. Kansas City, Missouri, ANA, 1980.

American Nurses' Association, Council of Community Health Nurses: Standards of Community Health Nursing Practice. Kansas City, Missouri, ANA, 1986.

American Public Health Association, Public Health Nursing Section: The Definition and Role of Public Health Nursing Practice in the Delivery of Health Care: A Statement of the Public Health Nursing Section. Washington, D. C., APHA, 1980.

Barnum, B. J. S.: Nursing Theory: Analysis, Application, Evaluation. Glenview, Illinois, Scott, Foresman/Little, Brown Higher Education, 1990.

Batra, C.: Professional issues: The future of community health nursing. *In* Cookfair, J. M., ed.: Nursing Process and Practice in the Community. St. Louis, Mosby Year Book, 1991, pp. 613–635.

Becker, M. H., and Maiman, L. A.: Models of health-related behavior. *In* Mechanic, D., ed.: Handbook of Health, Health Care, and the Health Professions. New York, The Free Press, 1983, pp. 539–568.

Chinn, P. L., and Jacobs, M. K.: Theory and Nursing: A Systematic Approach. 2nd Ed. St. Louis, C. V. Mosby, 1987.

Cummings, K. M., Becker, M. H., and Malie, M. C.: Bringing the models together: An empirical approach to combining variables to explain health actions. J. Behav. Med. *3*;123–145, 1980.

Dickoff, J., and James, P.: A theory of theories: A position paper. Nurs. Res. *17*;197–203, 1968.

Dreher, M. C.: The conflict of conservatism in public health nursing education. Nurs. Outlook *30*;504–509, 1982.

Eben, J. D., Nation, M. J., Marriner, A., and Nordmeyer, S. B.: Self-care deficit theory of nursing. *In* Marriner, A., ed.: Nursing Theorists and Their Work. St. Louis, C. V. Mosby, 1986, pp. 117–130.

Janz, N. K., and Becker, M. H.: The health belief model: A decade later. Health Educ. Q. *11*;1–47, 1984.

Jones, P. K., Jones, S. L., and Katz, J.: Improving follow-up among hypertensive patients using a health belief model intervention. Arch. Intern. Med. *147*;1557–1560, 1987.

Kennedy, A.: How relevant are nursing models? Occup. Health *41*;352–355, 1989.

Kirscht, J. P.: The health belief model and illness behavior. *In* Becker, M. H., ed.: The Health Belief Model and Personal Health Behavior. Thorofare, New Jersey, Charles B. Slack, 1974, pp. 9–26.

Maglacas, A. M.: Health for all: Nursing's role. Nurs. Outlook *36*;66–71, 1988.

Maiman, L. A., and Becker, M. H.: The health belief model: Origins and correlates in psychological theory. Health Educ. Monographs *2*;336–353, 1974.

McKinlay, J. B.: A case for refocusing upstream: The political economy of illness. *In* Jaco, E. G., ed.: Patients, Physicians, and Illness. 3rd Ed. New York, The Free Press, 1979, pp. 9–25.

Melnyk, K. M.: Barriers: A critical review of recent literature. Nurs. Res. *37*;196–201, 1988.

Milio, N.: A framework for prevention: Changing health-damaging to health-generating life patterns. Am. J. Public Health *66*;435–439, 1976.

Milio, N.: Primary Care and the Public's Health. Lexington, Massachusetts, Lexington Books, 1983.

Milio, N.: Promoting Health Through Public Policy. Philadelphia, F. A. Davis, 1981.

Orem, D. E.: Nursing: Concepts of Practice. 3rd Ed. New York, McGraw-Hill, 1985.

Pender, N. J.: Health Promotion in Nursing Practice. 2nd Ed. Norwalk, Connecticut, Appleton-Century-Crofts, 1987.

Rosenstock, I. M.: Historical origins of the health belief model. *In* Becker, M. H., ed.: The Health Belief Model and Personal Health Behavior. Thorofare, New Jersey, Charles B. Slack, 1974, pp. 1–8.

Salmon, J. W.: Dilemmas in studying social change versus individual change: Considerations from political economy. *In* Duffy, M., and Pender, N. J., eds.: Conceptual Issues in Health Promotion—A Report of Proceedings of a Wingspread Conference. Indianapolis, Indiana, Sigma Theta Tau, 1987, pp. 70–81.

Torres, G.: Theoretical Foundations of Nursing. Norwalk, Connecticut, Appleton-Century-Crofts, 1986.

Waitzkin, H.: A Marxist view of health and health care. *In* Mechanic, D., ed.: Handbook of Health, Health Care, and the Health Professions. New York, The Free Press, 1983, pp. 657–682.

Walker, L. O.: Toward a clearer understanding of the concept of nursing theory. Nurs. Res. *20*;428–435, 1971.

White, C. M.: A critique of the ANA social policy statement. Nurs. Outlook *32*;328–331, 1984.

Woods, N. F., and Catanzaro, M.: Nursing Research: Theory and Practice. St. Louis, C. V. Mosby, 1988.

Nursing Process in the Community

Upon completion of this chapter, the reader will be able to:

1. Discuss the major dimensions of a community.

2. Identify the major sources of information about a community's health.

3. Use epidemiological methods to describe the state of health of a community or aggregate.

4. Identify epidemiological study designs for researching health problems.

5. Formulate aggregate diagnoses.

Holly B. Cassells

The primary concern of nurses who take on the various roles of the community health nurse is to improve the health of the community. Community health nurses use all of the principles and skills of nursing practice as well as those of public health practice to aid the community.

But what is a community? Towns and cities come to mind immediately. And how can a nurse provide services to such a large and nontraditional "client"? A major aspect of the public health philosophy is applying approaches and solutions to health problems so that the greatest number of people receive the maximum benefit. In this way, efficient use of time and resources is achieved. Despite the desire to provide services to each individual in a community, the community health nurse recognizes the impracticability of this task. An alternative approach is to consider the community itself as the unit of service, i.e., to use the steps of the nursing process in working with the community as an entity.

This chapter addresses the first steps in adopting a community- or population-oriented practice. Before applying the nursing process, a community must be defined, and its characteristics must be described. Then, the assessment and diagnosis phase of the nursing process can proceed at the aggregate level.

THE NATURE OF COMMUNITY

Many dimensions are useful in describing the nature of community. The three dimensions addressed are the community as an aggregate of people, the community as a location in space and time, and the community as a social system.

Aggregate of People

Probably the most essential attribute of a community is that it is composed of people, in particular, people who share one or more common characteristics. For example, members of a community may share common features such as citizenship in the same city or membership in the same religious organization, and similar demographic characteristics or traits such as belonging to a specific age group or ethnic background. Elderly members of a senior citizens group frequently are of similar ages, are retired from the work force, and experience similar economic pressures. It is likely that this group also shares common life experiences, interests, and concerns. Having lived through the many societal changes of the past 50 years, they may also possess similar perspectives on current issues and trends. Many elderly persons share a concern for the maintenance of good health, pursuit of an active lifestyle, and securing of needed services to support a quality life. These shared interests can be translated into common goals and activities, which are defining attributes of community.

There are many human factors that help to delineate a community. One such set of "people factors" of particular importance to the community health nurse comprises health-related traits, or *risk factors*. Persons sharing a predisposition to disease or impaired health may identify themselves as a community, and join together in a group to learn from and support each other. Parents of disabled infants, persons with AIDS, and those at risk for a second myocardial infarction each may consider themselves to be a community. Even when these individuals are not organized, the nurse may recognize that they constitute a form of community or aggregate because of their unique needs.

When individuals come together because of a common problem, a "community of solution" may be said to have formed. These persons may have little else in common with each other but become united by a desire to redress such problems as a shared hazard from an environmental contamination, a shared health problem arising from a soaring rate of teenage suicide, or a shared political concern about an upcoming city council election. The community of solution often disbands after problem resolution, but may subsequently identify other common issues to impact.

Each of these shared features may exist among persons who are geographically dispersed or within close proximity of each other. However, in many situations, proximity facilitates the recognition of commonalities and the development of cohesion among members. This active sharing of features in turn fosters a sense of community among individuals.

Location in Space and Time

However, regardless of the extent to which features are shared, communities of people may be defined on the basis of geographic or physical location. The dimension of location is best exemplified by the traditional view of community as an entity delineated by geopolitical boundaries. These boundaries demarcate the periphery of cities, counties, states, and nations and are easily identified on maps. Citizens are also members of communities with perimeters that are indicated by less visible boundary lines, such as voting precincts, school districts, water districts, and fire and police protection precincts. Residents may claim membership in each of these entities simultaneously.

Census tracts, which also delineate subsets of larger communities, are used expressly for data collection and population assessment by the U.S. Bureau of the Census. Census tracts facilitate the organization of information about those residing in specific geographical locales in a community. In densely populated urban areas, residents of a tract are frequently part of a neighborhood described by data for one or more census tracts. Therefore, census tract data may be useful in defining and describing neighborhood communities, even though the residents may be unaware of the boundaries or their membership in a census tract (see "Census Data").

Finally, the geographic dimension encompasses less formalized types of community or areas that can be identified as communities yet lack official geopolitical boundaries. Neighborhoods may be defined by a geographical landmark e.g., the East Lake section of a town or the north shore area. Community neighborhoods may also be identified by a style of building construction or by a common time of development, e.g., Co-op City in New York, a housing subdivision on the edge of a city, or a section of historical homes in a central area of a town. Similarly, a dormitory, communal home, or summer camp may also be considered a community. Each shares a close geographical proximity in addition to other characteristics.

Communities are defined not only by location but also by the dimension of time. Their existence and defining characteristics change over time. Although some communities are considered very stable, most tend to change with the demographics and health status of the members, development or decline of the larger community, and various effects of many other factors.

Major Features of a Community

Aggregate of people
THE "WHO" — personal characteristics and risks

Location in space and time
The "where and when" — physical location frequently delineated by boundaries and influenced by the passage of time

Social system
The "why and how" — interrelationships of the aggregate as they fulfill community functions

---

Social System

The third major feature of a community relates to the linkages community members form with each other. By interacting in groups within a community, the essential functions of community are fulfilled. These functions provide members with socialization, role fulfillment, goal achievement, and support. Therefore, a community may be considered a social system, with its interacting members comprising various subsystems within the community. These subsystems are both interrelated and interdependent, i.e., they are impacted by each other as well as by various internal and external stimuli. These stimuli consist of a broad range of events, values, conditions, and needs.

Health care systems are an example of complex systems that are made up of smaller interrelated subsystems. Because health care systems interact and depend on other larger systems, such as the city government, they can also be subsystems. Changes in the larger system may not only directly impact that large system but also cause repercussions in many subsystems. For example, when local economic pressures in a community cause a health system to scale back its operations, many subsystems are impacted. When programs are eliminated or reduced, service to other health care providers is limited, groups who normally use the system may have reduced access, and families who themselves constitute subsystems in society may be denied needed care. Almost every subsystem in the community may be required to react and readjust to such a financial constraint.

Communities that are very complex systems receive varied stimuli. The ability of a community to respond effectively to changing dynamics is an indicator of productive functioning. Examination of the functioning of the community and its subsystems provides clues to existing and potential health problems.

Example of Systems Interrelationships
HEALTH PROBLEMS can have a severe impact on multiple systems. For example, the AIDS epidemic has required significant funds for direct services to AIDS clients as well as for public AIDS education and prevention. Simultaneously, it has made unrelenting demands on many communities already strapped for funds to meet basic health needs of its citizens. In San Francisco, the allocation of funds for AIDS programs has reduced funding for other programs such as immunizations, family planning, and well-child care.

ASSESSING THE COMMUNITY: SOURCES OF DATA

The essential feature of a community is its members. By traveling through a community and using each of the human senses, the community health nurse becomes familiar with the community and begins to understand its nature. It is through this down-to-earth approach to assessment, which has been called "shoe leather epidemiology," that the nurse begins to establish certain hunches or hypotheses about the community's health—its strengths as well as its potential health problems. For the community health nurse, these initial assessments will have to be better substantiated before a community diagnosis and plan can be formulated.

The use of certain public health tools becomes essential to a nursing practice that is aggregate focused. Demography and the analysis of statistical data provide descriptive information about the population. Epidemiology involves the analysis of data to discover the patterns of health and illness distributions in populations. Epidemiology also involves the conduct of research to explain the nature of health problems and identify aggregates at increased risk of developing these problems. The next section addresses these tools and describes

ways in which community health nurses can apply them to the assessment of the aggregate.

Census Data

Every 10 years, the U.S. Bureau of the Census undertakes a massive survey of all U.S. families. In addition to this decennial census, intermediate surveys are made to collect specific categories of information. These collections of statistical data describe the characteristics of the population of the nation as a whole as well as of progressively smaller geopolitical entities, e.g., states, counties, and census tracts. The census also allows description of large metropolitan areas that extend beyond formal city boundaries. These are called Standard Metropolitan Statistical Areas (SMSAs), and they consist of a central city with more than 50,000 people and the associated suburban or ring counties. In the 1980 census, data were reported for an even larger statistical entity called a Metropolitan Statistical Area (MSA), which consists of very large urban cities and their extended suburbs. A census tract, which is one of the smallest reporting units, usually is made up of 3,000–6,000 persons, most of whom share some similar characteristics such as ethnicity, socioeconomic status, or type of housing.

The census collects a broad range of information that is extremely helpful to community health nurses familiarizing themselves with a new community. Among the many demographic variables tabulated in the census are population size; distribution of age, sex, race, and ethnicity; socioeconomic status; and housing characteristics. Variables that describe the health of the community per se are not a part of census data. The comparison of data with those of other communities and of previous time periods is an essential part of analyzing the data and interpreting its meaning. By comparing data for one census unit, such as a census tract or a city, with those of another community or the nation as a whole, the nurse can identify the attributes that make each community unique. These attributes provide clues to the potential vulnerabilities or health risks of a community. For example, a community health nurse may discover from census reports that a district has many elderly persons. This directs the nurse toward further assessment of the social resources (housing, transportation, and community centers), health resources (hospitals and clinics capable of providing geriatric services), and health problems common to aging persons. By identifying the trends in the population over time, the community health nurse can then modify public health programs to more effectively meet the changing needs of that community.

Census Data Can Reveal "Hidden Pockets" of Need

CENSUS DATA are not only helpful in revealing dominant community features but also suggest the existence of small "hidden pockets" of persons who may have special needs. One nurse who initially assessed her community as an upper-middle-class community was surprised to find 20 families living below the poverty level, three of which did not possess running water in their homes. Did these families have particular needs that could be addressed by a community health nurse? Deviations from the central trend, therefore, can be very revealing and important in determining a community health nurse's practice priorities.

Vital Statistics

The official registration records of births, deaths, marriages, divorces, and adoptions form the basis of data included in vital statistics. These events are aggregated and reported annually for the preceding year by city, county, and state health departments. When compared with previous years, vital statistics provide indicators of growth or shrinkage in the population size. In addition to supplying information about the number of births and deaths, registration certificates record the cause of death, which is useful in determining morbidity and mortality trends. Similarly, birth certificates document the type of birth (e.g., whether cesarean) and the occurrence of any congenital malformations. This information is also important in assessing the health status of the community.

Other Sources of Health Data

The U.S. Bureau of the Census conducts numerous other surveys on subjects of interest to the government, such as crime, housing, and labor. Results of these surveys as well as the census and vital statistics reports are usually available in public libraries. The National Center for Health Statistics compiles annual National Health Survey data, which describe health trends in a national sample. Reports are published on the prevalence of disability, illness, and other health-related variables.

In addition to these important sources of information, community health nurses frequently can access a broad range of state and community government reports that contribute to the comprehensive assessment of a population. Local agencies, chambers of commerce, and health and hospital districts collect invaluable information on the health of the communities they serve. Local health systems agencies (discussed in Chapter 6) and other planning organizations also compile and analyze statistical data as part of the planning process. All of these formal and informal resources can be used by the community health nurse in learning about a community or aggregate (Table 5–1).

A community health nurse, however, may require data on certain community aspects for which no formalized collection has been undertaken. Therefore, it may be necessary for the nurse to perform the data collection, compilation, and analysis. For example, school nurses regularly aggregate data from student records to learn about the demographic composition of their population. Their ongoing surveys of classroom attendance and causes of illness are essential to an effective school health program. Thus, the school nurse is not only a consumer of existent data but also a researcher collecting original data for the assessment of the school community.

Calculation of Rates

Collection and compilation of large amounts of descriptive information about the aggregate have been discussed. So far, it has been assumed that data were in the form of counts or simple frequencies of events, e.g., the number of persons with a specific health condition. Community health practitioners interpret these raw counts by transforming them into rates. Rates are arithmetic expressions that allow one to consider a count of an event relative to the size of the population from which it is extracted, i.e., the population at risk. Rates are population proportions or fractions in which the numerator is the number of events occurring in a specified period of time. Events described by the numerator are necessarily included as part of the denominator. The denominator consists of all those in the same population at the same specified

Table 5–1
Community Assessment Parameters

Parameter	Importance to CHN	Sources of Information

Geography
  Topography
  Climate
	Influences nature of health problems and access to health care	Almanac
		Chamber of Commerce

Population
  Size
  Demographic character
  Trends
  Migration
  Density
	Describes population served; suggests their health risks and needs
	
	Suggests growth or decline
		Census documents
		Chamber of Commerce
		Local documents

Environment
  Water
  Sewage and waste disposal
  Air quality
  Food quality and access
  Housing
  Animal control
	Impacts quality of life and nature of environmental health problems
	
	Reflects community resources
	
	Suggests socioeconomic issues
		Local and state health departments
		Newspapers
		
		Local environmental action group
		
		Census documents

Industry
  Employment levels
  Manufacturing
  White vs. blue collar
  Income levels
	Impacts social class, access to health care, and resources
	Influences nature of health problems
		Chamber of Commerce
		Almanac
		Employment commission
		
		Census documents

Education
  Schools
  Types of education
  Literacy rates
  Special education
  Health services
  School lunch programs
  Access to higher education
	Influences socioeconomic status, access to health care, ability to understand health recommendations	Census documents
		School districts and nurse

Recreation
  Parks and playgrounds
  Libraries
  Public and private recreation
  Special facilities
	Reflects quality of life, resources available to community, concern for young and disadvantaged	Parks and recreation departments
		Newspapers

Religion
  Churches, synagogues
  Denominations
  Community programs
  Health-related programs
  Community organizing
	Influences values in community, organizing around common interests and concerns
	Reflects involvement of members, community skills, and resources for community needs
		Chamber of Commerce
		Newspapers
		Community center newsletters

Communication
  Newspapers
  Neighborhood news
  Radio and television
  Telephone
  Hotline
  Medical media
  Public service announcements
	Reflects concerns and needs of community
	Networks and resources available for health-related use
		Local libraries
		Newspapers
		
		Local health department
		Medical and nursing society

Parameter	Importance to CHN	Sources of Information

Transportation
  Intercity and intracity
  Handicapped
  Emergency transport
	Impacts access to services, food, and other resources
	Reflects resources available to community
		Local bus and train service
		Local hospital emergency service

Public services
  Fire protection
  Police protection
  Rape treatment centers
  Utilities
	Impacts security of community
	Reflects resources available
		Local police department

Political organization
  Structure
  Methods for filling positions
  Responsibilities of positions
  Sources of revenue
  Voter registration
	Reflects level of citizen activism and involvement, values, and concerns of citizenry
	Mechanism for nurse activism and lobbying
		Newspapers
		Local political party organization
		Local board of elections
		Local representatives

Community development or planning
  Activities
  Major issues
	Reflects needs and concerns of community
	Impacts level of involvement of professionals in issues
		Newspapers
		Local and state planning board
		Local community organizations

Disaster programs
  American Red Cross
  Disaster plans
  Potential sources of disaster
	Level of preparedness, coordination, and resources available
	Influences resources and plans
		Local American Red Cross office
		Local emergency coordinating council
		Local fire department

Health statistics
  Mortality
  Morbidity
  Leading causes of death
  Births
	Reflects health problems, trends, and state of community health
	Impacts resources needed and CHN services provided
		Local and state health department
		Health facilities and programs
		National vital statistics reports
		National Center for Health Statistics reports
		Morbidity and Mortality Weekly Report

Social problems
  Mental health
  Alcoholism and drug abuse
  Suicide
  Crime
  School dropout
  Unemployment
  Gangs
	Impacts health problems and types and amounts of services required
	Influences CHN program priorities
		Local and state department of social services
		Local mental health centers
		Local hotlines
		Libraries

Health manpower	Influences health resources available and nature of CHN practice	Local and state health planning agency Health professional organizations Telephone directory Community service directory
Health professional organizations	Provides support for CHN practice	

Community services
  Institutional care
  Ambulatory care
  Preventive health services
  Nursing services
	Reflects resources available	Local United Way organization
		Local voluntary service directory
		County hospital
		Local health department

CHN, community health nurse.

time period (i.e., per day, per week, or per year). This proportion is multiplied by a constant (k) that always is a multiple of 10, such as 1,000, 10,000, or 100,000. By using a constant, the resultant number is usually converted to a whole number, which is larger and easier to interpret. A rate can be reported as the number of cases of a disease occurring for every 1,000 or 100,000 persons in the population.

Using Rates in Everyday Community Health Nursing Practice

THE VALUE of rates is exemplified in the following school situation.

On completing tuberculosis screening in the Southside School, the community health nurse identified 15 students with newly positive tuberculin tests among the 500 students at risk of tuberculosis (those tested). The proportion of Southside School students affected was 15/500, or .03 (3%), or a rate of 30/1,000 students at risk for tuberculosis. Concurrently, the nurse conducted screening in the Northside School and again identified 15 positive tuberculin tests. This school, however, was much larger than the Southside School and had many more potentially at-risk students (900). To place the number of affected students in perspective relative to the size of the Northside School, the rate was calculated as 15/900, or 0.017 (1.7%), or a rate of 17/1,000 students at risk.

On the basis of this comparison, the nurse concluded that even though both schools had *equal numbers* of tuberculin conversions, Southside School had the *greater rate* of tuberculin test conversions. The nurse then could proceed to explore reasons for the difference in these rates.

$$\text{Rate} = \frac{\text{Numerator}}{\text{Denominator}} = \frac{\begin{array}{c}\text{Number of}\\\text{health events}\\\text{in a specified period}\end{array}}{\begin{array}{c}\text{Population in same}\\\text{area in same}\\\text{specified period}\end{array}} \times k$$

When raw counts are converted to rates, the community health nurse can make meaningful comparisons with rates from other districts or states, the nation as a whole, and a previous time period. These analyses assist the nurse in determining the magnitude of a public health problem relative to the experience of others and allow more reliable tracking of trends in the community over time.

Morbidity: Incidence and Prevalence Rates

The two principal types of morbidity rates (rates of illness) used in public health, are incidence rates and prevalence rates. *Incidence rates* describe the occurrence of new disease cases in a community over a period of time relative to the size of the population at risk of developing that disease during that same period.

$$\text{Incidence rate} = \frac{\begin{array}{c}\text{Number of new cases}\\\text{or events occurring}\\\text{in population}\\\text{in a specified period}\end{array}}{\begin{array}{c}\text{Population at risk}\\\text{during same}\\\text{specified period}\end{array}} \times k$$

Sometimes the incidence rate is considered the most sensitive indicator of the changing health of a community because it captures the fluctuations of disease in a population. Although incidence rates are valuable for following trends in chronic disease, they are particularly useful for detecting short-term acute disease changes such as those that occur with infectious hepatitis or measles, where the duration of the disease is typically short.

If a population is exposed to an infectious disease at a given time and place, a specialized form of the incidence rate, the *attack rate,* is used. Attack rates document the number of new cases of a disease in those exposed to the disease. A common example of the application of the attack rate is food poisoning; the denominator used to derive a rate is the number of persons exposed to a suspect food.

A *prevalence rate* is the number of all cases of a specific disease in a population at a given point in time relative to the population at the same point in time.

$$\text{Prevalence rate} = \frac{\begin{array}{c}\text{Number of existing}\\\text{cases in population in}\\\text{a specified point in time}\end{array}}{\begin{array}{c}\text{Population at}\\\text{same specified}\\\text{point in time}\end{array}} \times k$$

Note that those who recover from a disease are removed from the numerator, and that persons who are deceased are removed from the numerator (Fig. 5–1). Prevalence rates describe the number of per-

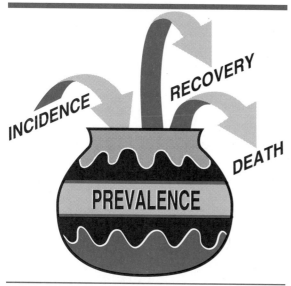

Figure 5–1
Prevalence pot: The relationship between incidence and
prevalence. (Redrawn from *A Study Guide to Epidemiology
and Biostatistics*, 3rd Ed., by R. F. Morton, J. R. Hebel, and
R. J. McCarter, p. 30, with permission of Aspen Publishers,
Inc., © 1990.)

sons with the disease at a specific point in time and
so are sometimes called point prevalences. For this
reason, they are frequently used in cross-sectional
studies. Period prevalences represent the number of
existing cases during a specified period or interval of
time and include old cases as well as new cases that
develop in the period of time.

Prevalence rates are influenced by two factors:
the number of people who develop a particular
condition (incidence) and the duration of the condition. A prevalence rate is derived by multiplying
incidence by duration. An increase in the incidence rate or the duration of a disease increases the
prevalence rate of a disease. With the advent of
life-prolonging therapies, e.g., insulin for treatment of type I diabetes mellitus, the prevalence of a
disease may increase without a change in the incidence rate. As can be seen, those who survive a
chronic disease but are not cured remain in the
"prevalence pot" (see Fig. 5–1). For conditions
such as cataracts, recent advances in surgical removal permit many persons to recover and thereby
move out of the prevalence pot. Although the incidence has not necessarily changed, the reduced du-

ration of the disease lowers the prevalence rate of
cataracts in the population.

Morbidity rates are not available for many conditions, and when available, may be subject to
under reporting. More widely available, routinely
collected rates of births and deaths (mortality rates)
are presented below.

Other Rates

There are numerous other rates that are useful in
characterizing the population. *Crude rates* summarize, for example, the occurrence of births
(crude birth rate), deaths (crude death rates), or
diseases (crude disease rates) in the general population. The numerator is the number of events and
the denominator is the average population size or
the population size at midyear (usually July 1).

Because the denominators of crude rates represent the total population and not the population at
risk for a given event, these rates are subject to
certain biases in interpretation. Crude death rates
are sensitive to the number of persons at the highest
risk of dying, in particular, the elderly. A relatively
older population probably will produce a higher
crude death rate than will a population in whom
the range is more evenly distributed. Conversely, a
young population will have a somewhat lower
crude death rate. Similar biases can occur for crude
birth rates, e.g., higher birth rates in young populations. This distortion results because the denominator reflects the entire population, not only the
population truly at risk of giving birth. Various
statistical tests consider age differences between
populations and are used to produce summary
rates, which are adjusted for age differences. Epidemiology textbooks provide discussions of direct
and indirect age standardization methods.

Age-specific rates are rates that characterize a
particular age group in the population, usually
with regard to deaths or births. By determining the
rate for specific subgroups of a population, the bias
due to the confounding factor of age is removed.
To characterize a total population using age-
specific rates, rates for each subgroup must be
computed because a single summary rate is not
being used. Specific rates for other variables, such
as race and sex, may be determined in a similar
fashion.

Numerous other rates are used in assessing different segments of the population; see Table 5–2

Table 5-2
Major Public Health Rates

Rate Denominator	Rates	Usual Factor	Rate for United States, 1990
Total Population	Crude birth rate $= \dfrac{\text{Number of live births during the year}}{\text{Average (midyear) population}}$	Per 1,000 population	16.7
	Crude death rate $= \dfrac{\text{Number of deaths during the year}}{\text{Average (midyear) population}}$	Per 1,000 population	8.6
	Age-specific death rate $= \dfrac{\text{Number of deaths among persons of a given age group in 1 year}}{\text{Average (midyear) population in specified age group}}$	Per 1,000 population	1.0 (5–14 years)* 26.1 (65–74 years)*
	Cause-specific death rate $= \dfrac{\text{Number of deaths from a stated cause in 1 year}}{\text{Average (midyear) population}}$	Per 100,000 population	366.2* (diseases of the heart) 202.1* (malignant neoplasms)
Women Aged 14–44	Fertility rate $= \dfrac{\text{Number of live births during 1 year}}{\text{Number of women aged 14–44 in same year}}$	Per 1,000 women aged 15–44	71.1
Live Births	Infant mortality rate $= \dfrac{\text{Number of deaths in 1 year of children aged less than 1}}{\text{Number of live births in same year}}$	Per 1,000 live births	9.1
	Neonatal mortality rate $= \dfrac{\text{Number of deaths in 1 year of children} <28 \text{ days}}{\text{Number of live births in same year}}$	Per 1,000 live births	5.7*
	Maternal mortality rate (puerperal) $= \dfrac{\text{Number of deaths from puerperal causes in 1 year}}{\text{Number of live births in same year}}$	Per 100,000 live births	7.9*
Rates Whose Denominators Are Live Births and Fetal Deaths	Fetal death rate $= \dfrac{\text{Number of fetal deaths in 1 year}}{\text{Number of live births and fetal deaths during same year}}$	Per 1,000 live births and fetal deaths	7.5†
	Perinatal mortality rate $= \dfrac{\text{Number of fetal deaths} \geq 28 \text{ weeks plus infant deaths} <7 \text{ days}}{\text{Number of live births and fetal deaths} \geq 28 \text{ weeks during same year}}$	Per 1,000 live births and fetal deaths	9.7†

* Estimates from National Center for Health Statistics: Births, marriages, divorces, and deaths for 1990. Monthly Vital Stat. Rep. *39*; 1991; and from National Center for Health Statistics: Births, marriages, divorces, and deaths for January 1991. Monthly Vital Stat. Rep. *40*; 1991.

† Rates from National Center for Health Statistics: Health, United States, 1990. Hyattsville, Maryland, Department of Health and Human Services, U.S. Public Health Service, Publication no. (PHS) 91-1232, 1991.

Table adapted from Mausner, J. S., and Kramer, S.: Mausner and Bahn Epidemiology: An Introductory Text. 2nd Ed. Philadelphia, W. B. Saunders, 1985, pp. 92–93.

for a summary and a standard epidemiology text-book for more detailed background information.

Concept of Risk

The concept of risk and risk factors is familiar to community health nurses whose practices focus on the prevention of disease. *Risk* refers to the probability of an adverse event, i.e., the likelihood that healthy persons exposed to a specific factor will acquire a specific disease. *Risk factor* refers to the specific exposure factor, which frequently is external to the individual, such as exposure to cigarette smoking, excessive stress, high noise levels, or chemicals in the environment. Risk factors may also be fixed characteristics of people, such as age, sex, or genetic makeup. Although these intrinsic factors are not alterable, certain lifestyle changes may reduce their impact as risk factors. For example, positive dietary practices and exercise regimens may modify the effects of aging as a risk factor for certain health conditions.

Epidemiologists describe the pattern of disease in the aggregate and quantify the effect of exposure to particular factors on the rate of disease. To identify specific risk factors, rates of disease for those exposed are compared with those of the nonexposed. One method for comparing two rates is by subtracting the rate of the nonexposed from that of the exposed. This measure of risk is called the *attributable risk*; it is the estimate of the burden of disease in a population. For example, if the rate of non–insulin-dependent diabetes were 5,000 per 100,000 persons in the obese population (those weighing more than 120% of ideal body weight) and 1,000 per 100,000 persons in the nonobese population, the attributable risk of non–insulin-dependent diabetes due to obesity would be 4,000 per 100,000 persons (5,000/100,000 minus 1,000/100,000). This means that 4,000 cases per 100,000 persons can be attributed to obesity. Thus, a prevention program designed to reduce obesity theoretically could eliminate 4,000 cases per 100,000 persons in the population. Therefore, attributable risks are particularly important in describing the potential impact of a public health intervention in a community.

A second measure of the excess risk caused by a factor is the *relative risk ratio.* To calculate a relative risk, the incidence rate of disease in the exposed population is divided by the incidence rate of disease in the nonexposed population. In the above example, a relative risk of 5 was obtained by dividing 5,000/100,000 by 1,000/100,000. This risk ratio suggests that an obese individual has a five-fold greater risk of diabetes than does a nonobese individual.

The relative risk ratio forms the statistical basis for the concept of risk factor. Relative risks are valuable indicators of the excess risk incurred by exposure to certain factors. They have been used extensively in identifying the major causal factors of many common diseases and so direct public health practitioners' efforts to reduce health risks.

Community health nurses may apply the concept of relative risk to suspected exposure variables to isolate risk factors associated with health problems in the community. For example, a community health nurse might investigate an outbreak of probable foodborne illness. The incidence rate for those exposed to potato salad in a school cafeteria can be compared with the incidence rate for those not exposed. The relative risk calculated from the ratio of these two incidence rates would indicate the amount of excess risk of disease that was incurred by eating potato salad. A relative risk might also be determined for other suspected foods and then compared with that for potato salad. Incidence rates for specific foods involved in foodborne illnesses are frequently called *attack rates.* A food with a markedly higher relative risk than other foods might be the causal agent in a foodborne epidemic; the identification of the causal agent (a specific food) is critical to the implementation of an effective prevention program, such as teaching proper food-handling techniques.

EPIDEMIOLOGY

Epidemiology is defined as the study of the distribution and determinants of health and disease in the community. It may be described as the principle science of community health practice, and as such, it entails specialized methods and approaches to scientific research. Community health nurses working to improve the health of the aggregate use epidemiological approaches in community assessment and diagnosis and in planning and evaluating effective community interventions. Discussed are the uses of epidemiology and its specialized methodologies.

Use of Epidemiology in Disease Control and Prevention

Although the origins of epidemiology may be traced to ancient times, formal epidemiological techniques were developed in the 19th century. The focus of early applications was on identifying factors associated with infectious disease and its epidemic spread in the community. By identifying factors critical to the development of disease, public health practitioners hoped to improve preventive strategies. Specifically, investigators attempted to identify differences among those who were stricken with a disease such as cholera or plague compared with those who remained healthy. These differences might include a broad range of personal factors such as age, socioeconomic status, and health status. Investigators also asked if there were differences in location or environment of ill persons compared with healthy individuals, and if these factors influenced the development of disease. Also examined was whether factors of time, such as when persons developed disease, contributed to disease etiology. Use of this **person-place-time** model organized epidemiologists' investigations of the pattern of disease in the community. The study of the amount and distribution of disease constitutes **descriptive epidemiology**.

An Example of the Epidemiological Approach
AN EARLY example of the use of the epidemiological approach is that of John Snow's investigation of an epidemic of cholera in the 1850s. He analyzed the distribution of person, place, and time factors by comparing the rates of death among people living in different geographical sectors of London. Snow noted that those using a particular water pump had significantly higher mortality rates due to cholera than those using other sources in the city. Although the cholera organism had not yet been identified, the clustering of disease cases around one neighborhood pump suggested new prevention strategies to public health officials, i.e., that cholera might be reduced in a community by controlling the contamination of drinking water sources (Snow, 1936).

In addition to investigating personal, place, and time factors related to disease, epidemiologists examined complex relationships among the many determinants of disease. This investigation of the causes, or etiology, of disease is called **analytic epidemiology**. Even before bacterial agents were identified, public health practitioners recognized that single factors alone were insufficient to cause disease. In exploring the cholera epidemics, for instance, Snow in 1855 collected data about social and physical environmental conditions that might favor disease development, in particular, contamination of local water systems and the pumps where people obtained water. He also gathered information about people who became ill, including their patterns of living, especially related to water use, their socioeconomic characteristics, and their health status. A comprehensive data base assisted Snow in developing a theory about the possible cause of the epidemic. As mentioned, Snow suspected that a single biological agent probably was responsible for the cholera infection, even though the organism, *Vibrio cholerae,* had not been discovered at that time. The comparison of death rates of those using one source of water with rates of those using a different water pump suggested an association between cholera and water quality.

By examining the interrelationships of host and environmental characteristics, the epidemiologist uses an organized method of inquiry to derive an explanation of disease. This model of investigation has been called the epidemiological triangle because of the three elements that must be analyzed: agent, host, and environment (Fig. 5–2). The development of disease is dependent on the extent of exposure to an agent, the strength or virulence of the agent, the host's susceptibility (either genetic or immunological), and the environmental conditions (including the biological, social, and physical environment) existing at the time of exposure to the agent (Table 5–3). The model implies that

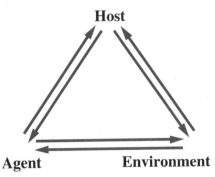

Figure 5–2
Epidemiological triangle.

Table 5–3
A Classification of Agent, Host, and Environmental Factors That Determine the Distribution of Diseases in Human Populations

Factors	Examples
Agents of Disease—Etiological Factors	
Nutritive elements	
Excesses	Cholesterol
Deficiencies	Vitamins, proteins
Chemical agents	
Poisons	Carbon monoxide, carbon tetrachloride, drugs
Allergens	Ragweed, poison ivy, medications
Physical agents	Ionizing radiation, mechanical
Infectious agents	
Metazoa	Hookworm, schistosomiasis, onchocerciasis
Protozoa	Amebae, malaria
Bacteria	Rheumatic fever, lobar pneumonia, typhoid, tuberculosis, syphilis
Fungi	Histoplasmosis, athlete's foot
Rickettsia	Rocky mountain spotted fever, typhus
Viruses	Measles, mumps, chickenpox, smallpox, poliomyelitis, rabies, yellow fever
Host Factors (Intrinsic Factors)—Influence Exposure, Susceptibility, or Response to Agents	
Genetics	Sickle cell disease
Age	—
Sex	—
Ethnic group	—
Physiological state	Fatigue, pregnancy, puberty, stress, nutritional state
Prior immunological experience	Hypersensitivity, protection
Active	Prior infection, immunization
Passive	Maternal antibodies, gamma-globulin prophylaxis
Intercurrent or preexisting disease	
Human behavior	Personal hygiene, food handling, diet, interpersonal contact, occupation, recreation, utilization of health resources
Environmental Factors (Extrinsic Factors)—Influence Existence of the Agent, Exposure, or Susceptibility to Agent	
Physical environment	Geology, climate
Biological environment	
Human populations	Density
Flora	Sources of food, influence on vertebrates and arthropods, as a source of agents
Fauna	Food sources, vertebrate hosts, arthropod vectors
Socioeconomic environment	
Occupation	Exposure to chemical agents
Urbanization and economic development	Urban crowding, tensions and pressures, cooperative efforts in health and education
Disruption	Wars, floods

From Lilienfeld, A. M., and Lilienfeld D.: Foundations of Epidemiology. New York, Oxford University Press, 1980, pp. 47–48.

when the balance among these three factors is altered, the rate of disease will change.

The epidemiological triangle is most applicable to conditions that can be linked to clearly identifiable agents such as bacteria, chemicals, toxins, and other exposure factors. With increased understanding of diseases that do not have single causal agents, other models have been developed that stress the multiplicity of environment and host interactions. An example of such a model is the "wheel model" (Fig. 5–3). The wheel consists of a hub that represents the host with all of its human characteristics such as genetic makeup, personality, and immunity. The surrounding wheel represents the environment and comprises biological, social, and physical dimensions. The relative size of each component in the wheel depends on the health problem being analyzed. Diseases dependent on heredity would be represented by a relatively large genetic core. Origins of other health conditions may be more dependent on environmental factors (Mausner and Kramer, 1985). Because the model allows for a multiple-causation rather than a single-causation theory of disease, it is more useful for analyzing complex chronic conditions and identifying factors that are amenable to their intervention.

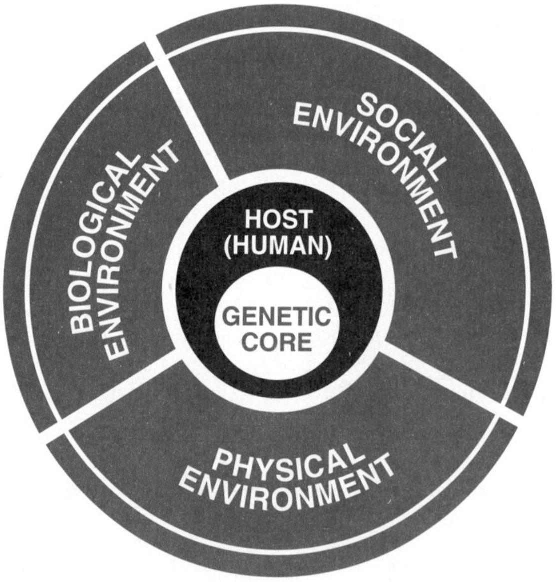

As the causative agents of many infectious diseases were discovered, subsequent public health interventions led to a decline in mortality due to widespread epidemics, particularly in the developed countries. As a result, the focus of public health efforts during the past few decades has shifted to the control of chronic diseases such as cancer, coronary heart disease, and diabetes. These chronic diseases tend to have multiple interrelated factors associated with their origins rather than a single causative agent. Epidemiologists, however, apply approaches to chronic diseases that are similar to those used in infectious disease investigation, thereby developing complex theories about chronic disease control. Of particular importance to chronic disease reduction is the identification of risk factors. As previously discussed, risk factors suggest specific prevention and intervention approaches that may effectively and efficiently reduce morbidity and mortality from chronic disease. For example, the identification of cardiovascular disease risk factors has suggested a number of lifestyle modifications that could reduce the morbidity risk before disease onset. Primary prevention strategies such as reduction of dietary saturated fats, smoking cessation, and hypertension control were developed as a response to previous

Figure 5–3
Wheel model of human–environment interaction. (Redrawn from Mausner, J. S., and Kramer, S.: Mausner and Bahn Epidemiology: An Introductory Text. 2nd Ed. Philadelphia: W. B. Saunders, 1985, p. 36.)

Coronary Heart Disease Risk Factors Supported by Epidemiological Data

- History or clinical picture of myocardial infarction or ischemia
- Male sex (males have three to four times the risk of women in midlife and twice the risk of elderly women)
- Cigarette smoking (currently smoking 10 or more cigarettes daily)
- Hypertension
- High total cholesterol levels (>240 mg/dL) High low density cholesterol (>160 mg/dL) Low high density cholesterol (<35 mg/dL)
- Diabetes mellitus
- History of cerebrovascular disease or occlusive peripheral vascular disease
- Severe obesity (>30% overweight)

Adapted from National Cholesterol Education Program: Report of the Expert Panel on Detection, Evaluation, and Treatment of High Blood Cholesterol in Adults. Bethesda, Maryland, NCEP, NIH Publication no. 89-2925, 1989.

epidemiological studies that identified them as risk factors.

Use of Epidemiology in Secondary and Tertiary Prevention Approaches

As discussed earlier, a principle goal of classic epidemiology is to identify etiologic factors of diseases so that the most effective primary prevention activities might be encouraged. Another aim of epidemiology, however, is to describe the course of disease over time. Observations of the disease process may suggest factors that aggravate or ameliorate its progress. This information also assists in determining usual treatment or rehabilitation patterns, i.e., secondary or tertiary prevention approaches.

Identifying disease in its earliest stages is a principle purpose of screening programs. Screening is usually classified as a secondary prevention activity because disease is discovered after a pathological change has occurred, ideally, early in the disease process (see "Levels of Prevention," Chapter 1). Epidemiologists use information obtained through screening of populations to determine rates of disease occurrence in the community and describe attributes and risk factors common to those with the disease compared with those who are disease free. In addition, systematic surveys as well as ongoing data collection provide important information about changing incidence and prevalence rates. National and regional compilations of these rates are given in vital statistic reports. Local ongoing surveys of the development of disease are also common. For example, public health departments continuously monitor the occurrence of many communicable diseases in communities, noting changes that may affect the health of citizens and to which a response by the health department is necessitated. School nurses tabulate illness rates according to disease and compare well with ill children. This provides epidemiological information about patterns and risk factors and may be helpful in protecting well children in the future.

Epidemiologists also describe the course of disease over time documenting secular trends in disease. Secular trends are changes that occur over a long period of time (years or decades), such as the declining incidence rate in cancer of the uterus and increase in cancer of the breast. Frequently, the associated patterns of treatment and intervention are also documented. In many instances, this information is derived from research studies conducted by clinicians. Cancer registries provide information about not only the incidence and prevalence of disease in a community but also its course, treatment, and associated survival rates. Community surveys of the disabled population that were undertaken to assess prevalence, may also be used to evaluate the adequacy of present services and project future needs.

Use of Epidemiology in Health Services

Epidemiology has been discussed regarding the determinants of disease in populations. However, epidemiological principles are also useful in studying the delivery of health care to populations, in particular, in describing and evaluating the use of health services by the community. For example, determining the relative number of health care providers in relation to the population size may assist in assessing the system's adequacy in providing care. Also of interest are the reasons that clients initially seek care, methods by which clients pay for their care, and clients' satisfaction with services. Regardless of whether these data are collected by community health nurses or health services researchers, they are essential information for those who strive to improve clients' access to quality health care.

Health Services Epidemiology
HEALTH SERVICES – focused epidemiology is exemplified by a 1980 study that showed that the poor tend to have higher hospitalization rates than the nonpoor (National Center for Health Statistics, 1981). Although this may imply greater access to health care, a 1981 study found that low socioeconomic status individuals tend to have more chronic disease, which may explain their higher hospitalization rates (Aday and Anderson, 1981).

Epidemiological studies can be used to evaluate quality of care. An example of this approach is a comparative study of a special geriatric inpatient evaluation ward that used an interdisciplinary program of elderly care (Rubenstein et al., 1984). The outcomes of interdisciplinary care were compared with those of the care usually received by elderly clients on the hospital ward. Patients in the special unit were found to have lower mortality rates, lower morbidity rates, and higher levels of patient satisfaction. One of the most important findings of this study was the lower costs incurred by clients on the special unit compared with those on other units. This latter finding suggests another aspect of health services epidemiology—the evaluation of the cost-effectiveness of health care and of specific interventions or modes of delivery.

Regarding the application of epidemiological findings, although it is essential that study results be incorporated into prevention programs for communities and at-risk populations, the philosophy of public health and its subspecialty of epidemiology dictates that application be extended to and translated into major health policy decisions (Ford, 1978). The aim of health policy planning is to achieve positive health goals and outcomes for the good of the majority of society. As a process designed to bring about desirable social changes, it is influenced not only by epidemiological factors, but also by history, politics, economics, culture, and technology. The complex interaction of these factors may explain the slow pace of application of epidemiological knowledge. An example of incomplete progress in implementing effective health policy is lung disease in the United States. The major risk factor, cigarette smoking, was identified and conclusively linked to high rates of lung cancer and heart disease as early as the 1950s (Doll and Hill, 1952). Implemented public policies designed to protect the community include taxation of cigarettes, warning labels on cigarette packages, and, most recently, restriction of smoking in public areas. Nevertheless, other aspects of health policy remain unmodified—in essence, promoting cigarette smoking. One example is the proliferation of billboard and media advertisements targeted to vulnerable segments of the population, i.e., adolescents and black and Hispanic males; this has been vigorously protested and debated in community forums. Recently, the U.S. government endorsed the opening of markets in Third World countries for the export of tobacco products; former Surgeon General Koop called it the export of "disease, death, and disability" (Chen and Winder, 1990, p. 659; see also Barry, 1991).

In 1976, Milio suggested other areas where public policy had not kept pace with epidemiological research findings. She asserted that public policy that provides consumers with healthier options such as improved safeguards in the workplace, enforcement of higher environmental standards, access to more nutritious food, and incentives to reduce alcohol consumption would significantly benefit the health of consumers. Today, these continue to be among the primary concerns of public health professionals.

In summary, there are innumerable areas where public health practitioners and epidemiologists have not yet effectively modified public policy in the interest of improved health. Exercising "societal responsibility" in the application of epidemiological findings is within the province of community health nurses, but as Gordis noted, will necessitate the active involvement of the citizen-consumer (1980). Community health nurses collaborating with community members can most effectively combine epidemiological knowledge and aggregate-level strategies to effect change on the broadest scale.

EPIDEMIOLOGICAL METHODS

Descriptive Epidemiology

Descriptive epidemiology focuses on the amount and distribution of health and health problems within a population. Its purpose is to describe the characteristics of persons who are protected from disease and of those who have a disease. Factors of particular interest include age, sex, ethnicity or race, socioeconomic status, occupation, family status, and many other variables. Epidemiologists use morbidity and mortality rates to describe the extent of disease and to determine risk factors that make certain groups prone to developing the disease.

In addition to **"person"** characteristics (or the "who"), the frequency of disease is described by the **place** of occurrence (or the "where"). For example, certain parasitic diseases such as malaria and schistosomiasis are known to occur in tropical areas. Other diseases may occur frequently in certain geopolitical entities; for example, gastroenteritis outbreaks often occur in communities with lax standards for water pollution. A third parameter that assists in defining disease patterns is **time** (or the "when"). Incidence rates may be tracked over a period of days or weeks (e.g., epidemics of infectious disease) or over an extended period of years (e.g., trends in the cancer death rate).

These person, place, and time factors can be used to form a framework for the analysis of a disease and may suggest variables that are associated with high versus low rates of disease. Hypotheses about the etiology of disease can then be generated from descriptive epidemiology and tested by analytic methods.

Analytic Epidemiology

Analytic epidemiology investigates the causes of disease by determining why a disease rate is lower in one population group than in another. Hypotheses generated from descriptive data are tested and either accepted or rejected based on results of analytic research. The epidemiologist seeks to establish a cause-and-effect relationship between a preexisting condition or event and the disease. To determine this relationship, two major types of research studies may be undertaken: *observational* studies and *experimental* studies.

Although observational studies are frequently used for descriptive purposes, they also are used in discovering the etiological factors of disease. By observing disease rates in groups of people that are differentiated on the basis of an experience or exposure, the investigator can begin to understand the factors that contribute to disease. To illustrate, differences in the rates of disease may occur in the obese compared with the nonobese, in smokers compared with nonsmokers, and in those with high levels of life stress compared with those with low levels. Variables that define characteristics, obesity, smoking, and stress are called *exposure* variables.

However, unlike experimental studies, observational studies do not allow the investigator to manipulate the specific exposure or experience or, often, to control or limit the effects of other extraneous factors that may influence the development of disease. For example, life stress is known to be related to depression. Those of low socioeconomic status also have high depression rates. Because persons of low socioeconomic status frequently experience greater life stresses, the relationship between stress and depression is difficult to assess. Therefore, the confounding factor of socioeconomic status makes it more difficult to demonstrate the effect of stress on depression.

The three major study designs used in conducting observational research are cross-sectional (Fig. 5–4), retrospective (Fig. 5–5), and prospective (Fig. 5–6).

OBSERVATIONAL STUDIES

Cross-sectional Studies

Cross-sectional studies, sometimes called *prevalence* or *correlational* studies, examine relationships between potential causal factors and disease at one point in time. Surveys in which information about the risk factor(s) and the disease are collected at the same time exemplify this design. Both the National Health and Nutrition Examination Survey (NHANES) and the subsequent Hispanic Health and Nutrition Examination Survey (HHANES) collected cross-sectional data on persons 1–72 years old regarding their current dietary practices and physical status (Delgado et al., 1990). The purpose of the two surveys was to detect nutritional deficiencies in the population. Although associations among disease and specific factors can be identified in a cross-sectional study, it is not possible to make causal inferences because the temporal sequence of events cannot be established; i.e., the cause preceded the effect. In the NHANES, for example, it is not possible to determine whether high salt intake preceded hypertension and thus is the causal factor, or whether the reverse is true. Therefore, cross-sectional studies have limitations with regard to discovering etiological factors of disease. However, they are useful in identifying preliminary relationships that may be further explored by other analytic designs and therefore may be thought of as hypothesis-generating studies.

Retrospective Studies

Retrospective studies compare a group of individuals known to have a particular condition or disease with a group of individuals who do not have the disease. The purpose of these studies is to determine whether cases (diseased group) differ in their exposure to a specific factor or characteristic relative to controls (nondiseased group). To make unambiguous comparisons, the cases are selected according to explicitly defined criteria regarding the type of case and the stage of disease. Controls are selected from among the general population and should have had the same opportunity of exposure

Time Dimension:

PRESENT

**Sample: Subjects sampled
from population-at-large
at one point in time**

Advantages

Quick to plan and conduct

Relatively inexpensive

May provide preliminary
indication of whether an
association between a risk
factor and disease exists

Provides prevalence data
needed for planning health
services

Hypothesis generating

Disadvantages

Cannot calculate relative
risk with prevalence data

Temporal sequence of factor
and outcome unknown

Figure 5–4
Cross-sectional, or prevalence, study.

Time Dimension:

PAST

**Sample: Subjects sampled
with regard to disease and
condition**

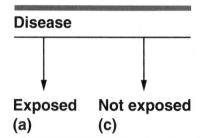

Disease

Exposed   Not exposed
(a)   **(c)**

History of exposure
(factors) from the
past

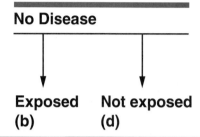

No Disease

Exposed   Not exposed
(b)   **(d)**

Advantages

Can calculate odds ratio (OR),
which is an estimate of
relative risk:

$$OR = \frac{a}{a+c} \div \frac{b}{b+d} \quad * \quad = \frac{ad}{bc}$$

(*If disease is rare.)

Requires fewer subjects than
prospective designs do

Possible to study multiple risk
factors presumed to be related
to a disease

Less expensive and difficult to
conduct than a prospective study

Disadvantages

Incidence of disease cannot
be calculated

Selection of control group is
difficult

Relies on recall or records
for exposure information
that is subject to bias

Exposure ascertained after
disease occurs (temporal
relationship)

Figure 5–5
Retrospective, or case–control, study.

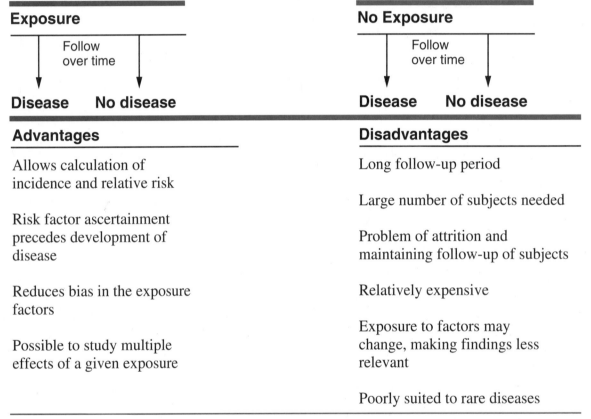

Time Dimension:

FUTURE

Sample: Healthy subjects sampled with regard to exposure or risk factor(s)

Exposure

Follow over time

Disease   **No disease**

No Exposure

Follow over time

Disease   **No disease**

Advantages

Allows calculation of incidence and relative risk

Risk factor ascertainment precedes development of disease

Reduces bias in the exposure factors

Possible to study multiple effects of a given exposure

Disadvantages

Long follow-up period

Large number of subjects needed

Problem of attrition and maintaining follow-up of subjects

Relatively expensive

Exposure to factors may change, making findings less relevant

Poorly suited to rare diseases

Figure 5–6
Prospective, or cohort, study.

as the cases, i.e., they are similar to the cases in as many ways as possible. Frequently, persons hospitalized for diseases other than the disease under study are selected as controls if they do not share the exposure or risk factor under study. For example, patients with heart disease may be selected as controls in a study of patients with lung cancer; however, this could introduce serious confounding because these patients often share the risk factor of smoking. To prevent the further introduction of bias into the study, the methods of data collection must be the same for both groups. For this reason, it is desirable for interviewers to remain unaware of whether subjects are cases or controls.

In retrospective studies, data collection extends back in time to determine previous exposures or risk factors. Study data are analyzed by comparing the proportion of subjects with disease (cases) who possess the exposure or risk factors with the corresponding proportion in the control group. A greater proportion of cases exposed than controls suggests an association of the disease with the risk factor.

Retrospective study designs are often used because they are better able than cross-sectional studies to address the question of causality. They also require fewer resources and time in data collection than prospective studies (discussed next). There are many examples of retrospective, or *case–control studies,* in the literature. One classic example is the investigation of risk factors for lung cancer by Doll and Hill (1952). They compared exposure rates for those diagnosed with lung cancer (cases) with those diagnosed with cancer of sites other than the chest and oral cavity (controls). Detailed smoking histories were taken on all subjects. Of the cases, a significantly higher proportion of those with lung cancer smoked compared with the control group. From this study, a hypothesis was developed that smoking might be etiologically related to lung cancer.

Prospective Studies

In prospective studies, a group of individuals who are considered free of a disease are followed forward in time to determine if and when disease occurs. These individuals, the *cohort,* are a group of persons who share a common experience within a defined time period. For example, a birth cohort consists of all persons born within a given period of time. The cohort is assessed with respect to an exposure factor suspected of being associated with the disease and is classified accordingly at the beginning of the study. The cohort then is followed for the development of disease. The disease rates for those with a known exposure are compared with rates for those who remain unexposed. Because subjects are followed prospectively, data collected over time can be summarized by incidence rates of new cases. As was indicated earlier, comparison of two incidence rates produces a measure of relative risk:

$$\text{Relative risk} = \frac{\text{Incidence rate among exposed}}{\text{Incidence rate among unexposed}}$$

The relative risk indicates the extent of excess risk incurred by exposure to a factor relative to nonexposure. A relative risk of 1 suggests no excess risk due to exposure, whereas a relative risk of 2 suggests twice the risk of developing disease if exposed to the particular factor versus no exposure.

Prospective studies, or *longitudinal, cohort,* or *incidence* studies, are advantageous designs in that more reliable information about the etiology of disease is obtained than in other study methodologies. The temporal relationship between the presumed causal factors and the effect can be more strongly established than in retrospective and cross-sectional studies. Calculations of incidence rates and relative risks provide a valuable indicator of the magnitude of risk created by exposure to a factor.

However, certain disadvantages are inherent in the prospective design. Following a cohort for periods of time is costly in terms of resources and staff and results in subject attrition. These logistical problems may be compounded by problems arising from the nature of chronic diseases. Frequently, chronic diseases have long latency periods between exposure and manifestation of the disease. Furthermore, the onset of chronic conditions may be sufficiently insidious as to make it extremely difficult to document the incidence of disease. In addition, as mentioned previously, many diseases do not have a unifactorial etiology but rather are influenced by many interacting factors. These problems do not negate the benefits of prospectively designed epidemiological studies; rather, they suggest a need for careful planning and tailoring of the study to the disease as well as to the study's purpose.

Numerous prospective studies can be found in the literature. In many cases, they have been instrumental in substantiating causal linkages between specific risk factors and disease. A classic example is an early cohort study of deaths due to lung cancer (Doll and Hill, 1956). Questionnaires were originally completed on a cohort of physicians in Great Britain. These subjects were then classified according to several variables but most importantly according to the amount of cigarettes smoked. A 4.5-year follow-up of death certificate data revealed an increased mortality rate due to lung cancer (as well as to coronary thrombosis) among physicians who smoked relative to those who did not smoke. The death rate for heavy smokers was 166/100,000 versus 7/100,000 for nonsmokers. Combining these two incidence rates in a measure of excess risk indicated that heavy smokers were 23.7 times more likely to develop lung cancer than nonsmokers (relative risk, 166/100,000 divided by 7/100,000, or 23.7). These findings in a prospective study provided strong epidemiological support for smoking as a risk factor for lung cancer.

Comparison of Time Factors in Retrospective and Prospective Study Designs

Cohort Study:

Girls with bacteriuria ⟶ Women with renal disease

Girls with sterile urine ⟶ Women without renal disease

Case–Control Study:

Girls with bacteriuria ⟵ Women with renal disease

Girls with sterile urine ⟵ Women without renal disease

PAST---------------PRESENT---------------FUTURE
(BEGINNING)

Comparison of time factors in prospective design (cohort) and retrospective design (case–control) approaches to studying the possible effect of childhood bacteriuria on renal disease in adult women.

Another well-known prospective study is the Framingham Study. Findings suggested that serum cholesterol level was associated with the future development of coronary heart disease (Kannel et al., 1971). This and other cohort studies formed the basis for later experimental studies aimed at reducing serum cholesterol through diet modification or drug therapy to ultimately lower the incidence rate of coronary heart disease.

EXPERIMENTAL STUDIES

Another type of analytic study is the experimental design (Fig. 5–7). In these epidemiological investigations, experimental methods are applied to questions regarding the effectiveness of interventions designed to modify the effects of risk factors, i.e., testing of treatment and prevention strategies. The investigator randomly assigns subjects who are determined to be at risk for developing a particular disease to an experimental or a control group. Only the experimental group is subject to the intervention, but both groups are observed over time for the occurrence of disease. Although theoretically it is possible to introduce an exposure or risk factor as the experimental factor, ethical considerations usually prohibit the use of human subjects for these purposes. Therefore, epidemiological studies of an experimental nature usually have been restricted to clinical trials of prophylactic and therapeutic measures. For example, experimental testing of vaccines for safety and efficacy is a common application of experimental studies.

The experimental design is also useful in investigating chronic disease. The Multiple Risk Factor Intervention Trial (MRFIT) tested a number of interventions thought to be effective in preventing heart disease: smoking cessation, reduction of dietary cholesterol, and treatment of hypertension (MRFIT, 1982). The control group was made up of similar high-risk men who were referred to their private physicians for routine medical care. This trial may be considered a public health trial because it tested a set of preventive actions within a community setting.

In contrast, the Coronary Primary Prevention Trial compared the effects of a cholesterol-lowering drug with those of a placebo in a clinical sample (Lipid Research Clinics Program, 1984). The cholesterol-lowering drug reduced the inci-

Time Dimension:

FUTURE

**Sample: Participants
randomized**

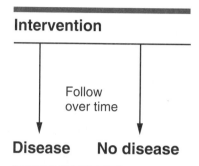

Intervention

Follow
over time

Disease   **No disease**

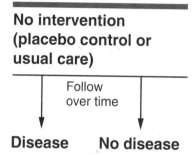

**No intervention
(placebo control or
usual care)**

Follow
over time

Disease   **No disease**

Advantages	Disadvantages
With randomization, gives confidence that outcome is due to treatment or intervention and not to other unknown factors	Often impractical to conduct in human populations
Provides strongest evidence that a factor is causal when an effect is seen	Requires relatively long time to conduct, and factors and/or disease may change unrelated to clinical trial

Figure 5–7
Experimental, or clinical trial, study.

dence of coronary heart disease by 19% after a 7-year follow-up. Thus, experimental studies are important in determining which of many possible preventive programs should be implemented. Although these studies are of a medical nature, experimental designs may be useful in evaluating community health nursing interventions such as determining the value of particular prenatal interventions in reducing the incidence of low-birth-weight infants, the effectiveness of a sex education program in preventing high rates of teenage pregnancy, or the feasibility of an AIDS prevention program among intravenous drug users. It is only through the conduct of research that optimal community interventions are identified.

APPLICATION OF THE NURSING PROCESS

The synthesis of assessment data into diagnostic statements about the health of the community is the second step of the nursing process. These statements specify the nature and etiology of the actual or potential community health problem. They necessarily direct the plans developed by community health nurses to resolve the problem. A formulation that assists in the writing of a community diagnosis was developed by Muecke (1984). The diagnosis consists of four components (Fig. 5–8): identification of the health problem or risk, aggregate or community affected, etiological or causal

Increased risk of _____
                        (disability, disease, etc.)

among _____ related to
             (community or population)

_____ as demonstrated
       (etiological statement)

in _____.
              (health indicators)

Figure 5–8
Format for community health diagnosis. (Redrawn from
Muecke, M. A.: Community health diagnosis in nursing. Pub-
lic Health Nurs. *1*;23–35, 1984. By permission of Blackwell
Scientific Publications.)

statement, and evidence or support for the diagnosis.

Assessment and Diagnosis

The process of collecting data, analyzing it, and
deriving community diagnoses is demonstrated in
the following example. The identification of a
client health problem on a home visit provided the
initial impetus for an aggregate health education
program. Data collection extended from the individual client level to a broad range of literature and
data about the nature of the problem in populations. Formulating a community level diagnosis
then provided direction for the ensuing plan.

THE REFERRAL

The school nurse in a local school district is frequently the person with the knowledge and resources to follow up student health problems with
the family at home. In the West San Antonio
School District, the school nurse sets aside several
hours each week for home visiting. Home visits are
initiated by a variety of mechanisms, but in this
situation a teacher expressed concern for a student
whose brother was dying of cancer. The student,
John, was a junior in high school and in a health
class had expressed his personal fears about cancer.
He generated much interest on the part of his class-

mates regarding their own risk of cancer and the
ways they might reduce that risk.

FAMILY ASSESSMENT

The school nurse visited John's family and learned
that the oldest son, age 25, was diagnosed 1 year
earlier with testicular cancer. Since then, he had
undergone a range of therapies that had been palliative but not curative, perhaps because the cancer
was advanced at the time of diagnosis. The nurse
spent time with the family discussing care for their
son, answering questions, and exploring support
available to them and their other children.

The next week at the school nurse staff meeting,
the nurse enquired about her colleagues' experiences with other young clients with this type of
cancer. Only one nurse remembered a young man
who had developed testicular cancer. None were
familiar with its prevalence, incidence, risk factors,
or prevention and/or early detection approaches.
The nurse recognized the high probability that high
school students would have similar questions and
could benefit from reliable information.

COMMUNITY ASSESSMENT

The school nurse embarked on a community assessment, searching for answers to the above questions. The first step was to collect information
about testicular cancer. The nurse reviewed the
nursing and medical literature for key articles discussing care of clients with this cancer and its diagnosis and treatment. *Epidemiological studies provided additional data regarding its distribution
pattern in the population and associated risk factors.* She learned that young men aged 20 to 35
were at greatest risk. No other major risk factors
were identified; however, young men who tend to
be healthy do not routinely seek regular health
care, including testicular cancer screening. They
also may be subject to the apprehensions frequently associated with conditions affecting sexual
function. These factors contribute to a delay in
prompt detection and treatment. Although only
6,100 new cases of testicular cancer were estimated
to be diagnosed in 1991 in the United States, it was
one of the most common tumors in young men
and is amenable to treatment if discovered early
(National Cancer Society, 1991).

Retrieval of Data

CURRENT DATA on the health of the population of the United States is found in many places. Finding the latest statistics available in an area of interest at the local, state, or national level can be a challenging experience for a student, community health nurse, graduate student, or even a nurse researcher. Statistics are necessary, however, for comparison purposes, in identifying the health status of an aggregate or population in a community. The following guidelines are suggested places to begin a search. As experience in gaining access to statistics in an area of interest increases, more resources will become known.

Reference Librarian. The best place to start is in a school or community library, or health sciences library if a large campus is available. Cultivate a relationship with the reference librarian and learn from the librarian how to obtain access to the literature of interest to you, for example, from government documents, or how to carry out literature searches by computer.

Government Documents. Local libraries have a listing of government depository libraries; these are libraries that have government documents available for use by the public. If the government document needed is not available at a local library, ask the reference librarian at the local library to contact a regional library or state library where an interlibrary loan of the document can be obtained. The Library of Congress in Washington, D.C., has a Directory of United States Government Depository Libraries. The number of the national reference service at the Library of Congress is 202/707-5522, or call the operator in Washington, D.C., for assistance.

Health, United States, 1990. This is an annual publication (*Health, United States, 1991,* etc.,) of the National Center for Health Statistics, which reports the latest health statistics for the United States. It presents statistics in areas such as the following: prenatal care, low birth weight, infant mortality, life expectancy, death rates, cancer incidence and survival, trends in AIDS, diabetes, overweight, hypertension, high serum cholesterol, substance use, air pollution, exposure to noise, health status and utilization, national health expenditures, health insurance, Medicaid, Medicare, health maintenance organizations,

hospital care, nursing home care, physician contacts, dental visits, diagnostic, surgical, and nonsurgical procedures, mental health services, and information on enrollment and graduates of health professions schools, including minorities and women. Graphs and tables are easy to read and interpret with accompanying texts. Many statistics are presented over a selected number of years so that trends may be seen. Also some statistics are presented using comparisons with other countries and for U.S. minority populations.

If this publication is not available locally, it may be ordered from the United States Government Printing Office (GPO), Superintendent of Documents, 732 N. Capitol Street, N.W., Washington, D.C. 20402. The telephone number is 202/783-3238, or the operator in Washington, D.C. may be called for assistance. A new edition of this publication is produced each spring and is available in paperback.

Morbidity and Mortality Weekly Report. This publication, known by its initials MMWR, is prepared by the Centers for Disease Control in Atlanta, Georgia. It provides weekly reports compiled by state health departments on numbers of cases of selected notifiable diseases such as AIDS, aseptic meningitis, encephalitis, gonorrhea, hepatitis, legionellosis, Lyme disease, malaria, measles (rubeola), meningococcal infections, mumps, pertussis, rubella, syphilis, toxic-shock syndrome, tuberculosis, tularemia, typhoid fever, typhus fever, and rabies, and deaths in 121 U.S. cities by age categories. It also reports accounts of interesting cases, environmental hazards, outbreaks, or other public health problems of interest. An annual index is helpful for locating articles and the latest statistics on areas of interest. It is published weekly by The Massachusetts Medical Society, 1440 Main Street, Waltham, MA 02154. It is found in local and state health departments and many local and health sciences libraries. A subscription is available from the aforementioned Massachussetts Medical Society.

Centers for Disease Control. Commonly called by its initials, the CDC, the Centers for Disease Control compiles information on the following topics: tobacco, violent and abusive behavior, educational and community-based programs, unintentional injuries, occupational safety and health, environmental health, oral health, diabetes and chronic disabling conditions, sexually transmitted diseases, immunization and infectious diseases, clinical preventive services, and surveillance and data systems. The Centers for Disease Control is located in Atlanta, Georgia 30333.

On the basis of these facts, the nurse reasoned that high school students were a potentially important target for a prevention program. Of importance to a comprehensive assessment, however, was clarifying what students did know, how comfortable they were discussing health problems of a sexual nature, and how interested they were in learning more. Therefore, the nurse's next step was to approach the junior and senior high school students and administer a questionnaire designed to elicit this information. The nurse also queried the health teacher regarding the amount of pertinent information about cancer and sexual development that the students received in the classroom. The nurse considered the latter an important prerequisite to dealing with a sensitive subject such as genital health. The health teacher reported that students did receive instruction about physical development and psychosexual issues. Students expressed a strong desire for more classroom time devoted to these subjects, including cancer prevention. They did not, however, have much knowledge of beneficial health practices related to cancer prevention.

COMMUNITY DIAGNOSIS

After collecting a broad range of assessment data, the nurse was able to document that a potential health need existed in the community of high school students. The next step of analyzing and synthesizing data culminated in a community diagnosis. For this aggregate, the community diagnosis was:

There is an increased risk of undetected testicular cancer among young men related to insufficient knowledge about the disease and the methods for preventing and/or detecting it at an early stage, as demonstrated by high rates of late initiation of treatment.

Planning

Clarifying the problem and its etiology provided direction for the nurse as she initiated the planning phase of the nursing process. Planning encompassed several activities, including the discovery of recommended health care practices regarding testicular cancer. The nurse also sought to determine the most effective and appropriate approaches for male and female high school students. Identifying helpful community agencies was an essential part of the process. The local chapter of the American Cancer Society offered consultative services and invaluable information and materials. The media center of a nearby nursing school and the faculty of this school were also very supportive of the development of the program.

After formalizing objectives, the nurse presented her plan to the teaching coordinator and principal of the high school. Their approval was necessary before any further investment could be made in the project. After eliciting their enthusiastic support, the nurse proceeded with more detailed plans. Classroom instruction methods and activities were selected and developed that would maximize involvement of high school students in their learning. A film and physical models for demonstrating and practicing testicular self-examination were also ordered. Group process exercises designed to relax students and assist them in being comfortable with sensitive subject matter were prepared. The nurse scheduled two 40-minute sessions dealing with testicular cancer as part of the junior-level health class. As a final step of the planning phase, evaluation tools were designed that assessed knowledge levels after each class session as well as the extent to which health practices were integrated into students' lifestyles at the end of the junior and senior years.

The nurse was now ready to proceed with implementation of a testicular cancer prevention and screening program. She had initiated the assessment phase by identifying an individual client and family with a health need, and she extended the assessment to the high school aggregate. Collection of data at the aggregate level (for both the general population and the local high school population) assisted in formulation of a community diagnosis.

The diagnosis directed the development of a community-specific health intervention program and its subsequent implementation and evaluation.

Intervention

Each of the two sessions was conducted as part of a health education class. Students participated in group exercises at the beginning of the class period and then were asked about their current knowledge about testicular cancer. A film was shown in the classroom; then, the nurse guided a discussion about cancer screening. In the second session, the use of testicular models was introduced, and the self-examination procedure was demonstrated. Students were supervised as they practiced the examination procedure on the models. Male students were advised about the frequency of the self-examination. Females discussed the need for young men to be aware of their increased risk, and a parallel was drawn with breast self-examination.

Evaluation

After implementation of the class sessions, the nurse administered the instruments that assessed the students' knowledge. It was gratifying that knowledge levels were very high immediately after the classes. In addition, students were pleased that the subject of testicular cancer was frankly discussed and that they had the opportunity to ask questions and get clear responses about such a sensitive subject. Feedback from teachers also was very positive. The nurse reported that her image as a knowledgeable health resource in the high school was enhanced.

Intermediate-term evaluation occurred at the end of the students' junior and senior years. A 15-minute evaluation was arranged during other classes. The integration of positive health practices and, in particular, testicular self-examinations into students' lifestyles was evaluated. As expected, the prevalence of regular self-assessment was significantly lower than knowledge levels at the end of the

school year. However, 30% of male students reported regularly practicing self-examinations at the end of 1 year, and 70% reported they had done a self-examination at least once during the past year.

For long-term evaluation, the compilation of incidence data is ideal and documents the reduction of a health problem in a community. Because testicular cancer is very rare, incidence data are not reliable and may not be feasible to collect. However, for other more prevalent conditions, the collection of objective statistics is helpful in revealing decreases and increases in disease trends, which in turn may be related to the strengths and deficiencies of health programs.

It is evident that epidemiological data and methods are essential to each phase of the nursing process. The community health nurse compiles a range of assessment data that support the nursing diagnosis. Epidemiological studies help in planning a program by establishing the effectiveness of certain interventions and the specificity of each for different aggregates. This information supports the nurse's implementation of tailored intervention strategies. Finally, epidemiological data are important for the community health nurse's documentation of program effectiveness, especially in the long term.

SUMMARY

Communities are formed for a variety of reasons and can be homogeneous or heterogeneous in their composition. To help assess the nature of a given community, community health nurses study and interpret data from sources such as the census, morbidity and mortality reports, vital statistics, and information from local government agencies. Through the use of epidemiological studies, they can glean valuable information about the causes and prevalence of health and disease in a community. Based on this information, the community health nurse is able to apply the nursing process—expanding assessment, diagnosis, planning, intervention, and evaluation from the individual client level to that of a targeted aggregate in the community.

L e a r n i n g
A c t i v i t i e s

1. Walk through your community neighborhood, and compile a list of variables that are important to describe with demographic and epidemiological data. Write down your hunches or preconceived notions about the nature of the population in this community for later comparison with the statistical data you collect.

2. Walk through your neighborhood and describe the information you gain through your senses, i.e., smells, sounds, and sights observed in this area. How do each relate to the community's health?

3. Compile a range of relevant demographic and epidemiological data for your community by examining census reports, vital statistics reports, city records, and other sources available in libraries and agencies.

4. Using the data you have collected, identify three health problems of this community and formulate three community health diagnoses.

REFERENCES

Aday, L. A., and Anderson, R. M.: Equity of access to medical care: A conceptual and empirical overview. Med. Care *19*(12suppl);4–27, 1981.

Barry, M.: The influence of the U.S. tobacco industry on the health, economy, and environment of developing countries. N. Engl. J. Med. *324*;917–920, 1991.

Chen, T. T., and Winder, A. E.: The opium wars revisited as US forces tobacco exports in Asia. Am. J. Public Health *80*;659–662, 1990.

Delgado, J. L., Johnson, C. L., Roy, I., and Trevino, F. M.: Hispanic Health and Nutrition Examination Survey: Methodological considerations. Am. J. Public Health *80*(suppl);6–10, 1990.

Doll, R., and Hill, A. B.: Lung cancer and other causes of death in relation to smoking. Br. Med. J. *2*;1071, 1956.

Doll, R., and Hill, A. B.: Study of the aetiology of carcinoma of the lung. Br. Med. J. *2*;1271–1285, 1952.

Ford, A. B.: Epidemiological priorities as a basis for health policy. Bull. N. Y. Acad. Med. *54*;10–22, 1978.

Gordis, L.: Challenges to epidemiology in the coming decade. Am. J. Epidemiol. *112*;315–321, 1980.

Kannel, W. B., Castelli, W. P., Gordon, T., and McNamara, P. M.: Serum cholesterol, lipoproteins and the risk of coronary heart disease: The Framingham Study. Ann. Intern. Med. *74*;1–12, 1971.

Lilienfeld, A. M., and Lilienfeld, D.: Foundations of Epidemiology. New York, Oxford University Press, 1980.

Lipid Research Clinics Program: The Lipid Research Clinics Coronary Primary Prevention Trial results: Parts 1 and 2. J.A.M.A. *251*;351–374, 1984.

Mausner, J. S., and Kramer, S.: Mausner and Bahn Epidemiology: An Introductory Text. 2nd Ed. Philadelphia, W. B. Saunders, 1985.

Milio, N.: A framework for prevention: Changing health-damaging to health-generating life patterns. Am. J. Public Health *66*;435–439, 1976.

Muecke, M. A.: Community health diagnosis in nursing. Public Health Nurs. *1*;23–35, 1984.

Multiple Risk Factor Intervention Trial Research Group: Multiple Risk Factor Intervention Trial. JAMA *248*;1465–1477, 1982.

National Cancer Society: Career Facts and Figures—1991. Atlanta, Georgia, American Cancer Society, 1991.

National Center for Health Statistics: Births, marriages, divorces, and deaths for 1990. Monthly Vital Stat. Rep. *39*;1991.

National Center for Health Statistics: Births, marriages, divorces, and deaths for January 1991. Monthly Vital Stat. Rep. *40*;1991.

National Center for Health Statistics: Health, United States, 1980. Hyattsville, Maryland, Department of Health and Human Services, U.S. Public Health Service, 1981.

National Center for Health Statistics: Health, United States, 1990. Hyattsville, Maryland, Department of Health and Human Services, U.S. Public Health Service, 1991.

National Center for Health Statistics: NHANES—Dietary Intake Findings, United States, 1971–1974. Hyattsville, Maryland, Department of Health, Education, and Welfare, NCHS, Vital Health Statistics: Series 11, data from the National Health Examination Survey No. 202, Publication no. (HRA) 77-1647, 1977.

National Cholesterol Education Program: Report of the Expert Panel on Detection, Evaluation, and Treatment of High Blood Cholesterol in Adults. Bethesda, Maryland, NCEP, NIH Publication no. 89-2925, 1989.

Rubenstein, L., Josephson, K. R., Wieflan, G. D., English, P. A., Sayre, J. A., and Kane, R. L.: Effectiveness of a geriatric evaluation unit. N. Engl. J. Med. *311*;1664–1670, 1984.

Snow, J.: On the Mode of Communication of Cholera. 2nd Ed. London, Churchill; reproduced in: Snow on Cholera. New York, Commonwealth Fund, 1936.

CHAPTER

6

Health Planning

Upon completion of this chapter, the reader will be able to:

1. Define what is meant by "aggregate as client."

2. Apply the nursing process within a systems framework to the larger aggregate.

3. Describe the steps in the health planning model.

4. Identify the level of prevention and the system level appropriate for nursing interventions with aggregates.

5. Compare and contrast goals and outcomes of health planning legislation from the Hill-Burton Act to the National Health Planning and Resources Development Act.

6. Identify the advantages of comprehensive health planning.

7. Describe the community health nurse's role in health planning.

Barbara S. Morgan
Patricia M. Burbank
Deborah A. Godfrey

Health planning for and with the community is viewed as an essential component of community health nursing practice. What does it really mean? At first glance, the terminology appears simple enough, but the underlying concept is more complex. Like many other components of community health nursing, it tends to vary somewhat when applied to different aggregate levels. Health planning with an individual or a family may focus on direct care needs and/or self-care responsibilities; at the group level, the primary goal may be health education; and at the community level, health planning may involve prevention of diseases within a population or control of environmental hazards.

An example may help to demonstrate the interaction of community health nursing roles with health planning for a variety of aggregate levels. Nancy Jones is the high school nurse in a small suburban community. In the course of her daily encounters with students, she notes an increasing incidence of school dropouts as a result of pregnancy. The nurse at the junior high confirms a corresponding increase among the younger teenagers. Current articles in nursing and other professional journals as well as in the general media proclaim what appears to be a national epidemic of unwed pregnant teenagers.

Why is this happening in an era of increased knowledge and more readily available and more effective contraceptive techniques? Nancy's assessment of the problem at the local level includes the following findings. The teenagers who are sexually active often do not use contraception on a regular basis because they want their actions to seem "spontaneous" rather than "planned." They also do not perceive themselves as vulnerable to pregnancy because of a variety of misconceptions regarding the reproductive process, e.g., "I will not become pregnant if I do not have regular periods or my boyfriend does not ejaculate inside me." Teenagers also find many contraceptive methods difficult or embarrassing to obtain. In addition, there is no family planning clinic in the area, and local physicians admit to reluctance to counsel or prescribe for teenagers without parental permission. The nurse also discovers that an attempt several years ago to institute a sex education class in the school system was stopped by a group of parents who felt this responsibility belonged in the home. Nancy's plan of action took all of these factors into consideration. Meetings with teachers and school officials indicated a willingness to deal with this sensitive issue within the school system if parents could be convinced of its validity. Parents revealed in meetings with her that they were not entirely comfortable with the topic and did need assistance with their teenaged children. They were concerned, however, about the possibility of the mechanics of reproduction being taught without any attention to the obligations involved in relationships and in making moral decisions. Their willingness to support such a program would be facilitated by participation in the planning of the curriculum and by the chance to meet the teacher(s) before the program began. This was a compromise from a previous plan to have parents sign a consent form for each teenager's participation. The students themselves felt this was stigmatizing and said they would attend only if it was required. The family planning agency in a nearby metropolitan area was asked to consider opening a part-time clinic in this suburb. A home tutoring program was proposed to maintain pregnant teenagers' education and encourage their return to school.

Implementation of such a plan is time consuming and requires dealing with many obstacles. The nurse enlisted the aid of school officials and other professionals in the community for this ambitious project. Time is needed to evaluate the long-term effectiveness in reducing the incidence of teen pregnancies. However, this example shows how nurses can and should become involved in health planning. Nancy identified an important need: teen pregnancy is a significant health risk for the individual and often predicts lower education and socioeconomic status, resulting in further health problems. Her assessment and planned interventions included individual teenagers, their parents and families, the school system, and the resources of the community.

This chapter will provide an overview of health planning from a nursing perspective, a model for student involvement in health planning projects, and a review of significant health planning legislation.

OVERVIEW OF HEALTH PLANNING

One of the major criticisms of current community health nursing practice involves the shift away from the community and larger aggregate focus to primary involvement with family caseload management or agency responsibilities. While focusing on the individual or family as the client, nurses must remember that these clients are members of a larger population group or community and are influenced by factors within this environment. By carrying out an assessment of the aggregate or community as a whole, important factors influencing the health of individuals and families can be identified, and interventions can be planned to meet these health needs (Fig. 6–1).

Historically, the community as client is not a new concept. The focus on the community as client is exemplified by Lillian Wald's work in New York City at the Henry Street Settlement in 1893–1895. She and others worked with the extremely poor immigrants in the area, caring for the ill in their homes while also working for social reform on a larger scale.

Figure 6–1
The community as client. Assessment parameters from Chapter 5 (Table 5–1) help identify the client.

> "THE 'CASE' element in these early reports of hers [Wald] got less and less emphasis; she instinctively went behind the symptoms to appraise the whole individual, saw that one could not understand the individual without understanding the family, saw that the family was in the grip of larger social and economic forces, which it could not control. . . . "
> (Duffus, 1938).

It is clear that the early beginnings of public health nursing itself incorporated not only the nurses' visits to people in their homes but also application of the nursing process to larger aggregates and communities to improve the health of a greater number of people. Silverstein (1985) identifies Wald's goals and those of public health nursing as health promotion and disease prevention for all people. To accomplish this, health planning at the aggregate or community level is necessary.

A recent trend from the mid-1960s through the present has been a shift from public health nursing with an emphasis on the community as the focus of care to community health nursing, which encompasses all nursing activities performed outside the hospital setting (Smith, 1984). In public health nursing from the time of Wald through the 1950s, the focus was on mobilizing communities to solve their own problems, treating primarily only the poor, and working to improve environmental conditions that fostered disease. Several social changes that began in the 1950s have altered the role of the nurse, including increases in family mobility, suburbanization, and government expenditures for a variety of health programs. Presently, community health nursing focuses on individuals and family

Table 6–1
Levels of Community Health Nursing Practice

Client	Example	Characteristics	Health Assessment	Nursing Involvement
Individual	Lisa McDonald	An individual with a variety of needs	Individual strengths, problems, needs	Client-nurse interaction
Family	Moniz family (five members)	A family system with individual and group needs	Individual and family strengths, problems, needs	Interactions with individuals and with family as a group
Group	Boy Scout troop; Alzheimer's support group	Common interests, problems, and/or needs; interdependency	Group dynamics, fulfillment of goals	Group member and/or leader
Population group	AIDS patients in a given state; pregnant adolescents in a school district	Large, unorganized group with common interests, problems, and/or needs	Assessment of common problems, needs, and vital statistics	Application of nursing process to identified needs
Organization	A work place; a school	Organized group in a common location with shared governance and goals	Relationship of goals, structure, communications to strengths, problems, and needs	Consultant and/or employee; application of nursing process to identified needs
Community	Italian neighborhood; Anytown, USA	An aggregate of people in a common location with organized social systems	Analysis of systems, strengths, characteristics, problems, and needs	Community leader, participant, health care provider

units, includes all social classes, and has no defined role in environmental health (Smith, 1984).

The larger aggregate is emphasized as the client or unit of care in an effort to reestablish the role of the nurse in improving the health care of groups. By becoming involved again in health care at the larger aggregate level, the community health nurse should not lose sight of nursing care at the individual and family levels but rather use information about communities and insight gained to understand the health problems of these individuals and families and ultimately work toward improving their health status (Table 6–1).

Before nurses can be expected to participate in health care planning, however, they must be knowledgeable about the process and comfortable with the concept of community as client or focus of care. It is essential that the "how-to" be an integral part of the undergraduate curriculum. If health planning is included in basic nursing education, the student becomes aware of not only the process but also the opportunities for professional involvement at many levels.

Recognizing the need to provide learning experiences for students in the investigation of community health problems, Hegge (1973) described the use of learning packets for independent study, and Ruybal et al. (1975) provided opportunities for students to apply epidemiological concepts in community program planning and evaluation. Neither approach, however, presented a complete model that used the nursing process as a framework for health planning.

In addition to the paucity in the literature of a comprehensive model, conversations with nurse educators have revealed a need for such a model. Although some programs have incorporated health planning into their curricula, this apparently is not universal. At a national conference of community health nursing educators held at the University of North Carolina in May 1983, much attention was given to the need for greater emphasis in undergraduate curricula on the larger community and aggregate focus and health planning. The majority of those attending, representing nursing programs throughout the country, acknowledged that their community health nursing courses focused on family theory and family clinical experiences and agreed with the need for increased emphasis on health planning at the larger aggregate level. Stanhope and Lancaster (1988) call this focus "population-focused practice" and discuss the need for introduction to this important area at the baccalaureate level.

HEALTH PLANNING MODEL

In a response to this need for a population focus, a model was developed that applies the nursing process within a systems framework to the larger aggregate, with the objective of improving the health of this aggregate (Fig. 6–2). Incorporated into a

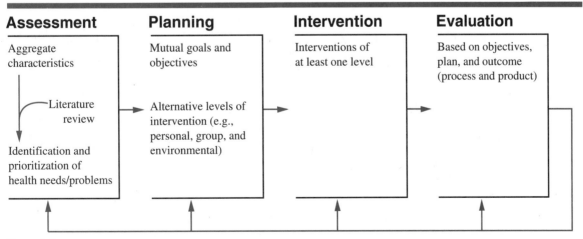

Figure 6–2
Health planning model.

health planning project, it can be used to assist students in viewing larger aggregates as the client and gaining knowledge and experience in the health planning process. The specific objectives are based on a model for group intervention by Hogue (1985). Use of the model requires careful consideration of each step in the process (Table 6–2).

Several considerations affect the choice of a specific aggregate for study. The community in which the nurse works may have extensive or limited opportunities appropriate for involvement; each community offers different possibilities for health intervention. An urban area, for example, might have a broader variety of industrial and business settings that need assistance, whereas a suburban community may offer a wider choice of family-oriented organizations such as boys' and girls' clubs, parent-teacher associations, and so on.

When selecting an aggregate for intervention, a nurse should also consider personal interests and strengths. Are you interested more in teaching preventive health or in planning for organizational change? Are your communication skills better suited to large or small groups? Do you prefer working with the elderly or with children? Thoughtful consideration of these and other vari-

---

Table 6–2
Health Planning Project Objectives

I. Assessment
  A. Specify level of aggregate selected for study (e.g., group, population group, or organization). Identify and provide a general orientation to the aggregate (e.g., characteristics of aggregate system, its suprasystem, and its subsystems). Include why this aggregate was selected and the method used for gaining entry.
  B. Describe specific characteristics of the aggregate, including:
    1. Sociodemographic characteristics—age, sex, race or ethnic group, religion, educational background and/or level, occupation, income, marital status, and so on.
    2. Health status—work or school attendance, disease categories, mortality, health care use, and measurements of population growth and population pressure (e.g., rates of birth and death, divorce, unemployment, drug and alcohol abuse). Select indicators appropriate for chosen aggregate.
    3. Suprasystem influences—existing health services available to improve health of aggregate and existing or potential impact (positive and negative) of other community-level social system variables on aggregate. Identify methods of data collection used.
  C. Provide relevant information gained from literature review, especially in terms of characteristics, problems, or needs that one would anticipate finding with this type of aggregate. Include comparison of health status of chosen aggregate with other similar aggregates, the community, the state, and/or the nation.
  D. Identify health problems and/or needs of specific aggregate based on comparative analysis and interpretation of data collection and literature review. Include input from clients regarding their perceptions of needs. Give priorities to health problems and/or needs and indicate how these priorities are determined.

II. Planning
  A. Select one health problem and/or need for intervention and identify ultimate goal of intervention. Identify specific, measurable objectives as mutually agreed on by student and aggregate.
  B. Describe alternative interventions necessary to accomplish objectives. Include consideration of interventions at each systems level where appropriate (e.g., aggregate system, suprasystem, and subsystems). Select and validate intervention(s) with highest probability of success. (Note: Intervention may include using existing resources and/or developing new resources).

III. Intervention
  A. Implement at least one level of planned intervention when possible. If intervention was not implemented, provide rationale.

IV. Evaluation
  A. Evaluate objectives, plan, and outcomes of intervention(s). Include aggregate's evaluation of project as well. Evaluation should include consideration of both process and product and of both appropriateness and effectiveness.
  B. Make recommendations for further action based on evaluation and communicate these to appropriate individuals or systems levels.

ables in interaction with the choices available in your community will facilitate beginning assessment of an appropriate aggregate.

Assessment

Gaining entry is not only a necessary first step but also an important one when establishing a professional relationship with the chosen aggregate. The nurse's communication skills are essential to establish contact and make a positive first impression. An appointment should be made for the first meeting to facilitate a welcome.

The nurse must initially clarify the nurse's position and organizational affiliation, knowledge, and skills; mutual expectations regarding what can be accomplished; and available time. Once entry has been established, negotiation continues in terms of maintaining a mutually beneficial relationship.

Meeting with the aggregate on a regular basis will allow for an in-depth assessment. Determination of sociodemographic characteristics (e.g., distribution of age, sex, race, and so on) may help to determine both health needs and appropriate methods of intervention. For example, adolescents need information regarding drug and alcohol use and abuse, nutrition, and the development of other-gender relationships. They usually do not enjoy being lectured to in a classroom-like atmosphere, but it requires much skill to get them involved and participating on a small-group level. The average educational level of an adult group will affect not only their knowledge base but also their comfort with formal versus informal learning settings. If the focus is an organization or a population, the aggregate members may be more diverse, and it may be more difficult to coordinate time and energy commitments. Information regarding sociodemographic characteristics may be gathered from a variety of sources, including the nurse's own observations, consultation with others who work with the aggregate (e.g., the nurse in a factory or school, a Headstart teacher, the resident manager in an elderly high-rise apartment building), records or charts if available, or members of the aggregate (verbally or via a short questionnaire).

In assessing the health status of the aggregate, it is important to consider both positive and negative factors. The presence of disease or unemployment may suggest specific health problems, but low rates of absenteeism at work or school may indicate that preventive interventions are more appropriate. The specific aggregate will determine which measures of health status are relevant. Immunization levels are an important index for children and usually ignored for adults; however, with the elderly, you might want to consider the need for influenza injections. Similarly, one would expect less incidence of chronic diseases with the young, whereas the elderly obviously have higher morbidity and mortality rates.

The suprasystem in which the aggregate is located may facilitate or impede health status. Differing organizations and communities provide various resources and services to their members. Some are obviously health related, such as the presence or absence of hospitals, clinics, private practitioners, emergency facilities, health centers, visiting nursing associations, and health departments. Support services and facilities are also important. For example, does the area provide group meal sites and/or meals-on-wheels to the elderly? Are there recreational facilities and programs for children, adolescents, and/or adults? The use of services is further determined by availability of transportation, reimbursement mechanisms or sliding-scale fees, community-based volunteer groups, and so on. Assessment regarding these factors requires exploration of public records (e.g., from town halls, telephone books, and community services directories) and talking with health professionals, volunteers, and key informants in the community. The nurse's role is to augment existing resources or possibly even create a new service; just duplicating what is already available to the aggregate is not the goal.

A literature review is an important means of comparing the aggregate with the "norm." During the winter, children in a Headstart setting, daycare center, or elementary school may appear to exhibit a high rate of upper respiratory infections. What does the pediatric literature indicate is a normal incidence for children of this age range in group environments? Is a factory's experience with on-the-job injuries within an average range for that type of manufacturing? If the aggregate appears especially healthy, what does available information say about the potential problems one might expect (e.g., developmental stage stresses for adolescents or work or family organization stresses for adults)? Comparison of the foregoing assessment with currently available research reports, statistics, and health information will help to determine and prioritize health problems and/or needs for the aggregate.

The last phase of the initial assessment is identification and prioritization of the health problems and/or needs of the specific aggregate. This should be directly related to both the assessment and the review of the literature and should include a comparative analysis of the two. It is also very important that this step reflect the incorporation of the aggregate members' perceptions of the need(s). Depending on the aggregate, this may come directly from aggregate members or from consultation with others who work with them (e.g., a Headstart teacher). Interventions are seldom successful if input from the clients has been omitted or ignored at this level. Last, the identified problems and/or needs must be prioritized to plan effectively.

The following factors should be considered when determining priorities:

- Aggregate's preferences
- Number of individuals in the aggregate who are or could be affected by this health problem
- Severity of the health need or problem
- Availability of potential solutions to the problem
- Practical considerations such as individual skills, time limitations, and available resources

In addition, priorities may be further refined by the application of a framework such as Maslow's (1968) hierarchy of needs (e.g., lower-level needs have priority over higher-level needs) or Leavell and Clark's (1965) levels of prevention (e.g., primary prevention may take priority for children, whereas tertiary prevention might be of higher priority for the elderly) (see Table 1–1, Chapter 1).

Assessment is ongoing throughout the nurse's relationship with the aggregate; however, once an initial assessment is complete, the nurse should proceed to the planning stage. It is particularly important at this step in the process to link it with the other stages, i.e., planning should stem directly and logically from the assessment and be realistic in terms of implementation.

Planning

Selection of the problem or need for intervention should be determined by the prioritization as described above. Then, the ultimate goal for intervention must be identified. For example, are you interested in increasing the aggregate's level of knowledge on a particular topic, or do you expect health behaviors to change as a result of your plan? It is important to be specific with the goals and objectives and make them measurable. This will facilitate not only the nursing intervention(s) but also the evaluation.

Planning the intervention is actually a multistep process. First, determine the level(s) (e.g., subsystem, aggregate system, and/or suprasystem) at which you plan to intervene. Second, plan interventions for each appropriate system level that will accomplish your objectives. Interventions may be focused on any of the three levels of prevention: primary, secondary, or tertiary. These levels apply to aggregates and communities as well as to individuals. Primary prevention consists of health promotion and activities directed at providing specific protection from illnesses or dysfunctions. Secondary prevention includes early diagnosis and prompt treatment to reduce the duration and severity of disease or dysfunction. Tertiary prevention is carried out when irreversible disability or damage has occurred. Rehabilitation and restoration of an optimal level of functioning is the goal of tertiary prevention. Plans should include goals and activities that reflect the level of prevention appropriate for the identified problem. Third, validate the practicality of the planned interventions according to available personal, aggregate, and suprasystem resources. Although teaching is often a major component of community health nursing, consider other potential forms of intervention (e.g., personal counseling, group process, game therapy, role modeling, or creation of a community service). Last, plan the scheduling of the intervention(s) with the aggregate to maximize participation (Table 6–3).

Levels of Prevention (Leavell and Clark, 1965)
Primary prevention (prepathogenesis):
   health promotion and specific protection

Secondary prevention (pathogenesis):
   early diagnosis and prompt treatment,
   disability limitation

Tertiary prevention (advanced pathogenesis):
   rehabilitation

Table 6–3
Systems Framework Premises

I. Each system is a goal-directed collection of interacting, interdependent parts (subsystems)

II. System as a whole continually interacting with and adapting to environment (suprasystem)

III. Hierarchical (suprasystem $\longrightarrow$ system $\longrightarrow$ subsystems)

IV. Each system characterized by:
- A. Structure—arrangement and organization of parts (subsystems)
  1. Organization/configuration—e.g., traditional versus nontraditional; greater variability (no right or wrong; no proper versus improper form)
  2. Boundaries—open versus closed; regulate input and output
  3. Territory (spatial and behavioral)
  4. Role allocation
- B. Functions—goals and purpose of system—activities necessary to ensure survival, continuity, and growth of system
  1. General
     - a. Physical—food, clothing, shelter, protection from danger, provision for health and illness care
     - b. Affectional—meeting emotional needs of affection and security
     - c. Social—identity, affiliation, socialization, controls
  2. Specific—each family also has own individual agenda regarding values, aspirations, cultural obligations, and so on
- C. Process/dynamics
  1. Adaptation—attempt to establish and maintain equilibrium; balance between stability and differentiation/growth; self-regulation and adaptation $\longrightarrow$ equilibrium/homeostasis
     - a. Within family—between family members
     - b. External—family interaction with suprasystem
  2. Integration—unity, ability to communicate
  3. Decision making—power distribution; consensus, accommodation, authoritarian

Intervention

The intervention stage may be the most enjoyable stage for both the nurse and the clients. Careful assessment and planning before this step should help to ensure the receptivity of the aggregate.

Generally, implementation of plans should proceed as previously set forth, but the nurse should also be prepared to be flexible in dealing with unexpected contingencies (e.g., bad weather, transportation problems, a smaller or larger group than anticipated, a competing event; see examples of unsuccessful student projects in the next section). If for some reason intervention becomes impossible, carefully consider the various potential causes of this.

Evaluation

Evaluation is an important component of understanding the success or lack of success of the project. It may include feedback from the participants (verbally or in writing) as well as the nurse's in-depth analysis. Evaluation includes reflecting on each previous stage to determine strengths and weaknesses; this is evaluation of the process. Were plans appropriate but based on an incomplete assessment? Was adequate input from the clients allowed for? Were the interventions realistic or unrealistic in terms of available resources? Evaluation also includes consideration of the product, or outcomes. Were the stated goals and objectives accomplished? Were the participants satisfied with the interventions? Are you comfortable with what was accomplished? It is important to be able to honestly and comprehensively evaluate both positive and negative aspects of each experience.

After the project is completed, the final step is often short-changed. Without communicating recommendations for follow-up to the aggregate and/or other appropriate persons, the impact of the intervention may be limited. Although not every experience lends itself to continuing activity, most at least indicate the need for additional interventions. These may be generated from within the aggregate or from community agencies and resources.

A comprehensive, fulfilling health planning project involves both careful consideration of each step in the process and a close working relationship with the aggregate.

HEALTH PLANNING PROJECTS

The following are examples of student projects using this health planning model with different types of aggregates: group, organization, popula-

Table 6–4
Interventions by Type of Aggregate and System Level

Project	Type of Aggregate	System Level for Intervention
Obese children	Group	Subsystem and aggregate system
Rehabilitation group	Group	Subsystem and aggregate system
Textile industry	Organization	Aggregate system and suprasystem
Housing for elderly	Population group	Aggregate system
Bilingual students	Group, organization, population group	Aggregate system and suprasystem
Crime watch	Community	Aggregate system and suprasystem

tion group, and community. The interventions with these aggregates occur at the three systems levels: subsystem, aggregate system, and suprasystem (Table 6–4).

Successful Projects

OBESE CHILDREN

While working in a Headstart setting, a student and the nurse identified two obese boys from the same family. After contacting their mother, the student made a home visit and learned that the parents were separated and the children spent time in each parent's home as well as with the grandparents. Obesity appeared to be a family problem; both parents were obese. The student worked with the boys individually and together, carried out teaching with the mother and grandparents, and met once with the boys' father. Both the boys' mother and grandparents were included in the planning. A variety of interventions were carried out, including a food diary with the adults, teaching regarding low-calorie snacks and menu planning, a food collage, and a "Food Land" game made up by the student

for the boys. Positive changes were noted in dietary patterns for the mother and boys by the end of the semester. The Headstart nurse was also kept informed of the family's progress so that continued reinforcement could take place after the student left the situation.

TEXTILE INDUSTRY

A student selected for study a textile plant with approximately 470 employees and no occupational health nurse. For data collection, she used Serafini's (1976) assessment guide for nursing in industry. Three major problems or needs were identified through collaboration with management and union representatives. First, the most common, costly, and chronic employee accident in the plant was lower back injury. Second, there was a generalized concern among employees about the possibility of undetected hypertension. Third, the first-aid facilities were disorganized and had no accurate inventory system. Interventions were then planned and implemented for all three identified areas.

On the suprasystem level, plans were formulated by the student with the company's physicians and communicated to management for enactment of an employee training program on proper lifting techniques. Concise and specific job descriptions and requirements were proposed to facilitate medical assessment of the health status of potential employees. In addition, the first-aid supplies were organized and clearly labeled, and an inventory system was developed. On the aggregate system level, a hypertension screening program was planned and conducted. Approximately 85% of the employees were screened, and 10 persons were identified with elevated blood pressure readings, conditions that were later diagnosed as hypertension.

As a result of the project, management representatives recognized that workers' health could be improved or maintained at optimal levels through a variety of nursing interventions. Consequently, the student was hired as an occupational health nurse upon graduation to facilitate this goal.

HOUSING FOR THE ELDERLY

Another project involved the residents of a housing complex for the elderly. The student met with 20 interested women and assessed their needs through a short questionnaire. Findings revealed that exercise was the highest-priority need. Investigation of existing resources revealed that the community's YWCA offered a senior exercise class that met three times a week at a cost of $1 per session. This information was shared with the population group, but use of the program was not considered feasible by members. The alternative plan on which they agreed was to have weekly sessions led by the student at the housing complex (aggregate system level intervention) using exercises described by Frenkel and Richard (1977).

In evaluating outcomes, subjective comments from the participants indicated they felt better about themselves as a result of exercising and maintaining their range of motion. It also was a positive experience for the student; not only did she learn more about the elderly in general, she also gained skill in applying the nursing process to a larger aggregate within a community.

BILINGUAL STUDENTS

Occasionally, a project will not only have an impact on the specific aggregate, but also have broader implications. One bilingual student, who was interested in a community with a large Portuguese subculture, chose as her aggregate students who were enrolled in the town's bilingual program within the school system. Included in her assessment were the specific group of students, members of the organizational level of the school system, and the population group of Portuguese-speaking residents in the town.

One problem identified through observation of the children and interviews with teachers and community residents was the lack of primary disease prevention for this subculture. Further assessment revealed the problem to be related to a lack of knowledge rather than to a lack of concern.

Interventions were limited to one grade level. Within that aggregate system, the children were taught many basics of healthy lifestyles, including nutrition, hygiene, and dental care. Information was presented in class in both Portuguese and English. The content was summarized in each language as well as in pictures and then was sent home to all parents.

When the local teachers communicated to their state-level coordinators what the student had been doing, the materials the student developed were incorporated into the bilingual programs throughout the state (suprasystem level).

CRIME WATCH

One student was concerned with the rising incidence of crime in a community and organized a crime watch program. This involved periodic meetings with local residents (aggregate system) as well as with the police. Interventions included posting signs in the neighborhood and more frequent police patrols (suprasystem level). The program increased the residents' awareness of potential problems as well as the need to be more concerned with neighborhood safety.

REHABILITATION GROUP

After working at a senior citizens' center for a few weeks, a student began a careful assessment of the clients served by the center. In addition to interviewing clients already active in the center, he made home visits to speak with homebound clients served by the center's social workers and Meals-on-Wheels program. A common need for socialization and rehabilitation was assessed among several of the homebound group. A significant factor in considering plans to meet this need was the center's recent purchase of a van equipped to transport handicapped people in wheelchairs. After the student further assessed the clients' health and functional status and determined mutual goals, four of these homebound clients expressed a desire to attend a rehabilitation program at the center, if one were available. A weekly program was initiated based on these clients' needs and included van transportation, a coffee hour, an exercise class, a noontime meal, and a craft class. After some initial reluctance to participate and the withdrawal of one man from the group, the group functioned very well. Progress was made toward meeting the goals of increased socialization and rehabilitation.

Unsuccessful Projects

When a project is not completed successfully, its failure can usually be related to problems with one or more stages of the nursing process. This is often not discovered until the evaluation phase. The fol-

Table 6–5	
Unsuccessful Projects	
Project	**Problematic Step of Nursing Process**
Headstart program	Assessment (gaining entry)
Prenatal clinic	Assessment of aggregate system
Group home for mentally retarded adults	Assessment (mutual identification of health problems and needs)
Safe Rides program	Planning (mutual identification of goals and objectives)
	Evaluation (recommendations for follow-up)
Manufacturing plant	Implementation

lowing examples of unsuccessful projects illustrate failures at different steps of the nursing process (Table 6–5).

HEADSTART PROGRAM

One problem that has occurred periodically is the lack of time to follow through with implementation. There may be many reasons for this, one of which is the initial problem of gaining entry. For example, a student who was aware that one community had a large number of low-income families decided to investigate the feasibility of beginning a Headstart program for the children in the area (a population group). After many frustrating weeks of telephone calls to leaders in the community (which often were not returned), she was finally able to locate the person in charge. By this time, the semester was almost completed. Needless to say, she was disappointed at the end result.

This example illustrates the importance of identifying a key informant early, i.e., someone who is familiar with the community, particularly if you are new to the area. Unfortunately, such persons are not always obvious, since they may not be considered community leaders. For example, although the key informant in one community may be the director of a neighborhood health center, in another community it may be the person in charge of a local thrift shop serving an underprivileged area.

PRENATAL CLINIC

After working for a few weeks in a prenatal clinic serving a primarily lower-income population, the student identified several needs she had observed among the clients. Realizing that she needed to gather information regarding what the clients perceived as their needs, she developed a questionnaire that listed several possible topics for discussion and left space for the clients to write in what they would like to learn more about. Also included were spaces for clients to fill in times when they would be able to attend a health education workshop and whether they had transportation available. After the student collected and tallied the questionnaires from 25 clients, she determined that infant feeding, whether breast or bottle, was the topic most frequently mentioned by the clients and that Tuesday evening was the best time. Transportation was not listed as a problem. With this information, the student set a date for her teaching project, made posters for the clinic, mailed notices describing the program to the clients, and planned her teaching. The evening of the program arrived and the student was extremely disappointed to find that no clients attended.

What happened? There are many possible reasons for such occurrences. One explanation offered by the student was that returning to the clinic in the evening was too much of an inconvenience, even though this was the time when most said they could attend. Possibly, health education may not have been a priority for this group of clients; the questionnaire assumed that it was important and merely asked about interests. Also, the neighborhood surrounding the clinic may not have been perceived as safe during the evening hours.

This example illustrates the importance of careful assessment and the possible results if assessment is incomplete. One recommendation that the student made was to communicate health education information to clients during clinic hours and use more individual counseling, posters, and other media within the clinic setting.

GROUP HOME FOR MENTALLY RETARDED ADULTS

Another example of an unsuccessful project involved a student who identified as her aggregate six women living in a group home for mentally retarded citizens in the community. From her observations, she noted that they were all overweight, and she decided that she would institute a weekly weight-reduction program for them. She then proceeded to meet with the women weekly, at which time she weighed them, discussed diets, and talked about the four food groups. At the end of an 8-week period, her evaluation revealed that not only had the women not lost weight but that a few of them had gained weight! The student had failed to consider the womens' perceptions of their needs and priorities. The women did not consider their weight a problem. Furthermore, their boyfriends provided positive reinforcement regarding their appearance.

SAFE RIDES PROGRAM

One student assessed a university student community through a questionnaire and identified the problem of drinking and driving.

Seventy-seven percent of those she surveyed stated that they had experienced driving while under the influence of alcohol, and 16.5% had been involved in an alcohol-related car accident. After identifying the problem, the student worked with the campus alcohol and drug resource center to plan and implement a Safe Rides program. This program, which was modeled after one in place in another state, provided student volunteers to answer a hot-line and drivers to pick up students who had driven themselves or ridden with another who was now unsafe to drive home. Student interest in the program was also determined. Many unforeseen complications were resolved, such as the need for liability coverage for all individuals participating in the program and funds to cover expenses such as gas reimbursement money. The student formulated a 12-hour, 3-week training program to prepare student volunteers for their involvement in Safe Rides. By the end of the semester, the Safe Rides program was ready to begin. However, by this time, the student—the prime motivating force—had graduated. Although others were committed and involved, apparently no provision had been made for another person to coordinate and follow through with the program after the student had left. Because the Safe Rides program really required on-going efforts at coordination, the program was never fully implemented in the student's absence.

MANUFACTURING PLANT

Even careful planning does not always eliminate all potential obstacles.

One student chose to work in an occupational setting involving heavy industry. Her entree into the organization was approved by both the occupational health nurse and the nurse's supervisor in personnel.

After reviewing the literature, working for several weeks with the nurse, and assessing the organization and the employees, the student identified the potential for back injury as a primary problem. Her plan was to decrease the risk factors involved in back injuries by distributing information about proper body mechanics to the workers in a teaching session. This plan was resisted, however, by the personnel manager. Despite his recognition of the need for such instruction, he initially resisted implementation because of an unwillingness to allow the employees to attend the session on company time. A compromise was reached by allowing attendance during coffee breaks, which would be extended by 5 minutes. Before the program could be implemented, however, it was cancelled by the personnel manager because negotiations for a new union contract were under way and there was a high probability of a strike. Consequently, management was unwilling to allow any changes in the usual routine.

The student had proceeded appropriately and even received clearance from the proper officials, but the union problems could not have been anticipated or circumvented. The student could only share her information and concern with the nurse and the personnel manager and encourage them to implement her plan when contract negotiations were completed.

Each of these projects addressed or was designed to address a particular level of prevention. Most of these examples focused on primary prevention and health promotion because they were conducted by students and were time limited (Table 6–6). However, for the community health nurse working on a regular basis with an aggregate (e.g., in the occupational health setting), interventions would be targeted for all three levels of prevention and at a variety of system levels. It is useful to view nursing interventions with aggregates within a matrix structure to ensure that all opportunities for intervention are being addressed. The matrix gives ex-

Table 6–6
Level of Prevention for Each Project

Primary Prevention	Secondary Prevention	Tertiary Prevention
Textile industry (first aid and back injury prevention)	Obese children	Rehabilitation group
Housing for elderly	Textile industry (blood pressure screening and counseling)	
Bilingual students	Group home for mentally retarded adults	
Crime watch		
Headstart program		
Prenatal clinic		
Safe Rides program		
Manufacturing plant		

amples of how the occupational health nurse may intervene at all systems levels and all levels of prevention (Table 6–7). In practice, most interventions occur at the individual level and include all levels of prevention. Interventions at the aggregate level usually are less frequent. For many occupational health nurses, time does not allow for intervention at the suprasystem level. However, indus-

tries are integral parts of the community system. Factors that affect the health of communities also affect the health of employees, and vice versa. Some industries take their reciprocal relationship with the surrounding community quite seriously. For nurses in these industries, interventions at the suprasystem level may become a reality, thus improving the health of both the community and the

Table 6–7
Occupational Health: Levels of Prevention for System Levels

System Level	Primary Prevention	Secondary Prevention	Tertiary Prevention
Subsystem (individual)	Yearly physical examination for each employee	Regular blood pressure monitoring and diet counseling for each employee with elevated blood pressure	Referral for job retraining for employee with a back injury
Aggregate/group system	Incentive program to encourage departments to use safety devices	Weight reduction group for overweight employees	Support group for employees who are recovering from problems with alcohol or drug use
Suprasystem (community)	Health fair open to the community as well as employees	Counseling and referral of members of community with elevated blood pressure or cholesterol based on health fair findings	Media advertising to encourage people with substance abuse problems to seek help, including community resources where assistance is available

workers. Although occupational health nursing has been used as an example here, a similar matrix can be constructed for interventions carried out by any nurse working with aggregate systems.

A review of the preceding projects illustrates the variety of opportunities available for health planning with aggregates. In addition, they exemplify the application of the nursing process within various types of aggregates at different systems levels and at each level of prevention. A review of these examples demonstrates the vital importance of each step of the nursing process. Assessments of aggregates must be thorough, as exemplified by the textile industry project. Assessment included answers to key questions about the aggregate's health and demographic profile as well as a comparison of this information with the picture of similar aggregates presented in the literature. Careful planning is a necessity, and mutual goals acceptable to both the nurse and the aggregate must be agreed on. The housing for the elderly and rehabilitation group projects illustrate such mutual planning. Interventions also need to include aggregate participation and be designed to meet the mutual goals, as exemplified by the Crime Watch project. Last, evaluation must include both process and product evaluation and be conducted with aggregate input as demonstrated by the bilingual student's project.

Health planning at the national level is another example of planning for aggregates. The national level can be considered a broader extension of the suprasystem level and as such impacts on each of the other levels described. National health planning has been minimally influenced by nurses but has a tremendous effect on nursing and nursing practice. Because of the necessity for understanding planning on a national level, a discussion of present health planning legislation will follow.

HEALTH PLANNING LEGISLATION
Early History

Although health planning activities existed in the United States before the 1940s, these were usually directed toward specific health problems, e.g., services for maternal and child health, provision of health care activities, and so on. Furthermore, these activities were usually initiated by private, nongovernment agencies such as the American Public Health Association or the American Cancer Society, with limited involvement by the federal government. For example, in the 1930s, Blue Cross and the United Fund in New York City were responsible for starting local health planning, but it was mostly provider oriented. The Health and Planning Council of New York was the agency formed to implement local health planning.

The federal government's involvement in health planning changed, however, at the end of World War II, when the government turned its attention to issues raised by the private sector (Table 6–8). At this point, there was a general shortage of hospital beds and a lack of coordination among hospitals.

Table 6–8
Federal Health Planning Legislation

Year	Legislation	Purpose
1946	Hill-Burton Act (PL 79-725)	Provided federal aid to states for hospital facilities
1965	Heart Disease, Cancer, and Stroke amendments (PL 89-239)	Established regional medical programs to make technology available to community health care providers
1966, 1967	Public Health Service Act amendments (PL 89-749, PL 90-174)	Together established "Partnership for Health Program" to promote highest level of health for all
1974	National Health Planning and Resources Development Act (PL 93-641)	Established Health System Agencies to increase accessibility, acceptability, continuity, and quality of health services; control rising costs of care; prevent unnecessary duplication of services

Rural areas were especially needy in terms of hospital beds as well as medical personnel (Braverman, 1978).

Hill-Burton Act

To address the need for better access to hospitals, Congress passed the Hospital Survey and Construction Act (Hill-Burton Act, PL 79-725) in 1946, which provided federal aid to states for hospital facilities. This is generally considered to be the first major effort by the federal government to promote health planning.

To be eligible for funds under the Hill-Burton Act for hospital construction and modernization, a state had to submit a plan documenting resources available and estimates of need. As a result, vast sums of money were spent; the outcome was an increase in the number of beds, with the majority in general hospitals.

Although the act and its amendments are often criticized for focusing too narrowly on construction, the act improved the quality of care in rural areas and introduced systematic statewide planning (Stebbins and Williams, 1972).

Regional Medical Programs

The Hill-Burton Act provided for planning related to construction, but the Heart Disease, Cancer, and Stroke Amendment of 1965 (PL 89-239) was more comprehensive and established regional medical programs. These programs were intended to make available to community health care providers the latest technology from existing medical centers for the treatment of the leading causes of death.

To achieve this, 56 health regions across the country were established and charged with evaluating the health needs within each region. Priorities, objectives, and regional programmatic approaches were then developed. As a result, not only was local participation in planning mandated, but also funds were provided for both planning and operating (Hyman, 1982).

Although regional medical programs have been credited with the regionalization of certain services and the introduction of innovative approaches to the organization and delivery of care, some observers have felt that the reforms were not comprehensive enough. Also, because the RMPs were not incorporated into existing federal and state pro-grams, there were both gaps and duplication in delivery of services, personnel training, and research (Stebbins and Williams, 1972).

Comprehensive Health Planning

To broaden the categorical approach to health planning that had characterized previous legislation, Congress signed into law the Public Health Service Act Amendments of 1966 (PL 89-749) relating to comprehensive health planning. Combined with PL 90-174, which was passed in 1967, these amendments created the "Partnership for Health Program." The objectives of the program were directed toward promoting and ensuring the highest level of health attainable for every person while at the same time not interfering with the existing patterns of private practice.

A two-level planning system was formulated to meet these objectives. The "A" agencies, with input from an advisory council in which health care consumers were in the majority, were to play a statewide coordinating role. Meanwhile, plans to meet designated local community needs were formulated by the "B" agencies.

Although the comprehensive health plans were the first of the programs previously described to mandate consumer involvement, many felt that they failed in their basic intent. Various reasons have been cited for the perceived failure, including inadequate funding, conflict avoidance in policy formulation and goal establishment, lack of political influence, and, most important, provider opposition (e.g., American Medical Association, American Hospital Association, and major medical centers). The mission appeared to be a discussion of what was wrong with health care delivery rather than providing mechanisms for action (De-Bella, et al., 1986; Roseman, 1972).

Certificate of Need

As a response to increases in capital investments and budgetary pressures, state governments developed the idea of obtaining prior government approval for certain projects through the use of a certificate of need. The first state certificate-of-need law was passed in New York State in 1964, requiring government approval of major capital investments by hospitals and nursing homes. Many, although not all, states followed with certificate-of-need laws (DeBella et al., 1986; Koff, 1988).

National Health Planning and Resources Development Act

Given the perceived failure of the comprehensive health planning program, the federal government focused on a new approach to health planning. Of great concern was the cost of health care expenditures, which had escalated since the end of World War II; the uneven distribution of services; the general lack of knowledge of personal health practices, and the emphasis on more costly modalities of care. The National Health Planning and Resources Development Act of 1974 (PL 93-641) combined the strengths of the Hill-Burton Act, regional medical programs, and the comprehensive health planning program to forge a new system of single-state and areawide health planning agencies.

The goals and purposes of the new law were increased accessibility, acceptability, continuity, and quality of health services; restraint of the rising costs of health care services; and prevention of unnecessary duplication of health resources. Of particular interest were the needs of the disadvantaged and the concern for providing quality health care. Not only would the provider and consumer be involved in the planning and improvement of health services, but also the system of private practice would be placed under scrutiny.

At the center of the program was a network of local health planning agencies that composed the health system agency, which developed a health systems plan for its geographical service area. These plans were then submitted to a state health planning and development agency, which integrated the plans into a preliminary state plan. This preliminary plan was then submitted to a statewide health coordinating council for approval. The law mandated that the council comprise at least 16 members appointed by the governor, with 60% of its members representatives of health system agencies and at least 50% consumers. One major function of this council was to prepare the state health plan that reflected the goals and purposes of the act. Once formulated, the tentative plan was presented at public hearings throughout the state for discussion and possible revisions.

Despite careful deliberations by health planners with input from consumers, the health system agency was not always blandly accepted at the grass roots level. For example, Rhode Island's state health plan was commended by federal officials as a considerable achievement and given high praise.

However, when the plan was first presented at seven public hearings throughout the state in 1980, approximately 10,000 persons attended, many essentially to protest two of the recommendations.

One recommendation was to move in the direction of a smaller number of larger hospitals, and the second was to reduce the number of hospital beds. In Newport, persons argued vehemently that if the maternity unit of the local hospital was closed and women were forced to deliver in other communities, there would be no more "native New-porters." The same recommendations precipitated a candlelight march in Westerly, a suburban community, with the slogan, "Save Our Hospital."

What happened? Why did a plan aimed at "promoting quality of care while constraining costs" meet with such resistance? In retrospect, planners agreed that although much time was spent introspectively developing the plan, the public was not prepared for the recommendations, which were very ambitious. Furthermore, there was a perception in the state that the council had more power than it actually had; finally, the hospital community went out of their way to discredit the plan. The second state health plan was presented in 1983 with the two recommendations substantially modified, and it was met with little or no opposition from the public. By this time, the functions of the council were better known, and the recommendations were more conservative.

Current Status of Health Planning

Under the Reagan administration, competition within the health care system was encouraged, and the emphasis was placed on cost shifting and cost reduction. This approach, combined with a cutback in funding, dealt a death blow to federal health planning.

As a result of the cutbacks, the role of health system agencies was redefined, and the federal government recommended their elimination. Because of a reduction in federal funding, some health system agencies did close. Those that remained experienced a decrease in staff, which resulted in a decrease in overall board functioning and a reordering of priorities. In an effort to compensate for the decrease in federal funding, some health system agencies sought nonfederal funding or tried to build coalitions to provide the power base necessary for change.

In summary, a lack of funding, the nature of the health system agencies' mandate, general instability within the agencies, and a tendency to maintain the status quo rendered accomplishments restricted and tentative (DeBella et al., 1986; Koff, 1988). As the decade of the 1980s ended, certificate-of-need reviews were still required in 33 states and the District of Columbia. Trends in these programs have been to liberalize the requirements for approval, conduct expedited reviews, and exempt certain projects from review (American Public Health Association, 1989).

For health planning to be effective given the current political climate, Tierney and Waters (1983) have indicated that a comprehensive approach at the state level with input from health care providers, insurers, business, labor, government, and consumers is necessary. Health planning as a process is too important to the future economic, social, and health needs of our nation to let the progress made since the Hill-Burton Act became law be negated by changes at the federal level.

NURSING IMPLICATIONS

One method of strengthening local and national health planning is through increased nursing involvement. Nurses' use of this health planning model facilitates a systematic approach to improving health care at the aggregate level. Through application of this model, aggregates from small groups through national population groups can be assessed; their health needs can be identified; and planning, intervention, and evaluations can be carried out. If nurses were to reemphasize the larger aggregate as client, the health of individuals and families as well as of groups would improve.

SUMMARY

Community health nurses have a responsibility to incorporate health planning into their practice. The unique talents and skills of nurses, augmented by the comprehensive application of the nursing process, can facilitate improvement of the health of populations at various aggregate levels. Health planning policy and process constitute a part of the knowledge base of the baccalaureate-prepared nurse. Systems theory provides one framework for application of the nursing process in the community. Interventions are possible at subsystem (individual), system (aggregate or group), and suprasystem (population or community) levels using all three levels of prevention.

Learning Activities

1. Assess a neighborhood or local community using exploratory techniques: drive through the area and identify types of houses, schools, churches, health related-agencies, and businesses; look for potential environmental/safety hazards; interview a clerk at the town hall, a senior citizen at a meal site or daycare center, a newspaper reporter, a visiting nurse, a police officer, a social worker, or a school nurse regarding the community; call the local, county, or state health department for morbidity and mortality statistics; and/or attend a town council or school committee meeting. Compare and contrast your findings with those of your classmates.

2. Construct a matrix similar to that of Table 6–7 using interventions from the school nurse setting.

3. As a class project, identify 10–15 questions that will elicit important health information from young adults. Have each student in your class write answers to these questions. Tally the students' responses and as a group, draw conclusions from this assessment. Identify problems or potential problem areas and construct a plan to solve or prevent these problems.

4. Attend a health system agency meeting or a meeting about health planning at the local level. Observe the number of health care providers and consumers present. Compare the issues being discussed with the goals of improving quality of care and reducing health care costs.

5. Interview a health planner at the state or local level to determine the status of comprehensive health planning and certificate-of-need review in your community and/or state.

REFERENCES

American Public Health Association: Most states continue health planning program. Nation's Health 19;24, 1989.
Braverman, J.: Crisis in Health Care. Washington, D.C., Acropolis Books, Ltd., 1978.
DeBella, S., Martin, L., and Siddall, S.: Nurses' Role in Health Care Planning. Norwalk, Connecticut, Appleton-Century-Crofts, 1986.
Duffus, R. L.: Lillian Wald: Neighbor and Crusader. New York, Macmillan, 1938.
Frenkel, L. J., and Richard, B. B.: Exercises to help the elderly live longer and stay healthier, and be happier. Nursing 77;58–63, 1977.
Hegge, M. L.: Independent study in community health nursing. Nurs. Outlook 21;652–654, 1973.
Hogue, C.: An epidemiologic approach to distributive nursing practice. In Hall, J. E., and Weaver, B. R., eds.: Distributive Nursing Practice: A Systems Approach to Community Health. 2nd Ed. Philadelphia, J. B. Lippincott, 1985, pp. 288–303.
Hyman, H.: Health Planning: A Systematic Approach. Rockville, Maryland, Aspen Systems Corp., 1982.

Koff, S.: Health Systems Agencies: A Comprehensive Examination of Planning and Process. New York, Human Sciences Press, Inc., 1988.
Leavell, H. R., and Clark, E. G.: Preventive Medicine for the Doctor in His Community. New York, McGraw-Hill, 1965.
Maslow, A. H.: Toward a Psychology of Being. New York, Van Nostrand Reinhold, 1968.
Roseman, C.: Problems and prospects for comprehensive health planning. Am. J. Public Health 62;16–19, 1972.
Ruybal, S. E., Bauwens, E., and Fasla, M. J.: Community assessment: An epidemiological approach. Nurs. Outlook 23;365–368, 1975.
Serafini, P.: Nursing assessment in industry. Am. J. Public Health 66;755–760, 1976.
Silverstein, N. G.: Lillian Wald at Henry Street, 1893–1895. Adv. Nurs. Sci. 7;1–12, 1985.
Smith, G. R.: Historical foundations and trends. In Schoolcraft, V., ed.: Nursing in the Community. New York, John Wiley & Sons, 1984, pp. 23–400.
Spradley, B. W.: Community Health Nursing: Concepts and Practice. 3rd Ed. Glenview, Illinois, Scott, Foresman, 1990.

Stanhope, M., and Lancaster, J.: Community Health Nursing: Process and Practice for Promoting Health. 2nd Ed. St. Louis, C. V. Mosby, 1988.

Stebbins, E. L., and Williams, K. N.: History and background of health planning in the United States. *In* Reinke, W. A., ed.: Health Planning: Qualitative Aspects and Quantitative Techniques. Baltimore, Maryland, Waverly Press, 1972, pp. 1–19.

Tierney, J. T., and Waters, W. J.: The evolution of health planning. N. Engl. J. Med. *308*;95–97, 1983.

Community Organization

Upon completion of this chapter, the reader will be able to:

1. Define community organization.

2. Identify major concepts, models, and strategies of community organization.

3. Discuss conceptual frameworks for community organization practice by community health nurses.

4. Define social action, social planning, and community development.

5. Explain appropriate use of community organization concepts and strategies in nursing care of aggregates.

6. Apply knowledge of community organization to primary, secondary, and tertiary prevention of priority community health problems.

Peggy Hickman

A universal goal of nursing is ensurance of access to basic health care for all people. The American Nurses' Association (ANA) (1985) declares that health care is a right and notes that community health nurses encounter many situations in which human rights and freedoms may be in jeopardy. The ANA states that a major responsibility of community health nurses is "to advocate for individuals and families, to identify and rectify gaps in health care services, and to influence health and social policies that are inconsistent with this basic right" (ANA, 1986).

Equal access to basic health care services is a human right affirmed by national and international nursing and health organizations. Basic health care services are defined by the World Health Organization (WHO) as the provision of the full range of resources essential to human

---

Basic Health Care Services as Defined by the World Health Organization (WHO, 1978)

- EDUCATION ABOUT prevailing health problems, including methods of prevention and control
- Promotion of adequate food supply and proper nutrition
- Provision of safe water and basic sanitation
- Maternal and child health care, including family planning
- Immunization against the major infectious diseases
- Prevention and control of locally endemic diseases
- Appropriate treatment of common diseases and injuries
- Provision of essential drugs

---

health. Of concern to nurses is the global reality that basic health care services are not equally accessible to all (ANA, 1985; Institute of Medicine, 1988; WHO, 1978). In some cases, access is limited by unequal distribution among aggregates of the resources needed to attain and retain health. Although an increase in resources does not ensure good health, the lack of resources is closely linked to poor health. Research and epidemiological surveillance has documented that as socioeconomic status decreases, overall morbidity and mortality increase (Blum, 1983; Kovner, 1990; Lee and Estes, 1990). In other cases, access to basic health

care services is limited by barriers such as distance, lack of transportation, time constraints, lack of knowledge or skills, and lack of services appropriate to the culture, religion, or language of the aggregate. Sometimes, basic health care services are unavailable or fragmented due to government policies, priorities, and procedures or because the various sectors of the community are unable to work together in a coordinated or collaborative manner. The WHO recognizes that the attainment of individual and aggregate health not only is a function of the health sector, but also requires action by all sectors of the community, including agriculture, animal husbandry, communication, education, food production, government, health, housing, industry, and public works. The WHO states that health is an integral part of the overall social and economic development of the community and that community members have the "right and duty to participate individually and collectively in the planning and implementation of their health care" (1978).

Much of the success of community health nursing practice is directly related to the nurse's skill in enabling individuals, aggregates, and communities to promote, protect, and restore their health through organized community efforts. The ANA explicitly states that community health nursing entails "the understanding and application of (a) concepts of public health and community, (b) skills of community organization and development, and (c) nursing care of selected individuals, families, and groups for health promotion, health maintenance, health education, and coordination of care" (1986). Within the remainder of this chapter, major concepts, models, and strategies of community organization will be presented and discussed in relation to community health nursing practice that is focused on promotion, protection, and restoration of the health of aggregates.

DEFINITION OF COMMUNITY ORGANIZATION PRACTICE

Community organization has been defined in a variety of ways, including as a process, an outcome, and a social structure (Christenson and Robinson, 1989; Cox, 1987). Definitions of community organization as a process include interactional processes related to developing competent community action systems and technical tasks such as community assessment, diagnosis, planning, implementation, and evaluation.

Community organization is practiced by professionals from a variety of disciplines, including nursing, and by volunteers in civic associations and social action groups. All share a common focus—the community—and interventions are oriented toward changing community institutions and solving community problems. Goals of community organization practice may include outcome goals, which specify the desired change or action being pursued, and process goals, which define adjunct outcomes desired as a result of the methods used to bring about a change (Table 7–1). Central to community organization practice is the concept of social justice, with resources being allocated in an equitable manner and priority given to individuals, families, and aggregates at the greatest risk or with the greatest need.

For the purposes of this discussion, community organization will be defined as the process whereby community change agents empower individuals and aggregates to solve community problems and achieve community goals. Within the context of community health nursing, this definition could be translated to specify that community organization is the process whereby the nurse empowers individuals, aggregates, and communities to solve priority community health problems and to achieve community goals such as universal access to basic health care services.

Table 7–1
Examples of Community Organization Goals for Child Health Promotion

Client Focus	Process Goal	Outcome Goal
Individual or family	Development of problem-solving skills	Healthy children
Aggregate	Development of collaborative planning skills by nurses and aggregate members	Establishment of a well-child clinic in a low-income neighborhood
Community	Community competence	Community health

COMMUNITY ORGANIZATION IN NURSING PRACTICE

The incorporation of community organization as a part of community health nursing practice is not new. Nursing history is rich with examples of civic-minded, community-oriented persons who have alleviated community health problems and social injustices by mobilizing effective community action systems. Florence Nightingale recognized the need for aggregate level intervention to bring about changes in health. As Nightingale focused on the promotion and restoration of health through improvement of the environment, she analyzed the power structure and intervened at the appropriate level to bring about change. In *Notes On Nursing* (1946, p. 247), Nightingale observed that the creation of a healthy environment is not the sole responsibility of the nurse and is better accomplished by involving other persons in the health-promoting activities.

The theme of community organization as a component of nursing practice was carried into 20th century community health nursing practice by organizations such as the National Organization for Public Health Nursing (NOPHN). A 1935 NOPHN nursing textbook identified general objectives for community health nursing practice, including education of individuals, aggregates, and communities "to protect their own health," to "adjust" social conditions affecting health, to "correlate" health and social programs for the welfare of the family and community, and to develop "adequate public health facilities."

Community organization is both implicit and explicit in current descriptions and standards of community health nursing practice. The ANA (1986) and the WHO (1974, 1978, 1985a, 1985b) identify community organization as a basic community health nursing skill, with the preferred approach to community organization being community development. The term "partnership" is used repeatedly by the ANA (1986) in the process criteria to describe the relationship between the community health nurse and the individual, aggregate, or community.

Primary Health Care

The best framework for incorporating community organization into community health nursing practice is primary health care (WHO, 1978). Primary health care refers to community-based provision of essential health care that is accessible to all members of the community (WHO, 1978). Essential health care includes the basic health care services described earlier in the chapter. Primary health care is based on scientifically sound methods and technologies that are practical, affordable, and socially and culturally acceptable. Community health services are based on prevailing community needs and social, political, economic, cultural, and religious characteristics. Within the context of primary health care, basic community health services should be made universally accessible to individuals and aggregates in the community through their full participation and "at a cost that the community and country can afford to maintain at every stage of development in the spirit of community self-reliance and self-determination" (WHO, 1978). Furthermore, primary health care "forms an integral part both of the country's health care system, of which it is the central function and main focus, and of the overall social and economic development of the community" (WHO, 1978).

The role of nursing in community-based primary health care has been well defined by international health organizations. The WHO (1974) describes nursing as a system of care consisting of community health nurses, midwives and other clinical specialists, paraprofessionals, teachers, researchers, administrators, and community members. The WHO (1974, 1985) and the Pan American Health Organization (1977) identify the role of the community health nurse, in partnership with the community, as that of assessing the health status of individuals, families, and communities; prioritizing health needs, identifying resources and groups at risk; planning ways to meet priority health needs; implementing health promotion, disease prevention, case-finding, and curative services in the community; promoting development of individual, family, and community competence to identify and meet their health needs; and evaluating community health services and outcomes. Primary health care is endorsed by the ANA (1986) as the preferred approach to community health nursing practice.

Primary health care sets the framework for community organization practice by nurses in several respects. First, it specifies the approach to community organization as one of partnership with individuals, aggregates, and all sectors of the community. Second, it indicates outcome goals of equitable distribution, appropriate technology, and focus on prevention and a process goal of community participation. Third, it defines the primary health care system as the preferred community organization structure. These three components — process, outcome, and structure — set the parameters for the choice of community organization models selected by nurses to guide their practice.

COMMUNITY ORGANIZATION CONCEPTS

Many community organization and community health nursing models share common roots in theories and concepts of social change and social interaction. The concepts of social systems, social change, and community participation will be discussed to provide a basis for understanding selected community organization models and their application to community health nursing practice.

Systems Theories

Social scientists view the community as a system with wholeness, boundaries, organization, openness, and feedback. Each community consists of interrelated subsystems, including aggregates and sectors. Aggregates are groups within the community that share common characteristics. Sectors are functional divisions of the community such as health, welfare, education, economics, energy, agriculture, religion, transportation, communications, business and industry, recreation, safety, and government and politics. Within systems theory, all sectors and aggregates of the community are interrelated. A change in one subsystem will affect all other subsystems as well as the community as a whole. Similarly, communities are parts of larger systems called suprasystems. Changes in the suprasystem will also affect a community system and its subsystem aggregates and sectors (Anderson and Carter, 1990).

When promoting the health of aggregates, the community health nurse may intervene at varied levels of the community system. The term "focal system" denotes the system level that is the primary focus of community care. However, within the community systems framework, the nurse must consider the focal system, its subsystems, and the suprasystem as a single entity when planning nursing care. Therefore, when planning health intervention in one aggregate or sector of the community, it is necessary to analyze the effects of the proposed change on all other components of the community. Furthermore, health promotion in the community cannot be achieved by the health care subsystem alone. Community health is brought about by the cooperative effort of all sectors of the community. Recognizing the multiple determinants of human health, the WHO (1978) recommends that health promotion be a collaborative effort of scientific health services, traditional health services, agriculture, animal husbandry, food, industry, education, housing, public works, communication, and all other sectors of community development.

A general nursing model fitting social systems theory is Neuman's health-care systems model. According to Neuman (1982), "Health or wellness is the condition in which all parts and subparts (variables) are in harmony with the whole man." At the aggregate level, Neuman's model indicates that community health nurses must assess all of the aggregates and sectors comprising the community, not just the traditional health sectors, as a part of the nursing process. Anderson and McFarlane's (1988) community-as-client model incorporates the concept of a multisectoral basis for health, similar to Connor's (1969) social compass, with Neuman's systems model (1982) providing an integrated system-oriented framework for community health nursing practice.

Social Change

Lewin (1951) identified a three-stage process of social change:

1. Unfreezing—the breakdown of existing mores, values, and traditions
2. Changing—the identification and internalization of new values and behavior patterns
3. Refreezing—the integration of the new values into the community mores and traditions

Lewin developed the concept of force field analysis as a model for analyzing the change process. Within the force field analysis model, the change process is affected by driving and restraining forces that promote or oppose a proposed change.

Change occurs when the strength or direction of the driving forces and/or retraining forces are changed. Although Lewin's research has much useful application to community health nursing practice, one must examine carefully the ethics of changing community values, mores, and traditions unless the community members freely initiated and directed the process.

Community Participation

Community participation has been identified as one of the variables associated with healthy communities and is incorporated into some definitions of community health (Lackey et al., 1987). Cottrell (1976), a social scientist, and Goeppinger (1982), a community health nurse, characterize competent, healthy communities as having

- Commitment
- Participation
- Articulateness
- Effective communication
- Conflict containment and accommodation
- Self-awareness and other awareness
- Clarity of situational definitions
- Management of relations with larger society.

Research has been conducted on the relationship between community participation and the change process. In a 1953 study of group communication patterns, Bavelas found that groups develop greater problem-solving skills when a participatory, rather than a directive, pattern of communication is used. The exception was in emergency situations, when directive communication was needed for immediate resolution of the problem.

Building on Bavelas' research, Hersey and Blanchard (1982) developed a model that identified two approaches to change—participatory and directive. In *participatory change,* members of the aggregate affected are involved in planning and problem solving at all levels of change process (Fig. 7–1). Hersey and Blanchard's research has found the participatory approach to be most effective when working with mature, competent communities that can take ownership of the change process. Although the participatory change process is slow, change effected is long lasting because community members develop a sense of ownership and commitment to the change. In contrast, *directive*

Participatory Approach

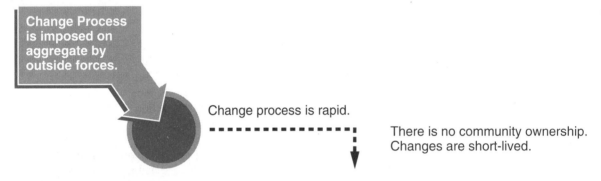

Directive Approach

Figure 7–1
Two approaches to change in a community. (Data from Hersey, P., and Blanchard, K.: Management of Organizational Behavior: Utilizing Human Resources. Englewood Cliffs, New Jersey, Prentice-Hall, 1982.)

change is imposed on the community by outside forces. Although the directive approach has the advantage of bringing about change more rapidly, without community ownership of the process, changes tend to be short lived. Community organization research reinforces Hersey and Blanchard's findings that community partnership in all aspects of the planning process increases the strength and longevity of the change (Daly and Angulo, 1990; Flynn et al., 1991; Jones and Harris, 1987). In applying community participation research to clinical practice, community health nurses should consider the situation, the nature of the aggregate, and the relative merits of speed versus longevity when planning community change strategies.

COMMUNITY ORGANIZATION MODELS

Over the years, several typologies of community organization practice have evolved. The typologies are based on a consideration of a variety of elements, including the character of the community action system, setting or locality, substance of the problem being addressed, character of the issues being generated, kind of aggregate most directly affected, organizational structures being developed, sponsor of the community organizing project, and role of the professional worker, in this case, the community health nurse (Kramer and Specht, 1975). The typology most frequently used by com-

Table 7–2
Nurses' Roles in Three Community Organization Models

Model	Major Concepts	Nurses' Roles
Social planning	Data collection Rational decision making	Fact gatherer Expert analyst Program implementer Facilitator
Social action	Polarization Confrontation/ conflict	Community activist Agitator Negotiator
Community development	Community involvement Self-direction Self-help	Enabler Teacher/educator

munity health professionals is the typology described by Rothman (1972). Rothman has synthesized the various definitions and approaches into three models of community organization practice — social planning, social action, and locality development, which is more commonly known to the health professional as community development. Each model will be described briefly in relation to nursing practice (Table 7–2).

Social Planning

In the social planning model, community decisions are based on fact gathering and rational decision making. Emphasis is placed on the task rather than on the process. Because rapid problem solution is the primary goal of social planning, the directive approach to social change that emphasizes "expert" planning is used. Roles of the community health nurse using a social planning approach would be facilitator, fact gatherer, expert analyst, and program implementer.

Social Action

In the social action model, community change is accomplished by polarization of the community around selected issues, followed by confrontation or conflict between persons with opposing viewpoints. Whether the concentration is on process or

goals, the major focus of social action is the transfer of power to the aggregate level (Alinsky, 1971). Social action organizers may be revolutionary or evolutionary (Archer et al., 1984). Revolutionary social activists focus on the transformation of society, whereas evolutionary social activists work within the existing social system. Within the social action model, the role of the community health nurse would be community activist, agitator, and negotiator.

Community Development

Community development is a model that places emphasis on community involvement, self-direction, and self-help in determining and solving problems (Rothman, 1972). The individual and aggregate skills learned during the problem-solving process are important elements of the solution to the problem. Within the community development model, the role of the community health nurse would be as an enabler and a teacher of problem-solving skills. Paterson and Zderad's humanistic model of nursing (1976) and Orem's self-care nursing model (1980) tend to support the concept of enablement as a major role of nursing.

The caveats related to the use of the social planning and social action models are similar to those discussed earlier in relation to social change and community participation theories. Based on current standards and frameworks for community health nursing practice, the preferred model for health promotion and protection is community development. However, Rothman's three models of community organization are not intended to be mutually exclusive. Collectively, the models represent a spectrum of approaches that take into account a wide range of variables affecting community organization practice. As such, the three models present community health nurses with alternative approaches to community organization based on the desired nursing role.

COMMUNITY ORGANIZATION STRATEGIES FOR NURSES

The selection of a community organization approach and strategy is dependent on the aggregate's social and cultural context, the nature of the issue or health problem being addressed, and the cultural and ethical values of the nurse serving as community organizer. Warren (1969) identifies three major community organization strategies for achieving social change—collaborative strategies, campaign strategies, and contest strategies. The three strategies correspond to Rothman's models of community organization practice.

Collaboration Strategies

According to Warren (1969), collaborative strategies are those that fit with the community development typology of community organization practice. Collaborative strategies are used in situations of issue consensus in which there is basic agreement or likelihood of basic agreement that an issue or problem should be resolved. Within collaborative strategies, the role of the nurse as change agent would be as an enabler or a facilitator.

During the assessment phase, the nurse and community members jointly identify community health needs and resources. Depending on the time frame and community context, the nurse gathers data from community members through surveys, town meetings, and interviews and presents the findings to community members for validation, prioritization, and decision making or teaches community members to conduct their own needs assessment. During the planning phase, the nurse fosters community decision making by facilitating community-controlled decision making and teaching problem solving and planning skills as necessary. When implementing the plan, the community health nurse may teach self-care to individuals, families, and aggregates; train community workers to prevent, detect, and treat selected health problems; or provide community-based nursing care when indicated. Collaborative approaches to evaluation of community health and nursing interventions can be fostered by involving community members in the design of evaluation mechanisms that are easy to implement and interpret.

Campaign Strategies

Campaign strategies are linked with the social planning approach to community organization. Campaign strategies are appropriate in situations where there are different opinions about the substance of an issue or the proposed solution of the issue, but the possibility of consensus. Within the campaign model, the role of the nurse as change agent is persuader and expert witness. As a community health expert, the nurse would use epidemiological methods to gather data and identify major problems and groups at risk. Based on the epidemiological diagnosis, the nurse would recommend solutions and plan appropriate nursing interventions. A major part of the implementation process may be "selling" the program to the community. Campaign methods include mass media campaigns, one-on-one persuasion, letters, endorsement by well-known people, public presentations, activation of support groups, and other persuasive techniques.

Contest Strategies

Contest strategies are most closely linked to social action approaches. Contest strategies, including social action, nonviolence, and civil disobedience, are appropriate when there is refusal of the power structures to recognize a problem or strong opposition to a proposed solution. The predominant role of the change agent is that of advocate, agitator, or contestant. Within the social action model, the nurse would address inequities in health and health care by working within the system to bring about change or by assisting the client to confront the system and force change. Although nurses may attempt to improve community health through confrontation tactics such as strikes or civil disobedience, more popular contest strategies in contemporary U.S. community health practice are political mobilization and legislation.

Social scientists indicate that in practice, no single community organization strategy is universally appropriate. Community organization strategies should be selected after careful consideration of the situation, the nature of the problem or issue being addressed, the social and political context, and the values and beliefs of both the aggregate and the community health nurse. In a review of major U.S. nursing theories, Meleis (1985) identified the roles of nurses. Based on Meleis' analysis of role definitions, it appears that social planning is the practice model most universally supported by nursing theories. This finding should give the nursing profession food for thought because community development is the community organization model considered by social science researchers to be most congruent with U.S. traditions, values, and beliefs

(Christenson and Robinson, 1989) and is recommended by international health and nursing organizations as most appropriate for nursing practice.

APPLICATION OF THE NURSING PROCESS THROUGH COMMUNITY ORGANIZATION

Nurses engaged in promoting, protecting, and restoring community health may select from several community organization models to guide their practice (see Table 7–2). The role of the nurse in relation to community health assessment, diagnosis, planning, intervention, and evaluation would vary according to the model selected to guide each phase of practice. The application of social planning, social action, and community development will be discussed briefly in relation to nursing process in the care of aggregates.

Social Planning

The nurse who has selected social planning would be a gatherer and analyzer of facts during community assessment. The community diagnosis would be based on empirical data and recommendations presented by the nurse. Planning would be a process of rational decision making by the nurse and other expert planners. The selected nursing interventions would be implemented and evaluated by the nurse. The relationship of the nurse to the community and its aggregates would be that of provider to consumer. In the late 20th century, the social planning model has been the model of community organization most frequently used by U.S. nurses in traditional community health agencies and organizations. The advantages of this approach are speed and control of the planning process. A major drawback is a lack of community or aggregate ownership of the goal or solution, often resulting in underuse or nonuse of community health nursing services.

**C a s e
S t u d y
1**

Social Planning for Tertiary Prevention of Drug Abuse

Assessment Epidemiological analysis conducted by a large urban health department indicated that substance abuse had reached epidemic proportions. In one of the health districts, nurses were involved in a program of prevention and early intervention for potential teen drug abusers. The program had been initiated at the local community's request and was financially supported by churches, businesses, and various civic organizations. Because of the success in primary and secondary prevention of drug abuse, county health planners proposed a program of tertiary prevention in the same district. Citing the same epidemiological data that had triggered the teen program, the county health department unilaterally planned a federally funded methadone maintenance program to rehabilitate hard-core heroin abusers.

Diagnosis Alteration existed in community/aggregate function due to heroin abuse.

Planning and Goal Long-term heroin abusers will become productive members of the community.

Interventions A methadone program was begun in the clinic that had the teen drug use prevention program. Community health nurses were called on to implement the new program in the community. Using a variety of campaign strategies, the nurses were able to convince the community to start a methadone program.

Outcomes Two years later, the drug programs were evaluated. County health planners judged the methadone program to be effective because a large number of addicts were enrolled in the program and were experiencing varying degrees of success in heroin withdrawal. However, the teen drug prevention program had disappeared. The methadone program had been linked by community residents to an increase of theft in the area of the clinic. Because of the presence of hard-core drug users in the clinic, parents, schools, and law enforcement agencies no longer referred teenagers to the prevention and early treatment program that was in the same building. All community funds for the teen program were withdrawn. Community mistrust of the health department, including the nursing staff, was high, and staff morale and satisfaction were low.

Evaluation A few adults in the methadone maintenance program ceased heroin use, maintained steady jobs, and were judged to be productive members of the community. Therefore, the goal of tertiary prevention was partially met in an aggregate of adults. However, the unintended outcome—the loss of primary and secondary prevention programs—resulted in an overall increase in heroin use in the community, primarily among teenagers and young adults.

Social Action

Within the social action model, the focus of nursing assessment would be on crystallization of issues. Prioritization of issues and selection of intervention strategies initially may be the nurse's prerogative. Later, community or aggregate members may be actively involved in selection and prioritization of issues and action to be taken. Interventions include polarization around issues to shift the balance of power within the community system and its suprasystems and subsystems. Evaluation would be conducted jointly by the nurse and aggregate members, possibly during "debriefing" sessions. The relationship of the nurse to the aggregate might be that of advocate, agitator, activist, powerbroker, or negotiator on behalf of the aggregate. The social action model is often selected by nurses desiring political action or policy changes by governments and corporations. An advantage of this approach is the ability to effect change for aggregates with scarce resources. A disadvantage is that polarization around issues is difficult to reverse and interferes with mutual problem solving should that option be desired in the future.

**C a s e
S t u d y
2**

Social Action in Primary Prevention for Older Adults

Assessment In recent years, state and federal budget crises have affected services for many aggregates. In one state, budget cuts threatened services for the elderly. Comprehensive health promotion was targeted for reduction or termination. In both urban and rural areas, elderly persons faced the potential loss of community-based programs of primary prevention.

Diagnosis Primary prevention was impaired, as evidenced by termination of community health promotion programs for the elderly.

Planning and Goal Community will promote, protect, and restore the health of all residents.

Interventions A social action approach using contest strategies was chosen. The State Nurses Association in conjunction with senior citizens' coalitions and the State Public Health Association organized a mass write-in and direct-contact campaign to inform legislators of potential health and political ramifications of the budget cut.

Outcome The campaign resulted in funds being returned to community health programs for the elderly.

Evaluation The community's capacity to provide primary prevention for aggregates of elderly citizens was restored.

Community Development

Within the community development model, community health assessment would encompass multiple sectors of the community system and focus on community or aggregate identification of perceived needs and potential resources. Diagnosis is based on the community's priorities. Nursing interventions would be focused on community self-help and capacity building, mobilization of resources, and integration of health care services. Direct care of individuals and aggregates may be provided when such services are related to promotion of health of the entire community. Evaluation is a joint process involving process, outcome, and context components. As a community developer, the nurse would approach community health practice with two goals. First, individuals and aggregates in the community would become active partners in carrying out each step of the nursing process. Second, as a result of the manner in which the nurse implements the nursing process, individuals and aggregates would acquire the skills and knowledge needed to promote, protect, and restore their community's health in the future. Nursing roles would include those of collaborator, enabler, empowerer, and partner. Advantages of this approach include broad-based solutions to complex community health problems and community ownership of health. A disadvantage is the length of time needed to effect change.

Case Study 3

Community Development for Primary and Secondary Prevention of Rural Health Problems

Assessment A nursing student was assigned to conduct a comprehensive community health nursing assessment of a rural Midwestern community. One of the important social structures within the community was an active Protestant church. The student chose a community development approach to the assignment and taught church members how to conduct and interpret a neighborhood survey. The survey indicated that a major community need was promotion of individual, family, and aggregate physical and mental health. In addition to identifying community health nursing needs, the student observed that the survey initiated linkages between church members and non–church member community residents.

Diagnosis Optimal community health with potential for achievement was evidenced by community participation in needs assessment.

Planning and Goal The community will engage in self-care by planning and implementing programs of primary prevention for all aggregates.

Interventions As a graduate, the former student returned to the community as a parish nurse. Church members, in partnership with the parish nurse, planned a series of programs to meet neighborhood health promotion needs. The nurse facilitated church leadership in the planning process and provided technical assistance regarding health promotion strategies.

Outcomes Church members, in consultation with community residents, began a weekly diet, exercise, and Bible study group for women; an after-school recreation program for grade-school children and teenagers; and a family counseling center. The program was implemented by the church, primarily using church and neighborhood personnel and resources. The nurse was called on at times to provide selected community health nursing services such as health teaching. However, ownership of the program belonged to those who had conducted the survey and planned and implemented appropriate solutions.

Evaluation Simple evaluation methods such as group attendance and perceived success in meeting personal health promotion goals indicated successful outcomes for the program. Furthermore, not only had selected neighborhood health needs been met by using collaboration strategies to carry out the nursing process, but the competence of the community had been improved as it became able to identify and solve its own health problems.

Selecting Community Organization Models

As noted earlier, the nurse is not confined to a single community organization model in the practice of community health nursing. All three models are useful. In a similar vein, the nurse may mix models used as situational variables change during the stages of the nursing process. The knowledge of community organization concepts, models, and strategies is part of the science of nursing. The skill with which the nurse uses these concepts, models, and strategies in community health practice is an art.

SUMMARY

Community organization is as a skill basic to effective community health nursing practice. The theoretical basis of community organization has been discussed. Primary health care has been presented as a framework for understanding the pertinence of community organization to community health nursing practice.

Guidelines for selection of community organization models and strategies appropriate to community health nursing have been suggested. Three models of community organization practice—social planning, social action, and community development—have been presented. Application of the three models to community health nursing practice has been discussed. Although all three models have use in nursing care of aggregates, the model preferred by community health and nursing organizations is community development. Community development emphasizes community participation and multisector collaboration in planning affordable, acceptable solutions to priority health problems.

Community organization is a powerful tool when used appropriately and skillfully by community health nurses. Communities empowered to mobilize effective community action systems for the promotion, protection, and restoration of health become full partners in achieving the goal of equal access to basic health care services. As all nurses have discovered, an important reason for incorporating community organization into community health nursing practice is very practical—it really works!

L e a r n i n g
A c t i v i t i e s

1. Identify and interview social planners, social activists, and community developers in your community. Compare the similarities and differences in their approaches to community organization.

2. Play a simulation game such as "The World Game," which demonstrates the interrelatedness of multiple community sectors.

3. Draw a model depicting your understanding of nursing and primary health care.

4. Conduct a mock community health planning forum in which various members of the groups are assigned different community organization roles. Discuss your observations and reactions after the exercise.

5. Write community health nurse job descriptions for each of the three models of community organization.

6. Write a "concept paper" discussing your views of the art and science of community organization in community health nursing practice.

REFERENCES

Alinsky, S. D.: Rules for Radicals: A Pragmatic Primer for Realistic Radicals. New York, Random House, 1971.

American Nurses' Association: Code for Nurses With Interpretive Statements. Kansas City, Missouri, ANA, 1985.

American Nurses' Association: Standards of Community Health Nursing Practice. Kansas City, Missouri, ANA, 1986.

Anderson, E. T., and McFarlane, J. M.: Community as Client. Philadelphia, J. B. Lippincott, 1988.

Anderson, R. E., and Carter, I.: Human Behavior in the Social Environment. New York, Aldine DeGruyter, 1990.

Archer, S. E., Kelly, C. D., and Bisch, S. A.: Implementing Change in Communities: A Collaborative Process. St. Louis, C. V. Mosby, 1984.

Bavelas, A.: Communication patterns in task oriented groups. *In* Cartwright, D., and Zander, A., eds.: Group Dynamics: Research and Theory. Evanston, Illinois, Roe, Peterson, & Co., 1953, pp. 669–682.

Blum, H. L.: Expanding Health Care Horizons. Oakland, California, Third Party Publishing, 1983.

Christenson, J. A., and Robinson, J. W., Jr.: Community Development in America. Ames, Iowa, Iowa State University Press, 1989.

Connor, D. M.: Understanding Your Community. Oakville, Ontario, Development Press, 1969.

Cottrell, L. S.: The competent community. *In* Kaplan, B. H., Wilson, R. N., and Leighton, A. H., eds.: Further Explorations in Social Psychiatry. New York, Basic Books, 1976, pp. 195–209.

Cox, F., Erlich, J. L., Rothman, J., and Troponan, J. E.: Strategies of Community Organization: Macropractice. Itasca, Illinois, F. E. Peacock, 1987.

Daly, J. M., and Angulo, J.: People-centered community planning. J. Comm. Dev. Soc. *21*;88–103, 1990.

Flynn, B., Rider, M., and Ray, D.: Healthy cities: The Indiana model of community development in public health. Health Educ. Q. *18*;331–347, 1991.

Goeppinger, J., Lassiter, P.G., and Wilcox, B.: Community health is community competence. Nurs. Outlook *30*;464–467, 1982.

Hersey, P., and Blanchard, K.: Management of Organizational Behavior: Utilizing Human Resources. Englewood Cliffs, New Jersey, Prentice-Hall, 1982.

Institute of Medicine: The Future of Public Health. Washington, D.C., National Academy Press, 1988.

Jones, E. R., and Harris, W. M.: Conceptual scheme for analysis of the social planning process. J. Comm. Dev. Soc. *18*;18–41, 1987.

Kovner, A. R.: Health Care Delivery in the United States. New York, Springer, 1990.

Kramer, R. M., and Specht, H.: Readings in Community Organization Practice. Englewood Cliffs, New Jersey, Prentice-Hall, 1975.

Lackey, A. S., Burke, R., and Peterson, M.: Healthy communities: The goal of community development. J. Comm. Dev. Soc. *18*;1–17, 1987.

Lee, P. R., and Estes, C. L., eds.: The Nation's Health. San Francisco, Boyd & Fraser, 1990.

Lewin, K.: Field Theory in Social Sciences. New York, Harper and Row, 1951.

Meleis, A. I.: Theoretical Nursing: Development and Progress. Philadelphia, J. B. Lippincott, 1985.

National Organization for Public Health Nursing: Manual of Public Health Nursing. New York, Macmillan, 1935.

Neuman, B.: The Neuman Systems Model: Application to Nursing Education and Practice. Norwalk, Connecticut, Appleton-Century-Crofts, 1982.

Nightingale, F.: Notes on Nursing. Philadelphia, J. B. Lippincott, 1946, p. 247. (Originally published in 1859.)

Orem, D. E.: Nursing: Concepts of Practice. New York, McGraw-Hill, 1980.

Pan American Health Organization: The Role of the Nurse in Primary Health Care. Washington, D.C., PAHO, 1977.

Paterson, J. G., and Zderad, L. T.: Humanistic Nursing. New York, Wiley, 1976.

Rothman, J.: Three models of community organization practice. *In* Zaltman, G., Kotler, P., and Kaufman, I., eds.: Creating Social Change. New York, Holt, Rinehart, & Winston, 1972, pp. 477–478.

Warren, R.: Types of purposive social change at the community level. *In* Kramer, R., and Specht, H., eds.: Readings in Community Organization Practice. Englewood Cliffs, New Jersey, Prentice-Hall, 1969, pp. 134–149.

World Health Organization: Community Health Nursing. Geneva, WHO, 1974.

World Health Organization: Primary Health Care. Geneva, WHO, 1978.

World Health Organization: A Guide to Curriculum Review for Basic Nursing Education. Geneva, WHO, 1985*a*.

World Health Organization: Primary Health Care in Industrialized Countries. Geneva, WHO, 1985*b*.

CHAPTER

8

The Home Visit

Upon completion of this chapter, the reader will be able to:

1. Discuss the purpose of the home visit.

2. Differentiate between the purpose of a public health nursing visit and that of a home health nursing visit.

3. Differentiate between the nursing interventions involved in a public health visit and those involved in a home health visit.

4. Use the nursing process in outlining the steps involved in conducting a home visit.

5. Discuss the process used in contracting with patients and their families to achieve health care goals.

Christine DiMartile Bolla
Jean Cozad Lyon

Home health visits are made by community health nurses from many different disciplines. The purpose of home visits by nurses is to provide nursing care to individuals and their families in their homes. The specific objectives and services provided by nurses vary depending on the type of agency providing services and the population served. Home visits are usually provided by nurses who work for public health departments, visiting nurse associations, home health agencies, or school districts. A school nurse, for example, may make visits to the homes of students who have poor academic performances because of health problems.

Community health nurses from clinics often conduct home visits as part of patient follow-up. Public health nurses make visits to follow-up patients with communicable diseases and provide health education and community referrals to patients with identified problems. Nurses working for home health agencies or through nursing registries make home visits, often to assist patients in their transitions from hospital to home but also as ordered by health care providers because of exacerbations of chronic conditions.

The focus of all home visits is on the individual for whom the referral is received. The nurse assesses the interaction of the individual with the family and provides education and interventions for the family as well as the client. The nurse evaluates how the individual and family interact as part of an aggregate group in the community. The need for referrals for community services is identified by the nurse and made as necessary.

Nurses who make home visits receive referrals from a variety of sources, including the client's physician or nurse practitioner, hospital discharge planner, school teacher, or clinic health care provider. Requests for nursing visits to assess and assist with the client's health care can also originate with the client or the client's family.

PUBLIC HEALTH NURSING

Specific services provided by public health nurses vary among states and counties within each state based on geographical location, population needs, and budget constraints. Although public health nurses serve aggregate groups in communities by providing health education and primary prevention services, home visits have increasingly become the vehicle of service provision (Oda, 1989). Client visits made by public health nurses vary and can include ante partum or postpartum visits to mothers with infants who are at high risk for complications or follow-up of clients with communicable diseases such as hepatitis and tuberculosis. Public health nurses also serve clients in rural areas where other health care services are not available.

Referrals for visits by skilled public health nurses are often made for individuals and families who are poor and have no health care benefits (employed persons and their dependents comprise more than 75% of Americans who have no health coverage [U.S. Department of Commerce, 1990]). However, not all public health nursing departments provide skilled nursing care to clients. In the event that the public health nursing service does not provide visits by skilled nurses, referrals for clients who require skilled nursing care, such as dressing or Foley catheter changes, are made to a home health agency. To facilitate appropriate client referrals, it is important for referral sources, such as the hospital, clinic, and health care providers, to be knowledgeable of the nursing services provided by the local public health nursing department and home health agencies. In some counties, the public health department has a home health nursing agency that is separate from the public health nursing service, and referrals are made to the agency that can best serve the client's needs.

HOME HEALTH CARE

The term "home health care" describes a system in which health care and social services are provided to homebound or disabled people in their home rather than in medical facilities (U.S. Department of Commerce, 1990). Clients referred for home

---

HOME VISITS have been an integral part of nursing for more than a century, originating with Florence Nightingale's "health nurses" in England. In the United States in 1877, the Women's Branch of the New York City mission sent the first trained nurses into the homes of the poor to provide nursing care. Under the direction of Lillian Wald, pioneering efforts were initiated to provide services to the poor in their homes in the late 19th century (Kalisch and Kalisch, 1978; Kelly, 1985).

health care require nursing services for assessment of physical, psychosocial, and functional needs (Lockhart, 1985). The nursing care provided is short term and intermittent, based on the needs of the individual client. Health care services are provided using a team approach that includes social workers and physical, occupational, and speech therapists, with the community health nurse serving as the case manager who coordinates all services and provides nursing care to the client.

Clients who receive home health services usually have health insurance that pays for the visits. This coverage can be in the form of Medicare, Medicaid, or private insurance. Individual county home health agencies may provide services to clients who do not have health insurance and do not qualify for Medicaid because of their income level or legal status. Provision of home health services to these aggregates is far from universal. Whether individuals who make home health referrals for uninsured clients are able to obtain the services depends on the policy of the county public health department.

CONDUCTING A HOME VISIT USING THE NURSING PROCESS

ASSESSMENT

Visit Preparation
It is important that the nurse making the home visit prepare for the visit by reviewing the referral form and any other pertinent information that is available concerning the client. The first home visit provides the nurse with the opportunity to establish a trust relationship with the client and family and to establish credibility as a resource for health information and community referrals in a nonthreatening environment.

The Referral
The referral (Fig. 8–1) is a formal request for a home visit. Referrals come from a variety of sources, including hospitals, clinics, health care providers, individuals, and families. The type of agency that receives the referral will vary depending on the client services that are needed. Public health referrals are made for clients who are in need of health education, e.g., infant care education and resource allocation, or for follow-up of clients with communicable diseases and their contacts.

Home health referrals are requested to provide short-term, intermittent skilled services and rehabilitation to clients. For example, a client who has had a stroke requires skilled nursing assessments, physical therapy visits for gait training, speech therapy for improvement of a speech deficit, and occupational therapy for retraining in activities of daily living such as bathing and cooking.

Review of the referral form before the first visit gives the community health nurse basic information about the client such as name, age, diagnosis or health status, address, telephone number, insurance coverage if any, reason for referral, and source of the referral, whether a clinician, health care provider, communicable disease service, hospital, client, or client's family.

Public health referrals usually provide information on the client's condition that necessitates public health nurse visits. An example is a client who is positive for tuberculosis, in which case the nurse is notified of the client's place of residence, type and location of employment, and any known contacts, including family and friends. Another example is a 16-year-old girl who is referred for ante partum visits because she is 7 months pregnant and has just initiated prenatal care.

Additional information provided in the home health referral includes current client medications, prescribed diet, other disciplines involved in the care of the client, physician's orders, and/or goal of care. This information is important because it gives the nurse a picture of the client.

Initial Telephone Contact
The client is contacted by the nurse and informed of the referral for service. The first telephone contact with the client or family consists of an exchange of essential information, including an introduction by the nurse, identification of the agency that has received the referral, and the purpose of the visit. After this initial information is exchanged, the client is informed of the nurse's desire to make the home visit, permission is received from the client, and a mutually acceptable time is set for the visit. Because the nurse is considered a guest in the client's home, it is important that the client understand and agree to the visit. The nurse verifies the client's address and asks for specific directions to the client's home.

During a home health visit, the client is requested to present evidence of insurance informa-

PATIENT NUMBER		□NEW □READMIT **INTAKE**	DATE LAST SEEN BY MD	CASE MANAGER

NAME: LAST FIRST M.I. | **TELEPHONE NO.:** | **SEX** M F | **BIRTHDATE** | **AGE** | **DATE OF 1st VISIT** M.D. AUTH. YES _____ NO _____

STREET ADDRESS: CITY: STATE: ZIP:

HOSP/SNF:

ADM. DATE:

DIRECTIONS:

DIS. DATE:

DIAGNOSES: PRIMARY #

1.

2.

3.

4.

DX KNOWN TO PT? _____

PHYSICIAN NAME: SPECIALTY:

ADDRESS:

TEL. NO.:

PHYSICIAN NAME: SPECIALTY:

ADDRESS:

TEL. NO.:

HOSP/SNF:

ADM. DATE:

DIS. DATE:

MEDICARE NO.

MEDI-CAL NO./SS #.

HISTORY:

AGENCY WORKER: TEL. NO.:

PAY SOURCES/ SERVICE REQUEST:

PHN	PT	ST	OT
NSW	HHA	HCA	PD

INS. CO.:

POLICY #:

GRP. #:

COV. CODE:

RELIGIOUS/CULTURAL PATTERNS/LANGUAGE/ PSYCHO-SOCIAL

EMERGENCY/FAMILY CONTACTS (BY PRIORITY)

TEL. NO.:

CONTACT PERSON:

NAME REL. HOME # WORK #

MEDICATIONS

#1

ADDRESS

#2

ADDRESS

PERTINENT HOSPITAL INFORMATION

DATE/TIME:_____

SKILLED ORDERS PER: _____

DIET/FLUIDS

ALLERGIES

EQUIPMENT: DME YES _____ NO _____

INTAKE SOURCE NAME	AGENCY	TEL. NO.
HOW DID YOU LEARN ABOUT OUR SERVICES?		
INTAKE RECEIVED BY	DATE	

Figure 8–1
Referral form. (Courtesy of Home Calls, Oakland, California.)

146

tion, such as a Medicare card or Medicaid stickers. The nurse should forewarn the client of this so the client or family can locate the information before the visit. If the client is unable to provide this verification, the nurse assists with these functions during the visit.

Not all clients have a telephone. If this is the case, the nurse rechecks the referral for a telephone number where messages can be left. (It is also worthwhile to contact the health care provider who made the referral to see if the telephone number was omitted unintentionally.) If the client does not have a telephone, the nurse may choose to make a drop-in visit. This type of visit consists of an unannounced visit to the client's home, during which the nurse explains the purpose of the referral, receives the client's permission for the visit, and sets up a time for a future visit with the client. The client may agree to the first visit while the nurse is there.

If the client is not at home for the drop-in visit, the nurse leaves an official agency card and a brief message asking the client to contact the agency to schedule a nursing visit. The nurse informs the referring agency that the visit was attempted but that the client was not available for contact. A formal agency letter, identifying the agency and the reason for the referral, is often sent to clients who are difficult to contact. The nurse's primary responsibility when unsuccessful in locating the client is to keep the clinic, physician, or referring agency informed of the nurse's efforts to establish contact with the client.

Environment

An environmental assessment begins as the nurse leaves the agency en route to the client's home. Specific questions asked by the nurse are (Keating and Kelman, 1988):

- How does the client's neighborhood compare with other neighborhoods in the area?
- Are there adequate shopping facilities, such as grocery stores, close to the client's home?

The nurse should also make note of the client's dwelling, that is, whether the client lives in a single-family home, in a single room in a home or hotel, in an apartment, or in a shared apartment or house. Specific assessments that are made include:

- Is the client's residence easily accessible by the client, given the client's age and functional ability? For example, if the client has limited endurance, can the several flights of stairs be negotiated when entering or leaving the dwelling?
- Are facilities for the handicapped available as necessary?
- Is the dwelling in an area with high rates of drug abuse or crime?
- Is the building or home secure?
- Does the client live alone? If so, how does the client get to the physician or clinic? How does the client purchase groceries?
- Does the client have food in the home? If so, who prepares the client's meals? Are the meals nutritious?
- Are there rodents, cockroaches, or other potential vectors of disease present in the client's home?
- Does the client's home have hot running water, heat, sanitation facilities, and adequate ventilation?
- Is the client's residence safe relative to the client's physical status, or is the home cluttered with debris and furniture?

Safety Issues

The nurse who makes home visits is aware of the environment and surroundings when making home visits. On occasion, the nurse may not feel safe entering a client's home environment (Cattran et al., 1986). For example, a nurse may arrive at a home and discover that the client lives in a drug house where drugs are being openly sold. In this situation, the nurse should not enter the home but may call the client and make arrangements for the client to meet at a local restaurant, the health agency, or some other public location. No nurse is expected to disregard personal safety in an effort to make a home visit.

Social Talk

When the nurse meets with the client, whether in the home or at another mutually agreeable location, the initial conversation revolves around social topics. The nurse assumes a friendly manner and asks general questions about the client, the client's family, and health care services that will benefit the client. These questions assist the nurse in assessing the client's needs and creates a comfortable atmosphere in which the nurse and client communicate.

Building Trust

Many of the clients in need of nursing visits do not trust the health care system and are not comfortable with a representative from an agency visiting in their home. For example, a client who is pregnant and does not have legal status in the United States will be hesitant to allow a nurse to visit because the client will be fearful of being reported to immigration authorities. The nurse's role in visiting this client is to focus on the health and safety of the client and her fetus. Thus, the nurse must build a trust relationship early in the visit, or the client will not allow additional visits. If a trust relationship is not established and the client believes that the nurse will report the client to immigration, it is highly probable that the client will move to another location to avoid future contact.

Physical Assessment

During the first home visit, the type of client assessment will vary depending on the purpose of the home visit. The public health nurse assesses the client's knowledge of the client's health status. The nurse identifies knowledge deficits and uses this information in the development of a plan of care.

Subjective information is obtained from the client and the client's family and includes the client's perception of the situation and what the client identifies as problems. The nurse assesses whether the client is isolated physically or socially from others and whether the client is a member of a close-knit, nurturing, supportive family or kinship network. The amount of support that the client perceives to be available may or may not be accurate, so the nurse asks several questions about the client's family, friends, and daily routine to assess the client's level of social support.

The home health nurse assesses the client's health knowledge and performs a physical assessment. The physical assessment of the client includes a review of all systems, with an emphasis on the systems affected by the client's presenting condition. The nurse obtains objective data through the use of essential physical assessment skills such as observation, palpation, auscultation, and percussion. The physical assessment also includes in-

formation regarding the client's functional status (Higgs and Gustafson, 1985). Assessment of the functional status is important for Medicare reimbursement and for the development of an individualized nursing care plan. This assessment includes information regarding the client's ability to ambulate, to perform activities of daily living independently, and to use assist devices such as a cane or wheelchair. Specific functional limitations, such as shortness of breath or muscle weakness, are assessed at this time. Information obtained during the assessment phase is used to identify nursing diagnoses and develop a plan of care.

DIAGNOSIS AND PLANNING

Develop a Plan for the Client and Family

After the assessment phase of the home visit, the nurse develops a plan of care for the client and the client's family. This plan is developed with the client and the family. Often, the nurse will develop a contract with the client that delineates the role and responsibilities of the nurse regarding the client's health and the role of the client and the client's family (Spradley, 1990). If during the planning phase the client expresses a disinterest in contracting to improve health, the nurse will be limited in possible interventions. Goals are identified that the client is willing to work toward with the nurse's assistance.

The goal of home visits for both public health and home health nursing is to involve the client in taking an active role in health promotion. The nurse is careful to not allow the client to become dependent on the nurse's interventions because the nurse's involvement is short-term.

Outline the Client and Family Roles

Written contracts are helpful for both the nurse and the client because the client's and nurse's roles in implementation of the plan are clearly delineated (Spradley, 1990). If either the client or the nurse forgets their role in the plan, the written contract is used as a reference. The contract can be modified by mutual agreement of the client and the nurse.

INTERVENTION

Implementation of the care plan begins during the first home visit. The nurse begins to provide the client and family with health information concerning the client's health status and availability of and access to community resources. In the case of the home health visit, the nurse provides skilled nursing care. At the end of the initial home visit, the nurse discusses with the client the need for another home visit. The nurse and client discuss the goal of the next visit, specifically, what the client is to do before the visit. The client and family are informed about any information or skills the nurse will provide during the next visit, and the nurse and client agree on a day for the next visit.

Referral for Community Services
During the first visit, the nurse provides the client and family with information regarding community resources, including the purpose of the resources, services provided, eligibility, any involved expense, and agency telephone numbers. Referrals depend on the availability of community resources, eligibility of the client for the services, willingness of the client to use the resources, and suitability of the resources for the client. Examples of such services include information about immunization clinics for children in the family, adult day health care or senior centers for elderly clients who could benefit from socialization, adult education classes or continuation high school for pregnant teen clients who have dropped out of high school, or Meals-On-Wheels services for clients who are not able to prepare lunches.

If necessary, the client or client's family may request assistance from the nurse in contacting the community resources. The client and family are encouraged to make the contacts, but if the client and family are unable to make the calls or do not speak English, the nurse needs to intervene on behalf of the client. By providing referral information during the first home visit, the nurse can follow-up during the next home visit on the success of the client or family in contacting and using community services.

Terminating the Visit
The nurse terminates the first visit when the assessment is completed and a plan for care is established with the client. The average first visit should not be longer than 1 hour. Much information is provided

to the client during that hour, and much information is collected by the nurse. Most clients are tired by the end of a 1-hour visit and often cannot retain any additional information provided by the nurse. It is preferable to set a date for another home visit to reinforce information provided and work progressively toward achieving goals.

EVALUATION

Evaluation of Progress Toward Goals
The evaluation process is continuous and allows the nurse to determine the success or progress toward the goals identified for the client. Input from the client is critical to determine whether the goals established are realistic and achievable for the client.

Modifications of the Plan as Needed
The evaluation process also allows the nurse and client or family to discuss what is working well and where modifications are needed in the plan. Evaluation occurs through open communication between the nurse and client, with the nurse asking questions about specific parts of the care plan. If a trust relationship exists, the client feels comfortable in telling the nurse if there are problems in the care plan.

When Goals Have Been Achieved
The overall purpose of home visits is to assist the client with the information and nursing care that is necessary for the client to function successfully without interventions by the nurse. When the care plan goals have been achieved, the nurse is no longer needed by the client. The client knows what community resources are available and how to access health care services for primary, secondary, and tertiary interventions.

APPLICATION OF THE NURSING PROCESS THROUGH HOME VISITS

Three case studies are presented. Two public health visits—one communicable disease follow-up and one involving an ante partum client—and one home health care visit—posthospitalization follow-up—are followed through case studies.

Case Study 1

Public Health Visit: Communicable Disease Follow-up

The public health nurse receives a referral from the county hospital to see Ray, a 57-year-old white man who was recently diagnosed with tuberculosis. The first purpose of the referral to the public health nurse is to meet with the client to ensure that he received the appropriate information about tuberculosis and is followed for medical care on a regular basis. The second purpose of the referral is for the public health nurse to meet with Ray and identify people with whom he has been in close contact. The nurse then establishes contact with these people, notifies them that they have been exposed to tuberculosis, and encourages them to have follow-up tests for tuberculosis from health care providers.

The nurse contacts Ray and establishes a time for the home visit. The nurse notes that he resides in a residential hotel in a lower-middle-class neighborhood of a large urban area. During the visit, the nurse discovers that the client is an unemployed construction worker. He has no knowledge of where he might have contracted tuberculosis. Ray assures the nurse that he is compliant with taking his medications. He gives the nurse the names of his friends with whom he plays poker every week at a hotel and tells the nurse that he has told these friends to be tested for tuberculosis. The nurse makes a note of the names, and later talks with them individually by telephone. During these subsequent conversations, the nurse is very careful to maintain the client's confidentiality. The nurse informs these individuals that they may have been exposed to tuberculosis and of the importance of testing for them, by either their health care providers or their local health department.

Ray indicates to the nurse that he has no family, and other than his friends at the hotel, he has minimal contact with other people. The nurse records this information onto the communicable disease form and returns the information to the public health department's communicable disease division.

Assessment

Assessment by the public health nurse of the client with a communicable disease involves assessment at the individual, family, and community levels.

Individual The public health nurse assesses whether the client receives appropriate information and regular medical care for tuberculosis and whether the client follows the prescribed treatment regimen.

Family Although Ray states that he has no family, his friends in the hotel constitute a working support network. The public health nurse is familiar with kinship networks and with their importance as alternative family systems (Stack, 1974). Nursing assessment of Ray's kinship network involves determining whether the members have been tested for tuberculosis. In addition, the public health nurse assesses the client's network for the following:

● Network composition
● Network's knowledge of tuberculosis
● Functional capacity
● Network stressors
● Network strengths and weaknesses

- Network's ability to provide support for Ray
- Health beliefs and practices
- Use of health services

Community The public health nurse is aware that the number of new cases of tuberculosis in the community has increased over the past 12 months. The public health nurse further notes that there has been an increase in the number of area residents immigrating from various Third World countries and that this population may be at increased risk for the development of tuberculosis (Dowling, 1991).

Diagnosis

Individual The public health nurse determines that Ray has a knowledge deficit regarding the disease process and transmission of tuberculosis.

Family Ray's support network demonstrates knowledge deficits related to the disease process and transmission of tuberculosis, location of communicable disease clinics, and the importance of screening for persons exposed to tuberculosis.

Community The public health nurse, in conjunction with case workers at the communicable disease clinic, formulates the following diagnosis for Ray's community: increased risk for development of tuberculosis among community residents, as evidenced by increased incidence of new cases of tuberculosis over the past 12 months.

Planning and Goals

Individual

Short-term Goal
- Client will verbalize knowledge of transmission of tuberculosis; signs and symptoms of complications of tuberculosis; purpose, administration schedule, and side effects of medications.

Long-term Goal
- Client will perform self-care activities related to treatment of tuberculosis and follow-up as necessary with appropriate health care professionals.

Family

Short-term Goal
- Support network members will demonstrate basic knowledge of cause and transmission of tuberculosis and will agree to be tested for tuberculosis.

Long-term Goal
- Support network members with positive test results will receive appropriate treatment.

Community

Short-term Goal
- Community members will demonstrate knowledge of increased incidence of tuberculosis in their community and of

available community resources for treatment and prevention of tuberculosis.

Long-term Goal
- Incidence of tuberculosis in the community will decrease over the next 3 years.

Intervention

Implementation of the plan of care for the client with tuberculosis occurs at the individual, family, and community levels.

Individual The public health nurse refers Ray to the communicable disease clinic of the local health department. Because tuberculosis is a reportable communicable disease, the public health nurse obtains information from the client regarding persons with whom he has been in close contact.

Family The public health nurse contacts members of Ray's support network and refers them to the communicable disease clinic as appropriate. The nurse provides these persons with information concerning transmission of tuberculosis and of the importance of early treatment and follow-up.

Community The public health nurse meets with professionals from the communicable disease clinic and from the health department and with members of the community to establish a program to raise public awareness regarding the increased incidence of tuberculosis in the community. The public will be informed of the importance of preventive measures, of the availability of community screening services for tuberculosis, and of existing health care resources in the community.

Evaluation

The client's and support network's knowledge of the disease process, transmission, treatment, and signs and symptoms of tuberculosis are indicators used in evaluating the plan of care. Confirmation of follow-up with the communicable disease clinic by the client and members of his support network can also be used for evaluation.

The incidence rate of tuberculosis in the community and the rate of use of tuberculosis clinics and related resources are measures that can be used to evaluate the effectiveness of interventions at the aggregate level.

Levels of Prevention

Primary prevention of communicable disease is directed to prevention of the occurrence of specific diseases such as tuberculosis. Programs that increase public awareness of the disease process and of the transmission, diagnosis, and treatment of tuberculosis constitute primary prevention activities. The goal of secondary prevention is early detection of existing conditions. Tuberculin skin testing and subsequent follow-up of positive test results are important secondary prevention measures. The tertiary level of prevention is aimed at reducing the effects and spread of tuberculosis. Referral for early, effective treatment and education of clients for self-care are important measures of tertiary prevention.

C a s e
S t u d y
2

Public Health Home Visit

Ante Partum Client The public health nurse receives a referral to see a 17-year-old black girl, Ali, who is referred by the county prenatal clinic. Ali is 5 months pregnant with her third pregnancy within the past year. Ali miscarried the previous two pregnancies during the first trimester.

When the nurse makes the home visit, she notes Ali to be 5 feet and 9 inches tall and 120 pounds. She resides in a two-room apartment with her boyfriend, who is the father of the baby. The nurse begins the first visit with social talk, asking Ali general questions about her employment, education, and duration of her residence in the area. Ali appears to be pleased that the nurse is interested in her. Once a trusting relationship is initiated, the nurse asks Ali how she feels about the pregnancy. Ali reveals that she is happy about the pregnancy but is worried that there will be problems because of her two previous miscarriages. She had not planned any of the pregnancies but did not use contraceptives to prevent the pregnancies. Ali's boyfriend works and is able to pay the rent and buy food for her. Ali dropped out of high school during her junior year but would like to complete her high school education. She has Medicaid coverage for her health care.

During the initial home visit, the nurse assesses that Ali is underweight and that she has several knowledge deficits in the areas of prenatal nutrition, infant care, breast-feeding, and contraception. The nurse also identifies the need for a referral to the public school for continuation of Ali's high school education. The nurse briefly discusses her assessment with Ali in a nonthreatening, nonjudgmental manner. The nurse informs Ali that if she is interested, she can schedule future home visits to provide Ali with more information and to answer Ali's questions. Ali agrees to future visits to discuss the topics that have been identified by the nurse during the assessment phase. The plan for future visits is mutually agreed on. As the visits progress, the nurse and Ali modify the plan based on evaluation of progress.

The nurse terminates home visits with Ali when the mutually established goals are achieved. The nurse schedules a postpartum visit with Ali after the baby is born to assess the infant care provided and to answer any questions that Ali has concerning infant care.

Assessment

Although it is important to perform an individual assessment of Ali, the public health nurse assesses Ali as a member of a family and as a member of the community. "Community" in this case refers to the aggregate of publicly insured adolescent pregnant women.

Individual Individual assessment of Ali reveals an underweight 17-year-old pregnant girl who is unable to demonstrate knowledge of nutrition in pregnancy, infant care, breast-feeding, contraception, or educational options for pregnant teenagers.

Family An individual assessment of Ali mandates the need for an assessment of the composition and function of Ali's family. The public health nurse will assess the following factors with regard to Ali's family (Logan, 1986):

- Family composition
- General support network
- Family and network patterns related to psychosocial and economic support of Ali
- Family and network attitude toward health
- Family and network beliefs regarding use of health-related services
- Beliefs and attitudes of family and network regarding infant care, breast-feeding, and nutrition
- Attitudes of father of baby regarding involvement with Ali and the baby, health beliefs, ability to assume role of parent, and knowledge of pregnancy and birth

Community The public health nurse is aware of the need to see the larger, aggregate picture. Identifying the aggregate as the pregnant adolescent community, the public health nurse uses the following techniques in an ongoing assessment (Bayne, 1985):

- Observations
- Resource analysis
- Key informant interviews
- Environmental indices

Using the above techniques, the public health nurse gathers information regarding the following:

- Educational and employment options for pregnant teens and teens with infants
- Availability of health services designed specifically for pregnant teenagers and their infants
- Availability of health services targeting low-birth-weight infants
- Availability of support groups for this aggregate
- Availability of teen parenting classes

Diagnosis

The public health nurse formulates nursing diagnoses based on thorough individual, family, and community assessments.

Individual The following individual nursing diagnoses were formulated for Ali:

- Knowledge deficit regarding nutrition in pregnancy, infant care and feeding, contraception, availability of community resources, and educational options for pregnant teenagers.
- Inadequate nutrition related to low-income status and inadequate knowledge of nutritional requirements of pregnancy

Family The public health nurse formulated the following diagnosis for Ali and her family:

- Lack of family support related to Ali living away from home
- Altered family communication patterns related to role confusion among family members

Community The public health nurse formulated the following diagnoses for the pregnant adolescent community:

- Minimal availability of health care services, parenting classes, contraception counseling, and educational opportunities for pregnant teenagers
- Lack of coordination of existing services

Planning

Planning health services and interventions for pregnant teenagers involves formulation of short-term goals and long-term goals for the individual, family, and community.

Individual

Short-term Goals
- Ali will gain at least 3 pounds per month (Olds et al., 1980).
- Ali will demonstrate knowledge of community resources for pregnant adolescents by next nursing visit.

Long-term Goal
- Ali will carry her infant to term without evidence of maternal or fetal complications.

Family

Short-term Goal
- Ali and her partner will attend teen parenting classes.

Long-term Goal
- Ali, her partner, and other family members will be able to perform mutually determined role responsibilities.

Community

Short-term Goals
- Increased community awareness of resources for pregnant teenagers.
- Increased awareness of contraception counseling services for adolescents.

Long-term Goals
- Establishment of effective, comprehensive prenatal health, contraception, and education services for pregnant teenagers.
- Decline in rate of teen pregnancies and birth of compromised neonates over next 24 months.

Intervention

Implementation of the individual plan of care for Ali involves visits by the public health nurse with referral to existing prenatal services for pregnant teenagers. Family intervention comprises referral of Ali and the father of the baby to a support group for pregnant teenagers and partners. Implementation of the plan of care for the aggregate of adolescent pregnant women includes the following:

- Meeting with community leaders
- Meeting with local school administrators and faculty to disseminate information for pregnant teenagers
- Formation of community organizing groups (Bayne, 1985)

Evaluation

Evaluation includes measures of nutritional status of individual teenagers and of the use of support groups and educational and nutritional services by teenagers and their families. Evaluation of the effectiveness of interventions at the aggregate level focuses on measurement of availability of options for pregnant teenagers, measures of teen awareness and use of services, and determination of changes in incidence rates of teen pregnancy and compromised neonates.

Levels of Prevention

Prevention of teenage pregnancy involves interventions at primary, secondary, and tertiary levels. At the primary level, prevention comprises activities that prevent teen pregnancy from occurring. The secondary level of prevention involves interventions for early detection of teen pregnancy and early intervention such as counseling for prenatal care and availability of pregnancy termination services. The goal of prevention at the tertiary level is to reduce the effects of adolescent pregnancy. Examples of tertiary prevention for pregnant teenagers include provision of prenatal education in areas such as nutrition, parenting, and infant care.

C a s e
S t u d y
3

Home Health Care Home Visit

Bea, a 48-year-old black woman, is referred to a visiting nurse service by her physician on discharge from a local acute care hospital. The referral indicates a primary diagnosis of "status post myocardial infarction" with a secondary diagnosis of "non–insulin-dependent diabetes mellitus." Information provided on the referral form indicates that Bea has had poorly controlled diabetes for the past 10 years. She has a history of hypertension, which is now controlled, and had a cerebrovascular accident 3 years ago with no residual functional impairment. Bea's medical and nursing care is paid by Medicaid. The following medications are listed on the referral form: 5 mg isordil q.i.d., 25 mg hydrochlorothiazide q.d., 5 mg micronase b.i.d., and 0.4 mg nitroglycerin sublingually as needed for chest pain. Bea's prescribed diet is a 1,500-calorie American Diabetic Association (ADA) diet with no added salt.

On the way to Bea's home, the nurse notes that the neighborhood is severely distressed as evidenced by overt drug activity. Many homes are in need of repair, and garbage litters the streets in most areas. There is an obvious lack of supermarkets and discount drug stores and only one small convenience market within walking distance of Bea's home.

After entering the home, the nurse initiates social talk with Bea, asking her open-ended questions about how she is doing now that she is home and if she is having any problems. Before proceeding further with the visit, the nurse obtains Bea's signature on the consent form, verifies the Medicaid number, and compares Bea's medications with those listed on the referral form. The nurse then performs a thorough physical, family, environmental, and functional assessment. This assessment reveals an obese black woman with stable vital signs who has been free of chest pain for more than 24 hours, has a visual impairment due to diabetes, and has experienced a random fingerstick blood glucose of 320 mg/dL.

Bea resides in a small, single-family dwelling. She has difficulty taking her medication because of poor visual acuity. Bea demonstrates a severe knowledge deficit regarding the purpose and side effects of her medications. She cannot identify the signs and symptoms of hyperglycemia or hypoglycemia. She is unable to select a 1,500-calorie diabetic diet and cannot discuss dietary sources of concentrated sugar, saturated fat, salt, and cholesterol.

Bea lives with her 18-year-old son and 15-year-old daughter. Her daughter assists Bea with her medications. The daughter is able to demonstrate the ability to give Bea her medications correctly.

Bea is a single parent with many friends and family members on whom she relies for support. She is active in her church. Bea ambulates with a cane due to muscle weakness and is unable to walk more than 15 feet without becoming tired. Her poor vision makes it difficult to negotiate the five stairs in front of her home without help.

The nurse establishes a plan of care with input and agreement from Bea. The nurse will visit Bea three times a week to assist Bea with the following:

- Assess fasting blood glucose level.
- Provide diet instruction to Bea and to her daughter, who prepares meals.
- Provide instruction on medications.
- Evaluate comprehension of the instruction.
- Assess Bea's physical status with emphasis on her cardiovascular system.

Referrals will be made to an ophthalmologist for evaluation of Bea's visual acuity, to a dietitian for personalized diet evaluation and instruction, and to a physical therapist for musculoskeletal strengthening and proper use of assist devices. Bea's family agreed to accompany her to a series of informational classes entitled "Living With Diabetes" that were sponsored by the community outreach department of a local hospital. There is no fee for attending the classes.

The nurse also assesses Bea's teenage children to determine how they are coping with their mother's illness. A plan and interventions are determined for the children based on the nurse's assessment.

Assessment

The nurse assesses Bea as an individual but extends the assessment to include Bea as a member of a family and a member of the community. Community in this case can be defined as the aggregate of blacks diagnosed with diabetes mellitus.

Individual Individual assessment of Bea should include the following:

- Fasting and random serum glucose
- Measurement of vital signs
- Nutritional history
- Bea's knowledge of disease process of non–insulin-dependent diabetes mellitus

- Bea's ability to safely administer medications
- Bea's ability to perform fingerstick glucose test and interpret results
- Evaluation of biological systems
- Bea's functional status

Family Assessment of Bea's family should include the following (Daniel, 1986):

- Family composition
- Family strengths and weaknesses
- Health status of family members
- Effects of family support on Bea's management of her diabetes and on Bea's use of health services
- Family members' perceptions of health and illness
- Family health promotion activities
- Family health care use patterns
- Family as open or closed system
- Family communication patterns
- Family use of community resources
- Roles of family members
- Family stressors
- Degree of family unity
- Income
- Cultural background
- Relationship of family to the community
- Family nutritional patterns/priorities
- Housing
- Safety

Community The community health nurse must be able to define the community targeted for assessment (Spradley, 1990). Community assessment of the aggregate of blacks with diabetes mellitus includes the following:

- Availability of culturally relevant health care for this aggregate
- Availability of educational services for blacks with diabetes
- Prevalence of diabetes mellitus in the community in general compared with the prevalence in the black community
- Availability of culturally relevant nutritional counseling and exercise programs for publicly insured citizens with diabetes

Diagnosis

The nursing diagnosis for Bea includes individual, family, and aggregate aspects. The community health nurse uses a holistic approach in formulating nursing diagnoses.

Individual Knowledge deficit regarding purpose and side effects of medications; knowledge deficit regarding selection of appropriate foods from 1,500-calorie ADA diet.

Family Family knowledge deficit regarding disease process and management of diabetes mellitus.

Community Lack of available education and screening services for publicly insured blacks with diabetes mellitus.

Planning

The plan of care for Bea, her family, and her community includes both long- and short-term goals.

Individual

Short-term Goal
- Client will verbalize five sources of concentrated dietary sugar by the third nursing visit.

Long-term Goals
- Fasting blood glucose will remain within normal limits.
- Client will ambulate in home without tiring.

Family

Short-term Goal
- Client's daughter will verbalize principles of 1,500-calorie ADA diet.

Long-term Goal
- Client and family will be able to effectively use available health care services.

Community Lack of readily accessible screening programs and culturally relevant educational programs for the aggregate of blacks at risk for developing diabetes mellitus.

Intervention

Implementation of the plan of care for Bea is carried out at the individual, family, and community levels.

Individual The community health nurse schedules visits over the next 8 weeks to instruct Bea in the purpose and side effects of her medications. In addition, the nurse teaches Bea about the signs and symptoms of hyperglycemia and hypoglycemia, and food selection for ADA diet and refers Bea to an ophthalmologist.

Family The community health nurse makes every effort to schedule visits when the client's daughter and other family and network members are present to provide the family with information regarding diabetic education classes and availability of health care facilities in the community.

Community

- Meet with local ADA representatives
- Meet with community leaders
- Advocate with local leaders for readily accessible screening programs and culturally relevant diabetes education for this aggregate
- Work with community leaders for formulation and implementation of programs to increase public awareness of signs and symptoms of diabetes mellitus

Evaluation

Evaluation of the plan of care for the individual, family, and aggregate in this case includes physiological measures of well-being, evaluation of the degree of comprehension and assimilation of health information by the client and her family, and survey of expanded options for blacks with diabetes mellitus.

Levels of Prevention

Prevention of diabetes mellitus and its complications is practiced at the primary, secondary, and tertiary levels.

Primary Primary prevention measures for diabetes mellitus consist of efforts to prevent the occurrence of the disease. Although diabetes mellitus is often a hereditary condition, alteration of risk factors such as obesity and lack of physical activity can delay and, in some cases, indefinitely postpone the development of non–insulin-dependent diabetes mellitus and its complications (Kiehn et al., 1976). Nutrition counseling for the prevention and reduction of obesity as well as exercise programs that promote establishment of regular routines of physical activity would be appropriate primary preventive measures.

Secondary The goal of secondary prevention is to detect disease in its earliest stage. Early case finding and early treatment are appropriate activities associated with secondary prevention for non–insulin-dependent diabetes mellitus. Increased availability of blood glucose screening, with referral to appropriate health care and nutritional counseling services, are fundamental components of secondary prevention.

Tertiary Tertiary prevention concerns the reduction of the effects of disease. Increasing the availability of support groups, health care resources, nutrition counseling, and self-care education programs for individuals with non–insulin-dependent diabetes mellitus are appropriate measures of tertiary prevention.

SUMMARY

This chapter presented information on performing both public health and home health nursing visits to clients in their homes. A general overview of the nursing process for clients in the home setting was presented and then expanded to include the individual, family, and community. Case studies were presented for clients with communicable disease, teen pregnancy, and diabetes. The home visit, the foundation of community health nursing, provides the forum for important interventions, not only with individuals and families but also with communities. The community health nurse has the responsibility to bring the concerns of individuals and families with whom she visits into the community.

Learning Activities

1. Make arrangements to accompany both a public health nurse and a home health nurse on home visits.

2. Interview a public health nurse about the types of client referrals received and ask what interventions are usually performed. Repeat this activity with a home health nurse. Ask both nurses what they like best about their jobs.

REFERENCES

Bayne, T.: The pregnant school-age community. *In* Higgs, A. R., and Gustafson, D. D., eds.: Community as Client: Assessment and Diagnosis. Philadelphia, F. A. Davis, 1985, pp. 129–134.

Cattran, J. M., Gala, J., and Kellogg, R. Family-centered nursing in the home. *In* Logan, B. B., and Dawkins, C. E., eds.: Family-Centered Nursing in the Community. Menlo Park, California, Addison-Wesley, 1986, pp. 431–460.

Daniel, L. L.: Family assessment. *In* Logan, B. B., and Dawkins, C. E., eds.: Family-Centered Nursing in the Community. Menlo Park, California, Addison-Wesley, 1986, pp. 183–208.

Dowling, P. T.: Return of tuberculosis: Screening and preventive therapy. Am. Family Phys. *43*;457–467, 1991.

Finnegan, L., and Ervin, N. E.: An epidemiological approach to community assessment. Public Health Nurs. *6*;147–151, 1989.

Higgs, A. R., and Gustafson, D. D., eds.: Community as Client: Assessment and Diagnosis. Philadelphia, F. A. Davis, 1985.

Kalisch, P. A., and Kalisch, B. J.: The Advance of American Nursing. Boston, Little, Brown & Co, 1978.

Keating, S. B., and Kelman, G. B.: Home Health Care Nursing. Philadelphia, J. B. Lippincott, 1988.

Kelly, L. Y.: Dimensions of Professional Nursing. New York, Macmillan Publishing, 1985.

Kiehn, T. G., Anderson, J. W., and Ward, K.: Beneficial effects of a high-carbohydrate, high-fiber diet on hyperglycemic diabetic men. Am. J. Clin. Nutr. *29*;895–899, 1976.

Lockhart, C. A.: Family-focused community health nursing services in the home. *In* Archer, S. E., and Fleshman, R. P., eds.: Community Health Nursing. 3rd Ed. Monterey, California, Wadsworth Health Sciences, 1985, pp. 272–294.

Logan, B. B.: Adolescent pregnancy. *In* Logan, B. B., and Dawkins, C. E., eds.: Family-Centered Nursing in the Community. Menlo Park, California, Addison-Wesley, 1986, pp. 635–667.

Oda, D. S.: Home visits: Effective or obsolete nursing practice? Nurs. Res. *38*;121–123, 1989.

Olds, S. B., London, M. L., Ladewig, P. A., and Davidson, S. V.: Obstetric Nursing. Menlo Park, California, Addison-Wesley, 1980.

Spradley, B. W.: Community Health Nursing: Concepts and Practice. 3rd Ed. Glenview, Illinois, Scott, Foresman/Little, Brown, 1990.

Stack, C.: All Our Kin. New York, Harper & Row, 1974.

U.S. Department of Commerce/International Trade Administration, Health and Medical Services: U.S. Industrial Outlook. Washington, D.C., U.S. Documents, 1990.

CHAPTER

9

Health Education

Upon completion of this chapter, the reader will be able to:

1. Select a learning theory, and describe its application to an individual, family, or aggregate.

2. Identify teaching skills or strategies that exemplify client-centered health education for individual, family, or aggregate as the client.

3. Identify resources of health education materials appropriate for a given individual, family, or community as client.

4. Compare and contrast Freire's approach to health education with an individualistic health education model.

5. Prepare a teaching plan and evaluation criteria for individual, family, and aggregate.

6. Discuss the role of the nurse as health educator within a political and social context.

Sandra DeBella

Nurses are health educators, and in many situations the role of the community health nurse is primarily that of educator. Part of a nurse's professional responsibility is to dispense vast amounts of health information (DeBella, 1988). The character of the information shared with clients varies, ranging from highly technical explanations of treatment or medication protocols to basic information regarding access to needed health care services. The commitment of the nursing profession to health promotion, health maintenance, and disease prevention supports the essential role of health education in community health nursing. Health education is primarily a specialized communication process, and nursing emphasizes the concepts of communication and process within its practice.

The community health nurse as health educator has specialized skills and the goal of establishing a partnership for health with the client. This partnership includes self-care for individuals and aggregates through empowerment to make health care choices; this perspective connotes a reciprocal relationship between the nurse and the client. This creates a climate of respect for the client, which fosters an understanding of the differences in client motivations. This perspective also presents the goal of assisting clients to achieve optimum well-being through their own actions and decisions. The broad concepts of empowerment that are implicit in this approach to health care and health education facilitate a client's ability to improve personal or aggregate living conditions; make informed decisions about personal, family, or community health practices; and use appropriate health care services.

Another professional goal of the community health nurse is to integrate health education into practice, recognizing that health education encourages the practice of healthy lifestyle behaviors that prevent both acute and chronic illnesses. Thus, health education is not just information dissemination but rather a process of facilitating health care decision making. The outcome of successful health education endeavors should be the change of selected behaviors to support healthier living.

The community health nurse sees health education as one of the categories of activities aimed at health promotion and disease prevention. Other categories are environmental health and safety measures and preventive health services such as family planning and immunization programs. Health education is a dimension of these other categories, and all of these activities must be integrated into a community to improve health and social conditions. The community health nurse also recognizes that counseling and education are complementary nursing functions.

HEALTH AS A PERSONAL VALUE WITHIN A SOCIAL CONTEXT

To understand health education, one must understand health and education and their respective implications. One definition of health is presented by the World Health Organization (WHO): "Health is a state of complete physical, mental, and social well being, not merely the absence of disease" (1958). This definition is accepted as a goal by many, yet it is controversial in its scope and direction. Health from this perspective is not the product of the health care system but rather a concept that reflects the values of society. This view of health is both qualitative and quantitative; health is measured both in numbers, e.g., physicians' visits, days of work missed, or years of life, and by factors such as satisfaction with life, hope, and personal and community goals (North Bay Health Systems Agency [NBHSA], 1980).

The health field concept introduced by Marc Lalonde, then Minister of the National Health and Welfare in Canada, is a framework that reflects this definition. This health field framework classifies the determinants of health as follows:

- Human biology, including the physical and mental aspects of health developed within an individual as a result of an individual's basic biology and organic makeup. Included are genetic inheritance, processes of maturation, and the internal systems of the body.
- Environment, including physical and other factors related to health that are external to the body and over which the individual has little control. Examples are food, drugs, air and water quality, noise pollution, communicable disease, garbage and sewage disposal, and much of the social environment.
- Health care organizations, including the quantity, quality, arrangement, nature, and relation-

ships of people and resources in the provision of health care. Usually referred to as the health care system, it includes providers, institutions, and services of a medical nature.

- Lifestyle, including the aggregate of decisions made by the individuals that affect their health and over which they more or less have control. Personal desires and habits that are not good from a health point of view create self-imposed risks. When these risks result in illness or death, the person's lifestyle can be said to have contributed to the illness (Lalonde, 1974).

This focus on lifestyle is based on two assumptions:

- Responsibility for personal health rests primarily with the individual, not with the government, physicians and hospitals, or third-party payor systems. Meaningful health policies must be directed toward increasing the individual's sense of responsibility for health and ability to understand and cope with health issues.
- If the individual's responsibility is to be effectively discharged, it must be supported by social policies designed to provide environmental protection, health information, and access to health care when needed (NBHSA, 1980).

As described in Chapter 4, another perspective is presented by Dr. Nancy Milio, a community health nurse educator who has for many years emphasized the need for community health nurses to be involved in policy making as direct care for populations. Her six propositions emphasize the need to recognize that all individual client health care decisions are made within a societal context. It is a challenge to the community health nurse to address both aspects of this perspective on health —the individual's responsibility and society's responsibility to support and inform the individual, family, or aggregate so they can make the best decisions for their well-being. For individuals and communities to take responsibility for health, education is a prerequisite.

Marilyn Ferguson sums up an approach to learning and its relationship to health when she states, "Learning is not only like health, it is health" (1980). According to Ferguson, if we are not learning and teaching, we are not awake and alive. She also points out some of the pitfalls of our

institutionalized educational system, which influences our approach to education in many different situations. Often, our system emphasizes being right at the expense of being open. "Dis-ease," or not feeling comfortable with ourselves, may begin in a classroom setting. In contrast with an educational system that seeks to adjust the individual to the society as it exists, humanistic educators maintain that society should value the uniqueness and autonomy of its members.

Health education is essential to any effort to promote healthful lifestyles. Our understanding of health education is as a holistic process with intellectual, psychological, and social dimensions relating to activities that increase the abilities of people to make informed decisions that affect their personal, family, and community well-being. This understanding of health education acknowledges the effectiveness of working with the family and the community in settings such as schools, community organizations, work settings, and peer groups.

COMMUNITY SETTINGS

A 1987 Centers for Disease Control report on the National Adolescent Student Health Survey noted that teenagers' understanding of health-related issues is related to the amount of time that schools devote to such topics. The implications for these findings suggest that schools, in particular middle schools and high schools, may be able to reduce the incidence of illness and death from preventable causes such as heart disease and sexually transmitted diseases by educating adolescents about healthier lifestyles. Because of the documented prevalence of sexually transmitted diseases in the adolescent population as well as the recognition that adolescence is a period of behavioral experimentation, adolescents are identified as a population at high risk for HIV infection.

Another 1987 survey of high school adolescents in San Francisco revealed that 92% of the students surveyed knew that sex was a primary means of transmission for HIV infection (DiClemente, 1989). However, only 60% of these students were aware that the use of condoms reduces the risk of HIV infection; 88% of the students surveyed stated that they believed that education was the best way to prevent AIDS, and they wanted AIDS education in their curriculum. The researchers conducting this survey made some very cogent conclusions regarding the need for AIDS education in our schools. Knowledge alone has not been demonstrated to be a powerful mediator of behavior change; however, it is an essential prerequisite for such change.

Health educators, including community health nurses, recognize the value of community groups such as schools in providing the type of education needed to address high-risk populations such as adolescents. They believe that HIV prevention curricula must go beyond conveying information and dispelling myths to fostering individual and group decision making as it relates to risk management and high-risk behaviors. Some of the educational strategies used successfully in these settings are classroom presentations and discussions, peer counseling, support groups, and self-help groups. This proactive perspective on health education can be adapted for many lifestyle health education groups, such as smoking cessation, nutrition and weight control, and exercise and stress reduction.

HEALTHIER LIFESTYLES

Since the mid-1960s there has been a growing awareness of the value of a healthy lifestyle. A lifestyle in which Americans eat more nutritious food, smoke less, maintain proper weight, and exercise regularly would improve health more than the use of physicians or medicine. Throughout the 1970s and 1980s, there was consistent awareness of the role of health education in supporting a healthier lifestyle. The Bureau of Health Education was established in 1974 to provide leadership and coordinate program development in the areas of smoking and health, community program development, and professional consultation. The National Center for Health Education was established in 1975 as an independent nonprofit organization to serve as a national focal point for public education. In 1976, the National Consumer Health Information and Health Promotion Act established the Office of Health Information and Health Promotion in the Office of the Assistant Secretary of Health to provide a national program of health information. In 1976, the Surgeon General's report *Healthy People* called for setting specific health objectives and goals for designated populations.

In the 1980s, during Surgeon General Everett Koop's tenure as the chief public health officer, he was very direct in his support of individual health through the support of social policies that created healthier social and physical environments. Koop fostered national policies that reflected changed attitudes toward lifestyle choices such as tobacco and alcohol use. Policies that prohibit smoking in public buildings, schools, hospitals, and theaters and during air flights of less than 2 hours' duration provide the social reinforcement to not smoke or to quit smoking. Koop's report in 1989 reinforced previous warnings about all types of tobacco use with the addition of noting smoking as an addiction. Social pressure is one of the most influential reasons given by people in their choice to quit smoking. Another example of a change in social attitudes that was formalized by Koop in a Spring 1989 report was a recommendation that the level of blood alcohol used as an index of the legal level of intoxication be reduced.

Another example of public policy informing individuals to assist them in making better personal health decisions is the 1989 California legislation that mandates that all retailers of alcoholic beverages post a warning sign about the hazards of drinking while pregnant.

HEALTH AS A CULTURAL VALUE

What constitutes health in any given society is determined by that group's values and perspective. Other chapters address the cultural determinants of health, so only a few examples will be presented here.

A "New Age" view of health might be defined as a health promotion attitude that strives for a balanced sense of well-being. Thus, health is viewed as a harmony of life forces or energies. Health as well-being promotes the peak experience of the individual or group. This view of health has come to express itself in many forms: a quest for physical fitness, a greater awareness of nutrition, the importance of stress management, and a concern for the preservation of natural resources such as air, water, and open space. This holistic view of health informs the attitudes and behaviors of many Americans and influences society in numerous ways ranging from support of alternate methods of healing to support of legislation for clean air and water.

This view challenges traditional science-based health care by placing health in a social, ecological, and political context rather than in a medical treatment context.

In contrast to this proactive New Age, or holistic, view of health is the health experience of the rural population of Rabun Gap in Appalachia. The life experiences and beliefs of this rural community were first chronicled for the public in the Foxfire books (e.g., Wiggington, 1968; Wiggington and Bennett, 1986), which grew out of a school project for the local students. Subsequent books describe their crafts, skills, and views of their community, providing a real feel for their culture. Several books contain chapters on home remedies. The remedies, although used by the community, are not presented as alternatives to modern medicine but rather to show the resourcefulness of a community isolated from traditional medicine. The healers and healing practices of this small, rural community represent a cultural experience of a highly independent, self-reliant group. One healer, Mrs. Youngblood, is an individual from this community who typifies a "mountain woman." She carries about her the air of gentle pride and of wisdom that results from having grown up with the severity of the harsh mountain life and its lack of modern conveniences. Her knowledge of herbal remedies and understanding of the body's natural healing powers are impressive (Wiggington, 1986). Many other cultural groups have their own healing traditions; the Mexican-American, Asian, and African-American health experiences are described in other chapters in this text.

These examples are presented to highlight the idea that the U.S. culture is composed of very disparate groups; our society is not homogenous, so our health care beliefs and practices are diverse. For the community nurse, this difference is reason for always seeking the client's view of health before proceeding with health education. When working with a client or community, it is imperative to understand the cultural values in which health beliefs are rooted.

LEARNING THEORIES AND STRATEGIES

The application of teaching principles to the process of communication creates teaching. Learning is a lifelong process of change. Theories of teaching and learning reflect different assumptions about the learner, the processes of teaching and learning, and the proposed goals of teaching and learning. Teaching is presented as a process that succeeds in enabling students to learn. The teaching process consists of five steps that parallel those of the nursing process:

Nursing Process	Teaching Process
Data collection Assessment Nursing diagnosis	Learning needs assessment Readiness to learn; motivation
Planning	Objectives and goals
Intervention	Teaching strategies and skills
Evaluation	Behavior change; better decision making

There are many learning theories. Some theories are more consistent with community health nursing's approach to client care; these will be explored in this chapter. Some learning theories, however, because of their theoretical perspective, are narrow in their application to community health nursing's emphasis on health education.

CONCEPTS OF TEACHING AND LEARNING

Health teaching is a specialized communication process that is directed toward improving the learner's health behaviors. Learning can be defined as a change in health behavior resulting from new information, new experiences, or practice (Blattner, 1981). Teaching comprises those activities that provide the new information, new experiences, or the opportunity to practice the new skill. Thus, teaching and learning are not separate activities, although the choice of emphasizing learning or teaching as the starting point involves being aware of the real, although subtle, difference between the two.

Theories of learning emphasize the relationship between the teacher and the learner as well as the nature of the material to be learned. The discussion of the following theories of learning serves to illustrate this point.

The *stimulus–response* learning theory originated in the 1920s in psychological experiments with animals. In these experiments, stimulation of a reflex response unrelated to the needs of the animal, e.g., salivating at the sound of a bell, was rewarded. This was the era of classic conditioning followed by the operant conditioning of B. F. Skinner. Operant conditioning involved animals acting on their environment, e.g., pushing buttons or pulling levers for food pellets. Conditioning does not include intent or motivation, only positive or negative reinforcement of the behavior. Operant conditioning is the theory behind learning strategies such as programmed learning, behavior modification, or aversion therapy. Feedback loops, positive reinforcement, and reinforcement to prevent skill extinction are all concepts garnered from stimulus–response learning theory (Bigge, 1980).

Cognitive field, or Gestalt learning theory, was proposed by Kurt Lewin in the 1940s. Lewin's cognitive theory of learning includes an existential approach to the world; the individual exists in the individual's chosen perceived reality. Meaningful learning takes place within the context of the learner's "life space." Life space contains the individual and the individual's psychological environment, goals sought, things avoided, and barriers to the goals. Cognitive field theory integrates biological, psychological, and sociological factors and acknowledges persons as neither dependent nor independent of their environment but as constantly interacting with it. The only reality persons can ever know or work with is their own interpretation of what is real. The cognitive field theory of learning suggests that the person usually chooses to do what seems best and that intellectual processes are deeply affected by personal goals (Bigge, 1980).

Another major learning theory adapted from psychology is the *humanistic learning* theory, as exemplified by Carl Rogers. Humanistic learning theory accepts the premises of cognitive field theory but places more value on the self-assessment and self-growth of the learner. Humanists are interested in explaining the relationship of humans to their world and to other people. Some major premises in humanistic learning theory are:

- Humans have a natural potential for learning.
- Significant learning takes place when the learner

perceives the subject as relevant to the learner's purposes.
- Learning that involves a change in self-organization is threatening and tends to be resisted.
- Learning is facilitated when the learner participates in the total process.
- Self-initiated learning that involves the whole person, feelings as well as intellect, is the most lasting and pervasive learning.
- Independence, creativity, and self-reliance are facilitated when self-evaluation is primary and evaluation by others is secondary.

Humanistic psychology's contribution to learning theory may be summarized by saying that the most socially useful learning in the modern world is learning the process of learning, which creates an openness to new experiences and change throughout life. In humanistic learning theory, an individual is seen as a whole person who lives with purpose and intent and for whom the meaningfulness of the individual's own experience is essential (Rogers, 1969).

The adult learning theories of Malcolm Knowles may be viewed as a particular adaptation of humanistic learning theory. Knowles identified the problem of pedagogy (teaching strategies) designed for knowledge transfer as problematic because they were designed for children, not for self-directing autonomous adults. He identified four major learning theory assumptions that distinguish the adult learner (Knowles, 1980):

- The adult has a self-concept that has developed from dependence to independence and from other directions to self-direction.
- Adults have accumulated life experiences that serve as a resource for the learning.
- Readiness to learn is related to developmental milestones.
- Learning is present oriented and problem directed for the adult.

Knowles contends that learning is an internal process that involves the person intellectually, emotionally, and physiologically. A critical part of adult learning is interacting with the environment. Therefore, a critical function of the teacher is to create an environment that allows numerous options for adult students (Table 9–1).

TEACHING STRATEGIES DERIVED FROM THEORIES OF LEARNING

The stimulus–response theory of learning offers the following specific principles that can be helpful in new learning situations, particularly in the acquisition of psychomotor skills (Redman, 1983):

- The learner should be actively involved in learning, i.e., in learning by doing and involving as many of the senses as possible (seeing, hearing, and feeling).
- Repetition is an important part of mastering a skill; overlearning can assist skill retention.
- Positive reinforcement is more motivating than negative reinforcement.
- Generalization, as well as discrimination, can be encouraged so that learning can be transferred.

Health programs that use behavior modification are adaptations of the stimulus–response theory, e.g., smoking cessation, weight reduction, and, sometimes, eating disorder and substance abuse treatment.

Cognitive field theory lends itself to situations in which intellectual development, discussion, synthesis, and critique are important elements of learning. Here, learning is considered in the context with purpose and individual goals. The organization of information is important; the direction of learning should be from simple to complex, from concrete to abstract, and from the part to the whole. The perceptual features of learning are also important. Therefore, the combination of sense experiences — sight, sound, touch, smell, and taste — with discussion or reading is included. The teacher's role is one of assisting the individual to discover the connectedness, or relationship, among concepts. The meaning of the concepts to the individual learner is most important. This

---

Table 9–1
Superior Conditions of Learning and Principles of Teaching

It is becoming increasingly clear from the growing body of knowledge about the processes of adult learning that there are certain conditions of learning that are more conducive to growth and development than others. These superior conditions seem to be produced by practices in the learning–teaching transaction that adhere to certain superior principles of teaching as identified below:

Conditions of Learning	Principles of Teaching
The learners feel a need to learn.	1. The teacher exposes students to new possibilities for self-fulfillment. 2. The teacher helps each student clarify his own aspirations for improved behavior. 3. The teacher helps each student diagnose the gap between his aspiration and his present level of performance. 4. The teacher helps the students identify the life problems they experience because of the gaps in their personal equipment.
The learning environment is characterized by physical comfort, mutual trust and respect, mutual helpfulness, freedom of expression, and acceptance of differences.	5. The teacher provides physical conditions that are comfortable (as to seating, smoking, temperature, ventilation, lighting, decoration) and conducive to interaction (preferably, no person sitting behind another person). 6. The teacher accepts each student as a person of worth and respects his feelings and ideas. 7. The teacher seeks to build relationships of mutual trust and helpfulness among the students by encouraging cooperative activities and refraining from inducing competitiveness and judgmentalness. 8. The teacher exposes his own feelings and contributes his resources as a colearner in the spirit of mutual inquiry.

Table continued on following page

Table 9–1
Superior Conditions of Learning and Principles of Teaching *Continued*

Conditions of Learning	Principles of Teaching
The learners perceive the goals of a learning experience to be their goals.	9. The teacher involves the students in a mutual process of formulating learning objectives in which the needs of the students, of the institution, of the teacher, of the subject matter, and of the society are taken into account.
The learners accept a share of the responsibility for planning and operating a learning experience and therefore have a feeling of commitment toward it.	10. The teacher shares his thinking about options available in the designing of learning experiences and the selection of materials and methods and involves the students in deciding among these options jointly.
The learners participate actively in the learning process.	11. The teacher helps the students to organize themselves (project groups, learning–teaching teams, independent study, etc.) to share responsibility in the process of mutual inquiry.
The learning process is related to and makes use of the experience of the learners.	12. The teacher helps the students exploit their own experiences as resources for learning through the use of such techniques as discussion, role playing, case method, etc.
	13. The teacher gears the presentation of his own resources to the levels of experience of his particular students.
	14. The teacher helps the students to apply new learnings to their experience, and thus to make the learnings more meaningful and integrated.
The learners have a sense of progress toward their goals.	15. The teacher involves the students in developing mutually acceptable criteria and methods for measuring progress toward the learning objectives.
	16. The teacher helps the students develop and apply procedures for self-evaluation according to these criteria.

From Malcolm S. Knowles: The Modern Practice of Adult Education: From Pedagogy to Andragogy, © 1980, pp. 57–58. Adapted by permission of Prentice-Hall, Englewood Cliffs, New Jersey.

learning with understanding is lasting and can be transferred to new situations. Goal setting by the learner serves as motivation for further learning. Success is a primary motivation and helps determine the learner's self-perception and future goals (Redman, 1983).

A public health nurse working, for example, in a family planning clinic with a group of adolescent girls might consider the cognitive field learning theory when planning her presentation. Questions that she would consider in planning for an information session with these girls would include the following:

- What is the developmental level of the girls (physically, psychologically, and socially)?
- What are their personal goals (e.g., intimacy, social acceptance)?

- What do they already know about contraception and safe sex?

The nurse's presentation will include a combination of experiences for the senses (touch, hearing, and sight). The following items will be presented for handling by the group:

- Diaphragm
- Contraceptive sponge
- Condoms
- Contraceptive jelly
- Birth control pills in different containers

The nurse will discuss with the participants their knowledge and experience with birth control. What do they know about the pros and cons of the various methods? The nurse will explore options and individual choices with the girls.

Lewin's work also provided the foundation for the health belief model, which is described in Chapter 4. Lewin conceptualized life space as negative, positive, and neutral regions. Diseases are conceived as regions of negative valence that can be expected to exert a force that moves the person away from a positive region. Preventive behaviors are strategies for avoiding negatively valued regions of illness and disease. The health belief model was developed in the early 1950s by Rosenstock, Hochbaum, and Kegeles and refined in the 1970s by Becker.

The following case is an example of the health belief model used as a framework for the health teaching of a newly diagnosed type II diabetic. Mrs. C is a 54-year-old woman who is 5 feet and 4 inches tall and weighs approximately 170 pounds. She is a part-time dispatcher at a local trucking company, and she is married with three grown children and one grandchild. She has been referred to the diabetic clinic by her physician, who recommends weight loss, exercise, and diet as primary means of controlling her diabetes. Mrs. C says that she thinks diabetes is a serious disease, but she did not know you could do anything about the disease once you had it. She has gained most of her weight during her pregnancies more than 20 years ago. She likes to cook, and she does not exercise. Her primary recreation is watching TV or movies with her husband and visiting her children on weekends. Mrs. C drinks only an occasional glass of wine or beer on social occasions. She loves desserts and does not care much for "fresh stuff."

The nurse working with Mrs. C over the next few months will explore her understanding of the nature and cause of her diabetes and assist her in acquiring the knowledge she needs to make health decisions about weight and exercise (Fig. 9–1). Be-

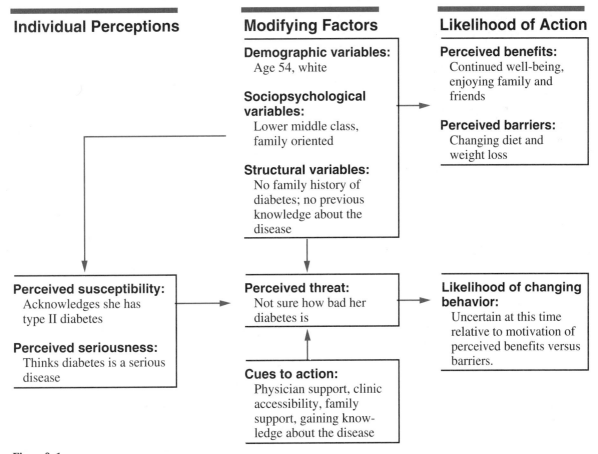

Figure 9–1
Application of the health belief model. (Modified from Becker, M. H., The health belief model and sick role behavior. *In* Becker, M. H., ed.: The Health Belief Model and Personal Health Behavior. Thorofare, New Jersey, Charles B. Slack, 1974.)

fore any behavior changes can be initiated that Mrs. C will successfully maintain, the client must believe the changes are worth the effort and will make a difference in her health outcome.

The previous learning theories make certain working assumptions about the learner and the teacher that must be critiqued for their appropriateness to the individual and aggregate learning situation.

In any teaching situation with an individual client or the aggregate as client, the community health nurse chooses health education theories that influence the learning situation. For example, when teaching a teenage mother how to breast-feed her baby, the nurse takes her cues from the individual client. What are this young mother's concerns? How comfortable is she while feeding the baby? What type of support does she have for her breast-feeding efforts? Does she have a successful role model, e.g., a mother, sister, or friend who has successfully breast-fed? What is this mother's world (cognitive field)? As the mother becomes more comfortable with her breast-feeding skills, the community health nurse provides positive reinforcement (stimulus–response). The nurse follows the client's lead in regard to what is important information for her to have about her baby (humanistic learning) while sharing with her the appropriate information about normal growth and development, safety, nutrition, and immuniza-

tions (adult learning). When the community health nurse is working with groups, health education models that go beyond the individual learning needs are used to address the political and social contexts of the group's learning needs. A health education program addressing clients with a chronic illness such as chronic obstructive pulmonary disease would consider the contributing causes of the clients' condition and the community resources available for their rehabilitation and would strongly support self-help groups.

HEALTH EDUCATION IN A SOCIAL CONTEXT

If health education is to balance the individualistic psychological emphasis of most learning theories, we must put the theories in a broader social context or use learning theories that address education within a socioeconomic perspective. Melanie Dreher points out the consequences for community nursing of the use of psychological or individualistic theories that are intended for clinical practice rather than for public or community health practice. In these theories, greater attention is given to the psychological symptoms of poor health than to the socioeconomic causes.

"RATHER THAN work at the organizational level to change the political institutions that permit poor housing, unsatisfactory waste disposal, and unsafe water to exist in a subculture of one of the wealthiest nations in the world, the priority of the public health nurse is to assist the victims of those institutions to make individual adjustments. . . . Rather than attempt to reorganize a health care system, that by their own admission is 'chaotic,' 'tortuous,' and 'confusing,' nursing educators emphasize the role of the public health nurse as a patient advocate to help *individual* clients negotiate that system" (Dreher, 1982).

Teaching Strategies for Individuals, Families, and Aggregates

Strategy
Discussion
Question and answer
Role play
Simulations
Peer counseling
Interviews
Lecture (most used but
   least effective)
Field trip
Brainstorming
   (generative themes)
Demonstrations
Audiovisuals
Pamphlets
Media
Task force groups
Health fairs

FREIRE'S EDUCATION MODEL

Paulo Freire's model of education is an example of applying the principles of social justice to the aggregate because it has as its foundation community self-determination and change for the culturally or economically disenfranchised. It is these populations that are also frequently at risk for health problems. Other health education models that address concepts of readiness to learn and motivation may not fit well with such disenfranchised populations. Freire's educational model, which involves education for empowerment and liberation, addresses these populations. Freire's educational approach was conceived in response to Third World oppression and therefore addresses oppression in its various forms in any society. *Conscientization* is one of the central concepts of Freire's education model. Conscientization means a critique of reality that brings to consciousness unacknowledged power relationships with the goal of constructing a world less distorted by relations of domination (Freire, 1973). Education is based on real human needs and concerns; learning is self-generated rather than merely receptive. Freire presents a pedagogy that combines reflection with action to produce new patterns of understanding. The act of liberation occurs when both teachers and learners recognize the learners' ability to pose their own problems and struggle to achieve their own solutions (Graman, 1988).

Freire's Model

Phase 1: Participant Observation
Process of *participant observation* — becoming familiar with the language and values of the group

Phase 2: Generative Themes
Small groups identify generative themes (key words suggestive of the concerns of the people)

Phase 3: Symbolic Meanings
Representation of the generative themes in images, pictures, or symbols

Phase 4: Decoding and Possible Solutions
Symbols, images, or pictures "decoded" by the group with a teacher/facilitator looking at the causes, consequences, and possible solutions of the problems represented by generative themes

---

In this problematizing of reality, learners identify their problems and come to recognize and understand the significance of these problems in relation to their own lives and the lives of others. Critical reflection and consciousness lead to an at-

tempt to overcome the problem and to deal with the conditions that provided the environment for the problem. Education, as the posing of questions or problems expressed in *generative themes,* is an attempt to connect the student's and teacher's realities in a learning experience. Freire defines a generative theme as a concrete representation of an idea, a value, a concept, or a hope as well as the obstacles that impede humankind's full humanization (Freire, 1971). Examples of generative themes are pictures, TV programs, videos, role plays, or any simulations that portray the problem under consideration in a social context. By engaging in dialogue about generative themes, learners connect concrete ideas, such as the cost of health care, problems with access to health care, and need for new forms of health care, to their specific health problem. This dialogue of concern takes place using the language and terms of the client-consumer rather than using the provider's language and frame of reference. Minkler and Cox (1980) presented an application of Freire's educational approach in a health context. They noted that this approach involves the perception of health and medical care within the total oppressive structure of society. Health reform is then viewed within a broader structural transformation. A major part of this transformation involves changing the relationship between providers and consumers and the oppressive elements of the status quo that impact on health through health education.

Sociopolitical Dimension

Freire's education model has been used extensively in literacy education (Freire, 1970*a*, 1970*b*; Grabowski, 1975; Graman, 1988) to empower people through their gain of literacy skills while engaging in a process that is socially liberating. Freire's model may be considered to expand on some of the elements of the cognitive field and humanistic theories of learning, including Knowles' adult education perspective. What Freire adds is a sociopolitical dimension to learning. Freire acknowledges the individual as primarily a social being; therefore, how an individual learns is as important as what the individual learns in determining the social meaning and value of education.

Freire's approach always includes the client's definition of the problem in the client's own terms.

This can be a valuable addition to a more traditional health education model that defines health care problems from the provider's perspective and presents client problems as noncompliance. A community health nurse can use this approach to health education to provide both content and process for politicizing individuals and communities regarding their health care rights. Advocacy within the Freire model of health education has new meaning; it means not only working at the immediate level of providing a knowledge base with which clients may make sound health care decisions but also working at the social structural level in which the health care problems are embedded. This approach to health education is political and acknowledges that health and health care are political issues. As many community health nursing leaders note (Anderson, 1988; Milio, 1983; Dreher, 1982), community health nurses must acknowledge the relationship between individual health and its social context.

Empowerment Education

Freire's approach to health education has been called empowerment education by some health educators. These health educators note that powerlessness can be linked to disease and that empowerment and control are supportive of health (Wallerstein and Burnstein, 1988). Freire's approach to health education complements and extends traditional health education approaches in at least two major areas. Knowledge is derived from the group or community through the process of conscientization, which takes the form of a participatory dialogue among equal partners. There are no experts and no recipients of knowledge, but rather there is a common exploration of the nature of the identified health problem. This participatory dialogue leads to positive, planned changes and action. The action may be on an individual, group, or community level and always recognizes the inherent mutual interaction of these levels. The role of the health educator is to contribute information as a resource after the problem themes have been identified and explored.

Two examples of Freire's approach being used for health education are presented. A cancer awareness project directed through the North Bay Health Resources Agency is an example of how Freire's educational model can direct and inform the character of a project, making it a vehicle of individual and community growth and understanding. The Cancer Awareness/Risk Reduction Project was a 3-year, three-tiered community education program that targeted four rural California counties. The project focused on the relationship of specific health behaviors (nutrition, smoking, and weight reduction) to cancer risk. The first level of community education was a general media awareness campaign that involved radio and local newspaper coverage and grocery-bag stuffers at selected major supermarkets. The second level of education was accomplished through presentations to groups requesting the opportunity to provide information more specific to their needs. Groups included employee groups, school parent groups, and seniors' groups.

The third level of education included a variety of community classes on health behaviors. The classes were created with the understanding that all of the participants were adult learners and that the value of health is relative to the social context of their lives. The 6-week nutrition program called "For the Health of It . . . Eat Right" presented factual knowledge about cancer and diet while assessing the participants' level of involvement. These classes provided the opportunity for the health educator to interact with the clients; identify their vocabulary, concerns, and symbols or metaphors; and then decode them with the clients looking for solutions. The goal of the project was to provide the community with tools with which to make health care decisions that were in their best interest and to enable both individuals and groups within the various rural communities to use available resources for their self-care. One of the outcomes of the third phase of this project was that some members of the community came to see themselves as more self-reliant and able to influence their local environment.

Cancer Awareness Project Using Freire's Model

PARTICIPANT OBSERVATION. Discussed with the group were their concerns relating to age, activity, and nutrition. What areas of nutrition information were important to them?

GENERATIVE THEMES. Bad foods are sweets, fried foods, junk food, and "goodies." Good foods are fruits, vegetables, fish, and lean meat. Fatty foods are desserts, munchies, and high cholesterol foods.

SYMBOLIC MEANINGS. How we learn to eat, what makes food pleasing, the fast food phenomenon, time to eat, and what does eating mean are examples.

DECODING AND POSSIBLE SOLUTIONS. What are meal times like? When do we eat, and why? What foods do we like, and why?

Freire's model emphasizes the centrality of language, communication, and client self-direction; it informed and created the character of the health education project so that it politicized and educated its designated population. This project was well served by Freire's model because a number of the participants became concerned about the broader context of cancer prevention through their initial involvement with individual lifestyle changes (DeBella, 1988).

Wallerstein and Burnstein (1988) presented another example of Freire's model in the Alcohol Substance Abuse Prevention Program (ASAP) for high school students in New Mexico. The program started in 1982 in a high-risk adolescent population. ASAP uses Freire's educational model, including the participation of the adolescents as co-learners with the health professionals, valuing the student's experience as a contribution to social knowledge about substance abuse, critical thinking by the students in raising their own questions, and group dialogue to explore root causes and motivate students to engage in creative actions that address problems in their community and society as a whole (Table 9–2).

HEALTH EDUCATION MODELS

Health education models reflect different teaching and learning theories and address individuals, families, or communities. The well known health belief model primarily focuses on the individual and was derived from Kurt Lewin's social psychology approach. The health promotion model of Pender is also primarily oriented to the individual, although the modifying effects of demographics and situational variables are noted (Fig. 9–2).

The Precede model (an acronym for Predisposing, Reinforcing and Enabling Causes to Educational Diagnosis and Evaluation) is a health education program planning approach (Figs. 9–3 and 9–4). The model, developed by Green et al. (1983), has seven phases and is multidisciplinary. The

Table 9–2
ASAP: An Example of Freire's Model

The ASAP model has the following affective, cognitive, behavioral, and social components as inspired by Freire:

ASAP is participant centered with the youth taking responsibility for asking questions and contributing personal experiences, feelings, and thoughts about strategies for change.

ASAP is small group centered with knowledge socially generated from dialogue about the patients and their own lives.

ASAP promotes active learning on an emotional level. Patient stories become a code to work through their feelings of sadness, empathy, and anger at the patient and at their own harsh lives and to emerge with a sense of expanded opportunities.

ASAP promotes active learning on a cognitive level, using the problem-posing methodology. Students identify the problems they see in the emergency center and jail, share their own family and community experiences, analyze the root causes, and pose alternatives for themselves, their peers, and communities.

ASAP promotes active learning on a behavioral (and cognitive) level, with assertiveness and communication techniques, role playing, and decision-making activities.

ASAP promotes connectedness and social support with others, building on natural empathy and values of community cooperation through small groups at the hospital, small group peer teaching, and annual recognition parties and ASAP/Students Against Drunk Driving chapters.

ASAP promotes a sense of self-achievement by engaging youth in assertiveness training and peer teaching.

ASAP promotes socially responsible leadership and transfer of decision making by supporting youth in peer teaching and in choosing their own arenas for action such as schoolwide campaigns against drinking and driving.

Modified from Wallerstein, N., and Burnstein, E.: Empowerment education: Freire's ideas adapted to health education. Health Educ. Q. *15*;379–394, 1988. Copyright © 1988 John Wiley & Sons, Inc. Reprinted by permission of John Wiley & Sons, Inc.

phases include epidemiology, the social and behavioral sciences, administration, and education. The model has two major premises: 1) health and health behavior are multifactorial, and 2) to ad-

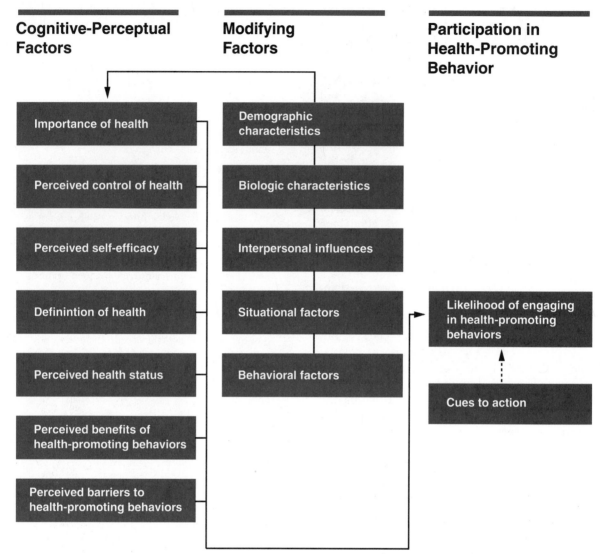

Figure 9–2
Health promotion model. (Redrawn from Pender, N. J.: Health Promotion in Nursing Practice. 2nd Ed. Norwalk, Connecticut, Appleton & Lange, 1987, p. 58.)

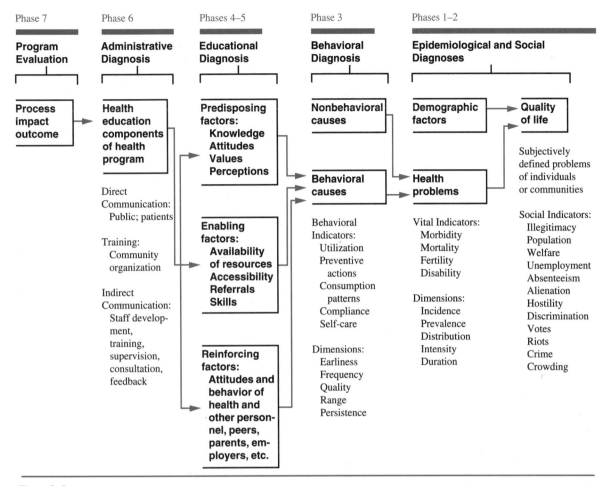

Figure 9–3
The Precede model (Redrawn from Green, I., et al.: Health Education Planning. Palo Alto, California, Mayfield Publications, 1980, p. 14.)

Phase 7	Phases 5–6	Phases 4–5	Phase 3	Phase 2	Phase 1
Program Evaluation	**Administrative Diagnosis**	**Educational Diagnosis**	**Behavioral Diagnosis**	**Epidemiological Diagnosis**	**Social Diagnosis**

Process

Health education components

A. Program objective

Predisposing factors

A. Knowledge

Nonbehavioral causes

Demographic variables

Quality of life

Impact

Behavioral causes

B. Attitudes

Patient

Health problem

Social implications

B. Client cognitive affective, and behavioral objectives

Outcome

C. Values

C. Program content

D. Perceptions

Community health nurse

Enabling factors

D. Implementation

Reinforcing factors

Figure 9–4
The Precede model planning form. (Redrawn from Green, I., et al.: Health Education Planning. Palo Alto, California, Mayfield Publications, 1980, p. 14.)

dress these multiple factors, health education must be multidimensional. It should also be noted that the Precede model is similar to the nursing process and the health teaching process in that it follows a step-by-step problem-solving progression from assessment to planning, implementation, and evaluation. The following is an application of the Precede model to the problem of intravenous drug abuse in a community:

Precede Schematic

Phase 1: Social diagnosis

Quality of life

Intravenous drug abuse

Social implications

Individual and social losses to the community (potential for crime)

Phase 2: Epidemiological diagnosis

Demographic variables (of intravenous drug users)

Age, sex, income, race, education

Health problems

Hepatitis B, HIV, tuberculosis

Phase 3: Behavioral diagnosis

Client: high-risk behaviors, low self-esteem, non-compliance

Community nurse: lack of knowledge about addiction as human behavior, lack of adequate treatment centers or programs for drug users

Phases 4 and 5: Education diagnosis and prioritizing

Predisposing factors

Knowledge about the characteristics and needs of intravenous drug users

Attitudes of the clients, the community, and the health care providers (punitive versus rehabilitative attitudes)

Values: intravenous drug user as person viewed as potential member of society or detriment to society

Perceptions

Clients (low self-esteem, worthlessness)

Family rejection, shame, or ignorance

Community (denial or disdain)

Health care team (ambivalent but motivated because of health risks to general population)

Enabling factors

Availability of education and rehabilitation programs

Mental health support services

Reinforcing attitudes

Community leaders, health care professionals, mental health professionals, law enforcement

Phases 5 and 6: Administrative diagnosis and prioritizing

Lack of community awareness of intravenous drug use and its consequences

Health education component

Community health education objectives for community leaders and the general public

Education for intravenous drug users for rehabilitation or clean needle use

Phase 7: Program evaluation

Process: Evaluated are the involvement and commitment of community leaders and mental health and other health care providers, availability of rehabilitation counselors, and cooperation of law enforcement.

Impact: Scope of the program determines objectives for the community and intravenous drug users.

Outcome: Health goal for the community will be to decrease HIV infection risk to the general population from intravenous drug users by increasing rehabilitation programs and/or needle exchange programs.

Social goals: Address the growing drug use problems by grass roots efforts such as self-esteem programs in schools, family strengthening programs, and community education programs.

The advantage of this health education planning model is that it is comprehensive and can serve as an action guideline for the community health nurse working within a community on selected health-related issues.

HEALTH EDUCATION RESOURCES

In planning health education programs for individuals, families, or aggregates, there is a vast array of educational materials that can be used to support the learning objectives and goals of the programs. The following provides limited reference to some of these sources. Teaching handbooks, such as Rankin and Duffy's *Patient Education: Issues,*

Principles and Guidelines, provide a rather comprehensive categorical source of educational resource material. The following is a summary of these categories:

- Professional organizations: There are more than 30 professional organizations, ranging from the American Association of Sex Educators, Counsellors and Therapists to the American Hospital Association, that provide printed as well as audiovisual materials at no or minimal cost.
- Hospitals, medical societies, and educational centers: The community health nurse should explore the region for medical centers.
- Volunteer and nonprofit organizations: These organizations have a specific focus or area of concern and can be outstanding resources for information and research in a particular area. Examples of volunteer organizations range from Alcoholics Anonymous and Alanon (and other derivations of these groups) to disease-specific groups such as the American Cancer Society, Diabetes Association, Arthritis Foundation, and Multiple Sclerosis Foundation. These, and other organizations of this nature, are excellent sources of information and support for clients, whether individuals or groups, who have identified problems.
- Commercial organizations: Pharmaceutical companies or medical supply companies may be excellent resources for specific information on medication or procedures. This information may be available in pamphlets or audiovisual material.
- Government sources: The U.S. government is a major publisher of health-related information through departments such as the Office of Consumer Affairs, Food and Drug Administration, Department of Health and Human Services, National Clearing House for Drug and Alcohol Abuse, National Institutes of Health, Public Health Service, and Department of Labor. State agencies may also be primary publishers of information related to a particular region or locale. State departments of health, mental health, aging, or social services can be excellent resources for a state perspective on a particular health problem. Through local libraries, counties and cities may also be good sources of local information on environmental, health, and safety issues.

A word of caution in choosing health education materials to use when working with client populations is necessary. Knowing a learner's level of motivation through the health belief model or another assessment tool may not be adequate in assessing the type of learning materials most appropriate to the client. One characteristic of client populations to note is their level of literacy. In many instances, populations at risk for health problems are also populations with limited literacy skills. An excellent resource when working with clients with lower literacy skills is *Teaching Patients With Low Literacy Skills* (Doak et al., 1985). This book complements Freire's model, which has been used primarily with populations with low levels of literacy. These authors documented the extent of the literacy problem in the United States and have found that as many as 20% of the population has a reading level of fifth grade or less. They also make the point that literacy is not necessarily a factor of intelligence but rather of educational opportunities versus barriers and disabilities. The elderly, refugees, and migrants are examples of populations who experience barriers to literacy. Doak et al. offer several ways to assess client literacy and have suggestions for dealing with limited literacy, such as rewriting of materials and using appropriate audio or visual materials. An example of the impact of literacy is demonstrated by several studies that have assessed the readability of contraceptive

---

Tips on Teaching Clients With Limited Literacy Skills (Doak et al., 1985)

TEACH THE smallest amount possible to do the job.

Make your point as vividly as you can.

Have the client restate and demonstrate the information.

Review repeatedly.

---

literature available to clients (Ledbetter et al., 1987; Swanson et al., 1988) and noted that the materials reviewed were not well matched to the clients' needs.

HEALTH EDUCATION EVALUATION

Although there are many proposed methods of teaching evaluation for individuals and groups, the basic evaluation of health education comes through changes in values, attitudes, and health behavior. All learning has cognitive, affective, and psychomotor components that are integrated and goal directed. Teaching is an activity that facilitates and stimulates the learning potential of the individual or aggregate. The teacher and learners come together in a safe environment to set learning goals and create opportunities for self-learning and self-evaluation. The teacher thus serves as a resource person who respects and enhances each learner's unique cultural background, belief system, and life experience. The goal of health teaching is to enable the health practitioner and client to enter each other's worlds, recognize mutual health values, and learn more about each other and themselves. Much of our daily behavior is preprogrammed, unexamined, unconscious behavior. When a person or group decides to become self-aware and re-sponsible for making desired personal or social changes, health education has been successful.

The purpose of health education is to help individuals and aggregates maximize their creative potential, examine and critique relevant issues, and live productively in their own unique way, making their contribution to society. As Marilyn Ferguson noted, "Only a community can offer holistic education; true education strengthens the capacity to make sense of one's life as it develops" (1980).

APPLICATION OF THE NURSING PROCESS

The following case studies and teaching plans are offered as examples of the use of selected teaching approaches that are appropriate for the individual, family, and community and their respective learning needs.

**C a s e
S t u d y
1**

Individual Teaching Care Plan

Situation: An individual with AIDS has experienced a significant amount of weight loss (tertiary prevention).

Assessment

Assess whether intake of nutrients is adequate to meet the caloric needs of an individual with chronic HIV infection.

Assess the potential for stomatitis or other gastrointestinal opportunistic infections.

Assess the economic status related to ability to obtain and prepare food.

Assess knowledge regarding nutrition.

Diagnosis

Altered nutrition: less than body requirements, related to anorexia.

Altered nutrition: less than body requirements, related to difficulty in obtaining and preparing food of appropriate texture for ability to eat.

Potential for infection related to inadequate nutrients.

Knowledge deficit.

Planning and Goals

Client will be able to obtain and prepare foods high in calories and of the appropriate texture to be satisfying.

Secondary gastrointestinal infections and/or amelioration of their symptoms will be prevented.

Intervention and Health Teaching

Discuss nutritional requirements for persons with HIV infection. Provide pamphlets and nutritional information, and develop lists of foods that appeal to client. Suggest different forms of favorite foods that are difficult to eat because of texture.

Review the clients's dietary intake for 1 week.

Potential referrals: Dietician, social worker, Visiting Nurse Service, and community-based AIDS programs that provide meals.

Evaluation

Client demonstrates weight maintenance or gain and identifies adequate sources of foods that are of an appropriate variety, with an emphasis on high-caloric, high-vitamin, low microbiologic foods.

C a s e
S t u d y
2

Family Teaching Care Plan

Situation: Home care for person with AIDS (secondary prevention).

Assessment

Assess family's fears that they may contract AIDS from client.

Assess degree of acceptance of the person with AIDS as family member with a chronic disease.

Assess nature of caregiver relationship with client.

Assess family's understanding of how HIV virus can be and cannot be transmitted and of Centers for Disease Control universal precautions.

Diagnosis

Knowledge deficit related to fear of transmission of HIV virus.

Planning and Goals

Unfounded fears will be alleviated.

Transmission of HIV virus will be prevented.

Intervention and Health Teaching

Teach family members about the communicability of HIV virus (casual contact versus sexual contact).

Review and reinforce universal precautions for caregivers from Centers for Disease Control.

Use home care guidelines.

Potential referrals: community-based AIDS support or respite group, public health department, Visiting Nurse Service.

Evaluation

Competent, comforting home care is provided for person with AIDS, with no infection of any family member.

Case Study 3

Community Teaching Care Plan

Situation: Increased rates of AIDS among intravenous drug users in community. High-risk drug use behaviors are prevalent.

Assessment

What are the attitudes and willingness of the community in dealing with the drug-using population?

Number of intravenous drug users versus the availability of treatment facilities.

Willingness of community to use fiscal and manpower resources to deal with drug users.

Diagnosis

Alteration in community self-concept.

Planning and Goals

Identify the magnitude of the drug use problem in the community and the public and private resources available to address it.

Intervention and Health Teaching

Identify the barriers to reaching intravenous drug users.

Plan community education programs at three levels: community leaders, general public, and intravenous drug users.

Choose appropriate community education model for each level.

Potential referrals: Federal, state, and local AIDS education organizations and funding sources for intravenous drug programs.

Evaluation

Each community education program should be evaluated. Community leaders should acknowledge, respond, and support community efforts to deal with the intravenous drug problem. The general public should understand the potential risk to the community. Intravenous drug users should participate in specialized treatment programs and education programs to decrease the risk of HIV transmission.

SUMMARY

Community health nurses use a variety of learning theories and health education strategies in their work with clients. It is important to match the appropriate theory or strategy to the client's learning needs and situation. It is also essential that the community health nurse recognize that health education is a political as well as social activity, even on a one-to-one individual level and certainly as it is directed toward improving the health of aggregates. Striving to achieve a partnership with clients to mutually choose health-related goals is the first step in making client-centered education a reality. Stimulus–response, cognitive field, and humanistic learning theories are examples of educational theories based in psychology that have primary application to individuals and families. The Precede model is presented as an example of an educational approach that relates health planning to the aggregate. Freire's learning theory is based on an analysis of the social context of health care problems. Through critical consciousness, the client becomes aware of his or her health care problem and selects a method of addressing that problem as the client reflects on the larger social issues that create the context for the problem. For example, smokers in a nonsmoking class could, while dealing with the immediate symptoms and problems of their smoking addiction and choosing the best solutions for their individual needs, reflect on the social climate that supported their smoking habit (movies, TV, and advertisements, particularly those of the 1950s and 1960s that glamorized smoking). They might also note the changes in society that have occurred, such as setting a goal of a smokeless community by the year 2000.

There are numerous sources of health education materials for the community health nurse working with individuals, families, and groups. The challenge to the community health nurse is to locate these materials and match them to the client's level of interest, understanding, and literacy. The health teaching process can be viewed as paralleling the nursing process, thereby providing a familiar way of organizing and planning health education.

Learning Activities

1. Discuss the differences and similarities between health education planned for individuals and programs planned for the aggregate.

2. Review your local newspaper for 1–2 weeks and identify some social issues (e.g., housing, employment, health insurance, runaways). How do these issues relate to health and health care in your community? What role could health education play in addressing any of these issues?

3. Gather information from media advertising (TV, radio, newspaper, or magazines). What is the message of the advertisement, and how is it being presented? What can we learn about presenting health education messages in the public media?

4. In groups of three or four students, choose a community or aggregate (e.g., your neighborhood, the homeless population, a group of seniors, or a group of young mothers looking for child care). Use the PRECEDE model to analyze their problem, and evaluate the process and your results.

5. Using the same community as studied in activity 4, apply Freire's model (identify with the members of the community, determine their generative themes in their own language, and problematize and prioritize the participants' view of their problem). Evaluate this process and your proposed results.

6. Compare the results of your processes and outcomes in activities 4 and 5. Identify the problems and/or limitations of either or both approaches.

REFERENCES

Anderson, E. T., and McFarlane, J. M.: Community as Client: Application of the Nursing Process. Philadelphia, J. B. Lippincott, 1988.

Becker, M. H., ed.: The Health Belief Model and Personal Health Behaviour. Thorofare, New Jersey, Charles B. Slack, 1974.

Bigge, M. L.: Learning Theories for Teachers. 2nd Ed. New York, Harper & Row, 1980.

Blattner, B.: Holistic Nursing. New York, Prentice-Hall, 1981.

DeBella, S.: The Community Health Nurse as Health Educator Using a Social Theorist's Perspective. 116th APHA annual meeting, Boston, November 14, 1988.

DiClemente, R. J.: Prevention of HIV infection among adolescents. AIDS Educ. Prevent. *1*;70–78, 1989.

Doak, C., Doak, L., and Root, J.: Teaching Patients with Low Literacy Skills. Philadelphia, J. B. Lippincott, 1985.

Dreher, M.: The conflict of conservatism in public health nursing education. Nurs. Outlook *30*;504–509, 1982.

Edwards, L.: Health education. *In* Edelman, C., and Mandle, C. L., eds.: Health Promotion Through the Life Span. St. Louis, C. V. Mosby, 1986.

Ferguson, M.: The Aquarian Conspiracy: Personal and Social Transformation in the 1980s. Los Angeles, J. B. Tarcher, Inc., 1980.

Flaskerud, J. H.: AIDS/HIV Infection: A Reference Guide for Nursing Professionals. Philadelphia, W. B. Saunders, 1989.

Freire, P.: Pedagogy of the Oppressed. New York, Herder and Herder, 1972.

Freire, P.: The adult literacy process as cultural action for freedom: Part 1. Harvard Educ. Rev. *40*;205–225, 1970*a*.

Freire, P.: Cultural action and conscientization: Part 2. Harvard Educ. Rev. *40*;452–477, 1970*b*.

Grabowski, S., ed.: Paulo Freire: A Revolutionary Dilemma for the Adult Educator. Syracuse, New York, Syracuse University, 1972.

Graman, T.: Education for humanization: Applying Paulo Freire's pedagogy to learning a second language. Harvard Educ. Rev. *58*;433–438, 1988.

Green, I., et al.: Health Education Planning. Palo Alto, California, Mayfield, 1983.

Hanchett, E. S.: Nursing Frameworks and Community as Client. Norwalk, Connecticut, Appleton & Lange, 1988.

Joint Committee on Health Education: New Definitions. Health Education Monograph No. 33. Washington D.C., U.S. Public Health Service, 1973.

Knowles, M. S.: The Modern Practice of Adult Education: Andragogy versus Pedagogy. 2nd Ed. Chicago, Follett Publishing Co., 1980.

Lalonde, M.: A New Perspective on the Health of Canadians: A Working Document. Ottawa, Canadian Ministry of National Health and Welfare, 1974.

Ledbetter, C., and Swanson, J.: Readability of Commercial Versus Generic Health Instructions: Condoms. Women's Health Care International. Austin, University of Texas, 1988.

Milio, N.: Promoting Health Through Public Policy. Philadelphia, F. A. Davis, 1983.

Minkler, M., and Cox, K.: Creating critical consciousness in health: Applications of Freire's philosophy and methods to the health care setting. Int. J. Health Serv. *10*;311–322, 1980.

North Bay Health Systems Agency: A Biannual Health Plan: A Proposed Health Agenda for Sonoma, Napa and Solano Counties, 1980–82. Petaluma, California, North Bay Health Systems Agency, 1983.

Pender, N.: Health Promotion in Nursing Practice. 2nd Ed. Norwalk, Connecticut, Appleton & Lange, 1987.

Rankin, S. H., and Duffy, K. L.: Patient Education: Issues, Principles and Guidelines. Philadelphia, J. B. Lippincott, 1983.

Redman, B. K.: The Process of Patient Education. St. Louis, C. V. Mosby, 1983.

Rogers, C.: Freedom to Learn. Columbus, Ohio, C. E. Merrill Co., 1969.

Swanson, J.: The Readability of Reproductive Health Materials: Commercial Versus Generic Contraceptive Instructions. 116th Annual APHA meeting, Boston, November 15, 1988.

Wallerstein, N., and Burnstein, E.: Empowerment education: Freire's ideas adapted to health education. Health Educ. Q. *15*;379–394, 1988.

Wiggington, E.: The Foxfire Book. New York, Anchor Press, 1968.

Wiggington, E., and Bennett, M.: Foxfire 9. New York, Anchor Press, 1986.

Wright, C.: Educating for community and liberation. Study Encounter *11*;1–12, 1975.

10

Policy, Politics, Legislation, and Public Health Nursing

Upon completion of this chapter, the reader will be able to:

1. Describe the role nurses have played in influencing the public's health through policy development.

2. Analyze public policy as the critical basis for protecting the public's health.

3. Identify the legislative process involved in establishing state or federal health policy.

4. Identify the political processes that influence health policy development.

5. Discuss political activities through which nurses can affect the health policies of their community and country.

Ruth F. Stewart
Madalon O'Rawe Amenta

This chapter will explore the relationship of health care politics and power to public health nursing. Because government is related to all aspects of health care, the focus will be on political action in relation to government. "Government" is the worksite of elected and appointed decision makers. Government determines

---

Politics: The Science of Government

DICTIONARY DEFINITIONS of politics refer to it as the science of government—the policies and aims of a nation, state, or other institution. The common elements in all of the definitions are power, capacity to influence, and authority in interpersonal or intergroup relationships. We also commonly recognize the allocation of always scarce resources as a function of politics.

Because resources are finite, the process of deciding who gets what, when, where, and how is critical to all groups, whether personal, professional, or societal. In a family with teenagers, a decision has to be made about who will get the car for the evening. In a community health nursing agency, decisions about continuing education opportunities, student preceptoring, salary increases, and promotion possibilities have to be made. In any work setting, there is continuous allocation of time, money, manpower, equipment, and supplies, and conflict inevitably arises among those competing to control them. Politics, influenced by the balance of power, determines the outcomes. According to Donna Diers, "Politics is the use of power for change" (Diers, 1985).

---

and frames the major policy issues that underlie the health care system, and the federal government pays for the largest proportion of the health care services delivered in the United States.

NURSES WHO MADE A DIFFERENCE

Two stories of political action by nurses will be related in this chapter. One story is famous, that of Florence Nightingale and her care of British foot soldiers in the Crimea in 1856. The other concerns a contemporary nurse who worked with Hispanic families living along Luckey Road in Monaco, Texas, in 1985. In each case, a nurse effectively used the political process to improve health conditions for clients. Nightingale's well-known sanitary reforms at Scutari saved thousands of lives. Carrie Long, a nursing student in Texas, acted to depollute the water supply and sewage disposal along Luckey Road, thus potentially reducing the risk of enteric infection.

Florence Nightingale: 1850s

The appointment of a woman to the position of Superintendent of the Nursing Staff by the Secretary of the British Army, Sir Sidney Herbert, was a radical move in the 1850s. He made the appointment in response to reports in *The London Times* that "the soldiers in Crimea die without the slightest effort to save them . . . [and the] sick appear to be tended by the sick, and the dying by the dying" (Kalisch and Kalisch, 1978). In contrast, French troops fighting alongside their British allies, were being admirably nursed by the Sisters of Charity.

Sir Herbert realized the need for drastic action and thought immediately and only of Nightingale, whose ability and commitment to nursing were widely recognized.

Although he knew Parliament would oppose sending women into the war zone, he took the risk and invited Nightingale to organize and supervise a nursing service for the wounded and ill soldiers. She readily accepted.

Nightingale recruited a group of 38 nurses and immediately went to Turkey. The situation they found at Scutari was, if anything, worse than that described. The Barrack Hospital was filthy, vermin ridden, and overcrowded, with 3,000–4,000 men occupying a space suitable for half that number. It was not surprising, therefore, that three fourths of the wounded soldiers contracted cholera, dysentery, and/or typhoid fever as a result of being hospitalized, not as a result of battlefield conditions.

Although the soldiers worshiped Nightingale, military and government officials blocked her efforts at every turn. The medical officers not only resisted the intrusion of the nurses but on a deeper level also resented the implication of incompetence that was inherent in Nightingale's proposed reforms. Although few of them cooperated with her, she persisted. Because she was from a wealthy and politically active family, she used her personal resources and influence in London to obtain food, dressings, and other necessary supplies. When the Nightingale nurses arrived, 60% of the patients were dying. At the end of the war, the mortality rate was reduced to slightly greater than 1% (Kalisch and Kalisch, 1978).

This dramatic change was not wrought by a miracle, but rather by Nightingale and her nurses counteracting neglect and outright sabotage through the canny use of power. She wielded great referent and connection power through her wealthy family and politically powerful friends. After the war, she achieved legitimate and expert power in her own right as a result of the extraordinary recognition accorded her by the British public for her humanitarian work at Scutari.

Carrie Long: 1980s

Luckey Road in Monaco, Texas, had not been lucky for the people who share the development built there by a contractor with an eye on a quick cash return. The boxlike wooden houses on small plots of land appealed to people seeking reasonably priced housing for their families. The contracts of sale required no down payment and offered a means for several poor Hispanic families to realize their dream.

These families were pleased to have electricity, running water, and indoor flush toilets. At first, they did not worry that their sewage drained into an open pit behind each house into which children or animals might fall. Nor did they realize that the hazards of this pit included the danger of acute and protracted infections and, perhaps, death.

These hazards were recognized, however, by Carrie Long, a student in a university community health nursing course who was working with the Saenz family. While doing the family assessment, she asked Mrs. Saenz about the household sewage. She thought she had misunderstood when told it drained into "a hole in the back" but knew that she had heard correctly when she visited the yard. Outside she found a 3-by-4 foot pit filled to the brim with raw sewage. Mrs. Saenz explained that it was not always so full; recent rains had raised the level.

Further data collected from neighbors confirmed that not only was this sewage situation commonplace, but also there were other problems. One family was transporting household water from 10 miles away because they could not get it piped into their house from the rural water supply. None of the families knew who was responsible for repairs and upkeep in the development. All they were sure of was where to mail the monthly payments —a lumber company's post office box. Only one family held a deed to their property.

Knowing that the problem was potentially explosive, Carrie began carefully collecting more data. She confirmed that Texas state law requires approved septic tanks for households in such rural areas and that the county health department has enforcement authority. Her companion concern, however, was that the families might be evicted and their plight made even worse if action were taken against the owners.

Carrie and two classmates had scheduled earlier, as part of their student project, a meeting with the county (administrative) judge to discuss health services and needs from the viewpoint of an elected official. During this meeting, she brought up the Luckey Road problems, and showed the judge pictures of the open-pit sewage. The pictures were "worth a thousand words." On seeing it, the judge expressed rage that such conditions existed within the county.

In discussing the situation, Carrie stressed her concern that the families not be evicted or harassed by the owners. They agreed that this would be a prime consideration in any corrective action. The judge asked for Carrie's cooperation, and after a conference with her instructor, she agreed to help.

Once she began working with the officials by providing the necessary names and addresses, the judge's office swung into action. They contacted the county health and the public works departments. The judge called on the media to raise public interest and support. A television mini-series exposé was planned with Carrie acting as liaison to the Luckey Road families. Since she suspected that her position as an "outsider" would hamper efforts to convince the families of her sincerity, she approached Don Martinez, a local leader who was well known for his strong religious convictions and commitment to helping others. Once aware of the situation, Mr. Martinez, better known as "Deacon," agreed to help.

In an effort to gather more information, the pair made house-to-house visits. Not only did they gain the cooperation of many neighborhood families, but some families agreed to describe their plight for the television production and to allow filming in and around their houses.

It was on this round of visits that Carrie met the Culebra family. Mr. Culebra's reaction to inquiries about sewage disposal was explosive, leaving no question about his anger and frustration. This family had to transport all water for household use 10 miles. Their water pipes, intact and laid to the road where the water main passed in front of the house, had been disconnected before they purchased the home. All efforts to get them reconnected, whether through assistance from the developer or the rural water board, had come to a dead end.

Mr. Culebra was especially upset because his wife had just returned from the hospital after having surgery, and she had to irrigate her drainage tubes twice daily. He was so angry that he reverted to Spanish during the conversation. Mr. Culebra agreed to tell his story on television.

Unfortunately, instead of arousing public concern, the television "exposé" failed miserably. Because the original investigative reporter had been subpoenaed in a court case at the time scheduled for filming, a substitute was assigned. The new reporter was not interested in the situation, let alone in portraying it sympathetically. He had the cameraman film a few shots of the Culebra's yard and open pit, but refused to go inside. Mr. Culebra was offended, later telling Carrie that the reporter thought "he was too good to go into a Hispanic's house."

The story that appeared on the evening news was a brief clip of the Culebra yard and pit, with Carrie describing the health implications. Public response was negligible. The program did, however, attract the attention of two affluent community members who told Carrie to "lay off" because sewage improvements would generate higher taxes.

To counter this argument, Carrie went to the county hospital for information. She learned that the amount of tax money spent for a 3-day hospital stay of one infant with severe diarrhea or one adult with surgical wound infection could be as high, if not higher, than the cost of installation of a septic tank. She learned that preventive health measures are a sound financial investment for society.

The judge's efforts with the health and the public works departments met with somewhat more success, a result of his legitimate power in county administration. Engineers, sanitarians, and others evaluated the situation and verified official records relating to the housing development. On one visit to the neighborhood, Carrie met by chance several of the public health inspectors. They were not eager to be involved and told her emphatically that any attempt to change conditions would be futile. She felt that they resented the meddling of nurses in their domain.

The inspectors' report, nevertheless, objectively and comprehensively documented the problems. Bureaucratic response outlining corrective action was slow, but there has been progress. The interest and support of Carrie and her nurse colleagues sustain hope for the Luckey Road residents that improvements will occur.

Power: The Key to Change

DESPITE THE common notion that power is inherently evil, it is, in reality, neutral. It attains value only in context. Power is the ability to change the behavior of others in desired ways, the ability to influence what others do, or, conversely, the ability to cause others to stop doing something. Parent power socializes worthy citizens; gang power promotes delinquent behavior. The term "power of the press" denotes the media's strong impact on thinking and, hence, behavior. The source of empowerment for any person or agency is its position or potential as perceived by others.

C a s e
S t u d y

Assessment

Carrie Long observed that open cesspools rather than adequate waste disposal existed in backyards of homes. She interviewed family and community members who lacked awareness of the potential danger and hazards to health and affirmed that no action had been taken by individuals, families, or the greater community to remedy the situation. The cesspools were located where people could fall into them. The nurse confirmed that state law required approved septic tanks in rural areas and that enforcement authority was the county health department. She verified that preventive measures are more cost-effective than a hospital stay for gastrointestinal disease or a wound infection.

Diagnosis

Individual

- Potential for injury related to open sewage pits
- Potential for infection related to open pits containing contaminated material

Family

- Impaired home maintenance management related to accumulated wastes
- Ineffective family coping related to stress resulting from care of injured or ill family members

Community

- Decreased ability to communicate due to imbalances in power between home buyers and contractor; at risk of community dysfunction due to inadequate systematic channels for linking families in potential crises to community resources
- At risk of environmental hazards due to inadequate inspection of new housing units by county authorities

Planning

Individual

- Children and adults need to immediately avoid pits.

Family

- Education, mutual goal setting, and collaboration will result in the family identifying hazards and using collective activity and support to eliminate hazards.

Community

- Dissemination to individuals, families, informal and formal leaders, and public officials in the community about the existence of the environmental hazards

- Coordination of efforts to bring pressure onto perpetrators of hazardous conditions and public officials responsible for taking action to eliminate hazards

Intervention

- Education and lobbying of individuals, families, and community members, including informal and formal leaders, politicians, health officials, and citizens, through the media regarding threat to health from environmental hazard in housing
- Follow-through with community members until corrective action is initiated

Evaluation

- Feedback from individuals, families, and community, including informal and formal leaders, politicians, health officials, and citizens, regarding knowledge and understanding of potential for injury and illness from environmental hazards
- Degree of coordination of efforts to bring pressure onto perpetrators of hazards to correct situation
- Outcomes of efforts taken for corrective action

Levels of Prevention

Primary

- Assessment, teaching, and referral related to prevention of accidents and infection related to environmental hazard

Secondary

- Screening for signs of infection and risk factors related to accident-prone behavior and/or environment
- Pressuring health officials to adequately inspect all new housing developments

Tertiary

- Coordinate processes that lead to correction of environmental hazard

---

Nurses: Agents of Change

Although historically nurses have been recognized as a necessary resource during wars and other emergencies, since the 1950s governments at all levels have begun to consider them indispensable in ordinary times (Aiken, 1982). The public now also recognizes nurses as necessary and valued national resources. In their advocacy role, nurses are seen as professionals whose knowledge, skill, and concern are used to promote society's well-being through a disciplined change process.

Because of their unique status in the lives of patients, because they are interpreters of the health care system to the public, and because their most basic professional activities are profoundly influenced by government-funded programs, public health nurses must know how to participate in the political process. To do this effectively, they need a sound knowledge of community, state, and national government organization and function and a clear understanding of how they interact as a system. They must know how to influence the cre-

Table 10–1
Sources for Legislative Information

Government Level	Information Available	Location
Federal	Background of members of Congress, committee assignments, terms of service	*Congressional Directory* Government Documents section of selected public or university libraries
	Congressional news, vote tabulations	*Congressional Quarterly Weekly Report* Government Documents section of selected public or university libraries
	Bills in process or legislated (bill number needed)	U.S. Congressperson U.S. Senator (may have local office)
	Health and nursing issues in U.S. Congress; American Nurses' Association political action committee *(The American Nurse)*	American Nurses' Association Washington Office 1101 14th St. N.W. Washington, D.C. 20005 (202) 789-1800
	Public health issues in U.S. Congress *(The Nation's Health)*	American Public Health Association 1015 15th St. N.W. Washington, D.C. 20005 (202) 789-5600
State	Bills in process or legislated (bill number needed)	State representative State senator (may have local office)
	Health and nursing issues in state legislature; state political action committees for nursing	State nurses association; for location, see *American Journal of Nursing* April directory issue

ation of health care legislation and how to contribute to the election and appointment of key officials. In addition, because policy is fundamental to governance, they need to know about the formulation of public policy and the acts of government and its agencies (Tables 10–1 and 10–2).

PUBLIC POLICY: BLUEPRINT FOR GOVERNANCE

Policy deals with values. It treats the "shoulds" of a situation (Diers, 1985). Policy articulates the guiding principles of collective endeavors, establishes direction, and sets goals. It influences and, in turn, is influenced by politics. Through the political process, policy directives may become realized or obstructed at any step along the way.

POLICY FORMULATION—THE IDEAL

In ideal circumstances, health care policy would be created by duly authorized bodies that would rationally—on the basis of valid evidence or data—determine what should be done. These groups would decide what would be right and then develop the political strategies to effect the desired outcomes (Diers, 1985). The question of whether a particular policy is advocated or adopted would depend on the degree that a group or the society as a whole might benefit without harm or detriment to subgroups (Spradley, 1985). Of all the seemingly limitless factors that might influence policy formation, group need and group demand should be the strongest determinants. The premises supporting the goals of health policy should be equitable dis-

Table 10–2
Sources for Electoral Information

Government Level	Information Available	Location
State	State government operations Political subdivisions Legislative information telephone number State election laws and procedures Campaign finance reports	Secretary of state, state capitol Alaska and Hawaii, office of Lieutenant governor, state capitol
County, municipal	Similar to above as appropriate to local government Political jurisdictions for each household address	County clerk, County court house, City clerk, City hall
General	Government information Political jurisdictions for each household address Names of current office holders in local jurisdictions	League of Women Voters 1730 M Street, N.W. Washington, D.C. 20005 (202) 296-1770 Telephone directory (major cities)

tribution of services and the assurance that the appropriate care is given to the right people, at the right time, and at a reasonable cost.

POLICY FORMULATION—IN THE REAL WORLD

"Real world" policy for health care, on the other hand, exemplifies both conflict and social change theories. It is the product of a continuous interactive process in which "interested" professionals, citizens, institutions, and other groups compete with each other for the attention of various branches of government (Aiken, 1982). The most obvious and prominent among these is the legislative branch, although policy is also made through executive orders, regulatory mechanisms, and court decisions. It may also issue from the recommendations of fact-finding commissions established by the legislative or executive branch. Occasionally, policy derives from formal planning. Sometimes, policy is created in the private sector. This occurs when private foundations mount demonstration projects in obvious areas of need (e.g., the homeless, high-risk adolescents) and, on the basis of the findings, official bodies act (Diers, 1985).

Health policy is rarely created through discrete, momentous determinations in relation to single problems or issues (Aiken, 1982). Most often, it evolves slowly and incrementally as an accumulation of many small decisions. It also changes slowly because changes in the social beliefs and values that underlie established policy develop within the context of actual service delivery. Most often, once a direct health care service is offered, especially an official, tax-funded service, it is difficult to discontinue it. Existing programs create tradition by establishing vested interest or a sense of entitlement on the part of the public or the recipients of the service as well as on the part of a bureaucracy that

An Example of Health Policy Formulation in the United States

THE NATIONAL Health Planning and Resource Development Act of 1974 (PL 93-641) was a major step in the direction of the statement of a coherent health policy for the United States (Diers, 1985). After almost 50 years of advocacy on the part of various health care, business, and citizen groups, health planning finally "got on the agenda." The law created a national network of local, regional, and state health planning organizations called health systems agencies and incorporated the certificate-of-need process. This policy initiative was short lived, however, because at its inception it was viewed by some, most notably, the American Medical Association, as restricting the freedom of health care providers in a competitive marketplace. Congress repealed public law 93-641 in the mid-1980s. Ironically, even though as an official policy directive national health planning is now defunct, the American Medical Association as well as the American Hospital Association are beginning to publicly endorse the planning concept (The American Nurse, January 1987).

---

invests itself not only in the delivery of the service but also in its own jobs, status, and income. This "tradition" also, in a natural effort at self-preservation, exerts political influence (Spradley, 1985).

STEPS IN POLICY FORMULATION

The tangible formulation of public policy begins with the most critical step — defining the problem and then "getting it on the agenda" (Aiken, 1982; Diers, 1985). The next step is the commitment of resources — most often, as indicated above, through the passage of legislation. Then, a regulatory schedule for the implementation of the law into program is formulated; finally, an evaluation process is designed that satisfies both regulatory and legislative remedies, should they be needed (Aiken, 1982).

POLICY ANALYSIS

Unlike advocacy, which is subjective, analysis of health policy is an objective process that identifies both the sources and consequences of decisions in the context of the factors that influence them (Spradley, 1985). Health policy analysis identifies those who benefit and those who experience a loss as the result of a policy. The following discussion of the evolution of legislation mandating payment for mammography touches on many of the dimensions set forth in the outline of an ideal health policy analysis model as developed by Spradley (Fig. 10–1).

The first step in the provision of insurance coverage for mammography screening in the United States was a 1986 congressional bill (sponsored by Representative Rose Oakar, D., Ohio) calling for mandatory reimbursement for annual mammography examinations as a voluntary option for

Medicare recipients (Broznan, 1986). Under its terms, the Medicare reimbursement structure for this "single best weapon against the undetected growth of breast cancer" was meant to serve as the model for the voluntary insurance sector. With the exception of some health maintenance organizations, private insurance plans did not include mammography because it is a diagnostic test rather than a procedure based on aggregate risk, as are other traditionally covered insurance benefits such as appendectomy.

Who would benefit from such coverage? One group of beneficiaries are women more than 40 years old, who are considered to be at risk. According to the 1987 National Health Interview Survey, 83% had not submitted to mammographic examination because of its cost (Thompson, 1989). Other beneficiaries, Oakar argues, are the taxpayers. Comparisons of her estimates of screening costs ($1.33 per person per month) with Medicare outlays for the treatment of breast cancer (approximately $680 million in 1984) demonstrate the potential long-term savings of public funds.

Who would lose? Others in testimony before a congressional subcommittee on the bill estimated that by the year 2000, at the 1986 rates, net costs would be in the range of $175 million and, therefore, prohibitively high.

A suggested solution was the exploration of methods of doing the testing more cheaply; the per-unit cost was $40–175 (Thompson et al., 1989). When less-expensive methods of technology and information management surrounding the procedure were ensured, it was argued, the benefit would probably be easier to "sell" to the Congress. Meanwhile, by May 1989, 21 states had passed breast cancer–screening legislation requiring third-party payments for the procedure. The Medicare Catastrophic Act that was to have been implemented in 1990 ensured 80% coverage of actual charges to a maximum of $50 for Medicare beneficiaries.

State mandates vary considerably as to types of insurance policies and what must be included, e.g., age limits, periodicity of examinations, quality control vis à vis sufficiently low-dose levels, and equipment standards (Thompson et al., 1989). As of early 1990 there still was no current effort to develop model legislation based on National Cancer Institute or American Cancer Society

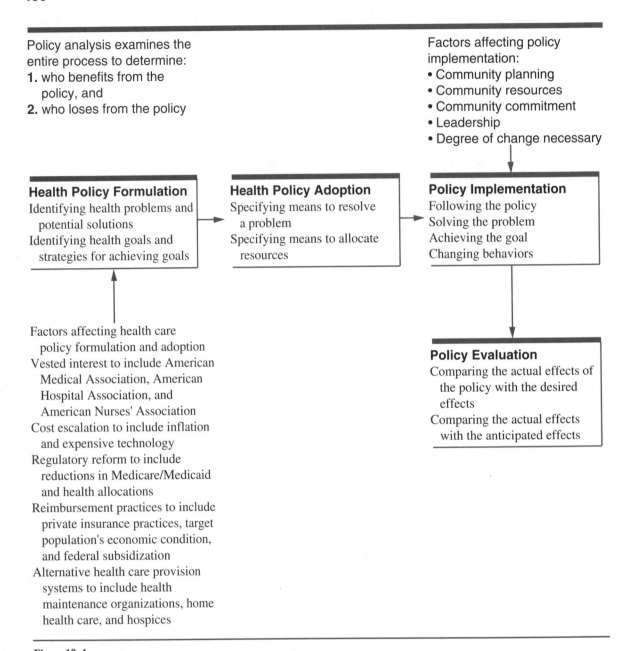

Policy analysis examines the entire process to determine:
1. who benefits from the policy, and
2. who loses from the policy

Factors affecting policy implementation:
• Community planning
• Community resources
• Community commitment
• Leadership
• Degree of change necessary

Health Policy Formulation
Identifying health problems and potential solutions
Identifying health goals and strategies for achieving goals

Health Policy Adoption
Specifying means to resolve a problem
Specifying means to allocate resources

Policy Implementation
Following the policy
Solving the problem
Achieving the goal
Changing behaviors

Factors affecting health care policy formulation and adoption
Vested interest to include American Medical Association, American Hospital Association, and American Nurses' Association
Cost escalation to include inflation and expensive technology
Regulatory reform to include reductions in Medicare/Medicaid and health allocations
Reimbursement practices to include private insurance practices, target population's economic condition, and federal subsidization
Alternative health care provision systems to include health maintenance organizations, home health care, and hospices

Policy Evaluation
Comparing the actual effects of the policy with the desired effects
Comparing the actual effects with the anticipated effects

Figure 10–1
Policy analysis model. (Redrawn from Spradley, B.: Community Health Nursing. 2nd Ed. Boston: Little, Brown & Co., 1985, p. 589.)

guidelines, even though both organizations are advocating comprehensive legislation and more and more women submit to the procedure every year, especially in the states that have the legislation. Through more discussion and sharing of the experience of current state laws and procedures, more uniform and equitable access to cost-effective screening for what is determined to be appropriate may emerge.

GOVERNMENT: THE HALLMARK OF CIVILIZATION

Government is broadly defined as the exercise of political authority, direction, and restraint over the actions of inhabitants of communities, societies, or states.

Government is crucial to human interdependence and the concomitant necessity for cooperative action. Among its purposes are the regulation of conditions beyond individual control, e.g., sewage treatment.

The delineation of the government's responsibility for health in the United States has evolved from statements of policy that express the values of the founders of the country. These statements have been issued in a series of historical documents. The earliest was the Mayflower Compact (1620), through which the Pilgrims committed themselves to making "just and equal laws" for the general good (Beard and Beard, 1944). The Declaration of Independence (1776) later established the doctrine of "inalienable Rights . . . Life, Liberty and the pursuit of Happiness" (Beard and Beard, 1944). The U.S. Constitution (1788), the bedrock of U.S. democracy as well as the supreme law of the land, established the responsibilities of the federal government, including the responsibility to "promote the general welfare." The following year, the first 10 amendments of the constitution, the Bill of Rights, ensured the sovereignty of the states in all areas not constitutionally reserved for the federal government. The Bill of Rights also emphasized specific individual freedoms (Hanlon and Pickett, 1984).

Intermediary policies have developed as needed to provide more specific guidance to government in its day-to-day operations. Some of these policies have been explicitly declared, and some have been implied through programs or other activities. An implicit policy basic to public health programming

is that the right to health of the majority must be preserved over individual freedoms. For example, a corporation may not dump hazardous wastes into the river that is a source of drinking water for a community.

Government Authority for the Protection of the Public's Health

The authority for the protection of the public's health is largely vested with the states, and most state constitutions specifically delineate this responsibility. Municipal subdivisions of states, such as counties, cities, or towns, usually have the power of local control of these services conferred by the state legislature (Fig. 10–2).

The responsibility of local, state, and federal governments for health services under varying conditions sometimes complicates attempts to determine the locus of political decision making. Because the supremacy of the state prevails in most situations, the state is a critical arena for political action. An example is the state's authority to license health professionals such as nurses and physicians as well as health care institutions such as hospitals, nursing homes, and daycare centers.

Each state establishes policies or standards for goods or services that impact the health of its citizens. As noted above, however, that authority may be affected by a number of factors. For example, the standards for pasteurization of milk sold within a state are determined by that state, but if the milk is to be sold in another state, it comes under the interstate commerce jurisdiction of the federal government. This could mean that a higher standard must be met, which in effect negates the state standard. On the other hand, where public health authority is delegated to political subdivisions within the state, they too may impose a standard that is higher (never lower) than that of the state (Hanlon and Pickett, 1984).

The federal government also has a strong influence on health services. Constitutionally, this authority is derived from the federal role in regulation of interstate commerce (e.g., meat inspection) and through broad interpretation of the general welfare clause (e.g., Medicare). Because states vary considerably in resources needed to provide health programs, significant de facto authority derives from the promise of revenues. Many of the programs

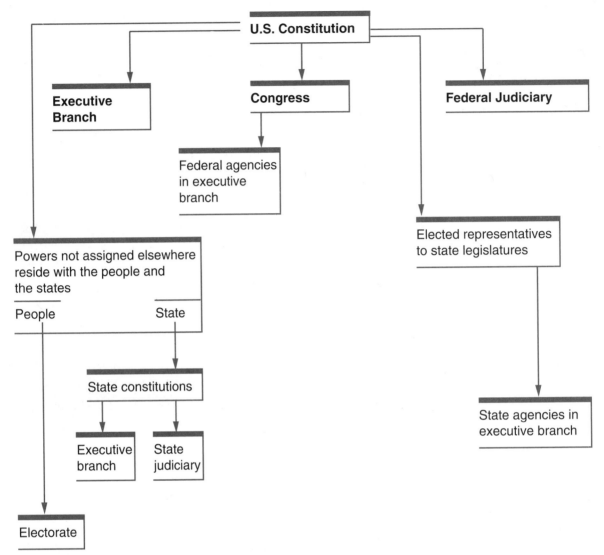

Figure 10–2
Mandate of powers. (Redrawn from Bagwell, M., and Clements, S.: A Political Handbook for Health Professionals. Boston: Little, Brown & Co., 1985, p. 23.)

discussed in this and other chapters are funded fully or partially through federal funds.

Conformance by states to federal program standards is voluntary, but the advantage of the revenue, which is withheld from the states if they do not comply, is seldom ignored. Programs such as control of sexually transmitted diseases and the statistical reporting system are standardized across the country because of the indirect but marked effect of federal funding.

Balance of Powers: Safeguard of Government

Decisions affecting the public's health are made not only at every level of government but also, as mentioned above, in each branch. The separation of powers is a principle as important to the health as it is to the economic or military status of the country.

The legislative branch (Congress at the federal level and the Legislature, General Assembly, or General Court at the state level) enacts the statutory laws that are the basis for governance. The laws, which are broad in scope, are administered and enforced by the executive branch through regulatory agencies. These agencies, in turn, define more specifically implementation of the statutes through rules and regulations known as regulatory or administrative law. The judiciary, the third branch of government, provides protection against oppressive governance and against professional malpractice, fraud, and abuse. Its function,

---

Checks and Balances on Immunization Requirements

IMMUNIZATION REQUIREMENTS for school attendance are an example of the checks and balances among the three branches of government. To protect the public welfare, most state legislatures have passed laws mandating that all primary school children be immunized against certain communicable diseases. The appropriate executive agency, usually the state health department, develops the regulations through which the law is implemented and enforced. The legislative branch has no further power over the administration of the law except to change it when necessary through amendment or repeal. The few parents who object to their children being immunized have recourse through the judicial system to have the law waived in their case.

---

through the courts, is to determine the constitutionality of laws, to interpret them, and to decide on their legitimacy when they are challenged (Beard and Beard, 1944). The courts also have jurisdiction over specific infractions of laws or regulations.

The Legislative Process: Politics in Action

The saying, "If you love the law and you love sausage, you shouldn't try to find out how either one is made," reflects a common cynicism about the decision-making process of public governance. For professional and business groups, it apparently does not pay to be too fastidious because most of them are knowledgeable about the process and adept at finding the points most sensitive to outside pressure. Medical and hospital associations are widely recognized for their shrewdness in this area. Until very recently, their success in influencing health care legislation has been remarkable. Many of the decisions that these associations have been successful influencing, however, have benefited their institutional interests, not consumers of health care or nurses as providers of that care.

HOW A BILL BECOMES A LAW

The procedure through which legislation must pass to eventually become law is similar for all U.S. legislative bodies. Once a concept has been drafted into legislative language, it becomes a bill, is given a number, and moves through a series of steps. The bill's passage is sometimes smooth, but more often than not, the bill may be extensively altered through amendments or even "killed" at various stages.

In the Congress and the 49 states that have a bicameral legislature, a bill must succeed through two legislative bodies, the House and the Senate. A bill that has moved successfully through the legislative process has one final hurdle—the chief executive's approval. The approval may be a clear endorsement, in which case the governor or president signs it. If the executive neither signs nor vetoes it, the bill may become law by default. An explicit veto conclusively kills the bill, which then can be revived only by a substantial vote of the legislature to override the veto. This is another example of the checks and balances of the government process (Archer and Goehner, 1982).

Issues that find their way into the legislative arena are commonly controversial, and proponents and opponents quickly align themselves. Because defeating a bill is much easier than getting one passed, the opposition always has the advantage. Health legislation, which usually requires preventive action (e.g., toxic waste management) or creates a new service (e.g., nursing center organizations for Medicare recipients), is at a disadvantage from several other standpoints as well.

Few elected officials are knowledgeable about the health care field. Although health is readily recognized as a national resource, it is not easily quantified into the economic terms that make the essence of an issue easy to grasp. Other disadvantages are the backgrounds, biases, and ambitions of each legislator. Frequently, the decision to run for public office is made in keeping with personal goals that are likely to differ considerably from health values or the public good.

Despite these obstacles, good health laws can be passed when concerned nurses and other health care workers understand the legislative process and use it effectively. For nurses, this is yet another mode of intervention on behalf of clients. It is as crucial to have legislation passed to reduce abuse of all children as it is to care physically and emotionally for the individual abused child.

The Nurse as Lobbyist: Persuasive Politics

To lobby is to try to influence legislators. A lobbyist is, by definition, a person who represents special interests (Kalisch and Kalisch, 1982).

terested in meeting only with their own constituents, i.e., those registered to vote in their political jurisdiction. The power of generating votes is the primary determinant of political influence!

The goal of the first contact with the official is to establish oneself as a concerned constituent as well as a credible source of information on health issues. The image of nurses as caring and helping people is a definite advantage here. In communities where nurses have already established strong political credentials, their colleagues will be more readily accepted. When a person establishes a reputation as a reliable and accurate resource, the influence as a lobbyist is substantially greater. This is simply an expression of the exchange principle, or quid pro quo, which is a firm political reality.

Legislators rely heavily on lobbyists for education on issues, and they usually want to hear from opposing sides before taking a position. Because of this dependence, the official must trust lobbyists to give accurate, even though predictably biased, in-

---

New Hampshire Nurses Learn to Lobby

NEW HAMPSHIRE nurses faced political reality when their licensing board was abolished. The sunset law, a good-government means of making boards and agencies accountable, requires periodic legislative reenactment of boards or they literally fade into the sunset. This occurred in New Hampshire during the 1981 legislative session.

Some New Hampshire legislators wanted to consolidate selected licensure under an umbrella board, and nurses became their initial target. Nurses believe they were selected because they were expected to be "clean, quiet, and cooperative and to leave by the servants' exit."

Nurses knew about the sunset review but expected the nursing board to be reauthorized with no problem. They assumed the legislators would appreciate the role of nurse li-

censure in protecting the public. However, the legislative session ended in June 1981 with no legislation for a nursing board.

A coalition of nurses rallied under the leadership of the New Hampshire Nurses' Association, calling itself the Coalition for Action in Nursing, and prepared for an upcoming special legislative session. They learned quickly how to lobby!

A friend in the state legislature, Representative Peter C. Hildreth (D), explained that "the swift passage of the bill to re-create the board of nursing was a direct result of the political clout of nurses. When they flexed their muscles, the politicians listened." And New Hampshire nurses are ensuring that politicians continue to listen! (American Nurses' Association, April 1982).

Influencing lawmakers to pass effective health legislation requires the participation of individual nurses as well as their organizations. The initial step in this process involves a telephone call to make an appointment with an elected official. Although there are exceptions, most officials are interested in

formation. And if a lobbyist does not have information requested, it should be obtained and given to the official quickly.

Each official represents a constituency with varied needs and interests, and each vote must be weighed within this context. It is important to realize that the positions taken by legislators will not always be to one's liking, and evaluation of their performance should be based on their overall voting patterns, not on their votes on isolated issues. Jesse Unruh, a political sage and former Speaker of the House of the California Legislature, explained, "Had I slain all my political enemies, I would have no friends today" (American Nurses' Association [ANA] Political Nurse, 1986). The ANA and the American Public Health Association (APHA) regularly tally and publish the records of each federal

candidate, thereby providing an opportunity to discuss issues of concern with constituents.

Telephone banks help a candidate identify supporters, opponents, and the critical "undecided" voter. These latter voters, who can make the definitive difference on election day, are courted by all candidates. The telephone interviews are highly structured and easily handled by inexperienced campaign workers. Direct contact with potential voters may occur later in the form of house-to-house "block walks" or election day poll work. The

---

The National Center for Nursing Research

THE NATIONAL Center for Nursing Research became a reality in November 1985 through broad-based bipartisan support in the U.S. Congress. The lop-sided vote to override President Reagan's veto of the center reflected the awareness of Congress of the contribution to health care made by the nursing profession. The center, within the National Institutes of Health (NIH), was a negotiated compromise from an earlier attempt to establish a separate Institute of Nursing Research.

During the floor debates preceding the successful override vote, numerous friends of nursing spoke passionately about the importance of nursing research. Senator Orrin

Hatch (R., Utah) reported a NIH researcher saying that "nurses are not a disease and at NIH we do disease research." The Senator's retort to his colleagues was that nursing research is ". . . related to health promotion, health education, and disease prevention. If that seems incompatible to the mission of NIH, then perhaps we should rename it The National Center for Disease."

Nurses are instrumental in educating their public officials as well as the public about nursing. As demonstrated by the creation of the National Center for Nursing Research, their political process clearly affects policy decisions in Washington.

---

legislator on all issues related to the organization's priorities. This information can be very helpful in evaluating elected officials.

The Political Process: Campaigning, a Means to an End

Helping someone win an election is a sure way of gaining influence. All candidates are grateful for campaign assistance and usually remember those who have helped. Although campaign contributions are commonly thought of as being financial, they can also take the form of campaign activities.

Because nurses are frequently unable to contribute much money, they can provide these invaluable services. For the novice, there are always veteran campaigners who are eager to help them "learn the ropes." Initially, one can address or stuff envelopes for mailings. One can also invite friends and neighbors for a social gathering to meet the

confidence this requires comes with experience and a strong commitment to the candidate and the cause.

Hosting a social function to allow nurse colleagues to meet the candidate is a welcome contribution to the campaign. Because nurses are substantial in number and their voting record is humanistic, they are valued as a political force. ANAPAC, the ANA political action committee (PAC), promotes awareness of this through its buttons and bumper stickers that proclaim that there are "5,000 nurses in every congressional district."

Nurses' Campaign Work Helps Win Elections
"CONGRESSWOMAN Jan Meyers (R., Kansas) and Senator Tom Harkin (D., Iowa) credit their successful 1985 elections to the financial and personal support they received from nurses in their states" (American Nurses' Association, 1985).

The federal Hatch Act, or a variation of it at other government levels, constrains government workers, including nurses, from certain political activities. The intent of this act was to protect employees from coercion by superiors. This protection, however, often affects personal freedom. In some situations, court decisions have ruled such prohibition against political activity an abridgement of free speech and thus unconstitutional. The armed forces have specified policies for their personnel (Archer and Goehner, 1982). All government employees should know about policies that may restrict their political activity.

The Power of Numbers

When nurses unite to influence health issues, they have enormous power. Comprising almost 1.9 million, they constitute the largest single discipline in health care (ANA, 1987).

This power of numbers is never more apparent than in the legislative process. A legislator carefully weighs the number of constituents supporting or opposing a bill before the legislator decides how to vote. A sizable block of constituents on one side of an issue can significantly affect that vote. "Representing the district" is important to a legislator for ethical reasons as well as for political pragmatism (Fig. 10–3).

PROFESSIONAL ASSOCIATIONS AND LOBBYING

Collective action by nursing and health care organizations such as ANA and APHA is critical to their goals. These associations monitor legislative activity related to health issues and link the process to their membership. This continual surveillance of the legislative environment is critical, as even seemingly minor amendments can have profound effects on health services.

Thorough monitoring requires the participation of people who are knowledgeable not only about nursing and health care but also about the political intricacies of the legislative process. The ANA and the APHA have full-time staff lobbyists who work with Congress. Many of their state constituent associations also work with state legislatures. However, regardless of how effective association lobbyists are in promoting the interests of nurses and society, they always need grass roots cooperation to deliver the real punch. In the final analysis, it is sufficiently high numbers of communications — letters and telephone calls — from individual constituents that have the greatest influence.

PACs

Since the 1970s, other important sources of collective influence have been PACs. These nonpartisan

Figure 10–3
The power of numbers. (With permission from Texas Nursing, September 1976. Copyright Texas Nurses Association, 1976.)

entities promote the election of candidates believed to be sympathetic to their interests. PACs are established by professional associations and business and labor groups under federal and state laws that stipulate how they may contribute financially to campaigns. The advantage of a PAC is that small donations from many members, when added together, make an impressive addition to a campaign fund in the name of an organization. This gains the attention of the candidate and earns good will for the group.

Cogent arguments are advanced — primarily by Common Cause, the self-styled citizens' lobby — against PACs. There is valid concern about the correlation of major PAC contributions and the legislator's votes on special interest legislation. As long as PACs are a reality of political life, however, nurses need to recognize their power and support those that are committed to electing candidates sympathetic to health care issues.

Most national associations of health care providers have PACs. Among the strongest are those representing hospitals, nursing homes, home health agencies, pharmaceutical interests, and insurance companies. A PAC that contributes considerable funds — non–health related as well as those that are health related — is the AMPAC, of the American Medical Association. State medical associations also have strong PACs. This means that organized medicine has a powerful influence on national and state elections and thus on health care legislation.

ANAPAC has been increasingly successful in raising funds and contributing to successful political races. In the 1988 elections, it endorsed 303 congressional candidates and contributed more than $291,800 to their campaigns. An impressive 89% of these races were successful (Ford-Roegner, 1988). State nurses associations have established PACs for participation in the state electoral process with equally remarkable results.

COALITIONS

When two or more groups join to maximize resources, thus increasing their impact and improving their chances of success in achieving a common goal, it is called a coalition. Coalitions of health care providers often work together on issues such as family violence and fluoridation of water supplies. An outstanding example of such cooperative action has been the establishment of rehabilitation programs for health professionals whose practice has been impaired by substance abuse or mental health problems.

Nursing and consumer groups often form coalitions to advance their shared interests in health promotion. The Grey Panthers is one consumer group that is a frequent and valued ally of nursing because of its concern for quality of life and health

---

Nurses Rally Against Registered Care Technologists

THE "INNOVATIVE solution to the shortage of bedside personnel" proposed by the American Medical Association (AMA) in 1988 enraged nurses and brought them together as had nothing else in history. The position of registered care technologist (RCT) was designed to "help" nurses and the nursing shortage through training individuals to "continuously monitor and implement physicians' orders at the bedside" and report to the physician. Although the AMA assured nurses that it had their practice needs in mind, nursing was not consulted about this. The legal and ethical implications to licensed nurses were not addressed.

The reaction by nurses and all major nursing organizations was instantaneous, universal, and volatile! Nurses unified to protect their patients and their role. Coalitions of nurses (licensed vocational, licensed practical, and registered) developed strategies to refute the AMA proposal and articulate the methods under way to increase the ranks of nurses.

Nurses were not alone in their concern for the quality of patient care by the RCTs, and many physician groups stood in opposition. Consumer groups, such as the American Association of Retired Persons, expressed opposition, and numerous major newspapers editorialized against the AMA.

Although the AMA continues to support its RCT plan, as of 1990, it had not begun any of the four proposed demonstration projects. Nurses realized their power possible through unity (Stewart, 1988).

care for the aging. Groups like the National Women's Political Caucus and the National Organization for Women share an interest in promoting the rights of women and are natural collaborators with nurses, for whom an issue is equity.

Political Action: One Public Health Nurse's Story

Joan Diamond, RN, a public health nurse in rural Texas, has been a long-time activist, both professionally and politically. She was acutely aware of the inequities that were causing higher-than-average communicable disease and infant mortality rates in her region. The affluence of most Texans stood in sore contrast to the poverty experienced by the people in her caseload. However, she knew that her nursing care interventions, regardless how skilled, could never improve individual client health without changes in the area's economic, environmental, and educational conditions.

These changes could never be realized unless the system designed to support the status quo was changed. Her frequent contacts with local appointed and elected officials were gaining her nothing except a reputation as "the nagging nurse." Rumblings of discontent from others in the area, however, were being heard by the district delegation to Austin, the state capitol. Out of this activist ferment emerged a young businessman who stood as a "reform" candidate for the state legislature.

Joan found Carl Findley's philosophy of government bracingly different from that of the incumbent and compatible with her own. All Findley knew about health care, however, was that he was "for it." He was, nevertheless, eager to learn, and he asked Joan to serve on his campaign advisory committee. He also asked her to develop a position paper that described the health problems in the district and established goals for improvement through his representation.

Joan consulted with clients and colleagues while writing the position paper and involved them in presenting it to the candidate for his approval — and education. Findley was pleased to have the information, especially the statistics that so convincingly documented the problems.

Meanwhile, Joan began actively recruiting colleagues to work in the campaign. The political ac-

tivity for most of these nurses had been limited to voting. They found the idea of political involvement both tantalizing and terrifying, but Joan was persuasive. She argued that if they really cared about promoting health, they should be helping to send a sympathetic and knowledgeable policymaker to Austin.

Under Joan's tutelage, the nurses, several of whom brought their children and friends to help, manned the campaign office for two nights a week. They prepared mailings, handled the telephone work, and dispatched yardsign crews. In addition, they organized neighborhood coffees and campaign rallies. They distributed and displayed bumper stickers advocating Findley's election. Several walked house-to-house in key neighborhoods handing out campaign leaflets and presenting themselves as nurses supporting Findley to get better health care for the district. They almost always had animated discussions with the residents.

Although the campaign was long and arduous, election day brought sweet reward; Findley won. In his victory address, he gave glowing praise to Joan and the other nurses for their contribution to his success.

Once in office, the Honorable Carl Findley's record showed he had learned that to be in favor of health meant working for better health legislation. He consulted regularly with Joan about health- or nursing-related legislation — a significant 200–250 bills of the approximately 2,000 bills filed in each legislative session! He also helped the Texas Nurses Association staff in lobbying his colleagues on health issues.

Findley is recognized by his constituents as representing the district well, and they reelected him six more times. As for the basic health issues of the people on her caseload that got Joan involved in politics in the first place, progress, albeit slow, has been made.

A major health initiative that received a great deal of attention in the Texas Legislature in 1985 was passed only because of Joan's influence with Findley. The Indigent Health Care Legislation was a bare bones effort to provide programs, especially perinatal and preventive services, for the poor. The need for state action had been well documented by a select committee of legislators, professionals (including one registered nurse), and businesspeople.

Coalitions pro and con were formed. The Texas Nurses Association aligned itself with public hospitals, community health centers, and numerous consumer groups to promote the program. When the final vote was imminent, Texas Nurses Association staff were astounded to learn that Findley was going to vote against it. They wasted no time in tracking down Joan in a North Texas Well Baby Clinic, and they told her the problem. She immediately called Findley, and her call was transferred to him on the floor of the House (an example of her power with him). At the very last minute, she was able to convince Findley that he should support the bill for the good of his district.

One vote is always important, but Findley's vote had special significance — it created a tie. This required the Speaker of the House to break the tie, which he did with a dramatic "aye." Without Findley's support, this bill would have been defeated by one vote. Because of Joan's professional concern and political activism, the poor of Texas received better health care.

NURSING AND THE HEALTH OF THE NATION: A SOCIAL CONTRACT

A profession derives its status from a contract with society to provide essential services under conditions of altruism and trust. Nurses are demonstrating this professionalism by serving the healthy and the sick and by serving future generations through their influence in promoting wellness as public policy. Nurses are a powerful political force.

If every public official had at least one nurse consultant to help put health issues in perspective, health policies would be improved. Although some nurses contribute to health policy development, more are needed. Both nurses and the public should be constantly attuned to opportunities to promote the appointment or election of nurses to policy-making positions.

An encouraging note is the increasing number of nurses winning elective office, whether school board or state house. The ANA reported that in January 1990, 46 nurses were serving in state legislatures and three were serving in major statewide offices.

Other nurses affect public policy through appointed positions in state and federal government. Sheila Burke, RN, as Chief of Staff for U.S. Senate Minority Leader Robert Dole (R., Kansas), was the highest ranking woman in the U.S. Senate administration. Carolyn Davis, RN, PhD, was President Reagan's appointee to a major health care policy-making position of Administrator of the Health Care Financing Administration from March 1981 through August 1985. Art Agnos, mayor of San Francisco, appointed five well-qualified nurses to major health policy positions in the city government. He was confident of their ability because of frequent contact with them during his prior tenure as a California assemblyman (personal communication; JoAnne Powell, March 1, 1990).

SUMMARY

Historically, nurses have been able to make significant differences in the quality of life experienced by the members of the communities they serve. The case study of Carrie Long presented in this chapter is an example of how one nurse gathered data and worked with residents, bureaucrats, and the media to effect change in a situation that was negatively affecting public health. By understanding how government works, how bills become law, and how legislators make decisions, nurses can influence policy decisions through individual efforts such as letter writing, participation in political campaigns, and selection of candidates who support policies conducive to improving the health and welfare of all citizens. When organized in lobbying groups, coalitions, and PACs, nurses can be a powerful force that brings about change in the delivery and quality of the health care of aggregates.

Learning Activities

1. Develop an "Insight" bulletin board with each class member contributing cartoons, anecdotes, and clippings about issues affecting public health or nursing.

2. Develop expertise on a current public health or nursing issue, including an understanding of the causes, effect on the public and possible solution(s). Influence its resolution through any of the following activities:

   - Write a succinct letter to the editor of a local paper.
   - Write a position paper and submit it to the "Opinion Page" of a local paper.
   - Write to elected or appointed officials whose jurisdiction could be influential on the issue.
   - Meet with an elected or appointed official to discuss the issue. (This can be done in groups of two or three.)
   - Call in to a radio talk show about the issue.
   - Volunteer to speak on the issue to appropriate consumer or professional groups.

3. Meet with an elected official for a 15-minute appointment in a group of two or three to ask about the official's concerns and priorities. If the official is not familiar with health issues, do not preach; instead, begin an educational process.

4. Invite an elected official who is sympathetic to nurses to speak to the local chapter of the National Nursing Students Association to discuss the political process and health policy.

5. Invite an elected official to spend a day with a public health nurse or nursing student in appropriate activities. (Take black-and-white pictures for press use.)

6. Invite a medical reporter from the press, radio, or television to observe public health nursing activities that would appeal to the public.

7. Participate in a group organized around a public health issue (e.g., disposable diapers, toxic waste, fluoride).

8. Serve as a volunteer in a campaign for a candidate who is supportive or potentially supportive of public health or nursing issues.

9. Serve as a volunteer for a political party of choice.

REFERENCES

Aiken, L.: Nursing in the 1980s. Philadelphia, J. B. Lippincott, 1982.

American Nurses' Association: New Hampshire nurses learn politics the hard way. Polit. Nurse 2;1, 1982.

American Nurses' Association: Veto victory. Polit. Nurse 5;1,4, 1985.

American Nurses' Association: Nurses, Politics and Public Policy (videocassette). Kansas City, Missouri, ANA, 1985.

American Nurses' Association: Building bridges over troubled waters. Polit. Nurse 6;6, 1986.

American Nurses' Association: Facts About Nursing. Kansas City, Missouri, ANA, 1987.

Archer, S., and Goehner, P.: Nurses: A Political Force. Monterey, California, Wadsworth, Health Sciences Division, 1982.

Bagwell, M., and Clements, S.: A Political Handbook for Health Professionals. Boston, Little, Brown & Co., 1985.

Beard, C. A., and Beard, M. R.: A Basic History of the United States. Philadelphia, The Blakiston Co., 1944.

Broznan, N.: Cost of mammography is a major deterrent. *The New York Times,* September 22, 1986, p. 19.

Cutchin, D. A.: Guide to Public Administration. Itasca, Illinois, F. E. Peacock, Publishers, Inc., 1981.

Diers, D.: Policy and politics. *In* Mason, D., and Talbott, S., eds.: Political Action Handbook for Nurses. Menlo Park, California, Addison-Wesley, 1985, pp. 53–59.

Deloughery, G. L., and Gebbie, K. M.: Political Dynamics: Impact on Nurses and Nursing. St. Louis, C. V. Mosby, 1975.

Ford-Roegner, P.: 89% of candidates endorsed by ANA-PAC win election. *Am. Nurse 20*;10–12, 1988.

Hanlon, J. J., and Pickett, G. E.: Public Health: Administration and Practice. St. Louis, Times Mirror/Mosby, 1984.

Kalisch, B. J., and Kalisch, P. A.: Politics of Nursing. Philadelphia, J. B. Lippincott, 1982.

Kalisch, P. A., and Kalisch, B. J.: The Advance of American Nursing. Boston, Little, Brown & Co., 1978.

Osgood, G. A., and Eliott, J. E.: Federal government. *In* Mason, D., and Talbott, S., eds.: Political Action Handbook for Nurses. Menlo Park, California, Addison-Wesley, 1985.

Spradley, B.: Community Health Nursing. 2nd Ed. Boston, Little, Brown & Co., 1985.

Stewart, R. F.: RCTs: A quick-fix boondogle. Heartbeat *1*;3–4, 1988.

Thompson, G. B., Kessler, L. G., and Boss, L. P.: Breast cancer screening in the United States: A commentary. Am. J. Public Health *79*;1541–1543, 1979.

Aggregates in the Community

CHAPTER

11

Child Health

Upon completion of this chapter, the reader will be able to:

1. Identify the major indicators of child and adolescent health status.

2. Describe social factors that contribute to declining child health status.

3. Discuss the individual and societal costs of poor child health status.

4. Discuss public programs targeted to children's health.

5. Apply knowledge of child health needs in planning appropriate, comprehensive care to children at the individual, family, and community levels.

Mary Brecht Carpenter
Susan Rumsey Givens

It is said that a nation's destiny lies with the health, education, and well-being of its children. If that is true, the future of the United States may be in jeopardy. In the United States, far too many children are not healthy. Every year, nearly 40,000 babies die before reaching their first birthday, and an additional 400,000 children develop chronic debilitating conditions that may limit their potential and productivity.

Poor child health status has long-term implications. Children who go to school sick or hungry, who cannot see the blackboard or hear the teacher, who abuse drugs or miss school frequently, or who are troubled by abusive parents or disruptive living circumstances often do not do as well as healthy children. It is then no surprise that so many of our nation's youth become trapped in the cycle of school failure, dropping out of school, delinquency, incarceration, teen pregnancy, and poverty.

This chapter will focus on the health needs of children and adolescents and the implications for community health nursing. Addressed will be indicators of child and adolescent health status, social factors that affect child health status, costs to the individual and society of poor child health, public programs targeted to children's health, and strategies to improve child health at the individual, family, and community levels.

INDICATORS OF CHILD HEALTH STATUS

Infant Mortality

Infant mortality is an important gauge of children's health status. It is often seen as a marker of the health and welfare of an entire community or society. The first year of life is the most hazardous until the age of 65. With a 1989 infant death rate of 9.8 deaths per 1,000 live births, the United States ranked an abysmal 22nd in infant mortality behind other industrialized nations including Japan, Sweden, Canada, and France (Table 11–1).

After two decades of steady improvement in infant mortality in the United States, progress has nearly stalled (Fig. 11–1). Black infants face a far greater risk of dying in their first year of life than do white infants, and a recent slowdown in the decline of black infant mortality has further widened the gap between black and white infant mortality (see

Table 11–1
Infant Mortality Rates: Ranking of the Developed Countries, 1989*

Rank	Country	Infant Mortality Rate†
1	Japan	4.59
2	Sweden	5.77
3	Finland	6.03
4	Singapore	6.61
5	Netherlands	6.78
6	Canada	7.20(c)
7	Switzerland	7.34
8	France	7.36
9	Hong Kong	7.43
10	Federal Republic of Germany	7.44
11	Ireland	7.55
12	German Democratic Republic	7.56
13	Norway	7.72
14	Australia	7.99
15	Spain	8.07‡
16	Austria	8.31
17	United Kingdom	8.42
18	Denmark	8.45
19	Belgium	8.64
20	Italy	8.80
21	Greece	9.77
22	United States	9.80
23	Israel	9.94
24	New Zealand	10.19

* Singapore and Hong Kong, not defined as "developed" by the United Nations, are included in the ranking since they have infant mortality rates below that of the United States rate.

† Number of infant deaths per 1,000 live births.

‡ Rate is for 1988.

From Office of International Statistics: National Center for Health Statistics, Infant Mortality Data Base (unpublished data). Hyattsville, Maryland, U.S. Public Health Service, 1989.

Fig. 11–1). Other minority groups, including Hispanics, Asians, and Native Americans, experience infant mortality rates much closer to that of whites.

Infant deaths are categorized according to age; neonatal represents infant deaths when less than 28 days old, and postneonatal represents infant deaths

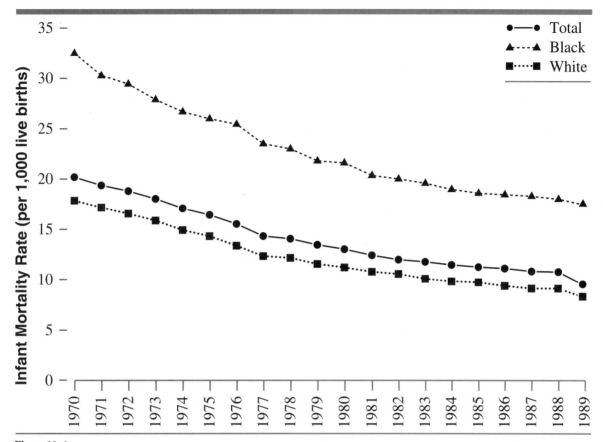

Figure 11–1
U.S. Infant mortality rate by race (1970–1989). (Redrawn from National Center for Health Statistics: Health: United States 1991. Hyattsville, Maryland, U.S. Public Health Service, 1991.)

when 28 days to 1 year old. The leading causes of death during the neonatal period are congenital anomalies, prematurity, and the effects of maternal complications. Leading causes of death during the postneonatal period are sudden infant death syndrome, congenital anomalies, injuries, and infection.

LOW BIRTH WEIGHT

Overall, the leading predictor of infant mortality is low birth weight (infants born weighing less than 5.5 pounds). Every year in the United States, more than 250,000 babies are born at low birth weight. Black infants are more than twice as likely as white infants to be born at low birth weight (National Center for Health Statistics [NCHS], 1990).

Although low-birth-weight infants comprise

only 7% of infants born, they account for nearly 60% of all the infant deaths (U.S. Congress, Office of Technology Assessment [OTA], 1988). Low-birth-weight infants are almost 40-fold as likely to die within the first 4 weeks of life; if raised in disadvantaged households, they have twofold to threefold the risk of physical and mental disabilities such as blindness, deafness, learning disabilities, and mental retardation (Institute of Medicine [IOM], 1985).

Despite the development of advanced technologies for keeping very small babies alive, the decline in the rate at which babies are born at low birth weight has stalled during the past 20 years (NCHS, 1990). Risk factors associated with low birth weight include lack of prenatal care, maternal smoking, alcohol and drug use, and low socioeconomic status.

LACK OF PRENATAL CARE

Associated with the high rate of infant death and sickness in the United States is the large number of women who do not receive early and regular prenatal care. Babies born to women who received no prenatal care are threefold as likely to be born at low birth weight and fourfold as likely to die as are babies of mothers who received first trimester care (IOM, 1985). One fourth of pregnant women in the United States fail to receive prenatal care beginning in the first trimester or they receive fewer than the 13 visits recommended by the American College of Obstetricians and Gynecologists (NCHS, 1990).

Through prenatal care, specific causes of infant morbidity and mortality such as sexually transmitted diseases, anemia, hypertension, poor maternal nutrition, and urinary tract infections are identified and treated. Health education and counseling provide women with the information they need to make lifestyle changes that will help ensure a healthy pregnancy. Comprehensive prenatal care is particularly important for low-income women because it helps them obtain needed social services such as the Special Supplemental Food Program for Women, Infants, and Children (WIC), food stamps, treatment for substance abuse, housing, child care, and job training.

SUBSTANCE ABUSE

Ideally, prenatal care begins when a woman is planning her pregnancy so that potential problems that can affect the development of a fetus in the very early stages of gestation can be identified and treated. For example, cigarette smoking and drug and alcohol use during the first trimester can harm the developing fetus before a woman even knows that she is pregnant. Likewise, in early pregnancy, uncontrolled chronic conditions such as diabetes can lead to congenital anomalies and developmental problems in the fetus.

SOCIOECONOMIC STATUS

Women who are poor; young; unmarried; or black, Hispanic, or Native American; or who have completed less than 12 years of education are less likely to obtain adequate prenatal care than are those who are older, married, white or Asian, and better educated. Women without health insurance are at greatly increased risk for not receiving prenatal care. Other barriers that block access to prenatal care include (IOM, 1985):

- Inadequate supply of health care providers and services
- Lack of coordinated, "user-friendly" services and inhospitable conditions
- Lack of knowledge and personal attitudes and lifestyle conditions that inhibit women from seeking prenatal care

Accidental Injuries

The causes of death among children change with age (see Fig. 11–1). After the first year, accidental injury (including motor vehicle injury, drowning, burning, and suffocation) is the leading cause of death. Injuries kill six times as many children as does cancer.

Motor vehicle accidents are a major cause of child deaths. Approximately one third of those killed are pedestrians. Approximately 500 children die each year from bicycle accidents; 80% of these deaths are the result of head trauma (American Academy of Pediatrics, 1990). Many of the children who survive serious motor vehicle accidents suffer severe permanent neurological damage. Nearly half of all motor vehicle accidents involving teenagers involve alcohol (National Highway Traffic Safety Administration, 1987).

Violence

Beginning in adolescence, suicide and homicide are major causes of death (Blum, 1987). Since 1978, suicide has been the leading cause of death among persons aged 15–24. Although suicide rates have increased for both white and black males aged 15–19, the rate for whites is more than twice that of blacks (Miller et al., 1989).

Homicide is the second leading cause of death for 15–24-year-olds in the United States, with black youth being at greatest risk. Since 1978, homicide has been the leading cause of death for black males aged 15–24 (NCHS, 1991).

"New Morbidities" of Youth

In addition to the dangers of accidents, suicide, and homicide, children, especially adolescents, are also confronted with a host of health-related problems, called the "new morbidities" of youth. These problems include teen sexuality and childbearing, sexually transmitted diseases (STDs) including AIDS, and substance abuse (OTA, 1991).

- Annually, almost 1 million girls become pregnant. The great majority of these pregnancies are unintended (NCHS, 1988). Teen childbearing poses significant health risks to the baby, including death, prematurity, low birth weight, and neglect.
- Sexually active teenagers have the highest rates of STDs among heterosexuals of all age groups. It has been estimated that one in every seven teenagers has an STD, thereby affecting approximately 2.5 million teenagers (Quackenbush, 1987).
- The U.S. Public Health Service estimated that childhood AIDS will soon become a major national public health problem. Nearly 3,500 children were projected to have AIDS by 1991, with another 20,000 being HIV infected (Koop, 1987).
- In a national survey, approximately one third of the responding adolescents reported having five or more alcoholic drinks at least once in the previous 2 weeks (U.S. Department of Health and Human Services [USHHS], 1990). In another national survey, almost 25% of adolescents reported having ever used an illicit drug (OTA, 1991).

Lead Poisoning

Lead poisoning is a preventable cause of death, mental retardation, cognitive and behavioral problems, and sensory and other disabilities in children. High levels of lead are also associated with lower class standing in high school, increased absenteeism, lower vocabulary and grammatical reading scores, poorer hand-eye coordination, and longer reaction times (Needleman et al., 1990). In the United States, one in every six children under the age of 6 has blood levels that are dangerously high, making lead poisoning the most prevalent disease of environmental origin among U.S. children (National Education Association, 1990).

Lead is an invisible threat. Sources of lead contamination include lead-based paint, water, food, soil, dust generated during restorations of older homes, and raising and lowering of windows

painted with lead-based paint. Before 1950, the use of lead-based paint was quite common, but the 1972 Lead Paint Poisoning Prevention Act severely limited the manufacture of lead-based paint. Nevertheless, an estimated 42 million housing units in the United States contain lead-based paint.

The neurotoxic properties of lead have been recognized for at least a century, but the nature and extent of subtle long-term effects are just being realized. Unlike the obvious signs of measles or polio, low-level lead poisoning is difficult to recognize in children. Children with elevated lead levels may be at a higher risk of dropping out of high school or have a reading disability. Exposure to lead, even in children who remain asymptomatic, may have enduring effects on school performance.

Immunizations

Although most serious communicable diseases can be prevented with immunizations, immunization rates among children in the United States are declining at an alarming rate. This decrease has resulted in increased outbreaks of once nearly eradicated diseases such as measles, rubella, and whooping cough.

Immunization status is particularly inadequate for poor and preschool children. One third of all poor children and one fourth of all preschoolers are not immunized against such common childhood diseases as measles, rubella, polio, and mumps. Nearly half of all measles cases occur in children under the age of 5 years (Centers for Disease Control [CDC], 1991a). In 1989, only 70–80% of 2-year-olds were immunized against measles, mumps, and rubella (Public Health Service, 1990). (See Chapter 23 for recommended immunization schedules.)

There are several reasons for the inadequate immunization rates. State immunization requirements vary, and most states do not have blanket immunization requirements for preschoolers. Therefore, preschoolers remain particularly vulnerable to outbreaks of measles, mumps, and pertussis. Poor children and their families may have difficulty paying for immunizations, and they are not likely to have insurance to help cover the expense. These children also often lack a primary care provider who can ensure that they obtain their immunizations on schedule.

Child Abuse and Neglect

Child abuse and neglect are other indicators of child health status. Approximately 1,000 U.S. children die each year from abuse and neglect (National Center on Child Abuse and Neglect, 1981). In 1987, almost 2.2 million official reports of child abuse or neglect were made to child protective service agencies. This number is expected to increase as the public becomes more attuned to reporting suspected abuse.

Most cases reported involved children under the age of 5, and dominant characteristics of their parents are substance abuse and having been abused themselves as children. A growing population of very young children are being raised by drug-abusing parents who are ill equipped to cope with the physical and psychological demands of caring for young children.

SOCIAL FACTORS AFFECTING CHILD HEALTH

As is true for all age groups, children's health is largely determined by social, nonmedical factors. However, because children, especially young children, are dependent on their families or others for their health and well-being, factors such as parents' or caretakers' education, income, and stability, and the security and safety of the home environment significantly impact children's physical and mental health and overall well-being.

Although most U.S. children are born healthy and remain so, many are not. Although some children at all income levels, of all races, and in all types of families suffer acute and chronic health conditions, those living in poor households or single-parent families, and those without health insurance coverage or of minority cultures are more likely to suffer from health problems. These at-risk children tend to have more developmental disabilities, are less likely to be immunized, and suffer more frequently from accidental injuries. Because their mothers are less likely to receive prenatal care, they are at higher risk for being born at low birth weight and of dying in their first year of life.

To successfully meet the health needs of at-risk children, the community health nurse must be cognizant of family and other social influences in a child's life and be prepared to address the child's health needs in that context.

Protective Factors

Beginning prenatally, a child's chances of being healthy are markedly improved when the mother obtains early and comprehensive prenatal care, eats a nutritious diet, and refrains from smoking, alcohol use, and illegal substance abuse. Women with adequate family incomes and health insurance, women who are married, and women who have at least a high school education are more likely to receive health care and practice healthy behaviors during pregnancy. When children eat nutritious diets, live in safe homes and neighborhoods, have supportive adults as role models, and practice healthy behaviors, many potential health problems can be prevented or minimized.

A child's access to health care also influences health and, although most children do receive immunizations, well child care, and acute care services, the gap is growing between those who can obtain timely health care and those who cannot (Johnson et al., 1991). A child's ability to obtain health care is affected by family income, place of residence, whether the child is in a one- or two-parent family, and whether one or both parents work in companies that offer health insurance.

Risk Factors

Just as family and community can offer important protection to support a child's health, serious risk factors may also be present that act as obstacles to good health. The most common risk factor is poverty, although being poor alone does not always mean a child is at risk. Compounding the risks of poverty, many poor children also live in unsafe neighborhoods filled with the danger and influence of crime and drugs. Being in single-parent families, having poor nutrition, and lacking positive and nurturing adult role models also increase health risks. A combination of these factors all too frequently contributes to a child's chances of being in poor physical or mental health.

POVERTY

Children are far more likely than adults to live in poverty (Fig. 11–2). In 1989, 12.6 million children lived in poverty,* representing 22.5% of children

---

* The federal poverty level for a family of three in 1992 was $11,570.

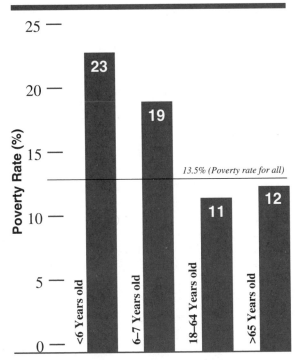

Figure 11–2
Poverty rates by age group (1987). (Redrawn from National Center for Children in Poverty: Five million children. New York, National Center for Children in Poverty, 1990. Prepared by Child Trends, Inc., Washington, D.C.)

under age 6 and 18.1% of children between the ages of 6 and 17. During the same year, the poverty rate for adults was 10.2%; for the elderly, it was 11.4% (Johnson et al., 1991). Children are more likely to be poor in America than in many other developed nations, including Canada, the United Kingdom, Sweden, and Australia (Smeeding et al., 1988).

Children in poverty experience more health problems than do their peers in higher income families (Klerman, 1991). Deaths from unintended injuries, child abuse, sudden infant death syndrome, and infectious diseases including AIDS are more common. Poor children also suffer more from low birth weight, asthma, dental decay, lead poisoning, and learning disabilities. The extreme living conditions of poor children who are also homeless, migrants, or in foster care usually compound their health problems. These social and economic burdens can create a sense of despair and hopelessness among parents and children that hinders healthy behaviors.

MATERNAL SUBSTANCE ABUSE

Whether an expectant mother smokes, drinks alcohol, or uses illicit drugs during pregnancy has profound effects on her infant's birth weight and neurological and physical development. The use of these substances cuts across all socioeconomic lines. Smoking is more common than alcohol and illicit drug use, and elimination of the use of tobacco among pregnant women would have significant results. A study by the U.S. Department of Health and Human Services found that if no women smoked during pregnancy, the rate of low birth weight would decrease by 25%, and the rate of infant mortality would decrease by 10% (Kleinman et al., 1988).

Although the effect of low alcohol consumption is uncertain, high levels of consumption by pregnant women are associated with spontaneous abortion, mental retardation of the child, low birth weight, and a cluster of congenital defects, including the nervous system dysfunction called fetal alcohol syndrome (FAS). In 1989, the U.S. Surgeon General reported that at least 5,000 infants were born with FAS annually and an additional 50,000 had fetal alcohol effects (National Commission to Prevent Infant Mortality [NCPIM], 1990). Alcohol abuse during pregnancy is the primary preventable cause of mental retardation in children (Lancet, 1983).

Illegal drug use by pregnant women has increased substantially in recent years with the introduction of crack cocaine. National estimates of drug-exposed newborns range from 100,000 to 375,000 per year (Chasnoff, 1988; U.S. General Accounting Office [GAO], 1990). Although poor, inner-city women often are perceived as more likely to be addicted to drugs, one study found that the problem of drug use during pregnancy is just as likely to occur among privately insured patients (13.1%) as among those relying on public assistance (16.3%). This study also found that illicit drug use among women is unrelated to race and socioeconomic status (Chasnoff, 1990).

Low birth weight and congenital anomalies are associated with drug use. Children born to crack-addicted mothers, in particular, are more likely to be of low birth weight and have long-term learning problems (Chavez et al., 1989). Drug use is also a major factor in the escalation of STDs among women and newborns because women often resort to prostitution to obtain money for drugs. In 1989, the syphilis rate in infants was the highest in several years, with 941 cases reported (CDC, 1991b). As tragic as this is, it is worsened by the dearth of treatment programs for addicted pregnant women and women with children.

SINGLE-PARENT HOUSEHOLDS

By far, children in households headed by single women are more likely to be in poverty. These children score lower on many health indicators than those living in two-parent homes (Klerman, 1991). Young women who become mothers before age 18 are less likely to graduate from high school and more likely to be single parents. Their incomes are often quite low; owing to this and a lack of social supports, their children's health may be less than optimal.

SOCIAL FACTORS AFFECTING ADOLESCENT HEALTH

All children's health is affected by social factors, but adolescents are faced with challenges to their health that are unique to this time of life. Although adolescence is usually considered a healthy time of life, it is the only age group in the United States not to have experienced an improved health status during the past 30 years (Blum, 1987).

This age group is increasingly confronted with violence in the form of accidents, suicide, and homicide as the leading causes of mortality. Teenagers also are facing health-related problems, such as substance abuse, teen sexuality and childbearing, and STDs including AIDS (OTA, 1991). Problems found more frequently among adolescents living in poverty include poor physical health, depression, pregnancy, and criminal victimization (National Commission on Children, 1991).

Whether an adolescent obtains needed health and other services is influenced by several factors such as attitudinal or behavioral obstacles presented by adolescents themselves, ability and willingness of health care providers to identify and treat their often complicated needs, and the broad array of social concerns that impact adolescent health.

Adolescence is a period of growing independence and experimentation with risk-taking be-

haviors. These changes affect the willingness of adolescents to discuss certain matters with parents and other authority figures, including health care providers. Confidentiality of services has been identified as important to an adolescent's willingness to obtain care, especially for sensitive matters such as sexual behavior, mental health, and substance abuse. Experts indicate that the traditional medical and health care system is unprepared to deal with adolescent health needs (Blum, 1987). Nevertheless, solutions to their unmet needs depend on how these issues are addressed.

In response to the inadequacies of traditional medicine to meet the complex health needs of the adolescent population, specialized service centers, such as school-based clinics and adolescent health clinics in hospital outpatient departments, have been created. These clinics serve largely low-income clients with multiple health and social needs, and their significance in meeting adolescent health needs is growing. In 1988, school-based or school-linked clinics served 120 junior and senior high schools nationwide, with most being located in low-income, inner-city areas. The number of clinics increased by 41% between 1987 and 1988 (Robert Wood Johnson Foundation, 1989).

COSTS TO SOCIETY OF POOR CHILD HEALTH

The best way to ensure the success and well-being of future generations is for each child to start life healthy and to have that health status maintained throughout childhood. Although many children are healthy, happy, and cared for by warm, loving families, too many children grow up with physical and emotional health problems that will impair their ability to reach their full potential. Any health problem — whether hunger, poor vision or hearing, increased blood levels of lead, asthma, anemia, dental caries, or teen pregnancy — can interfere with school attendance and a child's ability to grow and develop normally, to learn, and to succeed in life.

For no other age group is the prevention of health problems more significant or more cost-effective than for children. Each dollar spent on the prevention of physical and emotional problems in children is a sound investment.

Prenatal Care

Prenatal care, which costs as little as $600, can save hundreds of thousands of dollars by preventing conditions such as low birth weight that require expensive medical treatment after an infant has been born. The cost to our nation of low birth weight is astronomical. Health care costs for low-birth-weight infants average between $14,000 and $30,000. The total annual cost of neonatal intensive care for sick and small babies exceeds $2.5 billion. The IOM has calculated that every $1.00 spent on prenatal care for high-risk women can save more than $3.38 on the cost of providing direct medical care during the first year of an infant's life (IOM, 1985).

Immunizations

Another example of cost-savings can be seen in immunization programs that, in addition to saving money, can prevent disease, disability, and death. One estimate in 1983 revealed that the combined measles-mumps-rubella vaccination program saved $14.40 for every $1.00 spent on immunizations (White et al., 1985). Although the cost of immunizations has risen in recent years owing to liability concerns of vaccine manufacturers, there is no question that immunization is still cost-effective.

Lead Poisoning

Removal of the sources of lead in our environment is expensive but not nearly as expensive as the long-term consequences of lead poisoning. The CDC estimates that preventing a child's blood lead level from reaching dangerous levels saves $3,331 per child in avoided special education costs (Needleman, 1991).

Once discovered, lead can never be entirely removed from a child's body, nor can the neurological damage that has already been done be reversed. There is no cure for lead poisoning. Clearly, the most cost effective treatment is prevention.

Drug Abuse and Delinquency

Likewise, providing drug treatment for an addicted mother can save thousands of dollars in medical care, foster care, and special educational services for drug-exposed babies. According to one study, the median hospital charge for a drug-affected in-

fant was $5,500, and the median for nonexposed infants was $1,400 (U.S. General Accounting Office, 1990).

Adolescent Pregnancy and Parenting

Preventing pregnancy among school-aged mothers can reduce the rate of dropping out of school, welfare dependency, low birth weight, and infant mortality. It has been estimated that the public costs incurred in 1 year for all families that were started when parents were adolescents total $16.65 billion (costs of Aid to Families With Dependent Children program, Medicaid, and food stamps) (Burt and Levy, 1987).

PUBLIC HEALTH PROGRAMS TARGETED TO CHILDREN

A number of public programs have been established to address the health needs of children specifically, or in conjunction with a targeted population of the medically underserved or poor. In addition, local and state public health and social service agencies aim to protect the health of an entire community or state through programs such as water fluoridation, sanitation, and the control of infectious diseases. Furthermore, broad-based strategies, such as the elimination of lead-based paint, use of lead-free gasoline, and mandatory use of child safety seats in automobiles, serve to improve the health of children through community-wide approaches.

Medicaid

Poor children's ability to obtain health care services has improved since the introduction of Medicaid and its Early and Periodic Screening, Diagnosis, and Treatment (EPSDT) program. Medicaid is financed by state and federal governments and pays for health care services received by eligible individuals. In recent years, Congress has enacted expansions of Medicaid eligibility for pregnant women, infants, and children in an effort to improve the nation's infant mortality rate and children's health status.

Through EPSDT, children covered by Medicaid can receive a range of health and health-related services that far exceeds those usually covered by private insurance. Services include health, developmental, and nutritional screening; physical examinations; immunizations; vision and hearing screening; certain laboratory tests; and dental services. Unfortunately, not all poor children are eligible for Medicaid, and not all those eligible are enrolled. In 1991, Medicaid assisted only 59% of children living in poverty (National Commission on Children [NCC], 1991). Barriers standing in the way of reaching all eligible children include:

- Lengthy application forms and eligibility determination processes
- Stigma of welfare that is associated with Medicaid
- Increasing numbers of physicians unwilling to take Medicaid patients
- Unfriendly, overcrowded, and uncomfortable waiting rooms and public clinics

Medicaid does not provide access to health care for all those without private health insurance coverage. More than 34 million Americans, 8.3 million of whom are younger than age 18, are without any type of insurance. This represents approximately 13% of all children (NCC, 1991). Children without Medicaid or health insurance use fewer medical services than those who are insured, and they are less likely to receive their immunizations (NCC, 1991).

Direct Health Care Delivery Programs

Although Medicaid pays for the health care used by its recipients, several other public programs directly deliver health care services to underserved populations. Although some of these underserved populations are eligible for Medicaid, many are neither eligible nor do they have private health insurance.

MATERNAL AND CHILD HEALTH BLOCK GRANT

This program has its roots in a number of smaller, categorical grant programs that were consolidated in 1981. The grant was funded by Congress for $650 million in fiscal year 1992. Most of these funds are allocated to the states, which add their own funds and in turn provide funds to local public health clinics and other programs to deliver basic health care to pregnant women and children as well as additional services to children with special health care needs.

COMMUNITY AND MIGRANT HEALTH CENTERS PROGRAMS

The Community and Migrant Health Centers Programs began in 1965 as two of the early programs of the U.S. Office of Economic Opportunity. Through a network of approximately 550 centers that operate more than 2,000 clinics, these health centers provide comprehensive primary health care to more than 6 million low-income people, 2.1 million of whom are children under the age of 15. Fiscal year 1992 funding for these programs totaled $537.2 million.

NATIONAL HEALTH SERVICE CORPS

The National Health Service Corps (NHSC) is another federal program through which children receive primary health care services. The NHSC sends physicians, nurses, and other health care providers to underserved areas of the country. Through scholarships and loan repayment plans, the program assists students with medical, nursing, and other training in return for a certain number of years of service in a rural or urban underserved area. Since 1970, approximately 13,000 health care providers have been assigned, and many have worked in community and migrant health centers.

Although the NHSC funds were substantially reduced in the 1980s, in the past few years Congress has increased its funding to $101.1 million in fiscal year 1992 in response to the continued lack of health care providers, especially obstetric providers, in certain parts of the country.

SPECIAL SUPPLEMENTAL FOOD PROGRAM FOR WOMEN, INFANTS, AND CHILDREN

Although not exclusively a health program, WIC provides highly nutritious foods and nutrition education to low-income pregnant and breast-feeding mothers and their children under the age of 5. In addition, clients are encouraged to obtain prenatal care and preventive health care. Established in 1972, WIC has been one of the most successful, popular, and cost-effective public health programs. Women participating in WIC have less chance of delivering a low-birth-weight baby than similarly situated women not in the WIC program. One study found that for every $1.00 spent on WIC for pregnant women, the associated savings in the

Medicaid program during the first 60 days after birth ranged from $1.77 to $3.13 for both newborns and mothers (Food and Nutrition Service, 1990). Participation in WIC also increases children's chances of being immunized.

Despite its successes, all those eligible for WIC cannot be enrolled owing to funding limitations. With an annual appropriation of $2.6 billion, WIC serves approximately 4 million persons of an eligible population of more than 7 million (Johnson et al., 1991).

HEAD START

Head Start is a federally funded comprehensive early childhood program for low-income children ages 3–5. Head Start provides not only educational opportunities for children but also medical, dental, and mental health services and nutritional and social services. It strongly emphasizes parental involvement on a voluntary or paid-staff basis. Head Start is widely viewed as a successful program, although it does not reach all eligible children. Congress has been steadily increasing the funding level in recent years in an attempt to reach the goal of full enrollment by 1994. Considerable ground will have to be covered to reach this goal, however. In 1990, approximately 20% of eligible children were enrolled in Head Start (NCC, 1991).

STRATEGIES TO IMPROVE CHILD HEALTH

As pointed out earlier, most children in the United States are born healthy and remain so throughout childhood. However, this is not the case for all children. The protective factors operating in the lives of healthy children and the interventions they receive should be available to all children, but they are not.

Because child health is affected not only by medical factors but also by social and family concerns, responsibility for improving child health rests with parents, communities, employers, government, and health care professionals. Only as a child gets older can that individual be held responsible for practicing healthy behaviors and obtaining proper health care.

In an effort to involve nationwide activity and support for improving the health of children and of all Americans, the U.S. Public Health Service has established Health Goals for the Year 2000 (Public Health Service, 1990) (Table 11–2). The numerous

Table 11–2
Healthy People—2000: Selected Child Health Goals

Indicators	Goal	Year	Data
Child death rate	Reduce the death rate for children by 15% to no more than 28 per 100,000 children ages 1–14.	1987	33
Infant mortality rate	Reduce the infant mortality rate to no more than seven deaths per 1,000 live births.	1988	10.0
	Reduce the black infant mortality rate to no more than 11 deaths per 1,000 live births.	1988	17.6
Low-birth-weight infants	Reduce low birth weight to an incidence of no more than 5% of all live births.	1988	6.9%
	Reduce low birth weight to an incidence of no more than 9% of black live births.	1988	13%
Immunizations	Increase to 90% the percentage of children under the age of 2 who are fully immunized.	1989	70–80%
Alcohol and drug use	Reduce to 12.6% the proportion of children under the ages of 12–17 who have used alcohol, marijuana, or cocaine in the past month.	1988	25.2%
Suicide rate	Reduce suicides to no more than 8.2 per 100,000 youth ages 15–19.	1987	10.3

From U.S. Public Health Service, U.S. Department of Health and Human Services: Healthy People 2000. Washington D.C., U.S. Government Printing Office, Publication no. (PHS)91-50213, 1990.

goals and objectives that have been set for children provide opportunities to help an individual health care provider or a community, a state, or the nation focus on efforts that are needed to achieve optimal health for all children. To realize these goals, actions are needed at all levels of government and within families and communities.

Parent's Role

Even before conception, a mother's responsibility begins to ensure the health of her fetus. Before and during pregnancy, she must develop healthy behaviors, including proper nutrition and avoidance of smoking, alcohol, drugs, and other behaviors that could harm her fetus. This is particularly important in the early stages of gestation, when fetal organ systems are developing. It is also important for the mother to receive prenatal care early in pregnancy.

Parents must ensure that their children have a safe environment at home, in the neighborhood, and at school. They must protect their children from abuse and neglect and ensure that they attend school. Starting with breast-feeding, parents must give their children nutritious food and ensure that they are immunized, receive needed health care services, and acquire healthful lifestyles. One of a parent's most important jobs is to model healthy behaviors for their children.

Community's Role

Families need support from their community and society to fulfill their roles and responsibilities. Communities should create safe neighborhoods, support the development of community-based health programs, and promote community health education campaigns concerning prenatal care, smoking, nutrition, and other health topics. At individual and community levels, they can also sponsor health fairs, immunization drives, bicycle safety helmet campaigns, crime prevention and reduction programs, and other projects that help families develop healthy lifestyles and gain access to needed health services. Communities are well situated to encourage one-stop shopping for health and health-related services needed by children and families. Despite the number of health and social service programs that exist, they are usually poorly coordinated with each other, and there is little collaboration among the professional disciplines

(NCPIM, 1991). Communitywide initiatives to better organize services and reach out to families through public awareness campaigns and home visits can alert parents to the importance of immunizations, a safer environment, prenatal care, and other services and provide information on how to obtain these services.

As part of the community at large, the media should be involved with promoting child health. The media significantly influence children's lives and their perceptions of the world and themselves. From developing information campaigns about prenatal care and immunizations to discouraging violence and explicit sex in popular television programs, the media can have a profound effect on improving children's health and well-being.

Employer's Role

The private sector can play a role in improving the health of individual children or of the community in general. An employer can make health care more accessible to families with children by offering affordable health insurance that covers the employee and dependents. Employers also can provide for adequate sick and family leave and sponsor opportunities for employees to learn about healthy diets, healthy pregnancies, how to fight substance abuse, and ways to decrease stress. Businesses also can offer on-site child care and work with community leaders and public officials to initiate communitywide health promotion projects targeted to children.

Government's Role

The role of government in the United States in promoting or ensuring the health of children is more limited than it is in other countries. Most other countries have defined policies on children's health; the United States does not. Not only do such policies indicate that children are a priority of the government, but also they help shape the operation of programs and their method of funding.

In this country, state and federal governments have several public health programs, as discussed earlier, that provide assistance to children, especially to those at risk owing to poverty or other disadvantages. Despite the number of programs and the significant funds committed to each, many children with health problems do not receive the services they need; also, the various programs are not well coordinated, making access to them more difficult. Although these programs are not a substitute for a family's or caretaker's care and concern, they are important in protecting and promoting health and delivering services to those who would otherwise go without.

Effective programs for underserved populations should be expanded, and the managers and front-line workers such as community health nurses, social workers, physicians, and caseworkers should be encouraged to cross their program lines and professional orientations to collaborate and thereby assist children with problems that adversely impact their health. "One-stop shopping," i.e., user-friendly, accessible services for children and families, is an important concept for public programs to embrace so that children can receive services, especially preventive health and social services, before a problem becomes a crisis. Outreach efforts through programs such as home visiting should be an integral part of health initiatives to find children in need and draw them to the services they require.

Community Health Nurse's Role

Of all of the members of the community, the community health nurse is often the one most aware of children's health status, any barriers that stand between them and the care they need, and other factors that may be adversely affecting their health. Armed with this information and knowledge of the health and other resources available, it is the community health nurse's responsibility to advocate for improved individual and community responses to the needs of children, to participate in publicly funded programs, and to network with other professionals to improve collaboration and coordination of services.

One important role of the community health nurse is to help link community health services with the school system. Children must be healthy to learn, but often children arrive at the school door with vision, hearing, and other health problems that could have been prevented or alleviated with appropriate education, screening, and treatment. As children move out of the preschool years, sometimes their only connection with the health care system is through the school health nurse. School health nurses can be an important source of primary health care and health information for students and their families.

Community health nurses can act as catalysts to

Roles of the School Health Nurse

SCHOOL HEALTH nurses may be employed directly by the local school system or by city, state, or county governments. The nurse can play an important role in linking community health services with school-aged children. School health nurses may undertake some or all of the following responsibilities:

● Take part in curriculum selection or development
● Participate in in-service training
● Provide information regarding health service issues
● Identify health-related problems that affect school performance and/or attendance (symptoms of depression, lack of energy, drug abuse, child abuse)
● Promote staff wellness and physical fitness
● Provide classroom instruction
● Serve as a link to community health resources
● Facilitate integration of program components using student visits to nurse's office as teaching opportunities

From National School Boards Association: School Health: Helping Children Learn. Washington, D.C., NSBA, 1991. Copyright National School Boards Association reprinted with permission.

---

alert the health professional community, business leaders, religious groups, and voluntary organizations to the needs of children and the strategies that can improve their ability to obtain the services they need. Community health nurses, as individuals and groups, can also influence planning and implementing necessary changes in the health care system so that children's health is improved and national health goals for the year 2000 are achieved.

APPLICATION OF THE NURSING PROCESS

By applying the principles of the nursing process to the individual, family, and community, the community health nurse can more systematically and effectively provide child health services. Most communities offer a range of preventive and other important services needed by children. The community health nurse must thoroughly understand the needs of the individual child and family and be aware of available community resources to act as a catalyst for meeting child health needs.

Case Study

Jane Swanson, a community health nurse working for the county health department, received a telephone call from the high school nurse informing her that Sheila Parkhurst, a 16-year-old high school student from a low-income family, would be coming in that afternoon for a pregnancy test. Sheila had already missed three menstrual periods and was afraid to talk about this with her family, although she and the school nurse had a long discussion. She was going to ask her boyfriend to take her to the health department clinic for the pregnancy test after school.

Assessment

Sheila's pregnancy test was positive, and she was estimated to be 3½ months pregnant. She was upset and did not want to talk with Jane at the health department. Jane arranged to make a home visit the next afternoon.

Jane learned from the school nurse that Sheila felt at this time that she wanted to keep her baby. Knowing that a number of issues needed to be addressed at the first home visit, Jane prepared by developing a list of possible areas of assessment that covered individual, family, and community concerns. Her list included the following:

Individual

- Medical risk factors
- Emotional well-being
- Health-promoting and risk-taking behaviors
- Understanding of importance of obtaining preventive care services
- Understanding and acceptance of pregnancy
- Health insurance status
- Access to transportation

Family

- Adequacy of housing structure
- Safety of neighborhood
- Ability of family members to provide emotional support
- Ability of family to provide financial support

Community

- Prenatal and pediatric care
- Health and social services coordination
- Emotional guidance and counseling
- Educational opportunities for pregnant and parenting teenagers
- Job training
- Nutrition services such as WIC and food stamps
- Pregnancy and parenting education
- Child care availability

Assessment Data

Individual

- The client was already in the early second trimester of pregnancy, with no prenatal care. She was engaging in risk-taking behaviors (smoking, alcohol use, and poor eating habits).

- She desires to keep the baby and remain in school, yet she does not have a realistic understanding of the responsibilities of parenthood.

Family

- The family experienced disappointment with news of its only daughter's pregnancy, but the mother expressed a willingness to provide emotional support. The father, who was emotionally distant, expressed anger.

Community

- Jane determined that prenatal services were available but only during school hours.
- No parenting classes were available.
- No child care was available at the high school, making returning to school more difficult.
- Given her family income, Medicaid coverage and WIC services were probably available but would require lengthy and complex applications at the welfare office.

Diagnosis

Individual

- Altered health maintenance related to lack of prenatal care
- Knowledge deficit of effects of nutrition, smoking, and alcohol use on fetal development
- Altered parenting potential related to unrealistic expectations about parenting responsibilities

Family

- Altered family processes related to anger and disappointment over daughter's pregnancy

Community

- Lack of adequate prenatal and parenting services available to adolescents

Planning

To ensure that the action plan is complete, realistic, and successfully implemented, Jane must thoroughly identify the factors affecting Sheila's health and well-being. In addition, mutual goal setting among Sheila, her family, and Jane must be accomplished.

Individual

Long-term Goal

- Pregnancy outcome will be healthy.

Short-term Goals

- Sheila will obtain prenatal care.
- Sheila will express an understanding of the reasons to change nutrition and substance use habits.
- Sheila will plan with the nurse actions to change habits.

Long-term Goal

- Sheila will demonstrate successful parenting behaviors.

Short-term Goal

- Sheila will enroll in parenting class. (If classes are not available in time, reading material, films, videotapes, or visits with experienced parents may be used.)

Family

Long-term Goal

- Family's ability to handle crises will improve as evidenced by their ability to discuss problems and engage in mutual problem solving.

Short-term Goal

- Parents will display supportive behaviors such as accompanying Sheila to prenatal care appointments, helping her to engage in healthy behaviors, and assisting her to arrange child care so she can remain in school.

Community

Long-term Goal

- Accessible and user-friendly prenatal and other health care services targeted to adolescents will be established.

Short-term Goals

- Evening hours at the health department clinic will be extended to accommodate students and working families.
- Pregnancy and parenting classes will be provided in the community.
- A child care facility will be established in or near the high school.

Intervention

The immediate, mutually agreed-on goals established by the nurse, family, and individual must be addressed to help Sheila achieve a healthy birth outcome and begin her role as a successful parent. In addition, the nurse must act as an advocate for communitywide change to ensure that the needs of individuals are being met by the community in which they live. To achieve aggregate-level goals, the community health nurse must communicate the needs of individuals to program managers, community leaders, policymakers, and others in decision-making roles.

For example, the health department director may not be aware that prenatal services are not readily accessed by high-risk groups of women such as adolescents. By bringing this and possible solutions to the director's attention, clinic hours can be expanded to benefit both pregnant teenagers and pregnant working women.

Likewise, it is in the best interest of the pregnant teenager, her child, her family, and the community for her to remain in school and obtain her high school diploma. The community nurse is in an ideal role to stimulate dialogue about the consequences of dropping out of high school and to facilitate action around policies such as child care for parenting teenagers so that they may remain in school.

Evaluation

Evaluation strategies must involve both processes and outcomes on the individual, family, and community levels. For example, evaluating a strategy for an individual might entail considering processes (e.g., the number of prenatal appointments kept by the pregnant woman) or outcomes (e.g., whether the infant was born at full term). Evaluating a strategy at the community level would require assessing whether programs were established (such as an evening prenatal clinic) and whether the establishment of the programs led to improved outcomes such as a reduced rate of preterm births or a reduced rate of dropping out of school by adolescent mothers.

Levels of Prevention

For no other aggregate is prevention more important than for children. In particular, primary prevention strategies, such as early prenatal care, good nutrition, and healthy behaviors among pregnant women, help ensure that a child is born healthy and gets a healthy start in life. The costs to the child, family, and society for not implementing prevention strategies are astronomical.

Primary Primary prevention to a great extent depends on the age of the child. For the youngest children, strategies include preconceptional counseling and the practice of healthy behaviors by mothers before becoming pregnant and by parents and their children. Primary prevention also includes the prevention of unwanted pregnancy; this is especially important for adolescents.

Secondary Once pregnant, the mother must receive early and adequate prenatal care, practice healthy behaviors, obtain any other necessary social and supportive services, and prepare herself for becoming a parent. Although the woman is responsible for many of these practices, it also is incumbent upon the community to ensure that adequate preventive health services such as prenatal care, nutrition and dietary counseling, pregnancy and parent education, and social services are available. The community health nurse can alert community leaders to the individual and societal consequences of women not receiving prenatal care or of teenagers not being able to complete high school owing to child care responsibilities. This kind of information can help planners design programs and policies that are in the best interest of the individual and society.

Tertiary Tertiary prevention involves the rehabilitation of individuals and aggregates to maximize their potential functioning. In the case of adolescent pregnancy, the community health nurse is in an ideal position to initiate programs and services that will prevent future unwanted pregnancy among teenagers and will help the parenting teenager provide the best care possible to the child. These programs could include the establishment of parenting classes and support services to help adolescents complete their education; coordination of health and social services for the mother and her child, including family planning services; and well child care, immunizations, and nutrition services.

SUMMARY

Child health status remains an important indicator of the health of the nation. Despite worrisome data that reveal declining child health status, community health nurses can use their experience and "inside knowledge" of barriers to child health to educate others.

Rather than limiting their approach to caring only for the individual and family, community health nurses can maximize their roles to collaborate and forge alliances where needed to solve children's health problems. Nurses are authority figures in places where it may least be expected. Being on the front line of health care is a powerful and very real position to members of Congress, state legislators, mayors, and others. By creatively using this kind of power, community health nurses can contribute greatly to improving the health and well-being of all children.

Learning Activities

1. Examine infant mortality statistics in your community and compare the rates with state and national averages. Is infant mortality higher for particular ethnic groups within your community?

2. Imagine that you are a pregnant teenager without finances or available transportation and determine how you would obtain prenatal care.

3. Accompany a pregnant woman to a department of social services as she tries to establish Medicaid eligibility for herself and her unborn child.

4. Identify pregnancy and parenting education programs in your community that are available to low-income women.

5. Survey your local medical community to discover the extent to which physicians determine the children in their care that are at high risk for high blood levels of lead.

6. Determine the availability of immunizations to low-income children.

7. Survey businesses in your community to find out whether they offer maternity health insurance benefits, paid or unpaid maternity/paternity leave for new parents, and time off for prenatal care appointments. Use this information to develop a strategy to encourage the adoption of family-friendly policies and practices in the business community.

8. Communicate through writing letters or holding meetings about the needs of children with those in policy-making positions.

9. Develop working relationships with lay and consumer groups to address children's health needs in the community.

REFERENCES

Alcohol and the Fetus—Is zero the only option? Lancet *1*;682–683, 1983.

American Academy of Pediatrics: Injuries: Children's Number One Killer. Washington, D.C., AAP, 1990.

Blum, R.: Contemporary threats to adolescent health in the United States. J.A.M.A. *257*;3390–3395, 1987.

Burt, M. R., and Levy, F.: Estimates of public costs of teenage childbearing: A review of recent studies and estimates on 1985 public costs. *In* Hofferth, S. J., and Hayes, C. D., eds.: Risking the Future: Adolescent Sexuality, Pregnancy, and Childbearing. Volume II. Washington, D.C., National Academy Press, 1987, pp. 15–29.

Centers for Disease Control: Measles—United States 1990. M.M.W.R. *40*;369–372, 1991*a*.

Centers for Disease Control: Drug Abuse: The Crack Cocaine Epidemic: Health Consequences and Treatment. Washington, D.C., U.S. General Accounting Office, publication No. GAO/HRD-91-55FS, 1991*b*.

Chasnoff, I. J.: Hospital Incidence Study. *In* Perinatal Addiction Research and Education Update. Chicago, National Association for Perinatal Addiction Research and Education, 1988.

Chasnoff, I. J., Landress, H. J., and Barrett, M. E.: The prevalence of illicit drug or alcohol use during pregnancy and discrepancies in mandatory reporting in Pinellas County, Florida. N. Engl. J. Med. *322*;1202–1206, 1990.

Chavez, F. C., Mulinare J., and Cordero, H. F.: Maternal cocaine use during early pregnancy as a risk factor for congenital urogenital anomalies. J.A.M.A. *262*;795–798, 1989.

Editorial. Lancet *1*(8326); 1983.

Food and Nutrition Service, U.S. Department of Agriculture: The Savings in Medicaid Costs for Newborns and Their Mothers From Prenatal Participation in the WIC Program. Volume I. Washington, D.C., U.S. Government Printing Office, 1990.

Institute of Medicine: Prenatal Care: Reaching Mothers, Reaching Infants. Washington, D.C., National Academy Press, 1988.

Institute of Medicine: Preventing Low Birthweight. Washington D.C., National Academy Press, 1985.

Johnson, C. M., et al.: Child Poverty in America. Washington, D.C., Children's Defense Fund, 1991, pp. 1–39.

Kleinman, J. C., Pierre, M. B. Jr., Madans, J. H., et al.: The effects of maternal smoking on fetal and infant mortality. Am. J. Epidemiol. *27*;274–282, 1988.

Klerman, L. V.: Alive and Well? A Research and Policy Review of Health Programs for Poor Young Children. New York, National Center for Children in Poverty, Columbia University, 1991.

Koop, C. E.: Testimony Before the Select Committee on Narcotics Abuse and Control, U.S. House of Representatives, New York, July 27, 1987.

Miller, C. A., Fine, A., and Adams-Taylor, S.: Monitoring Children's Health: Key Indicators. 2nd Ed. Washington, D.C., American Public Health Association, 1989.

National Center for Children in Poverty: Five Million Children. New York, Columbia University, 1990.

National Center for Health Statistics: Advance report of final natality statistics, 1986. Monthly Vital Stat. Rep. *37*; 1988.

National Center for Health Statistics: Advance report of final natality statistics, 1988. Monthly Vital Stat. Rep. *39*(suppl 4); 1990.

National Center for Health Statistics: Firearm mortality among children, youth, and young adults 1–34 years of age, trends and current status: United States, 1977–88. Monthly Vital Stat. Rep. *39*(suppl):1–14, 1991.

National Center for Health Statistics: Advance report of final mortality statistics, 1989. Monthly Vital Stat. Rep. *40*(suppl 2); 3, 1992.

National Center on Child Abuse and Neglect: Study Findings: National Study of the Incidence and Severity of Child Abuse and Neglect. Washington, D.C., U.S. Government Printing Office, DHHS publication No. OHDS 81-30325, 1981.

National Commission on Children: Beyond Rhetoric: A New American Agenda for Children and Families. Washington, D.C., U.S. Government Printing Office, 1991.

National Commission to Prevent Infant Mortality: Troubling Trends: The Health of America's Next Generation. Washington, D.C., U.S. Government Printing Office, 1990.

National Commission to Prevent Infant Mortality: One-Stop Shopping: The Road to Healthy Mothers and Children. Washington, D.C., U.S. Government Printing Office, 1991.

National Education Association: Testimony before the Subcommittee on Toxic Substances, Environmental Oversight, Research and Development, U.S. Senate, July 27, 1990.

National Highway Traffic Safety Administration: Fatal Accident Reporting System, 1985. Washington, D.C., Department of Transportation, publication No. (HS) 806-566, 1987.

National School Boards Association: School Health: Helping Children Learn. Washington, D.C., 1991.

Needleman, H. L.: Childhood lead poisoning: A disease for the history text (editorial). Am. J. Public Health *18*;685–687, 1991.

Needleman, H. L., Schell, A., Bellinger, D., et al.: The long term effects of exposure to low doses of lead in childhood. N. Engl. J. Med. *322*;83–88, 1990.

Public Health Service, U.S. Department of Health and Human Services: Healthy People National Health Promotion and Disease Prevention Objectives. Washington, D.C., U.S. Government Printing Office, DHHS publication No. (PHS)91-50213, 1990.

Quackenbush, M.: (February 21, 1987). Testimony before Select Committee on Children, Youth and Families, U.S. House of Representatives, Berkeley, California, February 21, 1987.

Robert Wood Johnson Foundation: Making Connections: A

Summary of Robert Wood Johnson Foundation Programs for Adolescents. Princeton, New Jersey, RWJ, 1989.

Smeeding, T. M., Torrey, B. B., and Rein, M.: Patterns of income and poverty: The economic status of children and the elderly in eight countries. *In* Palmer, J. M., Smeeding, T. M., and Torrey, B. B., eds.: The Vulnerable. Washington, D.C., The Urban Institute Press, 1988.

United Nations Statistical Office: Population and Vital Statistics Report. New York, UNSO, 1990.

U.S. Congress, Office of Technology Assessment: Healthy Children: Investing in the Future. Washington, D.C., U.S. Government Printing Office, Publication no. OTA-H-345, 1988.

U.S. Congress, Office of Technology Assessment: Adolescent Health. Volume I: Summary and Policy Options. Washington, D.C., U.S. Government Printing Office, Publication no. OTA-H-468, 1991.

U.S. Department of Health and Human Services: 1989 National High School Senior Drug Abuse Survey. Washington, D.C., HHS News, 1990.

U.S. Department of Justice: Office of Justice Programs: Children in Custody, 1977–1987. Washington, D.C., U.S. Government Printing Office, 1988.

U.S. General Accounting Office: Drug Exposed Infants: A Generation at Risk. Washington, D.C., U.S. Government Printing Office, Publication no. GAO/HRD-90-138, 1990.

White, C., Koplan, J., and Orenstein, W.: Benefits, risks and costs of immunization for measles, mumps and rubella. Am. J. Public Health *75*;739–744, 1985.

CHAPTER 1

Women's Health

Upon completion of this chapter, the reader will be able to:

1. Discuss the incidence and prevalence of gender-specific health problems.

2. Determine the major indicators of women's health.

3. Relate the impact of poverty on the health of women.

4. Identify barriers to adequate health care for women.

5. Discuss the impact of public policy on the health of women.

6. Apply the nursing process to women's health concerns in the community.

7. Discuss reproductive health in relationship to the work place.

8. Examine prominent health problems among women of all age groups (from adolescence to old age).

9. Discuss primary, secondary, and tertiary prevention stages as they relate to women's health.

10. State the necessity for increased research efforts focused on women's health issues and their needs.

Donna Neal Thomas
Roma D. Williams

To achieve the goal of "health for all" by the 21st century, all women must have access to affordable and available health services. A significant number of women and their families face tremendous barriers in their attempts to gain access to health care. Knowledge deficits related to health promotion and disease prevention activities prevent women of all educational and socioeconomic levels from assuming responsibility for their own health and well-being.

The women's movement of the 1970s set high on its agenda a call for the reform of systems affecting the health of women. Women were encouraged to become involved not only as consumers of health services but also as establishers of health policy. Health professions, which were traditionally underrepresented by women, began to accept more women. Traditionally female-dominated professions such as nursing and teaching became more assertive in their demands to be recognized as full professions and to be recognized for their contributions to society.

In her preamble to a new paradigm for women's health care, Choi (1985) declared that collaboration and an interdisciplinary approach are necessary to meet the health care needs of women. She further stated that "essential to the development of health care for women are the concepts of health promotion, disease and accident prevention, education for self-care and responsibility, health risk identification and coordination for illness care when needed" (Choi, 1985).

This chapter will address the health of women as an aggregate, from adolescence through old age. Major indicators of health, health problems, and the socioeconomic, sociocultural, and health policy issues surrounding the health of women will be explored. Application of the nursing process to women's health concerns in the community setting and the identification of current and future research aimed at improving the health of women will be discussed.

MAJOR INDICATORS OF HEALTH

Women use health services at a much higher rate than men. Nevertheless, there are few data that truly allow for interpretation of the level of health. In the United States, data used to indicate the health status of any aggregate, whether men, women, or children, is indicative of the level of illness in our society. When the consumer becomes more vocal and assertive in expressing the desire to see that more of the health care dollar is directed toward health promotion and disease prevention than toward illness care, new systems may emerge for assessing the health status of the population.

LIFE EXPECTANCY

Females born in 1970 in the United States had an average life expectancy of 74.7 years. This is 7.6 years longer than males born in the same year. During the past decade, females continued to have the advantage in life expectancy. Male infants born in 1987 have a life expectancy of 71.8 years compared with 78.3 years for female infants (U.S. Bureau of the Census, 1989).

Racial background also influences life span. Since 1970, black females born in 1989 have added 6.3 years to their life expectancy; instead of the 69.4 years projected for longevity in 1970, the black female born in 1989 can expect to live 75.7 years. However, the life expectancy of white females born in 1989 is 79.1 years (U.S. Bureau of the Census, 1987).

The female sex has the advantage when it comes to longevity in most industrialized and nonindustrialized countries. Nevertheless, projections of life expectancy for female infants born in 2000 are less than that of male infants for infants born in Bangladesh, Bhutan, India, Nepal, Pakistan, and Papua New Guinea (Women—A World Report, 1985).

MORTALITY

Leading Causes of Death

Since 1960, the leading cause of death among men and women in the United States has been heart disease. However, the overall death rate related to diseases of the heart has shown a considerable decline during the past three decades. In 1960, 205.7 deaths per 100,000 women were due to heart disease, whereas in 1987, 121.7 deaths per 100,000 women were due to heart disease (U.S. Bureau of Census, 1990).

The five major causes of death in 1987 among women of all age groups are presented in Table 12–1.

Table 12-1
Five Leading Causes of Death Among Women for All Races and Age Groups in 1987

Age Group (Years)	Cause of Death (in Rank Order)
15-24	Accidents and adverse effects
	Suicide
	Malignant neoplasm
	Heart disease
	Cerebrovascular disease
25-44	Malignant neoplasm
	Accidents and adverse effects
	Heart disease
	Suicide
	Cerebrovascular disease
	Chronic liver disease and cirrhosis
45-64	Malignant neoplasm
	Heart disease
	Cerebrovascular disease
	Chronic obstructive pulmonary disease
	Accidents and adverse effects
65-74	Heart disease
	Malignant neoplasm
	Cerebrovascular disease
	Influenza and pneumonia
	Atherosclerosis

Adapted from U.S. Bureau of the Census: Statistical Abstract of the United States: 1988. 168th Ed. Washington, D.C., U.S. Government Printing Office, 1990, p. 81.

Table 12-2
Maternal Mortality Rate per 100,000 Live Births

Year	Total	White	Black	Other Nonwhite
1985	7.8	5.2	20.4	18.1
1986	7.2	4.9	18.8	16.0
1987	6.6	5.1	14.2	12.2

Maternal Mortality

Because of their reproductive capability, women are at risk for mortality related to pregnancy and childbirth as well as to spontaneous and legal abortion. Since the 1950s, maternal mortality has continued to decline in the United States. This reduction in maternal deaths can be in large part attributed to improved prenatal care and education of the woman, early detection of maternal risk factors, improved anesthesia, and antibiotics.

Since 1980, there has been a steady decline in maternal deaths among white women, from 6.7 deaths per 100,000 live births to 5.1 deaths in 1987 (Table 12-2). Although the decline has been much more dramatic for nonwhite women, their *infant* death rate is still more than twice that of white women (U.S. Bureau of the Census, 1990, p. 8). Multiple factors contribute to this increased mortality rate associated with pregnancy among non-

Barriers to Use of Prenatal Care

WOMEN WHO receive little or no prenatal care are at risk for higher mortality rates for themselves and their infants. Healthy People —2000 (U.S. Department of Health and Human Services, 1991) has set the goal for the nation's maternal mortality rate to be less than 3.3 deaths per 100,000 live births and to reduce the infant mortality rate to no more than seven deaths per 100,000 births.

Many of the factors associated with maternal deaths have also been related to infant deaths. Because of the wide disparity between deaths in white infants (8.9) and deaths in black (17.9), Native American (12.5) and Puerto Rican (12.9) infants, Healthy People—2000 has projected an infant mortality rate of no greater than 11, 8.5, and eight per 100,000 live births for each group, respectively, by the year 2000.

Reasons for women receiving insufficient prenatal care (Institute of Medicine, 1985):

● Financial constraints: absent or inadequate private insurance, lack of public funds for prenatal care, lack of support for public agencies providing maternity care services
● Lack of maternity care providers: inadequate numbers of physicians in some parts of the country, low participation of obstetrician/gynecologists in Medicaid and a decrease in obstetric care because of increasing malpractice premiums; inadequate use of nurse practitioners and nurse midwives
● Insufficient prenatal care in agencies where high-risk groups usually seek services (sites such as community health centers, hospital outpatient departments, and local health departments)

- Factors that make women disinclined to seek prenatal care: perceptions by the woman regarding the usefulness of prenatal care and of whether the environment where services are sought is supportive and pleasant, cultural values, and beliefs

- Inadequate transportation and child care services: distance to services and difficulty in arranging for babysitting
- Lack of systems to recruit hard-to-reach women into care: need to find and educate women regarding importance of care

white women. Major risk factors include inadequate access to prenatal care, poor nutrition, and substandard living conditions.

According to Jensen et al. (1989), the leading cause of maternal mortality is hypertensive disorders. Infection, hemorrhage, and other medical problems such as cardiovascular disease, diabetes mellitus, and trauma also are major factors.

In 1986, ectopic pregnancy was the reason for hospitalization for an estimated 73,700 women during their first trimester. Although the incidence of ectopic pregnancy has declined considerably, it remains the leading cause of maternal deaths during the first trimester. Teenagers are at high risk, especially nonwhite teenagers (Centers for Disease Control, 1989).

Mortality associated with legal abortion is rare. Complications that result in death are related to the type of procedure and the length of gestation at the time the procedure is performed. In addition, recognized or unrecognized health problems, anesthesia, hemorrhage, and infection have been identified as risk factors in abortion-related deaths (Hatcher et al., 1990).

Malignant Neoplasms

Cancer death rates among women increased from 136.4 per 100,000 women in 1960 to 175.1 per 100,000 women in 1985 (U.S. Bureau of the Census, 1987). The American Cancer Society (ACS) (1989) estimated that 236,000 deaths occurred among women as a result of cancer in 1988.

Of all deaths related to cancer, 20% were due to cancer of the breast in 1988. Women over the age of 65 accounted for 54% of cases (Centers for Disease Control, 1989). For women over the age of 50, breast cancer was the primary cause of death from cancer. In 1989, the ACS projected that deaths from lung cancer (49,000 cases) would surpass those from breast cancer (43,000 cases) in women.

Early diagnosis and prompt treatment are major factors in surviving many types of cancer. Approx-

imately 178,000 people were projected to die in 1989 because of late detection and delay in seeking treatment (ACS, 1989).

The Report of the Secretary's Task Force on Black and Minority Health (U.S. Department of Health and Human Services, 1985) examined cancer mortality rates among black, Asian and Pacific-Islander, Hispanic, and Native American women. The incidence of deaths from cancer of the lung was highest among Hawaiian women (31.5 deaths per 100,000 women), followed by Chinese (21.2 deaths); Hispanics (20.2 deaths), and blacks (20.1 deaths). The lowest rates were noted among Filipino (6.8 deaths), Native American (8.6 deaths), and Japanese (8.6 deaths) women.

There has been little change in 5-year survival rates for breast cancer since 1976. White women had a 75% survival rate, and black women had a 62% survival rate. Of cancers related to the reproductive tract, ovarian cancer has the lowest survival rate for either group — 37% for white women and 36% for black women (ACS, 1989).

With increased health education and early detection, many cancer deaths could be prevented. All women need to replace and avoid health-deteriorating practices by adopting health-promoting behaviors that foster a health-protecting lifestyle. Community health nurses play a major role in providing these services. An even greater role could be played if the financial constraints of many health departments did not result in inadequate staffing.

Cardiovascular Disease and Diabetes Mellitus

In the United States, more people die from cardiovascular disease than from any other condition. Women's age-adjusted death rate (127.3 deaths per 100,000 women) related to diseases of the heart were a little more than half that of men (247.7 deaths per 100,000 men) in 1985 (U.S. Bureau of the Census, 1987). Further declines in these rates are possible as individuals become more aware of risk factors and accept increasing responsibility for managing their own health and well-being.

For the leading causes of death, mortality rates among men are greater than among women in most categories, except diabetes mellitus. For this condition, black women have a higher rate (21.1 deaths per 100,000 women) than black men (17.7 deaths per 100,000 men) (U.S. Bureau of the Census, 1987). Diabetes mellitus–related mortality rates are 2.3 times higher for Native Americans than for the general population. Pima tribe members have the greatest prevalence of diabetes—10- to 15-fold higher than the overall U.S. rate (U.S. Department of Health and Human Services, 1985). Sex-specific information is not available.

Many of the conditions that lead to mortality among women are preventable. If they are detected early and treated, there could be a significant impact on both longevity and the quality of life.

MORBIDITY

Hospitalizations

The 1987 National Hospital Discharge Survey reported that more women than men were hospitalized. Yet, on average, the average length of hospitalization of men (6.9 days) exceeded that of women (6.2 days) until after the age of 65. For all ages, average inpatient stay for women (9.1 days) was longer than that for men (8.6 days), with delivery accounting for the most frequent reason for hospitalization. The longest average hospital stay (10.9 days) was for cerebrovascular disease, which occurred most frequently among women aged 65 years or older. Fractures accounted for an average of 9.4 days, malignant neoplasms for 8.3 days, and diseases of the heart for 7.2 days (U.S. Bureau of the Census, 1990).

After hospitalization for several of the above-mentioned conditions, referrals may be made to community health nurses to provide ongoing nursing care in the home. Because of the prospective payment system for hospitalization, there is an increasing demand for skilled nursing services to be provided in the home. Nurses practicing in home environments must be prepared to deliver high-tech as well as high-touch services.

Chronic Conditions and Limitations

Women are more likely than men to be limited in activity because of chronic conditions. Arthritis and rheumatism, hypertension, and impairment of back or spine are more likely to decrease women's activity level than they are to affect men who have similar conditions; almost twice as many women (24.6%) as men (12.4%) are limited in activity level because of arthritis and rheumatism. Nevertheless, more men than women are likely to have their activity limited because of heart conditions and impairment of lower extremities (U.S. Bureau of the Census, 1987).

Women who are age 65 years or older are more likely than men to have difficulty performing activities such as walking, bathing or showering, preparing meals, and doing housework (U.S. Bureau of the Census, 1987).

Functional limitations require home health care that is supervised and delivered by nurses practicing in community settings. Nursing interventions are planned and implemented based on functional assessments. The care plan facilitates optimal resumption of the individual's independence in personal care activities.

Surgery

With the exception of cesarean births and cardiac catheterizations, hysterectomy is the most frequently performed operation among women age 15 years or older. In 1986, 644,000 hysterectomies were performed in the United States; this represented a decline from 725,000 in 1975. Hysterectomy rates have been high among black women, i.e., 9–10% per 1,000 women. It has been projected that continuation of a trend toward increased hysterectomy rates means that more than 50% of U.S. women will have had a hysterectomy before they reach the age of 65 (Lowdermilk, 1986).

A woman may request a hysterectomy to improve her quality of life. However, some women have been counseled to have a hysterectomy when an alternative approach to resolving the problem might have been taken. For example, women of childbearing age with fibroid tumors have received hysterectomies when a myomectomy could have been done.

If there is the least doubt regarding the necessity for a hysterectomy, women are encouraged to obtain a second opinion; because of the importance of a second opinion, most insurance companies have indicated a willingness to pay for them. Community health nurses, functioning as advocates for women, could provide health education programs related to indications for hysterectomy and education regarding seeking a second opinion.

Birth by cesarean delivery is the most prevalent surgical procedure experienced by U.S. women. The highest rates occur among women over the age of 35 or less than 20 (Placek et al., 1983). The increase in cesarean births has been attributed to several factors, including progress in technology that facilitates monitoring of the fetus and fear by physicians of malpractice suits. Childbirth educators often include information related to the cesarean birth experience. In addition, classes may address the woman's role in avoiding cesarean birth (Young and Mahan, 1980).

Mental Health

The most frequently occurring interruption in the mental health of women is related to depression. Symptoms experienced range from feelings of sadness to thoughts of death (Weissman, 1980; Weissman and Klerman, 1982). Before World War II, women in their 40s were most likely to be diagnosed with depression. In more recent studies, women between the ages of 25 and 44 are identified as being at the greatest risk for developing depression (Klerman and Weissman, 1980; Weissman and Klerman, 1982).

Orr and James (1984) found that women of low socioeconomic status who were living alone with their children were at greater risk for depression than were women of higher socioeconomic status. The women in this study were found to be vulnerable to feelings of hopelessness and lowered self-esteem. Many women of this status are without emotional support or adequate financial support, and they often express a sense of frustration and futility.

Nurses practicing in community health settings should be aware of the signs and symptoms of depression. Referral sources for professional help within the community should be identified by the nurse.

Signs and Symptoms of Depression

THE WOMAN experiencing depression may display some of the following signs and symptoms (Smith, 1986):

- Mood disturbance and emotional distress
- Sad, blue, gloomy feelings
- Feelings of helplessness, hopelessness, being inadequate, worthlessness
- Loss of interest in work, friends, family, sex
- Low energy level
- Sleep pattern disturbances
- Loss of appetite or voracious appetite
- Feelings of heaviness in head or chest
- Crying easily and sighing often
- Complaining of headaches, backaches, constipation
- Difficulty in concentrating and making decisions
- Flat to hectic gaiety
- Everything drooping—mouth, eyes, posture (body language)

Family Configuration and Marital Relationship Status

Women are members of multiple family configurations, e.g., nuclear families, extended family units, single-parent units, families of group marriages, blended family units, adoptive family units, nonlegal heterosexual unions, lesbian family units, and others. Because of diverse family configurations, women's roles within the family are changing. Few women function in the traditional role; most function in whatever role is necessary to maintain their own and their family's integrity.

In 1989, more than 46.5 million families were maintained by single heads of households (U.S. Bureau of the Census, 1989). Single fathers were responsible for almost 1.8 million families. This contrasts with the 13.7 million families that were maintained by single women, with most of the women between the ages of 15 and 34. Families headed by women have increased by 65% since 1970. Table 12–3 lists characteristics of black and white female-headed households.

One contemporary family configuration is that of single women with one or more adopted children. Because there is no legal ban on single parent adoptions, an increasing number of single women

Table 12-3 Characteristics of Black and White Female-Headed Households		
Characteristic	**Black**	**White**
Median age (years)	38.1	42.2
Single (never married) (%)	35.9	15.1
Married and spouse absent (%)	23.2	15.7
Separated	20.3	12.6
Other (%)	2.9	3.0
Widowed (%)	18.8	27.0
Divorced (%)	22.1	42.2
No. of children per family	1.23	0.94

Adapted from U.S. Bureau of the Census: Statistical Abstract of the United States: 1988. 168th Ed. Washington, D.C., U.S. Government Printing Office, 1990.

Table 12-4 Median Annual Earnings by Family Type in Current Dollars for 1970, 1980, and 1988			
	Median Annual Income ($)		
Family Type	**1970**	**1980**	**1988***
Families maintained by a married couple	10,516	23,141	36,389
Families maintained by women	5,093	10,408	15,346
Families maintained by men	9,012	17,519	26,827

* Based on revised processing procedures: data not directly comparable with prior years.

From U.S. Bureau of the Census: Statistical Abstract of the United States: 1990. 110th Ed. Washington, D.C., U.S. Government Printing Office, 1988, p. 453.

are becoming adoptive parents, and they express joy in their new role.

An often-ignored family structure is that of the family headed by a lesbian parent. Unfortunately, some individuals cannot conceptualize how one can be a lesbian and a parent. However, some lesbians become parents and therefore are potential clientele. In most respects, their needs are similar to those of all mothers. Many large cities have lesbian/gay parent groups that provide support, anticipatory guidance, and strategies for coping in a heterosexually dominated society (Dickinson, 1990).

Court decisions have been 50/50 in favor of granting custody to gay parents. However, a lesbian single parent is more likely to have custody of her children than is the gay male single parent. Nevertheless, lesbians may become very fearful of losing custody of their children even though they may have been granted custody (Williamson, 1986).

The nurse who functions in the community setting is likely to work with families from diverse configurations. Early assessment of the strengths of family units can provide the nurse with a data base for positive nursing intervention that will enhance the family's levels of well-being.

Employment and Wages

Women are sole wage earners in 25–34% of the world's families (*Amazing but True,* 1985). Nearly half of the women in the U.S. labor force are working mothers with children less than 6 years of age.

Women predominate in positions such as librarians, secretaries, teachers, food service workers, welfare case workers, and nurses. A review of female-dominated versus male-dominated jobs discloses that there are inequities in wage and salary scales. Recent data indicate that women earn only $0.66–0.68 for every $1.00 earned by men (Sidel, 1991). In 1988, the median annual income for families maintained by women was $15,346 compared with $26,827 for those maintained by men (Table 12–4).

Eunice Cole, former president of the American Nurses' Association [ANA], said, "Nursing has traditionally been viewed as women's work and as such is undervalued" (ANA, 1984). In Illinois, it was demonstrated that charge nurses received as much as $12,540 less annually than did stationary engineers, whose primary duty was to run a boiler system. With the Hay system, which is a method for allocating points to education required, responsibility involved, and accountability, charge nurses scored 415 points compared with 181 points for the sanitary engineer (ANA, 1984). Some groups have said that the major battle of the last decade of the 20th century will focus on bringing about pay equity between the traditional female- and male-dominated jobs.

The aggregate fast becoming the poorest in the United States are women and their children. This phenomenon has been labeled the "feminization of poverty." The nurse working with these families should be aware of social services, child care programs, emergency services, and other resources for families in need. It is the community health nurse who will often act as case manager and advocate for families with social service agencies and other public entities.

OTHER FACTORS

Education and Work

"THE POSITION of women in a society provides an exact measure of the development of that society" (Gustav Geinger).

The United States is considered a highly developed country, but can it boast about the socioeconomic status of women? Perhaps U.S. women have a higher status compared with those in other countries, but against what standard does one measure? What are the social and economic factors influencing a woman's position in this country? Women's education and work will be explored.

According to the U.S. Bureau of the Census, in 1988 75.9% of women of age 25 years or older were high school graduates compared with 55.4% in 1970. Seventeen percent of women of this same age group had completed college in 1988; this was approximately twice the 1970 rate of 8.2%. Women earned 51.2% of masters degrees and 35.2% of doctorates in 1987, an approximate 10% increase over 1970 statistics.

Increasing numbers of women have been conferred degrees in traditionally male-dominated professions. Table 12–5 reflects the changes occurring in percentages of women receiving degrees in 1970, 1980, and 1987 (U.S. Bureau of the Census, 1990).

As more women enter the work force, it is not surprising that their former favorable mortality and morbidity rates change. The workplace is well known for providing stress from both the physical and social environments.

In addition to inequities outside the home, there are inequities within the home. Working women are less likely to have a spouse or partner to help with home and children (Duffy, 1982). Even when a spouse or partner is present, the burdens of

Table 12–5
Percentages of Women Receiving Degrees

Degree	Women Receiving Degrees (%)		
	1970	1980	1987
Medicine (M. D.)	8.4%	23.4%	32.4%
Dentistry (D. D. S. or D. M. D.)	0.9%	13.3%	24.0%
Law (LL. B. or J. D.)	5.4%	30.2%	40.2%
Theology (B. D., M. Div., or M. H. L.)	2.3%	13.8%	19.3%

housework and child care usually fall more heavily on women. These multiple role demands and conflicting expectations contribute to stress (Haas, 1982).

Milio, professor of health administration at the University of North Carolina, expresses concern for women as well as for the health and welfare of the unborn. What are the long-term effects on the woman's reproductive system in the workplace? If a woman becomes pregnant, the chances of her having maternity benefits are only 40%. The task of health care professionals, including occupational health nurses, is to work with management, unions, and other groups to develop programs in the workplace that will increase women's health-promoting options. A few of these options include educational programs, improved nutrition in the area of food service, exercise facilities, stress management clinics, and child care arrangements (Women's Health Risk, 1981).

Health Behavior

Women are beginning to seek information that will allow them to be in control of their own health. Since the early 1970s, women have met in self-help groups to develop a better understanding of their own health needs. According to Ruzek (1979), some of the health behaviors that women learn in self-help groups are recognition of the early signs of vaginal infections and sexually transmitted diseases, awareness of variations in female anatomy and physiology, importance of nutrition, breast self-examination (BSE), pregnancy testing, and contraceptive awareness.

Because of women's desire to become more knowledgeable of their own health, many books written for consumers are available in book stores, in public libraries and among the holdings of traditional women groups such as sororities, federated women's clubs, and others.

Pender's health promotion model synthesizes the literature on health promotion and wellness (Pender, 1987). She indicates that "health promoting behaviors are directed toward sustaining or increasing the level of well-being, self-actualization and fulfillment of a given individual or group" (Pender, 1987). This model can be used by the community health nurse in teaching health behaviors that lead to general health promotion among women.

Knowledge deficits prevail among women regardless of socioeconomic or educational level when it comes to an awareness of their own bodies. The authors of this chapter have found that regardless of whether a group comprises college-educated professional women or women employed as blue collar workers, many of the questions asked are the same. "Will I menstruate after I have a hysterectomy?" "When should I perform a breast self-examination?" "What can I do to prevent recurrent episodes of vaginitis?"

Nurses can play an instrumental role in helping women develop a greater sense of self-awareness. Furthermore, community health nurses can remove the cloak of mystery surrounding the woman's body and give permission to clientele to ask previously unmentionable questions.

Health Care Access

Approximately 32 million U.S. citizens are unable to receive medical care. This figure, although astronomical, does not include the 250,000 to 2 million homeless men, women, and children (U.S. Bureau of the Census, 1989). Owing to the nature of women's employment, they frequently lack health insurance and are not eligible for Medicaid benefits.

Individuals between the ages of 16 and 24 are disproportionately without any type of health insurance coverage. This young adult population comprises approximately 50% of those without insurance coverage. A further breakdown of women between the ages of 15 and 44 by race indicates that 28.5% of Hispanics, 21% of blacks, and 15% of whites are without coverage (Metropolitan Life, 1988). Lacking economic means for meeting the costs of health care, these women are not likely to seek health care delivery until they or a family member is in acute distress. Others may rely on home remedies, over-the-counter drugs, lay midwives, or other folk healers for health care.

Although the elderly are usually covered under Medicare, they often delay seeking health care. Elderly women usually receive a fixed income and may have difficulty with meeting the copayment required by Medicare. Many senior citizens have paid hospitalization insurance premiums for policies that fail to meet the gap.

Culture influences one's perception of health. It is essential that nurses become aware of the health practices of the diverse cultural groups that they serve, as demonstrated by the following example.

Lynn Saunders, a junior white nursing student, was assigned to make home visits to Joan Peabody, a 15-year-old black girl and her newborn baby boy. Joan lives with her mother, sibling, and grandmother. On a home visit, Joan informs Lynn that she is going to have to get her 6-week-old baby some "asafetida" for his "hives." The student was not familiar with this regimen and sought assistance from her instructor and a local pharmacist. The pharmacist informed the student of the safe dosage range. Joan said that giving a baby asafetida was common in her family.

Many folk practices surround the mystique of a woman's menstrual cycle. Various herbal teas are given to decrease dysmenorrhea and premenstrual syndrome, to regulate menstrual periods, and to provide greater comfort during menopause. Herbs may also be used in some cultures for vaginal and bladder infections (Rose, 1984).

TYPES OF PROBLEMS

Acute Illness

Females report a greater incidence of acute conditions than do males. According to Fogel and Woods (1981), most women will experience the acute pain of dysuria (painful urination) at some point in life. It is estimated that approximately 5% of primary care visits by women are prompted by symptoms suggestive of bacteriuria (Fowler, 1989). Women often experience their first urinary tract infection during pregnancy or soon after delivery. Nevertheless, the prevalence of infection directly correlates with age, increasing from about 1% to 6% between puberty and 60 years of age (Fowler, 1989). Another common problem — trigonitis, or "honeymoon cystitis" — frequently occurs with a change in sexual activity, usually from infrequent or no activity to more vigorous and frequent intercourse.

Other acute illnesses specific to the reproductive tract include pelvic inflammatory disease and other pelvic infections such as cervicitis, oophoritis, and vulvitis.

Chronic Disease

Included among chronic diseases affecting women throughout their life span are cardiovascular disease, hypertension, diabetes, arthritis, osteoporosis, breast conditions, and cancer.

There is clinical evidence to support that arteriosclerotic heart disease (ASHD) may have its beginnings in the second and third decades of a woman's life, although men are affected more often. Changing lifestyles are altering these statistics. Nonmodifiable risk factors for ASHD are family history and race.

Black women are more vulnerable than white women to ASHD and more frequently experience congestive heart failure and angina pectoris after myocardial infarction (Byyny and Speroff, 1990). Fortunately, there are several modifiable risk factors:

● Elevated serum lipid levels
● Habitual diet high in calories, total fats, cholesterol, refined carbohydrates, and sodium
● Hypertension
● Obesity
● Glucose intolerance
● Cigarette smoking

Modifiable risk factors considered minor in comparison are the following:

● Personality type
● Sedentary lifestyle
● Stress (Phipps et al., 1983)

Hypertension, defined as blood pressure of 140/90 mm Hg or greater, significantly increases the risk of serious morbidity and mortality from coronary heart disease. Essential hypertension is the most common type of chronic hypertensive disorder in women of childbearing age, accounting for 85% of such cases. It is also responsible for approximately one third of all hypertension cases during pregnancy.

Hypertension is more common in women than in men and affects more blacks than whites. Additional factors associated with primary hypertension are age of more than 35 years, family history of hypertension, obesity, cigarette smoking, and diabetes mellitus (Neeson and Stockdale, 1981).

Hypertension usually has an asymptomatic phase, so every woman, beginning in her teens, should be screened on an average of every 2 years. Diagnosis is crucial to prevent or modify the disease's possible complications.

According to Krowlewski and Warram (1985), there are 6 million known diabetics and 4 million undiagnosed diabetics in the United States. In previous years, community health nurses have worked to educate women to assume responsibility in their management of diabetes mellitus. More recently, community health nurses have been actively involved in educational and screening programs for groups at high risk. Included in these groups are individuals who have a family history of diabetes, who are obese, or who are elderly.

According to Cunningham et al. (1989), pregnancy is potentially diabetogenic. The condition may be aggravated by pregnancy, and clinical diabetes may appear in some women only during pregnancy. Consequently, considerable attention has been given to screening for diabetes in pregnancy. There is much controversy regarding the most effective method of screening for diabetes, but regardless of the selected method, the nurse is involved in explaining to the woman the purpose of the screening and how to prepare for the tests. In most public health settings, the nurse is responsible for explaining the results.

Arthritis, which afflicts an estimated 50 million people in the United States, is a major health concern for women. The incidence of osteoarthritis is slightly higher in females than in males, but rheumatoid arthritis afflicts three fold as many women as men (Byyny and Speroff, 1990). The cause of arthritis is not known; however, the recurring multiple factors in the development of arthritis include diet, environment, and stress. Nursing intervention focuses on aspects of prevention of joint deformity and modification of lifestyle if necessary.

Osteoporosis is a major disorder affecting women. This condition involves the diminishing of bone density. Conflicting estimates of its occurrence range from 25% to 50%. Although males may develop osteoporosis, it is more often associated with women and their loss of ovarian function. After menopause, white women are at highest risk for osteoporosis. In women, loss of bone begins at an earlier age and proceeds twice as rapidly as in men. Of the 200,000 women in the United States with osteoporosis who are over the age of 45, more than 40,000 will die from its complications (Notelovitz and Ware, 1985).

Although no cure has been found for osteoporosis, prevention strategies are important to begin early in life. Strategies involve an awareness of dietary practices such as maintaining a correct balance of calcium, vitamin D, and protein. In addition, more is being learned about the influence of exercise and its possible protective effect. Estrogen may be prescribed for both perimenopausal and postmenopausal women to maintain bone mass. The risks and benefits associated with estrogen replacement therapy must be discussed with the woman to facilitate her decision making.

Nurses in ambulatory health practices can encourage women to become more knowledgeable of the preventive aspects of osteoporosis. For women diagnosed with osteoporosis, nurses may assist in various aspects of management, e.g., education regarding prescribed medication, follow-up care, avoidance of complications, and dietary modifications as needed.

There has been an increasing incidence of breast cancer during the past 50 years. Presently, one of every nine women will develop breast cancer. Risk factors include age of more than 50, personal or family history of breast cancer, never having had children or having a first child after age 30, obesity, or a diet high in fat (ACS, 1991). Being a woman and aging are identified as the most significant risk factors for breast cancer.

In the battle against breast cancer, women must understand and practice early detection methods. The practice of monthly BSE should begin in high school. A breast examination by the woman's health care professional should be performed in addition to her annual pelvic and Pap smear. A baseline mammogram should be done around 35 years of age and every 1–2 years for women of age 40–49. Mammography, which is low-dose radiography, is not usually indicated for women less than age 35.

Once a woman reaches 50, an annual mammogram is recommended (ACS, 1991). Nurses in any setting where there is an aggregate of women should possess the skills for teaching BSE. Most

---

Resource Materials (Hane and Williams, 1991)

American Cancer Society Breast Cancer Resource Materials

BREAST CANCER: Nowhere to Hide (pamphlet)
Nowhere to Hide (video)
Breast Health (poster)
BSE — Special Touch (video, instructor's guide, and flip chart)
How to Do Breast Self-Examination (pamphlet)
A Woman's Guide to Mammography (pamphlet)

For additional resources, call 1-800-ACS-2345.

National Cancer Institute Breast Cancer Resources

A Mammogram Once A Year . . . For a Lifetime (video)
Smart Advice for Women 40 and Over: Have a Mammogram (pamphlet)
Guidelines for Screening Mammography

For additional resources, call 1-800-4-CANCER (in both English and Spanish).

---

chapters of the ACS regularly offer classes. Twenty percent of all malignant diseases in women occur in the genital tract. Carcinoma of the cervix, the most common, accounts for 21% of all new genital tract malignancies (Eisenkop et al., 1988). Because the cervix is accessible to cytologic study, mortality has decreased. Risk factors for cervical cancer include coitus before the age of 20, multiple sexual partners, history of human papilloma virus and other sexually transmitted diseases, or history of exposure to diethylstilbesterol in utero (DiSaia, 1983; Sherwen et al., 1991).

The decline in deaths due to cervical cancer is directly related to early detection through an annual pelvic examination that includes a Pap smear. In recent years, there has been debate regarding how often a woman should have a Pap smear. The American College of Obstetricians and Gynecologists recommends that women age 18 years or younger, if sexually active, receive an annual cytologic screening for cervical cancer. They state the test is inexpensive, causes no known harm, and has the capacity for a high degree of sensitivity (American College of Obstetricians and Gynecologists, 1980).

Carcinoma of the endometrium has increased significantly during the past three decades. It is most common in women during the sixth and seventh decades of life. Eighty percent of women with this condition are postmenopausal. Factors believed to be related to its occurrence are obesity, low parity, diabetes mellitus, and conditions in which there are high circulating estrogen levels uncountered by adequate progesterone levels. The most common sign of endometrial cancer, occurring in 90% of women, is abnormal vaginal bleeding. Women who are postmenopausal and experience vaginal bleeding should seek immediate gynecological evaluation (Eisenkopf et al., 1988). According to MacKay et al. (1983), a satisfactory screening method that would permit early diagnosis would do more to reduce mortality from this disease than would advances in treatment. Until that time, high-risk women should be identified and encouraged to seek ongoing monitoring.

More deaths in the United States are due to cancer of the ovary than to any other pelvic malignancy. The annual incidence of ovarian cancer usually ranges between 5 and 15 cases per 100,000 women. Approximately one in 70 women will develop this cancer; the rate increases fairly rapidly after age 40. Risk factors include increasing age, women who have never had children, and history of breast or endometrial cancer (ACS, 1991).

Early-stage detection of ovarian cancer is virtually impossible; when discovered, ovarian cancer has usually reached advanced stages. The health professional should be alert to ovarian enlargement with suspicion that ovarian malignancy may be present. After menopause, palpable ovaries are considered an abnormal finding and necessitate immediate diagnostic studies (MacKay et al., 1983).

Mental Health

The mental health of women is influenced by a variety of circumstances and conditions. Every day, women are called on to adapt to a changing environment. Although men live in the same stressful environment, according to Witkin-Lanoil (1984), women have some special stresses of their own:

"WOMEN MENSTRUATE, become pregnant and go through menopause. They sometimes have to justify their marital status to an employer and their sexual behavior to their family. They are expected to be full of energy at the end of a working day and prepared to keep going through the weekend. Women are expected to be sexy, but not sexual; to have a child, but remain childlike; to be assertive, but not aggressive; to hold a job, but not neglect their home" (p. 55).

Women face stressful decisions about career and family. Many women express anxiety in these decisions. Often, women describe their biological clock as ticking, and they feel pressured to make decisions regarding childbearing before they have fulfilled career goals.

Deciding to focus on a career may mean decreased authority and the suffering of stress in the workplace. Staats and Staats (1983) compared differences in stress levels between 82 women and 113 men who were employed in management and professional roles. Women identified higher stress levels in marital dissatisfaction, interpersonal conflict in the home, incompatibility within the family, marital discord, relationship with parents, criticism by friends, and worries over drug and alcohol problems. Furthermore, they reported more frequent episodes of nervous diarrhea, tension, and migraine headaches. They also indicated that they had problems in the past year for which they should have sought medical or mental health consultation.

Staats and Staats suggest that stress management programs for women include assertiveness training, cognitive skills training, and family therapy including role revision. These are recommended in addition to relaxation training, conflict resolution, and time-management activities.

Emotional state has been said to be influenced by ovarian function in women from the onset of menstruation to the cessation of menstrual periods. Depressive symptoms have been associated with menarche, premenstrual syndrome (PMS), postpartum, and the perimenopause (Gordon and Ledray, 1986). Depression is more prevalent among women than among men; however, some attribute this difference to women's role socialization rather than to biological differences (Radloff, 1980).

Although some health professionals view the perimenopause as a time of depression and dismay, many women consider this phase of development as a time of fulfillment and creativity. Thomas (1988) found in a study of midlife that although women experienced a high number of perimenopausal symptoms associated with depression, they also perceived themselves as leaders, as having talents in the visual and performing arts, and as possessing other abilities related to creative expression. It is suggested that nurses planning health promotion activities for an aggregate of midlife women draw on their client's creative energies and expressions as an intervention to decrease or prevent nonpathological depression.

Reproductive Health

Community health nurses provide a variety of services in the area of women's reproductive health from menarche through the postmenopausal phase. Nurses in collaboration with other health care professionals have identified a persisting group of preventable and correctable problems related to maternal-child health. Healthy People—2000 (U.S. Department of Health and Human Services, 1991) lists opportunities for improving maternal and infant health through reducing cigarette smoking and alcohol and other drug use, better nutrition, better socioeconomic opportunities including education, and decreasing environmental hazards.

One of the most important factors related to a woman's reproductive health focuses on the total life nutritional experience, from inception through infancy, childhood, and adolescence. Pregnancy may provide a motivational factor for developing an awareness of proper nutrition. During the nutritional assessment of a prenatal client, the community health nurse can take this opportunity to determine dietary habits and initiate a referral to the Special Supplemental Food Program for Women, Infants, and Children (WIC) program when necessary. The WIC program provides food vouchers for pregnant or breast-feeding women, infants, and children who are at nutritional risk.

Diet must be developed by taking into consideration factors other than kinds and amounts of foods. Other elements to consider include age, lifestyle, economic status, and culture. When counseling a pregnant adolescent, for example, it may be helpful to include the primary person responsible for meal preparation. However, the adolescent should not be ignored in the planning of her diet but rather should be asked to identify foods she likes from those recommended. The adolescent needs to be made aware of the impact of her nutrition on fetal growth and development. This information must be balanced with the young woman's individual needs.

The community health nurse has many opportunities to provide counseling in the area of family planning. Although the phrase "family planning" has come to imply planned limitation of pregnancies, another important aspect of family planning concerns couples attempting to increase their chances of conception. Infertility occurs in a surprising number of otherwise healthy adults. Approximately 15–18% of couples in the United States are unintentionally childless. Nevertheless, more than half of all pregnancies occurring in the United States are unintended (Hatcher et al., 1990). In her inaugural address as president of the American College of Obstetricians and Gynecologists, Klein (1984) stated:

"A FERTILE, sexually active woman using no contraception would, on the average, face 14 births or 31 abortions during her reproductive lifetime—a mind-boggling disruption of her life in this period of hoped-for independence and equality for women and in an era of disappearing economic value of children" (p. 287).

Community health nurses are in a strategic position to provide support and guidance for women in the control of their fertility. Numerous factors contribute to the decision of whether to use family planning methods. When counseling women on this matter, a holistic approach is needed. Factors such as age, pattern of sexual activity, cost, and access to health care as well as the woman's and her partner's values and beliefs must be considered. After a discussion with the nurse of benefits and risks, indications and contraindications, and advantages and disadvantages, the client selects a method that she believes to be safe and comfortable. The nurse's insistence on methods that are found to be a messy nuisance or that the woman fears may harm her may do more harm than good. These and other issues must be considered to ensure the greatest protection from unintended pregnancy.

Health care professionals often neglect to mention natural family planning as a method of family planning. Many consider this approach to be synonymous with the rhythm method. According to Rometta Hock (personal communication; University of Alabama in Huntsville, 1991), certified natural family planning practitioner, the fertility awareness method increases women's awareness of their own reproductive processes. This knowledge allows for feelings of empowerment and a sense of control of one's fertility. Women experience self-knowledge and thereby gain autonomy in relation to fertility. Family and community health care professionals need to have up-to-date information concerning natural family planning (Ponzetti and Hoefler, 1988).

Women who have decided that their family is large enough and do not wish to be concerned with temporary methods of fertility control select sterilization by tubal ligation. Surveys have indicated that for married couples over the age of 30, sterilization is the most commonly used method of fertility control (Hatcher et al., 1990). In no other phase of family planning is it more important that the client's decision be based on clear, complete information than it is for sterilization. The reversibility of sterilization procedures is not dependable; if a woman has any doubts about her future childbearing, she should be encouraged to use other methods of fertility control. It is hoped that research in the area of family planning will provide a number of safe options for all women that are designed to meet individual needs.

Sexually Transmitted Diseases and HIV

Sexually transmitted diseases are discussed in Chapter 23. In 1988, more than 700,000 cases of gonorrhea were reported, making it the most commonly reported communicable disease in the United States. However, genital chlamydial infections are the most common bacterial sexually transmitted disease in the United States, and case reporting is required in some states (Hatcher et al., 1990). A woman may acquire chlamydial infection along with gonorrhea. Benenson (1990) recommends treatment for both organisms when one is suspected.

The incidence of gonorrhea per 100,000 women aged 15–44 was 501 in 1989. Complications resulting from gonorrheal infection include pelvic inflammatory disease, sterility, and ectopic pregnancy (U.S. Department of Health and Human Services, 1991).

HIV infection is rapidly increasing among women and babies born to women in high-risk groups. Women at high risk for becoming HIV seropositive include the following:

● Intravenous drug users who share needles and/or syringes
● Prostitutes
● Those who have sex with partners who are infected
● Participants in unprotected sex

It is estimated that 20–35% of infants born to infected mothers develop HIV infection.

Community health nurses as well as other health providers, including physicians, nurse practitioners, nurse midwives, physician's assistants, and social workers, must be prepared to provide age-appropriate sexually transmitted disease prevention education. Risk-reduction objectives (U.S. Department of Health and Human Services, 1991) to decrease the spread of these diseases include the following recommendations:

● Reduce the proportion of adolescents who have engaged in sexual intercourse to no more than 15% by age 15 (baseline in 1988: 27% of girls reported in 1988) and not more than 40% by age 17 (baseline in 1988: 50% of girls).
● Increase use of condoms by partners of sexually active young women age 15–19 to 60% by year 2000 (baseline in 1988: 25%).

Accidents

Older women are at increased risk for accidents such as falls. Two thirds of accidental deaths in persons more than 65 years old are the result of falls (Yurick, 1984). Factors that may be responsible for this major cause of morbidity among the elderly are associated with an unsteady gait, reduced vision, or a hazardous environment. Because older women have an increasing number of falls, it is important to identify the preventable factors. Nurses, whether working with the elderly in the home or in institutional settings, must be knowledgeable of hazards that may be corrected to decrease the incidence of falls.

Women of all ages presenting a history of inadequately explained injuries need to be evaluated for possible battering. More than 1 million women seek medical care for injuries that result from physical battering by their husbands, ex-husbands, boyfriends, or lovers (U.S. Department of Health and Human Services, 1991). Women from all socioeconomic levels are affected. Nurses employed in community health settings need to know how to make assessments, provide support, and make referrals to agencies dealing with domestic violence.

Disability

According to Verbrugge (1990), compared with men women have more disabilities resulting from acute conditions but experience fewer disabilities resulting from chronic conditions because they report their symptoms earlier and receive necessary treatment. A disability may reduce the individual's activity; women report proportionately more days of restricted activity than do men. Women average 16.1 days of disability per year compared with 12.7 days for men (U.S. Bureau of the Census, 1990).

A frequently encountered disabling condition is dysmenorrhea. It is one of the most common concerns of women and affects approximately 50–60% of the female population between the ages of 15 and 24 (Sullivan, 1990). Although this is the time of its peak incidence, it continues to plague women throughout the reproductive years (MacKay et al., 1983). Brown (1982) found that at least 10% of women with dysmenorrhea are incapacitated for 1–3 days each month. Dysmenorrhea is the greatest single cause of absenteeism from school and work among young women. It is estimated that dysmenorrhea is the cause of the loss of 140 million working hours annually (Weiss, 1984). The economic impact of this condition is difficult to estimate.

Disabling conditions often limit the physical functional abilities of many women. The health care delivery system has often overlooked the unique needs of this aggregate. In planning care for disabled women, community health nurses should focus attention on enabling the woman to strengthen her capabilities. In addition, nurses should be sensitive to barriers in the clinical setting that affect the access of disabled women to health care services.

MAJOR LEGISLATION AFFECTING WOMEN'S HEALTH SERVICES

Several legislative acts have a direct or indirect impact on the health of women. Many changes have been made in the past decade that have the potential for improving the health and welfare of all women.

Public Health Service Act

The Public Health Service Act, passed in 1982, provides for the following activities:

● Biomedical and health services research
● Information dissemination
● Resource development
● Technical assistance
● Service delivery

During 1984, an inventory was made throughout the Department of Health and Human Services of government agencies provided for within the Public Health Service Act. The purpose of the inventory was to identify the extent of each agency's involvement in women's health concerns. The scope of activities includes general, reproductive, social, behavioral, and mental health among other female-specific health issues (Women's Health Report, 1985). Aggregates of women targeted by the Centers for Disease Control, a Public Health Service agency, encompassed those disabled by specific diseases, victims of sexual abuse and domestic violence, recent immigrants, and occupational groups.

In 1981, one agency within the Public Health Service, the Family Planning Assistance Program, assisted more than 4.5 million women in obtaining family planning services. The committee studying the prevention of low-birth-weight infants recommended the following in regard to the continuation of government support for family planning (Institute of Medicine, 1985, p. 128):

> "THE NEED for subsidized family planning remains significant and federal funds should be made generously available to meet documented needs. With regard to the particular relationship of family planning and low birthweight, it is important to stress that both young teenage status and poverty are major risk factors for low birthweight. . . . As such the program should be regarded as an important part of public effort to prevent low birthweight."

The focus of Public Health Service activities regarding women's health issues described most frequently in the inventory was health promotion and disease prevention with activities directed toward research, evaluation and analysis, and education and training operations. The task force responsible for the inventory recommended the continuation of monitoring and reviewing of activities concerning women's health by the Public Health Service. As advocates and as professionals directly involved with the health care of women, nurses should review the task force's complete report and thus encourage the implementation of goals set by the surgeon general for a complete nation of "healthy people," including healthy women.

Civil Rights Act

Title VII of the Civil Rights Act of 1964 prohibits discrimination based on sex, race, color, religion, or national origin in hiring or firing, wages, and fringe benefits. With the amendment of the act in 1978, discrimination was prohibited against pregnant women or conditions involving childbirth or pregnancy. This landmark legislation makes it unlawful for employers to refuse to hire, employ, or promote a woman because she is pregnant.

In addition, employee benefit plans that continue health insurance, income maintenance during disability or illness, or any other income support program for disabled workers will have to include disabilities due to pregnancy, childbirth, and other related conditions. If employers allow disabled employers to assume lighter or medically restricted assignments, the same considerations must be extended to the pregnant woman (Working Woman's Guide, 1984).

The amendment does not require employers to pay health insurance benefits for abortions or abortion-related care unless the mother's life is endangered or she has medical complications after an abortion. Employers are prohibited from firing or refusing to hire a woman because she has had an abortion.

Sexual harassment is a violation of the Civil Rights Act. Unwelcome sexual advances, requests for sexual favors, and other verbal or physical conduct of a sexual nature constitute harassment.

Social Security Act

The Social Security Act provides monthly retirement and disability benefits to workers and survivor benefits to families of workers covered by the system. Full retirement benefits are available to workers after 10 years of covered employment.

Recent changes in the Social Security Act permit a divorced person to receive benefits based on a former spouse's earning record when that spouse retires, becomes disabled, or dies if the marriage lasted at least 10 years. As of January 1985, a divorcee can receive spousal benefits at age 62 if her ex-husband is eligible for benefits—regardless of whether he is actually receiving them—and they have been divorced for at least 2 years.

Another benefit covered under Social Security is Medicare. Medicare consists of hospital insurance and medical insurance and includes payments for physicians, home health care, and other services and supplies after the deductible has been met (Working Woman's Guide, 1984).

Occupational Safety and Health Act

The Occupational Safety and Health Act enacted in 1970 ensured safe and healthful working conditions for workers in all businesses affecting commerce throughout the United States. Table 12–6 lists specific positions in which large numbers of

Table 12–6
Hazardous Occupations in Which Women Are Employed

Occupation	Health Hazard
Clerical workers	Organic solvents in stencil machines; correction fluids; rubber cement; ozone from copying machine
Textile and apparel workers	Cotton dust; skin irritants; chemicals
Hairdressers and beauticians	Hair, nail, and skin beauty preparations
Launderers and dry cleaners	Heat; heavy lifting; chemicals
Electronics workers	Solvents and acids
Hospital and other health care workers	Infectious diseases; heavy lifting; radiation; skin disorders; anesthetic gases
Laboratory workers	Biological agents: flammable, explosive, toxic, or carcinogenic substances; exposure to radiation; bites from and allergic reactions to research animals

women are employed and the potential for health hazards exist (Working Woman's Guide, 1984).

Reproductive risks associated with exposure to occupational health hazards are destined to increase because of the large numbers of women in the workplace. Potential parents exposed to certain health hazards may be at risk for unfavorable reproductive outcomes, including altered fertility, spontaneous abortion, congenital malformations, intrauterine growth retardation, and late fetal deaths.

Occupational health nurses, nurse practitioners, and community health nurses need to be cognizant of environmental hazards within the workplace. In taking health histories, data should be collected regarding the client's occupational environment to assess the potential risk to both general and reproductive health.

HEALTH AND SOCIAL SERVICES TO PROMOTE THE HEALTH OF WOMEN

Approximately 3.2 million women of childbearing age are assisted by Medicaid. It is a health insurance program for the poor exclusive of age eligibility, and it is administered by individual states.

Many of the women who are eligible for Medicaid are at high risk for poor pregnancy outcome, including low birth weight. Ideally, women who are at high maternal risk should be seen by a maternity care provider immediately after conception. Often, these women seek prenatal care late in the pregnancy or present at the emergency department when delivery is imminent without having received any prenatal care.

Consider the following example. Anita Rogers, a 16-year-old unemployed, single woman, comes to the Family Services Health Center seeking initial prenatal care at 36 weeks' gestation. She states that for a few days she has noted some brown discharge from her vagina. She tells the nurse practitioner that she knew that she should have begun prenatal care earlier, but when she called several physicians' offices, the receptionist told her that she should bring $50 for her first visit. She said that she did not have that much money, nor did her parents; her father was unemployed, and her mother worked at a cafe as a waitress. She also had difficulty with transportation.

Anita was sent to the hospital immediately for ultrasound. The ultrasound revealed triplets, but two of them had died in utero. Anita was hospitalized and soon began to hemorrhage. She delivered a 3-pound infant.

This case is not unusual among those most in need of high-quality prenatal care. However, barriers limit access to prenatal care. The Medicaid program allows for some access to care, but there is a need for greater public awareness of facilities and of maternity care providers who accept Medicaid.

Nurse practitioners, nurse midwives, and public health nurses may provide ambulatory perinatal care. One large metropolitan city has established a network for perinatal care. Nurses provide prenatal and postpartum care. Family practice residents, obstetric/gynecologic residents, and some private physicians deliver the women and accept referrals of women assessed as being at high risk. The women are assisted with obtaining Medicaid if they are eligible.

Women's Health Services

Since the mid-1970s, women have sought health services other than the conventional mode of care delivery. Many self-help groups have emerged, and new approaches to women's health services have been accepted. Because women have demanded a participatory role and have become more assertive, health care facilities, including physicians' offices, are more responsive to women's perceptions of their health needs. There has been a complete revolution in maternity care with the emergence of freestanding as well as hospital-based birth centers, family- and sibling-attended births, and so on.

The National Women's Health Network has been a strong advocate for women's concerns and has provided testimony before congressional hearings dealing with women's issues. This organization is concerned with patient rights, environmental safety, reproductive rights, warnings regarding the effects of alcohol and drugs on the developing fetus, and safety in relation to medical devices. For example, the network was instrumental in the worldwide recall of the Dalkon Shield intrauterine device.

Another concern is that of drug safety, especially concerning drugs that may have teratogenic or carcinogenic effects. For example, the network has attempted to identify women who may have been exposed to diethylstilbestrol in utero. These are just a few of the concerns of the network in regard to improving women's health (Charting a course, 1983).

The National Women's Health Network undertook a special project to encourage health promotion among black women. The Black Women's Health Project's coordinator, Byllye Avery, established self-help groups. The goals of these groups are "to raise the consciousness of women about the severity and pervasiveness of black women's health problems [and] to provide a comfortable, supportive atmosphere for women to explore health issues affecting them and their families."

The nationwide self-help groups have diverse interests. For example, in Monteocho Gordon, Florida, the focus is on reducing high blood pressure; in Chicago, the focus is on learning self-help skills.

HEALTH RESOURCES

American Cancer Society
1599 Clifton Road, N.E.
Atlanta, GA 30329

American Lupus Society
23751 Madison St.
Torrance, CA 90505
(213) 373–1335

Arthritis Foundation
1314 Spring Street, N.W.
Atlanta, GA 30309
(404) 872–7100
Check phone book for local chapters

Black Women's Health Project
Martin Luther King Community Center, Suite 157
Atlanta, GA 30120
(405) 659–3854

Boston Self-Help Center
18 Williston Road
Brookline, MA 02146
A counseling, consulting, and disability rights
organization staffed by and for people with disabilities

Coalition for the Medical Rights of Women
2845 24th Street
San Francisco, CA 94110
(415) 826–4401
A health advocacy and information resource;
publishes a monthly newsletter, Second Opinion

Command Trust Network
Breast Implant Information Service
256 South Linden Drive
Beverly Hills, CA 90212
(213) 556–1738

Gay Men's Health Crisis
129 West 20th Street
New York, NY 10011
(212) 807–6655

Gay Nurses' Alliance
44 St. Mark's Place
New York, NY 10003
An active group working for both gay rights and health
issues; provides educational resources

Health Research Group
2000 P Street, N.W.
Washington, D.C. 20036
(202) 872–0320
Publishes consumer-oriented books and manuals
on drugs, medical devices, occupational and
environmental health, health insurance and benefits
programs, and related topics

HERS (Hysterectomy Educational Resources and Services)
422 Bryn Mawr Ave.
Bala Cynwyd, PA 19004
(215) 667–7757
Provides information and counseling for women who have had hysterectomies and for those to whom hysterectomy has been recommended

Institutes for the Study of Medical Ethics
P.O. Box 17307
Los Angeles, CA 90017
(213) 413–4997
An active patients' rights group offering advocacy, documentation, and research; active in monitoring legislation

National AIDS Network
1012 14th Street, N.W.
Washington, D.C. 20005
(202) 347–0309
Referrals to local groups

National Women's Health Network
224 7th Street, S.E.
Washington, D.C. 20003
(202) 543–9222
A national consumer/provider membership organization; monitors and works to influence government and industry policies; publishes Network News

Paul VI Institute
6901 Mercy Road
Omaha, NE 68106-2604
(402) 390–9168
Information on the Creighton Model of the Ovulation Method/Natural Family Planning

Women and AIDS Resource Network
P.O. Box 020525
Brooklyn, NY 11202
(718) 596–6007

National Telephone Hotlines

American Cancer Society: (800) ACS–2345

National Cancer Institute: (800) 4–CANCER

National HIV/AIDS Information Line, Public Health Service, U.S. Department of Health and Human Services: (800) 342–AIDS

National Sexually Transmitted Disease Hotline, American Social Health Association: (800) 227–8922

Women's health consumers are requesting more emphasis in the area of well women's health care, i.e., health care aimed at well-being, health promotion, and disease prevention. Several nurses throughout the country have established collaborative practices with other health professionals to meet this demand for nonconventional services.

Other Community Voluntary Services

One of the major movements during the last decade has been that of networking. Networking has been described as a system of interconnected or cooperating individuals. It is the means by which women seek to advance their careers, improve their lifestyles, and increase their income, yet simultaneously help other women to be successful (Kleiman, 1980).

Business, professional, support, political and labor, artistic, sports, and health networks have been established throughout the United States. These multiple networks have enabled women to take on new identities and become empowered to achieve mutual goals.

Many private voluntary organizations spend money, time, and energy in attempting to increase health awareness among its members as well as provide direct services to the public. Most urban areas have crisis hot-lines where women volunteer to provide counseling to battered women, battering parents, rape victims, and those considering suicide as well as those with multiple other needs.

Helena Rowland arrives by taxi with her 2-year-old child at the Truth Safe House for Women. Her left eye is bloodshot, and her face is bruised and very edematous. It is obvious that she is about 6 months' pregnant. She states that "my old man got mad and started beating on me. When he left, I found a friend who gave me some money to come to this place. I just don't know what gets into him, but everytime I get pregnant he becomes even more abusive than usual. See my stomach? He kicked me right here [pointing to the left side of her abdomen]."

After the intake worker receives some preliminary information, Ms. Rowland is shown through the shelter and assigned a place for her and her baby to sleep. She is greeted by the other six women and their children (ranging in age from 2 weeks to 12 years).

The women are working together to prepare the evening meal. They tell Ms. Rowland to come back to the living room of the house because the nurse who comes to talk and assist them with personal and children's health concerns will be coming in a couple of hours.

One of the most effective low-cost, voluntary efforts to assist abused women involves the shelters and safe houses scattered throughout the United States. In 1985, 30 women per 1,000 couples suffered physical abuse by their male partners. The U.S. Department of Health and Human Services (1991) has set as an objective for the year 2000 to reduce the number of abused women to no more than 27 women per 1,000 couples. Many women needing shelter are often turned away from emergency housing. No more than 10% of women and their children will be turned away because of limited space if the nation meets the Healthy People objectives by the 21st century.

Women's organizations have a long history of voluntary involvement with the community. An increasing number have recently added to their agenda activities to improve pregnancy outcomes, to prevent teen pregnancy, and to support older women's rights. Organizations such as the Older Women's League, United Methodist Women, other religious denomination women's groups, Urban League, sororities, Junior League, YWCA, National Association of Colored Women's Clubs, and many others have made women's health a major item on their agenda.

C a s e
S t u d y

John Lawrence, an educator at the state women's correctional center, contacted the College of Nursing and expressed a concern for the health of the women at the prison. He indicated that many of the women were overweight, cared little about themselves, and lacked a general knowledge of how to maintain their health. He stated that there were pregnant women in the facility who were not aware of their role in ensuring a healthy pregnancy outcome.

Mr. Lawrence's call was followed by a call from Herman Martin, RN, who also expressed concern for the women's need for information regarding their personal hygiene. He was concerned that although the women were seen at the state-supported hospital for prenatal care, they were not permitted to attend prenatal classes. Although he was a Registered Nurse, Mr. Martin was not knowledgeable of women's health; his primary clinical focus was emergency and trauma care.

After gaining clearance by the prison officials and making an assessment of health care information needs, one of the faculty from the College of Nursing started offering classes during the summer. The next spring and each spring thereafter, junior nursing students were assigned to develop and carry out a 1-hour weekly health education and awareness session at the correctional facility.

Although each of these students expressed some initial anxiety toward the experience, each evaluated it as being a worthwhile learning experience.

The client is the aggregate of women prisoners at women's correctional center.

Assessment

- Lack of programs to promote health and prevent diseases among women prisoners

Diagnosis

- Knowledge deficit, health-seeking behaviors

Goal

● Improvement of health and well-being of incarcerated women (pregnant and nonpregnant)

Planning

● Provide health information through women's health education classes before the beginning of the spring semester.

Intervention

● Identify prison officials supportive of program and request input as to which women should be targeted for such a program.
● Meet with targeted women and assess level of knowledge regarding women's health.
● Survey what they perceive as learning needs, e.g., well women's care, women's anatomy and physiology, self-care in health promotion, health protection and disease prevention
● Each nursing student selects topic based on survey and develops a teaching plan for presentation to women prisoners (pregnant and nonpregnant) at least once during spring semester.

Evaluation

● Maintain record of attendance
● Seek feedback from women and prison officials regarding changes in self-care behavior regarding health
● Student response to learning experience

Levels of Prevention

Primary and Secondary The co-authors became involved in primary prevention as members of an ACS committee called Stop Cancer Among Minorities (SCAM). The SCAM committee members represented several ethnic groups from the settings of churches, schools, and health care agencies. The committee assessed the needs of a community that revealed a lack of knowledge of health promotion practices necessary to decrease the risk of cancer.

The committee planned a health fair to promote cancer awareness in the community. It was sponsored by the state chapter of the ACS and a local community health center. Nursing students and undergraduate faculty from the College of Nursing joined the committee to plan and implement the program.

Nursing students offered nutritious snacks (low in fat, high in fiber and complex carbohydrates) and discussed the relationship of diet to risk reduction for cancer. They also taught BSE and testicular self-examination. Other students shared the risks of starting to smoke and the benefits of quitting. There were seven booths associated with the seven danger signals of cancer.

Women's health care nurse practitioners, family nurse practitioners, and midwives from the community and the university baccalaureate nursing program as well as the clinic's medical staff joined together to perform breast and pelvic examinations for each woman. Pap smears were also performed and were sent for cytologic study to the state health department. Follow-up on Pap smear results was carried out by the health center's Director of Nursing Services.

Secondary The focus of secondary prevention is on early diagnosis or health maintenance for persons with chronic disorders. Junior-year nursing students from the College of Nursing involved in a community study identified a population at risk for the development of breast cancer. They gained permission to present a program on BSE to a group of nuns in a local convent. The students prepared themselves by becoming certified by the ACS as instructors in BSE. The ACS provided the students with current knowledge of breast cancer, its treatments, and early detection methods. The ACS also provided helpful films, pamphlets, and models for demonstration. Through the student's assessment, planning, and intervention, a group of women have been provided with skills for early detection of a life-threatening disease.

Tertiary Tertiary prevention consists of rehabilitation when sequelae of a condition have occurred. For example, Sandra Smith, a 55-year-old Native American, has had diabetes mellitus for the past 3 years. She attends an urban clinic for monitoring of her diabetes. After the physician examines her, he suggests that she have her annual pelvic examination. She is overdue for this, and she agrees to be seen by the women's health care nurse practitioner. Ms. Smith describes to the nurse symptoms of a yeast infection, e.g., increase in vaginal discharge and itching. Her examination and a wet mount confirmed the diagnosis of *Candida albicans,* a common problem of diabetic women. The woman learns about the nature, predisposing factors, and treatment of the infection.

ROLES OF THE COMMUNITY HEALTH NURSE

Direct Care

The community health nurse provides direct care in a variety of settings. Often, this is considered the "hands-on" nursing care given to a client in the home or a clinic. Direct care occurs many times every day in clinics such as sexually transmitted disease clinics. The following scene is representative of scenes that are repeated numerous times every day. Jane Beaumont is a 20-year-old white woman who has come to the clinic on the advice of her boyfriend. She appears confused and frightened. She states her boyfriend has "clap" and that he told her to go for treatment. She expresses little anger at this time and states that she knew he had other friends.

The nurse sees many opportunities for teaching, but if the client is too anxious she will be unable to integrate new information. The present goal of the nurse is to develop trust so that the young woman may return later for follow-up.

During the interview, the nurse gathers information regarding the behavioral aspects of sexuality, physical symptoms, the client's knowledge of sexual health, and the client's emotional responses to the problem. During the examination, chlamydia and gonorrhea cultures are taken from appropriate sites. After this, the nurse draws blood for serologic diagnosis of syphilis. She is diagnosed as having gonorrhea. The client also consents to testing for HIV after the nurse discusses risk factors with her.

After the examination and initiating treatment according to protocol, the nurse answers questions and stresses the importance of follow-up and future protection against sexually transmitted diseases. Ms. Beaumont asks why all this is necessary because she "feels OK." The nurse explains that 50–80% of all women have no complaints (symptoms) and feel "OK" even though the disease is present. The nurse asks her to return in 1 week for the test-of-cure culture. At this time, the nurse will also evaluate to determine whether the client understands her role in the prevention of sexually transmitted diseases, including HIV.

Counselor

The counseling role of the nurse occurs in almost every interaction in the area of women's health. Before beginning counseling in the area of reproductive health, it is essential for effective intervention that the nurse become aware of his or her value system, including how one's biases and beliefs about human sexual behavior affect the counseling role. In a representative scenario, Diana Cook comes to the family planning clinic reporting that she has missed two periods and "feels" pregnant. Ms. Cook is 33 years old and has two children, ages 9 and 12. Her pregnancy test is positive, and her pelvic examination is consistent with a 6–8-week pregnancy.

Ms. Cook had not planned this pregnancy, and she needs counseling regarding her options. The nurse realizes that this is a crisis in the life of this woman and that she will need support in whatever decision she makes.

RESEARCH IN WOMEN'S HEALTH

Women have long been the major users of the health care (illness care) system. However, there is little research that provides information that allows for prediction, explanation, or description of phenomena affecting the health of women. In the majority of cases, medical treatment for women is based on research for which the subjects were exclusively male. This is true even in conditions that are more prevalent among women.

Although depression occurs at almost twice the rate among women as among men, research on the effects and dosages of antidepressants was conducted among men. Recommendations for prescribing were made without consideration being given to women's biological differences (Women's Health Report, 1985).

The Office of Research on Women's Health was established in 1990 by the National Institutes of Health. Through a special task force, National Institutes of Health recommendations will be made for the research agenda for women's health for the next two decades (Healy, 1991).

Some of the areas for exploration and research among women are as follows:

- Health promotion
- Barriers to care
- Disease prevention
- Health education at various literacy levels
- Wellness across the life cycle
- Differences among women experiencing menopausal symptoms
- Dysmenorrhea
- Contraception, safe and effective
- Promotion of breast-feeding
- Infertility
- Coping with chronic illness such as lupus or arthritis
- Discomforts of pregnancy, including morning sickness
- Strengths of single female heads of households
- Adolescent sexuality
- Multiple role adaptation
- Menstrual cycle variations
- Control of obesity
- Substance abuse and its effect on pregnancy
- HIV infection and pregnancy
- Influence of diet on osteoporosis
- Effect of socialization to role
- Domestic violence

The Women's Health Initiative, a landmark study by the National Institutes of Health, was launched in 1991. This study will include women of all races and socioeconomic levels and will examine major causes of death, disability, and frailty. Specific conditions to be examined include heart disease and stroke, cancer, and osteoporosis (Healy, 1991).

Community health nurses can make a significant contribution toward the improvement of women's health through scholarly research either as principal investigators or through data gathering. Furthermore, they can become consumers of research and develop nursing interventions based on sound research and recommendations.

SUMMARY

Women's health care has multiple facets. There are many areas for community health nursing intervention.

Nurses are advocates and activists for women's health through their involvement in health policy-making as a profession. Along with other multidisciplinary and consumer groups, professional nurses are in the forefront of making changes in the health care delivery system that will promote an overall quality- and research-based health plan for women. Women are at the center of the health of the nation; therefore, if better models are developed for improving the health of women, the health of the entire nation will benefit.

Learning Activities

1. Integrate wellness principles and values into your personal and professional life.

2. Model to nonnursing students participatory (the woman as well as the health care provider) care to enhance wellness.

3. Survey examples from everyday life that support or encourage violence against women, e.g., magazines, books, and TV advertisements.

4. Survey lay magazine advertisements and determine the percentage of total pages that use a woman's image (including aging, menopause, overweight and obesity, and sexuality) to sell products.

5. Discuss with your female relatives the need for cancer screening based on ACS guidelines.

6. Discuss with your female relatives the need for a heart healthy nutritional plan based on American Heart Association guidelines.

7. Investigate community resources for sites that offer instruction in BSE, clinical examination, and use of dedicated mammography equipment (equipment used exclusively for radiographic examination of the breast).

8. Identify resources for mammograms for low-income women and whether the mammography facility is approved by the American College of Radiology (ACR).

9. Visit with a women's group in your community (e.g., business, church, sorority, parents without partners, and so on) to discuss their health care needs and concerns. From these data, develop research questions.

10. Call a family planning clinic and determine population served (eligibility), services offered, and costs.

11. Use the telephone directory to identify resources providing health care and psychosocial services to men, women, and children with HIV/AIDS.

12. Query a women's health care nurse practitioner or nurse-midwife regarding the changes they make in gynecological care of women with physical disabilities.

13. Review county or state health department statistics for leading causes of deaths among women of varying ethnic or racial groups.

14. Determine the percentage of women in your county who begin prenatal care during the first trimester.

15. Identify how the health care needs of women are met when they are in the correctional system in your county or state.

The authors wish to acknowledge the assistance of Debbie Gindhart in the preparation of their manuscript.

REFERENCES

Amazing but true. Savvy 6;9, 1985.

American Cancer Society: Cancer Facts and Figures—1989. Atlanta, Georgia, ACS, 1989.

American Cancer Society: Cancer Facts and Figures—1991. Atlanta, Georgia, ACS, 1991.

The American College of Obstetricians and Gynecologists: Periodic Cancer Screening for Women: Statement of Policy. Washington, D.C., ACOG, 1980.

American Nurses' Association: INA file lawsuit, charge unfair wages. Am. Nurse 16;11, 1984.

Association hails law for new mother/child Medicaid access. Nation's Health 14;1,5, 1984.

Benenson, A. S.: Control of Communicable Diseases in Man. 15th Ed. Washington, D.C., American Public Health Association, 1990.

Brown, M: Primary dysmenorrhea. Nurs. Clin. North Am. 17;145–153, 1982.

Byyny, R. L., and Speroff, L.: A Clinical Guide for the Care of Older Women. Baltimore, Williams & Wilkins, 1990.

Centers for Disease Control: Chronic disease reports: Deaths from breast cancer among women—United States, 1986. M. M. W. R. 38;565–569, 1989.

Centers for Disease Control: Ectopic pregnancy in the United States, 1970–1986. M. M. W. R. 38;1–10, 1989.

Charting a course for health and well being. Network News 8;2,8,9, 1983.

Choi, M.: Preamble to a new paradigm for women's health. Image 17;14–16, 1985.

Cunningham, F., MacDonald, P., and Gant, N. F.: Williams' Obstetrics. 18th Ed.: Norwalk, Connecticut, Appleton & Lange, 1989.

Dickinson, C.: In Lichtman, R., and Papera, S.: Gynecology: Well-Woman Care. Norwalk, Conneticut, Appleton & Lange, 1990.

DiSaia, P.: Neoplasia of the cervix. In Quilligan, E., ed.: Current Therapy in Obstetrics and Gynecology. 2nd Ed. Philadelphia, W. B. Saunders, 1983, pp. 191–195.

Duffy, M.: When a woman heads the household. Nurs. Outlook 30;46–47, 1982.

Eisenkop, S. M., Lowitz, B. B., and Casciato, D. A.: Gynecologic cancers. In Casciato, D., and Lowitz, B., eds.: Manual of Clinical Oncology. 2nd Ed. Boston, Little, Brown & Co, 1988, pp. 166–184.

Fogel, C., and Woods, N.: Health Care of Women: A Nursing Perspective. St. Louis, C. V. Mosby, 1981.

Fowler, J. E.: Urinary Tract Infection and Inflammation. Chicago, Year Book Medical Publishers, 1989.

Gordon, V. C., and Ledray, L. E.: Growth-support intervention for the treatment of depression in women of middle years. West. J. Nurs. Res. 8;263–283, 1986.

Haas, M.: Women, work and stress: A review and agenda for the future. J. Health Soc. Behav. 23;132–144, 1982.

Hane, N. L., and Williams, R. D.: Breast cancer: Office nurses—The best defense. Ob/Gyn Nurse Forum 2;2–6, 1991.

Hatcher, R., Stewart, F., Trussell, J., et al: Contraceptive Technology: 1990–1992. 15th Ed. New York, Irvington Publishers, 1990.

Healy, B.: Women's health, public welfare. J.A.M.A. 266;566–568, 1991.

Hock, R.: Personal communication, 1991.

Institute of Medicine: Preventing Low Birthweight. Washington, D.C., National Academy Press, 1985.

Jensen, M. D., Bobak, I. M., and Zalar, M. K.: Maternity and Gynecologic Care: The Nurse and the Family. 4th Ed. St. Louis, C. V. Mosby, 1989.

Kistner, R.: Gynecology: Principles and Practice. 3rd Ed. Chicago, Year Book Medical Publishers, 1979.

Kleiman, C.: Women's Networks. New York, Ballantine Books, 1980.

Klein, L.: Unintended pregnancy and the risks/safety of birth control methods. J. Obstet. Gynecol. Nurs. 13;287–289, 1984.

Klerman, G. L., and Weissman, M. M.: Depressions among women: Their nature and causes. In Guttentag, M., Salasin, S., and Belle, D., eds.: The Mental Health of Women. New York, Academic Press, 1980, pp. 57–92.

Krowlewski, A., and Warram, J.: Epidemiology of diabetes mellitus. In Marble, A., Krall, L., Bradley, R., et al., eds.: Joslin's Diabetes Mellitus. 12th ed. Philadelphia, Lea & Febiger, 1985.

Lowdermilk, D. L.: Reproductive surgery. In Griffith-Kenney, J., ed.: Contemporary Women's Health—A Nursing Advocacy Approach. Menlo Park, California, Addison-Wesley, 1986, pp. 603–621.

MacKay, E., Beischer, N., Cox, L., and Wood, C.: Illustrated Textbook of Gynecology. Philadelphia, W. B. Saunders Company, 1983.

Metropolitan Life and Affiliated Companies: Health insurance of women of childbearing age, United States, in 1985. Statistical Bulletin 69(4):16–23, 1988.

Neeson, J., and Stockdale, C.: The Practitioner's Handbook of Ambulatory OB/GYN. New York, John Wiley & Sons, 1981.

Notelovitz, M., and Ware, J.: Stand Tall! Every Woman's Guide to Preventing Osteoporosis. 2nd Ed. Gainesville, Florida, Bantam Books, 1985.

Orr, S. T., and James, S.: Maternal depression in an urban pediatric practice: Implications for health care delivery. Am. J. Public Health 73:363–365, 1984.

Pender, N. J.: Health Promotion in Nursing Practice. 2nd Ed. Norwalk, Conneticut, Appleton & Lange, 1987.

Phipps, W., Long, B., and Woods, N.: Medical-Surgical Nursing Concepts and Clinical Practice. 2nd Ed. St. Louis, C. V. Mosby, 1983.

Placek, P. J., Taffel, S., and Moien, J.: Caesarean section delivery rates: United States, 1981. Am. J. Public Health 73:861–863, 1983.

Ponzetti, J., and Hoefler, S.: Natural family planning: A review and assessment. Family Commun. Health 11(2):36–48, 1988.

Radloff, L. S.: Risk factors for depression: What do we learn from them? In Guttentag, M., Salasin, S., Belle, D., eds.: The Mental Health of Women. New York, Academic Press, 1980, pp. 93–109.

Rose, J.: Herbal treatments for women. In Weiss, K., ed.: Women's Health Care — A Guide to Alternatives. Reston, Virginia, Reston Publishing Company, 1984, pp. 235–245.

Ruzek, S. K.: Emergent modes of utilization: Gynecological self help. Nursing Dimensions 7:73–79, 1979.

Sherwen, L. N., Scoloveno, M. A., and Weingarten, C. T.: Nursing Care of the Childbearing Family. Norwalk, Connecticut, Appleton & Lange, 1991.

Sidel, R.: Women and children first: Toward a U. S. family policy. J. Health Care Poor Underserved 1:342–350, 1991.

Smith, L. S.: Psychologic concerns. In Griffith-Kenney, J., ed.: Contemporary Women's Health: A Nursing Advocacy Approach. Menlo Park, California, Addison-Wesley, 1986, pp. 156–175.

Staats, M. B., and Staats, T. E.: Differences in stress levels, stressors, and stress responses between managerial and professional males and females: Vector analysis — research education. Issues Health Care Women 4:165–176, 1983.

Sullivan, N.: Dysmenorrhea. In Lichtman, R., Papera, S., eds.: Gynecology: Well-Woman Care. Norwalk, Connecticut, Appleton & Lange, 1990.

Thomas, D. N.: Influences of Creativity, Depression and Psychological Well-Being on Physiological and Psychological Symptoms in Midlife Women. Unpublished dissertation, 1988.

U.S. Bureau of the Census, Statistical Abstract of the (United States: 1988. 108th Ed. Washington, D.C., 1987.

U.S. Bureau of the Census, Statistical Abstract of the United States: 1989. 109th Ed. Washington, D.C., 1989.

U.S. Bureau of the Census, Statistical Abstract of the United States: 1990. 110th Ed. Washington, D.C., 1990.

U.S. Department of Health and Human Services: Report of the Secretary's Task Force on Black and Minority Health. Washington, D.C., U.S. Government Printing Office, 1985.

U.S. Department of Health and Human Services: Healthy People — 2000. National Health Promotion and Disease Prevention Objectives — Public Health Service. Washington, D.C., U.S. Government Printing Office, 1991.

Verbrugge, L. M.: The twain meet: Empirical explanations of sex differences in health and mortality. In Ory, M. G., and Warner, H. R., eds.: Gender, Health and Longevity: Multidisciplinary Perspectives. New York: Springer Publishing, 1990.

Weiss, K.: Women's Health Care — A Guide to Alternatives. Reston, Virginia, Reston Publishing, 1984.

Weissman, M. M.: Depression. In Brodsky, A. M., and Hare-Mustin, R., eds.: Women and Psychotherapy. New York, Guilford Press, 1980, pp. 97–112.

Weissman, M. M., and Klerman, G. L.: Depression in women: Epidemiology, explanations, and impact on the family. In Notman, M. T., and Nadelson, C. C., eds.: The Woman Patient. Vol. 3: Aggression, Adaptations and Psychotherapy. New York, Plenum Press, 1982, pp. 189–203.

Williamson, M.: Lesbianism. In Griffith-Kenney, J., ed.: Contemporary Women's Health: A Nursing Advocacy Approach. Menlo Park, California, Addison-Wesley, 1986, pp. 278–296.

Witkin-Lanoil, G.: The reality of female stress. Health 16:54–60, 1984.

Women — A World Report. New York, Oxford University Press, 1985.

Women's Health — Report of the Public Health Service Task Force on women's health issues. Public Health Reports 100:73–106, 1985.

Women's health risk expected to increase. Am Operating Room Nurse J. 33:1181, 1981.

Working Woman's Guides to Her Job Rights. U. S. Department of Labor. Office of the Secretary. Women's Bureau. January, 1984.

Young, D., and Mahan, C.: Unnecessary cesareans. Ways to avoid them. Minneapolis, Minnesota, International Childbirth Education Association, 1980.

Yurick, A. G.: The nursing process and the activity of the elderly person. In Yurick, A. G., Spicer, B. E., Robb, S. S., and Ebert, N. J., eds.: The Aged Person and the Nursing Process. 2nd Ed. Norwalk, Connecticut, Appleton-Century-Crofts, 1984, pp. 5–32.

Men's Health

Upon completion of this chapter, the reader will be able to:

1. Identify the major indicators of men's health status.

2. Describe two major explanations for men's health status.

3. Discuss factors that impede men's health.

4. Discuss factors that promote men's health.

5. Describe men's health needs.

6. Apply knowledge of men's health needs in planning gender-appropriate nursing care for men at the individual, family, and community levels.

Janice M. Swanson

It is common knowledge that women live longer than men. Death rates for men are higher than for women for the major causes of death (National Center for Health Statistics [NCHS], 1991; Verbrugge and Wingard, 1987). However, despite increasing interest in health promotion and illness prevention, little attention has been paid to men's health. Although women's health is becoming a specialty area of practice and courses and programs in women's health are available in many colleges of nursing, courses, programs, and a specialty for men's health are not emphasized.

This chapter will focus on the health needs of men and the implications for community health nursing. Specific areas that will be discussed include men's health status, theories that attempt to explain men's health, factors that impede men's health, factors that promote men's health, men's health needs, meeting men's health needs, and planning gender-appropriate care for men at the individual, family, and community levels.

MEN'S HEALTH STATUS

Traditional indicators of health include rates of longevity, mortality, and morbidity.

Longevity and Mortality in Men

MAJOR DIFFERENCES between the sexes in rates of longevity and mortality show that men are disadvantaged despite marked increases in medical care and access to health services. In contrast, higher morbidity rates are experienced by women, who are more likely to use health services. Sex differentials have been associated with behavioral factors, which place men at greater risk of death. Antecedents of sex-linked behavior in men, however, are compounded by social and environmental factors of major public health concern. These factors, together with men's reluctance to seek preventive and health services, have marked implications for community health nursing.

Longevity

Rates of longevity are increasing for both men and women. We can expect to live more than 20 years longer than our forefathers and foremothers at the turn of the century. Infants born in the United States in 1988 can expect to live 74.9 years, whereas those born in 1900 lived an average of 47.3 years (NCHS, 1989, 1991). Although life expectancy has increased, the gender gap—differences between males and females—has also increased. Males born in 1988 will live an average of 71.5 years (NCHS, 1992). Females born in 1988, however, will live an average of 78.3 years. At the turn of the century, women lived an average of only 2 years longer than men. The gender gap increased from 5.5 to 7.8 years between 1950 and 1975, with females gaining over males each year. That trend reversed, and men started to catch up, as evidenced by a decline from 7.8 years in 1975 to 6.9 in 1987. Overall, however, differences in longevity rates between males and females suggest that males have become disadvantaged over the course of this decade.

The United States is the only Western industrialized nation that fails to report health and vital statistics by socioeconomic status (Navarro, 1989).

Standardized Terminology

IN THE fields of demography and sociology, the following terms are standardized:

Persons of all ages: Males, females

Children (younger than 18 years old): Boys, girls

Adults (18 years of age or older): Men, women

Sex: The distinction, biologically, between males and females

Gender: The attitudes and behavior of men and women that are shaped by socialization and have a potential to be changed

Role: The part one plays in society

Data from Skelton, R.: Man's role in society and its effect on health. Nursing 26;953–956, 1988; Verbrugge, L. M., and Wingard, D. L.: Sex differentials in health and mortality. Women Health 12;103–145, 1987.

In England, life expectancy is closely associated with socioeconomic status (Skelton, 1988). Reports of health and vital statistics in the United States by race and sex show that underserved populations in the United States, especially minorities, live significantly fewer years. For example, of those born in 1988, black males will live 64.9 years and white males will live 72.3 years; black females will live 73.4 years and white females will live 78.9

years (NCHS, 1991). Data for Hispanic populations have not been available until recently because they have been traditionally classified as white in the United States and considered an ethnic group. A shorter life expectancy for men is a phenomenon common to all contemporary industrialized countries (Tomasson, 1984). The United States lags behind a number of other countries, rating 22nd in life expectancy for men and 16th in life expectancy for women (NCHS, 1991).

Mortality

In addition to a shorter average life span, males in industrialized countries have higher death rates than do females (Tomasson, 1984). In the United States, males lead females in rate of mortality in each of the leading causes of death (Table 13–1). Men are nearly four times as likely as women to die from suicide, more than three times as likely to die

from homicide or legal intervention, and two to three times as likely to die from accident, chronic liver disease or cirrhosis, or chronic obstructive pulmonary disease. They are nearly twice as likely as women to die of diseases of the heart, pneumonia, or influenza and lead in deaths resulting from cancer, kidney disease, atherosclerosis, cerebrovascular disease, and diabetes (NCHS, 1990). The age-adjusted sex-to-mortality ratio for all ages has increased between 1950 and 1987 from 1.5 to 1.74 for whites and from 1.2 to 1.75 for blacks (U.S. Department of Health, Education, and Welfare [USDHEW], 1980; NCHS, 1990). Black men are more than three times as likely to die from accidents as are black women, 1.5-times as likely to die from diseases of the heart or from cancer, and 24% more likely to die from cerebrovascular disease. The highest sex-to-mortality ratios for both white and black men were for suicide, homicide, and legal intervention (NCHS, 1990).

Morbidity

In health interviews in which people are asked to report their view of their health status, men have consistently reported their health status higher than have women (Verbrugge and Wingard, 1987). In the National Health Interview Survey of 1990,

Table 13–1
Ratio of Age-Adjusted Death Rates Per 100,000 Population for the Leading Causes of Death by Sex in the United States for 1987

Cause of Death	Ratio of Male to Female
Suicide	3.9
Homicide and legal intervention	3.2
Accidents	2.7
Motor vehicle	2.6
All other	3.0
Chronic liver disease or cirrhosis	2.3
Chronic obstructive pulmonary disease	2.0
Diseases of the heart	1.9
Pneumonia or influenza	1.8
Malignant neoplasms	1.5
Nephritis, nephrotic syndrome, or nephrosis	1.5
Atherosclerosis	1.3
Cerebrovascular disease	1.2
Diabetes mellitus	1.1

Data compiled from National Center for Health Statistics: Health, United States, 1989. Hyattsville, Maryland, U.S. Public Health Service, 1990.

Sources of Data
National Center for Health Statistics
THROUGH THE National Vital Statistics System, the National Center for Health Statistics collects data from each state, the city of New York, the District of Columbia, the U.S. Virgin Islands, Guam, and Puerto Rico on births, deaths, marriages, and divorces in the United States.

National Health Interview Survey
The National Health Interview Survey is a continuing nationwide sample survey in which data are collected by personal interviews about household members' illnesses, injuries, chronic conditions, disabilities, and use of health services.

42.5% of men stated their health was "excellent" compared with 38.7% of women. However, 8.4% of men rated their health as "fair" or "poor" compared with 9.3% of women (NCHS, 1992).

Morbidity rates, or rates of illness, are very difficult to obtain and have been available usually only in Western industrialized countries (Waldron, 1983*b*). In the United States, for example, reports of analyses of morbidity by gender lag several years behind analyses of mortality by gender. Gender differences in morbidity reported here reflect the lastest available reports. Common indicators of morbidity are:

- Incidence of acute illness
- Prevalence of chronic conditions
- Use of medical and preventive care
- Use of other health services

Although variations exist, in general, women are more likely to be ill, whereas men are at greater risk for death.

ACUTE ILLNESS

The incidence rate is higher for women than for men for acute infective and parasitic disease, respiratory conditions, and digestive conditions (NCHS, 1987). The only exception is for injuries, which in 1986 were 24% greater for men. Acute conditions associated with the childbearing role of women are included. When these female conditions are excluded, however, the incidence rate for women is still 22% greater than that for men.

In the National Health Interview Survey 1986, men and women differed in their response to acute conditions. Women slowed their activities and rested in bed more often than men. The number of restricted-activity days per 100 persons for acute conditions is 35% greater for women than for men; similarly, the number of bed disability days per 100 persons is 55% greater for women than for men (NCHS, 1987). In this survey, an acute condition was considered a condition that lasted less than 3 months and either resulted in restricted activity or caused the patient to receive medical care.

CHRONIC CONDITIONS

A chronic condition was considered a condition that lasted at least 3 months or was listed as chronic from the onset, such as tuberculosis, neoplasm, or arthritis (NCHS, 1987). Women, in general, have higher morbidity rates than do men. Major sex-to-morbidity ratios are presented in Table 13–2.

Table 13–2
Morbidity Sex Ratios in the United States for 1986

Morbidity	Ratio of Male-to-Female Rate
Absence of extremities or parts of extremities	2.79
Gout	2.65
Emphysema	1.82
Ischemic heart disease	1.60
Intervertebral disc disorders	1.22
Hypertension	0.75
Asthma	0.66
Arthritis	0.63
Anemia	0.41
Diverticula of the intestine	0.37
Goiter or other disorders of the thyroid	0.27
Chronic enteritis and colitis	0.19
Migraines	0.15

From National Center for Health Statistics, Dawson, D. A., and Adams, P. F.: Current estimates from the National Health Interview Survey: United States, 1986. Vital Health Stat. Series 10, No. 164. DHHS Publication No. (PHS) 87–1592, Public Health Service, Washington, D. C., U.S. Government Printing Office, 1987.

Women are more likely than men to have a higher prevalence of chronic diseases that cause disability and limitation of activities but do not lead to death. Men, however, have higher morbidity as well as mortality rates for conditions that are the leading causes of death.

USE OF MEDICAL AND PREVENTIVE CARE

Medical Care

AMBULATORY CARE

Men seek ambulatory care less often than do women. According to the National Health Interview Survey 1986, the physician's office is the primary setting for ambulatory care for both men and women. Women had 6.1 physician contacts outside a hospital (physician's office, via telephone, as a hospital outpatient, home visit) in 1990, whereas men had 4.7 contacts (NCHS, 1992). Men are seen more frequently than women for conditions that correspond with their leading causes of mortality: ischemic heart disease, cerebrovascular disease, and injury (NCHS, 1983). On the other hand, women are seen more frequently than men for the chronic diseases found to be more prevalent among them. Visit rates for boys and girls less than 15 years old are about the same, but boys' visit rates for injury and poisoning are higher.

HOSPITAL CARE

The literature indicates that hospitalization rates also vary by sex. For example, in 1987, discharges from short-stay hospitals were higher for males (100.1 per 1,000 population) than for females (93.9 per 1,000 population) (NCHS, 1989; Verbrugge and Wingard, 1987). Males had more days of care (702.9 per 1,000 population) than females (605.7 per 1,000 population) and stayed longer (7.0 versus 6.5 days). Boys up to the age of 15 are hospitalized more than girls, but females aged 15–44 are hospitalized more often than males in this age group (Verbrugge and Wingard, 1987). When hospitalizations associated with reproduction are excluded, age-adjusted discharge rates for men and women are nearly the same. When sex-specific conditions are excluded (gynecological disorders in women and reproductive disorders in men), men's rates of hospitalization are a little higher than women's rates. Discharge rates increase for both men and women after the age of 45; rates for men, however, increase more rapidly. After age 65, men's discharge rates are higher than are those for women.

Preventive Care

Preventive examinations are necessary for early diagnosis of health problems. National health surveys indicate that women are more likely than men to receive physical examinations and to receive physical examinations while they are feeling well (NCHS, 1987; Verbrugge, 1982). Women's examinations are also more likely to be voluntary and recent than are men's examinations. On the other hand, examinations for men are more likely to be at the insistence of their employers. Women are more likely to have an ongoing source of care, a private physician, and are more likely to go to the private physician for care. Kovar (1980) asked men why they had no source of care. Men of all ages, more so than women, said simply that they do not need a source of care.

Other Health Services

Women are more likely to use prescription medications and to be admitted for psychiatric services to outpatient psychiatric settings such as community mental health centers that are federally funded and to be admitted for psychiatric services to private mental hospitals and psychiatric care units of nonfederal, general hospitals (NCHS, 1983, 1989). Women also are more likely to reside in nursing homes owing to their longer life expectancy. Rates of institutionalization in state and county mental hospitals for men, however, are greater than those for women.

THEORIES THAT EXPLAIN MEN'S HEALTH

It is clear that there is a gender gap in health. The data reviewed raise many questions for community health nurses to explore regarding sex differences in health and illness. Although men have shorter life expectancy and higher rates of mortality for all leading causes of death, women have higher rates of morbidity, including rates of acute illness and chronic disease, and use of medical and preventive care services. What theories exist to explain men's health status? Or, as asked by Verbrugge and Wingard (1987), how is it that "females are sicker, but males die sooner?" (p. 135). Is it simply that we aggregate more mortalities of men and more morbidities of women, or is it more a matter of how males and females respond to health problems? There are several explanations for this paradox.

Traditionally, adult health has been viewed within a developmental framework (Erickson, 1963); only later was there a focus specifically on the development of men (Levinson, 1978). Developmental theory has traditionally been used by nurses to explain individual behavior; less has been written about the many factors and combinations of factors that influence sex differences in the health and illness of populations.

Possible explanations proposed by Waldron (1976) and Verbrugge and Wingard (1987) attempt to account for sex differences in this important area:

- Genetics (inherited risks)
- Socialization (acquired risks)
- Orientations toward illness and prevention
- Reporting of health behavior

Genetics

Sex differences in mortality and morbidity are influenced by a number of genetic factors as well as environmental factors that underlie and interact with genetic factors (Waldron, 1983a, 1983b). From the moment of conception, males have long been considered the weaker sex. Fetal death rates for males are higher than for females, as are infant mortality rates and death rates due to congenital anomalies (NCHS, 1989; Verbrugge and Wingard, 1987). In addition, sex chromosome–linked diseases such as hemophilia, red–green color blindness, and certain types of muscular dystrophy are more common among males than among females (Verbrugge, 1982; Verbrugge and Wingard, 1987). Biological advantages for females may also exist due to the protective mechanism produced by estrogen against heart disease, although studies must be interpreted cautiously (Waldron, 1983a). In addition, Waldron (1976, 1982, 1983a) presents evidence that suggests genetic factors may contribute to sex differences in high-risk and aggressive behavior, mental and penal institutionalization, fatal accidents, and other violent deaths.

Socialization

A second theory for explaining sex differences in health is socialization. Acquired risks may be different between males and females owing to differences in work, leisure, and lifestyle. These differences may be influenced by sex role socialization.

More men than women are employed on a full-time basis in work environments outside the home. Usually, men's occupations are more hazardous than are positions held by women. Accidents on the job contribute significantly to higher accident rates and represent a major killer among men

(NCHS, 1989). Nonwhite men are more likely than are white men to volunteer for hazardous tasks to increase their pay (Robinson, 1985). Men's higher exposure to carcinogens at the work site is associated with higher rates of mesothelioma, coal worker's pneumoconiosis, acute leukemia, and cancer of the bladder (NCHS, 1989). Competition to succeed on the job contributes to hard-driving type A behavior in men, placing men at higher risk of ischemic heart disease (Waldron, 1982). Although occupational hazards to women's health are being identified, evidence indicates that unlike men, employment of U.S. women outside the home has had a positive effect on their health (Waldron, 1980).

Leisure, sports, and play activities also place men at high risk of injury. Waldron (1983b) states that "sex differences in socialization contribute to sex differences in risk-taking . . . behavior" (p. 1113). Greater risk taking by males is supported by boys' higher rates of accidents due to riskier play (Rivara et al., 1982), men's faster driving rates and

---

Four Dimensions of Stereotyped Male Sex Role Behavior

NO SISSY Stuff: **The need to be different from women**

The Big Wheel: **The need to be superior to others**

The Sturdy Oak: **The need to be independent and self-reliant**

Give 'Em Hell: **The need to be more powerful than others, through violence if necessary**

Data from David, D. S., and Brannon, R.: The male sex role: Our culture's blueprint of manhood, and what it's done for us lately. In David, D. S., and Brannon, R., eds.: The Forty-Nine Percent Majority: The Male Sex Role. Reading, Massachusetts, Addison-Wesley, 1976, p. 12.

---

higher rates of traffic violations and motor vehicle fatalities (Veevers, 1982), and men's greater use of illegal psychoactive substances, higher rates of alcohol consumption, and higher rates of cigarette smoking (NCHS, 1989).

Orientations Toward Illness and Prevention

Illness orientations, i.e., one's ability to note symptoms and take appropriate action, may also differ between the sexes. Boys in our society are socialized to ignore symptoms (Mechanic, 1964), whereas the reporting of symptoms may be more socially acceptable for girls. Women are more likely to cut down their activities when ill, to seek health care, and to report more details to health care providers (Verbrugge and Wingard, 1987).

Prevention orientations, i.e., one's ability to take action to prevent disease or injury, may also vary between the sexes. Women's higher likelihood of seeking preventive examinations includes routine reproductive health screening — the Papanicolaou test and breast examination. This examination includes some general screening, such as check of blood pressure and tests of urine and blood for chronic problems. Men do not have routine reproductive health checkups that include screening

that would also detect other health problems at an early stage.

Actual sex differences in preventive health behavior are variable and must be viewed with caution for two reasons: 1) little research has been carried out, and 2) the efficacy of many of the behaviors is still in question (Waldron, 1983*b*).

In the National Survey of Personal Health Practices and Consequences, women were more likely than men to report favorable practices in recency of health visits, blood pressure checks, dental flossing, and limiting of red meat intake for health reasons and as measured by the Alameda 5-Habit Index (measuring smoking, drinking, physical activity, weight, and hours of sleep) (Rakowski, 1988). On the other hand, men tended to spend more time in leisure time activities than did

---

Men's Reproductive Health Needs

REPRODUCTIVE HEALTH needs are beginning to be recognized as important to men's health as well as to women's health. Many sexually transmitted diseases (STDs) are at epidemic proportions in the United States and are a major health hazard for many men as well as women. There are sex differences in the incidence of STDs. It is well known that AIDS in the United States is more likely to occur in men; only 9.6% of persons with AIDS are women (NCHS, 1992). Less well known, perhaps, is that many STDs are considered to be intrinsically "sexist," as clinical evidence, more overt in men, is more likely to facilitate a correct diagnosis in men than in women (Perez-Stable and Slutkin, 1985). For example, rates of syphilis and gonorrhea are higher among men than among women as men are more likely to be treated for these STDs than are women (Centers for Disease Control, 1988; Perez-Stable and Slutkin, 1985).

Testicular cancer is the leading form of cancer in young men ages 15–35 and accounted for an estimated 6,100 new cases in 1991 (American Cancer Society, 1991). Cancer of the prostate is the third leading cause of death from cancer in men, accounting for about 15.7 deaths per 100,000 population in 1989 (NCHS, 1992).

Many occupational and environmental

agents associated with adverse sexual and reproductive outcomes in men have been identified and include pesticides, anesthetic gases in the operating room and dental office, inorganic lead from smelters, painting, printing, carbon disulfide from vulcanization of rubber, inorganic mercury manufacturing and dental work, and ionizing radiation from x-rays (see Chapters 24 and 25; Whorton, 1984; Cohen, 1986).

Many pharmacological agents, including prescription, over-the-counter, and recreational drugs, have been found to affect the reproductive outcomes or sexual functioning of men (Buffum, 1984; Cohen, 1986). Examples include drugs from the following categories: antihypertensives, antipsychotics, tricyclic antidepressants, MAO-inhibitor antidepressants, hormones, sedative-hypnotics, stimulants, carbonic anhydrase inhibitors, chemotherapy agents used in cancer treatment, opiates, and marijuana, tobacco, phencyclidine (PCP), and lysergic acid diethylamide (LSD).

A focus on gay men's health has come about largely through the advent of the AIDS epidemic. For the role of the clinician in assessment, education, counseling, and providing support related to the reproductive health of the gay male client, see Swanson and Forrest (1984).

women. No differences by sex were found in seat-belt use, and only a borderline difference was found regarding eating breakfast.

Other studies are also suggestive of sex differences in preventive health behavior. Women are more likely than men to take a vitamin regularly (Verbrugge and Wingard, 1987). Women are also more likely to brush their teeth and make dental visits than are men (NCHS, 1983, 1989; Verbrugge, 1982). In addition, women are more likely to have followed a weight reduction diet as more women report being overweight and are classified medically as obese (NCHS, 1989; Verbrugge, 1982). Both men and women engage in regular exercise, but the types of sports pursued by men tend to give them greater cardiovascular benefits (Verbrugge, 1982).

Verbrugge and Wingard (1987) state that females' illness and prevention orientations, in particular, their likelihood of seeking routine medical and dental care, contribute to their higher morbidity rates. These authors suggest two reasons for this phenomenon. First, women are the caretakers of the health of the family; they observe signs of illness, learn about sources of health care, set health care appointments and escort family members, and give direct care to ill family members. Second, women have more flexible schedules, which allow them to be the caretakers.

Reporting Health Behavior

A number of differences in how health behavior is reported may affect sex differentials (Verbrugge and Wingard, 1987). Most health surveys are conducted face-to-face or via telephone by women interviewers. Women may be better respondents than men, more likely to remember their health problems and actions, and more likely to talk with someone about aspects of their illness and health. A woman may respond more openly to another woman; a man may be more inhibited. Women are usually called on in health surveys to report the health behavior of men; therefore, women are proxies, and proxies have a tendency to underreport behavior (Montiero, 1976). Under these conditions, women may recall and report more health problems than do men. Men may be less willing to talk, may not recall health problems, and may lack a health vocabulary.

Discussion

INTERPRETING DATA

Verbrugge and Wingard (1987) caution that all four factors (inherited and acquired risks, illness and prevention orientations, and health-reporting behavior) must be taken into consideration when interpreting data. When only diagnostic data from examinations or laboratory tests are considered (a highly medical perspective), sex differentials are most likely the result of inherited and acquired risks. On the other hand, when data have the potential to be affected by social factors such as sex differences in illness and prevention orientations and health-reporting behavior, these factors should not be ignored. As the authors state, "A sex differential in emphysema partly reflects risks men and women incur, but also whether they are aware of the condition or feel like reporting it" (Verbrugge and Wingard, 1987, p. 134). Health interview data such as those from the National Health Interview Survey and the National Survey of Personal Health Practices and Consequences are the most common type of data available concerning a population's health; Verbrugge and Wingard (1987) caution that the social factors of sex differences in illness and prevention orientations and health-reporting behavior are therefore critical in interpreting health interview data.

Many issues are raised for community health nurses, who usually are women and usually interact with women clients. Because the data obtained and interpreted by community health nurses may be influenced by one or more of these factors, the following questions must be considered. What are the differences in reporting of health histories between male and female clients? How do data obtained by male nurses differ from those obtained by female nurses? What are the differences in data from health histories given by female "proxies" of absent members of the household or group and those given by the individual? What is the caretaking role of women in the family, and how can they be supported in the caretaking role? How do these questions apply to men in the caretaking role (e.g., parent, partner, or other caretaker of a person with chronic disease)?

In response to the question of why "females are sicker, but males die sooner," Verbrugge and Wingard (1987) provide several reasons. First, conditions that affect morbidity (e.g., arthritis and gout) do not significantly impact mortality, and conditions that affect mortality (e.g., heart disease) may not erupt as troublesome on a day-to-day basis. Second, there is a difference in how the sexes respond to their health problems. Although mortality is in large part the outcome of inherited or acquired risks, sex differences in illness and prevention orientations and the reporting of health behaviors suggest that social and psychological factors affect morbidity. Although males have higher prevalence and death rates for "killer" chronic diseases as well as for injuries and accident mortalities, females have higher prevalence rates for a greater number of nonfatal chronic conditions. In addition, adult women report higher rates of morbidity from acute conditions than do adult men. The authors state that "females' greater willingness and ability to take care of themselves when ill, to seek preventive help, and to talk about health all boost their morbidity rate" (Verbrugge and Wingard, 1987, p. 136).

SEX-LINKED BEHAVIOR

The largest sex differences in mortalities occur for causes of death associated with sex-linked behavior, which is more prevalent and encouraged in men in our society. Waldron and Johnson (1976) and, more recently, Harrison (1984) suggest that sex-linked behavior in men correlates with the following major categories of death:

- Smoking: lung cancer, bronchitis, emphysema, asthma
- Alcohol consumption: cirrhosis, accidents, homicide
- Poor preventive health habits and stress: heart disease
- Lack of other emotional channels: cirrhosis, suicide, homicide, accidents

Smoking, alcohol consumption, preventive health habits, and use of emotional channels are lifestyle factors that may be compounded by social and environmental conditions. These conditions include major public health concerns such as occupational hazards (e.g., carcinogens, stress) or unemployment and environmental hazards, both physical and psychological, such as massive adver-

Images of Men

MUCH HAS been written about the harmful, sex role–stereotyped images of women as passive, unintelligent, dependent sex objects, in print as well as in audio and visual media (Bird, 1970; Steinem, 1983). Less has been written about the damaging sex role–stereotyped images in the media's portrayal of men as aggressive, independent, and powerful, yet aloof (Allen and Whatley, 1986; Brannon, 1976). Community health nurses are in a position to overcome the traditional medical and scientific approach to men's health as the presentation of "facts" only (Ehrenreich, 1983) by marketing health information directly to men. Recognizing the difference between the damaging sex role–stereotyped images of men and the use of male culture as a way of communicating with men is important in marketing health concepts to men. For example, an early self-care book for men, *Man's Body: An Owner's Manual* (Diagram Group, 1976) uses language with which men can identify in their culture ("an owner's manual"). Another example of using this concept in marketing health information to men is an advertisement for seminars on fatherhood "Come to Our Fatherhood Seminar . . . Because Babies Don't Come With an Owner's Manual."

tising campaigns and the use of sex and sex roles to sell alcohol and tobacco in particular.

These concerns call for a major public health approach to men's health. These factors are compounded by men's lack of willingness to seek preventive care such as screening and to seek health care when a symptom arises.

Unemployment and Men's Health

ALTHOUGH UNEMPLOYMENT is not viewed as a major cause of mortality or morbidity, it is recognized as a health risk (Abraham and Krowchuk, 1986; Hibbard and Pope, 1987; Lewis, 1988). Consequences of unemployment include a loss of personal and social identity, a life crisis and major change, loss of income and/or poverty, and higher rates of illness (e.g., cardiovascular disease, hypertension, myocardial infarction, cerebrovascular accidents, cirrhosis, and psychosis). Other

increases noted are smoking, drinking, depression, aggression, and child abuse. The consequences of unemployment are felt not only at the individual level but also by the family and the community. Community health nurses may experience the deprivation associated with a community that experiences high rates of unemployment.

To counter these types of factors, research is needed to determine alternative methods of practice and education aimed at health promotion, health education, illness prevention, and political processes to create safer environments to enhance the growth and development of both males and females.

FACTORS THAT IMPEDE MEN'S HEALTH

Many factors have been viewed as barriers to men's health. Men's higher rates of mortality, greater risk taking, less use of the health care system, gaps in preventive health behavior, and differences in illness and health orientations and reporting of health behavior all contribute to a diminished health status for men. A number of other barriers have been proposed, including the patterns of medical care provided in the United States, access to care, and lack of health promotion.

Medical Care Patterns

DeHoff and Forrest (1984) state that "the usual pattern of medical care in this country—'the system'—has contributed indirectly to men's health problems" (p. 5). During his lifetime, a man is likely to come into contact, first, with a pediatrician; then, with a school nurse; next, with a college, military, or company physician; and, last, with a family practitioner, internist, or geriatrician by the time he develops chronic disease later in life. Many health professionals provide care for men with complex health needs in a wide variety of settings, yet these authors point out that men have no specialist to whom they can go for care that "feels right" for them. As medical care has become increasingly specialized, there has been a noticeable effort to reestablish general health care. This has been attempted by creating yet another specialty

—family practice—and by reincorporating the discrete specialties of internal medicine, pediatrics, obstetrics/gynecology, and geriatrics, into "primary care specialties." Men have been overlooked as new medical specialties have developed. Urologists, who may see men for genital abnormalities or diseases of the prostate, are not primary care physicians, and they also see women. The medical specialty andrology, which originated in Europe to treat problems of fertility and sterility, is considered too narrow in focus to treat "the whole man." Without a primary care specialty that focuses specifically on men's needs, many needs, such as sexual and reproductive problems and sex role influences on health and lifestyle, may not be attended to by anyone. In addition, these specialists and generalists have not received training that would enable them to focus on men's health needs specifically as occurs in women's health as a specialty area of practice.

Access to Care

MISSION ORIENTATION

Public interest in men's health has in large part focused on efforts necessary to maintain an effective work force (DeHoff and Forrest, 1984). Mission-oriented health care is a priority for large industries and organized sports. More general health care, however, may be provided through insurance programs. Perhaps the most complete care is currently offered by the military. However, marked deficiencies exist in the lack of a focus on prevention and health promotion at the individual and aggregate levels as well as in attention to policy regarding, for example, environmental hazards.

FINANCIAL CONSIDERATIONS

Another barrier to health care for men is financial ability. A man may receive an annual physical examination if he belongs to a health maintenance organization (HMO) or he is an executive or an airline pilot, but most insurance companies will reimburse only for a diagnosed condition—for pathology, not for preventive care. A man is more likely to be insured for acute or chronic illness conditions than for health education, counseling, or other types of preventive health care. Unlike women, who have annual gynecological examinations that include screening for other conditions and allow a woman to express other physical or psychological needs, men lack entree to the health care system for a physical examination on a routine basis.

TIME FACTORS

Men may not be as accessible as women to the health care system because of men's greater participation in the work force and because most men work during the time periods that usually correspond to when physicians are available, whether in private practice or in a clinic. Men also may be reluctant to take time from work for a medical visit, fearing loss of income or the stigmatization of being "weak," "ill," or "less of a man."

Lack of Health Promotion

A concept of health that considers health as merely the absence of disease is limiting. Traditional measures of mortality and morbidity, although reflective of the state of "health" of a population, fall short of desired health outcomes and tend to divorce the biological from the psychosocial (Choi, 1985). For example, the absence of overt pathology, even in the presence of behavioral risk factors such as smoking, alcohol consumption, obesity, and a sedentary lifestyle, is enough to give one a "clean bill of health." Physical recovery after impairment, illness, or injury is considered satisfactory. Prevention and health promotion are largely beyond the scope of the current system.

The disease focus of the present health care system is limited in addressing the precursors of today's mortalities. Many disciplines are needed to prevent today's health problems. Nursing's contribution to practice and research is instrumental in this process.

Community Health Nursing Services for Men
A MALE can be seen by a community health nurse in a well baby clinic, by a school nurse, an occupational health nurse, and finally by a community health nurse or home health nurse on a home visit for follow-up of a chronic disease. However, men are less likely to be seen by a community health nurse than are women. Not only is a major focus of many health departments maternal and child health, but also neither a medical nor a nursing speciality within a health department routinely exists to specifically address men's health. Preventive reproductive health care (family planning, prenatal care, and cancer screening) and associated general screening are not generally available for men. The hours of services offered by health departments do not usually provide ready access for men. The community health nurse's commitment to health for all requires an increased awareness of men's health issues in their social and cultural context and individual and group action that will improve men's physical, psychological, and social well-being.

Precursors of Mortalities
WHICH PRECURSORS OF today's mortalities are frequently not addressed by the present health care system?

Heart disease and stroke	Cancer
● Hypercholesteremia	● Sunlight
● Hypertension	● Radiation
● Diabetes mellitus	● Occupational hazards
● Obesity	● Water pollution
● Type A personality	● Air pollution
● Family history	● Dietary patterns
● Lack of exercise	● Cigarette smoking
● Cigarette smoking	● Alcohol
	● Heredity
	● Certain medical conditions

In a review, McKinlay and colleagues (1989) cite evidence to support the lack of impact of medical measures on mortality and morbidity in the United States. Coronary heart disease, cancer, and stroke are three conditions that account for two thirds of all mortality and the greatest use of resources. However, these authors contend that medical measures have not made substantial impact on mortality. An increase in life expectancy has occurred but usually has resulted in an increase in years of disability.

Mortality rates for coronary heart disease, the top killer, declined approximately 40% between 1968 and 1987 (McKinlay et al., 1989). The causes of the decline are not clear and have been associated with changes in risk behaviors. McKinlay and colleagues (1989) cite evidence that the effects of pharmacological intervention, emergency response in the community, coronary care units, and coronary bypass surgery have been negligible with the exception of some benefits from beta-blocking agents in post–myocardial infarction patients (Goldman and Cook, 1984).

Age-adjusted mortality rates for all types of cancer, the second top killer, increased slowly between 1950 and 1982 (McKinlay et al., 1989). Despite known environmental and personal risk factors for major cancers, funds and other resources have been allotted disproportionately into treatment and cure rather than into public health measures and primary prevention.

A Cancer Control Program (McKinlay et al., 1989)

ACCORDING TO Dr. Vincent DeVita, former director of the National Cancer Institute, adoption of a comprehensive cancer control program based on existing knowledge would require the following actions:

● Prevention, screening, early detection, and treatment
● Increased health promotion at the work place
● Dissemination through the media of prevention and control strategies
● Health education and screening by local voluntary organizations
● Reemphasized cancer control in education of health professionals
● Economic disincentives to smoking

The program would have the following outcomes:

● Decreased cancer mortality rates by 50% by the year 2000
● Savings of approximately 250,000 lives annually

Mortality rates for stroke have been declining since the turn of the century (McKinlay et al., 1989). Although the declines occurred well before antihypertensive therapy was available, McKinlay and associates (1989) cite evidence for the contribution of medical treatment to only about 12–25% of the decline since 1970.

Financial resources have been invested in traditional curative care rather than in public health action. An inordinate amount of funds is poured into the health care system each year, with only a minimum allotted to public health approaches (see Chapter 2). For example, in 1990, health expenditures accounted for 12.2% of the gross national product, an increase from 5.9% in 1965 (NCHS, 1992). Of every $1.00 spent on health care in 1990, approximately $0.57 went to hospital care and physician services, which are in large part curative in focus, and only $0.03 went to preventive government public health activities.

Social Demography and Social Epidemiology

EPIDEMIOLOGY is the method of research used to determine the nature and distribution of a health problem in a community (see Chapter 5). *Social demographers and social epidemiologists* study social and psychological factors that affect the distribution of health problems in a community. Factors associated with the occurrence of the problems can be identified, and resources can be focused on prevention. Social epidemiologists have identified men as a population at risk for premature death. What concentrated efforts can be made to improve men's health?

In view of the facts that finite resources have been allocated to traditional curative care rather than to public health and that the present health care system is limited in addressing the precursors of today's mortalities, the following question may be asked. Is medical care, or even another medical specialty, the answer to men's health needs when social, occupational, environmental, and "lifestyle" factors place men at risk?

Prevention and health promotion, when available, often are not applied at the aggregate and population levels. Nancy Milio (1983) asserts that healthy lifestyles are not a matter of free choice but rather result from opportunities that are not always equally available to people. As health policies shape opportunities for individuals and aggregates, environmental and occupational changes beyond the control of the individual are needed to improve the health of the population. Community health nurses can be involved in political activities that develop health policies that will make a difference for populations. Such activities are congruent with the philosophy of public health as health for all and a commitment to a social justice ethic of health care rather than a market justice ethic of health care. Examining men's health affords the community health nurse the opportunity to observe the impact of the market justice ethic of health care not only on the health of men in the United States but ultimately, because of men's traditional roles in the family, also on the health of women, family, and

---

Intervention at the Population Level: Economic Disincentives to Smoking (Summers, 1987)

IN 1982, an 8% increase in cigarette taxes was legislated. As a result:

- **2 Million adults stopped smoking.**
- **600,000 Teenagers were prevented from starting to smoke.**

A tax of an additional $0.20 could result in the reduction of:

- **500,000 premature deaths in adults who currently smoke**
- **the federal budget deficit by approximately $5 billion**

---

community. The community health nurse can play a vital role in contributing to a social justice ethic of health care, particularly in relation to promoting men's health.

FACTORS THAT PROMOTE MEN'S HEALTH

Factors that promote men's health can be found in the community, including interest groups in men and men's health, men's increasing interest in physical fitness and lifestyle factors, policy related to men's health, and health services for men.

Interest Groups in Men and Men's Health

Unlike the consumer movement that occurred on behalf of women's health in the 1960s and early 1970s, there is no consumer movement advocating men's health (Allen and Whatley, 1986). However, a small although viable men's consumer movement is beginning to be heard. The National Organization for Changing Men is interested in redefin-

ing the male role, particularly those aspects of the male role that are confining to the health and growth of men in our society. The American Assembly for Men in Nursing sponsors annual meetings that address issues such as men's health, men's work environments, research on men's health, and networking and support among men who are nurses. During the past decade, nursing has responded to consumer issues raised by feminists advocating a health care system sensitized to women's health care needs. Woods (1988) reviewed studies by nurses of women's health. Nurses are now pushing to define women's health beyond that limited to women's reproductive role (e.g., occupational risks). Nurses are also beginning to define and study men's health beyond that limited to men's occupational role (e.g., reproductive health) (Swanson and Forrest, 1984, 1987).

Men's Increasing Interest in Physical Fitness and Lifestyle

Although cardiovascular diseases are a major health hazard for men, research on the validity and usefulness of preventive and treatment modalities is an issue of considerable debate (Foreman, 1986). Men's interest in altering behavior that places them at risk of cardiovascular and other major diseases is increasing. For example, men's smoking behavior has changed dramatically. Between 1965 and 1985, the age-adjusted percentage of men who smoked decreased from 52% to 33% (NCHS, 1989). Men also report exercising as much as needed more frequently than do women (46% versus 37%); men also report participating more in active sports with a cardiovascular benefit such as jogging and running (NCHS, 1981).

Policy Related to Men's Health

Nurses are working to set policy related to men's health, particularly in the area of fatherhood (Hanson and Bozett, 1985). The Task Force on Male Involvement in Family Planning of the American Public Health Association (APHA) was instrumental in getting resolutions passed that called for greater access to family planning for men (1981) and that called for counting and reporting the number of men who seek care from federally funded family planning services (1987) (APHA, 1988). Men who seek care from federally funded

(Title X) family planning services in the United States are now counted and reported. A resolution on men's health submitted to the Governing Council of the APHA by the Medical Care Section, however, failed to pass in 1985.

Health Services for Men

Although Allen and Whatley (1986) argue that medicine "has largely focused on the problems of men" (p. 7), there is a lack of health care clinics tailored to the special needs of men, as have evolved to meet the special needs of women. The "well man clinic" model has been developed by male nurses in Scotland to expand the role of the public health nurse and the National Health Service in screening and health education of the marginal- and low-income man (Deans, 1988; Sadler, 1979). For a description of the well man clinic and a reproductive health clinic for men developed by public health nurses, see "New Concepts of Community Care."

MEN'S HEALTH CARE NEEDS

DeHoff and Forrest (1984) delineate men's health care needs that draw from both the biological and the psychosocial causes of men's distinctive health situation. According to these authors, men need the following:

- Permission to have concerns about health and to talk openly to others about them
- Support for the consideration of sex role and lifestyle influences on their physical and mental health
- Attention from professionals regarding factors that may cause illness or impact a man's expression of illness, including occupational factors, leisure patterns, and interpersonal relationships
- Information about how their bodies function, what is normal, what is abnormal, what action to take, and the contributions of proper nutrition and exercise
- Self-care instruction including testicular and genital self-examination
- Physical examination and history taking that include sexual and reproductive health and illness across the life-span
- Treatment for problems of couples, including interpersonal problems, infertility, family planning, sexual concerns, and sexually transmitted diseases
- Help with fathering, i.e., being included as a parent in the care of children
- Help with fathering as a single parent, in particular, with a child of the opposite sex, in addressing the child's sexual development and concerns
- Recognition that feelings of confusion and uncertainty in a time of rapid social change are normal and may mark the onset of healthy adaptation to change
- Adjustment of the health care system to men's occupational constraints regarding time and location of source of health care
- Financial ways to obtain the above

Additional health care needs of men are for primary prevention as well as for secondary and tertiary prevention at the individual, family, and community levels, to address the precursors of mortality that impact males so greatly. Because men are less likely than women to be seen as consumers in the health care system, alternative approaches must be developed that address their health needs. The most significant approaches in the future will be those that reach men in the community, in schools, in the work place, and in public settings. This calls for political processes that set policy, for health marketing techniques, and for advocacy.

MEETING MEN'S HEALTH NEEDS

Meeting the health needs of men requires approaches that extend beyond the traditional health care system model and include new concepts of community care. Interdisciplinary efforts are needed to address the many factors that impact the health of men. Major legislation and health and social services that meet the needs of men and women are complex and have been covered extensively in Chapter 3.

Traditional Health Services

Traditional health services for males are available in both government and private arenas. Services are usually diagnostic and treatment oriented rather than preventive. Government health services also stem from legislation, such as that reviewed in Chapter 3. Government health insurance programs include Medicare and workers' compensation. Government health assistance programs include Medicaid and maternal-child health services. Payment for health services may also be out-of-pocket or through private insurance such as Blue Cross–Blue Shield and HMOs. Health service programs that benefit men in particular are also sponsored by the government for specific population groups such as for veterans, military personnel, merchant marines, and federal employees.

Local and state health departments also provide services that benefit men as well as women and children. State departments of health provide policy and leadership and disburse state and federal funds for programs carried out by local health departments. These programs include the gathering of vital statistics, laboratory services, environmental and occupational health, and control of communicable disease, including venereal disease. Personal health services are usually operationalized through maternal-child health programs and programs for the disabled and elderly, although individual programs vary somewhat. For example, in 1983, 60% of federal family planning programs were carried out in health departments (Torres and Forrest, 1985). Although 20% of family planning provider agencies offered family planning services to men in 1983, approximately 1% of clients used such services (Torres, 1984; Select Committee on Population, 1978). Adult health activities in health departments are reflected in Chapter 3, Table 3–3 and Figure 3–4.

New Concepts of Community Care

Specific services for men within health departments are usually lacking in the United States, with the exception of family planning service models. An innovative public health nursing program directed at men has been started in Glasgow, Scotland, by two male health visitors (British term for public health nurses) from the National Health Service (NHS) (Deans, 1988; Sadler, 1979). Health visitors Bill Deans and Bob Hoskins set up a nurse-run well man clinic with the help of the NHS and the Scottish Council for Health Education. On home visits to a caseload of mothers and babies, Deans and Hoskins observed that fathers excused themselves and left for the local pub when they

arrived. Noting characteristics of the male population of their community such as overweight, heavy smoking, drinking, and high unemployment, they decided to modify their practice to the needs of their clients. One afternoon per week, the clinic, which is based on a nursing model rather than on a medical model, offers health screening, health education, and primary prevention to men. Marketing is important, and men are referred from general practitioners' and specialists' practices and recruited through newspaper advertisements. Clients with clinical signs and symptoms are referred back to their physicians. Lifestyle counseling and education are offered in areas such as fat and fiber content in diet, smoking, alcohol use, and exercise. Deans and Hoskins consider the clinic as a way of extending the health visitor's role as well as extending the NHS's efforts in health education with an aim to "nip potential diseases in the bud" (Sadler, 1979, p. 18). Deans and Hoskins are concerned that the NHS does not provide male services and are quite clear that "the unemployed chain-smoking husband needs as much care and health education from the health visitor as do his wife and baby" (Sadler, 1979, p. 18).

Public health nurses working in the Benton County Health Department in Corvallis, Oregon, responded to the challenge of teen pregnancy by launching a communitywide effort that included developing a men's health clinic and marketing reproductive health services directly to teenage boys and men (Fig. 13–1). Early efforts included establishing an advisory committee that included persons from churches, schools, and health care facilities. An extensive education program was launched in the high school by a public health nurse health educator and focused on decision-making processes and services available in the community. Later efforts involved establishing the clinic for men. The range of services is depicted by the flyer that tells about the clinic (see Fig. 13–1). Teenage boys were members of a consumer advisory committee established by the nurses that recommended the wording and format for advertisements about the clinic that were run in the high school newspaper. The advisory committee also recommended a format for flyers that would be attractive to males. Specifically, they requested a card with information about how to use condoms and about the clinic that would be small enough to

Serving All County Residents

Benton County Health Department

Men's Health Clinic

. . . care and treatment of health concerns unique to males . . .
757-6839

SERVICES AVAILABLE INCLUDE:

- ■ FREE CONDOMS
- ■ Information on birth control for men and their partners
- ■ Vasectomy counseling and referral
- ■ Full or partial payment of vasectomies for low income men
- ■ Diagnosis and treatment of sexually-related diseases
- ■ Medical treatment of genital and urinary problems
- ■ Counseling and support for concerns related to sexuality
- ■ Information for men involved in unplanned pregnancy
- ■ Opportunity to share in female partner's clinic visit
- ■ Books, pamphlets and information on men's issues relating to sexuality

ALL CARE AND COUNSELING IS STRICTLY CONFIDENTIAL

- ■ Teenagers welcome—parents' permission is not required
- ■ Staffed by nurse practitioners and registered nurses
- ■ No appointment necessary for condoms—self-serve, free

BENTON COUNTY HEALTH DEPARTMENT
530 NW 27th Street
Corvallis, Oregon 97330

757-6839

Rev. 9/87

Figure 13–1
Men's Health Clinic brochure, Benton County Health Department, Corvallis, Oregon. (Reprinted with permission.)

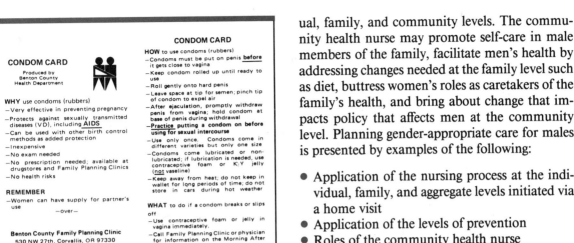

Figure 13–2
Condom card, Benton County Health Department, Corvallis, Oregon. (Reprinted with permission.)

discretely fit into their wallets yet be available to share with peers (Fig. 13–2). Since the first efforts were undertaken in 1977, public health nurses report a decrease in teen pregnancy from 10% to 4% in their targeted area (J. Ladd, personal communication, June 8, 1989). Benton County now reports the lowest teen pregnancy rate in Oregon.

APPLICATION OF THE NURSING PROCESS

Community health nurses are in an ideal position to address the health needs of men at the individual, family, and community levels. The community health nurse may promote self-care in male members of the family, facilitate men's health by addressing changes needed at the family level such as diet, buttress women's roles as caretakers of the family's health, and bring about change that impacts policy that affects men at the community level. Planning gender-appropriate care for males is presented by examples of the following:

● Application of the nursing process at the individual, family, and aggregate levels initiated via a home visit
● Application of the levels of prevention
● Roles of the community health nurse
● Research and men's health

Application of the nursing process to aggregates is facilitated by the use of systems theory, in which the nurse identifies the system and subsystems involved. The nurse may use a deductive or an inductive approach. A deductive approach would involve, first, carrying out a community assessment and identifying an area or areas such as a program needed by the community. Planning, implementation, and evaluation of the program would be carried out at the family or group level. An inductive approach, on the other hand, would involve entering the community system through a person or client via a referral about a problem or concern. Assessment of the individual would be followed by identification of those groups such as family and community to which the client belongs as well as assessment of those groups.

Case Study

Beth Lockwood, a community health nursing student at a health department, received a referral from the high school nurse to visit the Connors family to assess the mental health status of Richard Connors, a 16-year-old sophomore whose academic work in school had declined rapidly after the premature death of his father at age 46 from a myocardial infarction, which he suffered while cleaning the garage with Richard one evening after school. Efforts by Richard and the neighbors failed to revive Mr. Connors, for which Richard carries feelings of guilt. Household members include Mrs. Connors (44 years old) and Richard's sister, Yvonne, who is 12.

Assessment

The referral that Beth received to assess the Connors family after the premature death of Mr. Connors calls for an inductive approach to assessment. A deductive approach is used later by Beth, when her experience with the Connors family piques her concern about the status of men's health in the community in which her family resides. Beth must assess Richard, his mother, and his sister as household members of the

---

Gaining Skills Necessary to Address Men's Health Needs

ASSESSMENT SKILLS necessary to carry out screening activities with men to detect reproductive health needs may be lacking in nursing education. One community health nurse who worked in a rural health department felt unable to respond to male partners' requests for genital examinations when couples came to seek family planning services. The community health nurse requested to work for specified periods of time with a urologist and in a sexually transmitted disease clinic in a large urban area to gain the necessary skills. On return to the rural health department, she felt comfortable with male patients and taught the skills she had learned to nurse colleagues.

---

family. She must not stop with the immediate family, however, but continue to identify the other groups within the community to which each individual family member belongs. Viewing the community as a system and focusing on systems and subsystems will help Beth organize the data she collects during assessment. Knowing that "the whole is greater than the sum of its parts," Beth prepares for her visit by reviewing adolescent theories of development and family theory. Beyond individual assessment, she notes factors related to the development of sex role–related behavior that may impact on health. Examples of areas of assessment include the following:

- Family configuration, traditional or nontraditional
- Sex role–related behavior of parents, including work patterns in and out of home, division of household labor, and decision-making patterns
- Patterns of parenting—mothering, fathering, and substitute father figure(s)
- Ability of male children to disclose feelings to family members and others
- Degree of assertiveness in female children
- Ability of family members to give emotional and physical support during crises and noncrises
- Ability of family members to trade off role-related behavior during crises and noncrises
- Risk-taking health behaviors
- How stress and grief are processed
- Communal lifestyle patterns that place individual or family at risk (e.g., lack of exercise, poor diet, smoking, drinking)

- Family history of morbidity and mortality
- Health care–taking patterns of family members
- Preventive health behaviors
- How leisure time is spent

Assessment of other groups includes neighborhood and other peer groups, school environment, sports, and church and civic activities.

Diagnosis

Through induction, a nursing diagnosis is made for each individual and each system component, including family and the community. Examples of diagnoses follow.

Individual

- Loss of interest or involvement in activity related to conflicting stages of grief process secondary to premature death of father (Richard)
- Expressed dissatisfaction with parenting role related to feelings of helplessness and hopelessness secondary to premature death of husband (Mrs. Connors)
- Risk of interpersonal conflict due to prolonged, unrelieved family stress secondary to premature death of father (Yvonne)

Family

- Decreased ability to communicate related to family stress secondary to premature death of father
- At risk of family crisis related to disequilibrium

Community

- Inadequate systematic programs for linking families in crisis to community resources
- Inadequate systematic programs for populations at risk of premature death related to inadequate planning among community systems

Planning

Planning involves contracting and mutual goal setting and is an outcome of mutually derived assessment and diagnosis. A contract with the family alone is shortsighted and may provide little community benefit over time. Examples of other aggregates with whom a contract may be established include the following:

- The school subsystem that does not provide ongoing counseling but will meet periodically to evaluate pupil progression with family members
- The school subsystem that provides physical education in football, basketball, and baseball (nonaerobic, nonlifetime sports) but offers extramural aerobic, lifetime sports such as swimming and track after school hours
- The American Red Cross, which does not offer cardiovascular pulmonary resuscitation (CPR) courses on evenings or weekends but offers to consider doing so for a defined minimum-size community

Mutual goal setting requires collaboration regarding long- and short-term goals. Again, mutually defined needs and diagnoses are important to this process. Regardless of the diagnosis, each individual in the family and the subsystem must participate in developing a plan of care. Examples of goals follow.

Individual

Long-term Goal

- Individual family members will be able to trade off role-related behavior.

Short-term Goal

- Individual family members will express feelings related to abandonment and loss.

Family

Long-term Goal

- The family will exhibit increased ability to handle crisis as evidenced by ability to discuss roles and interdependencies.

Short-term Goal

- The family will identify specific ways to recognize and use support services.

Community

Long-term Goal

- Systematic programs will be established for populations at risk of premature death from coronary heart disease as evidenced by local planning bodies with ongoing evaluation of programs.

Short-term Goals

- Dissemination is provided to individuals, families, groups, and planning bodies in the community about the incidence of coronary heart disease.
- Existing programs are identified that address coronary heart disease.
- Existing programs are coordinated to bridge gaps and avoid duplication of effort.

Intervention

The nurse, family, and other aggregates each carry out interventions contracted during the planning phase to meet the mutually derived goals. Most importantly, the nurse empowers the family and community to develop the networks and linkages necessary to care for themselves.

Individual Individual counseling regarding loss and grief may be beneficial to each family member, but options may need to be explored, and referrals may need to be re-evaluated for members of the rural family. Education regarding preventive measures to combat risk factors for heart disease include those aimed at individual family members and address such areas as diet, exercise, smoking, alcohol use, and ways of handling stress.

Family Examples of interventions with the family include counseling, education, and referral aimed at promoting family self-care. For example, Beth's interventions with the Connors family are dependent on the family's ability to solve problems, to investigate community resources, and to create linkages between family and resources. Periodic family conferences at school and more inclusive family therapy may be initiated to enable the family to work through the death of Mr. Connors; this results in the development of new roles and the communication necessary to maintain family equilibrium. Education regarding preventive measures to combat risk factors for heart disease may need discussion at the family level as well as at the individual level (e.g., diet, exercise, smoking, alcohol use, and stress management).

Community Interventions must also be carried out with other aggregates. These may involve activities such as educating, facilitating program expansion, or tailoring programs to meet community needs. Intervention at the aggregate level calls for group and community work. The nurse carries out interventions at this level in several ways, for example, by communicating community statistics from a community analysis, relating anecdotes from families served, or linking family experience to program need by acting as an advocate and by bringing family members to board meetings or hearings on community health issues.

Education regarding preventive measures to combat risk factors for heart disease also includes those interventions aimed at the community. A rationale for the development of lifetime aerobic sports is needed not only by Richard but also by school districts. Exploring options with the school nurse and reviewing the school district health education curriculum would be beneficial. A community assessment of heart disease awareness, including determination of the availability of resources such as emergency response and CPR courses, is an aggregate intervention. Taking the outcome of the assessment in the form of statistics and the anonymous anecdotal story of the Connors family to planning bodies in the community also is intervention at the aggregate level. Creative programs used by other communities (e.g., teaching CPR within the school system) should be investigated and proposed.

Evaluation

Evaluation is multidimensional and ongoing. Using a systems approach to evaluation, the nurse evaluates each component of the system, from individual family member to family and community, in terms of goal achievement. Evaluation includes noting degrees of equilibrium established, degree of change, how the system handles change, whether the system is open or closed, and patterns of networking. Ongoing evaluation includes noting referrals and follow-up of the individual, the family, and other aggregates in use of resources.

Individual For example, use of resources such as support groups by the individual family member may be noted. These resources may include a support group for teens, a women's support group, support groups for those experiencing the loss of a spouse or other family member, reentry programs for women at a local junior college or university, and parents without partners.

Family Evaluation of the Connors family would also include follow-up of their use of support services specifically for the family, such as counseling options for the family as a unit. Evaluation would also focus on the family's ability to handle crises in the future.

Community Aggregate evaluation would focus on the community. For example, to what extent do school programs encourage sports options that promote lifetime aerobic activities and prevent premature death from heart disease? Are programs systematically planned in the community for populations that are at risk of premature death from heart disease?

Levels of Prevention

Society's expectations of men and women are in transition. Application of levels of prevention by the community health nurse must take into account men's health status, socialization of men, men's use of health care services, men's primary needs for prevention and health promotion, and the role of women as caretakers of the family's health.

Primary Because men are more likely to engage in risk-taking behavior than women and are less likely to engage in preventive behaviors, primary prevention must be marketed specifically to men. Examples of primary prevention for the Connors family are applied at the individual, family, and community levels:

Individual. Assessment, teaching, and referral related to diet and exercise behaviors

Family. Assessment and teaching related to food selection and preparation at home and fast-food restaurant food selection. Teach and role-model gender roles that allow male members of the family to use alternate expressions of emotion.

Community. Provision of CPR courses for members of the community; consultation with schools regarding need for aerobic activities in physical education and sports programs.

It is important to pull men from the family, work place, or other aggregates into involvement with family planning, education, antepartum and postpartum care, parenting, dental prophylaxis, and accident prevention. In addition, assessing need for immunizations and classes, e.g., retirement preparation, is considered action aimed at primary prevention.

Secondary Because men have higher mortality, morbidity, and health care use rates for many of the leading causes of death but are second to women in overall use of health care services including preventive physical examinations and screening, early diagnosis and prompt intervention must also be tailored to meet men's needs. Examples of secondary prevention regarding the Connors family include the following:

Individual. Screening for risk factors related to cardiovascular disease in the individual such as how the individual handles stress

---

Door Openers: Ways to Address Men About Health Concerns

STRATEGIES TO address men about health concerns include the following:

- Ask a man to talk about the last time he had a physical examination, what was done, why it was done, where, and what were the recommendations.
- Ask a man how he feels about his health insurance coverage, and if he lacks health insurance, ask what resources have been used for medical care for him and his family.
- Ask a man how he spends his leisure time, what he is doing to take care of himself, and what are his usual physical activities.
- Observe a man for signs of stress such as moist palms, nail biting, posture, and nervous movements. If signs of stress are present, ask how he is coping with an identified health problem, family problem, being unemployed, and so on.
- Observe a man for difficulty clearing airway (smoking) and flushing of the face (alcohol). Inquire as to habits of smoking and drinking and whether these habits have increased since the occurrence of the particular health or social problem.
- Involve men in decision making about health care to instill a sense of control of events.

Family. Screening for risk factors related to cardiovascular disease in the family such as how stress is processed by the family

Community. Organizing screening programs for the community such as health fairs

It is important to screen individuals and aggregates of men according to lifestyle risk factors, mortality at different age levels, morbidity, and occupational health risks.

Tertiary Activities that rehabilitate individuals and aggregates and restore them to their highest level of functioning are aimed at tertiary prevention. The nurse in the community is ideally situated to locate people in need of rehabilitation services. Evaluation and physical, mental, and social restoration services may be provided. Men in need of rehabilitation may have special needs because their disability impacts not only themselves but also their families and, ultimately, their communities. Financial assistance and vocational counseling, training, and placement may be priorities for the well-being of the family. Because of socialization, men may find it hard to admit they need help (Rappaport, 1985). Community health nurses who teach men with chronic disease to rest at specified periods during the day or to continue with medical regimens or speech or occupational therapy are providing tertiary prevention. Working with couples as a unit is also important, as caretaking patterns may shift owing to chronic disease and disability (Corbin and Strauss, 1984). Encouraging men to express their concerns about their health, their families, and their jobs as well as frustration with themselves is important. Examples of tertiary prevention with the Connors family are the following:

Individual. Assist individual family members in dealing with grief from the loss of father/husband.

Family. Assist family in dealing with grief and assuming alternate roles.

Community. Assist community in dealing with loss of fully functioning family by providing grief support services that include males or target males as well as females.

ROLES OF THE COMMUNITY HEALTH NURSE

Alternative approaches to reaching men will depend on creative marketing of multiple options for men. Community health nurses can fill multiple roles that address men's health now and in the future. Some examples follow.

Health Educator

Tailoring messages to the needs of men is imperative. Market surveys of brochures and posters designed for men or to include men may be crucial. For example, the "pregnant man" poster, which was designed to involve men in family planning services, may be accepted by one population yet found to be offensive by another. Health fairs for men are another example of health education efforts. Asking a car dealer to display a new car in which infant car seats are promoted may attract men to the fair. Emergency medical personnel can be asked to volunteer tours of emergency medical vehicles and give information at health fair sites to attract men and boys in particular.

Education can address the need for changing societal attitudes that encourage negative health behaviors, including risk taking among males regarding, for example, attitudes toward drinking, reckless driving, and wearing seat-belts. Teaching the caretaking role to both men and women is important. School programs that teach child care to boys open up new roles as nurturers and caretakers to fathers of the future. If such programs exist for girls in the community, what can be done to enlist support for parallel programs for boys?

Facilitator

The community health nurse may carry out the role of facilitator of change at several levels. Adult role models in the home and in the media may equate concern with health and health problems as "feminine" (Lewis and Lewis, 1977). Facilitating change by promoting healthy lifelong behaviors by parents and other family members is important. The community health nurse may also facilitate change at the aggregate level by assessing the community's needs and resources specifically designed for men, e.g., help for batterers (see Chapter 20).

Community health nurses working in an agency may review health education literature (e.g., family planning or parenting brochures) for sex role–related content and messages. Organizations that publish the literature can be contacted, and options can be offered based on feedback gathered by the nurses from the population they serve.

Facilitation of change also reaches the congressional district level; a community assessment may point out highway safety problems or a common occupational health hazard. Community organization efforts also need to be initiated and supported where indicated (see Chapter 7).

At the professional level, the community health nurse needs to join organizations and create awareness of men's health as an issue. A review of nursing and other professional literature for men's health and a review of indexes in nursing texts for men's health or men's reproductive health or fathering can be carried out.

RESEARCH AND MEN'S HEALTH

Will we allow men and women more options in the future (Lewis and Lewis, 1977)? As women progress into the work place, will their mortality rates be like those of men? Or will men be allowed to explore more flexible roles and live more like women? It is appropriate to ask how community health nurses can buffer the process by allowing more alternate choices for men in lifestyles as well as in health services. Charged with the public's health, community health nurses must ensure a safe work place and environment for both men and women. Community health nurses also provide for the disadvantaged, who may not have the economic freedom to choose from a range of options. Research directed toward men's health is an appropriate response to these concerns.

Nursing research is beginning to address health aspects of men's roles in the family, e.g., in family planning (Swanson, 1980, 1985, 1988), in childbearing (May and Perrin, 1985), and in parenting (Bozett, 1985; Hanson, 1985; Hanson and Bozett, 1985; Jones, 1985). Further research is needed on fathering and on gender effects on the delivery of health services. Structural components of service delivery such as hours and services for men and for couples are another area of research need. Research is also needed on new models of service delivery in both the public and the private sector. A cross-disciplinary approach is needed because approaches to men's health have social and psychological dimensions.

Last, research must include two approaches new to nursing: population-based research (Williams, 1988) and qualitative research (Chenitz and Swanson, 1986). Defining who in the community has hypertension, where they are, and the best method of reaching them is an example of population-based research (Williams, 1988). The latter, equally important approach, involves using qualitative research methods (e.g., interview and participant observation) to find out from men, couples, families, and groups, in their own words, about their experiences. Through this approach, researchers are better able to target research needs that are grounded in the experience of the people and reflect the complexity of human experience. Community health nurses can improve the health of the community by using knowledge that exists, by identifying problems for research, and by participating in research efforts.

SUMMARY

The gender gap is not new, nor is it confined to political arenas. The gender gap in health presents a serious paradox that has marked implications for community health nursing (Forrester, 1986; Swanson and Forrest, 1984). From birth on, men in industrialized countries have higher death rates and live shorter lives than do women (Tomasson, 1984). Although major advances in medical care and access to care have occurred in the United States during this century, men have suffered a disadvantage. However, the health of females appears to be worse than the health of males. Morbidity rates are higher for women because women are more likely to experience illness that does not cause death, to receive disability days, and to use health services (Verbrugge and Wingard, 1987). Evidence suggests sex differences in health may be related more to behavioral than to biological determinants, such as men's propensity to engage in risk-taking behaviors related to lifestyle. Antecedents of the largest sex differentials in mortality are associated with sex-linked behavior that is more prevalent in men—smoking, alcohol consumption, poor preventive health habits, stress, and lack of other emotional channels (Waldron, 1976). These factors, however, are compounded by social and environmental conditions of major public health concern: occupational and environmental hazards, both physical and psychological; unemployment; accidents, including motor vehicle and sport; suicide; and homicide. These concerns call for a major public health approach to men's health. These factors, compounded by men's lack of willingness to seek preventive and health care, have marked implications for community health nursing. Factors that impede men's health include medical care patterns based on acute care rather than on prevention. Factors that promote men's health include interest groups in men and men's health, men's increased interest in physical fitness and lifestyle, policy making related to men's health, and models of health services for men. Men's health care needs are psychosocial as well as medical, and they require prevention and health promotion marketed specifically for men. Current attempts to meet men's health care needs are made through the provision of both traditional and in-

knowledge that exists and by participating in research efforts.

Additional Reading — Men's Health

Bozett, F. W., and Forrester, D. A.: A proposal for a men's health nurse practitioner. Image: J. Nurs. Sch. *21*; 158–161, 1989.

Kus, R. J., and Bozett, F. W. A gay men's self-actualization group: A psychosocial nursing experience. Perspect. Psychiatr. Care *23*; 69–73, 1985.

MacIntyre, R.: Nursing loved ones with AIDS: Knowledge development for ethical practice. J. Home Health Care Pract. *3*; 1–10, 1991.

DiPasquale, J. A.: The psychological effects of support groups on individuals infected by the AIDS virus. Cancer Nurs. *13*; 278–285, 1990.

Wilson, S., and Morse, J. M.: Living with a wife undergoing chemotherapy. Image: J. Nurs. Sch. *23*; 78–84, 1991.

Gregory, D. M., Peters, N., and Cameron, C. F.: Elderly male spouses as caregivers: Toward an understanding of their experience. J. Gerontol. Nurs. *16*; 20–24, 1990.

Stoller, E. P.: Males as helpers: The role of sons, relatives and friends. Gerontologist *30*; 228–235, 1990.

Resources on Men's Health

The National Organization for Changing Men, P. O. Box 451, Watseka, IL 60970

The American Assembly for Men in Nursing, P. O. Box 31753, Independence, OH 44131

Putting the Boys in the Picture: A Review of Programs to Promote Sexual Responsibility Among Young Males, 1988, by Joy G. Dryfoos (a report to the Carnegie Corporation based on a survey of male involvement in family planning programs; contact Network Publications, P. O. Box 1830, Santa Cruz, CA 95061)

National Gay Task Force, 80 Fifth Avenue, New York, NY 10011

MENSNET (an online telecommunications system to foster communication about men's health, fathering, men's studies, and gay issues; contact Ron Mazur, P. O. Box 627, Northampton, MA 01061)

---

novative services. Community health nurses can plan gender-appropriate care for males by applying the nursing process to individuals, families, and communities using the three levels of prevention. Research related to men's health is in an early stage of development. Community health nurses can improve the health of the community by using

Learning Activities

1. Examine the vital statistics in your community and compare the sex-specific differences in mortality.

2. During a 1-week period, determine the frequency of newspaper articles in your major newspaper that identify the top 12 causes of mortality for men.

3. Survey the billboards in your community and determine the frequency of those that depict sex-linked behavior of men associated with risk-taking behavior.

4. Survey local businesses and industries in your community to find out what health promotion and prevention programs are available and used by men and women.

5. Select a family from your caseload that has a man in the household who is accessible to you. Select two "door openers" appropriate to initiate discussion of health concerns with this man. Devise a gender-appropriate nursing care plan that includes primary, secondary, and tertiary prevention for this man as an individual, for his family, and for the community in which he resides.

6. Select a family from your caseload that has a man in the household with whom you do not have ready access. Interview the woman caregiver in the household and obtain information by proxy about the man's health. If possible, arrange to meet the man for lunch, at work, or after work, and obtain information about his health. Compare the information obtained by proxy with that obtained from the client.

7. Review major nursing texts (e.g., medical-surgical) you have used as a student; examine the tables of contents and the indexes for content on men's health versus women's health.

REFERENCES

Abraham, I. L., and Krowchuk, H.: Unemployment and health: Health promotion for the jobless male. Nurs. Clin. North Am. *21*;37–47, 1986.

Allen, D. G., and Whatley, M.: Nursing and men's health: Some critical considerations. Nurs. Clin North Am. *21*;3–13, 1986.

American Cancer Society: Cancer Facts and Figures—1991. Atlanta, Georgia, ACS 1991.

American Public Health Association: Recording of males served by federally funded family planning programs. Policy statements. Am. J. Public Health *78*;204–205, 1988.

Bird, C.: Born Female: The High Cost of Keeping Women Down. New York, Pocket Books, 1970.

Bozett, F.: Gay men as fathers. *In* Hanson, S., and Bozett, F., eds.: Dimensions of Fatherhood. Beverly Hills, California, Sage, 1985, pp. 327–352.

Brannon, R. C.: No "sissy stuff": The stigma of anything vaguely feminine. *In* David, D., and Brannon, B., eds.: The Forty-Nine Percent Majority: The Male Sex Role. Reading, Massachusetts, Addison-Wesley, 1976, pp. 49–50.

Buffum, J. C.: Sexual and reproductive effects of pharmacologic agents. *In* Swanson, J., and Forrest, K., eds.: Men's Reproductive Health. New York, Springer, 1984, pp. 179–192.

Centers for Disease Control: Syphilis and congenital syphilis—United States, 1985–1988. M. M. W. R. *37*;486–489, 1988.

Centers for Disease Control: Update: Acquired immunodeficiency syndrome—United States, 1981–1988. M. M. W. R. *38*;229–236, 1989.

Chenitz, W. C., and Swanson, J. M., eds.: From Practice to Grounded Theory: Qualitative Research in Nursing. Palo Alto, California, Addison-Wesley, 1986.

Choi, M. W.: Preamble to a new paradigm for women's health care. Image: J. Nurs. Scholarship *17*;14–16, 1985.

Cohen, F. L.: Paternal contributions to birth defects. Nurs. Clin. North Am. *21*;49–63, 1986.

Corbin, J. M., and Strauss, A. L.: Collaboration: Couples working together to manage chronic illness. Image: J. Nurs. Scholarship *16*;109–115, 1984.

David, D. S., and Brannon, R.: The male sex role: Our culture's blueprint of manhood, and what it's done for us lately. *In* David, D. S., and Brannon, R., eds.: The Forty-Nine Percent Majority: The Male Sex Role. Reading, Massachusetts, Addison-Wesley, 1976, pp. 1–45.

Deans, W.: Well man clinics. Nursing *26*;975–978, 1988.

DeHoff, J. B., and Forrest, K.: Men's health. *In* Swanson, J., and Forrest, K., eds.: Men's Reproductive Health. New York, Springer, 1984, pp. 3–10.

Diagram Group: Man's Body: An Owner's Manual. New York, Paddington Press Ltd., 1976.

Ehrenreich, B.: The Hearts of Men: American Dreams and the Flight From Commitment. New York, Anchor Books, 1983.

Erickson, E.: Childhood and Society. New York, W. W. Norton and Co., 1963.

Foreman, M. D.: Cardiovascular disease: A men's health hazard. Nurs. Clin. North Am. *21*;65–73, 1986.

Forrester, D. A.: Myths of masculinity: Impact upon men's health. Nurs. Clin. North Am. *21*;15–23, 1986.

Goldman, L., and Cook, E. F.: The decline in ischemic heart disease mortality rates: An analysis of the comparative effects of medical interventions and changes in lifestyle. Ann. Intern. Med. *101*;825–835, 1984.

Hanson, S. M.: Single custodial fathers. *In* Hanson, S., and Bozett, F., eds.: Dimensions of Fatherhood. Beverly Hills, California, Sage, 1985, pp. 369–392.

Hanson, S. M., and Bozett, F., eds.: Dimensions of Fatherhood. Beverly Hills, California, Sage, 1985.

Harrison, J. B.: Warning: The male sex role may be dangerous to your health. *In* Swanson, J., and Forrest, K., eds.: Men's Reproductive Health. New York, Springer, 1984, pp. 11–27.

Hibbard, J. F., and Pope, C. R.: Employment characteristics and health status among men and women. Women Health *12*;85–102, 1987.

Jones, C.: Father-infant relationships in the first year of life. *In* Hanson, S., and Bozett, F., eds.: Dimensions of Fatherhood. Beverly Hills, California, Sage, 1985, pp. 92–114.

Kovar, M. G.: The elderly population: Use of medical care services by men and women in their middle and later years. Presented at the 108th Annual Meeting of the American Public Health Association, Detroit, October 1980.

Levinson, D.: The Seasons of a Man's Life. New York, Alfred A. Knopf, 1978.

Lewis, C. E., and Lewis, M. A.: The potential impact of sexual equality on health. N. Engl. J. Med. *297*;863–869, 1977.

Lewis, T.: Unemployment and men's health. Nursing *26*;969–974, 1988.

May, K. A., and Perrin, S. P.: Prelude: Pregnancy and birth. *In* Hanson, S., and Bozett, F., eds.: Dimensions of Fatherhood. Beverly Hills, California, Sage, 1985, pp. 64–91.

McKinlay, J. B., McKinlay, S. M., and Beaglehole, R.: A review of the evidence concerning the impact of medical measures on recent mortality and morbidity in the United States. Int. J. Health Serv. *19*;181–208, 1989.

Mechanic, D.: The influence of mothers on their children's health attitudes and behavior. Pediatrics *33*;444–453, 1964.

Milio, N.: Primary Care and the Public's Health. Lexington, Massachusetts, Lexington Books, 1983.

Montiero, L.: Monitoring Health Status and Medical Care. Cambridge, Massachusetts, Ballinger, 1976.

National Center for Health Statistics, Dawson, D. A., and Adams, P. F.: Current estimates from the National Health Interview Survey: United States, 1986. Vital Health Stat. Series 10, No. 164. DHHS Publication No. (PHS) 87-1592. Public Health Service. Washington, D. C.: U.S. Government Printing Office, 1987.

National Center for Health Statistics, Hing, E., Kovar, M. G., and Rice, D.: Sex differences in health and use of medical care, United States, 1979. Vital Health Stat. Series 3, No. 24. DHHS Publication No. (PHS) 83-1408, Public Health Service. Washington, D. C.: U.S. Government Printing Office, 1983.

National Center for Health Statistics, Schoenborn, C. A., Danchik, K. M., and Elinson, J.: Basic data from Wave I of the National Survey of Personal Health Practices and Consequences, United States, 1979. Vital Health Stat. Series 15, No. 2. DHHS Publication No. (PHS) 81-1163, Public Health Service. Washington, D. C.: U.S. Government Printing Office, 1981.

National Center for Health Statistics: Health, United States, 1987. Hyattsville, Maryland, U.S. Public Health Service, 1988.

National Center for Health Statistics: Health, United States, 1988. Hyattsville, Maryland, U.S. Public Health Service, 1989.

National Center for Health Statistics: Health, United States, 1989. Hyattsville, Maryland, U.S. Public Health Service, 1990.

National Center for Health Statistics: Health, United States, 1990. Hyattsville, Maryland, U.S. Public Health Service, 1991.

National Center for Health Statistics: Health, United States, 1991. Hyattsville, Maryland, U.S. Public Health Service, 1992.

Navarro, V.: Race or class, or race and class. Int. J. Health Serv. *19*;311–314, 1989.

Perez-Stable, E. J., and Slutkin, G.: Sexually transmitted diseases in men. *In* Swanson, J., and Forrest, K., eds.: Men's Reproductive Health. New York, Springer, 1985, pp. 71–142.

Rakowski, W.: Predictors of health practices within age-sex groups: National survey of personal health practices and consequences, 1979. Public Health Rep. *103*;376–386, 1988.

Rappaport, B.: Family planning: Helping men ask for help. *In* Swanson, J., and Forrest, K., eds.: Men's Reproductive Health. New York, Springer, 1985, pp. 245–259.

Rivara, F. P., Bergman, A. B., LoGerfo, J. P., et al.: Epidemiology of childhood injuries. Am. J. Disabled Child. *136*;502, 1982.

Robinson, J. C.: Racial inequality and occupational health in the United States: The effect on white workers. J. Int. Health Serv. *15*;23–34, 1985.

Sadler, C.: DIY male maintenance. Nurs. Mirror *160*;16–18, 1979.

Select Committee on Population: Fertility and contraception in the United States: U.S. House of Representatives final report. Washington, D. C., U.S. Government Printing Office, 1978.

Skelton, R.: Man's role in society and its effect on health. Nursing *26*;953–956, 1988.

Steinem, G.: Outrageous Acts and Everyday Rebellions. New York, Signet, 1983.

Summers, L. J.: A couple of good taxes. *The Boston Sunday Globe,* January 18, 1987.

Swanson, J.: Knowledge, knowledge, who's got the knowledge? The male contraceptive career. J. Sex Educ. Ther. *6*;51–57, 1980.

Swanson, J.: Men and family planning. *In* Hanson, S., and Bozett, F., eds.: Dimensions of Fatherhood. Beverly Hills, California, Sage, 1985, pp. 21–48.

Swanson, J.: The process of finding contraceptive options. West. J. Nurs. Res. *10*;492–503, 1988.

Swanson, J., and Forrest, K., eds.: Men's Reproductive Health. New York, Springer, 1984.

Swanson, J., and Forrest, K.: Men's reproductive health services in family planning settings: A pilot study. Am. J. Public Health 77;1462–1463, 1987.

Tomasson, R. F.: The components of the sex differential in mortality in industrialized populations, 1979–1981: Swedes, U. S. whites, and U. S. blacks. *In* Tomasson, R. F., ed.: Comparative Social Research. Greenwich, Connecticut, JAI Press, 1984.

Torres, A.: The effects of federal funding cuts on family planning services, 1980–1983. Family Planning Perspectives *16*;134–138, 1984.

Torres, A., and Forrest, J.: Family planning clinic services in the United States, 1983. Family Planning Perspectives *17*;30–35, 1985.

U.S. Department of Health, Education and Welfare. Health, United States, 1979. Hyattsville, Maryland, U.S. Public Health Service, 1980.

Veevers, J.: Women in the driver's seat: Trends in sex differences in driving and death. Population Res. Policy Rev. *1*;171, 1982.

Verbrugge, L. M.: Sex differentials in health. Public Health Rep. *97*;417–437, 1982.

Verbrugge, L. M., and Wingard, D. L.: Sex differentials in health and mortality. Women Health *12*;103–145, 1987.

Waldron, I.: An analysis of causes of sex differences in mortality and morbidity. *In* Gove, W., and Carpenter, G., eds.: The Fundamental Connection Between Nature and Nurture. Lexington, Massachusetts, Lexington Books, 1982, pp. 69–116.

Waldron, I.: Employment and women's health: An analysis of causal relationships. Int. J. Health Serv. *10*;435–454, 1980.

Waldron, I.: Sex differences in human mortality: The role of genetic factors. Soc. Sci. Med. *17*;321–333, 1983*a*.

Waldron, I.: Sex differences in illness incidence, prognosis and mortality: Issues and evidence. Soc. Sci. Med. *17*;1107–1123, 1983*b*.

Waldron, I.: Why do women live longer than men? Social Sci. Med. *10*;349–362, 1976.

Waldron, I., and Johnson, S.: Why do women live longer than men? J. Human Stress *2*;19–29, 1976.

Whorton, M. D.: Environmental and occupational reproductive hazards. *In* Swanson, J., and Forrest, K., eds.: Men's Reproductive Health. New York, Springer, 1984, pp. 193–203.

Williams, C.: Population-focused practice. *In* Stanhope, M., and Lancaster, J., eds.: Community Health Nursing: Process and Practice for Promoting Health. 2nd Ed. St. Louis, C. V. Mosby, 1988, pp. 292–303.

Woods, N. F.: Women's health. *In* Fitzpatrick, J., Tauton, R., and Benoliel, J., eds.: Annual Review of Nursing Research: Volume 6. New York, Springer, 1988, pp. 209–236.

14

Addressing the Needs of Families

Upon completion of this chapter, the reader will be able to:

1. State a personal definition of "family."

2. Identify characteristics of the changing family that have implications for community health nursing practice.

3. Describe strategies for moving from intervention at the individual level to intervention at the family level.

4. Describe strategies for moving from intervention at the family level to intervention at the aggregate level.

5. Discuss the application of one conceptual framework to studying families.

6. Discuss a model of care for communities of families.

7. Apply the steps of the nursing process to individuals within the family, to the family as a whole, and to an aggregate of which the family is a part.

Janice M. Swanson

Joe Hudson is a 74-year-old alcoholic who is being treated at an outpatient department in a large medical center. He lives in a hotel room in downtown Salt Lake City. He has one living relative of whom he is aware, a 76-year-old brother. Mr. Hudson states, "I had a falling out with my brother some 20 years ago. . . . I never hear from him. I reckon he's still in Boston, if he's alive at all." Mr. Hudson frequently falls out of bed, dislodging the telephone that the desk clerk has placed precariously close to the bed, which signals the desk clerk that something is amiss. The clerk then goes to Mr. Hudson's room and puts him back to bed. Mr. Hudson's source of income is a check sent him the first day of the month by an acquaintance, a minister, who lives in a town 75 miles away. The desk clerk cashes Mr. Hudson's check and assists him in paying his bill from the hotel, which provides congregate dining facilities.

Lai Chan is a Chinese refugee from Vietnam who moved with her family to San Francisco 3 months ago. Mrs. Chan is a single parent; Mr. Chan died in an automobile accident shortly after arriving in the United States. Mrs. Chan has two children—an 11-year-old son and a 5-year-old daughter. The family resides in a one-room efficiency apartment in the Tenderloin District in downtown San Francisco.

Jaime Gutierrez, a 72-year-old Mexican-American man, lives with his 36-year-old son, Roberto; his 34-year-old daughter-in-law, Patricia; and his three grandchildren, who are 14, 13, and 12 years old. Mr. Gutierrez was in good health until he fell from a tree while helping his son make roof repairs on the house in 1985. He suffered a concussion, right hemothorax, and fracture of T-11 and T-12. Confined to bed, he is receiving home health care. He requires intermittent catheterization but feels uncomfortable when the nurse suggests that his daughter-in-law is willing to carry out this procedure for him. Therefore, Roberto quit work to provide this personal care to his father. Consequently, the family of six lives on Mr. Gutierrez's retirement income, which consists of $239 from Social Security and $244 from a pension plan per month. Roberto would like to increase his job skills while at home. He has finished the 4th grade and has failed the G.E.D. twice. Patricia would also like to return to school and pursue job training. Although agreeable to Patricia's interests, Roberto is hesitant to support active steps taken by Patricia to initiate her plan.

These three families, which include today's broad contemporary definitions of family, are examples of families carried in caseloads by undergraduate community health nursing students. Assessments made by students during home, office, and hospital visits with these families triggered interventions that linked the families to resources provided by the community and, in turn, triggered questions about health needs of groups of families or larger aggregates living in the same communities.

Families have major health care needs that are not usually addressed by the health care system. Instead, the individual is the unit most frequently addressed by the health care system. This holds true for nursing interventions within the health care system. The majority of nurses work in hospi-

---

Nursing an Individual Client Versus Nursing a Family as Client

THESE AUTHORS discuss the similarities and differences between nursing an individual as client versus nursing a family as client. Using the Betty Neuman systems model as a guide, they present factors that contribute to the decision to use one approach versus the other. These factors include the following:

- **The perception of the client as to the need for nursing**
- **The nature of the stressors as affecting only one member of the family or other family members**
- **The risk of instability to the family as a whole posed by the health status of an individual member**
- **The feasibility of the family-nurse collaboration, i.e., the availability of family members and the availability of nursing time to meet with family members**
- **The knowledge and skill of the nurse**

Using a case study, the authors then make comparisons between an individual approach and a family approach by applying the nursing process to an individual client and to the family client.

Data from Ross, M. M., and Helmer, H.: A comparative analysis of Neuman's model using the individual and family as the units of care. Public Health Nurs. 5;30–31, 1988.

tals where interventions traditionally occur at the individual client level. Nurses, however, are on the forefront of a trend toward intervention at the family level.

The family is composed of many subsystems and, in turn, is tied to many formal and informal systems outside the family. The family is imbedded in social systems that have an impact on health, e.g., education, employment, housing, and more. Many disciplines are interested in the study of families; interdisciplinary perspectives and strategies are necessary to understand the impact of the family on health and the impact of the broader social system on the family. Traditionally, nursing, and even community health nursing, has relied heavily if not solely on theoretical frameworks for intervention with families from disciplines of psychology or social psychology, which target individuals (e.g., Duvall, 1977; Erikson, 1963; Festinger, 1957; Maslow, 1970; and Rogers, 1951). Dreher (1982) questions the usefulness of these frameworks for the public health nurse "who is ministering to the health of socially and economically diverse populations. . . . Such psychological themes often draw our attention away from broader social issues that are the essence of public health nursing" (p. 505).

Intended for clinical rather than for public health use, these models do not address why some social and economically advantaged populations are more likely to become self-actualized or why, in the experience of death, some populations experience greater mortality rates than other populations. Improvement, states Dreher (1982), must come about by addressing the socioeconomic conditions that make some families more dysfunctional than others and to alter the system itself that produces such inequities. Dreher cautions that socioeconomic causes cannot be interpreted as psychological symptoms. Thus, social and policy changes are necessary to alter the conditions under which families function. How community health nurses work with families within communities to bring about healthy conditions for families at the family, social, and policy levels will be addressed in this chapter. This chapter will focus on five areas:

- The changing family
- Approaches to meeting the health needs of families

- Family theory approach to meeting the health needs of families
- Extending family health intervention to larger aggregates and social action
- An example of the nursing process applied to a family

THE CHANGING FAMILY
Definition of the Family

Definitions of the family are many. Essentially, the term "family" as used here is defined as an aggregate made up of a body of units, the individuals that represent the whole sum, or the family. Definitions of the family vary by discipline, by the professional, and by distinct groups of families. For example, psychologists may define the family in terms of personal development and intrapersonal dynamics; the sociologist may define the family in terms of a "social unit interacting with the larger society" (Johnson, 1984, p. 333). Some professionals define the family in terms of kinship, by marriage, and by descent (Farber, 1973):

"[A family is] a cluster of people, whose relationship is stipulated by law in terms of marriage and descent, and whose precise membership varies according to the circumstances" (p. 2).

Other professionals define the family in terms of household membership, as "a primary group of people living in a household in consistent proximity and intimate relationships" (Helvie, 1981, p. 64). Most important, according to McGoldrick (1982), is the definition of "family" given by different family groups within the population:

"The dominant American (WASP) definition focuses on the intact nuclear family. Black families focus on a wide network of kin and community. For Italians, there is no such thing as the 'nuclear' family. To them family means a strong, tightly knit three- or four-generational family, which also includes godparents and old friends. The Chinese go beyond this and include in their definition of family all their ancestors and all their descendants" (p. 10).

The community health nurse interacts with communities made up of many types of families. When faced with the great diversity in the community, the community health nurse must formulate a personal definition of the family yet be aware of the changing definition of the family held by other disciplines, professionals, and family groups. The community health nurse who interacts with Mr. Hudson, the alcoholic who lives in a hotel, must have a broad conceptualization of the family. The surveillance activity of the hotel manager and the financial support of the minister-friend could both be accounted for in Jordheim's (1982) definition of the family as a "relationship community of two or more persons" (p. 61) whether from the same or different kinship groups.

Characteristics of the Changing Family

The characteristics of the U.S. family are changing. The typical family, the nuclear family, is defined as "a small group consisting of parents and their non-adult children living in a single household" (Farber, 1973, p. 2). The stereotypical view of this family as father, mother, and nonadult children is eroding. For example, in 1970, 85% of children under age 18 were living with two parents; in 1989, this proportion declined to 73% (Saluter, 1990). The proportion of children living with one parent increased during this time from 12% to 24%. More than twice as many white children (80%) as black children (38%) were living with two parents. Of Hispanic children, 67% were living with two parents.

Cohabitation has also increased over time. Cohabiting unmarried persons increased from 523,000 in 1970 to 2.8 million in 1989 (Saluter, 1990). In 1989, nearly one of every three of those households included children. Single parenting has also increased over time. In 1989, 15.5 million children were living with only one parent; of these, 13.7 million were mother-only households (Saluter, 1990). Thirty-nine percent of these children of single parent households lived with a parent who was divorced, 31% lived with a parent who had never been married, 20% lived with a parent who had been separated, 6% lived with a parent who was widowed, and 3% lived with a parent who was living apart from a spouse for other reasons. A homosexual family is made up of a cohabiting couple of the same sex who have a sexual relationship. The homosexual family may or may not have children.

Marked differences in income exist among these households. For example, mean annual income in 1989 for households with two parents was $42,500; for father-only households, $26,700; and for mother-only households, $15,700 (Saluter, 1990). Marked differences existed by race. Mother-only households had higher mean annual incomes among whites ($17,400) than among blacks ($12,900). Among mother-only households, 56% of white households and 36% of black households had incomes above the poverty level.

APPROACHES TO MEETING THE HEALTH NEEDS OF FAMILIES

Community health nursing has long viewed the family as an important unit of health care, with an awareness that the individual can be best understood within the social context of the family. Observing and inquiring about family interaction enable the nurse in the community to assess the impact and influence of family members on one another. Direct intervention at the family rather than the individual client level, however, is a new frontier for many nursing students, most of whom have experience in acute care settings before the community setting. A family model, largely a community health nursing or psychiatric/mental health intervention model, is now expanding into the areas such as birthing and parent-child, adult daycare, chronic illness, and home care. Nursing assessment and intervention must not stop with the immediate social context of the family, however, but must consider the broader social context of the community and society as well. As Dunn (1961) states, "the family stands in-between individual wellness and social wellness. You can't really have high-level wellness for either individuals or social groups unless you have well families."

Moving From the Individual to the Family

Community health and home care nurses have traditionally focused on the family as the unit of service; research shows, however, that most of these nurses continue to focus their practice on individuals residing in the home (Ford, 1979; Wright and Bell, 1981). Due to the current era of cost-containment, constraints on the community health nurse as well as on nurses working within hospitals and in other settings will increase. Reimbursement, for example, which is almost entirely calculated for services rendered to the individual, is a major constraint toward moving toward planning care for families as a unit. Therefore, a variety of creative approaches to meeting the health needs of families are needed, approaches reflecting interventions appropriate to the needs of the population as a whole.

FAMILY INTERVIEWING

Approaches to the care of families are needed and must be creative, flexible, and transferable from one setting to another. Community health nurses are generalists who bring previous preparation in communication concepts and in interviewing to the family arena. Wright and Leahey (1984) propose the realm of *family interviewing* rather than family therapy as an appropriate model. In this model, the community health nurse uses general systems and communication concepts to conceptualize health needs of families and a family assessment model to assess families' responses to "normative" events such as birth or retirement or to "paranormative" events such as chronic illness or divorce. Intervention is straightforward, as in asking a family to read a book about sex education of prepubescent teenagers, or dealt with through referral if the level of intervention is beyond the preparation of the nurse. For the purposes of this text, the model is extended to include intervention at the level of the larger aggregate. For example, the index of suspicion based on the health needs of a particular family for information would prompt the community health nurse to assess the need for similar information and the resources for intervention with other families in the community, in schools, churches, or other institutions. Family interviewing requires thinking "interactionally" not only in terms of the family system but also, in terms of larger social systems.

Creative family interviewing calls for interviewing families in many types of settings. The future prediction of decreased hospitalization supplemented by a wide variety of health care settings ranging from acute to ambulatory to community centers calls for flexible, transferable approaches. Clinical settings for family interviewing are reviewed by Wright and Leahey (1984) and include inpatient and outpatient ambulatory care and clinic settings in maternity, pediatrics, medicine, surgery, critical care, and mental health. According to these authors, community health nurses have many opportunities besides the traditional home visit to engage the family in a family interview. Community health nurses are employed in ambulatory care centers, occupational health and school sites, housing complexes, daycare programs, residential treatment and substance abuse programs, and in other official and nonofficial agencies. In each of these sites, community health nurses meet families and can assess and intervene at the family and community levels.

For example, the community health nurse can implement preventive programs for family units. The family is particularly appropriate as they experience similar risk factors—physiological, behavioral, and environmental. In a study conducted in a community hospital, Manley and Graber (1977) invited family members of patients with coronary heart disease to attend preventive screening and educational programs. Family members were evaluated for hypertension, smoking, and triglycerides. Findings were similar to those in large epidemiological studies: 25% had lipid abnormalities, 44% were overweight, 12% smoked, and 15.5% had previously undetected hypertension. Such programs can occur in community health settings and demonstrate the need to go beyond intervention with the individual family to groups of families, thus serving the population as a whole. A community health nurse working with Mexican-American families with diabetes could implement such a program, basing assessment on both needs of the individual families and biostatistics that reflect populations at risk. For example, the risk of diabetes in Mexican-Americans is four times that found in whites, and of all ethnic groups, Mexican-Americans are less likely to see a physician (Villareal and Trevino, 1985).

Involving family members in newborn assessments can aid the community health nurse in assessing the family's adjustment to the newborn and parenthood. It can be done in the home, clinic, or other health care center. Family members should be involved during the first contact or visit, and if they do not attend, a telephone call explaining the nurse's interest in them should take place (Wright and Leahey, 1984). More husbands and family members are becoming involved in the pregnancy and delivery phases of childbirth. Stranik and Hogberg (1979) describe a parent program that includes home visits and group sessions that provide

Home Visits by Nurses to Poor, Unmarried, Teenage Women Prompt More Rapid Return to School, Increase Employment, and Result in Fewer Subsequent Pregnancies

A PROGRAM of home visits by nurses is described that provided comprehensive care to poor, unmarried, and white teenagers bearing their first children in a semirural county in upstate New York. The study found that women who received home visits from the prenatal period through 2 years after the birth of their child were more likely than women who did not receive home visits to return to school more rapidly, to increase the number of months they were employed, to have fewer subsequent pregnancies, and to postpone the birth of their second child.

Data from Olds, D. L., Henderson, C. R., Tatelbaum, R., and Chamberlin, R.: Improving the life-course development of socially disadvantaged mothers: A randomized trial of nurse home visitation. Am. J. Public Health 78;1436–1445, 1988.

continuity of family involvement from prenatal through postpartum phases of care.

The community health nurse in the well baby clinic may often see parents for whom a family interview or home visit may be valuable. A general statement may be used to introduce the commonality of hurdles faced by new parents: "Many new parents face similar problems, which usually last only a short period of time. We find that bringing all of the family members together is important as the entire family is affected when a new baby comes into the home."

The community health nurse working with single parent families may face particular challenges. Mothers in single parent families report a higher incidence of children's academic and behavioral problems than do mothers in two-parent families. For example, in the National Health Interview Survey, 1988, researchers found that children 3–17 years of age living with a formerly married mother were more than three times as likely to have received treatment for emotional or behavioral problems in the preceding 12 months (8.8%) as children living with both biological parents (2.7%) (Dawson, 1991). It is important to remember, however, that children living in a nuclear family who experience severe conflict may have as many problems as children from a disrupted household. A study of single parent fathers found that 44% asked for help from other persons when dealing

with their children's feelings (Keshet and Rosenthal, 1980). Children in these families need a chance to express their concerns; the family interview is important in giving care to these families.

THE SCHOOL NURSE

The school nurse has a unique opportunity to compare the child in the school system—classroom, lunchroom, playground, and so on—with the child in the family system. The school nurse is increasingly becoming involved in planning special programs in the schools. Astute assessment of needs of children within the context of their families in interviews at school or in the home can lead to innovative interventions such as leading support groups for children with chronic illness. Other areas of assessment and intervention that benefit from a family approach include learning or behavioral problems and absenteeism (Wright and Leahey, 1984).

THE OCCUPATIONAL HEALTH NURSE

The nurse in the occupational health setting can also use a family approach to care to improve the health of the worker and contribute to overall productivity. For example, alcohol and chemical abuse account for much absenteeism in the workplace. Effective intervention with these families has been demonstrated (Steinglass, 1985). Assessment of occupational hazards may involve conducting reproductive histories in an effort to determine the effects of a chemical or agent on the reproductive capacity of the couple (Swanson, 1984). Toxic agents can also be transferred to family members from the workplace via clothes and equipment (Whorton, 1984). An awareness and high degree of suspicion of risks of occupational hazards common to industries in the community in which the community health nurse works are necessary. Obtaining an occupational history from all family members who have entered the workplace and referral for screening and health education of family members will contribute to unravelling occupational hazards and effects in the future. In addition, the community health nurse should be aware of the many family-related work issues that may trigger stress-related illness, such as promotion or loss of job and shift work.

INTERVENTION IN CASES OF CHRONIC ILLNESS

The community health nurse working with families coping with chronic illness in child, adult, or elder is aided by the family interview. As Glaser and Strauss (1975) state, chronic illness interjects change into various areas of family life:

"Sex and intimacy can be affected. Everyday mood and interpersonal relations can be affected. Visiting friends and engaging in other leisure time activities can be affected. Conflicts can be engendered by increased expenses stemming from unemployment and the medical treatment . . . different illnesses may have different kinds of impact on such areas of family life, just as they probably will call for different kinds of helpful agents" (p. 67).

Changes in family patterns, fears, emotional responses, and expectations of individual family members can be assessed in the family interview. Special needs of the primary caretaker—often, the spouse, daughter, or daughter-in-law—can be assessed (Archbold, 1980; Corbin and Strauss, 1984). The community health nurse making family visits to the elderly and terminally ill is able to assess intergenerational conflict and stress and to influence positively family interaction (Wright and Leahey, 1984).

Moving From the Family to the Community

Dreher (1982) states that the practice of public health nursing is distinct from that of other specialties in nursing because of its scope and orientation to the care of the public, not because of its practice setting. Preparation of the public health nurse, this author states, cannot be limited to "'following a family in the community'—paltry preparation for a career in caring for the health of the public" (p. 509). The care of entire populations is the major focus, as stated by Freeman (1963):

"The selection of those to be served . . . must rest on the comparative impact on community health rather than solely on the needs of the individual or family being served. . . . The public health nurse cannot elect to care for a small number of people intensely while ignoring the needs of many others. She must be concerned with the population as a whole, with those in her caseload, with the need of a particular family as compared to the needs of others in the community" (p. 35).

The challenge to the community health nurse, then, is to provide care to communities and populations and not to focus only on the levels of the individual and family. How does the community health nurse, who traditionally may carry a caseload of families, extend practice in the field with families to include a focus on the community? To do so, an aggregate, community, and population focus must serve as a backdrop to the entire practice.

For example, families must be viewed as components of communities. The community health nurse must know the community. As stated in Chapter 5, a thorough community assessment is necessary to practice in the community. By way of review, it is important to remember that communities must be compared not only in terms of differences in health needs but also in terms of differences in resources to effect intervention that will have an impact on policies and redistribute resources to ensure that the health needs of these communities and the families residing within them are met. As Dreher (1982) states:

"Data gathered about the physical, social, and demographic variables of the population being served are essential to provide an empirical basis for the development and delivery of nursing services. Unless these data, however, are viewed within a larger context—across communities—they will never serve to develop either the more encompassing

---

Sources of Data About the Community's Health
NATIONAL DATA are available from resources such as *Health, 1990* (National Center for Health Statistics, 1991, published annually), *Health Status of Minorities and Low Income Groups* (Department of Health and Human Services, 1991), and the *Morbidity and Mortality Weekly Report (M.M.W.R.)*. State data are also provided in these publications. More in-depth data at the state level may be obtained from state department of health publications that give mortality and morbidity statistics. Local data are available from the census, city planners, and city or county departments of health (see Chapter 5).

theories which explain the relationship between society and health or the policies which will be most effective in assuring health and health care" (p. 508).

Community health nurses must then compare city data with county data and then county data, state data, and national data. In addition, they may need to compare local census tract data and areas of a city or county with other areas of the city or county.

For example, community health nursing students in San Antonio, who were planning home visits to families of pregnant adolescents attending a special high school, compared local, state, and national statistics on infant mortality as a part of a community assessment. They found higher rates of infant mortality in San Antonio in census tracts on the south side of the city in which the population was predominantly Mexican-American. They also found the population to be younger, to have a higher rate of functional illiteracy among adults, to be less educated, to be more likely to drop out of high school, to have higher fertility rates, to have higher birth rates among adolescents, and to be more likely to be unemployed. They found that specific health needs varied among census tracts. Common major health needs of this subpopulation were thus identified from the community assessment, which assisted the students in planning care for these families. Their goals, for example, were broadened from carrying out interventions at the individual level to interventions at the family and community levels. In addition to targeting good perinatal outcomes for the individual teen parent, nursing students planned to include assessments of functional literacy at the individual and family levels, and arranged for group sessions in clinic waiting rooms that informed and referred individuals and family members to alternative resources to enable teen parents to complete school, take classes in English as a second language, and utilize resources for family planning and employment at the community level.

In addition to the cross-comparison of communities, the community health nurse also cross-compares the needs of the families within the communities and sets priorities. As the students mentioned above found that specific health needs varied between census tracts, so, too, the nurse in the community finds that specific health needs

---

Double Standard Tolerated in Public Health

A DOUBLE standard is tolerated in public health. Although the government is responsible for the maintenance of health, a minimal amount of health care is guaranteed each person due to the limitations of public resources. As Smith (1985) states:

"This prohibits discrimination based upon traits of persons that are not matters of free choice: for example, race, sex, and other congenital conditions; and wealth, poverty, or geographic location when these cannot be altered by the individual" (p. 143).

Thus, a minimum is established for all, yet as demonstrated with Medicare and Medicaid (see Chapter 3), unequal care exists due to differences in income (Medicare) and geographic location (Medicaid). In a market system, the wealthy can purchase all the health care services they desire; the poor cannot. The few supplemental resources provided by the government to ensure a minimum for all vary among communities, states, administrations, and countries.

---

vary among families. The nurse must account for time spent with families and choose those families on the basis of their needs compared with the needs of others in the community.

DELEGATION OF SCARCE RESOURCES

Although the community health nurse serves the community or population as a whole, fiscal constraints hold the nurse accountable for the best delegation of scarce resources. Time spent on home visits has traditionally allowed the community health nurse to assess the environmental, social, and biological determinants of health status among the population and the resources available to them. Fiscal accountability, nevertheless, means setting priorities. Anderson and her colleagues (1985) list the factors that impact public health nursing practice, especially home visits, as "the need to justify personnel costs in a time of fiscal constraint, the increasing number of medically indigent who turn to local public health services for primary care, and the change in reimbursement mechanisms by the federal government and some states" (p. 146).

In a period of cost-containment, the focus of community health nurses on prevention and health maintenance, areas difficult to justify, must carefully legitimate home visiting services by identifying aggregates in need of care. As stated in the definition of public health nursing by the Public Health Nursing Section of the American Public Health Association (1981):

"Identifying the subgroups (aggregates) within the population which are at high risk of illness, disability, or premature death and directing resources toward these groups is the most effective approach for accomplishing the goal of public health nursing" (p. 4).

Prioritizing groups at highest risk and using home visits to them in conjunction with planning for needs of larger aggregates are necessary. Hand-in-hand with this activity goes working for social and policy changes to alter the conditions that place these families at high risk. Little research has been done on the necessity for home visits in conjunction with group instruction or other agency-based care. Anderson and her colleagues (1985) report a study of the integration of public health nursing and primary care in northern California. They found that "the teaching component of primary care and the continuity of nursing care from hospital to clinic and home for patients served by county medical services was strengthened" (p. 146). Populations at high risk that may benefit from home visiting are being identified (Barkauskas, 1983; Brooten et al., 1986; Martinson et al., 1985; Olds et al., 1988). Evidence indicates that costs are cut by home visits for high-risk infants in combination with other support systems such as social and medical services (Brooten et al., 1986; State of California Health and Welfare Agency, 1982).

What are the approaches to meeting the health needs of families? Many schools of thought exist among community health, community mental health, and public health nursing professionals. Dreher (1982) states that the traditional basis for community health nursing intervention has a focus that has long endorsed psychological and social psychological theories to explain variations in health and patterns of health care, such as those set forth by Erikson (1963), Maslow (1970), Duvall (1977), Festinger (1957), Kubler-Ross (1975), and

Rogers (1951). She states that what is needed are "more encompassing theories which explain the relationship between society and health [and] the policies which will be most effective in assuring health and health care" (p. 508). To help bridge this gap, two approaches will be presented: meeting family health needs through the application of family theory; and extending family health intervention to larger aggregates and social action.

THE FAMILY THEORY APPROACH TO MEETING THE HEALTH NEEDS OF FAMILIES

There are many reasons why the community health nurse should work with families. Friedman (1981) lists the following five reasons:

- The belief that within the family unit, any "dysfunction" (e.g., separation, disease, or injury) that affects one or more family members probably will affect other family members and the family as a whole.
- The wellness of the family is highly dependent on the role of the family in every aspect of health care, from prevention to rehabilitation.
- The level of wellness of the whole family can be raised through care that reduces lifestyle and environmental risks by emphasizing "health promotion, 'self-care,' health education, and family counseling" (p. 4).
- Commonalities in risk factors and disease shared by family members can lead to case finding within the family.
- A clear understanding of the functioning of the individual can be gained only when the individual is assessed within the larger context of the family.

For example, 10-year-old Jean Wilkie was referred by her teacher to the school nurse. She was withdrawn, had no school friends, and was dropping behind in her school work. The school nurse talked to Jean in her office. Jean said that she had no friends because the other girls stayed overnight with each other "all the time" and that she did not want to bring her friends home because her father "drank all the time." The school nurse decided that Jean's problems needed assessment within the context of the family and arranged to visit the family at home. The father refused to participate in the family interview, but Jean's mother, her 13-year-old brother Peter, and Jean expressed concerns that the father had changed jobs several times in the past year, was frequently absent from work, and had been in two recent car accidents while "drinking." Thus, the school nurse was able to verify the family context as the basis of Jean's "problems" and to continue her family assessment and plan for intervention at the family level. In addition, she was prompted to assess the community's preventive efforts directed toward drinking and the ability to provide ongoing care for families of alcoholics.

Nurses have relied heavily on the social and behavioral sciences for approaches to working with families. Approaches that nurses have relied on heavily in studying the family include psychoanalytical, anthropological, systems or cybernetic, structural-functional, developmental, and interactional (for reviews, see Barker, 1981; Duvall, 1985; Nye and Berardo, 1966; Wright and Leahey, 1984). Three conceptual frameworks (systems, structural-functional, and developmental), often used by nurses in providing health care to families, will be described.

Systems Approach

The systems approach has been widely used in diverse areas such as education, computer science, engineering, and communication. General systems theory (see Chapter 3) is a way to explain how the family as a unit interacts with larger units outside the family and with smaller units inside the family (Friedman, 1981). The family may be affected by any disrupting force acting on a system outside it (suprasystem) or on a system within it (subsystem). Allmond and colleagues (1979) compare the family as a system with a piece of a mobile suspended from the air that is in constant movement with the other pieces of the mobile. At any time, the family, like any piece of the mobile, may be caught by a gust of air and become unbalanced, moving "chaotically" for a while; however, eventually, the stabilizing force of the other parts of the mobile will reestablish balance.

Wright and Leahey (1984) reviewed the literature on the application of general systems theory (von Bertalanffy, 1968, 1972, 1974) to the study of families. They found that little agreement exists on the basic concepts of systems theory, there has been

---

Major Definitions From Systems Theory

SYSTEM: "A GOAL-directed unit made up of interdependent, interacting parts which endure over a period of time" (Friedman, 1981, p. 73); a family system is not concrete. It is made up of suprasystems and subsystems and must be viewed in a hierarchy of systems. The system under study at any given time is called the focal, or target, system. In this chapter, the family system will be the focal system.

Suprasystem: The suprasystem is the larger system of which the family is a part, such as the larger environment or the community, e.g., churches, schools, clubs, businesses, neighborhood organizations, gangs, and so on.

Subsystem: Subsystems are the smaller units of which the family consists, such as sets of relationships within the family, e.g., spouse, parent-child, sibling, or extended family.

Hierarchy of Systems: The hierarchy comprises the levels of units within the system and its environment that in their totality make

up the universe. Higher-level units are composed of lower-level units, e.g., the biosphere is made up of communities, which are made up of families. Families are made up of family subsystems, and, in turn, family subsystems are made up of individuals, who are made up of organs, which are made of cells, and cells are made of atoms.

Boundaries: A boundary is an imaginary definitive line that forms a circle around each system and delineates the system from its environment. Auger (1976) conceptualizes the boundary of a system as a " 'filter' which permits the constant exchange of elements, information, or energy between the system and its environment. . . . The more porous the filter, the greater the degree of interaction possible between the system and its environment" (p. 24). Families with rigid boundaries may lack necessary information and resources pertinent to maintaining family health or wellness.

Open System: An open system interacts with its surrounding environment—it gives outputs and gets inputs necessary to survival. An exchange of energy occurs. All living systems are open systems. However, if a boundary is too permeable, the system may be too open to input new ideas from the outside and may be unable to make decisions on its own (Wright and Leahey, 1984).

Closed System: A closed system theoretically does not interact with the environment. This is a self-sufficient system; no energy exchange occurs. Although no system has been found that exists in a totally closed state, if a family's boundaries are impermeable, i.e., less open as a system, needed input or interaction cannot occur. An example is the refugee family from Vietnam living in San Francisco; they may remain a closed family for some time due to differences in culture and language.

Input: Input is information, matter, or energy that the open system receives from its environment that is necessary to survival.

Output: Output is information, matter, or energy dispensed into the environment as a result of receiving and processing the input.

Flow and transformation: The system's use of input may occur in two forms: some input may be used in its original state, and some input may have to be transformed before it is used. Both original and transformed input must be processed and flow through the system before being released as output (Friedman, 1981).

Feedback: Feedback is "the process by which a system monitors the internal and environmental responses to its behavior (output) and accommodates or adjusts itself" (p. 74) (Friedman, 1981). The system controls and modifies both inputs and outputs by "receiving and responding to the return of its own output" (p. 74) (Friedman, 1981). Internally, the system adjusts by making changes in its subsystems. Externally, the system adjusts by making boundary changes.

Equilibrium: Equilibrium is a state of balance or steady state that results from self-regulation or adaptation. As with the concept of a system as a mobile in the wind, balance is dynamic and, with change, is always reestablishing itself.

Differentiation: Differentiation is the tendency for a system to actively grow and "advance to a higher order of complexity and organization" (Friedman, 1981, p. 74). Energy inputs into the system make this growth possible.

Energy: Energy is needed to meet a system's demands. Open systems will require more input through porous boundaries to meet high energy levels needed to maintain high levels of activity.

---

little clinical application of systems concepts to families, and explanatory concepts of systems theory are not yet organized into a predictive theory.

CHARACTERISTICS OF HEALTHY FAMILIES

Pratt (1976) characterizes healthy families as "energized families," in the following ways:

- Members interact with each other repeatedly in many contexts.
- Members are enhanced and fulfilled by maintaining contacts with a wide range of community groups and organizations.
- Members make efforts to master their lives by becoming members of groups, finding information and options, and making decisions.
- Members engage in flexible role relationships, share power, respond to change, support growth and autonomy of others, and engage in decision making that affects them.

Role Relationships

WHEN EDNA Smith, a 64-year-old client with severe arthritis, was diagnosed with diabetes, her longtime friend, Frank Gardens, a widower of several years, moved in with her and assumed a caretaker role. The community health nurse assessed the dietary habits of Mr. Gardens and Mrs. Smith and found that Mr. Gardens did the shopping and the cooking because Mrs. Smith's mobility was severely restricted due to her arthritis. Because Mr. Gardens did the cooking, he purchased canned fruits and vegetables rather than fresh or frozen. Cooking, which was *a new role* for Mr. Gardens, was perceived by him as demanding. After several visits, he disclosed to the nurse that his resistance to preparing fresh or frozen fruits and vegetables came from "the time it takes to clean the darn things, cook 'em, store 'em and clean up the 'fridge when they go bad on ya." He stated unequivocally that it was stressful caring for Mrs. Smith and that he wanted to do it, but it was "much easier" to just "open a can" and "heat it in a pan" than to take the time and energy that preparation of fresh or frozen foods would require. The shift in roles that is often required of couples when one is diagnosed with a chronic illness can have an impact on the health of the family. For additional reading about how couples manage with chronic illness, see Corbin, J., and Strauss, A. L.: Unending Work and Care: Management of Chronic Illness at Home. San Francisco, Jossey-Bass, 1988.

The following conceptual frameworks have been found useful in studying the family. Community health nurses have found them helpful in assessing the characteristics of families and their strengths and weaknesses and in planning interventions.

Structural-Functional Conceptual Framework

With the structural-functional conceptual framework approach to the family, the family is viewed according to its structure or the parts of the system and according to its function, or what the family does.

STRUCTURAL

Wright and Leahey (1984) dichotomize aspects of family structure into internal and external structure. *Internal structure* of the family refers to the following four categories:

- Family composition, or who is in the family and changes in family constellation
- Rank order, meaning positions of family members by age and sex
- Subsystem or labeling the subgroups or dyads (e.g., spouse, parental, interest) through which the family carries out its functions
- Boundary, or who participates in the family system and how (e.g., a single parent mother who does not allow her 17-year-old son to let his girlfriend spend the night in their home)

External structure refers to the larger context of the family (Wright and Leahey, 1984). It includes the following five categories:

- Culture or way of life
- Religion

- Social class status and mobility
- Environment or larger neighborhood and home
- Extended family, including family of origin and family of procreation

FUNCTIONAL

Wright and Leahey (1984) also dichotomize *family functional assessment*, or how family members behave toward each other, into two categories: instrumental functioning and expressive functioning. *Instrumental functioning* refers to activities of daily living, e.g., elimination, sleeping, eating, or giving insulin injections. This area takes on important meaning for the family when one member of the family becomes ill or disabled and, unable to carry out daily functions for themselves, must rely on other members of the family for assistance. For example, an elder may need assistance getting into the bathtub, or a child may need to have medications measured and administered.

The second type of family functional assessment is *expressive functioning*, or affective or emotional aspects. This aspect has nine categories.

1. Emotional communication — is the family able to express a range of emotions, including happiness, sadness, and anger?
2. Verbal communication, which focuses on the meaning of words. Do messages have clear meanings rather than distorted meanings? Wright and Leahey (1984) give the example of masked criticism when a father states to his child, "Children who cry when they get needles are babies" (p. 56).
3. Nonverbal communication, which includes, e.g., any sounds, gestures, eye contact, touch, or inaction. An example is when a husband remains silent and stares out the window when his wife is talking to him.
4. Circular communication is commonly observed between dyads in families. A common example is the blaming, nagging wife and the guilty, withdrawn husband.
5. Problem solving refers to how the family solves problems. Who identifies problems — someone inside or outside the family? What kinds of problems are solved? What patterns are used to solve and evaluate tried solutions?
6. Roles refer to "established patterns of behavior for family members" (Wright and Leahey, 1984, p. 61). Roles may be developed, delegated,

negotiated, and renegotiated within the family. It takes other family members to keep a person in a particular role. Traditional roles are being challenged and are changing with economic and feminist changes; many women are entering the work force outside the home. Formal roles, with which the larger community agrees, may come into conflict with roles set by family and influenced by religious, cultural, and other belief systems.

7. Control refers to how the behavior of others is influenced. It is important to find out what the family rules are; who decides, enforces, and breaks them; and what are the consequences.

8. Alliances and coalitions are important within the family. What dyads or triads appear to occur repeatedly in the family? Who starts arguments between dyads? Who stops arguments or fighting between dyads? Is there evidence of mother and father against child? When does this change to parent and child against the other parent? The balance and intensity of relationships between subsystems within the family are important to note. Questions may be asked regarding the permeability of the boundary. Does it cross generations?

DEVELOPMENTAL

Nurses are familiar with developmental states of individuals from prenatal through adult. Duvall (1985), a noted sociologist, is the forerunner of a focus on *family* development. She identifies eight stages that normal families traverse from marriage to death.

Summary of Family Functional Assessment

  I. Instrumental functioning
    A. Activities of daily living
  II. Expressive functioning
    A. Emotional communication
    B. Verbal communication
    C. Nonverbal communication
    D. Circular communication
    E. Problem solving
    F. Roles
    G. Control
    H. Alliances and coalitions

Data from Wright, L. M., and Leahey, M.: Nurses and Families: A Guide to Family Assessment and Intervention. Philadelphia, F. A. Davis, 1984.

Family Life Cycle

1. **Beginning family (marriage)**
2. **Early childbearing family (eldest child is in infancy through 30 months old)**
3. **Preschool children (eldest child is 2.5–5 years old)**
4. **School-age children (eldest child is 6–12 years old)**
5. **Teenage children (eldest child is 13–20 years old)**
6. **Launching family (oldest to youngest child leaves home)**
7. **Middle-age family (remaining marital dyad to retirement)**
8. **Aging family (retirement to death of both spouses)**

Data from Duvall, E. M., and Miller, B. C.: Marriage and Family Development. 6th Ed. New York, Harper & Row, 1985.

Carter and McGoldrick (1980) emphasize that family development is more than development by phases of related children and adults; they believe the family is a "basic unit of emotional development, the phases and course of which can be identified and predicted" (p. 4). Wright and Leahey (1984) state that "it is an understanding of these phases and of the struggles encountered during them that the nurse requires to make a family assessment" (p. 38). The latter authors present the following developmental categories, which outline eight stages of family development and the tasks necessary for the family's resolution of each stage. The stages may be used by nurses to delineate family strengths and weaknesses.

ALTERATIONS IN FAMILY DEVELOPMENT: DIVORCE AND REMARRIAGE

Alterations to the life-cycle occur, as seen in previously reviewed statistics of separation, divorce, single parent families, and remarriage. Carter and McGoldrick (1980) identify phases involved in the processes of divorce, postdivorce, and remarriage (Tables 14–1 and 14–2). The family must engage in emotional work as a result of divorce, a process that may occur suddenly or be long and drawn out. Stern (1982a) interviewed stepfather families in their homes and conceptualized the integration of

Table 14-1
Dislocations of the Family Life Cycle Requiring Additional Steps to Restabilize and Proceed Developmentally

Phase	Emotional Process of Transition; Prerequisite Attitude	Developmental Issues
Divorce		
1. The decision to divorce	Acceptance of inability to resolve marital tensions sufficiently to continue relationship	Acceptance of one's own part in the failure of the marriage
2. Planning the breakup of the system	Supporting viable arrangements for all parts of the system	a. Working cooperatively on problems of custody, visitation, and finances b. Dealing with extended family about the divorce
3. Separation	a. Willingness to continue cooperative coparental relationship b. Work on resolution of attachment to spouse	a. Mourning loss of intact family b. Restructuring marital and parent-child relationships; adaptation to living apart c. Realignment of relationships with extended family; staying connected with spouse's extended family
4. The divorce	More work on emotional divorce: Overcoming hurt, anger, guilt, and so on	a. Mourning loss of intact family: giving up fantasies of reunion b. Retrieval of hopes, dreams, and expectations from the marriage c. Staying connected with extended families
Postdivorce Family		
1. Single-parent family	Willingness to maintain parental contact with ex-spouse and support contact of children and ex-spouse and ex-spouse's family	a. Making flexible visitation arrangements with ex-spouse and ex-spouse's family b. Rebuilding own social network
2. Single-parent (noncustodial)	Willingness to maintain parental contact with ex-spouse and support custodial parent's relationship with children	a. Finding ways to continue effective parenting relationship with children b. Rebuilding own social network

From Wright, L. M., and Leahey, M.: Nurses and Families: A Guide to Family Assessment and Intervention. Philadelphia, F. A. Davis, 1984, p. 52, as adapted from Carter, E., and McGoldrick, M.: The family life cycle and family therapy: An overview. *In* Carter, E., and McGoldrick, M.: The Family Life Cycle: A Framework for Family Therapy. New York, Gardner Press, 1980, pp. 3–28.

Stages and Tasks of Family Development

I. Marriage: The joining of families
   A. Establishment of couple identity
   B. Realignment of relationships with extended families to include spouse
   C. Decisions about parenthood
II. Families with infants
   A. Integration of infant(s) into family unit
   B. Accommodation of new parenting and grandparenting roles
   C. Maintenance of marital bond

III. Families with preschoolers
   A. Socialization of children
   B. Adjustment to separation by parents and children
IV. Families with school-age children
   A. Development of peer relations by children
   B. Adaptation by parents to their children's peer and school influences
V. Families with teenagers
   A. Development of increasing autonomy for adolescents

	Table 14–2	
	Remarried Family Formation: A Developmental Outline	

Steps	Prerequisite Attitude	Developmental Issues
1. Entering the new relationship	Recovery from loss of first marriage (adequate "emotional divorce")	Recommitment to marriage and to forming a family with readiness to deal with the complexity and ambiguity
2. Conceptualizing and planning new marriage and family	Accepting one's own fears and those of new spouse and children about remarriage and forming a step-family Accepting need for time and patience for adjustment to complexity and ambiguity of: a. Multiple new roles b. Boundaries: space, time, membership, and authority c. Affective issues: guilt, loyalty conflicts, desire for mutuality, and unresolvable past hurts	a. Work on openness in the new relationships to avoid pseudomutuality b. Plan for maintenance of cooperative coparental relationships with ex-spouse(s) c. Plan to help children deal with fears, loyalty conflicts, and membership in two systems d. Realignment of relationships with extended family to include new spouse and children e. Plan maintenance of connections for children with extended family of ex-spouse(s)
3. Remarriage and reconstitution of family	Final solution of attachment to previous spouse and ideal of "intact" family: Acceptance of a different model of family with permeable boundaries	a. Restructuring family boundaries to allow for inclusion of new spouse-stepparent b. Realignment of relationships throughout subsystems to permit interweaving of several systems c. Making room for relationships of all children with biological (noncustodial) parents, grandparents, and other extended family d. Sharing memories and histories to enhance stepfamily integration

From Wright, L. M., and Leahey, M.: Nurses and Families: A Guide to Family Assessment and Intervention. Philadelphia, F. A. Davis, 1984, p. 53, as adapted from Carter, E., and McGoldrick, M.: The family life cycle and family therapy: An overview. *In* Carter, E., and McGoldrick, M.: The Family Life Cycle: A Framework for Family Therapy. New York, Gardner Press, 1980, pp. 3–28.

    B. Refocus on midlife marital and career issues
    C. Beginning shift toward concern for the older generation
  VI. Families as launching centers
    A. Establishment of independent identities for parents and young adult
    B. Renegotiation of marital relationship
  VII. Middle-aged families
    A. Reinvestment in couple identity with concurrent development of independent interests

    B. Realignment of relationships to include in-laws and grandchildren
    C. Dealing with disabilities and death of older generation
  VIII. Aging families
    A. Shift from work role to leisure and semiretirement or full retirement
    B. Maintenance of couple and individual functioning while adapting to the aging process
    C. Preparation for own death and dealing with the loss of spouse and/or siblings and other peers

Data from Wright, L. M., and Leahey, M.: Nurses and Families: A Guide to Family Assessment and Intervention. Philadelphia, F. A. Davis, 1984.

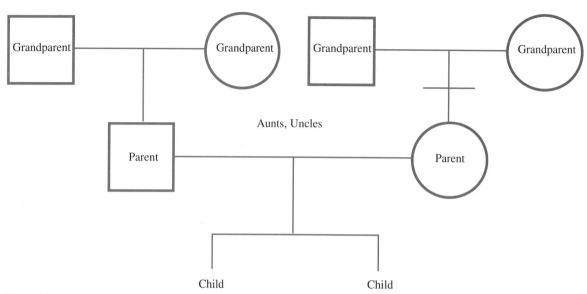

Figure 14–1
Genogram. (Redrawn from Wright, L. M., and Leahey, M.: Nurses and Families: A Guide to Family Assessment and Intervention. Philadelphia: F. A. Davis, 1984.)

Personal Goals of Recently Divorced Women
FROM DIVORCE records in three counties, the authors identified recently divorced women with children. Of 528 women contacted by mail and by telephone, 252 completed questionnaires and interviews. The women described eight categories of personal goals. The most frequently cited goals were, in order of frequency, independence, employment, and education. Older women were more likely to choose employment and environmental goals over mental health goals than were younger women.

Data from Duffy, M. E., Mowbray, C. A., and Hudes, M.: Personal goals of recently divorced women. Image J. Nurs. Scholarship 22;14–17, 1990.

the blended family once remarriage occurs as integration of two distinct family cultures. In addition, Stern (1982b) identified a set of affiliating strategies that can be taught to families that lead to stepfather-child friendship.

Assessment Tools

Many tools exist for the community health nurse to use in assessing the family (Friedman, 1981; Young, 1982; Wright and Leahey, 1984). Reviewed here are the genogram, the ecomap, and the family health tree.

GENOGRAM

The genogram is a tool that helps the nurse to outline the family's structure. It is a way to diagram the family constellation, or "family tree." It is possible to fill out the blank genogram (Fig. 14–1) for three generations of family members with the generally agreed on symbols (Fig. 14–2) to denote geneology. Children are pictured from left to right, beginning with the oldest child.

The community health nurse may use the genogram during an early family interview, starting with a blank sheet of paper and drawing a circle or a square for the person initially interviewed. The nurse tells the family that several background questions will be asked to gain a general picture of their family. Circles may be drawn around family members living in separate households (Fig. 14–3). The Chan family, a refugee family from Vietnam, is a nuclear family. With the death of Mr. Chan upon the family's arrival in San Francisco 3 months before the first home visit (see below), the family became a single parent family. Although Mr. Chan is no longer physically present in the family, his presence is still felt, as the nurse learns

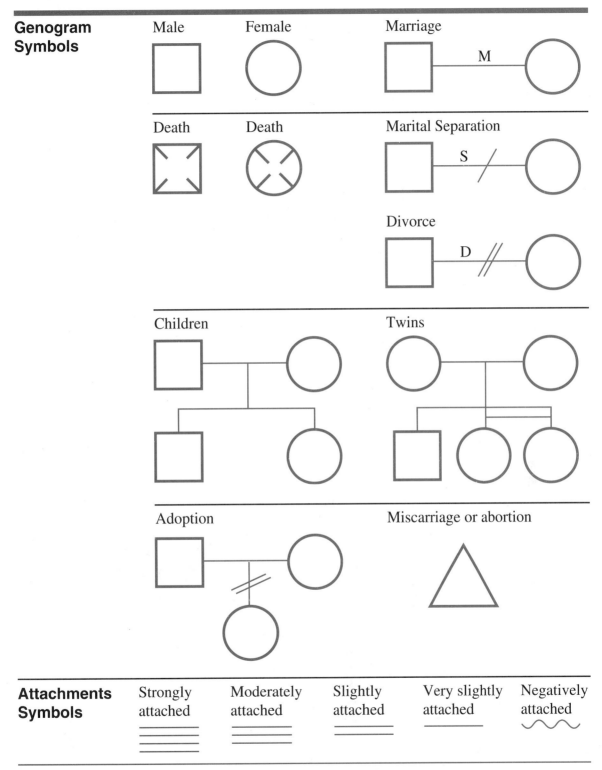

Figure 14–2
Genogram and attachment symbols. (Redrawn from Wright, L. M., and Leahey, M.: Nurses and Families: A Guide to Family Assessment and Intervention. Philadelphia: F. A. Davis, 1984.)

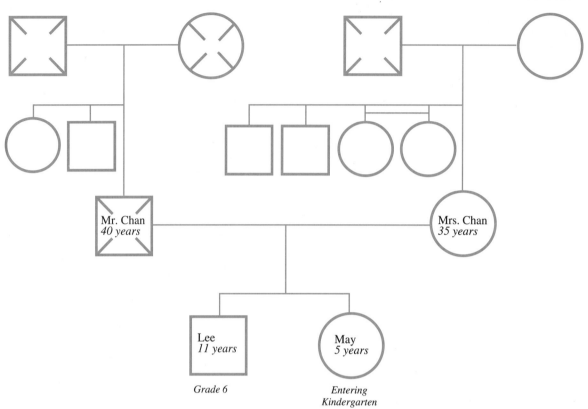

Figure 14–3
Sample genogram of Chan family.

the family has yet to express affectively their loss. Some families may be very cooperative in helping to fill out the genogram, freely relating significant information such as divorces and remarriages. Other families may be sensitive to such information, particularly when it is shown to recur with each generation.

FAMILY HEALTH TREE

The family health tree is another tool that is helpful to the community health nurse (Fig. 14–4). Based on the genogram, the family health tree provides a mechanism for recording the family's medical and health histories (Friedman, 1981; Diekelmann, 1977). Causes of death of deceased family members, when known, are important. Genetically linked diseases, including heart disease, cancer, diabetes, hypertension, sickle cell anemia, allergies, asthma, and mental retardation, can be noted. Environmental and occupational diseases, psychosocial problems such as mental illness and obe-

sity, and infectious diseases should also be noted. From health problems, familial risk factors can be noted. Risk factors can also be noted by inquiring about what family members do to prevent illness, such as having periodic physical examinations, Pap smears, and immunizations. Lifestyle-related risk factors can be assessed by asking what family members do to "handle stress" and to "keep in shape." The family health tree can be used in planning positive familial influences on risk factors, such as dietary, exercise, coping with stress, or pressure to have a physical examination.

ECOMAP

The ecomap (Fig. 14–5) is a tool that is used to depict a family's linkages to their suprasystems (Hartman, 1979; Wright and Leahey, 1984). As stated by Hartman (1978):

"The eco-map portrays an overview of the family in their situation; it depicts the important nurtur-

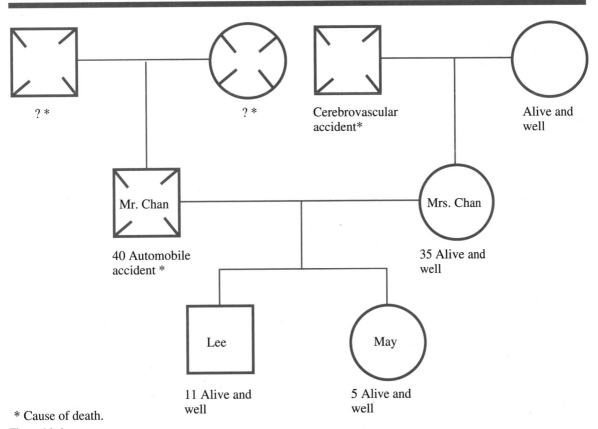

? *   ? *   Cerebrovascular accident*   Alive and well

Mr. Chan   Mrs. Chan

40 Automobile accident *   35 Alive and well

Lee   May

11 Alive and well   5 Alive and well

* Cause of death.

Figure 14–4
Chan family health tree. (Modified from Diekelman, N.: Primary Health Care of the Well Adult. New York, McGraw-Hill, 1977. Reproduced with permission of McGraw-Hill, Inc.)

ant or conflict-laden connections between the family and the world. It demonstrates the flow of resources, or the lacks and deprivations. This mapping procedure highlights the nature of the interfaces and points to conflicts to be mediated, bridges to be built, and resources to be sought and mobilized" (p. 467).

As with the genogram, the ecomap may be filled out during an early family interview, noting persons, institutions, and agencies significant to the family. Symbols used in attachment diagrams (see Fig. 14–2) may be used to denote the nature of the ties that exist. For example, in Figure 14–6, the Chan family ecomap suggests that few contacts occur between the family and the suprasystems. The community health nursing student was able to use the ecomap to discuss with the family the types of resources in the community and the types of relationships they wanted to establish with them.

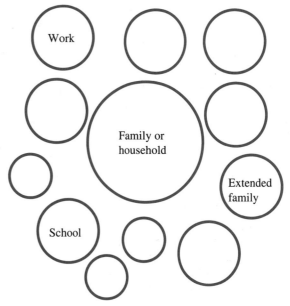

Work   Family or household   Extended family   School

Figure 14–5
Ecomap. (Redrawn from Hartman, A.: Diagrammatic assessment of family relationships. Soc. Casework 59;469, 1978.)

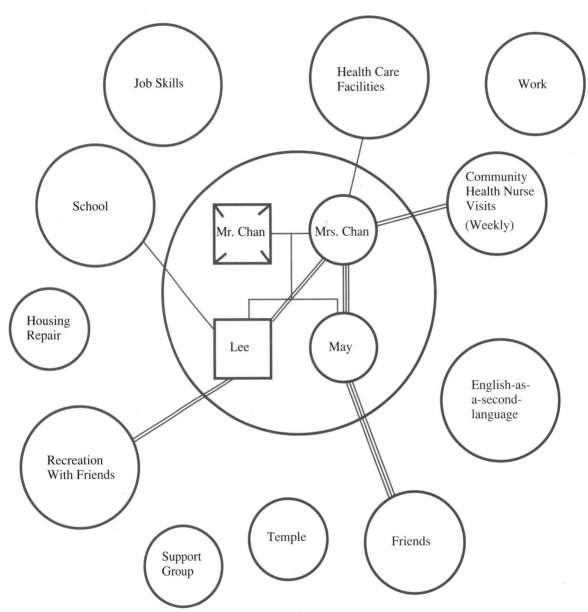

Figure 14–6
Sample ecomap of Chan family.

These tools for family assessment can be used with families in every health care setting to increase the nurse's awareness of the family within the community and to help guide the nurse and the family in the assessment and planning phases of care.

SOCIAL AND STRUCTURAL CONSTRAINTS

In addition to the standard tools reviewed above, an important aspect of family assessment and planning for intervention is the need to make note of the social and structural constraints that prevent families from receiving care, in particular, the health care they need. These constraints explain why some families differ in mortality rates, in ability to achieve "integrity" rather than "despair," or in ability to "self-actualize." Social and structural constraints are usually based in social and economic causes, which affect a wide range of conditions associated with major health indicators (mortality and morbidity), such as literacy, education, and employment. Families most frequently served by the community health nurse are the disadvantaged, those who are unable to buy health care from the private sector. Constraints to obtaining needed health and social services by these families are well documented, however, and may more often be due to characteristics of the health and social services rather than individual limitations of the family (Strauss, 1976, 1979). These constraints may be noted on the ecomap, as they influence each family's ability to interact with a specific agency. For example, in addition to noting the strength of the relationship between family and agency or institution, those constraints that prevent use or full use of the resource should be noted. Constraints include hours of service, distance and transportation, availability of interpreters, and criteria for receiving services such as age, sex, and income barriers. Specific examples include the different guidelines posed by each state for Medicaid and by each community for home-delivered meals to the homebound. Helping families understand constraints and linking them to accessible resources are necessary, but intervention at the family level is not sufficient. The common basic human needs of families in a community add up, and structural constraints faced repeatedly by families must be tallied by the community health nurse and compared with those of families in other communities. Intervention may then be planned and carried out at the aggregate level. A special health program targeting Asian refugee families in San Francisco was initiated by a public health nurse who noted recurring health-related problems among refugee families (M. Deasy, personal communication, 1985). Muecke (1984) reports the process of community health nursing diagnosis carried out by undergraduate community health nursing students among households in Seattle of Mien refugees from Laos. The following section is an overview of how community health nurses can extend intervention at the family level to larger aggregates and social action.

EXTENDING FAMILY HEALTH INTERVENTION TO LARGER AGGREGATES AND SOCIAL ACTION

Institutional Context of Family Therapists

Many theories exist to help bridge the gap between the application of nursing and family theory to the family and broader social action on the behalf of communities of families (Clements and Roberts, 1983; McGoldrick et al., 1982). Most family theorists view the family as a system that interfaces with outside suprasystems or institutions only when there is a problem to be addressed, such as in the school or a courtroom. Three approaches reviewed by Spiegel (1982) go beyond the family as a system to address the interaction between the family and the larger social system:

- The ecological approach
- Network therapy
- The transactional field approach

ECOLOGICAL APPROACH

The ecological approach indicts the specialization and fragmentation seen in the social and health service structure based on Western concepts of time and space. This approach focuses on a more complex and flexible structure. Helping families transcend rigid boundaries and intake procedures of agencies that they need to maintain themselves in their environment is essential (Spiegel, 1982; for a review, see Berry, 1980).

NETWORK THERAPY

Network therapy involves changing the network, be it extended family or friends who tend to maintain a dysfunctional status quo in the nuclear family. This is done by replacing the network with others from the wider systems who would be able to provide more support and therefore enhance the functioning of the family (Spiegel, 1982).

TRANSACTIONAL FIELD APPROACH

In this model, the approaches of "self-action" and "interaction," which are viewed by Spiegel (1982) to be linear and lead to " 'blame systems' or pejorative labels" (p. 35), are replaced with " 'transaction' which denotes system in process with system, where no entity can be located as first or final cause" (p. 35). The family as an institution, along with other institutions whether religious, educational, recreational, or government, is culturally anchored. That is, each holds to a "set of beliefs and values about the nature of the world and human existence known as Culture" (p. 36). An awareness of culture as it is expressed in each system, in particular, as it is expressed in mainstream U.S. values, versus the value patterns of the family is important. An awareness of the culture of origin, how the family's values are changing according to where they are in the process of acculturation, and the family's interpretation of the mainstream U.S. values is essential to viewing the transaction of systems with each other.

Models of Social Class and Health Services

Social class and race place major limitations on access to medical care. For example, the poor have long been known to use health services at lower rates than the middle class. In recent years, however, lower-income groups have exceeded the middle class in use of health services (National Center for Health Statistics, 1983, 1990). These differences are accounted for by the poor health of the low-income groups. When comparing groups of persons with the same severity of illness, poor persons have been reported to have the lowest rate of use of services (Kleinman et al., 1981; LaPlante, 1982). Approximately 15–20% of the U.S. population are uninsured or underinsured (Relman, 1987). Among a number of differences in access to

health care in the United States are race and region of the United States. For example, the number of physician contacts in 1991 by whites were 5.6 compared with 5.1 for blacks; 5.2 visits occurred in the Northeast compared with 5.6 in the South (National Center for Health Statistics, 1992).

Theoretical perspectives that underlie the reasons for these disparities are suggested by medical sociologists as a culture of poverty view of life that discourages self-reliance (Lewis, 1966) and a structural view that considers constraints to access to medical care (Duff and Hollingshead, 1968; Strauss, 1976, 1979).

CULTURE OF POVERTY

The *culture of poverty* view suggests that the relationship between social class and health services is due to a crisis-orientation, living-for-the-moment attitude, health beliefs that are culturally transmitted, a low value of health, lack of psychological "readiness," and individual predispositions such as an external locus of control (Riessman, 1984).

STRUCTURAL VIEW

The structural view considers two sets of constraints that limit use of medical care: material, such as money to buy services, and characteristics of health care settings for the poor in contrast to private office practices available for the nonpoor, such as hours available, waiting time, transportation, block appointments, specialty clinics, and disease-oriented rather than preventive care.

Research has looked at use of health care using attitudes and beliefs to test the culture of poverty explanation and using financial and systems barriers to test the structural explanation (Riessman, 1984). Although studies have acknowledged some problems methodologically and with generalizability, evidence supports the findings that unequal use of health care is more a result of the system of care rather than of individual characteristics of persons seeking care. For example, in a study in Washington, D.C., Dutton (1981) studied a predominantly black population that had to rely on settings such as public clinics, emergency departments and outpatient departments in hospitals versus those who used a prepaid group practice or private physicians. Dutton concluded that "poor and minorities face greater financial and organizational obstacles in seeking care. . . . Even within the *same* practice settings, the disadvantaged often face greater barriers than the more affluent and receive a different standard of care" (p. 423).

With recent cutbacks in services and the closing of public hospitals, increasingly more persons are forced to attend overcrowded public clinics where professionals have little control over the nature of their work and little time to establish ongoing relationships with clients. Riessman (1984) states that increasing clients' access to these kinds of services is not in itself sufficient. Instead, she notes changes called for by a new generation of medical sociologists, i.e., changes in the culture of medicine with its technological approach to human problems that separates the provider from the consumer and the consumer from a network of family and friends in society (Conrad and Schneider, 1980; Kotelchuk, 1976; Ehrenreich, 1978).

Models of Care for Communities of Families

Models exist to guide the community health nurse in providing care to communities of families in special need of services that improve access, equality between consumer and provider, and sensitivity to human need. Riessman (1984) reviews two models; one, initiated by consumer efforts, is an alternative childbirth center, *Su Clinica Familiar.* This center is located in the Rio Grande Valley in South Texas. It is situated in a "family-oriented rural health clinic" and serves mostly low-income Mexican-American agricultural worker families. Services (93%) were given by nurse-midwives between 1972 and 1979. Prenatal care and professionally assisted deliveries that encouraged family participation were made available to women who previously lacked access to care. Outcomes showed lower rates of prematurity than the state average, favorable birth weights, and positive Apgar scores.

A second model was initiated by a pediatrics department within an urban teaching hospital. This alternative delivery model offers home care for chronically ill children of poor, largely black and Hispanic families in New York City. A team focus that involved home visits by pediatric nurse practitioners was compared with usual in-hospital care. No difference existed between the families receiving home care and standard hospital care at 6 months in impact on the family and functional status of the child. Significant differences did exist

at 6 and 12 months, however, for psychological adjustment of the child and the mother's satisfaction with medical care, the home care group was favored.

Riessman (1984) states that these alternative programs are strategies to change the structural barriers that prevent access to care for low-income families. Professional role functions changed as nurses provided health care rather than physicians. Active self-care was promoted, and health and medical knowledge was shared. Assistance by family and social networks was encouraged. Riessman warns, however, that although both programs address aspects of the cultural critique of medicine, the programs do not "address the social determinants of disease." Neither program addresses the health-damaging conditions that poor persons face, such as poor housing, malnutrition, and environmental hazards at the workplace and in the community. Although these programs represent steps in the right direction, changes in access to medical and health services is not enough; social changes are also necessary.

Two health care delivery models to promote access to care for families are presented.

A block nurse program was initiated in St. Paul, Minnesota, by community health nurses (Martinson et al., 1985; Jamieson and Martinson, 1983). The program links registered nurses who live closest to families that have elders who need care with nursing services, medical supervision, and support services such as social work and volunteers. Based on a community needs assessment, census data showed that the 1-square-mile geographic area of St. Anthony's Park had a population of 6,969. Of this population, 12.5% (872) were age 65 or older. Of these elders, more than half lived in family households, one third lived in nonfamily households, and approximately one sixth lived in "group quarters." Annual incomes of households were below the poverty level ($7,500) for 26%, which accounted for approximately 5.2% of all elders living in the district.

Eighteen of more than 40 registered nurses who lived in the same district signed up to assist their elderly neighbors by making nursing services available to them to keep them out of hospitals and nursing homes. They were also involved in prevention and case finding. The nurses became roster nurses for the Ramsey County Public Health Nursing Service and completed 60 hours of gerontological nursing courses. Services are covered by Medicare, Medicaid, third-party insurance, and private funds. Private funding was needed because many of the nursing services needed by persons with chronic illness are not covered under current reimbursement guidelines. Careful documentation of services that are not covered will be useful to show the need for health policy and programs to cover services in the home that ultimately cut the cost of more expensive hospitalization and nursing home care.

With the projected increase of the elderly population and the early discharge from hospitals related to diagnosis-related groups to cut costs, the need for nursing services for this aggregate of elders is clear. Keeping persons with chronic illness in the home is a clear direction for the future.

A partnership for health program was initiated in Houston, Texas, by community health nurses (Mahon et al., 1991). The program links the general public, businesses, volunteer mothers, and a community health nurse with a targeted community of Hispanic mothers in need of early prenatal care. The peer education program trains volunteer Hispanic women to identify women at risk of late prenatal care, to provide culturally relevant information about resources in the community, and to give social support. Methods of providing information in culturally acceptable milieus was a priority. Examples include group meetings in a food pantry in the community, in the homes of the volunteers, or in the homes of the women at risk. During the first year of the program, 14 volunteer mothers contacted more than 2,000 women at risk of delayed prenatal care.

Clearly, these programs initiated by community health nurses also represent steps in the right direction to overcome barriers to medical and health services among the elderly and high-risk women. Major social determinants of health, however, such as poor housing, malnutrition, and poverty, call for even more proactive social change programs by nurses, the community, and the country.

APPLICATION OF THE NURSING PROCESS

The Home Visit

Home visiting is increasing in popularity in some contexts and coming under increased scrutiny in others. Providing health care in the home to persons with an identified health problem has been shown to be cheaper than hospital care (Berg and Helgeson, 1984; Brooten et al., 1986). The shift in financial structure to proprietary or for-profit corporations in home health care poses difficult questions for community health nursing. Although the home health care client has the same basic human needs now as before the shift to a market system, the shift creates an ethical dilemma — that of belief in market justice versus social justice. Questions about cost-effectiveness of home visiting to well families in face of limited public health resources have resulted in home visiting to largely high-risk populations such as primiparous mothers and their infants (Barkauskas, 1983), high-risk infants (Kaser et al., 1984), and infants at risk for developmental disabilities (Morris, 1985). As stated previously, setting priorities and visiting groups (families) in the community "at increased risk of illness, disability, or premature death" is necessary (Anderson et al., 1985, p. 146). Many considerations are made in conjunction with an agency's policy regarding home visits (see Chapter 8).

This section will present the application of the nursing process to a family on a home visit. The example will note the use of the home visit to identify a high index of suspicion of needs of larger aggregates within the community and consequent programs planned to meet those needs, which ultimately will benefit a population of families in the future.

The home visit is a crucial experience for both the student and the family (Berg and Helgeson, 1984). Important factors that may impact the home visit include the family's background experience with the health care system, the agency in which the student is working, the family's experience with previous students who have visited the family, and the background of the student. For example, student characteristics may vary; the student brings differing levels of knowledge of medical and nursing practice, of self, and of the community.

The student brings previous learning about families, family-related theory, the growth and development of members of different ages within a family, disease processes, and access to the health care system. Because curricula within schools of nursing vary, some students will also bring preparation in all specialties — medical-surgical, childbearing, parent-child nursing, and psychiatric/and mental health nursing—to the experience. Others may be taking basic clinical courses such as pediatrics and psychiatric/mental health nursing concurrently with community health. Thus, the need for review of appropriate theory, health education, and standard assessment tools for individuals and for families will vary.

The student's knowledge of self, previous life experience, and values are also important. Research reveals that conflict related to culture exists in the delivery of health care (Milio, 1975; see Chapters 16, 17, 18, and 19). Middle-class health care providers tend to prefer clients from the same social class (Papper, 1978). In a study of community health nurses' conceptions of low-income black, Mexican-American, and white family lifestyles and health care patterns, Erkel (1985) found respondents could not identify major health care delivery problems in giving care to different ethnic groups. Yet only half the respondents felt they could work equally well with each group. Students must recognize their strengths and weaknesses in these areas in preparation for entering a new community.

Knowledge of the community and level of comfort with a new environment, in particular, one outside the student's previous experience, are also important. Additional preparation by all students will be necessary before the first home visit is made, depending on the content of the referral.

Case Study

The first home visit is usually initiated by a referral. The source of a referral may be, for example, a clinic, a school, a private physician, or an agency responsible for the care of a particular aggregate. Doris Wilson received a referral to visit the Chan family from the Intercultural Agency, a private agency responsible for follow-up of refugees from Southeast Asia. The referral traditionally lists family members, names, and ages; address; telephone number; identifying characteristics of family; reason for referral; and response to referral.

The Chan family consists of Mrs. Chan, 35 years old; Lee, 11 years old; and May, 5 years old. The referral notes that the Chan family is a Chinese refugee family from Vietnam who have been in the United States 3 months. Mrs. Chan was recently widowed after her husband was killed in a hit-and-run automobile accident. Mrs. Chan speaks some English. The referral requests a home visit to assess health needs, immunization status, and knowledge of sources of health care.

Doris reviews previous learning in anticipation of her initial home visit and assessment of the family. She brings many skills such as interviewing, knowledge of pediatrics, and adult health, and specific nursing care skills. She reviews what is expected in terms of growth and development parameters for each family member. She also reviews the grieving process, its effect on the widow and the children, and supportive interventions. To

The Public Health Center is one setting in which community health nurses work.

The community health nurse reviews a referral before making a home visit.

As the nurse enters the neighborhood of her clients, she observes the density of housing, the bus services, and other aspects of the community.

The nurse visits a neighborhood store to assess the types and price of foods available.

Arriving at the client's apartment building.

Many nationalities are represented here. If she has difficulty locating the family, the nurse may seek help from the apartment house manager.

After knocking on the door, it is important for the nurse to announce who she is, as some people will not respond to a knock on the door for safety reasons.

The nurse presents her card from the health department and states the purpose of her visit.

The importance of social talk in establishing a relationship and trust is understood by the nurse and she takes time to chat with the family before beginning any tasks.

After first establishing a relationship with the adult, the nurse directs a question to a young child, who is far more comfortable on her mother's lap.

Periods of silence may be necessary while the client reflects on her thoughts and feelings.

The nurse may observe folk health practices during a home visit, which helps her learn more about the family health beliefs and needs.

A mutually agreed upon goal was keeping the daughter healthy.

Finding a source of dental care is agreed upon as a first priority, and a referral is made.

At the end of the home visit, the client accompanies the nurse to the elevator.

The nurse remains observant as she is leaving the client's apartment and notices children playing in a dark and poorly maintained hallway.

The client accompanies the nurse to the apartment building's front door.

The community health nurse returns to the health center and records the visit. Charting objectively and promptly and according to agency policy is part of the responsibility of making a home visit.

provide anticipatory guidance to the family, she will need to research areas in which she is lacking information or skill such as immunization needs, school requirements, and nutritional needs. She researches carefully the cultural health beliefs, values, and practices of the Chinese and Vietnamese (Erickson and Hoang, 1980; Muecke, 1983; Lappin and Scott, 1982; see Chapter 18). She collaborates with the Chinese community health nurse working in the health center for additional insight and guidance. She also investigates the health care resources and facilities available to refugee clients. She ensures that she has basic emergency telephone numbers to give to the family for ambulance, fire, and police service in their neighborhood. She reviews both agency policy and university or college policy regarding safety (see Chapter 8).

She engages in work on behalf of the family, known as *parafamily work,* to ready herself for the visit. If she has any questions about the family that must be answered (e.g., if the referral did not state the family's ability to speak English), she should contact the agency of referral. If necessary, she would then seek an interpreter through the agency to make the initial appointment and accompany her on home visits. She may also contact agencies with which she is unfamiliar that may provide needed services to the family. She will elicit from them information about criteria, location, available hours, and name of a contact for the family. Examples of such agencies for the Chan family include the local health department for immunizations, the medical center dental clinic for low-cost dental care, and several primary-care clinics at public and private hospitals. She will continue to do parafamily work throughout her visiting, as she contracts (see below) with the family and shares with them the exploration of resources.

Doris obtains a city map and rapid transit maps for both bus and subway. She familiarizes herself with the neighborhood in which the Chan family lives, where the nearest schools and hospitals are located, and the bus lines between the hospitals, other health care agencies, and where the family lives. She plans her own route and method of transportation to visit the family. She plans to visit during the day, if possible, but after school hours when Lee and May should be home.

She visits the neighborhood, engaging in a "community walk" in which she uses her five senses to observe and experience the community to familiarize herself before she makes her visit (see Chapter 5). She notes the high density of apartment housing, the high number of cars, the bus services, and the ages and numbers of people on the sidewalks. She notes children playing on the street, which is on a very steep hill. She notes that the busy, steep hill is the children's neighborhood, their community, their playground; that is where they spend their time. She also observes groups of older men clustered at streetcorners and talking. She observes the availability of grocery stores, largely "mom and pop" stores, and the lack of supermarkets. She enters one store near the Chan apartment and notes the availability and price of staples such as fresh produce, meat, rice, and milk; she plans to compare these prices with those of a supermarket in the suburbs. She also notes the location of the nearest pharmacy, private physician's offices, and clinics. The wide variety of entertainment available ranges from an elite theater to "adult" entertainment; she asks herself if these are types of entertainment her family may choose or could afford to choose.

Initial Contact Because Mrs. Chan has a telephone and speaks English, Doris calls for an appointment, announcing, "My name is Doris Wilson. I am a student community health nurse from the University, working with the San Francisco Health Department. The Intercultural Agency is concerned about how you and the children are doing and if you have found places to get health care. They have asked me to stop by and visit you. I would like to see Lee and May, too. I have time on Tuesday or Thursday at 3:00 P.M. It would probably take about an hour. Would 3:00 P.M. allow me to visit after school is out?"

As mentioned in Chapter 8, if families do not have telephones, the community health nurse may stop by the home and ask for an appointment for a later time that is convenient to the family. The nurse must be prepared for a visit, however, even when "dropping by" with a note, as the family may be very receptive, invite the nurse in, and proceed with a visit. When the family is not home, a card from the agency with a message asking them to call the nurse or setting a tentative time when the nurse will stop by again should be left on the door. Leaving personal cards or other messages in a mailbox is illegal. However, a note with a card may be mailed to the family. If there still is no response within 1 week, the nurse should return to the home and ask the apartment manager and neighbors if the family is still living in the residence. Apartment managers can aid in helping nurses locate families. How to deal with family members who are reluctant or never present for a family interview, particularly men and fathers, is reviewed by Wright and Leahey (1984). Letting reluctant family members know they have a unique and important view of the family, one only they can provide, is important. The nurse must also realize that some families will reject visits by not being at home at the arranged time, by simply not answering the door, by closing it once they identify who is there, or by asking the nurse not to return (Elkins, 1984).

Gaining Entrée Coordinating visits with bus schedules or parking meters is important to allow ample time for the student to devote complete attention to gaining entrée and carrying out a successful first home visit. Doris notes that there are many different names representing many different nationalities, including several families named "Chan," on the roster of the large apartment building and is thankful that the apartment number was noted on the referral. When Mrs. Chan answers through the speaker system, Doris announces clearly who she is, that she spoke with Mrs. Chan on the telephone, and that she is now here for the visit they agreed on.

Finding her way to the elevators and through the apartment maze, Doris walks down a darkly lit hallway, yet she notices a large hole in the hallway door with wooden splinters and makes a mental note of this environmental hazard. Doris knocks on the door, and states, "This is Doris Wilson, Mrs. Chan, the student community health nurse." It is important to announce who is knocking because for safety reasons, some people will not respond to a knock on the door. Mrs. Chan takes a moment to open the door, and Doris hears the shifting of several latches, a cue that safety may be a concern to the family. Doris realizes she is a guest, says hello, shakes Mrs. Chan's hand, and again states who she is, showing Mrs. Chan her university identification card and a card from the agency. She again states the purpose of her visit and sets the approximate time limit to the visit:

"I'm from the health department, and I'm a community nursing student at the university. The Intercultural Institute asked me to visit with you to talk about your family's immunizations and where you and your family might go to see a physician, nurse, or dentist. Here is my card with my name and office telephone number. I can stay about an hour, if that is all right with you."

She reassures the family that in the United States nurses make visits in the home and that she is not from the Immigration and Naturalization Service.

Assessment

Throughout the visit and on each succeeding visit, Doris assesses and reassesses the family in its home environment within its particular neighborhood in the community. Doris uses the conceptual framework of systems theory to organize her approach to the family. Her view of the community as a suprasystem and the family as a system composed of subsystems will help her not only to organize the data she collects during the assessment phase but also to carry out the other steps of the nursing process at the individual, family, and community levels. In assessing the family as client, Doris is aware that data about the family should be collected from as many members of the family as possible to accurately reflect its situation rather than from one individual only.

Developing rapport and trust between the community health nurse and the family is essential (Spradley, 1985). There may be a natural reluctance on the part of the student to enter the family's territory and to do so without "props" such as stethoscopes, blood pressure cuffs, and thermometers relied on so heavily in the acute care setting. There may be a tendency to immediately take the client's blood pressure, for example, so the nurse will feel more comfortable with something familiar to do. Leahy et al. (1982) state that the social phase of the home visit is very important; it is during this phase that rapport can begin to be established.

The importance of social talk in establishing a relationship and as a means of assessment cannot be overstressed. Morgan and Barden (1985) examined nurses' interactions with perinatal patients during home visits and found that the majority of the nurses' visits (53.8%) were categorized by nurse-observers as "asks for information" or "gives information." Very few visits (7.9%) were reported as "seems friendly." Patients, however, agreed that the nurses were friendly to them and to others present. Nurses appeared to be more critical of visits than were patients. When focused on allowing the family to express itself, the social phase can cut down on information asking and giving by the nurse, promote friendly interaction, and elicit data appropriate to the assessment phase.

In a study by Berg and Helgeson (1984) of students' first home visits, time spent socializing during the first home visit ranged between 5% and 100%; 13 of 15 students reported obtaining important data during the socializing phase of the visit. Important verbal and nonverbal cues can be noted, e.g., smiling, maintaining eye contact, shaking hands, and inviting the student to sit down. Environmental as well as behavioral cues, when noted and mentioned, can serve to elicit a family's history, biographical aspects, and biographical exchange between the nurse and the family. For example, noting photographs of family members, a record collection, types of books and magazines, or plants or pets can serve as cues that elicit much information about the family because such cues are based on the family's world, and their response interprets the meaning of that world as the family sees it. That is not to discount health-related cues such as bottles of Alka-Seltzer or commercial soups in the home of a family member on a low-sodium diet or herbal teas and folk treatments in the home of an immigrant, but the nurse should concentrate on establishing a trusting relationship before discussing health-related topics.

Fostering the relationship involves letting the family express their concerns before bringing up sensitive topics such as source of income. Agency assessment forms need not always be completed on the first visit; they can best be completed after the relationship is established. For example, Doris says hello to May, who is clinging to her mother, and to Lee, who is working on a puzzle, but knowing the respect due elders in Asian cultures, she directs her main conversation first to Mrs. Chan. Comments may be made about everyday topics such as the weather and about the family. "How long have you been here?" "Where is the rest of your family?" "What are the neighbors like?" The social phase, which should be repeated as an informal phase at the beginning of each visit, sets the stage for the rest of the visit. It is a way to informally check-in with the family to find out what is happening in their world, and it prepares the family for the more-focused phase of the visit by giving them a chance to renew their acquaintance with the nurse and to relax.

Having created a social footing on which the nurse and the family establish communication and rudimentary elements of trust, the focused phase of the visit allows the nurse and family to communicate more intensely around areas of concern to each and to determine needs, plans, and actions that need to be taken.

In this phase, the use of focused questions can elicit more details about the family important to assessment, such as the following. "Tell me how you got to San Francisco." (This may elicit a life review.) "Tell me, how do you spend your day?" (This may elicit activities of daily living or social interaction or lack thereof.) This question is repeated at different times with other members of the family.

In addition to gaining the information above, the community health nurse is able to observe family dynamics. This includes the relationships and patterns of communication among family members, roles that are taken, the division of labor or how things get done, and whether the family as a system is open or closed (see "The Family Theory Approach to Meeting the Health Needs of Families"). The nurse uses the five senses in making an ongoing assessment, attending to what is seen, heard, felt, smelled, and on occasion, even tasted.

Doris directs a question to May: "How old are you, May?" May, sitting on her mother's lap, grins and buries her face in her mother's shoulder, without verbally responding. Mrs. Chan states that May will be starting kindergarten in the fall, and she expresses her concern that May has not been to a dentist and that she would like to take her now so she will be ready for school. In addition, neither Lee nor Mrs. Chan has received dental hygiene. Mrs. Chan does not know if May needs an immunization. Mrs. Chan invites Doris into the kitchen where she keeps a shoebox full of papers. She shows Doris all their immunization records. Doris, prepared for the visit, assesses that May needs her fifth diphtheria-pertussis-tetanus immunization (second booster) and must have it before school starts.

A corner at the kitchen table in the small apartment gives Doris a chance to talk to Mrs. Chan alone.

"How are *you* doing, Mrs. Chan?" (Mrs. Chan is silent.) Nursing students bring communication and psychiatric skills with them to the community setting. The community health nurse knows to allow periods of silence while the client reflects on her thoughts and feelings.

"My husband is gone. . . ." [Mrs. Chan covers her face with her hands.]

"It must be hard to be alone . . . and with the children," Doris reflects. [Mrs. Chan shakes her head.] "I don't want to talk right now," she says. Doris realizes that support at a later date, once rapport is better established, is appropriate. A sensitive issue such as this cannot be pushed, but it must not be overlooked in the long term. Assessment will continue on a following visit, perhaps when the children are in school. She notes mentally that she will need to assess at a later date the children's response to their father's death.

Doris observes several unusual kinds of teas and asks Mrs. Chan if she uses any special medicines. Mrs. Chan shows Doris one of the special teas she uses when May has an upset stomach. She details that each of the different teas has a use for a specific ailment. An important exchange occurs, and Doris has the opportunity to learn of the folk health practices of the family.

Doris observes the kitchen, in particular, the techniques of food storage of new refugees. Many refugee families are unfamiliar with how to prepare foods for storage and are unaware of which foods need refrigeration. Assessment of these seemingly routine food-handling tasks and instruction requires tact and ingenuity.

Doris summarizes in her mind the following areas as appropriate to consider in her assessment of the Chan family:

Individual

- Language ability of individual members
- Sex role–related behavior of family members
- Lifestyle patterns that place individuals at risk, e.g., poor diet, inadequate exercise, use of alcohol or drugs, and so on
- Patterns of self-care in health and illness
- How leisure time is spent
- Utilization of preventive health services (physical examinations, dental hygiene, immunizations)

Family

- Family configuration; traditional beliefs and signs of acculturation
- Division of household labor and decision-making patterns

- Pattern of parenting
- Ability of family members to disclose feelings to each other and to others
- Ability of family members to give emotional and physical support to each other during times of crisis and of noncrisis
- How family members process grief
- Family history of morbidity and mortality
- Family interaction with groups in neighborhood and community

Community

- Resources available to the family, particularly Asian refugee families, in the community, such as school, sports, or religious activities
- Physical environment of apartment, building, and neighborhood
- Resources in the community for recreation and leisure
- Neighborhood safety

Diagnosis

Doris mentally makes a nursing diagnosis for each individual in the family and a tentative diagnosis for the family as a whole and poses community diagnoses. Ross and Helmer (1988) state that nursing diagnoses for the *individual* usually stem from using approaches such as a structural/functional framework, lifestyle, activities of daily living, and symptomatology. These authors state that nursing diagnoses for a *family* often differ from those for the individual and are developed from using approaches such as a systems framework, structural/functional framework, problems in communication or roles, and value conflicts.

Individual

- Alterations in health maintenance related to lack of routine dental hygiene (May, Lee, and Mrs. Chan)
- Alterations in health maintenance related to lack of immunizations for age (Carpenito, 1984) (May)
- Grieving related to loss of husband (Mrs. Chan)
- Knowledge deficit related to language and cultural differences (Mrs. Chan)

Family

- Alterations in health maintenance related to failure to seek health care despite awareness that such health care is needed
- At risk of family crisis due to prolonged stress secondary to premature death of father
- Alteration in family processes related to situational cross-cultural relocation
- Potential accidental wound related to faulty maintenance of apartment building environment

Community

- Inadequate systematic programs for linking Asian refugee families to community resources

● Inadequate systematic programs for maintaining environmental safety of apartment dwellers due to faulty upkeep of buildings

---

Sources of Nursing Diagnoses in the Community

THE FOLLOWING resources are available to aid in the formulation of appropriate nursing diagnoses in the community.

Alex, W. M.: Nursing diagnosis with the family and community. *In* Logan, B. B., and Dawkins, C. E., eds.: Family Centered Nursing in the Community. Menlo Park, California, Addison-Wesley, 1983, pp. 227–246.

Hamilton, P.: Community nursing diagnosis. Adv. Nurs. Sci. 5;21–36, 1983.

Houldin, A., Salstein, S., and Ganley, K.: Nursing Diagnoses for Wellness. Philadelphia, J. B. Lippincott, 1987.

Lee, H. A., and Frenn, M. D.: The use of nursing diagnoses for health promotion in community practice. Nurs. Clin. North Am. 22;981–986, 1987.

Martin, K. S., and Scheet, N. J.: The Omaha System: A Pocket Guide for Community Health Nursing. Philadelphia, W. B. Saunders Company, 1992.

Muecke, M. A.: Community health diagnosis in nursing. Public Health Nurs. 1;23–35, 1984.

Neufeld, A., and Harrison, M. J.: The development of nursing diagnoses for aggregates and groups. Public Health Nurs. 7;251–255, 1990.

Porter, E.: Administrative diagnosis—Implications for the public's health. Public Health Nurs. 4;247–256, 1987.

Porter, E.: The nursing diagnoses of population groups. *In* McLane, A., ed.: Classification of Nursing Diagnoses: Proceedings of the Seventh Conference. St. Louis, C. V. Mosby, 1987, pp. 306–314.

Planning

In Morgan and Barden's (1985) study of nurse-clients interaction on home visits, both nurses and clients "were uncertain as to whether or not they had agreed on goals to work toward" (p. 165). The authors conclude that the client should be more involved in the process of goal setting. Planning with the family is essential. Planning involves mutual goal setting between nurse and family; mutual setting of objectives to meet goals; prioritizing, or setting short- and long-term goals with the family; contracting, or establishing the division of labor between nurse and family that will meet the objectives; and evaluation of the process and outcome.

Contracting is defined as "any working agreement, continuously renegotiable, between nurse and clients" (Sloan and Schommer, 1991, p. 306). The purpose of the contract is to delineate jointly the change needed and how it will come about. Contracting carried out jointly will involve the family as an active participant. In a study of contracting by senior community health nursing students, Helgeson and Berg (1985) found that contracts were rated as important to the majority of students and families but were not appropriate to all. For example, written contracts were not appropriate for families who did not read or write. Written and oral contracts were not appropriate for families in crisis situations. And some families did not grasp the idea of a contract and did not agree to its use.

Individual

Short-term Goals

Doris planned and contracted verbally with Mrs. Chan around a mutually agreed-on goal: keeping May healthy so she will be ready for school. Receiving dental care for May was a priority for Mrs. Chan, who stated she would seek the immunization after the source of dental care was found. Doris agreed to Mrs. Chan's plan, realizing that the dental care may have a more visible, concrete outcome for the family and thus reinforce the benefits of the family's efforts in seeking this care. Doris offered a known resource to Mrs. Chan, the dental clinic at the medical center. Mrs. Chan felt she could take May by bus to the clinic but asked if Doris would call for an appointment for her "because I'm still afraid to speak on the phone." Doris answers, "I'll be glad to call. It can be difficult until you practice. I'll make this call and then you can try the next call, later, for the immunizations." An informal contract has now been established with the student calling first and giving Mrs. Chan support in her ability to try and make the second call, later, for the immunizations. Mrs. Chan and Doris then set a time frame in which Doris would call and make the appointment and inform Mrs. Chan, and Mrs. Chan agreed to keep the appointment time with May. A brief, reasonable, specific, and realistic contract is more likely to lead to the desired outcome. In addition, contracts must be continually reviewed, evaluated, and negotiated anew (Helgeson and Berg, 1985).

Long-term Goal

Doris noted mentally the long-term need of teaching the importance of immunizations.

Family

Short-term Goal

Short-term plans included assisting the family in expressing their feelings of loss in the grieving process.

Long-term Goal

Long-term plans included fostering the ability of the family to find and use appropriate support services for both physical and mental care.

Community

Short-term Goal

In addition to planning at the family level, Doris was aware that planning was needed at the community level. For example, she planned to identify existing programs that specifically addressed the physical and mental health needs of Asian refugees and to see if coordination of such programs included creating awareness of the programs in the referral systems of agencies such as the Intercultural Institute.

Long-term Goal

Planning at the community level also included an investigation into the process of how to initiate responsibility for obtaining repairs to the inner-city apartment in which the Chan family lives.

Intervention

Doris realized that many interventions would need to be carried out at the individual, family, and community levels.

Individual An example of an intervention at the individual level is referral for preventive health examinations for each family member.

Family At the family level, an example of an intervention is referral to a support group for the family's experience of grief.

Wright and Leahey (1984) categorize direct interventions offered by the nurse as those directed at family functioning at the following levels:

- cognitive
- affective
- behavioral

At the cognitive level, new information is provided to the family, usually educational, that promotes problem solving by the family. An example would be giving to Mrs. Chan the location of a dental care resource and information regarding the immunization needed by May. At the affective level, families are encouraged to express intense emotions that may be blocking their efforts at problem solving. An example would be Doris' planned validation of Mrs. Chan's emotions to allow her to work through the grieving process. Finally, at the behavioral level, tasks are negotiated to be carried out either during the family interview or as homework between visits. An example is the dental appointment to which Mrs. Chan will take May between visits. The nurse may also counsel a family to stop doing something it is doing, using changes in the same three areas above — providing information; encouraging the expression of affect that may be acting as a barrier, such as anger; and jointly assigning tasks to be carried out.

Community In addition, Doris realizes she has already used the referral process. She must engage in self-preparation and ongoing parafamily work to identify how the community is mobilized to provide physical and mental health care to families of refugees. Does anyone at the dental clinic speak Chinese or Vietnamese? Are there interpreters there and at the health department? At the clinics and the hospitals? If any exist, where are they? Where do most refugee families receive health care? Social support? Is there anyone working with widows? Are there any English-as-a-second language classes for Asians? Are there any job skills courses or programs for women approaching midlife? Questions such as these bring up many areas of assessment she will need to make with the Chan family and the community in the future, but her visit is over, and she must plan ongoing evaluation and terminate the visit.

Evaluation

Evaluation includes taking note of progress made during two phases: the on-going process of carrying out the contract, and the outcome at the termination of the relationship and the home visits (Helgeson and Berg, 1985).

Individual Doris reviews the basic informal contract with Mrs. Chan that will lead to an appointment and dental care for May. Doris will evaluate with Mrs. Chan the progress made during the next home visit.

Family Upon termination of visiting the family, Doris will evaluate the overall outcomes for the family in terms of changes in risk factors and health status. Using a systems approach, she will evaluate each component of the system, individual family members, dyads within the family, and the family as a whole in terms of goal achievement. For example, she will note if the family system is open or closed, the degree of equilibrium established, and the degree of change on the part of the family in finding and seeking care in the suprasystem.

Community In addition to evaluating the family system, she will also evaluate the ability of the suprasystem — the community — to provide culturally acceptable health resources and environmental safety needed by the family and will continue to intervene at the community level as needed to ensure that these resources are available to this and other families in the future.

Terminating the Visit

At the end of the home visit, Doris reviewed the needs that were identified and summarized the plan that each would carry out. Doris asked the family if they had any questions and instructed Mrs. Chan to call her at the number of the agency on the card she had given her upon entry to the home. They jointly agreed on a date and time for the next home visit, planning to meet earlier in the day before Lee was home from school, when May would have a neighbor with whom to play to allow them more privacy. Doris also set realistic expectations to the visits by telling Mrs. Chan that she would be available to visit her over the course of the next 12 weeks.

As she leaves, she notices that May and a friend are now playing in a darkly lit hallway. A large hole in the hallway door with wooden splinters reminds her that nurses in the community need to be aware of the environmental conditions that their families are encountering. With this information, to which most other health professionals do not have access, the nurse can act as an advocate and collaborator in mobilizing the community to take action in addressing housing and environmental health concerns. Mrs. Chan accompanies Doris to the entrance of the apartment building as she leaves.

Postvisit

The community health nurse is not finished with the visit. She must return to the agency and record the visit. Should Mrs. Chan call and need a visit before she returns to the field the following week, the community health nurse who responds to her call will know that a visit was made, what occurred, and what are the future plans. The observations made should be recorded objectively, and the charting carried out according to agency format and policy. A written referral may need to be made to the dental clinic. The referral from the Intercultural Institute must be answered and returned.

As she considers future plans for her visits, Doris feels overwhelmed, that she has only assessed the tip of the iceberg. She feels that there is much more she needs to know about Mrs. Chan, May, and Lee. She also feels she needs to carefully review how to assess the family as a whole. Are they a closed or open system? How does Mrs. Chan get support? What kind of friends does Lee have? What roles does he play in the family, now that he is without a father? How do culture and the process of acculturation affect family functioning? What are the family's resources, both financial and social?

In addition to questions about the family, Doris had many questions about other families who were faced with similar conditions. Cues from the home visit triggered thinking about the needs of larger aggregates: single parent refugee families; women in midlife without English-speaking skills, education, or job skills; and preteenagers and teenagers who enter U.S. schools with little English-speaking ability. What supports or group activities are available to meet their special needs?

Levels of Prevention

Society's expectations of the family are in transition. Application of the levels of prevention to families by the community health nurse must take into account the changing family configuration; the financial, emotional, and physical burdens often compounded in the single parent family; and the lack of resources such as health insurance or adequate health insurance experienced by many families today.

Primary Examples of primary prevention for the Chan family are applied at the individual, family, and community levels.

Individual. Assessment, teaching, and referral related to self-care behaviors such as immunization and dental hygiene

Family. Teaching, role-modeling, and reinforcing roles that allow family members to express feelings

Community. Providing health centers in the community where culturally acceptable preventive services are readily available to Southeast Asian refugees

Secondary Examples of secondary prevention for the Chan family are applied at the individual, family, and community levels:

Individual. Screening for dental caries, cervical cancer, and alterations in growth and development

Family. Screening for risk factors related to family dysfunction concerning how stress is processed by the family

Community. Organizing screening programs in community centers and distributing informative flyers in multiple languages in markets where non–English-speaking persons shop for native foods

Tertiary Examples of tertiary prevention for the Chan family are applied at the individual, family, and community levels:

Individual. Assist family members to express feelings related to grief in loss of father or husband. Assist family members to seek repair of dental caries.

Family. Assist family to deal with grief, assume flexible roles, and support each other in other ways.

Community. Assist community to provide support services for widows and families experiencing grief.

SUMMARY

This chapter has highlighted the community health nurse's work with families. Families have major health care needs that have been little addressed by the health care system. The nature of the family is changing, challenging traditional definitions and configurations. Approaches to meeting the health needs of families must go beyond that of the traditional health care system, which addresses the individual as the unit of care. Strategies are given for expanding notions of care from the individual to the family and from the family to the community. Common theoretical frameworks used to guide intervention with families from the disciplines of psychology or social psychology have been traditionally relied on by nurses. These frameworks often target individuals; frameworks are needed that go beyond the individual to the family and community and address social and policy changes needed to alter the social, economic, and environmental conditions under which families must function. Tools are provided for assessing the family and the family within the community. Provided are examples of the extension of family health intervention to larger aggregates, which involves social action to overcome constraints to accessing health services. Nonnursing and community health nursing models of care provided for communities of families are presented and critiqued. The nursing process is applied at the individual, family, and community levels on a home visit. Finally, examples of interventions by the community health nurse at individual, family, and community levels are presented.

L e a r n i n g
A c t i v i t i e s

1. With a group of three of your colleagues, each define the term "family". Compare your definitions and list similarities and differences. Develop a list of criteria for being a member of a family.

2. Complete a genogram for your family of origin. What are the high-risk factors in your family history? Current risk factors? Categorize current risk factors into physical, interpersonal, and environmental. Identify needed health education, and determine who needs the education. Identify sources of appropriate screening in the community for the risk factors identified.

3. Complete an ecomap for your current "family," however defined. What is your assessment as to the category of your family as an "open" or "closed" family system? What resources are currently used by your family for mental, physical, emotional, social, and community health? What referrals are needed?

RECOMMENDED READINGS

Austin, J. K.: Assessment of coping mechanisms used by parents and children with chronic illness. Am. J. Maternal Child Nurs. *15*;98–102, 1990.

Bappert, K. G.: Intervention strategies with multiproblem families: A structural-functional approach. J. Comm. Health Nurs. *6*;25–29, 1989.

Bomar, P. J.: Nurses and Family Health Promotion: Concepts, Assessment, and Interventions. Baltimore, Williams & Wilkins, 1989.

Bomar, P. J.: Perspectives on family health promotion. Family Comm. Health *12*;12–20, 1990.

Carey, R.: How values affect the mutual goal setting process with multiproblem families. J. Comm. Health Nurs. *6*;7–14, 1989.

Foster, R., Hunsberger, M. M., and Anderson, J. J.: Family-Centered Nursing Care of Children. Philadelphia, W. B. Saunders, 1989.

Fox, M. A.: The community health nurse and multiproblem families. J. Comm. Health Nurs. *6*;3–5, 1989.

Gilliss, C. L., Highley, B. L., Roberts, B. M., and Martinson, I. M.: Toward a Science of Family Nursing. Menlo Park, California, Addison-Wesley, 1989.

Logan, B. B., and Dawkins, C. E.: Family-Centered Nursing in the Community. Menlo Park, California, Addison-Wesley, 1986.

Lux, K. M.: Innovations in family and community health. Good health is good business: Prenatal health education in the work place. Family Comm. Health *12*;77–79, 1989.

Philips, B. U.: The forgotten family: An untapped resource in cancer prevention. Family Comm. Health *11*;17–31, 1989.

Swanson, J. M., Swenson, I., Oakley, D., and Marcy, S.: Community health nurses and family planning services for men. J. Comm. Health Nurs. *7*;87–96, 1990.

Vahldieck, R. K., Reeves, S. R., and Schmelzer, M.: A framework for planning public health nursing services to families. Public Health Nurs. *6*;102–107, 1989.

ADDITIONAL READINGS ON GAY PARENTING

Bozett, F. W.: Gay fathers: How and why they disclose their homosexuality to their children. Family Rel. *29*;173–179, 1980.

Bozett, F. W.: Parenting concerns of gay fathers. Topics Clin. Nurs. *6*;60–71, 1984.

Bozett, F. W.: Gay and Lesbian Parents. New York, Praeger, 1987.

Bozett, F. W.: Social control of identity by children of gay fathers. West. J. Nurs. Res. *10*;550–565, 1988.

Hanson, S. M., and Bozett, F. W., eds.: Dimensions of Fatherhood. Beverly Hills, California, Sage, 1985.

Hanson, S. M., and Bozett, F. W.: The changing nature of fatherhood: The nurse and social policy. J. Adv. Nurs. *11*;719–727, 1986.

Skeen, P., Walters, L., and Robinson, B.: How parents of gays react to their children's homosexuality and to the threat of

AIDS. J. Psychosoc. Nurs. Mental Health Serv. *26*;6–10, 1988.

Wismont, J. M., and Reame, N. E.: A lesbian childbearing experience: Assessing developmental tasks. Image: J. Nurs. Sch. *21*;137–141, 1989.

REFERENCES

Allmond, B. W., Buckman, W., and Gofman, H. F.: The Family is the Patient. St. Louis, C. V. Mosby, 1979.

American Public Health Association: The Definition and Role of Public Health Nursing in the Delivery of Health Care. Washington, D.C., APHA, 1981.

Anderson, M. P., O'Grady, R. S., and Anderson, I. L.: Public health nursing in primary care: Impact on home visits. Public Health Nurs. *2*;145–152, 1985.

Archbold, P.: Impact of parent caring on middle-age offspring. J. Gerontol. Nurs. *6*;79–85, 1980.

Auger, J. R.: Behavioral Systems and Nursing. Englewood Cliffs, New Jersey, Prentice-Hall, 1976.

Baines, E.: Caregiver stress in the older adult. J. Comm. Health Nurs. *1*;257–263, 1984.

Barkauskas, V. H.: Effectiveness of public health nurse home visits to primiparous mothers and their infants. Am. J. Public Health *73*;573–579, 1983.

Barker, P.: Basic Family Therapy. Baltimore, University Park Press, 1981.

Berg, C., and Helgeson, D.: That first home visit. J. Comm. Health Nurs. *1*;207–215, 1984.

Berry, J. W.: Ecological analyses for cross-cultural psychology. *In* Warren, N., ed.: Studies in Cross-Cultural Psychology. New York, Academic Press, 1980, pp. 157–189.

Blum, H. L.: Expanding Health Care Horizons. 2nd Ed. Oakland, California, Third Party Publishing Co., 1983.

Brody, H.: The systems view of man: Implications for medicine, science and ethics. Perspectives Biol. Med. *17*;71–91, 1973.

Brooten, D., Kumar, S., Brown, L., et al.: A randomized clinical trial of early hospital discharge and home follow-up of very-low-birthweight infants. N. Engl. J. Med. *315*;934–939, 1986.

Carpenito, L. J.: Handbook of Nursing Diagnosis. Philadelphia, J. B. Lippincott, 1984.

Carter, E., and McGoldrick, M.: The family life cycle and family therapy: An overview. *In* Carter, E., and McGoldrick, M., eds.: The Family Life Cycle: A Framework for Family Therapy. New York, Gardner Press, 1980, pp. 3–28.

Clements, I. W., and Roberts, F. B., eds.: Family Health: A Theoretical Approach to Nursing Care. New York, John Wiley & Sons, 1983.

Conrad, P., and Schneider, J. W.: Deviance and Medicalization: From Badness to Sickness. St. Louis, C. V. Mosby, 1980.

Corbin, J., and Strauss, A. L.: Collaboration: Couples working together to manage chronic illness. Image J. Nurs. Scholarship *14*;109–115, 1984.

Dawson, D. A.: Report on children with physical, mental, behavioral, and social problems, by family structure, 1988. Family Structure and Children's Health: United States, 1988. National Health Interview Survey. Vital Health Statistical

Series 10. No. 178. Washington, D.C., U.S. Government Printing Office, DHHS publication No. PH5 91-1506, 1991.

Department of Health and Human Services: Health Status of Minorities and Low Income Groups. Washington, D.C., U.S. Government Printing Office, DHHS publication No. (HRSA) 271-848/40085, 1991.

Diekelmann, N.: Primary Health Care of the Well Adult. New York, McGraw-Hill, 1977.

Dreher, M. C.: The conflict of conservatism in public health nursing education. Nurs. Outlook 30;504–509, 1982.

Duff, R. S., and Hollingshead, A. B.: Sickness and Society. New York, Harper & Row, 1968.

Duffy, M. E., Mowbray, C. A., and Hudes, M.: Personal goals of recently divorced women. Image J. Nurs. Scholarship 22;14–17, 1990.

Dunn, H. L.: High Level Wellness. Arlington, Virginia, R. W. Beatty, Ltd., 1961.

Dutton, D. B.: Children's health care: The myth of equal access. In The Report of the Select Panel for the Promotion of Child Health: Better Health for Our Children: A National Strategy. Volume 4. Washington, D.C., U.S. Government Printing Office, DHHS publication No. 79-55071, 1981, pp. 357–440.

Duvall, E. M.: Marriage and Family Relationships. 5th Ed. Philadelphia, J. B. Lippincott, 1977.

Duvall, E. M., and Miller, B. C.: Marriage and Family Development. 6th Ed. New York, Harper & Row, 1985.

Edwards, L. H., Eyer, J., and Kahn, E. H.: The use of partners in undergraduate public health nursing. Public Health Nurs. 2;213–221, 1985.

Ehrenreich, J.: Introduction: The Cultural Crisis of Modern Medicine. In Ehrenreich, J., ed.: The Cultural Crisis of Modern Medicine. New York, Monthly Review Press, 1978, pp. 1–35.

Elkins, C. P.: Community Health Nursing: Skills and Strategies. Bowie, Maryland, Robert J. Brady Co, 1984.

Erickson, R. V., and Hoang, G. N.: Health problems among Indochinese refugees. Am. J. Public Health 70;1003–1006, 1980.

Erikson, E.: Childhood and Society. 2nd Ed. New York, W. W. Norton and Co., 1963.

Erkel, E. A.: Conceptions of community health nurses regarding low-income black, Mexican American, and white families: Part 2. J. Comm. Health Nurs. 2;109–118, 1985.

Farber, B.: Family and Kinship in Modern Society. Glenview, Illinois, Scott, Foresman and Co., 1973.

Festinger, L.: A Theory of Cognitive Dissonance. Stanford, California, Stanford University Press, 1957.

Ford, L. C.: The development of family nursing. In Hymovich, D., and Barnard, M., eds.: Family Health Care—General Perspectives. 2nd Ed. New York, McGraw-Hill, 1979, pp. 88–105.

Freeman, R.: Public Health Nursing Practice. 3rd Ed. Philadelphia, W. B. Saunders, 1963.

Friedman, M. M.: Family Nursing: Theory and Assessment. New York, Appleton-Century-Crofts, 1981.

Friedman, M. M.: Family Nursing: Theory and Assessment. 2nd ed. New York, Appleton-Century-Crofts, 1986.

Glaser, B., and Strauss, A. L.: Chronic Illness and the Quality of Life. St. Louis, C. V. Mosby, 1975.

Hartman, A.: Diagrammatic assessment of family relationships. Social Casework 59;465–476, 1978.

Hartman, A.: Finding Families: An Ecological Approach to Family Assessment in Adoption. Beverly Hills, California, Sage, 1979.

Helgeson, D. M., and Berg, C. L.: Contracting: A method of health promotion. J. Comm. Health Nurs. 2;199–208, 1985.

Helvie, C. O.: Community Health Nursing: Theory and Process. New York, Harper & Row, 1981.

Jamieson, M., and Martinson, I.: Comprehensive care built around nursing can keep the elderly at home. Nurs. Outlook 33;271–273, 1983.

Janz, K. C., and Burgess, B.: Home health care. Stanford Nurse 7;7–9, 1985.

Johnson, R.: Promoting the health of families in the community. In Stanhope, M., and Lancaster, J., eds.: Community Health Nursing: Process and Practice for Promoting Health. St. Louis, C. V. Mosby, 1984, pp. 330–360.

Jordhein, A. D.: Alternative life-styles and the family. In Reinhardt, A. M., and Quinn, M. D., eds.: Family-Centered Community Nursing: A Sociological Framework. St. Louis, C. V. Mosby, 1980.

Kaser, M. T., Bappert, K. G., Carlson, A., Sharland, C., and Stein, M. M.: Community health nursing intervention with high risk infants: An innovative interdisciplinary approach. J. Comm. Health Nurs. 1;5–20, 1984.

Keshet, H., and Rosenthal, K.: Single-parent fathers: A new study. In Mussen, P., Conger, J., and Kagan, J., eds.: Readings in Child and Adolescent Psychology. New York, Harper & Row, 1980, pp. 184–188.

Kleinman, J., Gold, M., and Makuc, M.: Use of ambulatory care by the poor: Another look at equity. Med. Care 19;1011–1029, 1981.

Kotelchuk, D.: Prognosis Negative. New York, Random House, 1976.

Kubler-Ross, E.: Death: The Final Stage of Growth. Englewood Cliffs, New Jersey, Prentice-Hall, 1975.

LaPlante, M. P.: Have the disadvantaged really achieved equal access to medical care? A reconsideration. Paper read at Annual Meeting, American Public Health Association, Montreal, Canada, November 1982.

Lappin, J., and Scott, S.: Intervention in a Vietnamese refugee family. In McGoldrick, M., Pearce, J. K., and Giordano, J., eds.: Ethnicity and Family Therapy. New York, Guilford Press, 1982, pp. 483–491.

Leahy, K. M., Cobb, M. M., and Jones, M. C.: Community Health Nursing. 4th Ed. New York, McGraw-Hill, 1982.

Lewis, O.: The culture of poverty. Sci. Am. 215;19–25, 1966.

Mahon, J., McFarland, J., and Golden, K.: De madres a madres: A community partnership for health. Public Health Nurs. 8;15–19, 1991.

Manley, M., and Graber, A.: Coronary prevention program in a community hospital. Heart Lung 6;1045–1049, 1977.

Martinson, I. M., Jamieson, M. K., O'Grady, B. O., and Sime, M.: The block nurse program. J. Comm. Health Nurs. 2;21–29, 1985.

Maslow, A.: Motivation and Personality. 2nd Ed. New York, Harper & Row, 1970.

McGoldrick, M.: Ethnicity and family therapy: An overview. In McGoldrick, M., Pearce, J. K., and Giordano, J., eds.: Ethnicity and Family Therapy. New York, Guilford Press, 1982, pp. 3–30.

McGoldrick, M., Pearce, J. K., and Giordano, J.: Ethnicity and Family Therapy. New York, Guilford Press, 1982.

Milio, N.: The Care of Health in Communities. New York, Macmillan, 1975.

Miller, C. A., Coulter, E. J., Fine, A., Adams-Taylor, S., and Schorr, L. B.: 1984 update on the world economic crisis and the children: A United States case study. Int. J. Health Serv. 15;431–450, 1985.

Morgan, B. S., and Barden, M. E.: Nurse-patient interaction in the home setting. Public Health Nurs. 2;159–167, 1985.

Morris, J. M.: A descriptive study of the practice of community health nurses with infants at risk for developmental disabilities. J. Comm. Health Nurs. 2;53–60, 1985.

Muecke, M. A.: Caring for Southeast Asian refugee patients in the USA. Am. J. Public Health 73;431–438, 1983.

Muecke, M. A.: Community health diagnosis in nursing. Public Health Nurs. *1*;23–35, 1984.

Mundinger, M.: Home Care Controversy: Too Little, Too Late, Too Costly. Rockville, Maryland, Aspen Systems, 1983.

National Center for Health Statistics: Health, United States, 1982. Hyattsville, Maryland, U.S. Public Health Service, 1983.

National Center for Health Statistics: Health, United States, 1984. Hyattsville, Maryland, U.S. Public Health Service, 1985.

National Center for Health Statistics: Health, United States, 1989. Hyattsville, Maryland, U.S. Public Health Service, 1990.

National Center for Health Statistics: Health, United States, 1990. Hyattsville, Maryland, U.S. Public Health Service, 1991.

National Center for Health Statistics: Health, United States, 1991. Hyattsville, Maryland, U.S. Public Health Service, 1992.

Norris, P.: Women in poverty: Britain and America. Soc. Policy *14*;41–43, 1984.

Nye, I., and Berardo, F.: Conceptual Frameworks for the Study of the Family. New York, Macmillan, 1966.

Olds, D. L., Henderson, C. R., Tatelbaum, R., and Chamberlin, R.: Improving the life-course development of socially disadvantaged mothers: A randomized trial of nurse home visitation. Am. J. Public Health *78*;1436–1445, 1988.

Papper, S.: The undesirable patient. *In* Schwartz, H., and Kart, C., eds.: Dominant Issues in Medical Sociology. Reading, Massachusetts, Addison-Wesley, 1978, pp. 166–168.

Pratt, L.: Family Structure and Effective Health Behavior. Boston, Houghton Mifflin, 1976.

Riessman, C. K.: The use of health services by the poor: Are there any promising models? Soc. Policy *14*;30–40, 1984.

Rogers, C.: Client-Centered Therapy. New York, Houghton Mifflin, 1951.

Ross, M. M., and Helmer, H.: A comparative analysis of Neuman's model using the individual and family as the units of care. Public Health Nurs. *5*;30–31, 1988.

Saluter, A. F.: Marital status and living arrangements: March 1989. *In* Current Population Reports. Washington, D.C., U.S. Bureau of the Census, series P-20, No. 445, 1990.

Select Committee on Children, Youth and Families: U.S. Children and Their Families: Current Conditions and Recent Trends. Washington, D.C., U.S. House of Representatives, 1983.

Sloan, M. R., and Schommer, B. T.: The process of contracting in community health nursing. *In* Spradley, B. W., ed.: Readings in Community Health Nursing. Philadelphia, J. B. Lippincott, 1991, pp. 304–312.

Smith, J. B.: Levels of public health. Public Health Nurs. *2*;138–144, 1985.

Spiegel, J.: An ecological model of ethnic families. *In* McGoldrick, M., Pearce, J. K., and Giordano, J., eds.: Ethnicity and Family Therapy. New York, Guilford Press, 1982, pp. 31–51.

Spradley, B. W.: Community Health Nursing: Concepts and Practice. 2nd Ed. Boston, Little, Brown & Co., 1985.

State of California Health and Welfare Agency. High-risk Infant Follow-up Recommendations for Home Intervention Services for High-risk Infants and Their Families in California. Sacramento, Department of Health Services, Maternal and Child Health Branch, 1982.

Steinglass, P.: Family systems approaches to alcoholism. J. Substance Abuse Treatment *2*;161–167, 1985.

Stern, P. N.: Conflicting family culture: An impediment to integration in stepfather families. J. Psychosoc. Nurs. Mental Health Serv. *20*;27–33, 1982*a*.

Stern, P. N.: Affiliating in stepfather families: Teachable strategies leading to stepfather-child friendship. West. J. Nurs. Res. *4*;75–89, 1982*b*.

Stranik, M., and Hogberg, B.: Transition into parenthood. Am. J. Nurs. *79*;90–93, 1979.

Strauss, A. L.: Medical Ghettos. New Brunswick, New Jersey, Transaction, 1976.

Strauss, A. L.: Where Medicine Fails. New Brunswick, New Jersey, Transaction, 1979.

Swanson, J. M.: Taking the sexual, reproductive, and contraceptive histories. *In* Swanson, J., and Forrest, K., eds.: Men's Reproductive Health. New York, Springer, 1984, pp. 342–358.

U.S. Bureau of the Census: Characteristics of the Population Below the Poverty Level, 1981. Washington, D.C., U.S. Department of Commerce, Consumer Income Series P60, No. 138, 1983.

Villareal, S., and Trevino, F.: Testimony on health of Hispanics before the House Energy and Commerce Subcommittee, September 20, 1985.

von Bertalanffy, L.: General Systems Theory: Foundations, Development, Applications. New York, George Braziller, 1968.

von Bertalanffy, L.: The history and status of general systems theory. *In* Klir, G., ed.: Trends in General Systems Theory. New York, John Wiley & Sons, 1972.

von Bertalanffy, L.: General systems theory and psychiatry. *In* Arieti, S., ed.: American Handbook of Psychiatry. New York, Basic Books, 1974, pp. 1095–1117.

Warhola, C.: Planning for Home Health Services — A Resource Handbook. Washington, D.C., U.S. Government Printing Office, DHHS publication No. HRA 80-14017, 1980.

Whorton, M. D.: Environmental and occupational reproductive hazards. *In* Swanson, J., and Forrest, K., eds.: Men's Reproductive Health. New York, Springer, 1984, pp. 193–203.

Wright, L. M., and Bell, J.: Nurses, families and illness: A new combination. *In* Freeman, D., and Trute, B., eds.: Treating Families With Special Needs. Ottawa, The Canadian Association of Social Workers, 1981, pp. 199–205.

Wright, L. M., and Leahey, M.: Nurses and Families: A Guide to Family Assessment and Intervention. Philadelphia, F. A. Davis, 1984.

Young, R. K.: Community Nursing Workbook: Family as Client. New York, Appleton-Century-Crofts, 1982.

CHAPTER

15

Senior Health

Upon completion of this chapter, the reader will be able to:

1. Identify the major indicators of senior health.

2. Describe the problems associated with aging.

3. Discuss the factors that promote senior health.

4. Coordinate support services for the elderly.

5. Plan appropriate nursing care for seniors in the community.

6. Discuss allocation of resources for senior health.

Olive T. Roen

The first goal for the health of the nation in the year 2000 (Healthy People—2000, 1990) is to increase the span of healthy life. The achievement of this goal will be confirmed by the visibility of active elderly people who continue to make valuable contributions to all aspects of community life. Failure to meet the goal will be demonstrated by the number of elderly people whose life is restricted by physical and mental handicaps before succumbing to a premature death. Nurses working in the community care for the elderly in any state of health that allows them to stay outside the hospital or nursing home.

The goal of health care for the elderly is to maximize the ability to perform activities of daily living rather than to focus on cure of pathology (Hickey, 1983; Kennie, 1983). I once heard a wise old physician say that the challenge of aging is to live in symbiosis with one's infirmities. These statements are not meant to imply that no cure should be sought for illness in older people, but rather that many diseases associated with aging might be more amenable to compromise than to cure. Health care for the elderly draws on a far wider base than do the more defined protocols of acute care for younger people. Surgery and medication are important, but social disability requires social remedy, much of which is within the competence of the nurse. Health care for elders requires a team approach that includes professionals sometimes not thought of as health care providers, and the nurse not only is one of the most important members of the team but also may provide the leadership necessary for a care-based orientation (Hickey, 1983; Martinson, 1984a, 1984b; Parker and Secord, 1988).

Myths of Aging

1. People over the age of 65 years are old.
2. Most older people are in poor health.
3. Older minds are not as bright as younger minds.
4. Older people are unproductive.
5. Older people are unattractive and sexless.
6. All older people are pretty much the same.

Data from Dychwald, K., and Flower, J.: Age Wave. Los Angeles, Tarcher, 1989.

To introduce you to the challenges and opportunities of the field, this chapter will present an overview of the elderly population, a discussion of the major age-related problems, and a review of some solutions directed to the goal of an improved quality of life in old age.

MAJOR INDICATORS OF THE HEALTH OF THE ELDERLY

Demographically, aging is defined by chronological age. As an aggregate, the elderly are considered to be people aged 65 or older. This aggregate is divided into subgroups. People between the ages of 65 and 74 are called the "young old" (this subgroup may soon include people as old as 84), those aged 75–84 are called the "aged," and those aged 85 or older are called the "old old" (U.S. Senate Special Committee on Aging, 1988) or the "oldest old" (U.S. Bureau of the Census, 1989). The "frail elderly" are elderly people who are dependent on others for their day-to-day care. Although dependency needs vary according to health status, the U.S. Bureau of the Census (1984) classifies those aged 80 years or older as "frail elderly." It should be remembered that these ages are arbitrary and were originally defined to facilitate the administration of social programs. For example, in Germany in 1884, the age of 65 was determined to be the entrance to old age; that country began its national pension program at a time when far fewer people lived long enough to need provision for retirement. Other nations subsequently followed Germany's lead. Terms are still evolving, and to complicate matters further, people aged 50–55 and older may be called the "older population," especially by advertising and business marketing executives defining their target groups.

The Elderly Population in the United States

The aggregate of the elderly is the most rapidly expanding section of the United States population. In 1900, people more than 65 years old made up just 4% of the population. In 1980, this age group accounted for 11.3%, and by 2050, 21.8% of the U.S. population is projected to be of this age group. The very old will account for the most dramatic increase. In 1900, only 123,000 people, or 0.2% of the U.S. population, were age 85 or older. By 1980, this group increased to 2.24 million people, or 1%, and by 2050, more than 16.03 million people, or

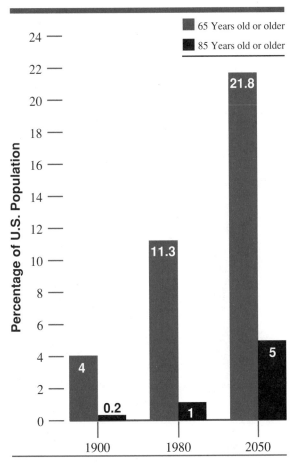

Figure 15–1
Actual and projected elderly population by specified age groups (1900–2050). (Redrawn from U.S. Senate Special Committee on Aging: Aging America: Trends and Projections, 1987–1988. Washington, D.C., Department of Health and Human Services, No. LR 3377(188)–D12198, 1988.)

more than 5% of the total population, are expected to be in this age group. This increase is due in large part to the increase in births before 1920 and after World War II, the control of communicable diseases, and a recent decrease in mortality among the middle-aged and elderly populations (U.S. Bureau of the Census, 1989; U.S. Senate Special Committee on Aging, 1988). The implications of this growth present a great challenge to future government policy-makers because the elderly are the greatest users of health services and, with advancing age, are in increasing need of various systems of support.

In 1990, there were more than 31 million people 65 years or older in the United States, 13 million aged 75 or older, and 3 million aged 85 or older. California had more than 3 million elderly residents, Florida and New York each had more than 2 million, and there were more than 1 million elderly residents in Pennsylvania, Texas, Illinois, Ohio, Michigan, and New Jersey. There were more than 1 million residents aged 75 and older in each state of California and New York (U.S. Bureau of the Census, 1992). The elderly are less likely to move than are other age groups; of those who do move, many seek homes in the South and Southwest for retirement. A small but significant number of retirees have begun to move back home, however, to be closer to family members. Agricultural states are likely to have a high proportion of elderly residents as younger people move away to seek opportunities elsewhere (U.S. Bureau of the Census, 1989; U.S. Senate Special Committee on Aging, 1988).

Mortality

Aging has a mortality of 100%. As a species, humans appear to have a natural life span of 85–100 years (Fries, 1980; Hayflick, 1974, 1980), but life always ends in death.

Mortality figures describe the quantity of life. In the United States, life expectancy at birth has increased from 49.2 years in 1900 to 75.0 years for those born in 1987. Life expectancy varies by sex and race, with the mortality rate for men exceeding that for women at every stage of life. The tendency of women to live longer than men is true of all ethnic groups, and it is not known if this is due to biological, environmental, or lifestyle differences. Of racial groups, whites have a greater life expectancy at birth (in 1987, 75.6 years for whites and 69.4 years for blacks) (U.S. Department of Health and Human Services, 1990b), but this ultimately changes. After age 80, life expectancy is higher for blacks than for whites (U.S. Department of Health and Human Services, 1988). Differences in life expectancy are decreasing, however, with decreases in socioeconomic variability. More research is needed on other lifestyle variables to determine their impact on longevity.

In 1986, the American Association of Retired Persons (AARP) reported 90% of elders to be white and 10% to be nonwhite. Hispanics comprise approximately 3% of the present elderly population but are the fastest growing segment. Minorities are projected to represent 30% of the elderly population by 2050.

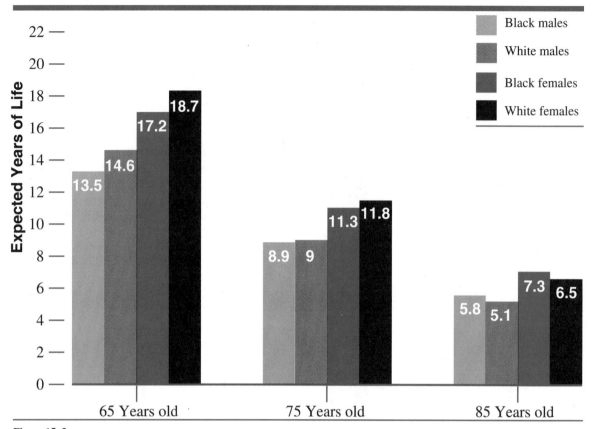

Figure 15–2
Life expectancy at specified ages by race and sex (United States, 1984). (Redrawn from National Center for Health Statistics: Health Statistics on Older Persons. Hyattsville, Maryland, Analytical and Epidemiological Studies. Series 3, No. 25, 1986.)

The leading cause of death for people more than 65 years old is heart disease. In 1988, the incidence of heart disease was 985.6 per 100,000 people of ages 65–74 and increased to a rate of 7,119.1 per 100,000 people at age 85 or older. Cancer is the second leading cause of death in this aggregate, with the largest increase in the 75- to 84-year-old group. It is replaced by cerebrovascular disease and stroke as the second leading cause of death in people more than 85 years old. The major acute causes of death are influenza, pneumonia, and accidents, with the incidence rates of all three increasing with age (U.S. Department of Health and Human Services, 1990*b*).

Morbidity

Morbidity statistics indicate the quality of life. They show where the U.S. population is on the wellness-illness continuum, and can direct the focus of the nurse in pursuit of better health for the aggregate. Most older people in the community describe their health as good to excellent, although many, if not most, of the elderly suffer from one or more chronic and degenerative diseases. Arthritis affects almost half the elderly population, followed in frequency by hypertensive disease. Hearing impairment and heart conditions afflict between one fourth and one third of the elderly. Other disabling conditions are orthopedic impairment, chronic sinusitis, cataracts and other vision problems, and diabetes (U.S. Department of Health and Human Services, 1988). Varicose veins, hemorrhoids, constipation, urinary tract diseases, hay fever, corns and callouses, and hernia of the abdominal cavity add to the list of common conditions.

Many elderly people are hospitalized for acute episodes of chronic conditions, often repeatedly for the same disease. Hospitalization is most often due to cardiac, circulatory system, digestive, or respiratory diseases or neoplasms. Only approximately 5% of the elderly receive nursing home care at any one time, but incidence of nursing home residence increases with age and loss of ability to provide self-care (U.S. Senate Special Committee on Aging, 1988).

It is interesting to note that older women report occurrences of both acute and chronic conditions more often than do elderly men; the only exception is for conditions that involve limitation of major activity. This apparently inconsistent finding that the longer-living female sex is also the less-healthy sex is interpreted in three ways. First, the diseases reported by men are more often chronic diseases that cause death, whereas diseases reported by women are more often acute diseases that respond to treatment. The second interpretation is that male morbidity is not fully reported and is actually much greater than the data show. Last, women are considered more likely to seek medical help when ill (U.S. Senate Special Committee on Aging, 1988).

Racial differences in morbidity in elderly people are not sufficiently documented, although more information is becoming available. Almost 47% of blacks and Hispanics of age 65 or older feel that they are in fair or poor health compared with less than 30% of whites (Ries, 1990). Much morbidity and mortality are related to socioeconomic factors. Reports from the National Indian Council on Aging in Albuquerque, New Mexico (Hispanic and Indian Elderly, 1989), demonstrate elevated death rates resulting from alcohol abuse, tuberculosis, diabetes, and pneumonia. Socioeconomic factors impact at least the first two of these diseases, possibly all of them.

Two opposing views of morbidity and aging are expressed by Fries (1980) and Schneider and Brody (1983). Fries proposed the ideal—that improved health in younger years will continue into old age and compress the degeneration associated with aging into a short period before death. This coincides with the Healthy People—2000 (U.S. Department of Health and Human Services, 1990*a*) goals for the United States. Schneider and Brody (1983) surveyed the present scene and suggested that more people will live longer with chronic diseases, which will require increased health care services as the population ages. Fries' view is an op-

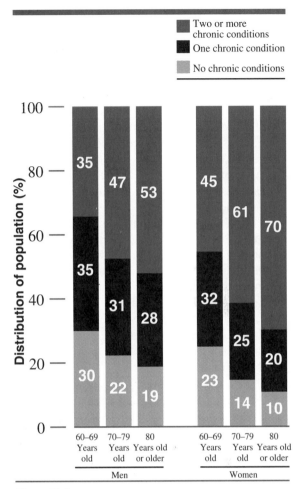

Figure 15–3
Percent distribution of population 60 years of age or older by number of chronic conditions according to age group and sex (United States, 1984). (Redrawn from National Center for Health Statistics: Aging in the Eighties: The Prevalence of Comorbidity and Its Association With Disability. Hyattsville, Maryland, Vital and Health Statistics, Series 3, No. 170, 1989.)

timistic prediction of long-term possibilities, whereas Schneider and Brody's opinion is based on the present reality and the foreseeable future. Taken together, they form their own continuum and are a useful goal and reference for the health care needs of the elderly as statistics on elderly health accumulate.

Health Behavior and Health Care

Continued good health is the major concern of the elderly (Archer et al., 1984). Health is considered good if lifestyle is not affected by physical or mental incapacity. Poor health threatens a feared dependence on others for the necessities of daily living, an embarrassing loss of body function, and loss of control over lifestyle, and warns of the imminence of death. Dr. Robert Butler, former head of the National Institute on Aging, said that the most necessary requirements for physical fitness are a nutritious diet and sufficient exercise to maintain good heart function and increase bone strength. He also emphasized the equal importance of social and psychological fitness, as manifest by a network of relationships and friends and continued goals for life (Today's senior citizens, 1984).

After 65 years of life, however, people do not arrive at the doorstep of old age unscarred but rather as a product of their genes, environment, and lifestyle. Habits, beliefs, attitudes, and values that have accumulated over the years may or may not promote health. Medical visits are expected. In 1986, the elderly made an average of nine visits to physicians compared with six or seven visits for those younger than 65 (U.S. Senate Special Committee on Aging, 1988).

Characteristics of Older Patients

Older patients are *not*:	Older patients *are:*
● Phony	● Punctual
● Well, but worried	● Flexible
● Chronically fatigued	● Polite
● Reckless	● Responsible
● Crybabies	● Postmenopausal

Adapted from Anderson, E. G.: Reflections on a practice going geriatric. Geriatrics 44(12);91–92, 1989.

The dental needs of the elderly are neglected. Despite need, the elderly are less likely to visit a dentist than are people younger than 65, usually because of financial reasons. Half of the elderly have no natural teeth, and about half of those with no teeth need dental care to ensure properly fitting dentures. Many of the elderly never visit the dentist. The loss of teeth leads to poor nutrition and causes a change in body image that leads to loss of self-esteem and withdrawal from the important supportive social network (Lebel, 1989).

The most common area of monitoring is blood pressure checks. Archer and colleagues (1984) reported a 1981 survey on the use of 14 services provided for the elderly in San Francisco. Blood pressure clinics headed the list. Apparently all ethnic and socioeconomic groups realize that blood pressure is important to health, although the parameters and reasons may not be understood. The advent of blood pressure machines in pharmacies and supermarkets has accelerated and supported this interest. Marion Laboratories estimate that 50% of blood pressure patients do not follow the medical advice they receive, so they made available a guide to wellness (Why Comply, 1990) to encourage people to take an active treatment role.

Growing older does not necessarily result in a decline in mental health comparable to that in physical health. Intellectual growth can continue; in the absence of disease, the lack of growth and challenge may predispose to decline and premature death. Growth is often related to high self-esteem as is given by continued success at work, although autonomy in employment may be a prerequisite (Dynamic elderly, 1984). Loss of autonomy or control almost always has a negative effect (Rowe and Kahn, 1987).

The lack of community mental health resources for the elderly is regretted by Hagebak and Hagebak (1983); the elderly are a sadly neglected and underserved group with special needs that are not understood by many therapists. They report that government programs intended to provide mental health services to the elderly have been weakened and underfunded to the point of being largely ineffective and that the provision of special services to the aged will be decided on a local level and be extremely fragmented and inadequate. Even if services are available, many elderly may be reluctant to seek them out owing to ignorance of the services offered, distrust, fear of being labeled mentally ill, or a belief that their condition is appropriate for their age.

Income

There is a direct relationship between income and the perception of health (U.S. Senate Special Committee on Aging, 1988) and feelings of loneliness (Cox et al., 1988).

In 1987, the median income for elderly people living alone was $8,390, and families headed by an elderly person had a median income of $20,810 that same year ($21,470 for whites, and $14,110 for blacks) (U.S. Bureau of the Census, 1989). In 1988,

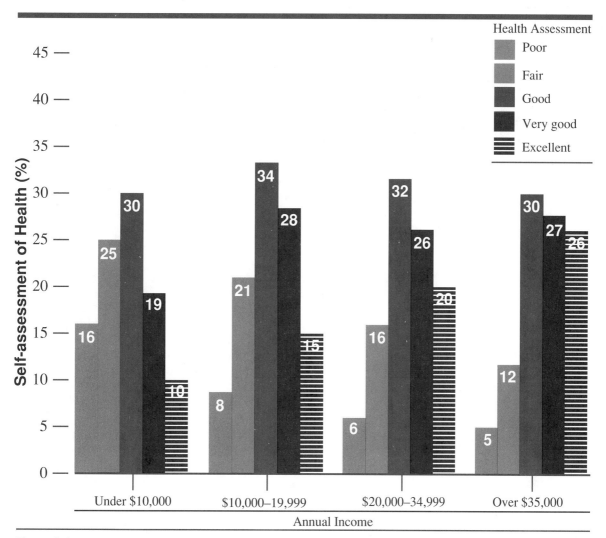

Figure 15–4
Self-assessment of health by income for persons 65 years of age or older (1989). (Redrawn from National Center for Health Statistics: Current estimates from the National Health Interview Survey, 1989. Hyattsville, Maryland, Vital and Health Statistics, Series 10, No. 176, October 1990.)

the average annual income for elderly Hispanics was $5,000–6,000, and for Native Americans, $3,500–4,500 (Rep. Bill Richardson, Hispanic and Indian Elderly, 1989).

Social Security benefits are the major source of income for the elderly, providing more than half of the total income for the majority of recipients. More than one third of recipients derive almost all of their income from this source. Earnings, interest on savings, and pension plans from other organizations provide other income (Facts and Figures, 1988).

Poverty is most likely to occur in households headed by women and minorities and among individuals not living with relatives (U.S. Bureau of the Census, 1989). Although a substantial number of elderly people live fairly close to the poverty level, most of the elderly are not considered poor. Reduction in family size as children leave home, lower taxes with lower income, and fewer or no work-related expenses may allow relatively more disposable income.

Many of the elderly want to work after retirement, but they usually prefer part-time work. The

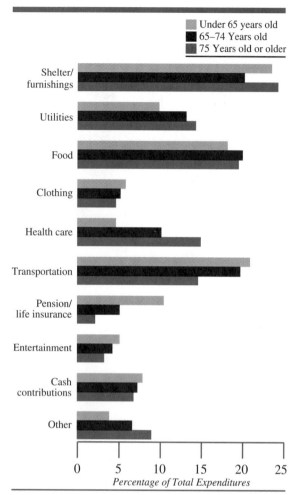

Figure 15–5
Consumer expenditures by type and age group (1984). (Redrawn from U.S. Bureau of Labor Statistics: Consumer Expenditure Survey: 1984 Interview. Washington, D.C., U.S. Department of Labor, Bulletin 2267, August 1986.)

companionship of other people and a feeling of purpose may be as important as the extra income.

In 1986, age-based mandatory retirement for most workers was abolished, but older people still face discrimination when competing with younger workers for jobs (U.S. Senate Special Committee on Aging, 1988).

Literacy and Education

As an aggregate, the elderly have had less formal schooling than later generations. In 1986, the median education received by the elderly was not quite 12 years. Almost half of the elderly had com-

pleted high school, and about one fifth had attended at least 1 year of college. Among the elderly, whites had higher educational levels than nonwhites (U.S. Senate Special Committee on Aging, 1988).

Almost 2% of the elderly report an inability to read and write. Functional illiteracy, which is the inability to read and write at an eighth grade level (the level of most newspapers and below the level of most government forms and health promotion material), is present in 20–25% of the population as a whole and probably is higher in the elderly, who have had less opportunity for formal schooling.

Marital Status, Relationships, and Living Arrangements

Women live longer than men, so it is not surprising that most older men are married (77%) and most older women are widowed (51%). Most elderly men live in a family situation, whereas most elderly women, especially those more than 75 years old, live alone. Widowed nonwhite women are more likely to live with other family members than are widowed white women (U.S. Senate Special Committee on Aging, 1988), but Alvin Korte warned those at the Hearing on Hispanic and Indian Elderly (1989) that the family was a fragile resource that was not always available and that the assumption that the elderly were held in high esteem and had strong intergenerational support was a myth. The increasing divorce rate of older people also contributes to the rising number of single elderly who maintain their own households.

However, most of the elderly live in an extended family situation. About 80% have one or more surviving children, live fairly close to at least one child, and have frequent contact with their child or children. Increasing numbers of the very old are dependent on children who also are elderly. Therefore, young family members may find themselves caring for two older generations. This can become an impossible burden, and the larger community may be increasingly called on to provide support.

Most elderly people own their own home, but an increasing number (currently about 25%) rent living space (U.S. Senate Special Committee on Aging, 1988). A significant number of elderly people cling tenaciously to inadequate housing. Many do not have a telephone, which can be a lifeline in case of emergency. Only about 5% of the elderly live in institutions such as nursing homes or boarding houses.

Religion

As people age, they become more committed to religious beliefs and participate more in church activities. More than 500,000 local churches and synagogues in the United States have a total membership of more than 140 million people. Only 4% of people between 50 and 69 years old and 3% aged 70 or older state that they have no religious affiliation.

Religious institutions have responded well to the needs of older people in their congregations and in the community at large by providing many services to assist them to continue to live at home and participate in community activities.

PROBLEMS OF THE ELDERLY

Most problems arise from the deterioration of physical and/or mental abilities possessed in the younger years. Harper (1985) stated that health in the elderly is not necessarily the absence of disease but rather the ability to live and function effectively in society and to exercise self-determination. The inability to do these things is perceived as a problem. This section will examine the impact made by various disorders on the performance of average activities of daily living by the elderly in the community.

Difficulties at Home

NUTRITION

Nutrition is a highly complex subject because food serves not merely the body but also the soul

---

Case Study: Nutrition
MRS. MILLER is an 84-year-old widow hospitalized with a history of weakness and weight loss. No organic condition was found that would explain these symptoms. One evening, Mrs. Miller told her nurse she could not shop for groceries any more, but Meals-on-Wheels delivered a hot meal on Monday, Wednesday, and Friday from which she "kept something back" to eat on the days on which no delivery was made. Mrs. Miller asked for reassurance that her nutrition was adequate.

(Schlenker, 1984). Recommended dietary allowances (RDAs) of nutrients for the elderly are currently controversial. The most recent RDAs for levels of essential nutrients required to meet the nutritional needs of healthy people were set by a subcommittee of the National Research Council in 1989, but special recommendations were not made for the elderly. Controversy centers on calcium and vitamin B-12 and B-6 requirements (Eastman, 1990) and on cholesterol levels (The latest word, 1990). Until specific RDAs are issued, recommendations apply to all adults over the age of 50.

Dietary Guidelines for Older People
THE FOLLOWING are recommended dietary allowances for daily intake for moderately active people aged 50 or older:

NUTRIENT	WOMEN	MEN
Calories	1,800	2,400
Protein	50 g	63 g
Vitamin A	4,000 I.U.	5,000 I.U.
Vitamin C	60 mg	60 mg
Thiamine	1 mg	1.2 mg
Riboflavin	1.2 mg	1.4 mg
Niacin	13 mg	15 mg
Calcium	800 mg	800 mg
Iron	10 mg	10 mg
Phosphorus	800 mg	800 mg
Fat	No more than 30% of total calories	
Cholesterol	Not to exceed 300 mg daily	
Sodium	Limit to 1,100–3,300 mg daily	
Fiber	Limit to 20–30 g daily, not to exceed 35 g	

Data from National Research Council: Recommended Dietary Allowances. 10th Ed. Report of the Subcommittee of the Tenth Edition of the RDAs, Food and Nutrition Board, Commission on Life Sciences. Washington, D.C., National Academy Press, 1989. Sodium recommendation from the American Heart Association; fiber recommendation from the National Cancer Institute.

If food is not appealing and there is no desire to eat, nutrition is not likely to be adequate. Even if prepared meals are delivered, they may not be eaten if food symbolizes family gatherings to a person now living alone or if cultural or religious tradition dictates that the ingredients would have been prepared differently. English tripe and onions cooked with milk is not interchangeable with highly spiced Tex-Mex menudo, and neither would appeal to other ethnic groups unaccustomed to such delicacies.

Loneliness, depression, grief, and anxiety are common reasons for altered eating habits. Too many old people exist on coffee and donuts and sink into malnutrition because such food satisfies hunger and is easily available when feelings of low self-esteem sap the energy required for the preparation of more nutritious food.

Kanak (1985) includes good nutrition with other self-care practices that provide maximum wellness. It is a major challenge for the nurse to identify the nutritional adequacy of food consumed by elderly clients and to piece together the resources available to meet deficiencies in shopping for food, preparing nutritious and appealing meals, and ingesting the food once it is prepared. Consistent good nutrition is probably the greatest single contribution to physical and mental health and gives the greatest return for the money and time invested. Malnutrition resulting from involuntary fasting leads to a delay in any healing process; lowering of the metabolic rate, body temperature, pulse rate, and blood pressure; dry and itchy skin; anemia; ulcerated mouth; abnormal heart rhythm; erosion of bone mineral; difficulty in walking; loss of sight and hearing; speech impairment; coma; and, ultimately, death (Graf, 1981).

Problems of Everyday Life for the Elderly

- Opening medicine packages
- Reading product labels
- Reaching things located high
- Fastening buttons, snaps, or zippers
- Vacuuming and dusting
- Going up and down stairs
- Cleaning bathtubs and sinks
- Washing and waxing floors
- Putting on clothes over one's head
- Putting on socks, shoes, or stockings
- Carrying home purchases
- Using tools
- If something happened at home, no one would know
- Using the shower or bathtub
- Tying shoelaces, bows, and neckties
- Moving around the house without slipping or falling

Data from Gallup Organization: Survey of New Product Needs Among Older Americans. Princeton, New Jersey, Gallup Organization, 1983.

DISABILITY

Disability turns routine activities of daily living into time-consuming challenges and is a source of constant irritation as mobility and communication with the outside world are affected. Obvious examples of disability are the breathlessness of emphysema, the residual deficiencies that follow a stroke, the deformities of arthritis and osteoporosis, and incontinence and the loss of vision and hearing. Many aids have been developed to compensate for these deficiencies; they can be contrived through ingenuity or obtained from medical equipment companies, the Sears catalog of aids for the handicapped, or mail-order catalogs such as "Comfortably Yours." *

Some Causes of Accidents in the Elderly

- Altered vision
- Aortic stenosis
- Cardiac arrhythmias
- Diabetes mellitus
- Generalized debility
- Hypothyroidism
- Medication reactions
- Nutritional deficiencies
- Orthostatic hypotension
- Peripheral vascular disease
- Sensory loss

Data from Escher, J. E., O'Dell, C., and Gambert, S. R.: Typical geriatric accidents and how to prevent them. Geriatrics 44(5);54–69, 1989.

ACCIDENTS

With aging, people become more vulnerable to injury and injury-related death (Schletty, 1984). For example, circulatory complications such as blood clots or respiratory infections such as pneumonia cause approximately 40,000 deaths annually in elderly persons after a hip fracture.

Reduced sensory perception, increased reaction time, circulatory changes resulting in dizziness or loss of balance, and confusion associated with dementia combine to make the elderly accident prone. Assessment of the environment and intervention to avoid accidents is typical primary prevention in community health care for both old and young clients. Simple measures that prevent accidents include eliminating environmental hazards, reducing the hot water heater setting to 120–

---

* Write to 2515 East 43rd Street, P.O. Box 182216, Chattanooga, TN 37422-7216, or phone (615) 867–9955.

125°F, checking the kitchen stove, and providing accessible fire extinguishers near fire hazards and a plan to escape in case of fire. A smoke detector should be installed in every home, but many older residences do not have them.

Accident Prevention at Home
THINK ACCIDENTS

Activities of daily living
Cognition
Clinical findings
Incontinence
Drugs
Eyes, ears, environment
Neurological deficits
Travel history
Social history

- Remove all loose rugs
- Tack down carpet edges
- Install secure handrails in the bathroom and wherever else needed
- Use a nonslip mat in the shower or bathtub
- Check stairs for stability, uniformity, and safety
- Eliminate clutter
- Avoid slippery floors
- Check the furnace and all heating devices (including the stove) to maintain proper functioning
- Lower hot water temperatures
- Label hot and cold water outlets and appliances with directions
- Install and maintain smoke detectors
- Check for proper storage of household chemicals, especially flammable substances
- Increase artificial lighting in all rooms

Data from Escher, J. E., O'Dell, C., and Gambert, S. R.: Typical geriatric accidents and how to prevent them. Geriatrics 44(5);54–69, 1989.

The telephone is literally a lifeline for the elderly, not only because help can be summoned directly but also because assistance can be sent if a scheduled call is not answered. Many churches provide a frequent, regular telephone call as a service to people in the area regardless of whether the recipient is a member of that particular congregation. Advance permission is obtained and provision is made for notifying a third person or entering the home if a call is not answered when expected.

Special Telephone Services

- Speakerphones for hands-free conversations
- Big-button telephones for easy dialing
- Memory phones for one-touch dialing
- Telephones compatible with hearing aids
- Four-number Dialer for quick access to emergency numbers
- Telecommunication Device for the Deaf (TDD) equipment
- Video communication terminal
- Artificial larynx
- Directel with "puff" activator for severe movement impairment

---

Information available from AT&T Special Needs Center, 2001 Route 46, Suite 310, Parsippany, NJ 07054-1315. Call toll free 1-800-233-1222.

MEDICATIONS

The elderly are substantial consumers of prescription drugs as well as over-the-counter medications and folk remedies. A National Medical Expenditure Survey reported that noninstitutionalized Medicare beneficiaries received a total of 486.6 million prescribed medications during 1987 at a total cost of $8.3 billion (Moeller and Mathiowetz, 1989). Out-of-pocket expenditures for outpatient prescription drugs are estimated to be approximately $300 for each person enrolled in Medicare in 1988 (U.S. Senate Special Committee on Aging, 1988). Because the Food and Drug Administration does not include the elderly in clinical trials, the effect of different drugs on the aging population is unknown, and drug dosage is achieved through trial and error. Little attention is given to possible drug–drug or drug–food interactions.

Even if the most appropriate medications are prescribed, they are often not used as directed. Medications may not be taken unless the person feels ill, they may be overconsumed because of the belief that more is better, they may be taken erratically due to loss of memory and lack of a system, or they may never be purchased if money is needed for other things. Monitoring drug therapy in the home is another challenge for community health nurses. Cameron and Gregor (1987) recommend a contingency contract established between nurse and client in which they work together to time medications to fit into the client's lifestyle. Black and King (1988) developed a flowchart to assist in identifying specific noncompliance problems and provide guided decision points for interventions to assist safe self-medication.

Alcoholism affects about 10% of the elderly population (Williams, 1984). It is difficult to diagnose because regular drinking will often be denied. Dependency may stem not only from consumption of the usual alcoholic beverages but also from the considerable alcohol content of some nonprescription sleep aids or "tonics." Alcohol reacts with other drugs and is itself a depressant, although the moderate and appropriate use of wine, beer, and spirits can stimulate the appetite and has a long history of use in medicine, especially in other cultures.

Schletty (1984) stated that more deaths from accidental poisoning occur among the elderly than among young children. In the elderly, poisoning results from the combined effect of drugs and alcohol or from an unintentional drug overdose following confusion or forgetfulness. Medications should not be kept by the bedside, outdated medications should be flushed down the drain, and a plan should be devised to assist the client in taking medications only as prescribed.

THERMAL STRESS

The ability to respond to thermal stress is impaired in the elderly, and emergency care may be needed for heat exhaustion or hypothermia (a core temperature at or below 95°F). A comfortable indoor climate can be maintained through air conditioning or heating. Therefore, the degree of thermal stress is a function of socioeconomic factors (Kolanowski and Gunter, 1983). The frail elderly and the obese are most vulnerable to heat exhaustion, and mortality increases with age, temperature, and duration of heat wave. The frail elderly are also at the greatest risk of hypothermia, which may occur with an environmental temperature of 65°F. Hypothermia may occur after accidents in the elderly, especially if a fall occurs at night when only lightweight nightclothes are worn and the victim is unable to call for help and must wait until someone arrives.

Funding exists to help pay winter fuel bills for low-income elderly, but it is much less frequently available for summer cooling. Local utility companies and human resource offices are good sources

of information. If transportation is not a problem, the nearest enclosed shopping mall can provide an agreeable climate as well as social stimulation. This should be seen as a temporary or short-term solution, however, as resources for climate control are identified by discussion with the affected individual, family, or community.

Illness and Hospitalization

PREVENTION: SCREENING

The elderly suffer repeated hospitalization for the exacerbation or loss of control of chronic disease or for symptoms of a new disease. Kennie (1984) discussed the importance of screening and case-finding programs to prevent or control chronic disease processes before they threaten the quality of life and, with clinical progression, become more expensive and difficult to treat. Well-planned and targeted screening programs with a health education component can be valuable tools in disease and disability prevention. However, screening programs have many limitations. Many elderly people do not have a regular physician and are lost to follow-up as work loads of health care teams increase. There is no reason to screen for problems that are not a health threat to the community if solutions cannot be offered. In many areas of the United States, screening programs may be available, but treatment has not been funded or does not exist. Agency-based screening programs also tend to attract those who are at lowest risk, mobile, motivated, and in the community. Disability, isolation, and lack of income are the causes or effects of more serious problems and require an expensive

---

Selected Potential Clinical Preventive Services for the Elderly

Immunizations

- Influenza
- Pneumonia
- Tetanus
- Hepatitis B

Screening

- Cancer screening
  - Breast (clinical examination, mammography)

- Colorectal (occult blood stool, sigmoid-oscopy
- Cervix and uterus (clinical examination, Pap smear, endometrial biopsy)
- Prostate (clinical examination, ultra-sound, laboratory tests
- Skin (clinical examination)

- Blood pressure measurement
- Vision examination and glaucoma screening
- Hearing tests
- Cholesterol measurements
- Diabetes screening
- Thyroid screening
- Asymptomatic coronary artery disease (exercise stress test)
- Osteoporosis (developing techniques)
- Dental health assessment
- Mental status/dementia
- Depression screening
- Multiple health risks appraisal/assessment
- Functional status assessment

Education and Counseling

- Nutrition
- Weight control
- Smoking cessation
- Home safety and prevention of injury
- Stress management
- Appropriate use of medications
- Exercise

From Office of Technology Assessment: The Use of Preventive Services by the Elderly: Preventive Health Services Under Medicare, Paper 2. Washington, D.C., Health Program, Office of Technology Assessment, Congress of the United States, 1989.

house-to-house screening program to effectively identify need.

PREVENTION: IMMUNIZATION

Pneumonia and influenza are two infectious diseases that result in increased mortality in the elderly. Vaccines are available for both diseases and are widely encouraged, especially for the frail elderly. Whether all elderly persons should be immunized against pneumonia and influenza is an ethical and economic consideration. Immunization itself carries risks, although they are minimal, and the decision of whether to be immunized may be made best by the informed individual. However, in time of epidemic, the cost to society of immunization is far less than the cost of treating these diseases and their associated complications.

Immunization Schedule for Adults Aged 65 or Older

- All persons in this age group should receive influenza vaccine each year. Contraindication: History of allergic reactions to eggs
- All persons in this age group should receive pneumococcal vaccine. Revaccination should be considered every 6 years.
- All elderly persons should be evaluated for completion of the primary series of vaccination against diphtheria and tetanus and receive booster doses of combined toxoids at 10-year intervals. Contraindication: History of severe reaction to previous dose
- The lifestyle, occupation, and special circumstances (including travel plans) of older adults should be assessed for consideration of other vaccines.

Data from American College of Physicians: Guide for Adult Immunization. 2nd Ed. American College of Physicians, 1990.

HOSPITALIZATION

For any age group, hospitalization is a major disruption of everyday life for the patient and family. In the hospital, the primary diagnosis is usually treated by seeking a cure for the pathology of an organ system, which, for the elderly, may make the overall situation worse (Harper, 1985; Kennie, 1983). Medical disorders of the elderly may be better treated by addressing functional problems and limiting many tests and procedures that weaken the body and produce limited information. An elderly person can be expected to be weaker and less alert after any hospitalization, and this should be considered by community nurses when planning care.

Polliack and Shavitt (1977) found that the need for hospitalization of elderly patients in Israel depended not only on the severity of the illness but also on physical, emotional, or social factors related to the availability of hospital and community services and the values of the society served. These factors and values led to a tendency of women to remain hospitalized longer than men and of elderly patients who lived alone to remain hospitalized longer than those who lived with someone. The

AIDS and the Elderly

- Ten percent of all persons with AIDS are age 50 or older
- By 1991, it is projected that 27,000 people over the age of 50 and 1,100 people over the age of 70 will be diagnosed with AIDS
- Projections are based on already identified HIV-positive carriers and their estimated lifespan
- Projections do not include unknown latent cases from sexual transmission, blood transfusions, or other known risk factors and may be underestimated
- Symptoms of AIDS may be expressed differently in the elderly
- AIDS, like syphilis, is described as a "great imitator," and could present as generalized fatigue and weight loss or with psychiatric symptoms that may be confused with dementia. Differential diagnoses from cancer and Alzheimer's disease are needed.

Data from Weiler, P. G.: Why AIDS is becoming a geriatric problem. Geriatrics 44(7);81–82, 1989.

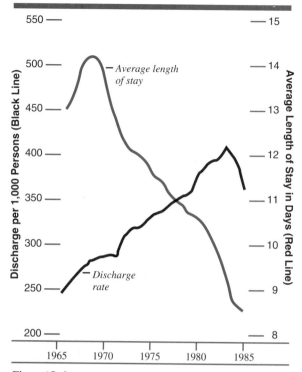

Figure 15–6
Trends in hospital use by persons 65 years or older (1965–1985). (Redrawn from National Center for Health Statistics: National Hospital Discharge Survey. Hyattsville, Maryland, Vital and Health Statistics, Series 13, various reports.)

importance of liaison among various services was demonstrated by the finding that hospital admission rates were lower when there was comprehensive and coordinated teamwork between physicians and nurses and when there were social and community facilities for primary medical care.

Because the U.S. medical model of health care serves acute illness better than chronic conditions, Brown (1990) says that many of the problems of the elderly can be attributed to the approach to care. Acute illness sanctions the "sick-role" behavior pattern and fosters dependency among client populations. These behaviors, which represent coping in a temporary situation, become permanent and inappropriate in chronic disease. Elderly people with serious chronic problems may become socially at risk, avoid medical treatment, reject diagnoses, increase conflict with health care providers, and suffer emotional stress that leads to psychosomatic symptoms.

In line with the attempt made in the 1980s to control health care costs through diagnosis-based prospective payment schedules for Medicare recipients, hospitals are pressured to discharge patients quickly, which means that more severe degrees of illness are now experienced by clients who are at home. Visiting nurses assist not only the client but also the family or household in understanding and complying with required treatment and the management of often complex equipment. This can severely strain the physical, financial, and emotional resources of the family, and the nurse should seek sources of respite care to relieve tension and burnout among family members.

Institutionalization

Institutionalization usually refers to the placement of persons who can no longer care for themselves in a nursing home or care facility from which they are not expected to return to an independent life in the community. Only about 5% of the elderly population live in nursing homes, but the proportion increases rapidly with age, from 1% of persons aged 65–74 to 6% of those aged 75–84 years and to more than 20% of those aged 85 or older (AARP and Administration on Aging, 1989). The median age of residents is 80, and the majority are widowed women. The larger number of women in nursing homes reflects the greater tendency of women to live alone, their poorer economic status, and their greater average age (U.S. Bureau of the Census, 1984). Approximately 50% of all institutionalized elderly in the United States suffer from some type of dementia and have lived at home with their family for 4–8 years from the time of the initial diagnosis until entering the nursing home (Gibson, 1984).

Mental Health of Elders

Positive

- Good relationships
- Friends
- Participation in activities
- Goals for the future
- Enjoyment of life

Negative

- Depression
- Isolation
- Confusion
- Disorientation
- Dementia

Rule out
    Poor nutrition
    Wrong use of medication
    Drug reaction or interaction
    Perception of "elderly role"
    Illness

More information is available in Aging America, 1988; Caring, August 1989 (entire issue).

Institutionalization is often a last resort when care of an aged relative has exhausted a family. Financial and emotional exhaustion may continue. Insurance policies for long-term care are becoming available, but they are expensive and of no assistance to those who are already old. Medicare does not provide for institutionalization, but when resources are spent, the resident becomes eligible for Medicaid. The issue of long-term care is that of most concern to older people at this time.

Death and Bereavement

Old age is a time of adjusting to loss. In the natural order of things, loss of parents is followed by loss of spouse, siblings, friends, and contemporaries, culminating in one's own death. A new phenomenon is the loss of adult children who have themselves become aged.

Funerals

THE USUAL procedure following death is to notify first the physician who will sign the death certificate and then the chosen funeral home. If death occurs at home, regardless of whether expected, the police or medical examiner's office must also be notified. This is still true at present even if a hospice is involved in care but may change as the hospice movement expands. An autopsy is rarely performed for a natural death unless requested by the medical examiner's office.

Many funeral homes are part of national chains, although their image is of individual family operation. Funeral homes and directors are licensed by each state and must comply with regulations set by federal, state, and local regulating agencies. They exist to provide any service a family wants within legal limits. A traditional funeral includes embalming and the cosmetic appearance of the body, viewing the deceased in the casket, a wake or rosary the evening before burial, and burial in the family-arranged plot. Above-the-ground entombment may take the place of burial. The funeral home will obtain the death certificate and other necessary papers, place newspaper notices, prepare clergy records, provide automobiles, and coordinate arrangements with the cemetery. The *average* cost of a traditional funeral in 1992 is about $5,200, plus $1,100 for the purchase, opening, and closing of the grave. Veterans of the armed forces may be buried in military cemeteries without charge for the grave.

Cremation usually is less expensive. A rigid container is all that is required, although a casket can often be rented if viewing is desired. A letter from the medical examiner's office authorizing cremation is usually required in addition to the other papers. Ashes are often interred in urn gardens or may be taken by relatives to scatter elsewhere.

Burial customs vary with religion or ethnic group. Funerals should be conducted in accordance with family wishes to avoid guilt feelings in the survivors. Funeral homes usually lose their association with the survivors after the burial, but personnel are often involved in crisis intervention and may refer survivors to therapy groups or inform such a group of a person in need.

From personal communication with Mr. Greg A. Medcalf, Assistant Manager, Sunset Memorial Park and Funeral Chapel, San Antonio, Texas, July 28, 1992.

The effects of bereavement in the elderly may not be expressed for some months after the death of a spouse and may continue for several years. Dimond (1985) believes that the usual view of death as a crisis should be superseded by the concept of grief resolution as a process during which the survivor learns to live without a spouse. Assessment of past experience and coping skills used in adjusting to a previous loss and identification of available support networks will assist in planning for care.

Many of the elderly turn to churches, synagogues, and other religious institutions at this time, and ministers, priests, rabbis, and other religious leaders have much experience in helping people through the grief process. Support groups for widows and widowers are often provided by religious organizations and usually are available for anyone in need. Other resources include secular support groups and private group or individual therapy.

The Community Environment

Assessment of the community for adequacy in meeting the needs of the elderly may produce some surprises. Neighborhoods generally considered highly desirable may not be so for all age groups. While increasing open space and protecting property values, restrictive zoning can result in long distances to grocery stores and a lack of public meeting places, sidewalks, nearby physician offices, and available public transportation (except for taxis). Inner-city residents may fare better than those in middle-class suburbs. Buses, sidewalks, corner shops, community centers, and churches keep the elderly fed and mobile.

Never assume the wealthy elderly can automatically provide care for themselves. Relying on a maid to shop and prepare meals is not much use if the maid does not arrive. Dismissing an unsatisfactory maid and hiring a new maid are traumatic experiences that require a great deal of energy and force a prolonged period of change. Independent wealth can provide a very pleasant situation, however, if someone is available to coordinate and supervise household staff or the staff is sympathetic to the needs of their employers.

Life can present most problems to the middle-class elderly. Often widowed, living alone in a house that has been home for many years but is now difficult to maintain, usually (if a woman) having had little employment experience but much volunteer involvement in various organizations, they find themselves in a role for which they are unprepared. Their life has often been directed to helping others, and they are uncomfortable receiving help themselves unless there is the possibility of contributing something in exchange. This may take the form of a cash payment for services provided, which is a satisfactory solution except when there really is not any money available. Many elderly with a seemingly middle-class lifestyle have become the genteel poor as fixed incomes fall further behind inflation and expenses continue to rise, including expenses for health care.

The need for mobility includes driving a car when this has really become no longer safe. We have all been behind "little old ladies" creeping down the highway. Police, however, are often sympathetic to elderly drivers, especially in small communities in which they are known. The police recognize the importance of mobility and assist as much as possible to keep their residents independent. Talk to police chiefs. Their goal is the smooth running of a community with no unpleasant surprises for residents. They know what happens in the community infrastructure and are very interested to hear about potential problems for community subgroups.

Abuse of the Elderly

Elder abuse is present in all parts of the United States — in private homes as well as other places. It is less likely to be reported than child abuse, but public and professional awareness of the problem is growing with more frequent media publicity and the establishment of shelters for the abused elderly in many communities.

A report (Elder Abuse, 1985) issued by the United States House of Representatives Select Committee on Aging, Subcommittee on Health and Long-Term Care supplemented by an article in *Parade* magazine (Robinson, 1985), describes the situation and offers some solutions. About 4% of the nation's elderly (more than 1 million people) may be victims of moderate-to-severe abuse. A typical victim is age 75 or older, in a position of dependency, and usually female (partly due to the longer life expectancy of women). Abusers are usually experiencing stress, possibly from alcoholism, drug addiction, marital problems, financial difficulty, or personality disorders. Either from shame or fear, abused elders are less likely to report abuse than are abused persons in other age groups, and the true incidence and prevalence rates of elder abuse are elusive (Fulmer, 1989).

Abuse generally falls into four categories: physical abuse (which ranges from hours of physical restraint to beating, burning, rape, and murder), psychological abuse (isolation, insult, threat, and fear), financial abuse (theft of money or property), and abuse by neglect (e.g., not providing needed new glasses, dentures, or clean clothes). The majority of states have laws requiring mandatory reporting of elder abuse; most are based on child abuse statutes, and most lack the ability to be enforced. Without federal assistance, inadequate funding is the rule. On the average, states spend about $25 for each child resident but only $2.90 per elderly resident for elderly protective services (Elder Abuse, 1985). Subcommittee recommendations include increased federal funding to the states (Social Services Block Grants) specifically to counteract elder abuse, the establishment of a National Center for Elder Abuse, and an increase in social services available to families caring for older persons. Immunity to prosecution would be granted to anyone reporting incidents of abuse.

Crime and the Elderly

The difference between abuse and crime is that crime is usually perpetrated by someone to whom the elderly victim has not granted access.

The elderly are easy targets for crime because physical frailty and mental confusion make them less likely to fight back. Fear of robbery was a common concern in the study population of Stein et al. (1984). The major crime against the elderly, however, is fraud; the promise of large sums of money if a "small deposit" (often equal to life savings) is made. Other crimes may be violent and quite predictable. Older neighborhoods are subject to deterioration before gentrification, and deteriorated neighborhoods usually suffer high crime rates. Elderly residents have often grown old with the neighborhood and do not wish to move from their familiar home regardless of how difficult life has become. However, the regular arrival of Social Security and pension checks and the pattern of movement from mailbox to home to bank invite interference.

It takes a long time for anyone to recover from being a victim of crime, and the elderly do not have much time. Physical injuries in the elderly take longer to heal than in younger people, but the emotional scars may last forever. The fear of being victimized is often enough to precipitate withdrawal, isolation, and depression. Economic and property loss may never be regained.

Security from crime is a major concern of the elderly and an important consideration for builders of retirement complexes. Direct deposit of checks, including Social Security checks, into bank accounts is recommended, transportation and a buddy system for shopping or social activities can be arranged, and education about crime prevention increased. The AARP offers a valuable pamphlet (Domestic Mistreatment of the Elderly: Towards Prevention—Some DOs and DON'Ts; order No. D 12885) that provides prevention suggestions on individual, family, and community levels.

Families of the Elderly

Most elderly people are usually happily connected with a family unit, but the increasing visibility of elder abuse is directing attention to the family dynamics that occur when the senior members of the family grow old.

Generally, up to the age of 75, most elderly people do more for their children than their children need to do for them (Gelman et al., 1985). If or when physical frailty becomes a problem, however, parent-child roles tend to become reversed, which can be a major source of stress for all. Daughters or daughters-in-law usually become the primary caregivers (Haug, 1985), sometimes at considerable financial as well as emotional cost. Lost wages are compounded by the loss of job-related benefits such as Social Security, a company-related pension, or medical insurance. A direct contribution to national well-being is made by the little appreciated and unreimbursed caregiver (Nissel, 1984).

A profile of family caregivers was developed by Montgomery (1984) during preliminary interviews with 300 families for a study on services for the families of the aged. Caregivers are spouses (37%) or adult children (53%). Most spousal caregivers are age 65 or older, with almost one third older than 75 years. Adult children are usually over the age of 50. Eighty percent of caregivers are female. Most assume total care of their elderly relative and have minimal social contact outside the home, often less than four contacts with other people each week.

The quality of life for the frail elderly may be substantially increased when care is given by a family member. There is a feeling of being wanted, of comfort, in familiar faces and surroundings (Haug, 1985). There is more freedom and personal control than is possible in any institution. With the increase of home health services, including house calls by physicians, accessible advice and treatment are more easily available, which satisfies both client and caregiver (Zimmer et al., 1985).

For the caregiver, benefits may be of a moral nature, such as the personal satisfaction of fulfilling a family obligation and the avoidance of the guilt of refusing to care for a parent or grandparent. Unfortunately, the benefits for the caregiver can be outweighed by the physical and emotional costs of caring for a sick elder who can only become more dependent until death is seen as a release for everyone (Gelman et al., 1985; Haug, 1985). The caregiver is three times more likely to report symptoms of depression than the recipient of care and four times more likely to report anger. Other expressed feelings include guilt, frustration, and sometimes desperation, as the needs of the elder conflict with and take precedence over the needs of the caregiver (Gelman et al., 1985). Stress arises from the increased work load; from intrafamily conflicts and social embarrassments caused by the elder's confused behavior; from the increased vigilance, worry, and concern that is the inevitable consequence of being responsible for someone who could hurt him- or herself or others; and from the interference caused by the elderly person's care in the marital, family, work, and community responsibilities of the caregiver (Beck and Phillips, 1983).

Alzheimer's disease is a major cause of caregiver stress. The national headquarters of the Alzheimer's Disease and Related Disorders Association (70 East Lake Street, Chicago, Illinois 60601) will give information about the disease and family support groups linked with affiliated chapters throughout the United States.

Many families care for their elders with very little outside support and a lack of awareness of existing social programs (Montgomery, 1984; Gelman et al., 1985). Family members are often so isolated from support systems that they are not aware such

---

Case Study: Jim C.

JIM C., a 72-year-old man, was admitted to a nursing home suffering from Alzheimer's disease. He was unable to walk, talk, or recognize members of his family. He was kept alive by nasogastric tube feeds. One day, his brother went to the nursing home and shot him. The sentence was 10 years' probation, which was terminated after 1 year. Jim's widow still grieves about the manner of his death and the disease that devastated the whole family.

---

support is needed until they become exhausted. The literature is unanimous in demanding support for caregivers by general public recognition of the problem, extension of existing programs, creation of new programs, and tax credits or financial reimbursement for care given by family members.

In response to obvious need, the provision of case management services for the elderly is a new and rapidly expanding industry that is not yet regulated by federal or state statutes (Katz, 1990). Services include the assessment and coordination of care for elderly people who may live at some distance from their children. These services are not usually covered by medical insurance but can bring great relief to overstressed family members. Social workers have been pioneers in the case management field, but opportunities exist for gerontological nurses. For more information, contact the National Association of Private Geriatric Care Managers (1315 Talbott Tower, Dayton, Ohio 45402). Case management programs provided by public and nonprofit agencies may be available in some areas.

SUPPORT FOR THE ELDERLY

Major Legislation

Legislation affecting the elderly takes innumerable forms as amendments are added to unrelated bills. The acts discussed here have the most direct impact.

THE SOCIAL SECURITY ACT

Originally passed in 1935, it has been amended 16 times. It is administered by agencies within the Department of Health and Human Services, including the Social Security Administration and the Health Care Financing Administration. Most working people are enrolled automatically in the Social Security program, which is financed by contributions from employers, employees, and the self-employed. Part of the Social Security contribution is designated for Medicare, which is the national program of health insurance for the elderly.

Social Security provides four different benefits, two of which are targeted directly to the elderly. Retirement benefits are paid at the full rate to persons retiring at age 65, providing they have met contribution requirements, and at 80% of that rate to persons retiring at age 62. If benefits are not claimed at age 65, an additional 3.5% is added for each year the benefits are not claimed until age 70. A spouse may claim the larger of spousal benefits or any benefits they may have earned in their own right. Ages when benefits are payable are scheduled to rise to reflect the increasing longevity of the population.

A benefit for survivors is the second provision of social security. Death at any age will bring a one-time "death payment" of $255, plus some income for surviving children below a specified age and possible widow or widower benefits from age 60 if claiming on the account of the late spouse or age 50 if totally and permanently disabled. Dependent parents are eligible for survivor's benefits if certain criteria are met.

A third provision of Social Security is disability payments for people unable to work during usual working years.

The fourth Social Security provision is Medicare hospital insurance benefits, which is divided into two parts. Part A is automatic and covers most of the cost of hospital care and certain kinds of care after discharge. There is a large deductible and co-payments to be made by the patient. Part B is for medical insurance. If a person elects this coverage, it helps pay for physicians' services, outpatient services, and some other medical items. The monthly premium for part B is $31.80 in 1992, and it usually increases each year.

The elderly poor are eligible for Medicaid coverage of the part B premiums and the deductibles and copayments if treatment is needed. The criteria vary from state to state and may be obtained from state Medicaid offices. Ask for information about the Qualified Medicare Beneficiary (QMB) program. For people who exceed the QMB limits, options are private Medigap insurance policies or joining a health maintenance organization (HMO) or competitive medical plan (CMP), which receives Medicare payments in exchange for providing care.

THE OLDER AMERICANS ACT

Signed into law by President Johnson in 1965, this act established the Administration on Aging within the Department of Health and Human Services. Its purpose is to identify the needs, concerns, and interests of older persons and to coordinate available federal resources to meet those needs. Amendments to the act in 1973 established area agencies on aging to provide local planning and control of programs, which must include nutrition services either as home-delivered meals or in communal settings. Multipurpose senior centers nationwide are sites for not only nutrition programs but also recreational, social, and health programs; housing assistance; counseling; and information services, all mandated by the act (Title III). Other requirements of the act are the development of employment opportunities for low-income elderly by means of the community service employment programs (Title V) and the establishment of programs for training personnel and supporting research (Title VI). Amendments passed in 1984 instruct area agencies on aging to plan for community-based programs to assist older people to remain in their homes and to provide supportive services to the victims of Alzheimer's disease and their families. National priority services for the elderly include transportation, home services, legal and other counseling services, and residential repair and renovation programs. The target population is persons over the age of 60 with the greatest economic or social needs, especially low-income minorities, but the provisions of the act benefit all older people through response to community needs.

When amending the Older Americans Act, Congress is particularly responsive to the recommendations of the decennial White House Conference on Aging. Last held in 1981, the White House has announced that the next Conference on Aging will be held in Washington, D.C., in 1993.

Government Agencies
ALMOST EVERY federal agency has a local office in addition to state and local agencies. For example:

- Social Security Administration
- Veterans Administration
- Mayor's Office for Senior Citizens
- Area Agencies on Aging: Each city, county, or state may have a different name for its agencies. Please look under the following listings to cross-reference:
  - Agency on Aging
  - Commission on Aging
  - Council on Aging
  - County Council on Aging
  - Department on Aging
  - Elderly Services
  - Human Services
  - Planning Council on Aging

Check your telephone book or call information for national, state, and local agency numbers.

From the National Council of Senior Citizens, 1331 F Street NW, Washington, D.C.

RESEARCH ON AGING ACT

The Research on Aging Act, 1974, created the National Institute on Aging within the National Institutes of Health. Its purpose is to conduct and support biomedical, social, and behavioral research and training related to the aging process and the diseases and other special problems and needs of the aged. Research goals are to enhance the quality of life, promote health and functional independence, increase understanding and effective treatment of the dementias (including Alzheimer's dis-ease), and develop leadership in working with the aged. The philosophy is to view aging as a fundamental human process about which much more knowledge is needed, with the aim of reducing current rates of morbidity and institutionalization. The National Institute on Aging is a source of grant funding for nurses conducting research on problems of aging.

OTHER LEGISLATION

A maze of legislation has an impact on the elderly population. Two important acts address people still in the work force, but they have tremendous implications for options and income available to the elderly. The Age Discrimination in Employment Act (ADEA), 1967, provided workers aged 40–65 with the same opportunities as younger employees for participation in employee benefit plans. In 1978, amendments raised the mandatory retirement age to 70 years, and in 1986 mandatory retirement at any age was abolished for almost all workers.

Employee pension rights in private pension plans were safeguarded by the Employee Retirement Income Security Act (ERISA), 1974, which set minimum federal standards for private plans. The Retirement Equity Act, 1984, increased protection for the surviving spouse or former spouse of pension eligible workers, and the Tax Reform Act, 1986, reduced vesting requirements for pension eligibility. These provisions will eventually increase the income of many elderly women as well as men. Public sector pension plans are subject to a somewhat different set of rules and are a complexity of variables that may leave employees and spouses less claim to benefits.

Services for the Elderly
FEDERAL PROGRAMS began with the Social Security Act in 1935. They concentrate on assessing need, planning programs to meet the need, developing program guidelines, implementing funding programs, and evaluating the results. Almost all federal programs are available to all of the elderly without income restriction, but because the poor elderly have the most need, most facilities are located in areas where poorer people have greater access. Examples are:

- Department of Health and Human Services
- Social Security Administration: Retirement benefits, survivor benefits, disability, Supplemental Security Income (SSI), guaranteed minimum income
- Health Care Financing Administration: Medicare, Medicaid
- Public Health Service: National Institutes of Health, National Institute on Aging
- Office of Human Development Services: Administration on Aging, Nutrition Program

for Older Americans, National Clearinghouse on Aging (information services)

- **Department of Agriculture:** Food stamps,
  provision of food for nutrition programs
- **Department of Housing and Urban Development:** Planned housing for the elderly; mul-
  tiunit apartment buildings may include a
  nutrition site, health clinic, and recreational
  facilities
- **Department of Transportation:** Urban Mass
  Transportation Administration: Funding for
  mass transportation services for the elderly
  with special needs, reduced fares during
  off-peak hours on public transportation
  systems receiving federal funds
- **Department of Labor:** Employment opportunities for unemployed people age 55 or
  older, investigates complaints of age discrimination
- **Veterans Administration:** Serves veterans
  of the Armed Forces and dependents of
  career personnel

Action

- **Peace Corps:** No upper age limit for
  healthy volunteers
- **Volunteers in Service to America (VISTA):**
  The "domestic Peace Corps," requires a
  proportion of its volunteers to be over the
  age of 55
- **Retired Senior Volunteer Program (RSVP):**
  Volunteers work in the nonprofit agency of
  their choice for reimbursement of expenses
- **Foster Grandparents Program**
- **Senior Companion Program:** Low-income
  elderly are reimbursed with a stipend and
  some benefits to be a companion to
  children or adults with special needs.
- **Small Business Administration:** Service
  Corps of Retired Executives (SCORE):
  Retired business executives assist new
  small business owners to establish and
  direct their business.

States, the original administrative units of
the nation, retain responsibility for many programs. In general, they administer and supplement federal programs within the state.
Acceptance of federal money means acceptance of federal guidelines for programs.
States vary most by the manner in which federal programs are supplemented.

- **Department of Human Resources:** Medicaid, SSI, and poverty programs of the Social Security Act; food stamps; protective
  services against abuse, case management,
  foster care for children and the aged, Medicaid eligibility for institutionalization, information, and referral
- **Departments of Health and Mental Health
  and Mental Retardation:** Licenses and controls health personnel and facilities, including long-term care facilities and nursing
  homes; may have special programs for
  older people
- **Department on Aging:** Administers funds
  provided by the Older Americans Act
  through designated regional area agencies
  responsive to local needs

Counties and cities incorporate federal and
state programs and may add more of their
own. City programs may have strict criteria
for eligibility and meet only a fraction of need.
They usually do not receive high priority in
the city budget, and services depend on the
city tax base and political philosophy. Examples of programs provided include assisted
homemaking and job placement, nutrition,
transportation, legal, financial, and other
types of counseling.

Thousands of other local programs exist,
sometimes serving a very limited area. They
are sponsored by various professional
groups, churches, businesses, and individuals, and they provide services such as telephone assistance, home-delivered meals,
and adult day care. Funding comes from
various sources. Directories that list local resources may be obtained from the United
Way, Junior League, Chambers of Commerce, and local religious agencies.

Organizations for the Elderly

The American Association of Retired Persons (AARP), 601 E Street N.W., Washington, D.C. 20049. Telephone: 1-202-434-2277.

Founded in 1958, AARP has more than 30 million members age 50 or older in almost 4,000 local chapters. Members receive *Modern Maturity* magazine bimonthly (the largest circulation magazine in the United States), and the *AARP News Bulletin* 11 times each year. A list of publications is available. AARP is involved in most issues affecting older people and has established the National Resource Center on Health Promotion and Aging to provide information and networking to health professionals across the country.

Gray Panthers, 1424 16th Street N.W., Suite 602, Washington, D.C. 20036. Telephone: 1-202-387-3111.

Founded in 1970 by Maggie Kuhn, Gray Panthers is an organization of people of all ages working together for social justice, to foster the concept of aging as lifetime growth, and to eliminate ageism. It strongly promotes adequate health care for all and has led fights against mandatory retirement and nursing home abuse. Gray Panthers awards grants to academicians, researchers, and creative artists over the age of 70 for continued work.

Older Women's League (OWL), 666 11th Street N.W., Suite 700, Washington, D.C. 20001. Telephone: 1-202-783-6686.

Formed in 1980 after a White House miniconference on older women and born from the double discrimination of age and sex, OWL's motto, "Don't Agonize — Organize," could be adopted for nurses. OWL fights for economic security for older women, widows, divorcees, caretakers, and displaced homemakers through job access and pension equity. *Gray Papers* and annual *Mother's Day* reports provide in-depth analysis of key issues. A list of publications is available.

National Council on the Aging (NCOA), 409 3rd Street S.W., Washington, D.C. 20024. Telephone: 1-202-479-1200.

Founded in 1950, NCOA was the first organization to give a national focus to the concerns of older people. It is an organization of professionals involved in all aspects of work with the elderly and is a national resource for information, training, technical assistance, advocacy, publications, and research on aging. NCOA projects have led to the Foster Grandparents program, Meals-on-Wheels, nutrition sites, and the training and placement of older low-income workers; it also has developed intergenerational programs in which the elderly help children. A list of publications is available.

National Council of Senior Citizens (NCSC), 1331 F Street N.W., Washington, D.C. 20004. Telephone: 1-202-347-8800.

Formed in 1961 during the struggle to enact Medicare, NCSC is an advocacy organization concerned with preserving and improving benefits for the aged by closely monitoring and initiating legislation. NCSC has strong connections with labor unions and a very active political action committee. Current priorities include a national health program.

Mature Outlook, Inc., 6001 North Clark Street, Chicago, Illinois 60660-9977. Telephone: 1-800-336-6330.

Part of the Sears organization, Mature Outlook reflects the new image of the elderly as healthy people with time and money to spend and a legitimate marketing target. For people age 50 or older, members receive discounts at Sears and a bimonthly magazine and newsletter.

NEW CONCEPTS OF COMMUNITY CARE

Across the country, new ways are being devised to meet the needs of the elderly. Four successful programs will be presented here.

The Nursing Home as Senior Center

The intense competition in the nursing home industry is inspiring exciting programs intended to give the facility greater visibility and deeper roots in the community. This example is based on the Chandler Center, a nonprofit retirement apartment and nursing home complex in San Antonio, Texas. It is a very attractive facility conveniently located in an area with a high elderly population. Its philosophy is to be a nursing home without walls, and the target population for its extended programs is the well elderly who can buy services. The senior center has its own building and staff to coordinate programs. It provides a meeting place and an opportunity for social activities and networking. One program exists to reduce aggravation and exploitation for people who need help at home and wish to hire a reliable contractor. The Chandler Center will assist in contacting an appropriate business, which then deals directly with the customer. Other programs are directed toward life enrichment and include the Institute of Lifetime Learning, which provides classes in languages, art, photography, and other subjects of interest to members. Day or vacation trips are organized, exercise and bridge groups meet, and invited speakers talk on topical subjects. Holidays bring special celebrations. Many activities are planned by members themselves, some of whom volunteer regular hours of help. The facility is also a meeting place for church groups and a chapter of AARP. Transportation is arranged for members who need assistance, and lunch is served daily. Meals at home are delivered on request.

Generations Together

Established in 1978 at the University of Pittsburgh Center for Social and Urban Research, Generations Together builds on the affinity of youth and age to develop programs using the strengths of one age group to meet the needs of the other age group in reciprocal relationships. Four distinct intergenerational programs give senior adults the opportunity to assist young people as resources to school teachers and students, as master artists offering their skills to children and youth, as child care aides, and as mentors to high school and university students. A fifth program organizes students aged 14–22 to provide direct services to senior citizens in need. Intergenerational child care includes visits by young children to older persons in senior centers or nursing homes. A variety of new demonstration projects are always evolving, and intergenerational activities have developed across the United States to meet community needs. Programs include intergenerational theater, literature discussion, and education of the homebound elderly in subjects such as psychology, politics, and mathematics by adult education students, as well as the more usual service projects.

Generations Together develops and investigates the impact of intergenerational programs in settings that are often multicultural and promote mutual growth and learning among youth and the elderly and support the philosophy of the continuity of life. Program assistance and a publication list are available from Generations Together (811 William Pitt Union, University of Pittsburgh, Pittsburgh, PA 15260).

Mutual Assistance: The Elderly Helping the Elderly

Religious organizations include many elderly persons in their congregations and are aware of their strengths and limitations. In many parts of the country, churches of different denominations are grouping together to combine resources to attack the social problems common to all.

The Jefferson Area Community Outreach for Older People (CO-OP) is a gathering of 11 churches representing most denominations, one synagogue, and a retirement community situated in a well-defined area in San Antonio, Texas. The target population is people age 60 or older who reside within the project area. Religious declaration or affiliation is not required. The purpose of the CO-OP is to promote and encourage independence for older people by establishing a neighborhood network of volunteers to provide mutual assistance, information, and services. A centrally located church provides office space. The CO-OP received a 3-year grant from the Robert Wood Johnson Foundation, but it is now funded by the participating organizations. The CO-OP philosophy is neighbor helping neighbor as needed on a voluntary basis. Services coordinated by the CO-OP include nutrition (home-delivered meals or church lunch programs), transportation, health education (used as a clinical site by nursing students), caregiver support and respite, increased social contact and involvement, counseling, home maintenance assistance, and information and referral. Members of all sponsoring organizations are asked to volunteer their time and talents in the service of those in need.

The CO-OP is affiliated with the National Federation of Interfaith Caregivers Inc. (P.O. Box 1939, Kingston, New York 12401).

The Social/Health Maintenance Organization Demonstration

Developed at Brandeis University's Bigel Institute for Health Policy, this research demonstration project studies the feasibility of providing the elderly with a single prepaid program of preventive, acute, and long-term services by integrating community-based care into the HMO model. Social/HMOs fill three critical gaps in Medicare and private insurance by supplying various long-term, in-home support services to assist members to remain in their homes as well as posthospital home or nursing home care that goes far beyond current Medicare criteria and 1–4 months of custodial nursing home care without restriction on setting or prior hospitalization. Benefits such as hearing aids, eyeglasses, and prescription medications are included.

Four sites (New York, Oregon, Minnesota, and California) enroll volunteer Medicare and Medicaid recipients within their service areas to reflect the local Medicare population by age, sex, marital status, living arrangements, and need for assistance with daily activities. Funding is by a Health Care Financing Administration premium equal to estimated Medicare costs plus a monthly premium from each member similar to the Medicare part B supplements. The pooling of finances and management of both short- and long-term care services have enabled the sites to break even financially and exceed target membership after 4 years of operation.

The purpose of the project is to provide information for policy and practice decision making for efficient and effective health care for elders. With common screening and assessment tools for the four sites, a 20,000-member data base has become the largest of its kind in the United States, with information on the biopsychosocial supports and needs of an elderly population. Further information is available from the Social/HMO Consortium (Bigel Institute for Health Policy, Heller Graduate School, Brandeis University, Waltham, Massachusetts 02254-9110).

APPLICATION OF THE NURSING PROCESS

A theory base applicable to the client's needs should provide the framework within which the nursing process is carried out. While theories themselves may be very complex, simplified versions distilled from major assumptions can assist the nurse in monitoring the health of the elderly and their responses to treatment. Social theories of aging have developed since the 1950s, usually in response to the concerns of a particular time in U.S. culture. Brown (1990) noted that they may be valid only in certain times and places and that they address specific issues related to aging rather than the experience of aging as a whole. Despite their limitations, theories may provide some guidelines for recognizing problems and planning appropriate care for elderly clients.

Selected Social Theories of Aging

Activity Theory
THE KEY to successful aging is the maintenance of optimal levels of activity from the middle years of life. This theory led to the establishment of many activity centers.

Disengagement Theory
As people age, their needs change from active involvement to withdrawal for contemplation about the meaning of life and impending death. As well as the withdrawal of the individual from society, there is the withdrawal of society from the aged. This academic theory caused great controversy.

Loss of Major Life Roles Theory
This theory challenged the disengagement theory by claiming disengagement was forced by denying older people societal roles, e.g., mandatory retirement from the work force. This led to the establishment of government programs to provide volunteer and work opportunities.

Continuity Theory

The unique personality and lifelong behavioral characteristics and habits of an individual continue into old age. This theory is an attempt to balance the extremes of the activity and disengagement theories.

Socially Disruptive Events Theory

If life is severely disrupted in a number of ways in a brief period of time (e.g., by retirement, loss of a spouse, and so on), social withdrawal becomes an appropriate response. This response should reverse with time. If disengagement becomes established, however, it becomes difficult to reverse.

Reconstruction Theory

Negative labeling of the elderly by society as well as self-labeling after negative life events led to a view of the elderly as incompetent and helpless.

Age Stratification Theory

This theory assumes that societies are inevitably stratified by age and class. The relative inequality of the elderly at any given time or situation depends on their typical life course experiences and are due mostly to the physical and mental changes that take place and the history of the time (e.g., wars) through which the cohort lived.

Modernization Theory

Loss of social status among the aged is a universal experience in all cultures in which modernization processes, which mostly affect the young and often involve new technology, are occurring.

Data from Brown, A. S.: The Social Processes of Aging and Old Age. Englewood Cliffs, New Jersey, Prentice Hall, 1990.

DATA COLLECTION SHOULD BE COMPLETE AND SYSTEMATIC. A standardized form provided by the agency is often helpful, but the nurse must understand the reasoning (theory base) behind the form to be able to adapt it to a situation outside the norm. Two common approaches are the *systems theory* and the *epidemiological triad.* With systems theory, the nurse examines a system, its subsystems and suprasystems, and its relationship with other systems. For example, if the primary focus is on the client as the system, the client's biological, psychological, and social subsystems may be examined as well as the client's suprasystems such as family interaction and neighborhood environment. The nurse is a part (subsystem) of the health care system that has a relationship with the client. The interaction between the client and the health care system provides data for evaluating and planning for desired outcomes. In the epidemiological approach, the host, agent, and environment are analyzed. This method is more easily used for one problem at a time. The client is the host, a particular problem is examined as the agent, and the environment includes all causes of and possible solutions for the problem that affects the host. A third method, which is the one used in the following example, is a problem-solving approach that identifies strengths and weaknesses and compensates for weaknesses. In practice, many theories are used concurrently; the principles of systems theory and the epidemiological triad can be identified in the following case study.

WHEN WORKING WITH THE ELDERLY, DATA MUST BE COLLECTED THAT TAKE INTO ACCOUNT AGING CHANGES AND ARE MEASURED AGAINST ELDERLY NORMS. Assessment categories for the elderly should include nutrition, elimination, activity, medication consumption, body protection, cognitive tasks, life changes, and the environment (Yurick, 1984). Nursing diagnoses stem from validated data.

ASSESSMENT OF THE FAMILY AND COMMUNITY OF A CLIENT FOLLOWS THE SAME SYSTEMATIC DATA COLLECTION METHODS. The community nurse is always aware of the health status of both the client's family and the agencies to which clients may be referred (e.g., whether an agency is effective in its stated purpose and has sufficient power, funding, and personnel). As information is gathered on clients and agencies, the larger community is assessed for its strengths and weaknesses. "Community" may be defined on the level that will most benefit the client. For an individual as client, community may be the street of residence, the neighborhood, or the area within the limits of available transportation. If the family is the client, the community will expand to include areas of interest to the family group. If the entire aggregate of the elderly is the client, community will have a national perspective. As the nurse builds a data base on different clients and neighborhoods, strengths and weaknesses of the town, state, and nation become apparent. Many community nurses eventually pursue health-related issues of personal interest to policy-making levels, developing a wide network of people in all aspects of health care in the process.

Formal nursing diagnoses are not well developed for use in the community, and nurses should be prepared to devise their own when necessary. Sharing and validation of nursing diagnoses with clients also are more complex in the community setting. A nursing diagnosis may be validated with an individual client, but validation may be more difficult for family and community diagnoses because members of each group may have different viewpoints. When making a diagnosis at the family or community level, the nurse should be as objective as possible and seek validation from other agencies or professionals working in the same area as well as from the individual client.

PLANNING CARE ALSO REQUIRES A THEORY BASE. Maslow's (1970) Hierarchy of Needs and Erikson's (1963) Eight Ages of Man are useful and familiar concepts. It must be remembered that Maslow felt that relatively few people would incorporate survival, security, belonging, and self-esteem needs to reach self-actualization. Realistically, the nurse should set goals aiming for belonging and increased self-esteem after the needs for survival and security are met. Erikson saw the task achievements of the elderly as integrity versus despair. Ego integrity is the comfort and acceptance of self as a unique and valuable being, the completed work of the trials and triumphs of life on an individual, and a sense of fulfillment that brings calmness before death. Despair results from failure to achieve integrity, frustration and anger at the passage of time, and a fear of approaching death.

IN COMMUNITY HEALTH, IT IS PARTICULARLY IMPORTANT FOR THE NURSE TO SET SHORT- AND LONG-TERM GOALS THAT ARE CONGRUENT WITH THE DESIRED OUTCOMES OF THE CLIENT. A community health nurse works in the environment of the client, which adds complexity to the process. The nurse is given power and respect, but patient compliance will not usually be good unless the patient sees some value in outcomes desired by the nurse. The client and the family and environment of the client will control the speed and depth of implementation of the nursing care plan.

EVALUATION, AS EVERY OTHER STEP OF THE PROCESS, IS A JOINT ACTIVITY OF THE CLIENT AND THE NURSE. It measures movement toward or away from a specified goal and gives dynamic feedback that affects planning and intervention. An elderly person may be slow to achieve progress because of arthritis, frailty, or nutritional status rather than because of deliberate noncompliance. Chronic illness has a long-term time frame, and the standard for evaluation may be the prevention of deterioration instead of the cure of the disease. Community problems may have an even longer time frame, or they may be solved fairly quickly if a general problem affects a small group and the solution is inexpensive.

C a s e
S t u d y

Mrs. Darren, a 75-year-old widow, was referred to the community health nurse by her physician, who did not feel she could sufficiently care for herself. Her diagnoses were hypertension, mild congestive heart failure, arthritis, and occasional confusion after transient ischemic attacks. A home visit was made by the nurse. Mrs. Darren lived in a rundown house in an inner-city neighborhood. It was raining and the roof was leaking, and the house had no functioning heat unit. A rat was seen scrambling in the garbage. Mrs. Darren told the nurse that she had no children and her only relative was a sister who lived with her family in another state. She was used to the neighborhood and knew her neighbors, but she was frightened of the teenagers she saw hanging around when she went by bus to the supermarket to cash her Social Security check. She had Supplemental Security Income, Medicare, Medicaid, and food stamps. She ate mostly bread, butter, and coffee, but she enjoyed fried chicken and oranges after going to the supermarket. Constipation was sometimes a problem, so she took a spoonful of laxative every night. She said she did not always remember if she had taken her medication and held out a small bottle containing an assortment of pills of different colors, shapes, and sizes.

Assessment

With Mrs. Darren as the system, or central planning focus, the nurse identified her biopsychosocial subsystem strengths and weaknesses and looked for actual or potential connections to her family and community suprasystems. Thinking of aging theories, the nurse felt Mrs. Darren was undergoing some forced disengagement due to her physical and social circumstances, which might be reversed if her health could be maintained and her links to the community strengthened. Part of the data-gathering process for Mrs. Darren would be to discover her previous pattern of living and her likes and dislikes (using the continuity theory as a basis for planning); the nurse would then assess the community for means to assist Mrs. Darren and then select the available community resources that would be most acceptable to her. On a practical rather than a theoretical level, the nurse also checked with Mrs. Darren's physician regarding the prescriptions and identified the assortment of pills by taking them to the pharmacist who filled the prescriptions.

By means of a problem-solving approach for data gathering, Mrs. Darren's assets were identified as:

- Being basically able to care for herself
- Receiving medical treatment
- Receiving income from various sources
- Being accustomed to the neighborhood and knowing her neighbors

Her liabilities were more extensive:

- Inadequate nutrition
- Confusion with medications and improper use of laxatives
- Condition of house, which was not supportive of health
- Threat of violence in neighborhood and possibility of attack for Social Security money
- Physical impairment resulting from age and illness
- No children or other family living nearby
- Probable progression of confusion
- Possibility of a major stroke at home while unattended

Diagnoses and Planning

Diagnoses and related short- and long-term goals address Mrs. Darren's situation, in which no close family lives nearby. Plans at the three levels of prevention are written for the diagnoses and include suggestions for intervention with families.

Individual

- Altered nutrition: less than body requirements, related to difficulty or inability to procure food

  Short-term Goal

  - Mrs. Darren will improve her diet to include RDA of nutrients including fiber and fluids as evidenced by diet recall and report regular bowel habits without the inappropriate use of laxatives.

  Long-term Goals

  - Mrs. Darren will maintain a nutritionally adequate diet through self-care and use of community programs as evidenced by a steady weight and normal tests for nutritional status during physical examinations.

  - Inconsistency in medication regimen related to forgetfulness and mild confusion

  Short-term Goal

  - Mrs. Darren will identify medications and know when to take them as evidenced by demonstration to nurse.

  Long-term Goals

  - Mrs. Darren will continue to take medications as ordered as evidenced by stabilization of disease processes and intermittent demonstration to nurse.

  - Potential for injury related to inadequate housing, possibility of robbery of Social Security money, and aging and progression of disease

  Short-term Goal

  - Mrs. Darren will improve her home to a level allowing healthy habitation, avoid robbery by varying her routine and using banking services, and expand her social network and maintain health care appointments.

  Long-term Goal

  - Mrs. Darren will explore sheltered housing for the elderly and continue contact with community health nurse and neighborhood friends.

Family

- Potential for injury to family unit related to unanticipated loss of interaction with Mrs. Darren due to her declining health and distance of residence

  Short-term Goal

  - Address of family members included in her record to facilitate emergency contact.

  Long-term Goal

  - Mrs. Darren will maintain family contact by mail, telephone, or possible visits.

Community

- Knowledge deficit of nutritional services related to lack of publicity of available nutritional programs for the elderly

  Short-term Goal

  - Identify existing community programs

  Long-term Goals

  - Publicity campaign to advertise nutrition services for the elderly in the community
  - Lack of support programs for medication consistency related to unrecognized need

  Short-term Goal

  - Identify existing programs and memory aides for consistency with medication regimen.

  Long-term Goals

  - Support community pharmacists in campaign to increase public awareness of need to take medications as prescribed.
  - Identify and support programs that will assist with provision of prescribed medications for people who have difficulty obtaining prescriptions due to lack of insurance, money, or transportation or other problems.

  - Lack of programs and resources for elderly residents of limited income related to cost of services and competition for limited funds

  Short-term Goal

  - Identify existing programs for the elderly in the community

  Long-term Goal

  - Community groups work together to maximize use of resources

Intervention

When the nurse discussed the nursing diagnoses and plans with Mrs. Darren, Mrs. Darren agreed with the short-term goals, but she was not sure she wanted to leave her home for other housing or to meet other people through community activities. However, she agreed that she would try to do so.

During the course of the next few visits, the nurse explained basic nutritional principles and helped make a shopping list and menus for 1 week. Together, they developed a plan to assist with medication scheduling. Referrals initiated by the nurse resulted in a greatly improved living situation. A financial advisor from the city's Supportive Services to the Elderly program encouraged Mrs. Darren to open a bank account for the direct deposit of her checks and showed her how to use it. A home health aide from the same program came for half a day each week to assist with shopping and cleaning. The sanitation department of the health district exterminated the rats, the roof was fixed by the local area agency on aging, and a church-sponsored group painted the house and cleaned the yard. A small heater was purchased from the Salvation Army store, and application was made to the utility company for help with bills during the winter months.

Mrs. Darren was encouraged to talk about her earlier life during the nurse's visits. She had been widowed soon after her marriage when her husband was killed serving with the army overseas, and she had never remarried. She lived in the neighborhood where she grew up, although it had deteriorated over the years. She had worked as a secretary until her retirement for a small company that had paid salaries each week in cash and had no pension plan. She had enjoyed the companionship and the quiet efficiency and routine of the office. Her sister had married a salesman and moved several times. She had four children, all grown now, but Mrs. Darren remembered visits to them when they were small, and they all exchanged letters and cards at Christmas. Mrs. Darren felt pleased with her accomplishments in life but ashamed of the circumstances in which she was now living, and she was reluctant to ask for help from community agencies about which she knew nothing.

With this information, the nurse planned to increase Mrs. Darren's social contacts by introducing her to a structured group that met frequently and offered several activities among which she might find something she enjoyed, and would be missed if she were unexpectedly absent. A neighbor was encouraged to invite her to a nutrition site, where she became involved in a domino-playing group. Mrs. Darren allowed her name to be put on the waiting list for an apartment for the elderly, but with the other changes this was no longer a priority, and a decision could be made when an apartment became available.

Evaluation

With the nurse as intermediary and coordinator of community services, Mrs. Darren easily accepted help with the problems related to security and survival. When her home improvements were completed, Mrs. Darren was able to maintain herself more comfortably with the help of the weekly visit from the home health aide. The establishment of orderly routine, the companionship at the nutrition site, and safer financial arrangements increased Mrs. Darren's feelings of belonging and self-esteem. The nurse reduced her home visits to Mrs. Darren but maintained contact with her during her visits to the health clinic for blood pressure checks and preventive health care arranged to supplement and coordinate with her medical care.

Discussion with the home health aide informed the nurse of proposed funding cuts to the city's supportive services to the elderly program, which would result in reduced services. The nurse spoke to the president of the district branch of the professional nurse's association, who notified the state level of the association to monitor funding on the state level and assisted the nurse in working with other local agencies for the elderly to establish a publicity campaign against the proposed funding cuts through letter writing to the editors of local newspapers, speaking at public hearings on the city budget, and speaking at city council meetings. Although funds were reduced, the cuts were much less severe than they would have been without the campaign, and most services were able to continue although with waiting time increased for admission of new clients.

Levels of Prevention

Primary

Goal
> Promotion of good nutrition

Individual

- Instruct on nutritional needs
- Plan shopping list and menus incorporating any prescribed diet for health problems

    Family

- Instruct on nutritional needs of family members by age, sex, or special needs

    Community

- Increase nutrition information where food is sold

    Goal
    > Consistency with medications as prescribed and prevention of medication error

    Individual

- Written and oral instructions when medications are dispensed, at level of understanding and in language of the client
- Repetition of instructions by client to health care provider

    Family

- Instruction repeated to family member

Community

- Community education program about understanding medications

  Goal
  Promotion of safety and prevention of injury

  Individual. See boxed information: Accident prevention at home.

- Immunizations as appropriate
- Use of community services for assistance to maintain property and prevent deterioration
- Network of friends and family

  Family

- Services of community health nurse or case manager
- Counseling availability
- Respite care availability

  Community

- Community education programs for the elderly
- Community health nurse awareness of potential hazards for elderly residents and intervention as needed

  Secondary

  Goal
  Assessment and treatment of nutrition-related disorders

  Individual

- Referral for assessment of possible nutrition-related disorders
- Hospitalization or prescribed nutritional supplements for illness resulting from inadequate nutrition

  Family

- Referral for nutritional assessment and counseling

  Community

- Emergency food supplies

  Goal
  Diagnosis and treatment of medication-related injury

  Individual

- Referral for apparent overmedication or undermedication symptoms
- Drug or food reactions

  Family

- Reassessment of understanding of medications

Community

- Twenty-four–hour poison hot-line
- Emergency department with 24-hour response
- Medical services

  Goal
    Response to injury

  Individual

- Medical services
- Social services
- Medical alert call systems

  Family

- Referral to the appropriate agency

  Community

- Emergency housing
- Emergency trauma and medical care
- Police and judiciary system

  ### *Tertiary*

  Goal
    Maintenance of improved nutrition

  Individual

- Use of community services

  Family

- Exchange family recipes
- Attend home economics classes

  Community

- Campaigns for nutritional awareness and healthy eating
- Healthy snacks in food machines
- Funding of community food services for aggregates or emergencies
- Services providing access to food, e.g. food banks, Meals-on-Wheels, food stamps
- Transportation to grocery stores or nutrition services

  Goal
    Maintenance of consistency with medications and medication changes

Individual

- Continued ability to explain current medications as prescribed
- Stability or progression toward wellness of disease process
- Use of commercial gadgets to assist memory
- Home health nurse to give medications if beyond capability of client (e.g., some injections)

Family

- Ability to explain and assist with medication administration

Community

- Outreach programs and publicity campaigns
- Twenty-four–hour availability of pharmacist for consultation

Goal
Maintenance of safe living in the community and delay the need for long-term care facilities and institutionalization

Individual

- Safety appliances
- List of agencies to call for various assistance needs
- Monitoring by community health nurse

Family

- Respite care
- Referrals as needed

Community

- Housing improvement programs
- Other programs to assist home living
- Direct banking services
- Police surveillance
- Telephone services
- Handicapped transportation services
- Sheltered housing and foster homes for the elderly
- Retirement communities
- Nursing homes and long-term care facilities

ALLOCATION OF RESOURCES FOR SENIOR HEALTH

Many different agencies provided assistance to keep Mrs. Darren functioning adequately in the community, and many more could have been used. The increasing number of older people and their needs for health care are stimulating discussion on the kind of services that should be provided. Netting and Williams (1989) identify four themes concerning ethical decision making in an aging society:

1. Autonomy versus beneficence—the rights, wishes, and competency of a client to accept or refuse professional advice
2. Issues of death, dying, and termination of treatment
3. The allocation of resources in an aging population
4. Family caregiving and/or the obligation to provide care

Readers are referred to the ethical literature for arguments on these themes. This section is intended only to raise a few questions about the allocation of resources to the elderly.

In a discussion of aggregates and health care, the issue of resource allocation is always in the forefront. Health care, for economic reasons alone, is a limited resource. Questions about the most effective distribution of health care resources among the claims of rival aggregates are issues of "rationing" and social justice.

Callahan (1987) felt that resources should be targeted to the young and that health resources available to people over the age of 65 should be limited "first at the level of public policy and then at the level of clinical practice and the bedside." The elderly would be reeducated to become less dependent on medical care and more accepting of a "natural life span" followed by a "tolerable death." In Callahan's view, the elderly should focus on the care of the young and future generations, not on their own cohort. Fry (1988) noted that the content of nursing education would change and that social concerns would take precedence over the individual when planning care for those over the age of 65 if this philosophy were adopted.

At first glance, this is a repugnant idea that considers the elderly to be disposable, as having outlived their productive value to society, and as now only consuming material resources. Obviously, many people over the relatively young age of 65 are highly productive and refute such generalization. Aging, however, is very individualistic, and public policy can be a useful scapegoat. For example, cardiopulmonary resuscitation (CPR) is often the entry into high-technological prolongation of a poor quality of life that many elderly fear. Research is establishing guidelines (Murphy et al., 1989; Podrid, 1989) to improve successful CPR rates in the elderly. A national policy limiting CPR to elderly clients with the greatest chance of a successful outcome could be well accepted, reduce legal action against institutional and individual health care providers, and reduce health care costs by using fewer resources.

CPR and the Elderly

- Cardiopulmonary resuscitation (CPR) is less successful for patients age 70 or older than for younger patients.
- CPR attempts lasting longer than 5 minutes are usually unsuccessful in the elderly.
- CPR is usually unsuccessful in elderly patients with several chronic or acute diseases.
- CPR is rarely effective for elderly patients with cardiopulmonary arrests that are out-of-hospital, unwitnessed, or associated with asystole or electromechanical dissociation.
- CPR is most successful for an elderly person who functioned independently with a normal mental status before the arrest, had a witnessed cardiac arrest with a vital sign detected at the onset, had ventricular tachycardia or fibrillation, responded within 5 minutes to cardiac massage, and regained consciousness promptly.

Data from Murphy, D. J., Murray, A. M., Robinson, M. D., and Campion, E. W. Outcomes of cardiopulmonary resuscitation in the elderly. Ann. Intern. Med. 111;199–205, 1989.

Because of unmet needs, especially in the areas of long-term care and outpatient support services, organizations advocating for the elderly are working actively for a national U.S. health program with universal access to care based on need. As a group, the elderly have already received favored status in access to care by the right to Medicare coverage at the age of 65. With the introduction of prospective payment systems in an attempt to control costs, the elderly have also experienced external control of health care and have been an experimental pilot group in many ways for the general population.

Some younger people have been concerned that the power of the elderly could divert resources from other aggregates such as mothers and children or persons with AIDS. Several grass roots organizations have been formed to express this concern, but the national Americans for Generational Equity group disbanded due to lack of support.

RESEARCH ON THE HEALTH OF THE ELDERLY

Topics for research may be identified throughout this chapter. Studies on the elderly and the process of aging are needed in all areas. How can we predict and plan for the welfare of the majority while allowing flexibility for the needs of outliers? Why are the elderly such a diverse group? What causes the different rates of physical and mental aging? How far can we go in defining this aggregate by age alone, or should some other standards be developed? There is an immediate need for studies to show how medication acts in older people and whether drug dosage or frequency should be different.

Different cultural and ethnic attitudes and practices concerning aging must be identified and incorporated into care. As increasingly active groups of the elderly gain increasing autonomy in health care decision making and control of their death and dying (including the right to refuse treatment), there is a danger that not all people will be well served (Kapp, 1989). When individuals are expected to claim the rights they have been given, many less-assertive older people, especially those from cultures in which decisions are made within the family rather than by an individual, may not claim the care they need. Health care delivery must be culturally sensitive.

Stein et al. (1984) conducted a study to identify stressors for elderly people living in the community. The subjects of this study lived in poor neighborhoods, had an annual income of $4,000–8,000, and had not completed high school. Immediate economic survival was identified as their utmost concern, specifically related to rising food costs and threatened cuts in Social Security. Fear of having to live in a nursing home, loss of sight, and

being robbed were other significant stressors. Concerns about health and disability, with the possibility of increased dependence, caused more distress than did the thought of death. Other concerns related to having to live with children, or having lived in the neighborhood for only a short period of time. This last concern may relate to unfamiliarity with the community, lack of peer support, and pervasive change. The authors concluded that their sample as a whole showed a generalized anxiety state about the future, and they suggested that perceived stress for the elderly should be measured in terms of anticipated events or emotions. If this is so, by prolonging uncertainty about the economic future, continued publicity about proposals to lower or tax Social Security benefits, Medicare, and other programs for the elderly is particularly cruel and stressful.

Research is also needed on motivation factors for the recruitment and retention of nurses to care for the elderly as well as the qualities needed to gain satisfaction in what can be a very difficult and challenging field.

ROLES OF THE COMMUNITY HEALTH NURSE

The first role (and duty) of the community health nurse is to be visible in the community and seen as a resource for health care for everyone. Nurses working with the elderly have the same roles as other community health nurses. At different times, as appropriate, roles include client advocate to the family and health care system and aggregate advocate to the community, educator of client and public, planner, case manager, facilitator, coordinator of care between agencies, observer, data collector, researcher, case finder, and provider of clinical nursing care. Nurses should also seek to be board members of organizations that affect their clients and to be political lobbyists. Given the constraints of working for government agencies on whatever level and within which most community health employment lies, this last may need ingenuity, which is characteristic of community health nurses.

SUMMARY

This chapter has taken a broad approach to the health of the elderly, who form the most diverse and rapidly increasing aggregate. Issues that affect the day-to-day life of the elderly are addressed: a functional body rather than the absence of disease; enough money and services to allow enjoyment of life; adequate food, housing, and mobility; the dignity of knowing each life has affected all those whom it has touched; and the respect due to those who, by nature of advanced age, are closer to the adventure of the end of this life. The purpose of public health is to improve life at all ages for all people, and each chapter in this textbook contrib-utes to that end, which, in effect, is a good life at a good age. The health of the elderly is a function of everything encountered in life—environmental health; occupational health; biological, psychological, spiritual, and social health; men's and women's health; and the history, politics, policy, and future of health—and nurses are major contributors to the entire field of health care. The health of the elderly begins in the prenatal clinic and ends at death, and nurses participate in each step of the way.

Learning Activities

1. As a group activity, review the case history of Mrs. Darren presented in this chapter. Discuss assessment using different theories. What other information would you like to have? What other services may the client need (e.g., dentistry)? Where would you find these services in your community?

2. Read your daily newspaper and a weekly newsmagazine. Keep a scrapbook of articles about legislation that affects the elderly. How many other news items or advertisements highlighted information of specific interest to older people (e.g., products, services, and so on)?

3. Talk to police chiefs in small towns or incorporated cities about the elderly in their communities. Ask what facilities are available for older people. Be prepared to discuss needs and offer solutions. Look for community strengths and weaknesses.

4. Talk to the minister or rabbi of a large church or synagogue. Ask about contributions to the congregation and the community made by elderly members and programs provided for older people. Look for networking of resources.

5. Go to a bookstore and review books describing travel and education opportunities available only to older people. Ask travel agents about their older clients. Are you surprised at their responses?

6. Visit a private retirement community. Talk to the social director and arrange to interview and record the reminiscences of some residents. Prepare a journal of interviews (and give copies to those interviewed). Do the same in a public-funded housing community for the elderly. Note the similarities and dissimilarities of the stories. Ask your community librarian for local history related by older people.

7. For your eyes only! Answer (in writing) the following questions:

   ● What are your personal feelings about growing old?

   ● How do you feel when surrounded by elderly people of various physical and mental abilities?

- What are the positive aspects of aging?

- What are the negative aspects of aging?

- Would you want, appreciate, enjoy, or recommend enthusiastically the care available to the elderly in your community? What would you provide if money were no object? What would be your priorities with limited funds? How would you initiate your first priority? Go ahead and try it!

REFERENCES

American Association of Retired Persons and the Administration on Aging, U.S. Department of Health and Human Services: A Profile of Older Americans, 1989. Publication no. PF 3049 (1289). D996. Washington, D.C., AARP, 1990.

Archer, S. E., Kelly, C. D., and Bisch, S. A.: Implementing Change in Communities: A Collaborative Process. St. Louis, C.V. Mosby, 1984.

Beck, C. M., and Phillips, L. R.: Abuse of the elderly. J. Gerontol. Nurs. 9(2);97–101, 1983.

Black, M., and King, M.: A new look at self-medication practices of the elderly: Clinical decision making for community health nurses. Family Comm. Health 11(3);1–8, 1988.

Brown, A. S.: The Social Processes of Aging and Old Age. Englewood Cliffs, New Jersey, Prentice Hall, 1990.

Callahan, D.: Setting Limits: Medical Goals in an Aging Society. New York, Simon and Schuster, 1987.

Cameron, K., and Gregor, F.: Chronic illness and compliance. J. Adv. Nurs. 12;671–676, 1987.

Cox, C. L., Spiro, M., and Sullivan, J. A.: Social risk factors: Impact on elders perceived health status. J. Comm. Health Nurs. 5;59–73, 1988.

Dimond, M.: Bereavement and the elderly: A critical review with implications for nursing practice and research. J. Adv. Nurs. 6;461–470, 1985.

Dynamic elderly. U.S. News and World Report, July 2, 1984, pp. 48–53.

Eastman, P.: Scientific squabble. AARP Bull. 31(3);8, 1990.

Elder Abuse: A National Disgrace. Report of the Subcommittee on Health and Long Term Care, May 10, 1985. Washington, D.C., Select Committee on Aging, Subcommittee on Health, U.S. House of Representatives, Publication no. H2-377.

Erikson, E. H.: Childhood and Society. 2nd Ed. New York, Norton, 1963.

Facts and Figures about Social Security. Washington, D.C., U.S. Department of Health and Human Services, 1988.

Fries, J. F.: Aging, natural death, and the compression of morbidity. N. Engl. J. Med. 303;130–135, 1980.

Fry, S. T.: Rationing health care to the elderly: A challenge to professional ethics. Nurs. Outlook 36(5);256, 1988.

Fulmer, T. T.: Mistreatment of elders: Assessment, diagnosis, and intervention. Nurs. Clin. North Am. 24;707–716, 1989.

Gelman, D., et al.: The family: Who's taking care of our parents? Newsweek, May 6, 1985, pp. 61–68.

Gibson, M. J.: Some societal responses to dementia in developed countries. Ageing Int. 11;11–16, 1984.

Graf, J. F.: Death by fasting. Science 2;18, 1981.

Hagebak, J. E., and Hagebak, B. R.: Meeting the mental health needs of the elderly: Issues and action steps. Aging 335–336;26–31, 1983.

Harper, M. S.: Refining leadership in an aging society. Sister Charles Marie Frank Lecture, Incarnate Word College, San Antonio, Texas, March 18, 1985.

Haug, M. R.: Home care for the ill elderly: Who benefits? Am. J. Public Health 75(2);127–128, 1985.

Hayflick, L.: The strategy of senescence. Gerontologist 14;37–45, 1974.

Hayflick, L.: The cell biology of human aging. Sci. Am. 242;58–65, 1980.

Hickey, K.: Impact of the elderly. Hospitals 57(9);103–104,107, 1983.

Hispanic and Indian Elderly: America's Failure to Care. Report on a Hearing before the Select Committee on Aging, House of Representatives, 101st. Congress, August 7, 1989, Albuquerque, New Mexico. Washington, D.C., U.S. Government Printing Office, Publication no. 101-730, Part 1.

Kanak, M. F.: Nutrition Education in the Elderly. Paper presented at the First International Conference on Health Education in Nursing, Midwifery, and Health Visiting, Harrogate, England, May 23, 1985.

Kapp, M. B.: Medical empowerment of the elderly. Hastings Center Rep. 19(4);5–7, 1989.

Katz, M. G.: Go the distance. AARP Bull. 31(7);10–12, 1990.

Kennie, D. C.: Good health care for the aged. J. A. M. A. 249;770–773, 1983.

Kennie, D. C.: Health maintenance of the elderly. J. Am. Geriatr. Soc. 32(4);316–322, 1984.

Kolanowski, A. M., and Gunter, L. M.: Thermal stress and the aged. J. Gerontol. Nurs. 9(1);13–15, 1983.

Lebel, J. O.: Health needs of the elderly. Dental Clin. North Am. (Geriatr. Dent.) 33;1–5, 1989.

Martinson, I.: Establishing a resource for care of the aged. J. Gerontol. Nurs. 10(10);11–14, 1984a.

Martinson, I.: Gerontology comes of age. J. Gerontol. Nurs. 10(7);8–17, 1984b.

Maslow, A. H.: Motivation and Personality. 2nd Ed. New York, Harper & Row, 1970.

Moeller, J., and Mathiowetz, A.: Prescribed Medicines: A Summary of Use and Expenditures by Medicare Beneficiaries. Washington, D.C., Department of Health and Human Services, Publication no. (PHS) 89-3448, 1989.

Montgomery, R. J. V.: Services for families of the aged: Which ones will work best? Aging 347;16–21, 1984.

Murphy, D. J., Murray, A. M., Robinson, M. D., and Campion, E. W.: Outcomes of cardiopulmonary resuscitation in the elderly. Ann. Intern. Med. 111(3);199–205, 1989.

Netting, F. E., and Williams, F. G.: Ethical decision making in case management programs for the elderly. Health Values 13(3);3–8, 1989.

Nissel, M.: The family costs of looking after handicapped elderly relatives. Ageing Soc. 4;185–204, 1984.

Parker, M., and Secord, L. J.: Case managers: Guiding the elderly through the health care maze. Am. J. Nurs. *88*;1674–1676, 1988.

Podrid, P. J.: Resuscitation in the elderly: A blessing or a curse? Ann. Intern. Med. *111*(3);193–195, 1989.

Polliack, M. R., and Shavitt, N.: Utilization of hospital inpatient services by the elderly. J. Am. Geriatr. Soc. *25*;364–367, 1977.

Ries, P.: Americans Assess Their Health: United States, 1987. Washington, D.C., National Center for Health Statistics, Vital and Health Statistics, Series 10, Publication no. 174, 1990.

Robinson, D.: How can we protect our elderly? *Parade Magazine,* February 17, 1985, pp. 4–7.

Rowe, J. W., and Kahn, R. L.: Human aging: Usual and successful. Science *237*;143–149, 1987.

Schlenker, E. D.: Nutrition in Aging. St. Louis, Times Mirror/Mosby, 1984.

Schletty, A. V.: Home injuries are not an accident. Aging *344*;31–35, 1984.

Schneider, E. L., and Brody, J. A.: Aging, natural death, and the compression of morbidity: Another view. N. Engl. J. Med. *309*;854–856, 1983.

Stein, S., Linn, M. W., Slater, E., and Stein, E. M.: Future concerns and recent life events of elderly community residents. J. Am. Geriatr. Soc. *32*;431–434, 1984.

The latest word on cholesterol. AARP Bull. *31*(3);2, 1990.

Today's senior citizens: Pioneers of a new golden era. *U.S. News and World Report* July 2, 1984, pp. 51–53.

U.S. Bureau of the Census: Demographic and Socioeconomic Aspects of Aging in the United States. Current Population Reports, Series P.23, Publication no. 138. Washington, D.C., U.S. Government Printing Office, 1984.

U.S. Bureau of the Census: Population Profile of the United States: 1989. Current Population Reports, Series P.23, Publication no. 159. Washington, D.C., U.S. Government Printing Office, 1989.

U.S. Bureau of the Census: 1990 Census of Population and Housing. Summary Population and Housing Characteristics, United States. Washington D.C., U.S. Department of Commerce, Economics and Statistics Administration. Publication no. 1990 CPH-1-1, March 1992.

U.S. Department of Health and Human Services: Health statistics on older persons: United States, 1986. Vital and Health Statistics, Series 3, No. 25, 1987. Washington, D.C., U.S. Government Printing Office, DHHS Publication no. (PHS) 87-1409, 1988.

U.S. Department of Health and Human Services: Healthy People — 2000: National Health Promotion and Disease Prevention Objectives. Washington, D.C., U.S. Government Printing Office, Publication no. (PHS) 91-50213, 1990*a*.

U.S. Department of Health and Human Services: Health United States, 1989. Washington, D.C., U.S. Government Printing Office, DHHS, National Center for Health Statistics, Publication no. (PHS) 90-1232, 1990*b*.

U.S. Senate Special Committee on Aging: Aging America: Trends and Projections. Washington, D.C., Department of Health and Human Services, Publication no. LR 3377 (188)-D12198, 1988.

Why Comply: Marion Guide to Wellness. New York, Marion Laboratories, 1990.

Williams, M.: Alcohol and the elderly: An overview. Alcohol Health Res. World *52*;3–9, 1984.

Yurick, A. G.: The nursing process and the aged person. *In* Yurick, A. G., Spier, B. E., Robb, S. S., and Ebert, N. J., eds.: The Aged Person and the Nursing Process. 2nd Ed. Norwalk, Connecticut, Appleton-Century-Crofts, 1984, pp. 5–32.

Zimmer, J. G., Groth-Junker, A., and McCusker, J.: A randomized controlled study of a home health care team. Am. J. Public Health *75*;134–141, 1985.

Special Needs of Aggregates

16

Cultural Diversity and Community Health Nursing

Upon conclusion of this chapter, the reader will be able to:

1. Discuss racial and cultural diversity in U.S. society.

2. Identify the cultural aspects of nursing care for culturally diverse individuals, groups, and communities.

3. Analyze the sociocultural, political, economic, and religious factors that impact on the nursing care of culturally diverse individuals, groups, and communities.

4. Compare health-related values, beliefs, and practices of the dominant cultural group with those of individuals and groups from culturally diverse backgrounds.

5. Apply the principles of transcultural nursing to community health nursing practice.

Margaret M. Andrews

According to the U.S. Bureau of the Census, one third of the U.S. population consists of individuals from racial, ethnic, and cultural subgroups, sometimes referred to as minorities. By the early part of the 21st century, individuals from culturally diverse backgrounds will account for 51.1% of the total U.S. population. For the first time in U.S. history, the nation's racial and ethnic subgroups will comprise a majority of the total population. If current demographic trends continue, the cultural diversity expected in the 21st century will be 23.4% Hispanic, 14.7% black, and 12% Asian (U.S. Bureau of the Census, 1990). At the same time, the Native American population is projected to remain at 0.6% or decrease slightly due to intermarriage (U.S. Bureau of the Census, 1983).

The number of immigrants and refugees in the United States is projected to continue to increase. In addition, people from other countries will probably continue to seek treatment in U.S. hospitals, particularly for cardiovascular, neurological, and cancer care, and U.S. nurses will continue to have the opportunity to travel abroad to work in a wide variety of health care settings in the international marketplace. In the course of one's nursing career, it is possible to encounter foreign visitors, international university faculty, international high school and university students, family members of foreign diplomats, immigrants, refugees, members of more than 130 different ethnic groups, and Native Americans from more than 500 federally recognized tribes. A serious conceptual problem exists within nursing in that without formal preparation nurses are expected to know, understand, and meet the health needs of culturally diverse individuals, groups, and communities.

Members of some cultural groups, most notably, blacks and Hispanics, are demanding culturally relevant health care that incorporates their specific beliefs and practices. There is an increasing expectation among members of certain cultural groups that health care providers will respect their "cultural health rights," an expectation that frequently conflicts with the unicultural, Western, biomedical world view taught in U.S. educational programs that prepare nurses and other health care providers.

Given the multicultural composition of the United States and the projected increase in the number of individuals from diverse cultural backgrounds, concern for the cultural beliefs and practices of people in community health nursing is becoming increasingly important. Nursing is inherently a transcultural phenomenon in that the context and process of helping people involves at least two persons who usually have different cultural orientations or intracultural lifestyles.

HISTORICAL PERSPECTIVE ON CULTURAL DIVERSITY

At no other time in the history of nursing have cultures been interacting and communicating with each other more frequently than today. However, nurses have been concerned with the cultural dimensions of care for many years. A brief historical overview of the ways in which nurses have responded to the health care needs of those from various cultural backgrounds follows.

Although the 19th century concept of culture was limited and thought to be associated primarily with physiological differences, Florence Nightingale's involvement in The Crimea and her concern with the fate of the Australian aborigines make her the first nurse in modern history to consider cultural considerations in nursing care. Concern for the health care needs of culturally diverse groups is also reflected in early 19th century U.S. history. In 1870, Linda Richards became the first nurse known to engage in international nursing when, under the auspices of the American Board of Missions, she established a school of nursing in Japan. In the early 1900s, Lillian Wald, Lavinia Dock, and other public health nurses provided nursing care for European immigrants, many of whom resided in low-income tenement houses in New York City.

In the 1960s and 1970s, many racial and ethnic groups, most notably, blacks and Hispanics, became increasingly concerned with their civil rights and raised the consciousness of the U.S. public. Influenced by the social and political climate, U.S. nurses responded with growing professional awareness and increased sensitivity to individual attitudes, values, beliefs, and practices about health, illness, and caring among culturally diverse clients. The nursing profession responded to the sociocultural and historical events of this era with the development of a new subspecialty called *transcultural nursing.*

In 1959, Madeleine Leininger, a nurse-anthropologist, used the term transcultural nursing to define the philosophical and theoretical similarities between nursing and anthropology. In 1968, Leininger proposed her theory-generated model; in 1970, she wrote the first book on transcultural nursing, *Nursing and Anthropology: Two Worlds to Blend* (Leininger, 1970). According to Leininger, transcultural nursing is "a formal area of study and practice focused on a comparative analysis of different cultures and subcultures in the world with respect to cultural care, health and illness beliefs, values, and practices with the goal of using this knowledge to provide culture-specific and culture-universal nursing care to people" (Leininger, 1978, p. 493). *Culture specific* refers to the "particularistic values, beliefs, and patterning of behavior that tend to be special, 'local,' or unique to a designated culture and which do not tend to be shared with members of other cultures" (Leininger, 1991, p. 491) whereas *culture universal* refers to the "commonalities of values, norms of behavior, and life patterns that are similarly held among cultures about human behavior and lifestyles and form the bases for formulating theories for developing cross-cultural laws of human behavior" (Leininger, 1978, p. 491).

The term *cross-cultural nursing* is sometimes used synonymously with transcultural nursing. The terms *intercultural* and *multicultural nursing* are also used, as is the phrase "ethnic people of color" (Branch and Paxton, 1976). Since Leininger's early work, many other nurses have contributed significantly to the advancement of nursing care of culturally diverse clients, groups, and communities, and some of their contributions will be mentioned in this chapter.

Culture

In 1871, the English anthropologist Sir Edward Tylor was the first to define the term "culture." According to Tylor (1871), culture refers to the complex whole including knowledge, belief, art, morals, law, custom, and any other capabilities and habits acquired by virtue of the fact that one is a member of a particular society. Culture represents a way of perceiving, behaving in, and evaluating one's world, and it provides the blueprint for determining one's values, beliefs, and practices.

Culture has four basic characteristics. It is

- Learned from birth through the processes of language acquisition and socialization
- Shared by all members of the same cultural group
- Adapted to specific conditions related to environmental and technical factors and to the availability of natural resources
- Dynamic

Culture is an all-pervasive, universal phenomenon, without which no human exists. Yet the culture that develops in any given society is always specific and distinctive, encompassing all of the knowledge, beliefs, customs, and skills acquired by members of the society. Within cultures, groups of individuals share beliefs, values, and attitudes that are different from those of other groups within the same culture. Differences occur because of ethnicity, religion, education, occupation, age, sex, and individual preferences and variations. When such groups function within a large culture, they are referred to as subcultural groups.

The term *subculture* is used for fairly large aggregates of people who share characteristics that are not common to all members of the culture and enable them to be thought of as a distinguishable subgroup. Ethnicity, religion, occupation, health-related characteristics, age, sex, and geographic location are frequently used to identify subcultural groups. Examples of U.S. subcultures based on ethnicity (i.e., subcultures with common traits such as physical characteristics, language, or ancestry) include blacks, Hispanics, Native Americans, and Chinese-Americans; those based on religion include members of the more than 1,200 recognized religions such as Catholics, Jews, Mormons, Muslims, and Buddhists; those based on occupation include health care professionals such as nurses and physicians, career military personnel, and farmers; those based on a health-related characteristic include the blind, hearing impaired, or mentally retarded; those based on age such as adolescents and the elderly; those based on sex or sexual preference include women, men, lesbians, and gay men; and those based on geographic location include Appalachians, Southerners, and New Yorkers.

The term *minority* refers to "a group of people who, because of their physical or cultural characteristics, are singled out from the others in the society in which they live for differential and unequal treatment, and who therefore regard themselves as objects of collective discrimination" (Wirth, 1945, p. 347). The concept of minority varies widely and is contextual. For example, men may perceive themselves to be a minority group within nursing, which is a female-dominated profession, whereas women are the minority in the male-dominated professions such as engineering. Although any group of individuals may perceive itself as a minority, there are four federally defined minority groups: blacks (including those of African, Haitian, or Dominican Republican descent), Hispanics (those of descent from a Spanish-speaking country such as Mexico, Cuba, or Puerto Rico); Asians (those of Japanese, Chinese, Filipino, Korean, Vietnamese, Hawaiian, Guamian, Samoan, or East Indian descent), and Native Americans (Eskimos or those from one of more than 200 Native American tribes). Because the term minority connotes inferiority, members of some of the groups mentioned object to its use and prefer terms such as ethnicity or cultural diversity.

Culture and the Formation of Values

According to Leininger (1978), *value* refers to a desirable or undesirable state of affairs. Values are a universal feature of all cultures, although the types and expressions of values differ widely. *Norms* are the rules by which human behavior is governed and result from the cultural values held by the group. All societies have rules or norms that specify appropriate and inappropriate behavior. Individuals are rewarded or punished as they conform to or deviate from the established norms. Values and norms along with the acceptable and unacceptable behaviors associated with them are learned in childhood (Herberg, 1989).

Every society has a *dominant value orientation,* a basic value orientation that is shared by the majority of its members as a result of early common experiences. In the United States, as in other cultures, the dominant value orientation is reflected in the dominant cultural group, which is made up of white, middle-class Protestants, typically those who came to this country at least two generations ago from Northern Europe. Because many members of the dominant cultural group are of Anglo-Saxon descent, they are sometimes referred to as WASPs (white Anglo-Saxon Protestants). Although the list is incomplete, summarized in Table 16–1 are 20 of the dominant U.S. value orientations as reflected in well-known proverbs.

In addition to the values identified from U.S. proverbs, the dominant cultural group places emphasis on educational achievement, science, technology, individual expression, democracy, experimentation, and informality (Herberg, 1989).

Although there is sometimes an assumption that the term white refers to a homogenous group of Americans, there is a rich diversity of ethnic variation among the many groups that constitute the dominant majority; origins include Eastern and Western Europe (Ireland, Poland, Italy, France, Sweden, Russia, and so on), as well as Canada, Australia, New Zealand, and South Africa (origins can ultimately be traced to Western Europe). Appalachians, the Amish, and other subgroups are also examples of whites who have cultural roots that are recognizably different from those of the dominant cultural group.

According to Kluckhohn and Strodtbeck (1961), there is a limited number of basic human problems for which all people must find a solution and five common human problems that concern values and norms:

1. What is the character of innate human nature? (human nature orientation)
2. What is the relation of the human person to nature? (person-nature orientation)
3. What is the temporal focus (time sense) of human life? (time orientation)
4. What is the mode of human activity? (activity orientation)
5. What is the mode of human relationships? (social orientation)

Regarding the first question, the innate human nature of people may be good, evil, or a combination of good and evil. Some consider human nature to be unalterable or able to be perfected only through great discipline and effort because they believe life is a struggle to overcome a basically evil nature. For others, human nature is perceived as fundamentally good, unalterable, and difficult or impossible to corrupt. According to Kohls (1984), the dominant U.S. cultural group chooses to believe the best

Table 16–1
Dominant Value Orientation

Proverb	Value
Cleanliness is next to godliness.	Cleanliness
A penny saved is a penny earned.	Thriftiness
Time is money.	Time thriftiness
Don't cry over spilt milk.	Practicality
Waste not, want not.	Frugality
Early to bed, early to rise, makes one healthy, wealthy, and wise.	Diligence, work ethic
God helps those who help themselves.	Initiative
It's not whether you win or lose, but how you play the game.	Good sportsmanship
A man's home is his castle.	Privacy, value of personal property
No rest for the wicked.	Guilt, work ethic
You've made your bed, now sleep in it.	Responsibility, retaliation
Don't count your chickens before they're hatched.	Practicality
A bird in the hand is worth two in the bush.	Practicality
The squeaky wheel gets the grease.	Aggressiveness; assertiveness
Might makes right.	Superiority of physical power
There's more than one way to skin a cat.	Originality, determination
A stitch in time saves nine.	Timeliness of action
All that glitters is not gold.	Wariness
Clothes make the man [or woman].	Concern for physical appearance
If at first you don't succeed, try, try again.	Persistence, work ethic
Take care of today, and tomorrow will take care of itself.	Preparation for the future
Laugh and the world laughs with you; weep and you weep alone.	Pleasant outward appearance

From Kohls, L. R.: Survival Kit for Overseas Living. Yarmouth, Maine, Intercultural Press, 1984.

about a person until that person proves otherwise. Concern in the United States for prison reform, social rehabilitation, and the plight of less-fortunate people around the world is reflective of the fundamental goodness of human nature, although human nature may also be viewed as a combination of good and evil.

Second, in examining the ways in which our person-nature relationship is perceived, there are three perspectives:

- Destiny, in which the human person is subjugated to nature in a fatalistic, inevitable manner
- Harmony, in which people and nature exist together as a single entity
- Mastery, in which it is believed that people are intended to overcome natural forces and put them to use for the benefit of humankind

Most Americans consider the human person and nature to be clearly separated (an incomprehensible perspective for many individuals of Asian heritage). The idea that one can control one's destiny is alien to many individuals of culturally diverse backgrounds. Many cultures believe that people are driven and controlled by fate and can do very little, if anything, to influence it. Americans, by contrast, have an insatiable drive to subdue, dominate, and control their natural environment (Kohls, 1984).

What does this values orientation have to do with health and illness? Consider three individuals who have recently been diagnosed with hypertension; each embraces one of the values orientations described. The person whose values orientation is destiny might say, "Why should I bother watching my diet, taking medication, and getting regular blood pressure checks? High blood pressure is part of my genetic destiny, and there is nothing I can do to change the outcome. There is no need to waste money on prescription drugs and health checkups." The person whose values orientation embraces harmony might say, "If I follow the diet prescribed and use medication to lower my blood pressure, I can restore the balance and harmony that were upset by this illness. The emotional stress I've been feeling indicates an inner lack of harmony that needs to be balanced." Finally, the person whose values orientation leads to belief in active mastery might say, "I will overcome this hypertension no matter what. By eating the right foods, working toward stress reduction, and conquering the disease with medication, I will take charge of the situation and influence the course of my disease."

Third, there are three major ways in which people can perceive time. The focus may be on the past, with traditions and ancestors playing an important role in the client's life. For example, many Asians, Native Americans, East Indians, and Africans hold beliefs about ancestors and tend to value long-standing traditions. In times of crisis, such as illness, individuals with a values orientation emphasizing the past may consult with ancestors or ask for their guidance or protection during the illness. The focus may be on the present, with little attention being paid to the past or the future. These individuals are concerned with the current situation, and the future is perceived as vague or unpredictable. Nurses may have difficulty encouraging these individuals to prepare for the future, e.g., participate in primary prevention measures. Last, the focus may be on the future, with progress and change highly valued. These individuals may express discontent with both the past and the present. In terms of health care, these individuals may inquire about the "latest treatment" and the most advanced equipment available for a particular problem.

The dominant U.S. cultural group is characterized by a belief in progress and a future orientation. This implies a strong task or goal orientation. This group has an optimistic faith in what the future will bring. Change is often equated with improvement, and a rapid rate of change is usually viewed as normal.

Fourth, this value orientation concerns activity. Philosophers have suggested three perspectives:

- Being, in which there is a spontaneous expression of impulses and desires that is largely non-developmental in nature
- Growing, in which the person is self-contained and has inner control, including the ability to self-actualize
- Doing, in which the person actively strives to achieve and accomplish something that is regarded highly

The doing is often directed toward achievement of an externally applied standard, such as a code of behavior from a religious or ethical perspective.

The Ten Commandments, Pillars of Islam, Hippocratic oath, and Nightingale pledge are examples of externally applied standards.

The dominant cultural value is action oriented with an emphasis on productivity and being busy. As a result of this action orientation, Americans have become very proficient at problem solving and decision making. Even during leisure time and vacations, many Americans value activity.

Finally, consider the cultural values orientations concerning the relationships that exist with others. There are three ways in which relationships may be categorized:

- Lineal relationships refer to those that exist by virtue of heredity and kinship ties. These relationships follow an ordered succession and have continuity through time.
- Collateral relationships focus primarily on group goals, and family orientation is all important. For example, many Asian patients will describe family honor and the importance of working together toward achievement of a group versus a personal goal.
- Individual relationships refer to personal autonomy and independence. These goals dominate; group goals become secondary.

The social orientation among the dominant U.S. cultural group is toward the importance of the individual and the equality of all people. Friendly, informal, outgoing, and extroverted, members of the dominant cultural group tend to scorn rank and authority, as demonstrated by, for example, nursing students who call faculty members by their first name, patients who call nurses by their first names, employees who fraternize with their employers, and so on. Members have a strong sense of individuality; however, family ties are relatively weak, as demonstrated by the high rate of separation and divorce in the United States. In many U.S. households, the family has been reduced to its smallest unit, the single parent family.

When making health-related decisions, clients from culturally diverse backgrounds rely on relationships with others in various ways. If the cultural values orientation is lineal, the client may seek assistance from other members of the family and allow a relative (e.g., parent, grandparent, elder brother) to make decisions about important health-related matters. If collateral relationships are valued, decisions about the client may be interrelated with the impact of illness on the entire family or group. For example, among the Amish, the entire community is affected by the illness of a member because the community pays for health care from a common fund, members join together to meet the needs of both the patient and the patient's family for the duration of the illness, and the roles of many in the community are likely to be affected by the illness of a single member. The individual values orientation concerning relationships is predominant among the dominant cultural majority in the United States. Decision making about health and illness is often an individual matter with the client being the sole decider, although members of the nuclear family may participate to varying degrees.

FAMILY

Despite the alarmingly high rate of divorce in the United States, the family remains the basic social unit. The essence of family consists of people living together as a unit. There are four major traditional categories of family:

- Nuclear (husband, wife, and child or children)
- Nuclear dyad (husband and wife alone, either childless or no children living at home)
- Single parent (either mother or father and at least one child)
- Extended family (includes grandparents, aunts, uncles, cousins, and sometimes individuals not biologically related). Minority families have traditionally been categorized as extended rather than nuclear.

Family Characteristics

In addition to structural differences in families cross-culturally, there may be accompanying functional diversity. For example, among extended families, kin residence sharing has long been recognized as a viable alternative to managing scarce resources, meeting child care needs, and/or caring for a handicapped or elderly family member. Sometimes the shared household is an adaptation for survival and protection.

In general, families with a culturally diverse heritage include not only a large number of adults but also a larger number of children than do families of the dominant cultural group. In a study of what the author referred to as successful rural black adolescents, Lee (1985) reported that the average number of children per home was five. Hispanics also tend to have higher fertility and birth rates than the non-Hispanic population (Ventura, 1987).

More than half (55.3%) of all black children under the age of 3 are born into single parent families. Among Puerto Ricans living in the United States, 44% of families are headed by single women (U.S. Bureau of the Census, 1985). Among black families, grandmothers have the most active involvement with the grandchildren when they live with their single adult daughter. This is not the case in families with two parents or in single parent families when the grandmother lives in a different household. Thus, black infants are exposed to a variety of other primary care providers and experience very different patterns of social interaction than do their counterparts in the dominant cultural group (Garcia Coll, 1990; Wilson, 1984).

In addition to a higher incidence of single heads of household, some cultural groups also have a higher incidence of teen parenting. Both blacks and Hispanics (especially Mexican-Americans and mainland Puerto Ricans) have higher percentages of births to mothers under the age of 20 (24% and 18%, respectively) than do whites (10%) (Ventura, 1987). Blacks also have a higher rate of adolescent pregnancy than whites, especially for births to unmarried teenagers. Adolescent pregnancies among whites have declined markedly in recent years as a result of sex education programs in schools, availability of contraceptives, and legalization of abortion.

The family constellations associated with teen parenting are unique and provide a special socialization context for infants. Hispanic teen mothers, for example, receive more child care help from grandmothers and peers than do white teen mothers (Garcia Coll, 1990). Among blacks and Puerto Ricans, the presence of the maternal grandmother ameliorates the negative consequences on the infant of adolescent childbearing. Among low-income black families, grandmothers who were more knowledgeable about infant development had adolescent daughters who were more knowledgeable if they were taking care of their infant. In addition, grandmothers are more responsive and less punitive in their interactions with the infant than are their daughters. These data suggest two mechanisms by which three-generational households can have an impact on the infant's development: by influencing the mother's knowledge about development and by providing other more responsive social interactions with infants (Garcia Coll, 1990, 1988, 1987).

Ethnic families are often characterized as being more conservative in terms of sex roles and parenting values and practices than are white families. For example, Japanese-American and Mexican-American families are family centered, enforce strict sex and age roles, and emphasize children's compliance with authority figures (Trankina, 1983; Yamamoto and Kubota, 1983). Thus, infants of culturally diverse backgrounds are involved in different family interactions than are infants from the dominant U.S. cultural group.

Relationships that may seem apparent sometimes warrant further exploration when interacting with clients from culturally diverse backgrounds. For example, the dominant cultural group defines siblings as two persons with either the same mother, the same father, the same mother and father, or the same adoptive parents. In some Asian cultures, a sibling relationship is defined as any infants who are breast fed by the same woman. In other cultures, certain kinship patterns, such as maternal first cousins, are defined as sibling relationships. In some African cultures, anyone from the same village or town may be called "brother" or "sister." Certain subcultures, such as Roman Catholics (who may be further subdivided by ethnicity into those who are Italian, Polish, Spanish, Mexican, and so on) recognize relationships such as "godmother" or "godfather" in which an individual who is not the biological parent promises to assist with the moral and spiritual development of an infant and agrees to care for the child in the event of parental death. The godparent makes these promises during the religious ceremony of baptism.

When providing care for infants and children, it is important to identify the primary provider of care as this individual may or may not be the biological parent. Among some Hispanic groups, for example, female members of the nuclear or extended family, such as sisters and aunts, are primary providers of care. In some black families, the

grandmother may be the decision maker and primary caretaker of children.

SOCIOECONOMIC FACTORS

Most families with racially or ethnically diverse backgrounds have a lower socioeconomic status than does the population at large, with a few exceptions (e.g., Cuban-Americans and some subgroups of Asian-Americans). Unemployment is consistently high among Native Americans with most reservations reporting an unemployment rate of approximately 30% (U.S. Senate Select Committee on Indian Affairs, 1985). Because the litany of inequalities is endless, a brief overview of the distribution of resources will be examined in general terms rather than in specific detail.

Distribution of Resources

Status, power, and wealth in the United States are not distributed equally throughout society. Rather, a very small percentage of the population enjoys most of the nation's resources, primarily through ownership of multibillion-dollar corporations, large pieces of real estate in prime locations, and similar assets. Using socioeconomic status as an indicator of status, power, and wealth, the U.S. population has traditionally been divided into three social classes: upper, middle, and lower. Socioeconomic status may be calculated by considering a wide variety of factors, but it is customarily determined by examining factors such as total family income, occupation, and educational level. In a less-formalized examination of socioeconomic status, factors such as age, sex, material possessions, health status, family name, location of residence(s), family composition, amount of land owned, religion, race, and ethnicity might be considered.

A disproportionate number of individuals from the racially and ethnically diverse subgroups are members of the lower socioeconomic class, whereas a larger percentage of members of the dominant cultural group (white Anglo-Saxon Protestants) belong to the upper and middle socioeconomic classes. Because the United States has socioeconomic stratification, the idealization of America as the land of opportunity often applies more to members of the upper and middle classes than to those in the lower class. The outcome of social stratification is social inequality. For example, it is well known that school systems, grocery stores, and recreational facilities vary significantly between the inner city and the suburbs.

For many years, health care settings have been the subject of study and concern regarding distribution of resources, with members of racial and ethnic minority groups clamoring with indignation at the inequalities. As the only industrialized, Western nation in the world without a national health care delivery system, the United States provides the best health care to those with the highest socioeconomic status and the worst health care to those with low socioeconomic status. Thus, in the United States, the quality of health care is determined largely by one's socioeconomic status, not by health status.

Education

One of the components considered in determining socioeconomic status is educational level. Native Americans and Alaskan natives who are at least 25 years old have an average of 9.6 years of formal education; this is the lowest rate for any major U.S. ethnic group (Brod and McQuiston, 1983). Laosa (1978, 1980) provided evidence suggesting that differences between white and Mexican-American maternal home teaching strategies can be accounted for by differences in levels of formal schooling rather than by cultural differences or economic indices. Mothers who had received more years of formal education inquired and praised more often than did mothers with less education. In contrast, the lower the mother's formal level of education, the more often the mother used modeling as a teaching strategy. Compared with white mothers, Hispanic mothers inquired and praised less often and used modeling, visual cues, directives, and negative physical control more often (Laosa, 1980). These differences disappeared entirely, however, when the mother's or father's educational levels were controlled statistically. In contrast, controlling the mother's or father's occupational status did not erase the cultural group differences in maternal teaching behavior. These studies contribute to our understanding of the ways in which educational level attained by people

from culturally diverse backgrounds affects the didactic aspects of the child-rearing environment (Garcia Coll, 1990).

Some data related to children will be used to examine the impact of socioeconomic factors on culturally diverse families. According to the 1985 Congressional Research Science, poverty rates among children of all ages were 43% for blacks, 40% for Hispanics, and 12% for whites. For the children of single mothers under the age of 30, poverty rates were 87% for Hispanics, 77% for blacks, and 65% for whites. Thus, the experience of growing up in poverty is often a large part of being a minority member of society. Research-based data about poverty among minorities are very scarce, however, especially those involved in analyzing the extent to which the problems associated with low socioeconomic status affect children, but it is known that residential segregation, substandard housing, unemployment, poor physical and mental health, prejudice, discrimination, and low self-image are all part of the cycle of poverty (Garcia Coll, 1990).

Lower social class status is associated with differences in parenting behaviors, home environment, and attitudes about health and illness. The care-giving environment of a large percentage of racially and ethnically diverse infants can be a function of culture as much as of socioeconomic status, and it is probably a combination of the two factors. For example, there are both racial and socioeconomic differences in methods of feeding (breast versus bottle), use of pacifiers, and age at weaning and toilet training (Garcia Coll, 1990).

The importance of other correlates of socioeconomic status, such as home language and family size, have also been studied. In a study that measured both the levels and the profiles of performance on measures of various abilities by children from Hispanic and white families of diverse socioeconomic levels, home language backgrounds, and family size, it was found that Hispanic and white children performed equally well when socioeconomic factors were controlled. However, the combination of low socioeconomic status and language minority status negatively affected the children's performance in areas such as verbal ability, quantitative ability, and short-term memory (Laosa, 1980).

CULTURE AND NUTRITION

Long after assimilation into the U.S. culture has occurred, clients from various ethnic groups will continue to follow culturally based dietary practices and to eat ethnic foods. Whenever a new group of immigrants arrives in the United States, it is common to see neighborhood food markets and ethnic restaurants established soon after arrival. Frequently, the ethnic restaurant is a meeting place for members of the cultural group to mingle, and customers from the dominant cultural group may be of secondary interest; thus, food is an integral part of cultural identity that may be even more significant than financial gain.

Nutrition Assessment of Culturally Diverse Groups

Among factors that must be considered in a nutrition assessment are the cultural definition of food, frequency and number of meals eaten away from home, form and content of ceremonial meals, amount and types of food eaten, and regularity of food consumption. Because potential inaccuracies may occur, the 24-hour dietary recalls or 3-day food records traditionally used for assessment may be inadequate when dealing with clients from culturally diverse backgrounds. Standard dietary handbooks may fail to provide culture-specific diet information because nutritional content and exchange tables are usually based on Western diets (Pennington, 1976). Another source of error may originate from the cultural patterns of eating; for example, among low-income urban black families, elaborate weekend meals are frequently eaten, whereas weekday dietary patterns are markedly more moderate.

Although community health nurses may assume that "food" is a culture-universal term, it may be necessary to clarify with the client what is meant by the term. For example, certain Latin American groups do not consider greens, an important source of vitamins, to be food and thus fail to list intake of these vegetables on daily records. Among Vietnamese refugees, dietary intake of calcium may appear inadequate because of the low consumption rate of dairy products common among members of this group. Pork bones and shells, however, are commonly consumed, thus providing adequate quantities of calcium to meet daily requirements.

Food is only one part of eating. In some cultures, social contacts during meals are restricted to members of the immediate or extended family. For example, in some Middle Eastern cultures, men and women eat meals separately, or women are permitted to eat with their husbands but not with other males. Among some Hispanic groups, the male breadwinner is served first, and then the women and children eat. Etiquette during meals, use of hands, type of eating utensils (e.g., chopsticks, special flatware), and protocols governing the order in which food is consumed during a meal all vary cross-culturally.

Dietary Practices of Selected Cultural Groups

Cultural stereotyping is the tendency to view individuals of common cultural backgrounds similarly and according to a preconceived notion of how they behave. However, not all Chinese like rice, not all Italians like spaghetti, not all Mexicans like tortillas, and so on. Nevertheless, aggregate dietary preferences among people from certain cultural groups can be described (e.g., characteristic ethnic dishes, methods of food preparation including use of cooking oils); the reader is referred to nutrition texts on the topic for detailed information about culture-specific diets and the nutritional value of ethnic foods.

Religion and Diet

Cultural food preferences are often interrelated with religious dietary beliefs and practices. As indicated in Table 16–2, many religions have proscriptive dietary practices, and some use food as symbols in celebrations and rituals. Knowing the client's religious practice as it relates to food makes it possible to suggest improvements or modifications that will not conflict with religious dietary laws.

Beyond the scope of this text is the issue of fasting and other religious observations that may limit a person's food or liquid intake during specified times (e.g., many Catholics fast and abstain from meat on Ash Wednesday and the Fridays of Lent,

Table 16–2 **Dietary Practices of Selected Religious Groups**	
Religion	**Dietary Practice**
Hinduism	All meats are prohibited.
Islam	Pork and intoxicating beverages are prohibited.
Judaism	Pork, predatory fowl, shellfish and other water creatures (fish with scales are permissible), and blood by ingestion (e.g., blood sausage, raw meat) are prohibited. Blood by transfusion is acceptable. Foods should be kosher (meaning "properly preserved"). All animals must be ritually slaughtered by a sochet (i.e., quickly with the least pain possible) to be kosher. Mixing dairy and meat dishes at the same meal is prohibited.
Mormonism (Church of Jesus Christ of Latter-day Saints)	Alcohol, tobacco, and beverages containing caffeine (e.g., coffee, tea, colas, and selected carbonated soft drinks) are prohibited.
Seventh-Day Adventism	Pork, certain seafood (including shellfish), and fermented beverages are prohibited. A vegetarian diet is encouraged.

Muslims refrain from eating during the daytime hours for the month of Ramadan but are permitted to eat after sunset, and Mormons refrain from ingesting all solid foods and liquids on the first Sunday of each month).

RELIGION AND CULTURE

Although it is impossible to be an expert on each of the estimated 1,200 religions practiced in the United States, knowledge of health-related beliefs and practices as well as general information about the religious observances is important in providing culturally sensitive nursing care. For example, it is important to have a general understanding of the religious calendar, including designated holy days, when planning home visits or scheduling clinic visits for members of a specific religious group. It is also useful to know the customary day or days of religious worship observed by members of the religion. Although the majority of Protestants worship on Sundays, the sacred day of worship may vary for other religious groups. For example, the Muslims' holy day of worship extends from sunset on Thursday to sunset on Friday, whereas for Jews and Seventh-Day Adventists, the day extends from sunset on Friday to sunset on Saturday. Roman Catholics may worship in the late afternoon or evening of Saturday or all day Sunday. Some religions may meet more than once weekly. In addition to regularly scheduled weekly religious service, most major religions also recognize special days of observance or celebration that last from 1 day (e.g., Christmas, Easter, Rosh Hashanah, and Janamasthtmi) to 1 month (e.g., Ramadan). Some days of commemoration or observation are based on a lunar calendar and some have rotating dates, so it is necessary to consult official information sources such as religious leaders or official calendars to verify exact dates. It is also important to ask clients what religious observations they adhere to as individual activity within the religious organization may vary widely.

As an integral component of the individual's culture, religious beliefs may influence the client's explanation of the cause of illness, perception of its severity, and choice of healer. In times of crisis, such as serious illness and impending death, religion may be a source of consolation for the client and family and may influence the course of action believed to be appropriate.

Religion and Spirituality

Religious concerns evolve from and respond to the mysteries of life and death, good and evil, and pain and suffering. In nursing, nurses frequently encounter clients who find themselves searching for a spiritual meaning to help explain the illness or disability. Some nurses find spiritual assessment difficult because of the abstract and personal nature of the topic, whereas others feel quite comfortable discussing spiritual matters. Comfort with one's own spiritual beliefs is the foundation to effective assessment of spiritual needs in clients.

Although the religions of the world offer various interpretations to many of life's mysteries, most people seek a personal understanding and interpretation at some time in their lives. Ultimately, this personal search becomes a pursuit to discover a supreme being (e.g., Allah, God, Yahweh, Jehovah, and so on) or some unifying truth that will render meaning, purpose, and integrity to existence (Cluff, 1986).

An important distinction must be made between religion and spirituality. *Religion* refers to an organized system of beliefs concerning the cause, nature, and purpose of the universe, especially belief in or the worhship of a god or gods. More than 1,200 religions are practiced in the United States. *Spirituality* is born out of each person's unique life experience and personal effort to find purpose and meaning in life. To assess the spiritual needs of culturally diverse clients, suggested guidelines are given in Table 16–3.

Prolongation of life, euthanasia, autopsy, donation of body for research, disposal of body and body parts (including fetus), and type of burial may be influenced by religion. You should use discretion in asking clients and their families about these issues and gather data only when the clinical situation necessitates that the information be obtained. Clients and families should be encouraged to discuss these issues with their religious representative when necessary. Before dealing with potentially sensitive issues, it is important to establish rapport with the client and family by gaining their trust and confidence in less-sensitive areas.

Developmental Considerations: Childhood

Illness during childhood may be an especially difficult clinical situation. Children as well as adults have spiritual needs that vary according to the child's developmental level and the religious climate that exists in the family. Parental perceptions

---

Table 16–3
Methods of Assessing Spiritual Needs in Culturally Diverse Clients

Environment

Does the client have religious objects in the environment?

Does the client wear outer garments or undergarments that have religious significance?

Are get-well greeting cards religious in nature or from a representative of the client's church?

Does the client receive flowers or bulletins from church or other religious institution?

Behavior

Does the client appear to pray at certain times of the day or before meals?

Does the client make special dietary requests (e.g., kosher diet; vegetarian diet; or diet free from caffeine, pork, shellfish, or other specific food items)?

Does the client read religious magazines or books?

Verbalization

Does the client mention a supreme being (e.g., God, Allah, Buddha, Yahweh, or other), prayer, faith, church, or religious topics?

Is a request made for a visit by a clergy member or other religious representative?

Is there an expression of anxiety or fear about pain, suffering, or death?

Interpersonal Relationships

Who visits the client? How does the client respond to visitors?

Does a church representative visit?

How does the client relate to nursing staff and to roommates?

Does the client prefer to interact with others or to remain alone?

Data from Boyle, J. S., and Andrews, M. M.: Transcultural Concepts in Nursing Care. Glenview, Illinois, Scott, Foresman/Little, Brown & Co., 1989.

---

about the illness of their child may be partially influenced by religious beliefs. For example, some parents may believe that a transgression against a religious law is responsible for a congenital anomaly in their offspring. Other parents may delay seeking medical care because they believe that first prayer should be tried. Certain types of treatment, e.g., administration of blood or of medications containing caffeine, pork, or other prohibited substances and selected procedures, may be perceived as cultural taboos, which are to be avoided by both children and adults.

Developmental Considerations: Old Age

Values held by the dominant U.S. culture, such as emphasis on independence, self-reliance, and productivity, influence aging members of society. Americans define people at the chronological age of 65 as old and limit their work; in some other cultures, persons are first recognized as being unable to work and then identified as being old. In some cultures, it is the wisdom, not the productivity, of the elderly that is valued; thus, the diminishment of one's activity level and reduction of physical stamina associated with growing old are accepted more readily without loss of status among culture members. Retirement is also culturally defined, with some elderly working as long as physical health continues and others continuing to be active but assuming less physically demanding jobs.

The main task of elderly persons in the dominant culture is to achieve a sense of integrity in accepting responsibility for their own lives and in having a sense of accomplishment. Individuals who achieve integrity consider aging a positive experience, make adjustments in their personal space and social relationships, maintain a sense of usefulness, and begin closure and life review. Not all cultures value accepting responsibility for one's own life. For example, among Hispanics, Asians, Arabs, and other groups, the elderly are often cared for by family members who welcome them into their homes when they are no longer able to live alone. The concept of placing an elderly family member in an institutional setting to be cared for by total strangers is perceived as an uncaring, impersonal, and culturally unacceptable practice by many cultural groups.

Elderly persons may develop their own means of coping with illness through self-care, assistance from family members, and social group support systems. Some cultures have developed attitudes and specific behaviors for the elderly that include humanistic care and identification of family members as care providers. The elderly may have special family responsibilities, e.g., the elderly Amish provide hospitality to visitors, and elderly Filipinos spend considerable time teaching the youth skills learned during a lifetime of experience.

Elderly immigrants who have made major lifestyle adjustments in the move from their homeland to the United States and/or from a rural to an urban area (or vice versa) may need information about health care alternatives, preventive programs, health care benefits, and screening programs for which they are eligible. These individuals may also be in various stages of "culture shock," which is a term used to describe the state of disorientation or inability to respond to the behavior of a different cultural group because of its sudden strangeness, unfamiliarity, and incompatibility to the newcomer's perceptions and expectations (Leininger, 1978).

CROSS-CULTURAL COMMUNICATION

Both verbal and nonverbal communication are important in community health nursing and are influenced by the cultural background of both the nurse and the client. Cross-cultural, or intercultural, communication refers to the communication process occurring between a nurse and a client who have different cultural backgrounds as both attempt to understand the other's point of view from a cultural perspective.

Nurse-Client Relationship

From the initial introduction to the client through termination of the relationship, community health nurses are in a continuous process of communication. Because beginning impressions are so important in all human relationships, cross-cultural considerations concerning introductions warrant a few brief remarks. To ensure that a mutually respectful relationship is established, it is important for the nurse to introduce himself or herself and indicate how the client should refer to the nurse, i.e., by first name, last name, or title. Having done so, the nurse should ask the client to do the same. This enables the nurse to address the client in a manner that is culturally appropriate and could avoid embarrassment in the future. For example, it is the custom among some Asian and European cultures to write the last name first; thus, confusion can be avoided in an area of extreme sensitivity, the client's name.

Both the community health nurse and the client are likely to bring cultural stereotypes to the nurse-client interaction. For example, when Ragucci

(1981) studied the views of Italian-Americans toward nurses, she found a very traditional expectation, with respondents usually expecting nurses to carry out physicians' orders without making independent health care judgments. Similarly, a study of Asian clients reveals that nurses are expected to provide medications, including injections, and to perform treatments ordered by physicians (Gould-Martin and Ngin, 1981) but not to provide psychosocial care. In Asia and in many parts of Africa, family members perform all support tasks such as bathing, feeding, and other comfort measures while nurses engage in strictly procedural activities such as changing dressings or administering medications.

One of the major challenges community health nurses face in working with clients from culturally diverse backgrounds is overcoming one's own *ethnocentrism.* Ethnocentrism is the tendency to view one's own way of life as the most desirable, acceptable, or best and to act in a superior manner to another culture. One must also beware of *cultural imposition,* which is the tendency to impose one's own beliefs, values, and patterns of behavior on individuals from another culture.

Space, Distance, and Intimacy

Both the client's and the nurse's own senses of spatial distance are significant throughout the home visit, with culturally appropriate distance zones varying widely. For example, nurses may back away from clients of Hispanic, East Indian, or Middle Eastern origin who invade personal space with regularity in an attempt to bring the nurse closer into the space that is comfortable to them. While nurses are uncomfortable with clients' close physical proximity, clients are perplexed by the nurse's distancing behaviors and may perceive the community health nurse as aloof and unfriendly. Summarized in Table 16–4 are the four distance zones identified for the functional use of space that are embraced by the dominant cultural group, including most nurses. Interactions between clients and nurses may also depend on the client's desired degree of intimacy, which may range from very formal interactions to close personal relationships. For example, some Southeast Asian clients expect those in authority, i.e., nurses, to be authoritarian, directive, and detached.

Table 16–4 **Functional Use of Space**	
Zone	**Remarks**
Intimate zone (0–1.5 feet)	Visual distortion occurs Best for assessing breath and other body odors
Personal distance (1.5–4 feet)	Perceived as an extension of the self, similar to a "bubble" Voice is moderate Body odors are inapparent No visual distortion Much of the physical assessment will occur at this distance
Social distance (4–12 feet)	Used for impersonal business transactions Perceptual information is much less detailed Much of the interview will occur at this distance
Public distance (12+ feet)	Interaction with others is impersonal Speaker's voice must be projected Subtle facial expressions are imperceptible

Data from Hall, E.: Proxemics: The study of man's spatial relations. *In* Galdston, I., ed.: Man's Image in Medicine and Anthropology. New York, International Universities Press, 1963, pp. 109–120.

The emphasis on social harmony among Asian and Native American clients may prevent the full expression of concerns or feelings during the interview. Such reserved behavior may leave the nurse with the impression that the client agrees with or understands an explanation. However, nodding or smiling by Asian clients may only reflect their cultural value for interpersonal harmony, not agreement with the speaker. Nurses may distinguish between socially compliant client responses aimed at maintaining harmony and genuine concurrence by obtaining validation of assumptions. This may be accomplished by inviting the client to respond frankly to your suggestions or by giving the client permission to disagree.

In contrast, Appalachian clients traditionally have close family interaction patterns that often lead them to expect close personal relationships with health care providers. The Appalachian client may evaluate the nurse's effectiveness on the basis of interpersonal skills rather than on professional competency. Appalachian clients are likely to be uncomfortable with the impersonal, bureaucratic orientation of most health care institutions. Clients of Arab, Latin American, or Mediterranean origin, often expect an even higher degree of intimacy and may attempt to involve the nurse in their family system by expecting participation in personal activities and social functions. These individuals may come to expect personal favors that extend beyond the scope of professional nursing practice and may feel it is their privilege to contact the nurse at home during any time of the day or night for care (Lipson and Meleis, 1983).

Overcoming Communication Barriers

Nurses tend to have stereotypical expectations of the client's behavior. In general, nurses expect behavior to consist of undemanding compliance, an attitude of respect for the health care provider, and cooperation with requested behavior throughout the examination. Although clients may ask a few questions for the purpose of clarification, slight deference to recognized authority figures, i.e., health care providers, is expected. Individuals from culturally diverse backgrounds, however, may have significantly different perceptions about the appropriate role of the individual and family when seeking health care. If you find yourself becoming annoyed that a client is asking too many questions, assuming a defensive posture, or otherwise feeling uncomfortable, you might pause for a moment to examine the source of the conflict from a cross-cultural perspective.

During illness, culturally acceptable "sick role" behavior may range from aggressive, demanding behavior to silent passivity. According to Hartog and Hartog (1983), complaining, demanding behavior during illness is often rewarded with attention among Jewish and Italian-American groups, whereas Asian and Native American patients are likely to be quiet and compliant during illness. During the interview, Asian clients may provide the nurse with the answers they think the nurse wants to hear, which is behavior consistent with the dominant cultural value for harmonious relationships with others. Thus, an attempt should be made to phrase questions or statements in a neutral manner that avoids foreshadowing an expected re-

sponse. Appalachian clients may reject a community health nurse whom they perceive as "prying" or "nosey" due to a cultural ethic of neutrality that mandates minding one's own business and avoiding assertive or argumentative behavior.

Nonverbal Communication

Unless one makes an effort to understand the client's nonverbal behavior, it is possible to overlook important information such as that which is conveyed by facial expressions, silence, eye contact, touch, and other body language. Communication patterns vary widely cross-culturally, even for seemingly "innocent" behaviors such as smiling and handshaking. Among many Hispanic clients, for example, smiling and handshaking are considered an integral part of sincere interaction and essential to establishing trust, whereas a Soviet client might perceive the same behavior by the nurse as insolent and frivolous (Tripp-Reimer and Lauer, 1987). Sex issues also become significant, e.g., among some groups of Middle Eastern origin, men and women do not shake hands or touch each other in any manner outside of the marital relationship. If the nurse and client are both female, however, a handshake is usually acceptable.

Wide cultural variation exists when interpreting silence. Some individuals find silence extremely uncomfortable and make every effort to fill conversational lags with words. In contrast, Native Americans consider silence essential to understanding and respecting the other person. A pause following a question signifies that what the speaker has asked is important enough to be given thoughtful consideration. In traditional Chinese and Japanese cultures, silence may mean that the speaker wishes the listener to consider the content of what has been said before continuing. The English and Arabs may use silence out of respect for another person's privacy, whereas the French, Spanish, and Soviets may interpret it as a sign of agreement. Asian cultures often use silence to demonstrate respect for elders (Boyle and Andrews, 1989; Tripp-Reimer and Lauer, 1987).

Eye contact is among the most culturally variable nonverbal behaviors. Although most nurses have been taught to maintain eye contact while talking with clients, individuals from culturally diverse backgrounds may misconstrue this behavior.

Asian, Native American, Indochinese, Arab, and Appalachian clients may consider direct eye contact impolite or aggressive, and they may avert their own eyes during the conversation. Native American clients often stare at the floor when the nurse is talking; this is a culturally appropriate behavior that indicates that the listener is paying close attention to the speaker.

In some cultures, including Arab, Hispanic, and black groups, modesty for women is interrelated with eye contact. For Muslim women, modesty is achieved in part by avoiding eye contact with men (except for one's husband) and keeping eyes downcast when encountering members of the opposite sex in public situations. In many cultures, the only woman who smiles and establishes eye contact with men in public is a prostitute. Hassidic Jewish men also have culturally based norms concerning eye contact with women. The male may avoid direct eye contact and turn his head in the opposite direction when walking past or speaking to a woman. The preceding examples are intended to be illustrative but not exhaustive.

Touch

Touching the client is a necessary component of a comprehensive assessment. Although there are benefits in establishing rapport with clients through touch, including the promotion of healing through therapeutic touch, physical contact with clients conveys various meanings cross-culturally. In many cultures, e.g., Arab and Hispanic, male health care providers may be prohibited from touching or examining all or certain parts of the female body. During pregnancy, the client may prefer female health care providers and may refuse to be examined by a man. Be aware that the client's significant other may also exert pressure on health care providers by enforcing these culturally meaningful norms in the health care setting.

Touching children may also have associated meanings cross-culturally. For example, Hispanic clients may believe in *mal ojo* ("evil eye")—an individual becomes ill as a result of excessive admiration by another. Many Asians believe that one's strength resides in the head and that touching the head is considered disrespectful. Thus, palpation of the fontanelle of an infant of Southeast Asian descent should be approached with sensitivity. It may be necessary to rely on alternative sources of information (e.g., assessing for clinical manifestations of increased intracranial pressure or signs of premature fontanelle closure). Although it is the least desirable option, you may have to omit this part of the assessment.

Sex

Violating norms related to appropriate male-female relationships among various cultures may jeopardize the therapeutic nurse-client relationship. Among Arab-Americans, a man is never alone with a woman (except his wife) and is usually accompanied by one or more other men when interacting with women. This behavior is culturally very significant, and failure to adhere to the *cultural code* (set of rules or norms of behavior used by a cultural group to guide their behavior and to interpret situations) is viewed as a serious transgression, often one in which the lone male will be accused of sexual impropriety. The best way to ensure that cultural variables have been considered is to ask the client about culturally relevant aspects of male-female relationships, preferably at the beginning of the interaction before you have an opportunity to violate any culturally based practices.

Language

When assessing non–English-speaking clients, the nurse may encounter one of two situations—choosing an interpreter or communicating effectively when there is no interpreter.

Non–English-Speaking Clients

Interviewing the non–English-speaking person requires a bilingual interpreter for full communication. Even the person from another culture or country who has a basic command of English may need an interpreter when faced with the anxiety-provoking situation of becoming ill, encountering a strange symptom, or discussing a sensitive topic such as birth control or gynecologic or urologic concerns. It is tempting to ask a relative, friend, or even another client to interpret because this person is readily available and is anxious to help. However, this is disadvantageous because it violates confidentiality for the client, who may not want personal information shared with another. Furthermore, the friend or relative, although fluent in ordinary language, is likely to be unfamiliar with medical terminology, clinic procedures, and medical ethics.

Whenever possible, a bilingual team member or trained medical interpreter should be used. This person knows interpreting techniques, has a health care background, and understands patients' rights. The trained interpreter also is knowledgeable about cultural beliefs and health practices and can help you bridge the cultural gap and advise you concerning the cultural appropriateness of your recommendations.

Although the nurse is in charge of the focus and flow of the home visit or client-nurse interaction, the interpreter is an important member of the health care team. Ask the interpreter to meet the client before the visit to establish rapport and learn the client's age, occupation, educational level, and attitude toward health care. This enables the interpreter to communicate on the client's level.

The nurse should allow more time for home and clinic visits with culturally diverse clients who require an interpreter. With the third person repeating everything, it can take considerably longer than interviewing English-speaking clients. It will be necessary to focus on the major points and to prioritize data.

There are two styles of interpreting: line-by-line and summarizing. Translating line-by-line ensures accuracy, but it takes more time. Both the nurse and the client should speak only a sentence or two and then allow the interpreter time to interpret. Use simple language, not medical jargon that the interpreter must simplify before it can be translated. Summary translation goes faster and is useful for teaching relatively simple health techniques with which the interpreter is already familiar. Be alert for nonverbal cues as the client talks; this can give valuable data. A good interpreter also will note nonverbal messages and communicate those to the community health nurse.

Summarized in Table 16–5 are suggestions for the selection and use of an interpreter.

Although use of an interpreter is the ideal, one may find oneself in a situation with a non–English-speaking client when no interpreter is available. Table 16–6 summarizes some suggestions for overcoming language barriers when there is no interpreter.

Table 16–5
Overcoming Language Barriers: Use of an Interpreter

Before locating an interpreter, be sure that you know what language the patient speaks at home because it may be different from the language spoken publicly (e.g., French is sometimes spoken by aristocratic or well-educated people from certain Asian or Middle Eastern cultures).

Avoid interpreters from a rival tribe, state, region, or nation (e.g., a Palestinian who knows Hebrew may not be the best interpreter for a Jewish client).

Be aware of sex differences between interpreter and client to avoid violation of cultural mores related to modesty.

Be aware of age differences between interpreter and client.

Be aware of socioeconomic differences between interpreter and client.

Ask interpreter to translate as closely to verbatim as possible.

An interpreter who is not a relative may seek compensation for services rendered.

HEALTH-RELATED BELIEFS AND PRACTICES

One of the major aspects of a comprehensive cultural assessment concerns the collection of data related to culturally based beliefs and practices about health and illness. Before determining if cultural practices are helpful, harmful, or neutral, the nurse must first understand the logic of the belief system underlying the practice and then be sure to fully grasp the nature and meaning of the practice from the client's cultural perspective.

Health and Culture

The first step in understanding the health care needs of clients is to understand one's own culturally based values, beliefs, attitudes, and practices. Sometimes this requires considerable introspection and may necessitate that one confront one's own biases, preconceptions, and prejudices about specific racial, ethnic, religious, sexual, or socioeconomic groups. Second, identify the meaning of health to the client, remembering that concepts are derived in part from the way in which members of

Table 16–6
Overcoming Language Barriers When There Is No Interpreter

Be polite and formal.

Greet the client using the last or complete name. Gesture to yourself and say your name. Offer a handshake or nod. Smile.

Proceed in an unhurried manner. Pay attention to any effort by the client or family to communicate.

Speak in a low, moderate voice. Avoid talking loudly. Remember that there is a tendency to raise the volume and pitch of your voice when the listener appears not to understand, and the listener may perceive that you are shouting or angry.

Use any words that you might know in the patient's language. This indicates that you are aware of and respect their culture.

Use simple words, such as "pain" instead of "discomfort."
Avoid medical jargon, idioms, and slang. Avoid using contractions such as "don't," "can't," and "won't." Use nouns repeatedly instead of pronouns. For example, say "Does Juan take medicine?" instead of "He has been taking his medicine, hasn't he?"

Pantomime words and simple actions while you verbalize them.

Give instructions in the proper sequence. For example, say "First wash the bottle. Second, rinse the bottle" instead of "Before you rinse the bottle, sterilize it."

Discuss one topic at a time. Avoid using conjunctions. For example, say "Are you cold [while pantomiming]?" "Are you in pain?" instead of "Are you cold and in pain?"

Validate if the client understands by having the client repeat instructions, demonstrate the procedure, or act out the meaning.

Write out several short sentences in English and determine the client's ability to read them.

Try a third language. Many Indo-Chinese speak French. Europeans often know three or four languages. Try Latin words or phrases.

Ask who among the client's family and friends could serve as an interpreter.

Obtain phrase books from a library or bookstore, make or purchase flash cards, contact hospitals for a list of interpreters, and use both formal and informal networking to locate a suitable interpreter.

their cultural group define health. Considerable research has been conducted on the various definitions of health that may be held by various groups. For example, Jamaicans define health as having a good appetite, feeling strong and energetic, performing activities of daily living without difficulty, and being sexually active and fertile (Mitchell, 1983). In a study of Italian women, Ragucci (1981) observed that health means the ability to interact socially and perform routine tasks such as cooking, cleaning, and caring for oneself and others. On the other hand, some individuals of Hispanic origin believe that coughing, sweating, and diarrhea are a normal part of living rather than symptoms of ill health—perhaps because of their high frequency in the client's country of origin. Thus, individuals may define themselves or others in their group as healthy even though the nurse identifies symptoms of disease.

Defining Illness From a Cross-Cultural Perspective

For clients, symptom labeling and diagnosis depend on the degree of difference between the individual's behaviors and those the group has defined as normal, beliefs about the causation of illness, level of stigma attached to a particular set of symptoms, prevalence of the pathology, and meaning of the illness to the individual and family.

Throughout history, humankind has attempted to understand the cause of illness and disease. Theories of causation have been formulated based on religious beliefs, social circumstances, philosophical perspectives, and level of knowledge. The following section will explore some of the more prevalent theories of illness causation.

CAUSES OF ILLNESS

There are three major perspectives from which disease causation may be viewed: biomedical (sometimes used synonymously with the term "scientific"), naturalistic (sometimes used synonymously with the term "holistic"), and magicoreligious. The first, the *biomedical,* or *scientific,* theory of illness causation, is based on the assumption that all events in life have a cause and effect, that the human body functions more or less mechanically (i.e., the functioning of the human body is analogous to the functioning of an automobile), that all life can be reduced or divided into smaller parts (e.g., the human person can be reduced into body, mind, and spirit), and that all of reality can be observed and measured (e.g., with intelligence tests and psychometric measures of behavior). Among the biomedical explanations for disease is the germ theory, which posits that microscopic organisms such as bacteria and viruses are responsible for specific disease conditions. Most educational programs for nurses and other health care providers embrace the biomedical or scientific theories that explain the cause of both physical and psychological illnesses.

The second way in which clients explain the cause of illness is from the *naturalistic,* or *holistic,* perspective, a viewpoint that is found most frequently among Native Americans, Asians, and others who believe that human life is only one aspect of nature and a part of the general order of the cosmos. Individuals from these groups believe that the forces of nature must be kept in natural balance or harmony.

Among many Asians, there is a belief in the *yin-yang theory* in which health is believed to exist when all aspects of the person are in perfect balance. Rooted in the ancient Chinese philosophy of Tao, the yin-yang theory states that all organisms and objects in the universe consist of yin or yang energy forces. The origin of the energy forces are within the autonomic nervous system, where balance between the opposing forces is maintained during health. Yin energy represents the female and negative forces, e.g., emptiness, darkness, and cold, whereas yang forces are male and positive, emitting warmth and fullness. Foods are classified as hot and cold in this theory and are transformed into yin and yang energy when metabolized by the body. Yin foods are cold, and yang foods are hot. Cold foods are eaten when one has a hot illness, and hot foods are eaten when one has a cold illness. The yin-yang theory is the basis for Eastern or Chinese medicine and is commonly embraced by Asian-Americans.

The naturalistic perspective posits that the laws of nature create imbalances, chaos, and disease. Individuals embracing the naturalistic view use metaphors such as the healing power of nature, and they call the earth "Mother." From the perspective of the Chinese, for example, illness is not seen as an intruding agent but rather as a part of life's rhythmic course and as an outward sign of the disharmony that is within.

Many Hispanic, Arab, black, and Asian groups embrace the *hot-cold theory* of health and illness, an explanatory model with its origin, in the ancient Greek humoral theory. The four humors of the body—blood, phlegm, black bile, and yellow bile—regulate basic bodily functions and are described in terms of temperature, dryness, and moisture. The treatment of disease consists of adding or subtracting cold, heat, dryness, or wetness to restore the balance of the humors.

Beverages, foods, herbs, medicines, and diseases are classified as hot or cold according to their perceived effects on the body, not on their physical characteristics. Illnesses believed to be caused by cold entering the body include earache, chest cramps, paralysis, gastrointestinal discomfort, rheumatism, and tuberculosis. Illnesses believed to be caused by overheating include abscessed teeth, sore throats, rashes, and kidney disorders.

According to the hot-cold theory, the individual as a whole rather than a specific ailment is significant. Those who embrace the hot-cold theory maintain that health consists of a positive state of total well-being, including physical, psychological, spiritual, and social aspects of the person. Paradoxically, the language used to describe this artificial dissection of the body into parts is a reflection of the biomedical/scientific perspective, not a naturalistic or holistic one.

The third major way in which people view the world and explain the causation of illness is from a *magicoreligious* perspective. The basic premise of this explanatory model is that the world is seen as an arena in which supernatural forces dominate. The fate of the world, and those in it, depends on the action of supernatural forces for good or evil. Examples of magical causes of illness include the belief in voodoo or witchcraft among some blacks and others from circum-Caribbean countries. Faith healing is based on religious beliefs and is most prevalent among selected Christian religions, including Christian Scientists; various healing rituals may be found in many other religions, such as Roman Catholicism, Mormonism (Church of Jesus Christ of Latter-day Saints), and others.

It is possible to have a combination of world views, and many clients are likely to offer more than one explanation for the cause of their illness. As a profession, nursing largely embraces the biomedical/scientific world view, but some aspects of holism have begun to gain popularity, including a wide variety of techniques for management of chronic pain such as hypnosis, therapeutic touch, and biofeedback. Belief in spiritual power is also held by many nurses who readily credit supernatural forces with various unexplained phenomena related to clients' health and illness states.

Culture and Healing

When self-treatment is unsuccessful, the individual may turn to the lay or folk-healing systems, to spiritual or religious healing, or to scientific biomedicine. All cultures have their own preferred lay or popular healers, recognized symptoms of ill health, acceptable sick-role behavior, and treatments. In addition to seeking help from the nurse as a biomedical/scientific health care provider, clients may also seek help from folk or religious healers. Some clients, such as Hispanics or Native Americans, may believe that the cure is incomplete unless healing of body, mind, and spirit is accomplished, although the division of the human person into parts is a Western concept. For example, an Hispanic client with a respiratory infection may ingest antibiotics prescribed by a physician or nurse practitioner and herbal teas recommended by a *curandero* and also say prayers for healing suggested by a Catholic priest.

The variety of healing beliefs and practices used by the many U.S. subcultural groups far exceeds the limitations of this chapter. It is important, however, for the nurse to be aware of alternative practices and recognize that in addition to folk practices, there are many alternative healing practices. Although it is dangerous to assume that all indigenous approaches to healing are innocuous, the majority of practices are quite harmless, regardless of whether they are effective cures.

Folk Healers

There are numerous folk healers. Hispanic clients may turn to a *curandero, espiritualista* (spiritualist), *yerbo* (herbalist), or *sabador* (equal to a chiropractor). Black clients may mention having received assistance from a *hougan* (voodoo priest or priestess), spiritualist, or "old lady" (an older woman who has successfully raised a family and specializes in child care and folk remedies). Native American clients may seek assistance from a *shaman,* or medicine man. Clients of Asian descent may mention that they have visited herbalists, acupuncturists, or bone setters. Each culture has its own healers, most of whom speak the native tongue of the client, make house calls, and cost significantly less than healers practicing in the biomedical/scientific health care system. In addition to folk healers, many cultures have lay midwives (e.g., *parteras* for Hispanic women) or other health care providers who meet the needs of pregnant women.

In some religions, spiritual healers may be found among the ranks of the ordained or official religious hierarchy ranks and are called priest, bishop, elder, deacon, rabbi, brother, sister, and so on. Other religions have a separate category of healer, e.g., Christian Science "nurses" (not licensed by states) or practitioners.

HEALTH, ILLNESS, AND CULTURAL DIVERSITY

Despite the unprecedented explosion in scientific knowledge and the tremendous resources available within the U.S. health care delivery system, members of the federally defined minority groups (i.e., blacks, Hispanics, Native Americans, and those of Asian/Pacific-Islander heritage) have not benefitted equally or equitably. In response to this lack of equality, Margaret M. Heckler, Secretary of the U.S. Department of Health and Human Services, established a Task Force on Black and Minority Health in 1984 to examine the nature of the disparities and propose solutions that would result in an overall improvement of health for members of the federally defined minority groups (Heckler, 1985).

Since the turn of the century, the overall health status of all U.S. citizens has improved greatly, primarily as a result of improved sanitation, better nutrition, and mass immunization that resulted in a drastic decline in infectious diseases. Since 1960, the U.S. population has experienced a steady decline in the overall death rate from all causes, and remarkable progress is being made in understanding the causes and risks for developing conditions such as heart disease and cancer. The decline in cardiovascular disease mortality from 1968 to 1978 alone improved overall life expectancy by 1.6 years. Advances in the long-term management of chronic diseases mean that conditions such as hypertension and diabetes no longer necessarily lead to premature death and disability, although some individuals do experience both, particularly those from culturally diverse backgrounds (Heckler, 1985). Concomitantly, advances in social and behavior sciences research and methodology have enabled us to better understand the behavioral underpinnings of health, identify effective strategies for disease prevention, maintain treatment regimens, and suggest ways to change behavior in favor of more healthful living habits.

Although tremendous strides have been made in the United States toward improving health and longevity, statistical trends show a persistent, distressing disparity in key health indicators among certain subgroups of the population. In 1983, life expectancy reached a new high of 75.2 years for whites and 69.6 years for blacks, producing a racial gap of 5.6 years. The life expectancy of blacks today was reached by whites in the early 1950s. Infant mortality rates have declined steadily for several decades for both blacks and whites. In 1990, the infant death rate for blacks was 17.6 deaths per 1,000 live births; this rate is twice the rate of 8.5 deaths per 1,000 live births for whites and similar to the 1960 rate for whites of 20 deaths (National Center for Health Statistics, 1991).

Causes of Disease in Minority Populations

In analyzing mortality data from 1979 to 1981, the Task Force on Black and Minority Health identified six causes of death that combined account for more than 80% of the mortality observed among members of the federally defined minority groups in excess of the white population. The Task Force on Black and Minority Health uses the term *excess deaths* to express the difference between the number of deaths actually observed in a minority group and the number of deaths that would have occurred in that group if it experienced the same death rates for each age and sex as the white population (Heckler, 1985).

Although the ranking of health problems according to excess deaths differs for each minority

population, the six health problems became overall priority issue areas. These six causes of death are cancer, cardiovascular disease and stroke, chemical dependency as measured by deaths due to cirrhosis of the liver, diabetes, homicides and accidents (unintentional injuries), and infant mortality.

In addition to excess deaths, special analyses of morbidity and health status indicators for minorities were developed by the Task Force on Black and Minority Health. These indices included prevalence rates of selected chronic and infectious diseases, hospital admissions, physician visits, limitation of activity, and self-assessed health status. Additional mortality indices included person-years of life lost, life expectancy, and relative risk of death by cause.

Some factors contributing to the health status of persons from culturally diverse backgrounds are not disease specific but have bearing on the overall health needs of each minority group. Among those that the Task Force on Black and Minority Health reviewed are demographic data characterizing minority groups, minority needs in education, health professionals, and health care services and financing (Heckler, 1985).

CULTURAL EXPRESSION OF ILLNESS

There is wide cultural variation in the manner in which certain symptoms and disease conditions are perceived, diagnosed, labeled, and treated. The disease that is grounds for social ostracism in one culture may be reason for increased status in another. For example, epilepsy is seen as contagious and untreatable among Ugandans, as cause for family shame among Greeks, as a reflection of a physical imbalance among Mexican-Americans, and as a sign of having gained favor by enduring a trial by a God among the Hutterites (Tripp-Reimer, 1984).

Bodily symptoms are also perceived and reported in a variety of ways. For example, individuals of Mediterranean descent tend to report common physical symptoms more often than do persons of Northern European or Asian heritage. Among Chinese, there is no translation for the English word "sadness," yet all people experience the feeling of sadness at some time in their life. To express emotion, Chinese clients sometimes somaticize their symptoms; for example, a client may complain of cardiac symptoms because the center of emotion in the Chinese culture is the heart. If the client has experienced a loss through, for example, death or divorce, and is grieving, the client may describe the loss in terms of a pain in the heart. Although some biomedical/scientific clinicians may refer to this as a psychosomatic illness, others will recognize it as a culturally acceptable somatic expression of emotional disharmony.

A discussion of pain will follow to illustrate the cultural variability that may occur with a symptom of significant concern to nurses.

Cultural Expression of Symptoms: Pain

To illustrate the manner in which symptom expression may reflect the client's cultural background, pain, an extensively studied symptom, will be used. Pain is a universally recognized phenomenon and an important aspect of assessment for clients of various ages. Pain is a very private, subjective experience that is greatly influenced by cultural heritage. Expectations, manifestations, and management of pain are all embedded in a cultural context. The definition of pain, like that of health or illness, is culturally determined.

The term "pain" is derived from the Greek word for penalty, which helps explain the long association between pain and punishment in Judeo-Christian thought. The meaning of painful stimuli for individuals, the way people define their situation, and the impact of personal experience combine to determine the experience of pain.

Much cross-cultural research has been conducted on pain. Pain has been found to be a highly personal experience that depends on cultural learning, the meaning of the situation, and other factors unique to the individual. Silent suffering has been identified as the most valued response to pain by health care professionals. The majority of nurses have been socialized to believe that in virtually any situation, self-control is better than open displays of strong feelings.

In a study by Davitz and Davitz (1981) of nurses' attitudes toward pain, it was discovered that the ethnic background of patients is relevant to the nurse's assessment of both physical and psycholog-

ical pain. Nurses view Jewish and Spanish patients as suffering the most and Anglo-Saxon/Germanic patients as suffering the least. In addition, nurses who infer relatively greater patient pain tended to report their own experiences as more painful. In general, nurses with an Eastern or Southern European or African background tend to infer greater suffering than do nurses of Northern European background. Years of experience, current position, and area of clinical practice are unrelated to inferences of suffering.

In addition to expecting variations in pain perception and tolerance, a nurse should expect variations in the expression of pain. It is a well-known fact that individuals turn to their social environments for validation and comparison. A first important comparison group is the family, which transmits cultural norms to its children.

The anthropologist Zborowski (1969) found that the meaning of pain and behavioral responses to the painful stimulus are culturally learned and culturally specific. Zborowski studied pain in four groups of men admitted to a veterans' hospital. The "old American" patients, defined as third-generation Americans, were found to be unexpressive; they reported pain, but emotional behavior was controlled. Complaining, crying, or screaming was viewed as useless or unnecessary. Both Jewish and Italian men were expressive in their pain response and asked for immediate pain relief by any means possible. Irish men viewed pain as a private event to be endured alone. This group was unemotional and nonexpressive of pain. In addition, when in pain, the old American and Irish groups tended to withdraw socially, whereas the Jewish and Italian groups preferred the company of friends and relatives.

Culture-Bound Syndromes

Clients may have a condition that is culturally defined, known as a *culture-bound syndrome*. Some of these conditions have no equal from a biomedical/scientific perspective, but others, such as anorexia nervosa and bulimia, are examples of the cultural aspects of illness among members of the dominant U.S. cultural group. Table 16–7 presents selected examples from among the more than 150 culture-bound syndromes that have been documented by medical anthropologists.

Table 16–7
Selected Culture-Bound Syndromes

Group	Disorder	Remarks
Whites	Anorexia nervosa	Excessive preoccupation with thinness, self-imposed starvation
	Bulimia	Gross overeating, then vomiting or fasting
Blacks	Blackout	Collapse, dizziness, inability to move
	Low blood	Not enough blood or weakness of the blood that is often treated with diet
	High blood	Blood that is too rich in certain components due to ingestion of too much red meat or rich foods
	Thin blood	Occurs in women, children, and the elderly; renders the individual more susceptible to illness in general
	Diseases of hex, witchcraft, or conjuring	Sense of being doomed by spell, part of voodoo beliefs
Chinese or Southeast Asians	*Koro*	Intense anxiety that penis is retracting into body
Greeks	Hysteria	Bizarre complaints and behavior because the uterus leaves the pelvis and goes to another part of the body
Hispanics	*Empacho*	Food forms into a ball and clings to the stomach or intestines, causing pain and cramping
	Fatigue	Asthma-like symptoms
	Mal ojo ("evil eye")	Fitful sleep, crying, and diarrhea in children caused by a stranger's attention, sudden onset
	Pasmo	Paralysis-like symptoms of face or limbs, prevented or relieved by massage
	Susto	Anxiety, trembling, and phobias from sudden fright
Native Americans	Ghost	Terror, hallucinations, sense of danger
Japanese	*Wagamama*	Apathetic childish behavior with emotional outbursts

CULTURE AND TREATMENT

After a symptom is identified, the first effort at treatment is often self-care. In the United States, an estimated 70–90% of all illness episodes are treated first, or exclusively, through self-care (Zola, 1979), often with significant success. The availability of over-the-counter medications, relatively high literacy level, and influence of the mass media in communicating health-related information to the general population have contributed to the high percentage of self-treatment. Home treatments are attractive because of their accessibility compared with the inconvenience associated with traveling to a physician, nurse practitioner, and pharmacist, particularly for clients from rural or sparsely populated areas. Furthermore, home treatment may

mobilize the client's social support network and provide the sick individual with a caring environment in which to convalesce. The nurse should be aware, however, that not all home remedies are inexpensive. For example, urban black populations in the Southeast sometimes use medicinal potions that cost much more than an equivalent treatment with a biomedical intervention (Tripp-Reimer and Lauer, 1987).

A wide variety of so-called nontraditional interventions are gaining the recognition of health care professionals in the biomedical/scientific health care system. Acupuncture, acupressure, therapeutic touch, massage, biofeedback, relaxation techniques, meditation, hypnosis, distraction, imagery, and herbal remedies are interventions that clients may use alone or in combination with other treatments.

CULTURAL NEGOTIATION

Although there are subtle differences in the two processes, *cultural negotiation* and *culture brokerage* are both considered acts of translation in which messages, instructions, and belief systems are manipulated, linked, or processed between the professional and the lay models of health problem and preferred treatment. In each act, attention is given to eliciting the client's views regarding a health-related experience, e.g., pregnancy, complications of pregnancy, or illness of an infant (Tripp-Reimer and Afifi, 1989). Katon and Kleinman (1981) described negotiation as a bilateral arrangement in which the two principal parties attempt to work out a solution. The goal of negotiation is to reduce conflict in a way that promotes cooperation.

Cultural negotiation is used when conceptual differences exist between the client and the nurse, a situation that may occur for one or more of the following reasons. The nurse and client may be using the same words but have different meanings, apply the term to the same phenomenon but have different notions of its causation, and have different memories or emotions associated with the term and its use (Tripp-Reimer and Brink, 1985).

In cultural negotiation, attention is given to providing scientific information while acknowledging that the client may hold different views. If the client's perspective indicates that behaviors would be helpful, positive, adaptive, or neutral in effect, it is appropriate for the nurse to include these in the plan of care. If, however, the client's perspective would result in behaviors that might be harmful, negative, or nonadaptive, the nurse should attempt to shift the client's perspective to that of the practitioner (Herberg, 1989; Spector, 1986; Tripp-Reimer and Afifi, 1989).

Because pregnancy and childbirth are social, cultural, and physiological experiences, any approach to culturally sensitive nursing care of childbearing women and their families must focus on the interaction between cultural meaning and biological functions (Greener, 1989; Kitzinger, 1982). Childbirth is a time of transition and a social celebration that is of central importance in any society; it signals a realignment of existing cultural roles and responsibilities, psychological and biological states, and social relationships. Child rearing is also a period during which culturally bound values, attitudes, beliefs, and practices permeate virtually all aspects of life for both the parents and the child.

SOLUTIONS TO HEALTH CARE PROBLEMS IN CULTURALLY DIVERSE POPULATIONS

The factors responsible for the health disparity between minority* and white populations are complex and defy simplistic solutions. Health status is influenced by the interaction of physiological, cultural, psychological, and societal factors that are poorly understood for the general population and even less so for minorities. Despite the shared characteristic of economic disadvantage among minorities, common approaches for improving health are not possible; rather, diversity within and among minorities necessitates activities, programs, and data collection that are tailored to meet the unique health care needs of many different subgroups. Despite these caveats, the Task Force on Black and Minority Health has made recommendations in the following six categories:

● Health information and education
● Delivering and financing health services
● Health professions development
● Cooperative efforts with the nonfederal sector
● Data development
● Research agenda

Health Information and Education

According to the Task Force on Black and Minority Health, minority populations are less knowledgeable or aware about some specific health problems than are whites, as demonstrated by the following examples.

● Blacks and Hispanics receive less information about cancer and heart disease than do nonminority groups.
● Blacks tend to underestimate the prevalence of cancer, give less credence to the warning signs, obtain fewer screening tests, and are diagnosed at later stages of cancer than are whites.

---

* The term "minority" is used because this section reports data from a federal study in which this term is used.

- Hispanic women receive less information about breast cancer than do white women. Hispanic women are less aware that family history is a risk factor for breast cancer, and only 25% of Hispanic women have heard of breast self-examination.
- Many professionals and lay persons, both minority and white, do not know that heart disease is as common in black men as it is in white men and that black women die from coronary heart disease at a higher rate than do white women.
- Hypertensive Japanese women and younger men (ages 18–49) are less aware of their hypertension than are the nonminority subgroups.
- Among Mexican-Americans, cultural attitudes regarding obesity and diet are often barriers to achieving weight control.

Programs to increase public awareness about health problems have been well received in several areas. For example, the Healthy Mothers/Healthy Babies Coalition, which provides an education program in both English and Spanish, has contributed to increased awareness of measures to improve the health status of mothers and infants. In addition, increased knowledge among blacks of hypertension as a serious health problem is one of the accomplishments of the National High Blood Pressure Education program. The success of these efforts indicates that carefully planned programs have a beneficial effect, but efforts must continue and be expanded to reach even more of the target population and to focus on additional health problems.

PLANNING HEALTH INFORMATION

Sensitivity to cultural factors is often lacking in the health care of minorities. Key concepts to consider in designing a health information campaign include meeting the language and cultural needs of each identified minority group, using minority-specific community resources to tailor educational approaches, and developing materials and methods of presentation that are commensurate with the educational level of the target population. Furthermore, because of the powerful influences of cultural factors over a lifetime in shaping people's attitudes, values, beliefs, and practices concerning health, health information programs must be sustained over a long period. Examples of the ways in which these concepts may be interwoven into health promotion efforts include the following:

- Involve local community leaders who are members of the cultural group being targeted to promote acceptance and reinforcement of the central themes of health promotion messages.
- Health messages are more readily accepted if they do not conflict with existing cultural beliefs and practices. Where appropriate, messages should acknowledge existing cultural beliefs.
- Involve families, churches, employers, and community organizations as a support system to facilitate and sustain behavior change to a more healthful lifestyle. For example, although hypertension control in blacks depends on appropriate treatment (e.g., medication), blood pressure can be improved and maintained by family and community support of activities such as proper diet and exercise.
- Language barriers, cultural differences, and lack of adequate information on access to care complicate prenatal care for Hispanic and Asian women who have recently arrived in the United States. By using lay volunteers to organize community support networks, programs have been developed to disseminate culturally appropriate health information.
- Homicide is the leading cause of death for young black men and one of the leading causes of death for Hispanic men and black women. It is a major contributor to the disparity in mortality rates between these groups and whites. Homicide prevention activities should include strategies such as behavioral modification interventions for handling anger and community-based programs to call attention to the extent and consequences of violence in black and Hispanic communities. In addition, the root cause of the underlying poverty should be examined, and programs to improve the overall financial status of minority groups should be implemented.
- The use of inhalants among young Hispanic and Native American groups should be dealt with through an appropriate and culturally sensitive health education campaign.

EDUCATION

Although printed materials and other audiovisual aids contribute to the educational process, client education is inherently interpersonal. The success of an educational effort for clients is often determined by the credibility of the source and is highly dependent on the skill and sensitivity of the nurse in communicating information in a culturally appropriate manner. Education programs are particularly critical and necessary for several health problems with the greatest impact on minority health, such as hypertension, obesity, and diabetes. For example, if diabetics could improve their self-management skills through education, an estimated 70% of complications (e.g., ketoacidosis, blindness, and amputations) could be achieved, thus saving much human misery as well as health care dollars.

Delivery and Financing of Health Services

Innovative models for delivering and financing health services for minority populations are needed. According to the Task Force on Black and Minority Health, models should increase flexibility of health care delivery, facilitate access to services by minority populations, improve efficiency of service and payment systems, and modify services to be more culturally acceptable.

The most commonly used indicators of adequacy of health services for a population include distribution of health care providers, but this is an inadequate measurement. The following exemplify the problem associated with health services for minorities:

- The disparities in death rates between minorities and whites remain despite overall increases in health care access and use.
- Language problems hinder refugees and immigrants when they seek health care.
- Blacks with cancer postpone seeking diagnosis of their symptoms longer than do whites, and delay initiation of treatment once diagnosed.
- A smaller proportion of black women than white women begin prenatal care in the first trimester of pregnancy (63% versus 76%); this factor is related to the high black infant mortality rate.
- The postneonatal death rate, which constitutes the majority of infant mortality for Native Americans and Alaskan natives, remains high. Postneonatal mortality implies an adverse environment for the infant and is thought to result from problems such as infectious disease, unintentional injury, and a lower rate of use of health care for these acute problems.

CONTINUITY OF CARE

Continuity of care is associated with improved health outcomes and is presumably greater when a client is able to establish an ongoing relationship with a care provider. The issue is central because many of the major killers of minorities, such as cancer, cardiovascular disease, and diabetes, are chronic rather than acute problems and require extended treatment regimens. Consider the following:

- A higher percentage of blacks and Hispanics than whites report that they have no usual source of health care (29% and 19% versus 13%).
- Refugees are eligible for special refugee medical assistance during their first 18 months in this country. After this, however, refugees who cannot afford private health insurance and are ineligible for Medicaid or state medical assistance may become medically indigent.
- Many Native Americans and Alaskan natives live in areas where the availability of health care providers is half that of the national average, and the Indian Health Service is often unable to provide coverage.

FINANCING PROBLEMS

Due to economic inequalities, members of minority groups tend to rely on Medicaid and charity for their health care needs. Elderly minority people are less likely than whites to supplement Medicare with additional private insurance (Heckler, 1986).

- Proportionately three times as many Native Americans, blacks, Hispanics, and certain Asian/Pacific-Islander groups as whites live in poverty.
- Proportionately twice as many blacks and three times as many Hispanics as whites have no medical insurance (18% and 26% versus 9%).
- Of those who had no insurance, 35% had not seen a physician during the past 12 months compared with 22% of those who had insurance.

Health Professions Development

Minority and nonminority health professional organizations, academic institutions, state governments, health departments, and other organizations from the public and private sectors should develop strategies to improve the availability and accessibility of health care professionals to minority communities (Heckler, 1985).

- Minorities (and whites) live in communities that do not usually conform to the specific geographic boundaries of political jurisdictions (e.g., states, counties, wards). Minority communities are not evenly distributed and often cross over these geographic boundaries. In contrast, record keeping and other processes for monitoring (and potentially influencing) the availability of health professionals and resources are usually determined by and restricted to these political boundaries.
- The size of a minority population, number of cultural subgroups, and demographic features such as pattern and distribution of minority communities are factors that influence the number of health profession students that each group might be expected to generate and the degree to which a minority group can support a cadre of health professionals in their community. With few exceptions, minorities are underrepresented as students and practitioners of the health professions. Although the number of minority nursing students has been steadily increasing, there still are proportionately more white nursing students.
- Differences in the availability of health personnel resources to minority communities are apparent regardless of the minority group being considered. Communities located in urban/metropolitan areas have significantly more professional resources.

Developing Strategies Within the Federal and Nonfederal Sectors

The Task Force on Black and Minority Health has recommended a review of programs having an impact on the actual or potential availability of health professionals to minority communities in an effort to improve collaboration. Activities to improve

minority health should involve participation of organizations at all levels — community, municipal, state, and national. The private sector can also serve as an effective channel for programs targeted to minority health projects. National organizations concerned with minorities such as the National Urban League and the Coalition of Hispanic Mental Health and Human Services Organization include health-related issues in their national agendas and are actively seeking effective ways to improve the health of minorities. Organizations such as these have a powerful potential for effecting change among their constituencies because they have strong community-level grass roots support.

Changes in health behavior frequently depend on personal initiative and are most likely to be triggered by health promotion efforts from locally based sources. Community involvement in developing health promotion activities can contribute to their success by providing credibility and visibility to the activities and facilitating their acceptance.

However, not all minority communities have the ability to identify their own health problems and initiate activities to address them. Support from the state and federal governments as well as private sector assistance is needed to assist with identifying and solving health-related problems afflicting the minority community (Heckler, 1985). There are many ways in which assistance may be provided to minority communities, including the use of technical assistance to identify high-risk groups and then help with planning, implementing, and evaluating programs to address the identified needs; specialized community services such as federally or privately funded demonstration projects for infants and the frail elderly; and programs supported by businesses and industries (e.g., AFL-CIO health promotion programs organized via unions).

Improving and Using Available Sources of Data

The Task Force on Black and Minority Health has recommended that existing sources of health data be improved by including racial and ethnic identifiers in data bases and oversampling selected minorities in national surveys. Analyses such as cross-comparisons from different data sets and specialized studies should be encouraged because they can contribute to understanding the health status and needs of minority populations. Unfortunately, many studies conducted in the past have failed to include data categories for culturally diverse groups and subgroups.

Research Agenda

Finally, the Task Force on Black and Minority Health recommends that a research agenda be developed to investigate factors affecting minority health, such as risk factor identification, risk factor prevalence, health education interventions, preventive services interventions, treatment services, and sociocultural factors and health outcomes.

COMMUNITY HEALTH NURSING AND CULTURALLY DIVERSE POPULATIONS

In a study by Bernal and Froman (1987), the degree of self-efficacy among 190 community health nurses caring for Puerto Rican, black, and Southeast Asian clients, the degree of influence of various background variables on the nurses' level of self-efficacy, and the difference in self-efficacy for caring for the three ethnic groups were examined. Using a cultural self-efficacy scale to determine their degree of confidence in caring for the three ethnic groups, the researchers reported that the highest confidence scores were found among community health nurses caring for (in rank order) blacks, Puerto Ricans, and Southeast Asians but that overall the nurses felt very inadequate in providing nursing care to those from ethnically diverse backgrounds.

Low scores were observed on items that included knowledge of health beliefs and practices as well as beliefs about respect, authority, and modesty. Higher scores were observed in using an interpreter correctly. Results suggest that community health nurses do not feel confident about caring for any of the three major ethnic groups. Furthermore, this perceived weakness occurred regardless of the nurses' education and demographic variables.

These results, although disappointing to those who consider cultural aspects of nursing care to be important, are not surprising. They show empirical support for the speculation made by the U.S. Department of Health and Human Services (1985)

that nurses are not being provided with the experiences needed to build confidence in the application of community health concepts to the care of culturally diverse populations. The purpose of this chapter is to provide an overview of the various components of culture that community health nurses need to provide culturally relevant and sensitive care to individuals, groups, and communities of various racial and cultural backgrounds.

ROLE OF THE COMMUNITY HEALTH NURSE IN IMPROVING HEALTH FOR CULTURALLY DIVERSE PEOPLE

This chapter has provided data detailing the health care problems of culturally diverse individuals, families, groups, and communities. Given the complexity of the problems and the wide variation in incidence and distribution of these problems within specific subgroups, there is no simple method of providing culturally sensitive community health nursing care to all clients.

The following principles may assist the community health nurse when working with culturally diverse clients:

- Conduct a cultural self-assessment.
- Conduct a culturological assessment (discussed later).
- Seek knowledge about local cultures.
- Recognize political aspects of culturally diverse groups.
- Increase cultural sensitivity.
- Recognize culturally based health problems.

First, because all nursing care is based on a systematic, comprehensive assessment of the client, it is important for the community health nurse to gather cultural data on clients from racially and ethnically diverse backgrounds. A culturological assessment refers to a systematic appraisal or examination of individuals, groups, and communities regarding their cultural beliefs, values, and practices to determine explicit nursing needs and intervention practices within the cultural context of the people being evaluated (Leininger, 1978). The term "culturological" is a descriptive reference to culture phenomena in their broadest sense.

In conducting a culturological assessment, the community health nurse should therefore be involved in determining and appraising the traits, characteristics, or smallest units of cultural behavior as a guide to nursing care. Culturological assessments tend to be broad and comprehensive because they deal with cultural values, belief systems, and ways of living now and in the recent past. However, the nurse can learn to appraise segments of these larger areas, such as a particular cultural value, and then relate this finding to other aspects, such as culture practices. Culturological assessments are as vital as physical and psychological assessments. The following section will summarize major data categories pertaining to the culture of clients and offer suggested questions that the nurse might ask to elicit needed information.

CULTUROLOGICAL ASSESSMENT

Brief History of the Ethnic and Racial Origins of the Cultural Group With Which the Client Identifies

- With what ethnic group or groups does the client report affiliation (e.g., Hispanic, Polish, Navajo, or a combination)? To what degree does the client identify with the cultural group (e.g., "we" concept of solidarity or a fringe member)?
- What is the client's reported racial affiliation (e.g., black, Native American, Asian, and so on)?
- Where was the client born?
- Where has the client lived (country, city) and when (during what years)? (If the client has recently relocated to the United States, knowledge of prevalent diseases in the country of origin may be helpful.)

Values Orientation

- What are the client's attitudes, values, and beliefs about birth, death, health, illness, and health care providers?
- Does culture impact the manner in which the client relates to body image change resulting from illness or surgery (e.g., importance of appearance, beauty, strength, and roles in cultural group)?
- How does the client view work, leisure, and education?

- How does the client perceive change?
- How does the client value privacy, courtesy, touch, and relationships with individuals of different ages, of different social class (or caste), and of the opposite sex?
- How does the client view biomedical/scientific health care (e.g., suspiciously, fearfully, or acceptingly)? How does the client relate to persons in a different cultural group (e.g., withdrawal, verbally or nonverbally expressive, or negatively or positively)?

Cultural Sanctions and Restrictions

- How does the client's cultural group regard expression of emotion and feelings, spirituality, and religious beliefs? How are dying, death, and grieving expressed in a culturally appropriate manner?
- How is modesty expressed by men and women? Are there culturally defined expectations about male-female relationships, including the nurse-client relationship?
- Does the client have any restrictions related to sexuality, exposure of body parts, or certain types of surgery (e.g., amputation, vasectomy, and hysterectomy)?
- Are there any restrictions against discussion of dead relatives or fears related to the unknown?

Communication

- What language does the client speak at home? What other languages does the client speak or read? In what language would the client prefer to communicate with you?
- What is the English fluency level of the client—both written and spoken? Remember that the stress of illness may cause clients to use a more familiar language and temporarily forget some English.
- Does the client need an interpreter? If so, is there a relative or friend whom the client would like to have interpret? Is there anyone whom the client would prefer to not interpret (e.g., member of the opposite sex, a person younger or older than the client, or a member of a rival tribe or nation)?
- What are the rules (linguistics) and modes (style) of communication?

- Is it necessary to vary the technique of communication during the interview and examination to accommodate the client's cultural background (e.g., tempo of conversation, eye contact, sensitivity to topical taboos, norms of confidentiality, and style of explanation)?
- How does the client's nonverbal communication compare with that of individuals from other cultural backgrounds? How does it affect the client's relationship with you and with other members of the health care team?
- How does the client feel about health care providers who are not of the same cultural background (e.g., black, middle-class nurse, or Hispanic of a different social class)? Does the client prefer to receive care from a nurse of the same cultural background, sex, and/or age?
- What are the overall cultural characteristics of the client's language and communication processes?
- With which language and/or dialect is the client most comfortable?

Health-Related Beliefs and Practices

- To what cause or causes does the client attribute illness and disease (e.g., divine wrath, imbalance in hot-cold or yin-yang, punishment for moral transgressions, hex, or soul loss)?
- What does the client believe promotes health (e.g., eating certain foods, wearing amulets to bring good luck, exercise, prayer, ancestors, saints, or intermediate deities)?
- What is the client's religious affiliation (e.g., Judaism, Islam, Pentacostalism, West African voodooism, Seventh-Day Adventism, Catholicism, or Mormonism)?
- Does the client rely on cultural healers (e.g., *curandero, shaman,* spiritualist, priest, minister, or monk)? Who determines when the client is sick and when the client is healthy? Who determines the type of healer and treatment that should be sought?
- In what types of cultural healing practices does the client engage (e.g., herbal remedies, potions, massage, wearing of talismans or charms to discourage evil spirits, healing rituals, incantations, or prayers)?
- How are biomedical/scientific health care providers perceived? How does the client and family perceive nurses? What are the expectations of nurses and nursing care?
- What comprises appropriate "sick-role" behavior? Who determines what symptoms constitute disease and illness? Who decides when the client is no longer sick? Who cares for the client at home?
- How does the client's cultural group view mental disorders? Are there differences in acceptable behaviors for physical versus psychological illnesses?

Nutrition

- What nutritional factors are influenced by the client's cultural background?
- What are the meanings of "food" and "eating" to the client? With whom does the client usually eat? What types of foods are eaten? What does the client define as food? What does the client believe comprises a "healthy" versus an "unhealthy" diet?
- How are foods prepared at home (e.g., type of food preparation; cooking oils used; length of time foods are cooked, especially vegetables; amount and type of seasoning added to various foods during preparation)?
- Do religious beliefs and practices influence the client's diet (e.g., amount, type, preparation, or delineation of acceptable food combinations such as kosher diets)? Does the client abstain from certain foods at regular intervals, on specific dates determined by the religious calendar, or at other times?
- If the client's religion mandates or encourages fasting, what does the term "fast" mean to the client (e.g., refraining from certain types or quantities of foods, eating only during certain times of the day)? For what period of time is the client expected to fast?
- During fasting, does the client refrain from liquids or beverages? Does the religion allow exemption from fasting during illness, and, if so, is the client believed to have an exemption?

Socioeconomic Considerations

- Who comprises the client's social network (i.e., family, peers, and cultural healers)? How do they influence the client's health or illness status?

- How do members of the client's social support network define "caring" (e.g., being continuously present, doing things for the client, or looking after the client's family)? What are the roles of various family members during health and illness?
- How does the client's family participate in the client's nursing care (e.g., bathing, feeding, touching, and being present)?
- Does the cultural family structure influence the client's response to health or illness (e.g., beliefs, strengths, weaknesses, and social class)? Is there a key family member whose role is significant in health-related decisions (e.g., grandmother in many black families or eldest adult son in Asian families)?
- Who is the principal wage earner in the client's family? What is the total annual income? (This is a potentially sensitive question that should be asked only if necessary.) Is there more than one wage earner? Are there other sources of financial support (e.g., extended family, investments)?
- What impact does economic status have on lifestyle, place of residence, living conditions, ability to obtain health care, and discharge planning?

Organizations Providing Cultural Support

- What influence do ethnic and cultural organizations have on the client's receiving health care (e.g., Organization of Migrant Workers, National Association for the Advancement of Colored People, Black Political Caucus, churches, schools, Urban League, and community-based health care programs and clinics)?

Educational Background

- What is the client's highest educational level obtained? Does the client's educational background affect the client's knowledge level concerning the health care delivery system, how to obtain the care needed, teaching and learning skills, and any written material that is distributed in the health care setting (e.g., insurance forms, educational literature, information about diagnostic procedures and laboratory tests, and admissions forms)?

- Can the client read and write English, or is another language preferred? If English is the client's second language, are materials available in the client's primary language?
- What learning style is most comfortable or familiar? Does the client prefer to learn through written materials, oral explanation, or demonstration?

Religious Affiliation

- How does the client's religious affiliation impact health and illness (e.g., death, chronic illness, body image alteration, and cause and effect of illness)?
- What is the role of client's religious beliefs and practices during health and illness?
- Are there healing rituals or practices that the client believes can promote well-being or hasten recovery from illness? If so, who performs these?
- What is the role of significant religious representatives during health and illness? Are there recognized religious healers (e.g., Islamic imams, Christian Scientist practitioners or nurses, Catholic priests, Mormon elders, and Buddhist monks)?

Cultural Aspects of Disease Incidence

- Does the client have any specific genetic or acquired conditions that are more prevalent in a specific cultural group (e.g., hypertension, sickle cell anemia, Tay-Sachs disease, or lactose intolerance)?
- Are there socioenvironmental diseases that are more prevalent among the client's specific cultural group (e.g., lead poisoning, alcoholism, AIDS, drug abuse, or ear infections)?
- Are there any diseases against which the client has an increased resistance (e.g., skin cancer in darkly pigmented individuals)?

Biocultural Variations

- Does the client have distinctive physical features that are characteristic of a particular racial or ethnic group (e.g., skin color or hair texture)? Does the client have any variations in anatomy that are characteristic of a particular racial or ethnic group (e.g., body structure, height, weight, facial shape and structure [nose, eye shape, facial contour], or upper and lower extremity shape)?

● How do anatomic and racial variations affect the assessment?

Developmental Considerations

● Are there any distinct growth and development characteristics that vary with the client's cultural background (e.g., bone density, psychomotor patterns of development, or fat folds)?

● What factors are significant in assessing children from the newborn period through adolescence (e.g., expected growth on standard grid, culturally acceptable age for toilet training, introducing various types of foods, sex differences, discipline, and socialization to adult roles)?

● What is the cultural perception of aging (e.g., is youthfulness or the wisdom of old age more highly valued)?

● How are elderly persons handled culturally (e.g., cared for in the home of adult children or placed in institutions for care)? What are culturally acceptable roles for the elderly?

● Does the elderly person expect family members to provide care, including nurturance and other humanistic aspects of care?

● Is the elderly person isolated from culturally relevant supportive persons or enmeshed in a caring network of relatives and friends?

● Has a culturally appropriate network replaced family members in performing some caring functions for the elderly person?

CULTURAL SELF-ASSESSMENT

Second, community health nurses can engage in a cultural self-assessment. Through identification of health-related attitudes, values, beliefs, and practices that are part of the cultural baggage brought to the nurse-client interaction, it is possible to better understand the cultural aspects of health care from the perspective of the client, family, group, or community. Everyone has ethnocentric tendencies that must be brought to a level of conscious awareness so that efforts can be made to temper ethnocentrism and view reality from the perception of the client.

INCREASE KNOWLEDGE ABOUT LOCAL CULTURES

Third, community health nurses can learn about the cultural diversity characteristic of the subgroup or subgroups that are most prevalent within their communities. Because it is impossible to know about all health-related beliefs and practices of the diverse groups served, it is reasonable to study selected ones. This cultural study may be accomplished by a review of nursing, anthropology, sociology, and related literature on culturally diverse groups; by in-services held at community health agencies, educational institutions in the community, or organizations serving minority groups; by enrolling in courses on transcultural or cross-cultural nursing and medical anthropology; and by interviewing key members of the subgroups of interest such as clergy members, nurses, physicians, and others to obtain information about the influence of culture on health-related beliefs and practices.

RECOGNIZE POLITICAL ASPECTS

Fourth, awareness of the political aspects of health care for culturally diverse groups and communities can enable community health nurses to have increased involvement in influencing legislation and funding priorities aimed at improving health care for specific populations. Recognized for their leadership role in community health matters involving culturally diverse groups, community health nurses may be invited by political leaders to participate in political decision making affecting the health of a targeted subgroup. Community health nurses should also be active politically, both individually and collectively, to be able to influence legislation affecting culturally diverse individuals, groups, and communities, and they should offer to serve on key community committees, boards, and advisory councils that impact the health of culturally diverse groups.

PROVIDE CULTURALLY SENSITIVE CARE

Fifth, when caring for individuals and families who have culturally diverse backgrounds, the community health nurse can assess, diagnose, implement, and evaluate nursing care in a manner that is culturally sensitive, relevant, and appropriate. To provide this culturally appropriate nursing care, it is necessary to be aware of the cultural similarities and differences between the nurse and the client, whether an individual, a family, a group, or a community, and to create a relationship of mutual respect on a foundation of effective cross-cultural communication. A guideline for gathering cultural data has been presented, and this guideline or a similar one may be used for identifying significant areas in which the nurse and client differ. Knowledge about biocultural variations in health and illness is particularly important when conducting cultural assessments.

RECOGNIZE CULTURALLY BASED HEALTH PRACTICES

Last, try to understand the nature and meaning of culturally based health practices of clients, groups, and communities. Once the practices are understood, a determination regarding their appropriateness in a particular context can be made. Generally, it is helpful to decide if a cultural practice is useful, neutral, or harmful to the client, group, or community. Helpful and neutral practices should be encouraged or "tolerated," whereas harmful practices should be discouraged. The classification of some cultural healing practices is not so easily determined. For example, many Southeast Asians practice coining, which is rubbing of a coin over body surfaces to expel bad winds that are believed to cause illness such as respiratory disorders. Because coining leaves abrasions on the skin, community health nurses are sometimes faced with an ethical dilemma when coining is practiced on young children; this practice may be construed by some members of the dominant cultural group as child abuse. This practice is not useful, so the deci-

sion must be made as to whether it is neutral or harmful.

The argument for the practice being neutral is based on the facts that the abrasions usually heal quickly and no harm is done to the child as a result of the practice and the practice is meaningful to parents who have much confidence in the healing powers that are associated with the practice of coining.

The argument can also be made that the practice is harmful. The red marks and skin abrasions caused by the coining constitute child abuse because the integumentary system is compromised; thus, the child is placed at increased risk for skin infection. Also, given that the child could require antibiotics or other medication for, in this example, a respiratory disorder, encouraging coining may prevent the child from receiving needed medical intervention and thus delay treatment, which may prove to be harmful.

As a solution, the community health nurse could suggest that parents combine traditional treatment with Western biomedicine; that is, the parents could use coining in conjunction with a biomedical intervention. Therefore, the healing will occur in a manner that has involved the use of both folk and professional health care systems.

SUMMARY

To provide community health nursing for individuals, groups, and communities representing the hundreds of different subcultures found in the United States, it is necessary to include cultural considerations in the nursing care. Guidelines for gathering data from clients of culturally diverse backgrounds have been suggested in this chapter and are interwoven throughout the text. Knowledge about culture-specific and culture-universal nursing care is foundational and is an integral component of community health nursing.

L e a r n i n g
A c t i v i t i e s

1. Examine the vital statistics of your community, and compare differences in morbidity and mortality rates for whites and racial and ethnic subgroups. What data are available according to racial and ethnic heritage, and what data would you like to see that are missing?

2. Visit an inner-city grocery store and compare quality, prices, customer services, and variety of products with those of a suburban grocery store.

3. Select a client from your caseload who comes from a racially or ethnically diverse background, and conduct a cultural assessment.

4. Interview someone from a racial or ethnic background that is different from your own to determine beliefs about illness causation, use of the lay and professional health care delivery systems, and culturally based treatments.

5. Review your local telephone directory for listings of ethnic restaurants. Dine at one. While dining, notice the types of available ethnic foods, ethnicity of servers and customers, evidence of cultural heritage in restaurant decor, and information about the culture available from the menu, placemats, or elsewhere in the restaurant. Ask the owner or manager about the history of the restaurant.

6. Attend religious services at a church, temple, synagogue, or place of worship for a religion different from your own.

7. Interview an official representative (e.g., priest, elder, monk, or bishop) from a religion with which you are unfamiliar. Ask about health-related beliefs and practices, healing rituals, support network for the sick, and dietary practices.

8. Watch primetime TV and note the racial and ethnic diversity that is present during the commercials. During the program, note the role played by racially and ethnically diverse characters. Are they heroes (heroines) or the "bad guys"? What are their occupations, socioeconomic status, religions, and lifestyles?

9. Skim a popular magazine for references to racially and ethnically diverse subgroups. What is being written? Is the nature of the article favorable or unfavorable?

REFERENCES

Bernal, H., and Froman, R.: Confidence of community health nurses in caring for ethnically diverse populations. Image *19*;201–203, 1987.

Boyle, J. S., and Andrews, M. M.: Transcultural perspectives in the nursing process. *In* Boyle, J. S., and Andrews, M. M., eds.: Transcultural Concepts in Nursing Care. Glenview, Illinois, Scott, Foresman and Co., 1989, pp. 67–92.

Branch, M. F., and Paxton, P. P., eds.: Providing Safe Nursing Care for Ethnic People of Color. New York, Appleton-Century-Crofts, 1976.

Brod, R. L., and McQuiston, J. M.: American Indian adult education and literacy: The First National Survey. J. Am. Indian Educ. *1*;1–16, 1983.

Cluff, C. B.: Spiritual intervention reconsidered. Topics Geriatr Rehab. *1*;77–82, 1986.

Davitz, L. L., and Davitz, J. R.: Cross-cultural inferences of physical pain and psychological distress. Nurs. Times *73*;521–523, 556–558, 1977.

Davitz, L. L., and Davitz, J. R.: Suffering viewed in six different cultures. Am. J. Nurs. *76*;1296–1297, 1976.

Garcia Coll, C. T.: Developmental outcome of minority infants: A process-oriented look into our beginnings. Child Dev. *61*;270–289, 1990.

Garcia Coll, C. T.: The consequences of teenage child-bearing in traditional Puerto Rican culture. *In* Nugent, J. K., Lester, B. M., and Brazelton, T. B., eds.: The Cultural Context of Infancy. Norwood, New Jersey, Ablex, 1988, pp. 111–132.

Garcia Coll, C. T., Sepkoski, C., and Lester, B. M.: Cultural and biomedical correlates of neonatal behavior. Dev. Psychobiol. *14*;147–154, 1987.

Gould-Martin, K., and Ngin, C.: Chinese Americans. *In* Harwood, A., ed.: Ethnicity and Medical Care. Cambridge, Massachusetts, Harvard University Press, 1981.

Greener, D. L.: Transcultural nursing care of the childbearing woman and her family. *In* Boyle, J. S., and Andrews, M. M., eds.: Transcultural Concepts in Nursing Care. Glenview, Illinois, Scott, Foresman and Co., 1989, pp. 95–118.

Hartog, J., and Hartog, E. A.: Cultural aspects of health and illness behavior in hospitals. West. J. Med. *139*;911–916, 1983.

Heckler, M. M.: Report of the Secretary's Task Force on Black and Minority Health. Washington, D.C., U.S. Government Printing Office, 1985.

Herberg, P.: Theoretical foundations of transcultural nursing. *In* Boyle, J. S., and Andrews, M. M., eds.: Transcultural Concepts in Nursing Care. Glenview, Illinois, Scott, Foresman and Co., 1989, pp. 3–66.

Katon, W., and Kleinman, A.: Doctor-patient negotiation and other social science strategies in patient care. *In* Eisenberg, L., and Kleinman, A., eds.: The Relevance of Social Science for Medicine. Boston, D. Reidel Publishing Co., 1981.

Kitzinger, S.: The social context of birth: Some comparisons between childbirth in Jamaica and Britain. *In* MacCormack, C. P., ed.: Ethnography of Fertility and Birth. New York, Academic Press, 1982, pp. 152–167.

Kluckhohn, F., and Strodtbeck, F.: Variations in Value Orientations. Evanston, Illinois, Row, Peterson & Co., 1961.

Kohls, L. R.: Survival Kit for Overseas Living. Yarmouth, Maine, Intercultural Press, 1984.

Laosa, L. M.: Maternal teaching strategies in Chicano and Anglo American families: The influence of culture and education on maternal behavior. Child Dev. *51*;759–765, 1980.

Laosa, L. M.: Maternal teaching strategies in Chicano families

of varied educational socioeconomic levels. Child Dev. *49*;1129–1135, 1978.

Lee, C. C.: Successful rural black adolescents: A psychological profile. Adolescence *20*;129–142, 1985.

Leininger, M.: Culture, Care, Diversity, and University: A Theory of Nursing. New York, National League for Nursing, Publication no. 15–2402, 1991.

Leininger, M.: Nursing and Anthropology: Two Worlds to Blend. New York, John Wiley & Sons, 1970.

Leininger, M.: Transcultural Nursing: Concepts, Theories, and Practice. New York, John Wiley & Sons, 1978.

Lipson, J., and Meleis, A.: Issues in health care of Middle Eastern patients. West. J. Med. *139*;854–861, 1983.

Mitchell, M.: Popular medical concepts in Jamaica and their impact on drug use. West. J. Med. *139*;841–847, 1983.

National Center for Health Statistics: Health, United States, 1990. Hyattsville, Maryland, U.S. Public Health Service, 1991.

Pennington, J. A.: Dietary Nutrient Guide. Westport, Connecticut, AVI, 1976.

Ragucci, A. T.: Italian Americans. *In* Harwood, A., ed.: Ethnicity and Medical Care. Cambridge, Massachusetts, Harvard University Press, 1981, pp. 56–84.

Spector, R.: Cultural Diversity in Health and Illness. Norwalk, Connecticut, Appleton-Century-Crofts, 1986.

Trankina, F. J.: Clinical issues and techniques in working with Hispanic children and their families. *In* Powell, G. J., ed.: The Psychosocial Development of Minority Group Children. New York, Brunner/Mazel, 1983, pp. 307–329.

Tripp-Reimer, T.: Reconceptualizing the construct of health: Integrating emic and etic perspectives. Res. Nurs. Health *7*;101–109, 1984.

Tripp-Reimer, T., and Afifi, L. A.: Cross-cultural perspectives on patient teaching. Nurs. Clin. North Am. *24*;613–619, 1989.

Tripp-Reimer, T., and Brink, P. J.: Culture brokerage. *In* Bulecheck, G. M., and McCloskey, J. C., eds.: Nursing Interventions: Treatments for Nursing Diagnoses. Philadelphia, W. B. Saunders, 1985, pp. 120–131.

Tripp-Reimer, T., and Lauer, G. M.: Ethnicity and families with chronic illness. *In* Wright, L. M., and Leahy, M., eds.: Families and Chronic Illness. Springhouse, Pennsylvania, Springhouse Co., 1987, pp. 77–99.

Tylor, E. B.: Primitive Culture. Vol. 1 and 2. London, Murray, 1871.

U.S. Bureau of the Census: General Population Characteristics —Part 1: United States Summary. Vol. 1. Washington, D.C., U.S. Government Printing Office, 1983.

U.S. Bureau of the Census: Persons of Spanish origin in the United States: March, 1985 (advance report). Washington, D.C., U.S. Government Printing Office, series P-20, No. 403, 1985.

U.S. Department of Health and Human Services: Consensus Conference Report on the Essentials of Public Health Nursing Practice and Education. Rockville, Maryland, U.S. Department of Health and Human Services, 1985.

U.S. Senate Select Committee on Indian Affairs: Indian Juvenile Alcoholism and Eligibility for BIA Schools (Senate Hearing 99-286). Washington, D.C., U.S. Government Printing Office, 1985.

Ventura, S. J.: Births of Hispanic parentage, 1983 and 1984. Monthly Vital Stat. Rep. *36*;1–19, 1987.

Wilson, M. N.: Mothers' and grandmothers' perceptions of parental behavior in three generational black families. Child Dev. *55*;1333–1339, 1984.

Wirth, L.: The problem of minority groups. *In* Linton, R., ed.: The Science of Man in the World Crisis. New York, Columbia University Press, 1945, pp. 347–372.

Yamamoto, J., and Kubota, M.: The Japanese-American family. *In* Powell, G. J., ed.: The Psychosocial Development of Minority Group Children. New York, Brunner/Mazel, 1983, pp. 237–247.

Zborowski, M.: People in Pain. San Francisco, Jossey-Bass, 1969.

Zola, I.K.: Oh where, oh where has ethnicity gone? *In* Gelfand, D., and Kutzik, A., eds.: Ethnicity and Aging: Theory, Research, and Policy. New York, Springer, 1979, pp. 14–36.

Cultural Influence in the Community: The Mexican-American Community

Upon completion of this chapter, the reader will be able to:

1. Identify the disease and health conditions prevalent among Mexican-Americans.

2. Describe two major reasons for the status of Mexican-American health.

3. Discuss factors that impede Mexican-American health.

4. Describe the folk health system that is unique to Mexican-Americans.

5. Apply knowledge of Mexican-American health in planning culturally relevant nursing care at the individual, family, and community levels.

Ricardo A. Martinez

There continues to be a lack of empirical data regarding the use of folk medicinal systems, the role of the family in the use of health services, and the role of specific characteristics such as language as a barrier to health care in the Mexican-American community. Presented in this chapter will be traditional Mexican-American concepts and beliefs that are more prevalent in the older segment of the population. Younger, better-educated Mexican-Americans may also adhere to traditional values and beliefs, but they may not overtly display them, in either family involvement or publicly.

This chapter will focus on the health needs of Mexican-Americans and implications for community health nursing. Discussed will be reactions to illness and its care, unique characteristics of Mexican-American families as they relate to health care, Mexican-American beliefs of disease causation, herbal medicine as it relates to nursing care, and the practitioner's role in improving cultural adaptation to health care in the community through improved access, language intervention, and health education efforts.

REACTIONS TO ILLNESS: UNDERSTANDING AS A PREREQUISITE

Disease is an ongoing problem that faces every component of a community. The influence of disease has shaped the destiny of civilizations. The presence of disease has led to the advent of new treatments with an indirect effect of increased life expectancy.

Illness is a social phenomena as well as a biological reaction. A community's health beliefs and attitudes about disease and illness have a direct effect on perceptions of illness and methods of coping. Every community develops methods and ways of coping that result in medical systems that are unique to a particular societal group and its culture.

Three categories of beliefs and associated reactions to disease and illness are scientific, nonscientific, and folk medicinal (Gemmill, 1973a,b).

The scientific reaction is characterized by a logical explanation of events in relation to a cause and an effect. The physician learns medical facts that are a compilation of experiments that lead to definite clinical application.

The nonscientific reaction stems from the ancient belief that illness may be caused by magic or a supernatural source. A positive side to nonscientific reaction is that illness can be "cured" by magic. In this regard, the reaction to both illness and cure is psychological.

Folk medicine has some basis in the scientific arena. Folk medicine is practiced throughout the world, including all parts of the United States. There are little statistical data confirming the incidence of folk medicine in the country, but anthropologists and sociologists have recognized a strong prevalence in many regions, especially minority communities.

Traditional medical practitioners may deny the presence of folk medicine. This denial or avoidance response in reaction to minority patient behavior has been called "clinical color blindness" (Gemmill, 1973a,b).

A practitioner who expresses clinical color blindness may also display clinical blindness to patient responses to illness. Unfortunately, patients who do not respond to health care within the practitioner's defined acceptable guidelines may be considered followers of nonscientific medicine.

The practitioner may also be "culturally partially sighted." In this situation, the provider tries to understand the patient's response to health care but is not open-minded, so responses to cultural variation in medical treatment are characterized by overt negative reactions.

The deliberate practitioner is one who is "culturally sighted." A cooperative environment exists between the practitioner and the patient. The goal of adequate health care is achieved regardless of medical beliefs or attitudes.

Nurses caring for patients from ethnic backgrounds may be categorized as culturally blind, but they may progress to culturally sighted if an effort is made to learn about ethnic behaviors in response to modern medical care. Nurses can understand particular folk medicinal systems as well as contributing systems such as families and language patterns.

The Mexican-American population has a strong folk medicinal system and is similar in some ways to the African-American and Native American cultures.

A BIOLOGICAL PERSPECTIVE: DISEASE PREVALENCE IN THE MEXICAN-AMERICAN COMMUNITY AND ACCESS TO HEALTH CARE

A continuing problem for health care practitioners is the lack of research regarding identification of health differences among minority groups or the prevalence of illness among certain populations.

The complexity of the disparity among minorities in health status has been recognized (U.S. Department of Health and Human Services, 1986). For example, Hispanics of Mexican or Cuban origin have low-birth-weight rates not significantly higher than rates for the white population despite the lower socioeconomic status of Hispanics. However, there is a clear pattern of less use of preventive services among adult Mexican-Americans, including prenatal care. In addition, Mexican-American children make fewer physician visits and receive fewer vaccinations than do white children (U.S. Department of Health and Human Services, 1986).

The first large-scale effort to measure the health of Mexican-Americans was the 1982–1984 Hispanic Health and Nutrition Examination from the National Center for Health Statistics (for a summary, see Lecca, Greenstein, and McNeil, 1987). The results of the survey appear to be consistent with the U.S. Department of Health and Human Services' report (1986). Only 19% of the Southwest Mexican-American women of child-bearing age used oral contraceptive pills. An additional 15% had had tubal ligation. Of interest was that these incidence rates were similar to those of the general population.

Vision, hearing, and dental examinations are not a frequent practice among Mexican-American children who failed such examinations. Of these children, at least one third had not had an examination within the past year. Of significance in the survey results was that fewer than 1% of Mexican-American children (4–11 years old) had lead toxicity levels; there may be a continuing decrease in environmental lead exposure.

Also of significance was the increase in cancer-screening practices among Mexican-American women. Eight of 10 Mexican-American women (20–74 years old) met American Cancer Society guidelines for periodic Pap smear. Three of four women met the breast examination guideline of a physician screening (U.S. Department of Health and Human Services, 1986). Some public health educational approaches geared to Mexican-Americans may be successful.

Despite lower socioeconomic status and higher rates of obesity and diabetes, cardiovascular disease rates are lower for Mexican-Americans than for whites (U.S. Department of Health and Human Services, 1986). In a 1987 special report from the Robert Wood Johnson Foundation, key indicators of access to health care among minorities were presented (Leon, 1987). Almost one third of Mexican-Americans were without a regular source of health care and had not had an ambulatory visit within the 12 months before the survey. Almost one fifth of Mexican-Americans had made an emergency visit within the 12 months before the survey, were without health insurance, and were in fair or poor health. In all of these categories, whites were reported as better off than the remainder of the population (Leon, 1987). Unlike previous national access surveys, which found Hispanics only slightly worse off than the national average, the 1986 national access survey found a considerable deterioration in their situation.

Socioeconomic conditions may be seen as both a cause and a result of Mexican-American health conditions. Poor health conditions may affect socioeconomic conditions in three ways:

- By causing an interruption in or termination of employment (especially significant for the head of a household)
- By preventing a person from learning or participating in activities that would increase income and education
- By causing a person to spend a disproportionate amount of income on maintaining health status or reducing disease or injury

Adverse socioeconomic conditions may affect health status in the following ways:

- By subjecting a person to unhealthy environmental conditions (e.g., crowded housing, lack of treated drinking water or proper sewage disposal)
- By depriving a person of the education necessary to understand preventive measures in disease

control and general physical well-being (e.g., lack of knowledge about nutrition, not understanding theory)

- By limiting the care received
- By barring a person from health care services (e.g., through racial discrimination or lack of transportation)
- By leading a person, through ignorance and desperation, to seek types of health care that might ultimately cause self-harm (Lyndon B. Johnson School of Public Affairs, 1979)

In view of the relationships between poverty and health, the socioeconomic status of a large portion of the Mexican-American population in South Texas indicates that there are many potential health problems. These problems may be summarized as follows:

- The low income of many Mexican-Americans gives them little money for medical services. Lack of funds may require the foregoing of medical services or reliance on assistance from others (i.e., family, friends, charities, or public funds).
- The lack of formal education among many Mexican-Americans suggests that they are less likely to be aware of or to practice modern preventive health care. And the low income of many, if not most, Mexican-Americans makes the practice of preventive health care difficult.
- Crowded housing and the lack of basic services, such as treated water and proper sewage disposal, result in a greater potential for spreading of communicable diseases among many Mexican-Americans. Lack of these facilities also makes preventive health practices difficult (Lyndon B. Johnson School of Public Affairs, 1979).

Consequently, a system of health care delivery that includes preventive health services and health education and is designed for relatively well-educated Mexican-Americans with a moderate income probably will not meet the needs of those with a low income. Rather, the development of an appropriate health system must be based on the health risks and health needs of the Mexican-American population and must take into account their age distribution, income, and education.

THE MEXICAN-AMERICAN FAMILY

The Mexican-American population in the United States is estimated to be 6–10 million. From one third to one half of the Mexican-Americans in the Southwest live either below the official level of poverty or immediately above it. Educational opportunities have been so restricted that this ethnic group is 3–4 years behind the educational attainment of the general population. Despite the economic and educational problems, Mexican-Americans continue to demonstrate unique socialization characterized by warmth and closeness that are the result of the family structure.

Literature that explains economic, educational, and other social characteristics of Mexican-Americans fails to provide a realistic understanding of Mexican-Americans in their daily lives. Some Hispanic writers, such as Octavio Romano-V., lash out at anthropologists and sociologists who present Mexican-Americans as an ahistoric group. Romano-V. insists that to correct the distortion of Mexican-American history, it is necessary to view Mexican-Americans in the contexts of a historical culture and an intellectual history instead of the stereotypical, static concepts of a traditional culture and nonintellectual history (Romano-V., 1986).

One way to discuss the Mexican-American family is to differentiate between traditional and non-traditional lifestyles. These characteristics may also be seen in other Hispanic groups or cultures.

Within the traditional framework, the family is seen as a close-knit group in which elders are the decision makers. It is not uncommon to see extended family members living with the nuclear family. All of the members regard the family as the main focus of social identification. Each member is a symbol of the family, and each must help maintain community respect for the family. It is within the family nucleus that one not only is disciplined but also receives love and understanding. And this love and understanding permeate outwardly to the extended family of grandparents, uncles, and aunts. If at all possible, the members of the family live in close proximity to each other and visit frequently. Each is concerned for the other and readily offers assistance when needed. However, family problems are for the family to solve, and "outside" help is seldom sought or desired.

The father is the unquestioned authority of the household. He is hard, unyielding, and strong. He often exemplifies these traits by demonstrating his ability to drink heavily and conquer members of the opposite sex *(machismo).* The members of his family must show him respect at all times, and failure to do so will invoke his wrath, usually in the form of a physical beating. His family is poor, but he provides for them as well as he can because it is his duty as head of the family to look after them (Stenger-Castro, 1978).

The mother is soft, nurturing, and self-sacrificing. Her place is in the home. Her responsibilities are to ensure that the household runs properly and to be in charge of the children's upbringing. She does not openly question her husband's actions. Any pain or suffering she experiences is considered concomitant to being female (Stenger-Castro, 1978).

The children are to be seen and not heard. They are expected to contribute to the running of the household. The girls help their mother with the household chores. The boys find jobs as soon as they are old enough so that they may contribute monetarily to the family. There are usually four or more siblings, and they must remember that the younger respect the older and that the female respects the male. Most find it easier to confide in their mother because their father is someone they respect but do not know very well. Typically, the children will have some schooling; some may finish high school, but they must not forget that their duty to the family takes precedence over personal ambition.

Murillo (1976) pointed out that because of the close interpersonal ties that exist among family members, the Mexican-American may temporarily forgo job, school, or other activities to meet family needs—which have priority.

The traditional family member is courteous and will demonstrate good manners, which may cause problems in communication. For example, a young Mexican-American boy translating for a white physician may not wish to convey to his mother a question such as "Why did you wait so long to obtain medical care?" or a question regarding her personal status. He may see this as rude or disrespectful.

The nontraditional Mexican-American has adopted acculturative patterns that may be the result of migration into white communities or improvement of educational level or economic status. The Mexican-American maintains characteristics such as close family ties, certain health beliefs, and recreational patterns.

The nontraditional Mexican-American may not engage in the traditional forms of recreation, such as group drinking and conversation but will still enjoy fiestas, *pachangas,* and *fandangos.* Traditional events such as debuts or *la quinceanera,* in which 15-year-old girls enter womanhood, are still practiced.

Cultural continuance in families is evident in the ways the members use terms of endearment and address their elders, the way they behave with their peers, and the way they use long-tested demeanor when responding to figures of authority. Young Mexican-Americans, some outwardly tough and aggressive and seemingly independent of family ties and restrictions, harbor tender feelings toward their *"jefitos"* and *"jefitas."* Although visible changing characteristics may appear to make contemporary lifestyles unstable and haphazard, the vulnerability of tough gang members is shown during family-oriented gatherings and celebrations, where all indifference and isolation are cast aside when the piñata is broken and "Las Mananitas," a Spanish song traditionally sung at birthdays that symbolizes rejoicing and life, accompanies a family ritual (Enrique, 1980).

It is important for one to remain alert and recognize the ways in which the Mexican-American culture is practiced and kept alive. It is exciting to hear a young couple, attired in symbolic fashions as they walk with their child and using the word *"jita"* in addressing the child. Another example of cultural continuance in the health care setting involves nursing interaction with an obstetric patient being first seen for prenatal care. The young Mexican-American patient may be very interested in diet and regular check-ups but will explain to the nurse specific folk medicinal habits that have been passed from generation to generation. In the best interest of patient care, the nurse should listen attentively and not be judgmental but rather allow cultural habits to be integrated with modern medical care.

Mexican-Americans are often viewed in a stereotypical manner. What may not be recognized is their unique methods of socialization and their rituals, celebrations, and festivities, which are of both historical and cultural importance. Whether Mexican-Americans are classified as traditional or nontraditional is a matter of individual perception and classification habits. Family loyalty scales and the assimilation processes mark individual differences and degrees of cultural continuance.

BELIEFS OF DISEASE CAUSATION AMONG MEXICAN-AMERICANS

Mexican-Americans typically view health or disease as an area in which God or some other extrahuman force has been influential, either directly or indirectly. Regardless of the causative agent, the explanation as to why the condition happened to the particular individual at a particular time is likely to be sought in the extrahuman realm. A particular cause of an illness may be that of *castigos,* or a punishment. *Castigos* are sanctions imposed by the supernatural and are used to explain certain conditions of ill health. This source is essentially benevolent and comes from God. The malevolent source, with or without the intermediation of evil, may be in the form of *brujas,* or witches (Clark, 1959). The ultimate source of disease is God, who is said to have placed illness and all other things in the world. Foster (1953) discussed ideas of disease causation that are based on natural phenomena, supernatural or physiologically untrue concepts, magical origins, and emotional concepts. Many recognized and named illnesses are due to a series of emotional experiences.

An important concept within the Mexican-American culture is that of *curanderismo,* or folk healing. *Curanderismo* is a complicated system of healing that involves the *curandero,* or healer, who acts as a diagnostician, counselor, or practitioner for many Mexican-Americans. The *curandero* is usually considered the wisest individual, having derived powers to heal from God.

Mexican-American folk medicine considers three types of causation: empirical, magical, and psychological (Saunders, 1954). In a study of Mexican-Americans in California, Clark (1959) discussed the theory of disease in this population in terms of diseases of "hot and cold" imbalance, diseases caused by dislocation of internal organs, diseases of magical origin, diseases of emotional origin, other folk-defined diseases, and "standard scientific" diseases.

Mexican-Americans can explain etiological factors associated with disease at two levels: the source of disease at the extrahuman level in its benevolent and malevolent forms (discussed earlier) and provoking agents, which are operative in the daily life processes. The following agents are considered to be provocations (Samora, 1961):

- Food: food that is spoiled; food that does not agree with one; green fruit; food given to one by a *bruja;* and food to which one is allergic
- Shock: being frightened; receiving unfavorable news, such as news about the death of a loved one
- Accidents of various sorts
- Bodily malfunction: general bodily malfunction; malfunction or displacement of specific organs
- Age: general greater susceptibility to illness with increasing age
- Abuse of the body: overindulgence in eating or drinking; debauchery
- Not taking care of one's self: vague and general acts of omission or commission
- Congenital: being born ill or deformed
- Hereditary: having inherited a tendency toward, or a susceptibility for, certain illnesses
- Contact with the elements: being in drafts; getting the feet wet; night air; too much sun
- Environmental, nonspecific: (an illness that is "going around"
- Contact with persons: *mal ojo* ("evil eye") given through admiration; individuals who practice *brujeria* (witchcraft) may hex or bewitch someone; individuals who are *enconosos* (malevolent) may aggravate an illness (this is not the same as causing an illness).
- Occupational causes: lifting heavy objects; working under unfavorable conditions such as excessive heat, dampness, or cold

The germ theory of disease is not recognized by all Mexican-Americans; this may be a function of educational and economic levels.

In a descriptive study conducted in 1978, the author surveyed 50 Mexican-American lower-income mothers of preschool-age children about their attitudes toward immunization. Study results indicated that these mothers tend to immunize their children primarily as a prerequisite to enter the public school system. They also felt that immunizing their children would produce fever, which they considered an "illness." They thought that it was in the best interest of the child not to have them go through this unnatural process.

Diseases are classified as being caused by certain factors or having a specific origin. The following sections describe diseases caused by the dislocation of internal organs, by emotions, and by magic.

Diseases Caused by Dislocation of Internal Organs

Caida de la mollera is a disease of infants that occurs when the fontanelle of the parietal or frontal bone of the cranium falls and leaves a "soft spot" that sometimes vibrates during breathing. It usually happens during breast-feeding or as a result of a sudden fall. The baby is usually spoon-fed during the illness (Rubel, 1960).

Treatment consists of putting salt on the fallen fontanelle and allowing it to remain for 3 days. As this is done, the curer presses against the roof of the baby's mouth to raise the depression. If not successfully treated, it can lead to "drying up," and death can occur. Normal feeding cannot be resumed until the fontanelle has been raised to its normal position. Along with this ritual, an herbal tea is administered in large amounts (Rubel, 1960).

Empacho is an infirmity of both children and adults that occurs when food particles become lodged in the intestinal tract and cause sharp pains. To treat this illness, the person lies face down on a bed with the back bared. The attending curer lifts a piece of skin from the waist and pinches it, listening for a snap from the abdominal region. Once the nature of the illness is established, this is repeated several times along the spinal column in hopes of dislodging the offending material.

Preparations of herbs such as *chichipaste, cascara sagrada, ajenjible* (or *jengibre*) (ginger), and rhubarb as well as drugs like *desempacho* are administered orally to penetrate, soften, and crumble the chunk of food. *Empacho* is usually not a serious infirmity, and prayer is usually not part of the curing process (Rubel, 1960).

Diseases of Emotional Origin

The mind–body dualism of modern medicine does not exist in traditional medicine. As a result, many physical diseases are tracked to emotional origins and treated psychosomatically.

Bilis, or bile, is a concept brought to Mexico by the Spanish, but it is of Greek origin. Originally, it was based on the ancient belief that the body was composed of four humors.

This belief maintains that the humors must remain in balance for a person to enjoy good health. Any highly emotional experience such as anger or fear may cause the humors to become unbalanced, and excess bile may flow into the bloodstream, producing a wide variety of illnesses.

In a study of Mexican-Americans in California, Clark (1959) stated: "The term 'bilis' is not always used to indicate a disease; sometimes it means simply that a person is nervous or upset about something. In its medical sense, however, bilis is a disorder which is diagnosed and treated like any other illness. Adults are said to be particularly susceptible to it. The illness always comes on after a person becomes very angry, especially if he flies into an uncontrollable rage. A day or two after this fit of anger, the attack occurs. The disorder produces symptoms of acute nervous tension, chronic fatigue and malaise" (Holland, 1978, p. 104).

Bilis is ordinarily treated with herbal remedies such as *negrita* and *sauco* (elder tree) that are consumed in the form of teas. Less severe cases are not treated.

Susto, or fright sickness, is another emotion-based illness that is very common in Mexico. All indications suggest that the concept is Indian rather than Spanish in origin.

Almost any disturbing or unstabilizing experience such as an unexpected fall, a barking dog, or a car accident may be sufficient to cause *susto* if part of the self separates from the body. In southern Mexican Indian groups in which this concept exists in a more aboriginal context, *susto* is attributed to a spirit loss. With the loss of spirit, cold air rushes in and takes over the body. A case in San Antonio dealt with the traumatic experience of a baby passing through the birth canal as causing *susto*.

In the early stages, *susto* is usually accompanied by colic, diarrhea, high temperature, vomiting, and several other symptoms. The person's appetite is lost, and the intestines slowly desiccate and will not allow food to pass through. If not cured in the early stages, the patient suffers long continuous periods of malaise, listlessness, and loss of appetite (Holland, 1978).

As the disease progresses, the patient is forced to withdraw from active participation in normal family and social activities and remain in bed. *Susto* is believed to sometimes be fatal.

Traditional curers usually resort to a combination of herbal and magicoreligious devices to treat *susto* (Holland, 1978). Among Mexican-Americans in Texas and virtually all Mexican Indian and peasant groups, the practitioner calls the spirit back into the patient's body to effect the cure. The illness is treated by brushing the body with *ruda* for nine consecutive nights. The brushing is performed to remove the cold air and allow the spirit, which is being summoned, to return to the body. This treatment is often accompanied by prayers and burning candles before images of saints, in either the home or church.

Diseases of Magical Origin

Mal ojo is assumed to be the magical origin of many illnesses, especially those afflicting children. According to this belief, some people are born with *vista fuerte* (strong vision) with which they unwittingly harm others with a mere glance. One of every set of twins inevitably possesses this power. It is believed that the glance toward a pregnant woman may cause an infant to become ill with fever because the "heat of the pregnancy" damages its tender spirit (Holland, 1978).

An infant with *mal ojo* sleeps restlessly, cries for no apparent reason, vomits, and has fever and diarrhea. *Mal ojo* can also be fatal. *Mal ojo* is treated by rubbing the body with an egg for three consecutive evenings. During this ritual, the healer will chant several prayers. The egg, with the heat captured in the shell, will be broken and left overnight, under the head of the bed. In the morning, if the egg appears to be "cooked," then *mal ojo* was the cause of the illness.

It is not uncommon in San Antonio for Mexican-American mothers to adorn their children with amulets, which are usually a "deer eyes," or *"ojos de venado"* (a legume seed from Mexico) as prevention of *mal ojo*. In addition, the color red, in the form of either string or yarn, may be tied to the child's wrist for protection. The nurse should not question the parent but rather accept this practice, especially if it is psychologically helping the mother.

Dano, or witchcraft, plays an important part in traditional Mexican disease concepts. Those with close ties to Mexican Indian and peasant cultures are generally credited with greater knowledge of witchcraft than are more assimilated Mexican-Americans. Witches are described as people who sell their souls to the devil in return for the power to harm others through magic (Holland, 1978). *Brujeria,* or witchcraft, should not be confused with *curanderismo,* or folk healing.

The Hot-Cold Syndrome

Exposure to excessive heat or cold may be the main cause of illness. Also, certain foods may be thought to cause illness if they generate heat or cold within the body.

Some of the illnesses believed to be caused by cold entering the body are listed below (Currier, 1978):

- Chest cramps: Cold air enters the chest when a person is overheated.
- Earache: A cold draft of air enters the ear canal.
- Headache: The coolness of mist or of the night air called *aigre* penetrates the head.
- Paralysis: A part of the body is "struck" by *aigre.* Stiffness, which is considered to be a partial, temporary paralysis, is ascribed to the same cause.
- Pain due to sprains: Such "cold pains" are the result of cold entering the damaged part.
- Stomach cramp: When the body is warm and not adequately covered, cold can enter from the air or from a body of water.
- Rheumatism: Cold from some outside source lodges in the afflicted bones.
- Teething: The pain of teething is a "cold pain" that originates in the coldness of the new white teeth that are growing in.
- Tuberculosis: Cold enters the body from water or carbonated beverages, especially when the body is overheated from work or travel.

The following are some of the illnesses believed to be caused by an overabundance of heat in the body:

- *Algondoncillo:* Heat rises from the center of the body to the mouth, causing the gums, tongue, and lips to turn white.
- *Dislipela:* Overexposure to the sun can cause the sun's heat to collect in the skin, resulting in an

outbreak of red spots on the hands, arms, or, less often, feet.

- Dysentery: Because it is accompanied by bloody stool and blood is intensely hot, dysentery is classified as a hot disease and may be caused by consuming too much hot food.
- Sore eyes: A person may overstrain the eyes, causing them to "work hard" and thus heat up; alternatively, cold, wet feet can cause the body heat to rise to the head and overheat the eyes.
- *Fogazo:* Heat rising from the center of the body causes the mouth and tongue to break out in tiny red spots. In contrast to *algodoncillo,* this is not a serious disease.
- Kidney ailments: Any pain in the kidneys is a hot pain; most kidney ailments are accompanied by itching feet or ankles, reddening of the palms of the hands, and fever.
- *Postemilla:* An abscessed tooth results from heat concentrating in the root of the tooth, evidenced by the fact that when the abscess bursts, it releases blood.
- Sore throat: Wet feet cause sore throat by driving body heat up into the throat.
- Warts and rashes: Regardless of the cause (a subject on which my informants refused to speculate), these ailments are the result of heat. Warts and rashes are irritating, and irritation is always ascribed to heat, never to cold.

The causes of diseases and the strong beliefs found among Mexican-Americans cannot be ignored and should be taken into consideration by health care providers. The Mexican-American should not be ridiculed for beliefs of disease causation but rather supported in recognizing the existence of disease, regardless of the cause. After all, illnesses have some basis for developing, and who is qualified to question the validity of certain beliefs? The underlying importance of recognizing the individual's beliefs is the ability to accept the belief and indirectly begin to educate on "real" causes of illness.

USE OF HERBAL MEDICINE AMONG MEXICAN-AMERICANS

Historically, the most important uses of herbs have been medicinal. For most of history, there have been limited resources for treating injuries and dis-

eases. Plant remedies have been the most continuous and universal form of treatment. Among Mexican-Americans, herbal medicine has strong cultural and historical ties to Indian, Aztec, and Spanish-Moorish societies.

In an extensive study of the healing herbs found in the upper Rio Grande Valley, Curtin (1947) cited numerous illnesses for which the Mexican population had devised treatment. Although these data will not be presented here in great detail, an effort was made to check the *curanderos'* familiarity with the medicines. As expected, the *curanderos* had used the great majority of the herbs described by Curtin for essentially the same symptom complexes.

The use of herbs by Mexican-Americans demonstrates the extent of both their nosological considerations and their pharmacopeia. The following is a list of medicinal herbs and the conditions they treat (Martinez, 1978, pp. 262–263):

- Rattlesnake oil *(aceite de vibora):* rheumatism
- Mineral water *(agua piedra):* kidney stones
- Garlic *(ajo):* diphtheria prevention, pain in the bowels, toothache, rabid dog bite, stomach trouble, snakebite, hypertension
- Cottonwood *(alamo sauco):* swollen gums, ulcerated tooth
- Cottonwood (a different generic herb) *(alamo de hoja redondo):* boils, broken bones
- Sweet basil *(albahaca):* hornet bite, colic
- Apricot *(hueso de albaricoque):* goiter, dryness of the nose
- Camphor *(alcanfor):* pain, rheumatism, headache, faintness
- Amaranth *(alegria):* heart trouble, tuberculosis, jaundice
- Alfalfa *(alfalfa):* bed bugs
- Filaree *(alfilerillo):* need for diuretic, rheumatism, gonorrhea
- Lavender *(alhucema):* phlegm, colic, vomiting, menopause
- Licorice *(yerba del lobo):* clotted blood
- Aster *(cosmose):* chest congestion
- Parsley *(amis):* painful shoulders, stomach troubles, colic
- Cocklebur *(cadillos):* diarrhea, rattlesnake bite
- Wild pitplant *(buchuheat):* pyorrhea, throat irritation, skin irritation
- Desert tea: headaches, cold, fever, kidney pain
- Scouring brush *(pingacion):* gonorrhea

In addition, the root *inmortal* is occasionally ground into powder for upper respiratory infection chest pain, fatigue, and tuberculosis. Spearmint *(yerba buena)* is good for childbirth, newborns, colic, and menstrual cramps. Cupping *(ventosa)* is good for muscle aches and, as a liniment, for the nerves.

A few herbs are used to treat psychiatric conditions, which opens the door for other types of treatment for such conditions. *Yerba del dapo,* an herb in the aster family, is used for *saltido,* or "jumping stomach," which appears to be a nervous kind of stomach disorder. The green plant is formed into a large ball, wrapped in a cloth, and placed on the navel to stop the throbbing. Some herbs are also used as love charms to enhance sexual performance and bring good fortune in the pursuit of love.

The use of herbs in combination with prayer and touch are seen in a variety of rituals associated with folk illnesses such as *susto* and *mal ojo.*

There are specific herbs or herbal preparations that may be used in the treatment of certain chronic conditions such as hypertension, diabetes, arthritis, and some malignancies. Even though few studies have been conducted on the efficacy or effects of these herbal preparations, most herbalists are aware of proper dosages. Nurses usually should allow patients to continue their herbal regimen, but at the same time they should encourage the use of modern medical care and practice.

Ruda is used to "sweep" the person during the ritual for *susto.* A tea of *cenizo* is administered after the ritual to enhance the warmth needed to draw the spirit back to the person. *Yerba buena* is administered as part of the ritual for *mal ojo.* Some herbs with a purgative effect are administered as part of the treatment for *empacho.*

If it were possible, it would be interesting to trace certain remedies now sold in pharmacies in extract form to the first application in the form of leaf, bark, or root. How have people come by this knowledge? Has knowledge been the result of repeated experimentation or of the coincidental application of the remedy?

In the 1890s, Don Pedro Jaramillo lived in the southern part of Texas near the Mexican village of Los Olmos. Legend says that God bestowed upon Jaramillo the power to *recetar* (prescribe) formulas to cure the sick. Many of his *recetas* included herbs. Because of his popularity and success in helping people, Jaramillo is still recognized as the "saint" of *curanderos* in Texas.

The use of medicinal herbs continues in modern societies, especially in Mexican-American communities. Stores continue to sell herbs, and their popularity has continued through the practice of *curanderismo.* Nurses should not be critical of the practice of herbal medicine but rather recognize it as an alternative health care system that supplements modern medical practice.

CULTURAL ADAPTATION TO HEALTH CARE IN THE COMMUNITY

Improving Access

It is well known that Mexican-Americans tend to fall into a lower economic level than the general population.

In 1981, the average income of Hispanic families was 70% of that of white families ($16,400 versus $23,500). A fourth of all Hispanic families fell below the U.S. Bureau of the Census' poverty level (Davis et al., 1983). In 1990, the percentage of all Hispanic families falling below poverty level had increased to 28.1 (National Center for Health Statistics, 1992).

Because of a lower economic level, certain conveniences available to other groups, such as transportation, may not be available to Mexican-Americans. Without adequate transportation, problems may arise in relation to access. For example, clinic appointments may be missed or impossible to keep because of inadequate public transportation.

In addition, because some households have no telephones, essential communication such as appointment reminders, contact of ill patients for follow-up care, and so on may be a problem.

Use patterns of Hispanics and other low-income persons compared with patterns of the white population and higher-income groups are manifested as follows (U.S. Department of Health, Education, and Welfare, 1979):

- A smaller proportion of Hispanics and low-income patients see a physician; the average number of physician visits per year is lower among Hispanics, but somewhat higher among low-income patients.

- Outpatient department use is greater among nonwhites and low-income patients.
- Short-stay nonfederal hospitalization rates are lower among Hispanics but higher among low-income patients.
- Length of hospital stay is longer for both Hispanics and low-income persons.
- Fewer Hispanics and low-income persons report to a physician versus a clinic as a regular source of care.

Improving access to health care for Mexican-Americans may include making appointment times convenient (e.g., evening and weekend hours), having satellite clinics in the community (close to the population being served), or working through neighborhood associations and churches to provide care and health education.

Mobile vans as portable treatment modules have been used in some communities as a way to improve access. However, in some communities, this may be seen as intimidating or intruding; a permanent facility may be more acceptable (Aranda, 1971).

More than 12% of Americans appear to have particularly serious trouble coping with the conventional health care system and obtaining care when needed. One fifth of Hispanic adults are medically disadvantaged, primarily because of financial problems, lack of health insurance, lack of a regular source of medical care due to financial problems, or lack of knowledge as to where to obtain care (Weisfield, 1983).

Reducing Language Barriers and Improving Communication

The most important differences between Hispanic folk medicine and scientific medicine that influence the choice of one over the other are as follows:

- Scientific medicine is largely impersonal.
- Scientific procedures are unfamiliar to the layperson.
- A passive role is played by family members in conventional health care.
- Considerable control of the situation is taken by professional health care providers.

In contrast, Mexican-American folk medicine is largely a matter of personal relations, familiar procedures, active family participation, home care, and a large degree of control of the situation by the patient or family. Given these differences, it is easy to understand why considerable motivation would be necessary for a Mexican-American to have strong preference for scientific medicine over a system that is more familiar and possibly psychologically more rewarding, or at least less punishing (Gemmill, 1973).

Techniques for reducing communication barriers may include recognition that low-income people have a tendency to express positive attitudes about modern health care that may not reflect their true attitudes. Also, to further reduce language barriers, communication between practitioners and patients should consist of dialogue-based rather than one-sided imperatives. This is particularly important because the patient and practitioner may not use the same words for the same meanings of disease processes, even within a similar language (Kay, 1979).

Guarneschelli et al. (1972) reported a case of subdural hematoma occurring in an infant secondary to the manipulations of a folk healer. The *curandera* had conducted the traditional healing ritual for "fallen fontanelle." The importance of reporting this case is appropriate; however, to label the phenomenon, as occurred in this report, a "variant of the battered child syndrome" was inappropriate. The parents sought treatment from a healer for a disease not recognized by conventional medicine. This could have been considered appropriate behavior in the context of their cultural belief. The parents sought a cure for their child's illness, and the *curandera* behaved in the accepted manner of the tradition of the art. The injury probably occurred as an accidental complication of the procedure.

This may be a good example of practitioners being "culturally blind" and not understanding the true meaning of folk medicine.

There has been much discussion in the literature regarding the need for bilingual and bicultural health practitioners, especially as a way of gaining the trust and confidence of patients. In addition to the need to transmit information in Spanish, there must be sensitivity in the patient–practitioner interaction. Scherwitz (1980) found that when practitioners spoke in Spanish, the medical recommendations increased in meaningfulness.

IMPROVING HEALTH EDUCATION AND HEALTH COMMUNICATION

According to the U.S. Department of Health and Human Services' report on black and minority health (1986), "Health promotion messages and health care to Hispanic groups are most effective when delivered within their social frame of reference, focusing on problems known to exist in the community."

Certain common elements appear to contribute to the success of many health programs. The key elements are as follows:

- Community involvement and outreach
- Program focus on comprehensive services, including disease prevention and health promotion
- Program ability to improve minority access to health services
- Cultural sensitivity to the group being served

Examples of health programs that have been successful in Mexican-American communities include community outreach; hypertension control; maternal and child health care; family planning, health education, promotion, and prevention; bicultural and bilingual health care; and Medicare/Medicaid (U.S. Department of Health and Human Services, 1986). In general, improved access to medical care was cited as a key element of a program's success; however, success was by no means limited to this element.

Case Study

Maria Garcia brings her 3-year-old child, Hector, to the hospital emergency department with a high temperature, chills, vomiting, and complaint of flank pain. She is registered at the desk and is questioned as to how payment will be made. Sra. Garcia does not have health insurance for her children. She explains that she will pay cash. The white receptionist demands that a deposit of $25.00 for emergency department services be made before treatment. Sra. Garcia obliges.

Sra. Garcia has two other children, 8 and 10 years old. Her husband is a carpenter, and he spends considerable time traveling to complete contracted jobs.

Sra. Garcia is directed to a waiting room. After 1½ hours of waiting, she is escorted to a treatment room by a white nurse. No communication takes place between the nurse and Sra. Garcia. The nurse asks the mother to hold the child while she takes his temperature. The nurse proceeds to place Hector in a tub of cool water; no explanation is given, and both Sra. Garcia and Hector are wondering what is going on. Sra. Garcia is alarmed that the nurse is doing this to her child. She strongly believes that his fever and symptoms are the result of being exposed to the cold morning air and that this submersion will only increase his complaints. The nurse begins to ask Sra. Garcia about the child's history. Very little is understood by Sra. Garcia, and the nurse makes no attempt to obtain a translator.

After 30 minutes of being in the tub, Hector is removed; his temperature is retaken. The nurse nods to Sra. Garcia as though she is saying, "He's okay." The nurse then says, "The doctor will be here in awhile."

Dr. Williams, a young white physician, walks in and in a very hostile manner asks Sra. Garcia why she had to bring him to the emergency department instead of a physician's office. Sra. Garcia was overwhelmed by his questions and felt guilty about the visit and her failure to bring him to the hospital sooner. Sra. Garcia explained to the physician that she had not had time and that she had been taking Hector to the *curandero,* who had been giving him some herbal tea to drink.

The physician explained to Sra. Garcia that the child needed to be hospitalized. She stated that she needed to consult with her husband about this and she would return after the decision had been made. The physician could not understand why she had to consult with her husband but agreed to let her go; he stressed the need for the child to be hospitalized.

That afternoon, Sra. Garcia discussed the need for hospitalization with her husband. Mr. Garcia felt that the physician did not know what he was talking about. He insisted that she see Pepito the *curandero* before going back to the hospital. She did, and Pepito concurred that seeking medical attention was probably the thing to do. Following hospitalization, the family was referred to the local health department for follow-up home visits by a public health nurse.

Study Questions

- Why was communication between Sra. Garcia and the health care professionals a problem?
- What could have been done to explain to Sra. Garcia the purpose of the cool bath?
- Why is the white health care professional considered the ultimate "all-knowing" individual?
- Explain disease causation and lack of knowledge of the germ theory as it has an impact on the interaction between the health care providers and the Garcia family.
- What significance was there in Sra. Garcia discussing the hospitalization with the husband?
- What significance was there in the Garcias obtaining a *curandero*'s opinion?

SUMMARY

This chapter presented an overview of the health needs and beliefs of Mexican-Americans and their implications for community health nursing. Major diseases and health conditions prevalent among Mexican-Americans were identified. Socioeconomic and culturally relevant reasons for the status of Mexican-Americans' health were reviewed. The folk health system, including common maladies and herbal medicine unique to Mexican-Americans, was described. How to improve cultural adaptation to health care in the community emphasized improving access to health care, reducing language barriers, and health education and communication. Finally, a case study was presented that serves as a stimulus for the generation of a culturally relevant nursing care plan for a Mexican-American family.

L e a r n i n g
A c t i v i t i e s

1. Develop a culturally relevant nursing care plan for this family, which includes assessment, nursing diagnoses, planning, intervention, and evaluation at the individual, family, and aggregate or community levels, for follow-up by the public health nurse.

2. Categorize these interventions that you generate into primary, secondary, and tertiary levels of prevention.

3. Find where in your community you could (a) take a beginning or advanced course in Spanish; (b) take a course in Spanish specifically designed for health professionals; and (c) refer Spanish-speaking clients to a course in English as a second language.

4. Consider the roles played by Hispanic actors and actresses during prime-time television. What percentage of the actors and actresses are of Hispanic origin? What messages are given about this population?

5. Identify through census data where persons of Hispanic origin reside in your city or town. Locate health care resources in those census tracts and compare them with health care resources available in census tracts populated largely by whites.

6. Locate a *curandero,* or healer, in the Hispanic community and make an appointment to discuss health beliefs, common illnesses, and their treatments. Ask how the *curandero* came to be a healer.

REFERENCES

Aranda, R. G.: The Mexican-American syndrome. Am. J. Public Health *61*;105, 1971.

Clark, M.: Health in the Mexican-American Culture. Berkeley, California, University of California Press, 1959, pp. 164, 197.

Currier, R. L.: The hot-cold syndrome and symbolic balance in Mexican and Spanish-American folk medicine. *In* Martinez, R. A., ed.: Hispanic Culture and Health Care. St. Louis, C. V. Mosby, 1978, p. 141.

Davis, C., Haub, C., and Willette, J.: U.S. Hispanics: Changing the face of America. Population Bull. *38*;3, 1983.

Enrique, H.: Retention of heritage through family ritual. Agenda *10*;6, 1980.

Foster, G.: Relationship between Spanish and Spanish-American folk medicine. J. Am. Folklore *66*;201–217, 1953.

Gemmill, R. H.: Cultural Differences in Medical Care. San Antonio, Texas, Academy of Health Sciences, U.S. Army, Publication no. GR51-240-008-06, 1973*a*, p. 29.

Gemmill, R. H.: Cultural Variation in Medical Care. San Antonio, Texas, Academy of Health Sciences, U.S. Army, Publication no. GR51-240-008-10, 1973*b*, pp. iii, xii.

Guarnaschelli, J., Lee, J., and Pitts, F.: Fallen fontanelle: A variant of the battered child syndrome. J.A.M.A. *222*;1545, 1972.

Holland, W.: Mexican-American medical beliefs: Science or magic? *In* Martinez, R. A., ed.: Hispanic Culture and Health Care. St. Louis, C. V. Mosby, 1978, p. 104.

Kay, M.: Lexemic change and semantic shift in disease names. Culture Med. Psychiatr. *3*;73–94, 1979.

Lecca, P. J., Greenstein, T. N., and McNeil, J. S.: A profile of Mexican-American health: Data from the Hispanic health and nutrition examination survey 1982–84. Arlington, Texas, Health Services Research, 1987.

Leon, M.: Special Report. The Robert Wood Johnson Foundation Serial Report No. 2. Princeton, New Jersey, The Robert Wood Johnson Foundation Communication Office, 1987, p. 6.

Lyndon B. Johnson School of Public Affairs: Socioeconomic conditions among Mexican-Americans in South Texas. *In* The Health of Mexican-Americans in South Texas, a report by the Mexican-American Policy Research Project. Austin, Texas, University of Texas, 1979, p. 11.

Martinez, R. A.: Hispanic Culture and Health Care: Fact, Fiction, Folklore. St. Louis; C. V. Mosby, 1978.

Murillo, N.: The Mexican-American family. *In* Hernandez, C. A., ed.: Chicanos: Social and Psychological Perspectives. edited by Carrol, St. Louis, C. V. Mosby, 1976, p. 22.

National Center for Health Statistics: Health, United States, 1991. Hyattsville, Maryland, Public Health Service, 1992.

Romano-V., O. I.: The anthropology and sociology of the Mexican-Americans: The distortion of Mexican-American history. El Grito II;14–16, 1986.

Rubel, A.: Concept of disease in Mexican-American culture. Am. Anthrop. *62*;797–799, 1960.

Samora, J.: Conception of health and disease among Spanish Americans. Am. Catholic Sociol. Rev. *22*;319, 1961.

Saunders, L.: Cultural Differences and Medical Care. New York, Russell Sage Foundation, 1954, p. 148.

Scherwitz, L.: The effect of language on physician patient interaction. (abstract) Washington, D.C., Research Proceedings Services, National Center for Health Services Research, Department of Health and Human Services Publication no. (PHS) 80-3288, 1980.

Stenger-Castro, E. M.: The Mexican-American: How his culture affects his health. *In* Martinez, R. A., ed.: Hispanic Culture and Health Care. St. Louis, C. V. Mosby, 1978. pp. 23–25.

U.S. Department of Health and Human Services: Report of the Secretary's Task Force on Black and Minority Health, Vol. VIII. Hispanic Health Issues. Washington, D.C., U.S. Department of Health and Human Services, January 1986, p. 5.

U.S. Department of Health, Education, and Welfare: Health Status of Minorities and Low Income Groups. Washington, D.C., DHEW, U.S. Public Health Service, Publication no. (HRA)-79-627, 1979, pp. 11–12.

Weisfeld, V.: Special Report. The Robert Wood Johnson Foundation Serial Report No. 1. Princeton, New Jersey, The Robert Wood Johnson Foundation Communication Office, 1983, pp. 3–11.

Cultural Influence in the Community: Southeast Asian Refugees

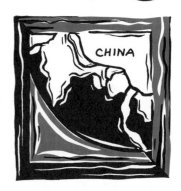

Upon completion of this chapter, the reader will be able to:

1. Discuss social, economic, and cultural issues that influence Southeast Asian refugees in the United States.

2. Discuss factors that impede the health of Southeast Asian refugees.

3. Identify specific areas of assessment for Southeast-Asian Americans.

4. Plan appropriate culturally relevant nursing care for Southeast Asian individuals, families, and communities.

Marjorie A. Muecke

In the past 6 years, over 500,000 refugees from Southeast Asia have settled in the United States.* Some 90% of them are under 45 years of age. Consequently, their first contacts with our health care system are usually through obstetrics, pediatrics, and emergency rooms. Whereas the first wave of Southeast Asian refugees in 1975 was generally well educated and familiar with Western ways, most of those arriving in the past 3 years have had little or no formal education and have led self-subsistent lives in rural and remote hill areas. Many of the recent arrivals have stayed in refugee camps for 3–5 years. Health problems such as tuberculosis, anemias, and dental and gum disease are much more prevalent among them than the first wave of refugees.[3]

This paper aims to ease the frustrations that physicians, nurses, and dentists commonly report in trying to work with the less-Westernized refugees and to promote refugee patients' adherence to health care plans. The focus is upon explaining behavior patterns and health care expectations that are common among Southeast Asian refugee patients. Disease conditions that are prevalent among this population are not discussed because they are treated in available literature.[3-20]

* From 1975 to December 1981, 565,757 refugees from Southeast Asia entered the United States.[1] While the United States has accepted more refugees from Southeast Asia than any other country, on a per-capita basis (number of Southeast Asian refugees per national population), the United States ranks third after Australia and Canada, and in terms of per-capita financial contributions to international refugee aid agencies, the United States ranks 12th.[2] The People's Republic of China and France rank second and third after the United States in terms of the total number of Southeast Asian refugees accepted for resettlement (265,588 and 71,931, respectively, as of April 30, 1981).[1]

This article is reprinted from the American Journal of Public Health, April 1983, Vol. 73, No. 4. ©1983 American Journal of Public Health. We thank Dr. Muecke and the American Journal of Public Health for allowing us to reprint the article.

It has been almost a decade since this article was originally published. In that interim, another one half million refugees from Southeast Asia have been resettled in the United States, in addition to immigrants from Vietnam and Amerasians.

Some of the examples provided in this text pertain to the mutual disorientation of newcomers and hosts toward each other and, therefore, may no longer pertain to Southeast Asian–Americans today. However, the point of the article — the painful mismatch between persons from Third World countries and U.S. society and the discomfort that this mismatch entails for both the refugee and the host — pertains to refugees coming into the United States for permanent resettlement in the 1990s. To date, these refugees are predominantly from the former Soviet Union, Ethiopia–Eritrea, highland Laos, Romania, Cuba, and Iran.

The author's areal focus in medical anthropology is mainland Southeast Asia.[21,22] She is a volunteer at the Seattle-King County Health Department's Refugee Screening Clinic; works with refugees in her teaching of undergraduate and graduate nursing and anthropology students at the University of Washington, Seattle; and consults extensively with health care professionals working with refugees. Many of the observations that follow are based upon personal experience.

BACKGROUND

The refugees have fled from three countries of mainland Southeast Asia: Cambodia, Laos, and Vietnam. The French held suzerainty over these countries from the late 19th century to 1954 and grouped them together under the label "Indochina." The French coined the term "Indochina" in a superficial attempt to unify the disparate groups in the area by emphasizing their heritage of Indic and Chinese influences. French control ended with the Geneva Agreements in 1954 and, with it, the political basis for the use of the term. To refer to the refugees as Southeast Asians is accurate but somewhat misleading in that the refugees have fled none of the countries of *insular* Southeast Asia, nor any of the mainland Southeast Asian countries of Burma, Malaya, Singapore, and Thailand. Nevertheless, "Southeast Asian" is used in this paper because we possess no other more accurate designation of this diverse group of refugees.

Although the refugees have only three national origins, they represent a wide variety of ethnic, language, and religious groups (Table 18–1). The extent of conversion to Christianity among the different groups has yet to be studied. Folk medical practices are less likely to be carried out by Christian than non-Christian refugees. Relationships among the different groups vary and often reflect a long history of sociopolitical conflict. Refugees in the United States generally choose first to be with their own ethnic group, second with Americans, and last with refugees from other groups.

Four characteristics of refugees distinguish the Southeast Asian refugees from other Asian groups who have resettled in the United States through immigration:

- They have come to the United States by second, not first choice; their first choice was almost in-

Table 18–1
Major Ethnic, Language, and Religious Identifications of Southeast Asian Refugees, by Country of Origin and Urban, Rural, or Hill Residential Background

Country of Origin	Urban, Rural, or Hill Background	Ethnic Group	Primary Language*	Religion
Cambodia	Rural	Cambodian (or Khmer)	Cambodian	Theravada Buddhism
	Urban (rural)	Cham	Cham	Islam (Sunni sect)
	Urban	Chinese	Teochiu, Cantonese†	Confucian-Taoism-Mahayana Buddism; Roman Catholicism
	Urban	Vietnamese	Vietnamese	(Same as Chinese)
Laos	Rural (urban)	Lao, Lu	Lao	Theravada Buddhism
	Rural	Thai Dam	Thai Dam; Lao	Animism‡
	Urban (rural)	Chinese	Chinese†	Mahayana Buddhism
	Hill	Lao Theung	Khmu; T'in; Lamet; Lao	Animism
		Hmong (or Meo or Miaw)	Hmong	Animism; some Christianity
		Mien (or Man or Yao)	Mien	Animism
Vietnam	Urban or rural	Vietnamese	Vietnamese	Confuscian-Mahayana Buddhism-Taoism; Roman Catholicism
	Urban	Chinese	Cantonese†	(Same as Vietnamese)

* Many refugees are fluent in more than one language.

† A variety of dialects/languages are spoken by the ethnic Chinese refugees, including the following: Teochiu (from Swatow), Cantonese, Hakka, Halnanese, Fukien, Hokkien, Toi Sanese, and among the educated, Mandarin.

‡ Although there are myriad interpretations of animism, they all involve the belief that anthropomorphic spirits may reside in organic material such as rice, trees, or earth, and can influence or determine human events and well-being.

variably to return to their native country if its political and economic conditions were similar to those that existed before the 1975 changes of government.

- They have come to the United States with little preparation, scant belongings, and no nest of compatriots to greet or help them.
- There is no realistic option for them ever to return to their homeland.
- They are survivors. Although statistics are not available, it is commonly estimated that for every refugee resettled, one died in flight.

CARING FOR SOUTHEAST ASIAN REFUGEE PATIENTS

Most Southeast Asians who come to the United States are likely to know some diseases that are recognized by Western medicine. The diseases they know, however, are often ones with which U.S. health personnel are unfamiliar because they are rarely seen in the United States, e.g., cholera, leprosy, malaria, smallpox, or tuberculosis. Complicating the poor cross-cultural correspondence of knowledge of disease, such medical basics as the germ theory and principles of anatomy and physiology are foreign to Southeast Asians who have not been educated, and there is no surgical tradition in Southeast Asia.

Nevertheless, when inconvenienced by sickness, most Southeast Asian refugees want to go to a doctor. Some common problems that they pose are that they rarely seek care when they are asymptomatic and few are familiar with our appointment system: some regard the most convenient doctor as the closest one not requiring an appointment and accepting medical coupons, i.e., a hospital emergency room. To cope with these and related problems, general guidelines follow for working with partially English-speaking Southeast Asian refugee patients who are in the early stages of integrating into U.S. culture.

The most important caveat is to seek the refugee patient's opinion whenever possible. This is necessary because cultural patterns are not predictive at the level of the individual and because the cultural orientations that the refugees have brought with them are undergoing rapid change. Not only are ethnic variations in practices, beliefs, and reactions common, they are complicated by variations in rural-versus-urban background, sex, and educational experience of the individual, as well as by group and individual variations in patterns of adjustment to life in the United States. There is also a tendency, particularly among refugees sponsored by Americans and among converts to Christianity, to renounce traditional religious and medical beliefs and practices. This is associated with the expectation of appearing less different from, and therefore more acceptable to, Americans. As such,

it is an example of Goffman's "passing" in order to hide the stigma of being a refugee.[23]

The First Encounter

A quiet, unhurried but purposeful demeanor is a part of normal professional decorum that is particularly reassuring to Southeast Asians because it symbolizes characteristics that are highly valued among them, such as wisdom, good judgment, and dignity.

When the patient is accompanied by relatives, addressing at least the initial conversation to the oldest of the group shows appropriate respect for elders; this person is also usually the ultimate decision maker for the patient.

Naming systems vary by ethnic group and can be very different from the Western system, fomenting consternation among record keepers. The surname is often placed first and may be a clan name (Hmong, Mien) or dynasty name (Vietnamese) rather than a family name (Table 18–2). Among

Table 18–2
Selected Common Characteristics of Southeast Asian Naming Systems by Ethnic Group

Ethnic Group	Usual No. of Names per Person	Common Surnames	Husband and Wife Share Surname	Example of a Name 1 = given name, 2 = middle name, 3 = surname
Cambodian	2	Chak, Chep, Samroul, San, Sok, Som, Vuthy	No	3 1 / Sovann Loeung
Chinese*	3	Chan, Chau, Ha, Lau, Lee, Lieng, Ly, Ong, Pho, Tang, Vuong	No	3 2 1 / Wang Din Wah
Hmong	2–4	Chang, Fang, Hang, Khang, Lee, Lor, Ly, Moua, Thao, Xiong, Vang, Vue, Yang	No	3 1 / Vang Koua
Lao	2	(varied: usually 3–5 syllables)	Yes	1 3 / Thongsouk Vongkhamkaew
Mien	2–4	Saechan, Saechao, Saelau, Saelee, Saelui, Saephan, Saetau, Saetang, Saetem, Saezulai	No	3 1 / Saeteun MuiChua
Vietnamese	3–4	Cao, Dinh, Hoang, Le, Luu, Ly, Ngo, Nguyen, Phan, Pho, Tran	No	3 2 1 / Nguyen thi Canh

* In Chinese publications, the family name precedes the given name (usually hyphenated): Chen Tai-chien or Chen, Tai-Chien. But in American and British journals, a Chinese name is usually anglicized and transposed: Tai Chien Chen or Chen, T. C. (see Council of Biology Editors Style Manual, 3d Ed., 1972, p. 156).

most groups except the Lao, the woman does not change her family (clan or dynasty) name at marriage. Among some groups, an individual may take additional names at certain points of the life cycle. Many refugees, however, are changing their names to conform to U.S. practice. Because of this and the wide ethnic variation in name systems, it is best to ask the patient what he or she wants to be called. To initiate contact, it is usually appropriate to address adults by title (Mrs., Mr., Dr.) plus first (given) name (see Table 18–2).

Provider attempts to obtain information through medical, health, and fertility histories of the less well educated Southeast Asian patient tend to be unproductive. This is because in Southeast Asia, medical patients are rarely told the names of their illnesses, of the medicines given, or of the diagnostic procedures performed on them; consequently, they rarely know what was done for them or why. Furthermore, refugee patients from rural or hill areas or with little formal education are not accustomed to the Gregorian calendar used in the West. Their methods for calculating ages may vary by up to 2 years from our method of counting birth as day 1. In addition, fertility histories are likely to underreport pregnancies and fetal losses because many people in Southeast Asia do not consider the fetus human, and some do not consider the newborn human until the baby is 3 days old (Hmong, Lao) or even older.

Interpreters

If the patient does not speak English easily, trained bilingual interpreters should be sought to ensure accurate two-way flow of information at the key decision-making points in the health care process, i.e., for history taking, when prescribing and evaluating diagnostic or therapeutic procedures that are new to the patient, and before any change in management, as from the intensive care unit to the medical floor in a hospital or from parenteral to oral medication. Without a trained bilingual interpreter at such points, intentions to provide for the patient's informed consent are thwarted, patient safety is jeopardized, and patient's noncompliance to medical regimen is likely.[24] Ideally, the interpreter should be bilingual and bicultural, treated as a colleague, and chosen both for competence in the language foreign to the health care professional and for familiarity with biomedicine.

When speaking through an interpreter, watching the patient (rather than the interpreter) will enable you to pick up behavioral cues. If the patient's responses do not fit your comment, check that you have made your meaning clear to the interpreter. Sometimes it will take an interpreter much longer to say in a Southeast Asian language what has just been said in English; this is often the sign that a cultural as well as a linguistic translation is being made. Sometimes the interpreter may appear to answer for the patient; this may be because he or she knows the information sought from having been that patient's interpreter on previous occasions.

If trained interpreters or bilingual health care providers are not made available for work with non– or partially English-speaking patients, the health care agency may be failing to meet the requirement of Title VI of The Civil Rights Act of 1964 for the provision of equal access to care, regardless of national origin.* Resettlement agencies (commonly called "VOLAGS" for "voluntary agencies") can provide information on the availability of interpreters in local areas. Each refugee's initial resettlement in the United States is organized by a VOLAG so the refugee should know the name of his or her VOLAG.†

Whether speaking through an interpreter or directly with a patient who is not sufficiently functional in English, ambiguity of meaning can be minimized in the following ways[25]:

- Using basic words and simple sentences and using nouns rather than pronouns
- Paraphrasing words that carry much meaning (e.g., "workup") in order to be precise about the specific meaning intended
- Avoiding use of metaphors, colloquialisms, and idiomatic expressions

---

* All agency recipients of federal funds, including Medicare, are subject to the stipulations of Title VI.

† The VOLAGS are American Council for Nationalities; American Fund for Czechoslovak Refugees; Buddhist Council for Refugee Rescue and Resettlement; Church World Service; International Rescue Committee; Iowa Refugee Service Center; Lutheran Immigration and Refugee Service; Tolstoy Foundation, Inc.; United Hias Service, Inc.; US Catholic Conference (USCC); World Relief Refugee Service; and Young Men's Christian Association. All but USCC are headquartered in New York.

- Learning and using basic words and sentences in the patient's language; this induces the patient or interpreter to take greater care in making their use of language accurate
- Inviting correction of your understanding of the matter at hand ("Am I understanding you correctly that . . .?")

Informed Consent

Obtaining a Southeast Asian refugee patient's informed consent prior to undertaking a medical procedure is difficult because cultural differences in health-related concepts often cannot be simply translated linguistically and because values of biomedicine might conflict with those of the patient's culture.[26] From an uninformed Southeast Asian perspective, diagnostic tests are baffling, inconvenient, and often unnecessary. Procedures such as circumcision or tonsillectomy, which biomedicine considers simple, are generally unknown. Any invasive procedure is frightening and may be believed to have long lasting and multiple effects. The prospect of surgery can be terrorizing. There is a great fear of mutilation that stems from widespread beliefs (among non-Christians) that souls are attached to different parts of the body and can leave the body, causing illness or death. This fear of mutilation extends through death, so that few Southeast Asians consent to autopsy unless they know and agree with the reasons for it in their own case.

Ensuring that a patient gives or withholds adequately informed consent to procedures guards his or her legal and ethical rights and can also prevent iatrogenic psychological distress and promote patient adherence to the medical regimen.[27] However, a belief that verbal statements in and of themselves can cause the event described to occur lingers among some peoples from Southeast Asia. As a result there is a tendency to avoid discussing problems, risks, and dangers. Explanations about why necessary procedures are recommended should be made routinely. For example, once the patient understands that the body continuously produces its own blood, that red blood cells live only 120 days, and that blood drawn from patients is used to help assess their physical status, the patient will usually consent to blood drawings for laboratory analysis.

However, the difficulties in achieving truly informed consent can be large. Reducing the number of procedures performed to a minimum is desirable. In some cases, cultural considerations may have to supersede usual policy for obtaining informed consent. For example, if the group to which the patient belongs believes that at death grandparents and parents become ancestors who should be worshipped and obeyed and who shape the well-being of living descendants, the children of the patient for whom a decision about terminating active intervention needs to be made may have difficulty consenting to terminate care. Such consent would be equivalent to contributing to the death of an ancestor, i.e., of one who would shape the survivors' fates.

The "Passive Obedient Patient"

Southeast Asians generally expect health professionals to be experts in diagnosis, treatments, and medications. Consequently, they tend not to contribute as much information as health care professionals want or consider essential.[28] According to many Southeast Asian cultural traditions, authority figures should not be questioned or opposed directly so as not to offend or embarrass them openly; they may, however, be discreetly disobeyed "behind their backs." That is, the passive obedience may be a culturally adaptive and sanctioned illusion of conformity. However, among some refugees in the United States, the tendency to passivity around authority figures is compounded by fear and ignorance of our legal system: suspicion that divulging personal information, as for a medical history, could jeopardize their legal rights is common. When the health problem is severe or complex, it may be useful to ask an intermediary who is close to the patient (e.g., VOLAG caseworker or the sponsor) to assist. Sometimes a refugee patient considers the doctor or nurse to be of such exalted status that the patient could do nothing other than obey.

The better a refugee patient understands reasons for a health professional's inquiries, the more direct and complete the responses tend to be. However, gaps in cross-cultural meaning may preclude refugees' understanding of medical rationales. The interpretation of organic signs and symptoms is not isomorphic across cultures[29,30]: points of major concern to health professionals may be irrelevant (exact age, medical or fertility history, causes of relatives' deaths) or unfamiliar (allergy, depression, virus, names of medications) to refugee patients. Values between two cultures may conflict (prolong life versus relieve suffering). The Southeast Asian refugee patient often copes with uncertainty and authority in a way — passive obedience — that is consonant with cultural heritage but frustrating to the norms of biomedicine. The refugee can protect self-esteem by concealing, through passivity, his or her own ignorance. The refugee believes that he or she can protect the health professional's status by concealing disagreements or incomplete understandings, i.e., by appearing obedient or compliant. Asking the patient to explain the issue at hand can reduce the illusional aspect of the patient's passive-obedient behaviors.

The "Noncompliant Patient"

Two common causes of failure to adhere to the medical or nursing regimen reiterate the need for bilingual and bicultural trained interpreters or for the assistance of refugee advocates or caseworkers: 1) the patient's misunderstanding of the medical regimen (e.g., taking the antimalarials chloroquine or Fansidar for a fever, as fevers in hill areas were commonly associated with malaria) and 2) the patient's inability to carry out behaviors that are prerequisite to observance of the medical regimen, such as locating and getting to the referral site or using the telephone to report new medical or nursing problems.

Ethnographic and clinical evidence suggest that noncompliance among Southeast Asian refugee patients is associated with the following patient perceptions: 1) cessation of symptoms, 2) inconvenience of observing the regimen, and 3) lack of cultural precedent for the regimen. Therefore, to help prevent noncompliance, the rationale(s) for continuing treatment after cessation of symptoms (or despite the absence of symptoms, as in prophylactic isoniazid treatment or antihypertensive therapy) should be made explicit to the patient. The patient should also be asked whether the patient knows of a cultural precedent for the proposed prescription and what there is about carrying it out that would be difficult for the patient. If the patient identifies no cultural precedent for it or identifies one that the patient values negatively or identifies barriers to its implementation, the necessity for the regimen should be reconsidered. If still indicated,

special efforts should be made to assist the patient in adhering to the regimen.

Constraints of Body Image

Notions of body image that are widespread among Southeast Asians but uncommon among Americans include reverence for the head, dispassionate acceptance of the female breast as the natural means for infant sustenance, and extreme privacy of the lower torso. The human head is regarded as the seat of life and therefore as highly personal, vulnerable, honorable, and untouchable except by close intimates. Procedures that invade the surface or an orifice of the head tend to frighten Southeast Asians with the thought that the procedures could provide exits for one's life essence. This is particularly true for infants on whom a scalp vein is used for intravenous lines because infants are considered at high risk for loss of life and because the lines are close to the soft fontanel from where it is believed that the soul may take easy exit. Explanation of the rationales for the procedures in question is necessary to allay undue anxiety.

Although breast-feeding in public is commonplace among rural and hill populations of Southeast Asia, the refugees quickly observe that it is unusual in the United States. Most refugee women prefer to bottle-feed their infants in the United States because of its perceived convenience and conformity to American norms.

The area of the body between the waist and knees is almost never exposed, even in privacy, by anyone other than young children. The loose hospital gown or physical examination of the genital area consequently can be deeply humiliating and unnerving to the Southeast Asian patient. Pelvic examinations of unmarried Southeast Asian women should not be undertaken routinely. When there is medical indication for a pelvic examination, the woman may want her husband to be present; if possible, the practitioner, and interpreter if one is needed, should both be female.

Social Supports

To be alone is frightening to many Southeast Asians. Offering to involve the patient's family as much as possible during the diagnostic and treatment program can help put them at ease; scheduling an entire family for care simultaneously can promote understanding and adherence as well. Different cultures dictate that different persons accompany the patient; e.g., at childbirth, a Chinese woman should have her mother-in-law in attendance, and a Hmong woman, her husband to bathe the newborn; for infants and children, either parent may assume what Americans term a mothering role.

Adult Southeast Asians are generally more comfortable with health care providers of their own sex rather than the opposite sex. This is particularly true for young and unmarried women.

If the option exists when making staff assignments or referrals for a Southeast Asian patient, ask if the patient would prefer an Asian service provider; often the patient would prefer a Filipino, Korean, or Japanese to an American even if the health care provider cannot speak a Southeast Asian language. However, because of political differences, persons from Laos and Cambodia might prefer not to have a Vietnamese nurse or physician.

Many non-Christian and non-Muslim Southeast Asians wear strings around their wrists and amulets on necklaces, ankle bands, or clothes. Although simple in appearance, such accoutrements can carry deep sacred and social meanings for the sick person and family. The wrist strings are believed to prevent soul loss, which in Laos and Cambodia is thought to cause illness. In a commonly practiced ritual, a soul-caller, respected elders, and kin symbolically bind the sick person's soul in the body by tying strings around the wrists (and, for infants, the neck, ankles, or waist). The strings thus signify both the spiritual wholeness and social support of the sick person. The soul-calling, wrist-tying ritual is also performed to bolster the strength of the ritualee in the face of major change, as at marriage or leaving home. If the strings or amulets must be removed for medical purposes, an explanation of the need to do so usually brings the patient's consent; some might want to keep the removed item.

Medication

Southeast Asians tend to define their health problems in terms of physical symptoms and to seek symptomatic treatment. They also tend to express emotional disturbances somatically; doing so enables them to avoid the heavy stigma that mental illness carries among Southeast Asians.[23,31]

The main reason most refugees from Southeast Asia go to a doctor is to get medicine for a symptom. They usually believe that Western medicine is very powerful and cures quickly. If they go to a doctor when sick and do *not* receive medicine, they are likely to feel cheated. Once given medicine which they find effective, however, they might reason, "Since I forgot to take one yesterday, I'll take two today," or, "If one pill is good, two are better." While most are familiar with the beneficial effects of Western medicine, few understand the risks of overdosages or underdosages.[28,32] This is related to the fact that all kinds of medicines were imported from the West and were widely available over the counter in Southeast Asian cities and towns. They were popular for quick relief of acute symptoms and usually self-administered by a people who could not read the foreign language in which the package instructions were written.

Underlying this conviction about the powerfulness of Western medicine to cure, however, is an anxiety that Western medicine might not be appropriate for Eastern people. Not only is the belief widespread that Asian bodies, diets, and behaviors are different from American, but also there is the, at times, perplexing knowledge that according to the Chinese "hot-cold" theory most Western medicines are classified as "hot," while most Southeast Asian herbal medicines are "cool." Such contradictions and uncertainties tend to heighten the Southeast Asian patient's concern about drug-induced idiosyncratic and side effects. Their concern often results in self-management of prescribed as well as over-the-counter medication. Prescriber efforts to explain the reason(s) for set dosages will increase the safety of the patient's tendency to self-medicate.

Traditional Self-Care Practices

Southeast Asians have traditionally dealt with illness through self-care and self-medication. When illness occurs in the United States, they practice self-care longer before seeking professional care than do Americans. This is related to their having had access to most drugs over the counter at low cost in Southeast Asia, to having had few hospitals and physicians, and to the high cost of Western medical care. Four major forms of self-care that are commonly performed by refugee patients in the United States are offerings to spirits, dermabrasive techniques, maintenance of hot-cold balance, and use of herbal medicines.

Theories of supernatural etiology and cures of illness are widespread among non-Christian Southeast Asians. Traditional treatment of illness includes a focus on the supernatural agent as well as on the body of the sick person. For example, among non-Christian Hmong, illness is interpreted as a visitation by spirits. It is commonly believed that a child becomes sick when its spiritual parents try to take it back; treatment consequently involves placation of the spiritual parents, and this may be done by offering them chicken at an altar in the home.[33] When sickness occurs in other persons, the head of household administers herbal remedies, having grown the herbs in a home garden. If sickness persists, a shaman may be called to enter a trance in order to communicate directly with offended spirits and to negotiate for the return of the sick person's soul; the negotiation is usually accompanied by a sacrifice of a pig or a chicken.

Because of the pervasive influence of China on the development of the peoples of Southeast Asia, Chinese medical tenets and practices have influenced the belief systems of most people from the area—the medical texts of Mien shamen were even written in Chinese. Chinese folk remedies that are widely practiced among the Vietnamese, Khmer, Hmong, and Mien (but not significantly among the Lao) include modifications of acupuncture, massage, herbal concoctions and poultices, and the dermabrasive practices of cupping, pinching, rubbing, and burning.

The dermal practices are the most common among the refugees (regardless of religion) but the least known by Americans. The dermal methods are perceived as ways to relieve headaches, muscle pains, sinusitis, colds, sore throat, coughs, difficulty breathing, diarrhea, or fever. In *cupping,* a cup is heated and then placed on the skin; as it cools, it contracts, drawing the skin and what is believed to be excess energy or "wind" or toxicity into the cup; a circular ecchymosis is left on the skin. *Pinching* and rubbing produce bruises or welts on the site of treatment; pinching may be at the base of the nose, between the eyes, or, like rubbing, on the neck, chest, or back. *Rubbing* involves an insistent rubbing of lubricated skin with a spoon or a coin, in order to bring toxic "wind" to the body surface.[34,35] A similar remedy is *burning*— touching a burning cigarette or piece of cotton to

the skin, usually the abdomen, in order to compensate for "heat" lost through diarrhea. These measures all produce changes in the skin and can be misread as signs of physical abuse by persons who are not sufficiently informed to make the differential diagnosis of cultural self-care.[36] The practices present a threat to the physical integrity of the person only if that person has a blood clotting disorder. They nurture the person's sense of being cared for and sense of security in being able to do something about disturbing symptoms. There is sound psychosociocultural reason to allow, or even support, these practices among the Indochinese.[35]

The above remedies are related to Chinese theories of health as a state of balance among the different components of the body and of the body with its environment. Illness prevention and treatment involve modification of food intake in order to maintain or restore equilibrium by rebalancing the body's component parts. Therapeutic adjustment of the diet requires consideration of the hot or cold nature of foods, cooking methods, and the person's ailment. The qualities hot and cold, like the polarities of energy called yin and yang, must be kept in balance to ensure health. Although the rules for classifying foods as hot or cold are difficult to decipher and seem to vary by informant,[37,38] most fruits and vegetables, along with fish, duck, and other things that grow in water, are cold, and most meats, sweets, coffee, and spicy condiments, such as garlic, ginger, and onion, are hot. Hot foods and beverages are thought to replace and strengthen one's blood; consequently, after surgery and childbirth, hot drinks are preferred, and cold drinks, jello, and juices are avoided. Many refugees in the United States have organic medicines for a wide variety of problems from impotence to mental illness and may take them simultaneously with prescribed medications. The Hmong and Chinese are particularly skilled herbalists.

Death and Depression

Southeast Asian and biomedical reactions to death often differ in two ways. First, the biomedical drive to prolong life conflicts with the general Southeast Asian preference for quality of life over length of life because of the expectation of less suffering in one's next reincarnation. Because of this expectation, they may seem to "give up" on relatives who are severely injured but survive an accident or on infants requiring intensive care because they were born prematurely. Second, almost all Southeast Asians want themselves and their relatives to die at home rather than in the hospital. At home they know they can give or receive the comfort of loved ones, comfort that they do not expect in the hospital. Furthermore, most believe that the spirit of a person who dies away from home is unhappy and so will cause trouble to the survivors long afterward.

Perhaps the greatest threat to refugee health is depression. It is related to the pervasive and overwhelming losses and changes that refugees have experienced in a relatively short time. These may leave the refugee confused and disoriented for years afterward.[39,40] Compounded with the sorrow and homesickness is the insecurity of isolation from their past and present environments. And on top of these are the role reversals, intergenerational conflicts, and reduced social status that commonly occur within each refugee ethnic group in the United States. Refugees, in general, are vulnerable and afraid in the United States. Because the health care system is one of the few culturally sanctioned sources of institutional support for them (the other sources—church and school—are not available

for all refugees) and because their access to informal U.S. social life is extremely limited, many adult refugees can be expected to seek care and attention on a long-term basis from health care providers.

SUMMARY

Resettlement of refugees from the Third World to the United States has occurred primarily in the last quarter of the 20th century. This chapter examines differences in expectations of resettlement among American health care providers and agencies and refugees who came from Cambodia, Laos, and Vietnam in the early 1980s.

Suggestions for facilitating communication and acceptance of differences are offered. These include guidelines for using language interpreters, for obtaining informed consent from refugee patients, and for dealing with death and depression. Characterization of Southeast Asian patients as "passive-obedient" and "noncompliant" is exposed as misleading stereotyping. Health-related issues crucial to many Southeast Asians, such as notions of the body, self-care, and needs for social support, are also identified and explained.

Learning Activities

1. Interview an Asian-American or recent Asian immigrant health care professional about the experience of being a minority in a European majority culture.

2. Watch prime-time television and check television listings to determine whether Asian-American characters are included. In what roles are Asian-Americans cast? What messages are being conveyed about Asian-Americans?

3. Identify an Asian-American cultural healer in the community, and schedule an appointment to discuss health beliefs and practices, treatments for various illnesses, and the preparation necessary to become a healer (i.e., how did the individual acquire his or her healing skills).

4. Using census data, identify the number, age, sex, and locations of residence for Asian-Americans in your city or area. Identify the health resources available in Asian-American neighborhoods and compare them with those available in other neighborhoods.

REFERENCES

1. Refugee Reports. Washington, D. C., American Council for Nationalities Service, 1982, pp. 3,4,8.
2. 1981 World Refugee Survey. New York, U. S. Committee for Refugees, Inc., 1981, pp. 40–41.
3. Catanzaro, A., and Moser, R. M.: Health status of refugees from Vietnam, Laos, and Cambodia. J.A.M.A. *247*;1303–1307, 1982.
4. Intestinal parasites (editorial). M.M.W.R. *347*;28–29, 1979.
5. Wiesenthal, A. M., Nickels, M. K., Hashimoto, K. G., et al.: Intestinal parasites in Southeast Asian refugees: Prevalence in a community of Laotians. J.A.M.A. *244*;2543–2544, 1980.
6. Malaria—U. S. 1980. M.M.W.R. *26*;413–415, 1980.
7. Trenholme, G. M., and Carson, P. E.: Therapy and prophylaxis of malaria. J.A.M.A. *240*;2293–2295, 1978.
8. Follow-up on tuberculosis among Indochinese refugees. M.M.W.R. *29*;47–53, 1980.
9. Tuberculosis among Indochinese refugees—US 1979. M.M.W.R. *29*;383–384, 389–390, 1980.
10. Tuberculosis drug resistance found among Indochinese. Refugee Rep. *2*;4, 1981.
11. Follow-up on drug resistant tuberculosis. M.M.W.R. *29*;602–604, 609–610, 1980.
12. Viral hepatitis type B. M.M.W.R. *29*;1–3, 1980.
13. Hepatitis B associated with acupuncture—Florida. M.M.W.R. *30*;1–3, 1981.
14. Centers for Disease Control: Health status of Indochinese refugees. Natl. Med. Assoc. *72*;59–65, 1980.
15. Skeels, M. R., Nims, L. J., and Mann, J. M.: Intestinal parasitosis among Southeast Asian immigrants in New Mexico. Am. J. Public Health *72*;57–59, 1982.
16. Yankauer, A.: Refugees, immigrants, and the public health (editorial). Am. J. Public Health *72*;12–14, 1982.
17. Peck, R. E., Chuang, M., Robbins, G. E., and Nichaman, M. Z.: Nutritional status of Southeast Asian refugee children. Am. J. Public Health *71*;1144–1148, 1981.
18. Erickson, R. V., and Hoang, G. N.: Health problems among Indochinese refugees. Am. J. Public Health *70*;1003–1006, 1980.
19. Feldstein, B., and Weiss, R.: Cambodian disaster relief: Refugee camp medical care. Am. J. Public Health *72*;589–594, 1982.
20. Davis, J. M., Goldenring, J., McChesney, M., and Medina, A.: Pregnancy outcomes of Indochinese refugees, Santa Clara County, California. Am. J. Public Health *72*;742–744, 1982.
21. Muecke, M. A.: Health care systems as socializing agents: Childbearing the North Thai and Western ways. Soc. Sci. Med. *10*;377–383, 1976.
22. Muecke, M. A.: An explanation of "wind illness" among the Northern Thai. Cult. Med. Psychiatry *3*;267–300, 1979.
23. Goffman, E.: Stigma: Notes on the Management of Spoiled Identity. Englewood Cliffs, New Jersey, Prentice-Hall, 1963.
24. Kline, F., Acosta, F. X., Austin, W., et al.: The misunderstood Spanish-speaking patient. Am. J. Psychiatry *137*;1530–1533, 1980.
25. Werner, O., and Campbell, D. T.: Translating: Working through interpreters and the problem of decentering. *In* Naroll, R., and Cohen, R., eds.: A Handbook of Method in Cultural Anthropology. New York, Columbia University Press, 1970, pp. 398–420.
26. Kunstadter, P.: Medical ethics in cross-cultural and multicultural perspective. Soc. Sci. Med. *14B*;289–296, 1980.
27. Miller, I. J.: Medicine and the law: Informed consent I–IV. J.A.M.A. *244*;2100–2103, 2347–2350, 2556–2558, 2661–2662.
28. Tran, Minh Tung: Indochinese Patients: Cultural Aspects of the Medical and Psychiatric Care of Indochinese Refugees. Washington, D. C., Action for South East Asians, 1980, pp. 54–72.
29. Kleinman, A.: Patients and Healers in the Context of Culture. Berkeley, California, University of California Press, 1980.
30. Leslie, C.: Medical pluralism in world perspective. Soc. Sci. Med. *148*;191–195, 1980.
31. Dunn, F. L.: Traditional Asian medicine and cosmopolitan medicine as adaptive systems. *In* Leslie, C., ed.: Asian Medical Systems: A Comparative Study. Berkeley, California, University of California Press, 1976, pp. 133–158.
32. Tran, Minh Tung: The Vietnamese refugees as patients. *In* A Transcultural Look at Health Care: Indochinese With Pulmonary Disease. Rockville, Maryland, The Lung Association of Mid-Maryland, 1980, pp. 26–40.
33. Chindarsi, N.: The Religion of the Hmong Njua. Bangkok, The Siam Society, 1976.
34. Golden, S., and Duster, M. C.: Hazards of misdiagnosis due to Vietnamese folk medicine. Clin. Pediatr. *16*;949–950, 1977.
35. Yeatman, G. W., and Viet, Van Dang: Cao gio (coin rubbing): Vietnamese attitudes toward health care. J.A.M.A. *244*;2748–2749, 1980.
36. Yeatman, G. W., Shaw, C., Berlow, M. J., et al.: Pseudobattering in Vietnamese children. Pediatrics *58*;616, 1976.
37. Breakley, G., and Voulgaropoulos, E.: Laos Health Survey: Mekong Valley 1968–1969. Honolulu, The University Press of Hawaii, 1976, p. 41.
38. Wu, Duh: Traditional Chinese concepts of food and medicine in Singapore. Singapore, Institute of Southeast Asian Studies, 1979.
39. Charron, D. W., and Ness, R. C.: Emotional distress among Vietnamese adolescents: A statewide survey. J Refugee Resettlement *1*;7–15, 1981.
40. Smither, R.: Psychological study of refugee acculturation: A review of the literature. J Refugee Resettlement *1*;58–63, 1981.

The African-American Community

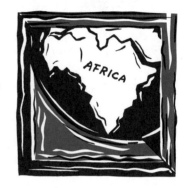

Upon completion of this chapter, the reader will be able to:

1. Identify the impacts of social, economic, and cultural trends in U.S. society on the health of African-Americans.

2. Assess the community health nursing needs of African-American individuals, families, and communities.

3. Describe the types of healers and cultural healing practices prevalent among African-Americans.

4. Identify ways in which community health nursing for African-American individuals, families, and communities can be provided with cultural sensitivity.

5. Analyze the major causes of excess morbidity and mortality among African-Americans.

6. Propose solutions to the community health problems facing African-American individuals, families, and groups.

Margaret M. Andrews
Lucretia Bolin

Early historical documents indicate that blacks first came to the North American continent in 1619, 1 year before the Pilgrims arrived at Plymouth Rock (Bennett, 1962). These early settlers were not slaves but rather free men and women who came to North America for the economic advantages promised by this resource-rich land. Between the time of their 17th-century arrival and 1860, however, more than 4 million slaves were brought to North America, primarily from the West Coast of Africa. Since then, blacks have come to the United States from other parts of Africa as well as many Caribbean nations.

Although 19th-century U.S. history reminds us of Civil War efforts to free black slaves, the 20th century will be noted by historians for the struggle of African-Americans to win equal civil rights — in virtually all aspects of life ranging from education to recreation. Despite the many strides made by legal mandate, widespread disparities between blacks and whites prevail. These disparities exist across a wide variety of contexts: serious inequalities exist in health care, such as diminished access to services, lower quality of care, fewer qualified health care providers available to meet the needs of African-American communities, and subtle racial discrimination in determining the allocation of human and material health care resources.

Table 19–1
Black Resident Population by State for 1990 and 1980

1990 Black Population Rank	State	1990 Black Population	1990 Percentage of State Population	1980 Black Population	1980 Percentage of State Population	Change from 1980 to 1990 (n)	Change from 1980 to 1990 (%)
1	New York	2,859,055	15.9	2,402,006	13.7	457,049	19.0
2	California	2,208,801	7.4	1,819,281	7.7	389,520	21.4
3	Texas	2,021,632	11.9	1,710,175	12.0	311,457	18.2
4	Florida	1,759,534	13.6	1,342,688	13.8	416,846	31.0
5	Georgia	1,746,565	27.0	1,465,181	26.8	281,384	19.2
6	Illinois	1,694,273	14.8	1,675,398	14.7	18,875	1.1
7	North Carolina	1,456,323	22.0	1,318,857	22.4	137,466	10.4
8	Louisiana	1,299,281	30.8	1,238,241	29.4	61,040	4.9
9	Michigan	1,291,706	13.9	1,199,023	12.9	92,683	7.7
10	Maryland	1,189,899	24.9	958,150	22.7	231,749	24.2
11	Virginia	1,162,994	18.8	1,008,668	18.9	154,326	15.3
12	Ohio	1,154,826	10.6	1,076,748	10.0	78,078	7.3
13	Pennsylvania	1,089,795	9.2	1,046,810	8.8	42,985	4.1
14	South Carolina	1,039,884	29.8	948,623	30.4	91,261	9.6
15	New Jersey	1,036,825	13.4	925,066	12.6	111,759	12.1
16	Alabama	1,020,705	25.3	996,335	25.6	24,370	2.4
17	Mississippi	915,057	35.6	887,206	35.2	27,851	3.1
18	Tennessee	778,035	16.0	725,942	15.8	52,093	7.2
19	Missouri	548,208	10.7	514,276	10.5	33,932	6.6
20	Indiana	432,092	7.8	414,785	7.6	17,307	4.2
21	District of Columbia	399,604	65.8	448,906	70.3	−49,302	−11.0
22	Arkansas	373,912	15.9	373,768	16.3	144	0.0
23	Massachusetts	300,130	5.0	221,279	3.9	78,851	35.6
24	Connecticut	274,269	8.3	217,433	7.0	56,836	26.1
25	Kentucky	262,907	7.1	259,477	7.1	3,430	1.3
26	Wisconsin	244,539	5.0	182,592	3.9	61,947	33.9
27	Oklahoma	233,801	7.4	204,674	6.8	29,127	14.2
28	Washington	149,801	3.1	105,574	2.6	44,227	41.9

THE AFRICAN-AMERICAN COMMUNITY

Sociodemographic Overview

African-Americans in 1990 constituted 12.1% of the U.S. population, up from 11.7% in 1980 (Table 19–1). The African-American population has increased 13.2% versus 6.0% for whites and 9.8% for the total population (Current Population Reports, 1991). Projections for the year 2000 are that African-Americans will account for 15% of the total population. An analysis of age composition among African-Americans indicates that 33.1% of the African-American population is less than 18 years of age and that 8.2% is 65 years of age or older. An

inverse gender phenomenon is reflected in these statistics, with males being overrepresented in the 18-year-old and under cohort and older women disproportionately represented in the 65-year-old and older cohort.

Economic Milieu

According to the most current data available from the U.S. Bureau of the Census (Current Population Reports, 1991), African-American family income represented 56% of white family income. The annual median income for white families in 1989 was $35,980, higher than the 1980 level of $23,520, whereas that for African-American families in

Table 19–1
Black Resident Population by State for 1990 and 1980 *Continued*

1990 Black Population Rank	State	1990 Black Population	1990 Percentage of State Population	1980 Black Population	1980 Percentage of State Population	Change from 1980 to 1990 *(n)*	Change from 1980 to 1990 (%)
29	Kansas	143,076	5.8	126,127	5.3	16,949	13.4
30	Colorado	133,146	4.0	101,703	3.5	31,443	30.9
31	Delaware	112,460	16.9	95,845	16.1	16,615	17.3
32	Arizona	110,524	3.0	74,977	2.8	35,547	47.4
33	Minnesota	94,944	2.2	53,344	1.3	41,600	78.0
34	Nevada	78,771	6.6	50,999	6.4	27,772	54.5
35	Nebraska	57,404	3.6	48,390	3.1	9,014	18.6
36	West Virginia	56,295	3.1	65,051	3.3	−8,756	−13.5
37	Iowa	48,090	1.7	41,700	1.4	6,390	15.3
38	Oregon	46,178	1.6	37,060	1.4	9,118	24.6
39	Rhode Island	38,861	3.9	27,584	2.9	11,277	40.9
40	New Mexico	30,210	2.0	24,020	1.8	6,190	25.8
41	Hawaii	27,195	2.5	17,364	1.8	9,831	56.6
42	Alaska	22,451	4.1	13,643	3.4	8,808	64.6
43	Utah	11,576	0.7	9,225	0.6	2,351	25.5
44	New Hampshire	7,198	0.6	3,990	0.4	3,208	80.4
45	Maine	5,138	0.4	3,128	0.3	2,010	64.3
46	Wyoming	3,606	0.8	3,364	0.7	242	7.2
47	North Dakota	3,524	0.6	2,568	0.4	956	37.2
48	Idaho	3,370	0.3	2,716	0.3	654	24.1
49	South Dakota	3,258	0.5	2,144	0.3	1,114	52.0
50	Montana	2,381	0.3	1,786	0.2	595	33.3
51	Vermont	1,951	0.3	1,135	0.2	816	71.9

The population counts set forth herein are subject to possible correction for undercount or overcount. The United States Department of Commerce is considering whether to correct these counts and will publish corrected counts, if any, no later than July 15, 1991.

Adapted from the U.S. Bureau of the Census: United States Population Estimates by Age, Sex, Race, and Hispanic Origin: 1980 to 1988. Series P-25, No. 1045. Washington, D.C., U.S. Government Printing Office, 1990; and Current Population Reports: The Black population in the United States: March 1990 and 1989. Series P-20, No. 448. Washington, D.C., U.S. Government Printing Office, 1991, pp. 1–17.

1989 was only $20,210, higher than the 1980 level of $14,460 (U.S. Bureau of the Census, 1983; Current Population Reports, 1991). These figures are misleading because they fail to show that African-American family incomes must be used to support more family members and that both husband and wife are employed in more African-American families than in white families and earn disproportionately less than their white counterparts. Furthermore, the U.S. Department of Labor indicated that the majority of female-headed African-American families live below the federally defined poverty level.

More than one third of the African-American population lives in poverty compared with 10% of the white population. In 1989, over 9 million (31%) of African-Americans were poor. Although 25% of poor African-Americans receive some form of public assistance, only 10% of poor whites receive such aid. African-American families are more than three times as likely to be poor in comparison with white families. Approximately 43.2% of all African-American children are members of these families. Less than 15% of white children live in households that are officially defined as poor. African-American families headed by females have the highest poverty rate, compared with African-American married couples and male-headed households (Current Population Reports, 1991).

Poverty statistics reflect employability, education, and opportunity for employment. Overall, the current trend reveals that African-Americans, regardless of gender, are more likely to be unemployed. The percentage of African-American men in the labor pool who were unemployed was 11.8 in 1989, compared with 4.8% for white men; the percentage was 10.8 for African-American women, compared with 4.0% for white women (Current Population Reports, 1991).

Even if African-Americans are employed, there is a great discrepancy in median earnings when contrasted with those of whites. In 1989, the median earnings of African-American men and women were 69% and 98%, respectively, of that of their white counterparts. African-American women earn comparatively less than African-American men. Based on the past rate of progress in integration of African-Americans into the labor force, it will take 90 years for African-American professionals to approximate the proportion of African-Americans in the population (Staples, 1982).

Education

The percentage of African-Americans graduating from high school is lower than that of whites. Just over 66% of African-Americans have completed high school, compared with 79.9% of whites. Disparities in rates of college enrollment and college completion also exist for African-Americans (Current Population Reports, 1992b). African-American women tend to have more education than African-American men. Furthermore, despite much rhetoric about equal opportunities for women in the workplace, there exists significant sexual discrimination in that women's earnings are much lower than men's.

College-educated whites face fewer barriers to career aspirations than do college-educated African-Americans, who are unemployed as frequently as white men who have not graduated from high school (U.S. Civil Rights Commission, 1982).

Changing Patterns of African-American Family Life

Like all of U.S. society, African-Americans have witnessed an era of sexual permissiveness, alternative family lifestyles, increased divorce rates, and reductions in fertility rate. Black women are twice as likely as white women to have engaged in sexual intercourse by age 19. Although the percentage for white females is lower, those who do have sex are engaging in premarital sex more often and have a larger number of sexual partners. However, greater numbers of sexually active African-American females are not using reliable contraceptives, and 41% are pregnant at any given time (Mindel et al., 1988).

As a result of increased premarital sexual activity among African-Americans, a significant number — more than half — of African-American children are born to single mothers. Racial differences in the number of infants born to single unwed mothers is widened due to the greater numbers of white (41%) than African-American (26%) women who have low-cost abortions. It is projected that the number of African-American infants born to single mothers will continue to increase as the percentage of births increases among African-American adolescent mothers (Cummings, 1983; Mindel et al., 1988; National Center for Health Statistics, 1991).

Married African-Americans face the same economic and cultural forces that undermine the marital stability of the general population. Between 1970 and 1991, the number of individuals who were divorced tripled, from 4.3 million to over 15 million (Current Population Reports, 1992a). There has been a general decline in the percentage of married African-Americans from 1970 (64%) to 1991 (44%). The proportion of divorced African-Americans rose from 4% to 11%, in comparison with a rise of 3% to 8% for whites. When the economic aspects are considered, the divorce rate of middle-class African-Americans is lower, and that is because chances for a stable marriage increase in parallel with family income and educational achievement (U.S. Bureau of the Census, 1990).

Roles

In recent years, the issue of sex roles has received considerable attention, with the debate centering on female subordination and male dominance and privilege. African-Americans must grapple with both racial discrimination and role identity issues.

African-American men are frequently stereotyped as "irresponsible, criminalistic, hypersexual, and lacking in masculine traits" (Staples, 1988, p. 312). Some of these stereotypes become self-fulfilling prophecies because the dominant society is structured in a way that prevents many African-American men from gaining equal access to social, economic, and political institutions, which hampers their participation and structural incorporation into the larger society (Cheung, 1991). Although mainstream culture has deprived many African-American men of the economic ability to perform what are considered stereotypic male work roles and functions, most function in a way that gains the respect of their children, peers, and community (Staples, 1988).

African-American women are struggling with issues such as equal pay for equal work, child care facilities, and female parity in the work force. Instead of joining the predominantly white, middle-class women's movement, many African-American women have formed their own organizations such as the Welfare Rights Organization, Black Women Organized for Action, and the Black Feminist Alliance.

Relationships between African-American men and women have had a unique evolution. Unlike the white family, which is characterized by a patriarchy historically sustained by the economic dependence of women, the African-American dyad is characterized by more equal roles and economic parity. The system of slavery did not permit African-American men to assume the superordinate role in the family constellation. In recent times, lower-class African-American women have tended to be the breadwinners (through employment or receipt of government aid), enjoy higher levels of education than their male counterparts, and hold dominant positions in their families. Thus, in African-American families, relationships between men and women depend on sociopsychological factors rather than an economic compulsion to marry and remain married.

Finding and keeping a mate are complicated by a number of psychosocial factors as well as structural restraints. First, there are more African-American females than males, making competition among women high. Second, although some African-American men are threatened by successful African-American women, further investigation reveals other underlying forces such as the need for security versus the desire for freedom and the quest for monogamous intimacy versus the seduction of sexual variety. The traditional exchange of feminine sexual appeal for male financial support is declining as women are able to define their own status and become economically independent. Research indicates that African-American wives are usually less satisfied with their marriages than are white wives. However, the source of their dissatisfaction is often associated with the problems created by poverty and racism (Staples, 1988).

The past decade witnessed a significant increase in interracial dating and marriage. Among the reasons for this change are the desegregation of the public school system, the work force, and other social settings.

Through the 1970s, the most typical interracial pairing involved an African-American man and a white woman with the male partner usually of higher socioeconomic status. This pattern was so common that it was described by social theorists as racial hypergamy. In essence, it was assumed that the higher-status African-American man was exchanging his socioeconomic status for the privilege of marrying a woman who belonged to a racial group that was considered superior. Contemporary interracial relations are much more likely to involve people with a similar educational background and occupational status (Staples, 1988). However, fewer than 5% of all marriages involving an African-American are interracial (Poussaint, 1983).

Rural Versus Urban African-Americans

As shown in Table 19–2, the majority of African-Americans live in metropolitan or urban areas, but significant numbers also reside in nonmetropolitan or rural parts of the country, particularly in the South. The rural and urban lifestyles are markedly different (see Chapter 27).

SOCIAL JUSTICE: AN AFRICAN-AMERICAN PERSPECTIVE

Self-Concept and Racial Identity

From early childhood, African-American children face the reality that racial identity and self-concept are interrelated. In the mid-1960s, the African-American consciousness movement began. This movement is known for its contribution to increased awareness of racial and cultural identity, including the "Black Pride" slogan and accompa-

nying changes in societal knowledge about the importance of racial identity issues.

The importance of race is maintained by both internal and external forces. Both African-Americans and non–African-Americans constantly reinforce the importance of racial identity as a societal issue. Among African-American families, "blackness" is sometimes viewed as part of the "we-versus-they" focus. Nobles (1973) described the "extended self" as "the self of one's people" and therefore "one's being is the group's being." Similarly, African-American children's racial self-esteem is strongly influenced by parental behaviors, particularly those of mothers during child rearing. The number of African-American cultural objects found in the home; the instruction of children about well-known African-American figures in history, sports, politics, and other realms of society; attitudes about African-American physical characteristics; attitudes about African-American activities; and the instruction of children about differential treatment of African-Americans in society all influence the African-American child's level of racial self-esteem (Orque et al., 1983; Lipscomb, 1975).

Racism

One of the major recurrent stresses in the lives of African-Americans is racism and its direct and indirect effects. Racism—organizational, institutional, and individual—handicaps the lives of African-Americans. It influences and shapes their life experiences over a variety of contexts. It is suggested that the occurrence of disparities across a variety of contexts is linked to the precarious relationship between African-Americans and whites. Past negative attitudes of whites toward African-Americans have contributed to the current social marginality and a lack of structural incorporation in the dominant culture.

According to Cheung (1991), racial discrimination exists particularly for visible racial and ethnic minority groups. Racial discrimination (i.e., racism), says Cheung (1991), "has always denied [African-Americans and other visible minorities] equal access to social, economic, and political institutions, thereby hampering their [participation] and structural incorporation into the larger society" (p. 593). Blocked opportunities to succeed, achieve, and obtain legitimate goals foster extreme

Table 19–2
Percentage Distribution of Whites and African-Americans by Geographical Area, 1990

Geographic Area	Distribution (%)	
	White (N = 206,983,000)	African-American (N = 30,392,000)
Total population	84.1	12.3
Northeast	21.1	17.4
Midwest	25.3	19.8
South	31.9	54.3
West	21.7	8.5
Metropolitan areas	76.4	83.8
Nonmetropolitan areas	23.6	16.2

Adapted from Current Population Reports: The Black population in the United States: March 1990 and 1989. Series P-20, No. 448. Washington, D.C., U.S. Government Printing Office, 1991, pp. 1–17.

conditions of stress, learned helplessness, and depression at individual and collective levels.

Persistent racial discrimination and disadvantaged conditions reinforce the current position of social marginality of African-Americans today. One of the byproducts of racial discrimination is continuing and persistent disparities in important indicators of living conditions, particularly in the areas of health, morbidity, and mortality.

COMMUNICATION AND LANGUAGE

During the past several decades, there has been increasing literature and interest centering around *black English,* especially its impact on the educational process of African-American children. Smitherman (1977) referred to black English as reflecting "linguistic-cultural African heritage and the conditions of servitude, oppression and life in America."

Black English has been referred to as black dialect, black creole, soul talk, Afro-American speech, Ebonics, and Afro, but regardless of the terminology used, it is a dialect spoken at some time by 80–90% of African-Americans and is essentially Euro-American speech with African-American meaning, nuance, tone, and gesture (Smitherman, 1977).

Development of Black English

During the period of slavery, West African slaves from different tribes developed a form of communication, known as pidgin, to communicate among themselves as well as with whites. Pidgin is a form of communication used when two persons speak two different languages and do not have a common third language *(lingua franca).* Because African languages were not used widely, offspring of the early slaves began to speak English pidgin, which eventually developed into a new language known as Creole. In this language, West African structure and idiom are retained, but English words are substituted (Smitherman, 1977; Orque et al., 1983).

Characteristics of Black English

Black English is a highly oral, stylized, rhythmic, spontaneous language. Smitherman (1977) developed an African-American language model that is divided into two aspects: linguistic and stylistic. The linguistic aspect focuses on grammatical structure and word usage, establishing rules of black English.

The stylistic aspect refers to the communication power of black English through various ritual forms or modes that give meaning to the sounds and grammatical structure (e.g., sermon, prayer, spiritual hymns, folk songs, toasts, verbal contests, voodoo curses, and so forth). All of these indicate the power of the spoken word among African-Americans, and many reflect cultural attitudes toward time, nature, the universe, life, death, and evil (Smitherman, 1973, 1977; Orque et al., 1983).

It is important to remember that variations in age, social class, educational level, and locale among African-Americans influence the communicative process. Some African-Americans, especially those from backgrounds of greater socioeconomic and educational achievements, may be "bilingual," i.e., be fluent (or at least knowledgeable of linguistic differences) in both English and black English. Blacks of middle- and upper-class socioeconomic status may or may not follow the cultural type presented; thus, each individual and family must be assessed rather than relying on sweeping generalizations and cultural stereotypes.

HEALTH BELIEFS AND PRACTICES
Traditional Beliefs About Health and Illness

The traditional views of health and illness stem from the African belief regarding life and the nature of being. To many Africans, life is a process rather than a state, and a person is viewed in terms of energy forces rather than matter. All things, whether living or dead, are believed to influence each other. Therefore, humans have the power to influence their own and others' destinies through the use of behavior, whether proper or otherwise, as well as through knowledge of the person and the world. In health, the person is in harmony with nature; illness occurs with disharmony. Traditional beliefs about health are holistic, with mind, body, and spirit being integrally interwoven (Spector, 1986).

Illness, or disharmony, is attributed to a number of sources, primarily demons and evil spirits, who act on their own accord. The goal of treatment, from the traditional African perspective, is to remove the harmful spirit(s) from the body of the ill person. Several methods are used by healers.

Several researchers have studied what health and illness mean to African-Americans; Thomas (1981) reported that from an African-American perspective, health is described as feeling good and having no problems or pains. Snow (1974) indicated that good health is classified with other kinds of good luck such as wealth or success. LaFargue (1972) reported that African-Americans define illness as "feeling bad" or an "inhibition of physical activity." In addition, Hines (1972) indicated that the absence of preventive health orientation among African-Americans results from a cultural emphasis on being oriented to the present rather than to the future. According to Snow (1974), illness is seen as undesirable, as are bad luck, poverty, domestic turmoil, or unemployment.

Illnesses are classified as natural or unnatural. In a natural illness, a person has inadequate protection and is affected by nature's forces (e.g., cold air entering the body or impurities in the air, food, or water). In an unnatural illness, evil influences such as witchcraft, voodoo (hoodoo), a hex, a fix, or rootwork may be blamed for problems ranging from nightmares to serious illness. In addition, illnesses may be sent by God as punishment for sin (e.g., moral transgressions by parents may be punished by the illness, or even death, of a child). An illness that is spiritual in origin must be cured by a spiritual healer; thus, physicians or other health care professionals are unable to help persons who are being punished by God (Snow, 1974). Traditionally, to maintain health, it was necessary to "read the signs." Natural phenomena such as the phases of the moon, seasons of the year, and planet positions affect the human body and its processes.

In a study of low-income African-Americans residing in Tucson, Arizona, Snow (1974) described their cultural healing system as a composite of rare elements of African origin, remnants from the folk and formal medicine practices of the 19th century, and selected beliefs from modern scientific health care, all interwoven with factors from Christianity, voodoo, and sympathetic magic. Three major themes developed from Snow's data:

- The world is a hostile and dangerous place.
- The individual is vulnerable to attack from external sources (e.g., nature, God, malice of relatives, friends, or strangers).
- The individual is helpless and must depend on outside help.

Cultural Health Practices

Traditionally, roots, herbs, potions, oils, powders, tokens, rituals, and ceremonies have been and continue to be used in many Southern communities. Historically, these practices arose to fill a void left by the inaccessibility and denial of health care by white physicians in the rural South and were carried over from West Africa. In urban areas today, there is more reliance on the practice of African-American cultural healers (e.g., priest/priestess or spiritualists), who focus more on the mystical component and psychological support and less on herbal or root medicine (Orque et al., 1983).

According to research by Snow (1974) and Bloch (1975), the general population, including African-Americans, predominantly self-treat illness. Oils, candles, incense, and aerosol room sprays may be purchased at special stores or through the mail and are used to repel evil. The numbers 3 and 9 are very powerful and are often used by African-Americans in both home remedies and magic rituals (Snow, 1974).

Voodoo (or hoodoo) has been practiced in the United States for more than 200 years and originated with the arrival of slaves from West Africa. The term has been attributed to two sources: it may be derived from a creole French word meaning "sorcerer," or it is a derivation of *Vodu,* a West African god. Voodoo refers to a belief system that involves the use of magic, both white (good) and black (bad), which may be used to bring health or illness to a person. Oils, powders, colored candles, and other objects are used in the practice of voodoo. Illness is attributed to a fix, hex, or spell that is placed on one person by another out of anger (Spector, 1986; Orque et al., 1983).

Other healing practices of African-Americans include the use of prayer, laying on of hands, "rooting," magic rituals, and specific diets.

The most common method of treating illness is prayer; laying on of hands is especially popular. Rooting, a practice derived from voodoo, is also used. In rooting, a person (usually a woman) is consulted about the cause or source of the illness and then prescribes a treatment that may consist of a wide variety of interventions including ingestion of home remedies, application of poultices, performance of rituals, and so forth.

Many African-Americans believe that health is maintained by a "proper" diet, which is defined as eating three nutritious meals a day, including a hot breakfast. Rest and a clean environment are also important. Laxatives may be used to keep the system "running" or "open."

Preventive measures may include the use of an amulet, talisman, or charm that is usually worn on the body for the purpose of attracting good health or preventing illness. Among the more prevalent objects worn for these purposes are copper or silver bracelets and *asafetida* (dried resinous material from roots of certain plants that resembles a sponge). Cod liver oil may be ingested to prevent colds, and a sulfur and molasses preparation is rubbed on the back in the spring to prevent illness as the new season begins.

Summarized in Table 19–3 are selected African-American folk illnesses as well as etiology, clinical manifestations, practitioners sought for a cure, and treatment.

CULTURAL HEALERS

Many African-Americans believe in the power of healers to heal and help others. It may be necessary to consult more than one healer, and the simultaneous use of healers of the body, mind, and spirit is not unusual among some traditional families. For example, an upper respiratory infection might require an antibiotic from a physician or nurse practitioner and an herbal remedy from the "old lady." In a study by Bloch (1975), African-Americans indicated that cultural healing remedies help a person to psychologically deal with discomforts but that when the interventions of cultural healers fail, a physician or nurse practitioner should be consulted.

Table 19–4 summarizes the types of cultural healers in the African-American healing system.

Biocultural Variations in Illness

Historically, there has been, and continues to be, a troubling disparity in the health status of African-Americans compared with that of white Americans. These troubling disparities continue to exist despite advances in medical technologies and treatments. The report on African-American and minority health issued by the U.S. Department of Health and Human Services noted that people from minority backgrounds suffer 60,000 "excess deaths" annually (Heckler, 1985). The six major contributors to the disparity between the African-American and white mortality rates are cancer, cardiovascular disease and stroke, diabetes mellitus, chemical dependency, homicide and accidents, and infant mortality. African-Americans also have higher rates of mortality from communicable diseases, including AIDS (U.S. Public Health Service, 1988).

African-Americans have a life expectancy of 69.1 years compared with 75.6 years for whites, a difference of 6½ years (National Center for Health Statistics, 1991). African-Americans have a disproportionately high incidence of hypertensive disease, diabetes, cancer, and glaucoma. One of every four African-Americans has hypertension, compared with one of every seven whites. African-American men aged 45–64 have a 41% higher mortality rate than white men, and the mortality rate for African-American women is more than twice that for white women. During the past 25 years, the rate of cancer mortality among whites has increased only 5% compared with 26% for African-Americans. Table 19–5 summarizes the annual total and "excess" deaths for African-Americans for selected causes of mortality.

INDICATORS OF HEALTH IN THE AFRICAN-AMERICAN POPULATION

Of the 2 million U.S. people who die each year, approximately 12% are African-Americans. According to the report on black and minority health (Heckler, 1985), the six federally identified categories of disease account for 41% (cardiovascular disease), 12% (infant mortality), 10% (cancer), 6% (homicide), 3% (cirrhosis), and 1% (unintentional injuries) of excess death among African-Americans. The disparity between the excess mortality rates of African-Americans and those of whites affects certain age groups more than others. Compared with whites, African-Americans have

Table 19–3
Folk Illnesses Among African-Americans

Illness	Cause	Symptoms	Healer	Treatment
High blood (too much blood)	Diet very high in red meat and rich food; belief that high blood causes stroke	Weakness Paralysis Vertigo or other signs/symptoms related to a stroke	Family member, friend, spiritualist, or self; the latter does this after referring to a Zodiac almanac.	Take internally lemon juice, vinegar, Epsom salts, or other astringent food to sweat out the excess blood. Treatment varies depending on what is appropriate according to the Zodiac almanac.
Low blood (not enough blood—anemia is conceptualized)	Too many astringent foods, too harsh a treatment for high blood; remaining on high blood pressure medication for too long	Fatigue Weakness	Same as for high blood	Eat rich red meat, beets. Stop taking treatment for high blood. Consult the Zodiac almanac.
Thin blood (predisposition to illness)	Occurs in women, children, and old people. Blood is thin until puberty, and remains so until old age except in women.	Susceptibility to illness	Individual	Individual should exercise caution in cold weather by wearing warm clothing or by staying indoors.
Rash appearing on a child after birth. No specific disease name —the concept is that of body defilement.	Impurities within the body coming out. The body is being defiled and will therefore produce skin rashes.	Rash anywhere on the body; may be accompanied by fever	Family member	Catnip tea as a laxative or other commercial laxative; the quantity and kind depend on the age of the individual.
Diseases of witchcraft, "hex," or conjuring	Envy and sexual conflict are the most frequent reasons for hexing another person.	Unusual behavior Sudden death Symptoms related to poisoning, (e.g., foul taste, weight loss, nausea, vomiting) A crawling sensation on the skin or in the stomach Psychotic behavior	Voodoo Priest(ess) Spiritualist	"*Conja*" is the help given the conjured person. Treatment varies, depending on the spell cast.

Adapted from Hautman, M. A.: Folk health and illness beliefs. Nurse Pract. *4*(4):27, 1979. © The Nurse Practitioner: The American Journal of Primary Health Care.

Table 19–4
Healers in the African-American Cultural Healing System

Healer	Preparation	Scope of Practice
"Old lady"	Usually an older woman who has successfully raised her own children and is knowledgeable in child care and folk remedies	Consulted about common ailments for advice on child care Found in rural and urban communities
Spiritualist	Called by God to help others No formal training Usually associated with a fundamentalist Christian church	Assists with problems that are financial, personal, spiritual, or physical Predominantly found in urban communities
Voodoo priest(ess) or Hougan	May be trained by other priest(ess) In the United States, the eldest son of a priest becomes a priest. The daughter of a priestess becomes a priestess if she is born with a veil (amniotic sac) over her face. Studies the art of voodoo during childhood (e.g., herbal medicines, bone reading, roleplay with animals, sign studying) under the mentorship of priest or priestess	Knowledgeable about properties of herbs and interpretation of signs and omens Able to cure illness caused by voodoo Uses communication techniques to establish therapeutic milieu like a psychiatrist Treats African-Americans, Mexican-Americans, and Native Americans
Root doctor	Knowledgeable in diagnosis of illness and treatment with roots, oils, candles, and ointments prepared from secret formulas Learns by apprenticeship with established root doctor.	Provides physical and emotional support Uses roots for treatment of various physical and psychological problems Uses and prescribes various home remedies such as poultices and application of oils

Data from Boyle, J. S., and Andrews, M. M., Transcultural Concepts in Nursing Care. Glenview, Illinois, Scott Foresman and Co., 1989; Hautman, M. A.: Folk health and illness beliefs. Nurse Pract. *4*:27, 1979; and Orque, M. S., Bloch, B., and Monrroy, L. S.: Ethnic Nursing Care: A Multi-Cultural Approach. St. Louis: C. V. Mosby, 1983.

twice the rate of infant mortality. The disparity is similar through age 24, and a sharp increase occurs thereafter through age 64. Thus, for infants and adults through middle age, excess deaths are most pronounced. In later life, African-Americans have lower mortality rates for many diseases than do whites.

Although the survival rate for African-Americans in later life is greater than that for whites, elderly African-Americans are more likely to endure greater rates of poverty and illness than their white counterparts (Johnson, 1991).

Homicide is a major cause of excess deaths occurring in African-American men of age 25–44. Homicide accounted for 38% of the male excess deaths and 14% of the female excess deaths below the age of 45. Excess deaths in African-Americans between the ages of 45 and 69 were mainly the result of cancer, heart disease, stroke, diabetes, or cirrhosis.

Diabetes mellitus is increasingly important as a cause of excess deaths among older African-American women. Although diabetes accounts for fewer than 2% of male excess deaths and 5% of female excess deaths (to age 70), it is a major risk factor for heart disease and if uncontrolled can lead to other serious consequences such as amputation and blindness.

Similarly, hypertension has serious health consequences if left untreated. It is the leading cause of renal failure and hypertension-related end-stage renal disease in African-Americans and a major concomitant of heart disease and stroke. Hypertension accounts for more than 5% of excess deaths among African-Americans. Cirrhosis of the liver accounts for more than 3% of excess deaths in men and 2% of excess deaths in women (to age 70). Many of the excess deaths in African-Americans could be prevented through preventive and public health activities.

Table 19–5
Average Annual Total and Excess Deaths in African-Americans for Selected Causes of Mortality

Causes of Excess Death	Excess Deaths in Males and Females (Cumulative to Age 70)	
	No.	%
Heart disease and stroke	18,181	30.8
Homicide and accidents	10,909	18.5
Cancer	8,118	13.8
Infant mortality	6,178	10.5
Cirrhosis	2,154	3.7
Diabetes	1,850	3.1
Subtotal	47,390	80.4
All other causes	11,552	19.6
Total excess deaths	58,942	100
Total deaths, all causes	128,635	
Ratio of excess deaths to total population		42.5
Percent contribution of six causes to excess death		80.4

Adapted from Heckler, M. M.: Report of the Secretary's Task Force on Black and Minority Health. Washington, D.C., U.S. Government Printing Office, 1985.

survival rate is 51% for whites and 38% for African-Americans. Of the 24 primary cancer sites for which survival data were available, African-Americans had a better 5-year survival rate than whites for only six—stomach, pancreas, kidney and renal pelvis, thyroid, brain, and bone marrow (and multiple secondary sites, for multiple myeloma). The breast cancer survival difference (64% for African-Americans and 76% for whites) is statistically significant, in part because of the large numbers of African-Americans who have lymph node involvement or direct extension of tumors to adjacent tissue at the time of diagnosis (stage IIIB). These data suggest that early detection might improve the overall survival rate for African-Americans. Factors that may contribute to poor cancer survival rates include lower socioeconomic status, later stage at diagnosis, delay in detection and treatment, treatment differences, biological factors such as immune competence and response, histological patterns of tumors, and nutritional status (Young et al., 1984; Berg, 1977; Page and Kuntz, 1980; Wilkinson, 1979). Educational levels, attitudes, awareness of cancer prevention strategies, and related health behaviors are also factors.

The scientific literature supports the hypothesis that the racial differences in cancer experience may be in large part attributable to social and/or envi-

Relative risks for specific causes of death in those less than age 45 are disturbingly high among African-Americans compared with whites. African-Americans in this age group have a relative risk of death from all causes nearly twice that of whites. Relative risk reflects the comparative likelihood of dying from a particular cause. The conditions for which relative risks of death are highest for African-Americans are tuberculosis, hypertension, homicide, and anemias.

CANCER

As shown in Table 19–6, 5-year relative survival rates for cancer of the esophagus, colon, rectum, larynx, lung, breast, cervix, and prostate are higher in African-Americans than in whites (American Cancer Society, 1990).

There are striking racial differences in survival rates for cancers of certain sites. Overall, the 5-year

Table 19–6
Cancer Relative 5-Year Survival Rates by Primary Site and Race, 1980–1985

Selected Primary Sites	Percentage	
	Whites	African-Americans
All sites	51	38
Esophagus	8	6
Colon	55	48
Rectum	53	39
Pancreas	3	5
Larynx	68	53
Lung and bronchus	13	12
Breast (female)	76	64
Cervix	67	59
Prostate	73	63
Multiple myeloma	26	29

Adapted from American Cancer Society: Cancer Facts and Figures–1990. Atlanta, Georgia, American Cancer Society, 1990.

ronmental factors rather than to inherent genetic or biological differences. This has major community health ramifications in terms of the accessibility, availability, use, quality, and continuity of health resources (e.g., state-of-the-art cancer screening, detection, treatment, and rehabilitation).

CARDIOVASCULAR DISEASE

Heart disease and stroke cause more deaths, disability, and economic loss in the United States than any other acute or chronic disease and are the leading causes of days lost from work. At all ages and for both sexes, cardiovascular and cerebrovascular diseases are major problems for the African-American population.

African-American men are almost twice as likely to die from stroke as are white men, and their death rate from stroke is more than twice that of other minorities. There is also a marked excess of hypertension, a major risk factor for stroke.

Recent studies show that among African-Americans 20–64 years old, there is an excess mortality from coronary heart disease. This is more marked in African-American women than in men. More white men are hospitalized for acute myocardial infarction than are African-American men —possibly because of the higher rate of sudden death in African-Americans before hospital admission or the decreased availability of emergency services such as ambulances and paramedical assistance in African-American communities.

The major risk factors for cardiovascular and cerebrovascular diseases are hypertension, elevated cholesterol levels, smoking, and obesity—factors that can be combatted by intensive public health efforts.

Hypertension

High blood pressure is much more common among African-Americans, especially men, than among other groups. Strides have been made, however, to lower systolic blood pressure. Between 1960 and 1980, mean systolic blood pressure decrease in African-American adults was greater than that in whites. By 1980, African-American adults were more likely to be aware of their elevated blood pressure than were whites. The improved control of hypertension has contributed significantly to the

general health of African-Americans, but continued efforts are necessary to increase awareness, treatment, and control of hypertension because there remains a significant excess of hypertension in African-American men and women.

Cholesterol

Mean total serum cholesterol levels are lower in African-American than in white adults. High density lipoprotein (the "good fat") cholesterol levels are consistently higher in African-American men than in white men. This finding does not hold true for African-American and white women.

Smoking

Mortality secondary to tobacco use is perhaps one of the most preventable causes of excess mortality in the general population. Smoking increases the risk of cardiovascular disease mortality. More African-American men than white men smoke, but the prevalence of heavy smoking is greater among white adults. However, trends in the literature demonstrate that tobacco companies have chosen to target minority populations. This is evidenced by advertisements directly aimed at African-Americans.

Obesity

Obesity, a known risk factor for cardiovascular disease, is more common among African-American women than any other group. Between the ages of 35 and 64, African-American women weigh an average of 10 pounds more than white women of the same age (Overfield, 1985).

Social, Cultural, and Economic Aspects

Because there is some evidence that African-Americans of higher socioeconomic status have a lower incidence of coronary heart diseases, the biological and genetic hypotheses concerning the increased incidence of cardiovascular diseases are being scrutinized. Studies of blacks in Africa and the Caribbean indicate that hypertension is less problematic than it is among blacks in the United States. The mechanisms by which socioeconomic status is associated with hypertension remain unclear. Hypertension has been related to residence in areas of high social stress and instability as well as to coping styles, education, and occupational insecurity. Hypertension-associated mortality rates also show linkages with social instability. The relationship between social factors and hypertension suggests that high blood pressure control in African-American communities can be improved by interventions that are not strictly biomedical but instead tap into the protective functions of social support that may attenuate the deleterious effects of stress in the lives of some African-Americans (Heckler, 1985; Keil et al., 1984; National Center for Health Statistics, 1991).

CHEMICAL DEPENDENCY

Alcoholism

Alcohol and drug-related problems are complex and involve a wide range of medical, social, and legal problems. Although few studies exist on the subject of alcohol and African-Americans there is evidence that alcohol abuse has a major impact on the health of African-Americans (Heckler, 1985). Using cirrhosis mortality statistics as an indicator of alcohol abuse, the rate of death for African-Americans is twice that for whites.

Overall, African-American drinking patterns are similar to those for the general population, with rates varying greatly by geographical location, sex, and religion. Accordingly, however, African-Americans in the general population experience and endure substance-related health problems to a greater extent than whites (Lee et al., 1991). The consequences of substance-related problems for African-Americans compared with whites appear to be graver in terms of arrests, homicides, unintentional mortality, and accidents. A higher percentage of abstainers and of heavy drinkers is found in the female African-American community than in female whites (51% versus 39% and 11% versus 7%, respectively). African-American and white men have similar drinking patterns. African-American boys of ages 14–17 drink less, have consistently higher abstention rates, and have consistently lower heavy drinking rates and alcohol-related social consequences than do their white counterparts. African-American males begin to have high rates of heavy drinking and social problems due to drinking after the age of 30 years; for white males, heavy and problem drinking is concentrated in the 18- to 25-year-old age group.

African-Americans are at disproportionately higher risk for certain alcohol-related problems such as esophageal cancer (10 times the rate of whites) and fetal alcohol syndrome.

Drug Abuse

African-Americans, particularly those living in major metropolitan areas, are at greater risk for drug abuse and its consequences. They have a higher rate of marijuana, cocaine, heroin, and illicit methadone use than do whites. The literature reveals changing trends in drug preference patterns among African-Americans (Harlow, 1990). This shift is heralded by an increase in cocaine-related morbidity and mortality among African-Americans. Harlow (1990) asserts that the rise in cocaine-related mortality was statistically significant when compared with the rates for either whites or Hispanics in 1986 and 1987. This disparity may reflect the use of more dangerous forms of cocaine, like crack, by the members of some African-American communities.

Using information from treatment programs, emergency departments, and medical examiners, the Drug Abuse Warning Network (DAWN) reports that African-Americans are more likely than whites to be involved with more dangerous drugs, to use more dangerous combinations of drugs, and to use more dangerous routes of administration. (New York City Police Department, 1982). African-Americans are three times as likely as whites to be receiving treatment for a drug abuse-related problem.

Primm and Wesley (1985) identify aggregate level factors that may explain the higher incidence of drug- and alcohol-related problems in some African-American communities. These factors are (1) history of racism, which imparts a psychological handicap; (2) poverty, unemployment, and a lack of career and job opportunities; (3) failure of law enforcement officials to eradicate drug trafficking in African-American communities; (4) the allure of and rewards for selling drugs; (5) powerlessness; (6) cultural and economic conditions that favor hustling and reject and devalue menial jobs; (7) social network influences and peer pressure; (8) frustration from confronting racism, discrimination, and rejection; and (9) high levels of stress at both the individual and community levels. To these factors one can add the lack of clear-cut cultural rules and ambiguous, ill-defined norms.

DIABETES

Diabetes mellitus is the seventh leading cause of death in the United States and is one of the major contributors to the disparity in health status between African-Americans and whites. The significance of diabetes as a health problem is increased by its association as a risk factor for other major diseases such as coronary heart disease, blindness, kidney failure, and peripheral vascular disease including vascular complications that may result in amputation.

The prevalence of diabetes is 33% higher in the African-American population than in the white population, with African-American women having a rate 50% higher than that of white women. The relationship between obesity and diabetes in African-American women is significant because the majority of African-American women with diabetes are obese. Mortality associated with diabetes increases with age in both whites and African-Americans. The perinatal mortality rate among African-American women with diabetes is three times that of white women with diabetes and 8.5 times that of nondiabetic white women.

Prevention of Diabetes and Its Complications

According to the American Diabetes Association, (1991), nearly one half of the cases of diabetes in the United States are likely to go unreported. Approximately 10.6 million Americans suffer from the disease.

Increased attention has been given to developing and identifying strategies that reduce the complications of diabetes. Significant advances have been made in both the treatment and management of diabetes during the past decade. Exemplary programs that provide continuing outpatient diabetes care to populations that are more than 80% African-American have operated in several urban areas. The major goal of these programs has been to prevent or delay the development and progression of complications in clients diagnosed with diabetes.

HOMICIDE AND UNINTENTIONAL INJURIES

Homicide

Although African-Americans comprise only 11.5% of the total population, they account for 43% of the homicide victims. African-American males have a 1-in-21 lifetime chance of becoming a homicide victim (versus a 1-in-131 chance for white males). Homicide is the leading cause of death of African-American males aged 15–44. In addition, they have the highest rate of committing homicide (69.2 per 100,000 versus 10.3 for white males). For African-American females, the chance of becoming a homicide victim is 1 in 104 (versus 1 in 369 for white females). African-American females have the second highest rate of homicide (12.9 per 100,000 compared with 3.1 for white females). This is particularly important for women who may become victims of battering, as in the case of domestic violence. The higher incidence of homicide rates for African-Americans is documented in all regions of the United States. However, these rates are particularly high in major metropolitan cities (Heckler, 1985).

Considered a public health problem, the high homicide rate can be related to social and psychological factors and external environments, including physical, historical, cultural, social, educational, and economic.

Although many of the factors related to homicide are similar in African-Americans and whites, some may be identified more closely with African-Americans occupying lower socioeconomic ranks. For example, both the perpetrator and victim are often found in urban areas characterized by low income, physical deterioration, a high dependence on public assistance, disrupted families, lack of social supports, ineffective sources of social support, a high proportion of young, single males, overcrowded and substandard housing, low rates of home ownership or single-family dwellings, mixed land use, and high population density (Heckler, 1985; President's Commission on Law Enforcement, 1967). More importantly, homicide brings with it a stigma that makes intervention extremely difficult. Prevention efforts must target the social factors that may play a role in the high incidence of homicide that terrorizes some urban African-American communities.

Primary, Secondary, and Tertiary Prevention of Homicide

In the case of homicide, primary prevention efforts must be directed at those social, cultural, technological, and legal aspects of the environment that facilitate perpetuation of the extraordinarily high homicide rates among African-Americans. Secondary prevention efforts should be directed to individuals manifesting early signs of behavioral and social problems that are related to increased risks for subsequent homicide. Family violence, childhood aggression, school violence, adolescent violence, alcoholism and drug abuse are important focal points for efforts aimed at secondary prevention of homicide. Tertiary prevention is concerned with situations in which a health problem is already well established but efforts can still be made to prevent further disability or death. In relation to homicide, the problems of greatest concern are types of serious violence that occur between eventual victim and perpetrator.

INFANT MORTALITY

Summarized in Table 19–7 are statistical data comparing patterns of childbearing of African-American women and white women (National Center for Health Statistics, 1992). For African-

American women, there are three components of excess risk for infant mortality:

- Increased risk of bearing a low-birth-weight infant (5.7% of white infants compared with 13.5% of African-American infants)
- Increased risk of neonatal death among normal-birth-weight infants
- Increased risk of postneonatal death, regardless of birth weight, relative to whites

These risks are related to, but not fully explained by, childbearing patterns. African-American women are more likely to give birth during adolescence, while single, or to have several births, all of which are more likely to be unintended and associated with adverse perinatal outcome.

A focal point in primary prevention of infant mortality is to improve services designed to help women, especially teenagers, avoid unwanted pregnancies. In 1989, 60% of African-American mothers received prenatal care in the first trimester compared with 78.9% of white mothers (National Center for Health Statistics, 1992). African-American mothers were more than twice as likely as white mothers (11.9% versus 5.2%) to receive either no care or care beginning in the third trimester of pregnancy. It is possible that there is a biological factor that influences birth weight and gives a different meaning to low birth weight for African-Americans than for whites, but research-based evidence is unavailable. Unfortunately, normal-birth-weight African-American infants have a higher rate of neonatal mortality than do white infants. This may reflect the prenatal care received, other health behaviors of the mothers, the quality of care in hospitals providing routine obstetric care, or other factors. To the extent that deaths occur after the baby is discharged from the hospital, excess deaths may reflect living conditions or health knowledge and health behavior on the part of the mother and her family.

Postneonatal mortality rates are higher among African-Americans for all major causes of death except congenital anomalies. Sudden infant death syndrome (SIDS) is the leading cause of postneonatal death, and research is continuing on causes and prevention. Accidents are another major cause of deaths and may be related to dimensions of living conditions, knowledge of health behaviors, or quality of care provided to children. Among all

Table 19–7
Childbearing Patterns of African-American and White Women, 1989

	White (Percent)	African-American (Percent)
Age of mother		
<18 years	3.6	10.5
18–19 years	7.2	12.9
Marital status		
Single mothers	19.2	65.7

Adapted from National Center for Health Statistics: Health: United States, 1991. Hyattsville, Maryland, U.S. Department of Health and Human Services, 1992.

groups, the mother's level of education is strongly associated with infant mortality, with those having lower educational levels experiencing higher rates of infant mortality.

The many risk factors associated with poor perinatal outcome among African-Americans that are related to low socioeconomic status include:

- Low income and inadequate insurance coverage, which often reduce access to appropriate health care
- Preexisting disease conditions
- Poor nutrition
- Inadequate housing and crowded living conditions
- Limited maternal education
- Stressful work environments
- Disrupted families and lack of social supports
- Problems of transportation and child care that impede use of services

Furthermore, populations with the worst pregnancy outcomes tend to have more teen mothers, more single mothers, and more unintended births.

When many of the social risk factors (education, marital status, trimester of first care, parity, age) are controlled, African-American women still have twice the risk of bearing low-birth-weight babies as do comparable whites.

AIDS

Infection with HIV constitutes a particularly severe public health problem in African-Americans. In 1991, nearly 32% of all cases reported to the Centers for Disease Control were African-American (National Center for Health Statistics, 1992). Among African-Americans with AIDS, between 1984 and 1991, 35.5% were homosexual or bisexual men, 39.5% were intravenous drug abusers, and 6.9% were both. In contrast, 76% of white AIDS cases were homosexual or bisexual men. Heterosexual transmission accounts for only 2.2% of the AIDS cases in whites but 7.6% in African-Americans. Women account for 20% of AIDS cases in African-Americans but only 16.4% among whites (National Center for Health Statistics, 1992).

Although 15% of U.S. children are African-American, 55.8% of AIDS cases occurring in those age 13 or younger are African-American. Three

fourths of these children contracted the disease at or near the time of birth from their HIV-infected mothers, and most are from families in which one or both parents are intravenous drug abusers (National Center for Health Statistics, 1992; U.S. Public Health Service, 1988).

The problem of AIDS is compounded by a variety of socioeconomic factors such as unemployment, lack of health insurance, poor overall health, educational disadvantages, and other poverty-related considerations. Because HIV infection in African-American populations combines one sensitive issue (race) with another (AIDS), it can be especially stigmatizing. AIDS is a sensitive issue because it is usually contracted through behaviors that have negative societal and moral connotations, e.g., drug abuse, homosexual behavior, and prostitution.

As indicated in Table 19–8, AIDS disproportionately affects men and women from culturally diverse backgrounds. For example, more than 72.4% of the women with AIDS are nonwhite, with 55.6% African-American (National Center for Health Statistics, 1992).

Educational programs and nursing interventions must be planned with consideration of the special needs of African-Americans who are at risk for contracting HIV infection and developing AIDS. Consideration must be given to the fact that

Table 19–8 Incidence of AIDS for Persons in the United States, 1991*	
Population	**No. of Cases**
All ages	33,477
Male (13 or more years of age)	28,941
White	16,066
African-American	8,360
Female (13 or more years of age)	4,029
White	1,038
African-American	2,322
Children (under 13 years of age)	507
White	114
African-American	306

* Through September 30, 1991.

Adapted from U.S. Department of Health and Human Services: Health: United States, 1990. Washington, D.C., U.S. Government Printing Office, 1991; and National Center for Health Statistics: Health, United States, 1991. Hyattsville, Maryland, U.S. Department of Health and Human Services, Public Health Service, 1992.

traditional sex roles and economic hardship make it difficult for many African-Americans to change the practices that put them at risk. For African-American women, for example, the use of condoms is not the woman's perogative; therefore, suggesting that she insist her partner use condoms without empowering her may lead to the inability to negotiate, continued failure to use condoms, and increased risk of physical abuse (Smeltzer and Whipple, 1991).

Serving the Aggregate Needs

The U.S. Public Health Service has proposed five strategies to address the issue of AIDS in minority (including African-American) populations:

- Expansion of human resources in an effort to control the spread of HIV
- Expansion of the knowledge base including additional surveys and research studies of AIDS in the African-American community
- Development of culturally appropriate communications through information, education, and outreach programs
- Alleviation of HIV-related discrimination and stigma
- Strengthening of community networks by better collaboration among local, state, and federal governments and community-based organizations and institutions.

NURSING CARE OF AFRICAN-AMERICAN INDIVIDUALS, FAMILIES, AND COMMUNITIES

When caring for African-American individuals, families, and groups, the nurse must consider five aspects to be able to give the best nursing care:

- Conducting a cultural self-assessment to identify personal beliefs
- Examining the cultural stereotypes held by society
- Increasing knowledge and skills in biocultural assessment
- Being aware of differences in cross-cultural communication
- Developing cultural sensitivity

Cultural Self-Assessment

When caring for African-American individuals, families, and groups, a nurse needs to engage in a cultural self-assessment to identify individual culturally based attitudes and beliefs about African-Americans, race, prejudice, racial discrimination, and related issues. Culturological self-assessment requires considerable self-honesty and sincerity and necessitates reflection on parents, grandparents, and other significant family members and close friends in terms of their attitudes toward African-Americans.

Cultural Self-Assessment

- How do your parents, grandparents, other family members, and close friends view people from racially diverse groups? What is the cultural stereotype of African-Americans? Does the cultural stereotype allow for socioeconomic differences, i.e., differentiate lower, middle, and upper classes?
- Have your interactions with African-Americans been positive? Negative? Neutral? Do you or significant others in your social network use any derogatory slang words when referring to African-Americans?
- How do you feel about going into a predominantly African-American neighborhood or into the home of an African-American family? Are you afraid, anxious, curious, or ambivalent?
- What stereotypes do you have about African-American men? Women? Children?
- What do you know about African-American culture? What are your stereotypical views about African-Americans and the following: Pregnancy, birth, and family planning? Child rearing practices? Teen years—menstruation, sex education? Adulthood—roles of men and women? Old age? Death?
- What culturally based health beliefs and practices do you think will characterize the African-Americans in your caseload? How are these different from your own culturally based health beliefs and practices?

If you are an African-American nurse, how do you feel about caring for other African-Americans? Are there socioeconomic differences between you and the African-American clients in your caseload? Do you believe that only other African-Americans can genuinely understand the needs of African-American clients? Or could a Hispanic, an Asian, or a white nurse provide culturally sensitive nursing care to African-American clients as well as you can?

Cultural Stereotypes

A nurse must examine the cultural stereotype of African-Americans held by other members of the nurse's culture. For example, if the nurse is of Hispanic origin, the nurse must consider what Hispanics, in general, say about African-Americans. The nurse must examine the recent interactions between the two cultures in the local community. Have African-Americans and Hispanics, for example, competed within the community for scarce economic resources, cooperated on a joint venture, or ignored each other? How would these factors impact on a nurse's professional interactions with African-Americans? How would a Hispanic community health nurse, for example, be received by an African-American family? What might be the clients' cultural stereotypes? How might negative stereotypes of Hispanics influence the professional nurse–client relationship with the African-American family? Some questions are suggested for your self-assessment.

BIOCULTURAL VARIATIONS IN ASSESSING AFRICAN-AMERICANS

The assessment of both standard and nonstandard biocultural variations among African-American clients requires a special note. A cursory head-to-toe overview of biocultural variations follows.

General Appearance

Cultural differences are found in the body proportions of individuals. In general, white men are 1.27 cm (0.5 inch) taller than African-American men, whereas white and African-American women are, on average, the same height. Ratios of sitting to standing heights reveal that African-Americans of both sexes have longer legs and

shorter trunks than whites. Because proportionately most of the weight is in the trunk, white men appear to be more obese than African-American men.

Despite their longer legs, African-American women are consistently heavier than white women at every age; African-American women weigh an average of 9.1 kg (20 pounds) more than white women between the ages of 35 and 64 (Overfield, 1985).

There are definite biocultural differences in bone length, as revealed by stature; African-Americans have longer legs and arms than whites. African-Americans tend to have wide shoulders and narrow hips, whereas Asians, for example, tend to have wide hips and narrow shoulders.

Biocultural differences are also demonstrated in the amount of body fat and the distribution of fat throughout the body, which may reflect dietary practices. In general, individuals from the lower socioeconomic class are more obese than those from the middle class, who, in turn, are more obese than members of the upper class. In addition to socioeconomic considerations, African-Americans tend to have smaller (1 mm) arm skinfold thicknesses than whites, but the distributions of fat on the trunk are similar.

Skin

The assessment of a client's skin is subjective and highly dependent on the nurse's observational skill, ability to recognize subtle color changes, and exposure to people with various gradations of skin color. Melanin, which is more abundant in African-Americans, protects the skin against harmful ultraviolet rays; this genetic advantage accounts for the lower incidence of skin cancer among African-Americans.

Mongolian spots, which are irregular areas of deep blue pigmentation, are usually located in the sacral and gluteal areas but sometimes occur on the abdomen, thighs, shoulders, or arms. Mongolian spots are a normal variation in children of African, Asian, or Latin descent. By adulthood, these spots become lighter, but they frequently are still visible. Mongolian spots are present in 90% of African-Americans and should not be confused with bruises. Recognition of this normal variation is particularly important when dealing with children who might be erroneously identified as victims of child abuse.

Other areas of the skin affected by hormones and, in some cases, differing for African-American clients are the nipples, areola, scrotum, and labia majora. In general, these areas are darker than other parts of the skin in both adults and children, especially among African-American clients. When assessing these skin surfaces, the nurse must observe carefully for erythema, rashes, and other abnormalities because the darker color may mask their presence.

Cyanosis is the most difficult clinical sign to observe in darkly pigmented people. Because peripheral vasoconstriction can prevent cyanosis, the nurse must be attentive to environmental conditions such as air conditioning, mist tents, and other factors that may lower the room temperature and thus cause vasoconstriction. Remember that for the person to manifest clinical evidence of cyanosis, the blood must contain 5 g reduced hemoglobin in 1.5 g of methemoglobin per 100 ml of blood, but laboratory data will not be available to demonstrate this in the community. Given that most conditions causing cyanosis also cause decreased oxygenation of the brain, other clinical symptoms, such as changes in level of consciousness, will be evident. Cyanosis usually is accompanied by increased respirations, use of accessory muscles of respiration, nasal flaring, and other manifestations of respiratory distress.

In both light- and dark-skinned clients, *jaundice* is best observed in the sclera. When assessing African-American clients, caution must be exercised to avoid confusing other forms of pigmentation with jaundice. Many African-Americans have heavy deposits of subconjunctival fat containing sufficient carotene to mimic jaundice. The fatty deposits become more dense as the distance from the cornea increases. The portion of the sclera that is revealed naturally by the palpebral fissure is the best place to accurately assess color. If the palate does not have heavy melanin pigmentation, jaundice can be detected there in the early stages (i.e., when serum bilirubin level is 2–4 mg/100 ml). The absence of a yellowish tint of the palate when the sclera are yellow indicates carotene pigmentation of the sclera rather than jaundice. If in doubt, you may inquire about light- or clay-colored stools and dark-golden urine as these often accompany jaundice.

Pallor in African-American clients is evident by the absence of the underlying red tones that normally give brown or black skin its luster. The brown-skinned person will manifest pallor with a more yellowish-brown color, and the black-skinned individual will appear ashen or gray. Generalized pallor can be observed in the mucous membranes, lips, and nail beds. The palpebra conjunctiva and nail beds are preferred sites for assessing the pallor of anemia. When inspecting the conjunctiva, you should lower the lid sufficiently to visualize the conjunctiva near the outer canthus as well as the inner canthus. The coloration is often lighter near the inner canthus.

Anemias, in particular, chronic iron deficiency anemia, may be manifest by "spoon" nails, which have a concave shape. A lemon-yellow tint of the face and slightly yellow sclera accompany pernicious anemia, which is also manifested by neurological deficits and a red, painful tongue. Fatigue, exertional dyspnea, rapid pulse, dizziness, and impaired mental function accompany most severe anemias.

Erythema is frequently associated with localized inflammation and is characterized by increased skin temperature. The degree of redness is determined by the quantity of blood present in the subpapillary plexus, whereas the warmth of the skin is related to the rate of blood flow through the blood vessels. When assessing inflammation in African-Americans, it is often necessary to palpate the skin for increased warmth, taut or tightly pulled surfaces that may be indicative of edema, and hardening of deep tissues or blood vessels. When palpating, the dorsal surface of the fingers will be most sensitive to temperature sensations.

The erythema associated with rashes is not always accompanied by noticeable increases in skin temperature. Macular, papular, and vesicular skin lesions are identified by a combination of palpation and inspection as well as the patient's description of symptoms. For example, clients with macular rashes will usually complain of itching, and evidence of scratching will be apparent. When the skin is only moderately pigmented, a macular rash may become recognizable if the skin is gently stretched. Stretching the skin decreases the normal red tone, thus providing more contrast and making the macules appear brighter. Some disorders are characterized by generalized rashes, which will be seen in the mouth upon inspection of the palate.

In African-American clients, *petechiae* are best visualized in the areas of lighter melanization such as the abdomen, buttocks, and volar surface of the forearm. When the skin is brown or very dark brown, petechiae cannot be seen in the skin. Most of the diseases that cause bleeding and microembolism formation, such as thrombocytopenia, subacute bacterial endocarditis, and other septicemias, are characterized by the presence of petechiae in the mucous membranes as well as the skin. Thus, the nurse should inspect for petechiae in the mouth, particularly the buccal mucosa, and in the conjunctiva.

Ecchymotic lesions caused by systemic disorders are found in the same locations as petechiae, although their larger size makes them more apparent in African-Americans. When differentiating petechiae and ecchymosis from erythema in the mucous membrane, pressure on the tissue will momentarily blanch erythema but not petechiae or ecchymosis.

Musculoskeletal System

The long bones of African-Americans are significantly longer, narrower, and denser than those of whites (Farrally and Moore, 1975). Bone density by race and sex reveal that African-American men have the densest bones, thus accounting for the relatively low incidence of osteoporosis in this population.

Curvature of the long bones varies widely among culturally diverse groups. African-Americans have markedly straight femurs compared with Native Americans, who have anteriorly convex femurs, and whites, who have intermediate shaped femurs. This characteristic is related to both genetics and body weight. Thin African-Americans and whites have less curvature than average, whereas obese African-Americans and whites have increased curvatures. It is possible that the heavier density of the bones of African-Americans helps to protect them from increased curvature due to obesity.

Table 19-9 summarizes reported biocultural variations in the musculoskeletal system.

Head

Perhaps one of the most obvious and widely variable cultural differences occurs with assessment of the hair. African-Americans' hair varies widely in texture. It is very fragile and ranges from long and

Table 19-9
Biocultural Variations in the Assessment of African-American Clients

Area of Variation	Remarks
Bone	
Frontal	Thicker in African-American men than in white men
Parietal occiput	Thicker in white men than in African-American men
Palate	Tori (protuberances) along the suture line of the hard palate. Problematic for denture wearers. Incidence rate is 20% for African-Americans and 24% for whites
Humerus	Torsion or rotation of proximal end with muscle pull, whites > African-Americans. Torsion in African-Americans is symmetrical; torsion in whites is greater on the right than on the left side
Vertebrae	Twenty-four vertebrae are found in 85–93% of all people. Racial and sex differences reveal 23 vertebrae in 11% of African-American females, a factor that may impact on low back pain.
Pelvis	Hip width is 1.6 cm (0.6 in) smaller in African-American, white, or Asian women
Femur	Convex anterior (Native American), straight (African-American), or intermediate (white)
Second tarsal	Second toe is longer than the great toe. Incidence rate is 8–12% for African-Americans and 8–34% for whites. Clinically significant for joggers and athletes who report increased foot problems
Height	White men are 1.27 cm (0.5 in) taller than African-American men
Composition of long bones	Longer, narrower, and denser in African-Americans than in whites. Osteoporosis rate is lowest in African-American men and highest in white women

Table continued on following page

Table 19–9
Biocultural Variations in the Assessment of African-American Clients *Continued*

Area of Variation	Remarks
Muscle	
Peroneus tertius	Responsible for dorsiflexion of foot
	Muscle is absent in 10–15% of African-Americans
	No clinical significance because the tibialis anterior also dorsiflexes the foot
Palmaris longus	Responsible for wrist flexion
	Muscle is absent in 12–20% of whites and 5% of African-Americans
	No clinical significance because three other muscles are also responsible for flexion

Based on data reported by Overfield, T.: Biologic Variation in Health and Illness: Race, Age, and Sex Differences. Menlo Park, California, Addison-Wesley, 1985; Boyle, J. S., and Andrews, M. M., eds.: Transcultural Concepts in Nursing Care. Glenview, Illinois, Scott, Foresman & Co., 1989.

straight to short, spiraled, thick, and kinky. The hair and scalp have a natural tendency to be dry and require daily combing, gentle brushing, and the application of oil.

Obtaining a baseline hair assessment is significant in certain disease states. For example, hair texture is known to become dry, brittle, and lusterless with inadequate nutrition. The hair of African-American children with severe malnutrition, as in the case of *marasmus* (total calorie deficiency) or *kwashiorkor* (protein calorie deficiency), frequently changes not only in texture but also in color. The African-American child's hair often becomes less kinky and assumes a copper-reddish color. Certain endocrine disorders are also known to affect the texture of hair.

Ears

Ceruminous glands are located in the external ear canal and are functional at birth. Cerumen is genetically determined and occurs in two major types: dry cerumen, which is gray, flaky, and frequently forms a thin mass in the ear canal; and wet cerumen, which is dark brown and moist. African-

Americans have a 99% frequency and whites have a 97% frequency of having wet cerumen (Overfield, 1985); individuals from other cultural backgrounds are more likely to have dry cerumen. The clinical significance of this occurs when examining or irrigating the ears. The nurse should be aware that the presence and composition of cerumen are not related to poor hygiene.

Mouth

Leukodema, a grayish-white benign lesion occurring on the buccal mucosa, is present in 68–90% of African-Americans but only 43% of whites (Martin and Crump, 1972). Care should be taken to avoid mistaking leukodema for oral thrush or related infections.

Oral hyperpigmentation also shows variation by race (Wassermann, 1974). Usually absent at birth, hyperpigmentation increases with age. By age 50, 10% of whites and 50–90% of African-Americans will show oral hyperpigmentation, a condition that is believed to be caused by a lifetime accumulation of postinflammatory oral changes (Overfield, 1985).

Teeth

Because teeth are often used as indicators of developmental, hygienic, and nutritional adequacy, the nurse should be aware of biocultural differences. The size of teeth varies widely; the teeth of whites are smallest, followed by those of African-Americans and then those of Asians and Native Americans. Larger teeth cause some groups to have prognathic, or protruding jaws, a condition that is seen most frequently in African-Americans. The condition is normal and does not reflect an orthodontic problem.

Agenesis (absence) of teeth varies by race, with absence of the third molar occurring in 9–25% of whites and 1–11% of African-Americans (Brothwell et al., 1963). Throughout life, whites have more tooth decay than do African-Americans. Complete tooth loss occurs more often in whites than in African-Americans despite the higher incidence of periodontal disease in African-Americans.

The differences in tooth decay between African-Americans and whites may be explained by the fact that African-Americans have harder and denser tooth enamel, which makes their teeth less susceptible to the organisms that cause caries. The increase in periodontal disease among African-Americans is believed to be caused by poor oral hygiene. When obvious signs of periodontal disease are present, such as bleeding and edematous gums, a dental referral should be initiated.

Thorax

Biocultural differences in the size of the thoracic cavity significantly influence pulmonary functioning as determined by vital capacity and forced expiratory volume (Oscherwitz et al., 1972; Lapp et al., 1974). In descending order, the largest chest volumes are found in whites, African-Americans, Asians, and Native Americans.

Secretions

The *apocrine* and *eccrine sweat glands* are important for fluid balance and thermoregulation. Approximately 2–3 million glands open onto the skin surface through pores. They are responsible for the presence of sweat. When contaminated by normal skin flora, odor results. Most Asians and Native Americans have a mild-to-absent body odor, whereas whites and African-Americans tend to have strong body odor. The amount of chloride excreted by sweat glands varies widely, and African-Americans have lower salt concentrations in their sweat than do whites.

LABORATORY TESTS

Biocultural variations occur with some laboratory tests, such as measurement of hemoglobin and hematocrit, serum cholesterol, serum transferrin, and two amniotic fluid constituents. The normal hemoglobin level for African-Americans is 1 g lower than for other ethnic groups, a factor that has implications in the treatment of anemia. The difference between African-Americans and whites with respect to *serum cholesterol* is quite interesting. At birth, African-Americans and whites have similar serum cholesterol levels, but during childhood, African-Americans have higher serum cholesterol levels than do whites (5 mg/100 ml). These differences reverse during adulthood, when African-American adults have lower serum cho-

lesterol levels than do white adults. This finding is important given the relationship of cholesterol to the occurrence of cardiovascular disease and the higher incidence of morbidity and mortality in African-Americans.

In a study of children 1–3½ years old, *serum transferrin* levels were found to differ between white and African-American children. The mean value was 200–400 mg/100 ml for white children and 341.4 mg/100 ml for African-American children (Roode et al., 1975). The higher serum transferrin levels in African-American children may be due to their lowered hemoglobin and hematocrit levels (Ritchie, 1979). Transferrin levels increase in the presence of anemia. If the hemoglobin and hematocrit levels are normally lower in African-Americans, then higher transferrin levels should be considered normal (Overfield, 1985).

The *lecithin-to-sphingomyelin ratio* is a laboratory measurement of the amniotic fluid, which indicates fetal pulmonary maturation. The ratio is used to calculate the risk of respiratory distress syndrome in premature infants. This ratio differs between African-Americans and whites, as does the pulmonary maturity it predicts (Olowe and Akinkugbe, 1978). African-Americans have higher ratios than do whites at 23–42 weeks of gestation. Lung maturity, as measured by a lecithin-to-sphingomyelin ratio of 2.0, is reached 1 week earlier in African-Americans than whites, i.e., at 34 versus 35 weeks. The risk of respiratory distress syndrome is 40–50% for a ratio score between 1.5 and 1.9 for premature white infants but not for premature African-Americans, who have a much lower risk of respiratory distress syndrome at the same low ratio scores. When the lecithin-to-sphingomyelin ratio is determined before induction of labor or elective cesarean section, the racial difference should be considered in making the decision (Overfield, 1985).

CROSS-CULTURAL DIFFERENCES IN COMMUNICATION

The nurse must be aware of cross-cultural differences in communication. For example, terms used by the client to describe symptoms of disease may include "sugar" (diabetes), "running off" (diarrhea), "locked bowels" (constipation), "low blood" or "tired blood" (anemia), "bad blood" (syphilis), and so forth.

The non–African-American nurse's language should be natural and congruent with the nurse's usual pattern of communication (i.e., attempts at using black English should be avoided as the client may interpret this as inappropriate and culturally insensitive). If the nurse is unclear about the meaning of a particular word or phrase, the nurse should ask for clarification by saying, "Tell me more about . . . ," or "You've used the word ____; could you tell me what that means to you?"

CULTURAL SENSITIVITY

When working with African-American groups or communities, every effort should be made to be culturally sensitive in recommendations and suggestions. It is often helpful to have proposed plans for a community project or program reviewed ahead of time by someone who is familiar with the culture of the population for whom the intervention is intended. The nurse might seek input from African-American nurses or other African-American members of the health care team in terms of cultural content. However, it must be remembered that socioeconomic factors may be even more significant than racial or ethnic affiliation, so a critique from an African-American colleague who is from a different socioeconomic class may fail to yield the desired outcome. A middle- or upper-class African-American professional from the suburbs may be unable to relate to the health care needs of lower-class urban or rural African-Americans. Whenever possible, key African-American community-based leaders should be part of the planning, implementation, and evaluation of projects or programs, and it is conventional practice to form an advisory council or board before undertaking major community health projects or programs. If the project or program is likely to impact a culturally mixed population, representatives from each target group should be asked to participate in proportion to their representation in the targeted community.

Cultural sensitivity includes understanding attitudes toward advice from health professionals. If African-American clients appear to be reluctant to follow the nurse's advice, the nurse should explore the possible cultural reasons.

CULTURAL HEALERS AND HEALTH PRACTICES

Whenever appropriate, cultural healers should be included in nursing care for African-American individuals, families, and communities. Cultural healers such as spiritualists, "old ladies," root doctors, and voodoo priests and priestesses frequently have the confidence and trust of many African-Americans in the community. Enlisting their support may be helpful in goal achievement for health projects or programs.

It may be useful to categorize culturally based health practices according to their effect on the client as helpful, neutral, or harmful. For example, the nurse might find it necessary to learn about *soul food,* a term that refers to various dishes shared by many African-Americans (although enjoyed by others as well) and derived from the practice of mixing leftover scraps with wild green plants and animal fat. With the assistance of a dietician, the nurse may want to identify the nutritional content of specific soul foods to assist the family in meeting the needs of members with conditions such as hypertension, diabetes, or heart disease. For example, many green vegetables are seasoned with salt pork (bacon) and thus may be harmful when eaten in large quantities by a client with hypertension or heart disease.

SUMMARY

It is imperative to note that we must continue to direct our efforts at improving the health of people of color as our population becomes more and more diverse. Unfortunately, in the foreseeable future, the health status of minority populations (i.e., people of color) will continue to be an arena of struggle, conflict, and challenge, as evidenced by the persistent documented disparities. This chapter has presented an overview of the social, economic, and cultural factors that have an impact on the health of African-Americans in contemporary U.S. society. Culturally based health beliefs, practices, and healers have also been described. The major causes of excess deaths for African-Americans as identified by the Secretary's Task Force on Black and Minority Health (Heckler, 1985)—cardiovascular disease, cancer, cirrhosis of the liver, diabetes, infant mortality, homicide, unintentional accidents, and communicable diseases including AIDS—have been presented along with some suggested approaches to decreasing their adverse impact on the health of African-Americans. The provision of culturally sensitive nursing care for African-American individuals, families, groups, and communities is important in community health nursing. The ways in which community health nurses can provide culturally sensitive, contextually relevant, and meaningful nursing care to African-American individuals, families, and communities have been suggested.

Learning Activities

1. Interview an African-American health care professional to ascertain the contextual experience of being African-American. Ask what the individual believes she or he has experienced both professionally and personally as a result of race.

2. Watch prime-time television and consider the parts played by African-American characters. What are their roles? What percentage of the actors are African-American? What message is being conveyed about race?

3. Using the guidelines suggested in Chapter 16, conduct an in-depth culturological assessment of an African-American client.

4. Identify an African-American cultural healer in the community, and schedule an appointment to discuss health beliefs and practices, treatments for various illnesses, and preparation necessary to become a healer (i.e., how the individual acquired the healing skills).

5. Using census data, identify the number, age, sex, and location of residence for African-Americans in your city or town. Identify the health resources available in African-American neighborhoods, and compare them with those available in predominantly white areas.

6. To learn more about the dietary patterns of African-Americans, the following references are suggested as background reading: Kittler, P., and Sucher, K. P.: Diet counseling in a multicultural society. Diabetes Educator *16*;127–131, 1989. U.S. Department of Agriculture: Cross-Cultural Counseling: A Guide for Nutrition and Health Counselors. Washington, D.C., U.S. Government Printing Office, 1986. After reading the background material, interview an African-American client in your caseload to discuss dietary practices.

REFERENCES

American Cancer Society: Cancer Facts and Figures—1990. Atlanta, Georgia, ACS, 1990.

American Diabetes Association: Diabetes: 1991 Vital Statistics. Alexandria, Virginia, ADA, 1991.

Bennett, L.: Before the Mayflower: A History of the Black American, 1619–1962. Chicago, Johnson, 1962, pp. 1–16.

Berg, J. W.: Economic status and survival of cancer patients. J. Chron. Dis. *39*;467–477, 1977.

Bloch, B.: Health Care From a Minority Point of View. San Francisco, University of San Francisco, 1975.

Brothwell, D. R., Carbonell, V. M., and Goose, D. H.: Congenital absence of teeth in human populations. *In* Brothwell, D. R., ed.: Dental Anthropology. New York, Pergamon Press, 1963, pp. 179–189.

Cheung, Y. W.: Ethnicity and alcohol/drug use revisited: A framework for future research. J. Addict. *25*;581–605, 1991.

Cummings, J.: Breakup of Black family imperils decades of gain. *The New York Times,* November 20, 1983, pp. 1–2.

Current Population Reports: The Black population in the United States: March 1990 and 1989. Series P-20, No. 448. Washington, D.C., U.S. Government Printing Office, 1991, pp. 1–17.

Current Population Reports: Marital status and living arrangements: March 1991. Series P-20, No. 461. Washington, D.C., U.S. Government Printing Office, 1992*a*, pp. 1–14.

Current Population Reports: Educational attainment in the

United States: March 1991 and 1990. Washington, D.C., U.S. Government Printing Office, 1992*b*, pp. 1–6.

Farrally, M. R., and Moore, W. J.: Anatomical differences in the femur and tibia between Negroes and Caucasians and their effect on locomotion. Am. J. Phys. Anthropol. *43*;63–69, 1975.

Harlow, K. C.: Patterns of rates of mortality from narcotic and cocaine overdose in Texas, 1976–1987. Public Health Reports *105*(5);455–462, 1990.

Heckler, M. M.: Report of the Secretary's Task Force on Black and Minority Health. Washington, D.C., U.S. Government Printing Office, 1985.

Hines, R. H.: The health status of Black Americans: Changing health perspectives. *In* Jaco, E. G., ed.: Patients, Physicians, and Illness. 2nd Ed. New York, Free Press, 1972, pp. 42–52.

Johnson, C.: The status of health care among black Americans: Address before the Congress of National Black Churches. J. Natl. Med. Assoc. *83*(2);125–129, 1991.

Keil, J. E., Loadholt, C. D., Weinrich, M. C., Sandifer, S. H., and Boyle, E.: Incidence of coronary heart disease in blacks in Charleston, South Carolina. Am. Heart J. *108*;779–786, 1984.

LaFargue, J. P.: Role of prejudice in rejection of health care. Nurs. Res. *2*;53–58, 1972.

Lapp, N. L.: Lung volumes and flow rates in black and white subjects. Thorax *29*;185–188, 1974.

Lee, J. A., Mavis, B. E., and Stoffelmayr, B. E.: A comparison of problems-of-life for blacks and whites entering a substance abuse treatment program. J. Psychoact. Drugs *23*(3);233–239, 1991.

Lipscomb, L. W.: Parental influence in the development of black children's racial self-esteem. D. A. I. *36*;567, 1975.

Martin, J. L., and Krump, E. P.: Leukoedema of the buccal mucosa in Negro children and youth. Oral Surg. *34*;49–58, 1972.

Mindel, C. H., Habenstein, R. W., and Wright, R.: Ethnic Families in America. New York, Elsevier Science, 1988.

National Center for Health Statistics: Health, United States, 1990. Hyattsville, Maryland, USDHHS, Public Health Service, 1991.

National Center for Health Statistics: Health, United States, 1991. Hyattsville, Maryland, USDHHS, Public Health Service, 1992.

New York City Police Department: Homicide Analysis. New York, Crime Analysis Unit, 1982.

Nobles, W. W.: Psychological research and the Black self-concept: A critical review. J. Social Issues *29*;11–31, 1973.

Olowe, S. A., and Akinkugbe, A.: Amniotic fluid lecithin/sphingomyelin ratio: Comparison between an African and a North American community. Pediatrics *62*;38–41, 1978.

Orque, M. S., Bloch, B., and Monrroy, L. S. A.: Ethnic Nursing Care: A Multicultural Approach. St. Louis, C. V. Mosby, 1983.

Oscherwitz, R.: Differences in pulmonary functions in various racial groups. Am. J. Epidemiol. *96*;319–327, 1972.

Overfield, T.: Biologic Variation in Health and Illness: Race, Age, and Sex Differences. Menlo Park, California, Addison-Wesley, 1985.

Page, W. F., and Kuntz, A. J.: Racial and socioeconomic factors in cancer survival: A comparison of Veterans' Administration results with selected studies. Cancer *45*;1029–1040, 1980.

Poussaint, A.: Black men — White women: An update. Ebony *38*;124–131, 1983.

President's Commission on Law Enforcement and Administration of Justice: The Challenge of Crime in a Free Society. Washington, D.C., U.S. Government Printing Office, 1967.

Primm, B. J., and Wesley, J. E.: Treating the multiply addicted black alcoholic. Alcohol. Treat. Q. *2*(3,4);155–178, 1985.

Ritchie, R. F.: Specific proteins. *In* Henry, J. B., ed.: Clinical Diagnosis and Management by Laboratory Methods. Philadelphia, W. B. Saunders, 1979, pp. 251–265.

Roode, H.: Serum transferrin values in white and black toddlers. South Afr. Med. J. *49*;319–321, 1975.

Smeltzer, S. C., and Whipple, B.: Women and HIV infection. Image: J. Nurs. Scholarship, *23*;249–256, 1991.

Smitherman, G.: White English in blackface, or who do I be? Black Scholar *1*;32–39, 1973.

Smitherman, G.: Talkin' and Testifyin': The Language of Black America. Boston, Houghton Mifflin, 1977.

Snow, L. F.: Folk medical beliefs and their implications for care of patients: A review based on studies among Black Americans. Ann. Intern. Med. *81*;82–96, 1974.

Spector, R.: Cultural Diversity in Health and Illness. Norwalk, Connecticut, Appleton-Century-Crofts, 1986.

Staples, R.: Black Masculinity: The Black Male's Role in American Society. San Francisco, Black Scholar Press, 1982.

Staples, R.: Black Americans. *In* Mindel, C. H., et al., eds.: Ethnic Families in America. New York, Elsevier Science, 1988, pp. 303–324.

Thomas, D. N.: Black American patient care. *In* Henderson, G., and Primeaux, M., eds.: Transcultural Health Care. Menlo Park, California, Addison-Wesley, 1981, pp. 209–223.

U.S. Bureau of the Census: America's Black Population, 1970 to 1982: A Statistical View, July, 1983. Washington, D.C. U.S. Government Printing Office, Series P10/P0P83, 1983.

U.S. Bureau of the Census: United States Population Estimates by Age, Sex, Race, and Hispanic Origin: 1980 to 1988. Washington, D.C., U.S. Government Printing Office, Series P-25, No. 1045, 1990.

U.S. Civil Rights Commission: Unemployment and Underemployment Among Blacks, Hispanics, and Women. Washington, D.C., U.S. Government Printing Office, 1982.

U.S. Public Health Service: Minority issues in AIDS. Public Health Rep. *103*(suppl 1 Rev.);91–93, 1988.

Wassermann, H. P.: Ethnic Pigmentation: Historical, Physiological, and Clinical Aspects. New York, American Elsevier, 1974.

Wilkinson, G. S.: Delay, stage of disease, and survival from breast cancer. J. Chron. Dis. *32*;365–373, 1979.

Young, J. L., Ries, L. G., and Pollack, E. S.: Cancer patient survival among ethnic groups in the United States. J. Natl. Cancer Inst. *73*;341–352, 1984.

Family Violence

Upon completion of this chapter, the reader will be able to:

1. Identify common types of abuse of children, women, and the elderly.

2. Describe the abusive patterns in child, woman, and elderly abuse.

3. Identify types of injury common in abusive situations.

4. Analyze assessment data to determine the risk of abuse in family members.

5. Identify long-term effects of violence on our society as a whole.

6. Describe the role of the nurse in primary, secondary, and tertiary prevention of abuse in family members.

7. Identify the legal requirements of a health professional in dealing with abuse situations.

Ann C. Watkins

Violence is rough or injurious physical force, action, or treatment. It surrounds us in our society. Results of violent behavior can be seen in large metropolitan areas as well as in small towns and rural populations. It can be seen on the streets, and it is hidden within family situations. What causes the violence so evident in our country today? Various reasons have been explored, ranging from too much violence on television to chemical imbalances in the brain. Another possible explanation is that we learn to become violent through the violent behavior of people around us.

or simply one too many in the family often was left to die from exposure or by some other means. It was not until early in the fifth century that infanticide was condemned. However, in many societies, that did not protect children. Children, especially first-born children, were often sacrificed for religious reasons. Children were seen as the property of the father, and he could do with them what he pleased.

Corporal punishment has consistently been used as a means of controlling children through the ages. Beethoven, who created beautiful music that has

---

Child Abuse

BEING A battered child means. . .
never knowing the consequences
of a gesture, facial expression or
request; sometimes a gift of
flowers is received affectionately,
and sometimes it's dashed down
with a shove and a
tirade of abuse. Sometimes a
request for a piece of gum is "a
good idea" and sometimes "it's
proof of your horrid greediness
and irresponsible lack of concern
over the cost of dental care!"
Sometimes looking sad is met
with friendly concern and
sometimes you're berated and
punished for being selfish and
ungrateful.
But you just never know. . .

laura

Photograph courtesy of Eric Rahkonen. Contra Costa Times, *Walnut Creek, California. Poem reprinted from Child Abuse and Neglect, Volume 2, C. Henry Kempe, An autobiography of violence, Pages 139–149, Copyright 1978, with permission from Pergamon Press Ltd, Headington Hill Hall, Oxford OX3 0BW, UK.*

The generational aspect of abuse within the family is explained in that way. Frustration can also be considered a possible cause of violence. Anger abounds in our society in individuals who have not been taught ways to control or deal with anger in a nonaggressive fashion.

HISTORY OF ABUSE

Violence is not limited to the 1990s. Humans have dealt with other humans violently since the beginning of time. Infanticide, or the killing of unwanted newborn children, has been practiced throughout history. Sickly or deformed children, a twin, a girl,

endured through the centuries, whipped his piano pupils with a knitting needle if they made mistakes. When Louis XIII was a child, he was whipped upon arising in the morning for the mistakes he had made the previous day. A schoolmaster in Germany kept track of the discipline he administered to his pupils during his career. He recorded 911,527 strikes with a stick, 124,000 lashes with a whip, 136,715 slaps with his hand, and 1,115,800 boxes on the ear (DeMause, 1975). Truly not an enviable record!

Even the nursery rhymes that are read to little children appear to condone violence against them. Consider this nursery rhyme from Mother Goose:

> "THERE WAS an old woman who lived in a shoe,
> She had so many children she didn't know what to do.
> She gave them some broth without any bread
> And whipped them all soundly and sent them to bed."

Wife beating was legal in the United States until 1824. Wives were seen as chattel of their husbands and could be beaten for such offenses as "nagging too much." The exploration of the problem of beating of women began in the United States with the civil rights movement in the 1960s. The expansion of the women's movement aided the lowering of the national tolerance for wife beating (Bell, 1977).

Until 1980, marital rape was not considered an offense in the United States. Currently, only 39 states have repealed or weakened the marital rape exemption, which dates back to an English common law of 1736. States that still do not consider marital rape a crime include Arizona, Idaho, Kentucky, Missouri, New Mexico, North Carolina, Oklahoma, South Carolina, South Dakota, Tennessee, and Utah (Campbell and Alford, 1989).

Abuse of the elderly has recently become recognized as a problem of great magnitude and also is not unique to the 20th century. In preindustrial Europe, it was common for legal documents to be drawn to allow the elder parent to continue to sit at the family table and use the front door. The problem is of greater magnitude today because persons are living longer so that there are more elderly. "By the year 2000, 15% of the U.S. population will be 65 or older, more than 3 million will be 85 or older, and 100,000 will be 100 or older" (Nornhold, 1990). Furthermore, younger adults are more concerned about their own lives than about accepting the obligations of caring for elderly relatives (Council of Scientific Affairs, 1987).

SCOPE OF THE PROBLEM

Violence takes a toll on our society. It affects countless families. The impact in 1 year is staggering. According to the American Humane Association's national study on child neglect and abuse, the rate of reported cases of child abuse and neglect has risen steadily since 1976. In 1976, there were

101 reported cases per 10,000 children. In 1985, there were 1,928 reported cases per 10,000 children. Of cases in 1985, 55.7% were cases of child neglect, and 44.3% were cases of maltreatment. In 11.7% of the cases, sexual abuse occurred. In 2.2% of the cases, there was serious physical injury (U.S. Bureau of the Census, 1989).

In a report issued in early 1990, the National Committee for Prevention of Child Abuse (NCPCA) reported a 10% increase in reported cases of child abuse and neglect in 1989, the greatest increase since 1985. This reflects a change in a trend of decreasing numbers of reported cases that began in 1986. This new increase more closely resembles that of the first half of the decade, when the annual increase averaged 11.4%. In 1989, there were 2.4 million reports of child abuse and neglect according to data from all states except one that failed to report. Thirty-eight states reported increases, six did not change, and only five reported a decrease. One thousand two hundred thirty-seven children died as a result of child abuse in 1989; this reflects a 38% increase in the 4 years since 1985. One child dies every 8 hours as a result of abuse. The NCPCA suggests that the greater proportion of the abuse reports reflect serious parental dysfunctioning, particularly in the large number of cases where substance abuse (primarily crack cocaine) was involved. In addition, there were more cases of extreme poverty and high levels of violence within the family situation (National Center for Child Abuse Prevention Research, 1990). Figure 20–1 compares the increase in reported abuse cases in the 10-year period from 1976 through 1985 with the 1989 increase.

A Family Violence Research Program has been conducted at the University of Rhode Island since the mid-1970s. Gelles and Straus (1987) completed a second survey of child maltreatment in 1985. They found that although the rates of reported cases of child maltreatment has increased more than 142%, the incidents of severe and very severe violence against children has actually decreased 47%. They attribute the increase in reporting to the revision of state laws, 24-hour hot lines for reporting abuse, and media campaigns. The decrease in severe violence was attributed to raising the consciousness of parents about the inappropriateness of violence.

Strauss (1978) reported the following in a national survey of domestic violence prepared for a

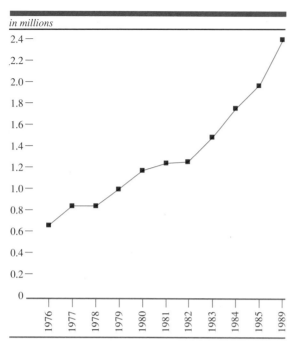

Figure 20–1
Reported cases of child abuse for 1976–1985 and 1989.
(From Statistical Abstract of the United States. 109th Ed.
U.S. Dept. of Commerce, Bureau of the Census. Washington, D.C., U.S. Government Printing Office, 1989.)

U.S. House of Representatives hearing on domestic violence:

> **"THE PREDOMINANT position of the family as a setting for violence seems to apply to every form of physical violence from slaps to torture and murder. In fact, some form of physical violence between family members is so likely to occur at some point in the life cycle that it can be said to be almost universal."**

Homicide is the ultimate form of violence. Statistics from the Uniform Crime Reports for the United States (1989) reveal that in 54.9% of the cases, the offender was known to the victim; individuals were killed by strangers only 12.4% of the time. Studies report that where an individual in an intimate relationship is killed, there has often been a history of physical abuse directed at the woman. This is true not only when a woman is killed; evidence suggests that when the man in an intimate relationship is killed, there is often a history of abuse of the woman who killed him (Mercy and Saltzman, 1989). Within the family, more than 1,000 women die each year at their husband's

hands, and more than 500 women kill their husbands each year (Raymond, 1989). The relationship of a murder victim to the assailant is shown in Fig. 20–2.

There is often a long history of violent tension between the victim and the offender before a domestic quarrel or petty argument results in death. The quarrel may be over an incident so petty that the general community is amazed that someone has died because of it (Goetting, 1988). Arguments were the most prevalent motive for homicides in 1988. Brawls occurring while under the influence of drugs and alcohol are included in the 18.9% of nonfelony murders (Fig. 20–3).

Domestic violence, or the battering of one partner by the other partner, has reached epidemic proportions in our society. Battering occurs in both married and unmarried couples and those in long- or short-term relationships. Battering has been reported in 12% of high school dating and in 38% of college dating (Bullock et al., 1989). Current estimates are that 2–6 million domestic partners are victims of abuse each year; this means that a violent act occurs every 5–16 seconds (Chez, 1988). The true scope of the problem is difficult to assess because of the large number of women who do not report the incidents. Timrots and Rand (1987) report that in a U.S. Department of Justice national crime survey covering a 5-year period, it was discovered that 48% of women had not reported incidents. The primary reason given by the victims for not reporting a crime is that the attack was a private or personal matter. According to Helton et al.

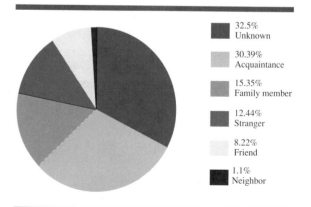

Figure 20–2
Relationship of a murder victim to offender. (Redrawn based on 1988 Uniform Crime Reports for the United States. Washington, D.C., U.S. Government Printing Office, 1989.)

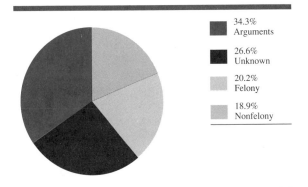

34.3%
Arguments

26.6%
Unknown

20.2%
Felony

18.9%
Nonfelony

Figure 20–3
Motives for homicides in the United States in 1988. (Redrawn based on 1988 Uniform Crime Reports for the United States. Washington, D.C., U.S. Government Printing Office, 1989.)

(1987), an estimated 1 of 34 U.S. women have been beaten at least once during their marriage; this proportion would increase if ex-spouses were included. In 7 of 10 cases of violence within the home, the violent act was committed by a woman's spouse or ex-spouse or boyfriend or ex-boyfriend. According to the U.S. Department of Justice, domestic violence is reoccurring in nature, and these women are likely to be victimized an average of three or more times during the year.

It is evident that the primary victim is usually a woman who is beaten by her male partner. The U.S. Department of Justice reports that three women are victims of violent crimes for every one man who is assaulted (Timrots, 1987). Chez (1988) reports that women are battered by men more than 90% of the time. "Domestic violence against women may be the single most common etiology for injuries in women presenting to the health care system" (McLeer et al., 1989). Battering of a man by a woman does occur, but research evidence suggests that the incidence is so low that it is not a health problem (Campbell and Humphreys, 1984). For the purposes of this chapter, abuse of the female partner in the relationship will be considered.

Abuse of the elderly, a problem that affects individuals from all socioeconomic groups, has also reached epidemic proportions (Butler, 1989). The problem of abuse of the elderly began to receive attention in 1981, when the U.S. House of Representatives Select Committee on Aging called abuse of the elderly "alien to the American ideal." The Select committee on Aging estimated that 4% of the U.S. elderly population were abused each year.

This represents approximately 1 million persons per year (Jones et al., 1988). The House Subcommittee on Elderly Health and Long-Term Care, a subcommittee of the Select Committee on Aging, reported in May 1990 that abuse of the elderly is on the rise. The incidence of abuse has increased from approximately 1 million victims annually in 1980 to 1.5 million victims annually in 1988 (approximately 5% of all older Americans). The survey found a range of abuse from the theft of Social Security checks to violent physical abuse, including rape and murder. The report cited that only one in eight cases is reported; one in five cases was reported in 1980 (House Subcommittee on Elderly Health and Long-Term Care, 1990). The Family Violence Project of the City and County of San Francisco reports that the most severe cases of violence seen by the project were assaults on the elderly (1989).

Violence takes its toll on the abused and the abuser—the victim and the perpetrator of the violence. In a report prepared for the U.S. Department of Health and Human Services in 1980, Barnett et al. listed some of the major effects of family violence (Table 20–1).

CHILD ABUSE
Dynamics of Abuse

Child abuse is physical or emotional injury, sexual assault, or exploitation of a child by another individual. It includes negligent treatment of a child by the person responsible for the child's welfare.

Causes of Child Abuse

During early research of what was then called the battered-child syndrome, Kempe and Helfer (1972) identified three factors that occurred in abusive situations.

First, the parent with the potential to abuse is likely to have been abused as a child, have low self-esteem, or have unrealistic expectations of a child's growth and development.

Second, the identified child is one who is seen as different by the parent. This includes but is not limited to premature infants, who were found to be abused twice as often as full-term infants, or children with an abnormality. A child of the "wrong sex" or a child who was hyperactive might also be a reason for identification.

Table 20-1
Major Effects of Family Violence

Effects on Adults	Effects on Children
Death by homicide (of either the abuser or victim)	Death by homicide
	Death by suicide
Death by suicide	Emotional injury (such as poor self-esteem)
Disabling injuries	Depression
Depression	Aggressive behavior toward others
Difficulty obtaining, maintaining, or adjusting to employment	Delinquency
	Poor school adjustment
Emotional abuse and deprivation	Learned victim/aggressor roles
Perpetuation of social isolation due to fear of disclosure	Runaway episodes
	Alcohol/drug experimentation
Continuing escalating violence if alternative behaviors are not learned	Early marriage
	Violent behavior in adult relationships
Breakup of the family	Expansion of violence into the community
Recurrence of violent behavior with a new partner	
Expansion of violence into the community	

Adapted from Barnett et al.: Family Violence: Intervention Strategies. Washington, D.C., U.S. Department of Health and Human Services, 1980.

Third, stress could be of a major or minor nature. The combination of these three factors create a favorable climate for abusive behavior (Kempe and Helfer, 1972).

These early findings have been substantiated by other researchers. Sangrund et al. (1974) wrote:

> "THE ETIOLOGY of child abuse appears to involve an interaction among three factors: personality traits of parents which contribute to abuse proneness, immediate environmental stress, and actual characteristics of the child which make him (or her) vulnerable for scapegoating" (p. 328).

Later studies also suggest that babies who were sick during the neonatal period and were difficult to care for caused them to be singled out by the parent. Failure to thrive was another finding at the time abuse was identified; many of these children continued to have growth retardation (Augoustinos, 1987).

The interrelationship of these three factors within a larger context has been examined through continued research. Various causation models have been proposed; one model is the Garbarino ecological model. It allows examination of the individuals involved—parent and child—within the family situation and under the influences imposed by society and culture. Its purpose is to provide a framework in which to understand the relationship among stress, social support systems, and child maltreatment (Howze and Kotch, 1984). The value is in not only looking at the causal relationships but also offering a framework for available supports and resources. Figure 20–4 demonstrates the Garbarino ecological model as adapted by Howze and Kotch.

Types of Child Abuse

There are four basic types of child abuse:

1. Physical abuse: a physical injury that is inflicted by other than accidental means on a child by another person
2. Child neglect (physical and emotional): negligent treatment or maltreatment of a child by a person responsible for the child's welfare; includes both acts and omissions on the part of the responsible person and failure to provide a loving environment in which a child can thrive, learn, and develop
3. Emotional maltreatment: willfully inflicting upon a child unjustifiable mental suffering, causing the child to be emotionally damaged
4. Sexual abuse: sexual activity between an adult and child; sexual assault or exploitation

The most common type of physical abuse is beating with an instrument, resulting in cuts, bruises, burns, and fractures. The types of injury vary only with the imagination of the adult. Parents often select a method to meet what they see as the disobedience of the child. This may produce a patterned injury that gives a clue to how the child was injured (Mittleman, 1987). Thus, a child who walks where he is not supposed to might have his feet dipped in scalding water, and the burns will cover the stocking area. A child who touches a light cord or light plug might be beaten with it, produc-

Cultural milieu (i.e., norms or values embraced that form the basis of our society)
- Attitudes toward violence
- Attitudes toward corporal punishment
- Attitudes toward child rearing
- View of the nature of the family
- View of the role of social and welfare institutions in supporting families
- Values placed on individualism, utility, merit, and technology

Social environment (i.e., factors relating to the structure of the community and society)
- Formal and informal social networks
- General community welfare
- Housing conditions
- Social integration
- Community agencies
- Economic resources
- Unemployment

Familial (i.e., factors present in the family systems that have an impact on family functioning)
- Marital stability
- Interaction between family members
- Special needs of family members (physical and emotional)
- Family structure
- Extended family relationships
- Family violence

Individual (i.e., factors that the individual takes with her or him into the family systems)
- Parent's perceptions of own childhood experience
- Parenting practices
- Physical and emotional health
- Tolerance of frustration
- Approach to problem solving
- Coping skills
- Self-image
- Focus of control
- Modernity

Figure 20–4
Garbarino's levels of predisposing factors of child abuse and neglect. (Based on adaptation from Child Abuse Neglect Int. J., Volume 8, Howze, D., and Kotch, J., Disentangling life events, stress, and social support: Implications for the primary prevention of child abuse and neglect. Page 403, Copyright 1984, with permission from Pergamon Press Ltd, Headington Hill Hall, Oxford OX3 0BW, UK.)

ing a looped or linear bruise pattern. A child who plays with matches or the stove might have his hand placed in the flame. A crying child or one who talks back might have hot pepper or Tabasco sauce poured in his mouth, or he might be suffocated with a pillow. Fear is a constant factor in the lives of these children.

Violent shaking of a baby is an example of abuse where a blow is not struck. However, shaking can cause serious and often permanent damage, including detached retinas, spinal cord injuries, and brain damage, because of hemorrhage and contusions caused by the brain striking the sides of the skull.

Young children ages 2–5 are the most frequently injured. Babies are in the greatest danger of severe injury or death because of their small size in contrast to the size of the punishing adult. The National Committee for the Prevention of Child Abuse reports (1989) that in the 15 states reporting the age of fatalities, 50% of the children were less than 1 year old. In two states (Massachusetts and Connecticut), 75% and 76%, respectively, of the fatalities were children less than 1 year old (National Center for Child Abuse Prevention Research, 1990).

Child neglect is a twofold problem. Physical neglect entails the failure to provide for basic needs, including safety, food, clothing, and shelter. In addition, failure to provide for the health needs of a child can also be construed as neglect. Emotional neglect is similar to emotional maltreatment in that results can be observed in the child. The cause is the lack of sensitivity and love shown by the parent for the child. The result is equally detrimental to the child.

Emotional maltreatment is a relatively new concept in the area of child abuse. The abuse has always occurred; however, there was very little concern about it or its consequences. It is difficult to strictly define but includes such acts as mental injury or commission of any act or acts that might affect the child's normal emotional development in a substantive way. The behavior evident in the child may demonstrate a substantial impairment in a normal range of performance and behavior. In observing children for emotional maltreatment, the nurse may observe signs such as an overly compliant or passive child. Equally as important is the child who is very aggressive or apt to fly into a rage. These children frequently do not keep up with the normal rate of physical, intellectual, and emotional development. Because emotional abuse almost always occurs in the home and is not witnessed by others and because the symptoms displayed by the child can occur in children who are not abused, treatment of these children is very difficult. Examples of emotional abuse include locking a child in a closet for a prolonged period of time, tying a child to a bedpost, or engaging in bizarre acts of torture. Subtle abuse might include acts of name calling such as "You're stupid," "You're a slut," or "You're bad or evil." Name calling can destroy a child's self-concept.

Sexual abuse is any sexual activity between an adult and a child, including use of a child for sexual exploitation, prostitution, or pornography. Incest is considered sexual relations between close family members such as father and daughter, mother and son, or siblings within the family. Sexual abuse often involves a person known to the child such as a relative or friend. It may occur over a prolonged period of time, and to ensure secrecy, threats to the child may be used to continue the abuse. Sexual abuse has many long-term consequences. Women who were sexually abused as children may suffer from depression, anxiety, and low self-esteem and experience sexual problems as adults (Bachmann et al., 1988). Men who were sexually abused as children also suffer from depression and frequently have difficulty maintaining an intimate emotional and sexual relationship with one person (Krug, 1989).

Of great concern are the large number of child abuse fatalities caused by violent and dependent drug users. Wyoming reported only 23% of substance abuse involvement in child abuse cases; however, in 50% of those cases, the child was killed (National Center for Child Abuse Prevention Research, 1990). It was recently reported that drugs were a factor in 50–90% of child welfare cases in California (DelVecchio, 1989). Drug addiction by the mother often results in the birth of an addicted infant and necessitates the placement of the infant because of the inability of the parents to provide adequate care. Furthermore, research suggests that successful treatment is unlikely if the parent is actively abusing drugs, so the children removed from their parents are unlikely to ever be safely reunited with their own family.

Failure to thrive is a term used to describe infants and children who fail to grow to expected standards of height and weight. In the context of this chapter, we consider only those who fail to thrive with no organic reason.

This syndrome frequently affects very young infants. The cause is usually found in the relationship between the person caring for the infant and the infant. It puts the child at risk for long-term effects of malnutrition and emotional deprivation, such as physical and mental development that remain below average (Johnson, 1979).

Bolton (1983) characterized parents of children who fail to thrive as dependent and isolated. They lived in an environment that lacked stimulation. They may have had poor relationships with their own parents and may have been rejected. They often view their children as abnormal when they are not. Many of the families have a multitude of internal and external stressors. They do not achieve an effective nurturing relationship with their child, and consequently the child fails to grow and develop properly (Bolton, 1983).

Some of the physical and behavioral indicators of child abuse and neglect are given (Table 20–2). The presence of any one of these indicators does not necessarily mean that a child is abused. However, it indicates the need for a thorough assessment of a child's situation.

ABUSE OF WOMEN

Dynamics of Abuse

Abuse of women is severe, deliberate, and repeated physical violence inflicted upon a woman by a man with whom she has or has had an intimate relationship.

Causes of Abuse

What causes an adult relationship to become violent? What characterizes the individuals who respond with violence to their mate or lover? Violence within a marriage or a close relationship is a problem that cuts across all class, racial, educational, and financial lines.

Studies of family violence show the generational aspect of abuse. A majority of batterers (more than 60%) were personally subjected to abuse when they were children. Violence was a way of life in their homes, and in more than 66% of their parents' marriages, violence played a significant role (Mehta and Dandrea, 1988). Several characteristics may suggest the propensity to violent behavior. Some characteristics are listed that may influence violent behavior between men and women in a close relationship.

In our society, men were often socialized to suppress feelings of sadness, loneliness, or confusion. More acceptable emotions were aggressiveness, assertiveness, or anger. Successful men in society often still have this macho image.

A man who batters his partner may purport to have a macho image; however, he often is extremely emotionally dependent on his wife for physical, mental, emotional, and moral support. His social isolation and few friends and outside interests combine to make him extremely vulnerable when anything competes with him for his wife's full attention. He is also often extremely jealous

---

Characteristics That May Influence Violence

PRESENT IN the history of the batterer
   Was a victim of child abuse
   Parents had a violent marriage
   Witnessed mother being beaten

Personal characteristics of the batterer
   Poor impulse control
   Unable to tolerate frustration
   Need to dominate (machoism)
   Possessive
   Externalizes blame
   Emotionally dependent upon wife
   Highly jealous
   Unable to trust
   Unrealistic expectations

Personal characteristics of the victim
   Low self-esteem and body image
   Rigid stereotyped sex roles
   Assumes total responsibility for the marriage
   Married young and had children early in the marriage
   Is pregnant

Family characteristics
   Family boundaries are rigid
   Socially and emotionally are isolated and withdrawn

---

and imagines infidelities. This makes him try to keep his wife socially isolated (Hiraki and Grambs, 1990).

Role of Self-Esteem

Physical and/or emotional abuse in childhood leads to the development of low self-esteem. In the case of battered women, diminished self-esteem is present in both the abused and the abuser. Their responses to this negative self-concept, however, are very different. When they become personally threatened by a situation occurring in their home, men respond with violence.

The woman who is battered also suffers from low self-esteem. She may see herself as deserving the beating because she did not live up to the man's expectations, even if the expectations were unrealistic. She may have been battered as a child and sought an early marriage as a means of escape from her own family situation. Low self-esteem may have led her to accept anyone who showed her affection. Sexual abuse may contribute to low self-esteem as well as to a poor concept of body image. In a recent study by Campbell (1989) of 193 bat-

Table 20–2
Physical and Behavioral Indicators of Child Abuse and Neglect

Physical Indicators	Behavioral Indicators
Physical abuse	**Physical abuse**
Unexplained bruises and welts:	Wary of adult contacts
In various stages of healing	Apprehensive when other children cry
Clustered or forming patterns	Extremes of behavior; aggressiveness or withdrawal
On several surface areas	Frightened of parents
Reflecting shape of article used	Afraid to go home
Unexplained burns:	Constantly on the alert for danger
Cigar or cigarette burns on soles, palms, back, or buttocks	Reports injury by parents
Immersion burns (socklike, glovelike, doughnut shaped on buttocks or genitalia)	
Rope burns on arms, legs, neck or torso	
Unexplained fractures:	
In various stages of healing	
Multiple or spiral fractures	
Unexplained lacerations or abrasions:	
To mouth, lips, gums, eyes	
To external genitalia	
Physical neglect	**Physical neglect**
Consistent hunger, poor hygiene, inappropriate dress	Begging or stealing food
Lack of medical or dental care	Consistent lack of supervision, especially in dangerous activities or for prolonged periods
Constant fatigue, listlessness, or falling asleep in class	Delinquency or stealing
	Early arrival and late departure from school
	Reporting no caretaker
Sexual abuse	**Sexual abuse**
Difficulty in walking or sitting	Withdrawal, fantasy, infantile behavior
Torn, stained, or bloody underwear	Bizarre, sophisticated, or unusual sexual behavior or knowledge
Genital pain or itching	Poor peer relationships
Bruises or bleeding from the external genitalia, vaginal or anal areas	Delinquency
Venereal disease, especially in preteenagers	Runaway
Pregnancy	Reporting of sexual assault
Emotional maltreatment	**Emotional maltreatment**
Failure to thrive	Habit disorders (sucking, biting, rocking)
Lag in physical development	Conduct disorders (antisocial, destructive)
Speech disorders	Neurotic traits (sleep disorders, inhibition of play)
	Psychoneurotic reactions (hysteria, obsession, compulsion, phobia)
	Behavior extremes
	Overly adaptive behavior:
	Inappropriately adult
	Inappropriately infant
	Developmental lags
	Attempted suicide

Adapted from the California Child Care Resource and Referral Network. San Francisco, 1982.

tered women, low self-esteem was found in women who were physically abused as well as in those who were both physically and sexually abused. The difference in total self-esteem was significant ($p < .05$), but the greatest difference between the two groups was in terms of body image. Sexually abused women had a significantly ($p < .1$) poorer concept of their body image than women who were not sexually abused.

Role of Isolation

Social isolation coupled with an idealized marriage and stereotyped roles that are difficult if not impossible to achieve help set the stage for violence. There is no escape because the boundaries of the family are very rigid. Secrecy and shame regarding the beatings impose an isolation. If jealousy is the cause of stress, the woman may not be able to socialize with others for fear of retribution by her husband. A very jealous husband may do all the shopping and control all of the money so the wife cannot do even simple things in society. The victim is trapped and does not reach out for help unless injury necessitates it. Even then, she may not share the cause of her injury.

Role of Pregnancy

In 1975, Gelles and Straus (1987) found that 25% of the female victims were beaten while they were pregnant. The Surgeon General's Workshop on Violence in 1986 recommended that all pregnant women be screened for abuse because pregnancy was such a high-risk period for battering. Data from studies indicate that battered women are three times more likely to be injured during pregnancy than are nonbattered women, and the consequence is often a spontaneous abortion (Mehta and Dandrea, 1988). Various studies indicate that 25–63% of women were battered while they were pregnant. They report blows to the abdomen, injuries to their breasts and genitalia, and sexual assault (Helton et al., 1987). The results of such violence are spontaneous abortion rates of 25–53% (Helton, 1989) and low-birth-weight babies. A study of pregnant women found the percentage of low-birth-weight babies born to battered women to be twice that of nonbattered women. When controlling for confounding variables between private and public hospital patients such as diet and prenatal care, battered private patients were four times more likely to deliver low-birth-weight babies. As

can be seen, pregnancy does not exclude women from the danger of beating. In fact, pregnancy may increase stresses within the family and provoke an attack.

Role of Alcohol

It is a myth that drug or alcohol abuse causes abuse of women. However, it is a fact that there is a high rate of involvement (50–80%) with drugs and/or alcohol in a violent relationship (Hiraki and Grambs, 1990). Consumption of drugs or alcohol may facilitate violent behavior by lessening inhibitions. The battered woman may also resort to the use of alcohol as a coping mechanism after battering begins or be enticed into the use of drugs or alcohol as a means of the man gaining control (King and Ryan, 1989). The danger in viewing alcohol or drugs as a cause for abuse is that treatment may be directed only toward correction of the alcohol or drug problem and the abuse problem is ignored. The suffering then continues, and danger in the relationship may continue to a point where there is loss of life.

Types of Abuse
PHYSICAL BEATING

Two studies of abuse of women document the types and severity of physical injury. Of 109 women interviewed by Dobash and Dobash (Campbell and Humphreys, 1984), 100 had more extensive injuries than bruises. These included fractures, head injuries with unconsciousness, and miscarriages. Eighty percent of the women had injuries sufficient for them to seek treatment.

A pilot study by Drake was done on 12 battered women (Campbell and Humphreys, 1984). Of the 12, 11 had been beaten while they were pregnant. Their injuries included 14 fractures, 7 multiple contusions, 7 head and facial lacerations, 7 incidences of hair being pulled out, 5 burns, 3 dislocated jaws, and 5 spontaneous abortions within 10 days of being beaten. A total of 52 injuries were present in the histories of the 12 women.

SPOUSAL RAPE

Spousal rape is forced sex in marriage. Campbell and Alford (1989) reported that "ten to fourteen percent of all married women and at least forty percent of battered wives in the United States have been raped by their husbands. In a study conducted by these nurses, they found that women had been forced into homosexual sex, sex with animals, were beaten, kicked or burned during sex and had been forced to 'endure other acts of extreme degradation'." Furthermore, in 5.2% of the cases of rape in the study, the children in the family had been physically involved by their fathers, and in another 17.8%, the children had witnessed the sexual attack on their mother.

Remaining in the Situation

Silence and secrecy characterize the problem of abuse of women. Beatings occur behind closed doors over a period of time, years perhaps, with the victim remaining with the offender. The offender is violent usually only at home, realizing that the behavior would not be tolerated anywhere else. Why do women remain in battering situations? The reason is not that they like being beaten; it is far more complex. It may involve loyalty, pity, duty, responsibility, or optimism. It may involve shame, denial, learned helplessness, confusion, and lack of energy. Economic dependence is also a potent factor. This is especially true of women who entered the relationship at a young age and do not have job skills.

Walker developed the cycle theory of violence (1979). It explains a common abusive pattern of violence followed by a period of no violence. There are three phases in the cycle: tension, explosion, and contrition. It partially explains why some women do not attempt to escape from the situation.

During the *tension* phase, there may be minor battering incidents. The woman will attempt to cope with these using techniques that may have been previously successful. She will deal with whatever caused the stress—e.g., dinner not ready on time, the house not clean, or the children arguing. She does not get angry with the abuser. Her lower self-esteem may, in fact, lead her to see reasons why the man's behavior was justified. He may have had a bad day at work, or he may have had too much to drink. She knows, however, that the incidents are not isolated. They will continue. Her goal is to keep the attacks at this level for as long a period of time as possible. This is a time of psychological denial. She denies she is angry with the abuser and tries to maintain an equilibrium so that his violence will not increase in either frequency or severity. This very act of denial is crippling and keeps

her from being able to cope and escape from the situation.

The second and most dangerous phase is the *explosive* phase. It is inevitable as tension builds and is characterized by rage out of control. It is usually shorter, ranging from hours to a day or more. It occurs in private, and the only option during this phase is for the woman to hide. She cannot exert any influence over the man's behavior. Walker reports that the man cannot seem to stop even if the woman is severely injured. After the attack is over, shock and disbelief occur in both the batterer and his victim. Unless the injury is severe, usually no medical help is sought. However, if the police are called, it is usually during this phase. The gravity of this explosive phase is seen in the fact that in 80% of all women murdered by their male partner, the police had been called to the home one to five times before the woman was killed (Walker, 1979).

The last phase is one of *loving kindness and contrition* by the batterer. He attempts to make up for his behavior with pleas and promises. Walker reports that women are most likely to flee during the beginning of this phase (1979).

Walker's cycle of violence can be expanded to be viewed like a wave. After the contrition phase, the man will often try to get the woman to "buy back" into the situation. Things will remain calm and even loving. If the woman remains in contact with her man, his pleas usually convince her to remain. If she does remain, the chances of him seeking help for his behavior are remote. The "same old situation" then exists, and the cycle will begin again with minor incidents and tension occurring until another explosion occurs, which is inevitable. The wave pattern of violence is shown (Fig. 20–5).

It is often difficult for health professionals who are attempting to help a battered woman to understand why the woman does not simply get out of the situation. King and Ryan (1989) reported that "the most potent reason that women stay with abusive partners is fear." The woman and her children are often threatened by the abuser if she tells or leaves. The legal system is cumbersome; often, women who seek help by restraining orders or other judicial means find that there may not be real safety in such methods. Other factors that keep a woman in an abusive situation are cultural (single parents are often discriminated against), religious (separation and divorce may be unacceptable), and

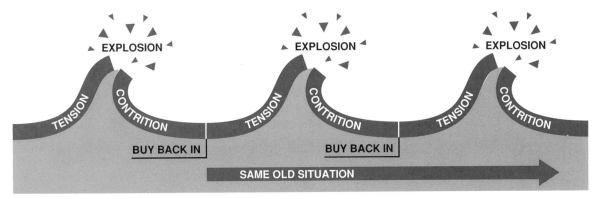

Figure 20–5
Wave pattern of violence. (Redrawn based on cycle of violence from The Battered Woman. By Lenore E. Walker. Copyright © 1979 by Lenore E. Walker. Reprinted by permission of HarperCollins Publishers.)

economical. Women who leave the abusive situation frequently face serious economic problems and may fall into poverty. This is especially true if they have children they must support and they married early and have no marketable job skills (King and Ryan, 1989).

Hiraki and Grambs (1990) identified women who are the most likely to leave a battering situation. These include:

- Women who have resources (money, friends, family, support)

- Women who have power (credit cards, a job, status outside the family)
- Women with no children
- Women who were not abused as children
- Women who did not see their mothers beaten
- Women who are in battering situations that are frequent and/or severe
- Women who have children who are starting to be beaten

Table 20–3 presents physical and behavioral indicators of assaults against women. The presence

---

Table 20–3
Physical and Behavioral Indicators of Assaults Against Women

Physical Indicators	Behavioral Indicators
Multiple abrasions or contusions to different anatomic sites	Timid and evasive behavior
	Fright
Injuries in various stages of healing	Low self-esteem
	Embarrassment
Injuries indicating failure to seek immediate care	Feelings of being trapped, powerless
Physical trauma in a pregnant woman	Passivity
	Jumpiness
Vague, nonspecific complaints such as anxiety, sleeplessness, headaches, insomnia, choking sensation, hyperventilation, and chest, back, or pelvic pain	Minimized serious injury
	Inconsistent description of the cause of the injury
	Drug or alcohol abuse (often overdose)
Severity of injuries vary	Depression
Rape	Frequent crying
	Suicide attempts
Trauma history (this may be the key)	
	Often accompanied by male partner who does not wish to leave her alone with medical personnel

Adapted from Barnett et al.: Family Violence: Intervention Strategies. Washington, D.C., U.S. Department of Health and Human Services, 1980.

of the indicators should alert the professional to carefully assess the situation for the presence of abuse.

ELDERLY ABUSE

Dynamics of Abuse

"Abuse is an act or omission by the one having the care, custody, or responsibility of an elderly person which results in harm or threatened harm to that person's health or welfare" (American Medical Association, 1985).

We are becoming a nation with an ever-increasing older population. As an increasing proportion of our population is elderly, their needs and care must be addressed. Elderly who can no longer care for themselves must have someone or someplace provide care. The generation of individuals in their 40s and 50s are often called the "sandwich generation"; they are no longer caring for their children and are beginning to care for their parents. Care of an aging parent may require sacrifice and commitment, as did care for children.

When an elderly parent can no longer care for himself or herself due to the physical or mental infirmities of age, there are several possible ways of dealing with the situation. One is to do nothing; this is an unsatisfactory way of dealing with the problem. A second way is for the parent to remain in the home and hire someone to provide care. This is often difficult to do and expensive; however, it may be most satisfactory to the elder. The third way is to place the elderly person in a retirement home or residential care facility. This also requires considerable financial obligation and may be resented by the elderly person. A fourth alternative is to take the elder into a family member's home. This is the least expensive other than doing nothing. An older person may see this as more satisfactory than a residential home for the elderly; however, it can place stress on the existing family situation.

With stress comes opportunity that may lead to abuse. This is especially true in families where violence is a response to stress. As young children in the home may experience physical abuse, so an elderly person whose demands or behavior causes problems may experience physical abuse. Stress in the primary caretaker can be caused by the needs of the elderly person exceeding the family's ability to meet them as well as by personal stresses of the caretaker such as the loss of a job, illness, or other family problems (Council on Scientific Affairs, 1987).

In 1983, Phillips began a nursing study on the relationship between the elderly and their caretakers. Her sample of 74 individuals was composed of individuals who were in good relationships and those who were in abusive and/or neglectful relationships. She considered a variety of demographic characteristics. There were 30 in the "abuse" group—60% women and 40% men. The mean age was 78.5. When exploring the relationship of the elderly person to the caregiver, she found that 46.7% involved a parenting relationship, 43.4% involved a birth parent, and 3.3% involved a stepparent. In only 26.7% of the cases was the abuser the spouse. Of the abused group, 36.7% were married, and 43.3% were widowed.

Campbell and Humphreys (1984) reported that studies had shown that the abuser was likely to be a member of the victim's family, usually one of their children who resided in the same household. They reported that physical abuse and neglect and emotional abuse are most likely to be caused by the victim's son and that emotional neglect or deprivation of rights were most likely to be caused by daughters. Both sons and daughters were equally guilty of financial abuse of the elderly.

The Council on Scientific Affairs of the American Medical Association reported in a 1987 study that the abuser is a relative in 86% of cases and lives with the elderly person in 75% of the cases. Approximately 50% of elder abusers are children or grandchildren of the victims, and approximately 40% are spouses.

In 1988, Jones et al. conducted a 28-month study of 118 patients who were abused. They found that 73% of the abusers were related to the victim. Sons and daughters were the most likely abusers, followed by grandchildren, spouses, and siblings. Seventy percent of the victims in their sample were widowed.

In a 1989 study, Godkin et al. concluded that a woman living alone with a male relative may be at greatest risk for abuse. In their sample, 80% of the victims were women, and 50% of the abusers were husbands or sons. They concluded that because the majority of the elderly are women, elder abuse is primarily a problem faced by them.

Findings of the House Subcommittee on Elderly Health and Long-Term Care (1990) found that the most common type of abuse was physical and financial, followed by denial of basic human rights and psychological abuse. Victims were likely to be age 75 or older and female. Abusers were most often adult children, typically sons who were abused by their parents when they were young (Subcommittee on Elderly Health and Long-Term Care, 1990).

Cognitive or physical impairment that prevents the elderly person from providing self-care is also a factor in the likelihood of abuse.

Types of Abuse

Types of abuse can be categorized as follows:

- Physical abuse: purposeful infliction of physical pain or injury, unnecessary physical restraint, or sexual molestation
- Physical neglect: withholding personal care, food, medications, or medical care or lack of supervision
- Emotional abuse: verbal assault, threats, provoking fear, isolation, intimidation, or humiliation
- Emotional neglect: withholding companionship
- Material abuse: theft or misuse of money or property
- Violation of rights: forceful removal from one's home (Fulmer and Wetle, 1986).

In 1983, the Consortium for Elder Abuse Prevention in the City and County of San Francisco prepared a protocol for service providers to provide more standard delivery of care. Their broad definitions of abuse can be helpful in understanding when an elderly person needs professional intervention in dealing with their life situation. They defined four types of elder abuse.

"*Physical abuse* is willfully inflicting upon an elder any cruel or inhuman corporal punishment or injury by any person who has the care of or custody of or who stands in a position of trust with an elder. This includes but is not restricted to physical beatings, sexual assault, unreasonable physical restraint, or prolonged deprivation of food and water.

"*Neglect* is the negligent failure of any person having the care or custody of an elder to exercise that degree of care that a reasonable person in a similar position would exercise." Neglect includes but is not limited to:

- "Failure to assist in personal hygiene or the provision of food and clothing for an elder
- Failure to provide medical care for the physical and mental health needs of the elder (does not include instances in which an elder refuses treatment)
- Failure to protect an elder from health and safety hazards
- Failure to prevent malnutrition

"*Fiduciary abuse* is when any person who stands in a position of trust with an elder willfully steals the money or property of that elder or secretes or appropriates the money or property of that elder to any use or purpose not in the due and lawful execution of the elder's trust.

"*Abandonment* is the desertion or willful forsaking of an elder by any person with the care or custody of that elder under circumstances in which a reasonable person would continue to provide care or custody."

Indicators of Abuse

A helpless elderly adult may be in the same vulnerable position as an abused child. Someone must become aware of the elder's problem for help to be received. Lists of possible indicators help the professional become aware of possible abusive situations. None is conclusive in itself, but they serve to alert the professional to perform further careful and full assessment. Table 20–4 lists the indicators of possible abuse of the elderly.

NURSING CARE OF VICTIMS OF FAMILY VIOLENCE

The nurse who cares for victims of family violence assumes many roles. The first role is that of a skilled clinician who is knowledgeable and has good assessment skills. Awareness of physical and behavioral characteristics of abuse of men, women, and children of all ages is crucial. The professional nurse often deals with the results of abusive behavior when individuals seek or are brought for treatment. The nurse is also in a position of dealing with individuals and families before abuse has occurred and can be a change agent for their improved care. She can educate families in

Table 20–4
Indicators of Possible Elder Abuse

Physical Indicators	Injury that has not been cared for properly
	Any injury incompatible with history
	Cuts, lacerations, puncture wounds
	Bruises, welts, discoloration:
	Bilaterally on upper arms
	Clustered on trunk but may be evident over any area
	Morphologically similar to an object
	Presence of old and new bruises at the same time
	Dehydration and/or malnourishment without illness-related cause; loss of weight
	Pallor
	Sunken eyes, cheeks
	Evidence of inadequate care
	Evidence of inadequate or inappropriate administration of medicine
	Eye problems, retinal detachment
	Poor skin hygiene
	Absence of hair and/or hemorrhage beneath the scalp
	Soiled clothing or bed
	Burns—cigarette, caustic, acid, friction, or contact with objects
	Signs of confinement (tied to furniture, bathroom fixtures, locked in room)
	Lack of bandages on injuries, evidence of unset bones
Family/Caregiver Indicators	Will not let the older person speak for self or see others without the presence of the caregiver
	Obvious absence of help, attitudes of indifference, or anger toward the elder
	Aggressive behavior
	Blaming the elder for things beyond the elder's control (incontinence)
	Previous history of abuse to others
	Problems with alcohol or drugs
	Indications of inappropriate sexual relationship
	Restriction of the activity of the elder within the family unit
	Conflicting accounts of incidents by the family and victim
	Unwillingness or reluctance to comply with service providers in planning for care of elder
	Withholding of security and affection

the care and nurturing of family members, growth and development of children, and needs of the elderly. Awareness of resources available to provide help is also essential. Communities will vary in services that are available. Nurses can be in the forefront in communities with few services as an advocate for those in need of services. Commitment to changing abusive patterns is essential in dealing with the results of violence.

Components of a comprehensive program for detection and treatment of abused individuals are given in Table 20–5.

The goal of primary prevention should be promotion of family wellness. Education plays a large part and ranges from education of children in grade schools regarding healthy family life to education of professionals to increase their awareness

of the problem of violence, facilitate case detection, and provide for early treatment. There is a strong need for community services so that there is a place to provide care for families before serious injury occurs to any member. There is also a need for a multidisciplinary approach that uses and coordinates the expertise of educational specialists and social welfare specialists as well as nurses, nurse practitioners, and medical personnel on a client's behalf. Nurses caring for families can meet with social workers, physicians, and community agency personnel for optimum planning.

The goal of secondary prevention in a comprehensive program is to provide support to families in stress, facilitating early diagnosis and treatment. A trauma center or family violence prevention agency with a centralized program is helpful. Fam-

Table 20–4	
Indicators of Possible Elder Abuse *Continued*	
Behavioral Indicators	Fear
	Withdrawal
	Depression
	Helplessness
	Resignation
	Hesitation to talk openly
	Implausable stories
	Confusion or disorientation
	Ambivalence/contradictory statements not due to mental disfunction
	Anger
	Denial
	Nonresponsiveness
	Agitation, anxiety
Financial Indicators	Unusual activity in bank accounts
	Activity in bank accounts that is inappropriate to the older adult, i.e., withdrawals from automated banking machines when the person has no way to get to the bank
	Power of attorney given when the person is unable to give a valid power of attorney
	Concern by relatives that too much money is being spent for the care of the older person
	Refusal to spend money on the care of the conservatee
	Recent acquaintances expressing undying affection for a wealthy older person
	Recent change of title of house in favor of a "friend" when the older person is incapable of understanding the nature of the transaction.
	Recent will when the person is incapable of making a will
	Placement not commensurate with financial ability of the elder
	Lack of amenities such as grooming items or clothing when the estate can afford to buy it
	Personal belongings (art, silverware, jewelry) missing
	Isolation of elder from old friends and family so that the elder becomes alienated from those who care and so becomes overly dependent on the caretaker
	Promises of lifelong care in exchange for willing or deeding of all property and money to caretaker
	Signatures of checks that do not resemble the elder's signature
	Checks and documents signed when the elder cannot write

Adapted from the Carlton, L.: Elder Abuse Prevention Protocol. San Francisco, San Francisco Prevention Task Force, 1983.

ily violence does not occur just between 9:00 A.M. and 5:00 P.M. on weekdays. Twenty-four–hour assistance may be crucial to protect victims. Shelters for victims to temporarily remove them from danger is helpful; abused women frequently feel they have nowhere to go. They may have little money and few marketable skills. A shelter can temporarily provide safety while they plan for their future.

The goal of tertiary prevention is to provide rehabilitative services to violent families. Because of the responsibility to report assault, there will be involvement of a social service agency or local law enforcement members if an injury has resulted in a report. There may be prosecution and punishment of the abuser and/or court-ordered removal of the victim from the family situation. Professional counseling services as well as self-help groups can be helpful to the family. Long-term follow-up and supervision may be necessary.

Nurses' Role in Care of Abused Children

Primary prevention focuses on the improvement of parent-child relationships from the beginning of that relationship until the child becomes an adult. In a nation where people are educated to perform many varieties of skills, we have yet to value the education necessary to be a successful parent. Individuals become parents by being handed a child; this does not necessarily qualify them for the responsibility. The fact that many children die from abuse underscores the need for early intervention

Table 20–5

Components of a Comprehensive Program to Reduce Family Violence for Individuals, Families, and the Community

Individuals	Family	Community
Primary prevention—Goal: Promotion of family wellness		
Birth control services for sexually active teens Family life education in schools, churches, and community centers Child care education for teenagers who babysit Preventive mental services for adults and children Training for professionals in early detection of violence	Parenting classes in hospitals, schools, and other community agencies Provision of bonding opportunities for new parents Social services for families Referral of at-risk families to community health nurses for follow-up services	Community education concerning family violence Development of community services such as crisis lines, respite placement for children, respite care for families with dependent elderly members, homemaker education, and evaluation
Secondary prevention—Goal: Diagnosis of and service for families in stress		
Nursing assessment for evidence of family violence in all health care settings Shelter or foster home placement for victims Social services for individuals or families Referral to community health agencies	Referral to self-help groups	Trauma center with 24-hour reporting, 24-hour response, 24-hour case intake, coordination with legal and medical authorities, coordination with voluntary agencies that have services, coordination with social services department responsible for provision of services Multidisciplinary committees to review cases and make recommendations for treatment Public authority involvement, police, district attorney, courts
Tertiary prevention—Goal: Reeducation and rehabilitation of violent families		
Professional counseling services for individuals and families	Parenting reeducation— formal training in child rearing	Foster homes Self-help groups Public authority involvement Follow-up care for known cases

with new parents, especially those who are very young. Early and careful assessment of parents for high-risk behaviors is essential in any preventive program.

Classes during pregnancy should focus on more than physical preparation for labor. Pregnant women need to know the dangerous effects of substance abuse on their unborn child and the potential life-long effects. In addition, the mother needs help to realize that substance abuse seriously limits a person's ability to parent. Including the realities of parenthood in prenatal classes and talking about fears and questions of the pregnant couple can begin to introduce positive concepts of parenting. Hospitalization and the postdelivery period are times of stress and role changes for all parents, especially for those who are a high risk for abusing. There are many things to learn such as diapering, breast- or bottle-feeding, or how to put the baby in a car seat. Parents also need to learn what to do when a baby cries and what to do when the baby will not stop crying. Care of the parent, such as an afternoon away from the child, should be included. For parents for whom it may be a hardship to pay a babysitter for an afternoon, other methods should be explored such as exchanging babysitting with a friend or joining a babysitting cooperative. The importance of touch, voice, and nurturing in the development of trust in the infant can be discussed. As children grow, there are opportunities for classes on child development, discipline, and development of skills. This can continue throughout the age span of the adolescent with the parent receiving help in how to deal with the teenager.

The perinatal period has been defined by Helfer (1987) as from 1 year before birth to 18–24 months after birth, and is a "window of opportunity" to strengthen the interaction of parents and child and thus decrease the danger of abuse. He suggests the following logic (Helfer, 1987, p. 567):

- Step 1: Child abuse and/or neglect occurs as a result of the breakdown in the interactional system between the caretaker (parent) and child.
- Step 2: Prevention of something bad usually requires enhancement of something good as a preceding event.
- Step 3: Teaching new parents the skill of communicating with their newly born has the potential of enhancing the interpersonal relationship or bond (something good).
- Step 4: An enhanced interpersonal relationship can lead to prevention of serious breakdown of the parent-child interaction and, in turn, lessen abuse, neglect, and sexual exploitation of one's children.

Parenting education is an important step in the prevention of abuse. Many communities, school districts, churches, and health departments have classes for parents. However, it is not uniformly available to parents from all socioeconomic groups.

Parenting education can also be done through extended visits from the community health nurse after the birth of a new child in a family. In a study by Olds et al. as reported by Dubowitz (1989), when a group of the highest-risk mothers (poor, unmarried teen mothers) were visited by a nurse for an extended period, the rate of child abuse was 4% compared with a rate of 19% for mothers who were not visited. Additional benefits were gained by the visited mothers; they showed greater use of community services, they had increased informal social support and improved dietary and smoking habits, and their pregnancies lasted longer and produced babies of higher birth weights.

To help alleviate the problem of abuse, greater emphasis must be put on prevention of abuse and not on just discovering abuse before the child is severely injured or killed.

Secondary prevention begins with the discovery that the child has suffered from dysfunctional parenting or has been injured. The community health nurse in the home or school may be the one to discover the injured child and institute the report to child protective or emergency services. It is necessary to help the parent understand that even though a report must be made, the nurse will remain available to the parent throughout the investigation and disposition of the case. The nurse can continue to support and educate the parent and help establish a positive parenting attitude.

Two areas of great concern are child care for working mothers and help for "latch key" children. A parent who is stressed in trying to balance work demands, home demands, and child care responsibilities needs day care for the children to provide safety, a richer environment for the child, and respite for the parent. Latch key children are home alone without supervision and have increased risk for abuse and neglect. The nurse can act as an advocate in the community to improve conditions for the working parent.

A crucial aspect of providing help and complying with medicolegal requirements is precise charting of the nurse's assessment when a child has been abused. Vague terms such as "apparently" or "appears" should not be used. The nurse should fully and completely record what she actually observes and refrain from providing opinions and interpretations. This is especially important because documentation may be used in court proceedings that may have direct bearing on the child's welfare.

Tertiary prevention deals with the very disturbed family and/or child. This may involve older children with any form of abuse, whether physical or sexual. Careful assessment of their needs and appropriate nursing care of their entire situation are essential.

The community health nurse may have a family referred by the court. The nurse may work with the parents while the child is out of the home in foster care following severe abuse and may provide ongoing care and supervision when a child is replaced with the family.

The nurse must be knowledgeable of support services within the community, including crisis lines, shelters, respite care, educational opportunities for parents, and public agencies that provide services. Parent support groups such as Parents Anonymous for individuals with parental stress or child abuse and Parents United for families dealing with sexual abuse are two such groups. Some groups offer support groups for the children. Sons and Daughters United is a group for children who have been sexually abused. Many of these groups are free and can be a great help to the parent and family in distress.

Tertiary prevention is important for children and adolescents who were sexually abused. These individuals may have problems that last into their adult life and do not go away unless treated. Many chronic problems resulting from sexual abuse respond to psychotherapy (Bachmann et al., 1988). Problems expressed by child sexual abuse victims are numerous and include anxiety, anger, attacks of hysteria, and somatic complaints such as headaches, abdominal distress, and concern with the genitourinary tract. Behaviorally, these individuals may have increased substance abuse, sexual deviance involving promiscuity, pregnancy, and prostitution. They may be truants or run away from home. Some are driven to self-mutilation (Bachmann et al., 1988).

Tertiary prevention may continue in the treatment of the adult woman who was sexually abused. Nurses who are dealing with gynecologic care of adult women and providing mental health nursing care may be particularly involved with patients who have a history of sexual abuse in their background. Depression is a common complaint, as are chronic complaints of sleep disorders. They often experience anxiety and low self-esteem. Self-destructive behavior and substance abuse may also be evident. Women who were abused often have chronic sexual problems involving fear of intimate relationships, dysfunctions of desire and arousal, and anorgasmia (Bachmann et al., 1988).

Problems of this magnitude need extensive treatment. The first step is discovery of the problem. It is here that nurses play an important role. Nurses must be knowledgeable, skillful, and caring in assessing their patients. A sense of trust must be established between the nurse and the patient. Nurses must be nonjudgmental and able to ask questions about abuse in a nonthreatening manner without expressing shock verbally or nonverbally at what they are told. It is these qualities that may lead a client to share a painful experience. After discovery of the problem, the patient should be referred to a mental health professional for long-term assistance. The nurse should remain available and in a supportive relationship with the patient.

Nurses' Role in Care of Abused Women

Campbell and Humphreys (1984) discuss primary prevention as involving intervention at a societal level, helping to change attitudes toward women. Women at risk must also be identified, and nursing care must be provided to both them and their potential abusers. Secondary prevention necessitates good case discovery for women who are in the beginning stages of the problem, and tertiary prevention is aimed at rehabilitation of a woman who has been severely beaten. Tertiary care may take place in shelters and/or mental health settings and may involve both physical and mental health care.

When dealing with an abused woman, the nurse should focus on the person first, not the problem. Accepting the woman as she is and developing a trusting relationship is important for the patient to confide in the nurse. Willingness to become involved and an ability to communicate and listen for both verbal and nonverbal cues are essential (Curry et al., 1988). The professional dealing with a battered woman must develop ways of asking difficult and perhaps embarrassing questions easily. Battering is violence, and violence is not allowable — it is a crime. Because it occurs within a family situation does not make it all right. Nurses must examine their own feelings so they can help uncover violence and reduce its effects on a battered woman. King and Ryan (1989) consider a primary goal of nursing intervention assisting the woman to reestablish a feeling of control and power in her life. It is crucial for the nurse to remain nonjudgmental and open to what the victim may tell her.

Assessment is facilitated if the woman is seen by herself. This sometimes presents a difficulty if the woman seeks treatment in the hospital and the man, if present, does not wish to leave her alone. It may require moving the patient to another area such as an examining room or the radiography department and giving a verifiable excuse to the husband that visitors are not allowed (Loraine, 1981).

Resources within the community should be made available to the patient. Bulletin boards in community health clinic waiting rooms can list telephone numbers of crisis lines and shelters. Nurses can carry cards in their pockets with referral numbers and give them to women about whom they are concerned to keep for reference. An exit plan is essential in providing comprehensive care;

it should be in the woman's hands before she leaves care. Table 20–6 is a sample exit plan used at an obstetric clinic when dealing with battered pregnant women. It could be made available to every woman receiving services to keep in case of emergency.

Long-term care is necessary for a battered woman. She can be helped to deal with the blame that is usually felt by asking her to describe the incidents that led to the abuse and helping her view them realistically. She should be asked to keep a log on a small calendar so she can see if the incidents of violence are increasing. The nurse should discuss what the client can do to prevent further violence (Helton, 1986). The nurse cannot solve the woman's problems, but the nurse can help her take responsibility for solving them. The woman must look at her situation in a realistic manner, express her anger, and work through depression. There

---

Table 20–6
Exit Plan for Battered Women

If you find that you or your children are in danger from your male partner, you must leave your home. If you decide to leave in anticipation of a battering incident or during or after one, advance planning can help.

Remember: If you feel a threat to your safety, get out of the situation even if you have not been able to plan ahead.

1. Pack changes of clothes for you and your children. Pack extra toilet articles, medicine, and an extra set of keys to the house and car. Ask a friend or neighbor to store the suitcase.
2. If possible, keep extra cash, your checkbook, and savings account book with a friend. You may need identification such as birth certificates, Social Security card, voter registration, utility bills, or driver's license to enroll your children in school or to arrange financial assistance.
3. Take something special for each child, such as a toy, book, or blanket.
4. Take any important financial records such as rent receipts or title to the car.
5. Know exactly where you could go—even in the middle of the night—and how to get there.

If you have been battered and are injured:
1. Go to any emergency department. If you are badly hurt, call an ambulance, the police, or a friend or relative.
2. Describe current and past battering incidents to the health care provider, especially if you are pregnant.
3. Get a copy of your medical record for any treatment you receive for injuries. It can help if the district attorney files charges for the assault.
4. If your physician prescribes medicine, ask for the name of the drug and ask why the physician wants you to take it. Be wary of tranquilizers; they may help you rest, but they will not solve your problem.

may be additional crises before she leaves the abusive situation that will require support (Curry et al., 1988). Maintaining contact with the individual and continuing support are essential for therapeutic nursing intervention. A feeling of acceptance by the nurse and support in the woman's ability to make decisions may also help raise her self-esteem.

Supportive, medicolegal, and safety considerations in provision of nursing care for the woman who has been abused are presented.

What To Do When You Suspect Abuse of a Woman

SUPPORTIVE CARE
  Interview her alone in a private setting.
  Establish a trusting relationship.
  Be interested.
  Take time to listen. Don't hurry.
  Ask her if she has been beaten.
  Ask her if it has happened before, how often and to what extent.
  Assure her that she is not alone.
  Help her set goals on what she has control over.

Medicolegal care
  Tell her that the abuse is against the law. She does not have to accept it; she has alternatives.
  Advise her how to make a police report.
  Carefully document your assessment.
  Make sure she has detailed medical documentation.
  Take photographs of her injuries.
  Give her a copy of the medical report.

Provision for safety
  Offer hospitalization if needed.
  Ask if she has a safe place to stay.
  Provide her with names and numbers of resources in her community.

Adapted from the Family Violence Project, unpublished data, San Francisco, District Attorney's Office, Hall of Justice, 1982.

Nurses' Role in Care of Abused Elderly

Many obstacles may be present for the nurse to overcome in assessing abusive situations in the elderly, including the reluctance to report abuse, the necessity for establishing a trusting relationship with the client, and ambiguous indications or lack of verifiable evidence. There are few clear indicators of elderly abuse. Simply differentiating the normal aging process from abuse may also be confusing for the nurse (Campbell and Humphrey, 1984).

An additional factor is that the client is an adult and as such should be able to control the client's affairs as much as the client is able. An adult should be able to live out life in the manner chosen freely and safely. Care should not overly restrict the individual's freedoms. Just as care is not forced on a battered woman, care should not be forced on an elderly adult. However, the elderly who because of senility cannot make informed choices may need similar protection, as would an abused child.

The focus of the nurse should be on the client and the client's needs. The needs of the family, community, and so on should not take precedence. The client should be allowed to make decisions for as long as the client can, even if the nurse does not agree that the decisions provide for safety.

In all care of the elderly, trust in the caregiver is an important part of treatment. A single nurse working with the client over a long period of time can promote the most favorable climate for improved care. It takes time to gain the client's confidence and build a trusting relationship. The nurse should also work with all family members or caregivers who provide care for the elderly client and help promote healthier relationships. Stress is usually a contributing factor to abuse. Helping the caregiver deal with their stress by finding respite care, a home health aide, or counseling may help. Most elderly victims live with the offender and are dependent on them; therefore, to help the victim, the nurse must also help the offender deal with the stresses that are causing or contributing to the abuse. The caregiver may also have problems such as mental illness or drug or alcohol abuse. Until these problems are dealt with, as long as the elderly person remains in the home, the abuse will most likely continue.

The right to privacy should be respected, as should confidentiality. However, in states where there is a mandatory reporting law for elder abuse, the nurse *must* comply with the law. For example, under the reporting law in California, the nurse must report cases of physical abuse, but the victim may withdraw consent to investigation or provision of services occurring as a consequence.

As the elderly population increases, more research is necessary to develop appropriate care.

Legal Responsibilities

CHILD ABUSE

The nurse has a legal responsibility in all states to report a case of suspected child abuse to the authorities named in the law. Confidentiality rules do not apply but are superseded by the legal duty to report. Although the laws may change in each state as to the specifics, all states set down the time limit by which time a report must be made without penalty. For example, in the state of California, a telephone report must be made immediately upon *suspicion or knowledge* and a written report must be made within 36 hours. Failure to comply can cause the nurse to be held civilly or criminally liable. In addition, punishment can be a fine of $1,000 or a maximum of 6 months in jail.

Each nurse should become familiar with the law in the state in which the nurse practices. If a nurse is unfamiliar with the law, a copy of the law can be requested from a state legislator. The local child protective division of the social service department is another resource for legal responsibility guidelines. The nurse could also call the local district attorney's office for interpretation of the law in that state.

California has been a pioneer in reporting legislation. As of January 1, 1985, any new employee of an agency who is legally mandated to report must sign a form stating knowledge of the reporting requirements and willingness to comply with the law.

SPOUSE ABUSE

To date, there is no mandatory law for reporting wife or husband abuse.

ELDERLY ABUSE

Forty-two states have mandatory reporting laws for reporting abuse of the elderly. Seven states advocate voluntary reporting—New York, Pennsylvania, Illinois, Wisconsin, Colorado, North Dakota, and South Dakota. New Jersey has no law dealing with reporting of abuse of the elderly (Tatara, 1990).

In states with less-than-optimum laws for reporting abuse, the nurse can act as an advocate for abuse victims lobbying vigorously for strengthening of the law.

APPLICATION OF THE NURSING PROCESS

There are many nursing diagnoses that can be related to the victim of abuse. Most of the diagnoses are psychologically oriented and deal with feelings and coping abilities. Physically oriented diagnoses will necessarily vary with the type of injury.

Psychologically and Physically Oriented Nursing Diagnoses for Victims of Violence

Psychologically Oriented
  Anxiety
  Family coping, disabling
  Family process, alteration in
  Hopelessness
  Knowledge deficit
  Powerlessness
  Posttrauma response
  Social isolation
  Thought processes, alteration in
  Violence, potential for

Physically Oriented
  Injury, potential for
  Impairment of skin integrity

C a s e
S t u d y

A 7.5-pound male infant was born to a 35-year-old mother. This was her second child; her other child was a 10-year-old daughter. The mother was noted by her obstetrician to be addicted to heroin and methadone; however, she denied use of any drugs during the latter part of her pregnancy. As a routine procedure, a toxicology screen was performed on the baby's urine immediately after birth. The report returned positive for heroin and cocaine.

An immediate social services referral was made, the baby was moved to a step-up nursery, and a police hold was placed on the infant. During the hospitalization, the mother displayed appropriate care and concern for her son, who began showing signs of severe withdrawal. The mother was devastated when she could not take her baby home. She continued to make daily visits to the nursery after discharge, accompanied by her husband or another family member.

One evening, she arrived with her husband and her daughter at dinner time. The family stopped in the cafeteria and brought several trays of food with them when they came to the nursery. They took the food into the room where discharged parents could take their newborns for visits. Their demeanor was appropriate, and the mother came into the nursery, changed her baby, and got a bottle for him. Shortly thereafter, she returned to the nursery carrying the baby and almost fell when she attempted to sit down in a rocking chair. The baby was placed back in the crib by the nurse, and the mother was escorted back to her family. The nurse observed the 10-year-old eating food from her tray and the parents' trays piled high with untouched food. The father was standing facing the wall, leaning against it, and rocking back and forth.

The mother was helped into a chair, and the nurse immediately called the social worker on call. When the social worker arrived and interviewed the mother, she admitted that they had taken cocaine after they had arrived at the hospital. The daughter reported to the social worker that she could get her parents home and indeed had done so many times. The parents were escorted from the hospital accompanied by their daughter. On the next day, Children's Protective Services was contacted about the family situation, in particular regarding the daughter. The newborn was temporarily placed in a foster home.

Assessment

The public health nurse's assessment and plans are based on the criteria shown in Table 20–2 for physical and behavioral indicators of physical or emotional violence or maltreatment. Figure 20–4 provides a framework for assessing individual, family, and community factors that may be present in an abuse situation. Assessment is validated with the family, and goals and interventions are mutually determined with the family.

Diagnosis

Individual

- Ineffective individual coping in care of children related to dependence/addiction to drugs
- Alteration in parenting, inability to provide safe care related to dependence/addiction to drugs
- Alteration of thought processes, inability to make competent decisions related to physiological changes due to drug intake
- Noncompliance to prohibition of drug use related to dependence/addiction

Family

- Ineffective/disabling family coping in care of children related to both parents' dependence/addiction to drugs
- Alteration in family process, inability to meet physical, emotional, and security needs of family members related to dependence/addiction of both parents to drugs

Community

- Need for public authority involvement to guarantee safety of the family's children
- Need for foster home to provide for care and welfare of the family's children
- Need for diagnosis, drug detoxification, and drug follow-up programs for both parents
- Need for follow-up care of family to assure safety of children when they are returned to parents' care

Planning

Individual

Short-term Goal

- Mother will acknowledge her dependence on drugs and will identify a drug treatment program in the city that is available to provide care to her

Long-term Goal

- The mother will enter a drug detoxification program

Family

Short-term Goal

- Both parents will acknowledge their dependence upon drugs and will identify a drug treatment program in the city that is available to provide care

Long-term Goal

- The children will be reunited with their family in their own home

Community

Short-term Goal

- A Child Protective Service case worker will open a file on the family and will begin a family evaluation

Long-term Goal

- Protective services for children will be maintained in the community through the combined efforts of local, state, and federal planning bodies
- The community will provide drug detoxification programs and will publicize their availability to those who need the service

Intervention

Interventions will be based on the components of a comprehensive program to reduce family violence for individuals, families, and the community. The public health nurse's assessment, nursing diagnosis, and goals will determine if primary, secondary, or tertiary interventions are needed.

Evaluation

Some examples of evaluation criteria based on the goals are:

- Ability to verbalize inability to care for children due to drug dependence
- Ability to identify options for drug treatment
- Ability to recognize and use community programs as necessary

SUMMARY

Violence occurs too commonly in our society. Not only has violence been used to solve problems since the beginning of our country's history, but violence is also used within the home to deal with stress and frustration.

Violence can be a generational problem. If it is not stopped, it may continue into the next generation. It is incredibly costly in terms of its toll on victims as well as on perpetrators. This self-perpetuating cycle causes indescribable pain to children, women, and elderly, who are the primary victims. And the abuser also is a victim. The ulti-mate victim is society, who must care for the results of the violent acts.

Nurses are involved in situations in which they can begin to change the pattern. Commitment to caring about the problem is a first step. Teaching alternate methods of dealing with stress, improved parenting relationships, and considerate care of the elderly is the beginning of primary prevention. If enough commitment is given to primary prevention, eventually, less and less care will have to be given to secondary and tertiary prevention. Ultimately, the generational cycle will be broken, and society as a whole will be stronger and more caring.

Learning Activities

1. Determine your professional responsibilities in your state by securing a copy of or reviewing the reporting laws for child abuse, battering of women, spousal rape, and abuse of the elderly.

2. Using the telephone book, find three community agencies (public or private) in your city that provide help in child abuse, woman abuse, and elderly abuse situations. Make a list of the telephone numbers to keep in the pocket of your uniform.

3. Call a child abuse warm line and/or hot line in your community and ask them what services they provide.

4. Call a battered women's shelter and determine the procedure for securing shelter placement for a battered woman and her children.

5. Visit a respite center for the elderly and observe the clients and the activities that are provided for them. What behaviors do you observe that would contribute to stress in the caretaker?

6. Follow the newspapers for 1 month and clip articles that deal with abuse of children, men, women, and elderly. Determine how many individuals were killed during that period in incidents of family violence.

REFERENCES

Augoustinos, M.: Developmental effects of child abuse: Recent findings. Child Abuse Neglect *11*;15–27, 1987.

Bachmann, G., Moeller, T., and Benett, J.: Childhood sexual abuse and the consequences in adult women. Obstet. Gynecol. *71*;631–642, 1988.

Bell, J.: Rescuing the battered wife. Hum. Behav. *6*;16–23, 1977.

Bloom, J. S., Ansell, P., and Bloom, M.: Detecting elder abuse: A guide for physicians. Geriatrics *44*;40–56, 1989.

Bolton, F., Jr.: When Bonding Fails. Beverly Hills, California, Sage Publications, 1983.

Brendtro, M., and Bowker, L.: Battered women: How nurses can help. Issues Mental Health Nurs. *10*;169–180, 1989.

Bullock, L., and McFarlane, J.: Birth-weight/battering connection. Am. J. Nurs. *89*;1153–1155, 1989.

Bullock, L., McFarlane, J., Bateman, L., and Miller, V.: The prevalence and characteristics of battered women in a primary care setting. Nurse Pract. *11*;47–54, 1989.

Butler, R.: Alert physicians can break the elder abuse cycle. Geriatrics *44*;11, 1989.

Campbell, J.: Women's responses to sexual abuse in intimate relationships. Health Care Women Int. *10*;335–346, 1989.

Campbell, J., and Alford, P.: The dark consequences of marital rape. Am. J. Nurs. *89*;946–949, 1989.

Campbell, J., and Humphreys, J.: Nursing Care of Victims of Family Violence. Reston, Virginia, Reston Publishing, 1984.

Carlton, L.: Elder Abuse Prevention Protocols. San Francisco, San Francisco Elder Abuse Prevention Task Force, 1983.

Chez, R. A.: Woman battering. Am. J. Obstet. Gynecol. *158*;1–4, 1988.

Commission on the Enforcement of Child Abuse Laws: Final Report. Sacramento, California, Office of the Attorney General California Department of Justice, 1985.

Council on Scientific Affairs: Elder abuse and neglect. J. A. M. A. *257*;966–967, 1987.

Curry, L., Colvin, L., and Lancaster, J.: Breaking the cycle of family abuse. Am. J. Nurs. *88*;1189–1190, 1988.

Daro, D.: Confronting Child Abuse. New York, The Free Press, 1988.

DelVecchio, R.: Childhood victims of crack — a S.F. crisis. *San Francisco Chronicle,* October 12, 1989, p. A11.

DeMause, L.: Our forebears made childhood a nightmare. Psych. Today *9*;85–86, 1975.

Dubowitz, H.: Prevention of child maltreatment: What is known. Pediatrics *83*;570–577, 1989.

Fulmer, T., and Wetle, T.: Elder abuse screening and intervention. Nurse Pract. *11*;33–38, 1986.

Gelles, R., and Straus, M.: Is violence toward children increasing? J. Interpersonal Violence *2*;212–222, 1987.

Goetting, A.: Patterns of homicide among women. J. Interpersonal Violence *3*;3–20, 1988.

Godkin, M., Wolf, R., and Pillemer, K.: A case-comparison analysis of elder abuse and neglect. Int. J. Aging Hum. Dev. *28*;207–225, 1989.

Helfer, R.: The perinatal period, a window of opportunity for enhancing parent-infant communication: An approach to prevention. Child Abuse Neglect *11*;565–579, 1987.

Helton, A., McFarlane, J., and Anderson, E.: Battered and pregnant: A prevalence study. Am. J. Public Health *77*; 1337–1339, 1987.

Hiraki, S., and Grambs, M.: Volunteer Manual on Marital Violence, 1990. (Available from Battered Women's Alternatives, Pacheco, California.)

House Subcommittee on Elderly Health and Long-Term Care: Elder Abuse: A Decade of Shame and Inaction. Washington, D.C., U.S. Government Printing Office, Committee publication No. 101-752, April 1990.

Johnson, S. H.: High-Risk Parenting. Philadelphia, J. B. Lippincott, 1979.

Jones, J., Dougherty, J., Scheble, D., and Cunningham, W.: Emergency department protocol for the diagnosis and evaluation of geriatric abuse. Ann. Emerg. Med. *17*;1006–1015, 1988.

Kempe, C. H.: An autobiography of violence. Child Abuse Neglect *2*;139–149, 1978.

Kempe, C., and Helfer, R. E.: Helping the Battered Child and His Family. Philadelphia, J. B. Lippincott, 1972.

King, M. C., and Ryan, J.: Abused women: Dispelling myths and encouraging intervention. Nurse Pract. *14*;47–58, 1989.

Krug, R.: Adult male report of childhood sexual abuse by mothers: Case descriptions, motivations and long-term consequences. Child Abuse Neglect *13*;111–119, 1989.

Langan, P., and Innes, C.: Crime and Justice Facts, 1985. Rockville, Maryland, Justice Statistics Clearing House, 1986.

Loraine, K.: Battered women: The ways you can help. RN *44*;23–28, 1981.

McLeer, S., Anwar, R., Herman, S., and Maquiling, K.: Education is not enough: A systems failure in protecting battered women. Ann. Emerg. Med. *18*;651–653, 1989.

Mehta, P., and Dandra, L.: The battered woman. Am. Family Physician *37*;193–199, 1988.

Mercy, J., and Saltzman, L.: Fatal violence among spouses in the United States, 1976—1985. Am. J. Public Health *79*;595–599, 1989.

Mittleman, R., Mittleman, H., and Wetli, C.: What child abuse really looks like. Am. J. Nurs. *87*;1185–1188, 1987.

National Center on Child Abuse Prevention Research: Current Trends in Child Abuse Reporting and Fatalities: The Results of the 1989 Annual Fifty State Survey. Working paper No. 808. Chicago, Illinois, March 1990.

Nornhold, P.: 90 Predictions for the 90's. Nursing 90 *20*;40, 1990.

Payne, J., Downs, S., and Newman, K.: Helping the abused woman. Nursing 86 *16*;53, 1986.

Phillips, L.: Abuse and neglect of the frail elderly at home: An exploration of theoretical relationships. J. Adv. Nurs. *8*;379–392, 1983.

Raymond, C.: Campaign alerts physicians to identify, assist victims of domestic violence. J. A. M. A. *261*;963–964, 1989.

Sandgrund, A., Gaines, R. W., and Green, A. H.: Child abuse and mental retardation: A problem of cause and effect. Am. J. Mental Deficiency *79*;327–330, 1974.

Straus, M.: National Survey of Domestic Violence: Some Preliminary Findings and Implications for Future Research. Prepared for hearings on Research Into Domestic Violence, U.S. House of Representatives, Subcommittee on Domestic and International Scientific Planning, Analysis and Cooperation, February 14, 1978.

The Random House College Dictionary. New York, Random House, 1982.

Timrots, A., and Rand, M.: Violent crime by strangers and nonstrangers (special report). Bur. Justice Stat. NCJ-103702. Washington, D.C., U.S. Government Printing Office, 1987, pp. 1–7.

U.S. Department of Commerce, Bureau of the Census: Statistical Abstract of the United States. Washington, D.C., U.S. Government Printing Office, 1989.

U.S. Department of Justice, Federal Bureau of Investigation: 1988 Uniform Crime Reports for the United States. Washington, D.C., U.S. Government Printing Office, 1989.

Walker, L. E. The Battered Woman. New York, Harper & Row, 1979.

CHAPTER 21

Mental Health

Upon completion of this chapter, the reader will be able to:

1. Describe the concept of aggregate mental health.

2. Describe how the nursing process is applied to promote the mental health of individuals and families in the community.

Mary E. Allen

This chapter will explore the concept of aggregate mental health as it relates to individuals and families in the community. The components of mental health for individuals include the absence of mental disease, normality of behavior, adjustment to environment, unity of personality, and correct perception of reality (Jahoda, 1955). Individuals do not function as isolated beings in this society; each individual is part of a network. That network may be a family or some other group to which the individual belongs (e.g., a group of single or widowed senior citizens who live in a common dwelling). Networks create systems. Family and group systems network through lines of communication, human bonds, and, as subsystems of communities, through societal norms.

When individuals experience mental illness, abnormal behavior, environmental maladjustment, disunity of personality, and altered perceptions of reality, the family or group to which the individual belongs is also affected. In many cases, the family or group may even enhance or intensify individual experiences. For example, alcoholism has been referred to as a family disease even though there may be only one alcoholic family member. The effects of alcoholism on a community manifest themselves through the noncontributions of the alcoholic to society as well as through the personally detrimental behaviors exhibited by the codependent significant others. For example, the adult children of alcoholics can suffer the influence of growing up in a codependent family system for generations to come. It is important in situations of this type that the nurse plan interventions with emphases on primary, secondary, and tertiary prevention. Primary prevention is implemented before the onset of an illness, with secondary prevention more appropriately being used after the onset of a particular illness. The focus of tertiary prevention is more rehabilitative in nature.

Families and other groups within a given community system collectively form an aggregate. *Aggregate mental health* may be defined as the degree to which families and groups contribute to enhance or intensify individual interaction along the mental health/mental illness continuum within a given environment.

COMMUNITY MENTAL HEALTH MOVEMENT

Historical Evolution

In general, the practice of psychiatry can be viewed in terms of three phases. The first phase of psychiatry, in which it is viewed as an independent science, began near the end of the 18th century and heralded a new empathic attitude toward mental illness. The second phase began approximately 100 years later as a result of the development of psychoanalysis by Sigmund Freud. The third phase hallmarked the coming of community psychiatry (Bellak, 1964). Community psychiatry differs from hospital-based psychiatry in that the emphasis is on practice in the community rather than treatment in institutional settings, and it acknowledges the importance of offering services within the context of community values, norms, and agencies.

Before 1960, the majority of mentally ill persons received treatment in isolation from their home communities. Having to travel great distances for treatment contributed to the difficulty of achieving mental health promotion and maintenance. The

---

History of Community Mental Health Movement
1963 — Funding of Community Mental Health Centers (CMHC) program through National Institute of Mental Health
1963 — CMHC Construction Act provided establishment of centers to replace custodial mental institutions
1975 — CMHC amendments increased the number of essential services from five to 12
1978 — Report of task panel on CMHC's assessment
1980 — Community Mental Health Systems Act
1981 — Omnibus Budget Reconciliation Act and repeal of Community Mental Health Systems Act

---

establishment of the Community Mental Health Centers Program of the National Institute of Mental Health (NIMH) was an attempt to alleviate some of these problems. The passing of appropriate legislation was the next step.

Legislation

A number of political forces contributed to the Community Mental Health Centers Construction Act of 1963. There was public concern about the quality of mental health care; leadership of mental health agencies was supportive of public concern; and a national mental health establishment was being maintained through federal fiscal support (Foley, 1975). The Community Mental Health Centers Amendments of 1975 and the Community Mental Health Centers Construction Act of 1963 provided for the establishment of community-based therapeutic centers to replace custodial mental institutions. Figure 21–1 summarizes these important events and legislation (Dowell and Ciarlo, 1983).

The NIMH identified the essential elements of comprehensive community mental health services:

- Inpatient services
- Partial hospitalization or at least day care service
- Outpatient services
- Emergency services provided on a 24-hour-a-day basis and available within at least one of the three services listed previously
- Consultation and educational services available to community agencies and professionals

Community Mental Health Events and Legislation

1963	Funding of Community Mental Health Centers (CMHCs) through the National Institute of Mental Health
1963	CMHC Construction Act provided establishment centers to replace custodial mental institutions
1975	CMHC amendments increased the number of essential services from 5 to 12

Figure 21–1
Community mental health events and legislation.

The goals of community mental health as a concept have been questioned (Amesbury, 1983; Lowery and Janulis, 1983). Financial cutbacks have impeded the development of the concept (Goplerud et al., 1983) with resultant program disintegration (Hagar and Kincheloe, 1983). Several questions raised about the goals of community mental health relate to implementation of the concept. For example, who is the patient? Who is the therapist? What is the therapeutic process? What is the goal? What is the theory? What is the role? However, the answers to many of these questions will depend on whether the patient is an individual, family, or aggregate; profession of the therapist; adopted school of thought for therapy; and existence of a prevention, promotion, or maintenance goal. Program disintegration results when these questions are not adequately addressed by the treatment team of the community mental health center. Continuity of care is then lost, and the patient suffers. Figure 21–2 delineates nine goals that have been used as the basis for organizing information about community mental health centers (Dowell and Ciarlo, 1983).

Who Pays for Community Mental Health Centers?
Federal block grants

- **Alcohol**
- **Drug abuse**
- **Mental health services**

Fee for service
State sources of funding

Of great importance is the evaluation of community mental health program effectiveness (Dowell, 1983). Particularly relevant to evaluation for the nurse working in the area of community mental health are discussions of intervention effectiveness (Brooker, 1984), role function, (Mereness, 1983) and emerging trends, issues, and problems of community psychiatric nurses (Leininger, 1983).

The concept of community mental health as operationalized by nurses has gained some support as evidenced by accounts of family support being offered in the home (East et al., 1983; Fagin, 1970)

Goals of Community Mental Health

1. Increase the range and quantity of public mental health services.

2. Make services equally available and accessible to all.

3. Provide services in relation to the existing needs in the community.

4. Decrease state hospital admissions and residents.

5. Maximize citizen participation in community programs.

6. Prevent development of mental disorders.

7. Coordinate mental health–related services in the catchment area.

8. Provide services as efficiently as possible.

9. Provide services that reduce suffering and increase personal functioning.

Figure 21–2
Goals of community mental health.

along with consultation services (Haylett and Rapport, 1964). There are reports of work with more specific populations such as the mentally handicapped (Cook, 1984) and schizophrenics (McGill et al., 1983).

Description of Deinstitutionalization

- Based on Humanitarian Philosophy
- Rejection of custodial hospital-based care
- Committment to community-based care
- Lowered costs to hospital
- Higher costs to communities not prepared for homeless chronically mentally ill

---

ASSESSMENT OF AGGREGATE MENTAL HEALTH

An ideal conceptual framework for the assessment of aggregate mental health includes components reflecting the application of systems theory, the nursing process, and a theoretical approach for the analysis of groups and families. These components provide the groundwork for a thorough assessment of the degree to which subsystems of families and groups contribute to enhance or intensify individual interaction along the mental health/illness continuum within a given environment, such as a catchment or service area.

Characteristics of a Catchment Area

- Geographically circumscribed
- One or more communities
- System of services for defined population
- Community-based mental health services

Nursing Process

The nurse uses the tools of the nursing process; assessment, nursing diagnosis, planning, intervention, and evaluation in her work with aggregates. The application of the nursing process is facilitated by good observational skills and the use of therapeutic communication techniques. Work with aggregates necessitates an ability to look beyond the individual client and consider the family and/or groups of which that person is a member, the client's environment, and the society as a whole. The nursing process serves as the organizing framework. The nurse's beliefs about humankind, society, nursing, mental health, and the environment in addition to the application of existing relevant theoretical frameworks serve as a guide for the placement of substantive material within the organizing framework.

Work with aggregates is facilitated by the application of a theory of group development. Direct patient care of individuals who are members of families and groups involves interaction in small groups. The usual size of a small group ranges from two to 10 members (Shaw, 1971). Small groups tend to be more predictable than large groups. To aid in the nurse's understanding of all groups, a wide variety of theoretical perspectives may be applied. Among the most common approaches to the analysis of groups are the psychoanalytical approaches, focusing on unconscious processes in group behavior; symbolic interactionism, focusing on meaning and identity in group behavior; systems analysis, examining exchange and equilibrium in group behavior; and theories that focus on temporal relationships in group behavior (Sampson and Marthas, 1977). A more eclectic theoretical approach that uses several of the common approaches to group analysis may be used to achieve the desired outcomes.

Role of the Community Mental Health Nurse

The role of the community mental health nurse working with aggregates may be defined in terms of educator, practitioner, and coordinator of services. As *educator,* the nurse instructs individuals, families, and/or groups through community organization about various aspects of preventive mental health, treatment of mental illness, and community management of individuals who are mentally ill yet function in the community. For example, the management of chronically mentally ill persons may cause disequilibrium for a particular community system. Providing education programs on the causes, symptoms, and treatment for chronicity may serve to dispel myths about this population. In addition, group and family education provides a ready support network for exchange of ideas related to disease management and an arena for the ventilation of shared feelings about chronicity and its impact on group and family networks.

As *practitioner,* the nurse works directly with individuals, groups, and families through the formation of a therapeutic relationship. For the master's prepared advanced practitioner, provision of individual, group, and family therapy facilitates the mental health of aggregates by collaborative identification of those dynamics that either contribute to, intensify, or enhance the individual's experience with the environment and the mental health/illness continuum.

The following list represents examples of reasons for referral to community mental health nurses:

- Discharge follow-up
- Assessment
- Drug monitoring
- Crisis intervention
- Parent education
- Preventive work

As a *coordinator* of services, the community mental health nurse not only functions as a referral source but also makes referrals to the following groups of professionals:

- Social work
- Psychology
- Psychiatry
- Occupational therapy
- Physical therapy
- Speech therapy
- Health departments

Mental illness may be accompanied by a wide variety of related health problems. As one of the few professionals who visits clients in community settings, such as the home or a halfway house, the nurse is in an excellent position to assess the physical and psychosocial status of the client and the environment.

U.S. Population of Chronically Mentally Ill
FROM 30% to 40% of all homeless people are chronically mentally ill.
An estimated 3 million homeless people are chronically mentally ill.

From Bawden, E. L.: Reaching Out to the Chronically Mentally Ill Homeless. J. Psychosocial Nurs. 28;6–13, 1990; and Hui, E., and Knecht, R.: Homeless teenagers on New York City streets. Imprint 38;55,57, 1991.

The Concept of Half-Way Houses
Congregate living benefits
Nonmedical provision of food, shelter, and limited personal care
Synonymous with:

- Residential care facility
- Board and care

- ● Community care homes
- ● Personal care homes
- ● Domiciliary homes
- ● Sheltered care facility
- ● Adult foster care
- ● Family homes
- ● Continuing care facilities
- ● Supervisory care homes
- ● Adult congregate living facilities

Adapted from Ross, V.: Protective living for the vulnerable. Geriatr. Nurs. 9;330–333, 1988.

Tools of Assessment

Commonly identified phases of any therapeutic relationship are initial or orientation, working, and termination. At the initial phase, the client and nurse get to know each other. An assessment is made to identify the needs of the client, and a contract is formulated to identify the responsibilities of both nurse and client in achieving the desired goals. At this stage, the nursing diagnosis reflects the mutually identified problems and needs of the client, whether individual, family, group, or community.

During the working phase, the client and nurse may actively become involved in the following activities:

- ● Identifying systemic patterns of behavior that are causing disequilibrium
- ● Identifying intrapersonal, interpersonal, and other system components interactions that may be detrimental to mental health
- ● Exploring ways to modify dysfunctional behavioral and environmental patterns
- ● Testing new and modified patterns for effectiveness
- ● Identifying problematic client-nurse-system boundary issues.

Termination is the final phase of the therapeutic relationship. At the beginning of a relationship, termination is discussed in terms of the length of time the nurse plans to work with the client on the formulated contract. Ideally, time boundaries should be built into therapeutic contracts through long- and short-term goal statements. During the termination phase, the nurse and client will summarize the outcomes of the relationship. The extent of goal achievement will be explored, and plans for continuity of care will be identified.

Boundary issues that may be problematic in therapeutic relationships can stem from excessive dependency on the part of the client or nurse, ineffective communication patterns, role ambiguity on the part of the client or nurse, and resistance to change.

C a s e
S t u d y

Application of the Nursing Process

John Davis is a 50-year-old white man who has been hospitalized in state mental institutions nine times in the last 30 years. Schizophrenia was the diagnosis each time he was admitted. He is single and presently lives with his 75-year-old widowed mother, Ann Davis, and her 60-year-old sister, Jane Capel. John has functioned adequately since his last hospital discharge 1 year ago. He takes his medication as prescribed, and his behavior may be described as manageable with brief periods of withdrawal. Ms. Capel works during the day as a bookkeeper and cooks meals in the evening for Mr. Davis and Mrs. Davis. In the past, Mrs. Davis has performed activities of daily living to a satisfactory degree. However, her eyesight has started to diminish, and she has experienced a slight hearing loss and periods of limited mobility related to an arthritic condition.

Ms. Capel has requested the assistance of the local public health department for two reasons. First, Mr. Davis has stopped taking his medication, stating, "I am cured." Since that time, he has begun to exhibit hallucinatory behavior, decreased ability to communicate effectively, and more prolonged periods of withdrawal. Mrs. Davis has been recently diagnosed as having Alzheimer's disease and is progressively more forgetful and disoriented, with diminished ability to perform the activities of daily living she once handled adequately.

The neighbors have been complaining to Ms. Capel when she comes home from work that Mrs. Davis' behavior is "strange," and they express the fear that Mr. Davis is becoming "sick" again. The neighbors avoid Ms. Capel except when they are complaining. She has started to feel less in control of the situation and has more frequent periods of anxiety and depression. She had hopes of an early retirement but now feels that is no longer possible given the situation of her family.

The local public health agency plans to send a professional nurse to visit this family. A student nurse will accompany the community mental health nurse.

Assessment

Assessment of aggregates in community mental health first involves identification of the community systems that comprise that aggregate and the boundaries of those systems. The boundaries may be cultural, ethnic, geographical, socioeconomic, or religious. A community study can assist the nurse in assessing a particular community system and the degree of interaction with other systems. When examining this case, questions related to identification of the following areas should be addressed:

Mental Health/Illness Problems Within the Community

- How is mental health defined by the family and members of the community?
- How is mental illness defined by the family and members of the community?
- Are people with psychiatric or mental health problems rejected or accepted by the community?
- How is rejection and/or acceptance exhibited by the community?
- Is the family labeled as abnormal or deviant by the community?
- What political or socioeconomic views support the acceptance or rejection of the family labeled as abnormal or deviant?
- What is the influence of culture, ethnicity, religion, and socioeconomic status on the prevailing definition of mental health or illness in terms of normality, adjustment to environment, unity of personality, and perception of reality?

Diverse Perspectives

- How do the subsystems of consumers, health care professionals, other professionals, government officials, law enforcement groups, business owners, and civic groups describe this family within the context of community?

Resources and Contributions of Various Groups

- What are the characteristics of the community environment?
- What age, sex, race, and family groupings are represented?
- To what degree are space and territoriality issues for the community?
- What is the relationship among income, occupational, and educational level groupings; strengths and concerns; and resulting mental health and illness?
- What community resources exist for this family, and where are they located?

Weaknesses or Neglected Areas

- How are family problems solved, and by whom?
- What is the family's decision-making process?
- Do all individuals in the family have a mechanism for expressing concerns?
- How effective is the mechanism?

Possible Points of Intervention

- How are nurses received by the family?
- If change is warranted, to what degree does the family system resist change?
- What groundwork must be laid before change can occur?
- Who are the power brokers within the family?
- Will power, tradition, or norms be affected by change?
- Who will benefit or suffer most from the change?

Evaluation of Intervention Effectiveness

- To what extent were long- and short-term goals met?
- Have problematic and dysfunctional patterns within the family system changed as a result of nursing intervention?
- To what extent did collaboration with other health professionals take place?
- Was a professional relationship maintained within ethical and legal boundaries?
- What is the longitudinal effectiveness of the nursing intervention?

When deciding whom to assess, the nurse may choose a *deductive* approach. When initially introduced to a community system with community as client, the nurse will want to use an approach to assessment starting with the more global concept of community working toward the individuals, families, and groups that make up that community. This deductive approach would start with a community study with the end result, for example, being a mental health prevention education program. A program of this type could lead to the identification of groups at high risk for mental illness, families in crisis, or individuals having difficulty coping with activities of daily living.

With an *inductive* approach, the nurse is introduced to the community system through work with an individual as client. The individual is the identified person within whom the problem is located. Assessment of the individual client will necessitate identification of the family, groups, and community to which the person belongs and subsequent assessment of those components.

In the case study, an inductive approach would be most appropriate. As identified patients, Mr. Davis is at greatest immediate risk, followed by Mrs. Davis. Ms. Capel is at risk as a consequence of her caregiver role and will also require some immediate attention to prevent the downward spiraling of her physical and mental health.

Diagnosis

Aggregate Versus Individual Diagnoses Nursing diagnosis is the identification of the actual or potential human responses to illness and factors that maintain the responses. Nursing diagnoses are not always illness oriented and, in the absence of illness, may be used to identify client strengths or positive responses to the human condition and the factors that maintain those responses.

Nursing diagnoses for more than one individual, such as a family, group, community, and aggregate, may be content-level or process-level nursing diagnoses. Content-level nursing diagnoses arise from a first-level assessment of the family, group, community, and aggregate and are a direct or indirect result of the initial assessment of individual content and subsequent determination of its meaning for the system components. Process-level nursing diagnoses arise from a second-level assessment of the system components and reflect the more abstract and dynamic responses of the family, group, community, or aggregate to process.

Examples of Aggregate Diagnosis

I. Case Study nursing diagnosis
  A. Individual nursing diagnosis—content level
    1. Decreased ability to perform activities of daily living related to self-discontinuance of antipsychotic medication secondary to schizophrenia (Mr. Davis)
    2. Decreased ability to perform activities of daily living related to mental confusion secondary to Alzheimer's disease (Mrs. Davis)
    3. Decreased ability to cope related to feelings of helplessness and hopelessness (Ms. Capel)
  B. Family nursing diagnosis
    1. Content level—decreased ability to perform shared activities of daily living related to uncontrolled disease processes
    2. Process level—potential family crises related to decreased equilibrium
  C. Community nursing diagnosis
    1. Content level—lack of understanding related to inadequate information about schizophrenia and Alzheimer's disease
  D. Aggregate nursing diagnosis
    1. Content level—lack of systematic programs for chronic populations related to inadequate planning among community systems and lack of funds

Through the process of induction, a diagnosis is made for each system component, culminating in an aggregate diagnosis. Note that the content-level diagnoses specially relate to the individual content of self-medication for schizophrenia, recently diagnosed Alzheimer's disease, and loss of personal control. The process-level diagnosis is more conceptually abstract and dynamic.

Planning Mental Health Promotion Activities

Mutual Goal Setting Mutuality in goal setting through collaboration with the agent and clientele is extremely important. The needs of the clientele must be clearly identified before formulation of nursing diagnoses and development of long- and short-term goals. The therapeutic relationship with clients is initiated during the contracting phase. If mutuality is built in early in the relationship, a good base will have been provided for the working and termination phases. No matter how confused, chaotic, or dysfunctional a family or group may appear, the individuals in those subsystems must be allowed to share in developing the plan of care.

In the case study, after individual and family diagnoses are validated with family members, examples of long- and short-term goals are as follows:

Individual

Short-term Goals

- Mr. Davis will adhere to prescribed medication regimen as evidenced by administering the correct drug by the correct route at the correct time
- Mr. Davis will verbalize the importance of taking prescribed medication to control symptoms of schizophrenia
- Mrs. Davis will maintain her current level of mental functioning in the areas of memory, orientation, concentration and judgment appropriate for the current stage of Alzheimer's disease
- Ms. Capel will identify ways to decrease her feelings of anxiety when they occur
- Ms. Capel will identify at least three ways to control impending feelings of depression

Long-term Goals

- Mr. Davis will have increased ability to perform activities of daily living as evidenced by grooming self, clearly communicating thought, and fewer periods of physical isolation
- Mrs. Davis will perform activities of daily living as evidenced by engaging in activities at her optimum level of functioning which are appropriate for the current stage of Alzheimer's disease

- Ms. Capel will have increased ability to cope as evidenced by verbalizing feelings of being more in control, and identifying retirement options

Family

Short-term Goals

- Family will acknowledge existence of failing health for several of its members
- Family will identify specific ways to cope with chronic disease
- Maintain a state of family equilibrium as evidenced by recognition and utilization of system support services as necessary

Long-term Goals

- The family will exhibit an increased ability to perform shared activities of daily living as evidenced by an ability to discuss present roles and duties and to redefine those roles as necessary
- Decreased potential for family crisis as evidenced by members' verbalizations of feeling more in control

Community

Short-term Goals

- Dissemination to individuals, families, and groups in the community about the incidence and management of schizophrenia
- Dissemination to individuals, families, and groups in the community about the diagnoses of Alzheimer's disease and the subsequent disease management

Long-term Goal

- Increased community understanding of chronic disease as evidenced by active participation in community education programs and decreased negative statements about the chronic population

Aggregate

Short-term Goals

- Identification of existing programs within various communities
- Coordination of existing community programs to eliminate duplication of services

Long-term Goal

- Establishment of systematic programs for chronic populations as evidenced by collaborative efforts of local, state, and federal planning bodies with ongoing evaluation of progress toward meeting the needs of the chronic population

Intervention

It is a good idea for the nurse to keep in mind alternative interventions if those originally planned are not successful. If rationales for interventions are carefully researched with an identification of why the intervention should work, there is a higher probability that the intervention will work.

There are a multitude of factors that could determine why some interventions work in one situation and do not work in another. These influencing factors could be related to demographic or environmental variables or to individual personality characteristics. Whatever the influencing factors, they must be taken into consideration before the implementation of interventions. Figure 21–3 presents examples of interventions for this case at the levels of primary, secondary, and tertiary prevention.

Evaluation

Components The problems associated with the measurement of community mental health nursing intervention has been identified in the literature (Brooker, 1984; Mereness, 1983; Leininger, 1983). Evaluation is the process for determining the extent of goal achievement in addition to the ongoing judgments about nursing effectiveness as interventions are implemented. Self-awareness involves a continuous examination of the extent to which the nurse's personality characteristics contribute to, intensify, or enhance the therapeutic relationship with the client. Self-evaluation through self-awareness is also part of the evaluation process.

Just as aggregates are multidimensional, so must be the evaluation by the nurse. Evaluation takes into consideration the system components of individual, group, family, and community. Evaluation of the following main points of nursing intervention are commonly considered in community mental health nursing (Brooker, 1984):

- Health education
- Drug supervision
- Supportive and practical help
- Counseling
- Psychotherapy
- Family therapy
- Behavior therapy
- Rereferral

In addition, for aggregates, the following areas merit evaluation:

- System equilibrium
- Homeostatic mechanisms
- Degree of change (positive, negative, openness, and closeness)
- Degree of networking (between-system components and within-system components)

Primary Prevention   **Goal:** Increased understanding of chronic disease

Individual	Family	Aggregate
Establish baseline level of knowledge	⟶	⟶
Establish learning capabilities	Identify family member(s) to receive education	Identify groups to target for education activities
Discuss application of learned knowledge to typical situations that could be encountered	⟶	⟶

Secondary Prevention   **Goal:** Increased ability to perform activities of daily living

Individual	Family	Aggregate
Establish baseline data on current level of performance for activities of daily living for impaired client	Identify with the family system the activities of daily living with which the impaired client will need assistance	Identify resources within the community that could offer supportive services to the family system
Model and role play facilitative communicative techniques	⟶	⟶

Tertiary Prevention   **Goal:** Adherence to prescribed medication regimen

Individual	Family	Aggregate
Discuss factors that contribute to the inability to adhere to the medication regimen	Discuss strategies that family can use to increase adherence by the impaired member	Satisfy the agency or institution that dispenses medication for the family and explore compliance aids with them

Figure 21–3
Example of interventions at primary, secondary, and tertiary prevention levels.

Discussion of Case Study Evaluation The evaluation of nursing interventions and the extent of goal achievement in this case will be multidimensional, occurring at individual, family, community, and aggregate levels. The nurse caring for this family has planned primarily secondary prevention interventions — those implemented after the onset of illness. These interventions are particularly relevant for Mr. Davis and Mrs. Davis. However, for Ms. Capel, the nurse has planned several interventions that can be classified as primary prevention, i.e., occurring before the onset of illness. The third classification is tertiary prevention — interventions designed to decrease any further declines in physical or mental health and to promote rehabilitation.

Evaluative questions relevant to the case are as follows:

Individual

- To what extent has there been an increase in Mr. Davis' ability to perform activities of daily living in the areas of grooming self, clearly communicating thoughts, and decreasing periods of isolation?
- To what extent does Mr. Davis adhere to the prescribed medication regimen as evidenced by administering the correct drug by the correct route at the correct time?
- Can Mr. Davis verbalize the importance of taking prescribed medication to control symptoms of schizophrenia?
- To what extent does Mrs. Davis perform activities of daily living that are appropriate to her optimum level of functioning and current stage of Alzheimer's disease?
- To what extent has Mrs. Davis maintained her current level of mental functioning in the areas of memory, orientation, concentration, and judgment?
- To what extent does Ms. Capel have an increased ability to cope as evidenced by verbalizing feelings of being more in control and identifying retirement options?
- To what extent can Ms. Capel verbalize ways to decrease her feelings of anxiety when they occur?
- Can Ms. Capel identify at least three ways to control her impending feelings of depression?

Family

- To what extent can the family exhibit an increased ability to perform shared activities of daily living as evidenced by an ability to discuss present roles and duties and define those that are necessary?
- Can the family acknowledge the failing health of several of its members?
- Can the family identify specific ways to cope with chronic disease?
- To what extent has the potential for family crisis decreased?
- To what extent is the family able to recognize and use system support services?

Community

- To what extent has the understanding increased of chronic disease by the community?
- To what extent has information about the incidence and management of schizophrenia been disseminated to individuals, families, and groups in the community?
- To what extent has information about the diagnosis and treatment of Alzheimer's disease been disseminated to individuals, families, and groups in the community?

Aggregate

- What types of systematic programs for chronic populations have been established?
- What types of programs currently exist within and outside of the community?
- To what extent are existing community programs coordinated to eliminate the duplication of services?

RESEARCH IN MENTAL HEALTH

Several research studies are pertinent to the case study presented in this chapter. Kane et al. (1990) explored the differences between two short-term, multifamily group intervention programs for relatives of hospitalized chronic schizophrenics in a nonequivalent comparison group design. A psychoeducational intervention consisted of interactive instructional activities, and the support group intervention consisted of nonstructured discussions. The analysis of covariance on adjusted posttest means indicated a differential treatment effect for depression and satisfaction for the psychoeducational groups. The authors' findings suggest that the process of a support group may not be compatible with a short time frame.

Taft and Barkin (1990) explored the use and misuse of psychotropic drugs in care for Alzheimer patients. The authors noted that family caregivers often report feelings of guilt associated with administering psychotropic drugs and may attribute the use of these to their own inability to cope. As noted, the role of the nurse is to establish and monitor therapeutic goals, to assess the incidence and severity of predictable side effects, and to provide a safe supportive environment that reduces the need for pharmacological interventions.

Several research studies have explored issues of importance to family caregivers. Bull (1990) examined factors influencing family caregiver burden and health outcomes during the transition from hospital to home. A repeated-measures design with triangulation of quantitative and qualitative methods was used to determine change in caregiver burden and health outcomes over time and to identify any change in the recipient's health status after hospital discharge. Forty-seven caregiver-recipient dyads completed three interviews and the study. The author found that recipient's physical health and functional ability before hospital discharge, the caregiver's physical health and functional ability, and the size of the social network after hospitalization were inversely related to burden at 2 weeks after discharge and that a greater burden at 2 weeks after discharge was associated with depression at 2 weeks and 2 months after discharge. The author notes that the findings may be helpful to health professionals who assist families in planning for care after hospitalization.

Biggs (1990) conducted a study to determine if there is agreement between family caregivers' and nurses' responses on the items and subscales of the Biggs Elderly Self-Care Assessment Tool (BESCAT). She felt that an assessment guide to be used by family caregivers would provide positive reinforcement oriented to what elderly family members can do in caring for themselves. The findings of the study indicated that there was an acceptable level of agreement between assessments of elderly self-care by family caregivers of dependent elderly and nursing assessments of the same self-care abilities.

Finally, Lindgren (1990) conducted a study to investigate the relationship between social support received by caregivers and the burden they experienced. An ex post facto correlational descriptive design was used to determine the relationships among variables. The sample consisted of 51 family caregivers, and all except one was age 50 or older. Burnout was measured by the Maslack Burnout Inventory, and social support was measured by the Norbeck Social Support Questionnaire. The major findings were that emotional exhaustion was only slightly related to social support but was significantly related to the situational variables of insufficient sleep, being cut off from friends, and social life change and that the caregivers' degree of emotional exhaustion was negatively related to length of caregiving service, perhaps indicating that caregivers with longer periods of time in that role had time to adapt to their situation.

SUMMARY

The purpose of this chapter was to explore the concept of mental health as it relates to groups of individuals and families in the community. The concept of aggregate mental health was described as well as a description of how the nursing process is applied to promote the mental health of individuals within families and groups in the community.

Learning Activities

1. Conduct a community study of the catchment or service area in which you live. Include the following:
   a. An identification of mental health problems within the community;
   b. Diverse perspectives on relevant issues (i.e., interviews with consumers and their families, professionals of health care, other professionals, government groups, police and law enforcement groups, business and civic groups, etc.);
   c. An identification of resources and the contributions of various groups to the coping strengths of the community related to mental health and other community concerns;
   d. An identification of weaknesses or neglected areas for mental health and other community concerns;
   e. An identification of possible points of intervention in community action;
   f. An identification of areas for further study.

2. Repeat the above study for an area in which a selected client resides.

REFERENCES

Amesbury, W. H.: The comprehensive mental health system: Is it achievable. Perspect. Psychiatr. Care *21*;31–33, 1983.

Bellak, L., ed.: Handbook of Community Psychiatry and Community Mental Health. New York, Grune & Stratton, 1964.

Briggs, A. J.: Family caregiver versus nursing assessments of elderly self-care abilities. J. Gerontol. Nurs. *16*;11–16, 1990.

Brooker, C. G.: Some problems associated with the measurement of community psychiatric nurse intervention. J. Adv. Nurs. *9*;165–174, 1984.

Bull, M. J.: Factors influencing family caregiver burden and health. West. J. Nurs. Res. *12*;758–776, 1990.

Cook, P.: Setting up a service for the mentally handicapped. Nurs. Times *80*;49–51, 1984.

Dowd, T. T.: Ethical reasoning: A basis for nursing care in the home. J. Comm. Health Nurs. *6*;45–52, 1989.

Dowell, D. A., and Ciarlo, J. A.: Overview of the Community Mental Health Centers Program from an evaluation perspective. Comm. Mental Health J. *19*;95–128, 1983.

East, P., Allman, H., and Harris, D.: Supporting the family. Nurs. Times *79*;70–71, 1983.

Fagin, C. M.: Family Centered Nursing in Community Psychiatry: Treatment in the Home. Philadelphia, F. A. Davis, 1970.

Foley, H. A.: Community Mental Health Legislation. Lexington, Massachusetts, D. C. Heath, 1975.

Goplerud, E. N., Walfish, S., and Apsey, M. O.: Surviving cutbacks in community mental health: Seventy-seven action strategies. Comm. Mental Health J. *19*;62–76, 1983.

Hagar, L., and Kincheloe, M.: The disintegration of a community mental health outpatient program, or off the back wards into the streets. Perspect. Psychiat. Care *21*;102–107, 1983.

Haylett, C. H., and Rapoport, L.: Mental health consultation. *In* Bellak, L., ed.: Handbook of Community Psychiatry and Community Mental Health. New York, Grune & Stratton, 1964, pp. 319–339.

Jahoda, M.: Toward a social psychology of mental health. *In* Kotinsky, R., and Witmer, H. L., eds.: Community Programs for Mental Health. Cambridge, Massachusetts, Harvard University Press, 1955, pp. 296–322.

Kane, C. F., DiMartino, E., and Jimenez, M.: A comparison of short-term psychoeducational and support groups for relatives coping with chronic schizophrenia. Arch. Psychiatr. Nurs. *4*;343–353, 1990.

Leichter, H. J., and Mitchell, W. E.: Kinship and Casework. New York, Russell Sage Foundation, 1967.

Leininger, M. M.: Community psychiatric nursing in community mental health—Trends, issues and problems. Perspect. Psychiatr. Care *21*;139–146, 1983.

Lindgren, C. L.: Burnout and social support in family caregivers. West. J. Nurs. Res. *12*;469–487, 1990.

Lowery, B. J., and Janulis, D.: Community mental health and the unanswered questions. Perspect. Psychiatr. Care *21*;156–158, 1983.

McGill, C. W., Falloon, I. R. H., Boyd, J. L., and Wood-Siveria, D.: Family educational intervention in the treatment of schizophrenia. Hosp. Comm. Psychiat. *34*;934–939, 1983.

Mereness, D.: The potential significant role of the nurse in community mental health services. Perspect. Psychiatr. Care *21*;128–132, 1983.

Sampson, E. E., and Marthas, M.: Group Process for the Health Professions. New York, John Wiley, 1977.

Scanlon, M. C., and Fleming, C. M.: Nurses come together to face ethical issues. Health Progr. *68*;46–48, 52, 1987.

Shaw, M. E.: Group Dynamics: The Psychology of Small Group Behavior. New York, McGraw-Hill, 1971.

Taft, L. B., and Barkin, R. L.: Drug abuse? Use and misuse of psychotropic drugs in Alzheimer's care. J. Gerontol. Nurs. *16*;4–10, 1990.

Substance Abuse

Upon completion of this chapter, the reader will be able to:

1. Discuss the historical trends and current conceptions of the etiology and treatment of substance abuse

2. Describe the current social, political, and economic aspects of substance abuse

3. Identify issues related to substance abuse in various populations encountered in community health nursing practice

4. Detail the typical symptoms and consequences of substance abuse

5. Apply the nursing process to substance abuse problems presented in a case study

6. Assess and describe the needs of special populations of substance abusers

Erika Madrid
Joanne M. Hall
Lucretia Bolin

Perhaps no other health-related condition has as many far-reaching consequences in contemporary Western society as does substance abuse. These consequences include a wide range of social, psychological, physical, economic, and political problems. The media bombards the public with accounts of crimes related to drug use and drug trafficking. A vast proportion of inmates in our overcrowded jails and prisons have substance abuse problems.

Women, children, and adolescents are now increasingly numbered among those affected by substance abuse problems. Babies are born addicted to crack cocaine or develop mental retardation due to fetal alcohol syndrome. Local and national efforts to change the situation often are inadequate and ineffective.

When in the past alcoholism and drug addiction were considered problems of the urban poor, they were virtually ignored by society as well as by most health professionals. Because substance abuse problems now pervade most levels of U.S. society, awareness is increasing. Community health nurses, in particular, must be aware of substance abuse problems because such problems are intertwined with the medical and social conditions of their clients.

This chapter will focus on assisting community health nurses to recognize substance abuse in their clients and in the larger community in which they function. Current conceptions of the etiology and treatment of substance abuse will be reviewed along with the most common symptoms of these disorders. Nursing interventions appropriate for assisting substance abusers will also be suggested to provide the community health nurse with tools for addressing these problems.

CONCEPTUALIZATIONS OF SUBSTANCE ABUSE

Conceptualizations of substance abuse and addiction have changed over the years more often for political and social reasons than for scientific ones. Some conceptualizations focus on the phenomenon of addiction, manifested by compulsive use patterns and the onset of withdrawal symptoms when substance use is abruptly stopped. Other views focus on the problems resulting from the substance use itself, regardless of whether an addictive pattern is present. Problematic conse-

quences of substance abuse include intoxication, psychological dependence, relational conflicts, employment or economic difficulties, legal difficulties, and health problems (Cahalan, 1988). For example, addiction need not be present for individuals to experience legal consequences of illicit drug use, driving while intoxicated, or alcohol or drug use–related domestic violence.

Definitions

The term "substance abuse" is relatively new, having come into common usage in the 1970s. Earlier conceptualizations generally focused on either alcoholism or drug addiction as singular addictive disorders. In contrast to the past, the most consistent current trend in theories about the use of substances and associated problems is the identification of core commonalities occurring in a variety of different substance use or compulsive behavior syndromes (Marlatt et al., 1988).

There remains a great deal of debate about how "substance use and abuse" should be defined and what substances should be included under this term. Traditional conceptualizations of substance abuse focus solely on alcohol and illicit "street drugs." Other conceptualizations include prescription medications such as tranquilizers or analgesics as abusable substances. In eating disorders like bulimia and compulsive overeating, food is viewed as the abused substance (Table 22–1).

In addition to varying in their abuse potential, substances vary in their degree of potential harm to those who consume them as well as to others in the immediate environment. Tobacco is an example of a substance that is considered unsafe to both the smoker and those who inhale the "second-hand" smoke in the environment.

Integrating the various opinions regarding the diagnosis of substance abuse, the American Psychiatric Association has classified in its most recent diagnostic manual (1987) psychoactive substance abuse disorders as either dependence or abuse. They define abusable substances as those that are psychoactive, i.e., that affect the nervous system.

The criteria for the diagnosis of dependence include a cluster of cognitive, behavioral, and physiological symptoms that are common to all categories of psychoactive substances. The symptoms indicate that the user has impaired control of the effect of the psychoactive substance and continues to use it despite adverse consequences. The symp-

Table 22–1
Classifications of Commonly Used and Abused Substances

Substance	Desired Effect	Possible Withdrawal Symptoms
Central Nervous System Depressants Alcohol Benzodiazepine Barbiturates Quaaludes	Euphoria Disinhibition Sedation	Anxiety Irritability Seizures Delusions Hallucinations Paranoia
Central Nervous System Cocaine Amphetamine	Euphoria Hyperactivity Omnipotence Insomnia Anorexia	Depression Apathy Lethargy Sleepiness
Opiates Morphine Methadone Dilaudid Fentanyl Heroin Percodan	Euphoria Sedation	Anxiety Irritability Agitation Nausea and Vomiting Diarrhea Yawning
Hallucinogens Marijuana MDMA (Ecstasy) LSD PCP	Hallucinations PCP: Violent dissociative effect	Depression Anxiety Sleep pattern disturbance

Adapted from Faltz, B., and Rinaldi, J.: AIDS and Substance Abuse: A Training Manual for Health Care Professionals. San Francisco, Regents of the University of California, 1987, p. 23.

toms of dependence include but are not limited to physiological tolerance and withdrawal. Dependence is classified by degree (mild, moderate, and severe). Substance abuse disorders can also be categorized as in partial or full remission (Table 22–2).

Psychoactive substance abuse is not as severe as dependence and does not include tolerance and withdrawal. It indicates maladaptive patterns of use and may be viewed as a precursor to psychoactive substance dependence (Table 22–3).

Etiology of Substance Abuse

The cost to U.S. society of alcohol and drug abuse is high. It is estimated that in 1988 the economic costs of alcohol abuse and drug abuse totaled $85.8 billion and $58.3 billion, respectively (Rice et al., 1990). These estimated losses reflect the costs of direct treatment and support, law enforcement ef-

forts, reduced productivity, lost earnings due to premature death, and the costs of accidents. Because substance abuse has had an impact on virtually every aspect of individual and communal life, it has been addressed by many institutions and academic fields. As a result, many theories have been developed to explain the etiology and scope of these problems and to offer solutions. Some theories address individual physiological, spiritual, and psychological factors. Others deal with social influences involving family, ethnicity, race, access to drugs, environmental stressors, economics, political status, culture, and sex roles.

In many theories, a combination of factors is cited as the underlying impetus for substance abuse. To date, no single factor or agent has been verified as causative of substance abuse as a general phenomenon (Peele, 1985). Therefore, depending on the etiological framework used, a variety of interventions have been devised to deal with the

---

Table 22–2
Diagnosis of Psychoactive Substance Dependence

Some symptoms of the disturbance have persisted for at least 1 month or have occurred repeatedly over a longer period AND at least three of the following must be present:

1. Substance often taken in larger amounts or over a longer period than the person intended
2. Persistent desire or one or more unsuccessful attempts to cut down or control substance use
3. A great deal of time spent in activities necessary to get the substance, take the substance, or recover from its effects
4. Frequent intoxification or withdrawal symptoms when expected to fulfill major role obligations at work, school, or home or when substance use is physically hazardous
5. Important social, occupational, or recreational activities given up or reduced because of substance use
6. Continued substance use despite knowledge of having persistent or recurrent social, psychological, or physical problems that are caused by or exacerbated by the use of the substance
7. Marked tolerance (need for markedly increased amounts of the substance to achieve the desired effect or markedly diminished effect with continued use of the same amount)
8. Characteristic withdrawal symptoms
9. Substance often taken to relieve or avoid withdrawal symptoms

Adapted from American Psychiatric Association: Diagnostic and Statistical Manual of Mental Disorders. Third Edition, Revised. Washington, D.C., American Psychiatric Association, 1987.

---

problem. Such interventions may not actually address the purported cause of the problem. To illustrate this, although alcoholism has been defined as a medical illness since 1955, contemporary interventions are often directed more toward moral reform or psychological change.

Although disease-oriented, medical model theorists have defined alcoholism as a loss of control over drinking or an individual malfunction, the etiology of the disease of alcoholism remains ambiguous (Brown, 1969; Jellinek, 1960; Keller, 1972. The genetic risk factor for alcohol problems appears at best to be modest (Naegle, 1988; Peele, 1986; Valliant, 1983). And genetic theories alone do not account for why certain ethnic, sex, or socioeconomic groups have a high incidence of prob-

lem drinking and alcoholism (Cahalan and Room, 1974).

The medical models of alcoholism and other substance abuse conditions also tend not to provide an understanding of commonalities among addictive behaviors (e.g., excessive drinking, gambling, eating, drug use, and sexual behavior). In reality, cross addiction or polydrug use is increasingly prevalent compared with abuse of a single substance (O'Donnell et al., 1976). Thus, specific biological medical models are giving way to multicausal models.

Another conceptual change regarding substance abuse is the increasing focus on not only persons who are using substances but also persons who are in close interactional proximity to these individuals. The concepts of coalcoholism, codependency, and the constellation of difficulties faced by the adult children of substance abusers exemplify how addiction can be viewed as a more global relational pattern. Adherents of this view observe that characteristic dysfunctional behavior patterns develop in those having significant, continual interaction with a substance abuser. These response patterns may become very problematic for these significant others and result in depression, excessive care taking of others, emotional repression, and development of their own compulsive patterns regarding work, food, spending, alcohol, and other drugs.

Table 22–3
Diagnosis of Psychoactive Substance Abuse

A. A maladaptive pattern of psychoactive substance abuse indicated by at least one of the following:
1. Continued use despite knowledge of having a persistent or recurrent social, occupational, psychological, or physical problem that is caused or exacerbated by the use of the psychoactive substance;
2. Recurrent use in situations in which use is physically hazardous.

B. Some symptoms of the disturbance have persisted for at least one month, or have occurred repeatedly over a longer period of time.

C. Never met the criteria for psychoactive substance dependence for this substance.

From American Psychiatric Association: Diagnostic and Statistical Manual of Mental Disorders. Third Edition, Revised. Washington, D.C., American Psychiatric Association, 1987.

Taking this idea one step further, addiction can be seen on a larger scale as a consciousness or propensity in communities that then becomes exaggerated by the interaction of cultures and social structures (Saleebey, 1986). This extension of the concept of addiction beyond alcohol or drug use per se treats it as a social and political problem rather than as an individual or familial problem (Wilson-Schaef, 1987).

Sociocultural and Political Aspects of Substance Abuse

In the community health sphere, substance abuse problems are not always easy to identify. The consequences of the sale and use of crack cocaine in an inner-city African-American neighborhood may be glaringly apparent through media attention. However, the silent ravages of alcohol abuse among elderly women are much less a focus of attention. Nurses must therefore incorporate the sociocultural and political dimensions of these phenomena, being critical of media trends.

The current dominant culture drinking norms in the United States are permissive (Pattison, 1984). Many traditional ceremonial, symbolic substance use patterns have been overshadowed by the influences of urbanization, consumerism, and mass culture. The consumption of mood-altering substances has become separated from family and food activities and is undertaken for the "use value" of a particular drug, i.e., what it can "do" for the individual. Past cultural definitions of these practices are inoperative, leaving a void regarding social expectations. These cultural conditions create ambiguity in determining clearly when a substance abuse problem exists. Each subculture may socially define abuse in a different way.

A particular drug experience can be understood as an ongoing interaction between the individual's subjective mood and the actual pharmacological effects of the drug. This interaction does not take place in a vacuum; rather, the expectations of what drugs will do are shaped by the culture of the user and involve the adoption of roles that are learned from more experienced users and reinforced by other social groups, including health care providers in some cases (Young, 1971).

Substances are also given economic value and are bought and sold as commodities in a variety of social arenas. The ways in which drugs, including medications and alcohol, are produced and dis-

tributed among the various segments of the population are determined largely by economic, cultural, and political conditions. The history of the use of cocaine is a good example of how these conditions are interrelated.

Crack Cocaine Epidemic

Once touted as a drug of great medicinal and religious significance, cocaine has become known as a highly potent and addictive substance. Cocaine abuse is currently perceived as a problem of epidemic proportions. The 1980s were called the "Decade of Cocaine." The Senate Judiciary Committee's study of cocaine abuse (National Institute of Drug Abuse, 1990) conservatively estimated that 2.2 million Americans use cocaine at least once a week.

The availability of cocaine has increased dramatically over the past decade. This increase began shortly after a change in drug control laws in the early 1970s that placed greater control on prescription drugs and focused less on street drugs. Trends regarding lifetime exposure, past year use, and past month use demonstrate that the western and northeastern areas of the United States have higher prevalence of cocaine use than do other regional areas (Abelson and Miller, 1985). Areas with greater population density also have greater reported lifetime exposure than do other areas. The highest at-risk group appears to be the young adult (age 18–25), with 6.8% reporting use.

Finally, increases have been documented in the number of cocaine-related emergency department visits. Emergency department admissions associated with cocaine use increased 3.5-fold between 1976 and 1981 (Kleber, 1988). One major consequence of increasing accessibility of cocaine and prevalence of its use is a 200% increase in deaths as well as a 500% increase in admissions to government treatment facilities since 1976 (Gold et al., 1986).

Cocaine is a powerful stimulant that can be inhaled, injected intravenously, or smoked. The newest form of cocaine (crack) is relatively inexpensive and has thus made cocaine available to the adolescent, young adult, and poor populations. This development has led to a greater number of complications and greater societal awareness of the pernicious effects of cocaine and other substance abuse. Reports in the literature and the media document a cocaine abuse crisis of unparalleled proportions precipitated by the underlying issues of poverty, unemployment, community disintegration, social and psychological isolation, and depression. The crisis is particularly evident in some African-American communities of major U.S. metropolitan areas.

Gross (1988) wrote that "nothing in the history of substance abuse has prepared us for the devastation that is caused by crack cocaine. Crack has destroyed entire communities by engulfing families in the web of crack sales or use. Parents who have teenage sons and daughters who have become entrepreneurs by selling crack are unable to refuse the help that this new wealth . . . brings" (p. 1). Crack is rapidly accelerating the destruction of the economically disenfranchised living in poor urban neighborhoods.

Crack cocaine has also been implicated in a number of medical complications such as seizure, stroke, myocardial infarction, psychosis resembling schizophrenia, and death. Even more alarming is the relationship between what Fullilove and Fullilove (1989) call "intersecting epidemics" (p. 146). The association between crack use as "chemical foreplay" and unprotected sexual interaction has resulted in a rising prevalence of sexually transmitted diseases, in particular, HIV infection. Bowser (1989) cites the common practice of bartering unsafe sex for drugs as a factor contributing to the rise in sexually transmitted disease prevalence in adolescent and young adult African-Americans. These youths are literally bartering their lives, as in Russian roulette, for crack cocaine.

Some women who engage in the abusive pattern of cocaine (crack) use who become pregnant are usually unable to stop their drug use without treatment. Cocaine use during pregnancy is associated with increased risk of spontaneous abortion, premature delivery, and abruptio placentae (Mena, 1990). Babies that have been addicted to cocaine in utero are hyperirritable, subject to seizures, possibly at increased risk for sudden infant death syndrome, and extremely difficult to care for. Long-term learning disabilities, behavioral problems, mental retardation, or physical handicaps are other potential consequences for these children of cocaine-using mothers (Snyder, 1985).

Typical Course of Addictive Illness: Focus on Cocaine

Perhaps the best approach to understanding the behavioral course and patterns of addictive illness is to view it on a continuum from initiation to dependency. It is, however, necessary to note that not all who initiate drug and/or alcohol use will progress in a linear fashion to dependency or display behaviors commonly associated with dependency. Data from surveys of high school seniors reveal that there is no clear evidence that all who use cocaine, or other substances, will progress to behaviors diagnostic of addiction. This supports the idea that addiction, or dependency, is not a unitary phenomenon with a single isolatable cause but rather the result of the multiplicative interaction among a host of variables.

Genetic and environmental vulnerabilities play important roles in the progression from initiation to continuation, transition, abuse, and, finally, addiction and dependency. No one ever plans to become dependent or addicted, nor do most people wish to be labeled as such. Individuals often describe a progression that began with socially mediated use. Such use appears to meet usual expectations and occurs in the context of social interactions. For some, the substance and setting will be reinforcing, priming the individual for a pattern of use. For others, the experience will be unpleasant enough to prevent further use. In the case of cocaine, the drug is thought to produce such strong feelings of euphoria, alertness, control, and increased energy that future use, particularly where access is high, is quite enticing (Daigle et al., 1988).

The continuation stage of substance abuse is a subsequent period in which substance use persists but does not appear to be detrimental to the individual. In cocaine abuse, continued use often occurs in a binge pattern (Gawin, 1988). Individuals are able to exercise some control over use, but use becomes more frequent. Use during this stage is not seen as problematic by either the individual or the social network.

However, drugs like cocaine are thought to be primary reinforcers that act on "reward pathways" within the brain. Evidence for this view comes from animal studies in which the animal with unlimited access will self-administer cocaine until exhaustion or death (Gawin, 1988; Rowbotham, 1988). This reinforcement phenomenon suggests that a sizeable portion of the human population is at risk for cocaine addiction. Perhaps we have witnessed so few cocaine-related fatalities in the past because of the high cost and illicit nature of the drug. However, crack is rapidly attenuating this effect; many crack users state that they "use until the money runs out or the drug runs out."

A critical point is the transition from substance use to substance abuse. There may be evidence to both the users and their social networks that the use of the substance is having adverse effects. During this stage, users may begin to use more often and in more varied settings. Rationalizations for use are commonly constructed during this stage to deny the seriousness and consequences of the substance use.

The social network may also play a role in allowing the substance abuse to continue. Spouses may call work to report that their partner is "sick." Social network members may compensate for the fact that the student is absent from school, the car payment is late, or an important appointment is cancelled or forgotten. These distress signals are quite common but often go unrecognized. One of the main reasons for this is that periods of use may be interspersed with periods of abstinence. This reinforces the individual's, and often the significant other's, perceived sense of control over the substance use, control that is in fact illusory.

In cocaine addiction, abstinence symptomatology plays a significant role in the progression from use to abuse and to dependency and addiction. Gawin (1988) discusses abstinence symptoms in the cocaine abuser as depression, lethargy, and anhedonia (inability to feel pleasure). In the genetically and environmentally primed individual, these symptoms determine the pattern of withdrawal from the drug. The marked depression experienced by the user when off cocaine, which resembles clinical depression, is contrasted with the recalled euphoria produced by the use of the drug. These factors, coupled with associational cues, help to initiate the vicious cycle of binge use with increased craving and continued self-administration to relieve symptoms.

The development of addiction or dependency is marked by changes in both behavior and cognition. There is an increasing focus on the substance and a narrowing of interests, social activities, and relationships. The process of becoming dependent or addicted requires the individual to negate evidence or information that may challenge the behavior or the rationalization of the behavior. There is a preoccupation with the substance and its procurement during this stage, even in the face of negative consequences. Intervention in this negative,

self-destructive downward spiral of the addiction stage is paramount. Although we have outlined the process of cocaine addiction, dependency on other substances, such as alcohol or narcotics, usually takes a similar course.

Typical Course of Addictive Illness: Stages in Continuum From Initiation to Dependency

I. Initiation
  A. First use of the substance
  B. Exposure frequently through family or friends

II. Continuation
  A. Continued more frequent use of substance
  B. Usually social use only with no detrimental effects

III. Transition
  A. Beginning of change in total consumption, frequency, and occasions of use
  B. More than just social use with beginning of loss of control

IV. Abuse
  A. Adverse effects and consequences to substance use
  B. Rationalizations for continued use and denial of adverse effects present in user and significant others
  C. Unsuccessful attempts at control of use

V. Dependency/Addiction
  A. Physical and/or psychological dependence on the substance marked by behavioral and cognitive changes
  B. Preoccupation with the substance and its procurement despite negative consequences
  C. Narrowing of interests, social activities, and relationships to only those related to the substance use

---

MODES OF INTERVENTION

As there are many theories about substance abuse, there also are a wide variety of intervention strategies. At the community level, there have been legislative measures to limit access to potentially addictive pharmaceuticals and illicit street drugs. The growing social demand for smoke-free environments in public buildings, restaurants, airplanes, and similar areas exemplifies how perceptions of tobacco and its risks have changed over the past 50 years. Alcohol taxes, zoning schemes for liquor outlets, a legal drinking age, and legal sanctions on driving while intoxicated are other examples of community efforts to prevent or contain substance abuse.

Educational programs administered through schools and penal institutions have also developed to prevent or foster early recognition of substance abuse. Television and radio have provided public service communications about the risks of substance abuse and the availability of treatment for these problems.

The formation of national associations, such as the National Council on Alcoholism, and the establishment of federal research entities, such as the National Institute on Drug Abuse and the National Institute on Alcohol Abuse and Alcoholism, have facilitated centralized efforts in the areas of education, research, and treatment. At the state level, there have also been legislative provisions to fund substance abuse treatment and rehabilitation.

Treatment

At the local level, a major proportion of the total effort has been invested in detoxification, residential, and, more recently, outpatient treatment programs. Detoxification is best described as a short-term treatment intervention designed most often to manage acute withdrawal from the substance. Detoxification involves medical management to attenuate the untoward side effects of the substance and to help stabilize the client.

Addressing acute withdrawal symptoms is of utmost importance, particularly in the case of the cocaine abuser who may experience extreme depression with suicidal ideation. Such feelings may actually cause the individual who is withdrawing from treatment to begin the vicious cycle of abuse again. Alcohol detoxification may have life-threatening medical consequences. Thus, detoxification may be one of the most crucial periods in the recovery process. Some detoxification programs are not medically supervised, but instead are administered by volunteer recovering addicts who offer social support. Nurses should be aware of the level of services offered in any detoxification program to make appropriate referrals.

Treatment programs vary but usually include group and individual therapy and counseling,

family counseling educational techniques, and socialization into 12-step groups. Some of these programs have also used techniques such as aversion therapy, disulfiram (Antabuse) therapy, methadone maintenance, hypnosis, occupational therapy, psychoanalysis, confrontation, assertiveness training, cognitive therapy, blood alcohol level discrimination training, and other behavior modification approaches.

There are basically two types of treatment programs: inpatient and outpatient. These programs may include a detoxification component. Treatment programs differ in other ways: they may be voluntary versus compulsory and pharmacologically based versus drug free (Brown, 1985). Although treatment in general is intricately tied to the concept of recovery, specific treatment approaches are guided by disciplinary philosophy. Thus, there are a variety of (sometimes contradictory) treatment approaches and models, as determined by the composition of staff and the philosophical approach to substance abuse problems.

Inpatient treatment isolates individuals from the external world and provides an opportunity to focus only on the substance abuse issues. Outpatient treatment, on the other hand, is appropriate for those who do not require such structure and protection; it is best suited to those with strong supportive social networks and high levels of motivation to recover.

Other types of treatment settings include the therapeutic community, which is a semistructured environment offering a supportive network of other recovering individuals. The classic example of a therapeutic community is that of Synanon, a society developed to reorient addicts to be socially productive. The therapeutic community helps to slowly integrate the individual into mainstream society.

Mutual self-help groups like Alcoholics Anonymous (AA), Cocaine Anonymous, and Narcotics Anonymous are therapeutic communities believed by many to be an essential component of the recovery process. These groups prescribe a program of introspection and personal growth with social support to maintain long-term abstinence. These programs endorse the disease concept of addiction, accept loss of control as its hallmark, and mandate total abstinence. Drug addiction and alcoholism are thus believed to be chronic in nature with acute periods of symptom exacerbation occurring with relapses to substance use. Treatment programs that demand total abstinence as the basis of recovery form a strong therapeutic alliance with mutual help groups.

Some important points regarding treatment are as follows:

1. Treatment should be tailored to the specific needs of the individual because not all addicts and alcoholics are the same.
2. Treatment should stress the importance of family interaction and attempt to engage important social network members in the process.
3. Treatment is not recovery but rather part of the recovery process and experience. As such, treatment programs must address the after-care needs of the client to maintain the gains made in treatment.
4. A comprehensive treatment approach will recognize the multifaceted nature of dependence and addiction and attempt to address these multiple influences within the course of the treatment and after discharge.

Research on treatment programs demonstrates that some treatment is better than no treatment but has not established significant differences in the rate of effectiveness of particular kinds of treatment programs (Miller and Hester, 1980; Sobel, 1978). Treatment evaluation depends also on the criteria used to measure effectiveness and the period of time over which the assessment takes place.

Examples of criteria that have been used are:

- Number of days abstinent
- Number of days without negative consequences of substance use
- Employability
- Days not absent from work
- Spouse's assessment of client's functionality
- Regular attendance at 12-step groups
- Compliance with follow-up appointments
- Absence of overt psychiatric symptoms
- Self-reports of progress

It is clear that treatment programs vary and that certain programs will be more culturally appropriate and effective than others for particular aggregates of individuals.

Other Approaches

Substance abuse problems are socially defined and frequently imputed to sufferers who are not complaining about their substance abuse (Szasz, 1985). Furthermore, the substance abuse treatment system has increasingly taken on social welfare and criminal justice tasks (Weisner, 1983). In this sense, substance abuse differs from many other health-related problems. Most states have laws pertaining to involuntary treatment of substance abusers. Employers and families are often enlisted to assist or coerce the identified client into accepting treatment. This aspect of substance abuse as a health concern raises some crucial questions for health care providers in terms of the encroachment of therapeutic intervention upon individual rights of privacy, informed consent, and self-determination (Peyrot, 1985).

On the individual level, substance abuse is dealt with in a number of ways, depending on the cultural and educational background and resources of the person, the attitudes of significant others, the degree of invasiveness of the effects of the substance use, and the visibility of alternatives. Some research has shown that a small percentage of individuals who recognize a harmful pattern of substance use are able to either stop using the substance or achieve a controlled, nonpathological pattern of use (Biernacki, 1986). There are those who, because of the impact of an important life change such as completion of education or getting married, appear to change from excessive use to social use of alcohol. Interventions have been developed to assist some individuals in achieving moderation (Marlatt et al., 1988).

Nevertheless, there are significant numbers of people who exhibit serious problems related to their use of mood-altering substances. These individuals are usually not able to stop or control their use without outside intervention. Historically, in U.S. society, the stigma against addicts and alcoholics has ensured that substance abuse problems are usually not recognized before they have become severe and/or chronic. In the case of alcohol research on the ability of identified problem drinkers to return to social alcohol use is still inconclusive. Consequently, most scientists and health care providers advocate abstinence from alcohol as the basis of recovery. We tend not to conceptualize a social use of illicit drugs because of the serious criminal implications involved.

Abstinence is difficult to maintain on a long term basis (after 1 year). Therefore, an important area of research and treatment is relapse prevention, a behavioral approach that aims to prepare the client for the relapse situation in the hope of preventing it or minimizing its negative impact on the entire recovery process (Marlatt and Gordon, 1986). Relapse prevention is a model that can be applied to alcohol, drug, and behavioral addictive problems such as overeating and compulsive gambling and can use either controlled use or abstinence as its goal.

Mutual Help Groups

Mutual help groups are associations that are voluntarily formed, are not professionally dominated, and operate through face-to-face supportive interaction focusing on a mutual goal. There are many mutual help groups, and they are usually organized by recovering substance abusers or those recovering from compulsive behavior patterns. The first of these was AA, which was founded in 1935. Initially, a small group of white male alcoholics found a way to stay sober 1 day at a time through meetings with others like themselves. The early AA members developed 12 steps to guide the recovery process (Kurtz, 1979). The process can be summarized as follows:

- Admission of defeat and surrender to a power higher than one's self
- Inventory of past shortcomings and strengths
- Spiritual practices (prayer and meditation)
- Willingness to change
- Making amends
- Extension of this process to all of one's life (Brown, 1985; Kurtz, 1979).

AA has been popularly viewed as relatively successful. Because it is nonprofessional and an ongoing source of assistance, it is an invaluable resource to the community. However, not all of those with alcohol problems find AA to be comfortable, culturally relevant, and socially supportive. Predominantly in large cities, women, people of color, gay men, and lesbians with alcohol problems have formed their own AA groups as well as other mutual help organizations for social support in recovery. Because of the realities of social discrimination and regional variation in customs, AA should not be considered a universal form of assistance for alcohol problems. However, it is surprising how many individuals from diverse social backgrounds find acceptance and support in AA.

Mutual Help Group Recovery Process

RECOVERY PROCESS involves the belief that recovery depends on the following main behavioral and cognitive changes.

1. Admission of defeat over control of addictive behavior and surrender to a power higher than one's self
2. Inventory of past shortcomings and strengths
3. Spiritual practices of prayer and meditation to help with the recovery process
4. Willingness to change self and behavior
5. Making amends to others wronged by addictive behaviors
6. Extension of this recovery process to the whole of one's life

---

Other 12-step programs have developed through adaptation of AAs approach to similar addictive problems. Narcotics Anonymous, Gamblers Anonymous, Debtors Anonymous, Cocaine Anonymous, Overeaters Anonymous, and Sex and Love Addicts Anonymous are examples. Because they became organized more recently than AA, these groups may not be as well known or as widely available or exhibit as much diversity among their membership as does AA. The 12 steps have also been applied to the syndromes of compulsive behavior and other difficulties experienced by the children, partner, and close associates of substance abusers. Alanon, Codependents Anonymous, and Adult Children of Alcoholics are examples of these groups. Although these groups initially had a predominance of female members, the trend is moving toward participation by equal numbers of men and women.

In general, 12-step meetings follow one of the following formats:

- Uninterrupted talk(s) by one or more speakers about "what it was like, what happened, and what it is like now"
- Discussion in which each person at the meeting has the opportunity to speak briefly
- Some combination of the first two options.

The customs shaping the actual format and sequence of the meeting vary according to group size, region of the country, ethnic and sex composition, and other cultural biases of the members. AA meetings are not standardized.

At least two mutual help groups have developed in response to their founders' negative experiences in AA or their failure to succeed in AA. Women for Sobriety was organized to replace or augment AA for women who tend to find AA inappropriately ego diminishing and often sexist in its literature and customs (Kirkpatrick, 1978). Secular Sobriety Groups were organized to meet the needs of atheists, agnostics, and others who are unable to accept the concept of or to depend on a "higher power" in their recovery from alcohol problems (Christopher, 1988).

Other mutual help groups that do not follow the 12 steps are available for a variety of addictive problems. Some of these, such as Weight Watchers, require more monetary commitment than does AA, which has no required dues or fees. Others have more involvement by professionals, such as Recovery Incorporated, which offers support to psychiatric clients. Any of these groups might also be considered resources for selected persons with substance abuse problems.

The organization and proliferation of mutual help groups may be one of the most important social developments of the 20th century. The groups comprise the most important human and ideological resource readily available to communities for the purpose of managing substance abuse. In the future, mutual help groups may begin to address prevention as well as become more involved with professional and government entities in the war on substance abuse. An example of such involvement can be seen in the neighborhood organization strategies devised by those whose immediate environment has become highly unsafe, flooded with illicit drugs, and subject to the effects of gang warfare. In this scenario, recovery has been redefined as the communal reclamation of living space through collective action; this is often achieved one building and one block at a time. These actions are important examples of how substance abuse can be responded to as a collective rather than as an individual problem.

Modes of Intervention for Substance Abuse
INDIVIDUAL AND Family Level

- Education
- Treatment: detoxification, inpatient, outpatient, residential
- Mutual help groups: Alcoholics Anonymous, Narcotics Anonymous, Cocaine Anonymous, Alanon, Narconon, and so on

Community Level

- Law enforcement measures to limit access and distribution of addictive substances ("street drugs")
- Alcohol taxes, zoning schemes for liquor outlets
- Legal drinking age and legal sanctions on driving while intoxicated
- Education programs at schools and penal institutions
- TV and radio public service communications concerning the risks of substance abuse and the availability of treatment

State and Federal Level

- Formation of national associations such as the National Council of Alcoholism
- Establishment of federal research entities such as the National Institute of Drug Abuse and the National Institute on Alcohol Abuse and Alcoholism (NIAAA) to centralize research, education, and treatment efforts
- Legislative provisions at the state level to fund substance abuse treatment and rehabilitation

---

SOCIAL NETWORK INVOLVEMENT
Family and Friends

The social network of the substance abuser can either be quite influential in helping the individual alter behavior or aid and abet the substance abuser in self-destruction. There is evidence for both positive and negative effects of social support in either mitigating or supporting the behaviors of substance abusers (Cronkite and Moos, 1980; Hall and Havassy, 1986; Jackson, 1954; Steinglass, 1985).

There is also evidence, particularly in the aggregate of adolescents and young adults, that substance use and abuse often occur in the context of social interactions. Alcohol and other substances may be used by adolescents as a social lubricant during an often-troubled developmental period (Abelson et al., 1985; O'Malley et al., 1985). Family treatment is considered essential in substance abuse because the family can be instrumental in enabling the continuation of substance abuse through protection and support of the individual during both using and inactive using time. In addition, the family has suffered the effects of the substance abuse emotionally, socially, economically, physically, and spiritually. For the substance abuser to return to an environment supportive of recovery, the family's wounds must be acknowledged and treated.

A term that deserves particular attention is "codependency." Beattie (1987) noted that the term "codependency" emerged in 1979 and has since become a common term in both the lay and professional arenas. Codependency is an ambiguous term, however, and is used differently by various disciplines and segments of the lay population. Perhaps its most comprehensive definition is that given by Subby (1984): Codependency is "an emotional, psychological and behavioral condition that develops as a result of an individual's prolonged exposure to, and practice of, a set of oppressive rules; rules which prevent the open expression of feelings as well as the direct discussion of personal and interpersonal problems" (p. 26).

Codependency is actually a new term for an interactional pattern that was recognized long ago by investigators (Jackson, 1954). There are definite and identifiable patterns of interaction that describe the alcoholic or addicted family system. Other researchers Stanton et al., 1978; Steinglass, 1985) supported the existence of these patterns in the family of the substance abuser and alcoholic. These behaviors help to maintain the family in a pattern that supports substance abuse and addiction.

There are mutual help groups for addressing codependency that are founded on the principles of AA, and provide opportunities to discuss the issues germane to the alcoholic or addicted family system or network. Families participating in treatment should also be encouraged to participate in these mutual help groups.

Codependency cannot be concretely defined the same way in each culture. Cultures and ethnic groups vary in the degree to which individuals are expected to anticipate the needs of others and care for them. The danger in applying a rigid definition of codependency in all cases is that it might unfairly and inappropriately pathologize some cultures value interdependency over individualism.

It is important for nurses to identify with each client the important members of the social network and to understand the ways in which these individuals provide support for the client. The nurse must also be cognizant of the fact that the concept of family does not refer only to nuclear families; it also includes alternative family systems. Whatever the constellation of family, significant others should be included in the treatment and intervention. Neither substance abuse, addiction, nor recovery occurs in a vacuum, and many relapses are precipitated by interpersonal conflicts.

Effects on Family Dynamics

Substance abuse has been called a family disease because it affects the entire family system, with potential adverse psychological and physical consequences for the family members in addition to the abuser (Bradshaw, 1988). Family theorists view families, whether the traditional nuclear form or an alternative, as social systems that try to stay in balance (Minuchin, 1974; Satir et al., 1975). They see families as either functional or dysfunctional depending on how well they fulfill the social tasks expected of them by our society. Substance-abusing families are frequently observed to be dysfunctional in clinical terms. However, its cultural and political factors should be considered, because families may have developed these patterns for historical reasons.

A functional family system is open and flexible and allows its members to be free to be themselves. In the nuclear family model, the parents model intimacy for the children, differences are negotiated, and communication is consistent and clear. In functional family systems, whether the traditional nuclear or other nontraditional forms, there is trust, individuality, and accountability among family members. All family members are able to get their needs met in a reasonable way.

On the other hand, dysfunctional families are closed systems with fixed, rigid roles. In the case of substance abuse, a major purpose of the system is to deny the substance abuse of the affected family member and keep this shameful family secret. In cases where a parent is the substance abuser, there may be only the appearance of intimacy between the parents. Generally, ego boundaries between the family members are weakened or nonexistent, with enmeshment of the members and an intolerance of individual differences. Rules are rigid, and communication is unbalanced, either always conflictual or always superficially pleasant.

All family functions are centered around the substance abuser, accommodating or compensating for the abuser's behavior (Brown, 1988). The individual needs of the other family members often go unmet. Denial is central to functioning of the family system. The spouse gradually takes over the functions of the substance abuser and control of the family. The children are cast into various roles in their struggle for survival in this environment, such as hero, junior parent, scapegoat, "little princess," peacemaker, or caretaker.

Adult children of these dysfunctional families often carry these roles and coping mechanisms into adult life. Many become substance abusers or the partners of substance abusers. The children of alcoholics have been found to be 3.5 times as likely to develop alcoholism (Cotton, 1979; National Institute on Alcohol Abuse and Alcoholism, 1985). They are also more likely to develop dysfunctional behavior patterns that can have serious consequences in their adult lives (Woititz, 1983). Frequently, they have difficulties with intimacy and parenting. Many have life long problems with depression and anxiety as well as physical illnesses often associated with depression and anxiety, such as ulcers, colitis, migraine headaches, and eating disorders.

Professional Enablers

Health care professionals have also contributed to the initiation and continuation of substance abuse and dependency in various ways. One obvious way is the physician's role in prescribing psychoactive medications. The medical model advocates the treatment of symptoms by medication, and the relief of pain, anxiety, and insomnia are no exceptions. The addictive potential of narcotic analgesics and antianxiety agents is often ignored if quick symptom relief is the main goal. Long-term goals for the treatment of the medical problems and nonmedication management of pain and anxiety are more thoughtful approaches that could be used.

Also, physicians and nurses are often first to see the physical effects of the substance abuse and are in an excellent position to intervene. By focusing on the health consequences of the substance abuse, they can often penetrate the person's denial and refer them into the appropriate treatment. Too often, this opportunity is missed because of the health care professional's reluctance to bring up this taboo subject. This reluctance may be based on the professional's inability to examine his or her own drinking and/or drug-taking behaviors or those of significant others.

In the past, many psychiatrists and psychotherapists have focused on the reasons why the person uses substances rather than on the dependency itself. The assumption was that insight would lead to a change in behavior. This approach has usually not proved to be effective, especially if the psychiatrist is concurrently prescribing other potentially addictive antianxiety medications or hypnotics. Complete abstinence from all mood-altering medication is a more effective model for preventing the cross-addiction common in substance abusers, i.e., substituting one substance for another, such as a benzodiazepine for alcohol. Exceptions to this approach are patients with serious medical conditions requiring pain medication and those who also have a second psychiatric disorder, such as schizophrenia, depression, or bipolar affective disorder, which requires appropriate medication.

VULNERABLE AGGREGATES

In viewing substance abuse problems from a community perspective, it becomes clear that there are special populations that are more likely to feel the impact of substance abuse problems more severely. Some groups are more susceptible to developing substance abuse problems, may tend to deteriorate more quickly in this process, or may have fewer sources of support for recovery compared with the traditional comparison group of middle-class, Euro-American, heterosexual men. These groups are therefore called "vulnerable aggregates," and they require special attention in terms of prevention, intervention, and rehabilitation strategies. The current arrangements for prevention, treatment, and mutual support are often not flexible enough to meet the needs of various vulnerable aggregates who are at risk of developing substance abuse problems and are often excluded or alienated from services by policies, provider attitudes, economic constraints, and social isolation.

Most often, substance abusers are young men of age 18–35, only a proportion of whom actually develop lifelong patterns of addiction. African-Americans, Hispanics, and Native Americans are thought to be especially at risk, although some Euro-American ethnic groups, such as Irish-Americans, are also more likely to develop problems, especially with alcohol (Day and Leonard, 1985). A complex web of factors, including ethnic practices, religious beliefs, economic conditions, availability of options and alternatives, and physiological susceptibility, influences the incidence and type of substance abuse that will be involved in each of these groups of men. For example, gay men have some unique difficulties, such as social ostracism and hostility, to face in adolescence as well as in adulthood.

Adolescence is a period of transition and social stress in which substances are often used for the first time. Substance abuse patterns may be established at this time because of the combined influences of peer pressure, the physiological immaturity of the user, social role pressures, a risk-taking orientation, and, frequently, the lack of other recreational alternatives.

Elderly men and women are considered vulnerable to substance abuse problems because of diminished physiological tolerance, the increased use of medically prescribed drugs, and the effects of cultural and social isolation that characterize industrial and postindustrial society.

Women

Perhaps the vulnerable aggregate, which has been receiving the most attention relevant to substance abuse in the past three decades, is women. This attention has been in response to the fact that women have been relatively neglected in substance abuse research. Within the population of women, there are smaller aggregates who are thought to be more severely affected by substance abuse problems (Johnson, 1987); these aggregates include women of color, low-income or no-income women, and working-class women whose increased risk stems from economic, social, and cultural factors. Lesbians are another aggregate of women in whom substance abuse is very problem-

atic because of its relationship with low self-esteem, stigmatization, and social isolation.

Many chemicals affect the bodies of women more quickly and destructively than they do men. Drug-dependent women report frequent physical and medical problems, with many of these problems related to their reproductive systems (Sutker, 1983). Also, alcoholism appears to have a more rapid progression in women than in men. Women tend to develop symptoms of alcoholic hepatitis and cirrhosis after fewer years than do men, in part because they metabolize alcohol at a different rate. Women have higher blood alcohol levels relative to body weight than do men, and estrogen has been shown to be able to change the rate of alcohol metabolism (Vourakis, 1983). Because of these occurrences, it is important to identify problem drinking and drug use early in women before they develop serious consequences.

Minorities

Ethnic and racial minorities bring to the treatment setting special challenges for the health care professional working in the field of substance abuse and dependency. These vulnerable aggregates are particularly susceptible to the effects of substance abuse and dependency because of their often-oppressed positions in the greater society. Under the strain of poverty, oppression, underemployment, decreased job opportunities, and racism, these aggregates find the escapism of substance abuse a preferable alternative to confronting the realities of a hostile and oppressive environment.

Theories of stress, social causation, and minority status all argue in favor of institutionalized racism as a factor in the generation of mental illness and substance abuse and dependency in these special aggregates (Dawkins, 1988). Cultural values and mores in some ethnic and racial minorities accept substance use for both economic and social reasons. Role modeling of substance use behavior provides acceptable guidelines for behavior within these communities. For example, in poor urban environments it is not uncommon for African-American aggregates to engage in substance use in public places on the street corners, in cars, outside of liquor stores and other store-front businesses, in public taverns, and in front of homes. Often, those within the community are quite aware of who buys, sells, or trades illegal substances.

In working with ethnic and racial minorities, it is important for the health care professional to recognize the sociopolitical and socioeconomic factors that impact on substance use, abuse, and dependency. These same factors will impact on help seeking, treatment, and outcome. Cultural sensitivity to the needs and issues germane to these vulnerable aggregates is a prerequisite to successful intervention and treatment.

Critics warn that traditional Euro-American modalities and treatment negate the ethnoracial minority experiences (Dawkins, 1988; Primm and Wesley, 1986; Ziter, 1987). Thus, treatment approaches geared toward a white society may be inappropriate and/or less effective for these vulnerable aggregates. Regarding the African-American aggregate, Ziter (1987) explained that because of the institutionalized racism and oppression in U.S. society, the environment for recovery may be contextually and experientially different than that of Euro-Americans, just as the environment that contributed to the initial abuse was different.

In the African-American community, there are several barriers to treating the substance abusing or addicted individual, such as:

- History of racism and the psychological handicap it creates on the individual's self-esteem and awareness
- Poverty, underemployment, and unemployment
- Availability and accessibility of both drugs and alcohol within the community
- Cultural and economic conditions that favor "hustling" over menial and low-paying jobs
- Allure of and economic rewards that come from selling drugs
- Inadequate social support for recovery as an alternative lifestyle and a tool of sociopolitical empowerment for the community and its inhabitants

Both external and internal constraints combine to cause and promote substance abuse and dependency within this aggregate.

Studies have identified that socioeconomic factors and social support have positive effects on treatment and outcome. Racial and ethnic minorities may represent a sizeable portion of the U.S. population that is economically disenfranchised. Limited financial resources may limit alternatives to public treatment settings, which are often understaffed, underfunded, and filled to capacity with long waiting lists.

Even if the individual completes treatment, returning to the original social environment may undermine any gains made within the treatment setting. The reinforcement for continuing substance use may be extremely powerful, and the social network of the individual may be nonsupportive. The individual needs a well-coordinated after-care program that addresses these issues.

The African-American recovering from substance abuse often returns to an environment where there is much pressure to use and multiple reinforcement of using behavior. Problems of continuing use by important members of the immediate and extended social network may undermine opportunities for continued behavioral change and abstinence. Thompson and Simmons-Cooper (1988) explain that "it becomes a challenge to be an OK individual in an environment where the prevalence of alcohol and drugs is highly visible, provides lucrative rewards and is tolerated within the community" (p. 29).

Recovery ideologies and programs may create an air of conflict and confusion and be disharmonic with the culture of the greater African-American community. As a result, African-Americans in recovery from substance abuse feel alienated and isolated. In early recovery, these feelings may be counterproductive to continued behavioral change and abstinence. Participation in groups such as AA may offer some support, but the African-American may sense that the discussion of underlying issues of racism and oppression may be perceived as irrelevant or inappropriate by the AA group. This further increases the individual's sense of isolation.

The treatment of ethnic and racial minority aggregates poses special challenges. The health care professional's value system will be challenged as well. Treatment providers must recognize that these vulnerable aggregates will encounter a host of barriers that will make treatment and long-term recovery extremely difficult. Some of these barriers are embedded in the historical and sociopolitical fabric of U.S. society and support the current conditions of racism and oppression. Other factors will be internal to the aggregate. To ignore the significance of either will lead to ineffectiveness in engaging the individual in treatment and promoting long-term recovery.

Recovery can be viewed as a tool of empowerment for these vulnerable aggregates. Substance abuse and dependency directly block opportunities for participation in the larger social system, further encapsulate and isolate the community and the individual, and support the negative valuations levied by a racist and oppressive society. This empowerment may be more meaningful to oppressed groups than a definition of recovery as "returning to the mainstream."

Other Aggregates

Substance abuse is considered the most common psychopathology in the general population. Within this category is a smaller aggregate of persons with one or more psychiatric diagnoses in addition to substance abuse itself (dual diagnoses). A study of individuals with alcohol or drug-dependence problems in the community found that 47% also had an additional psychiatric diagnosis (Helzer and Pryzbeck, 1988). These persons may be difficult to locate, lack understanding of how the two problems compound one another, be socially isolated and less likely to be employed, and be less readily identified by health care providers who fail to realize that both problems may coexist.

Treatment and integration of these dual-diagnosis persons into 12-step groups are often complicated when the need for the individual to take prescribed psychotropic medications is perceived as prescription drug abuse or as the substitution of one addiction for another. Special attention and flexibility are needed in meeting the needs of the dual-diagnosis aggregate, and such strategies are largely still in the developmental phase.

In assessing the risks for substance abuse and the extent of its impact in the real life of the community, it should be noted that frequently there are several bases for the vulnerability occurring in one individual or group. The adolescent, the low-income Hispanic male, the lesbian African-American mother receiving public assistance, and the Native-American family living on reservation land are all facing multiple sources of oppression

and vulnerability that contribute to an increased potential for substance abuse.

Special attention must be focused on the impact of the HIV epidemic and its relationship to substance abuse. Substance abusers are at increased risk of HIV-related health deficits in the following ways:

- Substances may cloud judgment, leading to high-risk sexual practices involving exchange of body fluids, such as sex without use of appropriate barriers like condoms.
- Intravenous drug use may involve the sharing of hypodermic needles.
- Chronic substance use (e.g., alcohol, heroin, amphetamines, nicotine, cocaine) impairs the immune system so that infection by HIV or by other pathogens that increase the chances of HIV infection is facilitated.
- Substance abuse may hasten physical and mental deterioration from the condition of seropositivity to an AIDS diagnosis and, eventually, a terminal condition.
- Chronic substance abusers generally have fewer supportive relationships available to them in the process of coping with the hardships that accompany HIV illness.
- Persons facing a stigmatizing, terminal, debilitating illness in themselves or a significant other are more prone to develop substance abuse problems in an attempt to cope with distress.

Last, substance abuse among health care professionals can also no longer be ignored. Physicians, nurses, dentists, and pharmacists are vulnerable to substance abuse, with the main addictions being to alcohol or narcotics (Bissell and Haberman, 1984). Although health care professionals are assumed to be "immune" to dependency because of their knowledge of medications, their increased access to drugs, belief in pharmaceutical solutions, and work-related stress they are at increased risk (Haack and Hughes, 1989; Shore, 1987). They are generally not addicted to street drugs but instead gain access to drugs through their work settings and divert medications for their own use. Their substance abuse often impairs their professional functioning; therefore, they frequently come to the attention of state regulatory boards.

Most states have rehabilitation programs for health care professionals that consist of treatment and monitoring during which they are allowed to retain their professional licenses. Despite their usually favorable recovery rate, it is difficult to get this population into treatment because of the pronounced denial and shame related to their substance abuse. However, the threatened loss of their professional license to practice may be a good motivator to break through their denial of the problem and encourage them to seek treatment.

Sexually Transmitted Diseases and Substance Abuse

THERE IS an increased risk for sexually transmitted diseases (e.g., HIV-related illness, herpes, genital warts, syphilis) among substance abusers for the following reasons:

1. Substances may cloud judgment, leading to high-risk sexual or drug practices involving exchange of body fluids, i.e., sex without appropriate barriers such as condoms.
2. Intravenous drug use may involve the sharing of hypodermic needles.
3. Chronic substance abuse impairs the immune system so chances of infection are increased.
4. Substance abuse may hasten the physical and mental deterioration of HIV-related illness.
5. Chronic substance abusers generally have fewer supportive relationships available to them to help in the process of coping with severe illness.

NURSING PERSPECTIVE ON SUBSTANCE ABUSE

Beginning during the Civil War, a substance abuse problem with which nurses were confronted but for which they had few solutions was patient addiction to medically prescribed narcotic analgesics such as codeine and morphine. Nurses often felt implicated in the development of these problems because of their role in administering these drugs at close intervals to patients in acute pain, who developed a craving for the euphoric effects of the drug that persisted after the need for analgesia had ceased.

Nurses have also encountered substance abuse in clients whose health problems are clearly related to alcohol abuse, such as liver cirrhosis, heart disease, neurological syndromes, and nutritional def-

icits. Unfortunately, in the past, alcohol problems were often not addressed in these health encounters because of the stigma of alcoholism and the lack of effective treatments.

The nursing literature did not clearly address substance abuse as a nursing problem until the late 1960s and not as a significant problem until the 1970s. Before this time, substance abuse was usually viewed as a moral problem or, if it involved illicit drugs, as a legal problem.

In the past decade, nursing has become more involved in the spectrum of compulsive behavior problems, including substance abuse. The American Nurses' Association Cabinet on Nursing Research (1985) asserts that substance abuse is a health problem of concern to nurses. A specialized organization, the National Nurses' Society on Addiction (NNSA), has been established with the philosophy that abuse of alcohol and other drugs, eating disorders, sexual and relational addiction, and compulsive gambling, working, and spending are closely related behavior patterns.

Nursing Diagnosis

The NNSA has been developing nursing assessment and interventions for the dependent client and has published two volumes of nursing care plans (1989, 1990). These plans adapt the nursing process to help individuals with various types of substance abuse and dependencies and physical and/or psychological problems associated with this abuse.

The nursing diagnoses from these volumes are based on four types of human responses to addictive disease: biological, cognitive, psychosocial, and spiritual. Common nursing diagnoses for clients with substance abuse and dependency problems (NNSA, 1989, 1990) are as follows:

- Alteration in comfort related to withdrawal symptoms
- Self-care deficits
- Hopelessness and depression related to substance abuse
- Powerlessness related to loss of control over use
- Knowledge deficit about addictive disease
- Dysfunctional family processes
- Alteration in self-concept and self-esteem
- Noncompliance related to denial of addictive disease

- Sleep pattern disturbance
- Anxiety
- Alteration in nutrition (less than body requirements)
- Social isolation
- Spiritual distress
- Ineffective individual coping
- Altered growth and psychosocial development
- Potential for violence
- Sensory-perceptual alterations related to withdrawal of the substance

Another concern that may be associated with women's alcohol problems is rape trauma syndrome. Women with histories of rape, sexual abuse, or childhood sexual trauma may develop heavy or problematic patterns of use of alcohol or other drugs as a means of compensating for posttraumatic stress symptoms in their daily lives (Bass and Davis, 1988; Covington and Kohen, 1984; Schaefer and Evans, 1987).

Community Health Nurses and Substance Abusers

The problem of substance abuse is so widespread that it affects every community and its inhabitants in varying degrees; the community health nurse is frequently concerned and involved with substance abusers or their significant others. Substance abuse nursing interventions with clients and their caregivers are necessary to ensure the success of other health interventions. Ignoring substance abuse problems frequently leads to lack of progress and clients' inability to carry out needed health practices. This is especially frustrating for the community health nurse and the other professionals who have collaborated on a comprehensive plan to allow an individual with a serious health problem to remain at home and avoid placement in an institution, for example.

Substance abuse or dependence either contributes to or complicates the course of many other illnesses and injuries. It is often a direct cause of many trauma injuries such as falls and car accidents. In high-crime, high-poverty areas, gunshot injuries may be secondary to involvement in illegal drug trade, burglaries, and robberies. Domestic violence injuries frequently occur when one or more of the family members are intoxicated.

Substance abuse can sometimes have lethal consequences when it occurs simultaneously with certain health problems such as sexually transmitted disease (e.g., AIDS), mental illness, pregnancy, and the medical problems of the elderly. Drug or alcohol use in someone with a sexually transmitted disease, in particular, AIDS, contributes to impaired judgment and the likelihood of unsafe sexual practices, i.e., sex without use of barriers such as condoms. In persons who are mentally ill, it can precipitate the onset and complicate the course of the illness. In depressive disorders, alcohol or drug use is frequently the factor that tips the scale toward a completed suicide. Alcohol or drug use during pregnancy has adverse consequences, as documented by the problems of the fetal alcohol syndrome infant and the crack cocaine syndrome infant, and can contribute to a stillbirth.

Drug and alcohol use can have disastrous results, particularly in the elderly population. As people age, their metabolism changes, and their tolerance for mood-altering substances diminishes. Many falls and fractures in this population are precipitated by alcohol consumption. Prescription medications, such as narcotic analgesics, tranquilizers, and hypnotics, can also contribute to changes in the level of consciousness and impair judgment. The complicated medication schedules required by many elderly patients demand full alertness to avoid inadequate doses or self-administered, unintentional overdoses.

Attitude Toward Substance Abusers

Although they are frequently recipients of nursing care in hospitals and community settings, nurses have historically had ambivalent attitudes toward alcoholics and drug addicts (Naegle, 1983). As part of the larger culture, the nurse may reflect the attitude that substance abuse is a stigmatizing, immoral behavior and, as a result, have difficulty providing care to these individuals. The moral view of substance abuse implies that individuals choose to get sick, injured, or addicted.

Strong negative feelings that conflict with nursing's humanistic stance may also stem from personal experiences. Being the emotionally or physically abused spouse or child of a substance abuser can have lasting effects on nurses' attitudes toward substance-abusing clients. On the other hand, alcohol or drug use by nurses to relieve stress or self-medicate dysphoric states may lead them to overidentify with the patient and deny the severity of the client's substance abuse.

Frequently, substance abusers are difficult clients in health care settings (Faltz and Rinaldi, 1987). When intoxicated, they may be obstreperous, uncooperative, and antisocial. When not intoxicated, they may exhibit none of these negative behaviors or be manipulative and demanding, using flattery or intimidation to hide drug-seeking behavior. Although nurses may initially be warm and understanding, once aware of manipulative attempts, they may have difficulty maintaining an accepting, nonjudgmental attitude. Realizing that recovery from substance abuse often comes very slowly can help nurses feel less pressured to get patients into treatment and be more able to simply raise consciousness by presenting the facts about addictive illness and leave the decision making to the client.

Nursing Interventions in the Community

How can community health nurses assist individuals, families, and groups experiencing substance abuse problems? First, they can provide an accurate assessment, which includes a family history and specific questions about personal drug and alcohol use (Fortin, 1983). They can be alert to environmental cues in the home that indicate substance abuse, such as empty liquor and pill bottles. An indication of prescription medication abuse is the patient's involvement with several physicians from whom narcotic analgesics and tranquilizers are obtained. This type of assessment can help with case finding and referral for treatment, even though the individual may have initially denied that there is a substance abuse problem.

Denial of substance abuse or dependence may range from completely blocked awareness of the entire problem to partial disavowal of the detrimental effects of the substance use and abuse. One of the primary tasks of intervention and treatment with the substance-dependent individual is to increase the individual's awareness of the problem.

Family and significant others can assist with this process by being more honest and direct with the individual about the detrimental effects of the substance abuse, especially as it has an impact on significant relationships. Before this occurs, the significant others have to overcome their own denial of the problems and its associated shame and guilt. Referrals to community education programs on substance abuse and dependence and mutual help groups such as Alanon and Narconon are interventions most useful to family and significant others.

The community health nurse may also include the social network to get the person into treatment. Although individuals who are forced to enter treatment may not be willing to admit the severity of the abuse and/or lack awareness, they can still benefit from exposure to the treatment program and eventually begin recovery from their dependency. Experiencing serious health consequences related to the dependency may constitute "hitting bottom" for the individual and may break through denial and/or collusion on the part of the family. The concept of hitting bottom is particularly important: this is not a mysterious process, but rather consists of a myriad of interacting forces that bring the individual to a point of despair. Hitting bottom may provide a window of opportunity for intervention. Behavioral prescriptions for abstinence will be ineffective if the cognitive structure that permits the behavior to continue is not also challenged. Therefore, capitalizing on cracks in the cognitive accounting system is essential.

The trust that develops in a caring nursing relationship can support disclosure of substance abuse problems and decrease denial in the client or family members. A realistic and positive attitude toward the person with substance abuse can provide families with hope. The nurse needs to have knowledge that recovery is possible and that community resources are available to help with that recovery. One of the primary roles of the community health nurse in helping substance abusers is to facilitate contact with helping agencies such as local treatment programs or mutual help groups. Collaboration with the client's physician is helpful should medical detoxification be necessary.

The other traditional community health nursing roles and interventions are also appropriate to use with substance abusers. Examples are as follows:

- Health teaching regarding addictive illness and addictive effects of different substances
- Providing direct care for abuse- and dependence-related medical problems
- Counseling clients and families about problems related to substance abuse
- Collaborating with other disciplines to ensure continuity of care

- Coordinating health care services for the client to prevent prescription drug abuse and avoid fragmentation of care
- Providing consultation to nonmedical professionals and lay personnel
- Facilitating care through appropriate referrals and follow-up

Application of the Nursing Process

Evelyn Weaver is a 72-year-old widow who was referred to the Visiting Nurse Association for follow-up after hospitalization for a seizure and fall she experienced in her home. Her hospital discharge diagnoses were ethyl alcohol abuse, seizure disorder, hypertension, and bruises and contusions on left arm and leg. Her discharge medications were 900 mg Dilantin p.o. at bedtime, 1 p.o. multivitamins q.d., 50 mg hydrochlorothiazide p.o. q.d., and 1 tablet Aldomet p.o. q.d.

Mrs. Weaver has lived alone in a two-bedroom house in a middle-class suburb for the 10 years since the death of her husband. Until 4 years ago, her daughter lived nearby with her two children and visited frequently. But after a bitter divorce, the daughter and the children moved several hundred miles away and visited only once or twice a year. Mrs. Weaver also had a married son in the area. He paid her bills once or twice a month but otherwise had minimal contact and appeared to be angry at her because of alcohol abuse. Mrs. Weaver's occupation had been primarily a homemaker and mother, and she tended to be socially isolated. She stopped driving after her last car accident, infrequently saw her two elderly cousins in town, and was not involved in any local community organizations.

Assessment

Individual In-home nursing assessment of the client was done by the visiting nurse, and information was obtained through the nursing interview and physical assessment. Mrs. Weaver admitted to an alcohol abuse problem but tended to minimize its severity. She reported she had stopped drinking for 2 days on her own and then had a seizure. She denied any past alcohol treatment such as counseling or AA meetings and said she was not interested in any now. She was abstinent from alcohol since her discharge from the hospital and thought that she would remain that way. She admitted to some loneliness and social isolation. She also reported sleep disturbances (i.e., difficulty falling asleep and staying asleep) and decreased nutritional intake with loss of appetite. She denied other psychoactive medication use, such as hypnotics, narcotic analgesics, or tranquilizers (benzodiazepines). She agreed to a social work referral to investigate attendant care and Meals-on-Wheels to help her.

Family Telephone contact with the client's daughter revealed that she was very concerned about her mother. She denied that alcohol abuse was her mother's problem but thought that poor nutrition and health practices were the cause of the hospitalization. She was anxious for the social work referral to get attendant care to assist her mother in the home. It took several calls and messages before the nurse was able to speak to the client's son. He said his mother was an alcoholic and that he had tried unsuccessfully in the past to get her to stop drinking. He was unwilling now to do more than visit her twice a month to pay her bills. He lived 1 hour away by car.

Community The middle-class suburb in which the client lived had no alcohol treatment services especially geared for the elderly. AA meetings and private substance abuse counselors were available, but none of them were willing to make home visits and deal with an elderly homebound client. The local senior center had no programs or education involving substance abuse and refused to allow AA meetings to be conducted in their building because they thought that their clients would be offended. The client's physician was aware of her alcohol abuse problem but did not know what to do to help her. Referral to an inpatient program for substance abuse was not possible because Mrs. Weaver refused to go.

Diagnosis

Individual

- Altered cardiovascular status secondary to hypertension
- Altered neurological status secondary to alcohol withdrawal seizures
- Knowledge deficit about addictive disease and effects of alcohol abuse
- Sleep pattern disturbance
- Alteration in nutrition (less than body requirements)
- Social isolation
- Ineffective individual coping related to inability to adjust to role of widow and maintain involvement in community activities
- Knowledge deficit about the effects and side effects of all of her medicine

Family

- Knowledge deficit about addictive disease and effects of excessive intake of alcohol
- Knowledge deficit of treatment approaches available for alcohol abuse and the recovery process
- Alteration in family process secondary to poor communication and denial of alcohol abuse in client

Community

- Knowledge deficit in senior center staff regarding the prevalence of alcohol abuse problems in the elderly population and adverse health effects of alcohol consumption in the elderly
- Knowledge deficits in community agencies that assist alcohol abusers (local AA and counselors) regarding the need to make home visits and provide services geared to the elderly

Planning

Planning for Mrs. Weaver's care involved collaboration with her family, her physician, the agency's social worker, and the community alcohol treatment resources. Health teaching and counseling were the main approaches used in assisting the client and her family directly. Indirect approaches involved networking with community agencies and supervising other caregivers.

Intervention

Individual

- Nursing visits two to three times weekly initially to monitor the client's medication issues or problems as related to maintaining an abstinence and/or medication dosing, cardiovascular status, neurological status, and nutritional status
- Social work referral to set up attendant assistance in the home and Meals-on-Wheels
- Health teaching regarding addictive illness, effects of excessive alcohol intake on the body, alcohol withdrawal seizures, no-added-sodium diet, and effect of medications
- Health teaching about all of the client's medications, their effects and side effects, and the necessity of following recommended dosing schedules
- Referral for alcohol treatment counseling and AA meetings when the individual is receptive

Family

- Continued contact with the client's daughter and son to involve them in her care
- Health teaching to the family on the course and treatment of addictive illness and the adverse effects of alcohol abuse in the client and the family as related to functioning, cohesion, and communication
- Role modeling by the visiting nurse of the use of clear, direct, and nonjudgmental communication about the client's alcohol abuse problems

Community

- List of local and national referral resources for clients with substance abuse problems made available to physicians with a particular focus on resources providing services for older age or elderly substance abusers
- Health teaching to community groups (e.g., senior center, AA fellowship, substance abuse counselors) regarding the prevalence of alcohol abuse in the elderly population and treatment and counseling approaches useful with this aggregate
- Collaboration with community organizations that do outreach with homebound elderly to assist in identification and referral
- Establishment of a referral network, i.e., phone hot-line, of concerned older age or elderly recovering individuals

Evaluation

Initially, interventions proceeded smoothly. Mrs. Weaver obtained attendant help for 2 hours three times weekly and Meals-on-Wheels. The visiting nurse filled her medi-set weekly. The attendant ensured that the client took her medications and ate her meals and assisted Mrs. Weaver with personal care. Mrs. Weaver remained abstinent from alcohol during this time but refused any treatment or counseling for her alcohol abuse problem. However, after about 3 weeks, she was rehospitalized after falling again at home. She was diagnosed with Dilantin toxicity; this occurred because she had surreptitiously been taking extra Dilantin at night to help her sleep.

After a few days, Mrs. Weaver was discharged from the hospital, and the case was reopened by the Visiting Nurses Association. Private attendant care and Meals-on-Wheels were also reinstated. This time, the physician discontinued the Dilantin and prescribed Antabuse with the understanding that the client receive alcohol counseling. The client did followup with the counseling referrals given to her by the visiting nurse, but her social situation did not change. She remained very isolated and refused AA involvement.

A third hospitalization occurred within a few weeks when Mrs. Weaver ingested alcohol in combination with the Antabuse. She became physically ill and required treatment. After this last hospitalization, the daughter decided to take action. She moved her mother, despite her initial resistance, into a retirement community that provided meals and social activities. The visiting nurse continued to follow the case in the new setting.

Initially, the client was angry and isolative at her new home. This changed after an attendant was hired to assist her with personal care and get her involved with the social activities at the community. The visiting nurse also set up medical follow-up with a new physician because she had moved too far away from the previous physician and informed the physician of the client's past medical and alcohol abuse problems. The situation remained stable for several weeks due to Mrs. Weaver's continued abstinence from alcohol. The visiting nurse continued to remain active in the client's care by arranging for aftercare, focusing on providing goal-specific social support for abstinence and general support for addressing the client's concerns and issues, particularly as related to feelings of isolating loss and transitions. Occasional lapses were framed as an opportunity for increasing the client's level of awareness about substance abuse–related problems and their cause.

Levels of Prevention

Primary

- Involves health teaching to individuals and groups on risk factors, early symptoms of substance abuse, adverse health and social consequences, addictive disease process, and treatment services available.
- Need to gear educative approaches especially to the more vulnerable aggregates (e.g., adolescents, minorities, mentally ill, women, and elderly)

Secondary

- Involves screening and early treatment approaches aimed at minimizing health and social consequences of substance abuse

- Involvement of physicians, nurses, and other health care professionals in various health care settings in this process
- Use of various screening and assessment tools as well as referrals to treatment services and mutual help organizations

Tertiary

- Involves more direct approaches (e.g., detoxification and inpatient or outpatient treatment) to halt the physiologically damaging effects of the substance abuse (e.g., liver disease, organic mental deficits, gastritis, and so on)
- Frequent use of medications to treat the symptoms of substance abuse–related disorders or as part of aversion therapy (e.g., Antabuse)
- Services provided by medical practitioners, treatment services, and mutual help organizations; generally advocate abstinence from the substance and improving the individual's health status

This case study illustrates the possible complexity and frustration involved in helping the substance abuser. Significant others and the medical community must be involved to assist the nurse in interventions. Often, the social situation, living situation, and/or social acquaintances also must change to maintain long-term recovery. However, with patience, persistence, and a caring, nonjudgmental attitude, the nurse can be effective in getting clients with substance abuse problems into recovery and improving their health status.

Intervention is effective if nurses believe that addiction treatment and recovery are possible and know the community resources available to aid with this process.

National Offices of Mutual Help or Resource Organizations

Al-Anon Family Groups, P.O. Box 862, Midtown Station, New York, NY 10018-0862, (212) 302-7240.

Alcoholics Anonymous, P.O. Box 459, Grand Central Station, New York, NY 10163, (212) 686-1100.

Drug and Alcohol Nursing Association, Inc., P.O. Box 6212, Annapolis, MD 21401, (301) 263-1131.

National Council on Alcohol, 12 W. 21st Street, New York, NY, 10010, (212) 206-6770.

National Institute on Alcohol Abuse and Alcoholism, 16-105 Parklawn Building, 5600 Fishers Lane, Rockville, MD 20857.

National Institute on Drug Abuse, 10-05 Parklawn Building, 5600 Fishers Lane, Rockville, MD 20857.

National Self-Help Clearinghouse, City University of New York, 33 West 42nd Street, New York, NY 10036.

Women for Sobriety Inc., P.O. Box 618, Quakertown, PA 18951, (215) 536-8026.

SUMMARY

This chapter has attempted to provide an overview of the complex, multifaceted phenomenon of substance abuse and its manifestations in the community. The focus has been on the social, economic, and political aspects of substance abuse as well as on the health-related ones. Substance abuse was related to the more general concept of addictive behaviors, not just those related to drug or alcohol abuse.

From the review of the various etiological theories, it is clear that there is no one causative factor in the development of the problem. Consequently, there is no one treatment approach to apply to all substance abusers. Cocaine addiction was presented in detail to illustrate the progression of substance use to abuse to dependency. Cocaine addiction is also a relevant example of the strong economic and social factors present in the development of dependency that must be taken into account in the recovery process.

A discussion of vulnerable aggregates focused on women and minorities. Resources for prevention and intervention at the individual, family, and community levels were outlined. Also, a case study applied the nursing process at these different levels.

Learning Activities

1. Attend a local AA, Narcotics Anonymous, or Cocaine Anonymous meeting and share your impressions with your classmates.

2. Attend a local Al-Anon, Narconon, or Adult Children of Alcoholics meeting and share your impressions with your classmates.

3. Visit a local treatment center that provides detoxification, inpatient, or outpatient treatment, and determine their treatment philosophy and what kind of services they provide to patients and their families.

4. Visit a treatment program for women, and determine how the particular needs of this population are assessed and addressed.

5. Learn about the local community college or high school's drug and alcohol education programs.

6. Contact your county or city's mental health services or substance abuse treatment services, and obtain a list of local treatment and education resources.

REFERENCES

Abelson, H. I., and Miller, J. D.: A decade of trends in cocaine use in the household population. *In* Kozel, N. J., and Adams, E. H., eds.: Cocaine Use in America. Rockville, Maryland, National Institute of Drug Abuse, NIDA Research Monograph No. 61, 1985, pp. 35–49.

American Nurses' Association Cabinet on Nursing Research: Directions for Nursing Research: Toward the Twenty-first Century. Kansas City, Missouri, American Nurses' Association, 1985.

American Psychiatric Association: Diagnostic and Statistical Manual of Mental Disorders. 3rd Ed. rev. Washington, D.C., American Psychiatric Association, 1987.

Bass, E., and Davis, L.: The Courage to Heal: A Guide for Women Survivors of Child Sexual Abuse. New York, Harper & Row, 1988.

Beattie, M.: Codependency No More: How to Stop Controlling Others and Start Caring for Yourself. New York, Harper & Row, 1987.

Biernacki, P.: Pathways From Heroin Addiction: Recovery Without Treatment. Philadelphia, Temple University Press, 1986.

Bissell, L., and Haberman, P.: Alcoholism in the Professions. New York, Oxford University Press, 1984.

Bowser, B. P.: Crack and AIDS: An ethnographic impression. J. Nat. Med. Assoc. *81*;538–540, 1989.

Bradshaw, J.: Bradshaw on the Family: A Revolutionary Way to Self-Discovery. Deerfield Beach, Florida, Health Communication, Inc., 1988.

Brown, S.: Treating Adult Children of Alcoholics: A Developmental Perspective. New York, John Wiley & Sons, 1988.

Brown, S.: Treating the Alcoholic: A Developmental Model of Recovery. New York, John Wiley & Sons, 1985.

Brown, R.: Vitamin deficiency and voluntary alcohol consumption. Q. J. Stud. Alcohol *30*;592–597, 1969.

Burkett, G., Yasin, S., and Palow, D.: Perinatal implications of cocaine exposure. J. Reprod. Med. *35*;35–42, 1990.

Cahalan, D.: Understanding America's Drinking Problem: How to Combat the Hazards of Alcohol. San Francisco, Jossey-Bass, 1988.

Cahalan, D., and Room, R.: Problem Drinkers Among American Men. New Brunswick, New Jersey, Rutgers Center for Alcohol Studies, 1974.

Christopher, J.: How to Stay Sober: Recovery Without Religion. Buffalo, New York, Prometheus, 1988.

Cotton, N. S.: The familial incidence of alcoholism: A review. J. Stud. Alcohol *40*;89–116, 1979.

Covington, S. S., and Kohen, J.: Women, alcohol and sexuality. Adv Alcohol Subs Abuse *4*;41–56, 1984.

Cronkite, R. C., and Moos, R. H.: Determinants of post treatment functioning of alcoholic patients: A conceptual framework. J. Consult. Clin. Psychol. 48;305–316, 1980.

Day, N. and Leaonard, K.: Alcohol, drug use and psychopathology in the general population. In Alterman, A., ed.: Substance Abuse and Psychopathology. New York, Plenum Press, 1985, pp. 15–44.

Daigle, R. D., Clark, H. W., and Landry, M. J.: A primer on neurotransmitters and cocaine. J. Psychoactive Drugs 20;283–295, 1988.

Dawkins, M. P.: Alcoholism prevention and black youth. J. Drug Issues 18;15–20, 1988.

Faltz, B., and Rinaldi, J.: AIDS and Substance Abuse: A Training Manual for Health Care Professionals. San Francisco, Regents of the University of California, 1987.

Fortin, M.: Community health nursing. In Bennett, G., Vourakis, C., and Woolf, D., eds.: Substance Abuse: Pharmacologic, Developmental and Clinical Perspectives. New York, John Wiley & Sons, 1983, pp. 209–223.

Fullilove, M. T., and Fullilove, R. E.: Intersecting epidemics: Black teen crack use and sexually transmitted diseases. J. Am. Med. Women's Assoc. 44;146–153, 1989.

Gawin, F. H.: Neuropharmacology of cocaine: Progress in pharmacotherapy. J. Clin. Psychiatr. 49(suppl);11–15, 1988.

Gold, M. S., Washton, A. M., Dackis, C. A., and Chatlos, J. C.: New treatments for opiate and cocaine users but what about marijuana? Psychiatr. Ann. 16;206–214, 1986.

Gross, S.: Report on crack. Presented to the San Francisco Health Commission, San Francisco, May 1988.

Haack, M., and Hughes, T., eds: Addiction in the Nursing Profession: Approaches to Intervention and Recovery. New York, Springer Publishing, 1989.

Hall, S. M. and Havassey, B. E.: Commitment to abstinence and relapse to tobacco, alcohol and opiates. In Tims, F. M., and Leukefeld, C. G., eds.: Relapse and Recovery in Drug Abuse. Rockville, Maryland, National Institutes of Drug Abuse, NIDA Research Monograph Series No. 72, 1986, pp. 118–135.

Helzer, J. E., and Pryzbeck, T. R.: The co-occurrence of alcoholism with other psychiatric disorders in the general population and its impact on treatment. J. Stud. Alcohol 49;219–244, 1988.

Jackson, J. K.: The adjustment of the family to the crises of alcoholism. Q. J. Stud. Alcohol 15;562–586, 1954.

Jellinek, E. M.: The Disease Concept of Alcoholism. New Haven, Connecticut, Hillhouse Press, 1960.

Johnson, E.: Substance abuse and women's health. Public Health Rep. 102(July–August suppl);42–48, 1987.

Keller, M.: On the loss of control phenomenon in alcoholism. Br. J. Addiction. 67;153–166, 1972.

Kirkpatrick, J.: Turnabout: Help for a New Life. Dubuque, Iowa, Kendall-Hunt, 1978.

Kleber, H. D.: Introduction to cocaine abuse: Historical, epidemiological and psychological perspectives. J. Clin. Psychiatr. 49(suppl);3–6, 1988.

Kurtz, E.: Not God: A History of Alcoholics Anonymous. Center City, Minnesota, Hazelden Educational Services, 1979.

Marlatt, G. A., Baer, J. S., Donovan, D. M., and Kivlahan, D. R.: Addictive behaviors: Etiology and treatment. Annu. Rev. Psychol. 39;223–252, 1988.

Marlatt, G. A., and Gordon, J. R.: Relapse Prevention: Maintenance Strategies in the Treatment of Addictive Behaviors. New York, Guilford Press, 1986.

Mena, M.: Perinatal substance abuse: An overview. Calif. Hosp. 4;27–33, 1990.

Miller, W. R., and Hester, R. K.: Treating the problem drinker: Modern approaches. In Miller, W. R., ed.: The Addictive

Behaviors: Treatment of Addiction, Drug Abuse, Smoking and Obesity, New York, Pergamon Press, 1980, pp. 11–141.

Minuchin, S.: Families and Family Therapy. Cambridge, Massachusetts, Harvard University Press, 1974.

Naegle, M.: The nurse and the alcoholic: Redefining a historically ambivalent relationship. J. Psychosocial Nurs. Mental Health Serv. 21;17–25, 1983.

Naegle, M. A.: Theoretical perspectives on the etiology of substance abuse. Holistic Nurs. Practice 2;1–13, 1988.

National Institute on Alcohol Abuse and Alcoholism: A Growing Concern: How to Provide Services for Children From Alcoholic Families. Washington, D.C., U.S. Government Printing Office, DHHS publication No. ADM 85-1257, 1985.

National Institute on Drug Abuse: Third Triennial Report to Congress: Drug Abuse and Drug Research III. Rockville, Maryland, Department of Health and Human Services, 1990.

National Nurses' Society on Addiction: Nursing Care Planning With the Addicted Client, Vol. I. Skokie, Illinois, National Nurses Society on Addictions, 1989.

National Nurses' Society on Addiction: Nursing Care Planning With the Addicted Client, Vol. II. Skokie, Illinois, National Nurses Society on Addictions, 1990.

O'Donnell, J. A., Voss, H. L., Clayton, R. R., Slatin, G. T., and Room, R.: Young Men and Drugs: A Nationwide Study. Rockville, Maryland, National Institute of Drug Abuse, NIDA Research Monograph 5, 1976.

O'Malley, P. M., Johnston, L. D., Bachman, J. G.: In Kozel, N. J., and Adams, E. H., eds.: Cocaine Use in America. Rockville, Maryland, National Institute of Drug Abuse, NIDA Research Monograph 61, 1985, pp. 50–75.

Pattison, E. M.: Sociocultural approaches to the problem of alcoholism. In Galanter, M., and Pattison, E. M., eds.: Psychosocial Treatment of Alcoholism. Washington, D.C., American Psychiatric Press, 1984, pp. 69–96.

Peele, S.: The implication and limitations of genetic models of alcoholism and other addictions. J. Stud. Alcohol 47;63–76, 1986.

Peele, S.: The Meaning of Addiction: Compulsive Experience and Its Interpretation. Lexington, Massachusetts, Lexington Books, 1985.

Peyrot, M.: Coerced voluntarism: The micropolitics of drug treatment. Urban Life 13;343–365, 1985.

Primm, B. J., and Wesley, J. E.: Treating the multiply addicted black alcoholic. Alcoholism Treatment Q. 2;155–178, 1986.

Rice, D., Kelman, S., Miller, L., and Dunmeyer, S.: The Economic Costs of Alcohol and Drug Abuse and Mental Illness: 1985. San Francisco, Institute of Health and Aging, University of California at San Francisco, 1990.

Rowbotham, M. C.: Neurological aspects of cocaine abuse. West. J. Med. 149;442–448, 1988.

Saleebey, D.: A social psychological perspective on addiction: Themes and disharmonies. In Watts, T. D., ed.: Social Thought on Alcoholism: A Comprehensive Review. Malabar, Florida, Robert E. Krieger, 1986, pp. 25–38.

Satir, V., Stachowiak, J., and Taschman, H.: Helping Families to Change. New York, Jason Aronson, Inc., 1975.

Schaefer, S., and Evans, S.: Women, sexuality and the process of recovery. J. Chem. Depend. Treat. 1;91–120, 1987.

Shore, J.: The Oregon experience with impaired physicians on probation: An eight year follow-up. J. A. M. A. 257;2931–2934, 1987.

Snyder, S., ed.: Cocaine: A New Epidemic. New York, Chelsea House, 1985.

Sobel, L. C.: Critique of alcoholism treatment evaluation. In Marlatt, G. A., and Nathan, P. E., eds.: Behavioral Approaches to Alcoholism. New Brunswick, New Jersey, Rutgers Center of Alcohol Studies, 1978, pp. 166–182.

Stanton, M. D., Todd, T. C., Hemp, D. B., Kirscher, S., and Van Dusen, J. A.: Heroin addiction as a family phenomenon: A new conceptual model. Am. J. Drug Alcohol Abuse 5;125–150, 1978.

Steinglass, P.: Family systems approaches to alcoholism. J. Substance Abuse Treatment 2;161–167, 1985.

Subby, R.: Inside the chemically dependent marriage: Denial and manipulation. In Subby, R., ed.: Codependency: An Emerging Issue. Deerfield Beach, Florida, Health Communication, Inc., 1984.

Sutker, P.: Drug dependent women: An overview of the literature. In Bescher, G., Reed, B., and Mondanaro, J., eds.: Treatment Services for Drug Dependent Women, Vol. I. Rockville, Maryland, National Institute of Drug Abuse, 1981, pp. 25–43.

Szasz, T.: Ceremonial Chemistry: The Ritual Persecution of Drugs, Addicts and Pushers. New York, Anchor Press, Doubleday, 1985.

Thompson, T., and Simmons-Cooper, C.: Chemical dependency treatment and black adolescents. J. Drug Issues 18;21–31, 1988.

Valliant, G. E.: The Natural History of Alcoholism: Causes, Patterns and Paths to Recovery. Cambridge, Massachusetts, Harvard University Press, 1983.

Vourakis, C.: Women in substance abuse treatment. In Bennett, G., Vourakis, C., and Woolf, D., eds.: Substance Abuse: Pharmacologic, Developmental, and Clinical Perspectives. New York, John Wiley & Sons, 1983.

Weisner, C.: The alcohol treatment system and social control: A study in institutional change. J. Drug Issues 13;117–133, 1983.

Wilson-Schaef, A.: When Society Becomes an Addict. San Francisco, Harper & Row, 1987.

Woititz, J. G.: Adult Children of Alcoholics. Hollywood, Florida, Health Communications, Inc., 1983.

Young, J.: The Drugtakers: The Social Meaning of Drug Use. London, Mac Gibbon & Key, 1971.

Ziter, M. L.: Culturally sensitive treatment of black alcoholics. Natl. Assoc. Social Workers 12;130–135, 1987.

CHAPTER 23

Communicable Disease

Upon completion of this chapter, the reader will be able to:

1. Discuss the routes of transmission of infection

2. Summarize the Centers for Disease Control recommended guidelines for universal precautions against the transmission of communicable diseases

3. Identify the protocols for notifiable diseases within the Centers for Disease Control monitoring and surveillance system and explain why the system is important

4. List three communicable diseases currently causing high morbidity in the United States, and identify the epidemiological indicators of racial and ethnic disparity

5. Specify which immunizations are required by law, and for what ages, and discuss their efficacy

6. Discuss the prevalence and danger involved in the acquisition of AIDS and other sexually transmitted diseases, and identify methods for control

Della Dash

As the world becomes more sophisticated and technologically advanced, increasing control can be asserted over what have historically been mysteries to be dreaded and feared. Epidemics have been eradicating entire civilizations for as long as there have been species, but finally there exists the capability to greatly reduce the alarming rates of morbidity and mortality caused by many of these infectious diseases.

Immunization, accomplished through the use of vaccines, may be the most important medical discovery. Entire generations can be prevented from painful death and debilitating deformity through the use of our vaccine power. Why, then, are so many people still dying of preventable infectious diseases? Treatments exist for many sexually transmitted diseases (STDs), yet why do syphilis and gonorrhea, for example, still exist? These are some of the questions that will be discussed in this chapter.

For years, not a single case of polio has been reported in the United States, but this is changing. In 1989, five cases of paralytic poliomyelitis were reported in the United States (Centers for Disease Control, 1989). Why are diseases like polio reappearing? In the past 150 years, we have made major advances in hygienic practices by designing water and sanitation facilities that contribute to the prevention of communicable diseases. With the recent cholera outbreak in Peru (May 1991), new attention is being paid to simple preventive measures that are taken for granted in the United States, a "developed" nation. The chlorine content has been doubled in potable water supplies, but, unfortunately, the people who are most likely to suffer the consequences of this recent epidemic are those who do not have access to clean water supplies for a variety of reasons, such as economic and political disparities. As the percentage of Americans living below the poverty level continues to increase, disparities in access to public health measures appear in growing proportions and are responsible in part for the recent increases in preventable communicable disease rates.

An estimated 34 to 37 million Americans (almost one seventh of the total U.S. population) do not have any health insurance. This statistic is magnified in the African-American and Hispanic communities and those living close to the poverty line (U.S. Bureau of the Census, 1990a). The children of these adults also have no health coverage other than Medicaid. Although it is required by law that all children attend school, and the schools require vaccination before entrance into these institutions, many children are not receiving the routine immunizations that are fundamental to the health, safety, and welfare of our young population as well as of the entire community as a whole.

In California, MediCal provides the necessary funding for the Child Disability Prevention Program or entry-level physical required by the schools as well as any vaccinations needed to bring that child up to date on their series. (Every state has their own program funded in part through Medicaid.) Between February 1985 and May 1987, one fifth of all U.S. children under the age of 6 were covered by Medicaid for at least 1 month (U.S. Bureau of the Census, 1990a). Although this is a gallant attempt to provide the basic health care requirements for one segment of society, it cannot adequately support the continuity or the depth of services necessary and should therefore not be used as a long-term solution for the provision of health promotion and disease prevention.

Many special interest groups, including nurses, are attempting to create a national health care system in the United States, and some states are already designing and implementing their own statewide programs to guarantee basic medical services for their constituents. The revision of health care priorities may be the most crucial aspect in the design of a new health care system. Emphasis must be placed on preventive care that provides a cost-effective system over time. Affordability of primary prevention is the key to a sustainable health care system, but it must be accomplished without compromising quality of care. If this new design in primary prevention is successful, the eradication of many communicable diseases could be accomplished, producing a healthier environment for everyone.

Two thirds of all employed nurses in the United States are currently working in hospital settings. However, projections for the future of nursing based on cost-containment and disease prevention health policies place increasing numbers of nurses in ambulatory care and other community-based health settings. In these areas, they will be better able to meet the health needs of the communities in which they work by providing much-needed health education and disease prevention programs designed to meet the specific health needs of each community.

Community health nurses provide health promotion and disease prevention programs related to the prevention and control of communicable diseases within the community. However, community health nurses do not work alone but rather are part of the multidisciplinary team that works together in the community to provide a front line of defense in preventing and controlling communicable diseases. These disciplines include sanitary engineering, public health, nursing, and medicine.

Most persons who contract communicable diseases are cared for at home and are seen on an outpatient basis. Community health nurses play a special role in the continuity of care provided for these persons as well as in prevention and control. For example, school nurses ensure vaccination of all children, occupational health nurses help keep industry safe for employees, STD clinic nurses provide health education and notifiable disease reporting, and nurse epidemiologists monitor surveillance systems and interpret data for appropriate planning of future interventions. It is important for each discipline to follow through with its role to provide the most comprehensive and effective care for the aggregate concerned.

This chapter will discuss modes of communicable disease transmission, prevention of transmission, reporting of communicable diseases, vaccine-preventable diseases and immunity, and STDs. The chapter will conclude with the application of the community health nursing process to a case study that illustrates the role of the community health nurse in prevention, case finding, reporting, and control as the needs of the individual, family, and other aggregates are addressed.

TRANSMISSION

There are three types of disease transmission in humans. Direct, indirect, and airborne are the routes available to all pathogens, and each can be interrupted if clearly understood and methods of prevention are adequately designed (Table 23–1). In addition, transmission can be vertical, or transplacental, or horizontal, occurring across a group of people such as within a family.

For any transmission to take place, there must be a human portal of entry *(host factor)* and a microbe from a source or reservoir *(agent factor)*. These two needs are different and very specific for each individual class of microbes; unfortunately, there are many possible routes for the spread and acquisition of communicable diseases in humans. Environmental factors such as crowding, pollution, and nutritional status may also influence the transmission of communicable diseases (see Chapter 24).

Direct Transmission

Direct transmission implies the immediate transfer of an infectious agent from an infected host or reservoir to an appropriate portal of entry in the human host through physical contact or droplets in the air.

Table 23–1 **Types of Transmission**	
Direct Transmission	**Indirect Transmission**
Physical contact	**Vehicle borne**
Biting	Fomites (toys)
Touching	Substances (food, blood)
Spitting	
Sexual contact	**Vector borne**
Fecal-oral	Mechanical
Anal intercourse	Biological
Oral-genital	
Airborne	**Airborne**
Dust and droplets	Dust and droplets
Droplet nuclei	Droplet nuclei

Direct, physical contact or spray from body fluids; indirect, vector or vehicle borne; airborne, aerosols and suspensions.

Data from Mausner, J. S., and Kramer, S.: Epidemiology: An Introductory Text. Philadelphia, W. B. Saunders, 1985.

Direct Transmission

Physical Contact
- Touching
- Kissing
- Sexual intercourse
- Biting

Droplets
- Spray that contacts a mucous membrane or other port of entry through sneezing, coughing, biting, singing, spitting, talking, or spray from urine

---

Spray from sneezing usually travels approximately 1 meter before the droplets fall on the ground. If someone is standing close enough, the droplets may make contact with an open wound or with mucous membranes such as eye conjunctiva, nose, or mouth, allowing the spread of infection to occur. This is why the exact distance a droplet can travel is of vital importance. This is one major route of transmission for some infectious diseases such as pulmonary tuberculosis. Once the pathogen reaches the lung and is established, it is extremely difficult to get rid of and is eventually fatal if not treated promptly and thoroughly.

Indirect Transmission

Indirect transmission is the spread of infection through vehicles such as inanimate objects, or *fomites,* and arthropods (vectors like mosquitos and ticks, which are known to be responsible for the transmission of communicable diseases).

Vehicle-borne or contaminated fomites can be any inanimate object, material, or substance that acts as a transport agent for the pathogen to be introduced into a suitable port of entry in the human host. Reproduction of the infectious agent may take place on or in the vehicle before the transmission of the pathogen. Fomites include toothbrushes, dirty dressings, any kind of equipment, cooking or eating utensils, toys, hairbrushes, linen, books, toilets, or currency, which is often overlooked but clearly responsible for pathogenic transmission. Everyone handles currency; it is passed back and forth without hands being washed during every business transaction, thus providing passage for microbes.

Last, substances can provide direct contact as indirect transmission occurs between the microbe and the human host in the form of food (milk, chicken, or water) that has been contaminated and taken directly into the digestive tract (fecal-oral route) or blood products (serum, platelets, and blood) and human transplants placed mechanically into the host via intravenous transfusion or surgery.

Vector-borne transmission can be carried out through biological and mechanical routes. The mechanical route does not involve multiplication or growth of the parasite or microbe within the vector itself. The parasite is transported as the vector mechanically carries the infectious agent in its intestinal tract, on its feet, or through its proboscis, or by the vector flying over or crawling on the human host or its food supply. In this way, the parasite is transported to its next victim.

Biological transmission occurs when the parasite grows or multiplies inside the vector or arthropod. This process is called *extrinsic incubation* and is defined as the period necessary for the reproduction of the parasite to take place within the arthropod, thus rendering it infective. This usually occurs within the intestinal tract or the circulatory system of the nonvertebrate host and must occur for the parasite to infect another person. The mode of transmission from the vector to the human host is often through a bite, a sting, or the deposit of fecal material on the skin at or near the puncture wound. This often causes an itching sensation,

---

Modes of Transmission

TO TEST your understanding of the previous information, try to identify which type of transmission is involved in the following:

1. A dog bite
2. The needle of an IV drug user
3. Biological warfare

---

which motivates the victim to rub or scratch the site and thus push the fecal material into the wound, where the parasite can easily enter the bloodstream of the host.

Airborne Transmission

Airborne transmission involves suspensions, particles of dust, aerosols, and droplet nuclei. The time frame in which an airborne particle can remain suspended greatly influences its virulence and infectivity. The size of the particle can also play an important role in how long it remains airborne and how successful it will be at penetrating the human lung. Particles of 5 micrometers or larger do not reach the lungs because they are trapped in the bronchial tree and eventually expelled. Particles of 1–5 micrometers may easily slide into the lung and be retained in the alveolar spaces. Studies have shown that particles of 2 micrometers or smaller have a 50% retention rate in the alveolar spaces, thus causing the greatest risk for infection (Mausner and Kramer, 1985). The smaller the particle, the less likely it is to settle out of the air too quickly, the greater the percentage of retention, the more virulent it will be, and the most likely it is to cause severe disease in the human host.

Droplet nuclei are small particles that separate from droplets through evaporation of water or fluid. Once this separation occurs, they can fall on the floor until they are kicked up as dust and inhaled into the lungs. If droplet nuclei are inhaled with the fluid still attached, they may separate in the respiratory tree and be inhaled into the alveolar space. Air conditioners and atomizers can cause particles to remain in the air for long periods of time, causing extreme risk if one person in a building has active pulmonary tuberculosis; research indicates that the mode of transmission for tuberculosis is droplet nuclei from airborne infections (Centers for Disease Control, 1990b). It is therefore important to have intact and reliable air filtration systems in all public buildings, especially in surgical suites and rooms reserved for isolation patients.

Dust is small particles from the soil that may include fungal spores, viruses, and bacteria. These particles become separated from the soil when blown into the air by wind or any other mechanical agitation such as that which occurs when shaking out linen or sweeping the floor. These activities can be hazardous if done improperly, thus spreading bacteria. This type of transmission can be extremely difficult to control as air quality deteriorates with growing urban and suburban populations, which are producing pollution at uncontrollable rates.

Prevention of Transmission

Prevention of transmission occurs at many levels. For example, the individual child must be taught hand washing and toilet hygiene; the family must know proper preparation and storage of food; and the community must provide a safe water supply and waste disposal system. Whether the community health nurse is teaching parents of infected children, day care workers, or caregivers of persons with AIDS, prevention of transmission is a major aspect of care. Guidelines developed for health professionals are available to assist the community health nurse in planning this care.

The Centers for Disease Control has devised guidelines for isolation precautions in hospitals (Garner and Simmons, 1983) that clearly define the techniques necessary to prevent the transmission of infectious organisms. These guidelines are applicable for hospitals and all other clinical environments such as health departments, community-based clinics, hospices, or even the home setting. Recommendations include hand washing; use of masks, gowns, and gloves; bagging and disposal of contaminated articles, equipment, linen, dishes, and soiled dressings; and protocol to be followed when handling laboratory specimens and used needles and syringes. It also outlines specifications for strict, contact, respiratory and tuberculosis isolation, as well as protocols for enteric, drainage and secretion, and blood and body secretion precautions. The guidelines define two types of isolation precautions: category-specific versus disease-specific. Each system has advantages and disadvantages, and every setting must determine the type of isolation precaution measures that are appropriate.

Universal blood and body fluid precautions, as outlined and recommended by the Centers for Disease Control, assume that all patients are infectious for HIV and other blood-borne pathogens, so all body fluids should be considered infectious, especially in emergency situations (Centers for Disease Control, 1987b). These precautions should be used by all health care personnel in every type of setting, including hospitals, clinics, and homes where there is provision of health care (Table 23–2).

Defining and Reporting Cases of Transmission

The Centers for Disease Control also produces the *Case Definitions for Public Health Surveillance* report (1990a), which describes in detail all of the diseases that must be reported to the Centers for Disease Control on a weekly basis, those that are kept under surveillance on a monthly basis, and those that are nonnotifiable but unusual and so should be reported when encountered. These classifications of diseases are defined according to confirmed cases, probable cases, laboratory-confirmed cases, clinically compatible cases, supportive laboratory results, epidemiologically linked cases, and diagnoses that meet the clinical case definition. Standardization of these definitions of disease is important for local, state, and national public health surveillance teams as it provides a baseline

---

Table 23–2
Universal Blood and Body Fluid Precautions

---

1. All health care workers should use appropriate barrier precautions to prevent skin and mucous membrane exposure when contact with blood or other body fluids of any patient is anticipated. Gloves should be worn for touching blood and body fluids and for performing venipuncture and other vascular access procedures. Gloves should be changed after contact with each patient. Masks and protective eyewear or face shields should be worn during procedures that are likely to generate droplets of blood or other body fluids to prevent exposure of mucous membranes of the mouth, nose, and eyes. Gowns or aprons should be worn during procedures that are likely to generate splashes of blood or other body fluids.

2. Hands and other skin surfaces should be washed immediately and thoroughly if contaminated with blood or other body fluids. Hands should be washed immediately after gloves are removed.

3. All health care workers should take precautions to prevent injuries caused by needles, scalpels, and other sharp instruments or devices during procedures, when cleaning used instruments, during disposal of used needles, and when handling sharp instruments after procedures. To prevent needlestick injuries, needles should not be recapped, purposely bent or broken by hand, removed from disposable syringes, or otherwise manipulated by hand. After they are used, disposable syringes and needles, scalpel blades, and other sharp items should be placed in puncture-resistant containers for disposal; the puncture-resistant containers should be located as close as practical to the use area. Large-bore reusable needles should be placed in a puncture-resistant container for transport to the reprocessing area.

4. Although saliva has not been implicated in HIV transmission, to minimize the need for emergency mouth-to-mouth resuscitation, mouthpieces, resuscitation bags, or other ventilation devices should be available for use in areas in which the need for resuscitation is predictable.

5. Health care workers who have exudative lesions or weeping dermatitis should refrain from all direct patient care and from handling patient care equipment until the condition resolves.

6. Pregnant health care workers are not known to be at greater risk of contracting HIV infection than are health care workers who are not pregnant; however, if a health care worker develops HIV infection during pregnancy, the infant is at risk of infection resulting from perinatal transmission. Because of this risk, pregnant health care workers should be especially familiar with and strictly adhere to precautions to minimize the risk of HIV transmission.

From Centers for Disease Control: Recommendations for prevention of HIV transmission in health-care settings. M. M. W. R. *36;*5–6, 1987*b*.

---

for comparison of data and monitoring of epidemiological trends across the country. Screening and intervention programs for disease control can readily be designed and implemented based on the data collected from adherence to this set of case definitions. It is important for the community health nurse to participate in this function because this nurse often is the only health care provider who will come into contact with many patients in the community who have no other access to health care.

The Centers for Disease Control also monitors national trends in reported communicable diseases. Reports by geographic region, state, and for the nation are published each week in the *Morbidity and Mortality Weekly Report.* Weekly and cumulative incidence totals of communicable disease and information on prevention and control are presented. Other topics include occupational and environmental hazards and unusual cases and outbreaks of disease (Table 23–3).

Knowledge of the principles and varied routes of transmission are essential to understanding and

---

Guide to Communicable Diseases
AN IMPORTANT resource for the community health nurse is an updated guide to communicable diseases:

Benenson, A. S.: Control of Communicable Diseases in Man. 15th Ed. Washington, D.C., American Public Health Association, 1990.

Table 23-3
National Notifiable Diseases Surveillance System (NNDSS)

List of All Notifiable Diseases

AIDS	Hansen disease	Rabies (animal
Amoebiasis	Hepatitis A	Rabies (human)
Anthrax	Hepatitis B	Rheumatic fever
Aseptic meningitis	Hepatitis (non-A, non-B)	Rocky Mountain spotted fever
Botulism (infant)	Hepatitis (unspecified)	Rubella
Botulism (wound)	Legionellosis	Salmonellosis
Botulism (unspecified)	Leptospirosis	Shigellosis
Brucellosis	Lyme disease	Syphilis (all stages)
Chancroid	Lymphogranuloma venereum	Syphilis (primary and secondary)
Cholera	Malaria	Syphilis (congenital)
Congenital rubella syndrome	Measles	Tetanus
Diphtheria	Meningococcal infections	Toxic shock syndrome
Encephalitis (post-chickenpox)	Mumps	Trichinosis
Encephalitis (post-mumps)	Pertussis	Tuberculosis
Encephalitis (post-other)	Plague	Tularemia
Encephalitis (primary)	Poliomyelitis (paralytic)	Typhoid fever
Gonorrhea	Psittascosis	Yellow fever
Granuloma inguinale		

Surveillance Maintained but Not Mandatory

Campylobacter infection	*Listeria monocytogenes* (listeriosis)
Chlamydia trachomatis infection	Mucopurulent cervicitis
Dengue fever	Nongonococcal urethritis
Genital herpes simplex virus infection	Pelvic inflammatory disease
Genital warts	Reye's syndrome
Giardiasis	Spinal cord injury
Haemophilus influenzae (invasive disease)	Varicella
Kawasaki syndrome	All other unusual outbreaks

controlling communicable diseases. Good hygienic practices are important, and hand washing is the principal defense against the transmission of infection. Nurses have an important role in breaking the chain of transmission. The identification and prevention of transmission of infectious organisms within the community must be accomplished. Community health nurses have a vital role in prevention, case finding, reporting, and control of communicable diseases. The reporting of notifiable diseases takes on new meaning for the community health nurse who works independently within the community as the liaison for each affected aggregate.

The following section will explore the communicable diseases that occur in various populations and can be prevented through the use of vaccines and appropriate technology. Epidemiological data will be used to define the scope of these problems in several different communities. Vaccine information is presented to assist the community health nurse in making appropriate decisions based on the aggregate targeted for such interventions. Polio, tuberculosis, measles, mumps, rubella, diphtheria, tetanus, pertussis, influenza, hepatitis B, and tuberculosis are communicable diseases that will be discussed.

VACCINE-PREVENTABLE DISEASES

The smallpox vaccine has not been given in the United States since 1971, and the last recorded case of naturally acquired smallpox was reported in Somalia in 1977 (Centers for Disease Control, 1991*d*). In 1980, the World Health Organization (WHO) declared smallpox completely eradicated

Table 23–4
Vaccination Status of U.S. Children in 1978 and 1985

Children Vaccinated for:	1978 (%)*	1985 (%)†
Measles	64	60.8
Mumps	51	58.9
Rubella	65	58.9

Statistics are for the United States only.

All percentages are for total number of children between the ages of 1 and 4.

* From Whaley, L. F., and Wong, D. L.: Nursing Care of Infants and Children. St. Louis, C. V. Mosby, 1983.

† From U.S. Bureau of the Census: Immunization Survey. Washington, D.C., U.S. Government Printing Office, 1990b, pp. 116–117.

worldwide. It is the first infectious disease that has been successfully eliminated. Many factors have contributed to this eradication, including the mode of transmission of the disease (close contact only), the location of smallpox in isolated areas, the ease of administration of the freeze-dried vaccine, the effectiveness of surveillance, the increased national priority, and the extent of community participation.

Immunity

The concept of *herd immunity* states that those not immunized will be safe if at least 80% of the population has been vaccinated. This is especially true for transmission of diseases that are found only in the human host and have no invertebrate host or other method of transmission, because without a virgin population to infect, the organism will be unable to live. Unfortunately, the U.S. Bureau of the Census reports that U.S. children have declining rates of immunization and, thus, a lack of protection through herd immunity (e.g., the most recent measles epidemic) (Table 23–4).

It is obvious that these issues must be addressed immediately, especially in areas of the United States with large populations of new immigrants (who may be infected with hepatitis B and tuberculosis), in urban and rural ghettos, and in the growing population of families with a lower socioeconomic status; the incidence of nonvaccinated children increases sharply in these groups. It is also important to assess which groups of U.S. children are not receiving their vaccination series routinely, and why they are not. Are they being excluded from this most important public health responsibility? Table 23–5 shows that black and other children have a much lower prevalence of complete vaccination series than their white counterparts.

The following technical information will provide details of the administration, dosage, schedule, risks, and care of vaccines. Different types of immunity will also be addressed, as well as the fears and misconceptions surrounding immunization practices.

There are several different kinds of immunity; each provides resistance to any of a number of specific infectious diseases. *Natural immunity* is an innate resistance to a specific antigen or toxin. *Acquired immunity* is derived from actual exposure to the specific infectious agent, toxin, or appropriate vaccine. *Active immunity* is present when the body can build its own antibodies, which provide protection from a bacterial or other antigenic substance. *Passive immunity* implies the temporary resistance that has been donated to the host

Table 23–5
Percentage of Children Vaccinated in 1985 by Age and Race

Vaccinated*	DTP (%)	Polio (%)	Measles (%)	Mumps (%)	Rubella (%)
All children age 1–4	64.9	55.3	60.8	58.9	58.9
White children age 1–4	68.7	58.9	63.6	61.8	61.6
Black and other children age 1–4	48.7	40.1	48.8	47.0	47.7
All children age 5–14	73.7	69.7	71.5	71.6	70.2
White children age 5–14	76.0	72.6	73.6	73.6	72.3
Black and other children age 5–14	64.0	57.5	62.6	63.2	61.4

* Three or more doses administered.

Data from U.S. Bureau of the Census: Immunization Survey, Washington, D.C., U.S. Government Printing Office, 1990b, pp. 116–117.

through transfusions of plasma proteins or from mother to neonate transplacentally and lasts only as long as the immunoglobulins remain in the bloodstream.

Active Immunization

Vaccines are either live and inactivated (attenuated) or killed; the virulence is removed from each, leaving only the antigenic property necessary to stimulate the human immune system to produce antibodies (Tables 23–6 and 23–7).

A *cold chain* is the system used to ensure that vaccines are kept below 8°C from the time they are manufactured until they reach the people to be vaccinated. There are many levels of a cold chain, including locations at the local, regional, and national areas to be served, and breaks can occur at

any of these levels due to, for example, bad roads, weather conditions, poor power supplies, and faulty thermometer readings. The importance of a cold chain is stressed because any improper storage that allows the vaccines to be exposed to high temperatures could cause them to lose their potency and render them completely useless. This becomes extremely difficult when distributing vaccines in rural areas that do not have access to electricity or cold storage. Many vaccine failures can be blamed on improper vaccine storage that has caused the loss of vaccine efficacy.

POLIO

Poliomyelitis vaccines are prepared by both live and killed virus and may cause dissimilar side effects. The live vaccine is a trivalent live attenuated

Table 23–6
Recommended Schedule for Immunization of Healthy Infants and Children*

Recommended Age†	Immunizations‡	Comments
2 Months	DTP, HbCV,§ OPV	DTP and OPV can be initiated as early as 4 weeks after birth in areas of high endemicity or during epidemics
4 Months	DTP, HbCV,§ OPV	2–Month interval (minimum of 6 weeks) desired for OPV to avoid interference from previous dose
6 Months	DTP, HbCV§	Third dose of OPV is not indicated in the United States but is desirable in other geographic areas where polio is endemic
15 Months	MMR,‖ HbCV¶	Tuberculin testing may be done at the same visit
15–18 Months	DTP,**†† OPV #	(See footnotes)
4–6 Years	DTP,§§ OPV	At or before school entry
11–12 Years	MMR	At entry to middle school or junior high school unless second dose previously given
14–16 Years	Td	Repeat every 10 years throughout life

* For all products used, consult manufacturer's package insert for instructions for storage, handling, dosage, and administration. Biologics prepared by different manufacturers may vary, and package inserts of the same manufacturer may change over time. Therefore, the physician should be aware of the contents of the current package insert.

† These recommended ages should not be construed as absolute. For example, 2 months can be 6–10 weeks. However, MMR usually should not be given to children younger than 12 months. (If measles vaccination is indicated, monovalent measles vaccine is recommended, and MMR should be given subsequently, at 15 months.)

‡ DTP, diphtheria and tetanus toxoids with pertussis vaccine; HbCV, *Haemophilus* b conjugate vaccine; OPV, oral poliovirus vaccine containing attenuated poliovirus types 1, 2, and 3, MMR, live measles, mumps, and rubella viruses in a combined vaccine; Td, adult tetanus toxoid (full dose) and diphtheria toxoid (reduced dose) for adult use.

§ As of October 1990, only one HbCV (HbOC) is approved for use in children younger than 15 months.

‖ May be given at 12 months of age in areas with recurrent measles transmission.

¶ Any licensed *Haemophilus* b conjugate vaccine may be given.

** Should be given 6–12 months after the third dose.

†† May be given simultaneously with MMR at 15 months.

May be given simultaneously with MMR and HbCV at 15 months or at any time between 12–24 months; priority should be given to administering MMR at the recommended age.

§§ Can be given up to the seventh birthday.

Adapted with permission from Report of the Committee on Infectious Diseases, 22nd ed. Copyright © 1991 American Academy of Pediatrics.

Table 23–7
Vaccine Routes, Dosages, and Requirements for Storage

Vaccine	Type	Dose and Route	Requirements for Storage (to Ensure Stability)
Trivalent oral poliovirus	Trivalent live virus	0.5 cc P.O.	Vaccine must be kept frozen and unopened
Inactivated poliovirus	Killed virus	1.0 cc S.Q.	2–8°C
Diphtheria	Toxoid	0.5 cc I.M.	2–8°C
Pertussis	Killed bacteria	0.5 cc I.M.	Do not freeze
Tetanus	Toxoid	0.5 cc I.M.	2–8°C
Measles-mumps-rubella	Live virus	1 Dose S.Q.	2–8°C; protect from light, reconstitute vaccine

Data from Howry, L. B., Bindler, R. M., and Tso, Y.: Pediatric Medications. Philadelphia, J. B. Lippincott, 1981.

virus vaccine that is administered orally to children under the age of 18 and used as primary inoculation for infants and children. Once swallowed, the vaccine attaches to the cellular mucosal lining of the intestines, where it colonizes and then enters the bloodstream to stimulate an antibody response. (For dosage and schedule, see Table 23–7.) Anyone recently immunized may excrete live attenuated virus or reverted wild-type virus in stool, so extra care should be taken when handling soiled diapers from these children because there is a risk of acquiring polio from this infectious waste. This vaccine may also cause paralysis within 2 months of inoculation, but the incidence is extremely rare — less than one in every 2 million doses given (Sherris et al., 1986) and much less than the risk of not vaccinating. The live vaccine is contraindicated for immunosuppressed persons or those presenting with acute gastritis and diarrhea. Intestinal disorder may inhibit the virus from attaching to the intestinal wall and thus nullify the inoculation. It is better to wait until the diarrhea subsides; if the child's return to the clinic is questionable, the dose can be given, and a second dose can be given if and when the child reappears after the gastritis clears up. For a variety of reasons, following recommended vaccination schedules is a major problem in both the United States and the developing world. Therefore, in both the United States and the developing world, it is recommended that the community health nurse administer all vaccines possible when the child visits the clinic, even if the child presents with fever. If there is a substantial risk of exposure to a pregnant woman who has not been previously immunized, she should receive the trivalent live attenuated oral polio virus vaccine

(Centers for Disease Control, 1988) because there is an increased risk of paralytic polio associated with pregnancy (Benenson, 1985).

MEASLES-MUMPS-RUBELLA

The measles-mumps-rubella vaccine is a combined live attenuated vaccine. The vaccine contains a small amount of neomycin, so the nurse administering it should inquire about sensitivity to the drug. Pregnant women should also avoid this live virus vaccine. Part of this vaccine may be cultured on chick embryo cells, causing an allergic reaction to anyone who has a known sensitivity to eggs. Any person receiving immunosuppressive therapy or suffering from an immunodeficiency disease should also avoid this inoculation.

Measles

Measles will be given special attention because it is the third largest infectious disease killer worldwide, exceeded only by diarrheal disease and malaria (Sherris et al., 1986). One percent of all world deaths annually are due to measles; this amounts to almost 2 million young people every year. In some areas of the world, one fourth of all children die from measles. This may be due to the fact that measles causes immunosuppression, so children who are already suffering from nutritional deprivation are more susceptible to opportunistic infections after they contract measles. The immune system of a child less than 15 months old is not mature enough to build reliable antibodies and provide lasting immunity after one measles inoculation. These young infants may also have remaining maternal antibodies that could interfere with their own antibody response. However, in endemic areas, it is important to administer the vaccine as early as 6 months and then repeat it when children are 12–18 months old; otherwise, they may die of measles before they reach 18 months.

Much of the European population is not immunized against measles because it is not required by law and there is not a strong immunization program set up to focus on measles. In Great Britain, more than 1,000 cases of measles are reported annually. Fewer than 20% of the children in France are vaccinated against measles. It was thought that most reported cases in the United States occurring over the past 10 years were imported, but it is now realized that this is not true and that only 1% of all U.S. measles cases in 1988 were imported (Johnson, 1989).

There are no subclinical cases of measles; every case is 100% visible, so this disease cannot hide itself. It is a disease that attacks only human beings and is spread by person-to-person contact without vector transmission. Measles is much more deadly when it attacks adults, contributing to the increase in measles-related mortality in the United States in 1989 (Table 23–8). The live attenuated measles vaccine may cause malaise and fever that can occur as long as 12 days after inoculation and may have a 1- to 3-day duration. Measles vaccine–related encephalopathy is rare, occurring in 1 of 1 million children. The vaccine is 98% efficacious, which renders measles totally preventable. It is the next disease targeted for world eradication, and plans by WHO have already been laid to cement this outcome.

In 1983, there were only 1,497 reported cases of measles in the United States, and 26 states reported

---

Why Are Measles Cases Increasing?

1. Preschool children are not yet immunized.
2. Some vaccines fail—especially those administered before 1975.
3. Some children are slipping through the system without being immunized.
4. Measles is attacking the older population and causing more deaths.

---

no cases of measles. By 1989, the number of reported cases had increased to 18,193, and measles-related mortality had increased to 22 cases. This represented a 12-fold increase in measles incidence over a 6-year time span. An epidemic was obvious.

Requirements for Worldwide Measles Eradication

1. A high level of immunization (at least 80%) must be achieved in the world population.
2. A strong international surveillance team must be ready to react to each reported case.
3. A strong immunization program must be internationally implemented to inoculate all people not yet immunized.

Mumps

The mumps vaccine may cause a mild fever a few weeks after inoculation. It is recommended that this vaccine be given after the age of 12 months and before the age of 12 years to reduce the chance of serious side effects. The mumps vaccine provides 96% protection for those immunized, but this leaves a small percentage of the inoculated population who have not seroconverted and have no real protection. If all children were inoculated with the mumps vaccine, then herd immunity would protect those who did not seroconvert. This is the goal.

Rubella

The incidence of rubella, previously called German measles, has greatly declined in the United States during the past decade (Benenson, 1985). It is recommended that all children over the age of 12 months receive this vaccine. Ninety-five percent seroconversion is achieved with one inoculation. A mild rash lasting 1 or 2 days may develop a few

---

Table 23–8
Annual Number of Reported Measles Cases and Deaths, 1983–1989

Year	No. of Reported Cases	Deaths
1983	1,497	4
1984	2,587	1
1985	2,822	4
1986	6,282	2
1987	3,655	2
1988	3,396	3
1989	18,193	22

Data from Centers for Disease Control: Summary of notifiable diseases —United States, 1989, M.M.W.R. *38*; 1–59, 1989.

days after this vaccine is given. Joint pain and swelling may also be experienced. Pregnant women who contract this disease should consider abortion secondary to the serious risk of fetal demise or malformations.

DIPHTHERIA-TETANUS-PERTUSSIS

Diphtheria-tetanus-pertussis (DTP) is a triple-antigen vaccine that combines diphtheria and tetanus toxoids with the pertussis vaccine. It is recommended for the initial vaccination series for children under the age of 7. Older children receiving their first inoculations should be administered adult toxoids and a separate pertussis vaccine because reactions to these drugs increase with age.

Diphtheria

Diphtheria toxoid will usually promote the formation of antibody against the toxoid for approximately 10 years. The vaccine may cause soreness at the site of injection, and fever may appear for 1 or 2 days.

Tetanus

Tetanus, previously called lockjaw, still occurs throughout the world. The tetanus bacillus can be found in soil that has been contaminated by animal excreta. This is a serious problem in areas where hygiene is poor and vaccination rates are very low. Neonatal tetanus is responsible for a large percentage of infant mortality in the developing world, primarily due to the use of contaminated instruments to sever the umbilical cord after birth.

The primary childhood series of tetanus is usually given as diphtheria-tetanus-pertussis in five successive doses. The tetanus toxoid may be given as a double antigen with diphtheria for children under the age of 6 years. After age 6 years, a child should be given the adult tetanus toxoid combined with a less potent dose of diphtheria toxoid. For adults, a booster of adult tetanus toxoid should be given every 10 years to provide consistent immunity from this disease. The vaccine may cause redness and swelling at the site of injection and fever for 1 or 2 days. The toxoid can also produce urticaria and general malaise.

Pertussis

Pertussis vaccine is recommended for children from 6 months to 6 years old but not for those over the age of 7 because the risks from receiving the vaccine increase with age. Reactions from the vaccine may include neurological symptoms, which should be reported immediately to a physician.

INFLUENZA

In the United States, influenza epidemics continue to occur with regular frequency. This causes continued serious concern for both public health and medical practitioners. The best defense is to review the information concerning the annually revised trivalent vaccine and encourage patients at risk to be inoculated. Each new epidemic brings a different and mutated strain of the virus, often more virulent than the last. Therefore, it is necessary to be revaccinated with the most current vaccine every autumn. All vaccine from previous years should not be reused but instead properly disposed. It is recommended that all persons over the age of 65; persons with chronic cardiac, pulmonary, or immunosuppressive diseases; and children (6 months to 18 years old) receiving long-term aspirin therapy be inoculated because these populations tend to be more susceptible to influenza-related complications and mortality (Centers for Disease Control, 1987a). Any person entering an endemic area should also be revaccinated annually.

HEPATITIS B

Many forms of hepatitis afflict people around the world, but the virus leading to the highest incidence of morbidity and mortality is hepatitis B virus. In the United States, there is an increasing number of persons who have active hepatitis B as well as carriers of the virus who continue to spread disease without showing signs of active infection. It has been estimated that in the United States, at least 15,000 people become carriers (approximately 23% are neonates) every year (Hollinger et al., 1990). This carrier status of chronic disease is extremely dangerous because severe damage to the liver may be occurring without obvious symptomatology to the patient (Sherlock, 1990). Eighty percent of all cases of primary liver cancer are due to hepatitis B virus (Maynard, 1990). Worldwide, there are approximately 300 million hepatitis B surface antigen (HBsAg) carriers, many of whom have no clinical signs of disease. The serological markers for hepatitis B virus in persons without a history of acute infection suggest that it is extremely common to have subclinical cases of disease (Sherlock, 1990). Undetected acute subclinical cases of hepatitis B virus infection could include as many as two thirds of all adult cases and most neonatal cases (Hollinger et al., 1990).

More than a decade ago, the target populations for contraction of the hepatitis B virus were homosexual men engaging in high-risk behavior, health care workers who were exposed to contaminated blood and body secretions, and people working in institutions for the developmentally disabled. Blood transfusions and dialysis were also responsible for a moderate percentage of hepatitis B infections. In the past decade, new groups have emerged as those at greatest risk—parenteral drug users, heterosexuals engaging in sexual contact with many different partners, and the large immigrant populations from Southeast Asia. This transformation is due in part to the aggressive change in behavior of homosexual men, the emergence of hepatitis B as an STD in the heterosexual population (Alter et al., 1990), the current immigration of groups with significant incidence of carrier status and active infection, and licensing of the hepatitis B vaccine in 1982. Vaccine coverage of health care workers along with changes in the use of universal isolation precautions for all blood and body secretions as recommended by the Centers for Disease Control in 1983 are responsible for much of the decrease of occupation-related cases of infection. The pool of regular blood donors has also changed, resulting in fewer transfusion infections. This is due to more rigorous screening of blood and the prohibition of high-risk donors.

Vaccination coverage has reached about 2.5 million people, 80% of whom are health care workers. It is estimated that only 7% of all people at risk for contracting this disease have been vaccinated.

After 6 months, approximately 90% of adults and 2% of infants and children experience clear-

---

Table 23–9
Universal Infant Hepatitis B Immunization Recommendations

For children born to mothers **not** infected with the hepatitis B virus

* Schedule one: Hepatitis B vaccine

First dose given soon after birth, before child is discharged from hospital
Second dose given between 1 and 2 months
Last dose given between 6 and 18 months
or
* Schedule two: Hepatitis B vaccine

First dose given between 1 and 2 months
Second dose given at 4 months
Last dose between 6 and 18 months

From CDC Fax Information Service, Document No. 361351 (November 19, 1992), based on recommendations of the Advisory Committee on Immunization Practice.

---

ance of serum HBsAg. The remainder of these children will become carriers for life, will continue to spread infection, and will have increased risk of mortality from chronic liver disease and hepatocellular carcinoma.

It is extremely important to continue effective implementation of the current programs for vaccination of all pregnant women who are seropositive for HBsAg, which indicates carrier status, and to provide all of their newborn infants with hepatitis B immune globulin and hepatitis B vaccine at birth. These neonates should then be followed up at 1 and 6 months with boosters to complete this series. It has been recommended that due to the high incidence of horizontal and vertical transmissions in Asian populations in the United States, all children born to Asian-American mothers should

---

Hepatitis B Carrier Status

1. Male-to-female ratio is 6:1 for carrier status.
2. Clearance of serum HBsAg level after 6 months occurs in approximately 90% of adults and 2% of infants and children.

Data from Sherlock, S.: Hepatitis B: The disease. Vaccine 8(suppl);S6–S8, 1990.

Vaccine Recommendations for Newborns of HBsAg-Positive Carrier Status Mothers
At birth
    Hepatitis B immune globulin (HBIG)
    Hepatitis B vaccine
At 1 month
    Hepatitis B vaccine booster
At 6 months
    Hepatitis B vaccine booster

Data from Hollinger et al.: Controlling hepatitis B virus transmission in North America. Vaccine 8(suppl);S122–S128, 1990.

be immunized against hepatitis B virus (Hollinger, 1990). It has been suggested that immunizing this population would be more cost effective than screening and testing before vaccinating those with positive screening results.

Several factors contribute to the success of a worldwide and/or a national eradication program for hepatitis B. In 1988, the cost for three doses of the vaccine in the United States was $62.04. The U.S. government has contract prices for all other required vaccines; these costs have been greatly reduced, primarily because of the large volume purchased. When the hepatitis B vaccine is required by law, it will become affordable for everyone. Until then, the cost of the vaccine alone, not including that of an organized program for administration and education, is prohibitive for those at highest risk of contracting this disease.

The second prohibitive factor is the presence of a carrier status with this disease. As long as there are carriers (300 million worldwide [Ghendon, 1990]), this disease can never be eradicated, only controlled. For eradication, there must be universal immunization of infants and adolescents (Alter, 1990). This can be accomplished by requiring the hepatitis B vaccine as part of the regular immunization schedule for all infants and children and insisting on more stringent coverage for this basic immunization series.

Non–follow-up with the second and third inoculations can also inhibit the success of seroconversion; therefore, strict programs for follow-up must be established. There will always be a small percentage of persons who do not seroconvert, even after three doses. However, if everyone received the series, then this small cohort would be protected through herd immunity.

A general lack of knowledge by physicians and the public at large regarding hepatitis B as an STD and the availability of a vaccine able to prevent it are other reasons for the continued spread of infection. It is the responsibility of physicians and nurses who work with populations at risk to provide education and encouragement to be vaccinated.

With the present-day stigma surrounding homosexuals and intravenous drug users, it has become more difficult to target these highly susceptible populations. Studies have also found that contrary to the success achieved in the gay community, the intravenous drug user population has not altered its behavior even after massive educational programs have been implemented.

The final hindrance for hepatitis B elimination comes from the increased number of sexual partners in the heterosexual community (including intravenous drug users). Hepatitis B can be considered an STD, and education is the only way to prevent the spread of infection because immunizing this entire population would be essentially impossible. This escalating risk factor is responsible for more transmission than can be attributed to the homosexual population (Alter, 1990).

From the following discussion, it becomes evident that worldwide eradication of hepatitis B virus is a major undertaking. The fact that the human hepatitis B virus has no vector or animal reservoir makes eradication possible. The existence of an effective vaccine along with the reliable screening of blood and its components for HBsAg offer optimism for the future. More research is needed to determine the duration of immunity from the vaccine and the interval required between boosters. The presence of a growing population with carrier status will continue to make eradication extremely difficult. However, with the global vaccination of all infants and children as well as high-risk populations, comprehensive worldwide eradication of new cases of hepatitis B can occur within the next 20–30 years (Ghendon, 1990). A dynamic approach to the design and implementation of an effective immunization policy with adherence to detailed protocol is necessary to reach these populations. A comprehensive educational program is necessary to teach the general public about the risks of contracting hepatitis B and the need for vaccinating against this disease. The present cost of the vaccine will continue to be a deterrent for those at highest risk for contracting the disease, but effective legislation can help remedy this situation.

PULMONARY TUBERCULOSIS

Although the incidence of pulmonary tuberculosis has slightly decreased during the past 10 years, it remains a menace to the public health of the United States. The rate of new tuberculosis cases (per 100,000 population) has slightly declined, but the incidence (in several minority ethnic groups) is increasing. The percentage of cases ranked by race and ethnicity in 1989 was highest for African-Americans between the ages of 25 and 44. Second in incidence were whites between the ages of 55 and 90. Hispanics ranked third, with their incidence also peaking in those age 25 to 44. Asian and Pacific-Islanders were fourth, and Native Americans and Alaskan Natives were last; for both groups, the incidence was highest in the young adult populations. More cases are developing annually among the new immigrant populations arriving in the United States. People born in the United States have lower rates of tuberculosis (as a group) than those who were born outside of the United States and then immigrated. Tuberculosis affecting immigrants usually occurs within 5 years of entering the United States (Centers for Disease Control, 1990c). There has been a dramatic increase in tuberculosis rates for health care workers, particularly of multidrug-resistant strains of tuberculosis, implicating nosocomial (hospital acquired) transmission or inappropriate drug therapy as the cause. Not only are pulmonary tuberculosis rates within the HIV-positive group increasing, but cases are presenting with radiographic features different from those of most people with the typical clinical manifestations of this disease (Mendelson and Adler, 1990). This is particularly dangerous because increased difficulty in identification of active tuberculosis cases leads to increasing rates of secondary exposure.

The best approach to tuberculosis control starts with an early detection program to isolate and treat identified cases of active tuberculosis. An effective screening program should be implemented to help identify those at risk for developing the disease. This should include the routine testing of all health care employees, teachers, and other professionals working in high-risk areas. Requirements and guidelines should be followed for health screening and follow-up of all aliens entering the country. Rapid diagnostic tools should be used to hasten identification of cases, and appropriate chemotherapeutic agents should be prescribed to ensure the reversal of active cases and/or the prevention of disease for those at risk. Health care facilities need to decrease the risks of airborne contamination through the use of air quality control measures and isolation protocols for identified active cases of tuberculosis. Public health nurses have a special task in completing home visits to ensure medication compliance for those on antituberculosis drugs and to provide follow-up screening for family and household members at risk for contracting tuber-

culosis from the resident being treated. An immediate epidemiological response to any outbreak of disease would help to arrest an impending epidemic. It has also been recommended that all HIV-positive persons and those in high-risk categories be suspected of having tuberculosis and routinely screened for disease. Vaccination with bacille Calmette-Guérin vaccine may be recommended in areas with high incidence and prevalence of tuberculosis transmission, particularly in some developing countries.

VACCINES FOR TRAVEL

For adults traveling outside of the United States into regions endemic for specific infectious diseases, vaccination is recommended (Table 23–10). There are many other vaccines available, and depending on the area, the season, and the likelihood of exposure, each vaccine should be considered. It is important for all people who will travel abroad to obtain the most current recommendations from

---

Immunization Guidelines

AS THE rate of health-related research increases, it is crucial that up-to-date sources of information regarding immunizations be checked periodically. Recommendations, policies, and procedures concerning immunization information are governed internationally by the World Health Organization and nationally (in the United States) by the Committee on Infectious Diseases of the American Academy of Pediatrics and the Advisory Committee on Immunization Practices of the U.S. Public Health Service. Occasionally, differences in opinions occur regarding information from these agencies, and it is extremely important for the community health nurse to thoroughly consider the population and the policies of the local health agency when interpreting these recommendations and procedures.

The implementation of these guidelines by physicians and nurses helps to protect the community from disease and disaster. When these recommendations are not followed, the public health system is jeopardized along with all of its constituents. A breakdown in this chain can leave children unimmunized, workers unprotected, and surveillance systems vulnerable to incomplete or inaccurate information.

Table 23–10
International Travel Vaccines Available and Recommended for Adults Entering Endemic Areas

Vaccine	Dosage	Interval
Cholera	1 Dose (0.5 cc)	Every 6 months
Hepatitis*	3 Doses (1.0 cc)	Unknown
Immune globulin†	1 Dose (5.0 cc)	Every 4–6 months
Influenza	2 Doses (0.5 cc)	First year given 4 weeks apart
	1 Dose (0.5 cc)	Every year
Japanese encephalitis	2 Doses (1.0 cc)	At 12 months; then every 4 years
Malaria‡	Prophylaxis—check for chloroquine resistance	Continuously while in endemic regions
Meningococcus A/C/Y/W-135	1 Dose	Every 3 years
Plague	2 Doses (0.5 cc)	6 Months apart
	1 Dose (0.5 cc)	1–2 Years after second dose (above)
	1 Dose (0.2 cc)	Years of possible exposure
Rabies, human diploid cell	3 Doses (1.0 cc)	Days 0, 7, and 21 or 28
	1 Dose (1.0 cc) pending titer check	At 2-year intervals— check titer if exposure remains possible
Tuberculosis bacille Calmette-Guérin vaccine	1 Dose (0.1 cc)	Once
Typhoid	2 Doses (0.5 cc)	4 Weeks apart
	1 Dose (0.5 cc)	Every 3 years
Yellow fever	1 Dose (0.5 cc)	Every 10 years

* Hepatitis vaccine can be Heptavax, Recombivax, or Engerix B.

† Immune globulin is also called gamma globulin.

‡ Many different kinds of malaria prophylaxis are available for the different strains of malaria. Currently, there is no vaccine available. Check status of chloroquine resistance in area.

    Data from Benenson et al.: Control of Communicable Diseases in Man. 14th Ed. Washington, D.C., American Public Health Association, 1985; Centers for Disease Control: Health Information for International Travel. Atlanta, Georgia, Centers for Disease Control, 1988; Ghendon: WHO Strategy for the global elimination of new cases of hepatitis B vaccine *8*(suppl);S129–132, 1990; Sherris et al.: Immunizing the World's Children. Population Rep. *L*;154–192, 1986; Wolfe et al.: Health Hints for the Tropics. 10th Ed. Washington, D.C., American Society of Tropical Medicine and Hygiene, 1989.

the Office of Overseas Travel at the Centers for Disease Control (Atlanta, Georgia). They publish an annual document, *Health Information for International Travel,* and provide a hot-line for international travelers [(404) 332-4559].

International Certificates of Vaccination, printed by WHO, usually on a heavy yellow paper, should be obtained from a physician when any of these vaccinations are administered, and this record of their administration should be carried at all times with the person's passport while traveling.

SUMMARY

Millions of lives are saved each year through immunization against the most common and deadly childhood diseases. Immunization against these diseases is safe and effective, but more attention must be focused on the distribution and delivery of vaccines in which the integrity has been maintained through the use of a cold chain. Measles is responsible for a large percentage of worldwide infant and child mortality, and it has been targeted as the next disease to be eradicated by WHO. Mumps and rubella are preventable through vaccination and should be administered as part of the infant schedule of inoculations. Diphtheria and pertussis remain serious causes of morbidity in developing countries, although they are preventable through the use of diphtheria-tetanus-pertussis vaccination. Neonatal tetanus is most often contracted at birth through contaminated instruments used to sever the umbilical cord. This is almost unknown in developed areas but remains a major cause of mortality in developing countries. Polio vaccines are administered orally, are very inexpensive, and provide long-term immunity from disease. Influenza virus changes virility every year, and those at risk of infection should be inoculated annually. Tuberculosis remains a disabling disease for many people throughout the world, and routine vaccination with bacille Calmette-Guérin vaccine may be recommended in areas of high endemicity. Hepatitis B has emerged as the greatest carrier threat to the public health of large numbers of people. The absence of a cure or adequate treatment for this disease brings public education to the center of preventive measures. For all of these diseases, prevention is the best cure.

SEXUALLY TRANSMITTED DISEASES

STDs that are transferred from host to recipient through sexual intercourse and/or sexual activity use a unique form of direct transmission. Along with the well-known diseases such as gonorrhea, syphilis, herpes, and trichomonas, many other microbes are now thought to be transmitted sexually due to the prevalence of alternative sexual practices such as oral-genital contact and anal intercourse. These specific activities increase the risk of fecal-oral contamination and infection. Diseases such as hepatitis B, AIDS, giardiasis, amebiasis, salmonellosis, and shigellosis are examples of this latest risk. Because of the prevalence and danger involved in the acquisition of these diseases, fecal-oral contamination will be discussed later. Incubation periods of selected STDs are listed in Table 23–11.

Chlamydia trachomatis

Chlamydia trachomatis, the bacterial organism responsible for causing chlamydial infections in humans, is often asymptomatic and leads to ocular, pulmonary, enteric, and genital tract infections. The latter group includes approximately 50% of nongonococcal urethritis in men and women and epididymitis in men. It is also responsible for obstructive infertility, ectopic pregnancy, and one third of all cases of pelvic inflammatory disease in women. It causes conjunctivitis in infants exposed at birth, leading to pneumonia in approximately 10% of infected cases. It is believed that infection rates in adolescent females may be as high as 40% in some populations (Martin, 1990). Currently, genital infections from *C. trachomatis* are not considered a notifiable disease by the Centers for Disease Control, although surveillance of the disease is being carried out.

The female organ most often infected by *C. trachomatis* is the endocervix; little or no inflammation is caused, so an asymptomatic infection results. Chronicity allows secondary scarring of the fallopian tubes to occur, resulting in permanent obstructive infertility and, possibly, ectopic pregnancies, which are life threatening. Studies have shown that a significant number of patients infected with *C. trachomatis* are also infected with *Neisseria gonorrhoeae.* Association with *Trichomonas vaginalis* has also been indicated.

It is for this reason that routine annual screening should be done on all sexually active patients, both male and female. Populations at high risk should receive special attention in the screening process and include sexually active adolescent females, women with multiple sexual partners, and African-Americans (African-American males are at a higher risk for asymptomatic disease than any other ethnic group) (Martin, 1990). Through routine screening, infections can be identified using new nonculture diagnostic tests that are readily available and not prohibitively expensive for rou-

Table 23–11 Incubation Periods of Selected Sexually Transmitted Diseases	
Sexually Transmitted Disease	**Incubation Period**
Chlamydia	Five to 10 days or longer
Gonorrhea	Approximately 2–7 days
Herpes simplex virus	Two to 12 days
HIV	Unknown, 6 months to 10 years
Human papillomavirus	Approximately 4 months
Syphilis	Ten days to 10 weeks; usually 3 weeks

Data from Benenson et al.: Control of Communicable Diseases in Man. 14th Ed. Washington, D.C., American Public Health Association, 1985.

tine use. Early identification and treatment of all sexual partners are advised to prevent long-term complications. Although treatment for *C. trachomatis* is easy, painless, and affordable, emphasis should be placed on prevention through health and sex education and the use of condoms during sex.

Neisseria gonorrhoeae

Neisseria gonorrhoeae is found only in the human host and can cause infertility through tubal occlusion (Goldsmith, 1990), perinatal infections, and even neoplasia if allowed to remain untreated. Unfortunately, gonorrhea is often asymptomatic in women and sometimes asymptomatic in men. Therefore, it is recommended that routine screening for gonorrhea be performed by the primary care physician during the annual physical examination of all sexually active individuals. It has also been recommended by the National Gonococcal Isolate Surveillance Project, which was implemented by the Centers for Disease Control in 1987, that all partners of infected individuals be screened and treated for gonococcal infections. There are many problems that have been identified as causing the recent upsurge of reported cases of infection by *N. gonorrhoeae*. The practice of sex-for-drugs within the poor urban population, the emergence of strains of gonococcal organisms that are resistant to antibiotics, and noncompliance with drug regimens for treating gonococcal infections are examples. However, the profound changes in the sexual behavior of homosexual men out of fear of contracting the AIDS virus has reduced the incidence of gonorrhea in this population. In addition, drugs have been developed that are better able to fight these infections with single doses.

From 1965 through 1975, there was a dramatic increase in the incidence of reported cases of gonorrhea—from almost 325,000 to nearly 1 million cases (Centers for Disease Control, 1989). This was due in large part to a new openness in sexual behavior among homosexuals and the community at large. The end of the war in Southeast Asia and the return of soldiers who had been sexually active overseas brought to the United States the exotic imported penicillin-resistant penicillinase-producing strain of *N. gonorrhoeae* (PPNG). By 1980, the incidence of reported gonorrhea leveled off; then, the AIDS epidemic hit the homosexual community, bringing with it changes in sexual behavior among middle-class white gay

men, which reduced the incidence of gonorrhea in this population. The result of the impending decade of increased drug use, occurring parallel to the AIDS epidemic, dramatically increased the incidence of gonorrhea in the poor urban population (Judson, 1990).

The dose of penicillin required to treat gonorrhea has increased since 1954, secondary to the organism's ability to mutate and adapt to elevated titration of modern chemotherapeutic regimens. It has therefore been necessary to develop new drugs to fight this organism with a single intramuscular injection (ceftriaxone or spectinomycin). It is recommended that follow-up occur with a second drug (doxycycline) administered orally for 7 days to protect against underlying chlamydial infection and prevent another resistant strain of gonorrheal organisms from developing.

One telephone survey of primary care physicians in Washington, D.C., an area of high incidence for both HIV and STD infections, found that the majority of physicians did not regard their patients to be at risk for developing gonorrhea and therefore did not routinely screen them or obtain detailed sexual histories (Bowman et al., 1991). Primary care physicians and nurses who work in STD clinics in the community must familiarize themselves with the latest information regarding STDs and their diagnoses and treatments. A complete sexual history should be taken from all sexually active patients, and routine screening should be carried out annually, because many cases of gonorrhea in women are asymptomatic and can cause serious irreversible consequences. Risk should be identified from the sexual history, and screening procedures should be carried out. Incidence should be reported to the local health department, and recommendations must be followed to reach all patients with active and potential infections.

Herpes Simplex Virus

Herpes simplex virus (HSV) afflicts approximately 700,000 new victims in the United States annually, and 90% of these genital infections are caused by HSV-2 (Peaceman and Gonik, 1991). Because many genital infections have the same clinical presentations, it is important to differentiate the causal virus with a culture. It takes about 1 week for lesions to appear after a person has become infected, although up to three of four persons may carry the antibody unknowingly, without having an outbreak. A primary herpetic infection is often extremely painful and debilitating. Treatment may decrease the duration of viral shedding, healing, and symptoms in primary outbreaks but is less effective in reducing the frequency and severity of recurrences. However, episodes may reappear at any time; it is uncertain what causes recurrences, but they have been attributed to a number of causes, including physical stimuli and increased levels of emotional stress. Due to the incurability of the disease, its unpredictability, and associated stigma, careful education is necessary, and counseling may be recommended (Swanson and Chenitz, 1989). The latency and reactivation of HSV are not clearly understood, and emphasis should be placed on prevention of HSV. A person presenting with active lesions should not engage in sexual intercourse until the lesions subside and should always use safer sex practices, including condoms and spermicides containing nonoxynol 9, during sex because asymptomatic viral shedding occurs in many infected individuals. Caution should be taken, however, because condoms and spermicides do not protect from perineal and extragenital lesions (Swanson and Chenitz, 1989).

Genital herpes is the most common cause of genital ulcers in the Western world. Genital ulcers place persons at high risk of infection with human immunodeficiency virus (HIV); therefore, persons with genital herpes are at high risk of HIV infection (Schmid, 1990).

Human Immunodeficiency Virus Infection

Acquired immunodeficiency syndrome (AIDS), caused by HIV infection, was first recognized in 1981 and has since become a leading cause of worldwide morbidity and mortality. In the United States, more than 100,000 AIDS-related deaths have been reported to the Centers for Disease Control since 1981; nearly one third were reported in 1990. During the 1980s, the demographic distribution of HIV/AIDS incidence was highest among homosexual or bisexual males and male or female intravenous drug users. In large urban areas such as San Francisco, New York City, and Los Angeles, HIV/AIDS was identified as the leading cause of death among adult men between the ages of 25 and 44 (Centers for Disease Control, 1991a).

Although the majority of AIDS/HIV-related deaths have occurred in the white population, the highest death *rates* have been reported in the African-American and Hispanic communities. According to the national AIDS surveillance program, AIDS-related deaths per 100,000 population in 1990 were 29.3 for blacks, 22.2 for Hispanics, 8.7 for whites, 2.8 for Asian/Pacific-Islanders, and 2.8 for American Indians/Alaskan Natives (Centers for Disease Control, 1991a). All cultures have attitudes, beliefs, and practices surrounding illness and death. Many cultures perceive illness as a result of immoral transgressions and that diseases of the blood are imbalances in a person's spiritual life (see Chapter 16). To educate about AIDS transmission, insight into these cultural dynamics surrounding blood and body secretions can greatly enhance the effectiveness of programming activities designed to reach specific segments of the population.

As we enter the 1990s, AIDS is escalating as a cause of death among women. In 1983, the first female cases of AIDS were reported; by 1990, the Centers for Disease Control reported that more than 10,000 U.S. women had died from AIDS. Fifty-five percent of all AIDS cases in women have been reported between 1989 and 1991, and 51% of these cases are among intravenous drug users. Most of these cases occurred in women of childbearing age, so integrating prevention, support, and treatment services into customary sites of care for women would enhance access for these women and thus reduce further incidence. At the Seventh International AIDS Conference in Florence, Italy, June 16–21, 1991, several studies were presented that focused on women and AIDS, a few of which will be presented here.

A recent study in New York City focused on women attending empowerment sessions. After the sessions, these women were more likely to feel they knew a lot about AIDS, were better able to protect themselves, and were more likely to have learned new ways to talk to their partners (Richie et al., 1991).

Another study in New York City recruited Latina women from the poorest section of the South Bronx to become AIDS educators for their peers. These women attended a culturally based program that was taught in Spanish and focused on empowerment and self-esteem. These peer educators were either HIV positive, recovering intravenous drug users, or homeless, or had a person with AIDS (called a PWA) in their family. This perspective gave them a sense of dedication to help their otherwise "unreachable" community (Cordova and Norwood, 1991).

These studies suggest that greater attention should be focused on women and AIDS. In some urban areas, such as New York City, HIV/AIDS has become a leading cause of infant and child mortality among black and Hispanic children, exceeding all other infectious diseases (Centers for Disease Control, 1991*a*). Because women of childbearing age can infect not only themselves but also their unborn children, information for empowerment and prevention must be better disseminated to reach those at risk.

Geriatric populations are also reporting high HIV/AIDS incidence rates, contracted predominantly from blood transfusions (Fillit, 1991). In 1989, 3% of all reported AIDS-related deaths in the United States occurred in people over the age of 60 (Centers for Disease Control, 1989). Statistics from 1991 show that 4% of AIDS cases occurred in people over the age of 70.

In 1989, 108 adolescent HIV/AIDS deaths were reported in the United States. Prevalence rates for people ages 11 to 24 have doubled each year since 1983 (Strunin, 1991). Studies on adolescent risk perception show "confusion about casual and sexual transmission of the virus"; therefore, many teenagers engage in unsafe sexual activity due to false beliefs about the transmission of HIV/AIDS. Reported rates of intravenous drug use vary in this population, as does the level of knowledge regarding AIDS and the beliefs surrounding this disease (Centers for Disease Control, 1990*d*). Studies assessing sexual and other health risk behaviors in adolescents are becoming more prevalent as the incidence of HIV/AIDS rises in this population. One study completed by the Centers for Disease Control and recently presented at the Seventh International AIDS Conference assessed adolescent (13 to 19 years old) client visits to publicly funded counseling and testing sites in 30 states. This study found that adolescents are more likely to be seen in STD, family planning, and prenatal clinics; are more likely to be African-American and female; and most often reported themselves to be at "heterosexual risk." They were also more likely to refuse HIV testing compared with adults and less likely to return for their results (or they delayed their return). It was concluded that further atten-

tion should be placed on risk assessment and HIV testing along with the provision of effective posttest counseling (Moore et al., 1991).

A second study done in Italy and presented at the AIDS conference suggested addressing health education to youth before they enter the "at risk" age to avoid behaviors due to lack of information. Television and mass media were identified as the most important sources of information (Guasticchi et al., 1991).

A study in France found that the image of condoms has improved but that condoms remain "masculine" objects and that educational efforts need to focus on the accessibility of condoms as well as the improvement of interpersonal skills (Spencer et al., 1991).

In the Madonna Project, conducted in Sweden, 30 people were dressed in red overalls (called the Red Army) and attended rock concerts and other public events where they sold condoms at a low cost and promoted the message to "Be Careful" or "Protect Yourself." This approach was particularly useful in reaching 50,000–60,000 youths at a

---

Centers for Disease Control 1991 Recommendations for Minimizing HIV Transmission for Health Care Workers

1. Follow universal precautions for all blood and body fluids.
2. Health care workers with weeping dermatitis or exudative lesions should not engage in direct patient care activities, contaminate patient care equipment or devices, or perform invasive procedures until lesions heal.
3. Exposure-prone procedures should be identified by each institution in which they are performed (medical, dental, or surgical).
4. Exposure-prone procedures should not be performed by HIV-infected health care workers, unless cleared by an expert review panel; then, prospective patients should be notified of the health care worker's positive HIV status.
5. Health care workers who perform exposure-prone procedures should be aware of their own HIV status.

Data from Centers for Disease Control: Recommendations for preventing transmission of human immunodeficiency virus and hepatitis B virus to patients during exposure-prone invasive procedures. M. M. W. R. 40;4–5, 1991c.

Table 23–12
Categories of Experimental Anti-HIV Drugs

Drug	Use in Postexposure Prophylaxis
Nucleoside analogues (ddI, ddC)	Significant toxicity such as peripheral neuropathy; potent in vivo
Hyperimmune globulin	Problematic secondary to variations in viral envelope protein
Vaccines	Thirteen being tried; field trials about to start, and WHO is in process of choosing sites. Success is probably years away; duration of immunity is still under experimental questioning. Probably never to be used for postexposure
Soluble CD4	Inhibitor of virus binding, in phase II clinical evaluation, long half-life, may be expensive, highly potent, and specific in vitro
Polyanions (dextran sulfate, heparin)	Inexpensive, short half-life, parenteral only, anticoagulation dangerous, moderate potency in vitro
Biological response modifiers (interferon)	Alpha clinically available in trial with AZT, toxicity with high doses, long-lived antiviral activity
Virus production and assembly inhibitors (protease inhibitor, N-butyl DNJ)	Highly potent in vitro; to prevent new viral formation in infected cells
GLQ223 (compound Q)	Early clinical trials very toxic; if used repeatedly may cause anaphylaxis

time and raising awareness of HIV/STD (Haglind et al., 1991).

Health care workers are not at increased occupational risk for contracting HIV/AIDS if they follow universal precautions for contact with blood and body secretions. The estimated HIV seropositivity rate among U.S. health care workers is 3%, which parallels the national HIV prevalence rate.

Several experimental treatments for AIDS, HIV infection, and postexposure prophylaxis are being studied in research laboratories around the world, but currently there is no cure. Some of these drug regimens have been approved by the Food and Drug Administration in the United States, and others have been given research permission on a limited basis for PWA.

Unfortunately, many of these drugs cause toxicity and/or severe side effects that render them incompatible for most individuals infected with HIV. Table 23–12 outlines these categories of experimental anti-HIV drugs and their use for postexposure prophylaxis (Flexner, 1991).

Statistics and projections for the prevalence of HIV/AIDS show that it will continue to rise into the next decade. Therefore, our goal must be to decrease the incidence rates for the transmission of AIDS/HIV in all segments of our population. Men, women, children, and the elderly have specific needs that must be addressed through creative and dynamic programming designed to educate and empower people so they can protect themselves against this deadly virus. Anything and everything should be tried to educate the public. It has been suggested that condom dispensers and clean-needle machines line up side-by-side next to automated teller machine banking systems and drive-through fast food lines. Surveillance systems should be enforced to assist in identifying populations at high risk and designing programs to meet the needs of these people. Prevention is our best chance of curbing the rates of this disease because a vaccine will take years to develop and probably would not be helpful for infected persons. Treatments for AIDS/HIV are continuously being sought, but there is no adequate treatment to cure a PWA. Current treatments focus on increasing the interval between the time of infection and the onset of illness. Unfortunately, toxic side effects make these drugs a poor choice for many infected individuals.

AIDS Information and Hot-line Numbers

AIDS/HIV-POSITIVE status is a notifiable disease, and incidence must be reported to the Centers for Disease Control on a weekly basis by all health departments in the United States. Several services are currently available for AIDS information and referrals. The National AIDS Information Clearinghouse, located in Rockville, Maryland, is a service funded by the Centers for Disease Control to provide professionals in the United States with AIDS information. They distribute a monthly HIV/AIDS Surveillance Report that gives detailed information on AIDS cases, and they provide free of charge references, referrals, and access to all government publications on AIDS. Their telephone number is (800) 458-5231.

The National HIV and AIDS Information Service, more commonly known as the National AIDS Hot-line, is also funded by the Centers for Disease Control and provides a 24-hour hot-line to the general public for information and education regarding the transmission and prevention of AIDS/HIV and referrals within a given geographic area. Callers are free to discuss medical symptoms, but the hot-line does not offer counseling or medical diagnosis, and the staff are not medically trained. They can refer callers to local services in their area through the use of their extensive data base for local, state, and national services offered throughout the United States. They can also send free information to callers requesting pamphlets on specific aspects of HIV/AIDS infection. Their telephone number is (800) 342-AIDS.

A TTY/TDD hot-line for access for the deaf to AIDS information exists for those who have a TTY machine; they also take calls through the operator for deaf relay service with type. This service is available from Monday through Friday from 10:00 A.M. to 10:00 P.M. EST. Their telephone number is (800) 243-7889.

The National HIV and AIDS Information Service also offers an SIDA hot-line for Spanish-speaking individuals who wish to obtain AIDS information. Spanish literature on AIDS is also available upon request. The SIDA hot-line is open 7 days a week from 8:00 A.M. to 2:00 A.M. EST. Their telephone number is (800) 344-7432.

Human Papillomavirus

There are at least 60 known types of human papillomavirus (HPV), ranging in virulence from benign common warts to genital warts (condyloma acuminatum) that may be malignant. The possible relationship between HPV and cancer has been studied extensively during the past 10 years. Many studies have demonstrated a strong association between the presence of genital warts and the development of histological changes in genital tissue. These changes vary from atypia to invasive carcinoma of the vagina, cervix, uterus, vulva, and penis (Zazove et al., 1990). Although the evidence is suggestive, several other risk factors have been identified and may occur before the development of a carcinoma. These risk factors include age, sexual practices, race, cigarette smoking, and sexual history. Unfortunately, a safe and effective cure is not in sight.

HPV may be the most common STD in the United States today, with 1–3% of all Pap smears intimating infection (Zazove et al., 1990). It has been estimated that 0.5–1.0% of all women show clinical signs of condyloma acuminatum and that at least 20 million women in the United States are infected with HPV (Brown et al., 1990). It is also estimated that the prevalence of disease in men parallels that found in the female population. With men, as with women, it is often difficult to tell if HPV is present, because often there are no clinical symptoms, and the virus can be localized internally on the genitalia. It is therefore possible to unknowingly spread infection.

There are several diagnostic tests for the detection of genital warts, many of which are extremely sensitive and reliable. They include clinical observation, facilitated by the use of acetic acid stain for detection of subtle lesions and colposcopy (androscopy in men); cytology and histology; and DNA hybridization (the most common is the Southern-blot test, which is not clinically available). Although there is no cure for genital warts, they can and should be treated as thoroughly as possible, and Pap smears should be done routinely to rule out the possibility of cervical dysplasia and carcinoma.

Treatments include the use of a resin called podophyllin; cryotherapy (with liquid nitrogen), which has been identified as the safest and most highly recommended treatment; laser therapy; 5-fluorouracil; and interferon. The use of condoms is advised for patients with condyloma acuminatum who will not practice abstinence while lesions are present.

Syphilis

There has been a slow and steady decline in the incidence of syphilis in the United States since 1947, but this trend drastically changed when a resurgence of primary and secondary cases of syphilis occurred in 1987. The highest incidence has occurred in poor urban areas among heterosexual African-Americans, where there is endemic crack cocaine use (Centers for Disease Control, 1991*b*). The recent epidemic is blamed on three major factors that must be addressed and remedied to stop this epidemic. The common root of these factors is the oppression of this population by a society that does not offer equal opportunity for education, employment, and health care, among other necessities, to all persons, which places this population at high risk. The first factor involves high-risk sexual behavior such as the practice of sex-for-drugs or sex-for-money to buy drugs, resulting in sex with multiple anonymous partners who cannot be easily identified and screened for disease. Second, persons in this group often have poor access to health care for screening and treatment of syphilis. Last, there is a low level of education at this socioeconomic level; this population experiences a high rate of unemployment and is predisposed to a definite disadvantage regarding knowledge and use of health education measures such as safer sex practices and clean needle use. This trend toward an increased incidence of syphilis among minority populations is of great concern because of its impact on the health of this community. For example, because of the lack of adequate prenatal care for most of these women, the incidence of congenital syphilis is also increasing.

Treponema pallidum is the organism or treponeme responsible for the infection known as syphilis, which affects only humans. It has three recognized stages of development. The primary stage, which presents with a painless lesion called a chancre, is of great importance because it often goes unnoticed, especially in women, because the lesion may be located inside the vagina and is not easily seen without clinical examination. If the infection is not cured at this stage, it will progress to secondary syphilis, which is responsible for a different set of highly infectious lesions. This stage will disappear spontaneously if untreated; the disease will show no clinical signs for long periods of time, often years, until a woman gives birth to a child with congenital syphilis or tertiary-stage syphilis appears with its irreversible destructive neurological signs and symptoms. Studies have shown that at least one third of all individuals sexually exposed to a person with infectious syphilis will become infected (Hutchinson and Hook, 1990).

Screening for syphilis at any stage of infection is easily accomplished with nontreponemal serologic tests such as the Venereal Disease Research Laboratory (VDRL) or the rapid plasma reagin (RPR) test. The fluorescent treponemal antibody-absorption (FTA-ABS) test, which is a treponemal serological test, should be used if either of the first two tests is positive to ensure the greatest reliability for exposing positive results at all stages of syphilis. All patients with positive results should be interviewed regarding their sexual history and encouraged to help locate those who may have been unknowingly infected. In most cases, treatment for syphilis involves a single intramuscular injection of long-acting penicillin G (benzathine penicillin). Prevention and screening are necessary, however, because the consequences of tertiary and congenital syphilis place a heavy burden on an already overwhelmed and often ineffective health care system. New programs are being designed that go directly into those areas hit hardest by this epidemic —crack houses and "crack trees" (networks used to distribute crack to the streets)—to provide screening and treatment by local health care professionals. This may be a way to reach a community that would not otherwise receive health care and would continue to spread infection, often unknowingly. For those at risk, safer sex practices should be taught, and condoms with spermicides containing nonoxynol 9 should always be worn during sexual activity.

Fecal-Oral Contamination

Fecal-oral contamination is the principal route of infection for many diseases and includes those that are sexually transmitted. One avenue for fecal-oral contamination is the use and ingestion of water supplies that have been polluted by infected fecal material. A potable water system is represented by the lack of high numbers of coliforms, which are the bacterial parts used to measure fecal contamination of water supplies. The percentage of coliforms found in the water usually represents the level of contamination from bacteria, amoebae, nematodes (worms), viruses, and other disease-spreading organisms. These organisms are responsible for the direct spread of infection of many water-borne diseases such as giardiasis, intestinal worms, hepatitis, diarrhea and dysentery, cholera, and typhoid fever.

Sexual activity (predominantly homosexual but also heterosexual) is now thought to be another pathway for fecal-oral contamination. Oral-genital and oral-anal sexual activities place people at high risk for infection from parasitic and bacterial organisms such as *Entamoeba histolytica,* which is a protozoan-causing amebiasis. *Giardia lamblia,* which causes giardiasis, is transmitted almost exclusively through fecal-oral contamination. Sexual transmission of giardiasis occurs with great frequency in the homosexual community.

Oral-fecal contamination of humans can occur through the use of polluted water sources as well as through unsafe sexual activity. Sexual transmission through oral-anal and oral-genital activities is responsible for many parasitic, helminthic, and protozoan infections thus predisposing those who engage in these sexual practices. Personal hygiene, environmental sanitation, and safer sexual practices represent the easiest and most cost-effective methods of preventing transmission of many parasitic and bacterial infectious diseases within the community. Safer sexual activity includes abstaining from such exercises or, more realistically, using barrier methods to greatly decrease the possibility for transmission of infectious organisms.

Community health nurses working with populations at high risk for contracting STDs should screen for risk factors and routinely refer clients for screening. Effective surveillance programs provide the best access to follow-up and treatment of STDs. If one infection is identified, that individual should be simultaneously screened for all other STDs. They should also be encouraged to inform their sexual partners of the identification of infection and the need for prompt screening and treatment.

The Fecal-Oral Transmission Cycle

1. On their vacation, Ben and Sue Duncan travel to a rural Mexican village. While in the village, they drink water from a contaminated stream.
2. Three weeks after having visited the village, Ben and Sue develop diarrhea. They are already home and back to work.
3. Ben works making ice cream at a very busy local ice cream parlor. While on the job, he runs to the bathroom and experiences an episode of diarrhea. He is very busy and forgets to wash his hands after defecating. He returns to work and continues making ice cream for the remainder of the evening.
4. Two weeks later, Lucy Gamble, who ate ice cream that Ben had made on the night he forgot to wash his hands after defecating, develops diarrhea.
5. The same night Lucy develops diarrhea, she engages in oral-genital sexual activity with her boyfriend, Joe Parkhurst.
6. Two weeks after the night Lucy developed diarrhea, Joe begins to suffer from diarrhea.
7. In this fashion, *Giardia lamblia* causes diarrhea in several people who are connected through poor hygienic and unsafe sexual practices.

Confidentiality and counseling should be offered at every session, and an objective, nonjudgmental attitude should be used when working with all populations. Individuals attending the program should be encouraged through patient education to remain selective in their choice of sexual partners, avoid high-risk behavior, and always use condoms with spermicides containing nonoxynol 9 or other barrier methods.

SUMMARY

STDs remain the second most prevalent infections known to humans; the first is the common cold. There are many organisms that are now considered an STD because of their mode of transmission (through sexual activity). Fecal-oral contamination from oral-genital and oral-anal sexual practices places persons at high risk of parasitic and bacterial infections. Asymptomatic *Chlamydia* infection is responsible for a large percentage of cases of female sterility. Untreated asymptomatic gonorrhea in women causes sterility through tubal occlusion. Many people do not consider themselves at risk for infection with gonorrhea, and therefore it can remain untreated for long periods of time, during which it continues to be spread unknowingly. Herpes virus is painful, and there is no cure, only medication to help decrease the acute episodes of infection. HIV is responsible for a large percentage of mortality in the male homosexual populations in the developed world and is quickly becoming a major killer in the developing world. Prevention is the only cure. HPV causes genital warts in men and women and has been associated with invasive carcinoma of the genital tract. There is no known cure for this virus, and it goes unnoticed in many individuals because it is often asymptomatic. The incidence of syphilis is increasing in the United States. However, syphilis can be easily treated if diagnosed. Many individuals do not realize they are infected and do not have routine screening. Increased surveillance programs must be instituted to make screening available and convenient for those who are at risk and would not otherwise receive medical care.

APPLICATION OF THE NURSING PROCESS

The following case study will demonstrate how a community health nurse applies the nursing process to a specific problem within the community in which she works. The community health nurse receives a referral from within the community. An assessment is carried out to identify the information necessary to provide accurate diagnoses. Nursing diagnoses and interventions are then outlined, including actual and potential problems, for each component of the community affected. A plan is drawn up by the community health nurse and the affected members of the aggregate. Implementation is carried out, followed by an evaluation of the entire nursing process. Primary, secondary, and tertiary preventive measures for the community are identified and can be put into practice to prevent future problems and epidemics.

Case Study

Miriam Beckwirth is a community health nurse at the local elementary school. Her job includes using the nursing process to work with students in a variety of functions such as teaching health education and lifestyle classes, seeing students in the school clinic when they are ill, and providing families with counseling for stressful episodes. She is also the liaison between the public health department and the school, and she ensures that all health department regulations are being met concerning child safety, nutrition, vaccination coverage, environmental safety, and mental health. It is her responsibility to report any unusual health-related occurrences such as suspected child abuse or the development of any infectious epidemic within the school or the larger aggregates. She is adept at using the nursing process to assess, plan, implement, and evaluate nursing care plans for each of her students to meet their individual needs, the related needs of their families, and selected needs of the larger community. She does this by addressing primary, secondary, and tertiary levels of prevention which she can influence positively.

Referral

Miriam received a telephone call from Mr. John Lemon, Jabril's third-grade teacher, stating that this normally healthy and very active 8-year-old Algerian-born boy was not able to participate in class because he was not feeling well. Mr. Lemon asked if he could send Jabril to see the nurse. Jabril has an older brother and a younger sister attending this school. Both siblings were attending their classes and not complaining of "feeling sick."

Assessment

To prepare for Jabril's visit, Miriam reviews the childhood illnesses with their classic signs and symptoms. Ten minutes later, Miriam receives Jabril in her office. A check of vital signs and an initial assessment finds that this child presents with a temperature of 101.6°F, red and inflamed eyes, a mild cough, and Koplik spots on his buccal mucosa. Jabril is irritable and complaining of general malaise ("feeling achy"). As Miriam questions the child, she learns that he has been feeling ill for approximately 15 hours and that no other person in the household is sick at the present time. She asks him about his sleeping pattern during the past week and reviews his nutritional intake.

Miriam pulls Jabril's chart to assess his immunization status and finds that he received a measles vaccine in Algeria on March 4, 1983. She then looks up his birthday and discovers he was born in North Africa on September 9, 1982. She calculates his age at the time of administration of the live attenuated measles vaccine to be 6 months.

Miriam then calls Jabril's mother, Mrs. Simcha Kamal and confirms the date of birth and the date of vaccination for Jabril. She tells Jabril's mother that Jabril is ill and needs further assessment by the family physician immediately.

Miriam telephones the Jabril's family physician, and the child is seen that afternoon. A blood sample is drawn in which the measles virus is isolated. A rise in antibody titers is also noted.

Four days later, Jabril develops a characteristic red blotchy rash that starts on his face; in the following days, the rash becomes generalized and lasts approximately 5 days. Jabril is diagnosed by the physician as having measles.

Diagnosis

Miriam begins writing a nursing care plan for Jabril based on several nursing diagnoses that fit his present condition (see boxed information).

Nursing Diagnoses and Nursing Interventions

For Jabril
  I. At risk for altered thermoregulation due to febrile condition; teach family to
   A. Monitor body temperature every 2 hours and record temperature.
   B. Administer analgesics and antipyretics as necessary and recommended by physician.
   C. Maintain hydration.
   D. Employ measures to reduce excessive fever when present.
    1. Remove blankets.
    2. Apply ice bags to axilla and groin.
    3. Initiate tepid water sponge bath.
    4. Maintain environmental temperature at a comfortable setting.

  II. Altered skin integrity due to measles lesions; teach family to
   A. Inspect skin condition.
   B. Offer Calamine lotion and antipruritic for itching.
   C. Use mild unabrasive soap and tepid water for hygiene.
   D. Remind child not to scratch lesions or rash.
   E. Encourage child to express feelings about skin condition.
   F. Explain reason for and treatment of skin condition to child, including usual duration.

  III. Altered oral mucous membrane due to Koplik spots; teach family to

A. Inspect child's oral cavity every morning, afternoon, and evening, and describe and document condition or change.
B. Provide supportive measures for mouth care.
   1. Assist child with oral hygiene before and after meals and as necessary.
   2. Use soft-bristled toothbrush or cotton applicator and mouthwash (avoid alcohol-based mouthwashes as these increase dryness and irritation and promote breakdown).
   3. Lubricate lips frequently.
C. Offer foods that are soft and bland, and avoid serving foods that irritate mucous membranes (hot, cold, spicy, fried, citrus).
D. Encourage oral fluids to maintain hydration and lubricate oral mucous membrane.

IV. Social isolation due to measles; teach family to
A. Involve child in setting goals and planning care.
B. Encourage child to perform activities of daily living independently.
C. Perform referrals for assistance if necessary.
D. Arrange for telephone so child can talk to friends.
E. Offer books, games, and television for diversional activity.
F. Child should engage in conversation with people not at risk for contracting measles.
G. Bring homework from school so child will not fall behind peers in class.

V. Disturbance of self-concept due to change in body image from rash; teach family to
A. Accept the child's perception of self.
B. Allow opportunities for child to verbalize feelings.
C. Provide positive reinforcement for child's efforts to adapt.
D. Teach child coping strategies.
E. Reinforce short duration of rash.
F. Arrange for child to interact with others who have similar problems if appropriate.

For Jabril's Family

I. Potential for disturbance in family coping due to acute illness
A. Allow time for family to discuss impact of child's illness and their feelings.
B. Facilitate family conferences; help family identify key issues and select support services, if needed.
C. Help child and family establish a visiting routine that will not tax child or family members.
D. Reinforce family's efforts to care for child.
E. Provide family with clear, concise information about child's condition. Be aware of what the family has already been told, and help them interpret information.
F. Help family support child's independence.
G. Provide emotional support to family by being available to answer questions.
H. Inform family of community resources available to assist in managing child's illness and provide emotional or financial support to the caretakers, e.g., if mother and father are both working and must take off time without pay to care for child.

II. Knowledge deficit related to vaccination schedule
A. Establish an environment of mutual trust and respect to enhance family's learning.
B. Negotiate with family to develop goals for learning.
C. Select teaching strategies (discussion, demonstration, role-playing, visual materials) appropriate for family's individual learning style.
D. Teach family about schedules of vaccines for childhood diseases, and have them demonstrate knowledge of vaccines and their schedules.
E. Encourage family to ask questions and discuss concerns.
F. Provide family with names and telephone numbers of resource people, agencies, or organizations to contact with questions or problems.

For Jabril's Classmates

I. Knowledge deficit related to measles infection
A. Establish an environment of mutual trust and respect to enhance children's learning.
B. Negotiate with children to develop goals for learning.
C. Select teaching strategies (discussion, demonstration, role-playing, visual ma-

terials) appropriate for the children's learning style.

D. Teach children about measles infection, and have them demonstrate knowledge of transmission, vaccination, and disease course of measles infection.

E. Teach how disease outbreaks can be dealt with in daily life.

F. Encourage children to ask questions and discuss concerns.

G. Provide children with names and telephone numbers of resource people, agencies, or organizations to contact with questions or problems.

II. Potential for altered skin integrity due to measles lesions

A. Encourage parents of classmates to inspect skin for signs of rash every day for 2 weeks if no other cases are reported in the area.

B. Encourage children to keep skin healthy by using proper hygienic practices and lotion daily and by avoiding irritating soaps or substances.

C. Educate children in preventive skin care and early recognition of rash and spots that occur with measles infection.

D. Encourage children to immediately report any skin eruptions or rashes.

III. Potential for infection due to measles

A. Minimize children's risk of infection by
1. Vaccinating all susceptible children.
2. Vaccinating all susceptible family members.
3. Vaccinating all susceptible community members.

B. Encourage early identification and reporting of infections to prevent further transmission.

C. Administer immune globulin when appropriate and recommended by child's physician.

D. Teach children to wash hands regularly after using the toilet and before meals.

E. Teach proper oral hygiene to children.

F. Ensure proper disposal of all tissues and contaminated materials within the school setting.

G. Provide adequate ventilation system within classrooms.

H. Report any suspicious cough or symptom to child's parents, and encourage them to have their child seen by the family physician.

Planning

After Jabril is seen by the physician and diagnosed, Miriam plans to make a home visit to jointly develop a plan of care with the family. She also begins formulating care plans for his family and the other children at the school. She must design each care plan for each component in mind if it is to serve their needs adequately. She must then report the case to the infectious disease branch of the local department of public health for surveillance. Then, she will review all nursing records of the children attending her school at the present time to ensure that no other students need to be revaccinated. If any student fits into this group, she must immediately revaccinate and monitor these children for signs of infection. A prophylactic dose of immune globulin may be given to these children by their family physician; however, administering immune globulin after the third day of incubation may prolong the incubation period without preventing disease. Because the exact date of exposure is unknown for these children, it may be unwise to administer immune globulin. Miriam then must notify the parents of all the children at the school so that other cases can be reported early. She realizes it is also important to ask parents to check the immunization status of all family members in the household.

Intervention

Miriam makes a home visit, and she and Mrs. Kamal develop the nursing care plan together. Mrs. Kamal identifies ways to offer supportive measures such as bedrest during the febrile period, antipyretics for the fever, dimming the lights for sensitive eyes, and providing a vaporizer in the child's room. Because Jabril is not a high-risk child, antibiotic therapy will probably not be necessary. Miriam warns Mrs. Kamal about the complications of measles and tells her that if she notices any of these signs or symptoms, she should take Jabril to the physician immediately. The complications she mentions include an earache (otitis media), any respiratory symptoms such as a severe cough or wheezing (pneumonia, bronchiolitis, obstructive laryngitis, and laryngotracheitis), and any neurological changes such as unsteady gait or memory disturbances (encephalitis).

Last and most important, Miriam informs Mrs. Kamal about the need for strict isolation from other children and adults who are not fully immunized against measles. This will include those who received live measles vaccine before the age of 12 months, those who are unsure of their age at vaccination, and those who were vaccinated before 1968 with an unknown type of vaccine. All persons within these categories should be revaccinated immediately; if they have come in contact with Jabril, they should also be in isolated for the next 12–14 days as this is the incubation period for measles and they could be spreading disease. Clinical signs of infection will not develop until after 1 or 2 weeks. Mrs. Kamal is also asked to make a complete list of everyone with whom Jabril has come in contact and the places he has been within the past 3 weeks. Miriam takes a complete history including the vaccination status of Jabril's siblings and parents. Mrs. Kamal is very eager to participate in this process because she is concerned about the health of her family.

The local department of public health is notified, and the case is appropriately reported and documented. A list of Jabril's contacts is given to the public health officer taking the information. It is up to this officer to contact those people who have been in close proximity with Jabril within the preceding 3 weeks. The officer will try to identify, isolate, and treat the individual who exposed Jabril and his schoolmates to the measles virus. Miriam prepares a note for all children to take home to their parents informing them of the measles case and alerting them to the signs and symptoms to be aware of within the family. She also encloses a form to help family members review vaccination schedules; this will ensure that this aggregate is protected against measles infection. Miriam then reviews all vaccination records for the children at the school. She is prepared to vaccinate any child currently in need of a booster against the vaccine-preventable childhood infections.

Evaluation

Five days after Miriam first examines Jabril, the public health officer at the department of public health telephones Miriam to inform her that they have isolated the original source of the measles virus. Apparently, the family living across the street from Jabril had some friends visit from Indonesia. These friends had a 1-year-old child who had not been vaccinated and developed measles upon arriving in the United States.

The child subsequently recovered but not before exposing several people at risk. This was an isolated incident, so only a few cases of clinical disease were caused. None of Jabril's classmates contracted measles. The benefit of this experience was the resulting emphasis placed on revaccinating those at risk and ensuring the health of this aggregate through more prudent vaccination adherence against preventable infectious diseases. This episode also displayed how important it is to have a reliable and efficient public health surveillance system.

Levels of Prevention

Primary The most effective method of prevention for measles is early vaccination of children at the age of 15 months. Any child vaccinated before the age of 12 months should be revaccinated at the age of 15 months. Any susceptible adults should be revaccinated.

Secondary A search for exposed individuals who are susceptible for infection from the measles virus should be implemented. Once these people are identified, they should be vaccinated to stop further transmission of measles. Isolation is impractical in a large community, but children should be kept out of school for at least 4 days after the appearance of a rash. The parents of children attending school should promptly and accurately report any suspicious family illness to the school nurse. All cases of measles should be reported early to the local health authority because reporting provides better control of outbreaks. Community health nurses should annually engage in continuing education activities to gain skills and increase their knowledge base so they can better serve their community.

Tertiary Community health nurses have the special task of intervening at individual, family, and aggregate levels by using the nursing process to assist with rehabilitation and restoration to baseline functioning, as presented in the case study. Surveillance systems should collect and relay health information and statistics from the local to the state and national levels.

SUMMARY

This chapter began by identifying threats to the health of the community and ways to keep the community free of infection. The community health nurse has the unique role of taking collective action with community members at the local, state, and national levels to preserve the health of aggregates.

Transmission of infectious agents is carried out through direct, indirect, and airborne contacts with human recipients. Understanding modes of transmission will help in design and use of effective methods to prevent the spread of infectious diseases.

Defining, reporting, and continuing surveillance of cases of infectious disease transmission are vital aspects of a national public health surveillance program. The information contributed from these activities provides baseline data for the monitoring of epidemiological trends, around which screening and intervention programs can be administered.

One major method of keeping communities free of infection is through the use of vaccines. There are different kinds of immunity, each lasting a specified amount of time, but the goal is for lasting immunity against infectious diseases. Vaccination, given in the correct dosage, route, and preparation, can provide lasting immunity to most individuals. Vaccine schedules for all ages should be adhered to, and vaccine integrity should be maintained through the use of a cold chain as well as checking expiration dates before use. Many individuals in areas around the world still suffer from vaccine-preventable infectious diseases, and mortality from these illnesses remains very high. Where eradication is not probable, control is the goal.

Hepatitis B is of growing concern because of the carrier status role in chronic disease and the severe damage to the liver that may occur without obvious symptoms.

STDs remain a very real threat to the community and have a unique form of transmission. Fecal-oral contamination offers a new route for many parasitic and infectious diseases. The sequelae from many of these diseases can leave men and women permanently infertile and/or predisposed to cancer. For many of these diseases, such as herpes simplex virus, HPV, and AIDS, there are no cures; prevention is the only method of control.

AIDS had predominantly been a disease of homosexual men, but it is now increasing in heterosexual populations. AIDS is also escalating as a cause of death among women.

For many infectious diseases, prevention is the only cure. Vaccines and safer sex practices have become the first line of defense. They are safe preventive measures that are more cost effective, in both economic and human terms, than not using these interventions.

Public health efforts are vitally important in combating the increasing trends of many infectious disease rates. Community health nurses have an important role in prevention, case finding, reporting, and other activities related to the control of communicable diseases within their communities.

L e a r n i n g
A c t i v i t i e s

1. Inquire about the reporting of notifiable diseases in your community. Who is responsible for the reporting process? To whom do they report, and how often?

2. Identify the type of universal precautionary measures used in your hospital or clinical setting.

3. Visit an STD clinic and find out what STDs are screened for and treated.

4. Find out what kind of vaccine services are available at your local health department and what form of follow-up is done.

5. Visit a testing laboratory to see how STD tests are done (e.g., VDRL, tests for gonorrhea).

6. Interview a teenager you know and find out about their feelings toward safer sex and their own personal risk evaluation.

7. Purchase a 1-year subscription to a public health nursing journal.

REFERENCES

Alter, M. J., Hadler, S. C., Margolis, H. S., et al.: The changing epidemiology of hepatitis B in the United States. Need for alternative vaccination strategies. J.A.M.A. *263*;1218–1222, 1990.

Alter, M. J., and Margolis, H. S.: The emergence of hepatitis B as a sexually transmitted disease. Med. Clin. North Am. *74*;1529–1541, 1990.

American Academy of Pediatrics: Report of the Committee on Infectious Diseases. 19th Ed. Elk Grove Village, Illinois, American Academy of Pediatrics, 1982.

Aral, S. O., and Holmes, K. K.: Sexually transmitted diseases in the AIDS era. Sci. Am. *264*;62–69, 1991.

Benenson, A. S.: Control of Communicable Diseases in Man. 14th Ed. Washington, D.C., American Public Health Association, 1985.

Bowman, M. A., Fredman, L., English, D. K., et al.: Screening for sexually transmitted diseases by primary care physicians. South. Med. J. *84*;294–298, 1991.

Brown, D. R., and Fife, K. H.: Human papillomavirus infections of the genital tract. Med. Clin. North Am. *74*;1455–1480, 1990.

Brunham, R. C., and Plummer, F. A.: A general model of sexually transmitted disease epidemiology and its implications for control. Med. Clin. North Am. *74*;1339–1352, 1990.

Centers for Disease Control: ACIP: Prevention and control of influenza. M. M. W. R. *36*;373–387, 1987a.

Centers for Disease Control: Recommendations for prevention of HIV transmission in health-care settings. M. M. W. R. *36*;5–7, 1987*b*.

Centers for Disease Control: Health Information for International Travel. Atlanta, Georgia, Centers for Disease Control, Division of Quarantine, Center for Prevention Services, publication No. 88-8280, 1988.

Centers for Disease Control: Summary of notifiable diseases: United States, 1989. M. M. W. R. *38*;1–59, 1989.

Centers for Disease Control: Case definitions for public health surveillance. M. M. W. R. *39*;1–44, 1990*a*.

Centers for Disease Control: Guidelines for preventing the transmission of tuberculosis in health-care settings, with special focus on HIV-related issues. M. M. W. R. *39*;1–29, 1990*b*.

Centers for Disease Control: Tuberculosis among foreign-born persons entering the United States. M. M. W. R. *39*;1–21, 1990*c*.

Centers for Disease Control: HIV-related knowledge and behaviors among high school students—Selected U.S. sites, 1989. M. M. W. R. *39*;385–397, 1990*d*.

Centers for Disease Control: Mortality attributable to HIV infection/AIDS—United States, 1981–1990. M. M. W. R. *40*;41–55, 1991*a*.

Centers for Disease Control: Primary and secondary syphilis —United States, 1981–1990. M. M. W. R. *40*;314–325, 1991*b*.

Centers for Disease Control: Recommendations for preventing transmission of human immunodeficiency virus and hepatitis B virus to patients during exposure-prone invasive procedures. M. M. W. R. *40*;4–5, 1991*c*.

Centers for Disease Control: Vaccinia (smallpox) vaccine: Recommendations of the Immunization Practices Advisory Committee (ACIP). M. M. W. R. *40*; 1–40, 1991*d*.

Chambers, C. V.: Sexually transmitted diseases. Primary Care *17*;833–850, 1990.

Cordova, R., and Norwood, C.: Unreachable low-income Latina women in a poor urban area themselves become AIDS educators. Presented at the Seventh International AIDS Conference, Florence, Italy, June 19–20, 1991.

Fillit, H.: Acquired immunodeficiency in the elderly: Normal, reversible, and irreversible causes. AIDS Med. Rep. *4*;20–24, 1991.

Flexner, C.: Management of occupational exposures to HIV: An update. AIDS Med. Rep. *4*;13–20, 1991.

Garner, J. S., and Simmons, B. P.: Guidelines for isolation precautions in hospitals. Infect. Control *4*(suppl);245–325, 1983.

Gellert, G. A., and Kaznady, S. I.: Melting the Iron Curtain: Opportunities for public health collaboration through international joint ventures. Br. Med. J. *302*;633–635, 1991.

Gerbert, B., Sumser, J., and Maguire, B. T.: The impact of who you know and where you live on opinions about AIDS and health care. Soc. Sci. Med. *32*;677–681, 1991.

Ghendon, Y.: WHO strategy for the global elimination of new cases of hepatitis B. Vaccine *8*(suppl);S129–S132, 1990.

Goldsmith, M. F.: Target: Sexually transmitted diseases. J. A. M. A. *264*;2179–2180, 1990.

Guasticchi, G., Autelitano, M., Barillard, S., and Fara, G. M.: Evaluation of knowledge on AIDS in Italy: A survey concerning young adults and school teachers. Presented at the Seventh International AIDS Conference, Florence, Italy, June 17–18, 1991.

Haglind, P., Ackerhans, M., and Falkenström, G.: The madonna project. Presented at the Seventh International AIDS Conference, Florence, Italy, June 19–20, 1991.

Hollinger, F. B., Bancroft, W. H., Dienstag, J. L., et al.: Controlling hepatitis B virus transmission in North America. Vaccine *8*(suppl);S122–S128, 1990.

Howry, L. B., Bindler, R. M., and Tso, Y.: Pediatric Medications. Philadelphia, J. B. Lippincott, 1981.

Hutchinson, C. M., and Hook, E. W.: Syphilis in adults. Med. Clin. North Am. *74*;1389–1414, 1990.

Johnson, R.: Program on measles, lecture series, Baltimore, Maryland, The Johns Hopkins University, 1989.

Judson, F. N.: Gonorrhea. Med. Clin. North Am. *74*;1353–1366, 1990.

Kellogg, B., Dye, C., Cox, K., and Rosenow, G.: Public health nursing model for contact follow-up of patients with pulmonary tuberculosis. Public Health Nurs. *4*;99–104, 1987.

Levine, G. I.: Sexually transmitted parasitic diseases. Primary Care *18*;101–127, 1991.

Martin, D. H.: Chlamydial infections. Med. Clin. North Am. *74*;1367–1384, 1990.

Mausner, J. S., and Kramer, S.: Epidemiology: An Introductory Text. Philadelphia, W. B. Saunders, 1985.

Maynard, J. E.: Hepatitis B: global importance and need for control. Vaccine *8*(suppl);S18–S20, 1990.

Mendelson, M. H., and Adler, J.: Resurgence of tuberculosis: Relationship to HIV infection and implications for infection control. Mount Sinai J. Med. *57*;221–224, 1990.

Moore, M., Cahill, K., Campbell, C., Kirby, C. D., and Valdiserri, R. O.: Failures and delays in returning for HIV test results at publicly funded clinics, U.S., 1989–1990. Presented at the Seventh International AIDS Conference, Florence, Italy, June 17–18, 1991.

Padian, N., Hitchcock, P. J., Fullilove, R. E., Kohlstadt, V., and Brunham, R.: Report of the NIAID study group on integrated behavioral research for prevention and control of sexually transmitted diseases. Sexually Transmitted Diseases *17*;200–210, 1990.

Peaceman, A. M., and Gonik, B.: Sexually transmitted viral disease in women. Postgrad. Med. *89*;133–140, 1991.

Richie, B., Safyer, S., Freudenberg, N., Rodriguez, I., and Florio, S.: An evaluation of an AIDS education empowerment program for incarcerated women. Presented at the Seventh International AIDS Conference, Florence, Italy, June 17–18, 1991.

Schmid, G.: Approach to the patient with genital ulcer disease. Med Clin North Am *74*;1559–1572, 1990.

Sherlock, S.: Hepatitis B: The disease. Vaccine *8*(suppl);S6–S8, 1990.

Sherris, J. D., Blackburn, R., Moore, S. H., and Mehta, S.: Immunizing the world's children. Population Rep. *L*;154–192, 1986.

Sobel, J. D.: Vaginal infections in adult women. Med. Clin. North Am. *74*;1573–1598, 1990.

Spencer, B., Lert, F., and Job-Spira, N.: From kisses to coitus. Presented at the Seventh International AIDS Conference, Florence, Italy, June 17–18, 1991.

Stanhope, M., and Lancaster, J.: Community Health Nursing. 2nd Ed. St. Louis, C. V. Mosby, 1988.

Strunin, L.: Adolescents' perceptions of risk for HIV infection: Implications for future research. Soc. Sci. Med. *32*;221–228, 1991.

Swanson, J., and Chenitz, W. C.: The prevention and management of genital herpes: A community health approach. J. Comm. Health Nurs. *6*;209–219, 1989.

Townsend, T. R.: Racial differences in rates of hepatitis B virus infection—United States, 1976–1980. J. A. M. A. *263*;29–30, 1990.

U.S. Bureau of the Census: Health Insurance Coverage: The Haves and Have-Nots. Washington, D.C., U. S. Government Printing Office, statistical brief, 1990*a*.

U.S. Bureau of the Census: Immunization Survey. Washington, D.C., U.S. Government Printing Office, Statistical Abstracts of the United States of America, 1990*b*, pp. 116–117.

U.S. Preventive Services Task Force: Counseling to prevent HIV infection and other sexually transmitted diseases. Am. Family Phys. *41*;1179–1184, 1990.

Whaley, L. F., and Wong, D. L.: Nursing Care of Infants and Children. St. Louis, C. V. Mosby, 1983.

Wolfe, M. S.: Health Hints for the Tropics. 10th Ed. Washington, D. C., American Society of Tropical Medicine and Hygiene, 1989.

Wooldridge, W. E.: Syphilis. Postgrad. Med. *89*;193–202, 1991.

Zazove, P., Caruthers, B. S., and Reed, B. D.: Genital human papillomavirus infection. Am. Family Phys. *41*;1279–1289, 1991.

Environmental Health

Upon completion of this chapter, the reader will be able to:

1. Describe broad areas of environmental health about which community health nurses must be informed, and name environmental hazards in each area.

2. Recognize the potential social, cultural, economic, and political factors affecting environmental health.

3. Apply the basic concepts of critical theory to environmental health nursing problems.

4. Identify aggregates at risk for particular environmental health problems.

5. Distinguish between environmental health approaches that focus on altering individual behaviors and those that aim to change health-damaging environments.

6. Formulate critical questions about environmental conditions that limit the survival and well-being of communities.

7. Understand the skills needed to facilitate community participation and partnership in identifying and solving environmental health problems.

8. Propose collective strategies in which community health nurses can participate to address the environmental health concerns of specific aggregates.

Patricia E. Stevens
Joanne M. Hall

Environmental health is of ever-increasing importance to community health nursing practice. Evidence accumulates that the environmental changes of the past few decades have profoundly influenced the status of public health. The safety, beauty, and life-sustaining capacity of the physical environment are unquestionably of global consequence. The ecological approach of the 1960s and 1970s tended to focus on clean water, clean air, and conservation of natural resources in specific locales. By the 1990s, it has become acutely apparent that the extinction of many species, diminishment of the tropical rain forests, proliferation of toxic waste dumps, effects of acid rain, progressive destruction of the ozone layer, shortage of landfill sites, consequences of global warming, development of deadly chemical and ballistic weapons, food adulteration by pesticides and herbicides, oceanic contamination through toxic dumping and petroleum spills, urban overcrowding, traffic congestion of thoroughfares, and an ever-growing number of industrial hazards posing health risks to workers are only a few of the urgent environmental difficulties we now face.

The purpose of this chapter is to explore the health of communities in relation to the environment. Environmental health is examined using critical theory as a framework for the discussion and a basis for described community health nursing practices. As was introduced in Chapter 4, critical theory is an approach that raises questions about oppressive situations, involves community members in the definition and solutions of problems, and facilitates interventions that liberate people from the health-damaging effects of environments.

Case examples are used throughout the chapter to illustrate how environmental health problems affect the everyday lives of aggregates. The term *aggregate* refers to a group that shares some common aspect, such as age, economic status, cultural perspective, gender, race, area of residence, chronic illness, and so on. Aggregates may be *communities* in which the members know and interact with each other, such as a barrio neighborhood or a labor union. Aggregates may also be "theoretically defined" categories of individuals who may or may not interact regularly with others in the defined group, as in "all crack cocaine users," "women with physical disabilities," or "all men over the age of 65."

Two other terms are used throughout the chapter. *Environment* is defined as the accumulation of physical, social, cultural, economic, and political conditions that influence the lives of communities. The *health* of communities depends on the integrity of the physical environment, humaneness of the social relations within it, availability of resources necessary to sustain life and manage illness, equitable distribution of health risks, attainable employment and education, cultural preservation and tolerance of diversity among subgroups, access to historical heritage, and sense of empowerment and hope (Table 24–1).

Table 24–1
Environmental Health Concepts

Concept	Definition
Aggregate	An aggregate is a group of people who share some common aspect, such as age, economic status, cultural background, gender, race, area of residence, chronic illness, and so on.
Community	Community is an aggregate in which the members know and interact with each other and have a collective identity, such as a *barrio* neighborhood or a labor union.
Environment	Environment is the accumulation of physical, social, cultural, economic, and political conditions that influence the lives of communities.
Health	Health of communities depends on the integrity of the physical environment, the humaneness of the social relations within it, the availability of resources necessary to sustain life and to manage illness, equitable distribution of health risks, attainable employment and education, cultural preservation and tolerance of diversity among subgroups, access to historical heritage, and a sense of empowerment and hope.

A CRITICAL THEORY APPROACH TO ENVIRONMENTAL HEALTH

Questioning what appears to be "given" in the environment and challenging "the way things have always been done" are the core dynamics of a critical way of thinking. For example, public buildings, schools, work places, and mass transportation systems are structures in the environment that are vital to people's everyday functioning. They are ordinarily taken for granted. The experiences of physically challenged persons, however, exemplify how that which has been taken for granted about the environment can be brought into question. Can disabled persons board the buses that run in our locales? Can wheelchair-using people enter public facilities? Can sight- or hearing-impaired children attend public schools and receive an equitable education? Will disabled persons be denied employment at a work place because hiring them would necessitate entrance ramps, wheelchair-accessible restroom facilities, and elevators?

Critical theory suggests that community health nurses should be vocally critical of obstructions in the environment that affect the safety and well-being of particular aggregates or deprive them of access to resources necessary for the pursuit of health. In identifying environmental sources of health problems, nurses must be involved with the communities that are affected. Rather than impose assessments of the problem, nurses should share their ideas and dialogue with community members: listening to what the community defines as problematic, helping to raise consciousness about environmental dangers, and assisting in bringing about changes.

Again, the experiences of disabled persons provide examples of how environmental health might be approached critically. Able-bodied people, often subconsciously, infantilize physically challenged individuals and assume that they are passive, powerless, and victimized by their physical incapacities. Community health nurses frequently approach members of this aggregate with intentions of assisting them to cope with their disabilities by arranging their immediate home environments to facilitate their activities of daily living. This may be an appropriate goal, but many disabled persons have identified broader problems such as architectural and discriminatory constraints in the environment that have systematically barred them from employment, education, housing, and health care. From their perspective, these may pose the most essential health problems. Many disabled persons "eschew the telethon's 'politics of pity' and abhor the 'poster child' image, demanding instead to be regarded as self-determining adults, capable of militant political action" (Anspach, 1979, p. 766).

As this situation suggests, only by being involved in open, respectful dialogues with the aggregates we serve can nurses learn how they perceive themselves, their health, and environmental influences. Helping communities become more aware of how the environment affects their health and assisting them to take actions to make needed changes in the environment is a very legitimate nursing action from a critical standpoint. The ultimate goal of the critical practice of community health nursing is the liberation of people from health-damaging environmental conditions.

Changes in environmental conditions achieved by people with disabilities and their advocates during the past two decades include federal legislation mandating accessibility of public facilities and services, changes in municipal building codes and state employment regulations, and increased enforcement of laws regarding nondiscrimination in hiring, educational opportunities, and health services. Collective actions were instrumental in the accomplishment of these environmental changes. Strategic organizing, litigation, testimony at public hearings, letter-writing campaigns, legislative lobbying, and mass demonstrations were some of the strategies used.

Because of its emphasis on collective strategies for change, a critical perspective can help nurses plan and implement aggregate-level interventions. Acting collectively can empower nurses to have a real impact on environmental health, as it has empowered disability rights activists to achieve their objectives. In the process of assessing environmental health problems, planning and implementing interventions, and evaluating the effectiveness of community-based actions, community health nurses should always be aware of physical surroundings as well as the effects on communities of cultural realities, social relations, economic circumstances, and political conditions. Several sources are available in the literature that discuss critical theory and its application to community health nursing (Allen, 1986; Butterfield, 1990; Freire, 1970; Hedin, 1986; Mies, 1983; Minkler and Cox, 1980; Stevens, 1989; Stevens and Hall, 1992; Thompson, 1987; Watts, 1990).

AREAS OF ENVIRONMENTAL HEALTH

Although many conceptual schemes are possible, we have divided the vast field of environmental health into nine subcategories: living patterns, work risks, atmospheric quality, water quality, housing, food quality, waste control, radiation risks, and violence risks (Table 24–2). The brief discussions of these areas of environmental health are only introductions to environmental health and focus on basic problems and strategies rather than on statistical detail. In the following sections, each of these nine areas of environmental health

is defined, several examples of problems relevant to each category are given, and vignettes that illustrate community health nursing responses to environmental health concerns are presented. Obviously, there are many environmental health hazards that are not specifically mentioned in this chapter, although they are no less important than the examples discussed. Table 24–3 lists some of the environmental health problems that are discussed.

Living Patterns

Living patterns are the relationships among persons, communities, and their surrounding environments that depend on habits, interpersonal ties, cultural values, and customs. Drunk driving, involuntary smoking (sidestream smoke), exposure to noise, unabated traffic, urban crowding, and the stress of increasing mechanization of daily life could pose environmental health problems be-

---

Table 24–2
Areas of Environmental Health

Area	Definition
Living patterns	Living patterns are the relationships among persons, communities, and their surrounding environments that depend on habits, interpersonal ties, cultural values, and customs.
Work risks	Work risks include the quality of the employment environment as well as the potential for injury or illness posed by working conditions.
Atmospheric quality	Atmospheric quality refers to the protectiveness of the atmospheric layers, the risks of severe weather, and the purity of the air available for breathing purposes.
Water quality	Water quality refers to the availability and volume of the water supply as well as the mineral content levels, pollution by toxic chemicals, and the presence of pathogenic micro-organisms. Water quality consists of the balance between water contaminants and existing capabilities to purify water for human use and plant and wildlife sustenance.
Housing	Housing, as an environmental health concern, refers to the availability, safety, structural, strength, cleanliness, and location of shelter, including public facilities and individual or family dwellings.
Food quality	Food quality refers to the availability and relative costs of foods, their variety and safety, and the health of animal and plant food sources.
Waste control	Waste control is the management of waste materials resulting from industrial and municipal processes and human consumption as well as efforts to minimize waste production.
Radiation risks	Radiation risks are health dangers posed by the various forms of ionizing radiation relative to barriers preventing exposure of humans and other life forms.
Violence risks	The environmental risks of violence include the potential for victimization through the violence of particular individuals as well as the general level of aggression in psychosocial climates.

Table 24–3
Examples of Environmental Health Problems

Area	Problems
Living patterns	Drunk driving Involuntary smoking Noise exposure Urban crowding Technological hazards
Work risks	Occupational toxic poisoning Machine-operating hazards Sexual harassment Repetitive motion injuries Carcinogenic work sites
Atmospheric quality	Gaseous pollutants Greenhouse effect Destruction of the ozone layer Aerial spraying of herbicides and pesticides Acid rain
Water quality	Contamination of drinking supply by human waste Oil spills in the world's waterways Pesticide or herbicide infiltration of ground water Aquifer contamination by industrial pollutants Heavy metal poisoning of fish
Housing	Homelessness Rodent and insect infestation Poisoning from lead-based paint "Sick building" syndrome Unsafe neighborhoods
Food quality	Malnutrition Bacterial food poisoning Food adulteration Disrupted food chains by eco-system destruction Carcinogenic chemical food additives
Waste control	Use of nonbiodegradable plastics Poorly designed solid waste dumps Inadequate sewage systems Transport and storage of hazardous waste Illegal industrial dumping
Radiation risks	Nuclear facility emissions Radioactive hazardous wastes Radon gas seepage in homes and schools Nuclear testing Excessive exposure to x-rays
Violence risks	Proliferation of handguns Increasing incidence of hate crimes Pervasive images of violence in the media High rates of homicide among young black males Violent acts against women and children

cause people live within sociocultural patterns that limit their ability to escape these realities (Berger et al., 1986; Greenberg, 1987; Harpham et al., 1988).

We are not referring to individuals' lifestyle choices, such as eating a diet rich in saturated fats, leading a largely sedentary life, or becoming emotionally involved with a substance abuser. Rather, living patterns reflect population exposure to environmental conditions that are affected by mass culture, social practices, ethnic customs, and technology.

For example, community responses to a massive toxic chemical spill are mediated by many cultural, psychological, social, and economic conditions in the residential areas affected (Vyner, 1988a). The technological hazard represented by the spill can be more difficult for communities to cope with than natural disasters. The human failure symbolized by technological hazards can evoke hopelessness, helplessness, and anger that manifests in heightened community stress and deepening personal depression (Vyner, 1988b). Difficulties in convincing state and federal officials of environmental health dangers and problems obtaining compensation for diseases and deaths caused by environmental toxins often result in revictimization of residents (Smets, 1988; Soble and Brennan, 1988). Leaving an area that poses potentially severe health risks from exposure to hazards may be hindered by the lack of low-cost housing and tightly knit social structures in the affected community. People may not be able to afford to move or willing to disrupt family and cultural roots to start over elsewhere, so they may live with the uncertainty and conflict. Long-term communitywide effects of division, animosity, distrust, cynicism, and despair often abound in such situations.

VIGNETTE

In an urban Chinese community, the economic aftershocks of a major earthquake cause the closure of many businesses. Some of these family businesses are forced to move to parts of the city less characterized by the use of Chinese languages. As a result of these moves, many elderly family members who do not speak English appear to be experiencing depression, characterized by a loss of appetite.

The community health nurses in the area begin visiting these elders, bringing interpreters with them. In their assessments, nurses focus on psychiatric symptoms and suggest ventilation of emotions. They encourage many of the elderly Chinese to attend a local senior center that is staffed and attended mostly by Euro-Americans. In some cases, they recommend psychiatric evaluations. In almost every instance, there is resistance to these interventions.

The nurses failed to establish an alliance with the very strong Chinese family organizations before imposing their solutions. They also neglected to investigate Chinese cultural patterns before attempting to assist them with the life pattern ramifications of the earthquake. Chinese people do not readily talk about feelings with outsiders, nor do they generally conceptualize distress in psychiatric terms. They interpret the presence of fatigue and disturbances in eating and sleeping patterns as physical illness. They expect health care personnel to recognize and help them with these physical symptoms. To suggest that socializing at clubs populated by English speakers would cure their illness seemed to them to be quite incredulous.

Work Risks

Work risks include the quality of the employment environment as well as the potential for injury or illness posed by working conditions. Environmental health problems posed by work risks include sexual harassment, occupational toxic poisoning, machine-operating hazards, electrical hazards, repetitive motion injuries, and work sites characterized by carcinogenic particulate inhalants (e.g., asbestos), dust pollutants (e.g., coal dust), and heavy metal poisoning (Cralley et al., 1990; MacKinnon, 1979; Regenstein, 1986; Rom, 1983; Smith, 1990; Stellman and Daum, 1973).

In the United States, more than 20 million injuries and 400,000 new cases of disease are recognized annually as work related (Marbury, 1987). These statistics do not reflect the health problems that are never reported (Berman, 1977). For example, a clerical worker leaves the office every day with a headache and back strain and, after 5 years on the job, develops carpal tunnel syndrome. A midwestern farmer suffers the loss of his hand by having it caught in his new hay-baler, not knowing that several other farmers in the state have been similarly injured using this same model of hay-baler. All male production workers who formerly worked for a chemical company producing a pesticide are found to be sterile. An operating room nurse has a miscarriage and remembers that many of her coworkers have also been unable to carry their babies to term. A dry cleaner often leaves work feeling light headed and dizzy from inhaling solvents all day at the shop, and one day she has a car accident on the way home.

VIGNETTE

Sanitation workers in an urban area have experienced an increasing incidence of puncture injuries in the process of transporting hazardous wastes from the public medical center. Several cases of hepatitis have resulted. As the story hits the newspapers, community health nurses are contacted by members of the city health commission and are instructed that they are to politically support the interests of the city and the medical center "at all costs." Subsequently, the sanitation workers' union contacts the community health nursing office and asks for information about available methods of safely packaging medical wastes. They also ask for a nurse to come and speak to their membership about immediate measures they can use to prevent further injuries on the job.

The nurses meet to resolve the conflict. Most agree that the union membership has pressing needs for education and support. Despite the city's demand for loyalty, they decide to "choose sides" with the workers and respond to their requests. They collectively draft a letter to the city health commission and arrange a meeting with the commissioners in which a small group of the nurses informs them of their plans to assist the sanitation workers. The health commission later holds a press conference, in which the actions of the nurses are depicted as mediational efforts that benefit both the union and the city. Eventually, a new medical waste disposal plan is jointly developed, and injured workers receive reasonable compensation in an out-of-court settlement.

Atmospheric Quality

Atmospheric quality refers to the protectiveness of the atmospheric layers, the risks of severe weather, and the purity of the air available for breathing purposes. Environmental dangers related to atmospheric quality include chlorofluorocarbon

destruction of the ozone layer, loss of carbon dioxide–consuming resources such as forests, tornadoes, electrical storms, smog, gaseous pollutants (e.g., carbon monoxide), excessive hydrocarbon levels, aerial spraying of herbicides, and acid rain (Connell, 1990).

The protectiveness of our atmospheric layers is diminishing (Regenstein, 1986; Woodwell, 1978). Chlorofluorocarbons, which are in widespread use for refrigeration, air conditioning, and aerosol propellants, remain in the atmosphere for a long time. These molecules cause depletion of the ozone layer of the atmosphere. The resulting "holes" in the ozone layer allow excess ultraviolet radiation to penetrate, with deleterious effects on living organisms. Another problematic atmospheric condition is increasing atmospheric carbon dioxide. This carbon dioxide allows sunlight to pass through to the earth but absorbs and traps part of the heat re-emitted by the earth. Thus, the surface temperature of the earth is heating up in what is called the "greenhouse effect," causing probably irreversible global climate changes and other catastrophic ecological consequences. Burning fossil fuels such as coal and oil releases carbon dioxide into the atmosphere, which stimulates the greenhouse effect. In addition, key processes that break down atmospheric carbon dioxide are being disrupted. The ongoing devegetation of much of the earth's surface, especially the cutting of the tropical rain forests, not only releases the carbon stored in the biomass but also eliminates sources of photosynthesis, the process by which plants absorb carbon and release oxygen. The rate at which the world's forests are being cut is almost inconceivable. This massive worldwide deforestation, combined with pollution, is wiping out countless species of animals and plants.

Severe weather conditions, another aspect of atmospheric quality that affects the public's health, can have quite dramatic results in the form of injury and loss of life, destruction of plants and wildlife, and property damage. Hazardous atmospheric pollutants threaten survival by causing lung cancer, chronic respiratory disease, and death as well as by exterminating animal and plant species (Rose, 1990). For instance, it is estimated that 50,000 lakes in the United States and Canada are "dead,"—i.e., devoid of fish and plant life due to acid rain (Perdue and Gjessing, 1989).

VIGNETTE

A sudden increase occurs in the number of emergency calls to a medical hot-line from residents of a particular urban neighborhood. These calls often involve elderly women who have collapsed in their homes. In one case, an asthmatic child developed severe dyspnea. One of the community health nurses comments that perhaps these problems are psychosocial manifestations of stress because the United States recently went to war in the Persian Gulf.

As the emergency calls continue, two other community health nurses note that respiratory difficulties are almost always implicated. These nurses decide to go to the neighborhood in question and look around. It happens to be nearing rush hour and within minutes all of the traffic on the nearby freeway is slowed to a crawl, apparently due to road construction. Through their direct observations and critical assessment, these nurses determine that several residential buildings in the area appear to be situated so that heavy car exhaust fumes stagnate around them. The nurses notify an environmental protection agency as well as the city transportation department to recommend further investigation and resolution of the problem.

One week later, the nurses return to the neighborhood and determine that the traffic is moving more efficiently, even though road construction continues. Within several weeks, the number of emergency medical calls more closely approximates the usual number of calls received.

Water Quality

Water quality refers to the availability and volume of the water supply as well as mineral content levels, pollution by toxic chemicals, and presence of pathogenic micro-organisms. Water quality consists of the balance between water contaminants and existing capabilities to purify water for human use and plant and wildlife sustenance. Problems of water quality include droughts, dosing of reservoirs with copper sulfate to reduce algae, contamination of drinking supply by human wastes, pesticide-contaminated aquifers, mercury-poisoned fish in the Great Lakes, lead leaching from water pipes, oil spills in the world's waters, water-borne bacteria, and toxicity caused by excessive chlorination.

Advances in water treatment technologies in industrialized countries such as the United States have controlled many water-related diseases such as cholera, typhoid, dysentery, and hepatitis A. However, disease outbreaks resulting from contamination by untreated ground water and inadequate chlorination are increasing in both urban and rural areas. Heavy metal and toxic chemical pollution can originate in the water treatment process or in the drinking water distribution system (Jackson et al., 1989; Krieps, 1989).

Some of the most serious problems are found in the sources of our drinking water (Hammer, 1975; J. Natl. Inst. Health Res., 1991; Lave and Upton, 1987). Microcontaminants escape landfills, effluent lagoons, and petroleum storage facilities to enter water supplies. Residential, commercial, and industrial outputs increase the pollutant load of surface water, such as rivers and lakes. Pesticides, herbicides, and carcinogenic industrial waste are infiltrating increasing amounts of ground water, the underground source of half of the U.S. population's drinking water. This is particularly tragic because ground water is uniquely susceptible to long-term contamination. Unlike river or lake water, once ground water becomes contaminated, there is no way to cleanse it.

VIGNETTE

In a midwestern farm community, there is growing concern about seepage of agricultural pesticides and herbicides into ground water. The situation is complicated by the fact that families obtain water from their own well rather than from a central municipal source. The families are aware of the long-range carcinogenic effects of many of the chemicals involved. Although family farmers have decreased their use of these chemicals, the large-scale agribusiness companies continue to use excessive amounts of these chemicals, sacrificing environmental integrity for larger crop yields.

County community health nurses lobby local officials to begin a comprehensive program to monitor ground water pollutants and enforce standards for herbicide and pesticide use. These officials are hampered by the powerful agribusiness companies that pressure them to stand back. Together, some of the county's farmers and the nurses organize grass roots information and support groups among rural families. Several projects are jointly started by the families and the nurses in coalition with environmental activist groups in the state. These projects include collecting samples from each family well for testing purposes, forming a local umbrella organization called "Water-Watch" to coordinate actions and communications, coordinating a research project with a federal health agency to track the health problems of a cohort of local residents who have had long-term consumption of these water sources, and disseminating an emergency plan for drinking water distribution should any wells be found to have toxic levels of pesticides, herbicides, or other pollutants.

Housing

Housing, as an environmental health concern, refers to the availability, safety, structural strength, cleanliness, and location of shelter, including public facilities and individual or family dwellings. Environmental health problems related to housing include homelessness; fire hazards; inaccessibility for disabled persons; illnesses caused by overcrowding, dampness, and rodent or insect infestation; poisoning from chipping lead-based paint; psychological effects of architectural design (e.g., low-cost high-rise housing projects); injuries sustained from collapse of building structures that are in disrepair; and winter deaths from inadequate indoor heating.

It is well known that poor housing conditions can spread infectious diseases (Harpham, et al., 1988), but what is becoming more apparent is that they can contribute to cardiovascular and respiratory disorders, cancers, allergies, and mental illnesses. A new term—"sick building"—has been used to describe a phenomenon in which public structures and homes cause toxic syndromes in their occupants because of building materials, poor ventilation, substances in furniture and carpeting, building operations, and/or cleaning agents (Greenberg, 1987; Kay, 1991b).

For example, commercial buildings with offices near underground parking garages may cause their workers to suffer carbon monoxide intoxication. The carcinogenic properties of formaldehyde, asbestos, and volatile organic compounds, which are common components of thermal insulation, cement, flooring, furnishings, and household con-

sumer products, are well known. However, much controversy is arising over the economic hardship that would be imposed on industry, government, business, and multidwelling owners should they be mandated to reduce concentrations of such toxic elements, by, for example, removing asbestos from buildings. Another sick building symptom is suffered disproportionately by the urban poor, who must turn on their gas stoves to supplement inadequate heating in their homes. In so doing they are exposed to chronic, and perhaps acute, levels of nitrogen dioxide, which can impair lung function and result in respiratory illness.

Health can be affected by not only the structure of housing but also the immediate surroundings in which it is situated, such as the neighborhood's population density, proximity to industry, safety of adjacent buildings, level of security, noise and pollution from nearby traffic, and so on (Kay, 1991c).

VIGNETTE

In a large northeastern city, an economic recession has led to massive unemployment, rising housing costs, and drastically reduced housing subsidies. Simultaneously, funding has been cut for several public health and mental health facilities. The result is that approximately 4,000 people are "houseless." This winter a dozen deaths have already occurred due to exposure to the elements. The local shelters are able to house a total of 500 persons each night, although none of these shelters accept women.

Community health nurses meet with local church groups who are committed to starting a shelter for women. This coalition acquires a building in an area near where many shelterless people congregate. They begin to offer accommodations for 75 women. After 3 months, the city takes over the women's shelter because of the churches' difficulties filling the beds and maintaining the project's financial solvency. The city changes the shelter to a dwelling for 50 men and 25 women because it has not been used sufficiently by women.

In evaluating what went wrong, the nurses consulted with several shelterless women as well as with workers from a popular soup kitchen. The answer was relatively simple. The women had not felt safe going to the shelter because of the area's high-crime reputation and lack of street lighting.

Eventually, a new coalition is formed, composed of the community health nurses, several women who are or had been shelterless, a representative from the police force, and the church groups. A new women's shelter is opened in a safer, well-lit neighborhood close to public transit lines.

Food Quality

Food quality refers to the availability and relative costs of foods, their variety and safety, and the health of animal and plant food sources. Food quality problems include malnutrition, bacterial food poisoning, carcinogenic chemical additives (e.g., nitrites, alar, cyclamate), improper or fraudulent meat inspection or food labeling, viral epidemics among livestock (e.g., cholera), food products from diseased animal sources, and disruption of vital natural food chains by eco-system destruction.

Foods can be contaminated by toxic chemicals as they pass along the food chain, eventually resulting in reproductive and mutagenic effects in humans (Regenstein, 1986). For instance, dioxin-containing weed killers are sprayed on range land. Cattle graze on the land, and the herbicide accumulates in their fatty tissue. The beef cattle are butchered, and their meat is sold at markets all along the West Coast. Dioxin shows up in human mother's milk in the western United States, and increasing numbers of children are born with birth defects in these same states.

A plethora of agrichemicals such as pesticides and fertilizers, materials from mechanical handling devices, detergents, and organic packaging materials can poison food. Unsuitable handling, storage, processing, and transport techniques can damage and contaminate foodstuffs. Food adulteration to increase the volume or weight of food or to improve its color or flavor is also problematic because adulterants are usually less nutritious and often harmful. Residues of antibiotics administered to animals remain in meat and milk products, causing people who consume them to develop resistance to a wide range of antibiotics that then are rendered ineffective in the treatment of human infections (Jackson et al., 1989; Krieps, 1989; Rose, 1990).

A new and potentially dangerous threat to food quality involves scientific gene mutations through "gene splicing," which produces livestock that grows faster and fattens more easily so that they can be slaughtered sooner and produce greater yields at a lower cost. This controversial genetic engineering is producing new animal species. The unregulated introduction of these genetically mutated species onto range land and into farm herds threatens the survival of food-producing animal species and has unknown consequences for human nutrition.

VIGNETTE

In a southern town with a population of 10,000, there is a large population of African-American farm workers and a smaller, but significant, number of Euro-American residents who are mostly employed as textile workers. Located well off the interstate arteries, the town experiences very high food costs due to shipping difficulties. Many families have tapered their diets, eating mostly bread, rice, beans, and eggs. Health assessments of school-aged children and toddlers indicate deficiencies of vitamins contained in fresh fruits and vegetables.

Local physicians, county health nurses, and the Parent-Teacher Association join forces to try to improve the nutritional situation. The most popular of the proposed solutions involves the idea of a community garden project. Land is leased from the county, and the project begins. Conflict arises when African-American community leaders realize that the mostly Euro-American textile workers have formed their own garden project, competing with the original garden project for the town's support. Racial tensions intensify.

The nurses and parents originally involved in setting up the project meet to avert a crisis. They decide to focus on reaching church leaders and women in both African- and Euro-American sectors of the town in the hope of supporting a dialogue and a just solution to the problem. Parents and church leaders spread the word in their respective communities. A community meeting is held at a time that is convenient for women in the town and at a neutral place that is deemed acceptable by both African-Americans and Euro-Americans.

Although tensions are strong enough to prevent the formation of a joint garden, each group feels successful and able to save face as a result of the solution reached in the meeting. Town funds are allocated on a per-capita basis to two gardening projects, and an agreement is reached that vegetable and fruit yields will be shared equitably depending on the yield from each site. Additional benefits of the cooperative plan are that the total garden space allotted is increased by 50% and a gardening "tool library" is started so that neither group needs to purchase all new tools.

Waste Control

Waste control is the management of waste materials resulting from industrial and municipal processes and human consumption as well as efforts to minimize waste production. Environmental health problems related to waste control include use of nonbiodegradable plastics, lack of efficient and affordable recycling programs, unlicensed waste dumps, sewage systems that are inadequate for actual population demands or in disrepair, industrial dumping of toxic wastes (e.g., Love Canal), exportation of hazardous radioactive medical wastes to Third World countries, coverups of illicit dumping, and nonenforcement of environmental protection legislation.

The increasing generation of trash by American consumers as well as improper treatment, storage, transport, and disposal of waste are of mounting concern (Carnes and Watson, 1989; Highland, 1983; Martin et al., 1987; Reinhardt and Gordon, 1991). Multiple problems exist. The increasing use of petroleum-based plastics in products such as disposable diapers creates grave ecological problems. Commercial and institutional wastes are routinely dumped with household waste in the same municipal incinerator, landfill, or sewer system. These commercial enterprises are generally exempt from the strict waste regulation applied to industry, although they often generate the same hazardous materials. Small businesses such as dry cleaners, photography laboratories, pesticide formulators, construction sites, and car repair shops use and discard a variety of substances that can cause serious public health problems. Solid waste landfills present a problem because methane gas accumulates in them as a byproduct of decomposing organic wastes. Without proper venting, the volatile gas can move through the soil and cause fires and explosions in nearby areas. Incineration of wastes is not the best solution because it causes particulate air pollution and is ineffective in the combustion of many hazardous wastes.

It is unknown how many hazardous waste sites exist in the United States; a conservative estimate is 22,000 (Greenberg and Anderson, 1984). Because of improper design, operation, or location of the waste sites, hazardous substances are spread through air, soil, and water to poison humans, animals, and plant life. Alarmingly, only a small percentage of hazardous wastes actually reach designated waste sites. The Environmental Protection Agency estimates that 90% of hazardous waste is improperly disposed of in open pits, surface impoundments, vacant land, farmlands, and bodies of water (Anderson, 1987).

VIGNETTE

In a city on the Mississippi River, an outbreak of shigellosis is traced to a group of high school students who have been swimming in a particular area of the river. It is found that the local meat-packing plant is releasing waste material, including human and animal feces, directly into the river.

After intervening to contain the shigella outbreak, the local community health nurses begin to assess the situation as a whole. Their research indicates that the meat-packing facility has been in violation of waste control laws for some time. City officials have imposed fines, which have been paid by the company, but the dumping has continued. A sign has been posted at the riverside that prohibits swimming.

Frustrated by their attempts to negotiate with the city and the plant, the nurses write a letter to both the local newspaper and the state capital newspaper, which has a wide readership across the state. In the letter, they voice concern about the community's health as well as the ecological integrity of the river. Their informative letter is published as a commentary in both papers, which prompts responses from two local environmental groups, several activist groups located downriver, and a national organization concerned with clean water. These groups are able to provide legal support, and a collective suit is brought against the meat-packing company. Subsequently, the company improves its waste treatment process to avoid being forced to pay a large award in the civil suit.

Radiation Risks

Radiation risks are the health dangers posed by the various forms of ionizing radiation, relative to barriers preventing exposure of humans and other life forms. Radiation risks include nuclear power emissions, radioactive hazardous wastes, medical and dental radiographs, radon gas seepage in homes, and wartime dangers of nuclear weaponry.

Nuclear industries are frought with environmental problems (Eisenbud, 1987; Merz, 1989). People and animals living in the vicinity of nuclear facilities such as power plants, waste storage sites, uranium-processing plants, nuclear weapons factories, and nuclear test sites have manifested increased rates of cancers, strokes, diabetes, cardiovascular and renal diseases, immune system damage, premature aging, infertility, miscarriages, and birth defects (Crosbie and Gittus, 1989; Walker, 1989). In addition, there is the ever-present risk of nuclear accidents in which large amounts of radioactivity are released into surrounding areas. It is not known what will be done with nuclear facilities after their three- or four-decade life spans are completed. By then, they will have become saturated with radioactivity as a normal part of their everyday operations and in some way will have to be decommissioned and decontaminated.

A safe way of disposing of nuclear wastes, which remain dangerously radioactive for hundreds of thousands of years, has not been devised. Much of the waste is currently stockpiled in interim collection centers. Not only is there a quandary about how, where, and when to dispose of nuclear wastes currently being generated, but radioactive materials that have already been improperly disposed must be managed. Countless drums of radioactive wastes dumped at sea or buried in the earth are leaking (Council on Scientific Affairs, 1989; League of Women Voters, 1985; Martin et al., 1987; Regenstein, 1986).

Millions of Americans are exposed to dangerous levels of radiation in their homes, schools, and work places (Probart, 1989; Sutcliffe, 1987). Radon is a radioactive decay product of radium that occurs naturally in certain kinds of phosphate- and uranium-containing rock such as granite and black shale. Radon can be present in building materials, drinking water, and soil. Radon gas diffuses into dwellings, mostly through soil, and is prevalent where uranium-bearing land is common. Radon seeps through basement walls, pipes, and cracks in the foundation and is trapped in buildings where there is inadequate ventilation.

Cumulative exposure to excessive or ill-performed radiographs can also cause radiation damage to the body (Wrenn and Mays, 1983). People who work with medical sources of radiation, such as radium or radioactive iodine, are at increased risk for cancers and birth-defective offspring. Older models of x-ray machines may emit excessive levels of radioactivity; all such equipment should be tested regularly for leakage.

VIGNETTE

During wartime, federal standards related to radioactive contamination of the environment and the public's "right to know" are suspended for military projects. In the middle of the U.S.-Iraq war, information "leaks" that a military installation in the southwestern desert, near Deserttown, plans test explosions of several new nuclear bombs, which they call nuclear "devices."

Local townspeople express concern, but no confirmation or denial of these plans is given by the military. The possible dates for the tests are also unknown. Residents begin to panic. Several families move. Others build makeshift shelters and begin stockpiling food. There is an increase in psychiatric hospitalization rates. A crisis is reached when a spate of three related adolescent suicides occurs in a period of 2 months. The entire community appears disorganized, helpless, and hopeless.

Town officials organize town meetings in which the public health nurses offer community education about the health effects of ionizing radiation and answer people's questions, but this does not raise morale among residents. The nurses decide to contact other communities that have faced similar threats to determine how they have dealt with them.

When these communities receive word of the situation in Deserttown, they organize a letter-writing campaign and a demonstration of their support. They converge on Deserttown for a weekend rally and celebration of solidarity. The youth of Deserttown extend this demonstration in the form of weekly vigils at the military site.

One year later, the community is more united and less depressed, and the adolescent suicide rate is significantly decreased. The nuclear threat remains.

Violence Risks

The environmental risks of violence include the potential for victimization through the violence of particular groups as well as the general level of aggression in psychosocial climates. Violence-fostered environmental health problems can arise from conditions such as extreme poverty, widespread unemployment, proliferation of handguns, pervasive media images of violence, lack of child abuse services, law enforcement's unwillingness to follow up on women's complaints of sexual molestation, and increasingly commonplace occurrence of hate crimes.

The potential for persons to be victims of violent crimes, including verbal abuse, harassment, battery, sexual assault, abduction, and murder, is at least partially determined by social, political, and economic characteristics of the environment (Brownmiller, 1975; Campbell, 1981). The phenomenon of urban youth gangs exemplifies a process in which poverty and powerlessness foster aggressiveness and territorial defensiveness in young males.

Social stigmatization of racial, ethnic, and religious minorities as well as lesbians and gay men can take the form of violent hate crimes against these groups. For example, official talk of registering, placing under surveillance, and possibly interning "suspicious" Arab-Americans during the U.S.-Iraq war was accompanied by an increase in malicious innuendos, threats, and violent crimes against Arab-Americans throughout the United States (Hall and Stevens, 1992). The relative political powerlessness of women and children makes them frequent targets of violence as well (Stevens and Hall, 1990). Media images promoting male aggressiveness and sexual dominance reinforce cultural norms of violence (Hanmer and Maynard, 1987).

It continues to be debated whether films, television, recorded music, and sexually explicit materials actually foster the commission of violent crimes. Regardless of whether they do, it is reasonable to conclude that these images influence the direction violent impulses take in terms of targets, e.g., women, children, and minorities (Linz et al., 1988; Sommers and Check, 1987). Most agree that key factors in the incidence and severity of violent aggression are the availability and regulation of ballistic weapons. Handguns, rifles, and automatic weapons are increasingly obtainable in U.S. communities. Communities face very difficult questions about how to curtail the violence in their environments. Increasing dependence on police forces, the penal system, and censorship tactics can produce a situation of diminishing returns; forceful repression may provoke an increase in social aggression.

VIGNETTE

At a prestigious private university, a survey reveals that more than 30% of the female students have experienced "date rape." The university appeals to its student health service to respond to this growing problem. The nurses at the health service are asked to organize classes for female students about self-defense and "what to do if raped."

One nurse voices opposition, pointing out that rape is a violent act perpetrated by men and is not a health matter that concerns only women. She suggests that male students be offered education about the bodily rights of others and classes about "how not to rape women." This causes a deep polarization among the nurses and other health workers at the student health service. Many feel the self-defense classes are useful even if they do not address the core problem. Others feel that to ignore male responsibility for rape is to encourage or condone a "climate of violence."

The self-defense classes are held but not well attended. One year later, the rates of date rape and other sexual assaults involving students at the university are even higher. In reevaluating their intervention, the nurses decide to mingle among the student body and to visit places where students hang out. They informally interview groups of students about what they think is involved in the high incidence of date rape. The consensus is that the fraternity culture on campus encourages heavy drinking and sexual aggressiveness on the part of male students. With these new data, the nurses approach university officials suggesting several services that should be offered to students and policy changes that should be made.

Together, the nurses and university staff develop new interventions. First, the university invites an alcohol problems researcher to institute an alcohol self-awareness research project as well as a bartender education program on campus. Second, the university requires that fraternity leaders participate in four weekend seminars about sexual assault and interpersonal violence. Third, incentives are given to fraternities based on how many of their members attend similar seminars, and commendations and prizes are extended for collective projects that demonstrate effectiveness in decreasing the number of date rapes and other violent crimes on campus. Last, a new policy is adopted in which the university pledges to vigorously pursue criminal and civil actions in all cases of sexual assault involving students.

EFFECTS OF ENVIRONMENTAL HAZARDS

Environmental effects on the public's health are quite complex and usually interconnected. For xample, nuclear power plant emissions can contaminate both water and air supplies, simultaneously involving water quality, atmospheric quality, and radiation risk. Overcrowded housing may exacerbate problems in managing human wastes, which may in turn taint food stuffs, all contributing to the spread of communicable disease.

Health-damaging effects of oppressive environments may be direct. A shiny, brightly colored radioactive medical waste product from the United States that has ended up in a Central American city dump may be picked up and played with by poor children who live nearby and scavenge for food in that dump (Schrieberg, 1991). The severe burns they suffer and the wine-colored spots on their skin are very direct effects of the illegally dumped toxic waste. Effects may also be indirect, as occurs with global warming (Baes et al., 1977). Farming regions will probably warm up, dry out, and become less productive. The sea level will probably eventually rise due to melting polar ice caps. The resulting coastal inundation and permanent flooding could force evacuation of lands now among the world's most desirable.

Effects of environmental hazards may be general or specific. The ramifications of massive unemployment, drought, and extensive smog cover, for example, are felt generally, whereas the particular housing needs of elderly persons using walkers or canes, the occupational risks faced by workers who repair electrical lines, and the mentally incapacitating effects of lead poisoning in children are experienced more specifically.

Environmental health effects can also be categorized as immediate, long range, or transgenerational. Burns, gunshot wounds, hurricane damage, and outbreaks of gastrointestinal distress among cafeteria customers are examples of immediate effects from health-damaging environments. Examples of long-term health effects include gradual occupational hearing loss, "black lung" in coal miners, and increased rates of cancer among migrant farm workers who were aerially sprayed with the pesticide DDT 15 years earlier (Archer and Livingston, 1983). Transgenerational effects occur with the radiation exposures of female factory workers at plutonium-processing plants that cause chromosomal anomalies and later result in birth defects in their offspring. Another transgenerational effect is seen in the repetition of domestic violence in successive family generations.

Some negative environmental health effects are reversible. For example, the lungs of nonsmokers who for years inhaled sidestream smoke from their smoking family members and coworkers can heal and be restored to healthy function if the smoke is eliminated. On the other hand, damage to human cells caused by radiation is irreversible. Many environmental dangers cause cumulative effects, as represented by heavy metal exposure. Over time, lead collects in the long bones and can be re-released into the body. Not only can it cause acute poisoning, but it later may cause additional damage (Fischbein, 1983).

EFFORTS TO CONTROL ENVIRONMENTAL HEALTH PROBLEMS

The 1970s were the decade of environmental concern. As cynicism toward institutions grew during the Vietnam era, legislative activism for environmental preservation exploded (Burger, 1989). Table 24–4 outlines the essential statutes. New agencies designed to regulate environmental conditions on a national level were created by Congress at that time, including the Environmental Protection Agency (EPA), Occupational Health and Safety Administration (OSHA), and Nuclear Regulation Commission (NRC).

Table 24–4 **Landmark Federal Environmental Legislation**	
Year	**Legislation**
1970	Clean Air Act
1970	Poison Prevention Packaging Act
1970	Occupational Health and Safety Act
1970	Hazardous Materials Transportation Control
1970	National Environmental Policy Act
1971	Lead-Based Paint Poisoning Prevention Act
1972	Federal Water Pollution Control Act Amendments
1972	Noise Control Act
1976	Resource Conservation and Recovery Act
1976	Toxic Substances Control Act
1977	Clean Water Act
1980	Low Level Radiation Waste Policy Act
1980	Comprehensive Environmental Response, Compensation, and Liability Act (Superfund)

The EPA has enormous responsibilities for protecting the environment and minimizing environmental risks to human health. Among its roles are setting standards for air and water quality, health surveillance and monitoring, evaluation of environmental risks, information acquisition, screening of new chemicals, basic research and training, data base maintenance, and establishing, evaluating, and enforcing regulatory efforts. In 1980, the EPA Superfund was established, which provided for a trust fund to be used in cleaning up toxic sites when those originally responsible were unable to pay for the cleanup (Burger, 1989; Greaves, 1983). However, there has been much controversy about the illegal squandering of funds related to this program.

The legislative activism of the 1970s was responsible for unprecedented movement toward a comprehensive national environmental policy, although the goal remains woefully unfulfilled. For example, improvements in air quality have been made through stricter automobile fuel and emissions standards, which are at odds with the American romance with the large car. Nevertheless, as a result, lead levels in urban air have decreased 87% since 1977 (Bingham and Meader, 1990). Tremendous dilemmas remain, however.

Many environmental problems are defined by historical events, such as the thalidomide crisis, the Love Canal episode, and the nuclear accident at Three Mile Island. Historical dynamics, social values, and powerful industry and business interests influence the attention paid to environmental problems as well as the economic commitment to their solutions (Reich, 1988). An example is the widespread agricultural use of neurotoxic organophosphate pesticides, which are known to cause lasting central nervous system damage (J. Natl. Inst. Health Res., 1991). Advocates for farm workers say the EPA should ban the use of pesticides registered in the highest toxicity category. Instead, the EPA has proposed new regulations that would require employers to provide general pesticide safety information to all farm workers. In addition, the EPA suggested regular testing to monitor blood levels of toxins of workers who apply the pesticides. However, monitoring would be required only for commercial applicators, i.e., those who apply chemicals as a business, not for farm workers who apply pesticides as one part of their duties. The EPA is said to have limited the scope of its monitoring requirement because of pressure from large agribusiness interests.

There has been inadequate scientific research for formulating environmental health policy, including a lack of baseline data and systems of routine surveillance (Walker, 1990). Health professionals and health science communities have few alliances with the environmentalists, conservationists, and consumers who pushed through the federal environmental legislation (Burger, 1989). There is also an inability or unwillingness to determine the damages caused by past practices because of the vast liability that would be incurred. Therefore, the impact of past hazardous waste management on present cancer clusters, for example, remains undetermined (Highland, 1983).

There are several other weaknesses in legislative efforts to control environmental problems. Legislation has sometimes been too detailed or inflexible, causing problems in the articulation of federal and local regulatory efforts (Walker, 1990). The laws often excuse industry and government from environmental clean-up because of the high costs involved, while communities suffer the health risks (Anderson, 1983). The EPA sets priorities for environmental problems, but resources to meet the identified needs are not provided (Walker, 1990). In addition, the EPA is dangerously behind its deadlines in addressing new contaminants. For example, current regulations allow some municipal water systems as long as 20 years to remove lead from service lines (Corn, 1991).

There is no federal regulation for recycling, although local communities have made great strides in this area. There is also no comprehensive ground water legislation similar to what has been adopted to preserve marine and surface waters (Bingham and Meader, 1990). The Occupational Health and Safety Act, as well as other statutes, was seriously weakened by the Reagan administration's deregulation of industry and defunding of environmental efforts throughout the 1980s (Bingham and Meader, 1990).

In general, most of the U.S. environmental health efforts have aimed for short-term goals rather than anticipating future needs and problems. In this regard, U.S. industries are underinvested in development of renewable resource technologies for the sake of transient profits. A crucial need also exists in the development of human resources in the area of environmental health (Walker, 1990). Nursing careers in environmental

health science would be an excellent move toward integrating health and environmental theory and practice at the community level.

Nurses need to work with the public toward more stringent and actively enforced environmental legislation and regulation as well as greater social control over corporations and other entities that are at fault for health-damaging environments. In the 1990s, government actions must include not only national but also worldwide environmental policies. Ozone depletion, global warming, and the destruction of tropical rain forests are among key global environmental health concerns. Community health nursing must expand its theory and practice to incorporate the reality that individual and community health depends ultimately on global environmental integrity. There are countless organizations working to preserve and protect the environment that could benefit from the active involvement and support of nurses; Table 24–5 lists several of these organizations.

APPROACHING ENVIRONMENTAL HEALTH AT THE AGGREGATE LEVEL

In the United States, the ideas of personal independence and individual responsibility for success and failure have always been very important. However, these values can lead nurses to blame individual clients for their health problems while overlooking glaring environmental hazards. By placing responsibility for the cause and cure of health problems exclusively on the individual, the belief is reinforced that all individuals are free to exert meaningful control over the quality and length of their lives (Becker, 1986). Such a perspective absolves society, government, industry, and business from accountability for changing pernicious conditions under which people live and work. Existing research evidence suggests that changing individual behaviors does not lead to significant reductions in overall morbidity and mortality in the absence of basic social, economic, and political changes (Freudenberg, 1984–1985; Milio, 1986). Emphasizing only public health interventions that attempt to modify deleterious personal habits through exercise programs, weight-loss regimens, smoking-cessation classes, and stress-reduction tactics fails to engage the broader environmental

---

Table 24–5
Environmental Organizations

American Farmland Trust
Animal Preservation League
Citizens for a Better Environment
Clean Water Action
Earth Regeneration Society
Forests Forever
Greenpeace
International Rivers Network
National Environmental Law Center
National Toxics Campaign
Natural Resources Defense Council
Ocean Alliance
Pesticide Action Network
Radioactive Wastes Campaign
Rainforest Action Network
Sierra Club
Toxics Coordinating Project
Trust for Public Land
U.S. Public Interest Research Group
Wilderness Society

origins of disease, injury, and ecological destruction (Salmon and Berliner, 1982).

Nursing is not alone in its focus on individual health-promoting interventions. With federal directives such as the 1979 Surgeon General's report (U.S. Department of Health and Human Services, 1979), most health agencies, health care institutions, and corporate workplaces have principally addressed the idea of "controllable risk" in the individual, with much less effort directed toward reducing risks in the environment. The government has also reduced its overall focus on environmental health. In the 1980s, the effectiveness and power of agencies such as the EPA and the National Institute for Occupational Safety and Health declined so that they are less able to study environmental health risks and enforce regulatory policies.

By focusing on the individual, other levels of intervention are overlooked (Zola, 1972). Interventions designed for individuals alone leave environments that "sicken" people unchallenged. Although environmental dangers posed by contamination of drinking water, carcinogenic food additives, loss of the ozone layer, and occupational hazards are often recognized as serious, the implication persists that little can be done about the inevitability of technological and industrial growth around the world (Crawford, 1977). Individuals therefore are compelled to simply accommodate environments that cause them illness and injury.

Recognition of the gravity and pervasiveness of environmental hazards can be overwhelming. Looking beyond the individual to recognize the environmental determinants of illness and wellness can be complicated and threatening. Intervening to improve the quality of air, water, housing, food, and waste disposal while reducing the risks of occupational injury, radiation, and violence requires basic social, economic, and political changes in the process. Bringing about changes in health-damaging environments must be an aggregate-level endeavor.

Community health nurses who base their practices on the principles of critical theory are better prepared to respond to all of these challenges. As the vignettes demonstrate, by focusing our efforts on organizing groups of people, we can facilitate community participation in identifying and solving environmental health problems and thus bring about changes that improve environments and eliminate hazards.

CRITICAL COMMUNITY HEALTH NURSING PRACTICE

What are some of the actions community health nurses might take to approach environmental health critically? As described in the vignettes, nurses take sides. They ask critical questions. Nurses become involved with the communities they serve, they form coalitions, and they become familiar with the use of various collective strategies. These areas of nursing intervention were developed and presented elsewhere (Stevens and Hall, 1992). In the interest of educating future practitioners about the critical practice of community health nursing as it applies to environmental health, each of these interventions is discussed in the following sections.

Taking a Stand, Choosing a Side

An old labor union folk song asks, "Which Side Are You On?" Acknowledging that there are multiple sides to issues about health and the environment does not mean that nurses can ultimately avoid taking a stand. Nurses have individual and collective decisions to make about whose interests they want to serve with their specialized knowledge and skills. To say that all should be served is certainly an ideal. However, the present reality is that consequences of hazardous environments are often experienced inequitably. Vulnerable groups are exposed to more health-damaging effects than are less vulnerable groups. Decisions nurses make about the positions they accept and the interventions they undertake have the potential to increase or decrease these inequities.

Community health nurses have a mandate to assist vulnerable aggregates who are less able to protect themselves from pollution, inadequate housing, toxic poisoning, unsafe products, and other hazards. Non–English-speaking refugees, racial minority children, the elderly, poor women, and illiterate manual laborers are just some of the groups in the United States who hold little power with which to broker with industry, government, business, and other large institutions for environmental changes and just compensations for harm suffered as a result of environmental hazards.

Environmental problems are clearly intertwined with social, political, and economic policies; barriers to resources; and the interests of those in positions of control. But how can nurses connect the immediate health problems experienced by particular groups and communities to this larger sphere of influences?

Asking Critical Questions

Consider the relationships between nonhealth policies and health. How do policies concerning ecological preservation, energy, housing, immigration, civil rights, crime, nutrition, minimum wage, occupational safety, and defense affect the well-being of people who live in the United States? Addressing the critical questions of who has access to resources in this country and whose interests are served in the system as it exists provides a way to include social, political, and economic factors in

---

Table 24–6
Critical Questions About Environmental Health Problems

What is the problem?
Who is defining the problem?
In what terms is the problem being described?
How are others in the situation viewing the problem?
What is the history of the problem?
How did things get the way they are?
What other situations are directly affected by this problem?
Who is impacted by the problem?
Whose health is being damaged because of the way things are?
Who benefits from the way things are?
Whose interests are served by current solutions?
What are the economic inequities in the situation?
Who has political power in the situation?
Who knows about the problem?
Who needs to know or know more about the problem?
How effective are current programs, strategies, and policies?
What are the barriers to help and relief from the problem?
What strategies have been used to try to alleviate the problem?
How successful have these strategies been?
What groups are already in place that might deal with this problem?
What resources are needed to solve the problem?
How accessible are the resources?
How can solutions be evaluated for effectiveness?

---

nursing assessments of the environment. Some patterns of questioning are useful in this endeavor. A sample set of questions is given in Table 24–6. These critical questions can be asked when approaching environmental health problems.

Dialogue resulting from critical questioning can frame the problem and assist in building collective strategies. Ideally, these questions should be explored collectively by those most directly impacted by the situation or problem. However, even one individual involved in the situation can begin to explore a problem from this perspective and define an initial basis for action.

Facilitating Community Involvement

Approaching community health from a critical perspective means working to improve health conditions while creating the context in which people can identify health-damaging problems in their environments. One important nursing goal is to help people learn from their own experiences and analyze the world with an aim to change it. It is essential that the people affected participate in a process of identifying and working to solve environmental problems.

To create this openness, nurses must abandon asymmetrical positions of leadership and instead join in mutual exchanges with community members that honor each individual's experience. The nurse's role changes from presenting solutions and directing lifestyle changes to asking critical questions of groups and assisting them to reflect on the problematic environmental realities of their lives. A second nursing role is to provide support, information, and expertise to groups to assist them in meeting their goals for environmental change. In each of these roles, nurses use the concept of solidarity, in which the relationship with the community and its individual members is maintained and nurtured despite disagreements that may occur over what is the best course of action.

Instead of trying to compel people to act in certain ways, nurses should assist aggregates in their own collective search for effective change strategies. Actions dictated from those outside the situation are often culturally inappropriate and therefore doomed to be ineffective. Lasting rapport with aggregates depends on honesty, fairness, and mutuality in interactions over extended periods of time.

With critical questions, community health nurses can assist community members in looking beyond immediate environmental problems to explore social, cultural, economic, and political circumstances that affect them. Nurses' knowledge of the scientific basis for health problems, insights about the historical origins of particular environmental hazards, technical skills, and expertise in communicating and organizing can be shared, not as a method of dominating but rather as a way to develop a mutual plan of action to deal with the problems that have been collectively identified. By addressing people's everyday concerns and targeting the problems they themselves identify, nurses situate their efforts in their clients' struggles.

Forming Coalitions

Another very important nursing task that arises from approaching environmental health from a critical perspective involves forming coalitions to bring about social change (Moccia, 1985). By initiating dialogue and building a strong base of collective support, nurses can insist on structural changes that eliminate hazards and improve the public's health. In dealing with health-damaging environments, nurses can approach already existing community organizations and family and friendship networks as well as help mobilize aggregate members who have not previously socialized or acted together. As a group, nurses can then expose hazards, assess needs, plan actions, report abuses, and secure appropriate resources, personnel, funding, and legislative changes.

Nurses can also be instrumental in organizing forums whereby community groups meet with the scientific experts who can help them gather evidence about health threats, with managers of businesses whose actions impinge on the economic life of the community, with heads of industry whose companies create ecological hazards, and with legislators who can bring community concerns to lawmaking bodies. Using available institutional resources, skills, and knowledge, nurses can also explore what is happening elsewhere. Making connections with groups in other locales who are struggling for similar environmental changes can enhance collective strength and solidarity. Press releases, media events, interviews, television spots, speeches, newsletters, and leaflets are important means of raising awareness among communities as well as calling the attention of outsiders to a situation at hand.

In working for various municipalities, agencies, and health care corporations, nurses may be constrained by the philosophies, policies, resources, and relations of these organizations. Although nurses may disagree with some of these organizational aspects, they are perceived by communities to be representatives of the organizations for whom they work. These institutional connections may cause problems for nurses working with groups who feel abandoned by the system, disregarded in policy decisions, or refused access to resources. Establishing alliances with disenfranchised communities is therefore a complex and often long-term process of building trust. Nurses must advocate for the fiscal, logistical, labor, and ideological support necessary for these processes. This means that in many cases, nurses will have to struggle collectively for institutional changes to develop resources to make the environment safer. When mobilizing aggregates for improvement of environmental health, it is essential that the process not be undermined by a withdrawal of resources because this will lead to further alienation and mistrust on the part of vulnerable groups.

It may appear that an "us–them" approach has been advocated in which one always aligns with the vulnerable against outside "enemies." This is an unfortunate oversimplification. When nurses build coalitions for improving environmental conditions, each issue or problem requires appropriate strategizing based on its own merits. Allies in a current struggle may have been adversaries in a previous struggle. For example, even though a bank refused to help farm families by granting farm loan extensions last month, it may still be an ally this month when a superhighway development project threatens its building as well as an adjacent poor neighborhood. An ally need not be in complete agreement with the core group's philosophy, political agenda, or moral beliefs. The federal government may be viewed as an adversary with regard to restrictive immigration policies but as an ally in its enforcement of the provisions of the Rehabilitation Act. There is virtually no person or faction that can be completely discounted as an ally, that will not ultimately be touched by some environmental health issue. It is a good idea to brainstorm about all the possible groups and factions in a locale that may have a stake in the outcome of an issue. A good coalition-building strategy is to have an eye on the future and envision how one struggle — one set of allies — can extend its network and subsequently form new coalitions for emerging issues.

Using Collective Strategies

A variety of collective strategies can be used by nurses in coalition with others to intervene at the aggregate level and facilitate liberating changes in a community's health. Organizing people to change health-damaging environments can be accomplished through combinations of coalition building; consciousness-raising groups; educational forums in neighborhoods, workplaces, schools, churches, and social clubs; seminars for health care providers, city officials, teachers, and employers; community needs assessments; dissemination of clinical research and policy analyses; use of mass media; canvassing; litigation; legislative lobbying; testimony at public hearings; demonstrations; and participatory research. Stotts (1991) demonstrated the use of several of these collective strategies in his community health nursing interventions aimed at limiting sidestream smoke or passive smoking in public buildings and worksites.

Although nurses have not traditionally used all of these collective strategies to intervene in community health matters, environmental hazards are multiplying geometrically, so they have a responsi-

bility to learn about them. If nurses have not been taught these types of organizational skills, they can learn from experts in the community who have had experience with conducting mass media campaigns, organizing demonstrations, canvassing neighborhoods, participating in class-action litigation, testifying at public hearings, and so on. There are also many books about political action that can be consulted.

One collective strategy that can be an effective aggregate-level community health nursing intervention is *participatory research,* sometimes called *action research.* Participatory research calls for nurses, community members, and other resource people to work together in identifying environmental health problems that should be investigated, designing the studies, collecting and analyzing the data, disseminating results, and posing solutions to the problems (Antonio, 1983; Chavis et al., 1983; Cook and Fonow, 1986; Freudenberg, 1984; Gordis, 1988; Mies, 1983). With the assistance of community health nurses, community members gather information on suspected environmental hazards, document their effects on health, educate their communities, persuade corporations to clean up, and lobby local, state, and federal governments for stricter regulations and better enforcement. The goal of the research process is not merely the production of knowledge but rather the generation of open discussion and debate that intensifies a community's conscious-

---

Participatory Research About Environmental Health
Research Project
Brown, P.: Popular epidemiology: Community response to toxic waste–induced disease. Sci. Technol. Hum. Value 12;78–85, 1987.

Abstract
The residents of Woburn, Massachusetts, working together with civic activists and some professionals, collected data confirming the existence of a leukemia cluster and demonstrated that it was traceable to industrial waste carcinogens that leached into their drinking water supply. These residents collectively took part in years of actions that led to successful civil suits against the corporations at fault. The actions of the Woburn citizenry offer a valuable example of lay commu-

nication of risk to scientific experts and government officials and demonstrate a concerted collective effort at investigation into disease patterns and their likely causes. This case, which drew national attention during the 1980s, has catalyzed similar efforts across the country and expands our knowledge of the effects of toxic wastes. The Woburn residents introduced evidence to show that the health effects of toxic wastes are not restricted to physical disease but also include emotional problems.

Using this case study of popular epidemiology, which involves community-propelled investigation, the author provides a framework for participatory research about environmental health.

ness of how its health is impaired by environmental constraints. The box on the preceding page presents an abstract of an article about popular epidemiology (Brown, 1987), which is a type of participatory research related to environmental health.

In towns across the United States, concerned residents are conducting surveys to determine how severe are the community health threats posed by factories that pollute waterways, nuclear power plants, aerial spraying of herbicides, vehicle exhaust pollution, off-shore oil drilling, and excessive lumbering (Freudenberg, 1984–1985). One such effort was very successful, as the following reveals.

In response to unregulated toxic contamination in Pennsylvania during the early 1980s, a coalition of tenant associations, environmental groups, senior citizens, labor unions, and Vietnam veterans who had been exposed to Agent Orange organized in Philadelphia. The Delaware Valley Toxics Co-

alition, as it was called, elicited the help of scientists and epidemiologists to write environmental impact reports about chemical contamination, implemented massive community and workplace education, staged protest demonstrations at polluting companies, organized testimony at public hearings, and helped draft legislation. The coalition also used the media creatively to publicize their concerns. For example, one labor union member sprayed from an unmarked canister into the city council chamber during public testimony. When the city council members protested, the unionist replied, "This can contains only air, but every day we have to work with chemicals we know nothing about." As a result of the coalition's efforts, the city of Philadelphia enacted the nation's first Right-to-Know law. The statute stipulated that workers and community residents had the right to know the names and health effects of chemicals used, manufactured, stored, or released into the air (Chess, 1983).

C a s e
S t u d y

Application of the Nursing Process

In December 1990, the *San Francisco Examiner* reported on an extensive problem of lead exposure in the city of Oakland, California (Kay, 1990). Some of the reported facts of this situation will be expanded to construct hypothetical nursing interventions.

Assessment

Oakland's community health nurses have long been involved with city residents and have been aware of high rates of lead poisoning in particular neighborhoods. In the wake of alarming newspaper articles about the dangerous incidence of lead exposure in the city, the nurses decide at a planning meeting to make lead exposure a priority. The community health nurses and several nursing students assigned to their department divide assessment tasks and uncover the following conditions.

A 1988 California study of lead exposure reported that approximately 50,000 California children have enough lead in their serum to lower intelligence, alter behavior, create neurological dysfunction, damage kidneys, and depress growth (Kay, 1990). It was found that one fifth of inner-city Oakland children have toxic levels of lead in their blood. Although the ubiquitous danger of lead poisoning has been known to city, state, and federal authorities for decades, they have failed to establish routine testing of children. They have not created programs to remove lead-based paint from existing structures, nor have they eliminated lead emissions from industrial sources and overcrowded freeways.

An economically depressed neighborhood in Oakland, hypothetically called "Rosario," is situated near numerous railways, freeways, and industrial yards. High numbers of African-American, Latino, and Southeast Asian residents live in the older homes that line the streets of Rosario. The concentration of lead in the soil of the neighborhood averages 1,200 parts per million (Kay, 1991a). A soil lead concentration of 500–1,000 parts per million is sufficient to cause dangerously high blood levels of lead in children (Kane, 1985). Lead levels are also significant in Rosario's drinking water because much of its plumbing consists of lead pipes that leach lead into standing water. Lead-based paint peels from most of the houses. Many heads of households who work in the nearby radiator shops, scrap metal yards, and battery-manufacturing plants carry lead dust home on their clothing and shoes. Isolated by language and economic circumstances, many Rosario residents do not know about the environmental health hazards to which they are being exposed.

Children absorb 50% of the lead they eat, drink, or breathe, whereas adults absorb only 10% (Kane, 1985). Children are more likely to come in contact with lead by playing in contaminated dirt and eating paint chips. Substandard nutrition also increases the absorption of lead. Lead in car exhaust and industrial emissions is inhaled and contaminates the ground near busy freeways and factories. Unfortunately, lead remains in soil for thousands of years (Needleman, 1980).

Lucia, a 7-year-old girl who lives in Rosario, developed a lead level several times as high as that needed to cause impairment of intelligence. Her hair fell out, and she became emaciated, weak, and often tearful. She had constant nosebleeds and fell down frequently. She was given painful and risky intravenous treatment with chelating agents over a period of 1 year, and most of her symptoms receded. But her mother says, "No one cleans up the area. People move in and out, but the poison remains here." In fact, local hospital spokespersons say that 25% of the children they treat for lead poisoning are repoisoned after they are sent home (Kay, 1990).

The state's Child Health Program, which provides health examinations for poor children, refuses to add lead tests to their routine examinations, even though the federal government now requires it as a condition for Medicaid funding (Nurse Week, 1991). California officials say that they provide testing when it is recommended by a physician, but private physicians in the city generally assume that lead poisoning is an East Coast phenomenon. Therefore, they often fail to recommend the blood test and are unlikely to recognize the syndrome of lead poisoning when it does occur. Furthermore, the Child Health Program reaches only about one third of those who are eligible. The governor recently vetoed $160,000 in funding for a lead-testing program for high-risk children in Oakland.

Based on this assessment, the city's community health nurses devise the following list of unresolved problems:

- Lead-screening programs for children are not in place.
- Private physicians are not recommending lead tests for vulnerable children.
- Health care providers at local public hospitals and clinics may not be recognizing lead-poisoning symptoms.

- Children are being repoisoned after treatment.
- Industrial and vehicular emissions are poorly controlled.
- No comprehensive plan for removal of lead-based paint from older structures in the city is under way.
- Many Rosario residents work in lead-related industries.
- Poverty and malnutrition are widespread in Rosario.
- Residents are poorly informed about lead hazards in the environment.
- Multiracial, multicultural, and language characteristics of Rosario make organizing and education efforts more complex.

Planning

Given their assessment, the community health nurses decide they must assist members of the Rosario community to force environmental changes that reduce lead-poisoning risks. They realize they should involve members of the Rosario community at planning meetings from the outset and make efforts to include African-American, Latino, and Southeast Asian community members. They contact neighborhood leaders, church leaders, ethnic clubs, the local Parent-Teacher Association, a senior citizen organization in the neighborhood, the Black Women's Health Project, and a local Latina women's political organization. In their initial meetings, they learn that there is a budding multicultural grass roots effort by People United for a Better Oakland (PUEBLO) (Kay, 1990) that is trying to go door to door educating Rosario residents about the dangers of lead.

With community members, the nurses discuss how all parties view the problem, what resources are available, how they might align with PUEBLO, who might serve as potential allies, what the community health nursing agency can do, how they might generate more community involvement, and what potential actions might be taken. The nurses also ask questions about what other circumstances are affecting Rosario residents. Community members express that they are still reeling from the damages caused by the previous year's earthquake. They also report that many of their neighbors are fearful of coming to the meetings or joining PUEBLO because they are undocumented workers and worry about deportation. In addition, the state highway commission is pressing for the construction of another freeway close to Rosario; everybody is worried about this. After several meetings, members decide to establish a permanent Rosario Coalition of which the nurses are an important part.

The nurses talk together about their competing priorities; the lead problem is only one of the issues they deal with. They reach the conclusion that they can most efficiently advocate for Rosario's residents by using their established ties with local physicians, nurses, and health care institutions. They allocate adequate funds and personnel to accomplish goals set by the coalition and establish a time frame for ongoing evaluation of the Rosario project. Nursing students and community health nursing faculty from the local university and college programs are encouraged to become involved in the interventions.

Intervention

The actions that the community health nurses in coalition with community members decide to take can be divided into interventions at the individual, family, and aggregate levels.

Individual

- Identify Rosario children who have been diagnosed and treated for lead poisoning, and plan follow-up nursing home visits in an attempt to prevent repoisoning.
- Add to the community health agency's child health assessment protocol several observations specifically designed to detect symptoms of lead poisoning and several questions aimed at establishing if there are specific risks for lead poisoning in the home.
- Coordinate with school nurses so that they can incorporate similar changes in their health assessment protocols.
- Establish an agreement with the state's Child Health Program that they will obtain lead levels on children if it is recommended, not only by physicians but also by school nurses or community health nurses.
- Together with members of the Rosario Coalition, prepare an educational pamphlet detailing the lead-poisoning risks that exist for Rosario residents. With the coalition's endorsement, the nurses mail the pamphlet to individual physicians and nurses who provide services to children in Oakland.
- Prepare translations of the pamphlet in languages and reading levels appropriate for Rosario residents and mail it to individual households.
- Follow up on pamphlet mailings with announcements of community health nurses' willingness to offer lead-poisoning education programs at churches, schools, hospitals, workplaces, medical association meetings, and nursing association meetings.

Family

- Initiate a family-to-family program in which a core group of Rosario community members attend educational meetings with the community health nurses. In these meetings, information is shared about the environmental origins of lead poisoning and its prevention, diagnosis, and treatment. These specially trained community members then take charge of the program, sharing their knowledge with extended family members and neighboring families.
- Coordinate with school nurses to establish a health education program in Rosario schools in which school-aged children are taught about lead poisoning. These children are then encouraged to take their knowledge home and teach younger preschool-aged brothers and sisters that they are not to eat dirt or paint chips.
- Investigate how community health nurses might be of more assistance to Rosario families in helping them apply for and obtain nutritional resources such as food stamps, Supplemental Food Program for Women, Infants and Children (WIC), food bank supplements, school lunch programs, and so on. With improvement of nutritional status, lead absorption might thus be decreased.

- Facilitate the formation of a support group for families with children who have suffered damage from lead poisoning. The community health nurses offer their offices for evening meeting space and serve as information resources about health care and social services as well as disability assistance from the government.

Aggregate

- With the Rosario Coalition, form broader coalitions with PUEBLO, Oakland churches, local nurses association, several preschool and day care centers, and the Oakland School Board to design a comprehensive, nonduplicative, cost-effective lead-screening program that will test all children in Oakland on a regular basis.
- Lobby state legislatures, municipal officials, local medical association, local hospitals, and city clinics regarding implementation of the plan.
- Contact the occupational health nurses at local lead-based industries to ascertain policies related to heavy metals, enforcement of regulations regarding lead disposal, and number of cases of lead poisoning among workers.
- Contact state environmental groups for advice on local efforts, and join with them in their fight for stricter regulation of lead emissions and toxic wastes.
- Contact researchers at a local university's environmental sciences program and request that they work with the coalition to conduct a house-to-house study of sources of lead poisoning. The nurses and other members of the coalition offer their cooperation in teaching Rosario residents about the questionnaires they will be expected to fill out and the data gathering that will be required involving soil, water, and paint samples. They also offer to coordinate the services of bilingual research assistants from the Rosario community.
- Contact local media (television, radio, and newspaper) about running a series of stories about local lead-poisoning risks. Nurses and other coalition members supply information and contacts for interviews and photographs.

Evaluation

In regular meetings of the original Rosario Coalition, the nurses facilitate evaluation of ongoing interventions. Among their many evaluation activities, the nurses keep track of both the number of lead-screening tests being done on Rosario children and the rates of lead poisoning and re-poisoning to see if their efforts in these areas are effective. They document participation levels at educational programs and family-to-family training sessions and interest in the nutrition referrals and support group, all of which appear to be successful.

The community health nurses also keep in close contact with the school nurses and the occupational health nurses. At one point, the occupational health nurses report that they are too overburdened in their jobs to do the necessary worker education concerning prevention of heavy metal poisoning. The community health nurses and coalition members offer to help. They set up an after-work educational program for foremen at the local industries and another program for union shop stewards. They hope that both groups will disseminate the information at their workplaces. The occupational health nurses are asked to report back with their observations of the success of the educational sessions.

The broader coalition's efforts at pushing through their plan for a comprehensive lead-screening program are met with a great deal of opposition from the state legislature, even though local officials support their plan. When repeated negotiations continue to fail, the coalition decides to align with environmental and civil rights groups who are suing the state of California for failing to provide federally mandated tests for lead poisoning in low-income children. They join as plaintiffs in the class-action suit. The community health nurses from Rosario give expert testimony in the case.

Examples of Levels of Prevention

Primary Prevention
EDUCATION OF the community regarding lead poisoning and lead hazards in the environment.

Secondary Prevention
Screening at-risk populations for exposure to lead/blood lead levels.

Tertiary Prevention
Follow-up treatment of persons with lead poisoning; removal of lead hazards from the community environment.

As the court case proceeds, some members of the state legislature begin to show more interest in a lead-screening program, and another vote is scheduled. The Rosario Coalition participates in a Lead Poisoning Awareness Day at the state capitol the week before the vote. They are active in the demonstration and give speeches about their local experiences. They visit the offices of individual legislators informing them of the situation in Rosario. Citing the tentative results from the environmental sciences' house-to-house research study as well as the statistics the community health nurses have been keeping about screening and poisoning rates proves to be very useful. This evidence strengthens the arguments coalition members make about the need for a comprehensive lead-screening program in the state. The coalition also shares these data with the national environmental groups with which they have been working. These groups use the data in testimony before federal legislators to secure federal funding for a new program to remove lead-based paint from existing structures.

SUMMARY

This chapter has provided a glimpse into the complex world of environmental health from a critical community health nursing perspective. The case study, vignettes, and examples have illustrated that nurses must evaluate the broader picture in assessing the environmental health status of communities and the vulnerable aggregates within them. In preventing, minimizing, and resolving environmental health problems, nurses must recognize patterns, detect subtle changes, identify underlying issues, and work collaboratively with a variety of other individuals and groups. In the past, environmental threats to health were usually suspected

Nurses Environmental Healthwatch

NURSES ENVIRONMENTAL Healthwatch is an organization that is involved in educating nurses about environmental concerns and nursing's role in bringing about a safe, healthy environment. Nurses Environmental Healthwatch may be contacted at 33 Columbus Avenue, Somerville, MA 02143.

only when other possible causes of illness had been ruled out. Nurses can expect this pattern to change drastically in future decades as environmental health moves increasingly to the forefront of the public health agenda.

Learning Activities

1. Identify a health-related problem associated with some aspect of the environment. It may be a problem you see in your community, one that you have read about, or a difficulty that a family you work with has identified. Examine the problem using the sample series of critical questions listed in Table 24–6. Without sharing your results, present the problem to a group of your peers and ask them to discuss it by responding to the same questions. Were there differences between your answers and those of the group? Were there similarities? On what points did everyone agree? Why? What questions caused the most disagreement? Why?

   Now repeat the entire activity by involving people other than nursing students in the group discussion. How did this discussion compare with the previous one and with your responses to the questions?

2. Attend meetings in which environmental hazards are discussed. If meetings or public forums are not available in your vicinity, write for information about the actions being taken in your state to fight environmental hazards. The reference librarians at your college or public library can suggest ways of contacting sources and supply addresses. Organizations that are likely to sponsor forums and provide information include those listed in Table 24–5 as well as the EPA, National Institute for Occupational Safety and Health, state and municipal agencies for environmental protection and occupational health, environmental caucuses of political parties, American Public Health Association, local public health department, farmers' organizations, and labor unions.

3. In this chapter, examples of how to use participatory research as an intervention in dealing with ecological hazards are described. In a group, brainstorm about possibilities for participatory action research projects in your locality. Try to think of examples from a variety of environmental health areas. Be creative in your planning. How might you mobilize community support and participation in

the research? What groups would you approach? What critical questions might you use to facilitate dialogue about the problem? What ideas do you have about the kinds of data that could be collected and how they could be used? How would you publicize your research results? What ramifications could the completed study have for community members, other communities in the state, and community health nurses in other locales?

4. Nurses may have to supplement their knowledge of collective strategies by reading books about political action and by learning from community members who are experienced in political organizing. Visit your college or public library to investigate books and journal articles outside the nursing literature. Compile a list of references related to one of these political strategies (e.g., grass roots organizing, legislative lobbying, community education, policy analysis, use of the media, coalition building, citizen surveys, public protest, letter-writing campaigns, or consciousness-raising groups). Exchange reference lists with your peers so you benefit from each other's efforts. Then, choose one or two books that interest you and read them.

REFERENCES

Allen, D. G.: Using philosophical and historical methodologies to understand the concept of health. *In* Chinn, P. L., ed.: Nursing Research Methodology Issues and Implementation. Rockville, Maryland, Aspen, 1986, pp. 157–168.

Anderson, R. F.: Human welfare and the administered society: Federal regulation in the 1970s to protect health, safety, and the environment. *In* Rom, W. N., ed.: Environmental and Occupational Medicine. Boston, Little, Brown & Co., 1983, pp. 835–864.

Anderson, R. F.: Solid waste and public health. *In* Greenberg, M. R., ed.: Public Health and the Environment: The United States Experience. New York, Guilford Press, 1987, pp. 173–204.

Anspach, R. R.: From stigma to identity politics: Political activism among the physically disabled and former mental patients. Soc. Sci. Med. *13A*;765–773, 1979.

Antonio, R. J.: The origin, development, and contemporary status of critical theory. Sociol. Q. *24*;325–351, 1983.

Archer, V. E., and Livingston, G. K.: Environmental carcinogenesis and mutagenesis. *In* Rom, W. N., ed.: Environmental and Occupational Medicine. Boston, Little, Brown & Co., 1983, pp. 63–74.

Baes, C. F., Goeller, H. E., and Olson, J. S.: Carbon dioxide and climate: The uncontrolled experiment. Am. Sci. *65*;310–319, 1977.

Becker, M. H.: The tyranny of health promotion. Public Health Rev. *14*(1), 15–25.

Berger, E. H., Ward, W. D., Morrill, J. C., and Royster, L. H., eds.: Noise and Hearing Conservation Manual. Akron, Ohio, American Industrial Hygiene Association, 1986.

Berman, D.: Why work kills: A brief history of occupational health and safety in the United States. Int. J. Health Serv. *7*;63–87, 1977.

Bingham, E., and Meader, W. V.: Governmental regulation of environmental hazards in the 1990s. Annu. Rev. Public Health *11*;419–434, 1990.

Brown, P.: Popular epidemiology: Community response to toxic waste-induced disease. Sci. Technol. Hum. Value *12*;78–85, 1987.

Brownmiller, S.: Against Our Will: Men, Women, and Rape. New York, Simon & Schuster, 1975.

Burger, E. J.: Human health: A surrogate for the environment: The evolution of environmental legislation and regulation during the 1970s. Regulat. Toxicol. Pharmacol. *9*;196–206, 1989.

Butterfield, P. G.: Thinking upstream: Nurturing a conceptual understanding of the societal context of health behavior. Adv. Nurs. Sci. *12*;1–8, 1990.

Campbell, J.: Misogyny and homicide of women. Adv. Nurs. Sci. *3*;67–85, 1981.

Carnes, S. A., and Watson, A. P.: Disposing of the U. S. chemical weapons stockpile. J. A. M. A. *262*;653–659, 1989.

Chavis, D. M., Stucky, P. E., and Wandersman, A.: Returning basic research to the community: A relationship between scientist and citizen. Am. Psychol. *38*;424–434, 1983.

Chess, C.: Winning the Right to Know. Philadelphia, Delaware Valley Toxics Coalition, 1983.

Connell, S. A.: And the children keep on dying: Parents say it must be pesticides. *San Francisco Chronicle*, June 10, 1990, pp. 3, 5.

Cook, J. A., and Fonow, M. M.: Knowledge and women's interests: Issues of epistemology and methodology in feminist sociological research. Sociol. Inquiry *56*;2–29, 1986.

Corn, D.: Precious bodily fluids. The Nation, 840, 1991.

Council on Scientific Affairs: Low-level radioactive wastes. J. A. M. A. *262*;669–674, 1989.

Cralley, L. V., Cralley, L. J., and Cooper, W. C., eds.: Health and Safety Beyond the Work Place. New York, John Wiley & Sons, 1990.

Crawford, R.: You are dangerous to your health: The ideology and politics of victim blaming. Int. J. Health Serv. *7*;663–680, 1977.

Crosbie, W. A., and Gittus, M., eds.: Medical Response to Effects of Ionizing Radiation. New York, Elsevier Applied Science Publishers, 1989.

Eisenbud, M.: Environmental Radioactivity From Natural, Industrial, and Military Sources. Orlando, Florida, Academic Press, 1987.

Fischbein, A.: Environmental and occupational lead exposure. *In* Rom, W. N., ed.: Environmental and Occupational Medicine. Boston, Little, Brown & Co., 1983, pp. 433–447.

Freire, P.: Pedagogy of the Oppressed (M. Bergman Ramos, translator). New York, Seabury Press, 1970.

Freudenberg, N.: Not in Our Backyard: Community Action for Health and the Environment. New York: Monthly Review, 1984.

Freudenberg, N.: Training health educators for social change. Int. Q. Comm. Health Educ. *5*;37–52, 1984–1985.

Gordis, L.: Epidemiology and Health Risk Assessment. New York, Oxford University Press, 1988.

Greaves, W. W.: Toxic substances control act. *In* Rom, W. N., ed.: Environmental and Occupational Medicine. Boston, Little, Brown & Co., 1983.

Greenberg, M. R.: Public Health and the Environment: The United States Experience. New York, The Guilford Press, 1987.

Greenberg, M. R., and Anderson, R. F.: Hazardous Waste Sites: The Credibility Gap. Piscataway, New Jersey, Center for Urban Policy Research, 1984.

Hall, J. M., and Stevens, P. E.: A nursing view of the U.S.–Iraq war: Psychosocial health consequences. Nurs. Outlook, *40*;113–120, 1992.

Hammer, M. J.: Water and Waste-Water Technology. New York, John Wiley & Sons, 1975.

Hanmer, J., and Maynard, M., eds.: Women, Violence and Social Control. Atlantic Highlands, New Jersey, Humanities Press International, 1987.

Harpham, T., Lusty, T., and Vaughan, P., eds.: In the Shadow of the City: Community Health and the Urban Poor. New York, Oxford University Press, 1988.

Hedin, B. A.: Nursing, education, and emancipation: Applying the critical theoretical approach to nursing research. *In* Chinn, P. L., ed.: Nursing Research Methology Issues and Implementation. Rockville, Maryland, Aspen, 1986, pp. 133–146.

Highland, J.: Hazardous waste: The environmental problem of the 1980s. *In* Rom, W. N., ed.: Environmental and Occupational Medicine. Boston, Little, Brown & Co., 1983, pp. 827–831.

Jackson, M. H., Morris, G. P., Smith, P. G., and Crawford, J. F.: Environmental Health Reference Book. Boston, Butterworth Publishers, 1989.

Kane, D. N.: Environmental Hazards to Young Children. Phoenix, Arizona, Oryx Press, 1985.

Kay, J.: State's kids still exposed to lead. *San Francisco Examiner,* December 9, 1990, pp. 1, 16.

Kay, J.: Ethnic enclaves fight toxic waste. *San Francisco Examiner,* April 9, 1991*a*, pp. 1, 8.

Kay, J.: Millions in U.S. exposed to toxic chemical risks. *San Francisco Examiner,* April 19, 1991*b*, p. 6.

Kay, J.: Minorities bear brunt of pollution: Latinos and blacks living in state's 'dirtiest' neighborhood. *San Francisco Examiner,* April 7, 1991*c*, pp. 1, 12.

Krieps, R., ed.: Environment and Health: A Holistic Approach. Brookfield, Vermont, Avebury, 1989.

Lave, L. B., and Upton, A. C., eds.: Toxic Chemicals, Health, and the Environment. Baltimore, Johns Hopkins University Press, 1987.

League of Women Voters Education Fund: The Nuclear Wastes Primer: A Handbook for Citizens. New York, Nick Lyons Books, 1985.

Linz, D. G., Donnerstein, E., and Penrod, S.: Effects of long-term exposure to violent and sexually degrading depictions of women. J. Personality Social Psychol. *55*;758–769, 1988.

MacKinnon, C.: Sexual Harassment of Working Women. New Haven, Connecticut, Yale University Press, 1979.

Marbury, M.: Worker health. *In* Greenberg, M. R., ed.: Public Health and the Environment: The United States Experience. New York, Guilford Press, 1987, pp. 76–104.

Martin, W. F., Lippitt, J. M., and Prothero, T. G.: Hazardous Waste Handbook for Health and Safety. Boston, Butterworth Publishers, 1987.

Merz, B.: Nuclear weapons facilities face attacks from environmentalists, government agencies. J. A. M. A., *262*;604–605, 1989.

Mies, M.: Towards a methodology for feminist research. *In* Bowles, G., and Klein, R. D., eds.: Theories of Women's Studies. Boston, Routledge & Kegan Paul, 1983, pp. 117–139.

Milio, N.: Promoting Health Through Public Policy. Ottawa, Ontario, Canadian-Public-Health Association, 1986.

Minkler, M., and Cox, K.: Creating critical consciousness in health: Applications of Freire's philosophy and methods to the health care setting. Int. J. Health Serv. *10*;311–322, 1980.

Moccia, P.: Collective strategies. *In* Mason, D. J., and Talbott, S. W., eds.: Political Action Handbook for Nurses: Changing the Workplace, Government, Organizations, and Community. Menlo Park, California, Addison-Wesley, 1985, pp. 181–189.

Needleman, H. L., ed.: Low Level Lead Exposure: The Clinical Implications of Current Research. New York: Raven Press, 1980.

Organophosphate pesticides: Neurotoxins threaten farm workers. J. Natl. Inst. Health Res. May, 21–24, 1991.

Perdue, E. M., and Gjessing, E. T., eds.: Organic Acids in Aquatic Ecosystems. New York, John Wiley & Sons, 1989.

Probart, C. K.: Issues related to radon in schools. J. School Health *59*;441–443, 1989.

Regenstein, L.: How to Survive in America the Poisoned. Washington, D.C., Acropolis Books, 1986.

Reich, M. R.: Social policy for pollution-related diseases. Soc. Sci. Med. *27*;1011–1018, 1988.

Reinhardt, P. A., and Gordon, J. G.: Infectious and Medical Waste Management. Chelsea, Michigan, Lewis Publishers, 1991.

Rom, W. N., ed.: Environmental and Occupational Medicine. Boston, Little, Brown & Co., 1983.

Rose, J., ed.: Environmental Health: The Impact of Pollutants. New York, Gordon & Breach Science Publishers, 1990.

Salmon, J. W., and Berliner, H. S.: Self-care: Boot straps or hangman's noose? Health Med. *1*;5–11, 1982.

Schrieberg, D.: Death from a healing machine: Radioactive waste goes on Mexican odyssey after sale of medical device. *San Francisco Examiner,* June 23, 1991, pp. 1, 12.

Smets, H.: Major industrial risks and compensation of victims: The role of insurance. Soc. Sci. Med. *27*;1085–1095, 1988.

Smith, B. E.: Black lung: The social production of disease. *In* Conrad, P., and Kern, R., eds.: The Sociology of Health and Illness: Critical Perspectives. 3rd Ed. New York, St. Martin's Press, 1990, pp. 64–77.

Soble, S. M., and Brennan, J. H.: A review of legal and policy issues in legislating compensation for victims of toxic substance pollution. Soc. Sci. Med. *27*;1061–1070, 1988.

Sommers, E. K., and Check, J. V.: An empirical investigation of the role of pornography in the verbal and physical abuse of women. Violence Victims *2*;189–209, 1987.

State sued for not providing tests for lead poisoning. *Nurse Week,* January 21, 1991, p. 5.

Stellman, J. M., and Daum, S. M.: Work is Dangerous to Your

Health: A Handbook of Health Hazards in the Workplace and What You Can Do About Them. New York, Vintage Books, 1973.

Stevens, P. E.: A critical social reconceptualization of environment in nursing: Implications for methodology. Adv. Nurs. Sci. *11*;56–68, 1989.

Stevens, P. E., and Hall, J. M.: Abusive health care interactions experienced by lesbians: A case of institutional violence in the treatment of women. Response Victimization Women Children *13*;23–27, 1990.

Stevens, P. E., and Hall, J. M.: Applying critical theories to nursing in communities. Public Health Nurs. *9*;2–9, 1992.

Stotts, R. C.: Application of the Salmon Model: A tale of two cities. Public Health Nurs. *8*;10–14, 1991.

Sutcliffe, C.: The Dangers of Low Level Radiation. Brookfield, Vermont, Avebury, 1987.

Thompson, J. L.: Critical scholarship: The critique of domination in nursing. Adv. Nurs. Sci. *10*;27–38, 1987.

U.S. Department of Health and Human Services: Healthy people: The Surgeon General's Report on Health Promotion and Disease Prevention. Washington, D.C., U.S. Government Printing Office, Publication no. (PHS) 75-55071, 1979.

Vyner, H. M.: Invisible Trauma: The Psychosocial Effects of Invisible Environmental Contaminants. Lexington, Massachusetts, Lexington Books, 1988*a*.

Vyner, H. M.: The psychological dimensions of health care for patients exposed to radiation and the other invisible environmental contaminants. Soc. Sci. Med. *27*;1097–1103, 1988*b*.

Walker, B.: Environmental health policies in the 1990s. J. Public Health Policy *11*;438–447, 1990.

Walker, J. S.: The controversy over radiation safety: A historical overview. J. A. M. A. *262*;664–668, 1989.

Watts, R. J.: Democratization of health care: Challenge for nursing. Adv. Nurs. Sci. *12*;37–46, 1990.

Woodwell, G. M.: The carbon dioxide question. Sci. Am. *238*;34–40, 1978.

Wrenn, M. E., and Mays, C. W.: Ionizing radiation. *In* Rom, W. N., ed.: Environmental and Occupational Medicine. Boston, Little, Brown & Co., 1983, pp. 667–686.

Zola, I. K.: Medicine as an institution of social control. Sociol. Rev. *20*;487–504, 1972.

CHAPTER 25

The Occupational Health Nurse: Roles and Responsibilities, Current and Future Trends

Upon completion of this chapter, the reader will be able to:

1. Describe the historical perspective of occupational health nursing.

2. Discuss emerging demographic trends that will influence occupational health nursing practice.

3. Identify the skills and competencies germane to occupational health nursing.

4. Apply the nursing process and public health principles to worker and work place health issues.

5. Discuss the role of state and federal regulations that impact occupational health.

6. Describe a multidisciplinary approach for resolution of occupational health issues.

7. Identify case studies, questions for group discussion, and learning activities.

Patricia Hyland Travers
Cherryl E. McDougall

Occupational health nursing, a branch of public health nursing, is defined by the American Association of Occupational Health Nurses (AAOHN) as:

" . . . the application of nursing principles in conserving the health of workers in all occupations. It emphasizes prevention, recognition, and treatment of illnesses and injuries and requires special skills and knowledge in the fields of health education and counseling, environmental health, rehabilitation and human relations" (American Association of Industrial Nurses [AAIN], 1976).

The evolution of occupational health nursing in the United States has mirrored the societal changes in moving from an agrarian to an industrial-based economy and, by 2000, to a service-based economy.

The concept of occupational health nursing dates to the late 1800s with the employment of Betty Moulder and Ada Mayo Stewart. Moulder was hired by a group of coal mining companies in 1888 to care for coal miners and their families (AAIN, 1976). Seven years later, the Vermont Marble Company hired Stewart to care for workers and their families; she is often referred to as the first "industrial nurse" because so much is known about her activities (Parker-Conrad, 1988). In 1897, Anna B. Duncan was employed by the John Wanamaker Company to visit sick employees at home; in 1899, a nursing service was established for employees of the Frederick Loeser department store in Brooklyn, New York (AAIN, 1976). The roots of occupational health nursing are entrenched in public health nursing practice with its initial focus on prevention, home care, and family-based health care.

At the turn of the century, the industrial revolution was well under way, and the concept of health care for employees spread rapidly throughout many states (Travers, 1987). Companies hiring industrial nurses in the early 1900s included the Emporium in San Francisco, Plymouth Cordage Company in Massachusetts, Anaconda Mining Company in Montana, Broadway Store in Los Angeles, Chase Metal Works in Connecticut, Hale Brothers in San Francisco, Filene's in Boston, Car-son, Pirie, and Scott in Chicago, Fulton Cotton Mills in Georgia, and Bullock's in Los Angeles (McGrath, 1946; Parker-Conrad, 1988).

The cost-effectiveness of providing health care to employees was achieving increased recognition. By 1912, after workers' compensation legislation had been instituted, there were 38 nurses employed by business firms (McGrath, 1946; Parker-Conrad, 1988). The following year, a registry of industrial nurses was initiated; in 1915, the Boston Industrial Nurses Club was formed, later evolving into the Massachusetts Industrial Nurses Organization. In 1916, the Factory Nurses Conference was organized, a group open only to graduate, state-registered nurses affiliated with the American Nurses' Association (ANA) (AAIN, 1976). These efforts indicated the identified need by practicing industrial nurses to explore the uniqueness of this evolving specialty area. More important, industrial nurses were practicing in single-nurse settings and recognized the importance of uniting as a group for the purpose of sharing ideas with peers practicing in the same nursing arena.

In 1917, the first educational course for industrial nurses was offered at Boston University's College of Business Administration, and in 1922, the Factory Nurses Conference changed its name to the AAIN, which reflected the evolving breadth and scope of the profession.

During and after the Depression years, many nurses lost jobs because management did not consider industrial nursing an essential aspect of doing business (Felton, 1985, 1986). The focus of health care for employees again changed as a result of many factors, including the impact of the two world wars. During World War I, the government demanded health services for workers at factories and shipyards holding defense contracts. Demographics in the work place were also dramatically different during World War II because of the increased numbers of women entering the work force. In 1942, the U.S. Surgeon General told an audience of nurses that the health conservation of the "industrial army" was the most urgent civilian need during the war (Felton, 1985). From 1938 through 1943, the number of occupational health nurses increased by more than 10,000. In 1942, 300 nurses from 16 states voted to create a national association, AAIN (AAIN, 1976). Catherine R. Dempsey, a registered nurse at Simplex Wire and

Cable Company in Cambridge, Massachusetts, was elected president of the national association. By 1943, approximately 11,000 nurses were employed in industry.

Nine years later, members of AAIN voted to remain an independent, autonomous association rather than merge with the National League for Nursing or the ANA. In 1953, another important step was taken toward formalizing this specialty area of nursing practice when the *Industrial Nurses Journal,* now called the *AAOHN Journal,* was published. In 1977, the organization changed its name to the AAOHN, the current professional organization for practicing occupational health nurses.

As work places have continued to change dramatically over the past few decades, the role of the occupational health nurse has become even more diversified and complex. Often working as the only on-site health professional, the occupational health nurse is in a unique position for developing surveillance programs, counseling employees, coordinating health promotion activities, setting up comprehensive referral networks, treating individuals for emergency and primary care health problems, consulting with business partners, and managing the overall occupational health service. Figure 25–1 depicts a model of occupational health nursing practice "within the context of societal and work setting influences" (Rogers, 1990).

The occupational health nurse is a worker advocate and has the responsibility to uphold professional standards and codes. However, the occupational health nurse is also responsible to management, is usually compensated by management, and must practice within a framework of company policies and guidelines (Rogers, 1990). Ethical dilemmas arise over many issues (i.e., screening, drug testing, informing employees regarding hazardous exposures, and confidentiality).

Occupational health nurses now comprise the largest professional group providing health care to employees in highly complex work environments. The roles of occupational health nurses are changing as a result of many factors, including rising health care costs, increased recognition of health effects associated with various exposures, emphasis on health promotion and wellness, health surveillance, AIDS, women's issues, ergonomics, reproductive issues, downsizing, and multicultural work forces. Table 25–1 outlines occupational health

nursing services currently mandated by State and Federal regulations as well as occupational health nursing services generally mandated by company policies.

Approximately 30,000 nurses are practicing in the occupational health setting in the United States; this represents 1.5% to 2% of the total nursing population. Approximately 50% of the 30,000 nurses work alone, making decisions regarding health and safety issues, influencing policy in health and safety, and planning and implementing a myriad of health programs. The majority of nurses practicing in the occupational health setting are prepared at the diploma level and have been practicing in the field of occupational health for a minimum of 12 years (Cox, 1989).

Rogers (1989) identified research priorities by polling a sample of AAOHN members. The survey identified the following research priorities deemed critical for shaping future OHN practice:

- Effectiveness of primary care at the work site
- Effectiveness of health promotion strategies
- Ethical issues
- Work-related health outcomes
- Health effects from chemical exposures
- Occupational hazards of health care workers
- Worker rehabilitation and return to work
- Cost effectiveness of occupational health nursing
- Quality assurance
- Impact of occupational health nursing programs on employee morale and productivity
- Ergonomics
- Influencing behavioral changes

Meeting the needs of employees in smaller businesses is another important practice and research priority. In 1982, approximately 60% of work sites in the United States were without occupational health and safety professionals (Public Health Service, 1989). The integration of occupational health principles into the curricula of schools of nursing, engineering, and management is critical. Because community health nurses may assume occupational health nursing roles, community health nurses must be knowledgeable about the specialty area of occupational health nursing. Municipalities, smaller companies, visiting nurse associations, and home care agencies may provide oppor-

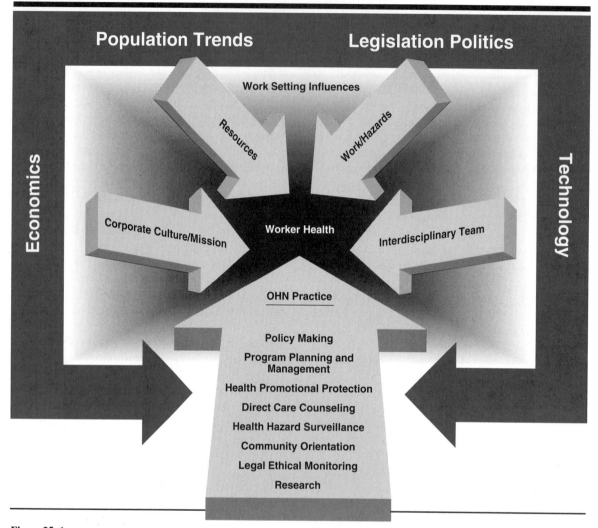

Figure 25–1
Occupational health nursing practice within the context of societal and work setting influences. (From Rogers, B.: Occupational health nursing practice, education, and research: challenges of the future. By permission of the American Association of Occupational Health Nurses, AAOHN Journal, Vol. 38, No. 11, pp. 536–543, 1990.)

Table 25–1
Occupational Health Nursing Services

Services Mandated by Federal and State Regulations

Safe and healthful work place
Emergency medical response
   First aid responder selection and training
   First aid space, supplies, protocols, and records
   Designated medical resources for incident response
Workers' Compensation
Confidentiality of medical records
Compliance with medical record retention requirements
OSHA compliance
   Medical personnel requirement (29 CFR 1910.15)
   Injury and illness reporting and recording
   Accident and injury investigation
   Cumulative trauma disorder prevention
   Employee access to medical and exposure records
   Medical surveillance and hazardous work qualification
   Personal protective equipment evaluation and training
   Infection control
   Employee Right-to-Know notification and training

Toxic Substances Control Act compliance
Community Right-to-Know compliance
Americans With Disabilities Act compliance
Rehabilitation Act: handicap, preplacement, fitness for duty evaluations, accommodations
Department of Defense, Department of Transportation, Nuclear Regulatory Commission, Drug-Free Workplace Act compliance
   Policy development
   Drug awareness education
   Drug testing, technical support
   Employee Assistance Program–type services
Threat of violence/duty to warn
VDT local regulations
State and local public health regulations
Nursing practice acts
Board of Pharmacy and Drug Enforcement Agency regulations
Continuing professional education required for licensure

Services Often Mandated by Company Policy

Clinical supervision of on-site health services
Health strategy development
Health services standards
   Space, staffing, and operational standards
   Occupational illness and injury assessment, diagnosis, treatment, and referral
   Nonoccupational illness and injury assessment, diagnosis, treatment, and referral
Disability and return-to-work evaluations and accommodations
Impaired employee fitness for duty evaluation

Preplacement evaluation and medical accommodation
Handicap evaluation, placement, and accommodation
Employee Assistance Program standards
International health: travel, medical advisory, and immunizations
Data collection and analysis
Medical consultation
Pregnancy placement in hazardous environments
Professional education and development
Audit and quality assurance

Services That Are Optional

Health education and health promotion
Medical screening for early detection and disease prevention

Physical fitness programs
Allergy injection programs

tunities for community health nurses to be involved in screening programs, health education activities, work place hazard evaluations, and other occupational health-related activities.

The occupational health nurse's strengths are embedded in assessment, planning, and implementation of health programs for populations, care plans for individuals, and health education activities for worker aggregates. Often, the lack of understanding or misperceptions about the occupational health nursing role has fostered the invisibility of the nurse, both within the nursing profession itself and within the business environment, thereby exacerbating the difficulties faced in being the sole guardian of health for workers in many companies (Travers, 1991). Empowered, well-trained, educated occupational health nurses will continue to impact crucial changes in the areas of primary, secondary, and tertiary prevention in occupational health. The roles and responsibilities of the occupational health nurse must be clearly articulated to lay persons, managers, workers, union representatives, colleagues in occupational health, nursing, and medicine so that occupational health nursing can continue to positively impact workers' health, contribute to decreasing health care costs, and foster reduction in health risks.

EMERGING DEMOGRAPHIC TRENDS

The direction of occupational health nursing is being influenced by sweeping transformations in industry, changing work force demographics, diversity of health care systems, integration of the world economy, shift in production from goods to services, and proliferation of advanced technologies (Johnston and Packer, 1987).

The focus of U.S. industry is moving away from large manufacturing facilities to smaller service-based businesses (Johnston and Packer, 1987). It is thought that work will be performed where and when the customer requires, which will force employers to make different demands on their employees. Flexible and varying work schedules and work sites may become more common than the daily trek to the same building for the 40-hour, 9:00-to-5:00 routine that has been the standard for many years. Of major importance will be the demand for an increase in skill level of all employees, even those who perform the most menial types of work. The ability to read, follow directions, and

perform mathematic calculations will be core requirements (Johnston and Packer, 1987).

The increasing availability of older workers as well as women, minorities, and immigrants will have far-reaching implications for employers and pose specific challenges for occupational health professionals.

There is expected to be an overall shortage of workers in the near future due to the slow gains in the U.S. population growth rate, which has been well below average for the past two decades (Johnston and Packer, 1987; Miller, 1989). In the 1980s, the population growth rate hovered around 1% per year. In the 1990s, the rate of gain is expected to be 0.75% of 1% per year (Miller, 1989). Between 1985 and 2000, the labor force will grow at a rate of 22% (from 115 to 141 million), which is the slowest rate since the 1930s. Miller (1989) suggested that human capital is becoming a more important resource for industry than financial capital. These trends are important to understand because of the direct impact on the national rate of economic growth, especially in the area of population-sensitive products, such as food, cars, housing units, household goods, and education services (Johnston and Packer, 1987).

Occupational Health Nursing Roles in Prevention

The median age of the U.S. work force is expected to increase from 35 in 1984 to approximately 39 in 2000. The number of workers age 35–54 will increase by more than 25 million (Johnston and Packer, 1987). Although there has been increased emphasis on health and fitness in the general population, the occupational health nurse's primary, secondary, and tertiary prevention strategies are expected to assume an even more important role in the prevention and treatment of chronic disease.

In the area of primary prevention, emphasis will continue to be placed on health promotion and disease prevention, including smoking cessation programs, nutrition counseling, cardiovascular health education and fitness, and cancer prevention.

With regard to secondary prevention, the occupational health nurse plans and implements health screening programs and health risk appraisals for early diagnosis and treatment of disease. Testing for cancer, hypertension, and cholesterol has been viewed as an effective screening tool. The occupational health nurse will increasingly be expected to document the return on investment for these and other related activities in the work place (Arthur D. Little, Inc., 1980; Chenoweth, 1989; Dees and Taylor, 1990; Williamson and Moore, 1987).

On a tertiary level, the occupational health nurse has played a critical role in the process of rehabilitation and return-to-work after all types of disabilities (Centineo, 1986). Yeater (1987) reported that 1981 disability costs were $184.6 billion. Knowledge of the work place, the ability to negotiate with the employer for appropriate accommodations, and comprehensive case management skills have been and will continue to be essential for the successful return to productive life of the disabled employee. Brown (1989) stated that a well-constructed case management plan can save 8% to 10% of paid disability claims.

Because older workers are more prone to chronic disease, the occupational health nurse can implement or monitor treatment protocols as well as assist workers to live and work at their optimum comfort level while managing their disease. Responsibilities for care of elderly parents or significant others will influence the balance of work and home for older workers. The occupational health nurse's role as a counselor, a referral resource for workers, and a consultant to management can influence future benefit changes.

Women in the Work Place

Over the next 15 years, women are expected to continue to join the work force in substantial numbers. By 2000, approximately 47% of the work force will be women, and 61% of U.S. women will be at work (Johnston and Packer, 1987). Women will comprise about three fifths of new entrants into the labor force between 1985 and 2000 (Johnston and Packer, 1987). Women's health and safety issues, such as maternal-child health, reproductive health, breast cancer education and early detection, stress, and work-home balance issues, will achieve heightened significance.

Thirty percent of women currently in the work force are between the ages of 16 and 44, and each year approximately 1 million babies are born to these women (Gates and O'Neill, 1990). The occupational health nurse can play a key role in the development and delivery of prenatal, postpartum, and childhood programs in the work place. Of primary importance will be the ability to serve as a change agent to initiate needed programs in the work environment. Employers must be educated regarding strategies to not only reduce health care costs for women and babies but also improve the work environment for mothers (Gates and O'Neill, 1990). Women who believe their employers are interested in the well-being of themselves and their families are more apt to be productive and satisfied employees (Gates and O'Neill, 1990).

Interest in work place safety and the relationship to reproductive outcome continues to grow as women of child-bearing years enter the work place in greater proportions than ever before. Although certain exposures to chemicals in the work place known to be mutagenic or teratogenic can be avoided, the vast majority of work place exposures have not been studied systematically (Pastides et al., 1988). Performing "walkthroughs" in the work place on a regular basis, recognizing potential and existing hazards, and maintaining communications with safety and industrial hygiene resources will continue to be critical work for the occupational health nurse (Table 25–2).

The role of employee advocate may expand as the occupational health nurse becomes increasingly involved in improvement of control strategies (e.g., engineering controls and/or work place accommodations for women who are pregnant or are attempting to conceive and must work in areas where potential reproductive hazards exist).

In 1988, breast cancer was surpassed only by lung cancer as the leading cause of cancer deaths in women (Owen and Long, 1989). Activities must continue to focus on prevention and early detection by increasing awareness of the incidence of breast cancer and providing accessible and affordable screening programs. The occupational health nurse will have an excellent opportunity to play a key role in reduction or morbidity and mortality associated with breast cancer, thereby supporting the National Cancer Institute's goals of a 50% cancer reduction by 2000 (Owen and Long, 1989).

Women may experience more stress than men in balancing their work and home roles. Child care continues to be the primary responsibility of women, and women still handle most of the household responsibilities; these cause women to experience a unique form of stress (Freedman and Bisesi, 1988). With more women entering and remaining in the work force, the occupational health nurse must be prepared to provide counseling and sup-

Table 25–2
Types of Occupational Hazards and Associated Health Effects

Category	Exposures	Health Effects
Chemical (routes of entry: inhalation, skin absorption, ingestion, and ocular absorption)	Solvents	Headache, central nervous system dysfunction
	Lead	Central nervous system disturbances
	Asbestos	Asbestosis
	Acids	Burns
	Glycol ethers	Reproductive effects
	Mercury	Ataxia
	Arsenic	Peripheral neuropathy
Biological (routes of entry: inhalation, skin contact/or puncture, ingestion, and ocular absorption)	Blood or body fluids	Bacterial, fungal, viral infections Hepatitis B
Physical	Noise	Hearing loss
	Radiation	Reproductive effects, cancer
	Vibration	Raynaud's disease
	Heat	Heat exhaustion, heatstroke
Psychosocial	Stress	Anxiety reactions and a variety of physical symptoms
	Work-home balance	
Ergonomics	Static or non-neutral postures	Cumulative trauma disorders
	Repetitive or forceful exertions	Back injuries
	Lighting	Headache, eye strain
	Shift work	Sleep disorders
Safety	Electrical	Electrocution
	Slips and falls	Musculoskeletal conditions
	Struck by or against object	

port for this employee population. Delivery of educational programs as well as implementation of support groups will be key adjuncts to the health and productivity of these women.

Minorities in the Work Place

Over the next 13 years, African-Americans, Hispanics, and other racial or ethnic groups will compose a large share of the expansion of the labor force (Johnston and Packer, 1987). Nonwhites will account for 29% of the net addition to the work force between 1985 and 2000 and more than 15% of the work force in 2000 (Johnston and Packer, 1987). As the number of minority and ethnic workers in the work force increases, so will the illnesses traditionally associated with these groups of workers (i.e., heart disease and stroke, hyperten-

sion, cancer, cirrhosis, and diabetes) (Rogers, 1990). Morris (1989) reported that in addition to basic health concerns for this population, available statistics indicate that minority workers have been disproportionately concentrated in some of the most dangerous work and therefore are at greater risk for developing any of the leading occupationally related disease and injuries as defined by the National Institute for Occupational Safety and Health (NIOSH) (Table 25–3).

The occupational health nurse will face challenges in developing programs that are culturally and linguistically appropriate. The occupational health nurse may be in an advocacy role to negotiate with the employer for changes in the work environment to reduce or eliminate existing or potential occupational exposures (Friedman-Jimenez, 1989).

Table 25–3
Ten Leading Work-Related Diseases and Injuries

Work-Related Disease or Injury	Examples of Effect
Occupational lung disease	Cancer, asthma
Musculoskeletal injuries	Back, upper extremity cumulative trauma disorders
Occupational cancers	Leukemia, bladder, skin
Trauma	Death, amputation, fracture
Cardiovascular diseases	Hypertension, heart disease
Reproductive disorders	Infertility, miscarriage
Neurotoxic disorders	Neuropathy, toxic psychosis
Noise-induced hearing loss	Loss of hearing
Dermatological conditions	Chemical burns, allergies
Psychological disorders	Neurosis, alcohol or substance abuse

Delivery and Access Issues Related to Health Care

Corporations have become driving forces in shaping the development of alternative approaches to health care (Rosen and Freedman, 1987). Rapidly increasing health care costs have spawned a number of alternative approaches to providing health care. Health maintenance organizations and preferred provider organizations are two of the more common health care management programs (Miller, 1989). It is important that the occupational health nurse remain informed about the various health care options available to the work force as rapid changes occur regarding corporate benefits. This is of particular importance when considering referral of a client to a community health resource. Participation in one of the managed care plans requires that treatment take place according to the organization's guidelines and within their health service delivery system. Managed care plans are replacing traditional indemnity plans. Access to care is strictly managed and, often, limited. As this trend continues, the role of the occupational health nurse will take on added importance. The nurse must be prepared to accept increasing responsibilities as a primary care provider.

AIDS in the Work Place

One health care issue that will continue to plague society is the AIDS epidemic. HIV infection poses a small but significant risk to health care workers. Roles of the occupational health nurse will continue to include education and counseling for workers with potential work place exposures as well as employees at risk because of personal behaviors (AAOHN, 1988). The occupational health nurse can influence employers to support workers with AIDS by improving benefits and making appropriate work place modifications to allow work continuance throughout the course of the disease.

AAOHN Year 2000 Recommendations

In cooperation with the U.S. Department of Health and Human Services, Public Health Service, the AAOHN has submitted recommendations to help define the national health objectives so that the following will occur by 2000 (AAOHN, 1988):

- Ninety percent of employers of 50 or more employees will provide access to programs of monitoring, intervention, and follow-up for chronic illnesses by qualified occupational health professionals, preferably occupational health nurses. These services should be at or convenient to the work site.
- Ninety percent of non–health care–related at-risk workers not protected by Occupational Safety and Health Administration (OSHA) regulations will be educated about HIV transmission and self-protective measures. This should be accomplished through education and information disseminated through public media, business, and trade association meetings and publications.
- Ninety percent of employers will develop a company policy that protects at-risk workers while safeguarding the confidentiality and employment (as appropriate) of HIV-positive employees.
- OSHA will implement a standard for protection against blood-borne pathogens using Centers for Disease Control guidelines for universal precautions to prevent transmission.

- Ninety percent of employers of health care workers whose work involves exposure to blood will offer voluntary, free, accessible vaccination against hepatitis B.
- Ninety percent of work places will provide access to health promotion and risk-reduction programs by qualified occupational health professionals who are knowledgeable about occupational health issues as well as health promotion. Occupational health nurses are ideal for this role.
- Every state health department will hire at least one occupational health nurse consultant for local industries. Presently, only a few states have such a consultant who can provide expertise and guidance in establishing and implementing occupational health services.

SKILLS AND COMPETENCIES

Although emergency care is still an important tenet of occupational health nursing, the current and future focuses are on a proactive approach with aims of prevention of illness and injury and promotion of health. Therefore, the occupational health nurse must possess the skills and competencies necessary to recognize and evaluate potential and existing health hazards in the work place. Skills in areas of management, knowledge of toxicology, ergonomics, epidemiology, environmental health, safety, record keeping, budgeting, counseling, and education are essential to meet the present and future demands of occupational health nursing practice.

To more readily define the breadth and scope of occupational health nursing practice, a skills and competency model was developed and implemented in 1990 (Travers et al., 1991). Examples of some of the skills and competencies of occupational health nursing practice are outlined according to eight defined areas of practice:

Management and Administration

- Managing budgets
- Hiring staff and management of staff performance
- Fostering professional development plans
- Developing program goals and objectives
- Business planning through knowledge of internal and external resources

- Providing comprehensive on-site services and programs
- Knowing of needs of business and employees
- Writing reports
- Performing audits and quality assurance
- Handling workers' compensation and disability
- Performing cost-benefit and cost-effectiveness analyses
- Allocating appropriate staff resources
- Being a leader in health-related issues
- Negotiating
- Facilitating work accommodations and return to work
- Coordinating medical response activities and site-disaster planning

Direct Care

- Applying the nursing process
- Delivering first aid and primary care according to treatment protocols
- Making a physical assessment
- History taking
- Medical testing
- Knowing immunization protocols
- Responding to medical emergencies
- Knowing trends in health-related issues

Health and Environmental Relationships

- Knowing plant operations, manufacturing processes, and job tasks
- Identifying potential and existing work place exposures
- Influencing appropriate and targeted recommendations for control of hazards in the work place
- Knowing toxicological, epidemiological, and ergonomic principles
- Understanding appropriate engineering controls, administration, and personal protective equipment specific to preventing exposure to health hazards in the work place
- Understanding roles and collaboration with other cross-functional groups as an integral part of a core multidisciplinary team

Legal and Ethical Responsibilities

- Knowing AAOHN Professional Standards of Practice and Code of Ethics

- Knowing state nursing practice act and ability to practice occupational health nursing within state guidelines
- Knowing federal regulations pertaining to occupational health
- Knowing the Americans With Disabilities Act, associated guidelines, and Affirmative Action and Equal Employment Opportunity legislation
- Knowing all aspects of medical record-keeping practices in compliance with nursing practice, state law, and standards of practice
- Knowing current legal trends related to negligence and malpractice cases in professional nursing and in the occupational health setting

Consultation

- Being a resource expert on health issues for employees and management
- Having broad knowledge of public health and occupational health principles and practices
- Creating effective professional and technical support networks both functionally and cross-functionally

Research

- Systematically collecting, analyzing, and interpreting data from different sources
- Recognizing trends in health outcomes by department, work area, or work process
- Planning, developing, and conducting surveys

Health Education

- Recognizing cultural differences and the relationship to health issues
- Using effective communication styles to match diverse employee/management audiences
- Making effective presentations
- Planning, developing, implementing, and evaluating health programs designed to meet the needs of specific employee groups or organizations
- Application of adult learning theory and principles to health education programs

Counseling

- Identifying employees' emotional needs, and providing support and counseling

- Making appropriate referrals and/or recommendations
- Listening
- Managing psychiatric emergencies

PRIMARY, SECONDARY, AND TERTIARY LEVELS OF PREVENTION

Like all community health professionals, the occupational health nurse's practice is based on the concept of prevention. Promotion, protection, maintenance, and restoration of worker health are the goals set forth in the AAOHN's definition of occupational health nursing. The levels can be further delineated into occupational and nonoccupational categories.

In the area of primary prevention, the occupational health nurse is involved in both health promotion and disease prevention. Patterson (1984, p. 5) documented that health promotion is defined by the American Hospital Association as: " . . . the process of fostering awareness, influencing attitudes and identifying alternatives so that individuals can make informed choices and changes in their behavior to achieve an optimum level of physical and mental health and improve their physical and social environment."

Disease prevention begins with recognition of a health risk, a disease, or an environmental hazard and is followed by measures to protect as many people as possible from harmful consequences of that risk (Clemen-Stone et al., 1987).

A variety of primary prevention strategies are used by the occupational health nurse. The most frequent method is one-on-one interaction. Because the occupational health nurse has daily contact with numerous clients for a myriad of reasons (e.g., assessment and treatment of episodic illness or injury, health surveillance), this is an important method of promoting health. The phrase "seize the moment" aptly describes the opportunity that presents with every client encounter. However, similar to community health nursing professionals, occupational health nurses plan, develop, and implement aggregate-focused intervention strategies. The occupational health nurse plans and implements programs such as weight reduction, AIDS awareness, ergonomics training, and smoking cessation. For overall health promotion, the nurse may plan and implement a health fair, which

Preplacement Medical Evaluation

Part 1 **Health Questionnaire**	Have you ever had problems with:	Yes	No
	Heart	___	___
	Circulation	___	___
	Infection	___	___
	Nerves	___	___
	Bones	___	___
	Muscles	___	___
	Lungs/breathing	___	___
	Vision/eyes	___	___
	Hearing/ears	___	___
	Allergies	___	___

If you have answered "Yes" to any of the above, please explain:

	Yes	No
Have you ever:		
Had an operation	___	___
Become sick from your work	___	___
Had a tetanus shot	___	___
Considered yourself disabled	___	___
(Within the past 5 years) consulted a physician	___	___

If you have answered "Yes" to any of the above, please explain:

Part 2
Physical Assessment

Vital signs _____

Height and weight _____

Vision test _____

Hearing test _____

Physical examination with review of systems _____

Laboratory tests appropriate to work place exposure _____

Part 3
Medical Summary
and Recommendations

Applicant is: _____ able to perform job

_____ able to perform job with restrictions

_____ not able to perform job

_____ on hold–awaiting more medical data

Diagnosis _____

Restrictions _____

Recommendations _____

Comments _____

Figure 25–2
Preplacement medical evaluation.

is a multifaceted health promotion strategy that usually includes a number of community health resources to provide expertise on a wide range of health issues and community services.

As part of an overall health and wellness strategy, the occupational health nurse may negotiate with the employer for an on-site fitness center or area with fitness equipment, or if cost or space is prohibitive, the employer may choose to partially subsidize membership to a local fitness center.

Types of nonoccupational programs included in the area of primary prevention are cardiovascular health, cancer awareness, personal safety, immunization, prenatal and postpartum health, accident prevention, retirement health, stress management, and relaxation techniques. Occupational health programs could include topics such as emergency response, first aid and cardiopulmonary resuscitation training, Right-to-Know training, immunization programs for international business travelers, prevention of back injury through proper lifting techniques, ergonomics, and other programs targeted to the specific hazards identified in the work place.

Secondary prevention strategies are aimed at early diagnosis, early treatment interventions, and attempts to limit disability. The focus at this level of prevention is on identification of health needs, health problems, and clients at risk (Clemen-Stone et al., 1987). A survey of eight countries (Murphy, 1989) showed that the major portion of the occupational health nurse's workday was devoted to prevention (40–80%) and that treatment and screening dominated prevention activities (18% and 16%, respectively).

As with primary prevention, the occupational health nurse uses a number of different strategies. By providing direct care for episodic illness and injury, the occupational health nurse is afforded the opportunity to conduct early assessments and provide treatment and/or referrals for a variety of physical as well as psychological conditions. Health screenings, which are designed for early detection of disease, can be offered at the work site by the occupational health nurse with relative ease and at minimal cost. Screenings may focus on vision, cancer, cholesterol, hypertension, diabetes, tuberculosis, and pulmonary function. Some other types of screening may be contracted with a vendor who uses mobile equipment to provide screenings such as mammography.

Secondary prevention efforts provided by the occupational health nurse include preplacement, periodic, and/or job transfer evaluations to ensure that the worker is being placed or is continuing to work in a job that is safe for that worker.

The preplacement evaluation is performed before the worker begins employment in a new company or is placed in a different job (Fig. 25–2). The evaluation is a baseline examination that consists of a medical history, an occupational health history (Fig. 25–3), and a physical assessment that should target the type of work that the client will be performing. For example, if the client is going to be lifting materials in a warehouse, special attention should be paid to any history of musculoskeletal problems. Strength testing and range of motion should be performed for all muscle groups. This type of examination would not be as important if the client were to be employed as a chemical engineer. The examination may also include medical tests to determine specific organ functions that may be affected by exposure to existing hazards in the client's work place. For example, if the client is working with a chemical that is a known liver toxin, baseline liver function tests may be appropriate to determine the current health status of the liver and its ability to handle this specific chemical exposure. The preplacement examination, however, must be carefully evaluated to ensure compliance with the Americans With Disabilities Act.

Periodic assessments usually occur at a regular interval (i.e., annual, biannual) and are based on specific protocols for those exposed to substances or irritants such as lead, asbestos, noise, or various chemicals.

Examinations of individuals transferring to other jobs are critical to document any changes in health that may have occurred while the client was working in a specific area or with a specific process. This is usually done to comply with OSHA regulations or NIOSH recommendations.

On a tertiary level, the occupational health nurse plays a key role in the rehabilitation and restoration of the worker to an optimal level of functioning. Strategies include case management, negotiation of work place accommodations, and counseling and support for workers who will continue to be affected by chronic disease (Moore and Childre, 1990).

The process of returning an individual to work begins with the onset of injury or illness. Regard-

Occupational Health History

Date: _____

Badge or Social Security Number: _____

Name: _____

Age: _____

Shift: _____

Job title: _____

Department: _____

How long in this job/area (months/years): _____

Average work hours/shift: _____

Physical requirements of work (hours/day):

        Lifting: _____

        Bending: _____

        Sitting: _____

        Repetitive movements: _____

        Standing: _____

        Twisting: _____

        Climbing: _____

Job description: _____
_____

Potential exposures:

        Chemical: _____

        Physical: _____

        Biological: _____

        Psychosocial: _____

        Ergonomic: _____

        Safety: _____

Personal protective equipment:

        Gloves: _____

        Glasses: _____

        Ear protection: _____

        Lab coat: _____

        Apron: _____

        Face shield: _____

        Goggles: _____

        Mask/respirator: _____

        Other: _____

Figure 25–3
Occupational health history.

Do you have a second job? _____

If yes, describe: _____

_____

_____

_____

_____

_____

Chief complaint: _____

Onset of symptoms: _____

Duration of symptoms: _____

Suspected cause: _____

Quality/severity of symptoms: _____

_____

_____

Aggravating factors: _____

_____

_____

Are there coworkers with similar symptoms? _____

Do symptoms change when not at work? _____

Past medical history: _____

_____

_____

_____

_____

_____

Current medications: _____

Hobbies: _____

Family health history: _____

_____

_____

_____

Smoking history: _____

Alcohol history: _____

Recreational drug use: _____

Exercise patterns: _____

Allergies: _____

Other comments: _____

_____

_____

Figure 25–3 *Continued*

Physical Demands Analysis

Job title _____   Department _____

Activity	Never	Rarely (5–10%)	Sometimes (10–40%)	Frequently (41–75%)	Always (75–100%)
Standing					
Walking					
Sitting					
Lifting					
10 lb. maximum					
20 lb. max., up to 10 lb. frequently					
50 lb. max., up to 25 lb. frequently					
100 lb. max., up to 50 lb. frequently					
>100 lb., 50 lb. or more frequently					
Pushing/pulling					
10 lb. maximum					
20 lb. max., up to 10 lb. frequently					
50 lb. max., up to 25 lb. frequently					
100 lb. max., up to 50 lb. frequently					
>100 lb., 50 lb. or more frequently					
Climbing					
Ladders					
Stairs					
Other (list)					
Balancing					
Stooping					
Kneeling					
Crouching					
Crawling					
Twisting					
Bending					
Reaching					
Overhead					
In front of body					
Handling					
Fingering					
Feeling					
Talking					
Ordinary					
Other					
Hearing					
Ordinary conversation					
Other sounds					
Vision					
Acuity: Near, 20 in. or less					
Acuity: Far, 20 ft. or more					
Depth perception three-dimensional					
Vision distance judgment					
Accommodation sharpness of vision/focus					
Color vision					
Field of vision (entire scope of vision/peripheral)					
Any other outstanding physical requirements not previously mentioned (list)					
Shift work					
Environmental conditions:					
Inside					
Outside					
Both					
Dust					
Fumes					
Hazards (describe)					

Figure 25–4

Physical demands analysis. (From Randolph, S. A., and Dalton, P. C.: Limited duty work: An innovative approach to early return to work. By permission of the American Association of Occupational Health Nurses, AAOHN Journal, Vol. 37, No. 11, p. 451, 1989.)

less of whether this involves an occupational or a nonoccupational condition, the occupational health nurse is the center of case management. The nurse works closely with the primary care provider to monitor the progress of the ill or injured worker and to identify and eliminate potential barriers in the return-to-work process. The nurse has a comprehensive understanding of the work place and of the physical requirements necessary for the client to work. The physical demands analysis (Randolph et al., 1989) is a useful tool in objectively assisting assessing the physical demands of any job (Fig. 25–4). Once the assessment is completed, the occupational health nurse can relay this information to the community health professionals caring for the client.

For workers needing special accommodations, the occupational health nurse can negotiate and facilitate those appropriate to the client's health limitations. The nurse is often the driving force behind the employer creating a "light-duty" pool. The goal of this type of program is to provide temporary work that is less physically demanding in nature than the client's regular work. This facilitates the client's return to the work place earlier than if required to wait until full strength was regained.

The occupational health nurse can monitor and support the health of clients returning to work while continuing to experience adverse health effects of chronic disease. For example, the client who is returning to work after sustaining a myocardial infarction may have blood pressure monitored on a routine basis. Counseling regarding adjustment to normal work life as well as support for behavior modification (i.e., smoking cessation) may also be provided.

IMPACT OF LEGISLATION ON OCCUPATIONAL HEALTH

Legislation and associated activities have influenced the practice of occupational health in the United States. Table 25–4 presents an historical perspective of some of the major legislation that have had and will continue to have a direct impact on the general practice of occupational health nursing. The Occupational Safety and Health Act, Workers' Compensation Act(s), and the Americans With Disabilities Act are highlighted.

The Occupational Safety and Health Act of 1970 was enacted 2 years after a major coal mining disaster occurred in West Virginia. The passage of this legislation came about because of worker health concerns, burgeoning environmental awareness, union activities, increased knowledge about work place hazards, and health concerns. The general duty clause of the act states that employers must "furnish a place of employment free from recognized hazards that are causing or likely to cause death or serious physical harm to employees." The act also identifies the roles of the various related government agencies, provides for the establishment of federal occupational safety and health standards, and identifies a structure of penalties, fines, and sentences for violations of regulations. The following organizations were formed under the provisions of the act:

- OSHA, under the jurisdiction of the Department of Labor, is responsible for promulgating and enforcing occupational safety and health standards.
- NIOSH, under the jurisdiction of the Department of Health and Human Services, is responsible for funding and conducting research, making recommendations for occupational safety and health standards to OSHA, and funding educational resource centers for the training of occupational health professionals.
- Occupational Safety and Health Review Commission, appointed by the president, is responsible for advising OSHA and NIOSH regarding the legal implications of decisions or action in the course of carrying out their duties.
- National Advisory Council on Occupational Safety and Health, appointed by the president, is a group of consumers and professionals who are responsible for making recommendations to OSHA and NIOSH regarding occupational health and safety.
- National Commission on State Workers' Compensation Laws, appointed by the president on a temporary basis, was a group that studied the adequacy of state workers' compensation laws and made recommendations to the president on their findings. This commission's work ended as of October 30, 1972.

OSHA has promulgated occupational health and safety standards, which are published in the

Table 25–4
Historical Perspective of Legislation Affecting Occupational Health in the United States

Year	Legislation	Year	Legislation
1836	First restrictive child labor law enacted (Massachusetts)	1965	McNamara-O'Hara Act (extends protection of the Walsh-Healy Act to include suppliers of government services)
1877	State legislation passed requiring factory safeguards (Massachusetts)	1966	Mine Safety Act (mandatory inspections and health and safety standards in mining industry)
1879	State legislation passed requiring factory inspections (Massachusetts)	1969	Coal Mine Health and Safety Act (mandatory health and safety standards for underground mines)
1886	State legislation passed requiring reporting of industrial accidents (Massachusetts)		
1910	State legislation passed requiring formation of an Occupational Disease Commission (Illinois)	1970	Occupational Safety and Health Act
		1970	Environmental Protection Agency established
		1970	Consumer Protection Agency established
1911	Workmen's Compensation Act passed (New Jersey)	1972	Equal Employment Opportunity Act
1935	Social Security Act passed (state and federal unemployment insurance program)	1972	Noise Control Act
		1972	Clean Water Act
1936	Walsh-Healy Act (federal legislation setting occupational safety and health standards for certain government contract workers)	1973	Health Maintenance Organization Act
		1973	Rehabilitation Act
1938	Fair Labor Standards Act (setting minimum age for child labor)	1976	Toxic Substances Control Act
		1976	Resources Conservation and Recovery Act
1948	All states have Workers' Compensation acts	1977	Federal Mine Safety and Health Act
1964	Civil Rights Act	1990	Americans With Disabilities Act

Code of Federal Regulations (CFR) and updated on a regular basis. Access to the most recent publication of these standards is a crucial occupational health nurse responsibility. The occupational health nurse must be knowledgeable of Title 29 of the code, part 1910 (29 CFR 1910) and other sections of the code that apply to specific hazards in the work place. For example, 29 CFR 1904 pertains to OSHA's record keeping requirements. This mandates the employer's responsibility to keep records of work-related injuries, illnesses, and deaths. These records must be posted in the work place for 1 month per year and made available for review by OSHA at any time. In many cases, the occupational health nurse has full responsibility for compliance with this standard. Under the act, any state has the right to implement their own occupational safety and health administration. The only requirement is that the state standards meet or exceed federal standards. California, Maryland, New York, and Michigan are states that have chosen to operate in this manner.

OSHA has 10 regional offices throughout the United States. Inspectors are assigned to each region to enforce the standards and provide consultation to industries.

An OSHA inspection can be initiated in one of several ways. Each office plans a schedule of routine visits to the industries in their respective regions. In the past, funding has been an issue, and inspections have not taken place in the quantity or frequency originally intended. An inspection can also be initiated if a major health or safety problem occurs at the work site such as a death, if five or more workers are sent to the hospital as a result of the same incident, or if there is a safety issue at the work place that has received publicity in the community. Inspection may also occur by employer request. This is not usually done unless the employer has an exemplary occupational health and safety program and wishes to participate in OSHA's voluntary inspection program. Inspection may also be initiated by an employee request due to concern about a suspected hazardous condition. In this case, OSHA is mandated to respond and must keep the employee's name confidential at the employee's request. In the past, penalties have been inconsequential, and rarely have sentences been served. However, recent events indicate that fines have increased, and OSHA has made public its intention to criminally prosecute company executives for serious and willful violations.

In many organizations, the occupational health nurse is the interface with the OSHA inspector. The nurse should know that employees or their union representatives have the right to walk around with the OSHA investigators. This requires the nurse to be knowledgeable about the potential hazards in the work place and about the appropriate control measures designed to eliminate or minimize exposure.

Workers' Compensation acts are state mandated and state funded. These programs provide income replacement and health care to workers who sustain a work-related injury, disability (temporary or permanent), or death. The Workers' Compensation acts also protect the employer in that the compensation received by the employee precludes legal suits against the employer. Each state regulates its own program and is unique to the state. The employer can self-insure, contract with commercial insurance carriers, or purchase a policy with the state-operated insurance fund. Workers receive an average of 66% of their take-home pay before taxes, and some disabled workers and their families are eligible for other benefit programs, including Old Age, Survivors, Disability and Health Insurance; Supplemental Security Income; or any other disability program that they may have purchased ei-

ther through the company or on an individual basis (Clemen-Stone et al., 1987).

In an era of sky-rocketing health care costs and a propensity for injured workers to engage the services of lawyers to represent them in negotiating lump-sum financial settlements, many employers are claiming that workers' compensation costs are crippling their ability to compete in an international marketplace. The occupational health nurse has a unique opportunity to support both the employee and employer in this arena. For the employee, the nurse may be the initial person to whom the work-related injury or illness is reported. Accurate assessment of the injury or illness and appropriate treatment are essential. Community resources must be identified so that the injured worker is provided with high-quality health care and appropriate medical follow-up. The occupational health nurse educates the employee regarding benefits under the Workers' Compensation Act and is often the one who files the claim. If the employee is disabled from work for a period of time, the nurse provides case management support and remains in contact with the employee until return to work. If the employer uses an insurance carrier, the nurse works closely with the claims adjuster to manage the case. The need for light duty or other work place accommodations is determined before the employee's return. In most cases, the nurse facilitates this process with the employer.

For the employer, the occupational health nurse provides the expertise in early intervention and case management. The goal is to limit the worker's disability while providing an opportunity for early return to work through appropriate work place accommodations. The desired outcome is a productive employee with optimum health and productivity plus reduced health care and workers' compensation costs.

The Americans With Disabilities Act, enacted by Congress in July 1990, is a comprehensive act that prohibits discrimination on the basis of disability. The core of this act requires employers to adjust facilities and practices for the purpose of making reasonable accommodations to enhance opportunities for individuals with disabilities (Kaminshine, 1991).

Employment provisions of this act began on July 26, 1992 for employers with 25 or more employees and are scheduled to begin in July 1994 for those with 15 or more employees. Provisions regarding access to public transportation and accommodations become effective in January 1993.

The act defines disability as "physical or mental impairment that substantially limits one or more major life activities; having record of such an impairment; or being regarded as having such an impairment" (Kaminshine, 1991, p. 249).

Physical or mental impairment guidelines are the same as those described in the Federal Rehabilitation Act and include "any physiologic disorder or condition, cosmetic disfigurement, anatomical loss affecting any of the major body systems, or any mental or psychological disorder" (p. 249). Major life activities include caring for self, walking, seeing, hearing and speaking (Kaminshine, 1991).

The Americans With Disabilities Act excludes conditions relating to sexual preference and gender identity, compulsive gambling, kleptomania, and pyromania. The act also denies protection for individuals who are currently involved in illegal drug use.

In particular, the occupational health nurse has responsibility in two areas. The first involves the duty to provide or facilitate reasonable accommodations. This is facilitated by the nurse's familiarity with the physical requirements of jobs in the work place. The second area of involvement involves pre-employment inquiries and health examinations. Pre-employment health examinations will be permitted only if phrased in terms of the applicant's general ability to perform job-related functions rather than in terms of a disability. The examination must be job related and consistently conducted for all applicants performing similar work. In consultation with legal counsel, the occupational health nurse must review all questionnaires to be used as part of the health examination (with exception of a drug-testing program) to ensure compliance with this act.

PROFESSIONAL LIABILITY

The occupational health nurse must also be aware of liability issues confronting the nurse because of the nature of working independently and the laws governing the employer-employee relationship (Lochlear-Haynes, 1990). Lochlear-Haynes described three legal issues germane to the employer-employee relationship:

- The client-nurse relationship
- The employment capacity of the occupational health nurse
- Any acts of negligence

The client-nurse relationship is confusing because the nurse is hired by the employer to provide services to the client. The concern is whether a professional relationship exists under the law or the relationship is based on a coworker status.

MULTIDISCIPLINARY TEAM WORK

As work places have become more complex, a diversity of experts have emerged in many functional and technical areas. To be successful, the occupational health nurse must recognize the need to work as part of an interdisciplinary team. The nurse may interact with occupational medicine professionals, industrial hygienists, safety professionals, employee assistance counselors, personnel professionals, and union representatives (Fig. 25–5). Community health professionals, insurance carriers, and other support agencies in the community are other critical linkages.

To illustrate the roles and collaborative efforts required to successfully resolve occupational health issues, two cases are described, and the roles and responsibilities of each interdisciplinary team member are briefly discussed.

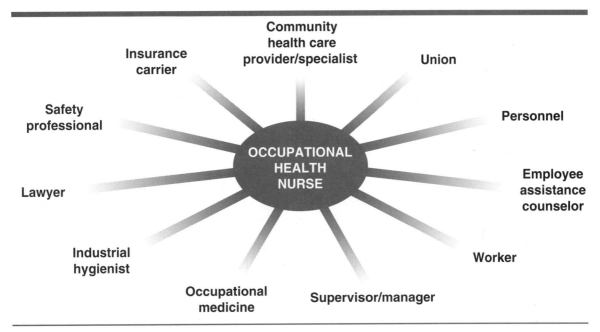

Figure 25–5
The occupational health nurse's professional links in the work place and community.

C a s e
S t u d y
1

A 23-year-old woman was recently transferred into a job that requires her to work with chemicals used in photolithography. She is newly married and might be pregnant, but this has not been confirmed. The client is concerned because the label on one of the pieces of equipment warns of possible reproductive effects. Also, she states that she has not felt well since transferring to this job, and she thinks it is a result of working with chemicals. There are no restrictions in this work area for pregnant women.

Occupational Health Nurse's Roles and Responsibilities

The OHN is probably the employee's first contact. The nurse listens to the employee's concerns and formulates a plan.

- Determine information by taking medical and occupational health histories. Perform a physical assessment, and discuss symptoms.
- Schedule a pregnancy test. If this is not a service provided by the occupational health nurse, referral must be made to the employee's health care provider. If the client does not have one, referral must be made to an appropriate community health resource. Ask the client to have the care provider document pregnancy test results.
- Assure the employee that investigation will ensue immediately, and state who will be involved (e.g., industrial hygienist, occupational health physician).
- Assess the work area or request that an industrial hygienist assess the area (e.g., leaking equipment, problems with ventilation).
- Request the most current industrial hygiene data appropriate to the area.

- Schedule the employee to see the occupational health physician once all data are collected regarding medical and industrial hygiene.
- Communicate any recommended work restrictions to supervisor and/or personnel department after the client is seen by the occupational health physician.
- Review the case in light of existing company policies, and influence changes as necessary.

Industrial Hygienist's Roles and Responsibilities

- Discuss the employee's concerns with the occupational health nurse and, as necessary, with employee.
- Provide the most current industrial hygiene data and analysis for the work area under investigation.
- If current data are not available, industrial hygiene monitoring must occur as soon as possible.
- Meet with the occupational health nurse and the occupational health physician as necessary for data communication and analysis.

Occupational Health Physician's Roles and Responsibilities

- Review the data with the occupational health nurse.
- View the work area and process.
- Discuss the data with industrial hygienist.
- Interview and examine the client.
- Make recommendations regarding the employee's health and safety.

Employee's Roles and Responsibilities

- Obtain pregnancy test and provide documentation of results to occupational health nurse.
- Communicate concerns to occupational health nurse and, as necessary, to industrial hygienist.
- Keep appointment with occupational health physician.
- Follow the recommendations of occupational health physician.

Supervisor/Manager's Roles and Responsibilities

- Allow investigation of work area by occupational health nurse and industrial hygienist.
- Follow the recommendations of occupational health physician.

Primary Community Health Care Provider's Roles and Responsibilities

- Before arriving at a diagnosis, confer with occupational health nurse and/or occupational medical consultant.
- Obtain all work place data relevant to case to help formulate appropriate treatment plan.
- Provide reproductive counseling to the family.
- Refer to appropriate specialists or community resources (i.e., March of Dimes, occupational or environmental pregnancy hot-lines).

Case Study 2

A supervisor calls the occupational health nurse and states that one of his employees appears to be incapacitated. The employee was functioning normally in the morning, but has appeared to be intoxicated since returning from lunch. The supervisor is concerned for the employee's safety as well as for the safety of others, and he is requesting assistance.

Occupational Health Nurse's Roles and Responsibilities

- Request that the supervisor accompany the employee to the occupational health nurse's office.
- Perform a physical assessment of the employee.
- Depending on the findings, the occupational health nurse will send the employee home with a family member, send the employee to a community care provider (hospital) for assessment via an ambulance, or if there is concern for personal safety, notify security.
- Notify the employee and supervisor that the employee needs to follow-up with the occupational health nurse upon returning to work.
- If the employee is sent to the hospital, alert the hospital to the reason for referral and request communication regarding assessment and disposition.
- On the employee's return to work, assess the employee's fitness for work; counsel, as appropriate, regarding alcohol or drug concerns; and make referral to appropriate resource (employee assistance counselor if available, or appropriate community health resource).
- Notify the supervisor when the employee is medically cleared to return to work.

Supervisor/Manager's Roles and Responsibilities

- Accompany the employee to the occupational health nurse's office.
- Consult with the personnel professional regarding company policy for this type of employee behavior.
- Do not allow the employee in the work place until medically cleared by the occupational health nurse.

Employee Assistance Counselor's Roles and Responsibilities

- Provide confidential counseling.
- Make appropriate decisions regarding referrals to community health resources.

Security's Roles and Responsibilities

- Protect the physical safety of all involved.

Community Health Resources' Roles and Responsibilities

- Emergency medical technicians or ambulance staff: Provide safe transport to the hospital.
- Hospital: Perform a medical assessment of worker and communicate results to occupational health nurse.
- Community counseling resource: Accept referral and provide counseling for worker as appropriate.

Employee's Roles and Responsibilities

- Present at the occupational health nurse's office for initial assessment.
- On return to work, discuss fitness for duty with the occupational health nurse.
- Accept referral for treatment.

Family's Responsibilities

- Accept responsibility that alcohol or substance abuse is a family issue by acknowledging the problem.
- Assist in directing the individual to appropriate care with community health care providers.
- Seek community resources for guidance and support (Alcoholics Anonymous, Al-Anon, Narcotics Anonymous, other local support groups).

**C a s e
S t u d y
3**

Forty percent of the 80 packers in department X are experiencing upper extremity symptoms that appear to be related to their job activities. An evaluation of their job tasks indicates that the workers are at risk for cumulative trauma disorders because of the repetitive, forceful motions combined with non-neutral postures and insufficient rest periods.

Occupational Health Nurse's Roles and Responsibilities

- Assess symptomatic individuals, and refer to an occupational medical consultant as appropriate.
- Conduct a walkthrough of the work area to assess job tasks by direct observation or videotaping.
- Evaluate OSHA 200 log, daily health services log, and Workers' Compensation and disability case statistics.
- Meet with department X manager to discuss the issues and propose solutions.
- Plan, develop, implement, and evaluate an ergonomics educational program for workers.
- Work with the multidisciplinary team to identify appropriate intervention strategies.
- Document cost-effectiveness of interventions.

Occupational Medical Consultant's Roles and Responsibilities

- Review data with the occupational health nurse.
- Diagnose the employee's condition, and make appropriate treatment recommendations (i.e., restricted work, application of ice, use of anti-inflammatory agents, referral).
- Conduct a walkthrough of work area.

Employee's Roles and Responsibilities

- Report symptoms to the occupational health nurse as soon as they occur.
- Adhere to the recommended treatment regimen.
- Attend educational sessions.

Supervisor/Manager's Roles and Responsibilities

- Meet with the occupational health nurse, medical consultant, and employees.
- Follow the recommendations of the multidisciplinary team.
- Recognize potential hazards (i.e., insufficient rest breaks, hazardous working conditions).
- Support decisions.

Health Care Provider's Roles and Responsibilities

- Accept referral from occupational medical consultant or occupational health nurse and evaluate data regarding the work place.
- Assess the employee, and develop a treatment plan.
- Communicate the plan to the occupational health nurse, and make recommendations for work restrictions.

SUMMARY

This chapter described the evolution of occupational health nursing during its first century of practice. Current and future demographics and business trends are described as they relate to this nursing specialty area. Aging workers, escalating health care costs, increasing numbers of women and minorities in the work force, and the competitive international marketplace are key factors shaping occupational health nursing practice.

Skills and competencies germane to occupational health nursing practice are identified. Critical work is also described in terms of primary, secondary, and tertiary prevention. For the community health nurse, knowledge of occupational health nursing practice is important because many companies, in fact, do not have on-site occupational health nurses and, therefore, must rely on community health nurses to support their occupational health and safety needs.

Legislative initiatives affecting occupational health nursing practice are identified, and the roles of colleagues in other occupational health specialty fields are discussed.

Case studies and learning activities are provided for the purpose of self-study or class discussion.

In conclusion, the occupational health nursing role is challenging and can have a tremendous impact on the quality and delivery of health care to workers and their families.

L e a r n i n g
A c t i v i t i e s

1. A large car manufacturer has consulted you to design a program to control respiratory disease among foundry workers. Workers in different areas of ferrous foundries are exposed to different respiratory hazards. The main problems are silica exposure and exposure to formaldehyde. The corporation would like to develop a pilot program for one of its foundries that will then be applied to its other foundries. Health and industrial hygiene data will be collected. Both the corporation and the workers support the project, and both see the project as having three purposes: detection of health effects in individuals who may benefit from intervention, determining the relationship of health effects to environmental exposures, and identifying control strategies as appropriate. Outline your pilot program. Discuss the implications of discovering adverse health effects among current workers. Describe the roles of the occupational health nurse, physician, industrial hygienist, safety professional, manager, and employee.

2. The fear of AIDS has created problems in many work sites. Some believe policies should exist; others believe HIV testing should be done at the work site. Still others affirm that education is the best approach for dealing with this extremely volatile issue.

- Is AIDS a concern for health care workers?
- Is AIDS a concern for occupational health nurses?
- Do you believe an AIDS policy should be in place at your company?
- Discuss what you would include in the policy.
- How has your nursing practice changed (if at all) as a result of AIDS?

3. A weight-loss program was conducted during August. Ten people participated in the 6-week program. The total weight loss for the group was 185 pounds. The following chart indicates the weight loss for the individuals.

Weight Before Program (pounds)	Weight After Program (pounds)
215	190
175	160
139	129
275	245
145	120
198	183
120	115
243	233
185	145
210	200

Is there a more effective way to show the results of the program? Assume you have been given this report by one of your peers for you to critique. Be as creative as you want, filling in any data, facts, figures, or other information that you feel is missing. Redesign a report that you would like to send to management.

4. Take an occupational history on five currently employed workers. Identify the occupation, associated job tasks, and potential health hazards. Describe control strategies that could minimize or eliminate the risk of adverse health effects.

5. Conduct a literature review to identify critical concepts in occupational health nursing, epidemiology, ergonomics, safety, industrial hygiene, and ethics.

REFERENCES

American Association of Industrial Nurses: The Nurse in Industry. New York, American Association of Industrial Nurses, 1976.

American Association of Occupational Health Nurses: AIDS Resource Guide: HIV Infections/AIDS in the Workplace. Atlanta, American Association of Occupational Health Nurses, 1988*a*.

American Association of Occupational Health Nurses: The year 2000: AAOHN health objectives for the nation. AAOHN J. *36*;285–288, 1988*b*.

Arthur D. Little, Inc.: Costs and Benefits of Occupational Health Nursing. Washington, D.C., U.S. Department of Health and Human Services, NIOSH Contract No. 210-78-0055, 1980.

Brown, K.: Containing health care costs: The occupational health nurse as case manager. AAOHN J. *37*;141–142, 1989.

Centineo, D.: Return-to-work programs: Cut costs and employee turnover. Risk Management *12*;44–48, 1986.

Chenowith, D.: Nurses' interventions in specific risk factors in high risk employees: An economic appraisal. AAOHN J. *37*;367–373, 1989.

Clemen-Stone, S., Gerber-Eigisti, D., and McGuire, S.: Comprehensive Community Health Nursing, 2nd Ed. New York, McGraw-Hill, 1987.

Cox, A. R.: Planning for the future of occupational health nursing: Part II. Comprehensive membership survey. AAOHN J. *37*;356–360, 1989.

Dees, J. B., and Taylor, J. R.: Health care management: A tool for the future. AAOHN J. *38*;52–58, 1990.

Felton, J. S.: The genesis of occupational health nursing: Part I. Occup. Health Nurs. *28*;45–49, 1985.

Felton, J. S.: The genesis of occupational health nursing: Part II. AAOHN J. *34*;210–215, 1986.

Freedman, S., and Bisesi, M.: Women and workplace stress. AAOHN J. *36*;271–274, 1988.

Friedman-Jimenez, G.: Occupational disease among minority workers: A common and preventable public health problem. AAOHN J. *37*;64–70, 1989.

Gates, D., and O'Neill, N.: Promoting maternal-child wellness in the workplace. AAOHN J. *34*;258–263, 1990.

Johnston, W., and Packer, A.: Workforce 2000: Work and Workers for the 21st Century. Indianapolis, Indiana, Hudson Institute, 1987.

Kaminshine, S.: New rights for the disabled: The Americans with Disabilities Act of 1990. AAOHN J. *39*;249–251, 1991.

Locklear-Haynes, T.: Public health in the workplace: Part II. Liability issues confronting the occupational health nurse. AAOHN J. *38*;78–79, 1990.

McGrath, B. J.: Nursing in Commerce and Industry. New York, The Commonwealth Fund, 1946.

Miller, M. A.: Social economics, and political forces affecting the future of occupational health nursing. AAOHN J. *37*;361–366, 1989.

Moore, P., and Childre, F.: Creative policy-making strategies for working with the healthy chronically diseased employee. AAOHN J. *38*;284–288, 1990.

Morris, L.: Minorities, jobs, and health: An unmet promise. AAOHN J. *37*;53–55, 1989.

Murphy, D.: The primary care role in occupational health nursing. AAOHN J. *37*;470–474, 1989.

Owen, P., and Long, P.: Facilitating adherence to ACS and NCI guidelines for breast cancer screening. AAOHN J. *37*;153–157, 1989.

Parker-Conrad, J. E.: A century of practice: Occupational health nursing. AAOHN J. *36*;156–161, 1988.

Pastides, H., Calabrese, E., Hosmer, D., and Harris, D.: Spontaneous abortion and general illness symptoms among semiconductor manufacturers. J. Occup. Med. *30*;543–551, 1988.

Patterson, J.: Health promotion: An overview for the workplace. AAOHN Update Series *1*;5, 1984.

Public Health Service: Promoting Health/Preventing Disease: Year 2000 Objectives for the Nation. Washington, D. C., U.S. Department of Health and Human Services, 1989.

Randolph, S. A., and Dalton, P. C.: Limited duty work: An innovative approach to early return to work. AAOHN J. *37*;446–452, 1989.

Rogers, B.: Establishing research priorities in occupational health nursing. AAOHN J. *37*;493–500, 1989.

Rogers, B.: Occupational health nursing practice, education, and research: Challenges for the future. AAOHN J. *38*;536–543, 1990.

Rosen, R. H., and Freedman, C.: Developing Healthy Companies Through Human Resources Management. Presented at the Prevention Leadership Forum, Washington Business Group on Health and Office of Disease Prevention, Washington, D.C., May 1987.

Travers, P. H.: *In* Cox, A. R., and Ryan, P., eds.: A Comprehensive Guide for Establishing an Occupational Health Service. Atlanta, Georgia, American Association of Occupational Health Nurses, 1987.

Travers, P. H.: Occupational health nursing in the 90's: Leveraging position and influence through assessment, networking, and communication. AAOHN Update Series *4*;1–8, 1991.

Travers, P. H., Bullwinkel, D., McDougall, C. E., and Powell, J.: Occupational health nursing in the 90's: Skills and competencies. Private in-house document, 1991.

Williamson, G. C., and Moore, P. V.: Health care cost containment: Current societal forces and health care trends. AAOHN J. *35*;444–448, 1987.

Yeater, D. C.: The occupational health nurse as disability manager. AAOHN J. *35*;116–118, 1987.

Home Health Care

Upon completion of this chapter, the reader will be able to:

1. Define home care.

2. Identify the types of home health agencies.

3. Discuss the sources of reimbursement for home care services.

4. Apply the nursing process to a home health client situation.

5. Identify the family or caregiver's role in home care.

6. Identify the goal of hospice home care for the terminally ill and their caregivers.

Jean Cozad Lyon
Theresa M. Stephany

The term "home health care" describes a system in which health care and social services are provided to home-bound or disabled people in their homes rather than in medical facilities (U.S. Department of Commerce). The Department of Health and Human Services set forth a definition of home health care that was developed by an interdepartmental work group:

"*Home health care* is that component of a continuum of comprehensive health care whereby health services are provided to individuals and families in their places of residence for the purpose of promoting, maintaining or restoring health, or maximizing the level of independence, while minimizing the effects of disability and illness, including terminal illness. Services appropriate to the needs of the individual patient and family are planned, coordinated, and made available by providers organized for the delivery of home care through the use of employed staff, contractual arrangements, or a combination of the two patterns" (Warhola, 1980).

Services coordinated in the home include not only skilled nursing care provided by registered nurses but also the services of physical, occupational and speech therapists, social workers, and home health aides. The broader home care industry definition of home health care includes supportive social services, respite care, and adult day care (Health Care Fin. Rev., 1988).

PURPOSE OF HOME HEALTH SERVICES

The primary purpose of home health services is to allow individuals to remain at home and receive health care services that would otherwise be offered in a health care institution, i.e., a hospital or nursing home setting (Harrington, 1988). The home health industry has grown tremendously over the past decade. The growth of home health services has been generated by numerous factors, including the increasing costs of hospital care and the subsequent introduction of the prospective payment system (PPS), by Public Law 98-21 of the Social Security Amendments in 1983. Under the PPS, hospitals receive a fixed amount of money based on the relative cost of resources used to treat Medicare patients within each type of diagnosis-related group (DRG) (Guterman and Dobson, 1986). Other third-party payers either pay for services or have negotiated preferred provider contracts with hospitals based on DRGs (U.S. Department of Commerce, 1990). These changes in the reimbursement system have provided motivation for hospitals to refine and improve their utilization review efforts to better control patient lengths of stay and facilitate discharges (Zander, 1988). Patients who are discharged from hospitals with the need for continuing, intermittent health care services are usually referred for home health services.

Compounding the hospitals' incentives to decrease patient lengths of hospital stay is the increasing number of elderly in the United States. By the year 2002, the number of people over the age of 65 is expected to be 45 million (Rice and Feldman, 1983). The number of people under the age of 65 who have physical disabilities, mental illnesses, or AIDS is also expected to increase (Shamansky, 1988). Therefore, there is a growing population of people whose lives can be sustained because of the introduction of highly technical care that can be provided at home, including ventilator support, total parenteral nutrition, advanced intravenous therapy, and dialysis (Shamansky, 1988). Because of the increase in the demand for home health care services, there has been substantial growth in the number of home care agencies.

TYPES OF HOME HEALTH AGENCIES

Home health agencies differ in their financial structures, organizational structures, governing boards, and populations served. The most common types of home health agencies are official (public), nonprofit, proprietary, chains, and hospital-based agencies.

Official Agencies

Official, or public, home health agencies are those that are organized, operated, and funded by local or state governments. These agencies may be part of a county public health nursing service or a home health agency that operates separate from the public health nursing service but is located within the county public health system. Official home health agencies are funded by taxpayers but also receive reimbursement from third-party payers, such as Medicare, Medicaid, and private insurance companies.

Nonprofit Agencies

Nonprofit home health agencies include all home health agencies that are exempt from paying federal taxes because of their tax status and reinvest any profits into the agency. Nonprofit home health agencies include independent home health agencies or hospital-based home health agencies. Not all hospital-based home health agencies are nonprofit, even if the hospital is classified as nonprofit. The home health agency can be established as a profit-generating service and thus serve as a source of revenue for the hospital or medical center. In this situation, the home health agency is categorized organizationally as for-profit, and federal taxes are paid on profits.

Proprietary Agencies

Proprietary home health agencies are those that are classified as for profit and pay federal taxes on profits generated. The number of proprietary agencies increased to 32% of all agencies by 1985 (Waldo et al., 1986). Proprietary agencies can be in the form of individual-owned agencies, profit partnerships, or profit corporations. Investors in proprietary partnerships or corporations receive financial returns on their investments made in the agencies, providing the agencies make a profit. A percentage of the profits generated are also reinvested into the agency.

Chains

A growing number of home health agencies are owned and operated by corporate chains (Harrington, 1988). These chains are usually classified as proprietary agencies, and may be part of a proprietary hospital chain. Agencies within chains have a financial advantage over single agencies in that the chains have lower administrative costs because many services are provided to all of the member agencies through a larger single corporate structure. For example, a multiagency corporation has greater purchasing power for supplies and equipment because of the volume purchased, and administrative services such as payroll and employee benefits can be provided for all chain employees by a single corporate office, thereby reducing duplication of these services. Criticism of proprietary and chain agencies includes concerns over the quality of services provided by agencies that are profit driven.

Hospital-Based Agencies

Since the implementation of the PPS in 1983, the number of hospital-based home health agencies has doubled (U.S. Department of Commerce, 1990). This trend is not surprising in light of the fixed reimbursement under PPS and the hospitals' incentive to decrease length of stay. By establishing home health agencies, hospitals are able to discharge to home patients who have skilled health care needs, provide the necessary services to the patient, and receive reimbursement through third-party payers, such as Medicare, Medicaid, and private insurance companies. The increasing number of home health agencies indicates that home health agencies are profitable endeavors and provide hospitals with a source of additional revenue (U.S. Department of Commerce, 1990).

Certified and Noncertified Agencies

Certified home health agencies meet federal standards and are therefore able to receive Medicare payments for services provided to eligible individuals (Harrington, 1988). Not all home health agencies are certified. The number of Medicare-certified home health agencies increased from 3,022 in 1980 to 6,005 in 1986 (National Association of Health Care, 1986). By June, 1988, there were approximately 11,000 home health agencies, which is an increase from 10,848 in 1987. Approximately 50%, or 5,500, of these agencies were Medicare certified (U.S. Department of Commerce, 1990).

Special Home Health Programs

Many home health agencies offer special, high-technology home care services. The motivation for offering high-technological services at home is both beneficial to the patient and financially advantageous. Through the implementation of these special programs, patients who require continuous skilled care in an acute or skilled nursing institution are able to return to their homes and receive care at home. From the financial perspective, skilled services provided at home are less costly to offer than hospitalization.

Examples of special services include home intravenous therapy programs for patients who require daily infusions of total parenteral nutrition or antibiotic therapy, pediatric services for children with chronic health problems, follow-up of premature infants who are at risk for complications, ventilator therapy, and home dialysis programs. The key to the success of all of these programs is the patient's, family's, or caregiver's ability to learn the care necessary for success of the home program and the motivation of these individuals to provide the care. If family or caregiver support is not available in the home, the patient cannot be considered a candidate for any of these programs, and other arrangements for care must be found.

Reimbursement for Home Care

Before the establishment of Medicare in 1965, individuals who required home health services paid cash for the services, and donations to the service agencies that provided the services helped to subsidize care for patients who were unable to pay (Kent and Hanley, 1990). Since 1965, individuals who are eligible for Medicare benefits under Title XVIII of the Social Security Act or for Medicaid benefits under Title XIX and those people with private health insurance can receive short-term, skilled health care services in their homes that are reimbursed by the federal government through the Medicare program. Provided services include nursing care, social service, physical therapy, occupational therapy, and speech therapy, and the program is tailored to the individual needs of the patient (Stuart-Siddall, 1986).

Public sources financed 75% of the home health services provided in 1988. More than half of the public spending was paid by Medicare; the remainder was paid by Medicaid. In 1988, Medicare paid for 30 million home visits, and supplies were furnished to Medicare beneficiaries at a cost of $1.8 billion (Health Care Financing Administration, 1989).

In 1989, the total expenditure for home health care services, excluding home health care products, was $9 billion. Spending for health care services has been increasing at an average annual rate of 20%. The rapid growth of the home health market is believed to be reflective of the following:

- Increasing proportion of persons of age 65 or older
- Lower average cost of home health care compared with institutional costs ($750 per month for routine skilled nursing care at home compared with $2,000 for care in an institution)
- Active support of insurers for home care
- Medicare promotion of home health care as an alternative to institutionalization (U.S. Department of Commerce, 1990, p. 49–4).

Payments made by patients or their families comprised 46% of the private financing (12% of total spending) for home health services. The remaining private financing was paid by private health insurance and nonpatient revenue (Health Care Finance Administration, 1990). It has been estimated that as many as 20% of industrywide home health care services provided by Medicare-certified and noncertified agencies is paid out-of-pocket (Rivlin and Wiener, 1988).

EDUCATIONAL PREPARATION OF HOME HEALTH NURSES AND NURSING STANDARDS

The American Nurses' Association (ANA) (1986) has established standards for home health nursing practice. These standards are differentiated into two levels of practice — that of the generalist home health nurse, who is prepared at the baccalaureate level, and that of the specialist nurse, who is prepared at the graduate level. According to the ANA, the generalist provides care to individuals and their families and participates in quality assurance programs. The generalist home health nurse must have community health assessment skills to diagnose complex biopsychosocial problems in families; teach health practices; counsel; and refer to other health care providers as necessary as well as high-technological nursing skills (Keating and Kelman, 1988).

The specialist home health nurse contributes additional clinical expertise to home health patients and their families, formulates health and social policy, and implements and evaluates health programs and services (ANA, 1986). Registered nurses with less than a baccalaureate education are not educationally prepared to meet the professional standards set forth for home health nursing and are encouraged to use the standards in providing care and in pursuing professional development.

Unfortunately, many home health agencies have not adopted the ANA standards for home health nursing and have hired nurses with less than baccalaureate preparation. Some of these home health agencies offer salaries that are lower than those offered to nurses employed in the acute hospital setting and thus cannot recruit educationally qualified nurses.

Albrecht's conceptual model (1990) for home care clearly identifies the educational content areas for students in undergraduate and graduate nursing programs with specialties in home health care. An underlying premise of the model is that professional satisfaction and effective patient outcomes depend on the education and experience of the home health nurse. Implications that are apparent in the model include the following:

- Nursing programs at the undergraduate and graduate levels must prepare competent providers of home health care.
- Curricula are to include concepts related to the suprasystem, health service delivery system, and home subsystem, which includes structural, process, and outcome elements.
- Students at the undergraduate level need at least one clinical observation or experience in a home health care agency.
- Graduate-level students need specific courses that cover concepts present in the model, including knowledge of education, preventive, supportive, therapeutic, and high-technology nursing interventions for home health care; a multidisciplinary approach to home health care; health law and ethics; systems theory; economics covering supply, demand, and productivity; and case management and coordination, finances, and organizational structure (Albrecht, 1990, p. 125).

NURSING PROCESS APPLIED TO HOME CARE

The home health nurse serves as a case manager for patients who receive care from staff of the home health agency or through contract services. The success of the case management plan is contingent on the ability of the nurse to use the nursing process to develop a plan of treatment that best fits the individual needs of the patient, the patient's family, or caregiver. The first step in the development of the plan of treatment and nursing care plan is the patient and family assessment.

The Albrecht nursing model for home health care (Fig. 26–1) provides a framework within which nurses, patients, and their families can interact to identify mutual goals of interventions and promote self-care capability of the patient at home (Albrecht, 1990). Three major elements that are used to measure the quality of home health care patient outcomes include structural, process, and outcome elements.

Structural elements include the client, family, provider agency, health team, and professional nurse. The process elements include three components—type of care, coordination of care, and intervention.

Outcome elements consist of patient and family satisfaction with care, quality of care, cost-effectiveness of care, health status, and self-care capability.

In the Albrecht model for home care, the relationship between the structural elements and the process elements directs the interventions that are implemented. The nurse executes the nursing process, including assessment, nursing diagnosis, planning, intervention, and evaluation, and then coordinates patient care (Albrecht, 1990).

Assessment

The home health nurse assesses the patient's physical, functional, and psychosocial status; physical environment; and social support during the first home visit. Information is collected through observations and questions asked of the patient and family or caregivers in the home environment. It is not unusual to find inconsistencies between information provided by the patient during hospitalization concerning the amount of physical or emotional support available from family and friends and the reality of the amount of support that is available to the patient in the home. The nurse validates or modifies the referral information received to reflect the actual home situation.

Often, contracts are jointly developed by the nurse and the patient and family to delineate the responsibilities of the patient, the family, and the agency for the provision of services. Data collec-

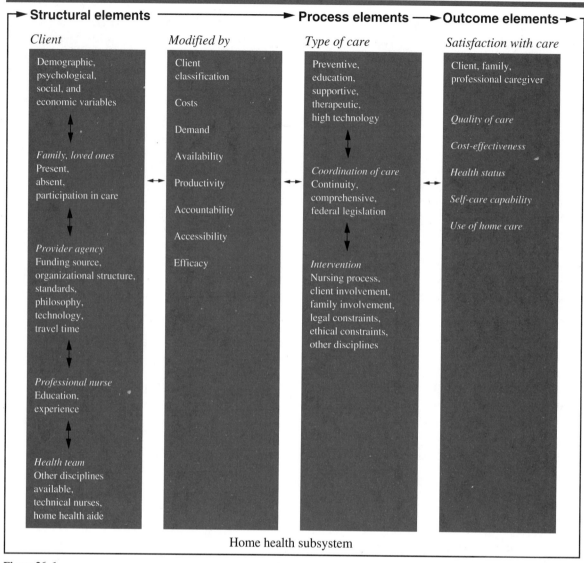

Figure 26–1
Albrecht nursing model for home health care. (Based on Albrecht, M. N.: The Albrecht model for home health care: Implications for research, practice and education. Public Health Nurs. 7(2);118–126, 1990. Reprinted by permission of Blackwell Scientific Publications, Inc.)

tion continues while the patient is receiving home health services. Changes in the patient's condition, environment, or social structure necessitate modifications in the plan of treatment and the nursing care plan.

There are differences between the plan of treatment and the nursing care plan. The plan of treatment includes the type of home health services to be received, the projected frequency of visits by each discipline (Albrecht, 1991), and the interventions that are needed. The nursing care plan addresses specific nursing interventions designed to treat the patient's actual or potential problems, with goals identified with measurable outcomes.

Diagnosis

After completion of the assessment, the nurse identifies the nursing diagnoses that address patient problems. Actual or potential problems are identified. The identification of nursing diagnoses serves as the basis for the nursing care plan. The nursing diagnosis information is communicated by the nurse case manager to the other members of the health care team involved in the patient's care, both informally and formally at weekly team conferences.

Planning

The assessment information and nursing diagnosis information serve as the foundation on which the nursing care plan and plan of treatment are developed for the patient. The plan identifies short- and long-term goals for the patient and is developed to have measurable outcomes. The plan will identify nursing interventions that are needed and additional home health services that are appropriate to enable the patient to achieve the identified goals. It is important that the patient and family be involved in the planning process to maximize the plan's success. Planning is a dynamic process that continues while the patient receives home health services. The plan is modified as needed depending on the patient's condition until the goals are met and the patient is discharged from the home health agency.

Intervention

Implementation of the home health plan begins when the initial planning stage is concluded. The nurse and other health care team members begin the home visits as planned, providing the services that were identified during the planning phase and written on the plan of treatment. The success of the interventions is based on many factors, including the patient's physical condition and the motivation or ability of the patient and the family to participate in the interventions.

Evaluation

The evaluation phase is when the nurse can determine if the goals established with the patient are realistic and achievable for the patient and the patient's family. It is through the collection of additional data during the evaluation phase that the nurse can identify the need for revisions in the nursing care plan and plan of treatment and intervene to make the necessary changes. An example is an elderly wife who, during the initial home visit, stated that she preferred to provide the physical care for her frail husband, who is nonambulatory. On a subsequent visit, the nurse assesses that the patient is not receiving the care that is required for the patient's personal care, specifically, bathing. The nurse discusses the problem with the wife and presents her with options that are available, including the services of a home health aide to provide personal care, including bathing, three times a week. A new plan is developed, and it includes the home health aide. The plan is implemented and evaluated during future visits.

Home Safety
PREVENTION OF injuries in the home by teaching and troubleshooting is the domain of the professional nurse. Months of expensive rehabilitation can be prevented by just a few minutes of the nurse's time and practical expertise.

Data from Tideiksaar, R.: Home safe home. Geriatr. Nurs. 10;280–284, 1989.

The establishment of a friendly working relationship with the family cannot be understated. Without the cooperation and agreement of the patient and family, any plan that is established is at risk for failure. With the cooperation of the patient and family, problems are identified early, and alternative or additional resources can be identified to facilitate the achievement of patient goals.

DOCUMENTATION OF HOME CARE

Ask any home health nurse to describe the most frustrating part of providing home health care, and the answer will probably revolve around documentation issues. Because of the prominent position that Medicare holds as a payer of home health care, the regulations set forth by the Health Care Financing Administration determine the home health industry's documentation. In 1985, the administration introduced forms 485, 486, and 487. These forms increased the documentation required by home health care providers from one page to three pages. Correct and accurate completion of these forms is the key to reimbursement (Galten, 1987). Payment or denial for visits made is based on the information that is presented on these three forms. If the nurse does not clearly document in the nursing notes the skilled care that is provided, the fiscal intermediaries will argue that the care was either not necessary or not done, and reimbursement will be denied. The home health nurse must have an excellent clinical foundation and the ability to identify and document actual and potential patient problems that require skilled nursing interventions (Morrissey-Ross, 1988).

No less important than documentation for reimbursement purposes is documentation of the care provided to record the quality of care received by the patient. The documentation of the home visit serves as record of the nurse's observations, assessment of the patient's condition, interventions provided, and the ability of the patient and family to manage the care at home. In addition, documentation of patient visits serves as a formal communication system among other home health professionals who also have interactions with the patient and family.

THE FAMILY OR CAREGIVER IN HOME CARE

The presence or absence of an involved family member or caregiver can make the difference between the successful completion of the plan of treatment, with the patient remaining in the home, and the need to transfer the patient to an extended-care facility or board-and-care facility. When a capable family member or caregiver is available to assist the patient, the home health nurse spends much of the visit time assessing the skills of the caregiver. The care provider is instructed by the home health nurse in the correct procedures for providing care and in recognizing the signs and symptoms of problems that are to be reported to the health care provider. The goal of the home health nurse's instruction is to provide the caregiver with the skills necessary to successfully care for the patient in the home without intervention of the nurse or other members of the home health team.

Patients who lack a family member or caregiver capable of learning the necessary care and providing the care present a special challenge for the home health nurse. When the patient lives alone and does not have caregivers, the nurse explores other resources available to supplement the patient's self-care activities in the home, such as a hired attendant for patients with extensive physical care needs and financial resources to pay for the attendant. Medicare and private insurance companies do not pay for attendant care. If the patient's income is low enough, in-home support services through the county may be an option. Other services that the nurse considers for the patient include Meals-on-Wheels. Friendly Visitors is a service in which a volunteer goes to the patient's home once a week or more often to provide socialization for the patient. Other options that are available in some communities include adult day health centers or senior service centers. Both of these options require arrangement for transportation of the patient to and from the centers. A variety of transportation methods are available in different communities, ranging from volunteers transporting patients to public transportation systems, such as minivans that provide door-to-door service. The type of services selected and referrals made are based on the individual needs of the patient and on the patient's level of functional ability.

Case Study 1

Susan Brown is a 40-year-old woman who was the driver in a single-car, roll-over accident 9 days ago. She was air-lifted to a trauma center and treated for multiple lacerations and abrasions, including a severe laceration to the left inner aspect of her arm. The referral for home health services made by the hospital at the time of discharge requested daily wound care to the infected left arm laceration by the home health nurse. Specific medical orders for wound care consist of removal of the arm brace, followed by wet-to-dry dressing changes using one-fourth strength Dakin's solution, wrapping the arm with gauze, and reapplication of the brace. Medications included one or two Vicodin tablets every 6 hours, as needed for pain, and 500 mg Keflex four times a day.

During the initial visit, the home health nurse identifies from data collected during the assessment four primary problems:

- The infected left arm laceration with large amounts of drainage related to introduction of bacteria
- Severe arm pain related to the injury
- Knowledge deficit related to inadequate understanding of self-administration of antibiotic
- Anxiety related to family communication problems

These problems are the basis of the nursing care plan for Susan (Carpenito, 1990; Sparks and Taylor, 1991).

Diagnosis

The patient had an infected left arm laceration related to introduction of bacteria secondary to wound, which was secondary to a motor vehicle accident.

Short-term Goals

- Keep laceration clean and debride wound through daily wet-to-dry dressing changes
- Encourage self-care in dressing changes

Long-term Goals

- Healed laceration without drainage or infection
- Full range of motion of the affected arm

Intervention

Because Ms. Brown has a moderate-to-large amount of yellow drainage from the laceration on her left arm, daily dressing changes are initiated, with additional dressings applied to contain the drainage. When the large amount of drainage persists for more than 3 days after initiation of the antibiotic therapy and the patient continues to have low-grade fevers (temperature of 99.2–99.8°F), the home health nurse notifies the physician, and a culture and sensitivity of the drainage is taken. An alternate antibiotic is prescribed based on the culture results. Ms. Brown and her mother are instructed to change the dressing, and they are supervised by the nurse.

Diagnosis

Pain related to arm injury

Short-term Goal

- Pain control through medication and relaxation techniques

Long-term Goal

- Pain free when arm injury is healed

Intervention

The assessment of Susan's arm pain includes a history of when the pain is most severe and the frequency of pain administration. The home health nurse assesses that the pain is most severe at night and recommends that Susan take two Vicodin tablets before going to bed and that she position her left arm in a position of comfort, supported by pillows to decrease edema. The nurse instructs Susan to lie down, rest, and listen to relaxing music during the day when the pain is intense to decrease the amount of arm pain through relaxation.

Diagnosis

Knowledge deficit related to inadequate understanding of self-administration of antibiotic

Short-term Goal

- Correct self-administration of antibiotic

Long-term Goal

- Infection resolved

Intervention

When the home health nurse asks Ms. Brown when she takes the Keflex, she explains that because the drug is prescribed to be taken four times a day, she takes the medication at 9:00 A.M., 1:00 P.M., 5:00 P.M., and 9:00 P.M. The nurse explains the purpose of the antibiotic and the importance of taking it every 6 hours to maintain an optimum blood level. Ms. Brown and the nurse agree on a schedule of 6:00 A.M., 12:00 noon, 6:00 P.M., and bedtime.

Diagnosis

Anxiety related to family communication problems

Short-term Goal

- Decreased anxiety through verbalization of feelings

Long-term Goal

- Anxiety resolved or controlled

Intervention

Ms. Brown's sister arrived from out-of-state to assist with her care after the accident. Within 3 days of her arrival, Ms. Brown's husband and sister got into an argument, and the sister left abruptly and returned home. This altercation is very upsetting to Ms. Brown, who is distraught over the communication problems between her husband and sister. The home health nurse encourages Ms. Brown to talk about her feelings concerning the dysfunctional relationship of her husband and sister and to discuss how she will address the situation with both her husband and her sister. The nurse stresses that the problem is between the husband and sister, and not with Ms. Brown, and that Ms. Brown should not feel guilty or responsible for the disagreement.

Ms. Brown has a large, supportive family, and a caregiver is available to assist her every day. Transportation to and from the physician's appointments is coordinated by her family and does not require the intervention of the nurse. The nurse remains involved with Ms. Brown until the infection is resolved, and the family is taught to provide the necessary wound care.

Referrals

Ms. Brown is referred for follow-up by her internist and orthopedist. She is also referred for a gynecologic appointment for evaluation of sudden onset of slight vaginal bleeding.

Ms. Brown's sister returned to her home, and no further confrontations occurred. The nurse suggests counseling for Ms. Brown if the relationship persists between her husband and sister or continues to cause Ms. Brown anxiety.

Hospice Home Care

The goal of home care for the terminally ill is to keep the client comfortable at home as long as possible and to provide support and instruction to caregivers. When the patient has been determined to be dying, the focus is no longer on cure but rather on comfort care. Some patients insist on staying home until they die; others leave that decision to their caregivers. Each family unit has different needs, and each must be supported in their decisions. In no case should home death be used as the standard by which excellence is determined, nor should home death be viewed as the ultimate measure of "successful" home care. It is vital to realize that caring for a terminally ill person includes caring for the family or caregivers and that not all caregivers desire for their loved one to die at home or are capable of having that occur. The goal of home death must be the goal of the patient and family, regardless of the personal preference of the nurse.

When caring for a terminally ill person at home, the hospice nurse must be skilled in physical and psychosocial care for both the patient and the caregiver. The patient is viewed as a whole person, not as an isolated disease. Caring for a terminally ill person at home demands that the family system be viewed as a unit.

Caring for the Caregiver

Although the dying patient is the focus of all nursing care, the experienced home care nurse knows that a careful assessment of the caregiver's mental and physical health is important. The spouse, lover, children, friends, and neighbors who have made the commitment to stay until the end need the nurse's time and attention as much as, if not more than, the patient. Although the wishes of the patient are important, all decisions regarding care are made with the health of the caregivers in mind. Caregivers need constant nurturing and praise for doing a terrific job. They cannot hear too often the words, "You're a great nurse to . . ." or "You're doing a wonderful job of taking care of . . . ."

Health of the Caregiver

GAYNOR FOUND that women with longer caregiving experience had more physical health problems than did those with less time caregiving, and that younger women found caregiving more psychologically burdensome than did older women. Nursing interventions must be directed toward preventing a decline in the caregiver's health and the development of a second patient who herself needs a caregiver.

From Gaynor, S. E.: The long haul: The effects of home care on caregivers. Image 22;208–212, 1990.

Caregivers need reassurance that their judgment is sound and to be reminded that they cannot do anything "wrong" if it is done for the patient's comfort. The caregivers need to know that they will not mistakenly overdose the patient and must repeatedly be reminded that the patient will not die because of something they did or did not do. Caring for the terminally ill requires that the home care nurse be willing to nurse the entire family; if the dying patient could articulate it, this is what the patient would ask.

PAIN CONTROL AND SYMPTOM MANAGEMENT

British hospice methods of pain control were introduced into the U.S. healthcare system about 15 years ago. They advocated avoidance of peaks and valleys in comfort by building a wall against the pain. In hospice nursing, pain medication is given in doses sufficient to keep the patient pain free and is given on a regular schedule to prevent pain from recurring before the next dose is given. Hospice methods of pain control are particularly well suited to home care. The vast majority of patients can be pain free until their deaths. The key to successful pain control for the terminally ill is to convince patients to take their medications on a regular basis, not just when they "cannot stand it any longer." By building up a wall against the pain, the patient need never hurt and never wait for relief. The nurse explains to patients that most pain medicines last about 4½ to 5 hours before completely wearing off. Patients are instructed to take their pain medication every 4 hours on a 24-hour basis to ensure a "margin of safety" so the medicine will not wear off before the next dose is due.

Pain is subjective and is whatever the patient says it is. Only the patient experiences the pain, and only the patient can judge the severity of the pain. To assist the patient in evaluation of the pain, an audiovisual aid, such as the Pain Assessment Ruler distributed by Roxane Laboratories (Fig. 26–2),

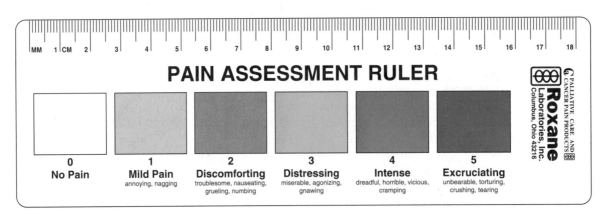

Figure 26–2
Pain assessment ruler. (Reproduced with permission from Roxane Laboratories, Columbus, Ohio.)

can be used. This pain-assessment tool allows the patient to indicate a color that best describes the pain: 0 is white and indicates no pain; 1 is light blue and indicates mild pain (e.g., annoying, nagging); 2 is yellow and indicates discomforting (e.g., troublesome, nauseating, grueling, numbing); 3 is apricot and indicates distressing (e.g., miserable, agonizing, gnawing); 4 is orange and indicates intense (e.g., dreadful, horrible, vicious, cramping); and 5 is red and indicates excruciating (e.g., unbearable, torturing, crushing, tearing). Because this pain-assessment scale uses both colors and words, it is appropriate for use with patients who cannot read.

Use of Morphine

MANY PATIENTS, especially the elderly, are afraid of becoming "junkies" or "druggies" and want to delay using morphine ". . . until I get really bad." Many believe that morphine signals ". . . the end of the line" and are amazed to learn that patients do well while receiving this drug for months, even years, before death occurs. Almost every family will need to be taught that addiction is not the same as tolerance and that their physicians will not ". . . cut off their supply if they take too much."

**C a s e
S t u d y:
2**

Ed McMillan is 64 years old and is dying of prostate cancer. He experiences urinary retention, chronic pain, weakness, constipation, and anorexia. He knows he does not have long to live, but he wants to go home to die and to be able to attend his youngest son's wedding in a nearby town.

Working together with Mr. McMillan and his wife, the home care nurse identifies four nursing diagnoses. Because of the patient's prognosis, only short-term goals are identified.

Diagnosis

- Urinary retention related to obstruction by the tumor

    Short-term Goal

    - Urinary drainage through a Foley catheter

Intervention

The nurse inserts an indwelling urinary catheter to alleviate urinary retention. The nurse instructs Mr. McMillan's family in catheter care and the signs and symptoms of a urinary tract infection to report to the nurse or physician.

Diagnosis

- Pain related to cancer

    Short-term Goal

    - Pain control

Intervention

Oral morphine sulfate (80 mg every 4 hours around the clock) for pain

Diagnosis

● Mobility impairment related to weakness from cancer

Short-term Goal

● Maximum mobility

Intervention

The nurse orders a walker and wheelchair to maximize Ed's mobility and instructs the family in proper use of the equipment.

Diagnosis

● Constipation related to morphine sulfate ingestion

Short-term Goal

● Regular bowel movements

Intervention

To prevent constipation, the nurse initiates a daily bowel regimen that includes monitoring fluid intake, introduction of a stool softener, and a laxative as needed.

The nurse requests that Mr. McMillan's physician order small doses of prednisone to temporarily improve the patient's poor appetite. The home care nurse also does a great deal of teaching.

The nurse instructs the family that it is common to lose one's appetite in advanced cancer. Despite the constant reassurance, Mrs. McMillan continues to do her best to feed her husband regularly, believing that "If only he'd eat, he'd get his strength back." The nurse continues her advocacy for Mr. McMillan by praising his wife for her loving care but repeating that it is normal for a patient with cancer to have a poor appetite. Because of the nurse's interventions, the patient is pain free, and his bowels move easily and regularly. With a leg bag instead of the usual catheter bag and the wheelchair for transportation, Mr. McMillan is able to attend his son's wedding.

When Mr. McMillan becomes too weak to stand, his home care nurse has an electric hospital bed set up in his home. The bed is strategically placed in the den, the center of family activity, and a home health aide comes to bathe him every other day. As his level of consciousness declines, the nurse helps his family keep him pain free by requesting morphine sulfate in rectal suppository form. When the patient's lungs begin to fill with fluid, the nurse suggests oxygen via nasal cannula and transdermal scopolamine patches to lessen his shortness of breath and decrease his secretions. The nurse visits daily while Ed is comatose to determine if the family is coping adequately and to offer suggestions as small problems arise. The home care nurse suggests that Mrs. McMillan's children help make funeral arrangements and get financial affairs in order before Mr. McMillan dies.

The patient dies peacefully in his own home, surrounded by his wife, children, and his many grandchildren. As was his wish, his corneas are donated for transplantation, and a memorial service is held in which family, friends, and former colleagues participate. Mr. McMillan's ashes are scattered at their weekend home in the mountains. After the initial bustle subsides, the home care nurse makes a follow-up bereavement visit.

Home care nurses who care for the terminally ill practice truly professional nursing. As case manager, the nurse draws on the expertise of the interdisciplinary team to obtain what the patient and family need at a most vulnerable time. Home care nurses are pivotal when caring for the dying because they are practical, knowledgeable, flexible, and family centered. Nurses have a long history of speaking for those who cannot speak for themselves. In patients' homes, nurses advocate for the terminally ill by offering unique skills in pain and symptom management and by sharing their hearts as well as their hands.

Learning Activities

1. Contact a local home health agency and interview the agency director. Ask what type of agency it is, the profit status, and whether it is Medicare certified. Report your findings to your classmates.

2. If possible, arrange to make home visits with a home health nurse.

3. Contact a local hospice and ask to spend a day with a home care hospice nurse.

4. Attend a team meeting in a home health agency or a hospice program to see how the roles of the various team members blend together to provide family-centered care.

5. Encourage an elderly person to do a "life review" discussing what accomplishment the person is most proud of and what the person would have done differently.

REFERENCES

Albrecht, M. N.: The Albrecht nursing model for home health care: Implications for research, practice, and education. Public Health Nurs. *7*;118–126, 1990.

Albrecht, M. N.: Home health care: Reliability and validity testing of a patient-classification instrument. Public Health Nurs. *8*;124–131, 1991.

American Nurses' Association: Standards of Home Health Nursing Practice. Kansas City, Missouri, American Nurses' Association, 1986.

Carpenito, L. J.: Nursing Care Plans and Documentation. Philadelphia, J. B. Lippincott, 1990.

Galten, R.: Documentation: The key to reimbursement. Caring *6*(2);68–69, 1987.

Gaynor, S. E.: The long haul: The effects of home care on caregivers. Image *22*;208–212, 1991.

Guterman, S., and Dobson, A.: Impact of the Medicare prospective payment system for hospitals. Health Care Fin. Rev. *7*;97–114, 1986.

Harrington, C.: Quality, access, and costs: Public policy and home health care. Nurs. Outlook *36*;164–166, 1988.

Health Care Financing Administration, Office of Research and Demonstrations: 40% Home Health Agency Skeleton File, 1989. Washington, D.C., Health Care Financing Administration, 1989.

Health Care Financing Review: National health expenditures, 1988. Health Care Fin. Rev. *11*;1–41, 1988.

Keating, S. B., and Kelman, G. B.: Home Health Care Nursing: Concepts and Practice. Philadelphia, J. B. Lippincott, 1988.

Kent, V., and Hanley, B.: Home health care. Nurs. Health Care *11*(5);234–240.

Morrissey-Ross, M.: Documentation: If you haven't written it, you haven't done it. Nurs. Clin. North Am. *23*;363–371, 1988.

National Association of Health Care: Report No. 164. Washington, D.C., National Association for Home Care, May 23, 1986.

Rice, D. P., and Feldman, J. J.: Living longer in the United States: Demographic changes and health needs of the elderly. Milbank Memorial Fund *61*;362–396, 1983.

Rivlin, A., and Wiener, J.: Caring for the Disabled Elderly. Washington, D.C., The Brookings Institution, 1988.

Shamansky, S. L.: Providing home care services in a for-profit environment. Nurs. Clin. North Am. *23*;387–398, 1988.

Sparks, S. M., and Taylor, C. M.: Nursing Diagnosis Reference Manual. Springhouse, Pennsylvania, Springhouse Corp., 1991.

Stuart-Siddall, S.: Home Health Care Nursing: Administrative and Clinical Perspectives. Chico, California, Aspen, 1986.

Tideiksaar, R.: Home safe home. Geriatric Nurs. *10*;280–284, 1989.

U.S. Department of Commerce/International Trade Administration: U.S. Industrial Outlook. Washington, D.C., U.S. Doc., 1990.

Waldo, D. R., Levit, K. R., and Lazenby, H.: National health expenditures, 1985. Health Care Fin. Rev. *8*;1–21, 1986.

Warhola, C.: Planning for Home Health Services: A Resource Handbook. DHHS Publ. No. (HRA) 80-14017. Washington, D.C., U.S. Public Health Service, Department of Health and Human Services, 1980.

Zander, K. S.: Nursing case management: Strategic management of cost and quality outcomes. J. Nurs. Admin. *18*;23–30, 1988.

CHAPTER 27

Rural Health

Upon completion of this chapter, the reader will be able to:

1. Identify the major indicators of rural health status.

2. Discuss the impact of rurality on access to health care.

3. Describe two major government resources supporting health care to the rural aggregate.

4. Devise nursing care plans for an individual, family, or aggregate within a rural area, and determine how their needs can be met with available resources.

5. Apply knowledge of rural health issues in promoting health care to the rural aggregate.

Charlene Olivia Lund

The rural community health nurse is willing to expend extra effort in providing nursing services to a rural population. The nurse meets the health needs of smaller populations distributed over a larger geographical area. Fewer resources are available compared with those found in an urban setting. For example, there are fewer telephones with which to contact primary care clinicians, and fewer convenient emergency clinics or hospitals. The rural community health nurse is challenged with greater autonomy in making decisions to provide comprehensive care to the rural individual, family, and community. The nurse must combine theories of community nursing practice with philosophies of public health to prevent problems and promote good health for the greatest number of rural people.

There is little information regarding rural health nursing in community health nursing texts. However, community health nursing has existed for more than a century in the United States and has included outreach to rural areas. Therefore, the rural community health nurse is foremost a community health nurse who follows the same nursing process and theory in providing health care to those in need. It is the characteristics, problems, and needs unique to a rural community that distinguish the rural community health nurse's role.

Practice settings for the rural community health nurse are often the same as those for the community health nurse; they include the county health department, primary care physician offices, community health centers, home health agencies, and others. The rural community health nurse is given authority by the employer, usually the local health department. The nurse functions independently, applying the nursing process in promoting and preserving health for rural aggregates.

This chapter will introduce the distinct nursing role of serving a rural community as a whole. A rural community's characteristics, problems, and potential solutions will be discussed in terms of primary, secondary, and tertiary prevention. Roles and functions of the rural community health nurse are presented with an emphasis on the roles of advocate for the community and of referral agent for the client, family, and community. A case study will be presented; the nursing process and self-care theory are applied to this case.

DEFINITION OF RURALITY

A clear definition of rurality is difficult. The concept of rurality encompasses numerous factors, including population density, types of employment, and cultural diversity. Although values and beliefs of rural populations often give the perspective of a rustic, simple, leisurely paced life, there is great variability in rural regions throughout the United States. Figure 27–1 is a U.S. map of rural, farm, and nonfarm areas.

Consider a town in the Appalachians, a Southwestern farming town, a recreational mountain town, and a Native American village. What are some of the characteristics common to each of these areas? How will this information affect the care provided by the rural community health nurse? This chapter will concentrate on farming communities with a particular emphasis on the migrant worker. However, this information can be extrapolated to other U.S. rural regions.

Population

According to criteria set by the U.S. Census Bureau, a Standard Metropolitan Statistical Area (SMSA) is defined by a population of 100,000 or more. The U.S. Bureau of the Census (1980) defines a rural area as any nonmetropolitan aggregate with less than 2,500 people residing in open country. "Open country" is considered to have a population density of one to six persons per square mile. By this definition, about 27% of the U.S. population is rural. For this chapter, any area populated with less than 15,000 people where residents must travel great distances to meet their health needs will be included in further discussions.

Population Trends

There has been a recent reversal in rural population trends from decades of decline to decades of substantial increase. In the period of 1970 through 1980, the population in nonmetropolitan areas increased by 15.8% compared with a growth of 9.8% in metropolitan counties (Browne and Hadwiger, 1982). This may have been a one-time aberration. However, even with these substantial increases, there are fewer resources. Many of these people go without health care or neglect their health needs.

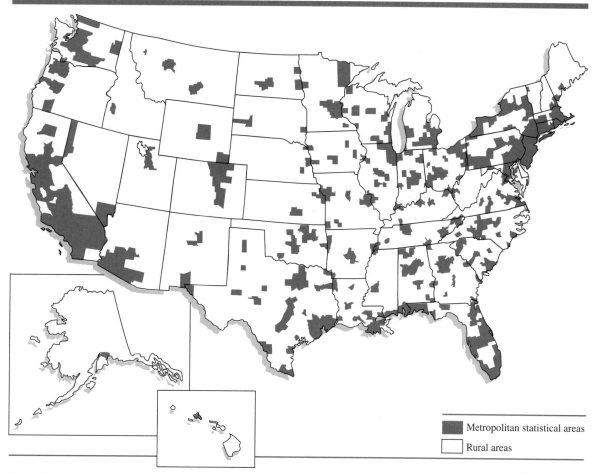

Figure 27–1
This map represents metropolitan statistical areas (MSAs), which include populations of 100,000 people. The reverse of this map represents all of rural America, farming and nonfarming areas. There would be even more light areas if this map had been divided by areas of less than 50,000 people. Population density thus plays an important part in the definition of rurality. (Adapted from U.S. Department of Commerce, Bureau of the Census, Metropolitan Statistical Areas. Stock No. 003-024-07228-9. Washington, D.C.: U.S. Government Printing Office, 1990.)

"Since the patient is a group, pulse and temperature readings are a series of statistical measurements: birth rates, death rates, incidence of particular diseases" (Tinkham and Voorhies, 1984, p. 184). The rural community health nurse can bridge the gap of needed health services for this growing rural community by acting as both a resource and a referral agent.

HISTORICAL PERSPECTIVE

There is a belief that health is a right of all persons and groups, not just of individuals in a hospital setting. As early as 1880, the nursing profession considered it a duty to reach out to persons unable to travel to or afford hospital care. This meant reaching out into the vast territories of rural United States.

In the 1950s, physicians began to specialize. Rural residents, who were used to seeing a "country doctor," had to go to cities to obtain health care. General practice in these areas was becoming increasingly scarce. Some resolution of the lack of primary health care services in rural communities began in 1965 with the creation of the position of the nurse practitioner. Nurse practitioners and physician assistants are often willing to relocate to rural areas and may be subsidized by government programs.

Several health manpower training acts, including the National Health Service Corps and Health for Underserved Rural Areas, attest to the value of the rural community health nurse. These programs subsidize advanced education in community health nursing to serve the rural aggregate.

Decreased financial resources have led to the curtailment and discontinuation of many health promotion programs, and the role of health care providers has come under increased scrutiny (Milio, 1984; Sienkiewicz, 1984). Rural health nursing practice must now include identification of subgroups or aggregates within the rural community who are at higher risk of illness or poor recovery.

Between 1886 and 1986, public health nursing as a profession has unfolded to become an exciting career. In 1923, Goldmark stated that "public health nursing has had a proud history, which portends a brilliant future" (p. 184). This is true today.

MAJOR INDICATORS AND PROBLEMS OF RURAL HEALTH

There are health problems unique to small rural communities. The chief difficulty is isolation of rural residents from the resources available in urban areas. Primary care clinicians are often scarce, and health departments are not always able to provide facilities or services to all rural aggregates within their geographical boundaries. Poor access to health services as a result of time factors, road conditions, or weather conditions compounds this problem.

The cost of health care is another concern. For the rural consumer, both access to and use of curative or preventive services are costly. Neither insurance nor Medicare is oriented to the concept of self-care versus curative services. In the long run, this may be more costly.

For the provider, professional liability costs are disproportionately high in relation to the income of the practice. This prohibits many clinicians from opening a solo practice in rural towns. Medicare reimburses rural health care providers at a lower rate than larger providers in urban areas.

"The amount of uncompensated care is increasing, further exacerbating the problem for those of our rural communities least able to pay the differences needed to provide vital health care services" (U.S. Senate hearing, 1988, p. 24).

Completing the cycle of depleted health provisions is the rapid disappearance of rural hospitals. Many legislative bodies have tried to find an answer to this health care problem in rural areas. In 1988, a special senate committee met regarding what they called the "Rural Health Care Challenge." They noted that the closure of 160 hospitals and the potential closure of 600 additional hospitals combined with unmet health care personal needs are hindering and may continue to hinder access to needed health care for years to come. There has been no viable solution.

Rural "hospitals are not the logical endpoint of today's trends in rural health care delivery," stated Bauer (1988, p. 83). He contends that emergency medical services can take the place of the emergency department at rural hospitals by delivering basic and advanced life support services at the scene in the shortest time possible and then sustaining the patient through transportation to a trauma center. Bauer also suggested that physical facilities for rural health care be located on a main highway, away from residential areas; be efficient; and perhaps be resourceful in using old jails and/or long-term care facilities. He also advocated a community infirmary to allow observation by health providers of rural residents for 1 or 2 days to determine whether transfer to a hospital is indicated.

Being aware of major problems in rural areas is important. The rural community health nurse must know the particular characteristics of a rural community because they indicate specific needs for nursing services. Indicators and rural characteristics include the following:

- Age, with an increase in the rural elderly population
- Education, with fewer high school graduates than in urban areas
- Family configuration, with more women heading households than ever before
- Economy, with a higher percentage of unemployed and lower incomes
- Transportation, with fewer (zero to one) cars per family

- Housing, with a higher percentage of dilapidated homes and more persons residing in small, substandard homes
- Resources, with more than one third of the 66 million rural Americans medically underserved

With a good understanding of the rural aggregate, the rural community health nurse can more easily act as a resource agent in times of need. For example, without readily available emergency services, the nurse may be called on to provide intensive physical or emotional emergency care. Knowledge of present emergency services can assist in this role. The nurse may then use expertise to assess other needs and prevent deterioration in other areas of health.

The concept of prevention is not well understood and appears to be out of the reach of most rural areas. Interestingly, the U.S. Surgeon General (1979) reported that as many as five of the 10 leading causes of death in 1976 were due to unhealthy behavior or lifestyle choices. The rural community health nurse can have a significant impact on many rural residents by educating them in risks endemic to their area and encouraging lifestyle changes.

Demographics

Rural population characteristics are distinct from the urban population in several ways. The rate of population growth in nonmetropolitan areas exceeded that of metropolitan areas for the first time in 1980. However, health care services have not paralleled rates of growth. Female and elderly populations are increasing in rural areas. The median age of the rural population has been increasing because of declining fertility, aging of the World War II baby boomers, and increasing longevity of people (U.S. Department of Agriculture, 1985). The exodus of rural youth to the cities where there are greater economic opportunities is another reason for the increased median age of rural populations. Last, mortality rates are lower, except for infants. All of these factors point to the increased need for rural community health nursing services.

Infant and maternal mortality rates are higher in areas where there is a decrease in the use of modern medical birthing facilities. Ninety-nine percent of all live births in the northern rural states were attended by a physician in a hospital compared with

---

Areas of Greatest Rural Health Needs

- **MORE RURAL households are now headed by Hispanics and African-Americans than by other cultural populations.**
- **More than 28% of rural households are headed by women.**
- **There is a lower educational status and a higher percentage of children and elderly in rural populations.**

Adapted from U.S. Department of Agriculture and Economic Research Service: Rural Conditions Chartbook: Rural Development Research Report 43, 1985.

85% in southern rural states. The lowest rate of use of modern medical facilities occurred among nonwhite mothers who had babies in Mississippi (Swanson and Swanson, 1976). However, rural residents consistently report lower demands for services. Perhaps it is the result of acceptance of many years without care so that rural residents no longer think of acquiring care. For example, a pregnant migrant worker may seek services only at the time of delivery to avoid cost and possibly forestall any problem with immigration services.

The rural community health nurse has more work than can be handled because the few new resources cannot meet the demand of the rapidly rising rural population. How does the nurse prioritize work? The nurse can concentrate efforts on meeting the health care needs of rural women and children, the rural elderly, and specific rural cultural groups.

Elderly Population

As in the general population, the elderly represent 12% of the overall rural population. Of all persons living in rural America, 7,775,760 (12%) are age 65 or older (U.S. Bureau of the Census, 1989). However, elderly men in rural areas outnumber those in urban areas, and elderly women in rural areas are fewer in number than their urban counterparts. This might reflect the rural lifestyle in which the unemployment rate is lower. Also, as rural women age and the family breaks up or members move away, the women retreat to the city, often to be institutionalized. In their rural isolation, women often sustain more accidents and injuries trying to maintain their independence. Families may be their only social and physical support (Pesznecker and Zahlis, 1986). Many of the rural elderly's problems are preventable, but they are not being prevented. Continuous rural health nursing services can help the elderly and are needed by this ever-growing population.

Economic Considerations

Rural America is rapidly departing from its heritage of agriculture- and resource-dependent industries (Browne and Hadwiger, 1982). Alternatives to low-skill industries and perpetually depressed local economies are being developed. However, many rural communities remain without resources or services because of extreme physical isolation, unattractive physical surroundings, or lack of leadership to promote change.

The rural poverty level is twice that of urban areas. In 1985, only 25% of the rural poor qualified for Medicaid versus 43% of the poor in inner cities (U.S. Senate committee report, 1988). With lower incomes and more financial insecurity, health care either becomes less important or impoverishes more people.

Rural Poverty and Economic Statistics

- **THERE ARE more than 11 million rural people with incomes below the poverty threshold; they account for 38% of the nation's poor.**
- **The median family earns about 80% of a metropolitan family's income.**
- **There are more unemployed and underemployed citizens in rural America.**
- **Agriculture shares approximately 10% of the total rural earning, much less than 50 years ago.**
- **Women, particularly Hispanics, are climbing in the labor force, yet making less money than men in equal positions.**

Data from Cornman, J. M.: Rural Poverty and Economic Development. Washington, D.C., National Rural Center, 1981.

Twelve cents of every dollar goes to health labor costs. Senator Kennedy stated that the United States will spend an amount for health care in 1990 equal to the total gross national product in 1980 if changes are not made (Sundwall, 1986). The rural community health nurse who understands the business of health care and the economics of the rural aggregate will be better prepared to listen to

---

Advantages of Community Participation

COMMUNITY INVOLVEMENT varies in U.S. Office of Equal Opportunity–sponsored health centers, ranging from local control to no participation. Participation by the community is an asset for several reasons. First, it may facilitate the attainment of program goals or better deployment of program resources. Second, it may expand the community's perspective and expectations of what the needs are and which plan is of greatest benefit or effect. Third, it may educate and ultimately change health providers' attitudes. Finally, it is morally imperative. "It can give firm, meaningful, unequivocal support to the democratic ethos that people should have the opportunity to participate in the decisions affecting their lives" (Hatch and Earp, 1976, p. 259).

---

rural community leaders when setting priorities to meet their health care needs.

Farming is a major rural business. However, it remains nonprosperous. Many farming populations are land rich and cash poor, thus foregoing elective expenditures such as health care. Fickenscher (1988, p. 132) stated "the most hazardous occupations are mining, farming, and forestry, all of which are rural. All are subject to cyclical swings and at present are having major difficulties." It stands to reason that health care is not a high priority with its high cost when cash is scarce.

Migrant Health Issues

Health values and beliefs are rooted in family and culture as well as in actual experiences with the health care systems. In rural areas, there can be a variety of subcultural aggregates, such as migrant workers, farmers, Native Americans, or even townsfolk. Too often, the nurse overlooks the cultural roots forming the perceptions of health. Sensitivity to cultural beliefs and lifestyles can assist in planning and implementing care appropriate to meet the special health needs of these aggregates.

One of the chief problems with many subcultures in the United States is an inability to be understood. It has been stated even among health care providers that various cultural groups are ignorant. What appears to be more true is that language barriers exist and that values placed on health and illness differ. There is a need to learn and incorporate the values and beliefs of subcultures into a firm working knowledge if influences on health behavior are to be achieved.

VIGNETTE: A rural community health nurse and a psychiatric social worker had seen many problems of alcoholism, teen pregnancy, and wife abuse in a small rural town. They diagnosed a need for increased independence among the Mexican-American women. They scheduled a "women's support group" and publicized it through the local paper. Their goal was to increase the awareness of the choices each woman would make in her life. No women showed up for the first meeting. The cultural family upbringing and belief in *machismo* would not allow them to change. The husbands had objected to the group because they were fearful of the impact such a group might have on their lives. The men foresaw a loss of authority.

This was a good learning experience in understanding and working with a subcultural aggregate. The next attempt to organize the group began by questioning the women to determine what health care needs they considered prominent. They, in turn, discussed their needs with their husbands. Six weeks later, a weight-reduction class that involved exercise and diet was started.

The health issues for migrant workers are numerous and include tuberculosis, alcoholism, malaria, malnutrition, anemia secondary to ova and parasites, hepatitis B, and typhoid fever. The National Health Service Corps has hired health personnel to train individuals within each cultural group to teach their group ways of improving health through lifestyle changes. The rural community health nurse can team up with these health care workers in making appropriate referrals for these subcultural groups to avoid duplicating services.

Migrant workers are the subculture most often dealt with in many regions of the United States. They migrate in all directions, from Florida, Texas, Mexico, and California to wherever a crew leader will hire them. Most of the migrants are Mexican or Mexican-American. Many Mexicans are in the United States illegally and remain undocumented

for purposes of the U.S. Bureau of the Census. They are rarely educated regarding health and disease prevention. Their priorities are having food to eat and shelter, not having the baby immunized or the family checked for tuberculosis. They often maintain their Hispanic tradition of keeping issues within the family to maintain their dignity and pride.

The migrant workers have more work-related accidents than the remainder of the population. They are constantly exposed to agricultural pesticides, snakes, and insects. Pneumonia and communicable diseases are other potential health problems prevalent in this group. Because cultural values provide powerful motivation and standards for behavior, it is crucial that the rural community health nurse learn these value systems to know how to bring about change.

The migrants are brought to the community but not into the community (Geary and Crane, 1985). Most permanent residents want the farm work completed quickly so the migrant way of life will not be so apparent. The camps are often difficult to find, and the crew leaders must approve of anyone leaving the site for medical or other reasons. This is a difficult and dehumanizing existence for these people.

Migrant health projects have begun in the southwest and western states as an extension of public health services to a population at great risk and very much in need of health care. Geary and Crane (1985) found that the projects bring services to those who seek help and search for those who do not. AIDS is increasing in this population; African-Americans and Hispanics comprise 40% of all persons with AIDS (Smith, 1988). Presently, the Centers for Disease Control has a study under way to determine the prevalence of HIV infection among migrant and seasonal farmworkers and their families.

The Mexican-American culture is characterized by a close-knit kin group. Because the mother is the primary health provider in the Mexican-American home, outside help is rarely requested. Illness is viewed as an imbalance in the body. Mexican-Americans believe that the degree of imbalance determines the severity of the condition (Reinert, 1986). Their objective is to decrease this imbalance. First, they will try teas, herbs, or other home remedies. Discussion of the symptoms will occur, first, among family and, later, among friends. Help from a folk healer, a *curandero,* may be elicited. If all else fails, they may seek a clinician. Rural community health nurses should elicit a client's view of illness and realize that they come with a set of concepts and interpretations about specific health problems.

Keeping adequate health records of this group has been another problem. It is necessary to inform the migrant workers of the importance of taking their health card to the next site. The nurse can then know what care has been given and what follow-up is needed.

The federal government attempts to reach many of these subcultural aggregates through special grants allocated to those providing curative, preventive, and social services. For example, the Indian Health Services was formed to assist Native Americans in obtaining increased access to care. These services are not limited to Native Americans; other groups that reside in the area can also benefit, such as migrant farmworkers and refugees from Southeast Asia.

Health Care Access and Use

The problem of access to rural health care services extends beyond the convenience of a location or facility. "It represents a complex interplay among beliefs, social organization, and patterns of behavior of health consumers as they relate to a complex health care system" (Hassinger, 1976, p. 164). Presently, one of every six Americans lives in an area lacking primary medical care. Approximately half of the 34 million persons lacking adequate health care live in rural areas (Department of Health, Education, and Welfare, 1978).

Health care in rural areas is affected by isolation and the poor economy. Despite the increase in numbers of physicians in towns with more than 25,000 residents (Rosenblatt, 1982) and a rapidly growing surplus of U.S. physicians, there has not been significant improvement in the geographical distribution of health personnel. The problem is maldistribution, not numbers of health care providers.

Staffing patterns of health care facilities can also impact the type of care available. Without a full staff and a team approach, comprehensive care is difficult, and preventive care is often impossible. General physicians cannot afford liability insurance. For example, annual insurance rates increased from $600 in 1985 to $8,000 in 1986 (Sundwall, 1986). There is an absence of consultations and a lack of backup physicians. All of these factors cause frequent physician turnover.

In most states, nurse practitioners are hired to work in shortage areas without legal backing of drug-dispensing laws. They must have the backup of physicians. Is it any wonder that clinicians experience burnout? The rural community health nurse can be the link between staff and patients, relieving the caseload of the clinician while providing more comprehensive care to the patient.

VIGNETTE: Carol Wynnewood, a rural community health nurse, arrived at her central county health department office at 8:00 A.M. She loaded her county car with the necessary items for the well child clinic she was to manage from 2:00 to 4:00 P.M. in a small rural town of 7,000. After reviewing and prioritizing her six cases, she called as many of these patients as possible to give them a general idea of the time of her visit.

Carol was unable to leave the office immediately per rules of safety for personnel (fog made visibility poor, which could endanger her life). By the time she was able to leave, her plans had changed. Another patient called with a more pressing problem: she was having trouble "catching her breath."

By the time Carol had arrived, this patient was experiencing sufficient difficulty in breathing that she required emergency transportation to the hospital, which was 45 miles away. Carol helped the patient remain calm until she could be transported. It was 12:20 P.M. when Carol left for her next visit, which was 10 miles away. She ate her lunch en route to check on a "premie" baby; she then headed to her clinic, which was 15 miles away.

The rural community health nurse faces many difficulties in providing thorough community nursing services. The first difficulty is a lack of time due to heavy caseloads and great distances between homes and rural communities. Second, the physical work setting is complex; each new case warrants a new environment. Finally, there is a need to abide by the bureaucratic rules and regulations that commit the nurse's time away from the rural aggregate.

As can be seen, the role of the rural community health nurse can be complex and can be complicated by many unpredictable factors. However, the job is exciting, challenging, and, at times, exhausting.

Residents of a rural community have their share of problems in acquiring health care services. Usually, there are great distances to travel over poorly kept roads. Rural residents spend an average of 30–40 minutes more to acquire health care than do residents of a metropolitan area (Elison, 1986). Longer waiting times and shorter visits with physicians cause much frustration. Many patients voice their displeasure with these factors and thus often select to receive no health care.

Health Care Resources

Agriculture remains a prime employer of migratory families in U.S. rural areas. In 1962, the Migrant Health Act reestablished federal aid for health services to migrant workers and their dependents. This grant provided funds from the U.S. Public Health Service to local and state agencies for services to migrant families.

The government helps special population groups through the U.S. Office of Economic Opportunity, which was established in 1964. This agency is responsible for neighborhood or community health centers, offering comprehensive ambulatory services to all low-income persons (Roemer, 1976, p. 14).

Numerous local, state, and federal programs are set up to increase the elderly's awareness of health in a positive way, encouraging successful aging. Some of these programs are the federally sponsored National Commission on Aging, community retirement groups, senior citizen activity centers, and Senior Actualization and Growth Exploration (SAGE). SAGE comprises four distinct programs. One of these programs instituted the National Association for Humanistic Gerontology in 1974 and has national networking. These groups as well as other resources cited throughout this chapter can assist the rural community health nurse in the role of rural community advocate.

ACTION FOR AND BY THE COMMUNITY

"In health efforts undertaken in and by rural communities, the initiative of the individual community must be captured by health planners through the active involvement of the community's residents" (Hatch and Earp, 1976, p. 243). Interventions for change will be successful depending on accurate assessment and joint cooperation among community leaders, the rural community health nurse, and other health planners. This will be discussed in "Preventive Nursing Care."

Although considered an asset, local participation alone cannot succeed in bringing about needed changes in relatively isolated and poor communities. Sainer et al. (1973) found that "when the black elderly took an active role in establishing their own social services, utilization improved because the elderly were able to establish those programs they felt were needed most" (p. 99). Community diagnosis and treatment are essential. This idea shifts the locus of orientation from customary professional care to the rural community for provision of their own health care.

A Guide for the Rural Community Health Nurse Regarding Legislation
FIRST, LEARN how and by whom the legislature is organized. Second, get involved in the legislative process by serving on community boards or committees. Finally, begin writing and/or presenting testimony before legislative committees.

The political activities of the rural community health nurse, then, involve working with community leaders, health-related groups, and groups at risk to accomplish relevant goals toward improved health for the aggregate.

Data from Clark, M. D.: Community Nursing. Reston, Virginia, Reston Publishing, 1984.

A community approach is concerned with the design and implementation of programs and policies to meet the health needs of identified populations. It "emphasizes working with the community to develop its ability for self-determination and self-reliance in health matters" (Gottshalk, 1980, p. 54). The rural community health nurse can assist the community through use of the nursing process and public health skills to take action for and by themselves in promoting health and preventing illness.

LEGISLATION AND POLITICAL ACTION

The future of nursing as well as health policy for the rural aggregate is dependent on legislative action. Rural community health nurses and rural residents must be aware of the power obtained through political action. They must develop a working knowledge of the health policy issues and politics of health care to articulate and meet their health needs. Since the 1950s, the federal government has extended aid for health facilities or increased manpower, enabling more of the underserved population to receive health care. Table 27–1 presents significant public health laws regarding rural health care.

Millions of dollars were spent in the 1970s to improve access to services in rural areas by enhancing provider recruitment. Rural communities are currently encouraged to obtain direct reimbursement by third-party carriers for primary care services provided by nurse practitioners. Consoli-

dation is recommended among program providers such as community health centers, Indian Health Services, and Veterans Administration hospitals to obtain the most from each health care dollar (Horowitz, 1986).

The political climate is ripe for programs offering a return to self-reliance. Although "self-responsibility cannot be legislated, it can be stimulated by an environment which gives value to self-reliant individuals. Holistic nursing is part of that environment" (Blattner, 1981, p. 61).

Several rural advocacy groups facilitate community participation, including the Rural American, the National Rural Center, the American Rural Health Association, and the National Rural Primary Care Association. Each group has the potential to strengthen lobbying efforts on behalf of rural citizens in America. "A community that has interest and monitors the performance and management of its health care programs will find its providers more responsive to local concerns" (Rosenblatt and Moscovice, 1982, p. 98).

If nurses want to be involved in policy making and health planning in support of needed changes in a rural community, they must be visible. By developing an operational knowledge of health

---

Table 27–1
Legislation Affecting Rural Populations

Year	Title and Summary
1957	Indian Health Assistance Act: Provided construction of health facilities for Native Americans.
1962	Migrant Health Act: Authorized federal aid for clinics serving migratory agricultural workers and families.
1968	Neighborhood Health Centers: Extended grant to migrant health services.
1970	Health Training Improvement Act: Provided expanded aid to allied health professions.
1971	Comprehensive Health Manpower Training Act: Increased federal programs for development of health manpower.
1973	Health Maintenance Organization and National Health Planning and Resource Development Act: Increased health insurance coverage for the rural population.
1974	Research on Aging: Established National Insitute on Aging within the National Institutes of Health
1976	National Consumer Health Information and Promotion Act: Provided necessary information and assistance to enable the individual to protect own health, i.e., self-responsibility.
1977	Rural Health Clinic Services Act: Provided medical services in areas with an insufficient number of physicians.
1981	Planned Approach to Community Health: Provided funding to states for delivery of preventive and health-promotive care to rural communities.
1986	Nurse Furnishing and Dispensing Bill in California: Permits nurse practitioners, under standardized procedures, affiliated with government agencies to furnish specified drugs or devices in clinics. Also allows registered nurses to dispense medicines in similar settings, children's health conferences, free clinics, and primary care facilities.

policy issues and politics and by becoming involved in the regional aggregate, the rural community health nurse can help a community attain their goals. The nurse must make realistic requests and always keep "table manners at health care smorgasbords" (Sundwall, 1986) to be most effective.

Bagwell (1980) stated, "It is encouraging to note that where nurses were able to develop a stronger sense of unity and common identity, they have been able to effect changes in practice acts that are more reflective of current health care demands" (p. 8). If a community can unite with the nurse and fight, the nursing profession will also be enhanced, although indirectly. To be heard, the rural community health nurse must be part of this decision-making process. Only through action will the rural community health nurse be visualized.

C a s e S t u d y

Application of the Nursing Process

Marta Diaz de la Rivera is a 43-year-old migrant worker. She moved to the United States from Mexico and married Jose Rivera 28 years ago. She has endured 13 pregnancies. She and Jose live with their two youngest daughters, who are ages 16 and 17, in a two-bedroom trailer home that is parked next to a migrant camp 15 miles from the nearest town. The other surviving seven children have married, although they remain in locations close to their parents and continue to travel with them as they work the fields.

For 2 months, Mrs. Diaz de la Rivera has been experiencing sweating episodes, a voracious appetite, and increased thirst. She appeared to be losing weight because her clothes were loose for the first time in 27 years. She felt run down and could not recover from a cold by treatment with teas and other familiar remedies. She thought her malady may be related to her 16-year-old daughter's recently announced pregnancy.

Experiencing a fainting spell finally prompted Mrs. Diaz de la Rivera to visit the nearest clinic, which was 25 miles away. She could not drive because she is illiterate, so one of her uncles brought her. Although not a Native American, she was seen at an Indian Health Service clinic.

The family nurse practitioner found blood sugar level of 289 mg%, weight of 200 pounds on a small-framed 5-foot-tall woman, and blood pressure of 158/94 mm Hg. Mrs. Diaz de la Rivera was diagnosed with diabetes mellitus, possible hypertension, and frank obesity. She had never heard of these diseases. She only knew that she was fat and worried a lot about her family. She had a tuberculin skin test and was told to return to the clinic in 2 days for a reading and chest x-ray, and in 1 week for clinical follow-up. Her only question was, "Can I go back to work today?"

Mrs. Diaz de la Rivera was sent home with the following recommended regimen:

- Stop work at least until return to clinic for follow-up.
- Inject insulin: 35 units NPH with 15 units Regular, every morning.
- Follow a 1,200-calorie American Diabetes Association weight reducing diet.
- Use a blood glucose-monitoring kit four times a day.
- Check and record blood pressure two or three times a day.

She was given pamphlets in the hope that her children could read them to her. Finally, she was to receive a home visit from a community health nurse within 24 hours.

A referral was called in to the county health department community health nurse supervisor, and a request was made for teaching regarding the complex medical regimen. A community health nurse received the referral that same afternoon and made her first visit the following morning. The nurse found that Mrs. Diaz de la Rivera had not begun the insulin injections. She was scared and lacked confidence in this new procedure. She did not understand why these shots were necessary, and she did not want to give them to herself. She had not understood that her symptoms were part of this uncontrolled disease; the family had had no time to read the pamphlets to her.

The community health nurse contacted the family nurse practitioner with a neighbor's telephone. She spoke about Mrs. Diaz de la Rivera and her home situation. Together, they worked out a care plan for the patient. The community health nurse returned to Mrs. Diaz de la Rivera's home to review the plan and obtain the patient's approval. Mrs. Diaz de la Rivera returned as scheduled to the clinic to find that she had had a positive purified protein derivative (PPD) reaction and thus would also need a chest radiograph and treatment for possible tuberculosis. Mrs. Diaz de la Rivera was even more worried, but she was willing to learn about how to care for herself and to try to prevent complications secondary to these illnesses.

Assessment

Data Collection

- Unaware of diseases and their chronicity or possible complications that could be prevented in the future
- Close-knit family
- Third-grade education in Mexico
- Speaks only Spanish
- Has unsuccessfully used methods of healing known to culture
- Traveled 25 miles to nearest health care facility
- Food is form of socialization; it is usually prepared by Mrs. Diaz de la Rivera and she is overweight

Planning

Community Diagnosis

- Ignorance of chronic health problems and their impact on self, family, and community
- Potential increased risk of tuberculosis for family and community
- Numerous uneducated or illiterate people among the migrants
- Language barrier
- Prevalence in use of cultural healers in migrant workers
- Few available health resources
- Prevalence of obesity
- Obesity in Mexican-American culture

Problem List

- Lack of knowledge of disease process, medications, diet, exercise, and other medical regimen
- Lack of health care education services regarding communicable disease
- Lack of programs to assist the illiterate
- Lack of bilingual health care workers
- Need to understand *curandero's* methods of healing
- Lack of health care services

Intervention

Prioritized Goals

- Increase knowledge regarding disease process
- Reduce impact of communicability
- Strengthen learning abilities
- Improve communication
- Improve cooperation between healing persons
- Increase resources
- Reduce risk of complications

Interventions

- Teach the client and her family about her diseases and their relationship with diet, activity, and activities of daily living.
- Test all family members.
- Teach all family members about tuberculosis.
- Use bilingual, pictures, and pamphlets.
- Obtain family help.
- Use interpreter from family, if possible.
- Discuss with *curandero* any methods she is using.
- Give information regarding regimen.
- Refer to community health worker to follow-up with care and instructions.
- Encourage support of family.
- Set up exercise program within the community.
- Refer to nutritionist.

Evaluation

- Family reads pamphlet and offers support and understanding to Mrs. Diaz de la Rivera
- All family receiving tuberculosis medication as necessary
- More confidence in knowledge
- Increased knowledge
- More bilingual helpers and translators
- The client feels respected
- Networking between resources

- Established trust with rural community health nurse
- More family nurse practitioners and mobile clinics with improved follow-up by patients
- Weight reduction
- Patient, family, and community health is improved
- Greater use of resources

Levels of Prevention

Primary Promotion of patient and family wellness

Individual

- Institute preventive health care of other chronic or communicable diseases.

Family

- Refer to community health nurse for education and follow-up.

Community

- Attend community education program regarding chronic diseases.

Secondary Reduce potential disability

Individual

- Educate patient regarding indicators of disease process.

Family

- Refer to community classes to learn more about chronic and communicable diseases.

Community

- Devise directory of available resources as they relate to education about chronic and communicable diseases.

Tertiary Encourage use of health services for evaluation and prevention of complications from chronic or communicable diseases.

Individual

- Educate Mrs. Diaz de la Rivera regarding foot care and signs and symptoms of neuropathy.

Family

- Refer to self-help group regarding diabetes mellitus.

Community

- Establish mobile health care unit to encourage routine evaluation for patients in this rural community.

Rural community health nurses must be familiar with the significant rural community issues, goals, perspectives, and needs. They need to be aware of the history, climate, job opportunities, and physical conditions in the geographical region being served. They must observe the interrelationships of the people in the community regarding their level of trust, support, and interaction. Finally, they must identify the needs of the rural aggregate in terms of the level of available health care.

Assessing the health care needs of a rural population requires collaboration with other disciplines and community leaders. This assessment identifies individuals, families, and aggregates at increased risk of illness, disability, or premature death. Interventions for the rural community are planned to reduce those at risk by developing needed resources that impact the greatest number of people. Finally, evaluation determines which activities and interventions have been successful or have made a significant contribution to the health status in terms of cost, benefits, and goal attainment.

The rural community health nurse assesses the need for nursing services by diagnosing deficits in relation to demand. More than the presence of a health problem is required. It is necessary to prioritize health problems for community action based on incidence, prevalence, and mortality. If a high accident rate is associated with a local main road, if half the community drinks alcohol to excess, or if there is a high rate of use of psychotropic drugs, the public should be informed so that community action can be taken. The nursing care plan must be designed and managed using innovative methods to meet the nursing goals for the rural aggregate.

Aggregate Support: Self-Care Theory

The deliberate behavior of initiating and performing actions on behalf of one's own health and well-being is defined as self-care. A self-care approach to rural health nursing is a dynamic, ongoing process that leads to community participation in making quality decisions regarding their own health. The rural community health nurse can apply this theory through the nursing process.

First, problem identification, an assessment of the community's ability to meet its health responsibilities, is made by looking at how the community functions as a whole. Assessment, then, would be the community diagnosis of health needs, de-

mands, and deficits. Planning, the second phase of the nursing process, would be the design of interventions to meet the goal of increased self-care for the entire aggregate. Implementation would increase the knowledge, skills, and motivation of the rural aggregate. Last, evaluation would monitor groups and involve judgments about the sufficiency and efficiency of the nursing action taken. Continuous evaluation helps determine whether health is impeded or fostered by the present process and indicates needed changes.

In providing health care for the rural aggregate, the rural community health nurse engages a holistic view, focusing on the preventive, nurturative, and health-promotive activities of the collective group. The self-care approach necessitates collaboration between the nurse and the rural community. The key to effective functioning is interaction — an exchange of materials, energies, and information through communication.

In self-care nursing for the rural aggregate, the belief is that the greater the community's ability to carry out its own care, the greater the level of health and satisfaction for the entire community. "Nursing care is designed either to increase the client's self-care abilities when this is possible or to compensate for limitations in client's own ability to meet the identified therapeutic self-care demand when it is not" (Hanchett, 1988, p. 17). The rural community health nurse encourages and collaborates with the rural population to take an active role in preventing illness and assume the primary responsibility for their own health. Providing support through the development of mutual help groups is one component of the extensive network for social and health services that may enhance self-care for the aggregate. Although many rural communities are now demanding relevant health services in which they can have an active role (Archer, 1982), there are many others who value health less and thus have a decreased awareness of their own potential for preventing problems. The rural community health nurse can educate these aggregates and thus promote increased wellness for everyone.

At times, government involvement has not strengthened the rural community's capacity for self-help. Early reliance has often resulted in dependence. As a result, the community becomes vulnerable to changes in government policies and programs and bureaucratic will. The rural community health nurse's actions and representation have been very sensitive to individual and community self-sufficiency, practicing the theory of self-care in a holistic manner and thereby potentiating high-level wellness for the aggregate.

Because everyone has a personal resource with which to achieve health, the community's resources will be a conglomerate. The nurse attempts to recover these resources and mobilize the community toward increased health and wellness. Therefore, applying self-care to the community means evaluating and improving health via lifestyle modification, effective coping styles, social support systems, and improved resources for the community as a whole. "Age, developmental level, life experience, sociocultural orientation, health and available resources affect ability to engage in purposeful self-care activities" (Orem, 1985, p. 35). The rural community health nurse is challenged to be part of this dynamic process.

Preventive Nursing Care

Preventive nursing activities are those that maintain and promote health and prevent further health disruption. Primary, secondary, and tertiary preventive activity levels, characteristic of rural community health nurses, are not mutually exclusive.

Primary prevention takes place before a health problem occurs, dealing with health-promotive activities before the onset of illness. This involves the earliest possible nursing intervention. The goal is to decrease the number of specific environmental risk factors in protection of the whole aggregate. As part of the community system, the rural community health nurse represents the public health department in focusing energies to promote optimum health and minimize or eliminate the loss of health. Mutual aid is an important vehicle of primary health care and health promotion. Nurses are an appropriate group to implement primary care services, which constitute the first element of a continuing health care process.

Secondary prevention most often occurs with the onset of the signs and symptoms of an acute illness, as occurred to Marta Diaz de la Rivera. It is not surprising that the rural community health nurse most often receives referrals for services at this level. If diagnosis and treatment interventions occur sufficiently early in the course of the condition, there can be a reduction in potential disabil-

ity. Secondary prevention focuses on the collaboration with the clinicians and patients to decrease impairments caused by the disease.

Tertiary prevention usually occurs after primary or secondary prevention. This level of care focuses on those suffering damage from a previous physical or mental illness condition. It could apply to the rural aggregate when several persons are adjusting to similar chronic conditions. Self-help groups could be started with assistance from health care providers to gradually decrease the physical or emotional reactions and increase activities. Stroke victims are one example of a population in whom tertiary prevention could minimize loss of function and return the entire aggregate to an optimal level of wellness.

The difference between secondary and tertiary preventive care lies in the focus of the problem as viewed by family members (Freidemann, 1983). In secondary prevention, the family sees the patient as passive and in need of care, whereas in tertiary prevention, the focus is on the patient's initiative to gain strength and regain previous skills and abilities. The rural community health nurse can be the impetus in keeping communication open in the family and within the rural community.

The Role of the Rural Community Health Nurse

The chief purpose of rural health nursing is to assist rural populations in achieving their full potential via good health. The rural community health nurse has a more independent and challenging role than the traditional hospital nurse in acting as part of health promotion and maintenance systems within a rural community. The role calls for creativity and resourcefulness beyond that needed in most urban areas.

As Freidemann (1983, p. V) stated, "Many nursing students today come to this subject of rural or community health nursing with the belief that it is less important and less exciting than 'real' nursing . . . the kind that takes place in emergency rooms and intensive care units where nursing the acutely ill patient is often a matter of life or death." With the movement toward preventive health care, the expansion of outpatient care services, diagnosis-related groups, and the prospective payment systems, there has been a sudden shift of patients from acute care settings to home care agencies. The rural community health nurse is challenged to be part of the community team comprising community participants, other health care providers, and administrators. Through outpatient and home health services, the nurse promotes and preserves the health of the rural aggregate working to make major health decisions.

In the case study, the rural community health nurse helped coordinate and develop resources to meet the needs of Mrs. Diaz de la Rivera and her family for care and health instruction. Through the development of mutual trust among individuals, families, and other rural resources, the nurse can carry out the role of community health advocate.

Rural Community Health Nurse Functions

- PROVIDES DIRECT nursing care in the home
- Facilitates health promotion for the aggregate
- Procures medical equipment and medicines as needed
- Acts as advocate for the community in assisting with communication and feedback
- Optimizes client use of and access to health care services
- Functions as a referral agent to client and community
- Acts as liaison between community and their health care providers
- Becomes a health resource to and for the aggregate
- Identifies health problems early through screening tests
- Teaches and counsels the community system health promotion

- Becomes liaison between families and community resources
- Organizes social support systems for individual and families
- As consultant, enables independence of mutual help groups
- Reduces risk factors and improves health of those at risk
- Fosters meaningful community involvement in attaining health-related goals
- Facilitates communication process between families and communities
- Demonstrates a sensitivity to variant groups in rural areas
- Evaluates programs serving the rural residents

The rural community health nursing role is demonstrated most clearly through the provision of primary, secondary, and tertiary preventive care to the rural aggregate. Descriptions of the multiple functions of the rural community health nurses are listed. These general roles are shared with the community health nurse but must be applied to the unique rural aggregate.

Two of the most significant roles for the rural community health nurse are those of referral agent and liaison for the community. As a referral agent, the nurse explores available resources and directs clients to these resources. This is a challenging role because of the limited supply of resources in rural areas. The rural community health nurse can advise self-help groups of the availability of nurses to serve as "temporary" consultants, speakers, or members of advisory boards on an invitation-only basis. Should an emergency occur, the appropriate resource could be mobilized to assist those in need.

The nurse can also advance health promotion and primary care through linkage with community help groups.

To communicate and problem solve with other disciplines, the rural community health nurse will need scientific rationale and creative skills. As advocate to the community, the nurse can help "organize and present grievances to governing bodies, insisting on consumer membership within decision-making bodies, and become involved in political activities at local, state and national levels" (Gulino and LaMonica, 1986, p. 84).

Many Americans are interested in improving their health. This may make the role of the rural community health nurse easier as individuals desire to participate in health promotion issues within their own community. More attention is being paid to sound nutrition and improved exercise. However, unique subcultures often involve a focus on diseases rather than on how to change the situation and reduce risk of illness; the rural community health nurse remains challenged to keep a clear focus on early prevention and on the entire community's desire for change.

Braden (1984, p. 411) stated, "Community health nurses who persistently provide quality service during the 10,000th home visit, who consistently address themselves to the needs of multiple-problem aggregates, who assertively advocate for quality provision of comprehensive, coordinated health care, who seek vantage points that can provide objectivity, who introspectively assess their own personal and professional attributes and who aggressively look for knowledge and skills, are the nurses who *will* make the difference."

RESEARCH IN RURAL HEALTH

Research in rural areas has been conducted for many years by many members of the behavioral science professions. Nursing research is a newer phenomenon, especially for the rural community health nurse. More recent studies have taken place in the community health nursing field, and these can be extrapolated to the role of the rural community health nurse. A descriptive approach has been used in defining the community health nurse and the nurse's role (Gulino and LaMonica, 1986), collaboration of the community health nurse with other health care providers (Pesznecker et al., 1982), and definitions of health behaviors (Laffrey et al., 1986). Each descriptive study gives the field of community health nursing more foundation on which to build.

Rural Efforts to Assist Children at Home is a service and training project that provides specialized health care and supportive services to chronically ill children in a 16-county area of Florida (Pierce and Weiss, 1986). Nurses who live in these rural communities are specially trained to serve as case managers to design and implement complex care plans in the home environment. They use the problem-oriented record, which has made it easier to evaluate their effectiveness. The study by Pierce and Weiss considers the problem-oriented record system of recording to provide information for future nurses.

More research is needed for and by rural community health nurses. Urbano et al. (1985) estab-

lished a research process to be used by community health nursing agencies. Their protocol provides objective guidelines for cost-effectiveness, organizational policies, and the use of nurse investigators, agencies, and research subjects. The steps listed can be used as a standard procedure for nursing research in rural areas as well as the encouragement needed for more rural community health nurses to contribute to nursing as a science and a profession.

SUMMARY

Rural community health nurses require a sound theoretical knowledge base as well as communication, caring, and problem-solving skills to make a significant contribution to the health of a rural community. Rural community health nurses are unique and have the potential to offer the continuity, comprehension, and coordination of services that are needed in a rural community. Understanding community organization and its development assists the rural community health nurse in helping the aggregate to articulate their health needs. The nurse plans health care programs and services and evaluates them in relation to their impact on health. Bolstered by experiences, nurses apply these skills to the community and watch health promotion in progress.

Rural health problems are numerous and are the result of lifestyle, cultural, and health beliefs. These problems include heart conditions, chronic arthritis, hypertension, visual impairment, mental illness, and alcohol abuse with resultant drinking-and-driving mortalities. The prevalence of the problems in rural compared with city life shows the increased need for rural mental health services and curative, preventive, and health-promotive activities. The rural community health nurse can be a facilitator of these services and a liaison for the rural aggregate.

Effective service delivery to the rural community is challenging, time consuming, and rewarding. The community constitutes the ebb and flow through the health network and brings meaning to the role of the rural community health nurse. The ultimate effect of a sensitive, sincere, and fully functioning rural community health nurse is improved community health status and an eagerness to work toward increased wellness of all ages and subcultures that make up the rural aggregate.

Learning Activities

1. Examine the vital statistics within your county, if possible, and compare the inhabitants' age, wage index, and health care facilities with those of the inhabitants of the county seat.

2. Over a 1-month period, determine the frequency of newspaper articles in your major newspaper that discuss health and/or health care compared with a rural newspaper.

3. Survey businesses and industries in your rural community to determine what health services are offered or covered by a company for its employees. (Note whether this is seasonal work.)

4. Select a family in your caseload that resides in a rural community. Devise a nursing care plan for each individual and family as a unit. Determine how their needs can be met with available resources. (If this is difficult, imagine the experiences of each rural community comprised of families and individuals with varied needs.)

5. Review periodicals related to rural health. Identify the top three issues discussed regarding inaccessible or unaffordable health care in the rural area.

REFERENCES

American Nurses' Association: Standards of Community Health Nursing Practice. Kansas City, Missouri, ANA, 1974.

Archer, S. E.: Marketing Public Health Nursing Services. Presented at the American Public Health Association; Montreal, Canada, 1982.

Bagwell, M.: The nursing network—A united front. Nurs. Leadership 3;5–8, 1980.

Bauer, J. C.: Trends in Rural Health Care Delivery: Progressive Non-hospital Alternatives. In LaVonne, S., and Walzer, N., eds.: Financing Rural Health Care. New York, Praeger, 1988, pp. 83–97.

Blattner, B.: Holistic Nursing. Englewood Cliffs, New Jersey, Prentice-Hall, 1981.

Braden, C.: The Focus and Limits of Community Health Nursing. Norwalk, Connecticut, Appleton-Century-Crofts, 1984.

Brown, W. P., and Hadwiger, D. F.: Rural Policy/Problems: Changing Dimensions. Lexington, Massachusetts, Lexington Books, 1982.

Clark, M. D.: Community Nursing. Reston, Virginia, Reston Publishing, 1984.

Cornman, J. M.: Rural Poverty and Economic Development. Washington, D.C., National Rural Center, Sept. 15, 1981.

Elison, G. T.: Frontier Health Care. Presented at the National Rural Health Care Association Conference, San Diego, California, May, 1986.

Fickenscher, K. M.: Maximizing Resources in a Restrained Environment. In Straub, L., and Walzer, N., eds.: Financing Rural Health Care. New York, Praeger, 1988, pp. 129–147.

Freidemann, M. L.: Manual for Effective Community Health Nursing Practice. Monterey, California, Wadsworth Health Sciences Division, 1983.

Gabel, J., Cohen, H., and Fink, S.: American's views on health care. Health Affairs Spring 8(1):103–108, 1989.

Geary, J., and Crane, J.: Following the migrant stream. In Hall, J. E., and Weaver, B. R., eds.: Distributive Nursing Practice: A Systems Approach to Community Health. Philadelphia, J. B. Lippincott, 1985, pp. 506–517.

Goldmark, J.: Nursing and Nursing Education in the United States. New York, Macmillan, 1923.

Gottshalk, J.: Nursing and Community Development. In Flynn, B., and Miller, M., eds.: Current Issues in Nursing. St. Louis, C. V. Mosby, 1980, pp 47–68.

Gulino, C., and LaMonica, G.: Public Health Nursing: A Study of Role Implementation. Public Health Nurs. 3;80–91, 1986.

Hanchett, E. S.: Nursing Frameworks and Community as Client; Bridging the Gap. San Mateo, California, Appleton & Lange, 1988.

Hassinger, E. W., and Whiting, L. R.: Rural Health Services: Organization, Delivery, and Use. Ames, Iowa, Iowa State University Press, 1976.

Hatch, J., and Earp, J.: Consumer Involvement in the Delivery of Health Services. In Hassinger, E. W., and Whiting, L. R., eds.: Rural Health Services. Ames, Iowa, Iowa State University Press, 1976, pp. 243–259.

Horowitz, D.: Frontier Health Care. Presented at the National Rural Health Care Association Conference, San Diego, California, May 1986.

Laffrey, S. C., Carol J. L., and Winkler, S. J.: Health behavior: Evolution of two paradigms. Public Health Nurs. 3;92–100, 1986.

Marriner, A.: Management moves. Nurs. Success 3;8–13, 1986.

Milio, N.: Chains of impact for Reaganomics on primary care policies. Public Health Nurs. 1;65–73, 1984.

Morris, E. W., and Winter, M.: Housing. In Dillman, D. A., and Hobbs, D. J., eds.: Rural Society in the U.S.: Issues for the 80's. Boulder, Colorado, Westview Press, 1982, pp. 196–204.

Orem, D. E.: Nursing Concepts of Practice. New York, McGraw-Hill, 1985.

Pesznecker, B., Draye, M., and McNeil, J.: Collaborative Practice Models in Community Health Nursing. Nurs. Outlook *30*;298–302, 1982.

Pesznecker, B. L., and Zahlis, E.: Establishing mutual-help groups for family-member care givers: A new role for community health nurses. Public Health Nurs. *3*;29–38, 1986.

Pierce, P. M., and Weiss, D. E.: REACH: Monitoring home-based nursing support. Nurs. Management *17*;33–36, 1986.

Reinert, B. R.: The health care beliefs and values of Mexican-Americans. Home Healthcare Nurse *4*;36–44, 1986.

Rodman, A. D., Misak, J. E., and Taylor, C. L.: HIV seroprevalence in migrant and seasonal farmworkers. Migrant Health (Clin. Suppl.) *5*(4):3–4, 1988.

Roemer, M. I.: Rural Health Care. St. Louis, C. V. Mosby, 1976.

Rosenblatt, R. A., and Moscovice, I. S.: Rural Health Care. New York, John Wiley & Sons, 1982.

Sainer, J., Schwartz, L., and Jackson, T.: Steps in the development of a comprehensive delivery system for the elderly. Gerontologist *13*;98–102, 1973.

Sienkiewicz, J. I.: Patient classification in community health nursing. Nurs. Outlook *32*;319–321, 1984.

Smith, D.: Primary care implications of HIV infection. Migrant Health Newsline (Clin. Suppl.) *5*(4):1–3, 1988.

Sullivan, J. A.: Directions in Community Health Nursing. Cambridge, Massachusetts, Blackwell Scientific Publications, 1984.

Sundwall, D.: Current Legislative Issues in Rural Health. Presented at the National Rural Health Care Association Conference, San Diego, California, May 1988.

Swanson, B. E., and Swanson, E.: Public policy of rural health. *In* Hassinger, E. W., and Whiting, L. R., eds.: Rural Health Services. Ames, Iowa, Iowa State University Press, 1976, pp. 137–163.

Talbot, D. M.: Assessing the needs of the rural elderly. J. Gerontol. Nurs. *11*;39–43, 1985.

Tinkham, C. W., Voorhies, E. F., and McCarthy, N. C.: Community Health Nursing. Norwalk, Connecticut, Appleton-Century-Crofts, 1984.

Urbano, M. T., Dolan, J. B., Von Windeguth, B. J., and Brellis, H. K.: Establishing a research process for community health nursing agencies. Home Healthcare Nurse *3*;18–22, 1985.

U.S. Bureau of the Census and Department of Agriculture: Current Population Reports: Rural and Rural Farm Population. Washington, D.C., U.S. Bureau of the Census, series P-20, publication No. 439, 1989.

U.S. Bureau of Census: Characteristics of Rural and Farm Related Population. Washington, D.C., U.S. Bureau of the Census, publication No. PC 80-2.9 C, Vol. 2, 1980.

U.S. Congress: Staff paper from Health Program Office of Technology Assessment re Rural Health Care by Hewitt, M. Washington, D.C., U.S. Government Printing Office, Congress Print No. Y3.722/2: 2R88, July 1989.

U.S. Department of Agriculture and Economic Research Service: Rural Conditions Chartbook: Rural Development Research Report 43, 1985.

U.S. Department of Health, Education and Welfare: Healthy People: the Surgeon General's Report on Health Promotion and Disease Prevention Background Papers. Washington, D.C., U.S. Government Printing Office, DHEW (PHS) publication No. 79-55071A, 1979.

U.S. Senate hearing before the Committee on the Budget: 100th Congress, 2nd Session. Senate Hearing No. 100-724. Washington, D.C., May 1988, pp. 1–140.

U.S. Senate: Staff report to Special Committee on Aging: The Rural Health Care Challenge. Washington, D.C., U.S. Government Printing Office, Senate Print No. 100-145, October 1988.

5

The Future of Community Health Nursing

Upon completion of this chapter, the reader will be able to:

1. Identify three forces that threaten life and health worldwide.

2. Define population-focused nursing.

3. Describe Cuba's model of population-focused nursing.

Janice M. Swanson
Karen A. Swanson

Health, our most valuable possession, is a primary concern in every society, and nurses, as health care providers, are becoming aware of their responsibility to help ensure the valuable possession of health in persons of all societies. To carry out this responsibility, community health nurses must be aware of forces that threaten health and study models of health care delivery in other countries that may promote the well-being of the greatest number of people.

This chapter will highlight selected health problems and challenges that health care professionals and citizens face and share. Then, a model of population-focused health care delivery by nurses in Cuba is presented. This model can serve as an inspiration to community health nurses as they endeavor to ensure the health of all persons in their communities.

Among the many health issues that merit attention and study because of their global effects and threat to human life are population growth, environmental stressors, and disease.

In any society, large populations create pressure. For example, in developing countries, feeding a population may become problematic if famine or problems with international trade occur. Malnutrition, disease, or death may be the outcome. Pressures from population growth are also felt in industrialized nations. Although food may be plentiful, overcrowding may lead to pollution, stress, and violence.

World population growth is often overlooked as a health-related problem, yet current rapid growth presents a threat to the health and economies of many nations. The exponential nature of world population growth is evident in information from the World Health Organization (WHO) (1990) (Fig. 28–1). In 1800, after 2–5 billion years of human existence, the world population was only about 1 billion people. In the next 130 years, from 1800 to 1927, it grew to 2 billion, and in only 33 more years, from 1927 to 1960, it reached 3 billion. In less than half of that time, the 14 years from 1960 to 1974, the fourth billion was added, and astonishingly, it took only the 13 years from 1974 to 1987 to add the fifth billion. Furthermore, WHO estimates that by 1998, the world population will grow to 6 billion; by 2005, to 7 billion; and by 2015, to 8 billion.

In 1987, when the world population reached 5 billion, distribution was uneven; 52% lived in only

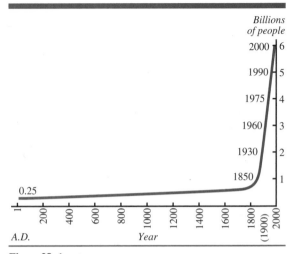

Figure 28–1
The J-shaped curve of world population growth. (Redrawn from Environmental Science: An Introduction by G. Tyler Miller, Jr. © 1986 by Wadsworth, Inc. Reprinted by permission of current copyright owner, Boston: Jones and Bartlett Publishers.)

five countries: China, India, U.S.S.R., the United States, and Indonesia. One third of the world's population were children, and 6% were elderly (age 65 or older).

Between 1985 and 1990, the world population grew by 87 million per year, with distribution remaining uneven; 81 million lived in developing countries and approximately 6 million lived in developed countries (WHO, 1990). During the same period, 50 million people died each year — 39 million in developing countries and 11 million in developed countries (WHO, 1990). Life expectancies were 73.4 years in developed countries and only 59.7 years in developing countries.

As the world's population grows, there is a rising global trend toward urbanization; people live closer together and migrate to urban areas for employment. In 1975, for example, 38.5% of the world's population lived in urban areas. By 1990, the proportion of urban dwellers swelled to 42.7%, and this proportion is expected to reach 60.5% by 2025. With increasingly dense living arrangements, the health of the general population is threatened by environmental stressors and disease.

An important component of both individual and world health is the relationship between humans and their environment. Environmental stressors can be categorized into four types:

- Stressors that directly assault human health, e.g., lead poisoning
- Stressors that damage society's goods and services, e.g., air pollution's effects on buildings
- Stressors that damage the quality of life, e.g., noise and litter
- Stressors that interfere with ecological balance and other forms of life (Banister et al., 1988)

Air, water, and land pollution are among the consequences of environmental stressors. For example, the chemical pollutant carbon monoxide makes up 50% of the worldwide air pollution problem, and other primary pollutants, such as nitrogen monoxide, sulfur oxides, particulates, and hydrocarbons, combine with carbon monoxide to create 90% of pollution worldwide (Banister et al., 1988). One contributing factor to water pollution is that only 66% of the world's urban population and 17% of rural areas have sanitation facilities (Banister et al., 1988).

Agricultural, industrial, residential, and commercial wastes increase land pollution. For example, chemical fertilizers have displaced natural fertilizers; synthetic pesticides have displaced natural means of pest control; and petrochemical products, such as detergents, synthetic fiber, and plastics, have replaced soap, cotton, and paper. Throwaway goods have replaced reusable goods and increased trash for disposal. Production technologies are contributing to worldwide environmental stress.

Because disease patterns vary throughout the world, primary causes of mortality differ in developed and developing countries. Primary causes of mortality in developed countries are cardiovascular disease, cancer, respiratory disease, stroke, violence, and accidents, whereas primary causes of mortality in developing countries are infections, malnutrition, and violence (Fry, 1985). Through improved sanitation, nutrition, and medical care, developed countries, once plagued with high rates of infectious disease, have overcome high rates of deaths due to these diseases. However, developed countries are now plagued by chronic diseases such as coronary heart disease, respiratory disease, and cancer (Banister et al., 1988).

Among the infectious diseases that contribute to high rates of mortality in developing countries are hepatitis B, rheumatic heart disease, hookworm infection, and endemic malaria; these diseases claim the lives of millions (Banister et al., 1988). Worldwide, 2 million children die annually from measles, and 600,000 children die from whooping cough; poliomyelitis affects 275,000 children, and tuberculosis affects as many as 10 million persons annually (Henderson, 1987).

AIDS is one disease that is shared globally. Ten percent of the population of central Africa is estimated to be infected, and in early 1990, between 5 and 10 million persons worldwide were thought to be infected with HIV (Banister et al., 1988; WHO, 1990). The U.S. Surgeon General estimates that 100 million people worldwide could die from AIDS by 2000 (Banister et al., 1988).

Promoting health worldwide is humankind's biggest challenge. In response to this challenge, WHO created a program of low-technology health care called "Health for All by the Year 2000," which is designed to prevent disease in poor countries. Only 10% of a poor country's gross national product is needed to reach this goal of health through clean air, vaccination, contraception, essential drugs, and mother and child health care (Banister et al., 1988). The program is population based and designed to take the majority of the health care out of urban areas and disperse it throughout communities. It is designed to reach an entire population and build health services based on the needs of the people through their involvement in the formation of policy and planning. In effect, it calls for people-oriented technologies rather than specialized medical technologies in efforts to enable communities to become self-reliant.

When it comes to health care practices, developed countries, which are heavily dependent on specialized medical technologies, are not appropriate models for developing countries. In fact, the health care policy in many developed countries is currently making health care inaccessible to the general public. Even in countries with socialist governments, medical costs increase annually, and citizens are faced with paying supplemental medical fees. In Great Britain, inequalities in health between the upper and lower classes are increasing despite a National Health Service (Townsend, 1990). In the United States, health care is exceeding 12% of the gross national product, yet between an estimated 34 to 37 million uninsured Americans cannot afford health care. Because the market-based developed countries treat health care as a commodity to be bought and sold, they focus on

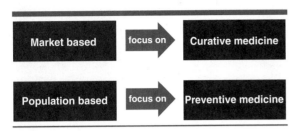

Figure 28–2
Health care approaches.

curative medicine because it creates more capital than does preventative medicine. Therefore, market-based health care systems lead to a goal opposite that of health for all by 2000 (Fig. 28–2).

Given the two basic health care systems—market based and population based—it is evident which paradigm nursing must seek out, implement, and finally establish to better promote health throughout the world. Although no one model of health care delivery will be effective in every country, the following account describes the health care system of one country that successfully implemented health care for all in the face of heavy economic sanctions. In 1985, Cuba was recognized for reaching the WHO goal of health for all (American Public Health Association, 1985). This country has proved to the world that health care does not have to be a privilege but can be provided as a basic human right.

REFERENCES

American Public Health Association: Edward Barsky Award presented to Sergio Del Valle, Cuban Minister of Health, at the Physician's Forum. Government Responsibility and the People's Health. Presented at the 113th annual meeting of the American Public Health Association. November 18, 1985.

Banister, E. W., Allen, M., Fadl, S., Bhakthan, G., and Howard, D.: Contemporary Health Issues. Boston, Jones and Bartlett, 1988.

Fry, J.: Common Diseases: Their Nature, Incidence and Care. 4th Ed. Boston, MTP Press, 1985.

Henderson, R. H.: EPI: Shots that save lives. World Health. Jan./Feb.; 4–7, 1987.

Townsend, P.: Widening inequalities of health in Britain: A rejoinder to Rudolph Klein. Int. J. Health Serv. *20*;363–372, 1990.

World Health Organization: Global Estimates for Health Situation Assessment and Projections 1990. Geneva, World Health Organization, 1990.

Nursing in Cuba: Population-Focused Practice*

Janice M. Swanson

THE AUTHORS of this chapter traveled to Cuba in 1992. The continuing progress of the model of "Health for All," achieved by Cuba in 1985, is evident in the following statistics, reported by Cuba's Ministry of Public Health, 1990.

Life expectancy continues to increase and was 75.2 years in 1989. Infant mortality also continued to decline and reached 11.1 deaths per 1,000 live births in 1989. In the 1990–1991 school year, 7,970 nurses were enrolled in the baccalaureate nursing program from which they will receive their *licenciatura* degree. The distribution of the neighborhood home/clinics, which places a nurse-physician team with every 120 families in the community, is completed in more than half of the country. All nurses must participate in carrying out a research or other scholarly project annually to ensure promotion and increased wages (L. Placeres Abreu, personal communication, April 29, 1992).

In the United States, nursing practice occurs largely within the prevailing model of health care delivery, that of fee-for-service for those who seek care. In Cuba, nursing practice occurs within a model of health care delivery that is distributed geographically and available to the entire population at no cost.

In the United States, population-focused nursing practice is a widely advocated approach within community health nursing to improve the health of the entire population (Williams, 1984). Williams (1984) defined a population focus as the fundamental distinction of community health nursing. Community health nursing practice synthesizes knowledge from the public health sciences and nursing theory to improve the health of all the people in the community (American Public Health Association, 1981). A population focus has the following characteristics: (1) nursing needs are approached in a scientific manner; (2) problems are defined and solutions proposed at the population or subpopulation level; (3) the focus includes more

than one subpopulation, that is, numerous and overlapping populations extending to the entire community; (4) attention is extended to those in need who do not seek care as well as those who do; and (5) concentration is on matching the health needs of a community and its resources (Williams, 1984).

Examples of population-focused community health nursing practice in the United States include the following: (1) Dreher's (1984) district nurses who served whole townships in New England; (2) public health nurses serving on reservations in the Indian Health Service; (3) the American Nurses' Association (ANA) proposed legislation for community nursing centers (Gleeson, 1984); and (4) block nursing in Minnesota, matching elders with health care needs and nurses in a geographic area (Martinson et al., 1985).

While each program presents a facet of population-focused practice, each experiences constraints to serving all the people in the community. Although comprehensive in outlook, programs are limited to serving only selected segments of the population. In Cuba, community health nursing is population-based practice that integrates a population focus, mobilization of the community for health, primary care, community health care, and home health care. That is, it is comprehensive and practiced within a geographic base, nationwide, extending to and serving all the persons in the community.

The system of health services that provides health care on a geographic basis to all is called *medicine in the community* (Danielson, 1979, 1985). Little is known, however, about nursing's evolution of population focus since the time of the revolution (Garfield, 1981; Swanson, 1981).

This paper describes Cuba's approach to population-focused nursing practice in the community. Information is based on travel to Cuba in 1978 and 1985; formal interviews arranged by the Ministry of Public Health with a nurse from that Ministry and a director of a school of nursing, both of which were tape recorded; interviews with leaders and members of community organizations, health workers, patients, and citizens; a review of Cuban nursing journals at the Biblioteca Nacional de Medicina (National Library of Medicine) in 1985; field visits to hospitals, both urban and rural, polyclinics, a neighborhood home/clinic, and a school of nursing; and visits to a work site, schools, churches, and homes.

---

*Adapted from Public Health Nursing, Vol. 4, No. 3, pp. 183–191, 1987. Reprinted by permission of Blackwell Scientific Publications, Inc.

THE ETHICS OF HEALTH CARE IN THE UNITED STATES AND CUBA

Market Justice

The United States' ideology of health, derived from a capitalist industrial system, subscribes to a market-justice model of health care delivery. In this model, people are entitled only to what they have achieved through their own individual efforts (Beauchamp, 1986). Health care is seen as a consumer good, dispensed by individual physicians and purchased by the consumer. In 1983, the United States spent 10.8% of its gross national product on health care. Yet, despite soaring expenditures in the health marketplace, considerable numbers of its citizens are in poor health and receive little or no health care at all (National Center for Health Statistics, 1984; President's Commission for the Study of Ethical Problems in Medicine and Biomedical and Behavioral Research, 1983). Available health care services in the United States are oriented to acute care, fragmented, poorly distributed, and not accessible to all. With cost containment a goal in this country, growth is expected to continue among models such as health maintenance organizations (HMOs), preferred provider organizations (PPOs), and other primary care facilities offering outpatient/ambulatory care centers, home health, and other community health agencies (Curtin, 1985). Predictions are that nurses will move out of hospital employment into alternative delivery systems such as these and others to meet a growing proportion of health needs, particularly in the areas of disease prevention and health promotion, as well as cost containment (Curtin, 1985). Neither the current nor predicted delivery system of health care in the United States is population based, however, and thus both fail to provide services to all the people in the community. They subscribe to the prevailing market model, that of fee-for-service, which is limited to those who seek services and can afford them.

Public Health as Social Justice

Public health ascribes to health as a basic right of all people and to disease prevention as the primary goal of health care. In a social justice model, the government, charged with furthering the health and welfare of its citizens, is responsible to see that everyone receives needed basic health care to the extent that public resources allow. Before the revolution in 1959, Cuba also had a market model of health care, with a large portion of the population without access to health care services. The revolution brought equity in basic necessities of living such as income, jobs, nutrition, and health protection. Cuba, a socialist society, subscribes to the social justice model of health. This model ensures that all persons are entitled to health protection and welfare, the burden of which is shared collectively to prevent "powerful forces of environment, heredity or social structure" from keeping this reality from some while allowing disproportionate access to others (Beauchamp, 1986).

Since 1959 the government of Cuba has taken full responsibility for the health of its people. In 1983, 7.8% of its national budget was spent on health care (Danielson, 1985). In contrast to the market model in the United States, Cuba guarantees universal health care coverage to all persons at no cost. Cuba was recognized for already having achieved the World Health Organization's goal of "health for all by the year 2000" at the annual meeting of the American Public Health Association in 1985 (American Public Health Association, 1985). It has evolved a model of health care with a focus on prevention. Through a geographically based network, preventive health care services are population focused and thus serve all the people in the community.

CHANGES IN HEALTH STATUS SINCE THE REVOLUTION

As in many developing countries, Cuba at the time of the revolution was faced with low rates of life expectancy at birth (age 57 years in 1958), high rates of infant mortality (70 deaths per 1,000 live births), high rates of mortality from infectious disease (94.4 per 1,000 population), high rates of illiteracy (one in four adults), unemployment, poor housing, and malnutrition (Halebsky and Kirk, 1985; Valdes-Brito and Henriquez, 1983). Through active participation of the people, both social change and health care services greatly improved the health status of the population (Danielson, 1979, 1985; Garfield, 1981). Life expectancy has increased more than 16 years and infant mortality has fallen by more than one half from 1958 to 1982 (Danielson, 1985). Major causes of mortality shifted from infectious diseases to chronic diseases (Ministerio de Salud Publica, 1983). Acute diarrheal disease, the major cause of infant death in 1962, fell to be the fifth cause of infant death in 1983 (Ministerio de Salud Publica, 1983). The incidence of tuberculosis, typhoid fever, and tetanus has decreased, and poliomyelitis, malaria, and diphtheria have been eradicated (Ministerio de Salud Publica, 1983; Valdes-Brito and Henriquez, 1983).

Social action brought about major social change that was needed for development and improvement in health status. For example, rates of adult illiteracy decreased from 25% to 4% in 1961 as a result of a year-long, countrywide literacy campaign by young persons, many of whom later became nurses (Kozol, 1978; Garfield, 1981). Slums were redeveloped, new housing was built, and existing housing was improved through the use of volunteers; unemployment was all but eliminated. Essential foods were rationed and prices were lowered to guarantee minimum nutritional levels for all. Educational and employment opportunities, in addition to child care and family planning, brought about marked change in the status of women (Halebsky and Kirk, 1985).

POPULATION-BASED NURSING PRACTICE

How the health care system and the professionalization of nursing evolved since the time of the revolution are reported in depth elsewhere (Danielson, 1979, 1985; Garfield, 1981). The population focus for nursing practice in Cuba as it grew within the health care system is highlighted here. This growth has been incremental. Succeeding phases incorporate practice from the previous phase(s), yet each is distinguished by practice that has extended to the entire population. Early mobilization efforts in the community preceded the addition of primary care and community health care in the geographically based polyclinic (community health center). Most recently, polyclinics serve as backup resources to the even more finely distributed neighborhood home/clinics that, in addition to the above areas of practice, integrate home health care.

Early Mobilization of the Community for Health: 1959–1964

At the time of the revolution, "nursing as a whole was employed and dominated by . . . private medicine" (Garfield, 1981, p. 65). During a period of transition, the Ministry of Public Health took comprehensive authority in all health matters (Danielson, 1985). Major changes included the following: public health, hospitals, and pharmacy services were regionalized; all medical care was free in public institutions; and preventive and rural health care programs were created.

The shift in the larger health care system to an ideology of public health affected nursing. One of the earliest changes was the demand for nursing's involvement in the community to help carry out the major philosophy of the new system: (1) to guarantee all persons the right to health; (2) to implement the government's full responsibility for the health of the people; (3) to carry out prevention as a primary goal of health care; and (4) to increase community participation in health. The community, from village to city, was organized block by block into organizations such as the Committees for the Defense of the Revolution (CDRs) and the Federation of Cuban Women (FMC), to which almost all citizens belong. Mobilization of citizens to participate in sanitation and immunization campaigns through the block organizations was facilitated by health education and preventive activities by nurses.

For example, in 1960 sanitary brigades of nurses were organized to help community groups such as the CDR and the Association of Small Farmers (ANAPs) improve environmental hygiene. To reduce infectious and parasitic disease, they undertook neighborhood efforts to clean up litter and garbage, to eliminate mosquito-breeding sites around homes, to wear shoes, and to boil drinking water (Tesh, 1986). Nurses and other health professionals were involved in coordinating early immunization campaigns carried out largely by mass organizations such as the CDR and FMC. The organizations took information to persons in the community, such as neighbors, day-care centers, and other organizations. Mass media including television, radio, and newspapers helped to educate the people about diseases that could be prevented by vaccines. Health commissions formed at local, regional, provincial, and national levels by the Ministry of Public Health planned for transport, storage, and distribution of vaccines. Through joint efforts, the entire at-risk population of Cuba was immunized against polio in 1 day (Gilpin and Rodriguez-Trias, 1978).

Nurses worked closely with organizations such as the CDR and the FMC for help in obtaining early attention to many health needs (Junco et al., 1980). For example, the FMC worked in neighborhoods to educate women and girls about sexuality, the need for early pregnancy testing, prenatal care, hospital births, and cervical tests.

In 1962, nursing was placed under the administrative control of the Ministry of Public Health (Garfield, 1981). By 1964, demands on the profession were again increased, as close to half of Cuba's 6,300 physicians and many nurses had fled the island by then, most to the United States. Expansion of hospitals, especially in rural areas, also created a need for more nurses. Nursing education was formalized and expanded during this period to meet these needs (Garfield, 1981; Danielson, 1985).

The Polyclinics: Integrating Primary Care and Community Health: 1965–1985

The years between 1965 and 1985 were marked by the consolidation of services under the Ministry of Public Health and the distribution of primary care and community health centers throughout the country. Consolidation included incorporation of existing private practice and prepaid medical plans into the public sector, and takeover of the remaining private hospitals by the Ministry of Public Health, both of which occurred by 1970 (Danielson, 1985; Garfield, 1981). A system of national health planning was also begun.

GEOGRAPHICALLY DISTRIBUTED PRIMARY CARE/COMMUNITY HEALTH CENTERS

Polyclinics, or community health centers, are distributed geographically throughout the island. Each one addresses the health needs of a specific catchment area of approximately 25,000 persons, divided into geographic sectors, or service areas of about 3,000 persons. Services are available to ev-

eryone in the community and cover every geographic area in the country. A range of services is located in the polyclinic: clinical, community health, social, and environmental. Thus, the same organization that provides clinical and social services also provides typical public health services such as sanitation and community health. In addition, polyclinics interact and work with the community through an area health commission with representatives elected by the community organizations, lay institutions, and lay health workers.

The expansion of the public health system created new demands on nurses. The first point of contact with the health care system, the polyclinics, whether urban or rural, offered both primary and community care dispensed by interdisciplinary teams. A field nurse, sanitarian, and at times a social worker were assigned to each geographic sector. Nurses worked as teammates with physicians in primary care specialties: pediatrics, obstetrics-gynecology, and internal medicine. Danielson (1985) listed nine programs that were the responsibility of polyclinic personnel: "women's health, child health, adult medical care, dentistry, control of infectious diseases, environmental services, food control, school health services, and occupational and labor medicine" (p. 51). In early years, however, new nursing graduates educated in hospitals were little prepared for work in the polyclinics, particularly in rural areas. Garfield (1981, p. 67) stated:

"MOST RURAL centers were staffed at this time by one physician (a new graduate also) and a 'visiting nurse.' The doctor staffed the health center proper; the nurse was responsible for nearly all outside care: traveling to hold clinics in nearby villages, emergency care of those too ill to travel to the health center, vaccinations, and follow-up home care. Thus, the new nurse had a tremendous amount of responsibility in the care of her community. In many ways, she functioned like the country doctor of old, grabbing her black bag and riding off on horseback to make house calls."

In 1974, the medicine in the community model was developed that further geographically distributed the nurse-physician primary care specialist teams in the community by sector. These teams were made responsible for the health needs of overlapping populations in each sector, with each one serving a population of the sector by focus of specialization.

Primary care is both curative and preventive. Thus, the physician and nurse teams spend approximately 12 hours each week in the community, making home visits or working with community groups. Teams for each sector include lay activists in health and a sanitarian, as well as social workers, psychologists, dentists, and statisticians. They are responsible for those in the community who do not seek services as well as those who do. Therefore, persons in high-risk categories such as elders, adolescents, and those with chronic disease have high priority and are followed using standardized protocols, called *dispensarization.*

With the focus of health care planning at the regional level, polyclinics are administratively independent from hospitals. Hospitals, also distributed at provincial and regional levels, are viewed as backup to the front line of prevention, the polyclinics. This allows the polyclinics, as the first point of contact with the health care system, "to define, orient, and protect the relationship of the health area population to the system of hospital and specialist services" (Danielson, 1985, p. 51). Thus, a process of intraconsultation occurs whereby patients, rather than being referred to a distant consultant from the hospital, meet with the consultant and the polyclinic team for referral for hospital care. Patients are then followed up by the primary team as it continues to arrange and participate in intraconsultations.

PROBLEMS ARE DEFINED AND SOLUTIONS ARE PROPOSED AT THE POPULATION OR SUBPOPULATION LEVEL

Examples of problems being defined and solved at the population or subpopulation level include a change brought about by consumers and one by administration. Parental resistance to a policy that forbade parents from spending the night with hospitalized children was voiced through regularly scheduled meetings between polyclinic team members and the community members in their assigned sector. A trial period allowing parents to stay with their ill children was implemented nationwide when the benefits, particularly to nursing staff, were realized. These benefits included pediatric patients who ate better, were more likely to take their medication, and responded to personal care given by a parent. The second example concerns a review of pediatric hospital readmissions in 1970 that pointed to discontinuity of care (Danielson, 1985). A program was initiated to discharge patients not to their parents alone, but to the parents and to the polyclinic. Follow-up of children in the community was assigned to a specific health worker.

A formal structure for community input into health policy comes from representatives in each polyclinic of *Poder Popular* (People's Power), a legislative branch of government set up for the people in 1977. When problems arise in the community or the needs of the community call for change in the delivery of health care, polyclinics and hospitals are held accountable by elected representatives of People's Power, who make up municipal assemblies. In turn, representatives are elected at provincial and national levels for the purpose of giving further input into health policy formation (Waitzkin, 1983).

NURSES IN THE COMMUNITY ORGANIZATION

With other team members, nurses continue to work with the mass or community organizations in health matters, extending the unit served from that of the individual and family to that of the community and population. Their participation in the mass organizations was reviewed by Junco et al. (1980). According to these authors, nurses have the responsibility of working with the mass organizations "to influence and educate in health matters, children, adolescents and adults" (p. 17). More specifically, nurses are responsible in the areas of educating the family in health matters, preventing accidents, providing sex education, offering nutritional education, and encouraging children to participate in matters of health.

Education of the family in health matters is coordinated with the CDR and extends to the community. Programs include teaching in areas of nutrition, prenatal care, prevention of infant mortality, vaccinations, sanitation, donation of blood, control of the mosquito *Aedes aegypti,* and other health activities. Programs include accident prevention in the home, school, and work place and in transit. Emphasis is placed on children going to and from school and playing in the streets.

Sex education is coordinated with the FMC and is carried out to promote the equality of women and to do away with the prejudices based on lack of information among parents, friends, and teachers who lack true scientific information needed by children and young people. Nutrition education emphasizes programs in the following areas: prenatal nutrition, identification and control of malnutrition in each sector into which the FMC brigade and nurse goes, how to achieve good nutrition from food products available in stores, and education of children and youth in children's organizations such as the Pioneers about good food habits. The participation of children in matters of health includes work with many organizations including the CDR, FMC, Pioneers, and others.

NURSING NEEDS ARE APPROACHED IN A SCIENTIFIC MANNER

To ensure that prevention of disease and promotion of health are extended to the entire population, nurses in Cuba must approach nursing needs and program planning scientifically. The following examples, from a review of the Cuban nursing literature from 1977 to 1985, show how nurses have done this.

Nurses are responsible for immunization programs on national, provincial, and municipal levels as well as in polyclinics (La Fortuna et al., 1980). They must plan an effective program of vaccination for all ages in all locations, including infant care centers, schools, and places of work. Careful statistics are gathered monthly and reports tallied yearly from each area to ensure a balance between supply and demand and to ensure that immunizations are kept current for all diseases of children and adults. It is nursing's responsibility to start vaccinations on all newborns that come to the polyclinic, to keep inoculations current for children, to correspond regarding vaccinations in all sectors, and to plan an effective program of vaccination for all areas.

In addition, nurses have conducted studies examining a wide range of nursing needs and focusing on specific populations ranging from large geographic areas of the country to a catchment area served by a polyclinic and even a particular sector. One study using population data examined the health needs of a population at risk, adolescents, in six municipal areas over a period of 6 months (Rivero et al., 1980). The authors described percentages of births to adolescents, interruptions of pregnancy, the incidence of syphilis and gonorrhea, rates of *dispensarization,* and "antisocial" behavior. Recommendations were made for nursing intervention and evaluation in the community.

Another study, targeting a catchment area, examined biopsychosocial factors in adolescent mothers 13 to 16 years of age (Ariosa and González, 1980). This survey included 86.4% of the population and focused on comparisons of urban versus rural areas. The study described age at first intercourse, use of contraception, rates of marriage, rates of abandonment of husband after birth, and number of visits in the home for health and sex education by nurses or *brigadas sanitarias* before pregnancy. Recommendations were made for nurses in the community to work more closely with community organizations such as the FMC and with the sanitary brigades to educate those who are most frequently in the homes of young people to prevent teen pregnancy. It also noted societal changes still needed to alleviate differences that exist on socioeconomic levels and in urban and rural areas and the impact of divorce on young people.

Neighborhood Home/Clinics: 1985–Future

A major change in philosophy of health care delivery at the community level was announced by Fidel Castro at the Second National Congress of Hygiene and Epidemiology in Havana in 1985 (De la Osa, 1985). A move is being made from the prior emphasis on primary care medical specialists in the polyclinics to a more generalist, family- and community-oriented approach called integral medicine. Even more finely dispersed in the community, the new model of health care places the nurse together with the physician in each neighborhood of 120 families. Located approximately eight blocks apart, a combination home and clinic will be the base for the nurse-physician team. A trial initiated in 1984 in an area of Havana was very successful and will be implemented throughout the island in 12 years (Castro, 1985).

ATTENTION TO THOSE IN NEED WHO DO NOT SEEK HEALTH CARE AS WELL AS THOSE WHO DO, AND MATCHING HEALTH NEEDS TO RESOURCES

The focus of the new program is primary, secondary, and tertiary prevention for all members of the family, neighborhood, and community. Risk factors in the community are defined, and attempts to prevent health problems occur through several avenues. First, primary care services are dispensed to the families in the home/clinics in the morning. Second, home visits are made by the nurse-physician team in the afternoon. This effort is to decrease use of hospital beds and to teach families how to care for ill, injured, or disabled members. Neighborhood emergency calls at night are limited by the team's skill in risk assessment and ability to educate the neighborhood in self-care. Group health education models are tested and applied according to risk factors in the population: obesity, drinking, smoking, and hypertension (Molinert et al., 1985). For example, a program of health education and systematic aerobic exercises was carried out in the trial area 5 days per week with a group of persons 54–74 years old. When compared with a control group at the end of 10 months, the program participants showed a significant decrease in use of hypertensives and tranquilizers, lowered blood pressure, decreased intake of salt, and a trend toward reduction in weight (only the last did not reach statistically significant levels).

The teams are backed up by the polyclinics where more specialists have been placed, including in dermatology, psychiatry, general surgery, urology, and ophthalmology, as well as the community health programs and personnel mentioned earlier. The borders for the area polyclinics have been realigned to make parallel those of the neighborhood home/clinics with those of the FMC, CDR, and the People's Power organizations to facilitate community input into health programs.

EDUCATIONAL PREPARATION FOR POPULATION-BASED NURSING

Special preparation for nurses to carry out a population-based practice in the neighborhoods and in the polyclinics in Cuba is not necessary, according to X. Rodriguez (personal communica-

tion, October 18, 1985), a nurse in the Department of Nursing, Ministry of Public Health. Nurses in Cuba do not need special education in public health, as public health is the cornerstone of their entire education. The curriculum is set by the Ministry of Education and the Ministry of Public Health and is based on current health profiles of the population. Not always so, Garfield (1981) reviewed the professionalization of nursing in Cuba and stated that early nursing education, largely given by physicians in hospitals, exaggerated medical specialization and devalued primary care. In 1972, nursing education allowed experience in the polyclinics for the first time. By 1976, nursing instructors emphasized theory-based nursing.

Today, most basic education still takes place in the traditional 3-year program rather than the university, but the emphasis begins with preventive health. Students take their beginning courses in mathematics, biostatistics, epidemiology, nutrition, diet therapy, community nursing, community medicine (public health), physics, chemistry, anatomy, physiology, microbiology, Spanish, Marxism, and physical education, according to a director of a school of nursing in Havana (G. Molinet, personal communication, September 8, 1978). In polyclinics, students' clinical experiences introduce them to the social and environmental determinants of health. They rotate to homes, schools, child care centers, and work places, dealing with preventive care and being exposed to interdisciplinary team work. In the hospital, they learn the backup system of care when the front line of primary care and prevention breaks down. The usual specialities include medical-surgical nursing, parent-child nursing, obstetrics, and psychiatry. Before a nurse can specialize in an area such as pediatrics or obstetrics, the nurse must return to the community and serve an additional 2 years; the postbasic specialization course takes 1 year (G. Molinet, personal communication, September 8, 1978; Garfield, 1981). Since 1977, a university-level program for nurses, called *licenciatura en enfermería,* similar to our baccalaureate program, has been instituted (Garfield, 1981). It offers a 4-year series of study after the postbasic program and 3 years of service in such areas as administration, teaching, and research. By 1983, only 135 graduates had received their *licenciatura* degree; in the school year 1983–1984, 1,073 nurses were enrolled in this program (Ministerio de Salud Publica, 1983). The need for baccalaureate preparation for nursing was expressed at the congress on hygiene and epidemiology in October 1985 by Castro, who announced a new goal of the nation to be to upgrade all nurses to have a baccalaureate degree.

CRITIQUE OF COMMUNITY HEALTH NURSING WITHIN THE CUBAN HEALTH CARE SYSTEM

Reviews and critiques of the Cuban health care system and nursing in the system have been reported by Danielson (1979, 1985) and Garfield (1981), respectively. Cuba, as a developing country, does not have a nurse-to-population ratio comparable to that in the United States. Currently, however, nursing in Cuba compares well with nursing in neighboring developing countries. For example, Cuba had a nurse-to-population ratio of 26.5 per 10,000 in 1983 (Ministerio de Salud Publica, 1983). In Central America, the number of nurses per 10,000 population was 6.4 in 1979, approximately one tenth that in the United States (Garfield and Rodriguez, 1985).

Many questions about nursing in Cuba, and particularly community health nursing as it is integrated into the total health care system, remain to be answered. Much of the health care literature about that country focuses heavily on the role of medicine and its practice in the community (Danielson, 1979, 1985). Little is known about the independent role of the community health nurse. Garfield (1981) stated it is necessary to view the characteristics of professionalism — autonomy and independence — in Cuba within a socialist framework ". . . by its *interactive* rather than *autonomous* character" (p. 72). Medicine and nursing do not experience independent practice but operate within a team concept for the good of the community. The early move toward medical specialization as evidenced in the early polyclinics tended to fracture care and may have not valued nursing's contribution (Garfield, 1981). This model is giving away to a more holistic model in the neighborhood/home clinics that views the human being as integrated physically, socially, and psychologically in the context of family and community. More needs to be known about the specific roles of the nurse in relationship to the roles of the other team members.

Another area, still largely unknown, is how the new generation of professional nurses of today, all of whom have received an educational base and core of experience that includes biostatistics, epidemiology, and public health and community health nursing, makes operational community health content in institutional settings such as hospitals. In a health care system that fully embraces prevention and health promotion, should not the nurse in the hospital carry out full prevention protocols? Are needs for such assessed and planned on an individual or aggregate basis, that is, by individual patient, by unit or ward, or by area? Or is such activity unnecessary because it is carried out in each geographic sector through the polyclinics? How does the nurse in the hospital work with families, carry out discharge planning, and work together with community polyclinic teams to provide continuity of care? How in the future will the neighborhood nurse be included in these areas? It is also necessary to know more about the articulation among the roles of nurses, other team members, lay health workers, and community members in carrying out health education and promoting self-care. As Cuba is now faced with a profile of mortality from chronic diseases, it is also appropriate to ask who is to take responsibility for the precursors of chronic disease, creating lifestyle changes and ensuring occupational and environmental health and safety — the individual or the state (Tesh, 1986)? What is the role of nursing in bringing about such changes? Finally, how do nurses and other health care team members specifically address chronic disease risk factors through community organizing, which has been a key factor in preventing infectious disease?

The initiation of neighborhood nursing will increase the need for nurses in the community and will make added demands on them. These new demands raise the question as to the adequacy of educational preparation of nurses to meet wider practice, leadership, and research roles. As nurses in practice in the community face a profile of chronic disease mortality and morbidity, they will be called upon to enhance the quality of life of both the ill and the well at individual, family, and community levels. As Garfield (1981) warned, primary and tertiary prevention will fall more and more to nurses in the home and neighborhood, as physicians are not on their "home turf" in non-clinical settings. Demands for nursing leadership will rise as the need to coordinate primary care, home care, and group health education increases. Working together with community organizations and coordinating programs based on the community's determination of needs is a role that has traditionally fallen to nursing, and it should grow in the future model of neighborhood care. New graduates must be prepared in new practice and leadership arenas, and preparation of nurses at the graduate level should be expanded in the future.

The demands for nursing research will also increase as the need for more population-focused epidemiological studies, surveys, and evaluations of preventive health education programs expand. More advanced preparation in the sciences of public health, particularly biostatistics and epidemiology, will be necessary.

IMPLICATIONS FOR COMMUNITY HEALTH NURSING IN THE UNITED STATES

Community health nursing in the United States is facing a crisis: by definition, it is committed to a socially just equity model — to provide the unmet health needs of the total population — in a system that follows the market model — allowing access to health care only for those who can pay.

With the corporatization of U.S. medical care (Starr, 1982), community health nursing is increasingly faced with the entrepreneurial or corporate business market model of health care. In this model, nurses are encouraged to "capitalize" on present trends in health care in the United States and join ". . . competitive health marketplace ventures" (Dugan, 1985, p. 23). On the other hand, community health nurses have also been presented the equity model, as in the block nursing program (Martinson et al., 1985). Ideological differences among nations generate different systems of health care delivery. In the United States, free enterprise is valued over distributive justice and will no doubt continue to shape the delivery of community health services; however, community health nursing in this country can be more relevant and effective in the future. For example, expansion of equity models such as that piloted by Martinson et al.

(1985) could help community health nurses work toward social equity and the development of the population-focused model. Yet constraints to expanding the match of unmet health care needs to health resources on a geographical basis to reach the entire population are many.

First, the United States lacks a commitment to equality in health status and the necessary social programs needed to bring it about, e.g., to change rates of illiteracy, levels of education and employment, and the status of women, although many work toward such changes.

A second constraint is the educational preparation of nurses. Unlike Cuba, few nurses receive public health preparation at undergraduate levels. Only 31.4% of students who entered nursing programs in 1981–1982 enrolled in baccalaureate programs (ANA, 1984). Traditionally, these are the only programs providing basic preparation in community health nursing. At the graduate level, 12.9% of students entering programs in 1981—1982 elected a major in public health nursing, up from 6.6% in 1978 (ANA, 1984). Yet according to a recent survey (Kornblatt, et al., 1985), only half of all National League for Nursing–accredited graduate community health nursing programs required a course in epidemiology. In keeping with this educational tradition, few nurses in community health nursing practice are prepared in public health. While the numbers of nurses working in community health service agencies increased 32.9% between 1974 and 1979 ". . . over half (56.7%) of the nurses employed for community health work in state and local agencies, excluding boards of education, had incomplete or no public health nursing education" (ANA, 1983, pp. 57–58).

The challenges to community health nursing are as follows: (1) to make operational to the fullest extent possible the ethic of public health, or social justice, from which our definition is synthesized; (2) to educate by requiring continuing education in the basics of community health nursing and the public health sciences within our own community health nursing ranks; (3) to require RN-to-BSN programs for community health nurses who lack a baccalaureate degree and make these programs accessible; (4) in view of predicted changes in the health care system, to reexamine the World Health Organization's earlier recommendation of community as the core of all basic nursing education (World Health Organization 1974; Flynn, 1984); and (5) to teach those in practice and education to carry out population-focused research and practice.

Research is needed. A magnet study in community health nursing that identifies models of excellence of population-focused practice, identifying who works in these agencies and what attracted them, is recommended. Furthermore, we must have studies designed to determine if and how nursing in various community settings such as the home, school, and work place influence the health of populations.

Cuba's ability as a developing country to forge ahead into new population-focused frontiers in nursing will be of continuing interest to our profession. Additional study of community health nursing in Cuba could benefit nurses in the United States as well as in other countries who seek "health for all." Will neighborhood nursing be as effective in helping to bring down rates of chronic disease as it was in bringing down rates of infectious disease? Will it improve the quality of life of the chronically

ill in the home and the families who give home care? What will be the long-term benefits other than cost effectiveness? Answers to these questions will come about through further observation and exchange between nurses in Cuba and nurses in the United States and other countries.

ACKNOWLEDGMENT. The author gratefully acknowledges the assistance of Richard Garfield in commenting on a draft of this article.

SUMMARY

This chapter focused on the issue of world health. Selected health problems faced by health professionals and citizens worldwide were presented: population growth environmental stressors, and disease. A model of population-focused health care delivery in Cuba highlighted the role of nurses in the community and serves as an inspiration to community health nurses as they work toward achieving the World Health Organization's goal of "Health for All by the Year 2000" in their respective communities.

Learning Activities

1. Discuss the advantages and disadvantages of limiting population growth.

2. Look up and compare the incidences of AIDS and deaths due to AIDS in Africa and in Cuba versus those in the United States. How do the incidences of AIDS and deaths due to AIDS in Cuba compare with those in Africa? With those in the United States? What might account for the differences?

3. Compare population-focused nursing in Cuba with community health nursing in your community. How are they the same, and how do they differ?

4. Look up and compare the rates of life expectancy and infant mortality in Cuba versus the rates in the United States. What factors do you think might account for the similarities in rates between the developing (Cuba) and the developed (United States) countries?

5. Investigate the efforts made to immunize the population of your county. How do these differ from Cuba's efforts after the revolution?

REFERENCES

American Nurses' Association: Facts About Nursing 1982–83. Kansas City, Missouri, American Nurses' Association, 1983.

American Nurses' Association: The Economic and Employment Environment: Recent Developments and Future Opportunities. Kansas City, Missouri, American Nurses' Association, 1984.

American Public Health Association: The Definition and Role of Public Health Nursing in the Delivery of Health Care: A Statement of the Public Health Nursing Section. Washington, DC, American Public Health Association, 1981.

American Public Health Association: Edward Barsky Award presented to Sergio Del Valle, Cuban Minister of Health, at the Physician's Forum. Government Responsibility and the People's Health: Program and Abstracts. Presented at the 113th annual meeting of the American Public Health Association, Washington, D. C., November 18, 1985.

Ariosa, M. F., and González, F. P.: Estudio de algunos factores bíopsico-social en la madre precoz 13–16 anos. [The study of some bio-psychosocial factors in the premature mother 13–16 years of age.] Actualidad en Enfermería 4;23–45, 1980.

Beauchamp, D. E.: Public health as social justice. In Mappes, T. A., and Zembaty, J. S., eds.: Biomedical Ethics. New York, McGraw-Hill, 1986, pp. 585–593.

Castro, F.: La Experiencia Cubana del Médico de la Comunidad y la Participación Popular en la Protección de la Salud. [The Cuban experience of medicine in the community and the participation of the people in the protection of health.] Address to the Second Congress of Hygiene and Epidemiology, Havana, Cuba, October 15, 1985.

Curtin, L.: Where will all the money go? Nurs. Management 16;7–9, 1985.

Danielson, R.: Cuban Medicine. New Brunswick, New Jersey, Transaction Books, 1979.

Danielson, R.: Medicine in the community. In Halebsky, S. and Kirk, J. M., eds.: Cuba: Twenty-Five Years of Revolution, 1959–1984. New York, Praeger, 1985, pp. 45–61.

De la Osa, J. A.: El médico de la familia ha introducido tal revolución. . . . [The family physician has introduced such a revolution. . . .] Granma, pp. 1, 3, 4, October 16, 1985.

Dreher, M.: District nursing: The lost benefits of a population-based practice. Am. J. Public Health 74;1107–1111, 1984.

Dugan, A. B.: Expanding nursing's practice terrain: Imperatives for future viability. Public Health Nurs. 2;23–32, 1985.

Flynn, B. C.: Public health nursing education for primary health care. Public Health Nurs. 1;36–44, 1984.

Garfield, R.: Nursing, health care and professionalism in Cuba. Soc. Sci. Med. 15A;63–72, 1981.

Garfield, R., and Rodriguez, P.: Health and health services in Central America. J.A.M.A. 254;936–943, 1985.

Gilpin, M., and Rodriguez-Trias, H.: Looking at health in a healthy way. Cuba Rev. 8;3–15, 1978.

Gleeson, S.: Community nursing centers: Definition and status in the legislature. J. Comm. Health Nurs. 1;65, 1984.

Halebsky, S., and Kirk, J. M., eds.: Cuba: Twenty-Five Years of Revolution, 1959–1984. New York, Praeger, 1985.

Junco, F. J., Garcia, D. H., de la Cruz, F. C., Oviedo, M. R., Valdes, Y. M., and Pedroso, A. G.: La enfermera y la parti-cipación de las organizaciones de masas en las tareas de salud. [The nurse and the participation of the mass organizations in the tasks of health.] Actualidad en Enfermería 4;16–22, 1980.

Kornblatt, E. S., Goeppinger, J., and Jagger, J.: Epidemiology in community health nursing education: Fit or misfit? Public Health Nurs. 2;104–108, 1985.

Kozol, J.: A new look at the literacy campaign in Cuba. Harvard Educ. Rev. 48;341–377, 1978.

La Fortuna, L. J., Romero, Z. B., and Torres, J. F.: Programa nacional de immunizaciones: Participación de enfermería. [The national immunization program: Participation of nursing.] Actualidad en Enfermería 4;23–32, 1980.

Martinson, I. M., Jamieson, M. K., O'Grady, B., and Sime, M.: The block nurse program. J. Comm. Health Nurs. 2;21–29, 1985.

Ministerio de Salud Publica: Informe Anual. Havana, Republica de Cuba, 1983.

Ministry of Public Health: Public health in figures. Havana, Republic of Cuba, 1990.

Molinert, H. T., Abrines, J. R., Henriquez, P. A., et al.: La experiencia cubana del médico de la comunidad y la participación popular en la protección de la salud. [The Cuban experience of medicine in the community and the participation of the people in the protection of health.] Presented by Fidel Castro at the meeting of the Second Congress on Hygiene and Epidemiology, Havana, Cuba, October 15, 1985.

National Center for Health Statistics: Health: United States, 1984. Washington, D. C., U.S. Government Printing Office, DHHS publication No. 85-1232, 1985.

President's Commission for the Study of Ethical Problems in Medicine and Biomedical and Behavioral Research: Securing Access to Health Care: A Report on the Ethical Implications of Differences in the Availability of Health Services, Vol. 1: Report. Washington, D. C., U.S. Government Printing Office, 1983.

Rivero, B. P., Botel, M. L., Garcia, N. P., and Venta, E. M.: La enfermera en la medicina en la comunidad: Riesgo de adolescente. [The nurse in community medicine: Adolescent at risk.] Actualidad en Enfermería 4;5–22, 1980.

Starr, P.: The Transformation of American Medicine. New York, Basic Books, 1982.

Swanson, J. M.: Birth planning in Cuba: A basic human right. Int. J. Nurs. Stud. 18;81–88, 1981.

Tesh, S.: Health education in Cuba: A preface. Int. J. Health Serv. 16;87–104, 1986.

Valdez-Brito, J. A., and Henriquez, J. A.: Health status of the Cuban population. Int. J. Health Serv. 13;479–486, 1983.

Waitzkin, H.: Health policy and social change: A comparative history of Chile and Cuba. Soc. Probl. 31;235–248, 1983.

Williams, C. A.: Population-focused practice. In Stanhope, M., and Lancaster, J., eds.: Community Health Nursing: Process and Practice for Promoting Health. St. Louis, C. V. Mosby, 1984, pp. 805–815.

World Health Organization: Community Health Nursing. Geneva, World Health Organization, Technical Report Series No. 558, 1974.

CHAPTER

29

Community Health Nursing: Making a Difference

Upon completion of this chapter, the reader will be able to:

1. Discuss how being a member of an aggregate influences health.

2. Predict community health issues of the future based on shared characteristics of aggregates.

3. Describe actions needed by community health nurses to assure future trends and changes in the health care system that will benefit the consumer of health care.

Mary Albrecht
Janice M. Swanson

For most individuals, hospitalization is only a temporary state that focuses on a diagnosed state of deficiency. Nursing's focus goes beyond the traditional concept of health as the absence of disease, a definition that reflects health in medical or disease terms. Nurses have long been concerned with prevention and health-promotion activities with individual patients, their families, and groups in hospital settings, e.g., childbirth preparation, parenting classes, or diabetes classes. Community health nursing extends the definition of health and, hence, nursing action to social units at the community, aggregate, and population levels.

Considering the individual in terms of the aggregate of which the individual is a member is important in community health nursing. Common characteristics such as sex, age, education, income level, and occupation are shared by many persons in the community. These characteristics impact the health of families and communities and are important in determining their needs. Shared characteristics of aggregates also aid in intervention to meet the health needs of aggregates. Social interaction, political activity, and trends determine health priorities and allocation of resources that impact the health of aggregates at local through national levels. The following examples will show the impact that being a member of an aggregate has on health.

Socioeconomic Status

Health is affected by socioeconomic status in several ways. Those of lower socioeconomic status have higher rates of morbidity and mortality than their counterparts of higher socioeconomic status. According to the World Health Organization (WHO), life expectancy is reduced by poverty through increased rates of infant mortality, developmental limitations, chronic disease, and traumatic death. The incidence of heart disease is 25% higher for persons with low incomes, and the likelihood of having cancer increases as family income decreases (Department of Health and Human Services [DHHS], 1990). Also, rates of infectious disease, including HIV infection, are more common among those of lower socioeconomic status (DHHS, 1990). The importance of these facts becomes evident when one considers that one of eight U.S. families lives below the federal poverty level (DHHS, 1990).

Sex

Whether one is male or female in the United States will affect health. Generally, women have had higher morbidity or disease rates, whereas men have had higher mortality or death rates (Bomar, 1989). Although remarkable strides have been made since the turn of the century in increasing longevity in men and women, there continues to be a gap between the life expectancies of the two groups. This gap has increased from 2.0 years in 1900 to a high of 7.8 years in 1979 (National Center for Health Statistics, 1990). Since then, this gap has steadily decreased to 7.4 years in 1980, and it reached 6.8 years in 1988 (National Center for Health Statistics, 1990). The major causes of death that have led to the downward trend of the gap between the sexes have been malignant neoplasms and diseases of the heart, which have increased for women and decreased for men since 1987 (National Center for Health Statistics, 1990). The driving force behind this trend may be attributed to

---

Community Health Nurses Make a Difference Through Programs: Volunteer Outreach to Prenatal Populations at High Risk

PUBLIC HEALTH nurses initiated a community-based program to reach prenatal populations at high risk of low birth weight. Volunteer neighborhood outreach workers were recruited and trained by the public health nurses. The neighborhood outreach workers got in touch with residents of targeted low income communities through personal contact, use of flyers, giving presentations in the community, and attending events such as baby showers. Program data were collected that showed the impact of the program on the community: home visits, telephone assistance, number of persons contacted at community presentations, and educational materials prepared and distributed. The authors review the successes and shortcomings of the outreach program and recommend a plan for program evaluation.

Data from May, K. M., McLaughlin, F., and Penner, M.: Preventing low birth weight: Marketing and volunteer outreach. Public Health Nurs. 8;97–104, 1991.

women entering the work force and, in turn, increasing the stress in their lives as well as to women smoking more cigarettes.

Age

Age is an important determinant of health and is closely linked to mortality. For example, according to WHO, the leading cause of death in childhood is unintentional injuries. This is also true for adolescents, for whom three fourths are related to motor vehicle accidents and more than half involve alcohol (DHHS, 1990). Patterns of morbidity also vary by age. More than 22% of people age 65 or older have a limitation in a major activity (DHHS, 1990). These are not "sick" individuals; essentially, they are "well" persons who experience periodic exacerbations that may require hospitalization. Most require acute care only periodically, yet medical care is designed to focus on acute care—attending to physiological needs associated with disease—rather than on care at all times. The real needs, especially for the chronically ill population, are for distributive, continuous care in the forms of health monitoring, supervision, and periodic home health or homemaker services. Most persons over the age of 65 live at home or with family members; nursing homes are used by 5% or less of the elderly population at any time (DHHS, 1990). Nursing homes, serving mostly the frail elderly, are also designed according to an acute care model that focuses on meeting the physical needs of patients rather than on their interpersonal social and environmental needs. The health and surveillance needs of this aggregate will continue to grow in the future.

Race and Ethnicity

Differences in health status and access to health services by race and ethnicity also exist. These differences can be partially attributed to inequalities of income, education, and geography. For example, in 1989, among U.S. women experiencing live births, white women were less likely to have no prenatal care or to initiate prenatal care during the third trimester (5.2%) than African-American women (11.9%), American Indian or Alaskan Native women (13.4%), and women of Hispanic origin (13%) (National Center for Health Statistics,

1992). Also, the incidence rate of AIDS among blacks is more than threefold that of whites (DHHS, 1990).

Social Interaction

Relationships are also important to health and may determine one's membership in an aggregate. According to WHO, social support is a necessary factor in promoting health and functional independence. Retirement, the loss of a spouse or close friend, or a change in social role can affect support systems and social contact, and all are risk factors for disease and functional independence (DHHS, 1990). Also, those who find themselves surrounded by smokers find it difficult to quit smoking, and factors such as modeling and support from friends are associated with engagement in exercise (Kottke, 1992). In addition, in dense populations, person-to-person transmission of a disease increases even if the agent is not highly infectious (Brock and Madigan, 1991). Families can also play a significant role in health promotion. Families influence personal health habits and physical environment. Participation by children in activities outside of the family has been shown to have a positive effect on health-promoting behaviors; this participation is monitored by the family (Bomar, 1989).

Geography/Politics

Where one lives (e.g., geography) may have an impact on the health of an aggregate beyond traditional geographically related phenomena, such as earthquakes, weather, or lack of certain minerals in the soil. Political factors have an impact on the delivery of health care services at all levels. For example, Medicaid is a government program that supplies supplementary funds for welfare and health care for persons of low income. Medicaid availability varies from state to state depending on local political climate, which is a factor in setting priorities. As a consequence, Medicaid assistance is not available to citizens of all states and varies widely. Currently, in Washington, Christine Gebbie, Secretary of Health and a leader in public health nursing, and others are working on a comprehensive health care bill that would organize a statewide program of universal health care that in-

---

Community Health Nurses Make a Difference Through Programs: Immunizations at the Mall

ONE COUNTY in the southwestern United States began back-to-school immunization programs at shopping malls during the month of August in the early 1960s. In 1986, the county health department delegated community health nursing to focus on primary prevention activities and to take responsibility for managing the immunization programs. In 1987, the community health nurses conducted the mall immunization programs and continued to do so, increasing services (offering immunizations for adults as well as children) and the number of immunizations given, for each year through 1989. A survey was conducted to assist the county health department in determining baseline information and marketing techniques for reaching more of the population. Questions asked were (1) where immunizations were usually obtained; (2) how they learned about the program at the mall; and (3) if the client would return to the mall program in the future. As a result, the mall immunization program was increased (additional sites and hours); marketing of the program was also increased; and reassessment of the mall immunization programs is now conducted on an annual basis. The program has implications for cost-effective strategies for providing immunizations for vaccine-preventable diseases.

Data from Guzzetta, P. J., Russell, C. K., and Bell, L. E.: Immunization mall programs. J. Commun. Health Nurs. 7;159–166, 1990.

cludes prevention and system development (Hine, 1992). In the future, residency in a state such as Washington may affect the health of that population.

COLLECTIVE ACTIVITY FOR HEALTH

Being a member of an aggregate with shared characteristics, whether age, ethnicity, or geographic factors, may have a marked effect on health. Shared characteristics of aggregates that may impact health are known as risk factors, because they place an aggregate at risk. These factors are key to the community, to public health, and to community health nursing as they form the basis for assessment, planning, intervention, and evaluation. While using the nursing process on behalf of individual health is important, it is carrying out the nursing process, using the same steps, at the aggregate level, that has the potential to make changes based on characteristics of the aggregate. Whether the needs are based on age or social or environmental characteristics, change at the aggregate level will make the broadest impact on health of the population as a whole. For example, elders in the Tenderloin (the congested, inner-city area) of San Francisco had to expose the lack of heat in their hotel on a collective basis before there was sufficient attention paid to this problem to cause the city to take action toward change. Likewise, the disabled population in San Francisco organized to call attention to their rights to have equal opportunity in housing, education, and employment. These activities require community organization that involves planning and political activity by aggregates within the community.

DETERMINANTS OF HEALTH

In keeping with modern concerns, research is showing that individual, social, and environmental factors rather than medical care are the real determinants of health and that intervention at these levels is possible and makes a difference. For example, in 1979, the Centers for Disease Control suggested that contributions to decreasing premature mortality from the 10 leading causes of death were environmental factors (20%), hereditary factors (20%), lifestyle (50%), and medical services (10%) (Gay et al., 1983). Note that only 10% is associated with medical services. The many and varied determinants of health and their uneven impact on the health of aggregates and communities have been the focus throughout this book.

CONFUSION REGARDING HEALTH, HEALTH CARE, AND MEDICAL CARE

As discussed in Chapter 1, "health" is viewed on a continuum from illness to peak potential. Health is fluid and changing in accordance with the goals and potential of aggregates within an environment.

Community Health Nurses Make a Difference Through Research: Empowering Families and Evoking Authority

A QUALITATIVE research study was conducted in which 30 expert public health nurses practicing in Washington State were asked to describe "clinical examples in which they made a difference in the outcome of high-risk maternal/child cases visited at home" (p. 101). Interviews were tape-recorded, transcribed, and analyzed. Twenty-one practice competencies were identified from the public health nurses' anecdotes from home visits to 95 families. Two of the 21 competencies were described in this article: (1) *empowerment* through encouraging family self-help, and (2) *coercion* by assuming responsibility for child protection, that is, using authority to shield children from violence and neglect. Although these competencies represent what the author calls "polarities," the public health nurse synthesizes them through skills in "fostering autonomy" and applying "persuading strategies" when compelled to do so, as when child protection is necessary. Working with vulnerable groups, public health nurses assure their right to "protection and sustenance" (p. 104). According to the author, further research is needed that will reveal how expert public health nurses carry out these competencies, and a theory that would explain these supposed contradictions.

Data from Zerwekh, J. V.: The practice of empowerment and coercion by expert public health nurses. Image J. Nurs. Schol. 24;101–105, 1992.

Health is achieved in multiple, complex ways. Medical care is truncated or falls far short of addressing the whole; it cannot address the complexity of factors that determine health. The focus of medical care, as practiced by physicians, is on the diagnosis and treatment of disease.

Health care, on the other hand, requires effort from the individual, family, community, and societal levels—including self-care, medical care, education, and political and environmental action. The focus of health care is on the promotion of health and prevention of disease. Pouring more funds into medical care will not solve societal health problems such as alcoholism and AIDS; it must be balanced with community organizing and advocacy that bring about change in the larger determinants of health. Perhaps the greatest question facing our nation is, when the determinants of health are multiple and complex and require intervention from many levels (e.g., education, economic, political science), is it ethical to continue to fund medical care for disease determination and

---

Community Health Nurses Make a Difference Through Research: Strategies and Supports for Drug-Exposed Infants at Home

THE PURPOSE of this study was to identify effective public health nurse interventions for use with caregivers providing for drug-exposed infants at home. Fifteen newborn infants with positive toxicology screens for PCP, cocaine, or both and 15 newborn infants without a positive toxicology screen (control group) were assessed, and 13 of the noncontrols were followed on home visits over 12 months. Findings of the study were consistent with previous studies in that infants exposed to drugs were small at birth and prone to "hypertonicity, infections, irritability, an increased need to suck, spitting up, flatulence, and a high-pitched cry" (p. 37). Strategies identified to meet these early problems were swaddling, small feedings, use of pacifiers, soy formula or iron-free formula, evaluation of calories consumed, and waking the baby to eat when necessary. By 6 months of age, most of the infants evinced fewer problems. The study also identified the needs of the caregivers, birth mothers, family/household, and public health nurse working with these families. The authors recommended further research, including the need to follow both the drug-exposed infants and the control group longitudinally.

Data from Saylor, C., Lippa, B., and Lee, G.: Drug-exposed infants at home: Strategies and supports. Public Health Nurs. 8;33–38, 1991.

The Future of Public Health: Where Are the Views of Public Health Nurses?

IN 1988, the Committee for the Study of the Future of Public Health (CSFPH) opened their report with a list of problems that demanded aggregate action and demonstrated the importance of public health in the United States today. These problems included AIDS, health care for the indigent, injuries, teen pregnancy, high blood pressure, smoking, substance abuse, hazardous waste, and Alzheimer's disease (CSFPH, 1988). But does this list reflect the concerns of the modern public health nurse? The committee of 22 members included 12 physicians, but only one nurse, and although the nursing profession is dominated by women, only one third of the committee were female (Ward 1989). Certainly there are some commonalities of opinion, but it is interesting to consider how these and other views expressed by the committee might have changed if the committee had contained 12 nurses and one physician. With greater representation by nurses, the health care system as a whole can work toward successfully achieving the public health concerns of the future.

---

treatment at great expense to the near exclusion of public health and the social and environmental components of health care?

HEALTH AS A RIGHT

Today, health is mistakenly viewed as a right, by many in the United States, not a privilege. Yet health is not a right in the United States, as evidenced by the major indicators of health in the United States which are far below those of many other western countries. Access to medical care is also not a right in the United States. Funds go to medical care in the United States rather than to prevention and health promotion because medical care is a large industry that generates revenue. However, instead of generating revenue and creating an industry in the United States, health promotion and prevention cut back the market or need for the largest U.S. industry: medical care. For health care to be truly health nurturing, there must be a sense of shared interests and community. When public support is scarce or fragmented, the health prospects for mainstream America are grim and insecure. Health care professionals and consumers must work together to determine appropriate goals for health care and institute broad public health measures to prevent and decrease morbidity (Callahan, 1989). Gebbie stated, "The number one issue for nursing leaders around the U.S. should be a system to implement and to finance an effective health and illness care system for all people, not simply those who can pay for it" (Hine, 1992, p. 7).

The answer lies not in providing equal access to a medically driven model in which energy of health

---

Nursing's Agenda for Health Care Reform

FORTY-TWO nursing organizations have endorsed *Nursing's Agenda for Health Care Reform,* including the Association of Community Health Nursing Educators, the American Association of Occupational Health Nurses, and the National Association of School Nurses, Inc. *Nursing's Agenda* calls for health care reform that would offer a basic "core" of health services to be made available to all on a geographical basis and delivered in familiar places such as homes, schools, and work places.

The core of care of nursing's proposal for health care includes the following:

● Primary health care will be delivered to all in community-based settings

● 1A standard, federally defined package of care will be available that provides essential health care services to all, financed through public and private sources
● Phasing in of the most essential services with priorities focusing on pregnant women and children and vulnerable populations with little access to the current health care system
● Changes in planning health services needs based on nationally changing demographics
● Reduction of health care costs
● Case management
● Long-term care
● Insurance reforms to assure access to all
● Ongoing review by public and private sectors

Data from National League for Nursing: Nursing's Agenda for Health Care Reform. New York, National League for Nursing, 1991, pp. 1–23.

professionals is concentrated downstream, where the focus is on rescuing the bruised and broken from the raging river of injury, illness, and disease. Rather, the answer lies in providing equal access to a preventive model like Cuba's, in which health professionals work to promote healthy communities upstream, by keeping them from falling into the river through collective activity (McKinlay, 1979).

Most recent proposals for national health insurance would provide greater access to downstream care for all America (Ward, 1990), whereas what is needed are proposals that would provide equal access to upstream care. For example, why should vast amounts of money be spent on neonatal intensive care rather than on preventing the need for such care through more cost-effective prenatal services and education, employment, and housing for communities at risk of low birth weight and high infant mortality?

One major proposal for changes in health care is Nursing's Agenda for Health Care Reform. This proposal would provide primary health care on a geographical basis to all in familiar, community-based settings. Community health nurses who work to support such a proposal by educating the public and their peers, lobbying local, state, and national legislators, and supporting nursing's voice in health care reform will hasten affordable upstream care for all in the United States.

Case Study

Karen Capel, a community health nursing student making her first home visits during field experiences in community health, visited a young family. Mrs. Dana Pritchett was at home with her 5-week-old baby and a 3-year-old preschooler; her two older children were in school. Her husband, a construction worker in a small town 3 hours away, came home to be with the family on weekends. This is Mrs. Pritchett's first experience with breast-feeding; she stated, "I want to see what it's like, because this is the last one. My husband had a vasectomy." When Karen asked how she was doing, Mrs. Pritchett replied, "Oh, the baby eats fine, I just get scared. . . . It's not safe here at night in this neighborhood, but what can I do? I get real scared."

Miguel Hernandez, another student, visited an elderly couple, the Simpsons. Mrs. Simpson is caretaker of her husband, who has a history of congestive heart failure, is hypertensive, and at times is confused. A home health aide assists Mrs. Simpson in the care of her husband daily, but the family is considering institutionalization due to Mrs. Simpson's diminishing ability to continue to care for him at home, a plan that she resists. The student notes that Mr. Simpson's blood pressure is elevated, he is short of breath, and his ankles are edematous. When checking Mr. Simpson's medications, Miguel notes a discrepancy in the date of the last refill for the patient's diuretic, and in the number of pills remaining in the bottle. When asked if Mr. Simpson has difficulty taking his "water pills," Mrs. Simpson stated, "I don't give them to him in the afternoon. . . . How can I take good care of him when I have to be up at night, putting him on the pan?"

On a home visit to Ms. Jane Fuller, a middle-aged woman, for follow-up hypertension, Karla Sanders, a student, met members of the extended family. Ms. Fuller's daughter, who is 23 years old, had many questions for Karla. She stated she had had a stroke in her teen years, was taking medication for hypertension, and had frequent migraines. Concerned, she asked Karla, "Does feeling anxious have to do with my not having sex because my husband's in jail?"

From the author's files.

SUMMARY

Factors such as child bearing, separation, and chronic disease impact the health of every individual, the health of the family, and, ultimately, the health of the community. Problems reflected by concerns such as safety, crime, and institutionalization are complex in nature. Addressing family and community needs associated with concerns such as those expressed in the case study vignettes is also complex. Although individuals and family members had received nursing and/or medical care during their last contact with the health care system, identifying and meeting individual, family, and community health needs from traditional medical and health care settings, such as hospitals, offices, and clinics only, is a limited if not impossible, task. Likewise, identifying and meeting individual, family, and community health needs while making only home visits is also limiting. The com-

plex problems facing the health of the community today such as those identified by students in the vignettes — separation, crime, chronic disease — require social action, such as that brought by community organizations and political activity, by a collective, or by groups of people, action that results in social change. Although hospital, office, clinic, and home visits are important, the complexity of health problems seen by practitioners have an impact on the family and the community and at times extend to the state, national, and international levels. Health teaching and monitoring a medical regimen as noted in the above examples are necessary but not sufficient interventions to ensure the health of an individual, a family, and a community. This is true due to many reasons, including the following:

- Health is a complex, dynamic, multifaceted phenomenon.
- Individuals are members of a group and aggregates such as families, neighborhoods, schools, churches, and other institutions that are organized to comprise communities.
- The organization of the community has an impact on health of individuals, families, communities, aggregates, and populations.
- To increase the health of aggregates, the community must identify its needs and organize to meet its needs.
- By working with families and other aggregates in the community to identify their needs and to organize and to meet their needs, community

---

Examples of Future Community Health Issues of Concern to Community Health Nursing

Increasing diversity of the population

Increasing proportion of the population living in poverty

Increasing proportion of the population uninsured or underinsured for heatlh care

Increasing longevity and proportion of the population over 65 years of age and living with a chronic disease

Infant mortality rates worsening in comparison with other developed and some developing countries

Increasing environmental pollution and concerns

Continuing hazards at the work place

Responses Needed by Community Health Nursing to Future Community Health Issues

Increased knowledge and practice of population-focused nursing

A baccalaureate degree as a basis for community health nursing practice

Increased diversity of community health nursing students and practitioners

Community health nursing centers geographically based and accessible to all, offering prevention-oriented primary care

Increased community organizing, advocacy, and political activity

---

Additional Readings

Griffith, H. M., Evans, M., Irvin, B., et al.: Nurses' perspectives on a national health plan. Nurs. Outlook *39*;178–182, 1991.

Henderson, V. A.: National health insurance: If not now, when? (editorial). Public Health Nurs. 2;59, 1985.

Navarro, V.: Why some countries have national health insurance, others have national health services, and the U.S. has neither. Soc. Sci. Med. *28*;887–898, 1989.

Pender, N. J., Barkauskas, V. H., Hayman, L., et al.: Health promotion and disease prevention: Toward excellence in nursing practice and education. Nurs. Outlook *40*;106–120, 1992.

Ward, D.: National health insurance: Where do nurses fit in? Nurs. Outlook *38*;206–207, 1990.

Yiu Matuk, L. C., and Horsburgh, M. E.: Rebuilding public health nursing practice: A Canadian perspective. Public Health Nurs. 6;169–173, 1989.

health nurses help promote the health of the population.

Today, more than ever, community health nursing can be the cornerstone of health care delivery and make a difference. In the United States, the change to a prospective system of reimbursement based on diagnosis-related groups has shortened hospital stays and increased the need for community-based health care. Groups and aggregates cared for in the community now require a broad range of nursing services. Fiscal realities and social demands appear likely to mandate the continued growth of community-based care for the foreseeable future. Health care reform that results in upstream care will mandate the continued growth of community-based care over the long term.

**L e a r n i n g
A c t i v i t i e s**

1. Discuss with your classmates how being a member of an aggregate influences an aspect of your personal health. Give an example.

2. Discuss why and how community health nurses make a difference. Give examples of possible community health nursing interventions for the three case study vignettes at (1) the individual level, (2) the family level, and (3) the aggregate or community level.

REFERENCES

Bomar, P.: Nurses and Family Health Promotion: Concepts, Assessment, and Intervention. Baltimore, Williams & Wilkins, 1989.

Brock, T., and Madigan, M.: Biology of Microorganisms. Englewood Cliffs, New Jersey, Prentice-Hall, 1991.

Callahan, D.: What Kind of Life? New York, Simon and Schuster, 1989.

Committee for the Study of the Future of Public Health, Institute of Medicine: The Future of Public Health. Washington, D.C., National Academy Press, 1988.

Department of Health and Human Services: Healthy People, 2000: National Health Promotion and Disease Prevention. Washington, D.C., U.S. Government Printing Office, DHHS publication No. (PHS) 91-50212, 1990.

Gay, J. R., Jacobs, B. J., and Kent, C. B.: The Technological Explosion in Medical Science: Implications for the Health Care Industry and Public 1981-2001. New York, Spectrum Publications, 1983.

Guzzetta, P. J., Russell, C. K., and Bell, L. E.: Immunization mall programs. J. Commun. Health Nurs. 7;159–166, 1990.

Hine, A.: Inspiring a new view of public health. Sigma Theta Tau Int. Reflections 17;7–8, 1992.

Kottke, T.: The "intervention index": Insufficient information. J. Clin. Epidemiol. 45;17–19, 1992.

May, K. M., McLaughlin, F., and Penner, M.: Preventing low birth weight: Marketing and volunteer outreach. Public Health Nurs. 8;97–104, 1991.

McKinlay, J. B.: A case for refocussing upstream: The political economy of illness. In Jaco, E. G., ed.: Patients, Physicians, and Illness. 3rd ed. New York, The Free Press, 1979, pp. 9–25.

National Center for Health Statistics: Advance Report of Final Mortality Statistics, 1988: Monthly Vital Statistics Report. Hyattsville, Maryland, U.S. Public Health Service, 1990.

National Center for Health Statistics: Health, United States, 1991. Hyattsville, Maryland, U.S. Public Health Service, 1992.

National League for Nursing: Nursing's Agenda for Health Care Reform. New York, National League for Nursing, 1991.

Saylor, C., Lippa, B., and Lee, G.: Drug-exposed infants at home: Strategies and supports. Public Health Nurs. 8;33–38, 1991.

Ward, D.: Public health nursing and the future of public health. Public Health Nurs. 6;163–168, 1989.

Ward, D.: National health insurance: Where do nurses fit in? Nurs. Outlook 38;206–207, 1990.

Zerwekh, J. W.: The practice of empowerment and coercion by expert public health nurses. Image J. Nurs. Schol. 24;101–105, 1992.

Standards of Community Health Nursing Practice

Standard I. Theory

The nurse applies theoretical concepts as a basis for decisions in practice.

Standard II. Data Collection

The nurse systematically collects data that are comprehensive and accurate.

Standard III. Diagnosis

The nurse analyzes data collected about the community, family, and individual to determine diagnoses.

Standard IV. Planning

At each level of prevention, the nurse develops plans that specify nursing actions unique to client needs.

Standard V. Intervention

The nurse, guided by the plan, intervenes to promote, maintain, or restore health, to prevent illness, and to effect rehabilitation.

Standard VI. Evaluation

The nurse evaluates responses of the community, family, and individual to interventions in order to determine progress toward goal achievement and to revise the data base, diagnoses, and plan.

Standard VII. Quality Assurance and Professional Development

The nurse participates in peer review and other means of evaluation to assure quality of nursing practice. The nurse assumes responsibility for professional development and contributes to the professional growth of others.

Standard VIII. Interdisciplinary Collaboration

The nurse collaborates with other health care providers, professionals, and community representatives in assessing, planning, implementing, and evaluating programs for community health.

Standard IX. Research

The nurse contributes to theory and practice in community health nursing through research.

Reprinted with permission from Standards of Community Health Nursing Practice, © 1986, American Nurses' Association, Washington, D.C.

Standards of Home Health Nursing Practice

Standard I. Organization of Home Health Services

All home health services are planned, organized, and directed by a master's-prepared professional nurse with experience in community health and administration.

Standard II. Theory

The nurse applies theoretical concepts as a basis for decisions in practice.

Standard III. Data Collection

The nurse continuously collects and records data that are comprehensive, accurate, and systematic.

Standard IV. Diagnosis

The nurse uses health assessment data to determine nursing diagnoses.

Standard V. Planning

The nurse develops care plans that establish goals. The care plan is based on nursing diagnoses and incorporates therapeutic, preventive, and rehabilitative nursing actions.

Standard VI. Intervention

The nurse, guided by the care plan, intervenes to provide comfort, to restore, improve, and promote health, to prevent complications and sequelae of illness, and to effect rehabilitation.

Standard VII. Evaluation

The nurse continually evaluates the client's and family's responses to interventions in order to determine progress toward goal attainment and to revise the data base, nursing diagnoses, and plan of care.

Standard VIII. Continuity of Care

The nurse is responsible for the client's appropriate and uninterrupted care along the health care continuum, and therefore uses discharge planning, case management, and coordination of community resources.

Standard IX. Interdisciplinary Collaboration

The nurse initiates and maintains a liaison relationship with all appropriate health care providers to assure that all efforts effectively complement one another.

Standard X. Professional Development

The nurse assumes responsibility for professional development and contributes to the professional growth of others.

Standard XI. Research

The nurse participates in research activities that contribute to the profession's continuing development of knowledge of home health care.

Standard XII. Ethics

The nurse uses the code for nurses established by the American Nurses' Association as a guide for ethical decision making in practice.

Declaration of Alma-Ata

The International Conference on Primary Health Care, meeting in Alma-Ata this twelfth day of September in the year Nineteen hundred and seventy-eight, expressing the need for urgent action by all governments, all health and development workers, and the world community to protect and promote the health of all the people of the world, hereby makes the following Declaration:

I

The Conference strongly reaffirms that health, which is a state of complete physical, mental and social wellbeing, and not merely the absence of disease or infirmity, is a fundamental human right and that the attainment of the highest possible level of health is a most important world-wide social goal whose realization requires the action of many other social and economic sectors in addition to the health sector.

II

The existing gross inequality in the health status of the people, particularly between developed and developing countries as well as within countries, is politically, socially and economically unacceptable and is, therefore, of common concern to all countries.

III

Economic and social development, based on a New International Economic Order, is of basic importance to the fullest attainment of health for all and to the reduction of the gap between the health status of the developing and developed countries. The promotion and protection of the health of the people is essential to sustained economic and social development and contributes to a better quality of life and to world peace.

IV

The people have the right and duty to participate individually and collectively in the planning and implementation of their health care.

V

Governments have a responsibility for the health of their people which can be fulfilled only by the provision of adequate health and social measures. A main social target of governments, international organizations and the whole world community in the coming decades should be the attainment by all peoples of the world by the year 2000 of a level of health that will permit them to lead a socially and economically productive life. Primary health care is the key to attaining this target as part of development in the spirit of social justice.

VI

Primary health care is essential health care based on practical, scientifically sound and socially acceptable methods and technology made universally accessible to individuals and families in the community through their full participation and at a cost that the community and country can afford to maintain at every stage of their development in the spirit of self-reliance and self-determination. It forms an integral part both of the country's health system, of which it is the central function and main focus, and of the overall social and economic development of the community. It is the first level of contact of individuals, the family and community with the national health system bringing health care as close as possible to where people live and work, and constitutes the first element of a continuing health care process.

VII

Primary health care:

1. reflects and evolves from the economic conditions and sociocultural and political characteristics of the country and its communities and is based on the application of the relevant results of social, biomedical and health services research and public health experience;
2. addresses the main health problems in the community, providing promotive, preventive, curative and rehabilitative services accordingly;
3. includes at least: education concerning prevailing health problems and the methods of preventing and controlling them; promotion of food supply and proper nutrition; an adequate supply of safe water and basic sanitation; maternal and child health care, including family planning; immunization against the major infectious diseases; prevention and control of locally endemic diseases; appropriate treatment of common diseases and injuries; and provision of essential drugs;
4. involves, in addition to the health sector, all related sectors and aspects of national and community development, in particular agriculture, animal husbandry, food, industry, education, housing, public works, communications and other sectors; and demands the coordinated efforts of all those sectors;
5. requires and promotes maximum community and individual self-reliance and participation in the planning, organization, operation and control of primary health care, making fullest use of local, national and other available resources; and to this end develops through appropriate education the ability of communities to participate;
6. should be sustained by integrated, functional and mutually supportive referral systems, leading to the progressive improvement of compre-

hensive health care for all, and giving priority to those most in need;
7. relies, at local and referral levels, on health workers, including physicians, nurses, midwives, auxiliaries and community workers as applicable, as well as traditional practitioners as needed, suitably trained socially and technically to work as a health team and to respond to the expressed health needs of the community.

VIII

All governments should formulate national policies, strategies and plans of action to launch and sustain primary health care as part of a comprehensive national health system and in coordination with other sectors. To this end, it will be necessary to exercise political will, to mobilize the country's resources and to use available external resources rationally.

IX

All countries should cooperate in a spirit of partnership and service to ensure primary health care for all people since the attainment of health by people in any one country directly concerns and benefits every other country. In this context the joint WHO/UNICEF report on primary health care constitutes a solid basis for the further development and operation of primary health care throughout the world.

X

An acceptable level of health for all the people of the world by the year 2000 can be attained through a fuller and better use of the world's resources, a considerable part of which is now spent on armaments and military conflicts. A genuine policy of independence, peace, détente and disarmament could and should release additional resources that could well be devoted to peaceful aims and in particular to the acceleration of social and economic development of which primary health care, as an essential part, should be allotted its proper share.

*   *   *

The International Conference on Primary Health Care calls for urgent and effective national and international action to develop and implement primary health care throughout the world and particularly in developing countries in a spirit of technical cooperation and in keeping with a New International Economic Order. It urges governments, WHO and UNICEF, and other international organizations, as well as multilateral and bilateral agencies, non-governmental organizations, funding agencies, all health workers and the whole world community to support national and international commitment to primary health care and to channel increased technical and financial support to it, particularly in developing countries. The Conference calls on all the aforementioned to collaborate in introducing, developing and maintaining primary health care in accordance with the spirit and content of this Declaration.

Reproduced, by permission, from Alma-Ata 1978. Primary Health Care. Report of the International Conference on Primary Health Care. Alma-Ata, USSR, 6–12 September 1978. Geneva, World Health Organization, 1978 ("Health for All" Series, No. 1), pp. 2–6.

Recommendations of the U.S. Preventive Services Task Force

The U.S. Department of Health and Human Services convened the U.S. Preventive Services Task Force in 1984. The mandate of this nonfederal, multidisciplinary expert panel was to evaluate the effectiveness of clinical preventive services — screening tests, counseling interventions, immunizations, and chemoprophylactic regimens — based on a systematic review of scientific evidence in published clinical research. The 481-page report of the Task Force, the Guide to Clinical Preventive Services, was published in 1989. The following eight tables are a summary of the Task Force recommendations found in the Guide.

The tables are organized by age group and provide general guidelines in working with individuals, families, and aggregates to encourage disease prevention by providing baseline measures necessary for followup.

The notes following each table identify **high-risk categories.** Many of the preventive services in the tables are recommended only for members of high-risk groups and *are not considered appropriate* in the routine examination of all persons in the age group.

Table 1
Birth to 18 Months

Schedule: 2, 4, 6, 15, 18 Months*

Leading Causes of Death:
Conditions originating in perinatal period
Congenital anomalies
Heart disease
Injuries (nonmotor vehicle)
Pneumonia/influenza

Screening

Height and weight
Hemoglobin and hematocrit[1]
HIGH-RISK GROUPS
   Hearing[2] (HR1)
   Erthrocyte protoporphyrin
      (HR2)

Parent Counseling

Diet
Breastfeeding
Nutrient intake, especially iron-rich
   foods

Injury Prevention
Child safety seats
Smoke detector
Hot water heater temperature
Stairway gates, window guards, pool
   fence
Storage of drugs and toxic chemicals
Syrup of ipecac, poison control tele-
   phone number

Dental Health
Baby bottle tooth decay

Other Primary Preventive Measures
Effects of passive smoking

Immunizations & Chemoprophylaxis

Diphtheria-tetanus-pertussis
   (DTP) vaccine[3]
Oral poliovirus vaccine
   (OPV)[4]
Measles-mumps-rubella
   (MMR) vaccine[5]
Haemophilus influenzae
   type b (Hib) conjugate
   vaccine[6]
HIGH-RISK GROUPS
   Fluoride supplements
      (HR3)
First Week
Ophthalmic antibiotics[7]
Hemoglobin electrophoresis
   (HR4)[7]
T4/TSH[8]
Phenylalanine[8]
Hearing (HR1)

Remain Alert for:
Ocular misalignment
Tooth decay
Signs of child abuse or
   neglect

This list of preventive services is not exhaustive.
It reflects only those topics reviewed by the U.S. Preventive Services Task Force. Clinicians may wish to add other preventive services on a routine basis, and after considering the patient's medical history and other individual circumstances. Examples of target conditions not specifically examined by the Task Force include:

   Developmental disorders   Metabolic disorders
   Musculoskeletal malformations   Speech problems
   Cardiac anomalies   Behavioral disorders
   Genitourinary disorders   Parent/family dysfunction

---

* Five visits are required for immunizations. Because of lack of data and differing patient risk profiles, the scheduling of additional visits and the frequency of the individual preventive services listed in this table are left to clinical discretion (except as indicated in other footnotes.)

1. Once during infancy.   2. At age 18-month visit, if not tested earlier.   3. At ages 2, 4, 6, and 15 months.   4. At ages 2, 4, and 15 months.
5. At age 15 months.   6. At age 18 months.   7. At birth.   8. Days 3 to 6 preferred for testing.

Table 1
Birth to 18 Months *Continued*

High-Risk Categories

HR1 Infants with a family history of childhood hearing impairment or a personal history of congenital perinatal infection with herpes, syphilis, rubella, cytomegalovirus, or toxoplasmosis, malformations involving the head or neck (e.g., dysmorphic and syndromal abnormalities, cleft palate, abnormal pinna); birthweight below 1500 g; bacterial meningitis; hyperbilirubinemia requiring exchange transfusion; or severe perinatal asphyxia (Apgar scores of 0–3, absence of spontaneous respirations for 10 minutes, or hypotonia at 2 hours of age).

HR2 Infants who live in or frequently visit housing built before 1950 that is dilapidated or undergoing renovation; who come in contact with other children with known lead toxicity; who live near lead processing plants or whose parents or household members work in a lead-related occupation; or who live near busy highways or hazardous waste sites.

HR3 Infants living in areas with inadequate water fluoridation (less than 0.7 parts per million).

HR4 Newborns of Caribbean, Latin American, Asian, Mediterranean, or African descent.

Table 2
Ages 2–6

Schedule: See Footnote*

Leading Causes of Death:
Injuries (nonmotor vehicle)
Motor vehicle crashes
Congenital anomalies
Homicide
Heart disease

Screening

Height and weight
Blood pressure
Eye exam for amblyopia and
 strabismus[1]
Urinalysis for bacteriuria
HIGH-RISK GROUPS
 Erythrocyte protopor-
  phyrin[2] (HR1)
 Tuberculin skin test (PPD)
  (HR2)
 Hearing[3] (HR3)

Patient & Parent Counseling

Diet and Exercise
Sweets and between-meal snacks,
 iron-enriched foods, sodium
Caloric balance
Selection of exercise program

Injury Prevention
Safety belts
Smoke detector
Hot water heater temperature
Window guards and pool fence
Bicycle safety helmets
Storage of drugs, toxic chemicals,
 matches, and firearms
Syrup of ipecac, poison control tele-
 phone number

Dental Health
Tooth brushing and dental visits

Other Primary Preventive Measures
Effects of passive smoking
HIGH-RISK GROUPS
 Skin protection from ultraviolet
  light (HR4)

Immunizations & Chemoprophylaxis

Diphtheria-tetanus-pertussis
 (DTP) vaccine[4]
Oral poliovirus vaccine
 (OPV)[4]
HIGH-RISK GROUPS
 Fluoride supplements
  (HR5)

Remain Alert for:
Vision disorders
Dental decay, malalign-
 ment, premature loss of
 teeth, mouth breathing
Signs of child abuse or ne-
 glect
Abnormal bereavement

This list of preventive services is not exhaustive.
It reflects only those topics reviewed by the U.S. Preventive Services Task Force. Clinicians may wish to add other preventive services on a routine basis, and after considering the patient's medical history and other individual circumstances. Examples of target conditions not specifically examined by the Task Force include:

Developmental disorders   Behavioral and learning disorders
Speech problems   Parent/family dysfunction

---

* One visit is required for immunizations. Because of lack of data and differing patient risk profiles, the scheduling of additional visits and the frequency of the individual preventive services listed in this table are left to clinical discretion (except as indicated in other footnotes).

1. Ages 3–4.   2. Annually.   3. Before age 3, if not tested earlier.   4. Once between ages 4 and 6.

Table 2
Ages 2–6 *Continued*

High-Risk Categories

HR1 Children who live in or frequently visit housing built before 1950 that is dilapidated or undergoing renovation; who come in contact with other children with known lead toxicity; who live near lead processing plants or whose parents or household members work in a lead-related occupation; or who live near busy highways or hazardous waste sites.

HR2 Household members of persons with tuberculosis or others at risk for close contact with the disease; recent immigrants or refugees from countries in which tuberculosis is common (e.g., Asia, Africa, Central and South America, Pacific Islands); family members of migrant workers; residents of homeless shelters; or persons with certain underlying medical disorders.

HR3 Children with a family history of childhood hearing impairment or a personal history of congenital perinatal infection with herpes, syphilis, rubella, cytomegalovirus, or toxoplasmosis; malformations involving the head or neck (e.g., dysmorphic and syndromal abnormalities, cleft palate, abnormal pinna); birthweight below 1500 g; bacterial meningitis; hyperbilirubinemia requiring exchange transfusion; or severe perinatal asphyxia (Apgar scores of 0–3, absence of spontaneous respirations for 10 minutes, or hypotonia at 2 hours of age).

HR4 Children with increased exposure to sunlight.

HR5 Children living in areas with inadequate water fluoridation (less than 0.7 parts per million).

Table 3
Ages 7–12

Schedule: See Footnote*

Leading Causes of Death:
Motor vehicle crashes
Injuries (nonmotor vehicle)
Congenital anomalies
Leukemia
Homicide
Heart disease

Screening	Patient & Parent Counseling	Chemoprophylaxis
Height and weight Blood pressure *HIGH-RISK GROUPS* Tuberculin skin test (PPD) (HR1)	**Diet and Exercise** Fat (especially saturated fat), choles- terol, sweets and between-meal snacks, sodium Caloric balance Selection of exercise program **Injury Prevention** Safety belts Smoke detector Storage of firearms, drugs, toxic chem- icals, matches Bicycle safety helmets **Dental Health** Regular tooth brushing and dental visits **Other Primary Preventive Measures** *HIGH-RISK GROUPS* Skin protection from ultraviolet light (HR2)	*HIGH-RISK GROUPS* Fluoride supplements (HR3) **Remain Alert for:** Vision disorders Diminished hearing Dental decay, malalignment, mouth breathing Signs of child abuse or neglect Abnormal bereavement

This list of preventive services is not exhaustive.
It reflects only those topics reviewed by the U.S. Preventive Services Task Force. Clinicians may wish to add other preventive services on a routine basis, and after considering the patient's medical history and other individual circumstances. Examples of target conditions not specifically examined by the Task Force include:

Developmental disorders	Behavioral and learning disorders
Scoliosis	Parent/family dysfunction

* Because of lack of data and differing patient risk profiles, the scheduling of visits and the frequency of the individual preventive services listed in this table are left to clinical discretion.

Table 3
Ages 7–12 *Continued*

High-Risk Categories

HR1 Household members of persons with tuberculosis or others at risk for close contact with the disease; recent immigrants or refugees from countries in which tuberculosis is common (e.g., Asia, Africa, Central and South America, Pacific Islands); family members of migrant workers; residents of homeless shelters; or persons with certain underlying medical disorders.

HR2 Children with increased exposure to sunlight.

HR3 Children living in areas with inadequate water fluoridation (less than 0.7 parts per million).

Table 4
Ages 13–18

Schedule: See Footnote*

Leading Causes of Death: Motor vehicle crashes, Homicide, Suicide, Injuries (nonmotor vehicle), Heart disease

Screening

History
Dietary intake
Physical activity
Tobacco/alcohol/drug use
Sexual practices

Physical Exam
Height and weight
Blood pressure
HIGH-RISK GROUPS
    Complete skin exam
        (HR1)
    Clinical testicular exam
        (HR2)

Laboratory/Diagnostic Procedures
HIGH-RISK GROUPS
    Rubella antibodies (HR3)
    VDRL/RPR (HR4)
    Chlamydial testing (HR5)
    Gonorrhea culture (HR6)
    Counseling and testing for
        HIV (HR7)
    Tuberculin skin test (PPD)
        (HR8)
    Hearing (HR9)
    Papanicolaou smear
        (HR10)[1]

Counseling

Diet and Exercise
Fat (especially saturated fat), cholesterol, sodium, iron,[2] calcium[2]
Caloric balance
Selection of exercise program

Substance Use
Tobacco: cessation/primary prevention
Alcohol and other drugs: cessation/
    primary prevention
        Driving/other dangerous activities
            while under the influence
        Treatment for abuse
HIGH-RISK GROUPS
    Sharing/using unsterilized needles
        and syringes (HR12)

Sexual Practices
Sexual development and behavior[3]
Sexually transmitted diseases: partner
    selection, condoms
Unintended pregnancy and contraceptive options

Injury Prevention
Safety belts
Safety helmets
Violent behavior[4]
Firearms[4]
Smoke detector

Dental Health
Regular tooth brushing, flossing,
    dental visits

Other Primary Preventive Measures
HIGH-RISK GROUPS
    Discussion of hemoglobin testing
        (HR13)
    Skin protection from ultraviolet
        light (HR14)

Immunizations & Chemoprophylaxis

Tetanus-diphtheria (Td)
    booster[5]
HIGH-RISK GROUPS
    Fluoride supplements
        (HR15)

Remain Alert for:
Depressive symptoms
Suicide risk factors (HR11)
Abnormal bereavement
Tooth decay, malalignment, gingivitis
Signs of child abuse and
    neglect

This list of preventive services is not exhaustive.
It reflects only those topics reviewed by the U.S. Preventive Services Task Force. Clinicians may wish to add other preventive services on a routine basis, and after considering the patient's medical history and other individual circumstances. Examples of target conditions not specifically examined by the Task Force include:

Developmental disorders	Behavioral and learning disorders
Scoliosis	Parent/family dysfunction

---

* One visit is required for immunizations. Because of lack of data and differing patient risk profiles, the scheduling of additional visits and the frequency of the individual preventive services listed in this table are left to clinical discretion (except as indicated in other footnotes.)

1. Every 1–3 years.   2. For females.   3. Often best performed early in adolescence and with the involvement of parents.   4. Especially for males.   5. Once between ages 14 and 16.

Table 4
Ages 13–18 *Continued*

High-Risk Categories

HR1 Persons with increased recreational or occupational exposure to sunlight, a family or personal history of skin cancer, or clinical evidence of precursor lesions (e.g., dysplastic nevi, certain congenital nevi).

HR2 Males with a history of cryptorchidism, orchiopexy, or testicular atrophy.

HR3 Females of childbearing age lacking evidence of immunity.

HR4 Persons who engage in sex with multiple partners in areas in which syphilis is prevalent, prostitutes, or contacts of persons with active syphilis.

HR5 Persons who attend clinics for sexually transmitted diseases; attend other high-risk health care facilities (e.g., adolescent and family planning clinics); or have other risk factors for chlamydial infection (e.g., multiple sexual partners or a sexual partner with multiple sexual contacts).

HR6 Persons with multiple sexual partners or a sexual partner with multiple contacts, sexual contacts of persons with culture-proven gonorrhea, or persons with a history of repeated episodes of gonorrhea.

HR7 Persons seeking treatment for sexually transmitted diseases; homosexual and bisexual men; past or present intravenous (IV) drug users; persons with a history of prostitution or multiple sexual partners; women whose past or present sexual partners were HIV-infected, bisexual, or IV drug users; persons with long-term residence or birth in an area with high prevalence of HIV infection; or persons with a history of transfusion between 1978 and 1985.

HR8 Household members of persons with tuberculosis or others at risk for close contact with the disease; recent immigrants or refugees from countries in which tuberculosis is common (e.g., Asia, Africa, Central and South America, Pacific Islands): migrant workers; residents of correctional institutions or homeless shelters; or persons with certain underlying medical disorders.

HR9 Persons exposed regularly to excessive noise in recreational or other settings.

HR10 Females who are sexually active or (if the sexual history is thought to be unreliable) aged 18 or older.

HR11 Recent divorce, separation, unemployment, depression, alcohol or other drug abuse, serious medical illnesses, living alone, or recent bereavement.

HR12 Intravenous drug users.

HR13 Persons of Caribbean, Latin American, Asian, Mediterranean, or African descent.

HR14 Persons with increased exposure to sunlight.

HR15 Persons living in areas with inadequate water fluoridation (less than 0.7 parts per million).

Table 5
Ages 19–39

Schedule: Every 1–3 Years*

Leading Causes of Death: Motor vehicle crashes, Homicide, Suicide, Injuries (nonmotor vehicle), Heart disease

Screening

History
Dietary intake
Physical activity
Tobacco/alcohol/drug use
Sexual practices

Physical Exam
Height and weight
Blood pressure
HIGH-RISK GROUPS
    Complete oral cavity exam
      (HR1)
    Palpation for thyroid
      nodules (HR2)
    Clinical breast exam (HR3)
    Clinical testicular exam
      (HR4)
    Complete skin exam (HR5)

Laboratory/Diagnostic Procedures
Nonfasting total blood cho-
  lesterol
Papanicolaou smear[1]
HIGH-RISK GROUPS
    Fasting plasma glucose
      (HR6)
    Rubella antibodies (HR7)
    VDRL/RPR (HR8)
    Urinalysis for bacteriuria
      (HR9)
    Chlamydial testing (HR10)
    Gonorrhea culture (HR11)
    Counseling and testing for
      HIV (HR12)
    Hearing (HR13)
    Tuberculin skin test (PPD)
      (HR14)
    Electrocardiogram (HR15)
    Mammogram (HR3)
    Colonoscopy (HR16)

Counseling

Diet and Exercise
Fat (especially saturated fat), cholesterol,
  complex carbohydrates, fiber, sodium,
  iron,[2] calcium[2]
Caloric balance
Selection of exercise program

Substance Use
Tobacco: cessation/primary prevention
Alcohol and other drugs:
    Limiting alcohol consumption
    Driving/other dangerous activities
      while under the influence
    Treatment for abuse
HIGH-RISK GROUPS
    Sharing/using unsterilized needles and
      syringes (HR18)

Sexual Practices
Sexually transmitted diseases: partner selection, condoms, anal intercourse
Unintended pregnancy and contraceptive
  options

Injury Prevention
Safety belts
Safety helmets
Violent behavior[3]
Firearms[3]
Smoke detector
Smoking near bedding or upholstery
HIGH-RISK GROUPS
    Back-conditioning exercises (HR19)
    Prevention of childhood injuries (HR20)
    Falls in the elderly (HR21)

Dental Health
Regular tooth brushing, flossing, dental visits

Other Primary Preventive Measures
HIGH-RISK GROUPS
    Discussion of hemoglobin testing (HR22)
    Skin protection from ultraviolet light
      (HR23)

Immunizations

Tetanus-diphtheria (Td)
  booster[4]
HIGH-RISK GROUPS
    Hepatitis B vaccine
      (HR24)
    Pneumococcal vaccine
      (HR25)
    Influenza vaccine[5] (HR26)
    Measles-mumps-rubella
      vaccine (HR27)

Remain Alert for:
Depressive symptoms
Suicide risk factors (HR17)
Abnormal bereavement
Malignant skin lesions
Tooth decay, gingivitis
Signs of physical abuse

This list of preventive services is not exhaustive.
It reflects only those topics reviewed by the U.S. Preventive Services Task Force. Clinicians may wish to add other preventive services on a routine basis, and after considering the patient's medical history and other individual circumstances. Examples of target conditions not specifically examined by the Task Force include:

Chronic obstructive pulmonary disease
Hepatobiliary disease
Bladder cancer
Endometrial disease

Travel-related illness
Prescription drug abuse
Occupational illness and injuries

---

* The recommended schedule applies only to the periodic visit itself. The frequency of the individual preventive services listed in this table is left to clinical discretion, except as indicated in other footnotes.

1. Every 1–3 years.   2. For women.   3. Especially for young males.   4. Every 10 years.   5. Annually.

Table 5
Ages 19–39 *Continued*   High-Risk Categories

HR1 Persons with exposure to tobacco or excessive amounts of alcohol, or those with suspicious symptoms or lesions detected through self-examination.

HR2 Persons with a history of upper-body irradiation.

HR3 Women aged 35 and older with a family history of premenopausally diagnosed breast cancer in a first-degree relative.

HR4 Men with a history of cryptorchidism, orchiopexy, or testicular atrophy.

HR5 Persons with family or personal history of skin cancer, increased occupational or recreational exposure to sunlight, or clinical evidence of precursor lesions (e.g., dysplastic nevi, certain congenital nevi).

HR6 The markedly obese, persons with a family history of diabetes, or women with a history of gestational diabetes.

HR7 Women lacking evidence of immunity.

HR8 Prostitutes, persons who engage in sex with multiple partners in areas in which syphilis is prevalent, or contacts of persons with active syphilis.

HR9 Persons with diabetes.

HR10 Persons who attend clinics for sexually transmitted diseases; attend other high-risk health care facilities (e.g., adolescent and family planning clinics); or have other risk factors for chlamydial infection (e.g., multiple sexual partners or a sexual partner with multiple sexual contacts, age less than 20).

HR11 Prostitutes, persons with multiple sexual partners or a sexual partner with multiple contacts, sexual contacts of persons with culture-proven gonorrhea, or persons with a history of repeated episodes of gonorrhea.

HR12 Persons seeking treatment for sexually transmitted diseases; homosexual and bisexual men; past or present intravenous (IV) drug users; persons with a history of prostitution or multiple sexual partners; women whose past or present sexual partners were HIV-infected, bisexual, or IV drug users; persons with long-term residence or birth in an area with high prevalence of HIV infection; or persons with a history of transfusion between 1978 and 1985.

HR13 Persons exposed regularly to excessive noise.

HR14 Household members of persons with tuberculosis or others at risk for close contact with the disease (e.g., staff of tuberculosis clinics, shelters for the homeless, nursing homes, substance abuse treatment facilities, dialysis units, correctional institutions); recent immigrants or refugees from countries in which tuberculosis is common; migrant workers; residents of nursing homes, correctional institutions, or homeless shelters; or persons with certain underlying medical disorders (e.g., HIV infection).

HR15 Men who would endanger public safety were they to experience sudden cardiac events (e.g., commercial airline pilots).

HR16 Persons with a family history of familial polyposis coli or cancer family syndrome.

HR17 Recent divorce, separation, unemployment, depression, alcohol or other drug abuse, serious medical illnesses, living alone, or recent bereavement.

HR18 Intravenous drug users.

HR19 Persons at increased risk for low back injury because of past history, body configuration, or type of activities.

HR20 Persons with children in the home or automobile.

HR21 Persons with older adults in the home.

HR22 Young adults of Caribbean, Latin American, Asian, Mediterranean, or African descent.

HR23 Persons with increased exposure to sunlight.

HR24 Homosexually active men, intravenous drug users, recipients of some blood products, or persons in health-related jobs with frequent exposure to blood or blood products.

HR25 Persons with medical conditions that increase the risk of pneumococcal infection (e.g., chronic cardiac or pulmonary disease, sickle cell disease, nephrotic syndrome, Hodgkin's disease, asplenia, diabetes mellitus, alcoholism, cirrhosis, multiple myeloma, renal disease, or conditions associated with immunosuppression).

HR26 Residents of chronic care facilities or persons suffering from chronic cardiopulmonary disorders, metabolic diseases (including diabetes mellitus), hemoglobinopathies, immunosuppression, or renal dysfunction.

HR27 Persons born after 1956 who lack evidence of immunity to measles (receipt of live vaccine on or after first birthday, laboratory evidence of immunity, or a history of physician-diagnosed measles).

Table 6
Ages 40–64

Schedule: Every 1–3 Years*

Leading Causes of Death: Heart disease, Lung cancer, Cerebrovascular disease, Breast cancer, Colorectal cancer, Obstructive lung disease

Screening

History
Dietary intake
Physical activity
Tobacco/alcohol/drug use
Sexual practices

Physical Exam
Height and weight
Blood pressure
Clinical breast exam[1]
HIGH-RISK GROUPS
Complete skin exam (HR1)
Complete oral cavity exam (HR2)
Palpation for thyroid nodules (HR3)
Auscultation for carotid bruits (HR4)

Laboratory/Diagnostic Procedures
Nonfasting total blood cholesterol
Papanicolaou smear[2]
Mammogram[3]
HIGH-RISK GROUPS
Fasting plasma glucose (HR5)
VDRL/RPR (HR6)
Urinalysis for bacteriuria (HR7)
Chlamydial testing (HR8)
Gonorrhea culture (HR9)
Counseling and testing for HIV (HR10)
Tuberculin skin test (PPD) (HR11)
Hearing (HR12)
Electrocardiogram (HR13)
Fecal occult blood/sigmoidoscopy (HR14)
Fecal occult blood/colonoscopy (HR15)
Bone mineral content (HR16)

Counseling

Diet and Exercise
Fat (especially saturated fat), cholesterol, complex carbohydrates, fiber, sodium, calcium[4]
Caloric balance
Selection of exercise program

Substance Use
Tobacco cessation
Alcohol and other drugs:
Limiting alcohol consumption
Driving/other dangerous activities while under the influence
Treatment for abuse
HIGH-RISK GROUPS
Sharing/using unsterilized needles and syringes (HR19)

Sexual Practices
Sexually transmitted diseases: partner selection, condoms, anal intercourse
Unintended pregnancy and contraceptive options

Injury Prevention
Safety belts
Safety helmets
Smoke detector
Smoking near bedding or upholstery
HIGH-RISK GROUPS
Back-conditioning exercises (HR20)
Prevention of childhood injuries (HR21)
Falls in the elderly (HR22)

Dental Health
Regular tooth brushing, flossing, and dental visits

Other Primary Preventive Measures
HIGH-RISK GROUPS
Skin protection from ultraviolet light (HR23)
Discussion of aspirin therapy (HR24)
Discussion of estrogen replacement therapy (HR25)

Immunizations

Tetanus-diphtheria (Td) booster[5]
HIGH-RISK GROUPS
Hepatitis B vaccine (HR26)
Pneumococcal vaccine (HR27)
Influenza vaccine (HR28)[6]

Remain Alert for:
Depressive symptoms
Suicide risk factors (HR17)
Abnormal bereavement
Signs of physical abuse or neglect
Malignant skin lesions
Peripheral arterial disease (HR18)
Tooth decay, gingivitis, loose teeth

This list of preventive services is not exhaustive.
It reflects only those topics reviewed by the U.S. Preventive Services Task Force. Clinicians may wish to add other preventive services on a routine basis, and after considering the patient's medical history and other individual circumstances. Examples of target conditions not specifically examined by the Task Force include:

Chronic obstructive pulmonary disease
Hepatobiliary disease
Bladder cancer
Endometrial disease

Travel-related illness
Prescription drug abuse
Occupational illness and injuries

---

* The recommended schedule applies only to the periodic visit itself. The frequency of the individual preventive services listed in this table is left to clinical discretion, except as indicated in other footnotes.

1. Annually for women.   2. Every 1–3 years for women.   3. Every 1–2 years for women beginning at age 50 (age 35 for those at increased risk).   4. For women.   5. Every 10 years.   6. Annually.

Table 6
Ages 40–64 *Continued*   High-Risk Categories

HR1 Persons with a family or personal history of skin cancer, increased occupational or recreational exposure to sunlight, or clinical evidence of precursor lesions (e.g., dysplastic nevi, certain congenital nevi).

HR2 Persons with exposure to tobacco or excessive amounts of alcohol, or those with suspicious symptoms or lesions detected through self-examination.

HR3 Persons with a history of upper-body irradiation.

HR4 Persons with risk factors for cerebrovascular or cardiovascular disease (e.g., hypertension, smoking, CAD, atrial fibrillation, diabetes) or those with neurologic symptoms (e.g., transient ischemic attacks) or a history of cerebrovascular disease.

HR5 The markedly obese, persons with a family history of diabetes, or women with a history of gestational diabetes.

HR6 Prostitutes, persons who engage in sex with multiple partners in areas in which syphilis is prevalent, or contacts of persons with active syphilis.

HR7 Persons with diabetes.

HR8 Persons who attend clinics for sexually transmitted diseases; attend other high-risk health care facilities (e.g., adolescent and family planning clinics); or have other risk factors for chlamydial infection (e.g., multiple sexual partners or a sexual partner with multiple sexual contacts).

HR9 Prostitutes, persons with multiple sexual partners or a sexual partner with multiple contacts, sexual contacts of persons with culture-proven gonorrhea, or persons with a history of repeated episodes of gonorrhea.

HR10 Persons seeking treatment for sexually transmitted diseases; homosexual and bisexual men; past or present intravenous (IV) drug users; persons with a history of prostitution or multiple sexual partners; women whose past or present sexual partners were HIV-infected, bisexual, or IV drug users; persons with long-term residence or birth in an area with high prevalence of HIV infection; or persons with a history of transfusion between 1978 and 1985.

HR11 Household members of persons with tuberculosis or others at risk for close contact with the disease (e.g., staff of tuberculosis clinics, shelters for the homeless, nursing homes, substance abuse treatment facilities, dialysis units, correctional institutions); recent immigrants or refugees from countries in which tuberculosis is common (e.g., Asia, Africa, Central and South America, Pacific Islands); migrant workers; residents of nursing homes, correctional institutions, or homeless shelters; or persons with certain underlying medical disorders (e.g., HIV infection).

HR12 Persons exposed regularly to excessive noise.

HR13 Men with two or more cardiac risk factors (high blood cholesterol, hypertension, cigarette smoking, diabetes mellitus, family history of CAD); men who would endanger public safety were they to experience sudden cardiac events (e.g., commercial airline pilots); or sedentary or high-risk males planning to begin a vigorous exercise program.

HR14 Persons aged 50 and older who have first-degree relatives with colorectal cancer; a personal history of endometrial, ovarian, or breast cancer; or a previous diagnosis of inflammatory bowel disease, adenomatous polyps, or colorectal cancer.

HR15 Persons with a family history of familial polyposis coli or cancer family syndrome.

HR16 Perimenopausal women at increased risk for osteoporosis (e.g., Caucasian race, bilateral oopherectomy before menopause, slender build) and for whom estrogen replacement therapy would otherwise not be recommended.

HR17 Recent divorce, separation, unemployment, depression, alcohol or other drug abuse, serious medical illnesses, living alone, or recent bereavement.

HR18 Persons over age 50, smokers, or persons with diabetes mellitus.

HR19 Intravenous drug users.

HR20 Persons at increased risk for low back injury because of past history, body configuration, or type of activities.

HR21 Persons with children in the home or automobile.

HR22 Persons with older adults in the home.

HR23 Persons with increased exposure to sunlight.

HR24 Men who have risk factors for myocardial infarction (e.g., high blood cholesterol, smoking, diabetes mellitus, family hisotry of early-onset CAD) and who lack a history of gastrointestinal or other bleeding problems, and other risk factors for bleeding or cerebral hemorrhage.

HR25 Perimenopausal women at increased risk for osteoporosis (e.g., Caucasian, low bone mineral content, bilateral oopherectomy before menopause or early menopause, slender build) and who are without known contraindications (e.g., history of undiagnosed vaginal bleeding, active liver disease, thromboembolic disorders, hormone-dependent cancer).

HR26 Homosexually active men, intravenous drug users, recipients of some blood products, or persons in health-related jobs with frequent exposure to blood or blood products.

HR27 Persons with medical conditions that increase the risk of pneumococcal infection (e.g., chronic cardiac or pulmonary disease, sickle cell disease, nephrotic syndrome, Hodgkin's disease, asplenia, diabetes mellitus, alcoholism, cirrhosis, multiple myeloma, renal disease or conditions associated with immunosuppression).

HR28 Residents of chronic care facilities or persons suffering from chronic cardiopulmonary disorders, metabolic diseases (including diabetes mellitus), hemoglobinopathies, immunosuppression, or renal dysfunction.

Table 7
Ages 65 and Over

Schedule: Every Year*

Leading Causes of Death: Heart disease, Cerebrovascular disease, Obstructive lung disease, Pneumonia/influenza, Lung cancer, Colorectal cancer

Screening

History
Prior symptoms of transient ischemic attack
Dietary intake
Physical activity
Tobacco/alcohol/drug use
Functional status at home

Physical Exam
Height and weight
Blood pressure
Visual acuity
Hearing and hearing aids
Clinical breast exam[1]
HIGH-RISK GROUPS
   Auscultation for carotid bruits
      (HR1)
   Complete skin exam (HR2)
   Complete oral cavity exam
      (HR3)
   Palpation for thyroid nodules
      (HR4)

Laboratory/Diagnostic Procedures
Nonfasting total blood cholesterol
Dipstick urinalysis
Mammogram[2]
Thyroid function tests[3]
HIGH-RISK GROUPS
   Fasting plasma glucose (HR5)
   Tuberculin skin test (PPD)
      (HR6)
   Electrocardiogram (HR7)
   Papanicolaou smear[4] (HR8)
   Fecal occult blood/Sigmoidoscopy
      (HR9)
   Fecal occult blood/Colonoscopy
      (HR10)

Counseling

Diet and Exercise
Fat (especially saturated fat), cholesterol, complex carbohydrates, fiber, sodium, calcium[3]
Caloric balance
Selection of exercise program

Substance Use
Tobacco cessation
Alcohol and other drugs:
   Limiting alcohol consumption
   Driving/other dangerous activities
      while under the influence
   Treatment for abuse

Injury Prevention
Prevention of falls
Safety belts
Smoke detector
Smoking near bedding or upholstery
Hot water heater temperature
Safety helmets
HIGH-RISK GROUPS
   Prevention of childhood injuries
      (HR12)

Dental Health
Regular dental visits, tooth brushing, flossing

Other Primary Preventive Measures
Glaucoma testing by eye specialist
HIGH-RISK GROUPS
   Discussion of estrogen replacement
      therapy (HR13)
   Discussion of aspirin therapy
      (HR14)
   Skin protection from ultraviolet
      light (HR15)

Immunizations

Tetanus-diphtheria (Td)
   booster[5]
Influenza vaccine[1]
Pneumococcal vaccine
HIGH-RISK GROUPS
   Hepatitis B vaccine
      (HR16)

Remain Alert for:
Depression symptoms
Suicide risk factors (HR11)
Abnormal bereavement
Changes in cognitive function
Medications that increase risk of falls
Signs of physical abuse or neglect
Malignant skin lesions
Peripheral arterial disease
Tooth decay, gingivitis, loose teeth

This list of preventive services is not exhaustive.
It reflects only those topics reviewed by the U.S. Preventive Services Task Force. Clinicians may wish to add other preventive services on a routine basis, and after considering the patient's medical history and other individual circumstances. Examples of target conditions not specifically examined by the Task Force include:

Chronic obstructive pulmonary disease	Travel-related illness
Hepatobiliary disease	Prescription drug abuse
Bladder cancer	Occupational illness and injuries
Endometrial disease	

---

* The recommended schedule applies only to the periodic visit itself. The frequency of the individual preventive services listed in this table is left to clinical discretion, except as indicated in other footnotes.

1. Annually.   2. Every 1–2 years for women until age 75, unless pathology detected.   3. For women.   4. Every 1–3 years.   5. Every 10 years.

Table 7	
Ages 65 and Over *Continued*	High-Risk Categories

HR1 Persons with risk factors for cerebrovascular or cardiovascular disease (e.g., hypertension, smoking, CAD, atrial fibrillation, diabetes) or those with neurologic symptoms (e.g., transient ischemic attacks) or a history of cerebrovascular disease.

HR2 Persons with a family or personal history of skin cancer, or clinical evidence of precursor lesions (e.g., dysplastic nevi, certain congenital nevi), or those with increased occupational or recreational exposure to sunlight.

HR3 Persons with exposure to tobacco or excessive amounts of alcohol, or those with suspicious symptoms or lesions detected through self-examination.

HR4 Persons with a history of upper-body irradiation.

HR5 The markedly obese, persons with a family history of diabetes, or women with a history of gestational diabetes.

HR6 Household members of persons with tuberculosis or others at risk for close contact with the disease (e.g., staff of tuberculosis clinics, shelters for the homeless, nursing homes, substance abuse treatment facilities, dialysis units, correctional institutions); recent immigrants or refugees from countries in which tuberculosis is common (e.g., Asia, Africa, Central and South America, Pacific Islands); migrant workers; residents of nursing homes, correctional institutions, or homeless shelters; or persons with certain underlying medical disorders (e.g., HIV infection).

HR7 Men with two or more cardiac risk factors (high blood cholesterol, hypertension, cigarette smoking, diabetes mellitus, family history of CAD); men who would endanger public safety were they to experience sudden cardiac events (e.g., commercial airline pilots); or sedentary or high-risk males planning to begin a vigorous exercise program.

HR8 Women who have not had previous documented screening in which smears have been consistently negative.

HR9 Persons who have first-degree relatives with colorectal cancer; a personal history of endometrial, ovarian, or breast cancer; or a previous diagnosis of inflammatory bowel disease, adenomatous polyps, or colorectal cancer.

HR10 Persons with a family history of familial polyposis coli or cancer family syndrome.

HR11 Recent divorce, separation, unemployment, depression, alcohol or other drug abuse, serious medical illnesses, living alone, or recent bereavement.

HR12 Persons with children in the home or automobile.

HR13 Women at increased risk for osteoporosis (e.g., Caucasian, low bone mineral content, bilateral oophorectomy before menopause or early menopause, slender build) and who are without known contraindications (e.g., history of undiagnosed vaginal bleeding, active liver disease, thromboembolic disorders, hormone-dependent cancer).

HR14 Men who have risk factors for myocardial infarction (e.g., high blood cholesterol, smoking, diabetes mellitus, family history of early-onset CAD) and who lack a history of gastrointestinal or other bleeding problems, or other risk factors for bleeding or cerebral hemorrhage.

HR15 Persons with increased exposure to sunlight.

HR24 Homosexually active men, intravenous drug users, recipients of some blood products, or persons in health-related jobs with frequent exposure to blood or blood products.

Table 8
Pregnant Women[1]

First Prenatal Visit

History
Genetic and obstetric history
Dietary intake
Tobacco/alcohol/drug use
Risk factors for intrauterine growth retardation
  and low birthweight

Laboratory/Diagnostic Procedures
Blood pressure
Hemoglobin and hematocrit
ABO/Rh typing
Rh(D) and other antibody screen
VDRL/RPR
Hepatitis b surface antigen (HBsAg)
Urinalysis for bacteriuria
Gonorrhea culture
HIGH-RISK GROUPS
  Hemoglobin electrophoresis (HR1)
  Rubella antibodies (HR2)
  Chlamydial testing (HR3)
  Counseling and testing for HIV (HR4)

Nutrition
Tobacco use
Alcohol and other drug use
Safety belts
HIGH-RISK GROUPS
  Discuss amniocentesis (HR5)
  Discuss risks of HIV infection (HR4)

Remain Alert for:
Signs of physical abuse

Follow-Up Visits
Schedule: See Footnote*

Screening
Blood pressure
Urinalysis for bacteriuria

Screening Tests at Specific Gestational Ages

14–16 Weeks:
  Maternal serum alpha-fetoprotein (MSAFP)[2]
  Ultrasound cephalometry (HR8)

24–28 Weeks:
  50 g oral glucose tolerance test
  Rh(D) antibody (HR9)
  Gonorrhea culture (HR10)
  VDRL/RPR (HR11)
  Hepatitis B surface antigen (HBsAg) (HR12)
  Counseling and testing for HIV (HR13)

36 Weeks:
  Ultrasound exam (HR14)

Counseling
Nutrition
Safety belts
Discuss meaning of upcoming tests
HIGH-RISK GROUPS
  Tobacco use (HR6)
  Alcohol and other drug use (HR7)

Remain Alert for:
Signs of physical abuse

This list of preventive services is not exhaustive.
It reflects only those topics reviewed by the U.S. Preventive Services Task Force. Clinicians may wish to add other preventive services on a routine basis, and after considering the patient's medical history and other individual circumstances. Examples of target conditions not specifically examined by the Task Force include:

Counseling on warning signs and symptoms
Physical findings of abdominal and cervical examination

Childbirth education
Teratogenic and fetotoxic exposures
Tay-Sachs disease

* Because of lack of data and differing patient risk profiles, the scheduling of visits and the frequency of the individual preventive services listed in this table are left to clinical discretion, except for those indicated at specific gestational ages.

1. See also Tables 4–6 for other preventive services for women.   2. Women with access to counseling and follow-up services, skilled high-resolution ultrasound and amniocentesis capabilities, and reliable, standardized laboratories.

Table 8
Pregnant Women *Continued*   High-Risk Categories

HR1 Black women.

HR2 Women lacking evidence of immunity (proof of vaccination after the first birthday or laboratory evidence of immunity.)

HR3 Women who attend clinics for sexually transmitted diseases, attend other high-risk health care facilities (e.g., adolescent and family planning clinics), or have other risk factors for chlamydial infection (e.g., multiple sexual partners or a sexual partner with multiple sexual contacts).

HR4 Women seeking treatment for sexually transmitted diseases; past or present intravenous (IV) drug users; women with a history of prostitution or multiple sexual partners; women whose past or present sexual partners were HIV-infected, bisexual, or IV drug users; women with long-term residence or birth in an area with high prevalence of HIV infection in women; or women with a history of transfusion between 1978 and 1985.

HR5 Women aged 35 or older.

HR6 Women who continue to smoke during pregnancy.

HR7 Women with excessive alcohol consumption during pregnancy.

HR8 Women with uncertain menstrual histories or risk factors for intrauterine growth retardation (e.g., hypertension, renal disease, short maternal stature, low prepregnancy weight, failure to gain weight during pregnancy, smoking, alcohol and other drug abuse, and history of a previous fetal death or growth-retarded baby).

HR9 Unsensitized Rh-negative women.

HR10 Women with multiple sexual partners or a sexual partner with multiple contacts, or sexual contacts of persons with culture-proven gonorrhea.

HR11 Women who engage in sex with multiple partners in areas in which syphilis is prevalent, or contacts of persons with active syphilis.

HR12 Women who engage in high-risk behavior (e.g., intravenous drug use) or in whom exposure to hepatitis B during pregnancy is suspected.

HR13 Women at high risk (see HR4) who have a nonreactive HIV test at the first prenatal visit.

HR14 Women with risk factors for intrauterine growth retardation (see HR8).

From Healthy People 2000: National Health Promotion and Disease Prevention Objectives. Washington, D.C., U.S. Department of Health and Human Services, Public Health Service, 1991. Available from the Superintendent of Documents, Washington, D.C., U.S. Government Printing Office, DHHS Publication no. (PHS) 91-50212.

Healthy People 2000

A government publication, *Healthy People 2000: National Health Promotion and Disease Prevention Objectives,* contains a national prevention strategy for improving the health of the citizens of the United States over the 1990–2000 decade. Health professionals from numerous disciplines, health advocates, and consumers contributed to the objectives aimed for by the year 2000. These persons testified at public hearings, wrote letters and papers, and organized and attended informational forums. Their commitment is reflected in the objectives, which focus on the prevention of major chronic illnesses, injuries, and infectious diseases. Premature deaths, disease, and disabilities will be prevented as these goals are attained. For all of us and for health policy makers, the strategy makes clear that we must invest in prevention. We can no longer afford to treat diseases and injuries that could have been prevented. The costs are too great in terms of our fiscal resources and in terms of human misery.

To reach the targets set for the year 2000, all Americans, not just health professionals, will need to make a concerted effort to change the underlying environmental and political conditions that will lead to the promotion of health and prevention of disease.

In *Healthy People 2000,* norms for health conditions for the U.S. population and targets for the year 2000 for each health condition are presented by major topic areas. Comparing the norm and the targets with conditions in your community can help in making a nursing diagnosis and in planning at the aggregate level. This Appendix V consists of two sections: Age-Related Objectives and Special Population Objectives, from which Key Health Status Objectives are excerpted. The complete document is available from U.S. government document offices and bookstores. The full citation is given at the end of the Appendix.

A. KEY AGE-RELATED OBJECTIVES

Children

The target for reducing deaths among infants and children:

Reduce the death rate for children by 15 percent to no more than 28 per 100,000 children aged 1 through 14, and for infants by approximately 30 percent to no more than 7 per 1,000 live births. (Baseline: 33 per 100,000 for children in 1987 and 10.1 per 1,000 live births for infants in 1987)

KEY HEALTH STATUS OBJECTIVES TARGETING CHILDREN

2.4   Reduce growth retardation among low-income children aged 5 and younger to less than 10 percent. (Baseline: Up to 16 percent among low-income children in 1988, depending on age and race/ethnicity)

6.3   Reduce to less than 10 percent the prevalence of mental disorders among children and adolescents. (Baseline: An estimated 12 percent among youth younger than age 18 in 1989)

7.1a   Reduce homicides among children aged 3 and younger to no more than 3.1 per 100,000. (Age-adjusted baseline: 3.9 per 100,000 in 1987)

7.4   Reverse to less than 25.2 per 1,000 children the rising incidence of maltreatment of children younger than age 18. (Baseline: 25.2 per 1,000 in 1986)

Incidence of Types of Maltreatment (per 1,000)	1986 Baseline	2000 Target
7.4a Physical abuse	5.7	<5.7
7.4b Sexual abuse	2.5	<2.5
7.4c Emotional abuse	3.4	<3.4
7.4d Neglect	15.9	<15.9

9.3a   Reduce deaths among children aged 14 and younger caused by motor vehicle crashes to no more than 5.5 per 100,000. (Baseline: 6.2 per 100,000 in 1987)

9.5a   Reduce drowning deaths among children aged 4 and younger to no more than 2.3 per 100,000. (Age-adjusted baseline: 4.2 per 100,000 in 1987)

9.6a   Reduce residential fire deaths among children aged 4 and younger to no more than 3.3 per 100,000. (Age-adjusted baseline: 4.4 per 100,000 in 1987)

9.8a   Reduce nonfatal poisoning among children aged 4 and younger to no more than 520 emergency department treatments per 100,000. (Baseline: 650 per 100,000 in 1986)

11.1b Reduce asthma morbidity among children aged 14 and younger, as measured by a reduction in asthma hospitalizations to no more than 225 per 100,000. (Baseline: 284 per 100,000 in 1987)

11.4   Reduce the prevalence of blood lead levels exceeding 15 μg/dL and 25 μg/dL among children aged 6 months through 5 years to no more than 500,000 and zero, respectively. (Baseline: An estimated 3 million children had levels exceeding 15 μg/dL, and 234,000 had levels exceeding 25 μg/dL, in 1984)

Special Population Target

Prevalence of Blood Lead Levels Exceeding 15 μg/dL & 25 μg/dL	1984 Baseline	2000 Target
11.4a Inner-city low-income black children (annual family income <$6,000 in 1984 dollars)	234,900 & 36,700	75,000 & 0

13.1   Reduce dental caries (cavities) so that the proportion of children with one or more caries (in permanent or primary teeth) is no more than 35 percent among children aged 6 through 8 and no more than 60 percent among adolescents aged 15. (Baseline: 53 percent of children aged 6 through 8 in 1986–87; 78 percent of adolescents aged 15 in 1986–87)

14.1   Reduce the infant mortality rate to no more than 7 per 1,000 live births. (Baseline: 10.1 per 1,000 live births in 1987)

Special Population Targets

Infant Mortality per 1,000 Live Births	1987 Baseline	2000 Target
14.1a Blacks	17.9	11
14.1b American Indians/Alaska Natives	12.5	8.5
14.1c Puerto Ricans	12.9	8

Note: Infant mortality is deaths of infants under 1 year; neonatal mortality is deaths of infants under 28 days; and postneonatal mortality is deaths of infants aged 28 days up to 1 year.

17.8*   Reduce the prevalence of serious mental retardation in school-aged children to no more than 2 per 1,000 children. (Baseline: 2.7 per 1,000 children aged 10 in 1985–88)

20.3d* Reduce Hepatitis B (HBV) among children of Asians/Pacific Islanders to an incidence of no more than 1,800 cases. (Baseline: An estimated 8,900 cases in 1987)

20.8   Reduce infectious diarrhea by at least 25 percent among children in licensed child care centers and children in programs that provide an Individualized Education Program (IEP) or Individualized Health Plan (IHP). (Baseline data available in 1992)

20.9   Reduce acute middle ear infections among children aged 4 and younger, as measured by days of restricted activity or school absenteeism, to no more than 105 days per 100 children. (Baseline: 131 days per 100 children in 1987)

---

* Indicates duplicate objectives, which appear in two or more priority areas.

20.10   Reduce pneumonia-related days of restricted activity as follows:

	1987 Baseline	*2000 Target*
Children aged 4 and younger (per 100 children)	27 days	24 days

KEY RISK REDUCTION OBJECTIVES TARGETING CHILDREN

1.3*   Increase to at least 30 percent the proportion of people aged 6 and older who engage regularly, preferably daily, in light to moderate physical activity for at least 30 minutes per day. (Baseline: 22 percent of people aged 18 and older were active for at least 30 minutes 5 or more times per week and 12 percent were active 7 or more times per week in 1985)

1.4   Increase to at least 20 percent the proportion of people aged 18 and older and to at least 75 percent the proportion of children and adolescents aged 6 through 17 who engage in vigorous physical activity that promotes the development and maintenance of cardiorespiratory fitness 3 or more days per week for 20 or more minutes per occasion. (Baseline: 12 percent for people aged 18 and older in 1985; 66 percent for youth aged 10 through 17 in 1984)

1.5   Reduce to no more than 15 percent the proportion of people aged 6 and older who engage in no leisure-time physical activity. (Baseline: 24 percent for people aged 18 and older in 1985)

1.6   Increase to at least 40 percent the proportion of people aged 6 and older who regularly perform physical activities that enhance and maintain muscular strength, muscular endurance, and flexibility. (Baseline data available in 1991)

2.10   Reduce iron deficiency to less than 3 percent among children aged 1 through 4 and among women of childbearing age. (Baseline: 9 percent for children aged 1 through 2.4 percent for children aged 3 through 4, and 5 percent for women aged 20 through 44 in 1976–80)

3.5   Reduce the initiation of cigarette smoking by children and youth so that no more than 15 percent have become regular cigarette smokers by age 20. (Baseline: 30 percent of youth had become regular cigarette smokers by ages 20 through 24 in 1987)

Special Population Target

Initiation of Smoking	*1987 Baseline*	*2000 Target*
Lower socioeconomic status youth†	40%	18%

†*As measured by people aged 20–24 with a high school education or less*

3.8   Reduce to no more than 20 percent the proportion of children aged 6 and younger who are regularly exposed to tobacco smoke at home. (Baseline: More than 39 percent in 1986, as 39 percent of households with one or more children aged 6 or younger had a cigarette smoker in the household)

8.3   Achieve for all disadvantaged children and children with disabilities access to high quality and developmentally appropriate preschool programs that help prepare children for school, thereby improving their prospects with regard to school performance, problem behaviors, and mental and physical health. (Baseline: 47 percent of eligible children aged 4 were afforded the opportunity to enroll in Head Start in 1990)

9.12a   Increase use of occupant protection systems, such as safety belts, inflatable safety restraints, and child safety seats, to at least 95 percent of children aged 4 and younger who are motor vehicle occupants. (Baseline: 84 percent in 1988)

13.8   Increase to at least 50 percent the proportion of children who have received protective sealants on the occlusal (chewing) surfaces of permanent molar teeth. (Baseline: 11 percent of children aged 8 and 8 percent of adolescents aged 14 in 1986–87)

20.11   Increase immunization levels as follows:

Basic immunization series among children under age 2: at least 90 percent. (Baseline: 70–80 percent estimated in 1989)

Basic immunization series among children in licensed child care facilities and kindergarten through post-secondary education institutions: at least 95 percent. (Baseline: For licensed child care, 94 percent; 97 percent for children entering school for the 1987–1988 school year; and for post-secondary institutions, baseline data available in 1992)

Pneumococcal pneumonia and influenza immunization among noninstitutionalized, high-risk populations, as defined by the Immunization Practices Advisory Committee: at least 60 percent. (Baseline: 10 percent estimated for pneumococcal vaccine and 20 percent for influenza vaccine in 1985)

Hepatitis B immunization among high-risk populations, including infants of surface antigen-positive mothers to at least 90 percent. (Baseline data available in 1992)

21.2a   Increase to at least 90 percent the proportion of infants up to 24 months who have received, as a minimum within the appropriate interval, all of the screening and immunization services and at least one of the counseling services appropriate for their age and gender as recommended by the U.S. Preventive Services Task Force. (Baseline data available in 1991)

21.2b   Increase to at least 80 percent the proportion of children aged 2 through 12 who have received, as a minimum within the appropriate interval, all of the screening and immunization services and at least one of the counseling services appropriate for their age and gender as recommended by the U.S. Preventive Services Task Force. (Baseline data available in 1991)

KEY SERVICE AND PROTECTION OBJECTIVES TARGETING CHILDREN

1.8   Increase to at least 50 percent the proportion of children and adolescents in 1st through 12th grade who participate in daily school physical education. (Baseline: 36 percent in 1984–86)

1.9   Increase to at least 50 percent the proportion of school physical education class time that students spend being physically active, preferably engaged in lifetime physical activities. (Baseline: Students spent an estimated 27 percent of class time being physically active in 1983)

5.8   Increase to at least 85 percent the proportion of people aged 10 through 18 who have discussed human sexuality, including values surrounding sexuality, with their parents and/or have received information through another parentally-endorsed source, such as youth, school, or religious programs. (Baseline: 66 percent of people aged 13 through 18 had discussed sexuality with their parents; reported in 1986)

6.14   Increase to at least 75 percent the proportion of providers of primary care for children who include assessment of cognitive, emotional, and parent-child functioning, with appropriate counseling, referral, and followup, in their clinical practices. (Baseline data available in 1992)

7.13   Extend to at least 45 States implementation of unexplained child death review systems. (Baseline data available in 1991)

7.14   Increase to at least 30 the number of States in which at least 50 percent of children identified as neglected or physically or sexually abused receive physical and mental evaluation with appropriate followup as a means of breaking the intergenerational cycle of abuse. (Baseline data available in 1993)

7.15   Reduce to less than 10 percent the proportion of battered women and their children turned away from emergency housing due to lack of space. (Baseline: 40 percent in 1987)

8.9   Increase to at least 75 percent the proportion of people aged 10 and older who have discussed issues related to nutrition, physical activity, sexual behavior, tobacco, alcohol, other drugs, or safety with family members on at least one occasion during the preceding month. (Baseline data available in 1991)

9.15   Enact in 50 States laws requiring that new handguns be designed to minimize the likelihood of discharge by children. (Baseline: 0 States in 1989)

13.12   Increase to at least 90 percent the proportion of all children entering school programs for the first time who have received an oral health screening, referral, and followup for necessary diagnostic, preventive, and treatment services. (Baseline: 66 percent of children aged 5 visited a dentist during the previous year in 1986)

14.11   Increase to at least 90 percent the proportion of all pregnant women who receive prenatal care in the first trimester of pregnancy. (Baseline: 76 percent of live births in 1987)

Special Population Targets

Proportion of Pregnant Women Receiving Early Prenatal Care	*1987 Baseline*	*2000 Target*
14.11a Black women	61.1†	90†
14.11b American Indian/Alaska Native women	60.2†	90†
14.11c Hispanic women	61.0†	90†

†*Percent of live births*

14.16   Increase to at least 90 percent the proportion of babies aged 18 months and younger who receive recommended primary care services at the appropriate intervals. (Baseline data available in 1992)

17.15   Increase to at least 80 percent the proportion of providers of primary care for children who routinely refer or screen infants and children for impairments of vision, hearing, speech and language, and assess other developmental milestones as part of well-child care. (Baseline data available in 1992)

17.16   Reduce the average age at which children with significant hearing impairment are identified to no more than 12 months. (Baseline: Estimated as 24 to 30 months in 1988)

17.20   Increase to 50 the number of States that have service systems for children with or at risk of chronic and disabling conditions, as required by Public Law 101–239. (Baseline data available in 1991)

21.4   Improve financing and delivery of clinical preventive services so that virtually no American has a financial barrier to receiving, at a minimum, the screening, counseling, and immunization services recommended by the U.S. Preventive Services Task Force. (Baseline data available in 1992)

Adolescents and Young Adults

The target for reducing deaths among adolescents and young adults:

Reduce the death rate for adolescents and young adults by 15 percent to no more than 85 per 100,000 people aged 15 through 24. (Baseline: 99.4 per 100,000 in 1987)

KEY HEALTH STATUS OBJECTIVES TARGETING ADOLESCENTS AND YOUNG ADULTS

2.3*   Reduce overweight to a prevalence of no more than 20 percent among people aged 20 and older and no more than 15 percent among adolescents aged 12 through 19. (Baseline: 26 percent for people aged 20 through 74 in 1976–80, 24 percent for men and 27 percent for women; 15 percent for adolescents aged 12 through 19 in 1976–80)

4.1b   Reduce deaths among people aged 15 through 24 caused by alcohol-related motor vehicle crashes to no more than 18 per 100,000. (Baseline: 21.5 per 100,000 in 1987)

5.1   Reduce pregnancies among girls aged 17 and younger to no more than 50 per 1,000 adolescents. (Baseline: 71.1 pregnancies per 1,000 girls aged 15 through 17 in 1985)

Special Population Targets

Pregnancies (per 1,000)	*1985 Baseline*	*2000 Target*
5.1a Black adolescent girls aged 15–19	186†	120
5.1b Hispanic adolescent girls aged 15–19	158	105

†*Nonwhite adolescents*

6.1a*   Reduce suicides among youth aged 15 through 19 to no more than 8.2 per 100,000. (Baseline: 10.3 per 100,000 in 1987)

6.1b* Reduce suicides among men aged 20 through 34 to no more than 21.4 per 100,000. (Baseline: 25.2 per 100,000 in 1987)

6.2* Reduce by 15 percent the incidence of injurious suicide attempts among adolescents aged 14 through 17. (Baseline data available in 1991)

6.3 Reduce to less than 10 percent the prevalence of mental disorders among children and adolescents. (Baseline: An estimated 12 percent among youth younger than age 18 in 1989)

7.1 Reduce homicides to no more than 7.2 per 100,000 people. (Age-adjusted baseline: 8.5 per 100,000 in 1987)

Special Population Targets

Homicide Rate (per 100,000)		*1987 Baseline*	*2000 Target*
7.1b	Spouses aged 15–34	1.7	1.4
7.1c	Black men aged 15–34	90.5	72.4
7.1d	Hispanic men aged 15–34	53.1	42.5
7.1e	Black women aged 15–34	20.0	16.0
7.1f	American Indians/Alaska Natives in Reservation States	14.1	11.3

7.7a Reduce rape and attempted rape of women aged 12 through 34 to no more than 225 per 100,000. (Baseline: 250 per 100,000 in 1986)

9.3b Reduce deaths among youth aged 15 through 24 caused by motor vehicle crashes to no more than 33 per 100,000. (Baseline: 36.9 per 100,000 in 1987)

19.1b Reduce gonorrhea among adolescents aged 15 through 19 to an incidence of no more than 750 cases per 100,000. (Baseline: 1,123 per 100,000 in 1989)

KEY RISK REDUCTION OBJECTIVES TARGETING ADOLESCENTS AND YOUNG ADULTS

1.3* Increase to at least 30 percent the proportion of people aged 6 and older who engage regularly, preferably daily, in light to moderate physical activity for at least 30 minutes per day. (Baseline: 22 percent of people aged 18 and older were active for at least 30 minutes 5 or more times per week and 12 percent were active 7 or more times per week in 1985)

1.4 Increase to at least 20 percent the proportion of people aged 18 and older and to at least 75 percent the proportion of children and adolescents aged 6 through 17 who engage in vigorous physical activity that promotes the development and maintenance of cardiorespiratory fitness 3 or more days per week for 20 or more minutes per occasion. (Baseline: 12 percent for people aged 18 and older in 1985; 66 percent for youth aged 10 through 17 in 1984)

Special Population Target

Vigorous Physical Activity	*1985 Baseline*	*2000 Target*
1.4a Lower-income people aged 18 and older (annual family income <$20,000)	7%	12%

2.8 Increase calcium intake so at least 50 percent of youth aged 12 through 24 and 50 percent of pregnant and lactating women consume three or more servings daily of foods rich in calcium, and at least 50 percent of people aged 25 and older consume two or more servings daily. (Baseline: 7 percent of women and 14 percent of men aged 19 through 24 and 24 percent of pregnant and lactating women consumed three or more servings, and 15 percent of women and 23 percent of men aged 25 through 50 consumed two or more servings in 1985–86)

3.5 Reduce the initiation of cigarette smoking by children and youth so that no more than 15 percent have become regular cigarette smokers by age 20. (Baseline: 30 percent of youth had become regular cigarette smokers by ages 20 through 24 in 1987)

Special Population Target

Initiation of Smoking	*1987 Baseline*	*2000 Target*
3.5a Lower socioeconomic status youth†	40%	18%

†*As measured by people aged 20–24 with a high school education or less*

3.9   Reduce smokeless tobacco use by males aged 12 through 24 to a prevalence of no more than 4 percent. (Baseline: 6.6 percent among males aged 12 through 17 in 1988; 8.9 percent among males aged 18 through 24 in 1987)

Special Population Target

Smokeless Tobacco Use	*1986–87 Baseline*	*2000 Target*
3.9a American Indian/Alaska Native youth	18–64%	10%

4.5   Increase by at least 1 year the average age of first use of cigarettes, alcohol, and marijuana by adolescents aged 12 through 17. (Baseline: Age 11.6 for cigarettes, age 13.1 for alcohol, and age 13.4 for marijuana in 1988)

4.6   Reduce the proportion of young people who have used alcohol, marijuana, and cocaine in the past month, as follows:

Substance/Age	*1988 Baseline*	*2000 Target*
Alcohol/aged 12–17	25.2%	12.6%
Alcohol/aged 18–20	57.9%	29%
Marijuana/aged 12–17	6.4%	3.2%
Marijuana/aged 18–25	15.5%	7.8%
Cocaine/aged 12–17	1.1%	0.6%
Cocaine/aged 18–25	4.5%	2.3%

4.7   Reduce the proportion of high school seniors and college students engaging in recent occasions of heavy drinking of alcoholic beverages to no more than 28 percent of high school seniors and 32 percent of college students. (Baseline: 33 percent of high school seniors and 41.7 percent of college students in 1989)

Note: Recent heavy drinking is defined as having 5 or more drinks on one occasion in the previous 2-week period as monitored by self-reports.

4.11   Reduce to no more than 3 percent the proportion of male high school seniors who use anabolic steroids. (Baseline: 4.7 percent in 1989)

5.4*   Reduce the proportion of adolescents who have engaged in sexual intercourse to no more than 15 percent by age 15 and no more than 40 percent by age 17. (Baseline: 27 percent of girls and 33 percent of boys by age 15; 50 percent of girls and 66 percent of boys by age 17; reported in 1988)

5.5   Increase to at least 40 percent the proportion of ever sexually active adolescents aged 17 and younger who have abstained from sexual activity for the previous three months. (Baseline: 26 percent of sexually active girls aged 15 through 17 in 1988)

5.6   Increase to at least 90 percent the proportion of sexually active, unmarried people aged 19 and younger who use contraception, especially combined method contraception that both effectively prevents pregnancy and provides barrier protection against disease. (Baseline: 78 percent at most recent intercourse and 63 percent at first intercourse; 2 percent used oral contraceptives and the condom at most recent intercourse; among young women aged 15 through 19 reporting in 1988)

Note: Strategies to achieve this objective must be undertaken sensitively to avoid indirectly encouraging or condoning sexual activity among teens who are not yet sexually active.

7.9   Reduce by 20 percent the incidence of physical fighting among adolescents aged 14 through 17. (Baseline data available in 1991)

7.10   Reduce by 20 percent the incidence of weapon-carrying by adolescents aged 14 through 17. (Baseline data available in 1991)

8.2   Increase the high school graduation rate to at least 90 percent, thereby reducing risks for multiple problem behaviors and poor mental and physical health. (Baseline: 79 percent of people aged 20 through 21 had graduated from high school with a regular diploma in 1989)

13.8   Increase to at least 50 percent the proportion of children who have received protective sealants on the occlusal (chewing) surfaces of permanent molar teeth. (Baseline: 11 percent of children aged 8 and 8 percent of adolescents aged 14 in 1986–87)

Note: Progress toward this objective will be monitored based on prevalence of sealants in children at age 8 and at age 14, when the majority of first and second molars, respectively, are erupted.

18.4a*   Increase to at least 60 percent the proportion of sexually active, unmarried young women aged 15 through 19 whose partners used a condom at last sexual intercourse. (Baseline: 26 percent in 1988)

Note: Strategies to achieve this objective must be undertaken sensitively to avoid indirectly encouraging or condoning sexual activity among teens who are not yet sexually active.

18.4b*   Increase to at least 75 percent the proportion of sexually active, unmarried young men aged 15 through 19 who used a condom at last sexual intercourse. (Baseline: 57 percent in 1988)

Note: Strategies to achieve this objective must be undertaken sensitively to avoid indirectly encouraging or condoning sexual activity among teens who are not yet sexually active.

21.2c   Increase to at least 50 percent the proportion of adolescents aged 13 through 18 who have received, as a minimum within the appropriate interval, all of the screening and immunization services and at least one of the counseling services appropriate for their age and gender as recommended by the U.S. Preventive Services Task Force. (Baseline data available in 1991)

KEY SERVICES AND PROTECTION OBJECTIVES TARGETING ADOLESCENTS AND YOUNG ADULTS

1.8   Increase to at least 50 percent the proportion of children and adolescents in 1st through 12th grade who participate in daily school physical education. (Baseline: 36 percent in 1984–86)

1.9   Increase to at least 50 percent the proportion of school physical education class time that students spend being physically active, preferably engaged in lifetime physical activities. (Baseline: Students spent an estimated 27 percent of class time being physically active in 1983)

5.8   Increase to at least 85 percent the proportion of people aged 10 through 18 who have discussed human sexuality, including values surrounding sexuality, with their parents and/or have received information through another parentally-endorsed source, such as youth, school, or religious programs. (Baseline: 66 percent of people aged 13 through 18 have discussed sexuality with their parents; reported in 1986)

5.10*   Increase to at least 60 percent the proportion of primary care providers who provide age-appropriate preconception care and counseling. (Baseline data available in 1992)

8.9   Increase to at least 75 percent the proportion of people aged 10 and older who have discussed issues related to nutrition, physical activity, sexual behavior, tobacco, alcohol, other drugs, or safety with family members on at least one occasion during the preceding month. (Baseline data available in 1991)

Adults

The target for reducing deaths among adults:

Reduce the death rate for adults by 20 percent to no more than 340 per 100,000 people aged 25 through 64. (Baseline: 423 per 100,000 in 1987)

KEY HEALTH STATUS OBJECTIVES TARGETING ADULTS

1.1*   Reduce coronary heart disease deaths to no more than 100 per 100,000 people. (Age-adjusted baseline: 135 per 100,000 in 1987)

Special Population Target

Coronary Deaths (per 100,000)	1987 Baseline	2000 Target
1.1a Blacks	163	115

3.2*   Slow the rise in lung cancer deaths to achieve a rate of no more than 42 per 100,000 people. (Age-adjusted baseline: 37.9 per 100,000 in 1987)

5.2   Reduce to no more than 30 percent the proportion of all pregnancies that are unintended. (Baseline: 56 percent of pregnancies in the previous five years were unintended, either unwanted or earlier than desired, in 1988)

Special Population Target

Unintended Pregnancies	1988 Baseline	2000 Target
5.2a Black women	78%	40%

6.4   Reduce the prevalence of mental disorders (exclusive of substance abuse) among adults living in the community to less than 10.7 percent. (Baseline: One-month point prevalence of 12.6 percent in 1984)

7.1   Reduce homicides to no more than 7.2 per 100,000 people. (Age-adjusted baseline: 8.5 per 100,000 in 1987)

Special Population Targets

Homicide Rate (per 100,000)	1987 Baseline	2000 Target
7.1b Spouses aged 15–34	1.7	1.4
7.1c Black men aged 15–34	90.5	72.4
7.1d Hispanic men aged 15–34	53.1	42.5
7.1e Black women aged 15–34	20.0	16.0
7.1f American Indians/Alaska Natives in Reservation States	14.1	11.3

10.1   Reduce deaths from work-related injuries to no more than 4 per 100,000 full-time workers. (Baseline: Average of 6 per 100,000 during 1983–87)

Special Population Targets

Work-Related Deaths (per 100,000)	1983–87 Average	2000 Target
10.1a Mine workers	30.3	21
10.1b Construction workers	25.0	17
10.1c Transportation workers	15.2	10
10.1d Farm workers	14.0	9.5

13.6   Reduce destructive periodontal diseases to a prevalence of no more than 15 percent among people aged 35 through 44. (Baseline: 24 percent in 1985–86)

16.1*   Reverse the rise in cancer deaths to achieve a rate of no more than 130 per 100,000 people. (Age-adjusted baseline: 133 per 100,000 in 1987)

17.9   Reduce diabetes-related deaths to no more than 34 per 100,000 people. (Age-adjusted baseline: 38 per 100,000 in 1986)

Special Population Targets

Diabetes-Related Deaths (per 100,000)	1986 Baseline	2000 Target
17.9a Blacks	65	58
17.9b American Indians/Alaska Natives	54	48

Note: Diabetes-related deaths refer to deaths from diabetes as an underlying or contributing cause.

20.3*   Reduce viral hepatitis as follows:

(Per 100,000)	*1987 Baseline*	*2000 Target*
Hepatitis B (HBV)	63.5	40
Hepatitis A	31	23
Hepatitis C	18.3	13.7

20.4   Reduce tuberculosis to an incidence of no more than 3.5 cases per 100,000 people. (Baseline: 9.1 per 100,000 in 1988)

KEY RISK REDUCTION OBJECTIVES TARGETING ADULTS

2.5*   Reduce dietary fat intake to an average of 30 percent of calories or less and average saturated fat intake to less than 10 percent of calories among people aged 2 and older. (Baseline: 36 percent of calories from total fat and 13 percent from saturated fat for people aged 20 through 74 in 1976–80; 36 percent and 13 percent for women aged 19 through 50 in 1985)

2.6*   Increase complex carbohydrate and fiber-containing foods in the diets of adults to 5 or more daily servings for vegetables (including legumes) and fruits, and to 6 or more daily servings for grain products. (Baseline: 2½ servings of vegetables and fruits and 3 servings of grain products for women aged 19 through 50 in 1985)

4.8   Reduce alcohol consumption by people aged 14 and older to an annual average of no more than 2 gallons of ethanol per person. (Baseline: 2.54 gallons of ethanol in 1987)

5.7   Increase the effectiveness with which family planning methods are used, as measured by a decrease to no more than 5 percent in the proportion of couples experiencing pregnancy despite use of a contraceptive method. (Baseline: Approximately 10 percent of women using reversible contraceptive methods experienced an unintended pregnancy in 1982)

15.4   Increase to at least 50 percent the proportion of people with high blood pressure whose blood pressure is under control. (Baseline: 11 percent controlled among people aged 18 through 74 in 1976–80; an estimated 24 percent for people aged 18 and older in 1982–84)

15.6   Reduce the mean serum cholesterol level among adults to no more than 200 mg/dL. (Baseline: 213 mg/dL among people aged 20 through 74 in 1976–80, 211 mg/dL for men and 215 mg/dL for women)

17.11   Reduce diabetes to an incidence of no more than 2.5 per 1,000 people and a prevalence of no more than 25 per 1,000 people. (Baselines: 2.9 per 1,000 in 1987; 28 per 1,000 in 1987)

KEY SERVICES AND PROTECTION OBJECTIVES TARGETING ADULTS

8.5   Increase to at least 50 percent the proportion of postsecondary institutions with institutionwide health promotion programs for students, faculty, and staff. (Baseline: At least 20 percent of higher education institutions offered health promotion activities for students in 1989–90)

16.11   Increase to at least 80 percent the proportion of women aged 40 and older who have ever received a clinical breast examination and a mammogram, and to at least 60 percent those aged 50 and older who have received them within the preceding 1 to 2 years. (Baseline: 36 percent of women aged 40 and older "ever" in 1987; 25 percent of women aged 50 and older "within the preceding 2 years" in 1987)

16.12   Increase to at least 95 percent the proportion of women aged 18 and older with uterine cervix who have ever received a Pap test, and to at least 85 percent those who received a Pap test within the preceding 1 to 3 years. (Baseline: 88 percent "ever" and 75 percent "within the preceding 3 years" in 1987)

16.13   Increase to at least 50 percent the proportion of people aged 50 and older who have received fecal occult blood testing within the preceding 1 to 2 years, and to at least 40 percent those who have ever received proctosigmoidoscopy. (Baseline: 27 percent received fecal occult blood testing during the preceding 2 years in 1987; 25 percent had ever received proctosigmoidoscopy in 1987)

21.2   Increase to at least 50 percent the proportion of people who have received, as a minimum within the appropriate interval, all of the screening and immunization services and at least one of the counseling services appropriate for their age and gender as recommended by the U.S. Preventive Services Task Force. (Baseline data available in 1991)

Older Adults

A target for reducing the proportion of people aged 65 and older who are limited in two or more activities of daily living:

Reduce to no more than 90 per 1,000 people the proportion of all people aged 65 and older who have difficulty in performing two or more personal care activities (a reduction of about 19 percent), thereby preserving independence. (Baseline: 111 per 1,000 in 1984–85)

KEY HEALTH STATUS OBJECTIVES TARGETING OLDER ADULTS

6.1c* Reduce suicides among white men aged 65 and older to no more than 39.2 per 100,000. (Age-adjusted baseline: 46.1 per 100,000 in 1987)

9.3c Reduce deaths among people aged 70 and older caused by motor vehicle crashes to no more than 20 per 100,000. (Baseline: 22.6 per 100,000 in 1987)

9.4a Reduce deaths among people aged 65 through 84 from falls and fall-related injuries to no more than 14.4 per 100,000. (Baseline: 18 per 100,000 in 1987)

9.4b Reduce deaths among people aged 85 and older from falls and fall-related injuries to no more than 105 per 100,000. (Baseline: 131.2 per 100,000 in 1987)

9.6b Reduce residential fire deaths among people aged 65 and older to no more than 3.3 per 100,000. (Baseline: 4.4 per 100,000 in 1987)

9.7 Reduce hip fractures among people aged 65 and older so that hospitalizations for this condition are no more than 607 per 100,000. (Baseline: 714 per 100,000 in 1988)

Special Population Target

Hip Fractures (per 100,000)	1988 Baseline	2000 Target
9.7a White women aged 85 and older	2,721	2,177

13.4 Reduce to no more than 20 percent the proportion of people aged 65 and older who have lost all of their natural teeth. (Baseline: 36 percent in 1986)

Special Population Target

Complete Tooth Loss Prevalence	1986 Baseline	2000 Target
13.4a Low-income people (annual family income <$15,000)	46%	25%

17.1* Increase years of healthy life to at least 65 years. (Baseline: An estimated 62 years in 1980)

Special Population Targets

Years of Healthy Life	1980 Baseline	2000 Target
17.1a Blacks	56	60
17.1b Hispanics	62	65
17.1c People aged 65 and older	12†	14†

†*Years of healthy life remaining at age 65*

17.3 Reduce to no more than 90 per 1,000 people the proportion of all people aged 65 and older who have difficulty in performing two or more personal care activities, thereby preserving independence. (Baseline: 111 per 1,000 in 1984–85)

Special Population Target

Difficulty Performing Self-Care Activities (per 1,000)	1984–85 Baseline	2000 Target
17.3a People aged 85 and older	371	325

Note: Personal care activities are bathing, dressing, using the toilet, getting in and out of bed or chair, and eating.

17.6a Reduce significant hearing impairment among people aged 45 and older to a prevalence of no more than 180 per 1,000. (Baseline: Average of 203 per 1,000 during 1986–88)

17.7a Reduce significant visual impairment among people aged 65 and older to a prevalence of no more than 70 per 1,000. (Baseline: Average of 87.1 per 1,000 during 1986–88)

20.2 Reduce epidemic-related pneumonia and influenza deaths among people aged 65 and older to no more than 7.3 per 100,000. (Baseline: Average of 9.1 per 100,000 during 1980 through 1987)

20.10 Reduce pneumonia-related days of restricted activity as follows:

	1987 Baseline	*2000 Target*
People aged 65 and older (per 100 people)	48 days	38 days

KEY RISK REDUCTION OBJECTIVES TARGETING OLDER ADULTS

1.3* Increase to at least 30 percent the proportion of people aged 6 and older who engage regularly, preferably daily, in light to moderate physical activity for at least 30 minutes per day. (Baseline: 22 percent of people aged 18 and older were active for at least 30 minutes 5 or more times per week and 12 percent were active 7 or more times per week in 1985)

1.5a Reduce to no more than 22 percent the proportion of people aged 65 and older who engage in no leisure-time physical activity. (Baseline: 43 percent in 1985)

20.11 Increase immunization levels as follows:

Pneumococcal pneumonia and influenza immunization among institutionalized chronically ill or older people: at least 80 percent. (Baseline data available in 1992)

21.2f Increase to at least 40 percent the proportion of adults aged 65 and older who have received, as a minimum within the appropriate interval, all of the screening and immunization services and at least one of the counseling services appropriate for their age and gender as recommended by the U.S. Preventive Services Task Force. (Baseline data available in 1991)

KEY SERVICES AND PROTECTION OBJECTIVES TARGETING OLDER ADULTS

2.18 Increase to at least 80 percent the receipt of home food services by people aged 65 and older who have difficulty in preparing their own meals or are otherwise in need of home-delivered meals. (Baseline data available in 1991)

8.8 Increase to at least 90 percent the proportion of people aged 65 and older who had the opportunity to participate during the preceding year in at least one organized health promotion program through a senior center, lifecare facility, or other community-based setting that serves older adults. (Baseline data available in 1992)

13.14b Increase to at least 60 percent the proportion of people aged 65 and older using the oral health care system during each year. (Baseline: 42 percent in 1986)

16.11 Increase to at least 80 percent the proportion of women aged 40 and older who have ever received a clinical breast examination and a mammogram, and to at least 60 percent those aged 50 and older who have received them within the preceding 1 to 2 years. (Baseline: 36 percent of women aged 40 and older "ever" in 1987; 25 percent of women aged 50 and older "within the preceding 2 years" in 1987)

Special Population Targets

Clinical Breast Exam & Mammogram:	*1987 Baseline*	*2000 Target*
Ever Received—		
16.11a Hispanic women aged 40 and older	20%	80%
16.11b Low-income women aged 40 and older (annual family income <$10,000)	22%	80%
16.11c Women aged 40 and older with less than high school education	23%	80%

| 16.11d | Women aged 70 and older | 25% | 80% |
| 16.11e | Black women aged 40 and older | 28% | 80% |

Received Within Preceding 2 Years—

16.11a	Hispanic women aged 50 and older	18%	60%
16.11b	Low-income women aged 50 and older (annual family income <$10,000)	15%	60%
16.11c	Women aged 50 and older with less than high school education	16%	60%
16.11d	Women aged 70 and older	18%	60%
16.11e	Black women aged 50 and older	19%	60%

16.12b   Increase to at least 95 percent the proportion of women aged 70 and older with uterine cervix who have ever received a Pap test, and to at least 70 percent those who received a Pap test within the preceding 1 to 3 years. (Baseline: 76 percent "ever" and 44 percent "within the preceding 3 years" in 1987)

16.13   Increase to at least 50 percent the proportion of people aged 50 and older who have received fecal occult blood testing within the preceding 1 to 2 years, and to at least 40 percent those who have ever received proctosigmoidoscopy. (Baseline: 27 percent received fecal occult blood testing during the preceding 2 years in 1987; 25 percent had ever received proctosigmoidoscopy in 1987)

16.14   Increase to at least 40 percent the proportion of people aged 50 and older visiting a primary care provider in the preceding year who have received oral, skin, and digital rectal examinations during one such visit. (Baseline: An estimated 27 percent received a digital rectal exam during a physician visit within the preceding year in 1987)

17.17   Increase to at least 60 percent the proportion of providers of primary care for older adults who routinely evaluate people aged 65 and older for urinary incontinence and impairments of vision, hearing, cognition, and functional status. (Baseline data available in 1992)

17.18   Increase to at least 90 percent the proportion of perimenopausal women who have been counseled about the benefits and risks of estrogen replacement therapy (combined with progestin, when appropriate) for prevention of osteoporosis. (Baseline data available in 1991)

B. KEY SPECIAL POPULATION OBJECTIVES

OBJECTIVES TARGETING PEOPLE WITH LOW INCOME

1.4a   Increase to at least 12 percent the proportion of lower-income people aged 18 and older (annual family income less than $20,000) who engage in vigorous physical activity that promotes the development and maintenance of cardiorespiratory fitness 3 or more days per week for 20 or more minutes per occasion. (Baseline: 7 percent in 1985)

1.5c   Reduce to no more than 17 percent the proportion of lower-income people aged 18 and older (annual family income less than $20,000) who engage in no leisure-time physical activity. (Baseline: 32 percent in 1985)

2.3a*   Reduce overweight to a prevalence of no more than 25 percent among low-income women aged 20 and older. (Baseline: 37 percent for low-income women aged 20 through 74 in 1976–80)

2.4   Reduce growth retardation among low-income children aged 5 and younger to less than 10 percent. (Baseline: Up to 16 percent among low-income children in 1988, depending on age and race/ethnicity)

2.4a   Reduce growth retardation among low-income black children younger than age 1 to less than 10 percent. (Baseline: 15 percent in 1988)

2.4b   Reduce growth retardation among low-income Hispanic children younger than age 1 to less than 10 percent. (Baseline: 13 percent in 1988)

2.4c   Reduce growth retardation among low-income Hispanic children aged 1 to less than 10 percent. (Baseline: 16 percent in 1988)

2.4d   Reduce growth retardation among low-income Asian and Pacific Islander children aged 1 to less than 10 percent. (Baseline: 14 percent in 1988)

2.4e   Reduce growth retardation among low-income Asian and Pacific Islander children aged 2 through four to less than 10 percent. (Baseline: 16 percent in 1988)

2.10a   Reduce iron deficiency to less than 10 percent among low-income children aged 1 through 2. (Baseline: 21 percent in 1976–80)

2.10b   Reduce iron deficiency to less than 5 percent among low-income children aged 3 through 4. (Baseline: 10 percent in 1976–80)

2.10c   Reduce iron deficiency to less than 4 percent among low-income women of childbearing age. (Baseline: 8 percent of women aged 20 through 44 in 1976–80)

2.10e   Reduce the prevalence of anemia to less than 20 percent among black, low-income pregnant women. (Baseline: 41 percent of those aged 15 through 44 in their third trimester in 1988)

3.5a   Reduce the initiation of cigarette smoking by lower socioeconomic status youth so that no more than 18 percent have become regular cigarette smokers by age 20. (Baseline: 40 percent of youth with a high school education or less had become regular cigarette smokers by ages 20 through 24 in 1987)

8.3   Achieve for all disadvantaged children and children with disabilities access to high quality and developmentally appropriate preschool programs that help prepare children for school, thereby improving their prospects with regard to school performance, problem behaviors, and mental and physical health. (Baseline: 47 percent of eligible children aged 4 were afforded the opportunity to enroll in Head Start in 1990)

11.4a   Reduce the prevalence of blood lead levels exceeding 15 μg/dL and 25 μg/dL among inner-city low-income black children (annual family income less than $6,000 in 1984 dollars) to no more than 75,000 and zero, respectively. (Baseline: An estimated 234,900 had levels exceeding 15 μg/dL, and 36,700 had levels exceeding 25 μg/dL, in 1984)

13.4a   Reduce to no more than 25 percent the proportion of low-income people (annual family income less than $15,000) aged 65 and older who have lost all of their natural teeth. (Baseline: 46 percent in 1986)

13.5a   Reduce the prevalence of gingivitis among low-income people (annual family income less than $12,500) aged 35 through 44 to no more than 35 percent. (Baseline: 50 percent in 1985–86)

14.9a* Increase to at least 75 percent the proportion of low-income mothers who breastfeed their babies in the early postpartum period, and to at least 50 percent the proportion who continue breastfeeding until their babies are 5 to 6 months old. (Baseline: 32 percent at discharge from birth site and 9 percent at 5 to 6 months in 1988)

16.11b Increase to at least 80 percent the proportion of low-income women (annual family income less than $10,000) aged 40 and older who have ever received a clinical breast examination and a mammogram, and to at least 60 percent those aged 50 and older who have received them within the preceding 1 to 2 years. (Baseline: 22 percent of women aged 40 and older ever in 1987; 15 percent of women aged 50 and older "within the preceding 2 years" in 1987)

16.12d Increase to at least 95 percent the proportion of low-income women (annual family income less than $10,000) aged 18 and older with uterine cervix who have ever received a Pap test, and to at least 80 percent those who received a Pap test within the preceding 1 to 3 years. (Baseline: 80 percent "ever" and 64 percent "within the preceding 3 years" in 1987)

17.2a   Reduce to no more than 15 percent the proportion of low-income people (annual family income of less than $10,000 in 1988) who experience a limitation in major activity due to chronic conditions. (Baseline: 18.9 percent in 1988)

21.2g   Increase to at least 50 percent the proportion of low-income people who have received, as a minimum within the appropriate interval, all of the screening and immunization services and at least one of the counseling services appropriate for their age and gender as recommended by the U.S. Preventive Services Task Force. (Baseline data available in 1991)

21.3c   Increase to at least 95 percent the proportion of low-income people who have a specific source of ongoing primary care for coordination of their preventive and episodic health care. (Baseline: 80 percent in 1986, as 20 percent reported having no physician, clinic, or hospital as a regular source of care)

22.4   Develop and implement a national process to identify significant gaps in the nation's disease prevention and health promotion data, including data for racial and ethnic minorities, people with low incomes, and people with disabilities, and establish mechanisms to meet these needs. (Baseline: No such process exists in 1990)

Note: This objective applies to each special population.

OBJECTIVES TARGETING BLACKS

2.3b*   Reduce overweight to a prevalence of no more than 30 percent among black women aged 20 and older. (Baseline: 44 percent for black women aged 20 through 74 in 1976–80)

2.4a   Reduce growth retardation among low-income black children younger than age 1 to less than 10 percent. (Baseline: 15 percent in 1988)

2.10e   Reduce the prevalence of anemia to less than 20 percent among black, low-income pregnant women. (Baseline: 41 percent of those aged 15 through 44 in their third trimester in 1988)

3.4d*   Reduce cigarette smoking to a prevalence of no more than 18 percent among blacks aged 20 and older. (Baseline: 34 percent in 1987)

4.2a   Reduce cirrhosis deaths among black men to no more than 12 per 100,000 black men. (Age-adjusted baseline: 22 per 100,000 in 1987)

5.1a   Reduce pregnancies among black adolescent girls aged 15 through 19 to no more than 120 per 1,000 black adolescents. (Baseline: 186 per 1,000 for non-white adolescents in 1985)

5.2a   Reduce to no more than 40 percent the proportion of all pregnancies among black women that are unintended. (Baseline: 78 percent of pregnancies in the previous 5 years were unintended, either unwanted or earlier than desired, in 1988)

5.3a   Reduce the prevalence of infertility among black couples to no more than 9 percent. (Baseline: 12.1 percent of married couples with wives aged 15 through 44 in 1988)

7.1c   Reduce homicides among black men aged 15 through 34 to no more than 72.4 per 100,000 black men. (Baseline: 90.5 per 100,000 in 1987)

7.1e   Reduce homicides among black women aged 15 through 34 to no more than 16.0 per 100,000 black women. (Baseline: 20.0 per 100,000 in 1987)

8.1a*   Increase years of healthy life among blacks to at least 60 years. (Baseline: An estimated 56 years in 1980)

8.11   Increase to at least 50 percent the proportion of counties that have established culturally and linguistically appropriate community health promotion programs for racial and ethnic minority populations. (Baseline data available in 1992)

9.1b   Reduce deaths among black males caused by unintentional injuries to no more than 51.9 per 100,000 black males. (Age-adjusted baseline: 64.9 per 100,000 in 1987)

9.4c   Reduce deaths among black men aged 30 through 69 from falls and fall-related injuries to no more than 5.6 per 100,000 black men. (Baseline: 8 per 100,000 in 1987)

9.5c   Reduce drowning deaths among black males to no more than 3.6 per 100,000 black males. (Age-adjusted baseline: 6.6 per 100,000 in 1987)

9.6c   Reduce residential fire deaths among black males to no more than 4.3 per 100,000 black males. (Age-adjusted baseline: 5.7 per 100,000 in 1987)

9.6d   Reduce residential fire deaths among black females to no more than 2.6 per 100,000 black females. (Age-adjusted baseline: 3.4 per 100,000 in 1987)

11.1a   Reduce asthma morbidity among blacks, as measured by a reduction in asthma hospitalizations to no more than 265 per 100,000 blacks. (Baseline: 334 per 100,000 blacks and other non-whites in 1987)

11.4a   Reduce the prevalence of blood lead levels exceeding 15 μg/dL and 25 μg/dL among inner-city low-income black children (annual family income less than $6,000 in 1984 dollars) to no more than 75,000 and zero, respectively. (Baseline: An estimated 234,900 had levels exceeding 15 μg/dL, and 36,700 had levels exceeding 25 μg/dL, in 1984)

13.1c   Reduce dental caries (cavities) so that the proportion of black children aged 6 through 8 with one or more caries (in permanent or primary teeth) is no more than 40 percent. (Baseline: 61 percent in 1986–87)

13.2c   Reduce untreated dental caries so that the proportion of black children with untreated caries (in permanent or primary teeth) is no more than 25 percent among children aged 6 through 8 and no more than 20 percent among adolescents aged 15. (Baseline: 38 percent of black children aged 6 through 8 in 1986–87; 38 percent of black adolescents aged 15 in 1986–87)

14.1a   Reduce the infant mortality rate among blacks to no more than 11 per 1,000 live births. (Baseline: 17.9 per 1,000 live births in 1987)

14.1e   Reduce the neonatal mortality rate among blacks to no more than 7 per 1,000 live births. (Baseline: 11.7 per 1,000 live births in 1987)

14.1h   Reduce the postneonatal mortality rate among blacks to no more than 4 per 1,000 live births. (Baseline: 6.1 per 1,000 live births in 1987)

14.2a   Reduce the fetal death rate (20 or more weeks of gestation) among blacks to no more than 7.5 per 1,000 live births plus fetal deaths. (Baseline: 12.8 per 1,000 live births plus fetal deaths in 1987)

14.3a   Reduce the maternal mortality rate among blacks to no more than 5 per 100,000 live births. (Baseline: 14.2 per 100,000 live births in 1987)

14.4b   Reduce the incidence of fetal alcohol syndrome among blacks to no more than 0.4 per 1,000 live births. (Baseline: 0.8 per 1,000 live births in 1987)

14.5a   Reduce low birth weight among blacks to an incidence of no more than 9 percent of live births and very low birth weight to no more than 2 percent of live births. (Baseline: 12.7 and 2.7 percent, respectively, in 1987)

14.9b*   Increase to at least 75 percent the proportion of black mothers who breastfeed their babies in the early postpartum period, and to at least 50 percent the proportion who continue breastfeeding until their babies are 5 to 6 months old. (Baseline: 25 percent at discharge from birth site and 8 percent at 5 to 6 months in 1988)

14.11a   Increase to at least 90 percent the proportion of pregnant black women who receive prenatal care in the first trimester of pregnancy. (Baseline: 61.1 percent of live births in 1987)

15.1a*   Reduce coronary heart disease deaths among blacks to no more than 115 per 100,000 blacks. (Age-adjusted baseline: 163 per 100,000 in 1987)

15.2a   Reduce stroke deaths among blacks to no more than 27 per 100,000 blacks. (Age-adjusted baseline: 51.2 per 100,000 in 1987)

15.3a   Reverse the increase in end-stage renal disease (requiring maintenance dialysis or transplantation) among blacks to attain an incidence of no more than 30 per 100,000 blacks. (Baseline: 32.4 per 100,000 in 1987)

15.5b   Increase to at least 80 percent the proportion of black hypertensive men aged 18 through 34 who are taking action to help control their blood pressure. (Baseline: 63 percent of aware black hypertensive men aged 18 through 34 were taking action to control their blood pressure in 1985)

16.11e   Increase to at least 80 percent the proportion of black women aged 40 and older who have ever received a clinical breast examination and a mammogram, and to at least 60 percent those aged 50 and older who have received them within the preceding 1 to 2 years. (Baseline: 28 percent of black women aged 40 and older "ever" in 1987; 19 percent of black women aged 50 and older "within the preceding 2 years" in 1987)

17.2c   Reduce to no more than 9 percent the proportion of blacks who experience a limitation in major activity due to chronic conditions. (Baseline: 11.2 percent in 1988)

17.9a   Reduce diabetes-related deaths among blacks to no more than 58 per 100,000 blacks. (Age-adjusted baseline: 65 per 100,000 in 1986)

17.10a   Reduce end-stage renal disease due to diabetes among blacks with diabetes to no more than 2 per 1,000 blacks with diabetes. (Baseline: 2.2 per 1,000 in 1983–86)

17.10c   Reduce lower extremity amputations due to diabetes among blacks with diabetes to no more than 6.1 per 1,000 blacks with diabetes. (Baseline: 10.2 per 1,000 in 1984–87)

17.11e   Reduce diabetes among blacks to a prevalence of no more than 32 per 1,000 blacks. (Baseline: 36 per 1,000 in 1987)

18.1b   Confine annual incidence of diagnosed AIDS cases among blacks to no more than 37,000 cases. (Baseline: An estimated 14,000–15,000 cases diagnosed in 1989)

19.1a   Reduce gonorrhea among blacks to an incidence of no more than 1,300 cases per 100,000 blacks. (Baseline: 1,990 per 100,000 in 1989)

19.3a   Reduce primary and secondary syphilis among blacks to an incidence of no more than 65 cases per 100,000 blacks. (Baseline: 118 per 100,000 in 1989)

20.4b   Reduce tuberculosis among blacks to an incidence of no more than 10 cases per 100,000 blacks. (Baseline: 28.3 per 100,000 in 1988)

21.2h   Increase to at least 50 percent the proportion of blacks who have received, as a minimum within the appropriate interval, all of the screening and immunization services and at least one of the counseling services appropriate for their age and gender as recommended by the U.S. Preventive Services Task Force. (Baseline data available in 1991)

21.3b   Increase to at least 95 percent the proportion of blacks who have a specific source of ongoing primary care for coordination of their preventive and episodic health care. (Baseline: Less than 80 percent in 1986, as 20 percent reported having no physician, clinic, or hospital as a regular source of care)

21.8   Increase the proportion of all degrees in the health professions and allied and associated health profession fields awarded to members of underrepresented racial and ethnic minority groups as follows:

	1985–1986 Baseline	2000 Target
Blacks	5%	8%

Note: Underrepresented minorities are those groups consistently below parity in most health profession schools — blacks, Hispanics, and American Indians and Alaska Natives.

OBJECTIVES TARGETING HISPANICS

2.3c*   Reduce overweight to a prevalence of no more than 25 percent among Hispanic women aged 20 and older. (Baseline: 39 percent for Mexican-American women aged 20 through 74, 34 percent for Cuban women aged 20 through 74, and 37 percent for Puerto Rican women aged 20 through 74 in 1982–84)

2.4b   Reduce growth retardation among low-income Hispanic children younger than age 1 to less than 10 percent. (Baseline: 13 percent in 1988)

2.4c   Reduce growth retardation among low-income Hispanic children aged 1 to less than 10 percent. (Baseline: 16 percent in 1988)

3.4e*   Reduce cigarette smoking to a prevalence of no more than 18 percent among Hispanics aged 20 and older. (Baseline: 33 percent in 1982–84)

5.1b   Reduce pregnancies among Hispanic adolescent girls aged 15 through 19 to no more than 105 per 1,000 Hispanic adolescents. (Baseline: 158 per 1,000 in 1985)

5.3b   Reduce the prevalence of infertility among Hispanic couples to no more than 9 percent. (Baseline: 12.4 percent of married couples with wives aged 15 through 44 in 1988)

7.1d   Reduce homicides among Hispanic men aged 15 through 34 to no more than 42.5 per 100,000 Hispanic men. (Baseline: 53.1 per 100,000 in 1987)

8.1b*   Increase years of healthy life among Hispanics to at least 65 years. (Baseline: An estimated 62 years in 1980)

8.11   Increase to at least 50 percent the proportion of counties that have established culturally and linguistically appropriate community health promotion programs for racial and ethnic minority populations. (Baseline data available in 1992)

13.2d   Reduce untreated dental caries so that the proportion of Hispanic children with untreated caries (in permanent or primary teeth) is no more than 25 percent among children aged 6 through 8 and no more than 25 percent among adolescents aged 15. (Baseline: 36 percent of Hispanic children aged 6 through 8 in 1982–84; 31–47 percent of Hispanic adolescents aged 15 in 1982–84)

13.5c   Reduce the prevalence of gingivitis among Hispanics aged 35 through 44 to no more than 50 percent. (Baseline: 74 percent among Mexican Americans; 79 percent among Cubans; 82 percent among Puerto Ricans; in 1982–84)

14.1c   Reduce the infant mortality rate among Puerto Ricans to no more than 8 per 1,000 live births. (Baseline: 12.9 per 1,000 live births in 1984)

14.1f   Reduce the neonatal mortality rate among Puerto Ricans to no more than 5.2 per 1,000 live births. (Baseline: 8.6 per 1,000 live births in 1984)

14.1j   Reduce the postneonatal mortality rate among Puerto Ricans to no more than 2.8 per 1,000 live births. (Baseline: 4.3 per 1,000 live births in 1984)

14.9c*   Increase to at least 75 percent the proportion of Hispanic mothers who breastfeed their babies in the early postpartum period, and to at least 50 percent the proportion who continue breastfeeding until their babies are 5 to 6 months old. (Baseline: 51 percent at discharge from birth site and 16 percent at 5 to 6 months in 1988)

14.11c   Increase to at least 90 percent the proportion of pregnant Hispanic women who receive prenatal care in the first trimester of pregnancy. (Baseline: 61.0 percent of live births in 1987)

16.11a   Increase to at least 80 percent the proportion of Hispanic women aged 40 and older who have ever received a clinical breast examination and a mammogram, and to at least 60 percent those aged 50 and older who have received them within the preceding 1 to 2 years. (Baseline: 20 percent of Hispanic women aged 40 and older "ever" in 1987; 18 percent of Hispanic women aged 50 and older "within the preceding 2 years" in 1987)

16.12a   Increase to at least 95 percent the proportion of Hispanic women with uterine cervix who have ever received a Pap test, and to at least 80 percent those who received a Pap test within the preceding 1 to 3 years. (Baseline: 75 percent "ever" and 66 percent "within the preceding 3 years" in 1987)

17.11b   Reduce diabetes among Puerto Ricans to a prevalence of no more than 49 per 1,000 Puerto Ricans. (Baseline: 55 per 1,000 aged 20 through 74 in 1982–84)

17.11c   Reduce diabetes among Mexican Americans to a prevalence of no more than 49 per 1,000 Mexican Americans. (Baseline: 54 per 1,000 aged 20 through 74 in 1982–84)

17.11d   Reduce diabetes among Cuban Americans to a prevalence of no more than 32 per 1,000 Cuban Americans. (Baseline: 36 per 1,000 aged 20 through 74 in 1982–84)

18.1c   Confine annual incidence of diagnosed AIDS cases among Hispanics to no more than 18,000 cases. (Baseline: An estimated 7,000–8,000 cases diagnosed in 1989)
         Note: Targets for this objective are equal to upper bound estimates of the incidence of diagnosed AIDS cases projected for 1993.

20.4c   Reduce tuberculosis among Hispanics to an incidence of no more than 5 cases per 100,000 Hispanics. (Baseline: 18.3 per 100,000 in 1988)

21.2i   Increase to at least 50 percent the proportion of Hispanics who have received, as a minimum within the appropriate interval, all of the screening and immunization services and at least one of the counseling services appropriate for their age and gender as recommended by the U.S. Preventive Services Task Force. (Baseline data available in 1991)

21.3a   Increase to at least 95 percent the proportion of Hispanics who have a specific source of ongoing primary care for coordination of their preventive and episodic health care. (Baseline: Less than 70 percent in 1986, as 30 percent reported having no physician, clinic, or hospital as a regular source of care)

21.8   Increase the proportion of all degrees in the health professions and allied and associated health profession fields awarded to members of underrepresented racial and ethnic minority groups as follows:

	1985–1986 Baseline	*2000 Target*
Hispanics	3%	6.4%

Note: Underrepresented minorities are those groups consistently below parity in most health profession schools — blacks, Hispanics, and American Indians and Alaska Natives.

OBJECTIVES TARGETING ASIANS AND PACIFIC ISLANDERS

2.4d   Reduce growth retardation among low-income Asian and Pacific Islander children aged 1 to less than 10 percent. (Baseline: 14 percent in 1988)

2.4e   Reduce growth retardation among low-income Asian and Pacific Islander children aged 2 through four to less than 10 percent. (Baseline: 16 percent in 1988)

3.4g*   Reduce cigarette smoking to a prevalence of no more than 20 percent among Southeast Asian men. (Baseline: 55 percent in 1984–88)

8.11   Increase to at least 50 percent the proportion of counties that have established culturally and linguistically appropriate community health promotion programs for racial and ethnic minority populations. (Baseline data available in 1992)

20.3d*   Reduce Hepatitis B (HBV) among children of Asians and Pacific Islanders to no more than 1,800 cases. (Baseline: An estimated 8,900 cases in 1987)

20.4a   Reduce tuberculosis among Asians and Pacific Islanders to an incidence of no more than 15 cases per 100,000 Asians and Pacific Islanders. (Baseline: 36.3 per 100,000 in 1988)

21.2j   Increase to at least 50 percent the proportion of Asians and Pacific Islanders who have received, as a minimum within the appropriate interval, all of the screening and immunization services and at least one of the counseling services appropriate for their age and gender as recommended by the U.S. Preventive Services Task Force. (Baseline data available in 1991)

22.4   Develop and implement a national process to identify significant gaps in the nation's disease prevention and health promotion data, including data for racial and ethnic minorities, people with low incomes, and people with disabilities, and establish mechanisms to meet these needs. (Baseline: No such process exists in 1990)

OBJECTIVES TARGETING AMERICAN INDIANS AND ALASKA NATIVES

2.3d*   Reduce overweight to a prevalence of no more than 30 percent among American Indians and Alaska Natives. (Baseline: An estimated 29–75 percent for different tribes in 1984–88)

2.10d   Reduce the prevalence of anemia to less than 10 percent among Alaska native children aged 1 through 5. (Baseline: 22–28 percent in 1983–85)

3.4f*   Reduce cigarette smoking to a prevalence of no more than 20 percent among American Indians and Alaska Natives. (Baseline: An estimated 42–70 percent for different tribes in 1979–87)

3.9a   Reduce smokeless tobacco use by American Indian and Alaska Native youth to a prevalence of no more than 10 percent. (Baseline: 18–64 percent in 1987)

4.1a   Reduce deaths among American Indian and Alaska Native men caused by alcohol-related motor vehicle crashes to no more than 44.8 per 100,000 American Indian and Alaska Native men. (Age-adjusted baseline: 52.2 per 100,000 in 1987)

4.2b   Reduce cirrhosis deaths among American Indians and Alaska Natives to no more than 13 per 100,000 American Indians and Alaska Natives. (Age-adjusted baseline: 25.9 per 100,000 in 1987)

6.1d*   Reduce suicides among American Indian and Alaska Native men in Reservation States to no more than 12.8 per 100,000 American Indian and Alaska Native men. (Age-adjusted baseline: 15 per 100,000 in 1987)

7.1f   Reduce homicides among American Indians and Alaska Natives in Reservation States to no more than 11.3 per 100,000 American Indians and Alaska Natives. (Age-adjusted baseline: 14.1 per 100,000 in 1987)

8.11   Increase to at least 50 percent the proportion of counties that have established culturally and linguistically appropriate community health promotion programs for racial and ethnic minority populations. (Baseline data available in 1992)

9.1a   Reduce deaths among American Indians and Alaska Natives caused by unintentional injuries to no more than 66.1 per 100,000 American Indians and Alaska Natives. (Age-adjusted baseline: 82.6 per 100,000 in 1987)

9.3d   Reduce deaths among American Indians and Alaska Natives caused by motor vehicle crashes to no more than 39.2 per 100,000 American Indians and Alaska Natives. (Age-adjusted baseline: 46.8 per 100,000 in 1987)

13.1b   Reduce dental caries (cavities) so that the proportion of American Indian and Alaska Native children aged 6 through 8 with one or more caries (in permanent or primary teeth) is no more than 45 percent. (Baseline: 92 percent in primary teeth and 52 percent in permanent teeth in 1983–84)

13.1d   Reduce dental caries (cavities) so that the proportion of American Indian and Alaska Native adolescents aged 15 with one or more caries (in permanent or primary teeth) is no more than 70 percent. (Baseline: 93 percent in permanent teeth in 1983–84)

13.2b   Reduce untreated dental caries so that the proportion of American Indian and Alaska Native children with untreated caries (in permanent or primary teeth) is no more than 35 percent among children aged 6 through 8 and no more than 40 percent among adolescents aged 15. (Baseline: 64 percent of American Indian and Alaska Native children aged 6 through 8 in 1983–84; 84 percent of American Indian and Alaska Native adolescents aged 15 in 1983–84)

13.5b   Reduce the prevalence of gingivitis among American Indians and Alaska Natives aged 35 through 44 to no more than 50 percent. (Baseline: 95 percent in 1983–84)

13.11b*   Increase to at least 65 percent the proportion of American Indian and Alaska Native parents and caregivers who use feeding practices that prevent baby bottle tooth decay. (Baseline data available in 1991)

14.1b   Reduce the infant mortality rate among American Indians and Alaska Natives to no more than 8.5 per 1,000 live births. (Baseline: 12.5 per 1,000 live births in 1984)

14.1i   Reduce the postneonatal mortality rate among American Indians and Alaska Natives to no more than 4 per 1,000 live births. (Baseline: 6.5 per 1,000 live births in 1984)

14.4a   Reduce the incidence of fetal alcohol syndrome among American Indians and Alaska Natives to no more than 2 per 1,000 live births. (Baseline: 4 per 1,000 live births in 1987)

14.9d*   Increase to at least 75 percent the proportion of American Indian and Alaska Native mothers who breastfeed their babies in the early postpartum period, and to at least 50 percent the proportion who continue breastfeeding until their babies are 5 to 6 months old. (Baseline: 47 percent at discharge from birth site and 28 percent at 5 to 6 months in 1988)

14.11b   Increase to at least 90 percent the proportion of pregnant American Indian and Alaskan Native women who receive prenatal care in the first trimester of pregnancy. (Baseline: 60.2 percent of live births in 1987)

17.2b   Reduce to no more than 11 percent the proportion of American Indians and Alaska Natives who experience a limitation in major activity due to chronic conditions. (Baseline: 13.4 percent in 1983–85)

17.9b   Reduce diabetes-related deaths among American Indians and Alaska Natives to no more than 48 per 100,000 American Indians and Alaska Natives. (Age-adjusted baseline: 54 per 100,000 in 1986)

17.10b   Reduce end-stage renal disease due to diabetes among American Indians and Alaska Natives with diabetes to no more than 1.9 per 1,000 American Indians and Alaska Natives with diabetes. (Baseline: 2.1 per 1,000 in 1983–86)

17.11a   Reduce diabetes among American Indians and Alaska Natives to a prevalence of no more than 62 per 1,000 American Indians and Alaska Natives. (Baseline: 69 per 1,000 aged 15 and older in 1987)

20.3g*   Reduce hepatitis B (HBV) among Alaska Natives to no more than 1 case. (Baseline: An estimated 15 cases in 1987)

20.4d   Reduce tuberculosis among American Indians and Alaska Natives to an incidence of no more than 5 cases per 100,000 American Indians and Alaska Natives. (Baseline: 18.1 per 100,000 in 1988)

20.7a   Reduce bacterial meningitis among Alaska Natives to no more than 8 cases per 100,000 Alaska Natives. (Baseline: 33 per 100,000 in 1987)

21.2k   Increase to at least 70 percent the proportion of American Indians and Alaska Natives who have received, as a minimum within the appropriate interval, all of the screening and immunization services and at least one of the counseling services appropriate for their age and gender as recommended by the U.S. Preventive Services Task Force. (Baseline data available in 1991)

21.8   Increase the proportion of all degrees in the health professions and allied and associated health profession fields awarded to members of underrepresented racial and ethnic minority groups as follows:

	1985–1986 Baseline	2000 Target
American Indians and Alaska Natives	0.3%	0.6%

OBJECTIVES TARGETING PEOPLE WITH DISABILITIES

1.5b   Reduce to no more than 20 percent the proportion of people with disabilities who engage in no leisure-time physical activity. (Baseline: 35 percent of people with disabilities aged 18 and older in 1985)
         Note: For this objective, people with disabilities are people who report any limitation in activity due to chronic conditions.

2.3e*   Reduce overweight to a prevalence of no more than 25 percent among people with disabilities. (Baseline: 36 percent for people aged 20 through 74 who report any limitation in activity due to chronic conditions in 1985)

6.5a   Reduce to less than 40 percent the proportion of people with disabilities aged 18 and older who experienced adverse health effects from stress within the past year. (Baseline: 53.5 percent in 1985)

8.3   Achieve for all disadvantaged children and children with disabilities access to high quality and developmentally appropriate preschool programs that help prepare children for school, thereby improving their prospects with regard to school performance, problem behaviors, and mental and physical health. (Baseline: 47 percent of eligible children aged 4 were afforded the opportunity to enroll in Head Start in 1990)

9.11   Reduce the incidence of secondary disabilities associated with injuries of the head and spinal cord to no more than 16 and 2.6 per 100,000 people, respectively. (Baseline: 20 per 100,000 for serious head injuries and 3.2 per 100,000 for spinal cord injuries in 1986)
         Note: Secondary disabilities are defined as those medical conditions secondary to traumatic head or spinal cord injury that impair independent and productive lifestyles.

9.22   Extend to 50 States emergency medical service and trauma systems linking prehospital, hospital, and rehabilitation services in order to prevent trauma deaths and long-term disability. (Baseline: 2 States in 1987)

14.15   Increase to at least 95 percent the proportion of newborns screened by State-sponsored programs for genetic disorders and other disabling conditions and to 90 percent the proportion of newborns testing positive for disease who receive appropriate treatment. (Baseline: For sickle cell anemia, with 20 States reporting, approximately 33 percent of live births screened (57 percent of black infants); for galactosemia, with 30 States reporting, approximately 70 percent of live births screened)

17.14   Increase to at least 40 percent the proportion of people with chronic and disabling conditions who receive formal patient education including information about community and self-help resources as an integral part of the management of their condition. (Baseline data available in 1991)

17.19   Increase to at least 75 percent the proportion of worksites with 50 or more employees that have a voluntarily established policy or program for the hiring of people with disabilities. (Baseline: 37 percent of medium and large companies in 1986)

17.20   Increase to 50 the number of States that have service systems for children with or at risk of chronic and disabling conditions, as required by Public Law 101-239. (Baseline data available in 1991)

21.21   Increase to at least 80 percent the proportion of people with disabilities who have received, as a minimum within the appropriate interval, all of the screening and immunization services and at least one of the counseling services appropriate for their age and gender as recommended by the U.S. Preventive Services Task Force. (Baseline data available in 1991)

From Healthy People 2000: National Health Promotion and Disease Prevention Objectives, Washington, D.C., U.S. Department of Health and Human Services, Public Health Service, 1991. Available from The Superintendent of Documents, Washington, D.C., U.S. Government Printing Office, DHHS publication No. (PHS) 91–50212.

INDEX

Note: Page numbers in *italics* refer to illustrations; page numbers followed by t refer to tables.

AA (Alcoholics Anonymous), 514
Abuse. See specific category, e.g., *Child abuse.*
Accidental injuries, as child health status indicator, 214
  as senior health problem, 338–339
    causes of, 338
    prevention of, 339
    telephone services for, 339
  as women's health problem, 245
Accidental poisoning, as senior health problem, 340
Acquired immune deficiency syndrome (AIDS). See also *Human immunodeficiency virus (HIV).*
  adolescents and, 552
  condom use and, 552–553
  education and, 165–166
  educators in, 551–552
  elderly and, 342, 552
  high-risk drug use behaviors and, case study in, 183
  home care for, case study in, 182
  in African-American community, 449–450
    educational programs and, 449–450
    incidence of, 449, 449t
    socioeconomic factors and, 449
    strategies to address in, 450
  in work place, 605
  incidence of, 551
    in ethnic and racial minorities, 551
    in women, 551
  infant and child mortality and, 552
  information and hotline numbers for, 554
  weight loss prevention in, case study in, 181–182
  world health and, 665
Activity theory, of aging, 352
Addictive illness, 510–511
Adolescent(s), AIDS and, 552
  education and, 165–166
  Healthy People 2000 objective(s) for, 715–718
    health status and, 715–716
    reducing deaths as, 715

Adolescent(s), *(Continued)*
    risk reduction as, 716–718
    services and protection as, 718
  pregnancy in, case study of, 224–228
    child health problem prevention and, 219
  substance abuse in, 518
Adolescent health, social factors affecting, 218
African-American community, 433–457
  AIDS in, 449–450
    educational programs and, 449–450
    incidence of, 449, 449t
    socioeconomic factors and, 449
    strategies to address in, 450
  biocultural variations in, 451–455, 453t-454t
    ears and, 454
    general appearance and, 451
    head and, 453–454
    illness and, 441
      excessive deaths and, 441, 444t
      health status disparity and, 441
      life expectancy and, 441
    laboratory tests in, lecithin-to-sphingomyelin ratio in amniotic fluid and, 455
      serum cholesterol and, 455
      serum transferrin and, 455
    mouth in, 454
    musculoskeletal system in, 453
    secretions in, 455
    skin in, 451–453. See also *Skin.*
    teeth in, 454–455
      absence of, 454
      decay of, 454–455
      periodontal disease and, 455
      size of, 454
    thorax in, 455
  cancer in, 444t, 444–445
  cardiovascular disease in, 445–446
    cholesterol and, 445
    hypertension and, 445
    obesity and, 445
    smoking and, 445
    social, cultural, and economic aspects of, 445–446

African-American community *(Continued)*
changing family life patterns in, 436–437
chemical dependency in, 446–447
alcoholism as, 446
drug abuse as, 446–447
communication and language in,
black English in, 439
differences in, 455–456
cultural healers in, 441, 456
types of, 441, 443t
cultural sensitivity and, 456
diabetes mellitus in, 447
prevalence of, 447
prevention of, 447
economic milieu of, 435–436
education in, 436
health beliefs and practices in, 439–441
cultural, 440–441
diet in, 441
folk illnesses in, 441, 442t
historical, 440
preventive measures in, 441
rooting in, 440–441
voodoo in, 440
traditional, 439–440
health indicators in, 441, 443–444
cirrhosis of liver and, 443
diabetes mellitus and, 443
elderly and, 443
excessive deaths and, 441, 443
homicide and, 443
hypertension and, 443
relative risks and, 444
Healthy People 2000 objectives for,
725–727
historical, 434
homicide in, 447–448
incidence of, 447
prevention of, 448
socioeconomic status and, 447–448
infant mortality in, 448–449
childbearing patterns and, 448, 448t
prevention of, 448
risk factors for, 449
sudden infant death syndrome and,
448–449
laboratory tests in, 455
nursing care in, 450–451
aspects of, 450
cultural self-assessment and, 450–451
cultural stereotypes and, 451
rural vs. urban in, 438, 438t
sex roles in, 437–438
finding and keeping mates and, 437
interracial dating and marriage and,
437–438
men and, 437
women and, 437

African-American community *(Continued)*
social justice and, 438–439
racism in, 438–439
self-concept and racial identity in,
438
sociodemographic overview of, 434t–435t, 435
substance abuse treatment barriers in,
519
Age Discrimination in Employment Act,
348
Age stratification theory, 353
Aggregate, definition of, 568
Aggregate-focused practice, 10–11
occupational nurses in, 11
private association–employed nurses
in, 11
school nurses in, 11
Aging. See also *Elder abuse; Elderly;
Senior health.*
myths of, 330
selected social theories of, 352–353
AIDS. See *Acquired immune deficiency
syndrome (AIDS).*
Alaska Native community, *Healthy People 2000* objectives for, 729–731
Albrecht nursing model, for home health
care, 629, *630*
Alcohol, Drug Abuse, and Mental
Health Administration, 53
Alcohol abuse. See *Substance abuse.*
Alcoholics Anonymous (AA), 514
Alma Ata, declaration of, 691–693
Alma Ata Charter of 1978, 61
Alma-ATA, declaration of, economic
and social development in, 691
government responsibility in, 691
health as right in, 691
health care planning in, 691
inequality of health status in, 691
international cooperation in, 692
national policy formulation in, 692
primary health care in, 691–692
world's resources usage in, 692
Alzheimer's disease, families of elderly
and, 346
American Association of Retired Persons, 350
American Indian community, *Healthy
People 2000* objectives for, 729–731
Americans With Disabilities Act, 615–616
disability definition in, 616
exclusions of, 616
occupational health nurse responsibilities in, 616
physical or mental impairment guidelines in, 616
pre-employment health examinations
under, 616

Americans With Disabilities Act
  (Continued)
  provisions of, 615
  timing in, 615–616
Amniotic fluid, lecithin-to-sphingomye-
    lin ratio in, biocultural variations
    of, 455
Anemia, African-American skin color
    and, 452
Arteriosclerotic heart disease, among
    women, 240
Arthritis, among women, 240
Atmospheric quality, atmospheric car-
    bon dioxide and, 573
  chlorofluorocarbons and, 573
  dangers related to, 573
  definition of, 573
  environmental health and, 573–574
  severe weather conditions and, 573
  vignette of, 573
  worldwide deforestation and, 573

B*ilis*, in disease causation beliefs, 413
Biomedical theory, of disease causation,
    388–389
Birth weight, low, as child health status
    indicator, 213
Blacks. See *African-American community.*
Block nurse program, 309–310
Breast cancer, among women, 240
  in African-American community, 444

C*aida de la mollera*, in disease causation
    beliefs, 413
Cancer, human papillomavirus and, 554
  in African-American community,
    444t, 444–445
  in women, 234
  men's health and, 268
  of breast, 240
  of endometrium, 242
  of ovary, 242
  of testicles, 263
  of uterine cervix, 241–242
Carbon dioxide, atmospheric quality
    and, 573
Carcinoma. See *Cancer.*
Cardiopulmonary resuscitation (CPR),
    elderly and, 363
Cardiovascular disease, in African-
    American community, 445–446
  cholesterol and, 445
  hypertension and, 445
  obesity and, 445
  smoking and, 445
  social, cultural, and economic
    aspects of, 445–446
  in women, 234–235
*Case Definitions for Public Health Sur-
    veillance*, 537

Case management, 48
Case-control studies. See *Retrospective
    studies.*
Census data, 84–85
  comparison of data and, 84
  "hidden pockets" of need and, 85
  information categories in, 84
  information range in, 84
Centers for Disease Control, 52, 105–
    106
  in prevention of disease transmission,
    guidelines for, 537
Cerebrovascular accident, men's health
    and, 268
Cervix, uterine, cancer of, 241–242
Chandler Center, elder care and, 351
Child abuse, 463–467
  as child health status indicator, 216
  by drug users, 466
  causes of, 463–464
    Garbarino ecological model in, 464,
      465
  dynamics of, 463
  emotional maltreatment in, 464, 466
    behavior due to, 466
    definition of, 464
    examples of, 466
  failure to thrive syndrome and, 466–
    467
  neglect in, definition of, 464
    emotional, 466
    physical, 466
  nurse's legal responsibilities in, 481
  nursing care in, 475–478
    primary prevention in, 475–477
      parent-child relationship and,
        475–476
      parenting education and, 477
      perinatal period and, 477
      pregnancy classes and, 476–477
    secondary prevention in, 477
      precise charting of assessment
        and, 477
      working parents and, 477
    tertiary prevention in, 477–478
      community support services and,
        478
      discovery and, 478
      sexual abuse and, 478
  physical, 464–466
    ages at risk of, 465–466
    beating with instrument as, 464–465
    definition of, 464
    violent shaking as, 465
  physical and behavioral indicators of,
    467, 468t
  sexual, 464, 466
    definition of, 464, 466
    incest as, 466
    long-term consequences of, 466
  types of, 464–467

Child health, 211–229
  case study in, 223–228
  indicator(s) of, 212–216
    accidental injuries as, 214
    child abuse and neglect as, 216
    immunizations as, 215
    infant mortality as, 212–213. See
        also *Infant mortality.*
    lack of prenatal care as, 214
    lead poisoning as, 215
    low birth weight as, 213
    "new morbidities" of youth as, 214–
        215
    socioeconomic status as, 214
    substance abuse as, 214
    violence as, 214
  poor, costs to society of, 218–219
  problem prevention in, adolescent
        pregnancy and parenting and, 219
    drug abuse and delinquency and, 219
    immunizations and, 219
    lead poisoning and, 219
    prenatal care and, 219
  public program(s) targeting, 219–221
    Community and Migrant Health
        Centers Programs as, 220
    direct health care delivery in, 220–
        221
    Head Start as, 221
    maternal and child health block
        grant in, 220
    Medicaid in, 219–220
    National Health Service Corps in,
        220
    Special Supplemental Food Pro-
        gram for Women, Infants, and
        Children (WIC) in, 220–221
  social factor(s) affecting, 216–218
    maternal substance abuse as, 217–
        218
    poverty as, 216–217, *217*
    protective factors as, 216
    risk factors as, 216
    single-parent households as, 218
  strategies to improve, 221t, 221–223
    community health nurse's role in,
        223
    community's role in, 222
    employer's role in, 222
    government's role in, 222–223
    parent's role in, 222
Childbearing, patterns of, 448, 448t
Children, *Healthy People 2000* objec-
        tives for, 711–715
    health status in, 711–713. See also
        Child health.
    reducing deaths in, 711
    risk reduction in, 713–714
    service and protection in, 713–714
  immunity and, 540, 540t
Children's Bureau, 42

Chlamydia trachomatis, 549–550
  in women, 549
  infections resulting from, 549
  screening for, 549
Chlorofluorocarbons, atmospheric qual-
        ity and, 573
Cholesterol, cardiovascular disease and,
        in African-American community,
        445
  serum, biocultural variations in, 455
Cigarette smoking, cardiovascular dis-
        ease and, in African-American com-
        munity, 445
Cirrhosis of liver, in African-American
        community, 443
Civil Rights Act, women's health and, 246
Clinical trial study, 102–103, *103*
  common application of, 102
  description of, 102
  examples of, 102–103
Cocaine, crack, 509–510
Code of Federal Regulations, in occupa-
        tional health, 614
Codependency, 516
Cognitive field learning theory, 168
  teaching strategies derived from, 169–
        170
    examples of, 170–172, *171*
Cohort studies. See *Prospective studies.*
Communicable disease(s), 533–563
  sexually transmitted disease as, 549–
        551. See also *Sexually transmitted
        disease.*
  transmission of, 535–539
    agent factor in, 535
    airborne, 536–537
      air filtration systems and, 537
      droplet nuclei in, 537
      particle size in, 536–537
    defining and reporting cases of,
        537–539
      breaking chain of transmission in,
        539
      National Notifiable Diseases Sur-
        veillance System in, 538, 539t
      national trends monitoring in, 538
      required case types in, 537
    direct, 535–536
    fomites in, 536
    host factor in, 535
    indirect, 536
    prevention of, 537
      Centers for Disease Control
        guidelines in, 537
      universal blood and body fluid
        precautions in, 537, 538t
    types of, 535, 535t
    vector-borne, 536
      biological route of, 536
      mechanical route of, 536
    vaccine-preventable, 539–549

Communicable disease *(Continued)*
    active immunization in, 541–549
      cold chain in, 541
      recommended schedule for, 541, 541t
      vaccine routes, dosages, and storage requirements in, 541, 542t
    diphtheria as, 544
    diphtheria-tetanus-pertussis as, 544
    hepatitis B as, 544–546. See also *Hepatitis B.*
    immunity in, 540–541. See also *Immunity.*
    immunization guidelines in, 547
    influenza as, 544
    measles as, 542–543
      age for immunization against, 542–543
      deaths due to, 542, 543t
      European populations and, 543
      world eradication of, 543
    measles-mumps-rubella as, 542
    mumps as, 543
    pertussis as, 544
    polio as, 541–542
    pulmonary tuberculosis as, 546–547
      incidence of, 546–547
      prevention of, 547
      screening program for, 547
    rubella as, 543–544
    smallpox as, 539–540
    tetanus as, 544
    travel and, 547–548, 548t
Communication, black English in, 439
    cross-cultural differences in, African-American community and, 455–456
Community, African-American. See *African-American community.*
    as aggregate of people, 82
      common characteristics in, 82
      "community of solution" in, 82
      risk factors in, 82
    as location in space and time, 82–83
      census tracts in, 83
      geopolitical boundaries in, 83
      neighborhood definition in, 83
    as social system, 83–84
      changing dynamics in, 84
      subsystems in, 83
    assessment of, concept of risk in, 91
      epidemiology in, 91–103. See also *Epidemiology.*
      parameters in, 85, 86t-87t
      sources of data in, 84–91
        calculation of rates in, 85, 88. See also *Rate(s).*
        census data in, 84–85. See also *Census data.*

Community *(Continued)*
      government surveys and reports in, 85, 86t-87t
      vital statistics in, 85
    environment of, elderly and, 344
    in child health improvement, 222–223
    major features of, 83
    Mexican-American. See *Mexican-American community.*
    nature of, 82–91
    Southeast Asian. See *Southeast Asian refugees.*
Community and Migrant Health Centers Programs, 220
Community health, broadened view of, 5
    current U.S. health policy and, 4
    definition of, 6, 50
    focus of, 6
    future of, 684
    historical evolution of, 17–21
    mission of, 4
    narrow view of, 4
    social justice and, 4, 7
Community health nursing, aggregate-focused practice in, 10–11
    occupational nurses in, 11
    private association–employed nurses in, 11
    school nurses in, 11
    case study in, 685
    critical, 583–587
      asking critical questions in, 584, 584t
      facilitating community involvement in, 584–585
      forming coalitions in, 585–586
      taking a stand in, 583–584
      using collective strategies in, 586–587
        Delaware Valley Toxics Coalition and, 587
        participatory research and, 586–587
    cultural diversity and. See *Cultural diversity.*
    definitions of, 4, 7, 9
      American Nurses' Association and, 9
      American Public Health Association and, 9
      Freeman and, 7
    future issues in, 686
    goal of, 4
    historical, 9
    home visit in, 144
    in child health improvement, 222–223
    in men's health, 280–281
      facilitating in, 280–281
      health education in, 280
    in women's health, 252–253
      counseling in, 253
      direct care in, 252–253
    levels of practice in, 112t, 113

Community health nursing *(Continued)*
nursing theory and. See *Nursing theory.*
population-focused practice in, 10
generalist application of, 10, *10*
scientific approach in, 10, 11t
specialist application of, 10, *10*
problem delineation in, microscopic
vs. macroscopic approach to, 70
program(s) in, immunizations at mall
as, 682
volunteer outreach to prenatal populations as, 680
research in, empowering families and
evoking authority in, 683
strategies and support for drug-
exposed infants and, 683
services for men in, 267
standards of, 689
team care and, 6
Community organization, 129–141
community participation in, 133–134
change process and, 133–134
directive, 133–134, *134*
participatory, 133, *134*
concepts of, 132–134
definition of, 130–131
as process, 130–131
goals of, 131, 131t
in nursing practice, 131–132
historical aspects of, 131
primary health care in, 131–132
models of, 134–135, 135t
basis of, 134
community development in, 135
case study of, 139–140
selection of, 140
social action in, 135
case study of, 138–139
social planning in, 135
case study of, 137–138
nursing strategies in, 135–137
campaign, 136
collaboration, 136
contest, 136–137
social change in, 133
systems theory in, 132–133
focal system and, 132
interrelated subsystems and, 132
intervention and, 133
Neuman's health-care systems
model and, 133
Continuity theory, of aging, 353
Coronary heart disease, men's health
and, 267–268
Coronary Primary Prevention Trial,
102–103
Correlational studies, 97, *98*
CPR (cardiopulmonary resuscitation, elderly and, 363
Crack cocaine, 509–510

Critical social theory, 76–78
application of, 77
basis of, 76
challenging assumptions about preventive health through, *77*, 77–78
data collection and analysis in, 77
manufacturers of illness in, 78
methodological approaches in, 77
politicoeconomic interventions in, *77*,
77–78
Cross-cultural nursing, 373
Cross-sectional studies, 97, *98*
Cuba, population-focused practice in,
667, 669–673. See also *Population-
focused practice, in Cuba.*
Cultural brokerage, 394
Cultural diversity, 371–404
community health nursing role and,
398–399
cultural self-assessment and, 402
culturally based health practices recognition and, 403
culturally sensitive care and, 402–403
culturological assessment and, 398–
402
biocultural variations in, 401–402
communication in, 399–400
cultural sanctions and restrictions
in, 399
definition of, 398
developmental considerations in,
402
disease incidence in, 401
educational background in, 401
health-related beliefs and practices in, 400
history of ethnic origins of client's
culture in, 399
nutrition in, 400
religious affiliation in, 401
socioeconomic considerations in,
400–401
support organizations in, 401
values orientation in, 399
increasing knowledge about local
cultures and, 402
political aspects and, 402
cross–cultural communication in,
383–387
non–English-speaking clients and,
386–387
interpreter selection for, 386–387,
387t
no interpreter and, 387, 388t
nonverbal, 385–386
eye contact in, 385–386
silence in, 385
nurse-client relationship and, 383–
384
cultural stereotypes in, 383–384

Cultural diversity *(Continued)*
    ethnocentrism in, 384
    initial contact in, 383
    overcoming barriers in, 385
    sex in, 386
    space, distance, and intimacy in, 384t, 384–385
    touch in, 386
  culture specific in, 373
  culture universal in, 373
  disease causation in minority populations and, 391
  excessive deaths in, 391
  expression of illness in, 391–393
    culture-bound syndromes and, 392–393, 393t
    pain and, 392
    symptoms and, 392
  family in, 377–378
  health care delivery in, inequality in, 390
  health indicators and, disparity in, 391
  health-related beliefs and practices in, 387–390
    defining illness in, 388–390
    disease causation in, 388–390
      biomedical theory of, 388–389
      hot-cold theory of, 389
      magicoreligious perspective on, 389
      naturalistic theory of, 389
      yin-yang theory of, 389
    folk-healers in, 390
    healing and, 390
  historical perspective on, 372–377
    in 19th century, 372
    transcultural nursing and, 372–373
  nutrition and, 380, 381t
    assessment of, 380
    dietary practices in, 380
    religion and diet in, 380, 381t
  religion and, 381–383. See also *Religion.*
  socioeconomic factor(s) in, 378–379
    education as, 379
    resources distribution as, 378–379
  solutions to health care problems and, 394–398
    continuity of care in, 396
    developing strategies in, 397
    financing in, 396
    health education and, 395–396
    health information in, 394–395
      increasing, 395
      lack of, 394–395
      planning, 395
    health professions development in, 397
    health services delivery in, 396
    research agenda in, 398

Cultural diversity *(Continued)*
  sources of data in, 397–398
  treatment of illness in, 393
Cultural negotiation, 394
Culture, characteristics of, 373
  definition of, 373
  minority, 374
  subculture in, 373
  values formation in, 374–377
    activity orientation in, 376
    common human problems in, 374
    dominant value orientation in, 374, 375t
    health-related decisions in, 375–376, 376–377
    human nature orientation in, 374–375
    norms in, 374
    person-nature orientation in, 375
    social orientation in, 376
      collateral relationships as, 376
      individual relationships as, 376
      lineal relationships as, 376
    time orientation in, 376
    value definition in, 374
Culture specific, definition of, 373
Culture universal, definition of, 373
Curanderismo, in disease causation belief, 412
Cyanosis, African-American skin color and, 452

Dano, in disease causation beliefs, 414
Department of Health, Education, and Welfare, 42. See also *Department of Health and Human Services.*
Department of Health and Human Services, 51–53, *52*
  agencies in, 51, *52*
  Health Care Financing Administration in, 51
  Office of Human Development Services in, 51
  Social Security Administration in, 51–52
  U.S. Public Health Service in, 52–53. See also *U.S. Public Health Service.*
Depression, among women, 236
  in Southeast Asian refugees, 430
  signs and symptoms of, 236
Developmental stages, screening procedures and, 56, 57t
Diabetes mellitus, in African-American community, as health indicator, 443
  prevalence of, 447
  prevention of, 447
  in women, 235, 240
  pregnancy and, 443

Diphtheria, 544
Diphtheria-tetanus-pertussis (DTP) vaccine, 544
Discharge planning, 48
Disease, communicable. See *Communicable disease.*
    history of, stages of, 14–17, *14*
    prevention of, levels of, 7, *7*, 8t
Disengagement theory, of aging, 352
Diversity, cultural. See *Cultural diversity.*
Divorce and remarriage, 299, 300t–301t, 302
Drinking water, quality of, 574
Drug abuse. See *Substance abuse.*

Ear(s), biocultural variations in, 454
Early and Periodic Screening, Diagnosis, and Treatment Program, child health and, 219–220
Ecchymotic lesions, African-American skin color and, 453
Ecomap, in family health, 304–307, *305–306*
Education, 164–184. See also *Learning; Teaching.*
    adolescents and, 165–166
    AIDS and, 165–166
    evaluation in, 180–181
    Freire's model of, 172–175. See also *Freire's education model.*
    health promotion model of, 175, *176*
    healthier lifestyles and, 166
    in African-American community, 436
    in child abuse prevention, 477
    in community settings, 165–166
    in culturological assessment, 401
    in social context, 172
    learning theories and strategies in, 167
    models of, 175–179
    nursing process application in, case studies in, 181–183
    Precede model of, 175, *177*, 179
        planning form for, *178*
        schematic for, *179*
    purpose of, 181
    relationship to health of, 165
    resources for, 179–180
        commercial organizations as, 180
        government sources as, 180
        material selection in, 180
        medical centers as, 180
        professional organizations as, 180
        volunteer and nonprofit organizations as, 180
    socioeconomic status and, 379
    substance abuse programs in, 512
    theory selection in, 172
Elder abuse, 344–345, 472–473. See also *Aging; Senior health.*
    abandonment in, 473

Elder abuse *(Continued)*
    categories of, 345
    dynamics of, 472–473
    fiduciary, 473
    indicators of, physical and behavioral, 473, 474t–475t
    neglect in, 473
    nurse's legal responsibilities in, 481
    nursing care in, 480
        focus of, 480
        restrictive care in, 480
        right to privacy and, 480
    physical, 473
    types of, 473
    typical victim in, 344
Elderly, *Healthy People 2000* objectives for, 721–723
    health status in, 721–722. See also *Senior health.*
    reducing activities of daily living limitation in, 721
    risk reduction in, 722
    services and protection in, 722
Empacho, in disease causation beliefs, 413
Employee Retirement Income Security Act, senior health and, 348
Endemic disease, definition of, 17
Endometrium, cancer of, 242
Environment, definition of, 568
Environmental health, 567–594
    aggregate level approach to, 582–583
    areas of, 570t, 570–580
    atmospheric quality in, 573–574
        carbon dioxide and, 573
        chlorofluorocarbons and, 573
        dangers related to, 573
        definition of, 573
        severe weather conditions and, 573
        vignette of, 574
        worldwide deforestation and, 573
    case study of, 587–592
    concepts of, 568, 568t
    critical community health nursing in, 583–587. See also *Community health nursing, critical.*
    critical theory approach to, 569–570
        change in, collective strategies for, 569
        core dynamics of, 569
        goal of, 569
        problem identification in, 569
    environmental organizations and, 582, 582t
    food quality in, 576–577
        definition of, 576
        "gene splicing" and, 576
        problems related to, 576
        toxic chemical contamination and, 576
        vignette of, 576–577
    hazards to, effects of, 580
    housing in, 575–576

Environmental health *(Continued)*
    definition of, 575
    problems related to, 575
    "sick building" phenomenon and,
        575
    vignette of, 575–576
    living patterns in, 570, 572
        definition of, 570, 572
        vignette of, 572
    participatory research about, 586
    problems in, 570, 571t
        control of, 580–582
            Environmental Protection Agency
                in, 581
            factors influencing, 581
            legislation in, 580, 581t, 581–582
            nursing careers in, 582
            scientific research and, 581
        radiation risks in, 577–578
            definition of, 577–578
            excessive or ill-performed radio-
                graphs and, 578
            nuclear industries and, 578
            nuclear waste disposal and, 578
            problems posed by, 578
            radon and, 578
            vignette of, 578
        violence in, 579–580
            ballistic weapons availability and,
                579
            problems posed by, 579
            social stigmatization and, 579
            vignette of, 579–580
        waste control in, 577
            definition of, 577
            hazardous waste sites and, 577
            problems related to, 577
            vignette of, 577
        water quality in, 574–575
            definition of, 574
            drinking water sources and, 574
            problems of, 574
            vignette of, 574–575
            water-related diseases and, 574
        work risks in, 572–573
            definition of, 572
            health problems posed by, 572–573
            vignette of, 573
Environmental Protection Agency, 581
Epidemic disease, definition of, 17
Epidemiology, 91–103
    analytical, 92, 97–103
        definition of, 92
        experimental research in, 102–103,
            103
            common application of, 102
            description of, 102
            examples of, 102–103
        observational research in, 97–102.
            See also *Observational research.*
        research studies in, 97
    chronic disease control in, 94–95

Epidemiology *(Continued)*
    definition of, 91
    descriptive, 92, 96–97
        definition of, 92
        "person" characteristics in, 96
        place of occurrence in, 96
        purpose of, 96
        time factor in, 96–97
    early focus in, 92
    historical, 92
    in disease control and prevention, 92–
        95
    in health services, 95–96
        adequacy of system evaluation in, 95
        cost-effectiveness evaluation in, 96
        health policy planning in, 96
        quality of care evaluation in, 95–96
    in secondary and tertiary prevention
            approaches, 95
        ongoing data collection in, 95
        screening programs in, 95
        secular trends documentation in, 95
    investigative models of, epidemiologi-
            cal triangle in, *92*, 92–94, 93t
        "wheel model" in, 94, *94*
Erythema, African-American skin color
        and, 452

Failure to thrive syndrome, child abuse
        and, 466–467
Family, as client, individual client vs., 288
    categories of, 377
    changing life patterns of, in African-
            American community, 436–437
    characteristic(s) of, 377–378
        changing, 290
        ethnicity in, 378
        number of children as, 377
        primary care provider as, 378
        relationship definition in, 378
        shared households in, 377
        teen parenting in, 377–378
    cultural diversity and, 377–378
    definition of, 289–290
    dysfunctional, 516–517
    extended, 377
    functional, 516
    in Mexican-American community,
            410–412. See also *Mexican-
            American community, family in.*
    moving from individual to, 290–293
        chronic illness intervention in, 293
        family interviewing model in, 291–
            292
        occupational health nurse in, 292
        school nurse in, 292
    moving to community from, 293–295
        scarce resources delegation in, 294–
            295
    nuclear, 377

Family *(Continued)*
  nuclear dyad, 377
  single-parent, 377
Family health, assessment tool(s) in,
    302–307
    ecomap as, 304–307, *305–306*
    family health tree as, 304, *305*
    genogram as, 302–304, *302–304*
    social and structural constraints
      and, 307
  developmental approach to, 299
    divorce and remarriage in, 299, 300t–
      301t, 302
    family life cycle in, 299
    stages and tasks in, 300–301
  extending intervention in, 307–310
    ecological approach to, 307
    network therapy and, 308
    transactional field approach to, 308
  functional approach to, 298–299
    expressive, 298–299
    instrumental, 298
  models of care for communities in,
    309–310
    block nurse program in, 309–310
    home care for chronically ill chil-
      dren in, 309
    Partnership for Health Program in,
      310
    Su Clinica Familiar in, 309
  needs of, meeting, 290–295
  reasons for working with family in, 295
  social class and health services models
    in, 308–309
    cultural poverty in, 308
    structural view in, 308–309
  structural approach to, 298
    external, 298
    internal, 298
  systems approach to, 296–298
    definitions in, 296–297
    healthy family characteristics in,
      297–298
Family health tree, 304, *305*
Family interviewing model, 291–292
  health care settings in, 291
  newborn assessments in, 291–292
  preventive programs in, 291
  single-parent families in, 292
Family Support Act, 43
Family violence, 459–485. See also
    Child abuse; Elder abuse; Women
    abuse.
  history of, 460–461
  major effects of, 463, 464t
  prevention of, 474–475
  reduction of, comprehensive program
    for, 474, 476t
  scope of, 461–463
    battering in, 462–463
    child abuse in, 461, *462*
    homicide in, 462, *462–463*

Family violence *(Continued)*
  victims of, abused children as, 475–478
    abused elderly as, 480
    abused women as, 478–480
    nursing care of, 473–480
Fecal-oral contamination, sexual activity
    and, 556
  sexually transmitted disease and, 555–
    556
  transmission cycle in, 556
  water supplies in, 556
Folk medicine, 408
Fomite, in disease transmission, 536
Food and Drug Administration, 52
Food quality, definition of, 576
  environmental health and, 576–577
  "gene splicing" and, 576
  problems related to, 576
  toxic chemical contamination in, 576
  vignette of, 576–577
Freire's education model, 172–175
  advocacy in, 174
  alcohol substance abuse prevention
    program using, 175, 175t
  cancer awareness project using, 174–
    175
  conscientization in, 173
  empowerment education in, 174
  foundation of, 172
  generative themes in, 173
  phases of, 173
  problem definition in, 173–174
  sociopolitical dimension of, 173–174
Funerals, procedure following death and,
    343

Garbarino's ecological model, of child
    abuse, 464, *465*
Generations Together, elder care and, 351
Genogram, in family health, 302–304,
    302–304
Gestalt learning theory, 168
Government, 50, 51–59
  agencies for elderly in, 348
  as authority for public health protec-
    tion, 197–198
  as hallmark of civilization, 197
  balance of powers in, 198–199
  federal level of, 50, 51–53
    organization in, 50, 51–53, *52.* See
      also *Department of Health and*
      Human Services; U.S. Public
      Health Service.
    scope of, 53
  in child health improvement, 222–223
  local level of, 56–59
    community health services in, 56, 57t
    direction of, 56
    environmental health services in, 56
    functions and services of, 58, 58t, *59*

Government *(Continued)*
    mental health services in, 56
    organization in, 56
    personal health services in, 56
    responsibilities of, 56
    scope of, 56–59
    services determination in, 58
  mandate of powers of, 197, *198*
  state level of, 53, 55–56
    assessment activities in, 55
    assurance activities in, 55
    organization in, 53
    policy development activities in, 55
    scope of, 53, 55t, 55–56
    specific duties of, 55t, 55–56
Gray Panthers, 350
Greenhouse effect, atmospheric quality
    and, 573

Hazardous waste sites, 577
Head, biocultural variations in, 453–454
Head Start program, 120, 221
Health, aggregate membership impact
    on, 680–682
    age in, 681
    geography and politics in, 681–682
    race and ethnicity in, 681
    sex in, 680–681
    social interaction in, 681
    socioeconomic status in, 680
  as cultural value, 166–167
  as personal value, 164–165
  collective activity for, 682
  community. See *Community health.*
  definitions of, 5–6, 44
    community health nursing in, 5
    community in, 5–6
    World Health Organization in, 5
  determinants of, 44, 164–165, 682
  disease prevention levels and, 7, *7*, 8t
  environmental. See *Environmental
      health.*
  evolution of, 14–21
    aggregate impact on, 14–17. See
        also *History of disease.*
  men's. See *Men's health.*
  mental. See *Mental health.*
  "New Age" view of, 166–167
  of adolescent. See *Adolescent health.*
  of child. See *Child health.*
  of family. See *Family health.*
  of seniors. See *Senior health.*
  preventive approach to, 6–7
  promotion of, 6–7
  public. See *Community health; Public
      health subsystem.*
  right vs. privilege in, 684–685
  rural. See *Rural health.*
  sex differences in, 261
    theories of explanation for, 261–266
      genetics in, 262

Health *(Continued)*
      illness and prevention orienta-
          tions in, 262–264
      interpreting data in, 264–265
      reporting health behavior in,
          264
      sex-linked behavior in, 265–266
      socialization in, 262
    women's. See *Women's health.*
    world. See *World health.*
Health Amendments Act, 42
Health belief model, 72–74, 171, *171*
    application of, 73–74
    core dimensions of, 72
    limitations of, 74
    major concepts of, 72
    Milio's framework for prevention and,
        76
    patients' behavior in, 74
    premise of, 72
    variables and relationships in, 73, *73*
Health care, home. See *Home health care.*
    in Cuba, at time of revolution, 668
      changes in, 668–669
      social action and, 669
      social justice model in, 668
    market justice model in, 668
    medical care vs., 683–684
    primary, 131–132
      community organization and, 132
      definition of, 131–132
      nursing role in, 132
    reform of, nursing's agenda for, 684
Health care services, access to, 130
    limitations of, 130
    basic, World Health Organization def-
        inition of, 130
Health care system, 41–62
    components of, 44–45, *45*
    focus of services of, 44
    funding in, 43
    future of, 59–62
      orientation shift in, 60
      patterns influencing, 59–60
      public health subsystem in, 61–62.
          See also *Public health subsystem.*
    goals of, 44
    major legislation and, 42–44. See also
        Legislation.
    measurable outcomes of, 44
    orientation of, 4
    private health subsystem in, 44, 45–
        50. See also *Private health subsys-
        tem.*
    public/environmental health subsys-
        tem in, 44–45, 50–59. See also
        Public health subsystem.
Health Goals for Year 2000, 221t, 221–
    222
Health maintenance organization
    (HMO), 43
    social, 352

Health Objectives Planning Act, 43
Health Objectives Planning Act 2000, 43, 60
Health planning, 109–126
  community as client in, 111, *111*
  focus of care shift in, 112–113
  levels of practice in, 112t, 113
  nursing education in, 113
  nursing implications in, 126
  overview of, 110–113
Health planning model, *113*, 113–117
  aggregate selection in, 114–115
  assessment in, 115–116
    identification and prioritization of health needs in, 116
    initial contact in, 115
    literature review in, 115–116
    positive and negative factors in, 115
    sociodemographic characteristics determination in, 115
    suprasystem of aggregate in, 115
  evaluation in, 117
  implementation in, 117
  planning stage in, 116–117
    goals and objectives of, 116
    intervention in, level of, 116
      practicality of, 116
      scheduling of, 116, 117t
    levels of prevention in, 116
  project objectives in, 114, 114t
Health planning projects, 117–123
  levels of prevention in, 121, 122t
    occupational health and, 122, 122t
  successful, 118–119
    bilingual students in, 119
    crime watch in, 119
    housing for elderly in, 118–119
    obese children in, 118
    rehabilitation group in, 119
    textile industry in, 118
  systems levels in, 118, 118t
  unsuccessful, 119–123, 120t
    group home for mentally retarded adults in, 120–121
    Head Start program in, 120
    manufacturing plant in, 121
    prenatal clinic in, 120
    safe rides program in, 121
Health promotion education model, 175, *176*
Health Resources and Service Administration, 52
Health subsystem, private. See *Private health subsystem.*
  public. *Public health subsystem.*
Healthy People 2000, 711–732
  age-related objectives in, 711–723
    adolescents and young adults in, 715–718
      health status objectives targeting, 715–716

Healthy People 2000 (Continued)
      risk reduction objectives targeting, 716–718
      services and protection objectives targeting, 718
      target for reducing deaths among, 715
    adults in, 718–721
      health status objectives targeting, 718–720
      risk reduction objectives targeting, 720
      services and protection objectives targeting, 720–721
      target for reducing death among, 718
    children in, 711–715
      health status objectives targeting, 711–713
      risk reduction objectives targeting, 713–714
      service and protection objectives targeting, 714–715
      target for reducing deaths among, 711
    older adults in, 721–723
      health status objectives targeting, 721–722
      risk reduction objectives targeting, 722
      services and protection objectives targeting, 722–723
      target for reducing activities of daily living limitation among, 721
  special population objectives in, 723–732
    African-Americans in, 725–727
    American Indians and Alaska Natives in, 729–731
    Asians and Pacific Islanders in, 729
    Hispanics in, 725–729
    people with disabilities in, 731–732
    people with low income in, 723–725
Healthy People: The Surgeon General's Report on Health Promotion and Disease Prevention, 43
Heart Disease, Cancer, and Stroke Amendment of 1965, 124
Hepatitis B, 544–546
  carriers of, 544–545
  in Asian-American population, 545–546
  infant immunization against, 545
  populations at risk for, 545
  vaccination coverage for, 545, 545t
  worldwide eradication of, 546
Herpes simplex virus, 550–551
Hill-Burton Act, 42, 124
Hispanic community. See also *Mexican-American community.*

Hispanic community *(Continued)*
 Healthy People 2000 objectives for,
  727–729
Hispanic Health and Nutrition Examination Survey, 15
Historical evolution of community
  health, 17–21
 bubonic plague in, 18–19
 classical times in, 17–18
 Elizabethan Poor Law in, 19
 Greece in, 17
 Industrial Revolution in, 19–20
 inoculation in, 20
 Middle Ages in, 18–19
 prehistoric times in, 17
 Renaissance in, 19
 Rome in, 18
 18th century in, 19–20
 19th century in, 20–21
History of disease, stages of, *14*, 14–17
 hunting and gathering in, 15–16
 industrial cities in, 16
 limitations of, 15
 preindustrial cities in, 16
 present day in, 16–17
 settled village in, 16
HIV. See *Human immunodeficiency
  virus (HIV)*.
HMO (Health Maintenance Organization), 43
 social, 352
Holistic theory, of disease causation, 389
Home health care, 625–639. See also
  Home visit.
 agencies in, certified and noncertified,
  627
  corporate chains in, 627
  hospital-based, 627
  nonprofit, 627
  official, 626–627
  proprietary, 627
  special home health programs in,
   627–628
  types of, 626–628
 Albrecht nursing model for, 629, *630*
 case study in, 633–635
 definition of, 626
 documentation of, 631–632
  for quality of care, 632
  for reimbursement, 631–632
  Health Care Financing Administration forms in, 631–632
 educational preparation in, 628–629
  ANA standards for, 628
  curricula content in, 629
  levels of practice in, 628
 family or caregiver in, 632
 for chronically ill children, 309
 growth of, 626
 home safety in, 631
 hospice in, 635–637

Home health care *(Continued)*
 caring for caregiver in, 635–636
 case study in, 637–639
 focus of, 635
 pain control and symptom management in, *636*, 636–637
 hospital length of stay and, 626
 nursing process applied to, 629–631
  assessment in, 629–630
  diagnosis in, 631
  evaluation in, 631
  implementation in, 631
  planning in, 631
 purpose of, 626
 reimbursement for, 628
  Medicare in, 628
  prior to Medicare, 628
  private financing in, 628
  public sources in, 628
Home health nursing, standards of, 690
Home visit, 143–161. See also *Home
  health care.*
 assessment in, 145–148
 building trust in, 148
 by community health nurses, 144
 care provided in, 145
 case studies in, 149–160, 311–325
 client and family role outlining in, 148
 community services referral in, 149
 diagnosis in, 148
 environment in, 147
 evaluation in, 149
 focus of, 144
 historical, 144
 implementation in, 148–149
 in family health, 310–311
 initial telephone contact in, 145, 147
 physical assessment in, 148
 plan development in, 148
 plan modification in, 149
 preparation for, 145
 purpose of, 144
 referrals for, 144, 145, *146*
 safety issues in, 147
 social talk in, 147–148
 termination of, 149
 unannounced, 147
Homicide, in African-American community, 447–448
 as health indicator, 443
 incidence of, 447
 prevention of, 448
 socioeconomic status and, 447–448
Hospice care, 635–637
 caring for caregiver in, 635–636
 case study in, 637–639
 focus of, 635
 pain control and symptom management in, *636*, 636–637
Hot-cold theory, of disease causation,
  389

Housing, definition of, 575
    environmental health and, 575–576
    "sick building" phenomenon in, 575
    vignette of, 575–576
Human immunodeficiency virus (HIV).
        See also *Acquired immune defi-
        ciency syndrome (AIDS)*.
    experimental anti-HIV drugs and,
        553, 553t
    health care workers and, 553
    in women's health problems, 244
    substance abuse and, 520
    transmission of, decreasing incidence
        rates for, 553
        recommendations for minimizing,
            552
Human papillomavirus, 554–555
    cancer and, 554
Humanistic learning theory, 168
Hypertension, among women, 240
    in African-American community, 443
        cardiovascular disease and, 445

Illness, acute, in men's health, 260
    in women's health, 239–240
    addictive, 510–511
        abstinence symptomatology in, 511
        behavior and cognition changes in,
            511
        continuation stage in, 510
        genetic and environmental vulnera-
            bilities in, 510
        social network role in, 511
        transition from use to abuse in, 511
    biocultural variations in, 441
        excessive deaths and, 441, 444t
        health status disparity and, 441
        life expectancy and, 441
    expression of, cultural diversity in,
        391–393
        culture-bound syndromes in,
            392–393, 393t
        pain in, 392
        symptoms in, 392
    reactions to, 408
    senior health and, 340–341
        immunization and, 341
        screening programs and, 340–341
        selected potential clinical preventive
            services in, 340–341
    treatment of, cultural diversity in, 393
Immunity, 540–541
    acquired, 540
    active, 540
    children and, 540, 540t
    herd, 540
    natural, 540
    passive, 540–541
Immunization, as child health status in-
        dicator, 215

Immunization *(Continued)*
    for travel, 547–548, 548t
    hepatitis B in, 545, 545t
    in child health problem prevention, 219
    in senior health, 341
    schedule for elderly adults in, 341
Incidence studies. See *Prospective studies.*
Infant mortality, AIDS and, 552
    as child health status indicator, 212–
        213
    categorization of, 212–213
    in African-American community,
        448–449
        childbearing patterns and, 448, 448t
        prevention of, 448
        risk factors in, 449
        sudden infant death syndrome and,
            448–449
    leading causes of, 213
    rates of, 212, 212t
    U.S. rates by race of, 212, *213*
Influenza, 544
Institute of Medicine, future of public
        health report of, 60–61
    recommended duties for state health
        departments of, 55, 55t
Intercultural nursing, 373
International Conference on Primary
        Health Care, declaration of, 691–
        693. See also *Alma Ata* entries.

Jaundice, African-American skin color
        and, 452
Jefferson Area Community Outreach for
        Older People (CO-OP), 351

Knowles learning theory, 168, 169t-170t

Lead poisoning, as child health status in-
        dicator, 215
    and child health problem prevention,
        219
    sources of, 215
Learning, cognitive field theory of, 168
    conditions of, 169t-170t
    definition of, 167
    humanistic learning theory in, 168
    Knowles' adult learning theory in,
        168, 169t
    stimulus-response theory of, 168
    theories of, teaching strategies derived
        from, 169–172
Legislation, concerning mental health,
        489, 489–490
    environmental health and, 580, 581t,
        581–582
    health planning, 123–126
        certificate of need in, 124

Legislation *(Continued)*
  Children's Bureau in, 42
  comprehensive, 124
  current status of, 125–126
  Department of Health, Education,
    and Welfare in, 42
  early history in, 123t, 123–124
  Family Support Act in, 43
  Health Amendments Act in, 42
  Health Objectives Planning Act in, 43
  Hill-Burton Act in, 42
  National Health Planning and Re-
    sources Act in, 43
  Occupational Safety and Health Act
    in, 43
  Omnibus Budget Reconciliation Act
    in, 43
  Public Health Service Act in, 43
  Pure Food and Drugs Act in, 42
  regional medical programs in, 124
  Shepard-Towner Act in, 42
  Social Security Act in, 42–43
  Tax Equity and Fiscal Responsibil-
    ity Act in, 43
  Year 2000 Objectives in, 43–44
  in occupational health, 613–616,
    614t
  process of, 199–200
    bill becoming law in, 199–200
  rural health in, 650t, 650–651, 655
    advocacy groups in, 650
    nurse's role in, 650–651, 655
    provider recruitment in, 650
  sources of information on, 193t
  substance abuse in, 511–512
Leukoderma, 454
Liver, cirrhosis of, in African-American
  community, 443
Living patterns, definition of, 570, 572
  environmental health and, 570, 572
  vignette of, 572
Lobbyist, campaigning and, 201–202
  coalitions and, 203–204
  definition of, 200
  education role of, 200
  nurse as, 200–201
  political action committees and, 202–
    203
  power of numbers and, *202*, 202–204
  professional associations and, 202
Long, Carrie, political action and, 189–
  192
  case study in, 191–192
Longevity, among men, 258–259
  among women, 232
  race and sex in, 258–259
  senior health and, 331–332, *332*
  standardized terminology in, 258
Longitudinal studies. See *Prospective
  studies.*
Loss of major life roles theory, of aging,
  352

M*al ojo*, in disease causation beliefs, 414
Mammography, insurance coverage for,
  195, 197
  recommended frequency of, 241
Maternal and child health block grant,
  220
Mature Outlook, Inc., 350
Measles, 542–543
  case study in, 557–562
  deaths due to, 542, 543t
  immunization against, age for, 542–543
    European population and, 543
  world eradication of, 543
Measles-mumps-rubella immunization,
  542
Medicaid, 46
  child health and, 219–220
  in women's health promotion, 247–248
Medicare, 46
Medications, in senior health problems,
  339–340
Melanin, African-American skin and, 451
Men's health, 257–283
  case study in, 273–280
  community health nurse's role in,
    280–281
    facilitator as, 280–281
    health educator as, 280
  factor(s) that impede(s), 266–269
    access to care as, 266–267
      financial considerations in, 266–
        267
      mission orientation in, 266
      time factors in, 267
    lack of health promotion as, 267–269
      cancer in, 268
      coronary heart disease in, 267–268
      financial resources in, 268
      precursors of mortalities in, 267
      stroke in, 268
    medical care patterns as, 266
  factor(s) that promote(s), 269–270
    health services for men as, 270
    interest groups as, 269
    physical fitness and lifestyle as, 269
    policy as, 269–270
  images of men and, 265
  indicators of, 258–260
    longevity as, 258–259
    morbidity as, 259–260
      acute illness and, 260
      chronic conditions and, 260, 260t
      sources of data and, 259
    mortality as, 259, 259t
  medical care usage in, 260–261
    ambulatory care in, 260–261
    hospital care in, 261
  meeting needs in, 270–273
    new concepts in, 271–273, *272–273*
    traditional health services in, 270–
      271
  needs in, 270

Men's health *(Continued)*
nursing home residence in, 261
prescription medications usage in, 261
preventive care usage in, 261
psychiatric services usage in, 261
reproductive health needs in, 263
research in, 281
strategies to address men about, 279
theories of explanation in, 261–266
genetics in, 262
illness and prevention orientations in, 262–264
interpreting data in, 264–265
reporting health behavior in, 264
sex-linked behavior in, 265–266
socialization in, 262
unemployment and, 265–266
Mental health, 488–502
assessment of, 490–492
conceptual framework for, 490
nursing process in, 490–491
tools of, 492
case study in, 492–501
community health nurse's role in, 491–492
as coordinator, 491
as educator, 491
as practitioner, 491
concept of half-way houses in, 491–492
goals of, 489, *490*
historical evolution in, 488
in senior health, 334, 343
legislation concerning, *489*, 489–490
local government services in, 56
morbidity among women and, 236
program effectiveness in, 489
research in, 501–502
services in, at local government level, 56
women's health problems in, 242–243
Mexican-American community, 407–420
case study of, 418–419
cultural adaptation to health care in, 416–417
improving access in, lower economic level and, 416
use patterns and, 416–417
reducing language barriers in, 417
disease causation beliefs in, 412–415
curanderismo and, 412
emotional origin of, 413–414
bilis in, 413
susto in, 413–414
God's role in, 412
hot-cold syndrome in, 414–415
immunization and, 412–413
internal organ dislocation in, 413
caida de la mollera and, 413
empacho and, 413
magical origin in, 414
dano and, 414
mal ojo and, 414

Mexican-American community *(Continued)*
provoking agents in, 412
disease prevalence in, 409–410
potential problems and, 410
socioeconomic conditions and, 409–410
family in, 410–412
literature and, 410
nontraditional framework of, 411
cause of, 411
cultural continuance in, 411
traditional framework of, 410–411
children's role in, 411
father's role in, 411
mother's role in, 411
health education improvement in, 418
Healthy People 2000 objectives for, 727–729
herbal medicine use in, 415–416
chronic conditions and, 416
historical, 415
modern society and, 416
psychiatric conditions and, 416
specific herbs in, 415–416
successful health programs in, 418
Milio's framework for prevention, 74–76
application of, 76
choice availability in, 75
health belief model and, comparison between, 76
health-sustaining resources in, 75
national level policy-making in, 75
propositions of, 75
Minority, definition of, 374
Modernization theory, of aging, 353
Mongolian spots, African-American skin color and, 451–452
Morbidity, among men, 259–260
acute illness and, 260
chronic conditions and, 260, 260t
sources of data and, 259
among women, 235–238
chronic conditions and limitations and, 235
depression and, 236
employment and wages and, 237t, 237–238
family configuration and marital relationship status and, 236–237, 237t
hospitalizations and, 235
mental health and, 236
surgery and, 235–236
incidence and prevalence rates in, 88–89
senior health and, 332–333, *333*
sex ratios in, 260t
Morbidity and Mortality Weekly Report, 105, 538
Morphine, use of, in hospice care, 637

Mortality, among infants. See *Infant mortality.*
  among men, 259, 259t
  among women, cardiovascular disease in, 234–235
    diabetes mellitus in, 235
    leading causes of, 232–233, 233t
    malignant neoplasms in, 234
  as women's health indicator, 232–235
  maternal, 233t, 233–234
  senior health and, 331–332, *332*
Mouth, biocultural variations in, 454
Multicultural nursing, 373
Multiple Risk Factor Intervention Trial (MRFIT), 102
Multiservice models, 48
Mumps, 543
Musculoskeletal system, biocultural variations in, 453
Myocardial infarction, post, case study in, 156–160

National Center for Nursing Research, 201
National Council of Senior Citizens, 350
National Council on Aging, 350
National Health Planning and Resources Development Act, 43, 125
National Health Service Corps, 220
National Institutes of Health (NIH), 52–53
National Notifiable Diseases Surveillance System (NNDSS), 538, 539t
National Nurses' Society on Addiction (NNSA), 521
National Women's Health Network, 248
Naturalistic theory, of disease causation, 389
Neisseria gonorrhoeae, 550
Neuman's health-care systems model, 133
Nightingale, Florence, political action and, 188–189
Nurse(s), as agents of change, 192–193, 193t–194t
  as lobbyist, 200–201. See also *Lobbyist.*
  occupational health, 292. See also *Occupational Health Nursing.*
  school, 292
Nursing, community health. See *Community health nursing.*
  cross-cultural, 373
  health of nation and, 205
  hospital employment in, community health employment vs., 4
  in primary health care, 132
  intercultural, 373
  occupational health. See *Occupational health nursing.*
  transcultural, 372–373

Nursing and Anthropology: Two Worlds to Blend, 373
Nursing process, application of, 103–107
  with elderly, 352–354
    aging changes in, 353
    care planning in, 354
    case study in, 354–362
    data collection in, 353
    evaluation in, 354
    family and community assessment in, 353–354
    short- and long-term goals in, 354
  assessment and diagnosis in, 104–107
  community assessment in, 104
  community diagnosis in, 106
  data retrieval in, 105–106
    Centers for Disease Control and, 105–106
    government documents and, 105
    Health, United States, 1990 and, 105
    Morbidity and Mortality Weekly Report and, 105
    reference librarian and, 105
  evaluation in, 107
  family assessment in, 104
  intervention in, 107
  planning in, 106–107
  referral in, 104
  community diagnosis statement in, 103–104, *104*
  community organization application of, 137–140
  health planning projects and, 117–123
  teaching process and, 167
Nursing theory, definitions of, 68–69
  format for review of, 71–78
  goal of, 69
  locus of change in, individual as, 71–74. See also *Health belief model; Self-care deficit theory.*
    society as, 74–78. See also *Critical social theory; Milio's framework for prevention.*
  microscopic vs. macroscopic approach in, 69–70
  scope of, 70–71
Nutrition, cultural diversity and, 380, 381t
  assessment in, 380
  dietary practices in, 380
  religion and diet in, 380, 381t
  in culturological assessment, 400
  senior health and, 337–338
  case study in, 337
  dietary guidelines in, 337

Obesity, cardiovascular disease and, in African-American community, 445

Observational research, 97–102
  cross-sectional studies in, 97, *98*
  prospective studies in, *100*, 101–102
    advantages of, 101
    comparison of time factors in retro-
      spective and, 102
    definition of, 101
    disadvantages of, 101
    examples of, 102
    relative risk in, 101
  retrospective studies in, 97, *99*, 101
    case selection in, 97
    control selection in, 97, 101
    data collection in, 101
    example of, 101
    purpose of, 97
    use of, 101
Occupational health nursing, 597–621
  AAOHN year 2000 recommendations
    in, 605–606
  aggregate-focused practice in, 11
  AIDS in work place in, 605
  case studies in, 617–621
  definition of, 598
  delivery and access issues in, 605
  emerging demographic trends in, 602–
    606
    focus of U.S. industry in, 602
    slow population growth in, 602
  historical, 598–599
  leading work-related diseases and inju-
    ries in, 604, 605t
  legislation in, 613–616, 614t
    Americans With Disabilities Act as,
      615–616. See also *Americans
      With Disabilities Act.*
    Occupational Safety and Health Act
      as, 613–615. See also *Occupa-
      tional Safety and Health Act.*
    Workers' Compensation Acts as, 615
  minorities in work place in, 604
    culturally and linguistically appro-
      priate programs for, 604
    dangerous work and, 604, 605t
    increasing numbers of, 604
  misperceptions about role of, 602
  model of, 599, *600*
  multidisciplinary team work in, 616,
    617t
  prevention roles in, 602–603, 607–613
    aging work force in, 602
    older workers in, 603
    primary level of, 602, 607, 609
      disease prevention in, 607
      health promotion in, 607
      nonoccupational programs in,
        607, 609
      strategies in, 607, 609
    secondary level of, 602–603, 609
      focus of, 609
      occupational health history in,
        609, *610–611*

Occupational health nursing *(Continued)*
    preplacement medical evaluation
      in, *608*, 609
    strategies in, 609
  tertiary level in, 603, 609, 613
    monitoring in, 613
    physical demands analysis in,
      612, 613
    return-to-work process in, 609, 613
    special accommodations needs in,
      613
    strategies in, 609
  professional liability in, 616
  research priorities in, 599
  responsibilities in, 599
  services of, 599, 601t
  skill and competency(ies) in, 606–607
    consultation as, 607
    counseling as, 607
    direct care as, 606
    health and environmental relation-
      ships as, 606
    health education as, 607
    legal and ethical responsibilities as,
      606–607
    management and administration as,
      606
    research as, 607
  small businesses and, 599, 602
  women in work place and, 603–604
    breast cancer and, 603
    prenatal, postpartum, and child-
      hood programs for, 603
    work place safety and reproductive
      outcomes for, 603, 604t
    work-home balance issues for, 603–
      604
Occupational Safety and Health Act, 43,
    613–615
  inspection under, 614–615
  organizations formed under, 613
  provisions of, 613
  standards publication of, 613–614
  women's health and, 246–247, 247t
Older Americans Act, 347
Older Women's League (OWL), 350
Omnibus Budget Reconciliation Act, 43
On Lok Senior Health Services Commu-
    nity Organization, 48
Oral hyperpigmentation, 454
Osteoporosis, 240
Ottawa Charter for Health Promotion, 61
Ovary, cancer of, 242

Pallor, African-American skin color and,
    452
Pandemic disease, definition of, 18
Papillomavirus, human, 544–555
  cancer and, 554
Parent(s), single, 292, 377
  teenagers as, 377–378

Partnership for Health Program, 124
Patient Education: Issues, Principles and Guidelines, 179–180
Penicillin, for *Neisseria gonorrhoeae* infection, 550
Pertussis, 544
Petechiae, African-American skin color and, 453
Poisoning, accidental, as senior health problem, 340
  lead, as child health status indicator, 215
    in child health problem prevention, 219
    sources of, 215
Policy, analysis of, 195–197
    mammography screening example of, 195, 197
    model for, 195, *196*
  formulation of, 193–195
    example of, 194–195
    ideal in, 193–194
    reality in, 194–195
    steps in, 195
Poliomyelitis, 541–542
Political action, Carrie Long's history of, 189–192
  Florence Nightingale's history of, 188–189
  power and, 190
  public health nurse's story in, 204–205
Politics, definition of, 188
Population-focused practice, 10
  characteristics of, 667
  generalist application of, 10, *10*
  in Cuba, 667, 669–673
    critique of, 674–675
      educational preparation adequacy in, 674–675
      hospital nursing in, 674
      nurse-to-population ratio in, 674
      nursing research demands in, 675
      team concept in, 674
    early mobilization of community in, 669–670
      community organization in, 669
      immunization campaigns in, 669–670
      new system philosophy in, 669
    educational preparation for, 673–674
    neighborhood home/clinics in, 672–673
      focus of, 673
      group health education models in, 673
      integral medicine in, 672–673
      polyclinics and, 673
      problem prevention in, 673
    nurses in, 671–672
      family health education and, 671–672
      immunization programs and, 672

Population-focused practice *(Continued)*
      nutrition education and, 672
      sex education and, 672
      studies conducted by, 672
    polyclinics in, 670–672
      geographically distributed primary care in, 670–671
      hospitals and, 671
      interdisciplinary teams in, 670
      nurse-physician primary care specialist teams in, 670–671
      primary care in, 671
      problem definition and solution in, 671
      range of services offered by, 670
      rural centers in, 670
    problem definition and solution in, 671
    U.S. community health nursing implications of, 675–676
      challenges and, 675–676
      educational preparation of nurses and, 675
      equality in health status and, 675
      market justice model and, 675
      research in, 676
  scientific approach in, 10, 11t
  specialist application of, 10, *10*
Precede education model, 175, *177*, 179
  planning form for, *178*
  schematic for, 179
Pregnancy, adolescent, case study in, 224–228
    child health problem prevention and, 219
  battered women and, 469
  case study in, 153–156
  crack cocaine use during, 510
  diabetes mellitus and, 240
Prenatal care, barriers to use of, 233–234
  in problem prevention, 219
  lack of, as child health status indicator, 214
Prevalence studies, 97, *98*
Private health subsystem, 44, 45–50
  competition and fragmentation in, 47–48
  coordination improvement efforts in, 48–49
    case management in, 48
    discharge planning in, 48
    multiservice models in, 48
    prioritization of care in, 48–49
  cost-containment concerns in, 46–47
    insurance premiums and, 47
    payment system and, 47
    profit vs. nonprofit sectors and, 47
  future of, 49–50
  Medicaid/Medicare and, 46
  personal care models in, 45–46
  services in, 45
  voluntary agencies in, 49

Promoting Health, Preventing Disease: Objectives for the Nation, 43
Prospective studies, *100*, 101–102
  advantages of, 101
  comparison of time factors in retrospective and, 102
  definition of, 101
  disadvantages of, 101
  examples of, 102
  relative risk in, 101
Public Health Service Act, 43
  women's health and, 245–246
Public health subsystem, 44–45, 50–59
  focus of, 50
  future of, 60–62
    ecological model in, 61
    Health Objectives Planning Act 2000 in, 60, 61
    health promotion in, 61
    influences on, 60
    Institute of Medicine's report on, 60–61
  government role in, 50, 51–59. See also *Government.*
  social justice principle in, 50–51
    inequity in access to health care in, 51
    social justice vs. market justice models in, 50–51
Pulmonary tuberculosis, 546–547
  incidence of, 546–547
  prevention of, 547
  screening program for, 547
Pure Food and Drugs Act, 42

Radiation risks, dangers posed by, 578
  definition of, 577–578
  environmental health and, 577–578
  excessive or ill-performed radiographs in, 578
  nuclear industries and, 578
  nuclear waste disposal and, 578
  radon and, 578
  vignette of, 578
Radiograph(s), excessive or ill-performed, environmental health and, 578
Radon, in environmental health, 578
Rate(s), age-specific, 89
  attack, 88
  calculation of, 85, 88
  crude, 89
  definition of, 85
  incidence, 88
  major public health, 89, 90t
  prevalence, 88–89, *89*
  usage of, 88
Reconstruction theory, of aging, 353
Regional medical programs, 124
Religion, cultural diversity and, 381–383
  developmental considerations in, 382–383

Religion *(Continued)*
  childhood in, 382
  old age in, 383
  home visits in, 381
  influence of, 381
  spirituality and, 381–382, 382t
  in culturological assessment, 401
Remarriage, divorce and, 299, 300t–301t, 302
Research on Aging Act, 348
Retirement Equity Act, 348
Retrospective studies, 97, *99*, 101
  case selection in, 97
  comparison of time factors in prospective and, 102
  control selection in, 97, 101
  data collection in, 101
  example of, 101
  purpose of, 97
  use of, 101
Risk, 91
  attributable, 91
  definition of, 91
  relative risk ratio in, 91
Risk factor(s), 91
  in chronic disease control, 94–95
Rubella, 543–544
Rural health, 641–659
  access and use in, 648–649
    difficulties of, 648–649
    health personnel distribution and, 648
    nurse practitioners and, 648
    vignette in, 648
  action for and by community in, 649–650
  areas of greatest need in, 645
  case study in, 651–654
  community experience in, 167
  definition of rurality in, 642–643, *643*
    population in, 642
    population trends in, 642–643
  demographics in, 645
  economic considerations in, 646
  elderly population in, 645–646
  health care resources in, 649
  historical perspective in, 643–644
  indicators of, 644–645
  legislation for, 650t, 650–651, 655
    advocacy groups in, 650
    nurse's role in, 650–651, 655
    provider recruitment in, 650
  migrant health issues in, 646–648
    adequate health records and, 648
    federal grants for, 648
    inability to be understood in, 646–647
    Mexican-American culture in, 647–648
    migrant worker in, 647
    projects in, 647
    vignette in, 647

Rural health *(Continued)*
  nurse's role in, 656–658
    community liaison in, 657
    focus of care in, 657–658
    functions of, 657
    hospital nurse vs., 656–657
    preventive care in, 657
    purpose in, 656
    referral agent in, 657
  preventive nursing care in, 656
  problem(s) in, cost as, 644
    decrease of hospitals as, 644
    isolation as, 644
    professional liability costs as, 644
  research in, 658
  self-care theory in, 655–656
    definition of, 655
    government involvement in, 655–
      656
    interaction in, 655
    problem identification in, 655

Screening programs, developmental
    stages and, 56, 57t
  in disease prevention, 95
  in senior health, 340–341
Secular trends, 95
Self-care deficit theory, 71–72
  application of, 72
  definitions of concepts from, 71
  general theory of nursing in, 71
  premise of, 72
  theoretical foundations of, 71
Senior health, 329–366. See also *Aging;*
    Elder abuse; Elderly.
  action for elderly in, 349
  cardiopulmonary resuscitation and,
    363
  case study in, 354–362
  characteristics of older patients in, 334
  community health nurse role in, 364
  demographics in, 330–331, *331*
  government agencies for elderly in, 348
  in rural areas, 645–646
  indicator(s) of, 330–337
    blood pressure monitoring as, 334
    dental needs as, 334
    health behavior and health care as,
      333–334
    income as, 334–336, *335–336*
      employment and, 335–336
      poverty and, 335
      social security and, 335
    literacy and education as, 336
    marital status and living arrange-
      ments as, 336–337
    mental health as, 334
    morbidity as, 332–333, *333*
    mortality as, 331–332, *332*
    religion as, 337

Senior health *(Continued)*
  legislation and, 346–350
    Age Discrimination in Employment
      Act in, 348
    Employee Retirement Income Secu-
      rity Act in, 348
    Older Americans Act in, 347
    Research on Aging Act in, 348
    Retirement Equity Act in, 348
    Social Security Act in, 347
    Tax Reform Act in, 348
  mental health in, 343
  new concepts in community care in,
    351–352
    Chandler Center as, 351
    elderly helping elderly as, 351–352
    Generations Together as, 351
    Jefferson Area Community Out-
      reach for Older People as, 351–
      352
    nursing home as senior center as, 351
    social/HMO demonstration as, 352
  organizations for elderly in, 350
  problem(s) in, 337–346
    accidental poisoning as, 340
    accidents as, 338–339
      causes of, 338
      prevention of, 339
      telephone services for, 339
    AIDS as, 342, 552
    alcoholism as, 340
    community environment as, 344
    crime as, 345
    death and bereavement as, 343–344
    disability as, 338
    elder abuse as, 344–345
      categories of, 345
      typical victim in, 344
    everyday life and, 338
    families of elderly and, 345–346
      Alzheimer's disease and, 346
      caregivers in, 345–346
      case management services and, 346
      quality of life and, 346
      role reversal in, 345
    hospitalization as, 341–342, *342*
      approach to care and, 342
      cost controls and, 342
      socioeconomic factors and, 341–
        342
      test and procedure limitation in,
        341
    illness as, 340–341
      immunization and, 341
      screening programs and, 340–341
      selected potential clinical preven-
        tive services in, 340–341
    institutionalization as, 342–343
    medications as, 339–340
    nutrition as, 337–338
      case study in, 337
      dietary guidelines in, 337

Senior health *(Continued)*
 thermal stress as, 340
 research in, 364
 resources allocation in, 363–364
  ethical decision making in, 363
  national health program in, 363–364
 services for elderly in, 348–349
 subgroups in, 330
Sexually transmitted disease, among
  men, 263
 Chlamydia trachomatis infection as,
  549–550
  screening for, 549–550
  women and, 549
 crack cocaine and, 510
 fecal-oral contamination in, 555–556
  sexual activity and, 556
  transmission cycle in, 556
  water supplies and, 556
 hepatitis B as, 546
 herpes simplex virus infection as, 550–
  551
 HIV infection as, 551–554. See also
  Acquired immune deficiency syn-
  drome (AIDS); Human immuno-
  deficiency virus (HIV).
 human papillomavirus infection as,
  554–555
  cancer and, 554
 incubation periods for, 549, 549t
 Neisseria gonorrhoeae infection as, 550
 syphilis as, 555
 women's health problems and, 244
Shepard-Towner Act, 42
"Sick building" phenomenon, 575
SIDS (sudden infant death syndrome), in
  African-American infant mortality,
  448–449
Single-parent family, 292, 377
Skin, biocultural variation(s) in, anemias
  as, 452
 cyanosis as, 452
 ecchymotic lesions as, 453
 erythema as, 452
 hormone effect on, 452
 jaundice and, 452
 melanin as, 451
 Mongolian spots as, 451–452
 pallor as, 452
 petechiae as, 453
Smallpox, 539–540
Smoking, cardiovascular disease and, in
  African-American community, 445
Sobriety Groups, secular, 515
Social change, campaign strategies in, 136
 collaboration strategies in, 136
 community development model in, 135
  case study of, 139–140
 contest strategies in, 136–137
 directive, 133–134, *134*
 nurses as agents of, 192–193, 193t-194t

Social change *(Continued)*
 participatory, 133, *134*
 process of, 133
 social action model in, 135
  case study of, 138–139
 social planning model in, 135
  case study of, 137–138
Social Security Act, 42–43
 senior health and, 347
 women's health and, 246
Social theory, critical. See *Critical social*
  theory.
Socially disruptive events theory, of
  aging, 353
Southeast Asian refugees, 421–430
 background of, 422–423, 423t
 caring for, attitudes toward death in,
  429–430
  body image constraints in, 427
  depression in, 430
  first encounter in, 424t, 424–425
  informed consent in, 426
  medication in, 428
  noncompliant patient in, 427
  passive obedient patient in, 426–427
  problems in, 423–424
  social supports in, 427–428
  traditional self-care practices in,
  428–429
   dermabrasive practices as, 429
   hot-cold balance in, 429
   supernatural etiology and cures
   as, 429
  using interpreters in, 425–426
 Healthy People 2000 objectives for, 729
 knowledge of disease of, 423
 naming systems of, 424, 424t
Special Supplemental Food Program for
  Women, Infants, and Children
  (WIC), 220–221
Spirituality, 381–382, 382t
Spouse abuse, nurse's legal responsibilities in, 481
Stimulus-response learning theory, 168
 teaching strategies derived from, 169
Stroke, men's health and, 268
Su Clinica Familiar, in family health,
  309
Subculture, definition of, 373
Substance abuse, 505–529
 alcohol in, in senior health problems,
  340
  prevention program using Freire's
  education model in, 175, 175t
  women abuse and, 469
 as child health status indicator, 214
 case study in, 482–484, 524–528
 child abuse and, 446
 conceptualizations of, 506–511
 course of addictive illness in, 510–511.
  See also *Illness, addictive.*

Substance abuse *(Continued)*
  crack cocaine in, 509–510
    increased availability of, 509–510
    medical complications and, 510
    pregnancy and, 510
    sexually transmitted diseases and, 510
    social effects of, 510
  definitions in, 506–507
  diagnosis of abuse in, 507, 508t
  diagnosis of dependence in, 506–507, 508t
  effects on family dynamics of, 516–517
    abuser centeredness and, 517
    adult children of abusers and, 517
  etiology of, 507–509
    alcoholism in, 508
  family and friends in, 515–516
    codependency and, 516
    identification of, 516
    patterns of interaction of, 516
    treatment for, 516
  in African-American community, alcohol in, 446
    drugs in, 446–447
  in child health problem prevention, 219
  intervention mode(s) in, 511–515
    educational programs as, 512
    legislation as, 511–512
  maternal, child health and, 217–218
  mutual help groups in, 514–515
    Alcoholics Anonymous as, 514
    prevention and, 515
    recovery process in, 514
    secular Sobriety Groups as, 515
    12-step programs in, 514
    Women for Sobriety as, 515
  national offices of mutual help or resource organizations in, 529
  nursing perspective on, 521–529
    attitude toward substance abusers in, 522–523
    community health nurses in, 522
      course of illness and injuries as, 522
      elderly and, 522
      ignoring substance abuse problems and, 522
      simultaneous health problems and, 522
    diagnosis and, 521–522
    nursing interventions in community and, 523–524
      accurate assessment in, 523
      denial breakdown in, 523
      helping agencies contact facilitation in, 524
    rape trauma syndrome in, 522
  professional enablers in, 517
    cross-addiction prevention and, 517
    intervention position of, 517

Substance abuse *(Continued)*
    psychoactive medication prescriptions and, 517
  sexually transmitted disease and, 521
  social network involvement in, 515–517
  sociocultural and political aspects of, 509
  substance classifications in, 506, 507t
  treatment of, 512–513
    detoxification in, 512
    evaluation criteria in, 513
    individual level in, 513
    inpatient, 512
    involuntary, 513
    mutual self-help groups in, 512–513
    outpatient, 512
    principles regarding, 513
    relapse prevention in, 514
    therapeutic community in, 512
    withdrawal symptoms in, 512
  vulnerable aggregates in, 517–521
    adolescence and, 518
    basis for vulnerability and, 520
    dual diagnoses and, 520
    elderly and, 518
    ethnic and racial minorities and, 518–520
      African-American treatment barriers in, 519
      after-care programs in, 519
      sociopolitical and socioeconomic factors in, 519
      substance use acceptance in, 518–519
      tool of empowerment approach in, 520
      treatment approaches in, 519
    health care professionals and, 520–521
    HIV epidemic and, 520
    typical abuser and, 518
    women and, 518
Sudden infant death syndrome (SIDS), in African-American infant mortality, 448–449
Susto, in disease causation beliefs, 413–414
Sweat glands, biocultural variations in, 455
Syphilis, 555

Tax Equity and Fiscal Responsibility Act, 43
Tax Reform Act, senior health and, 348
Teaching, definition of, 167
  principles of, 169t-170t
  process of, 167
  strategies of, derived from theories of learning, 169–172

Teaching *(Continued)*
　　for individuals, families, and aggre-
　　　gates, 172
*Teaching Patients With Low Literacy
　　Skills,* 180
Teenager(s), as parents, 377–378
Teeth, biocultural variation(s) of, 454–
　　455
　　agenesis as, 454
　　decay as, 454–455
　　periodontal disease as, 455
　　size as, 454
Testicle(s), cancer of, 263
Tetanus, 544
Thermal stress, as senior health problem,
　　340
Thorax, biocultural variations in, 455
Transcultural nursing, 372–373
Transferrin, serum, biocultural varia-
　　tions in, 455
Treponema pallidum, 555
Tuberculosis, case study in, 150–152
　　pulmonary, 546–547

Universal blood and body fluid precau-
　　tions, 537, 538t
U.S. Preventive Services Task Force,
　　mandate of, 694
　　recommendations of, 694–710
　　　ages 2–6 in, 697t-698t
　　　ages 7–12 in, 699t-700t
　　　ages 13–18 in, 701t-702t
　　　ages 19–39 in, 703t-704t
　　　ages 40–64 in, 705t-706t
　　　ages 65 and over in, 707t-708t
　　　birth to 18 months in, 695t-696t
　　　pregnant women in, 709t-710t
U.S. Public Health Service, Agency for
　　Toxic Substances and Disease Reg-
　　istry in, 53
　　Alcohol, Drug Abuse, and Mental
　　　Health Administration in, 53
　　Centers for Disease Control in, 52
　　Food and Drug Administration in, 52
　　Health Goals for Year 2000 in, 221t,
　　　221–222
　　Health Resources and Service Admin-
　　　istration in, 52
　　National Institutes of Health in, 52–53
　　regional offices of, 53, *54*
Uterine cervix, cancer of, 241–242

Vaccination. See *Immunization.*
Violence, as child health status indicator,
　　214
　　family. See *Family violence.*
　　risk of, ballistic weapons availability
　　　and, 579

Violence *(Continued)*
　　environmental health and, 579–580
　　problems posed by, 579
　　social stigmatization and, 579
　　vignette of, 579–580
Vital statistics, in community assess-
　　ment, 85
Voluntary agencies, 49

Waste control, definition of, 577
　　environmental health and, 577
　　hazardous waste sites in, 577
　　health hazards and, case study in,
　　　191–192
　　problems related to, 577
　　vignette of, 577
Water quality, definition of, 574
　　drinking water sources and, 574
　　environmental health and, 574–575
　　problems related to, 574
　　vignette of, 574–575
　　water-related diseases and, 574
WIC (Special Supplemental Food Pro-
　　gram for Women, Infants, and Chil-
　　dren), 220–221
Women abuse, 467, 469–472
　　alcohol and, 469
　　causes of, 467
　　characteristics that may influence, 467
　　dynamics of, 467
　　leaving situation in, 471
　　nurse's legal responsibilities in, 481
　　nursing care in, 478–480
　　　assessment in, 479
　　　community resources in, 479
　　　exit plan in, 479, 479t
　　　focus in, 478–479
　　　long-term, 479–480
　　　medicolegal, 480
　　　prevention in, 478
　　　safety provision in, 480
　　　supportive care in, 480
　　physical and behavioral indicators of,
　　　471t, 471–472
　　pregnancy and, 469
　　remaining in situation in, 470–472
　　　cycle theory and, 470
　　　　explosive phase in, 470
　　　　loving kindness and contrition
　　　　　phase in, 470
　　　　tension phase in, 470
　　　reasons for, 470–471
　　　wave pattern of violence and, 470,
　　　　471
　　self-esteem and, 467, 469
　　social isolation and, 469
　　type(s) of, 469–470
　　　physical beating as, 469
　　　spousal rape as, 469–470

Women's health, 231–256
  AIDS and, 551
  community health nurse's role in, 252–253
    counseling as, 253
    direct care as, 252–253
  in prison, case study of, 250–252
  indicator(s) of, 232–239
    education and work as, 238, 238t
    health behavior as, 238–239
    health care access as, 239
    life expectancy as, 232
    morbidity as, 235–238. See also *Morbidity.*
    mortality as, 232–235. See also *Mortality.*
  major legislation affecting, 245–247
    Civil Rights Act in, 246
    Occupational Safety and Health Act in, 246–247, 247t
    Public Health Service Act in, 245–246
    Social Security Act in, 246
  problem(s) in, 239–245
    accidents as, 245
    acute illness as, 239–240
    arteriosclerotic heart disease as, 240
    arthritis as, 240–241
    breast cancer as, 241
    chronic disease as, 240–242
    diabetes mellitus as, 240
    disability as, 245
    endometrium cancer as, 242
    HIV as, 244
    hypertension as, 240
    mental health as, 242–243
    osteoporosis as, 241
    ovarian cancer as, 242
    reproductive health as, 243–244
      family planning and, 243–244
      nutrition and, 243
    sexually transmitted disease as, 244, 549

Women's health *(Continued)*
    uterine cervical cancer as, 241–242
  promotion of, health and social services in, 247–252
    health resources and, 248–249
    Medicaid as, 247–248
    National Women's Health Network as, 248
    networking as, 249
    safe houses as, 249–250
  research in, 253–254
Women's Health Initiative, 253
Work risks, definition of, 572
  environmental health and, 572–573
  problems posed by, 572–573
  vignette of, 572
Workers' Compensation Acts, 615
World health, 664–676
  AIDS and, 665
  Cuba in, population-focused practice in, 667. See also *Population-focused practice, in Cuba.*
      health care delivery distribution in, 667
  environmental stressors in, 664–665
    air pollution and, 665
    land pollution and, 665
    water pollution and, 665
  health care approaches in, 665–666, *666*
  "Health for All by Year 2000" and, 665
  population distribution in, 664
  population growth and, 664, *664*
  primary causes of mortality in, 665
World Health Organization, basic health care services as defined by, 130
  definition of health by, 5

Year 2000 Health Objectives, 43–44, 61
Yin-yang theory, of disease causation, 389

ISBN 0-7216-1312-8

90069